Let's Get Natural with Herbs

by
Debra J. Rayburn

Library of Congress Cataloging-in-Publication Data
Rayburn, Debra - 1961 -
"Let's Get Natural With Herbs" by Debra Rayburn
The most complete A to Z reference guide to utilizing herbs for health and beauty to ensure their safe and effective use and their preparation. Five different cross-referencing indices.
1. Herbs 2. Herbology 3. Alternative Healing
I. Rayburn, Debra, 1961 - II. Title

Library of Congress Catalog Number:2006937486
ISBN: 978-1-886940-95-6

Cover Art and Layout by www.enki3d.com
Book Design: Julia Degan
Book Set in: Times New Roman, Allegro BT

Published by

OZARK
MOUNTAIN
PUBLISHING

PO Box 754
Huntsville, AR 72740

www.ozarkmt.com
Printed in the United States of America

Author's and Publisher's Disclaimer and Special Notice to the Reader

The information in this book is an examination of the mechanisms of herbal and other nutritional therapies that may hold promise as adjunctive treatments to orthodox (conventional) medical approaches, and is not meant to give specific recommendations of advice for the treatment of particular illness, nor is it intended to be a replacement for good medical diagnosis and treatment. This reference book is not provided in order to prescribe, treat, prevent, cure, or diagnose any injury, illness, condition, or problem of the body. It is intended only as a reference guide for use in the comprehensive management of the individual's health, and is for suggestion and educational purposes only. The author cannot be held responsible for claims arising from the erroneous identity of any herbs or plants, for any adverse reactions or effects resulting directly or indirectly from the suggested preparation methods or procedures, from the inappropriate use of any brew, concoction, mixture, preparation, remedy, or therapeutic regimen, from any undetected errors, or from the reader's misunderstanding of the text, nor does the author directly or indirectly dispense any medical advice or prescribe the use of medicinal herbs and plants as a form of treatment. Therefore, before undertaking any form of self-diagnosis or self-treatment with the use of any of the herbs, plants or mentioned remedies or therapies within this book, it is suggested that the reader seek the expertise of a qualified healthcare professional for diagnosis, treatment, and guidance in the selection of particular therapeutic modalities. Although there has been exhaustive research done on all sources to ensure the accuracy and completeness of the information contained in this book, the author assumes no responsibility for errors, inaccuracies, omissions, or any inconsistencies found herein.

Acknowledgements

Special Thanks to:

Dolores Cannon for her faith in my manuscript.

Julia, my editor, for all her laborious work in getting my manuscript edited and ready for publish.

John with enki3d.com for his beautiful artwork appearing on the front cover.

DEDICATION

This book is dedicated to my children Crystal and Erik, whose love and strength I have drawn upon throughout my writing. To Jon, my husband, and to Buddy, my Boston terrier who snores contentedly on the floor next to me as I write. I love you all dearly!

Table of Contents

FORMULARY 479
Therapeutic 480
Over 130 medical ailments ranging from abscess to yeast infection are organized alphabetically, and the formulas that can be used to remedy them.
Baby Care 535
Gentle formulas for use on baby's delicate skin, including baby bath, powder, and diaper rash ointment.
Child Care 536
Problems such as bad dreams, colds, minor wounds, or an upset tummy can be treated safely and effectively at home.
Skin Care 538
Body packs, facial rinses, lotions, skin cleansers, and moisturizers for dry, normal, and oily skin.
Hair Care 548
Conditioners, shampoo, and rinses to help restore and maintain healthy hair.
Oral Hygiene 551
Tooth cleansers, brightners, polishers, and breath fresheners to promote and maintain oral health.
Fragrance 552
Easy perfume, potpourri, and sachet formulas you can make yourself.
Household Cleaners 553
Non-toxic bleach, cleaners, polishes, upholstery shampoo, and wax for household use.
Insect Repellents 556
Effective natural insect repellents for indoor and outdoor use.
Pet Care 558
Flea and tick repellents, pet baths, and other formulas to help care for pets. Also includes a list of herbs that are toxic to pets and livestock.
Dyeing with Plants 560
Instructions on preparing plants for use in dyeing, materials needed, and a list of plants and their dye colors.

APPENDICES 567
Appendix I Herbs by Common Name 568
Reference list that will help find an herb for which you know only the common name.
Appendix II Herbs by Scientific Name 573
Reference list that will help find an herb or plant for which you know only the scientific name.

Glossary of Medical Terminology 578
Botanical Index 596
General Index 636
References for Additional Reading 673
Websites 676

Introduction

A miracle indeed, that a creation of such beauty and simplicity
can be utilized in the healing and wellbeing of all
Debra Rayburn

Many of us are familiar with herbs used as flavoring agents in culinary, however, archaeological evidence indicates that for thousands of years, numerous cultures around the world have relied upon the healing power of the plant kingdom. Today, a growing number of individuals continue to utilize herbs for their medicinal properties to promote and maintain health. Approximately 30% of all drugs currently prescribed in the United States contain at least one active ingredient derived from herbs. The remaining ingredients are chemically synthesized. The World Health Organization (WHO) estimates that herbs are utilized as the primary medicines by about two-thirds of the world's population, and that 80% of the world's population currently use some form of herbal medicine.

We use medicinal herbs all the time without realizing it. Perhaps you started your day with a stimulating cup of coffee, found a breath freshening sprig of parsley on your plate while dining out, or enjoyed an after dinner mint intended to help ward off indigestion. Medicine cabinets throughout the U.S.A. and other parts of the world are filled with prescription and over the counter (OTC) drugs that have botanical roots. OTC pain medications originated from the herb meadowsweet, which contains the constituent salicin, a well-known pain reliever. Many brands of toothpaste contain the antibacterial properties of mint, and the constituent thymol, derived from the herb thyme, is one of the active ingredients contained in a well-known brand of mouthwash.

With all the information out there, some orthodox (conventional) practitioners in the United States are still largely unaware of successful herbal remedies. A renewed interest in all forms of alternative medicine is occurring in healthcare, which is resulting in greater acceptance of natural therapies in mainstream medical circles. And at the forefront is botanical medicine, a system that focuses on promoting health and wellness with natural therapies. In the past thirty years, there have been tremendous advances in the understanding of how botanical therapies, work as well as the use of these natural substances to promote health and wellness. It is obvious that this emerging trend toward the use of herbs for medicines will persist and be a major part of medicine in the future. Botanical medicine is a method of healing that employs various medicinal herbs and plants to empower an individual to achieve the highest possible level of health. Botanical medicine's roots go back thousands of years as it draws on the healing wisdom of many countries including Egypt, China, India, and Greece. In all parts of the world, each culture has its own herbal traditions that have evolved over time. The traditional medicine system of China known as Traditional Chinese Medicine developed from the ancient beginnings of shamanistic medicine. Ayurvedic Medicine is the traditional medicine system of India and Nepal, and is the third largest medical system in the world. Eclectic Medicine is an extension of early American Herbal Medicine traditions and is still practiced today by naturopaths and herbalists in Europe and the U.S. Sharing its roots with eclectic medicine is Naturopathic Medicine, which includes acupuncture, botanical medicine, homeopathy, nutrition, oriental medicine, and other therapies. A licensed physician that has completed university training in standard western medicine, and has then gone on to receive additional degrees in the methods and philosophies of natural healing is known as a Holistic M.D. Medical Herbalists, also called Phytotherapists are trained through university programs and are present in Europe as well as the U.S, They are generally required to study both traditional uses of herbs as well as basic medical sciences of anatomy, biochemistry, nutrition, etc.

You may be wondering how botanical medicine differs from orthodox medicine. Conventional (orthodox) medicine focuses primarily on treating the symptoms, whereas botanical medicine addresses the whole person, focusing not only on the symptoms but on the underlying condition as well. The effects of herbal medicines may not be noticed as rapidly as when using conventional drugs. The reason for this is because botanicals work with the body not against it to strengthen, cleanse, and build the body systems gradually. When using nature's medicines you are often healthier, have fewer recurring illnesses, and tend to remain that way longer. Herbal medicines are often used as adjuvants to conventional medicines. What this means is that herbal remedies are used to compliment, complete, or support conventional medicines. This is especially true with a more severe problem that requires pharmacological or surgical intervention, such as cancer, congestive heart failure, Parkinson's disease, angina, or certain types of trauma.

There is really but one healing force in existence, and that force is nature itself, the inborn restorative power of the individual to overcome illness. The practical application of these natural agencies, when appropriately suited to the individual, is a true sign that the art of healing has been elaborated by the aid of compatible treatments. In the last two decades botanical medicine has experienced a tremendous revival, largely as a result of public awareness of the role that diet and lifestyle play in chronic conditions. Ultimately, botanical medicine may prove most useful in the deterrence of illness. The health benefits and cost effectiveness of a wellness oriented therapy program has been clearly demonstrated. One study found that participants in these types of programs reduced their number of days of disability by forty-five percent, their number of days spent in hospital by fifty percent, and the amount of money they spent on healthcare services by seventy-five percent.

I have always been fascinated by reports of healings utilizing nature's gift to us: the plant kingdom. As an herbalist, researcher, and writer, I have encountered many individuals who are confused by the rapidly growing herbal marketplace. Most of these individuals sincerely want to believe in the power of botanical medicines, but want clarification as to the proper applications and uses of these natural remedies. *Let's Get Natural with Herbs* contains a great deal of information that can be utilized as a self-help guide for minor ailments and for wellness oriented therapy programs.

This book was written not only for my own personal use, but also for the purpose of dispelling some of the misconceptions about medicinal herbs and plants, and to help bring about a closer reunion of people and plants. Botanical medicine has an ageless ability to heal the whole person and help one achieve an improved state of health and wellness. It is my hope that this book will further assist those who already practice natural healing, and encourage a greater interest in those who feel the stirrings of the healer within themselves.

Nature gives us all we need for health and wellbeing.
Open yourself to the magnificent power of the plants, and let the healing begin!

Debra Rayburn

GUIDELINES AND PRECAUTIONS

A sea of bluebells, their leaves quivering in the breeze, flow over the forest floor in waves of amethyst and sapphire. Their sweet fragrance, lovely color, and warmth bring a joy that is nearly unbearable. The clear sky above answers the lovely color by capturing and reflecting it like the radiant gleams of stained glass.

Debra Rayburn

Herbal Therapy Guidelines

Most herbs when used properly are the safest remedies available, and seldom does one experience any addiction, adverse or allergic reactions, dependence, or withdrawal symptoms from the correct use of herbs. A major area of concern is the belief that herbs are harmless. This, however, is not true. Herbs that have enough activity to be considered useful are often the ones that may pose the greatest danger. Herb use may be dangerous for many reasons: the quantity of plant material in a preparation may vary, the herb being used to treat a condition or problem has been contraindicated, or the herb has no activity and causes harm by delaying treatment with more suitable herbs. If herbs are misused or one fails to observe the cautions, they could cause an adverse reaction, system imbalance, poisoning, or possible fatality. Also, some persons may opt to discontinue use of their pharmaceuticals and start using nothing but herbs. For your own safety, please don't do that. One should initiate herbal use only where possible, particularly if health conditions are severe, as an abrupt switch in the course of your healthcare therapy could be dangerous. Remember that herbs tend to work gradually, and they generally take anywhere from one to six weeks to build up in your system, so benefits or results may not be noticeable until that time.

Herb Identification and Dangerous Plants

For the most part herbs can be identified accurately, however, there are a number of herbs that are *very* similar in appearance, and many herbs, especially in the absence of flowers, may resemble something quite different. Some species are toxic in part or in whole, and when ingested can cause breathing difficulties, arrhythmia, mouth and throat irritation, nausea, serious illness, ulcerations, vomiting, or even death. When handled or used topically (externally) some herbs may cause various skin irritations. It is important to be absolutely certain of identification prior to handling or ingesting any herb. If you do not have complete confidence and knowledge as to the identification of an herb in the wild it is always safest to purchase them from a reputable merchant. Educate yourself on the particular aromas and tastes of certain herbs, and if there is *any* uncertainty in identification, do not use it.

Adverse Effects

The vast majority of cases where herbs have caused adverse reactions or harm have usually occurred in those individuals who have ingested very large amounts, or who have used the herb for an extended period of time. If mild adverse reactions such as diarrhea, headache, or nausea occur within 1-2 hours of taking any herb, discontinue its use and shortly thereafter, the symptoms will generally subside. When a health condition is an immediate threat to life, treatment by a physician is the best choice. These guidelines apply to all of the herbs and conditions listed in this book. Prior to the use of medicinal herbs and plants or any other alternative therapy, consult a healthcare professional, especially if you have any of the following symptoms:

*Chest pain or arrhythmia *A lump or mass that appears anywhere on the body *A persistent cough or one with bloody, greenish, or yellowish colored mucus *Difficulty breathing or swallowing *A fever that registers over 102° F *A known or suspected bone fracture, eardrum punctures, poisoning, or stroke *A severe allergic reaction, burn, deep/gaping wound, hypertension, or infection *Loss of consciousness *Uncontrolled bleeding, diarrhea, or vomiting *Nipple discharge (other than during lactation) *Long-term or persistent symptoms *Acute, persistent, or unbearable pain.

Laxative and Emetic Herbs

Some herbs have very strong actions, which can result in very strong reactions. Emetic herbs, which induce vomiting, and laxative herbs, which cause bowel evacuation, are useful when these responses are expected as part of the therapy. However, when these responses are not expected it can provide a very uncomfortable condition. While emetic and laxative use helps to stimulate the elimination of wastes, they also have a tendency to reduce the body's energy levels; therefore, they should never be administered for extended periods of time, or used by persons who are already in a weakened condition.

General Precautions

Always check with your physician before using any botanical product, especially if you are taking a prescription or over the counter (OTC) medication. Also inform your herbalist about any prescription or OTC medications you may be taking. Many herbal remedies contain substances that can interact with other medications you may be taking. Be aware that the Food and Drug Administration (FDA) regulates botanical products only as food supplements, not drugs, therefore, labels on these products *don't* contain information regarding risks, adverse reactions, or the possibility of serious interactions with other substances. Due to incredible expense, the majority of herbal products sold in the United States have *not* been scientifically tested. Their alleged benefits are largely based on unconfirmed reports. This does not mean that they do not work; it merely indicates that for many herbs there are no clinical trials or research citations to back them up. Commercial botanical products may contain ingredients other than those listed on the label. For example, several batches of siberian ginseng capsules were found to include a nonlisted herb that contained male hormone-like chemicals. The amount of the active ingredient will fluctuate between commercial brands and perhaps even from bottle to bottle within a particular brand. Be cautious of commercial products that promise to *cure* a specific health condition. *Don't* use herbal remedies for those medical conditions that are serious, potentially serious, or are a threat to life. Avoid botanical preparations if you are pregnant or suspect that you may be pregnant as herbal effects on the developing fetus are unknown. Also it is best to avoid use of herbal preparations if you are breast-feeding as the herbs medicinal effects can be transferred to baby in this way too. Purchase your herbs or commercial herbal products from a reputable company, and remember that nine out of ten times, the clerk at the health food store is a salesperson, not a trained herbalist.

Commonly Asked Questions

What is an Herb?

An herb is any vegetative growth having no woody tissue that withers to the ground after each season's growth, and can be used for medicinal purposes, as a flavoring or seasoning agent, or a household remedy.

What is an herbalist?
An herbalist is a practitioner of and contributor to the field of botanical medicine. Found in all parts of the world, herbalists include holistic medical practitioners, homeopaths, native healers, naturopaths, nutritionists, pharmacists, shaman, scientists, writers, and many others to numerous to mention.

What is botanical medicine?
Botanical medicine is the art and tradition of using herbal remedies to promote health and prolong a healthy life. All over the world, each culture has its own herbal traditions that have evolved over time.

What are dietary supplements and can they actually help?
The term dietary supplement as defined by Congress in the Dietary Supplement Health and Education Act (DSHEA) of 1994 is a product taken by mouth that contains a dietary ingredient intended to supplement the diet. The ingredients of dietary supplements may include substances such as herbs or other botanicals, amino acids, vitamins, minerals, organ tissues, glandulars, and/or enzymes. They are available in a variety of forms including capsules, liquids, powders, softgels, and tablets, as well as energy bars. Whatever their form, the DSHEA places them in a special category of foods, not drugs, and requires they be labeled as a dietary supplement. Supplements should not be used as a substitute for the variety of foods important to a healthy diet. Even if you consume a wide variety of foods, it's difficult to make sure that you are getting all the vitamins, minerals, and other nutrients your body requires. If you are 50 + years of age, your nutritional needs could change. Informed food choices are the initial place to begin, making sure your diet includes a variety of foods while watching your caloric intake. Supplements in conjunction with fortified foods may help you obtain the appropriate amount of nutrients. Your physician and/or dietitian can assist you with these decisions. Together they can work with you to achieve a balance between the foods and nutrients you need.

Is it safe to use herbs during pregnancy?
The safety of herbs has not been determined for use during pregnancy, therefore, it is recommended that the use of herbs be discontinued if you are pregnant, think you may be pregnant, or are planning to become pregnant. Many herbs contain emmenagogue (stimulates menstruation), oxytocic (stimulates uterine contractions), or abortifacient (induces abortion) properties. Any substance, which has a strong effect on the body, should be used with extreme care as these same substances can also have a direct affect on the developing fetus. Topical applications should be used in place of ingested remedies only when *absolutely* necessary, and under the guidance and supervision of a trained healthcare professional. Consult your healthcare professional prior to taking any botanical preparations during this time. Also, the safety of many over-the-counter vitamin and mineral supplements during pregnancy has not been verified. As with any supplement not absolutely necessary for health, your safest course is to avoid it during pregnancy.

Can women who are breast-feeding use herbs?
Because of the potential for serious adverse reactions in nursing infants, women who are breast-feeding should avoid the use of herbs as the effects can be passed on to the infant directly through the breast milk. Topical applications should be used only when *absolutely* necessary, and under the guidance and supervision

of a trained healthcare professional. If you apply ointments to the breast, be sure to wash the breast and nipple thoroughly prior to breast-feeding as the medicinal effects can be passed to baby this way too. Consult your healthcare professional prior to taking any botanical preparations during this time. Also, the safety of many over-the-counter vitamin and mineral supplements during breast-feeding has not been verified. As with any supplement not absolutely necessary for health, your safest course is to avoid it during breast-feeding.

If I am scheduled for surgery, should I be concerned about the medicinal herbs or other dietary supplements I am taking?

Some supplements can have unwanted effects before, during, and after surgery. It is *very* important to tell your physician, surgeon, and anesthetist about the vitamins, minerals, herbs, and any other supplements you are taking before surgery. You will most likely be asked to stop taking these products at least 2-3 weeks prior to the procedure to avoid the possibility of potentially dangerous supplement-drug interactions including changes in heart rate and/or blood pressure or increased risk of bleeding, all of which could adversely affect the outcome of your surgery.

Are herbs, other supplements, and prescription drugs safe to take together?

First and foremost, check with your healthcare professional before adding to your prescription drug medications or changing over to alternatives. Many individuals often take prescription drug medicines along with herbal medicines or other supplementation. When using herbs or other supplements with prescription drugs it is *very* important to be aware of interactions. If you are taking any form of prescription drug, it is important that you educate yourself to the possible herb-supplement-drug interactions that could occur. Again, it is very difficult to predict any adverse reactions that could occur with the combined use of herbs, other supplements, and drugs. Medicinal plants and herbs as well as the information in this book are not meant to replace prescription drugs; instead, they're intention is to be used with them as an auxiliary, when possible. Herbs and other supplements may help to extend the effects of prescription drugs, thus enabling lower dosages, as well as helping to soften any adverse reactions that are common with many prescription drugs. Some herbs may increase or decrease nutrient absorption as well as prescription medications. For example, Saint John's Wort may lessen the effectiveness of some prescription drugs for certain cancers, depression, heart disease, HIV, or seizure conditions. Some herbs contain large amounts of mucilage or other types of fiber, which may inhibit the absorption of certain types of medications. Herbs that strengthen digestion and absorption may increase the absorption of some medications. Many supplements can change the way drugs are processed and eliminated in the liver. They can have an effect on liver enzymes, and can also change the blood levels of drugs. *Anticoagulants*: Some herbs and other supplements contain blood-thinning properties. Prescription drugs, some herbs, over the counter (OTC) medicines, and certain vitamin supplements, such as vitamin E, can each thin the blood. Taking any of these products alone or together can increase the possibility of internal bleeding or stroke (apoplectic). If you are taking anticoagulants be sure to have a healthcare professional monitor your coagulation-time to determine how fast your blood coagulates (clots). If your coagulation time changes by more than a few seconds, you could be in danger of hemorrhaging or at an increased risk of stroke (apoplectic). *Glycosides*: Some herbs contain cardiac glycosides. Foxglove is probably one of the best-known cardiant plants. Herbal supplements containing cardiac glycosides may over-stimulate the heart, and should be avoided if you are taking prescription cardiac drugs. *Hypertension*: Individuals who have a history of high blood pressure should avoid herbs and other supplements that constrict the blood vessels or stimulate the heart. If you are taking herbs or other supplements along with your prescription blood pressure drug, be sure to have your physician monitor you closely to see if your blood pressure medication dosage needs to be modified.

Can I administer herbs to my child?
Yes, some herbs are gentle enough to administer to children for short periods of time. Herbs are not recommended for use in children under the age of 10 years old.

What is the activity/rest principle?
Most herbs when used long-term and in small quantities are quite safe, however, there are some herbs that will suddenly increase in intensity of action. This increase can become harmful if the herb is taken regularly without a rest. To avoid cumulative effects, a general recommendation is the activity/rest principle, one would use herbs for six days then take one day off, six weeks then take one week off, six months then take one month off. Rest periods are important in that they enable the integration of the herbs into the physiology.

Can the elderly use herbs?
Yes, however, since the health of the aged is generally more delicate, and they are usually more sensitive to herbs and prescription drugs, smaller quantities consisting of one half to one third the adult dosage should be administered.

How do I know if I'm allergic to any particular herb?
Certain herbs may cause a hypersensitive (allergic) reaction in some individuals. Generally, it is impossible to predict a reaction of this nature in advance, however, most reactions are mild. Discontinuing use of the herb will usually stop the reaction. As with any adverse reaction, if discontinuing the herb does not stop the reaction, obtain prompt medical attention. A wide variety of hypersensitive symptoms including anaphylaxis, blood problems (anemia, coagulation problems, infection), bruises, burn-like peeling of the skin, chills, debility, difficulty swallowing, digestive complaints, fatigue, fever, headache, hives, hypotension, itchy/watery eyes, joint pain, mucous membrane irritation, muscle and blood vessel inflammation (severe), photosensitivity, photodermatosis, respiratory distress, runny nose, shortness of breath, sneezing, skin rash, swelling of the face/lips/or tongue, and wheezing can occur either singly or together in groups. The following easy at home allergy test will help you determine if you are allergic (sensitive) to a specific substance contained in a medicinal herb or plant (it sometimes works for food allergy as well).
Allergy Test: To perform this test, scratch the skin with a sterilized needle or pin and a sample of the (allergen) substance (i.e. oil, resin). If the scratch creates an undesired irritation within 30-60 minutes, you are likely to experience an undesireable reaction to the herb. Note: The scratches should be at least one-half (½) inch long and should not draw blood. It is important to be aware that some herbs will cause a particular sensation upon administration, or application, that is *not* an allergic reaction. For example, purple coneflower (echinacea) causes a mild, unharmful tingling sensation on the tongue; lobelia causes a scratchy feeling at the back of the throat; cloves cause a numbing sensation of the tongue; and cayenne causes a slight

burning sensation during bowel evacuation. Familiarizing yourself with an herb's normal sensory effect will help you to rule out what might be mistaken as a hypersensitive (allergic) reaction.

Why does the FDA say some herbs are unsafe?

The Food and Drug Administration (FDA) continually surveys the available literature pertaining to the pharmacology of medicinal plants and herbs, and have suggested that some botanicals are unsafe. While herbs generally do have an excellent safety record, there is no such thing as total safety with herbs. Indeed many herbs are poisonous; in fact about 5% of all poisonings are caused by the ingestion of herbs. The majority of these poisonings occur when adults or children ingest household or outdoor plants. Parents should educate themselves as to the recognition of dangerous plants, and children should be instructed never to ingest a plant unless a qualified adult has first taught them how to identify and use it. It is important to understand that these plants were not judged unsafe on the basis of proper usage, but only based on the report of abuse or misuse, on the occurrence of a severe adverse reaction, or the presence of a known carcinogenic substance.

Is it true that carcinogenic herbs cause cancer?

All medicines, whether natural or synthetic, contain substances that when taken in large enough amounts are toxic, and these substances are in effect very weak carcinogenic agents. It was once thought that if you ingested even the tiniest amount of any carcinogen, you would be at a significant risk for developing cancer. The chairman of the Biochemistry Department of the University of California at Berkeley, Bruce Ames, Ph.D, has long been one of the nation's leading carcinogen researchers. In the early 1980's, Dr. Ames shocked the world with the news that the dry weight of nearly all herbs used for food or medicinal purposes accounts for approximately 10% of *naturally* occuring carcinogens. Dr. Ames supposition was that herbs had evolved their toxic chemical constituents as protection against insects and disease causing microorganisms. According to estimates by Dr. Ames, a typical individual ingests 10,000 times more naturally occurring carcinogens than synthetic carcinogens. So, why hasn't each and every one of us developed cancer? It's because analytical study has discovered that most herbs used either as food or for medicinal purposes also contain chemical constituents that protect against cancer. Naturally occurring cancer-blocking chemicals include, but are not limited to vitamins such as A, C, and E, which help to offset the harmful effects of these toxic substances. It's not possible to protect ourselves from these carcinogenic chemicals, as we ingest them in almost everything we consume. For example, the chemical constituent safrol, found in sassafras, has been classified as carcinogenic. This same carcinogen is also found in many common flavoring agents such as basil, black pepper, nutmeg, and turmeric that are used in everyday culinary. The use of the whole plant helps to negate or offset any side effects that may occur from any one particular constituent found in the plant. It must be remembered that while a particular herb's chemical constituent may be considered carcinogenic when isolated and concentrated, as part of the combination of complex elements in the whole herb it is usually quite safe.

What should I do in the event of overdose or poisoning?

The first thing to do is contact your local poison control center immediately. In the event of a suspected overdose or poisoning the most important step, if it has not already occurred on its own, is to eliminate the suspected material from the stomach. This means that if the person is alert, and has not vomited, the antidotes to be employed are emetics, which induce vomiting. If you decide to use syrup of ipecac as the emetic, follow the directions for dosage and administration on the bottle. Vomiting should generally occur within 15-20 minutes. After the person has vomited, be sure to give them plenty of water to replenish their fluid levels. If the person does not vomit or if they are in a drowsy state, get them to the nearest hospital emergency room immediately. DON'T attempt to induce vomiting if the person is drowsy as they could aspirate (inhale) the vomit into their lungs.

I've never had to contact a Poison Center, what do I tell them?
Here is the toll-free number for the Poison Center: 800-222-1222. Local numbers are listed in your telephone directory. When you contact a poison control center, give the person who answers the phone the following information:

*Person's age and weight
*Common and scientific plant names (if known) or name of other supplement
*Amount ingested (if known).

If the ingested herb is unknown and the person vomits, it is important to save this and bring it to the hospital emergency room as this may have plant parts in it that could help in the identification of the plant material ingested and prove helpful in antidote administration.

Also, if the person is drowsy or unconsciousness, do not attempt to induce vomiting, get them to the nearest medical emergency room!

PREPARING BOTANICALS FOR USE

The quiet garden holds a beautiful assortment of roses that grow daintily at the end of long stalks. The bright blossoms of apricot, cream, orange, red, and yellow are radiant, the long buds glimmer like pointed flames against the vibrant green hedge, and the thick scent is full of golden summer memories.

Debra Rayburn

Collecting Herbs

To achieve maximum potency, herbs are collected at various times of the year. Remember that wild herbs tend to be much more potent than cultivated varieties. Herbs are best collected during dry weather as they contain more oils and/or resins during this time. Rainy weather can diminish the effects of an herb's constituents, and a wet herb has a tendency to spoil much quicker than if it were collected in dry weather. Early mornings after the dew has evaporated, or early evening before the dew has formed are the best times of the day to gather your herbs. Use herbs that grow nearest to you. Many illnesses that are contracted in a particular area are somewhat dependent upon the environmental conditions. The plants that grow in that particular area have a tendency to take on the characteristics of their environment, which make them quite useful in treating those health problems associated with the climate or conditions of that area. The best places to collect herbs are open fields or wooded areas. Always gather plants that are strong and healthy looking. Avoid collecting plants that are near highways or roads, plants that are in stagnant water, and those that are in close proximity to industrial buildings, heavily populated residential areas, or other areas that may be contaminated. Do not collect plants that are beginning to wilt, plants that show signs of insect damage, or plants that have dark or discolored areas as this may be caused by a fungus. The golden rules of collecting are:

*Endangered or rare plants should not be collected. For example, a plant that is considered common in one state may be an endangered species or protected in another *Fewer than (10) ten plants growing in one single area should not be gathered. Collect plants that are numerous or in numbers greater than ten, and then harvest no more than ⅓ of those plants that are growing furthest away from the main (mother) plant *Fill in any holes you have dug when gathering roots *Don't trespass onto private property. Be sure to get permission from the landowner first.

Times of Year

The recommended times of year when herbs are ready for collection are as follows. *Aerial* (above ground portion of the herb): before the flowering season or prior to the buds opening. *Bark* (inner, outer, or root): in the autumn after the leaves have fallen, or just prior to the buds opening in the spring. Outer and inner bark should be collected from smaller branches, as removing large sections around the tree's circumference will destroy the tree. *Bulbs*: late autumn, or after the plant's leaves have begun to wither. *Buds*: after they have formed, but prior to their opening. *Flowers*: during the flowering season. *Fruit*: when ripe. Avoid fruit that is damaged, has been lying on the ground, or shows signs of insect infestation. *Leaves*: after the flowering and fruit season is over. Avoid stripping the leaves from the entire plant, as this will destroy it. *Roots*: late fall or early spring. *Seeds*: after the flowering season when they have ripened. The best way to collect seeds is to lay something on the ground around the plant such as a newspaper to catch the seeds as they fall. Or, just prior to the seeds ripening, loosely tie a piece of very lightweight material, such as gauze, over the flower head to catch the seeds. Avoid collecting seeds that are blackened, have black spots on them, or are moldy looking as this could be caused by a fungus.

Drying Herbs

Proper drying is very important in order to retain the herb's color and properties. Freshly harvested herbs generally have moisture contents of anywhere between fifty to eighty percent, and unless they are used within that same day, must be dried prior to storage. To remove any dirt, wash or rinse herbs under *cold* running water. Gently scrub the outer bark and roots, then cut them into small pieces. Remove the inner bark in strips, thread it onto heavy thread or wire, and hang it up to dry. The three common drying methods are: *Outdoor Drying* requires that herbs be spread out on a drying screen. Make sure the screen you use is made out of a rust-free material such as fiber or steel mesh (an old steel mesh screen door raised up on cement blocks or saw horses works well). Put your herbs in a shady well-ventilated area and let them dry until the leaves crumble easily. *Indoor Drying* is as easy as bunching herbs together and tying a piece of string tightly around the stems. Hang the bunch upside down in a dust free, well-ventilated room that is out of direct sunlight and let them dry until the leaves crumble easily. *Oven Drying* (requires constant monitoring throughout the drying process) is a quick way to dry your herbs, and calls for a low temperature setting of no greater than 140 degrees F. Herbs (with the exception of oven drying) will generally take anywhere from three to six days to dry thoroughly. Once your herbs have dried, put them into airtight containers that have been labeled and dated. Store the containers out of direct sunlight in a cool, dry place. Dried herbs generally maintain their full potency for approximately one year.

The Art of Formulation

An appropriately combined formula is essential, and the art of formulation lies not only in the selection of the most effective herbs to use for the condition, but also in determining how those herbs should be used. Countless herbal preparations have been ruined simply because the user did not prepare them or use them to the best of their advantage. This naturally discourages most people from trying herbs again. It is important that the preparations be given sufficient trial for results. Certain herbs need to be prepared and administered correctly in order to derive benefits. For instance, boneset is generally taken as a hot infusion upon retiring to induce perspiration, and in the morning taken as a cold infusion for use as a laxative. Powdered slippery elm when taken as an enema is soothing to the bowels, but it is basically ineffective if the bowels are not flushed clean prior to injection of the herbal solution. Chamomile or sage when used as an after meal beverage tea can be steeped in a cup of hot water for only a few minutes prior to drinking it, however, when these herbs are used for medicinal purposes they need to be made into a stronger infusion. When used as a hair application sage and chamomile require a strong decoction, and sage decocted in an iron kettle will yield a much darker hair dye. Each preparation method gives a different result. An herb does not yield the same principles by decoction as by infusion. By means of decoction, the extractive, resinous, and bitter principles are extracted, whereas by infusion a large quantity of aromatic and volatile principles are obtained. Generally, in chronic conditions, most herbalists prefer to combine several different herbs rather than using a single herb, which may be too strong in its action or because the effects desired cannot be obtained by the use of any single herb. This combination or compound formula encourages healthy system functions and assists the body to heal itself. A general guideline for chronic conditions would be to use the appropriate preparation for approximately one month to every year since the condition began, and 1-6 grams of a compound formula can usually be taken 2-3 times per day. For acute conditions, the herbalist will use fewer herbs, maybe even just one. For example, purple coneflower (echinacea) is often times used singly at the onset of symptoms and continued until the symptoms abate. Preparations for extremely acute conditions may be taken as often as every 15-20 minutes. It is important to continue to take the preparation for 1-2 weeks after all symptoms have disappeared, as this will help to prevent any secondary infection or recurrance of the condition.

Principles of Formulation

The main principles of formulation are based upon four categories of herbal function. *Primary Herbs* contain the chief or primary properties required to address the condition and main symptoms, and it determines the basic action of the formula. Include large amounts of anywhere from one to three herbs that possess these properties. For example, expectorant for respiratory conditions, depurative for blood cleansing, etc. Any herb can be used as a primary, and the choice of which herbs to use will depend on the condition. The primary herbs make up the bulk of and will predominate your formula by approximately 80%. *Supporting Herbs* help to support the functions of as well as develop and enhance the effects of the primary herbs. It is important that inclusion of these secondary herbs does not dilute or lessen the activity of the primary herbs. An example of herbs that provide the properties required for secondary or supporting herb inclusion include stimulant herbs such as ginger or cayenne, which promote action of the primary herbs; carminative herbs such as fennel or cumin, which provide gentle action and protection; antispasmodic herbs such as lobelia, valerian, or hops relax the body; and demulcent herbs such as marshmallow, slippery elm, or irish moss, which soothe and provide protection. Secondary or supporting herbs will make up about 10% of your formula. *Assisting Herbs* are sometimes added to address the secondary symptoms of a condition, and are also used to further enhance the effects of the primary herbs, as well as helping to reduce the harsher effects (if any) of the primary and secondary herbs. Assisting herbs will make up approximately 5% of your formula. *Conducting Herbs* are added in small amounts to help mask the bitter taste of other herbs, direct assimilation, and help to offset any adverse effects. The inclusion of conducting herbs maximizes utilization of the other herbs thus helping to harmonize the entire formula. An example of herbs that would provide the properties required for conducting herb inclusion would be licorice, jujube, and cayenne. Conducting herbs will make up about 5% of your formula.

Forms of Herbal Preparation

Many conditions can be alleviated quicker when treatment is administered both externally (topically) as well as internally. Containers used for preparation should be glass, stainless steel, or clay, and they should be sterilized prior to putting any preparations in them.

Author Disclaimer: Administration and/or application suggestions found in this section are to be used as general guidelines only. The potency of individual preparations as well as the seriousness of the condition, the person's age, metabolism, diet, and weight are subject to substantial variation. Adjust administration and/or application accordingly.

Note: Preparations that are administered via subcutaneous or intravenous injections are recommended for professional use only.

Bath

Herbal baths are tub baths to which infusions or decoctions have been added. They are used for softening, scenting, or moisturizing the skin; opening or closing pores; reducing inflammation or pain; stimulating the system; relieving itching; easing muscular aches; etc. *Warm Bath*: A warm bath has a temperature of approximately 90-95° F and is used once a day for about ten minutes. Fill the bath halfway (about to the navel) to three quarters full. This warm bath is useful for such things as helping one feel calm and relaxed, hypotension, soothing nervous tension, or easing menopausal/menstrual problems. *Hot Bath*: A hot bath has a temperature of approximately 100-113° F and is used once a day for about five to eight minutes. Fill the bath halfway (about to the navel) to three quarters full. The hot bath is useful for treating a cold or flu and is generally followed by bundling up in blankets to promote perspiration and help eliminate body wastes. *Cold Bath*: A cold bath has a temperature of approximately 55-65° F and is used once a day for about five to fifteen seconds. Fill the bath halfway (about to the navel). This cold half-bath will help to stimulate the system causing increased heart action, with the heart slowing down after the initial shock, and is useful for such things as headache, insomnia, or nervous conditions. Add 2-4 cups herbal infusion or decoction directly into the bath water, or you can place whole plant material inside of a small muslin bag and hang it under the faucet letting the water run over it. Avoid hot baths if you have congestive heart failure (CHF).

Body Pack

A body pack is a mixture of herbs and other various ingredients that are made into a paste and applied to the body. As the mixture dries, it draws the impurities to the surface of the skin where they cling to the pack and are removed when the pack is rinsed off. Cleanse your body thoroughly prior to applying the body pack. Spread a thick mixture over your body making sure to avoid the eyes and mucous membranes. Let the mixture remain on your body for 15-20 minutes or until the mixture is dry and your body feels tight. Rinse or shower your body with warm water thoroughly until all of the pack is removed. Pat dry. Follow with a moisturizing lotion if needed. Apply once a month.

Bolus

A bolus is a suppository that is made using powdered herbs and is inserted into the rectum to assist in the healing of those conditions such as hemorrhoids, itching, etc. Add ½ part slippery elm powder to your selected powdered herbs. Warm cocoa butter over low heat using a double boiler. Remove from heat and mix in enough of the cocoa butter with your powdered herbs until they reach a firm consistency. Place the mixture on waxed paper and let it cool slightly. Once the mixture has cooled to where you can comfortably handle it, roll it into several small tubular shapes about the size of your little finger, and then cut each tube into 1-inch size pieces. Refrigerate all the pieces until they harden. Once hardened, remove the amount required from the refrigerator and allow it to warm up a bit prior to insertion. Insert 2-3 of the pieces into the rectum prior to bedtime. It is advisable to wear some form of protective undergarment while using a bolus, as the body's heat will cause the bolus to melt. Insert a fresh bolus each night for 5 days. At the end of the five-day period use a rectal cleansing rinse or enema of 2-4 cups warm water.

Candied Rose Petals (*confectio rosae*)
Rub or soak fresh red rose petals with warmed rose water. Lightly coat each petal with fine white sugar. Lay petals on a cookie sheet and heat in oven on a low setting until dried. Drying time varies so it is important to monitor closely so petals do not burn.

Capsules
Capsules contain the ground or powdered form of the crude herb and are less potent than tinctures. They keep indefinitely, are convenient to take, and they allow the ingestion of those herbs that have a bitter or offensive taste. To begin, you will need empty capsules. These can usually be purchased at your local health food store and come in a range of sizes with 00 being the most commonly used. Filling empty capsules with herbs is fairly easy. To put powdered herbs into the capsule, pull the capsule apart and press the open end of the capsule halves into the powdered herbs filling both halves. Put the capsule back together making sure it is tight. Capsules, usually tasteless, can be swallowed whole, or they may be open and mixed with applesauce or a cream-style cereal such as oatmeal.

Castor Oil Pack
Castor oil packs help stimulate the lymphatic system to draw away toxins. Applied externally, a castor oil pack is useful for glandular swelling, cysts, skin eruptions, abnormal growths, cancers, and hard swellings. To prepare a castor oil pack, purchase a good quality castor oil. Soak a cotton pad or piece of flannel in the oil and apply it as a moist pack over the affected area. Cover the pack with a thin layer of plastic and leave in place for 30-60 minutes. Placing a hot water bottle or heating pad on top of the pack will help stimulate absorption.

Compress
A compress is used to relieve fever, pain, or inflammation, or to promote the healing of an injury. Compresses can be applied either cold or hot. Prepare a strong infusion or decoction (refrigerate several hours or overnight for a cold compress). Place a piece of cloth or toweling into the liquid until it is saturated. Wring the toweling out until it no longer drips, and apply it as cold or as hot as possible directly onto the affected part of the body. The toweling for a cold compress will need to be re-saturated about every half-hour or when the toweling warms to body temperature. A hot compress will need to be re-saturated when the toweling feels cool. Placing a hot water bottle or heating pad on top of the compress will help to retain the heat.

Crude Herb
Collected, dried, cut, and sifted are the original way herbs have been prepared since ancient times. This form of herb has its advantages as you can actually see, smell, and taste the herb. Crude herbs can often be found in herb shops all over the world. Herbs in their crude forms are used to make many forms of herbal concoctions.

Decoction
A process using heat to draw out a plant's properties. This method ensures the release of the properties into the water and is mainly used with heavier plant material such as bark, roots, seeds, or nuts.

Decoctions are stronger than infusions and are used externally or internally to alleviate a wide variety of conditions. The herb to water ratio is generally one ounce of herb to one pint of water. Place whole, broken or chopped up herbs into a pan and cover with water. Bring water to a boil, then cover pan and let simmer for 20-25 minutes. Strain prior to use.

Douche

Administered vaginally, a douche will cleanse, disinfect, and soothe vaginal problems. Prepare a decoction or infusion. Strain and cool to body temperature. Fill a douche bulb, insert it into the vagina and squeeze slowly and gently until all the formula is expressed into the vaginal cavity (it is best to do this while straddling the toilet, standing in the bathtub, or lying down with a container such as a bedpan underneath you, as the formula will run back out of the vagina). Avoid using a douche if you are pregnant or suspect you are pregnant.

Electuary

An old fashioned way of administering unpalatable herbs to children, the elderly, those persons who enjoy taking herbal medicines but don't care for the often times bitter taste, or persons who cannot/will not swallow a capsule or pill. Mix a small amount of herb with honey, peanut butter, or maple syrup until it reaches a soft-mass consistency.

Enema

An enema is not only used to relieve the discomforts of constipation, it is also used to cleanse the colon or administer nutrition to a person who can take food no other way. For a cleansing enema, insert an enema tube into the rectum and administer 2-6 cups of plain warm water 2-3 times a day or until elimination takes place, or for a nutritional enema, substitute an herbal infusion in place of the water (it is best to do this while straddling the toilet, or lying down with a container such as a bedpan underneath you). Allow the liquid to come back out when it needs to. Don't try to retain the liquid inside for as long as possible, as this may create unnecessary discomfort or possibly cause the colon to balloon.

Enflcuragc

The process of extracting oils from flowers by placing them on a fatty body such as purified lard. Spread a ½ inch of lard onto a glass tray (ridges can be made in the lard to further assist absorption). Sprinkle fresh flowers over the lard. Renew the flowers each morning. Repeat this process (may take several days) until the lard fully absorbs as much of the oils as to make it very aromatic. Scrape the lard off the glass tray. Melt the lard at the *lowest* temperature possible. Strain.

Eye Drops

Place fresh plant material into a juicer to extract the plants juice. Dried plant material can also be used when made into an infusion first. Strain the juice through a fine cloth several times. Add an equal amount of vegetable glycerin and 15-20% boric acid to preserve the mixture. Put into a small dropper bottle. Apply one to two drops per eye as needed.

Extracts

A preparation obtained by combing an herbal substance and a solvent (grain alcohol, vegetable glycerin, water, vinegar, etc.), and then evaporating the solution down to the required concentration, or to a complete or approximate dryness. Bottles are often mislabeled as extracts when indeed they are actually tinctures, and many books refer to extracts and tinctures as being one and the same. Extracts have about the same advantages and disadvantages as tinctures, and although they start out the same, the end result of an extract is a much more concentrated form. Always prepare extracts at the lowest temperature possible as to high of a temperature may destroy the constituents and the volatile plant oils. Dried or fresh plants may be used. When using fresh plants, you may wish to wilt them (spread them out on a newspaper) for several hours. This process reduces their water content thus reducing spoilage. Extracts are made in liquid, granular, or solid form. They range in concentration from 2 to 100 times that of tinctures. The strength of the extract should be listed on the bottle in the form of a ratio. The first number of the ratio tells you how much herb is present, and the second number tells you how much solvent is in the preparation. Ratios for extracts can range anywhere from 4:1 to 10:1 and up. Since extracts are quite concentrated, they can have a bitter taste and it is perfectly acceptable to mix them with tea or water.

Note: Rubber stoppers, which I personally don't recommend, are sometimes used to cap the containers of extracts. They have a tendency to break down and impart a rubbery taste to the mixture.

An *Alcohol Extract* is a preparation containing grain alcohol either as a preservative or a solvent, and herbs, of such strength that one (1) one cubic centimeter (cc.) of the solution closely represents the activity of one (1) one gram of the dry, powdered herb. To make this type of extract, add one to four ounces of plant material to one pint of grain alcohol (don't use isopropyl rubbing alcohol as it is VERY toxic). This ratio can be adjusted dependant upon the amount of mixture you choose to make. Let it sit for 2-4 weeks. Shake the container and stir the contents twice daily. When the mixture is ready, strain it through a fine strainer or paper filter and allow it to evaporate down to the desired concentration. To make a *Cold Extract*, place twice the amount of plant material as would be generally used for an infusion into a non-metallic container. Pour over enough cold water to cover the plant material and let it sit for 12-14 hours. Strain. An *Acetic Extract* is a preperation made with 100% vinegar or other acetic menstrum (solvent), and combined with herbs in the same degree of strength as an alcohol extract. To prepare a *Powdered Extract*, cook herbs as teas in a large vat. The solid residue is removed and the remaining liquid is evaporated down, dried, and pulverized until only powder remains. Powdered extracts are about four times as potent as crude herbs, they store well, and the chemical concentrations discourage the growth of bacteria. An *Aqueous Extract* is a preperation made with 100% water as the menstrum, and combined with herbs in the same degree of strength as an alcohol extract. Adding plant material to water and simmering until the liquid is reduced to half makes a Heated Extract. Strain the solution into a non-metallic container and cover until it has cooled to body temperature. Once cooled, uncover the container and let the strained extract evaporate until it reaches the desired concentration. This evaporation process can be repeated and will yield a more potent extract each time. A *Fluidglycerate* is a preperation made with 50% each of vegetable glycerin and distilled water, combined with herbs in the same degree of strength as a fluidextract. A *Solid Extract* is prepared by evaporating a solution of the active part of an herb. To make this type of extract, use the isolated chemical constituent of an herb and evaporate it down to the required consistency. This type of extract is extremely potent and recommended for professional use.

Eyewash

Eyewash is a preparation used externally that can be helpful for itchy, red, or puffy eyelids, which may characterize conjunctivitis. To prepare eyewash, make an infusion or decoction. Cool and strain prior to use. Tilt your head toward the same side as the infected eye. *Slowly* pour the eyewash over the infected eye starting at the inside corner. To avoid transfer of infecton or reinfection, use fresh eyewash for each eye.

Facemask

A facemask is a mixture of herbs and other various ingredients that are made into a paste and applied to the face. As the mixture dries, it draws the impurities to the surface of the skin where they cling to the mask and are removed when the mask is peeled or rinsed off. To apply a facemask, cleanse your face thoroughly prior to applying the facemask. Spread a thick mixture over your face making sure to avoid the mouth and eye area. Let the mixture remain on your face for 10-15 minutes or until the mixture is dry and your face feels tight. Rinse your face with warm water thoroughly until all of the pack is removed. Pat dry. Use a moisturizing lotion if needed. Recommended application is once a month.

Flower Water

Flower water's soothing, refreshing, and astringent properties make it useful for face and body spritzs, skin wash, hair rinse, etc. To prepare flower water you will need 2 cups of freshly picked flower petals such as rose, lilac, or elder (the flower petal to water ratio depends on the color and fragrance desired), and 1-quart of *cold* water. Put the flower petals into an enamel saucepan and pour over water. Bring the water almost to a boil. Remove container from heat, let cool, and strain. Refrigerate any unused portion. Discard after 2-4 days.

Footbath

Footbaths are useful for ephidrosis (excessive perspiration) or skin infection. Make an infusion or a decoction. Cool until water temperature is comfortable (usually around 108° F or 43° C). Do not put your feet into very hot or scalding water. Pour cooled infusion or decoction into a basin or tub large enough to accommodate the hands or feet. Immerse the feet for 15-20 minutes two to three times a day until condition improves. Avoid footbaths if there are open wounds.

Gargle/Mouth Rinse

Gargles and mouth rinses are helpful to alleviate halitosis, gum/mouth/throat irritation, or periodontal disease. Make an infusion or a decoction. Cool. Gargle or swish liquid around in mouth for approximately one minute. Do not swallow.

Ghee (Clarified Butter)

Ghee is mainly used in treating inflammatory conditions, fever and ulcer. Ghee is an excellent base to use in ointments, or added to pastes. To make ghee heat one pound of raw unsalted butter on low heat until the white fats separate from the oil. Skim off the white fat, which is the ghee, and store in the refrigerator for later use.

Herbal Ash

Herbal ash, made from the carbonized residue of nonpoisonous herbs, plants, and wood (shavings), and is mainly used an antidote to absorb various non-caustic poisons that have been inadvertently ingested. There are a few variations to this preparation, but I find this one is the easiest. Put dried, crushed or crumbled, plant material into a large pan (preferably cast iron or one that will be used specifically for this method as the pan will end up scorched). Set the dried plant material on fire using only a match (Don't use any lighter fluid etc.), and burn until it has been reduced to ashes. Add approximately 1 to 1 ½ teaspoons of the ashes to a glass of water. You can also put the ashes into a gelatin capsule and take it in this way; however, the absorption effect is not as quick. Administer every hour (gradually tapering the dosage) until symptoms abate. Place any remaining ash in a sealed container and keep it handy, as it will keep indefinitely.

Herbal Tobacco

Some herbs are smoked therapeutically to relieve respiratory conditions, as an aid to tobacco smoking cessation, as an alternative to tobacco, for ceremonial use, or to simply help one to relax. Smoke able herbs contain no nicotine and are non-addicting. They can be smoked singly or in combination with other smoke able herbs. Place a small amount of the selected herbs into a waterpipe, which helps cut down on the harshness that sometimes accompanies herbal smoking. For use as a therapeutic application, inhale and fill the lungs with smoke, then fully exhale (do this six to ten times for a single treatment). Peppermint or spearmint is usually added to all smoke blends for its cooling menthol taste. *Bidis* are non-tobacco cigarettes, generally smoked in India, which include the herbs of spearmint, pleurisy root, jimson weed, marjoram, bitter orange, basil, and poppy. Bidis contain 65 mg. of scopolamine and 16 mg. of atropine per cigarette. Due to their nauseating effects when smoked alone, jimsonweed and lobelia should always be combined in *very* small amounts with other smokable herbs.

Infusions

Infusions are used externally or internally and relieve a wide variety of ailments. The aerial or aboveground portions (flowers, leaves, buds, fruits) are generally the parts that are used. The general herb to water ratios are as follows. Dried Herbs: *Weak Infusion*: add ½ ounce of herbs to one pint of water. *Normal Infusion*: add one ounce of herbs to one pint of water. *Strong Infusion*: add two ounces of herbs to one pint of water. Fresh Herbs: *Weak Infusion*: add one handful of herbs to one pint of water. *Normal Infusion*: add three handfuls of herb to one pint of water. *Strong Infusion*: add six handfuls of herb to one pint of water. Whether you choose fresh or dried herbs for use in your infusional formulas, the guidelines below will assist you in determining the appropriate method and proportions. Covering the container helps to retain the herb's properties. Strain prior to use. A *Cold Infusion* is generally prepared using powdered herbs (whole herbs can also be used), which are already partially broken down and will sufficiently extract their constituents when mixed into cold water. Stir powdered herbs into cold water or place whole herbs in a container and cover them with cool water. Set in a warm or sunny place for 2-3 hours, or leave them overnight. Certain herbs are better extracted in cool water as some of their properties may be damaged by heat. This process ensures the release of the more delicate properties into the water. Preparing a *Hot Infusion* is as easy as placing herbs and water into a pan. Bring the water to a slow boil, turn off the heat, cover, and steep from 10-15 minutes up to several hours. This method allows the aromatic principle of the herb to remain intact. An *Infusional Decoction* requires the preparation of an infusion, then, pour the entire infusion over the heavier plant material such as roots, bark, seeds, or nuts. Bring the mixture to a boil, reduce the heat and simmer the entire mixture for an additional 15-20 minutes.

Inhalation Therapy

Inhalation therapy is used primarily for respiratory conditions helping relieve allergy, colds, asthma, sinusitis, and bronchitis. Inhalation (Steam) Therapy: Helps remove toxins, soften and soothe the skin, unclog pores, etc. Put herbs into a bowl (glass or metal works best). Pour over very hot water. Drape a towel over your head (helps contain the steam) and lean over the bowl. Inhale the steam for no longer than 5 minutes. Follow with a facial rinse of cool water. Steam 1-2 times a week. Inhalation Therapy may also be used in the form of atomization (spray), or simply put a few drops on some cotton or a hankerchief, from which the vapor may be inhaled.

Juice

Juices are made by washing fresh herbs or fruits under cold running water, cutting them up into pieces, and running them through a juice extractor until they turn into a liquid. If you are using dry herbs, cover them with water and let them soak for 18-24 hours. To hand juice herbs, cut up and mash the plant material, then place it in a piece of cheesecloth and squeeze the pulp to release the juice into a container or a drinking glass. Some common herbs used to make juice are fruits, garlic, lemons, limes, onions, or parsley.

Leach (Lixiviate)

Leeching is a process performed prior to eating or using certain nuts. It consists of separating soluble from insoluble matter (the removal of tannic acid and certain toxic substances) by using cold water to dissolve or wash out the soluble matter. Grind the nuts (wear gloves if you have sensitive skin). There are two leaching methods one can use. The first method is to put the freshly ground nuts in a tight-weave mesh or cheesecloth bag. Place the bag under cold running water and rinse numerous times to wash away the excess tannic acid (this process may take several hours). The second method is to soak the freshly ground nuts in cold water overnight, then boil them for half an hour and strain off the water. Spread the nuts out to dry. Once dried, reduce them to a meal and toast in a pan. The meal is then ready for use.

Liniment

Liniments are used externally for muscle and joint pain, skin irritations, sprain, and bruises, as well as for disinfecting wounds (minor). They are prepared in the same way as tinctures, but since they are for external uses only, isopropyl alcohol is used. Macerate powdered, cut, or whole herbs in isopropyl alcohol for approximately 2 weeks (powdered herbs generally take 3-4 days). Elixirs, volatile oils, extracts, or tinctures can also be added to the mixture. Strain prior to use. Gently massage into area of discomfort.

Maceration
The maceration process blends the herbs healing properties with the liquid. The herb to liquid ratio is generally one small handful of herbs to 2-3 ounces of liquid. Place dried or fresh (bruise fresh herbs before placing into the liquid) herbs into a liquid such as alcohol, water, or oil, and let sit for 6-8 days. Strain prior to use.

Medicinal Tea
Medicinal teas can be made from most herbs and are not the same as beverage teas. Beverage teas (like the kinds you purchase in the grocery store) are extremely weak and generally have little if any therapeutic value. Medicinal teas, prepared by infusion or decoction, are very strong therapeutically due to the retention of their active constituents, and are extremely useful for acute and chronic conditions. To make a pot of medicinal tea, place approximately one ounce of selected dried herbs (if using fresh herbs, double the amount of herb) loosely inside of a stainless steel pot. Pour over enough water (about one pint) to cover the herbs and let them soak for ten minutes. Cover pot and place on stovetop. Simmer herbs for twenty to twenty five minutes. Strain and pour into a cup. Tea can be served hot, cold or iced depending on the purpose, and may be sweetened with honey or stevia.

Moxibustion Therapy
Moxibustion Therapy has been used since ancient times to ease pain and facilitate healing. It consists of dried, finely shredded mugwort down (from the leaves) that is rolled into either a cigar-shaped tube known as a *Moxa Stick* (or burning stick), or formed into several small pyramid-shaped cones. The cones once lit and smoldering are placed on the energy centers or affected areas of the body and allowed to burn down to the body, or the tube, once lit and smoldering, is passed slowly over the energy centers or affected areas on the body. This therapy helps to promote blood circulation, relaxation of the underlying nerves, immune system stimulation, reduction of pain, and helps facilitate whole body healing. To separate the down from the leaves, heat the leaves until they are very warm, and then rub them between your hands until only the cottony fibers remain. Once the down is formed in the shape you want, light it on fire, and immediately extinguish the flame, allowing the down to smolder. The advantage of using mugwort is that it burns quickly and at a low temperature.

Oils
Herbal oils ease burns, earache, muscle and joint pain, skin problems, wounds, etc., and are used in enemas, douches, ointments, and massage, as well as hair and skin care formulas. When preparing oils, powdered, dried, or fresh whole herbs may be used. If using fresh herbs, make certain that the herbs are free of any extra moisture. You may want to wilt the herbs prior to use by putting them in a dry, warm place overnight to ensure that all the moisture is gone prior to use. There are several different methods to preparing medicated oils. A few of them include the *Stovetop Method*, which requires constant monitoring and the decoction of approximately one part herbs in sixteen parts of water until all the water has evaporated. Combine 2 ounces of herbs with one cup of oil. Let this mixture stand for one to two days, strain again and bottle. To prepare the *Standard Method* place herbs into a container and pour over

base oil making sure herbs are covered and submerged. Set the mixture on a countertop and let stand for 2-4 weeks. Strain prior to use. The *Sun Method* is similar to the standard method in that the herbs are placed in a container and covered with base oil. The container is then covered and placed in a warm, sunny spot. Let the herbs macerate in the oil for approximately 2-4 weeks. Strain prior to use. Store in a cool, dark area. The *Oven Method* requires constant monitoring. Put herbs into an oven safe container and cover with base oil (or you may use canning jars). Place the container or jars in a larger pan with enough water to cover the bottom half of the container or jars. Turn oven on lowest heat setting and allow mixture to macerate for several hours. Check frequently, don't allow oil and herbs to overheat and burn. Let cool and strain prior to use. There are many base oils to choose from when preparing your medicated oil. Base oils that may be used include *Sweet Almond Oil* (light yellowish color/subtle almond scent) penetrates quickly to beautify, nourish, and pamper all skin types, and maintains a shelf life of approx. 8-10 months. *Hazelnut Oil* (light brownish color/subtle nutty scent) is used for skin that is damaged or dry, and has a shelf life of 6-8 months. *Jojoba Oil* (dark brownish color/odorless) is a natural emulsifier and due to its high vitamin E (a natural preservative) content will not turn rancid. It nourishes, softens, and smoothes all skin types, and is also used in hair conditioner and shampoo formulas. Due to its SPF 4 (sun protection factor) it is often added to suntan lotion formulas. *Wheat Germ Oil* (reddish color/strong scent) heals, nourishes, soothes, and supports skin regeneration. It is used for aging or dry skin. Due to the high lecithin content as well as the presence of vitamins A, D, and E, this oil is a natural preservative, and has a shelf life of 8-12 months. Adding a small amount (10-20 %) of wheat germ oil to your other base oils will help to extend their shelf life. *Coconut Oil* (solid white to semi clear/subtle coconut scent) improves and increases the moisture absorption of damaged, dry skin and is also used in hair, massage, and sun care formulas. It is a solid at room temperature and will liquefy when the container is placed in warm water. It has a shelf life of approximately 8-12 months. *Saint John's Wort Oil* (ruby red color/mild scent) is generally prepared using either olive, sweet almond, or jojoba as a base oil. It has a shelf life of approximately 12 months, and is used in all types of skin care formulas, as well as the application of a few drops to the forehead and temples for depression. *Olive Oil* (pale color/strong scent) is a wonderful disinfectant and wound healer. It has a shelf life of approximately 12 months, and works well for infected skin and arthritic or rheumatoid conditions. *Aloe Vera Oil* (pale color/ mild scent) moisturizes and rejuvenates damaged, dry, infected, or tired skin, and is used for various skin problems such as eczema and psoriasis. It has a shelf life of approximately 10-12 months. Herbal oils generally store for 8-12 months. Avoid the use of and discard any oils that have a foul odor or the presence of mold.

Ointment (Salve)
Ointments help ease and remedy many skin conditions such as bites, dry skin, irritations, and minor burns and wounds. Applied externally to the area of discomfort, the body absorbs the healing properties of the ointment through the skin. Decoct herbs in water until fully extracted (20-25 minutes). Strain. To prepare the base heat approximately one pint of oil. Add approximately 1½ ounces of melted beeswax. Add the decoction or mix about one ounce of powdered herbs into the base (it may turn dark in color) until it reaches the desired consistency. Preserve each ounce of base by adding 1-3 drops of vitamin E oil or a small amount (one teaspoon per quart of ointment) of gum or tincture of benzoin. If the ointment is to thick add a few more drops of oil, and if the ointment is too runny add a bit more

beeswax. Cool and pour into containers. When ointment has thickened to a cold cream consistency it is ready for use. Ointments last for several months.

Paste

Herbal pastes are useful for a variety of ailments and are made from herbs that have been mixed with honey, oil, or ghee. Pastes can be eaten directly from a spoon, stirred into an infusion or decoction, or used as in a poultice/plaster. Pastes maintain their potency for a long period of time if they are refrigerated, and if the paste is made using honey only, it will keep indefinitely with no refrigeration necessary. Using a mortar and pestle or an electric grinder, mash herbs into a paste consistency. A small amount of water, or honey may be necessary with the use of dry herbs.

Pessary

A pessary is an herbal suppository that is inserted into the vagina and assists in the healing of those conditions such as vaginitis, moniliasis, etc. A vaginal pessary is generally made close to the same circumference as your ring finger. Add ½ part slippery elm powder to your selected powdered herbs. Warm cocoa butter over low heat. Remove from heat and mix in enough cocoa butter with your powdered herbs until they reach a firm consistency. Place the herbal mixture onto waxed paper and roll into a small tubular shape. Cool the rolled mixture slightly and cut into one or two inch lengths. Refrigerate until hard. Once hardened, remove from the refrigerator and allow it to warm up a bit prior to insertion. Insert all of the pieces into the vagina just prior to bedtime (it is advisable to wear a sanitary pad or some form of protective undergarment while using a pessary, as the body's heat will cause the pessary to melt). The next day use a vaginal douche consisting of 2-4 cups warm water. General recommendations are to insert a fresh pessary each night for 1 week.

Pills

Pills consist of the ground or powdered form of crude herbs. They are taken for convenience and are actually quite easy to make. There are two methods for making pills. The first method is to mix powdered herbs with a little water or honey until it resembles a paste-like consistency. Roll or form this mixture into small oval, round, or desired shapes. The second method, requiring a bit more time, is to decoct herbs down to a paste-like consistency. Scrape this paste off the bottom of the container and roll it into small, grain-size pellets. Dry for 24-48 hours prior to ingestion. Pills, having a bit of a taste, can be swallowed whole or crushed and mixed with applesause or a cream-style cereal such as oatmeal.

Plaster

Plasters are used externally to relieve muscle and joint pain, etc. Mix powdered herbs with slightly warmed olive oil until it reaches a semimedium paste-like consistency. Spread the mixture onto a thin piece of material such as muslin, cotton, or gauze and fold cloth over so mixture is covered and will not come in direct contact with the skin. Place the plaster directly over the area of discomfort. Leave on for no longer than 10-5 minutes. Do not apply plasters directly over varicose veins. Avoid applying plasters if you have a circulatory problem.

Poultice

A poultice is a source of moist heat that can last for several hours and assists the body in absorbing the healing properties of the herbs through the skin. Used externally to relieve pain, inflammation, insect bites or stings, bruises, sprain, etc. Fresh or dried herbs can be used. Make an infusion, or mix powdered herbs with hot water until it forms a thick paste. Spread the mixture onto a thin piece of material such as muslin, cotton, or gauze and fold cloth over so mixture remains inside. Use a rolling pin to roll over the cloth dampening it with the moisture from the herbs inside. Place the poultice directly over area of discomfort. Cover the poultice with a hot water bottle and lay a woolen or very thick towel over the hot water bottle to retain the heat. Leave on for 20-25 minutes.

Powder

Powders begin as dried crude herbs, which are ground into a powder form using a morter and pestle or an electric herb grinder. Powders are the best way to achieve an even mix of herbs for use in capsules, or stirring them directly into infusions or decoctions. They are more efficiently utilized since they are already partially broken down, and less quantity of herb is needed than when using whole herbs. Powders will generally maintain their potency for six to eight months, and can be mixed with honey, oil, or ghee.

Sitz Bath

Used to relieve infection (bladder, prostate), hemorrhoids, or vaginal discomforts. Make an infusion. Run bath water (as hot as is comfortable) until water is hip deep. Add approximately two quarts of an infusion to bath water. Soak for 20-30 minutes. Avoid taking a hot bath if you have congestive heart failure.

Skin Wash

Skin washes are used for inflammation, sweating, acne, or skin problems. Prepare an infusion and let cool. Pour into a basin. Dip a clean washcloth into infusion and wash infected or irritated area. Pat dry.

Snuff

Snuff inhaled through the nostrils will help to clear and open nasal passages. To prepare an *Herbal Snuff*, powder herbs until they reach a talcum powder consistency. Take a small pinch of the powdered herb between your thumb and index finger and inhale this into the nasal passages. A *Salt-Water Snuff* is prepared by mixing 1 teaspoon of salt into a cup of warm water. Place 3-4 drops into each nostril.

Solution

A solution is a liquid that consists of a mixture of two or more solutes (substances) that are dissolved in a solvent. *Aqueous Solution*: A solution in which distilled water is the solvent. *Alcohol Solution* (ethyl hydroxide): A solution in which grain alcohol is the solvent. *Ethereal Solution* (ethyl oxide): A solution in which ether is the solvent. *Fiftieth-Normal Solution* (N/50 or 0.02): A solution $^1/_{50}$ (one-fiftieth) the strength of a normal solution. *Half-Normal Solution* (N/2): A solution half the strength of a normal solution. *Hundreth-Normal Solution* (N/100 or 0.01): A solution $^1/_{100}$ (one-hundreth) the strength of a normal solution. *Normal Solution* (N/1): A solution containing in each 1,000 cc. 1 gram equivalent weight of the active substance. *Standard Solution*: A solution that contains in each quart (liter) a definate amount of any regent. *Thousandth-Normal Solution* (N/1000 or 0.001): A solution $^{1}/_{1000}$ (one-thousandth) the strength of a normal solution. Solution Examples: *Normal Saline Solution*: Dissolve 0.9% of sodium chloride (common table salt) in distilled water and administer via intravenous injection following hemorrhage or severe diarrhea. *Thymol Solution*: A 1:1000 solution of thymol oil to be applied topically for use as an antirheumatic and antiseptic.

Spray

Sprays are used externally as facial spritzs, for sunburn or windburn, insect bites or stings, as an insect repellent, for skin problems, etc. Make a decoction, extract, or an infusion (diluted volatile oils may also be added). Put liquid into a spray bottle. Shake well before using. Avoid eye and mucous membrane areas if using volatile (essential) oils.

Syrup

Syrups are quite tasty and more readily taken by children or the elderly. They help soothe and coat the throat, and are quite useful for respiratory discomforts such as cough, bronchitis, sore throat, etc. A syrup base consists of honey, brown sugar, glycerin, or maple syrup. To make syrup using the no heat method, mix 2-3 tablespoons of base with 1 teaspoon of powdered herbs and administer in this form. To make *Herbal Syrup* using the heat method, boil base in a pint of infusion until it resembles a syrupy consistency. To make *Plain Syrup* using the heat method, boil base in one pint of water and mix in powdered herbs.

Tinctures

An herb placed in grain alcohol or vegetable glycerin is known as a tincture. The alcohol draws out the active properties of the herb, concentrates it, and helps preserve it. Tinctures are convenient to administer, assimilate quickly, and are easily digested. Tinctures assist in the detoxification of the body's tissues and are great for use as preventive therapy. They can be taken as drops in tea or water, used in a compress, or applied during massage therapy. The strength of the tincture should be listed on the bottle in the form of a ratio. The first number of the ratio tells you how much herb is present, and the second number tells you how much solvent is in the preparation. Ratios for tinctures range from 1:2 to 1:5 and up. The herbs full taste comes through in the alcohol and can be strong or unpleasant, so it is perfectly acceptable to mix them with tea or water. Alcohol-based tinctures have an indefinate shelf life. Note: Rubber stoppers, which I personally don't recommend are sometimes used to cap the containers of tinctures. They have a tendency break down and impart a rubbery taste to the mixture.

Alcohol Tinctures are generally 50% alcohol and 50% water. To make an *Alcohol Tincture* you will need one to four ounces of plant material, a glass container, and a pint of grain alcohol. Vodka is usually the alcohol of choice as it naturally contains the appropriate alcohol to water ratio, although brandy, gin, or rum can be used (don't use isopropyl-rubbing alcohol as it is VERY toxic). Dried or fresh plants can be used for making your tinctures. Avoid using plants that have been exposed to car emissions, pesticides, or other toxic substances. Remove any dirt and break the plant into small pieces allowing the alcohol to absorb more effectively. Place 1-4 ounces of herbs in a large glass jar and cover with approximately eight to twelve ounces (or about an inch above the herbs) with alcohol. Shake the mixture to expose all the plant surfaces to the alcohol, then label and date the jar. If your tincture is made using dried herbs, you may notice that they absorb quite a bit of alcohol in the first few days. If this occurs, simply add more alcohol to cover the herbs again. Shake your tincture twice daily for two weeks. Strain your mixture through a piece of muslin or a paper filter (this may need to be done a couple of times). Pour the tincture (a small funnel comes in handy here) into smaller amber or dark colored glass bottles (preferably ones with a dropper) filling them half full, then fill the remaining half with distilled water, shake, and your tincture is ready for use. Most alcohol tinctures have a potency life of 3-6 years. An *Aqueous Tincture* is a preperation made with 100% distilled water as the menstrum (solvent) combined with herbs in the same degree of strength as an alcohol tincture. A *Glycerite Tincture* is an alcohol-free preparation made with 50% each vegetable glycerin and distilled water combined with an herbal substance in the same degree and strength as an alcohol tincture. Glycerite tinctures have a potency life of 1-2 years, and are an excellent choice for elderly or children's remedies because of its sweet taste, as well as for those individuals who are recovering alcoholics or who do not care for the taste of alcohol. Make sure your glycerite tinctures are made with 100% vegetable glycerin. An *Acetic Tincture* has a shorter potency life (6-12 months) than tinctures prepared with alcohol or glycerin. Acetic tinctures are primarily used for those who have sensitivity to alcohol or glycerin, or when they will be administered for a long period of time. To make an acetic tincture, follow the same instructions as for making an alcoholic tincture, only substitute vinegar in place of the alcohol. Make sure the herbs are completely submerged in the vinegar. A *Glycerinated Tincture* is an alcohol tincture to which a small amount (¼ tsp to 1oz. bottle) of vegetable glycerin has been added.

Administration, Dosage, and Duration of Treatment

Administration Guidelines

As with other pharmaceuticals, herbs should be administered at certain times of the day, because the correct time of day could be important in attaining maximum benefit. Herbs that are administered on an empty stomach are effective in treating conditions such as the common cold, diarrhea, or flu. Herbs that are administered before meals are effective for intestinal toning or weight reduction. After meal herbs are effective for complaints such as indigestion. Herbs that are administered between meals are effective for nervous or urinary problems, and those conditions occuring in children or the elderly are effectively treated with herbs that are administered with food.

Dosage Guidelines

Dosage guidelines for herbal preparations have been established over the years, however, these guidelines for quantity and frequency may need to be adjusted to each individual based on a variety of factors, such as age, the seriousness of the condition or problem, dietary habits, metabolism, stress levels, weight, the specific nature of the respective preparation, and the concomitant use of other herbs or drugs. Because of individual body differences incredible results may be achieved from using one specific herb, conversely, for another individual that same herb may offer little or no result. Dosages typically involve what is referred to as a therapeutic range. If the dosage says 1-3 grams, 1 gram would be the lowest amount of herb taken to have an effect, and 3 grams would be the highest, safest amount to take of that herb. It is recommended that you start out with the lowest doasage, and if all goes well and you experience no adverse reactions then gradually increase the dosage up to the highest, suggested amount for that particular herb. Herbs take time to work, and the length of time herbs are used will depend on whether they're being used as a therapy to ease symptoms, a tonic to refresh and energize, or both. A general recommendation when using herbs is the activity/rest principle, whereby one would use herbs for six days then take one day off, six weeks then take one week off, six months then take one month off. Rest periods are very important in that they enable the integration of the herb into the physiology. When utilizing herbs both externally as well as internally one can attain greater healing benefits. There are five common methods of determining herbal dosages. *Pharmacologic*: In this method the amount of an herbal preparation is sufficient to induce specific, noticeable, strong, continued changes. *Physiologic*: This method recommends the minimum dosage of an herb required to induce a physiologic change. For example, a laxative would be administered *only* until a change in bowel activity occurs. *Homeopathic*: The homeopathic method is based on the principle of 'like cures like'. For example, an herbal preparation that causes dysuria and renal damage in high doses is given in very low doses to remedy urinary tract infection and kidney disease. *Folk Medicine*: A method based on ancient knowledge of plant use. Herbalists use mild, nontoxic herbs in large amounts, and collect only those plants that grow freely and close at hand. Also called wise woman herbalism. *Age and Weight*: The age method is useful for children and is based on inner-system maturity (the ability to metabolize, utilize, and eliminate herbs). The weight method (similar to Clark's rule) is useful for individuals who fall outside the average weight range, requiring an increased or decreased dosage.

Children's Dosage Guidelines

When administering herbal remedies to children, it is very important to decrease the dosage. To do this you can use the child's weight as a guide. Only mild herbs should be administered to children over the age of 10, and herbal remedies should never be administered to infants. The following guideline will assist you in calculating the approximate dosage for children.

Clark's Rule:

Take the child's weight in pounds and divide it by 150. This conversion will give you the approximate fraction of the adult dosage to be administered to a child. Example: A child of 50 pounds. Divide 50 by 150. This will give you 50/150 or ⅓ the adult dosage.

Elderly Dosage Guidelines

Since the health of the aged is generally more delicate, and they are usually more sensitive to herbs and prescription drugs, smaller quantities consisting of one half to one third the adult dosage should be administered.

Duration of Treatment Guidelines

The duration or period of treatment can vary according to the illness. *Acute* conditions such as the flu or common cold are of short duration, and require smaller, more frequent dosages. Administration is generally 4-6 times a day, and formulas requiring the use of a dropper should be administered each hour for 5-6 days or until symptoms abate. Improvement should begin to be noticeable within 2-4 days. A recurring condition or one that lasts for a long duration such as cancer is referred to as chronic, and requires the formula to be administered slowly over a longer period of time. Administration is generally 3-4 times a day, and formulas requiring the use of a dropper should be administered each hour for 30 days or until symptoms abate. *Chronic* conditions generally require one month of treatment for each year since the onset of the problem. Improvement should begin to be noticeable in as little as 1-4 weeks. If no sign of improvement is noticeable within these time periods, refrain from further treatment and reformulate your remedy. Herbal therapy should be continued for at least one to two weeks after the symptoms have abated to insure a complete recovery and help ward off any reoccurrence.

Equivalents

The following information should prove useful in measuring and dispensing herbal formulas as well as helping to determine how long a bottle of extract or tincture will last depending on the dosage. Remember, accuracy of measure will vary when using liquid herbal remedies. For example, ten drops of one tincture may not equal the volume of a different tincture due to glycerin content, sediment, herbs or plants used, etc. Also, keep in mind that the formation of a single water droplet is much larger than a single droplet of an extract or tincture, and the volume of a combination (contains multiple herbs or plants) tincture or extract containing vegetable glycerin will also change. The following equivalents or conversions are approximate.

Miscellaneous Measures (includes fluid ounces and other liquid measures)

3 grams = 1 teaspoon
16 grams = 1 ounce or 480 grains
60 drops = 1 teaspoon
1 tablespoon = 3 teaspoons
2 tablespoons = 1 fluid ounce
4 tablespoons = ¼ cup
8 tablespoons = ½ cup
12 tablespoons = ¾ cup
16 tablespoons = 1 cup or 8 fluid ounces
1 ounce = 16 drachms
2 cups = 1 pint or ½ quart
4 cups = 2 pints or 1 quart
1 pint = 16 fluid ounces or ½ quart
2 pints = 1 quart
8 pints = 1 gallon

1 quart = 32 fluid ounces or 2 pints
2 quarts = ½ gallon
½ ounce = 15 cc.
½-1 ounce = 15-30 cc.
1 ounce = 30 cc.
1¾ ounces = 50 cc.
2 ounces = 60 cc.
3½ ounces = 100 cc.
1 quart = 1000 cc.
1 pint = 500 cc.
1½ pints = 750 cc.
8 ounces = 250 cc.

Tincture and Extract Equivalents

10 milliliters of water = 280-290 drops
10 milliliters of a single tincture = 440 drops
10 milliliters of a combination tincture = 447 drops
4 milliliters of a tincture or extract = 1 teaspoon

Bottle Equivalents

A 2-ounce bottle has a longer dropper and contains more fluid than a one-ounce dropper.
A 1-ounce bottle of single or combination tincture or extract holds on average 29.57 milliliters of fluid.
A 1-ounce bottle = 7.5 teaspoons.
A 1-ounce bottle holds an average of 1,000-1,200 drops.
A 1-ounce bottle of tincture will last on average 10-12 days if administration is one dropperful three times a day.
A 1-ounce bottle of tincture will last on average 18-20 days if administration is twenty drops three times a day.

Dropper Equivalents

A 1-ounce dropper holds an average of 30-40 drops.
A 2-ounce dropper holds an average of 40-50 drops.
A 1-ounce dropperful = 1 milliliter = ¼ teaspoon = 30-40 drops.

Capsule Equivalents

1 "00" size gelatin capsule = approximately 10 grains or 650 milligrams.
2 "00" size gelatin capsules = approximately 1 teaspoon.
45-50 "00" size gelatin capsules = approximately one ounce of powdered herb.
1 "0" size gelatin capsule = approximately 8 grains or 500 milligrams.
60-70 "0" size gelatin capsules = approximately one ounce of powdered herb.
2 "00" size gelatin capsules = approximately 1 teaspoon of tincture.

MONOGRAPHS

Standing lonely in the heart of the forest is a tall, beautiful, pale-lilac orchid. Shining upon it is a gleaming ray of sunshine. The orchid, reaching upwards toward the brilliant light that is pouring down, embraces its warmth. Clusters of tiny, red, wild strawberries with three-fold leaves and small dainty white blossoms are grouped around its base.

Debra Rayburn

Medicinal Herbs and Plants

The monographs contain comprehensive profiles of over 450 medicinal herbs and plants and their therapeutic applications. The following herbs may be used singly or combined into a formulation. These monographs provide an introduction to many botanicals that may be difficult to find in any other source.

How To Best Use This Section
Medicinal herb and plant monographs are divided into the following sections. **Common Name:** Each monograph begins with the botanicals most widely accepted common name. **Pronounciation:** Pronounciations are given inside parenthesis directly across from the common name. **Latin Name:** The Latin name also known as the binomial or scientific name is directly beneath the common name in italics and parentheses. The Latin name generally uses something about the herb's history, geographic location, or historical use, and is always expressed as two words. The first word is the genus and the second word is the species. There may be different species in one genus. Latin names are changed occasionally to reflect recent discoveries relating to chemistry, genetics, morphology, or occasionally due to disagreements between botanists. Although common name usage may be simpler, the same common names can sometimes be used for several different herbs, which can lead to confusion in identification. When using herbs, comparing the scientific names will help assure which plant is which. **Synonyms/Related Species:** Provides synonyms (other names) the herb is known by. Some of the synonyms listed are antiquated and others are no longer in acceptance. They are included here as a matter of historical record. Also, some monographs include botanical and Latin names of closely related species from the same genus that grow in widely divergent habitats and are located in various regions worldwide. Related species are very similar in their properties and pharmacological activity, and are often used interchangeably. **Family/Class:** Refers to the technical class or family as well as the common class or family name. For example, peppermint belongs to the labiatae (mint) family. **Floral Emblem:** A flower or plant that has been adopted by a state, etc., which represents a visible symbol of that specific area. **Habitat:** Provides the regions where the herb has established itself or is cultivated. **Flavor:** The general flavor or taste of the herb. Some herbs may have more than one flavor. For example, an herb's flavor may start out as sour, then become sweet. Keep in mind that each individual's taste buds differ, and an herb tasting sour to one person may taste bitter to another. **Parts Used:** Refers to the parts of the herb that are used medicinally. **Properties:** Lists the herb's properties (i.e. antibiotic). **Constituents:** Provides information on the active chemical compounds found in the herb. **Historical Uses:** Here you'll find uses for which the herb has been deemed effective. **Discussion:** This section consists of concise information that is intended to more fully round out your understanding of the herb. **Cautions/Contraindications:** Alerts to any cautions regarding herbs that should be avoided by certain individuals, or in the presence of certain medical conditions such as depression*, recommendations for professional usage, or restrictions on use. **Adverse Reactions:** Refers to undesireable reactions (when known) that could occur from herbal misuse. Mild adverse reactions such as headache or nausea generally require the reduction of dosage or discontinuance of use. Severe or life threatening reactions such as abdominal pain of unknown origin, anaphylaxis, cardiac arrhythmia, cardiac arrest, convulsions, cyanosis, diarrhea (bloody or severe), hemafecia (blood in the stool), hematemesis (vomiting of blood), hematochezia (the

passage of bloody stools), hematuria (blood in the urine), paralysis, projectile vomiting, vomiting of bile, etc. require immediate medical attention. **Herb/Drug Interactions:** Refers to herb and pharmaceutical drug interactions (when known) that could occur with combined use. **Herb/Herb Interactions:** Refers to interactions (when known) that could occur between the combined uses of certain herbs. **Preparations/Dosage:** Refers to preparation methods and adult dosage guidelines. Remember, dosage in herbal therapy typically involves a range. If the dosage says 1-3 grams, 1 gram would be the lowest amount of herb taken to have an effect, and 3 grams would be the highest, safest amount to take of that herb. It is recommended that you start out with the lowest dosage in the range, and if all goes well and you experience no adverse effects then gradually increase the dosage up to the highest, suggested amount for that particular herb. This range should be individualized, depending on the seriousness of the condition as well as the specific nature and potency of the respective preparation. Administration may require a graduation of dosage, especially for children, the elderly, or those persons in an already weakened condition. These adult dosage guidelines are based on an average adult weighing 140-150 pounds with normal metabolism. **Isolation:** refers to the separation of some of the herb's chemical constituents for use either on their own, in solution, or in a combination formula. This process is generally reserved for those persons advanced in herbal preparation and having knowledge of chemistry.

Note: Widely varying geographical locations, climactic circumstances, and/or herbs introduced as alien or cultivated species (having escaped from a garden or having become naturalized) can have an effect on an herb's overall appearance, range of occurrence, and growth habit. For these reasons, botanical descriptions are not included in the Medicinal Herbs and Plants Monographs section.

*Depression: The following monographs containing the word depression are implied for occasional mild to moderate depression only. Seek immediate medical attention if depression is severe and/or associated with suicidal thoughts or tendencies.

Author Disclaimer: As with all research investigation, conclusions regarding the efficacy or usefulness of the medicinal herbs and plants discussed in this section are based on the prevalence of currently existing information and cannot be considered absolute or conclusive. The author does not guarantee that any herb or plant within these pages will consistently demonstrate the effects properties attributed to it. Also, the author does not guarantee that adverse reactions, cautions, consequence of overdose, or contraindications are included in the summary information presented here. The medicinal herb and plant monographs merely report general botanical findings. The dosage information found in the herbal monograph section is to be used as a general guideline only. Adjust dosages accordingly. And as always, before beginning or adding *any* new therapy program to your daily routine, be sure to consult a healthcare professional.

Abscess Root (ab ses·root)
(*Polemonium reptans*)

Synonyms/Related Species: Blue Bells, Greek Valerian, Showy Jacob's Ladder (*polemonium pulcherrimum*), Sticky Jacob's Ladder (*polemonium viscosum*), Tall Jacob's Ladder (*polemonium acutiflorum*), Western Jacob's Ladder (*polemonium occidentale*).
Family/Class: Polemoniaceae (phlox).
Habitat: Alaska, the Alpine and Subalpine zones, Europe, and North America.
Flavor: Sour/sweet.
Parts Used: Root.
Properties: Alterative, antiphlogistic, aromatic, astringent, diaphoretic, expectorant, hemostatic, and stimulant.
Constituents: Glycosides and saponin.
Historical Uses: Arrhythmia, bleeding, bronchitis, colds, cough, diarrhea, distemper (pestilential), emaciation, epilepsy, fever (ephemeral), gastrointestinal problems, hemorrhoids, hydrophobia (rabies in humans), hysteria, inflammation, insect bites or stings, laryngitis, lesion (tubercle), lung problems, mucus, respiratory conditions, scrofula, snakebite, tuberculosis, and ulcer (fistula, tuberculous).
Discussion: May clear and open bronchial passages; promote perspiration; reestablish healthy system functions.
Cautions/Contraindications: Avoid use if pregnant or breast-feeding.
Adverse Reactions: Diarrhea (possibly bloody), gastrointestinal cramps (severe), nausea, and/or vomiting.
Herb/Drug Interactions: This herb could cause an interaction (possibly severe) when taken with the following drugs: None known.
Preparations/Dosage: Crude Herb: 3-6 grams. Extract: 5-10 drops (0.333-0.666 cc.) one to two times per day. Infusion: ½-1 cup per day. Tincture: 10-15 drops (0.666-1 cc.) one to three times per day.

Acacia (e·kā she)
(*Acacia senegal*)

Synonyms/Related Species: Acacia Gum (*acacia nilotica*), Akakia, Albizzia Tree, Asiatic Acacia, Babul, Black Catechu (*acacia catechu-nigrum*), Black Wattle, Cape Gum, Catechu, Cutch, Egyptian Thorn, Green Wattle Tree, Gum Acacia, Gum Arabic, Indian Gum (*acacia arabica*), Kordofan Gum, Locust Tree, Mogadore Gum (*acacia gummifera*), Oriental Acacia, Senegal Gum, Shittah Tree, Thorny Tree, and Wattle Bark (*acacia decurrens*).
Family/Class: Leguminosae (legume).
Habitat: Afghanistan, Africa, the Amazon, Angola, Arabia, Asia, Australia, Beluschistan, Egypt, India, Iran, Morocco, and Myanmar (formerly Burma).
Flavor: Bitter/sweet.
Parts Used: Bark, gum.
Properties: Antibiotic, antiphlogistic, astringent, demulcent, emetic, expectorant, hemostatic, nutritive, stimulant, and tonic.
Constituents: Arabin (arabic acid), catechin (catechuic acid), gallic acid, glycoprotein, minerals (calcium, magnesium, potassium), monosaccharides, mucilage, polysaccharides, quercetin, and tannic acid.

Historical Uses: Abscess, asthma, bleeding, colds, colitis, congestion (uterine, vaginal), cough, croup, diarrhea, dietary supplement, digestive complaints, dysentery, ear problems, fever (ephemeral, enteric), gargle/mouth rinse, gastrointestinal problems, gleet, gonorrhea, hemorrhage (metrorrhagia), hemorrhoids, infection (bacterial, sexually transmitted, urinary tract), inflammation, lesion (tubercle), leukorrhea, malnutrition, mucus, nosebleed, periodontal disease, pharyngitis, pneumonia, respiratory conditions, scrofula, sexually transmitted diseases (STDs), skin problems, sore throat, stomatitis, substitute for oak bark, survival food, toothache, tuberculosis, typhoid, ulcer (bouveret, duodenal, fistula, gastric, peptic, tuberculous), urethritis, and vaginitis.
Discussion: May clear and open bronchial passages; inhibit or destroy development and growth of bacteria and other microorganisms; provide dietary supplementation; restore normal tone to tissues; serve as a nutritional adjuvant to therapeutic programs; soothe mucous membrane irritation.
Cautions/Contraindications: Avoid use if pregnant or breast-feeding. May interfere with the absorption of certain prescription drugs and vitamins.
Adverse Reactions: Constipation, diarrhea, hematuria (blood in the urine), nausea, and/or vomiting.
Herb/Drug Interactions: This herb could cause an interaction (possibly severe) when taken with the following drugs: None known.
Preparations/Dosage: Crude Herb (bark): 3-6 grams. Decoction (bark): ½ cup per day. Extract (bark): 5-10 drops (0.333-0.666 cc.) one to two times per day. Gum (powdered): 3-9 grams. Combine gum with water. Adding licorice, marshmallow, or slippery elm will help to make it more pleasing to the palate. Take ½-1 teaspoon per day. Acacia can be used as a survival food. As little as six to eight ounces of the gum can suffice for food and drink, and support an adult for approximately twenty-four hours.
Did You Know? Acacia has been used in the food industry to provide texture and body to processed foods.

Aconite (ak e·nīt)
(*Aconitum napellus*)

Synonyms/Related Species: Bikh, Bish, Blue-Flowered Monkshood (*aconitum uncinatum*), Blue Rocket, Columbian Monkshood (*aconitum columbianum*), Deadly Aconite, Friar's Cap, Helmet Flower, Indian Aconite (*aconitum laciniatum*), Japanese Aconite (*aconitum japonicum*), Mohri (*aconitum chasmanthum*), Mountain Monkshood (*aconitum delphinifolium*), Mousebane, Nepal Aconite, Russian Aconite (*aconitum orientale*), Western Monkshood (*aconitum columbianum*), White-Flowered Monkshood (*aconitum reclinatum*), and Wolf's Bane (*aconitum lycotonum*).
Family/Class: Ranunculaceae (buttercup).
Habitat: The Alps, Asia, Britain, the Carpathians, England, Europe, Germany, the Himalayas, Japan, Nepal, North America, Portugal, the Pyrenees, Russia, and Sweden.
Flavor: Bitter.
Parts Used: Leaves, root.
Properties: Analgesic, antiphlogistic, antispasmodic, cardiac depressant, counterirritant, diaphoretic, diuretic, mydriatic, narcotic, sedative, stimulant, and tonic.

Constituents: Aconine, aconitic acid, aconitine, ajacine, atropine, benzaconine, delphinine, indaconitine, inulin (starch), japaconitine, mesaconitine, picraconitine, protoanemonin, and pseudaconitine.

Historical Uses: Aneurysm, arthritis, asthma, Bell's Palsy, cardiovascular conditions, cerebrospinal hyperemia, colds, colic, constipation, enuresis (urinary incontinence), erysipelas, fever (ephemeral, rheumatic), flatulence, gout, inflammation, iritis, laryngitis, lumbago, migraine, muscle and joint pain, nervous conditions, neuralgia, numbness, pain, pericarditis sicca, pleurisy, pneumonia, respiratory conditions, rheumatism, sciatica, skin problems, spasmodic conditions, tachycardia, tonsillitis, urinary problems, whooping cough, and wounds (minor).

Discussion: May diminish or reduce functional activity of the heart; enhance circulatory system, intestinal system, and urinary system functions; lessen the vascularity of the iris; produce pupil dilatation; promote perspiration and urine flow; reduce the frequency of nighttime urination; restore normal tone to tissues; stimulate the sympathetic nerves and depress the cerebrospinal nerves; strengthen the respiratory system.

Cautions/Contraindications: Avoid use if pregnant or breast-feeding, or if you have hypertension. May cause numbness or prickling of fingers when collecting. Not for long-term use. Prolonged use may lead to a tolerance to the accumulation of tropine-alkaloids in the parasympathetic system; thus more of the herb is required to achieve the same effects. Use under professional guidance/supervision.

Adverse Reactions: Arrhythmia, atropinism (atropine poisoning), bradycardia, cardiac failure, confusion, convulsions, cold/clammy skin, confusion, depression of the central and peripheral nerves, diarrhea, difficulty swallowing, dizziness, enuresis (urinary incontinence), fainting, giddiness, headache, hypotension, irritability, labored breathing, limb pain, muscle cramps (severe), nausea, paralysis, restlessness, salivation, a sensation of suffocation, skin surface numbness, stomach cramps and pain (severe), stupor, tingling and numbness of the lips/mouth/tongue, slurring of speech, staggering, tachycardia, visual disturbances, vomiting, and/or possible death.

Herb/Drug Interactions: This herb could cause an interaction (possibly severe) when taken with the following drugs: None known.

Preparations/Dosage: External/topical uses only.

Isolation: Atropine: Soluble in alcohol and sparingly so in water. Average dose of $^{1}/_{150}$ grain (0.4 mg.) for use as a mydriatic and narcotic. Atropine sulfate: Soluble in water. Average dose of $^{1}/_{120}$ grain (0.5 mg.) for use as a mydriatic and narcotic.

Adrue (ad·ru a)

(*Cyperus articulatus*)

Synonyms/Related Species: Chufa, Cyperus, Guinea Rush, Nutgrass, and Sedge Root.

Family/Class: Cyperaceae (sedge).

Habitat: Egypt, India, and Jamaica.

Flavor: Pungent/bitter.

Parts Used: Root.

Properties: Antiemetic, antifungal, antispasmodic, aphrodisiac, carminative, emmenagogue, nutritive, and tonic.

Constituents: Cyperene, cyperol, cyperone, pinene, sesquiterpenes, and volatile oil.

Historical Uses: Allergy (food), amenorrhea, candida, colds, depression (mild/moderate), dietary supplementation, digestive complaints, dysmenorrhea, flatulence, flavoring agent, food source (root), gastritis, indigestion, infection (fungal), influenza, irritable bowel syndrome (IBS), liver problems, malnutrition, menstrual problems, menorrhagia, metabolic problems, moniliasis, mood swings, pain, spasmodic conditions, and vomiting.
Discussion: May aid digestion; arouse sexual impulses; enhance liver function; provide dietary supplementation; restore normal tone to tissues; serve as a nutritional adjuvant to therapeutic programs; stimulate menstruation.
Cautions/Contraindications: Avoid use if pregnant or breast-feeding.
Adverse Reactions: Nausea and/or vomiting.
Herb/Drug Interactions: This herb could cause an interaction (possibly severe) when taken with the following drugs: None known.
Preparations/Dosage: Crude herb: 3-9 grams. Root (cooked/dried/raw): Can be ingested freely. Tincture: 10-30 drops (0.666-2 cc.) one to three times per day.

Agave (e·gä vē)

(Agave americana)

Synonyms/Related Species: American Aloe, American Century, Century Plant, Flowering Aloe, Maguey, Mexican Tree of Life and Abundance.
Family/Class: Agavaceae (agave).
Habitat: Europe, Italy, Mexico, North America, Portugal, and Spain.
Flavor: Bitter.
Parts Used: Leaves, root.
Properties: Abortifacient, alterative, anti-inflammatory, diuretic, laxative, nutritive, and vasodilator.
Constituents: Gitogenin, hecogenin, manogenin, and saponin.
Historical Uses: Alopecia, arthritis, burns (minor), constipation, dietary supplementation, hormone therapy, indigestion, inflammation, jaundice, lesion (tubercle), liver problems, malnutrition, poisoning (sepsis), sexually transmitted diseases (STDs), scrofula, syphilis, toothache, tuberculosis, ulcer (fistula, syphilitic, tuberculous), and wounds (minor).
Discussion: May dilate the blood vessels; induce abortion; promote bowel evacuation and urine flow; provide dietary supplementation; reestablish healthy system functions; serve as a nutritional adjuvant to therapeutic programs and serve as an adjuvant to hormone therapy programs; stimulate peristalsis.
Cautions/Contraindications: Avoid use if pregnant or breast-feeding, or if you have appendicitis, an obstruction (intestinal), colitis, or Crohn's disease. Do not confuse this plant with true aloe (*aloe barbadensis*). Do not administer to children under the age of 12 years. May interfere with vitamin absorption. May cause dermatitis, photosensitivity, or photodermatosis in susceptible individuals.
Adverse Reactions: Deficiency (potassium), diarrhea (possibly bloody), gastrointestinal cramps (severe), hemorrhage, liver damage (often characterized by jaundice), nausea, vasodilatation, and/or vomiting.
Herb/Drug Interactions: This herb could cause an interaction (possibly severe) when taken with the following drugs: None known.

Preparations/Dosage: Crude Herb: 1-3 grams. Decoction: ½-2 ounces per day. Extract: 5-10 drops (0.333-0.666 cc.) one to two times per day. Extract (powdered): Average dose in substance 1-5 grains (0.066-0.324 gm.). Pulque (fermented juice): 1-2 cups per day. Root (powdered): In capsule form. Take 1-2 per day. Tincture: 15-30 drops (1-2 cc.) one to three times per day.

Agrimony (ag re·mō nē)
(*Agrimonia eupatori*)

Synonyms/Related Species: Aigremoine, Argemōnē, Church Steeples, Cockeburr, Cocklebur, Common Agrimony, Egrimoyne, Garclive, Liverwort, Philanthropos, Sticklewort, and Stickwort.
Family/Class: Rosaceae (rose).
Habitat: England, North America, and Scotland.
Flavor: Bitter/tangy.
Parts Used: Leaves, root.
Properties: Analgesic, antibiotic, anticarcinogen, antilithic, antiphlogistic, antiviral, astringent, diuretic, hemostatic, lithotriptic, and tonic.
Constituents: Coumarin, flavonoids, glycosides, minerals (iron, silicon), polysaccharides, silicic acid, tannic acid, vitamins (B_3 niacin (nicotinic acid), and K), and volatile oil.
Historical Uses: Acne, appendicitis, bleeding, bronchitis, bruises, calculus, cancer (breast, ovarian), colitis, congestion (lung, uterine, vaginal), conjunctivitis, cough, diabetes, diarrhea, dysentery, dysmenorrhea, enuresis (urinary incontinence), fever (ephemeral, enteric, rheumatic), gallbladder problems, gallstones, gargle/mouth rinse, gastrointestinal problems, gout, hematochezia (passage of bloody stools), hematuria (blood in the urine), hemorrhage, hemorrhoids, hives, infection (bacterial, bladder, viral), inflammation, jaundice, kidney stones, lesion (tubercle), leukemia, leukorrhea, lithemia, liver problems, menstrual problems, mucus, muscle and joint pain, pain, periodeontal disease, rheumatism, scrofula, skin problems, snakebite, sores, sore throat, sprain, tuberculosis, tumors (multiple myeloma), typhoid, ulcer (bouveret, duodenal, fistula, gastric, peptic, tuberculous), urethritis, vaginitis, warts (digitate, filiform, fugitive, glabra, mother, plana juvenilis, plantar, seborrhoeic, vulgaris), and wounds (minor).
Discussion: May decrease the effect of carcinogens; dissolve calculi; enhance digestive, gallbladder, liver, and urinary system functions; inhibit or destroy development and growth of bacteria and other microorganisms; prevent the development of calculus or stones; reduce excessive lithic acid (uric acid) and urate levels in the blood, tophi, and urine, and the frequency of nighttime urination; restore normal tone to tissues; soothe the mucous membranes; stimulate the immune system; strengthen the urinary system.
Cautions/Contraindications: Avoid use if pregnant or breast-feeding, or if you have hyperthyroidism, lupus, myasthenia gravis, rheumatoid arthritis (RA), Sjögren's syndrome, or any other autoimmune disease. May cause constipation if taken with prunes or psyllium.
Adverse Reactions: Nausea and/or vomiting.
Herb/Drug Interactions: This herb could cause an interaction (possibly severe) when taken with the following drugs: None known.
Preparations/Dosage: Crude Herb: 6-12 grams. Crude Herb (powdered): Average dose in substance 30-60 grains (2-4 gm.). Decoction: ½-1 cup per day. Infusion: 1-2 cups per day. Tincture: 10-30 drops (0.666-4 cc.) one to three times per day.

Alder (ôl der)
(*Alnus glutinosa*)

Synonyms/Related Species: Common Alder, English Alder, Green Alder (*alnus viridis*), Mountain Alder (*alnus incana*), Oregon Alder, Owler, Red Alder, Scottish Mahogany, Smooth Alder, and Tag Alder (*alnus serrulata*).
Family/Class: Betulaceae (birch).
Habitat: Alaska, the Alpine and Subalpine zones, Africa, Alaska, Asia, Britain, Europe, and North America.
Flavor: Bitter.
Parts Used: Bark.
Properties: Alterative, antiphlogistic, astringent, emetic, hemostatic, insect repellent, laxative, and tonic.
Constituents: Flavonoids, resin, saponins, tannic acid, and triterpenes.
Historical Uses: Asthma, bleeding, diarrhea, fever (ephemeral, rheumatic), fleas (leaves), gargle/mouth rinse, hematuria (blood in the urine), hemorrhage, hemorrhoids, inflammation, indigestion, lesion (tubercle), muscle and joint pain, pharyngitis, rheumatism, scrofula, sore throat, strep throat, syphilis, tuberculosis, and ulcer (fistula, syphilitic, tuberculous).
Discussion: May increase circulation; promote bowel evacuation; purify the blood; reduce tissue inflammation; reestablish healthy system functions; restore tone to the tissues; stimulate peristalsis.
Cautions/Contraindications: Avoid use if pregnant or breast-feeding.
Adverse Reactions: Diarrhea (possibly bloody), gastrointestinal cramps (severe), nausea, and/or vomiting.
Herb/Drug Interactions: This herb could cause an interaction (possibly severe) when taken with the following drugs: None known.
Preparations/Dosage: Crude Herb: 3-6 grams. Bark (powdered): Average dose in substance 8-12 grains (0.51-0.78 gm.). Decoction: ¼-½ cup per day. Extract: 5-10 drops (0.333-0.666 cc.) one to two times per day. Infusion: ½-1 cup per day. Tincture: 10-15 drops (0.666-1 cc.) one to three times per day.

Alfalfa (al·fal fe)
(*Medicago sativa*)

Synonyms/Related Species: Buffalo Grass, Buffalo Herb, Chilean Clover, Father of all Herbs, Lucerne, Purple Medick, and Yellow Lucerne (*medicago falcata*).
Family/Class: Leguminosae (legume).
Habitat: Europe, the Middle East, North America, and the Yukon Territory.
Flavor: Bitter/salty.
Parts Used: Aerial.

Properties: Alterative, anticarcinogen, anticoagulant, antiphlogistic, antiscorbutic, aromatic, diuretic, emmenagogue, hemostatic, hypotensive, nutritive, tonic, and vasodilator.
Constituents: Alkaloids (betaine (lycine), stachydrine, trigonelline), amino acids (canavanine), chlorophyll, coumarin, fatty acids (oleic, palmitic, stearic), fixed oils (olein, palmitin, stearin), flavonoids, genistein, glycosides, lutein, minerals (calcium, iron, magnesium, phosphorus, potassium, silicon, sodium, sulfur), phytoestrogen, protein, saponin, silicic acid, and vitamins (A, B_6 (pyridoxine), B_{12}, C, D, E, K, M (folic acid).
Historical Uses: Abscesses, acne, addiction (alcohol, narcotic), allergy, amenorrhea, anemia, appendicitis, appetite loss, arteriosclerosis, arthritis, asthma, athlete's foot, beverage, bladder problems, burns (minor), bursitis, cancer (breast, prostate, uterine), Celiac disease, colitis, constipation, cramps, cystitis, diabetes, dietary supplementation, digestive complaints, eczema, edema, emaciation, endometriosis, fatigue, fever (ephemeral, rheumatic), gastritis, gastrointestinal problems, glandular problems, gout, halitosis, hemorrhage, hemorrhoids, hormonal imbalances, hot flashes, hypertension (mild/moderate), hypercholesteremia, hypoestrogenism, infection, inflammation, insomnia, jaundice, liver problems, malnutrition, menopausal/menstrual problems, muscle and joint pain, nausea, nosebleed, periodontal disease, prostatitis, rheumatism, scurvy, ulcer (duodenal, gastric, peptic), urinary problems, and whooping cough.
Discussion: May balance the hormonal system; build capillary strength; cause blood vessel dilatation; cleanse the whole system; decrease the effect of carcinogens; delay or reduce coagulation of the blood; enhance the digestive system and food assimilation; increase strength, white blood cell counts, and vitality; lower cholesterol levels; maintain bone density; nourish and purify the blood; promote urine flow; protect against breast tissue tumors, heart disease, stroke (apoplectic), and tooth decay; provide dietary supplementation; reduce blood pressure levels; replace vitamin K that has been depleted by the use of antibiotic, cholesterol lowering, or seizure drugs; reestablish healthy system functions; reverse immune depression caused by the use of cancer drugs; serve as a nutritional adjuvant to therapeutic programs; slow the progress of arteriosclerosis; stimulate appetite, the immune system, and menstruation.
Cautions/Contraindications: Avoid use if pregnant, or if you have an estrogen dependant cancer, or if you have a history of estrogen dependant cancers, or if you have a deficiency (autoimmune), a fever, lupus, or premenstrual syndrome (PMS). Estrogen containing substances may contribute to abnormal blood coagulation, migraine, and could promote the development of certain types of estrogen dependant cancers. May cause the recurrence of lupus in persons in whom the condition has become dormant. Some persons may experience bleeding or increased clotting time when using this herb with anticoagulant drugs or aspirin. Unsprouted alfalfa seeds contain high levels of the toxic amino acid known as canavanine; therefore eat only seeds that have sprouted. Be sure to rinse sprouts thoroughly prior to eating.
Adverse Reactions: Bleeding (possibly serious), coagulation problems, diarrhea, edema, gastritis, indigestion, irritable bowel syndrome (IBS), nausea, and/or vomiting.
Herb/Drug Interactions: This herb could cause an interaction (possibly severe) when taken with the following drugs: Anticoagulant drugs, Hormones and Synthetic Substitutes (i.e. conjugated estrogens, contraceptives, and other hormonal replacement therapy (HRT), Hypotensive drugs, Salicylates, and Subsalicylates.
Preparations/Dosage: Crude Herb: 3-9 grams. Infusion: 1 cup per day.
Isolation: Betaine: Average dose of 2-4 grains (0.13- 0.26 gm.) for use as an emmenagogue.

Allspice (ôl spīs)
(*Pimenta racemosa*)

Synonyms/Related Species: Clove Pepper, Jamaican Pepper, Pimenta, Pimento, Pimienta, Pimiento, Spanish Paprika, Sweet Pepper, West Indian Allspice, and Wild Allspice.
Family/Class: Myrtaceae (myrtle).
Habitat: The Caribbean, Central America, Portugal, South America, and the West Indies.
Flavor: Pungent.
Parts Used: Berry.
Properties: Analgesic, anesthetic (local), antibiotic, antifungal, antioxidant, antiperiodic, antiphlogistic, antiviral, aromatic, carminative, counterirritant, malariacidal, parasiticide, and stimulant.
Constituents: Carvene (limonene), caryophyllene, chavicol, eucalyptol (cineol), eugenol (eugenic acid), fatty acids (oleic, palmitic, stearic), fixed oils (olein, palmitin, stearin), gum, phellandrene, resin, tannic acid, and volatile oil.
Historical Uses: Ague, athlete's foot, asthma, bronchitis, colds, colitis, cough, cystitis, chronic fatigue syndrome (CFS), congestion (uterine, vaginal), diarrhea, digestive complaints, diphtheria, dizziness, dysentery, earache, epilepsy, Epstein Barr Virus (EBV), erectile dysfunction, fever (ephemeral, herpetic, rheumatic), fibromyalgia, flatulence, flavoring agent, halitosis, herpes, hiccups, hypotension, hysteria, indigestion, infection (bacterial, fungal, viral), infertility, inflammation, kidney problems, leukorrhea, malaria, mononucleosis (infectious), muscle and joint pain, nausea, neuralgia, pain, palsy, parasites (malarial plasmodia, ringworm), periodontal disease, poisoning (food), respiratory conditions, rheumatism, sexually transmitted diseases (STDs), skin problems, spasmodic conditions, substitute for cloves, toothache, ulcer (peptic, syriac), urethritis, urinary problems, vaginitis, vomiting, warts (digitate, filiform, fugitive, glabra, mother, plana juvenilis, plantar, seborrhoeic, vulgaris), and wounds (minor).
Discussion: May aid digestion; increase circulation; inhibit oxidation and inhibit or destroy development and growth of bacteria and other microorganisms.
Cautions/Contraindications: Avoid use if pregnant or breast-feeding, or if you have cancer or have a history of cancer. May increase the effectiveness of antiviral drugs. Do not administer allspice to children under the age of twelve years. May cause dermatitis in susceptible individuals. Not for long-term use.
Adverse Reactions: Convulsions, depression, diarrhea, mucous membrane irritation, nausea, skin problems, and/or vomiting.
Herb/Drug Interactions: This herb could cause an interaction (possibly severe) when taken with the following drugs: Antiviral drugs.
Preparations/Dosage: Berries (powdered): Average dose in substance 5-30 grains (0.333-2 gm.). Oil of Allspice (*oleum pimentae*): 1-5 drops (0.066-0.333 cc.) per day in water or on a sugar cube. Pimento Water (*aqua pimentae*): Combine 5 parts bruised or crushed berries with 1 pint of water. Distill down to half of the original volume. Take 1-2 fl. ounces per day.
Isolation: Eucalyptol: 5 drops (0.333 cc.) in atomization or inhalation for respiratory conditions.

Aloe (al ō)
(*Aloe barbadensis*)

Synonyms/Related Species: Aluwe, Barbados Aloe, Cape Aloe (*aloe ferou*), Curacao Aloe (*aloe chinensis*), Cape Barbados Aloe, First-Aid Plant, Kumari, Medicine Plant, Mocha Aloe

(*aloe abyssinica*), Musambra Aloe (*aloe vulgaris*), Saber, Socotrine Aloe (*aloe perryi*), South African Aloe (*aloe latifolia, aloe saponaria,* and *aloe tenuior*), True Aloe, Turkey Aloe, Uganda Aloe (*aloe ferox*), and Zanzibar Aloe.
Family/Class: Liliaceae (lily).
Habitat: Africa, Arabia, the Island of Barbados, Egypt, India, the Mediterranean, and the Island of Socotra.
Flavor: Bitter.
Parts Used: Leaves, juice/gel.
Properties: Alterative, analgesic, anthelmintic, antibiotic, anticarcinogen, antiphlogistic, antifungal, antiviral, astringent, demulcent, emetic, hemostatic, hypotensive, laxative, lithotriptic, parasiticide, stimulant, teniacide, teniafuge, tonic, vasodilator, vermifuge, and vulnerary.
Constituents: Aloins (barbaloin, nataloin, socaloin, and zanaloin), anthracene, anthraquinone, emodin, flavonoids, glycoprotein, lecithin, minerals (calcium, iron, manganese, potassium, sodium, zinc), mucilage, organic acid, polysaccharides, resin, saponin, and sterols.
Historical Uses: Abscess, acne, acquired immune deficiency syndrome (AIDS), allergy, alopecia, amenorrhea, anemia, asthma, bladder problems, bleeding, bruises, burns (minor), bursitis, calculus, callouses, cancer (lung, skin), candida, canker sores, colic, colitis, conjunctivitis, constipation, corns, cramps, Crohn's disease, diabetes mellitus, digestive complaints, diverticulitis, dryness conditions, dysentery, ear infection, eczema, fever (ephemeral, herpetic, rheumatic), frostbite, gallstones, gastritis, gastrointestinal problems, hangover (caused by alcohol consumption), headache, hemorrhoids, hepatitis, herpes, human immunodeficiency virus (HIV), hypertension (mild/moderate), indigestion, infection (fungal, viral), inflammation, influenza, insect bites or stings, irritable bowel syndrome (IBS), kidney stones, lesion (tubercle), liver problems, menopausal/menstrual problems, moniliasis, muscle and joint pain, nervous conditions, pain, parasites (pinworm, ringworm, tapeworm), poison ivy/oak, premenstrual syndrome (PMS), pruritus, psoriasis, radiation burns/exposure, rash, rheumatism, scrofula, sexually transmitted diseases (STDs), shingles, skin problems, sores, stomachache, sunburn, surgery (recovery), tuberculosis, ulcer (duodenal, fistula, gastric, peptic, stasis, tuberculous), vaginitis, warts (digitate, filiform, fugitive, glabra, mother, plana juvenilis, plantar, seborrhoeic, vulgaris), wounds (minor), and wrinkles.
Discussion: May balance blood sugar, lipid, and skin's pH levels; cause blood vessel dilatation; decrease blood flow to frozen tissues and the effect of carcinogens; dissolve calculi; enhance cardiovascular system, female hormonal system, immune system, intestinal system, liver, and spleen functions; increase circulation and the absorption of nutrients through the digestive tract; promote bowel evacuation; reduce the risk of cancer (lung) in those individuals who smoke; moisturize sun aged skin; protect against carcinogens and radiation; reduce blood pressure levels; repair cell damage; restore normal tone to tissues; soothe mucous membrane irritation; speed healing; stimulate fertility (in women), pancreatic insulin levels, peristalsis, and the growth of healthy kidney cells; offset the negative effects of chemotherapy and radiation therapy drugs.
Cautions/Contraindications: Avoid use if pregnant or breast-feeding, or during menstruation, or in cases of enteritis, obstruction (intestinal), or rectal bleeding. Do not confuse this plant with agave (*agave americana*). Do not consume more than one quart of aloe juice daily. Do not administer to children less than 12 years of age. May interfere with prescription drug absorption. Not for long-term use.
Adverse Reactions: Diarrhea, gastrointestinal cramps, potassium loss, nausea, skin problems, and/or vomiting.

Herb/Drug Interactions: This herb could cause an interaction (possibly severe) when taken with the following drugs: Antidiabetic drugs, Corticosteroids, and Hypotensive drugs.
Preparations/Dosage: Extract: 5-10 drops (0.333-0.666 cc.) one to two times per day. Extract (powdered): Average dose in substance 1-5 grains (0.066-0.324 gm.). Gel/Juice: 1-2 teaspoons per day mixed with water or apple juice. Tincture: 5-30 drops (0.333-2 cc.) one to three times per day.
Isolation: Aloin: Average dose of ¼ grain (0.015 gm.) used as a laxative.
Did You Know? Some aloe plants have been discovered towering as high as 30-60 feet with a stem circumference measuring as much as 10 feet.

Alpine Cranberry (al pīn kran ber ē)

(*Vaccinium vitis-idaea*)

Synonyms/Related Species: Cowberry, Grouseberry (*vaccinium scoparium*), Lingonberry, Mountain Cranberry, Red Bilberry, and Whortleberry.
Family/Class: Ericaceae (heath).
Habitat: North America.
Flavor: Bitter/sweet.
Parts Used: Berries, leaves.
Properties: Analgesic, antiphlogistic, antiscorbutic, antiviral, diuretic, lithotriptic, and urinary antiseptic.
Constituents: Arbutin, avicularin, flavonoids, glycosides, hydroquinone, proanthocyainidine, pyroside, quercitrin, tannic acid, ursone (ursolic acid), and vitamin C.
Historical Uses: Calculus, fevers (ephemeral, rheumatic), gallstones, gout, inflammation, kidney stones, muscle and joint pain, pain, rheumatism, scurvy, substitute for bearberry (leaves), urinary problems, and viral infection.
Discussion: May dissolve calculi; promote urine flow.
Cautions/Contraindications: Avoid use if pregnant or breast-feeding, or if you have gastric sensitivity. Do not administer to children less than 12 years of age. May increase the absorption of lansoprazole, omeprazole, and protein-bound vitamin B_{12}. May cause allergic reactions or dermatitis in susceptible individuals. Not for long-term use.
Adverse Reactions: Diarrhea, nausea, and/or vomiting.
Herb/Drug Interactions: This herb could cause an interaction (possibly severe) when taken with the following drugs: GI drugs, Renal drugs.
Preparations/Dosage: Crude Herb: 3-6 grams. Decoction (leaves): ½ cup per day. Infusion (leaves): ½-1 cup per day.
Isolation: Arbutin: Average dose of 5-15 grains (0.333-1 gm.) for use as a diuretic and urinary antiseptic.

Alumroot (al em·root)

(*Heuchera parvifolia*)

Synonyms/Related Species: Common Alumroot, Crevice Heuchera (*heuchera micrantha*), Round-Leaved Alumroot (*heuchera cylindrical*), Richardson's Alumroot (*heuchera richardsonii*), and Smooth Alumroot (*heuchera glabra*).
Family/Class: Saxifragaceae (saxifrage).

Habitat: The Alpine and Subalpine zones, and North America.
Flavor: Bitter.
Parts Used: Root.
Properties: Antibiotic, antifungal, astringent, expectorant, hemostatic, and parasiticide.
Constituents: Tannic acid.
Historical Uses: Alopecia, bleeding, cancer (skin), cervicitis, colds, congestion (uterine, vaginal), diarrhea, dysentery, eyewash, fever, gargle/mouth rinse, gastroenteritis, heart disease, hemorrhoids, hepatitis, infection (bacterial, fungal), influenza, jaundice, lesion (tubercle), leukorrhea, liver problems, mucus, muscle and joint pain, parasites (ringworm, scabies, trichomonas), periodontal disease, pruritus, rash, respiratory conditions, scrofula, snakebite, sores, sore throat, tuberculosis, ulcer (duodenal, fistula, gastric, peptic, stasis, tuberculous), vaginitis, vomiting, and wounds (minor).
Discussion: May clear and open bronchial passages; encourage hair growth; enhance colon, lung, and spleen functions; inhibit or destroy development and growth of bacteria and other microorganisms; protect against heart disease; reduce both the rate of growth and the rate of reproduction of trichomonas; serve as an adjuvant to help reduce excessive salivation in epilepsy.
Cautions/Contraindications: Avoid use if pregnant or breast-feeding.
Adverse Reactions: Gastric irritation, hematuria (blood in the urine), and/or liver damage (often characterized by jaundice).
Herb/Drug Interactions: This herb could cause an interaction (possibly severe) when taken with the following drugs: None known.
Preparations/Dosage: Root (powdered): 3-9 grams.

Amaranth (am e·ranth)
(*Amaranthus hypochondriacus*)

Synonyms/Related Species: Floramor, Flower Gentle, Flower Velure, Lady Bleeding, Love Lies Bleeding (*amaranthus caudatus*), Pirewort, Prince's Feather, Red Cockscomb, Spleen Amaranth, Strawberry Blite, Velvet Flower, and Wild Amaranth (*amaranthus blitum*).
Family/Class: Amaranthaceae (amaranth).
Habitat: Africa, Britain, France, Greece, India, Java, and the United States.
Flavor: Sour/sweet.
Parts Used: Leaves.
Properties: Alterative, antacid, astringent, diuretic, hemostatic, and nutritive.
Constituents: Minerals (calcium, iron, phosphorus, potassium), protein, saponins, tannic acid, and vitamins (A, B_1 (thiamine), B_2 (riboflavin), B_3 (niacin), C (ascorbic acid).
Historical Uses: Acidity (gastric), bleeding, canker sores, colds, colic, congestion (uterine, vaginal), diarrhea, dietary supplementation, dysentery, gargle/mouth rinse, gastrointestinal problems, hemorrhage (metrorrhagia), hemorrhoids, inflammation, influenza, leukorrhea, malnutrition, menorrhagia, menstrual problems, nosebleed, periodontal disease, pruritus, skin problems, snakebite, sore throat, sores, sputum cruentum (bloody sputum), ulcer (duodenal, gastric, peptic), vaginitis, vomiting, and wounds (minor).
Discussion: May enhance digestive and urinary system functions; neutralize acidity; promote urine flow; provide dietary supplementation; reestablish healthy system functions; serve as a nutritional adjuvant to therapeutic programs.
Cautions/Contraindications: Avoid use if pregnant or breast-feeding.

Adverse Reactions: Nausea and/or vomiting.
Herb/Drug Interactions: This herb could cause an interaction (possibly severe) when taken with the following drugs: None known.
Preparations/Dosage: Crude herb: 3-9 grams. Extract: 5-10 drops (0.333-0.666 cc.) one to two times per day. Infusion: 1-2 cups per day. Tincture: 15-30 drops (1-2 cc.) one to three times per day.

Angelica (an·jel i·ke)
(*Angelica atropurpurea*)

Synonyms/Related Species: American Angelica, Archangel, Chinese Angelica Root (*angelica sinensis*), Dawson's Angelica (*angelica dawsonii*), Dong-Quai, European Angelica (*angelica archangelica*), Garden Angelica, Goutweed, Masterwort, Pinnate-Leaved Angelica (*angelica pinnata*), Purple Angelica, Sharp-Toothed Angelica, Spanish Angelica (*angelica heterocarpa*), Tang kuei, Tang kwei, White Angelica (*angelica arguta*), Wild Angelica (*angelica sylvestris*), and Wild Archangel.
Family/Class: Umbelliferae (parsley).
Habitat: Asia, Europe, Iceland, Lapland, North America, Prussia, Scotland, Spain, and Syria.
Flavor: Pungent/bitter.
Parts Used: Root, seeds.
Properties: Abortifacient, alterative, analgesic, antibiotic, anticoagulant, antifungal, antiperiodic, antiphlogistic, antispasmodic, aromatic, astringent, carminative, depurative, diaphoretic, diuretic, emmenagogue, expectorant, hemostatic, hypotensive, laxative, malariacidal, parasiticide, sedative, stimulant, stomachic, tonic, and vasodilator.
Constituents: Caffeic acid, coumarin, fatty acids (angelic), ferulic acid, flavonoids, inulin (starch), minerals (calcium), monosaccharides, polysaccharides, psoralens, resin, saponins, sterols, tannic acid, valerianic acid, vitamins (A, B_{12}, E (alpha-tocopheral), and volatile oil.
Historical Uses: Abscess, addiction (alcohol), plague, allergy, amenorrhea, anemia, angina, anorexia, appetite loss, arrhythmia, arteriosclerosis, arthritis, asthma, auditory problems, bleeding, bronchitis, bruises, cardiovascular conditions, chills, cirrhosis, cold extremities, colds, colic, constipation, cough, cramps, cystitis, cysts (ovarian), debility, dehydration, diabetes, diarrhea, digestive complaints, dysmenorrhea, escherichia coli (e-coli), exhaustion, eye problems, fever (ephemeral, enteric, intermittent, rheumatic), flatulence, flavoring agent, gastritis, gout, headache, hepatitis, hot flashes, hypertension (mild/moderate), hypoglycemia, hypotonia, indigestion, infection (bacterial, fungal, viral), infertility, inflammation, influenza, insomnia, insufficiency (venous), irritable bowel syndrome (IBS), lesion (tubercle), leukemia, lumbago, lung problems, malaria, menopausal/menstrual problems, migraine, muscle and joint pain, nausea, nephritis, nervous conditions, neuralgia, pain, parasites (malarial plasmodia, scabies), pleurisy, premenstrual syndrome (PMS), prolapse (rectal, uterine), prostatitis, pruritus, psoriasis, respiratory conditions, rheumatism, scrofula, skin problems, sores, spasmodic conditions, tenesmus, tinnitus, toothache, tuberculosis, tumors, typhoid, ulcer (bouveret, duodenal, fistula, gastric, peptic, tuberculous), urinary problems, visual disturbances, vitiligo, vomiting, weight loss, and wounds (minor).
Discussion: May aid digestion; calm the nerves; cause blood vessel dilatation; clear and open bronchial passages; counteract the effect of histamine; delay or reduce coagulation of the blood; enhance brain cells, intestinal system, and stomach functions; increase blood sugar levels,

circulation, libido, red blood cell counts, and sperm cell motility and viability; induce abortion; inhibit or destroy developement and growth of bacteria and other microorganisms and inhibit the release of serotonin; nourish and purify the blood; promote bowel evacuation, perspiration, the proliferation and differentiation of various blood components, including blood growth, and urine flow; reduce blood pressure levels, fractures in female athletes with irregular menstrual cycles and in persons taking prescription steroid drugs, the formation of arterial plaque, and the mortality rate of Rh-type incompatibility; protect healthy white blood cells during chemotherapy treatments; reestablish healthy system functions; restore normal tone to tissues; stimulate appetite, menstruation, metabolism, peristalsis, the production of insulin, and uterine contractions; strengthen the muscles and internal organs.

Cautions/Contraindications: Avoid use if pregnant or breast-feeding, or if you experience menorrhagia, or if you have cancer, diabetes, or heart disease, or at the first symptom of a herpes infection or recurrence. Do not apply to open wounds. Do not confuse this plant with poison hemlock (*conium maculatum*). May cause photosensitivity or photodermatosis in susceptible individuals. Some persons may experience bleeding or increased clotting time when using this herb with anticoagulant drugs or aspirin. Not for long-term use.

Adverse Reactions: Arrhythmia, bleeding (possibly serious), coagulation problems, diarrhea (possibly bloody), fluctuations in blood pressure levels, gastrointestinal cramps (severe), hematuria (blood in the urine), nausea, respiratory distress, and/or vomiting.

Herb/Drug Interactions: This herb could cause an interaction (possibly severe) when taken with the following drugs: Anticoagulant drugs, Hypotensive drugs, Salicylates, and Subsalicylates.

Preparations/Dosage: Crude Herb: 3-6 grams. Decoction (root): ¾-1 cup per day. Extract (cold/root): 1-1½ cups per day. Extract (root): 10-15 drops (0.666-1 cc.) one to two times per day. Infusion (seeds/crushed): ½-1 cup per day. Root (powdered): Average dose in substance ¼-½ teaspoon. Tincture: 10-30 drops (0.666-2 cc.) one to three times per day.

Angostura (ang ges·toor e)

(*Galipea cusparia*)

Synonyms/Related Species: Angustura, Cusparia Bark, and True Angustura.

Family/Class: Rutaceae (rue).

Habitat: South America and the West Indies.

Flavor: Bitter.

Parts Used: Bark.

Properties: Emetic, febrifuge, laxative, stimulant, and tonic.

Constituents: Alkaloids, angusturine, cusparine, galipine, galipoidine, galipoline, glucoside, and volatile oil.

Historical Uses: Diarrhea, dysentery, edema, fever (ephemeral), flavoring agent (for bitters), and gastrointestinal problems.

Discussion: May promote bowel evacuation; restore normal tone to tissues; stimulate peristalsis.

Cautions/Contraindications: Avoid use if pregnant or breast-feeding. Do not confuse this plant with the poisonous, odorless nux vomica (*strychnos nux-vomica*) also known as false angostura, or the poisonous copalchi bark (*strychnos pseudoquina*) of South America, or (*croton tiglium*) of Asia.

Adverse Reactions: Diarrhea (severe), nausea, and/or vomiting.

Herb/Drug Interactions: This herb could cause an interaction (possibly severe) when taken with the following drugs: None known.
Preparations/Dosage: Bark (powdered): Average dose in substance 5-15 grains (0.333-1 gm.). Decoction: ½-1 cup per day. Extract: 5-15 drops (0.333-1 cc.) one to two times per day. Infusion: 1-2 cups per day. Tincture: 15-20 drops (1-1.25 cc.) one to three times per day.
Did You Know? Some natives of South America still use angostura bark for fishing. They place the bark into a basket and drag the basket through the water. The bark releases its constituents into the water and stupefies the fish. The fish are then plucked from the water surface.

Anise (an is)
(*Pimpinella anisum*)

Synonyms/Related Species: Aniseed Stars, Badiana, Chinese Anise, Common Aniseed, Dipinella, Indian Anise, Pimpinel Seed, Star Anise, and Sweet Cumin.
Family/Class: Umbelliferae (parsley).
Habitat: Africa, Asia, Bulgaria, Crete, Egypt, England, Europe, France, Germany, Greece, India, Italy, Malta, Russia, Spain, South America, and Turkey.
Flavor: Pungent/sweet.
Parts Used: Seeds.
Properties: Analgesic, antibiotic, anticarcinogen, antifungal, antiphlogistic, antispasmodic, aromatic, carminative, depurative, diaphoretic, diuretic, emmenagogue, expectorant, narcotic, parasiticide, stimulant, and tonic.
Constituents: Anethol, carbohydrates, coumarin, creosol, fatty acids (arachidonic, linoleic, linolenic, oleic, palmitic, stearic), fixed oils (olein, palmitin, stearin), lipids, minerals (calcium, iron, magnesium, potassium), monosaccharides, mucilage, phytoestrogen, pinene, protein, sterols, vitamins (B, choline), and volatile oil.
Historical Uses: Appetite loss, asthma, belching, bronchitis, cancer (prostate), candida, cholera, cirrhosis, colds, colic, convulsions, cough, cramps, digestive complaints, diminished sex drive, diphtheria, edema, epilepsy, fever (ephemeral, rheumatic), flatulence, flavoring agent, gastritis, halitosis, headache, hepatitis, hiccups, indigestion, infection (bacterial, fungal), inflammation, influenza, insomnia, irritable bowel syndrome (IBS), liver problems, menopausal problems, moniliasis, mucus, muscle and joint pain, nausea, nervous conditions, pain, parasites (lice and their nits, scabies), perfume, pneumonia, potpourris, respiratory conditions, rheumatism, sachets, sinusitis, sore throat, spasmodic conditions, substitute for licorice, and vomiting.
Discussion: May aid digestion; cleanse the intestinal tract; clear and open bronchial passages; decrease the effect of carcinogens; inhibit or destroy developement and growth of bacteria and other microorganisms; prevent the deposition of fat in the liver; promote perspiration and urine flow; regenerate damaged liver cells; restore normal tone to tissues; serve as an adjuvant to some prostate cancer therapies; stimulate appetite, glandular secretions, libido, and menstruation.
Cautions/Contraindications: Avoid use if pregnant, or if you are allergic to anise or anethol, or if you have an estrogen dependent cancer, or if you have a history of estrogen dependant cancers, or if you are taking oral contraceptives. Do not confuse this plant with poisonous Japanese anise (*illicium landeolatum*). Estrogen containing substances may contribute to abnormal blood coagulation, migraine, and could promote the developement of certain types of estrogen dependant cancers. Not for long-term use.

Adverse Reactions: Abdominal pain, cancer (breast), coagulation problems, diarrhea, dizziness, edema, insufficiency (circulatory), migraine, nausea, seizure conditions, skin problems, stupor, and/or vomiting.
Herb/Drug Interactions: This herb could cause an interaction (possibly severe) when taken with the following drugs: Hormones and Synthetic Substitutes (i.e. conjugated estrogens, contraceptives (oral, etc.), and other hormonal replacement therapy (HRT).
Preparations/Dosage: Crude Herb: 3-6 grams. Infusion: 1-1½ cups per day. Oil of Anise (*oleum anisum*): Average dose 2-5 drops (0.133-0.333 cc.) in water or on a sugar cube. Seeds (powdered): Average dose in substance 10-15 grains (0.666-0.98 gm.). Tincture: 10-15 drops (0.666-1 cc.) one to three times per day.
Isolation: Creosol: Average dose of ½-2 drops (0.025-0.1 cc.) for use as an antimicrobic.
Did You Know? The ancient Egyptians cultivated anise for use as a fragrance and spice.

Apple (ap el)
(*Pyrus malus*)

Synonyms/Related Species: Crab-Apple Tree and Wild Apple.
Family/Class: Rosaceae (rose).
Floral Emblem: Arkansas and Michigan.
Habitat: The Caucasus, Britain, Europe, France, North America, Norway, Rome, Switzerland, and other regions.
Flavor: Sweet/sour.
Parts Used: Bark, fruit (seeds removed).
Properties: Analgesic, antibiotic, anticarcinogen, antioxidant, antiphlogistic, antiscorbutic, antiviral, carminative, laxative, lithotriptic, and nutritive.
Constituents: Amygdalin, amyl valerate, carbohydrates, cyanide, enzymes, gallic acid, inulin (starch), iron, magnesium, malic acid, monosaccharides, pectic acid, pectin, phlorhizin, phloroglucin, phosphates, phosphorous, phosphoric acid, protein, quercetin, sodium, tannic acid, tartaric acid, and vitamins (A and C (ascorbic acid).
Historical Uses: Allergy, arteriosclerosis, arthritis, asthma, beverage (ale/cider), calculus, cancer (bladder, breast, colon, ovarian), canker sores, cataracts, Celiac disease, constipation, deserts, diabetes, diabetic retinopathy, diarrhea, dietary supplementation, eczema, edema, emphysema, erysipelas, eye inflammation, fasting, fever (ephemeral, enteric, herpetic, rheumatic), gallstones, gout, headache, heart disease, herpes, hives, human immunodeficiency virus (HIV), indigestion, infection (viral), inflammation, insomnia, jams/jellies, kidney stones, liver problems, macular degeneration, malnutrition, mastitis, migraine, muscle and joint pain, pain, poisoning (heavy metal), polio, prostatitis, rheumatism, scurvy, sexually transmitted diseases (STDs), skin problems, sore throat, typhoid, ulcer (bouveret), wounds (minor), and wrinkles.
Discussion: May aid digestion; balance blood sugar levels; cause glycosuria by blocking the reabsorption of glucose; decrease the effect of carcinogens; dissolve calculi; eliminate heavy metals from the body; increase collagen production; inhibit oxidation; offset the negative effects of chemotherapy and radiation therapy; prevent histamine secretion; protect the eye lens and retinal cells from toxins, the skin from ultraviolet damage, and protect against heart disease; provide dietary supplementation; reduce arterial plaque formation and acidity (gastric); repair nervous system damage; serve as a nutritional adjuvant to therapeutic programs and may serve as an adjuvant to cancer, diabetes, and hypercholesteremia, drug therapies; stop or slow abnormal cell growth; strengthen capillary linings.

Cautions/Contraindications: Avoid excessive use if pregnant or breast-feeding. Apple seeds contain cyanide and are toxic.
Adverse Reactions: Constipation or diarrhea.
Herb/Drug Interactions: This herb could cause an interaction (possibly severe) when taken with the following drugs: Antibiotic drugs, Calcium Channel Blocker drugs, and Immune Suppressive drugs.
Preparations/Dosage: Decoction (bark): ¾-1 cup per day. Fruit (fresh): May be ingested freely. Infusion (fruit peels): 1-3 cups per day. Juice (fruit): May be ingested freely.
Did You Know? There are over 300 varieties of apple tree species, which grow in all fifty of the United States, as well as other regions, and the cultivated species of apple have the same properties as the wild varieties.

Apricot (ā pri·kot)
(*Prunus armeniaca*)

Synonyms/Related Species: Abricot, Albricoque, and Al-Birqūq.
Family/Class: Rosaceae (rose).
Habitat: Armenia, Asia, China, Britain, Egypt, England, France, the Himalayas, Italy, North America, Syria, and other regions.
Flavor: Sweet.
Parts Used: Fruit (with pit/stone removed), inner kernel of the pit/stone.
Properties: Anticarcinogen, antispasmodic, demulcent, expectorant, nutritive, sedative, and tonic.
Constituents: Amygdalin, carbohydrates, fatty acids (arachidonic, linoleic, linolenic, oleic, palmitic, stearic), fixed oils (olein, palmitin, stearin), hydrocyanic acid, iron, laetrile, magnesium, phosphorus, potassium, sodium, vitamins A, B_2 (riboflavin), B_3 niacin (nicotinic acid), and volatile oil.
Historical Uses: Cancer, colds, dietary supplementation, flavoring agent, food source, malnutrition, mucus, respiratory conditions, skin problems, spasmodic conditions, and substitute for oil of almonds.
Discussion: May clear and open bronchial passages; decrease the effect of carcinogens; enhance intestinal and lung functions; provide dietary supplementation; restore normal tone to tissues; serve as a nutritional adjuvant to therapeutic programs and as a natural source of laetrile; soothe mucous membrane irritation.
Cautions/Contraindications: Avoid use if pregnant or breast-feeding. The pit/stone contains hydrocyanic acid and is extremely poisonous; use only the inner kernel.
Adverse Reactions: Edema, hydrocyanism (hydrocyanic acid poisoning), nausea, and/or vomiting.
Herb/Drug Interactions: This herb could cause an interaction (possibly severe) when taken with the following drugs: None known.
Preparations/Dosage: Fruit (fresh): May be ingested freely. Infusion (crushed/powdered kernel): ½-1 cup per day. Juice (fruit): May be ingested freely. Inner Kernel (powdered): 3-5 grams in formulas.

Araroba (ar e·rōbe)
(*Andira araroba*)

Synonyms/Related Species: Bahia Powder, Brazilian Araroba, Brazil Powder, Chrysarobin, Crude Chrysarobin, Goa, Goa Powder, Ringworm Powder, Voucapoua Araroba, and Zebrawood.
Family/Class: Leguminosae (legume).
Habitat: India and South America.
Flavor: Bitter.
Parts Used: Resin (powdered).
Properties: Antioxidant, emetic, parasiticide, teniacide, and teniafuge.
Constituents: Bitter principle, chrysarobin, and resin.
Historical Uses: Acne, dermatitis, dhobi itch, eczema, hemorrhoids, parasites (ringworm, tapeworm), pruritus, psoriasis, skin problems, and sore nipples.
Discussion: May inhibit indirect oxidation of glucose phosphate in certain skin conditions; soothe nipple soreness.
Cautions/Contraindications: Avoid use if pregnant or breast-feeding. Do not apply or use goa powder in its crude form. Not for long-term use.
Adverse Reactions: Conjunctivitis, delirium, diarrhea (severe), fever, gastrointestinal irritation, mucous membrane irritation, nausea, skin problems, and/or vomiting.
Herb/Drug Interactions: This herb could cause an interaction (possibly severe) when taken with the following drugs: None known.
Preparations/Dosage: Decoction: ⅛-¼ cup per day. Resin (powdered): Average dose in substance ½ grain (0.0333 gm.).

Arborvitae (är ber·vī tē)
(*Thuja occidentalis*)

Synonyms/Related Species: African Arborvitae (*thuja articulata*), American Arborvitae, Chinese Arborvitae (*thuja orientalis*), Hackmatock, Lebensbaum, Swamp Cedar, Thuia du Canada, Thuja, Tree of Life, Western Red Cedar (*thuja plicata*), and Yellow Cedar.
Family/Class: Cupressaceae (cypress).
Habitat: Africa, Britain, China, Europe, Japan, and North America.
Flavor: Bitter.
Parts Used: Bark (inner), branches (new growth), leaves.
Properties: Abortifacient, analgesic, anticarcinogen, antifungal, antiphlogistic, antiviral, astringent, counterirritant, diaphoretic, diuretic, emmenagogue, expectorant, hemostatic, laxative, nervine, parasiticide, sedative, and stimulant.
Constituents: Flavonoids, glycoprotein, levo-fenchone, lignin, monosaccharides, mucilage, pinene, pinipicrin, polysaccharides, resin, tannic acid, thujone, volatile oil, and wax.
Historical Uses: Amenorrhea, anemia, anxiety, arrhythmia, arthritis, bleeding, bronchitis, burns (minor), cancer (breast, colon, lung, uterine), cardiovascular conditions, colds, constipation, cough, cystitis, debility, diarrhea, diuria (frequent daytime urination), dysentery, edema, fever (ephemeral, herpetic, rheumatic), glandular problems, gout, herpes, impetigo, infection (bacterial, fungal, viral), inflammation, insomnia, mucus, muscle and joint pain, neuralgia, pain, parasites (scabies), psoriasis, respiratory conditions, rheumatism, sexually transmitted diseases (STDs), skin problems, strep throat, and warts (digitate, filiform, fugitive, glabra, mother, plana juvenilis, plantar, seborrhoeic, venereal, vulgaris).

Discussion: May calm the nervous system; clear and open bronchial passages; decrease the effect of carcinogens; enhance cardiovascular system, immune system, glandular system, lung, and spleen functions; increase tolerance to chemotherapy and radiation therapy; induce abortion; promote bowel evacuation, perspiration, and urine flow; offset the negative effects of inoculations or vaccines; reduce the persistent urge to urinate; stimulate menstruation, peristalsis, and uterine contractions; strengthen the urinary system.
Cautions/Contraindications: Avoid use if pregnant or breast-feeding, or if you have diarrhea. Not for long-term use. Use with professional guidance/supervision.
Adverse Reactions: Coma, convulsions, diarrhea (severe), flatulence (excessive), gastritis, gastrointestinal problems, hemorrhage (mucous membrane), indigestion, irritable bowel syndrome (IBS), loss of consciousness, nausea, paralysis, reduced blood pressure levels, spasmodic conditions, vomiting, and/or possible death.
Herb/Drug Interactions: This herb could cause an interaction (possibly severe) when taken with the following drugs: None known.
Preparations/Dosage: Branches or Leaves (powdered): Average dose in substance 10-20 grains (0.666-1.333 gm). Crude herb: 6-12 grams. Decoction: ¼ cup per day. Extract: 3-5 drops (0.2-0.333 cc.). Infusion (cold): 1 tablespoon one to two times per day. Tincture: 5-10 drops (0.333-0.666 cc.) one to three times per day. Oil of Arborvitae (*oleum thujae*): Average dose 1-5 drops (0.066-0.333 cc) in water or on a sugarcube.

Arbutus, Strawberry Tree (är·byoot'es, strô ber ē trē)
(*Arbutus unedo*)

Synonyms/Related Species: European Arbutus, European Strawberry Tree, Madroño, Pacific Madroñe (*arbutus menziesii*), and Wild Strawberry Tree.
Family/Class: Ericaceae (heath).
Habitat: Algiers, Europe, Greece, Ireland, the Mediterranean, North America, and Spain.
Flavor: Bitter.
Parts Used: Bark, leaves.
Properties: Antiphlogistic, astringent, diuretic, emetic, expectorant, hemostatic, narcotic, stomachic, and urinary antiseptic.
Constituents: Arbutin and tannic acid.
Historical Uses: Bleeding, burns (minor), colds, cramps, diabetes, fever (ephemeral, rheumatic), gargle/mouth rinse, impetigo, infection (urinary tract), inflammation, insomnia, muscle and joint pain, pain, respiratory conditions, rheumatism, sores, sore throat, strep throat, stomachache, ulcer (gastric), urinary problems, and wounds (minor).
Discussion: May clear and open bronchial passages; enhance stomach function; increase strength; promote urine flow.
Cautions/Contraindications: Avoid use if pregnant or breast-feeding.
Adverse Reactions: Confusion, nausea, stupor, and/or vomiting.
Herb/Drug Interactions: This herb could cause an interaction (possibly severe) when taken with the following drugs: None known.
Preparations/Dosage: Crude Herb: 1-3 grams. Decoction (bark): ¼-½ cup per day. Infusion (bark or leaves): ½-1 cup per day.
Isolation: Arbutin: Average dose of 5-15 grains (0.333-1 gm.) for use as a diuretic and urinary antiseptic.

Arbutus, Trailing (är·byoot'es, tra'lin)
(*Epigaea repens*)

Synonyms/Related Species: Gravel Plant, Ground Laurel, Ground-Sweet, Mountain Pink, Wild Mayflower, and Winter Pink.
Family/Class: Ericaceae (heath).
Floral Emblem: Massachusetts.
Habitat: Britain and North America.
Flavor: Bitter/pungent.
Parts Used: Leaves.
Properties: Analgesic, antibiotic, antifungal, antilithic, antiphlogistic, antispasmodic, astringent, depurative, diuretic, hemostatic, lithotriptic, oxytocic, stimulant, tonic, urinary antiseptic, and vasoconstrictor.
Constituents: Arbutin, flavonoids, gallic acid, malic acid, monotropein, myricitrin, quercetin, tannic acid, ursone (ursolic acid), and volatile oil.
Historical Uses: Alkaline urine, arthritis, bleeding, bronchitis, calculus, candida, cramps, cystitis, diabetes, diarrhea, digestive complaints, dysentery, dysmenorrhea, edema, enuresis (urinary incontinence), escherichia coli (e-coli), fever (ephemeral, rheumatic), gallstones, gastritis, gleet, gonorrhea, gout, hematuria (blood in the urine), hemorrhage, hemorrhoids, herbal tobacco, hives, indigestion, infection (bacterial, bladder, fungal, sexually transmitted, urinary tract), inflammation, insufficiency (pancreatic), irritable bowel syndrome (IBS), kidney problems, kidney stones, lithemia, liver problems, lumbago, menopausal/menstrual problems, menorrhagia, moniliasis, mucus, muscle and joint pain, nephritis, pain, prostatitis, pyelitis, rash, rheumatism, sexually transmitted diseases (STDs), spasmodic conditions, spleen problems, syphilis, ulcer (syphilitic), urethritis, uterine problems, weight loss, and wounds (minor).
Discussion: May constrict the blood vessels; dissolve calculi; enhance liver, stomach, and urinary system; inhibit or destroy developement and growth of bacteria and other microorganisms; enhance cardiovascular system, intestinal system, and liver functions; prevent the development of calculus or stones; promote urine flow; reduce excessive lithic acid (uric acid) and urate levels in the blood, tophi, and urine, and the frequency of nighttime urination; restore normal tone to tissues; stimulate uterine contractions; strengthen the urinary system.
Cautions/Contraindications: Avoid use if pregnant or breast-feeding, or if you have chronic kidney disease, ulcer (duodenal, peptic), or if you have gastric sensitivity. Do not adminiter to children under 12 years of age. Do not administer simultaneously with food or medications that increase lithic acid levels. May interfere with the absorption of atropine (when taken by mouth), codeine, ephedrine, pseudoephedrine, and theophylline drugs. Not for long-term use.
Adverse Reactions: Aggravation of acid reflux disease, liver damage (often characterized by jaundice), mucous membrane irritation, nausea, tinnitus, and/or vomiting.
Herb/Drug Interactions: This herb could cause an interaction (possibly severe) when taken with the following drugs: Autonomic drugs, Diuretic drugs, Medications/Products containing ephedra or pseudoephedrine, Opiate Agonists/Narcotic drugs, and Theophylline drugs.
Preparations/Dosage: Crude Herb: 3-6 grams. Infusion: 1-2 cups per day.
Isolation: Arbutin: Average dose of 5-15 grains (0.3-1 gm.) for use as a diuretic and urinary antiseptic.

Areca Nut (ar i·ke nut)
(*Areca catechu*)

Synonyms/Related Species: Adekka, Betel Palm, East Indian Palm, Malabar Nut (*areca dicksoni*), Pinang, and True Betel Nut (*areca aleeraceae*).
Family/Class: Palmaceae (palm).
Habitat: Africa, Asia, Australia, Ceylon, China, India, Malacca, Siam, and Sumatra.
Flavor: Bitter.
Parts Used: Nut/seed.
Properties: Anthelmintic, aromatic, astringent, cardiac depressant, carminative, diuretic, hemostatic, laxative, miotic, sialogogue, teniacide, teniafuge, tonic, and vermifuge.
Constituents: Alkaloids, arecane, arecoline, fatty acids (oleic, palmitic, stearic), fixed oils (olein, palmitin, stearin), gallic acid, guavacine, guracine, gum, lignin, tannic acid, and volatile oil.
Historical Uses: Bleeding, colic, constipation, dentifrice, parasites (pinworm, roundworm, schistosoma, tapeworm), periodontal disease, and schistosomiasis.
Discussion: May aid digestion; cause pupil contraction; diminish or reduce functional activity of the heart; promote bowel evacuation, saliva secretion, and urine flow; restore normal tone to tissues; stimulate peristalsis and the vagus nerve.
Cautions/Contraindications: Avoid use if pregnant or breast-feeding. Do not confuse this plant with betel nut (*piper betle*). Chewing slices of the nuts will cause a euphoric effect and stain the mouth, lips, and feces a red color. May cause cancer (oral) when used long-term. Not for long-term use. Use with professional guidance/supervision.
Adverse Reactions: Bradycardia, cardiac failure, nausea, salivation (increased), spasmodic conditions, tremors, vomiting, and/or possible death.
Herb/Drug Interactions: This herb could cause an interaction (possibly severe) when taken with the following drugs: None known.
Preparations/Dosage: Crude herb: 3-6 grams. Decoction: ¼-1 cup per day. Extract: 1 drachm (4 cc.). Nut/Seed (powdered): 1-2 teaspoons used as a teniacide for tapeworm.
Isolation: Arecoline hydrobromide: Used in a 1% solution for use as a miotic, or as an anthelmintic in veterinary medicine.

Arnica (är ni·ke)
(*Arnica montana*)

Synonyms/Related Species: Alpine Arnica (*arnica angustifolia*), Common Arnica, European Arnica, Hairy Arnica (*arnica mollis*), Heart-Leaved Arnica (*arnica cordifolia*), Lake Louise Arnica (*arnica louiseana*), Lawless Arnica (*arnica diversifolia*), Leafy Arnica (*arnica chamissonis*), Leopard's Bane, Long-Leaved Arnica (*arnica longifolia*), Meadow Arnica (*arnica fulgens*), Mountain Arnica (*arnica latifolia*), Mountain Tobacco, Parry's Arnica (*arnica parryi*), Rydberg's Arnica (*arnica rydbergii*), Slender Arnica (*arnica gracilis*), Streambank Arnica (*arnica amplexicaulis*), and Wolfsbane.
Family/Class: Compositae (composite).
Habitat: Alaska, the Alpine and Subalpine zones, Asia, England, Europe, North America, Russia, Scandinavia, Scotland, Siberia, and the Yukon Territory.
Flavor: Bitter.
Parts Used: Flower, root.

Properties: Analgesic, antibiotic, antiphlogistic, cardiant, demulcent, diaphoretic, diuretic, expectorant, stimulant, and vulnerary.
Constituents: Arnicin, coumarin, fatty acids (angelic, arachidonic, linoleic, linolenic), glycosides, phulin, sesquiterpene lactones, tannic acid, vitamins (choline), and volatile oil.
Historical Uses: Alopecia, angina, arthritis, bronchitis, bruises, cardiovascular conditions, carpal tunnel syndrome, chilblains, cirrhosis, colds, cough, diphtheria, dislocations, edema, epilepsy, fatigue, fever (ephemeral, rheumatic), foot soak, fractures, gout, hemorrhage (metrorrhagia), infection (bacterial), inflammation, insect bites or stings, liver problems, motion sickness, muscle and joint pain, pain, myocarditis, palsy, phlebitis, respiratory conditions, rheumatism, seizure conditions, sprain, trauma (postoperative), and wounds (minor).
Discussion: May clear and open bronchial passages; enhance circulatory system function; inhibit or destroy developement and growth of bacteria and other microorganisms; prevent the deposition of fat in the liver; promote perspiration and urine flow; reduce the effects of postoperative tissue trauma; soothe mucous membrane irritation; speed healing; stimulate the cardiovascular system and white blood cells.
Cautions/Contraindications: Avoid use if pregnant or breast-feeding. Always apply arnica in a diluted form. Do not apply to broken skin or open wounds. Do not confuse this plant with aconite also known as wolf's bane (*aconitum napellus*). Not for long-term use. Use with professional guidance/supervision.
Adverse Reactions: Abdominal pain, arrhythmia, blisters, cardiac failure, coma, debility, diarrhea, gastroenteritis, inflammation, nausea, nervousness, pruritus, rash, skin problems, and/or vomiting.
Herb/Drug Interactions: This herb could cause an interaction (possibly severe) when taken with the following drugs: None known.
Preparations/Dosage: External uses only. Infusion (flowers): ⅛-¼ cup applied topically as an external wash. Tincture (flowers or root): 10-30 drops (0.666-2 cc.) diluted and applied topically.
Did You Know? Arnica has been used for over 400 years in America and Europe for a variety of conditions.

Arrowroot (ar ō·root)
(*Maranta arundinacae*)

Synonyms/Related Species: Araruta, Aru-Root, Bahia, Bermuda Arrowroot, Brazilian Arrowroot (*maranta palmata*), East Indian Arrowroot (*maranta ramosissima*), Indian Arrowroot, Maranta Arrowroot, Maranta Starch, Para-Arrowroot, and West Indian Arrowroot (*maranta allouya*).
Family/Class: Marantaceae (arrowroot).
Habitat: Africa, Bengal, Central America, India, Mauritius, Java, the Philippines, and South America.
Flavor: Bland.
Parts Used: Root.
Properties: Demulcent and nutritive.
Constituents: Albumin (albumen), fiber, gum, inulin (starch), and monosaccharide.

Historical Uses: Convalescence, diarrhea, dietary supplementation, dysentery, gangrene, gastrointestinal problems, insect bites or stings, malnutrition, poisoning (non-caustic), scorpion stings, substitute for kudzu root, and wounds (minor).
Discussion: May provide dietary supplementation; serve as a nutritional adjuvant to therapeutic programs and serve as an antidote for non-caustic poisons; soothe mucous membrane irritation.
Cautions/Contraindications: Avoid use if pregnant or breast-feeding.
Adverse Reactions: None known.
Herb/Drug Interactions: This herb could cause an interaction (possibly severe) when taken with the following drugs: None known.
Preparations/Dosage: Root starch (powdered): 3-6 grams. To extract the starch, crush and leach the roots in water. Strain or sieve the milky liquid into a container and let settle. Add clean water, mix, let settle, and strain again. Dry starch on cookie sheets in the sun (be sure to protect it from insects). Use as a thickening agent for soups and gravy.

Artichoke, Cardoon (är te·chōk, kär·doon)
(*Cynara cardunculus*)

Synonyms/Related Species: Artichoke Thistle, Carduus, Spanish Cardoon, and Tours Cardoon.
Family/Class: Compositae (composite).
Habitat: France, Italy, and Spain.
Flavor: Bitter.
Parts Used: Inner leaf stalks and the top portion of the stalk.
Properties: Antiphlogistic, aphrodisiac, carminative, depurative, diuretic, hepatic, and nutritive.
Constituents: Albumin (albumen), caffeic acid, chlorogenic acid, cynarin, cynaropicrin, cynaratriol, enzymes, flavonoids, grossheimin, gum, inulin (starch), iron, monosaccharides, phosphorus, potassium, rutin, sesquiterpene lactones, tannic acid, vitamin B_3 niacin (nicotinic acid), and volatile oil.
Historical Uses: Albuminuria, anemia (postoperative), appetite loss, arteriosclerosis, arthritis, dietary supplementation, digestive complaints, fever (ephemeral, rheumatic), gallbladder problems, indigestion, inflammation, jaundice, kidney problems, liver problems, malnutrition, muscle and joint pain, rheumatism, and weight loss.
Discussion: May aid digestion; arouse sexual impulses; cleanse the whole system; lower fat, cholesterol, protein, and triglyceride levels; prevent calculi and hemorrhage in persons with hypertension; promote urine flow; protect the liver; provide dietary supplementation; reduce capillary fragility; serve as a nutritional adjuvant to therapeutic programs; stimulate peristalsis.
Cautions/Contraindications: Avoid use if pregnant or breast-feeding, or if you have an obstruction (biliary). May cause allergic reactions and dermatitis in susceptible individuals.
Adverse Reactions: Nausea, obstruction (biliary), and/or vomiting.
Herb/Drug Interactions: This herb could cause an interaction (possibly severe) when taken with the following drugs: None known.
Preparations/Dosage: Inner Leaf Stalks and the Top Portion of the Stalk: Blanched and used in stews, soups, and salads.

Artichoke, Globe (är te·chōk, glōb)
(*Cynara scolymus*)

Synonyms/Related Species: Alcarchofa, Al-Kharšūf, Articiocco, and Garden Artichoke.
Family/Class: Compositae (composite).

Habitat: Africa, Arabia, the Canary Islands, Greece, Italy, the Mediterranean, North America, and South America.
Flavor: Bitter.
Parts Used: Flowerbuds.
Properties: Antiphlogistic, aphrodisiac, carminative, depurative, diuretic, hepatic, and nutritive.
Constituents: Albumin (albumen), caffeic acid, chlorogenic acid, cynarase, cynarin, cynaropicrin, cynaratriol, enzymes, flavonoids, grossheimin, gum, inulin (starch), iron, monosaccharides, phosphorus, potassium, rutin, sesquiterpene lactones, tannic acid, vitamin B_3 niacin (nicotinic acid), and volatile oil.
Historical Uses: Albuminuria, anemia (postoperative), appetite loss, arteriosclerosis, arthritis, dietary supplementation, digestive complaints, fever (ephemeral, rheumatic), food/vegetable (flower heads picked before maturity), gallbladder problems, indigestion, inflammation, jaundice, kidney problems, liver problems, malnutrition, muscle and joint pain, rheumatism, and weight loss.
Discussion: May aid digestion; arouse sexual impulses; cleanse the whole system; lower fat, cholesterol, protein, and triglyceride levels; prevent calculi and hemorrhage in persons with hypertension; promote urine flow; protect the liver; provide dietary supplementation; reduce capillary fragility and cholesterol levels; serve as a nutritional adjuvant to therapeutic programs; stimulate peristalsis.
Cautions/Contraindications: Avoid use if pregnant or breast-feeding, or if you have an obstruction (biliary). May cause allergic reactions and dermatitis in susceptible individuals.
Adverse Reactions: Nausea, obstruction (biliary), and/or vomiting.
Herb/Drug Interactions: This herb could cause an interaction (possibly severe) when taken with the following drugs: None known.
Preparations/Dosage: Flowerbuds: Boiled or eaten raw as a vegetable.

Artichoke, Jerusalem (är te·chōk, ji·roo se·lem)
(Helianthus tuberosus)

Synonyms/Related Species: Alcarchofa, Al-Kharšūf, Articiocco, Bengali, Hindoo, and Sunflower Artichoke.
Family/Class: Compositae (composite).
Habitat: Africa, Arabia, England, India, Italy, and North America.
Flavor: Bitter/bland.
Parts Used: Tubers.
Properties: Antiphlogistic, aphrodisiac, carminative, depurative, diuretic, hepatic, and nutritive.
Constituents: Albumin (albumen), gum, inulin (starch), levulin, iron, monosaccharides, phosphorus, potassium, and vitamin B_3 niacin (nicotinic acid).
Historical Uses: Albuminuria, anemia (postoperative), appetite loss, arteriosclerosis, arthritis, dietary supplementation, digestive complaints, fever (ephemeral, rheumatic), gallbladder problems, indigestion, inflammation, jaundice, kidney problems, liver problems, malnutrition, muscle and joint pain, rheumatism, and weight loss.
Discussion: May aid digestion; arouse sexual impulses; cleanse the whole system; lower fat, cholesterol, protein, and triglyceride levels; prevent calculi; promote urine flow; protect the liver; provide dietary supplementation; serve as a nutritional adjuvant to therapeutic programs; stimulate peristalsis.

Cautions/Contraindications: Avoid use if pregnant or breast-feeding, or if you have an obstruction (biliary). May cause allergic reactions and dermatitis in susceptible individuals.
Adverse Reactions: Obstruction (biliary).
Herb/Drug Interactions: This herb could cause an interaction (possibly severe) when taken with the following drugs: None known.
Preparations/Dosage: Tubers: Boiled, peeled, and eaten as a vegetable.

Asafetida (as e·fet e·de)
(*Ferula asafoetida*)

Synonyms/Related Species: Asa, Assafoetida, Azāfoetida, Devil's Dung, Food of the Gods, Gum Asafoetida, Iranian Asafetida (*ferula assa-foetida*), Kandaharre Hing, and Persian Asafetida (*ferula persica*).
Family/Class: Umbelliferae (parsley).
Habitat: Afghanistan, Asia, India, Iran, Pakistan, Persia, and Turkey.
Flavor: Bitter/pungent.
Parts Used: Gum resin (from the root).
Properties: Abortifacient, antifungal, antispasmodic, aromatic, carminative, counterirritant, expectorant, laxative, sedative, stimulant, and stomachic.
Constituents: Ferulic acid, gum, mucilage, resin, sulfur, and volatile oil.
Historical Uses: Allergy (food), amenorrhea, anxiety, asthma, bronchitis, candida, chorea, chronic fatigue syndrome (CFS), colds, colic, convulsions, cough, croup, depression (mild/moderate), digestive complaints, Epstein Barr Virus (EBV), fibromyalgia, flatulence, flavoring agent, gastritis, hypercholesteremia, hypoglycemia, hysteria, indigestion, infection (fungal), insect bites or stings, insomnia, irritable bowel syndrome (IBS), moniliasis, mood swings, mononucleosis (infectious), mucus, nervous conditions, pneumonia, respiratory conditions, spasmodic conditions, substitute for garlic, and whooping cough.
Discussion: May aid digestion; clear and open bronchial passages; enhance liver, spleen, and stomach functions; induce abortion; promote bowel evacuation; reduce cholesterol levels; regulate blood sugar levels; stimulate the alimentary tract, the mucous membranes, peristalsis, and uterine contractions.
Cautions/Contraindications: Avoid use if pregnant or breast-feeding. May cause dermatitis in susceptible individuals.
Adverse Reactions: Belching, convulsions, diarrhea, flatulence, headache, mucous membrane problems, nausea, and/or vomiting.
Herb/Drug Interactions: This herb could cause an interaction (possibly severe) when taken with the following drugs: None known.
Preparations/Dosage: Gum resin (powdered): 100mg.-1 gram. Emulsion: 4 parts asafetida to 100 parts water. Infusion: 1-2 cups per day. Pill Form: 3 grains of gum resin to a pill. Take 1 pill per day. Tincture: ½-1 teaspoon per day.

Ash (ash)
(*Fraxinus excelsior*)

Synonyms/Related Species: American White Ash (*fraxinus americana*), Basket Ash, Black Swamp Ash (*fraxinus nigra*), Blue Ash, Common Ash, Curl-Leaved Ash, English Ash, European Ash, Green Ash (*fraxinus lanceolate*), Hance Ash (*fraxinus rhynchophylla*), Hoop Ash, Oregon Ash (*fraxinus latifolia*), True Ash Tree, Water Ash, and Weeping Ash.
Family/Class: Oleaceae (olive).
Habitat: England, Europe, and North America.
Flavor: Bitter.
Parts Used: Bark (trunk/root), leaves, samaras (ash-keys).
Properties: Analgesic, antioxidant, antiphlogistic, astringent, depurative, diaphoretic, diuretic, hemostatic, laxative, lithotriptic, tonic, and vasodilator.
Constituents: Esculin, calcium, coumarin, flavonoids, fraxetin, fraxidin, fraxin, fraxinol, gum, malic acid, mannitol (mannite), mucilage, quercetin, rutin, sterols, tannic acid, terpenes, and volatile oil.
Historical Uses: Ague, arthritis, bladder problems, bleeding, calculus, diarrhea, dysentery, edema, eye problems, fever (ephemeral, rheumatic), flatulence, gallstones, gout, inflammation, jaundice, kidney stones, leprosy, liver problems, muscle and joint pain, pain, psoriasis, rheumatism, spleen problems, substitute for peruvian bark and senna, warts (digitate, filiform, fugitive, glabra, mother, plana juvenilis, plantar, seborrhoeic, vulgaris), weight loss.
Discussion: May cause blood vessel dilatation; cleanse the liver; dissolve calculi; inhibit oxidation; prevent hemorrhage in persons with hypertension; promote bowel evacuation, perspiration, and urine flow; reduce capillary fragility; restore normal tone to tissues.
Cautions/Contraindications: Avoid use if pregnant or breast-feeding.
Adverse Reactions: Nausea and/or vomiting.
Herb/Drug Interactions: This herb could cause an interaction (possibly severe) when taken with the following drugs: None known.
Preparations/Dosage: Crude Herb: 3-6 grams. Decoction (bark): ½-1 cup per day. Infusion (leaves and/or samaras): 1-2 cups per day.
Isolation: Esculin: Average dose of 10-15 grains (0.66-1 gm.) for use as a febrifuge. Mannitol hexanitrate: Average dose of 15-60 mg. (¼-1 grain) for use as a vasodilator.

Ash, Mountain (ash, moun ten)
(*Sorbus americana*)

Synonyms/Related Species: American Mountain Ash, European Mountain Ash (*sorbus aucuparia*), Rowan, Rowan Tree, Service Tree Ash (*sorbus domestica*), Sitka Mountain Ash (*sorbus sitchensis*), Sorb Apple, and Western Mountain Ash (*sorbus scopulina*).
Family/Class: Rosaceae (rose).
Habitat: Asia, Europe, Newfoundland, North America, Siberia, the Subalpine zones, and the Yukon Territory.
Flavor: Bitter.
Parts Used: Bark (inner), fruit (seeds removed).
Properties: Antiperiodic, antiphlogistic, antiscorbutic, aromatic, astringent, demulcent, depurative, diuretic, hemostatic, laxative, and malariacidal.

Constituents: Amygdalin, bitter substances, citric acid, fatty acids (oleic, palmitic, stearic), fixed oils (olein, palmitin, stearin), glycosides, hydrocyanic acid, malic acid, monosaccharides, sorbitol, sorbose, tannic acid, tartaric acid, and vitamin C (ascorbic acid).
Historical Uses: Ague, angina, arthritis, beverage, bleeding, calculus, colds, congestion (uterine, vaginal), dandruff, diabetes, diarrhea, diuria (frequent daytime urination), fever (ephemeral, intermittent, rheumatic), gallbladder problems, gallstones, gargle/mouth rinse, gastrointestinal problems, gout, hemorrhoids, indigestion, inflammation, kidney problems, kidney stones, laryngitis, leukorrhea, malaria, menstrual problems, mucus, muscle and joint pain, nausea, parasites (malarial plasmodia), respiratory conditions, rheumatism, scurvy, sore throat, stomachache, substitute for cinchona bark, tonsillitis, urinary problems, and vaginitis.
Discussion: May dissolve calculi; promote bowel evacuation and urine flow; purify the blood; reduce the persistent urge to urinate; soothe mucous membrane irritation; stimulate metabolism and peristalsis; strengthen the urinary system.
Cautions/Contraindications: Avoid use if pregnant or breast-feeding. Do not confuse this tree with common ash (*fraxinus spp.*). Not for long-term use. The seeds of the fruit contain hydrocyanic acid and are extremely poisonous.
Adverse Reactions: Diarrhea (severe), gastroenteritis, hematuria (blood in the urine), hydrocyanism (hydrocyanic acid poisoning), nausea, and/or vomiting.
Herb/Drug Interactions: This herb could cause an interaction (possibly severe) when taken with the following drugs: None known.
Preparations/Dosage: Crude Herb: 1-3 grams. Decoction (bark): ¼-½ cup per day. Extract (cold): 1 cup per day. Fruit (dried/powdered): Used as flour. Jelly (fruit): 1 tablespoon. Juice (fruit): 1 teaspoon.

Ash, Prickly (ash, prik lē)
(X*anthoxylum americanum*)

Synonyms/Related Species: Northern Prickly Ash, Sichuan Pepper Tree (*xanthoxylum alatum*), Southern Prickly Ash (*xanthoxylum clavaherculis*), Suterberry, Toothache Bush, Toothache Tree, and Yellow Wood.
Family/Class: Rutaceae (rue).
Habitat: Asia and North America.
Flavor: Pungent.
Parts Used: Bark (root), berries.
Properties: Alterative, analgesic, anthelmintic, antibiotic, anticarcinogen, anticoagulant, antiperiodic, antiphlogistic, antispasmodic, aromatic, astringent, carminative, counterirritant, depurative, diaphoretic, emmenagogue, hemostatic, lithotriptic, malariacidal, parasiticide, sialogogue, stimulant, tonic, and vermifuge.
Constituents: Alkaloids, benzoic acid, berberine, coumarin, fagarine, gum, monosaccharides, resin, tannic acid, vanillic acid, volatile oil, xanthoxylene, and xanthoxylin.
Historical Uses: Abdominal pain, abscess, ague, anemia (sickle cell), appetite loss, arrhythmia, arthritis, asthma, bleeding, bronchitis, calculus, cancer, chilblains, cholera, cold extremities, colic, cramps, cystitis, diarrhea, digestive complaints, edema, fever (ephemeral, enteric, hankow, intermittent, rheumatic), flatulence, flavoring agent, gallbladder problems, gallstones, gastralgia, gastrointestinal problems, gout, headache, hemorrhoids, hypotension, indigestion, infection (bacterial), inflammation, insufficiency (circulatory, venous), kidney stones, lesion (tubercle),

lethargy, liver problems, malaria, menopausal/menstrual problems, muscle and joint pain, pain, nausea, nervous conditions, paralysis, parasites (malarial plasmodia, pinworm, roundworm, scabies, schistosoma), periodontal disease, pruritus, rheumatism, schistosomiasis, scrofula, sexually transmitted diseases (STDs), skin problems, sore throat, sores, spasmodic conditions, syphilis, toothache, tuberculosis, typhoid, ulcer (bouveret, duodenal, fistula, gastric, peptic, stasis, syphilitic, tuberculous, varicose), varicose veins, vomiting, and wounds (minor).
Discussion: May aid digestion; decrease the effect of carcinogens; delay or reduce coagulation of the blood; depress excitability and conduction in the auricular muscle; dissolve calculi; enhance kidney, spleen, and stomach functions; increase circulation; inhibit or destroy development and growth of bacteria and other microorganisms; promote perspiration and saliva secretion; purify the blood; restore normal tone to tissues; stimulate appetite and menstruation.
Cautions/Contraindications: Avoid use if pregnant or breast-feeding, or if you have enteritis or gastroenteritis. Some persons may experience bleeding or increased clotting time when using this herb with anticoagulant drugs or aspirin.
Adverse Reactions: Bleeding (possibly serious), coagulation problems, nausea, salivation (increased), and/or vomiting.
Herb/Drug Interactions: This herb could cause an interaction (possibly severe) when taken with the following drugs: Anticoagulant drugs, Salicylates, and Subsalicylates.
Preparations/Dosage: Crude Herb (bark): 2-5 grams. Bark (powdered): Average dose in substance 8-10 grains (0.51-0.666 gm.). Decoction (bark and/or berries): 1 cup per day. Extract (berries): 10-30 drops (0.666-2 cc.). Extract: 3-8 drops (0.2-0.5 cc.) one to two times per day. Tincture: 5-20 drops (0.333-1.25 cc.) one to three times per day.
Isolation: Xanthoxylin: Average dose of 1-2 grains (0.066-0.133 gm.) for use as a simple bitter. Benzoic acid: Average dose of 5-15 grains (0.333-1 gm.) for use in bronchitis and cystitis.

Ash, Wafer (ash, wā fer)
(*Ptelea trifoliata*)

Synonyms/Related Species: Hoptree, Hop Trefoil, Ptela, Three-Leaved Hoptree, Swamp Dogwood, and Wingseed.
Family/Class: Rutaceae (rue).
Habitat: Europe and North America (predominantly the juniper/piñon belt and the ponderosa belt).
Flavor: Bitter/pungent.
Parts Used: Bark (root).
Properties: Anthelmintic, antibiotic, antifungal, antiperiodic, antiphlogistic, carminative, demulcent, depurative, laxative, lithotriptic, malariacidal, stimulant, stomachic, tonic, and vermifuge.
Constituents: Alkaloids, amino acids (arginine), berberine, coumarin, dictamnine, kokusaginin, marmesine, phellopterin, pimpinellin, ptelein, resin, sodium, skimmianine, and volatile oil.
Historical Uses: Ague, appetite loss, asthma, calculus, candida, chills, digestive complaints, fever (ephemeral, intermittent, rheumatic), gallstones, gastritis, gastrointestinal problems, gout, indigestion, infection (bacterial, fungal), inflammation, irritable bowel syndrome (IBS), kidney stones, lesion (tubercle), lung problems, malaria, moniliasis, muscle and joint pain, parasites (malarial plasmodia, pinworm, roundworm), rheumatism, scrofula, stomachache, substitute for hops, tuberculosis, ulcer (fistula, tuberculous), and wounds (minor).

Discussion: May aid digestion; dissolve calculi; enhance digestive system, liver, and stomach functions; increase vitality; inhibit or destroy developement and growth of bacteria and other microorganisms; promote bowel evacuation; purify the blood; restore normal tone to tissues; smooth and soften the skin; soothe mucous membrane irritations; stimulate appetite and peristalsis.
Cautions/Contraindications: Avoid use if pregnant or breast-feeding.
Adverse Reactions: Nausea and/or vomiting.
Herb/Drug Interactions: This herb could cause an interaction (possibly severe) when taken with the following drugs: None known.
Preparations/Dosage: Crude Herb: 3-6 grams. Bark (powdered): Average dose in substance 10-30 grains (0.666-2 gm.). Infusion: 1 cup per day. Tincture: 5-20 drops (0.333-1.25 cc.) one to three times per day.

Ashwagandha (äsh·wô·gän·dä)
(*Withania somnifera*)

Synonyms/Related Species: Indian Ginseng.
Family/Class: Solanaceae (nightshade).
Habitat: The Himalayas, India, North America, Pakistan, and Sri Lanka.
Flavor: Bitter/sweet.
Parts Used: Root.
Properties: Analgesic, antibiotic, anticarcinogen, antifungal, anti-inflammatory, aphrodisiac, astringent, hemostatic, hypnotic, narcotic, sedative, and tonic.
Constituents: Alkaloid, esters, saponins, solanine, and somniferine.
Historical Uses: Acidity (gastric), Alzheimer's disease, anxiety, arthritis, athletics, bleeding, bodybuilding, cancer, carpal tunnel syndrome, chronic fatigue syndrome (CFS), convalescence, deficiency (autoimmune), diminished sex drive, Epstein Barr Virus (EBV), erectile dysfunction, exhaustion, fatigue, fibromyalgia, infection (bacterial, fungal), infertility, inflammation, insomnia, memory/cognitive problems, mononucleosis (infectious), muscle and joint pain, nervous conditions, neuralgia, neurasthenia, pain, premature ejaculation, and weight loss.
Discussion: May arouse sexual impulses; calm the nerves; decrease the effect of carcinogens; enhance endurance, sexual stamina, virility, and vitality as well as immune and nervous system functions; give an instant charge of energy without the use of synthetic stimulants; impart a sense of well being and strength; improve memory and cognition; increase red and white blood cell and platelet counts; inhibit or destroy developement and growth of bacteria and other microorganisms; offset the negative effects of chemotherapy and radiation therapy; prevent suppression (immune) caused by exposure to strong chemical agents, and may restore immunity after exposure or treatment with such drugs; promote restful sleep and tissue regeneration; reduce cognitive deficit; restore normal tone to tissues.
Cautions/Contraindications: Avoid use if pregnant or breast-feeding, or if you have acute sexual anxiety. May result in ataxia and drowsiness when taken with other sedatives. This plant is related to belladonna.
Adverse Reactions: Ataxia, confusion, diarrhea (possibly bloody), gastrointestinal cramps (severe), lethargy, nausea, stupor, and/or vomiting.
Herb/Drug Interactions: This herb could cause an interaction (possibly severe) when taken with the following drugs: Anxiolytic drugs and Sedative drugs.

Preparations/Dosage: Root (powdered): Average dose in substance ¼-½ grain (0.015-0.0333 gm.). Tincture: 1-3 drops (0.06-0.2 cc.) one to three times per day.

Asparagus (e·spar e·ges)
(*Asparagus officinalis*)

Synonyms/Related Species: Shatavari, Sparrowgrass, Tian-Men-Dong, and Wild Asparagus.
Family/Class: Liliaceae (lily).
Habitat: Africa, Asia, England, Europe, Greece, North America, Poland, Russia, and Siberia.
Flavor: Sweet/bitter.
Parts Used: Root, stem, tips.
Properties: Antacid, anticarcinogen, antiphlogistic, cardiant, demulcent, diaphoretic, diuretic, expectorant, laxative, lithotriptic, nutritive, sedative, and tonic.
Constituents: Amino acids (aspartic acid), asparagosides, carbohydrates, enzymes, fats, flavonoids, glycosides, inulin (starch), iron, magnesium, monosaccharides, mucilage, phosphorus, quercitrin, resin, rutin, sulfur, tannic acid, vitamin B_3 niacin (nicotinic acid), and volatile oil.
Historical Uses: Acidity (gastric), acquired immune deficiency syndrome (AIDS), arthritis, bronchitis, burns (minor), calculus, cancer (breast), chronic fatigue syndrome (CFS), colds, congestion (lung), convulsions, cramps, cough, dietary supplementation, dysmenorrhea, Epstein Barr Virus (EBV), exhaustion, fatigue, fever (ephemeral, rheumatic), fibromyalgia, gallstones, gastrointestinal problems, gout, human immunodeficiency virus (HIV), infection (bladder), inflammation, insufficiency (adrenal), kidney stones, lesion (tubercle), malnutrition, menopausal/menstrual problems, mononucleosis (infectious), mucus, muscle and joint pain, nausea, respiratory conditions, rheumatism, sciatica, scrofula, sputum cruentum (bloody sputum), thirst, toothache, tuberculosis, ulcer (fistula, tuberculous), urinary problems, and wounds (minor).
Discussion: May calm the nerves; clear and open bronchial passages; decrease the effect of carcinogens and postoperative adhesions; dissolve calculi; enhance cardiovascular system, female hormonal system, lung, and kidney functions; improve mental clarity; neutralize acidity; promote bowel evacuation, fertility (women), perspiration, and urine flow; prevent hemorrhage in persons with hypertension; protect against chemical and environmental stressors; provide dietary supplementation; reduce capillary fragility; restore normal tone to tissues; serve as a nutritional adjuvant to therapeutic programs; soothe mucous membrane irritation; stimulate the cardiovascular system, immune system, and peristalsis.
Cautions/Contraindications: Avoid use if pregnant or breast-feeding, or if you have edema or nephritis. May cause allergic reactions or dermatitis in susceptible individuals.
Adverse Reactions: None known.
Herb/Drug Interactions: This herb could cause an interaction (possibly severe) when taken with the following drugs: None known.
Preparations/Dosage: Crude herb: 6-12 grams. Decoction (root): ½-1 cup per day. Juice (fresh): 1-2 tablespoons per day. Stems/tips: Cooked as a vegetable.

Avens (av inz)
(*Geum urbanum*)

Synonyms/Related Species: Bennet's Root, Blessed Herb, Chocolate Root, City Avens, Clove Root, Colewort, Cure All, Drooping Avens, European Avens, Gariophilata, Goldy Star, Guem, Harefoot, Herba Benedicta, Herb Bennet, Indian Chocolate, Jealousy Plant, Large-Leaf Avens (*geum macrophyllum*), Minarta, Nodding Avens, Old Man's Whiskers (*geum triflorum*), Pesleporis, Prairie Smoke, Purple Avens, Ross' Avens (*geum rossii*), Rough Avens, Star of the Earth, Throat Root, Water Avens (*geum rivale*), Water Flower, Way Bennet, Wild Rye, and Yellow Avens (*geum aleppicum*).
Family/Class: Rosaceae (rose).
Habitat: Alaska, the Alpine and Subalpine zones, Asia, Britain, England, Europe, Ireland, North America, Russia, Scotland, Siberia, and the Yukon Territory.
Flavor: Sour/sweet.
Parts Used: Leaves, root.
Properties: Anesthetic (local), antibiotic, antifungal, antiperiodic, antiphlogistic, antiviral, aromatic, astringent, carminative, depurative, diaphoretic, diuretic, hemostatic, malariacidal, stimulant, stomachic, and tonic.
Constituents: Eugenol (eugenic acid), gein, gum, resin, saponins, tannic acid, vitamins (choline), and volatile oil.
Historical Uses: Abscess, acid reflux, age spots, ague, amenorrhea, appetite loss, bleeding, bronchitis, bruises, chills, cirrhosis, congestion (uterine, vaginal), conjunctivitis, convalescence, debility, diarrhea, digestive complaints, diphtheria, dysentery, fatigue, fever (ephemeral, herpetic, intermittent), flavoring agent, freckles, gargle/mouth rinse, gastritis, gastrointestinal problems, halitosis, headache, hemorrhage (metrorrhagia), hemorrhoids, herpes, human immunodeficiency virus (HIV), indigestion, infection (bacterial, fungal, viral), inflammation, insufficiency (venous), leukorrhea, liver problems, malaria, menorrhagia, mucus, parasites (malarial plasmodia), rash, respiratory conditions, sore throat, substitute for peruvian bark, ulcer (stasis, varicose), vaginitis, and varicose veins.
Discussion: May aid digestion; enhance stomach function; inhibit or destroy development and growth of bacteria and other microorganisms; prevent the deposition of fat in the liver; promote perspiration and urine flow; purify the liver; restore normal tone to tissues; stimulate appetite.
Cautions/Contraindications: Avoid use if pregnant or breast-feeding.
Adverse Reactions: Diarrhea (possibly bloody), gastrointestinal cramps (severe), nausea, and/or vomiting.
Herb/Drug Interactions: This herb could cause an interaction (possibly severe) when taken with the following drugs: None known.
Preparations/Dosage: Crude Herb: 3-6 grams. Leaves and Root (powdered): Average dose in substance 15-30 grains (0.98-2 gm.). Decoction (root): ¼-½ cup per day. Extract (leaves): 5-10 drops (0.333-0.666 cc.) one to two times per day. Extract (root): 3-5 drops (0.2-0.333 cc.) one to two times per day. Infusion (leaves): 1 cup per day. Infusion (root): ½ cup per day. Tincture (root): 5-10 drops (0.333-0.666 cc.) one to three times per day.

Ayahuasca (ī ä·wäs kä)
(*Banisteria caapi*)

Synonyms/Related Species: Banisteria, Caapi, Cappi, Natem Pinde, South American Creeper, and Yagé.
Family/Class: Malpighiaceae (malpighia).
Habitat: South America.
Flavor: Bitter.
Parts Used: Root, stem.
Properties: Aphrodisiac, hallucinogen, and stimulant.
Constituents: Alkaloids, banisterine, ellagic acid, flavonols, harmaline, harmol, harmine, inulin (starch), iridoids, monosaccharides, proanthocyanidins, quercetin, saponins, and yageine.
Historical Uses: Angina, encephalitis lethargica, paralysis (cerebral), and Parkinsonism.
Discussion: May arouse sexual impulses; stimulate the central nervous system.
Cautions/Contraindications: Avoid use if pregnant or breast-feeding. Ayahuasca is a monoamine oxidase inhibitor (MAOI) herb. The combined use ayahuasca with sedative, tranquilizer, antihistamine, narcotic, or tricyclic antidepressant drugs will cause hypertensive crisis. The combined use of ayahuasca with amphetamines, cocaine, LSD, alcohol (including wine) avocados, unripe bananas, and dairy products (including aged cheese) will cause hypotensive crisis. It is recommended that no other drugs be used in combination with or within a ten-hour period of the use of ayahuasca.
Adverse Reactions: Cardiac failure, confusion, diarrhea (possibly bloody), dizziness, excitability, exhaustion (extreme), fainting, gastrointestinal cramps (severe), hypertensive crisis (severe rise in blood pressure levels), nightmarish hallucinations, nausea, psychosis, hypotensive crisis (arrhythmia, breathing difficulty, chills, severe drop in blood pressure levels), respiratory failure, stupor, vomiting, and/or possible death.
Herb/Drug Interactions: This herb could cause an interaction (possibly severe) when taken with the following drugs: Amphetamine drugs, Antidepressant drugs, Antihistamine drugs, Anxiolytic drugs, Cardiac drugs, Migraine drugs, Monamine Oxidase Inhibitors (MAOIs), Opiate Agonists/Narcotic drugs, Sedative drugs, and Tranquilizer drugs.
Preparations/Dosage: Aphrodisiac Use: To prepare, crush the root and/or stem in a morter (usually with other psychoactive herbs). Boil in a small amount of water for 6-8 hours. Strain and reduce the liquid to $^{1}/_{10}$ the original volume. Beginners should start with 1 ounce and slowly work their way up to 4 ounces. Physical adverse effects occurring upon use may include nausea and possible vomiting. Effects begin about one hour after ingestion and continue for approximately six to eight hours.
Isolation: Harmine: Average dose ⅓ - ⅔ grain (0.02-0.04 gm.) administered intramuscularly or subcutaneously for paralysis (cerebral) and parkinsonism.
Note: 4 ounces of liquid typically contains 500 mg of harmaline alkaloid. Since the harmaline alkaloid is poorly absorbed through the gastrointestinal system, one can take 25-100 mg. of harmaline hydrochloride and use it as a snuff, producing almost immediate results, however, using it in this way will produce a burning sensation of the nostrils and throat and will leave the user with cold-like symptoms for several days. The best way to administer this alkaloid is to place 25-100 mg. of this substance under the tongue or between the cheek and gum where it will be readily absorbed with little or no physical adverse effects. Fasting for 12-16 hours may help to offset any nausea.

Azedarach (e·zed e·rak)
(*Melia azedarach*)

Synonyms/Related Species: Africa Lilac, Āzād dirakht, Bead Tree, Chinaberry Tree, China Tree, Hagbush, Holy Tree, Hop-Tree, Indiai, Indian Lilac Tree, Margosa, Neem Tree, Nim, Nimba, Persian Lilac, Persian Noble Tree, Pride of China, Pride of India, and Pride Tree.
Family/Class: Meliaceae (mahogany).
Habitat: Africa, Asia, Australia, Europe, France, India, Indonesia, Spain, Sri Lanka, and the United States.
Flavor: Bitter.
Parts Used: Bark (root), fruit/seed (oil).
Properties: Antibiotic, antifertilizin, antifungal, antiperiodic, antiphlogistic, antiprotozoan, antiviral, aphrodisiac, astringent, emetic, emmenagogue, hemostatic, insect repellent, laxative, malariacidal, narcotic, parasiticide, tonic, vermifuge, and vermin repellent.
Constituents: Flavonoids, margosate, margosic acid, resin, tannic acid, terpene, and volatile oil.
Historical Uses: Abscess, ague, bleeding, bot fly, candida, contraceptive (male/female), cramps, cutworms, ear infection, fever (ephemeral, intermittent, rheumatic), hysteria, infection (bacterial, fungal, viral), inflammation, leprosy, malaria, moniliasis, mosquitos, moths, muscle and joint pain, parasites (amebas, lice and their nits, malarial plasmodia, scabies, trichomonas), periodontal disease, pruritus, rheumatism, sexually transmitted dieases (STDs), skin problems, syphilis, vermin, ulcer (duodenal, gastric, peptic, syphilitic), and wounds (minor).
Discussion: May arouse sexual impulses; enhance colon, lung, and skin functions; inhibit development or destroy growth of bacteria and other microorganisms, and inhibit malaria in the parasite stage; neutralize fertilizin (fertilization); promote bowel evacuation; protect against mosquito bites (when mixed with coconut oil); reduce both the rate of growth and the rate of reproduction of protozoa; restore normal tone to tissues; serve as a long lasting, non-toxic, agricultural spray; slow mosquito breeding (when combined with urea); stimulate menstruation and peristalsis.
Cautions/Contraindications: Avoid use if pregnant or breast-feeding. Not for long-term use.
Adverse Reactions: Diarrhea, nausea, stupor, and/or vomiting.
Herb/Drug Interactions: This herb could cause an interaction (possibly severe) when taken with the following drugs: None known.
Preparations/Dosage: Crude Herb (bark): 3-9 grams. Bark (powdered): Average dose in substance 10-20 grains (0.666-1.333 gm.). Decoction (bark): ½-1 ounce (15-30 cc.) per day. Seed Oil (*oleum melia fructus*): Dilute with a good quality vegetable oil and apply topically for lice, scabies, and other skin problems. Tincture: 10-30 drops (0.666-2 cc.) one to three times per day.

Bael (ba el)
(*Aegle marmelos*)

Synonyms/Related Species: Aegle, Bel, Bengal Quince, Bilwa, Cydonium, Indian Bael, Kydōnion Mēlon, Quince, Qwince, and Vilwa.

Family/Class: Rosaceae (rose).
Habitat: Asia and India.
Flavor: Sour.
Parts Used: Bark (root), fruit (ripe/unripe).
Properties: Anthelmintic, anticoagulant, astringent, carminative, hemostatic, laxative, and vermifuge.
Constituents: Alkaloids, coumarins, fatty acids (oleic, palmitic, stearic), fixed oils (olein, palmitin, stearin), inulin (starch), mucilage, pectic acid, pectin, saccharides, and tannic acid.
Historical Uses: Ancylostomiasis, bleeding, colic, constipation, diarrhea, digestive complaints, dysentery, inflammation, irritable bowel syndrome (IBS), nervous conditions, and parasites (hookworm).
Discussion: May aid digestion; delay or reduce coagulation of the blood; promote bowel evacuation; stimulate peristalsis.
Cautions/Contraindications: Avoid use if pregnant or breast-feeding, or if you have a coagulation problem. Some persons may experience bleeding or increased clotting time when using this herb with anticoagulant drugs or aspirin. Not for long-term use.
Adverse Reactions: Bleeding (possibly serious), coagulation problems, diarrhea (severe), nausea, and/or vomiting.
Herb/Drug Interactions: This herb could cause an interaction (possibly severe) when taken with the following drugs: Anticoagulant drugs, Salicylates, and Subsalicylates.
Preparations/Dosage: Decoction (bark): ½-2 ounces per day. Fruit (pulp/ripe): May be ingested freely for use as a laxative. Fruit (pulp/half-dried/unripe): May be ingested freely for use in diarrhea.

Balsam Of Peru (bôl sem uv pe·roo)
(*Myroxylon Pereirae*)

Synonyms/Related Species: Peru Balsam, Peruvian Balsam Tree, and Trinidad Balsam (*myroxylon frutescens*).
Family/Class: Leguminosae (legume).
Habitat: Central America (primarily San Salvador) and Trinidad.
Flavor: Bitter.
Parts Used: Oleoresin.
Properties: Antibiotic, antiphlogistic, carminative, diuretic, expectorant, parasiticide, stimulant, and stomachic.
Constituents: Cinnamein, cinnamic acid, coumarin, gum, peruol, peruvin, resin, vanillin (methyl pyrocatechinic acid), and volatile oil.
Historical Uses: Asthma, bronchitis, bruises, burns (minor), colds, congestion (uterine, vaginal), cough, dandruff, diarrhea, digestive complaints, dry skin, ear infection, eczema, fever (ephemeral, rheumatic), freckles, frostbite, gangrene, gastrointestinal problems, gleet, hemorrhoids, hypotension, indigestion, infection (bacterial), inflammation, laryngitis, lesion (tubercle), leukorrhea, mucus, muscle and joint pain, parasites (acarus and its eggs, ringworm, scabies), perfume, prurigo, pruritus, respiratory conditions, rheumatism, scrofula, skin problems, sore nipples, tuberculosis, ulcer (duodenal, fistula, tuberculous), vaginitis, and wounds (minor).

Discussion: May aid digestion; clear and open bronchial passages; increase blood pressure levels; inhibit or destroy development and growth of bacteria and other microorganisms; promote urine flow; soothe nipple soreness; stimulate the cardiovascular system and gastric secretions.
Cautions/Contraindications: Avoid use if pregnant or breast-feeding, or if you have an ulcer (gastric, peptic). Do not confuse this plant with balsam of tolu (*myroxylon balsamum*). May cause allergic reactions, dermatitis, photosensitivity, or photodermatosis in susceptible individuals. Not for long-term use.
Adverse Reactions: Hematuria (blood in the urine), nausea, and/or vomiting.
Herb/Drug Interactions: This herb could cause an interaction (possibly severe) when taken with the following drugs: None known.
Preparations/Dosage: Oleoresin (emulsion): 10-15 drops (0.666-1 cc.) diluted and applied topically. Oleoresin (in syrup): 10-30 drops (0.666-2 cc.).
Isolation: Cinnamic acid: Hypodermic dose 1-10 drops (0.066-0.666 cc.). Used externally and internally in tuberculosis.

Balsam Of Tolu (bôl sem uv te·loo)
(*Myroxylon balsamum*)

Synonyms/Related Species: Tolu Balsam Tree.

Family/Class: Leguminosae (legume).
Habitat: South America.
Flavor: Sweet.
Parts Used: Resinous exudate.
Properties: Antibiotic, antiphlogistic, diuretic, expectorant, parasiticide, stimulant, and stomachic.
Constituents: Cinnamein, cinnamic acid, resin, toluene, vanillin (methyl pyrocatechinic acid), and volatile oil.
Historical Uses: Asthma, bronchitis, bruises, burns (minor), colds, congestion (uterine, vaginal), cough, dandruff, diarrhea, dry skin, ear infection, eczema, fever (ephemeral, rheumatic), freckles, frostbite, gangrene, gleet, hemorrhoids, hypotension, incense, infection (bacterial), inflammation, laryngitis, lesion (tubercle), leukorrhea, mucus, muscle and joint pain, parasites (acarus and its eggs, ringworm, scabies), perfume, prurigo, pruritus, respiratory conditions, rheumatism, scrofula, skin problems, sore nipples, tuberculosis, ulcer (duodenal, fistula, gastric, peptic, tuberculous), vaginitis, and wounds (minor).
Discussion: May clear and open bronchial passages; elevate blood pressure levels; inhibit development or destroy growth of bacteria and other microorganisms; promote urine flow; soothe nipple soreness.
Cautions/Contraindications: Avoid use if pregnant or breast-feeding. Do not confuse this plant with balsam of peru (*myroxylon pereirae*). May cause allergic reactions, dermatitis, photosensitivity, or photodermatosis in susceptible individuals. Not for long-term use.
Adverse Reactions: Hematuria (blood in the urine), nausea, and/or vomiting.
Herb/Drug Interactions: This herb could cause an interaction (possibly severe) when taken with the following drugs: None known.
Preparations/Dosage: Syrup: 1-2 drachms (4-8 cc.). Tincture: 10-30 drops (0.666-2 cc.) one to three times per day.

Isolation: Cinnamic acid: Hypodermic dose 1-10 drops (0.066-0.666 cc.). Used externally and internally in tuberculosis.

Bamboo (bam·boo)
(*Bambusa arundinacea*)

Synonyms/Related Species: Bambu.
Family/Class: Graminaceae (grass).
Habitat: Asia, India, and Malaysia.
Flavor: Sweet.
Parts Used: Leaves, root, shoots (young).
Properties: Alterative, antiemetic, antiphlogistic, antispasmodic, astringent, depurative, diuretic, hemostatic, sedative, and tonic.
Constituents: Minerals (potassium, silicon), polysaccharides, silicic acid, and tannic acid.
Historical Uses: Asthma, bleeding, bronchitis, colds, convulsions, cough, enuresis (urinary incontinence), fever, gallbladder problems, infection (urinary tract), inflammation, mucus, spasmodic conditions, urinary problems, urodialysis (suppressed urine), uropenia (scanty urine), and vomiting.
Discussion: May cleanse or purify whole system; clear and open bronchial passages; enhance cardiovascular system, gallbladder, liver, respiratory system, stomach, and urinary system functions; promote urine flow; reestablish healthy system functions; restore normal tone to tissues.
Cautions/Contraindications: Avoid use if pregnant or breast-feeding.
Adverse Reactions: Nausea and/or vomiting.
Herb/Drug Interactions: This herb could cause an interaction (possibly severe) when taken with the following drugs: None known.
Preparations/Dosage: Crude Herb: 3-9 grams. Decoction: ¼-½ cup per day. Infusion: ½-1 cup per day. Shoots (young): May be eaten.

Banana (be·nan e)
(*Musa paradisiaca*)

Synonyms/Related Species: Mandingo Banana and Mawzah.
Family/Class: Musaceae (banana).
Habitat: Africa, Arabia, Asia, Brazil, the Canary Islands, Egypt, Florida, India, Japan, the Pacific Islands, and other subtropical and tropical regions.
Flavor: Sweet.
Parts Used: Fruit (ripe/unripe), leaves, root starch (prior to flowering), shoots (young).
Properties: Antacid, caustic, demulcent, hypotensive, nervine, nutritive, stimulant, and vasodilator.
Constituents: Albuminoids, amino acids (tryptophan), carbohydrates, disaccharide, fiber, inulin (starch), minerals (chlorine, iron, magnesium, potassium, sodium), monosaccharides, protein, and vitamins (A, B, B_6 (pyridoxine), B_{12}).
Historical Uses: Acidity (gastric), addiction (food, tobacco), anemia, constipation, depression (mild/moderate), digestive complaints, dry skin, fatigue, gastritis, gastrointestinal problems, goiter, hangover (caused by alcohol consumption), hypertension (mild/moderate), indigestion, insect bites or stings, irritable bowel syndrome (IBS), melancholy, memory/cognitive problems,

mood swings, nausea, premenstrual syndrome (PMS), seasonal affective disorder (SAD), skin problems, snakebite, ulcer (duodenal, gastric, peptic), warts (digitate, filiform, fugitive, glabra, mother, plana juvenilis, plantar, seborrhoeic, vulgaris), and weight loss.
Discussion: May calm the nervous system; cause blood vessel dilatation; help reduce food cravings, and help the body recover from the effects of nicotine withdrawal; improve cognition, concentration, memory, mood, and wellbeing; increase energy levels; normalize the heart rate; neutralize acidity; provide nutrition; reduce blood pressure levels and the risk of stroke (apoplectic); regulate blood sugar levels and the body's water balance; restore normal bowel action; soothe mucous membrane irritation; stimulate the production of hemoglobin.
Cautions/Contraindications: None known.
Adverse Reactions: None known.
Herb/Drug Interactions: This herb could cause an interaction (possibly severe) when taken with the following drugs: Hypotensive drugs.
Preparations/Dosage: Fruit (fresh): May be freely eaten, or roasted/baked/broiled/fried, or dried and ground into flour, or used as substitute for potatoes and added to soups/stews. Root (starch): Eaten/used as a food source or as a thickener for gravy/sauces. Shoots (young): Cooked as a vegetable. Hangover Remedy: A quick way to cure a hangover (caused by alcohol consumption) is with a banana and honey milkshake. The banana helps to soothe an upset stomach, the honey helps to build up depleted blood glucose levels, and the milk re-hydrates your entire system. Insect Bites/Stings: Rub the inside of a banana peel against the bite or sting to help reduce itching, and inflammation. Warts: Place the inside of a banana peel over the warts and tape it in place. Repeat as necessary.

Baneberry (bān ber ē)

(*Actaea spicata*)

Synonyms/Related Species: Adder's Eyes, Adder's Mouth, Adder's Root, Adderwort, Bugbane, European Baneberry, Herb Christopher, Necklace Berry, Rattlesnake Herb, Red Baneberry (*actaea rubra*), Red Cohosh (*actaea spicata*), Snake-Berry, and Western Baneberry.
Family/Class: Ranunculaceae (buttercup).
Habitat: Alaska, the Alpine and Subalpine zones, Britain, New Foundland, North America, and the Yukon Territory.
Flavor: Bitter.
Parts Used: Root.
Properties: Antiphlogistic, antispasmodic, astringent, counterirritant, emetic, emmenagogue, hallucinogen, laxative, narcotic, sedative, vermin repellent, and vulnerary.
Constituents: Aconitic acid, actein, glycosides, protoanemonin, and volatile oil.
Historical Uses: Abscess, asthma, colds, cough, emaciation, fever (ephemeral, rheumatic), inflammation, menstrual problems, muscle and joint pain, nervous conditions, respiratory conditions, rheumatism, sexually transmitted diseases (STDs), snakebite, spasmodic conditions, syphilis, ulcer (syphilitic), vermin, and wounds (minor).
Discussion: May promote bowel evacuation; speed healing; stimulate peristalsis.
Cautions/Contraindications: Avoid use if pregnant or breast-feeding. Do not confuse this plant with black hellebore (*helleborus niger*). May cause dermatitis in susceptible individuals. The berries are poisonous. Not for long-term use. Use with professional guidance/supervision.

Adverse Reactions: Arrhythmia, blistering of the mouth and throat, cardiac failure, circulatory failure, convulsions, diarrhea (bloody), dizziness, fainting, gastrointestinal problems, hallucinations, headache, hematuria (blood in the urine), increased pulse rate, kidney failure, nausea, respiratory failure, salivation, stomach cramps (severe), stupor, suppression (vagus nerve), vomiting, and/or possible death.
Herb/Drug Interactions: This herb could cause an interaction (possibly severe) when taken with the following drugs: None known.
Preparations/Dosage: Root (powdered): Average dose in substance 1-3 grains (0.066-0.2 gm.). Tincture: 1-5 drops (0.066-0.333 cc.) one to two times per day.

Barberry (bär ber ē)
(*Berberis vulgaris*)

Synonyms/Related Species: Barbaris, Berberry, California Barberry, Common Barberry, Darlahad, Holly-Leaved Barberry, Holy Thorn, Indian Barberry (*berberis asiatica*), Jaundice Bush, Mountain Grape (*berberis aquifolium*), Nepal Barberry (*berberis aristata*), Opthalmic Barberry, Otitogue, Oregon Grape Root, Pipperidge, Rocky Mountain Grape, and Sow Berry.
Family/Class: Berberidaceae (barberry).
Floral Emblem: Oregon.
Habitat: Africa, Asia, Ceylon, England, Europe, India, Ireland, North America, and Scotland.
Flavor: Sour.
Parts Used: Bark (stem/root), berry.
Properties: Alterative, analgesic, antibiotic, anticarcinogen, antifungal, antioxidant, antiperiodic, antiphlogistic, antiscorbutic, antiviral, astringent, depurative, diuretic, emmenagogue, hemostatic, hepatic, hypoglycemic, hypotensive, laxative, lithotriptic, malariacidal, parasiticide, sedative, stimulant, tonic, and vasodilator.
Constituents: Acetic acid, albumin (albumen), alkaloids, anthocyans, berbamine, berberine, chlorogenic acid, citric acid, gum, hydrastine, inulin (starch), isocorydin, mahonine, malic acid, minerals (copper, iron, manganese, phosphorous, silicon, sodium, zinc), oxycanthine, phosphoric acid, resin, silicic acid, tannic acid, wax, and vitamin C (ascorbic acid).
Historical Uses: Abscess, acne, ague, anemia (alcoholic), hangover (caused by alcohol consumption), appetite loss, arthritis, bleeding, bronchitis, bruises, burns (minor), calculus, cancer, candida, cardiovascular conditions, cholera, cirrhosis, colds, congestion (uterine, vaginal), conjunctivitis, constipation, cough, degenerative conditions, diabetes, diarrhea, debility, digestive complaints, dysentery, eczema, escherichia coli (e-coli), eyewash, fever (ephemeral, enteric, herpetic, intermittent, rheumatic), flatulence, gastrointestinal problems, infection (bacterial, bladder), gallstones, gargle/mouth rinse, gastritis, gastrointestinal problems, glandular problems, halitosis, hemorrhage, hepatitis, herpes, hyperglycemia, hypertension (mild/moderate), hypertrophy (spleen), indigestion, infection (fungal, urinary tract, viral), infertility, inflammation, irritable bowel syndrome (IBS), jam/jelly, jaundice, kidney problems, kidney stones, lesions (psoriatic, tubercle), leukorrhea, liver problems, malaria, malnutrition, moniliasis, mucus, muscle and joint pain, nausea, nephritis, pain, parasites (malarial plasmodia, ringworm), periodontal disease, pneumonia, premenstrual syndrome (PMS), pruritus, psoriasis, rash, respiratory conditions, Raynaud's disease, rheumatism, rheumatoid arthritis (RA), scrofula, scurvy, sexually transmitted diseases (STDs), sinusitis, skin problems, sore throat, spasmodic conditions,

spermatorrhea, spleen problems, syphilis, tuberculosis, tumors, typhoid, ulcer (bouveret, fistula, peptic, syphilitic, tuberculous), uterine problems, vaginitis, vomiting, wounds (minor).

Discussion: May aid digestion; cause blood vessel dilatation; cleanse the whole system; decrease the effect of carcinogens as well as the heart rate; dissolve calculi; enhance gallbladder, intestinal system, and thyroid functions; inhibit oxidation and inhibit or destroy developement and growth of bacteria and other microorganisms; promote bowel evacuation and urine flow; protect the liver; purify the blood; reduce blood pressure levels, blood sugar levels, and lesions (psoriatic); reestablish healthy system functions; restore normal tone to tissues; serve as an effective agent against bacteria that have become antibiotic resistant; stimulate the appetite, gastric secretions, immune system, menstruation, myocardium, peristalsis, and uterine contractions; stop or slow abnormal cell growth.

Cautions/Contraindications: Avoid use if pregnant or breast-feeding, or if you have anemia, diabetes, chronic diarrhea, gallstones, gastritis, gastrointestinal problems, heart disease, hypothyroidism, indigestion, irritable bowel syndrome (IBS), Raynaud's disease, chronic respiratory conditions, or in cases of poisoning (food). Do not use for longer than two weeks. May increase bilirubin levels, and interfere with prescription tetracycline antibiotic absorption. May reduce the absorption of antibiotic drugs. May interfere with amino acid L-histidine supplements, vitamin B_6 supplements, and sperm cell maturation. May cause sterility in males. Not for long-term use. Use with professional guidance/supervision.

Adverse Reactions: Arrhythmia, cardiac failure, convulsions, decreased myocardium (heart muscle) and respiratory functions, diarrhea, dizziness, fainting, hypotension, increased bilirubin (red bile pigment) levels, nausea, and/or vomiting.

Herb/Drug Interactions: This herb could cause an interaction (possibly severe) when taken with the following drugs: Antibiotic drugs, Antidiabetic drugs, Anxiolytic drugs, Hypotensive drugs, and Sedative drugs.

Preparations/Dosage: Crude herb (bark/berry): 3-6 grams. Bark (powdered): Average dose in substance ¼ teaspoon. Decoction: ½-1 cup per day. Extract: 3-5 drops (0.2-0.333 cc.) one to two times per day. Extract (solid): Average dose in substance 5-10 grains (0.324-0.666 gm.). Tincture: 5-15 drops (0.333-1 cc.) one to three times per day.

Isolation: Berberine: Average dose of the alkaloid or its salts 1-5 grains (0.066-0.324 gm.) for use as an antiperiodic and tonic, and for abscess.

Barley (bär lē)

(*Hordeum vulgare*)

Synonyms/Related Species: Foxtail Barley (*hordeum jubatum*), Scotch Barley, and Squirrel Tail Barley.

Family/Class: Graminaceae (grass).

Habitat: Alaska, Britain, North America, and the Subalpine zone.

Flavor: Sweet.

Parts Used: Grain, leaves (young), malt, sprouts (germinated seed).

Properties: Antibiotic, anticarcinogen, antifungal, antigalactic, antiphlogistic, antispasmodic, antiviral, carminative, demulcent, diuretic, nutritive, sedative, and tonic.

Constituents: Albumin (albumen), alkaloid, amylase, cellulose, chlorophyll, coumarin, enzymes, fatty acids (oleic, palmitic, stearic), fixed oils (olein, palmitin, stearin), flavonoids, gramine, hordein, hordenine, inulin (starch), invertase, maltose, minerals (calcium, chlorine, iron, magnesium, manganese, phosphorous, potassium), monosaccharides, mucilage, pectic acid, pectin, phospholipid, phosphoric acid, polysaccharides, prolamines, protein, tannic acid, and vitamins (B_1 (thiamine), B_3 niacin (nicotinic acid), B_6 (pyridoxine), B_{12}, C, E, M (folic acid).

Historical Uses: Abdominal pain, abscess, acne, acquired immune deficiency syndrome (AIDS), allergy (pollen), anemia, appetite loss, arthritis, belching, bronchitis, candida, cancer, colitis, cough, diarrhea, dietary supplementation, digestive complaints, eczema, fever (ephemeral, enteric, hay, herpetic, rheumatic), food stagnation, gallbladder problems, gastrointestinal problems, gout, hepatitis, herpes, human immunodeficiency virus (HIV), infection (bacterial, fungal), inflammation, jaundice, kidney problems, leprosy, lesions (tubercle), liver problems, lung problems, malnutrition, mastitis, moniliasis, muscle and joint pain, nausea, pimples, poisoning (heavy metal), psoriasis, respiratory conditions, rheumatism, scrofula, sexually transmitted diseases (STDs), skin problems, spasmodic conditions, syphilis, tuberculosis, tumors, typhoid, ulcer (bouveret, duodenal, fistula, gastric, peptic, syphilitic, tuberculous), urinary problems, and viral infection.

Discussion: May aid digestion; balance metabolism; decrease the effect of carcinogens; diminish or suppress lactation; enhance colon, digestive system, lung, and spleen functions; eliminate heavy metals from the body; increase vitality and strength; inhibit or destroy development and growth of bacteria and other microorganisms; promote urine flow; provide dietary supplementation; purify the blood; restore normal tone to tissues; serve as a nutritional adjuvant to therapeutic programs; soothe mucous membrane irritation.

Cautions/Contraindications: Avoid use if pregnant or breast-feeding. Do not harvest or use barley that has been infected with ergot fungi as it may cause poisoning.

Adverse Reactions: Congestion (cerebrospinal), cramps (possibly severe), ergotism (chronic poisoning caused by eating or using ergot diseased grain), hypertension (possibly severe), nausea, spasmodic conditions, and/or vomiting.

Herb/Drug Interactions: This herb could cause an interaction (possibly severe) when taken with the following drugs: None known.

Preparations/Dosage: Crude herb (powdered): 5-10 grams. Barley Juice (young barley leaves): 1-2 cups per day. Barley Water: Combine 1 part pearl barley (washed) to 9 parts water. Boil for 15-20 minutes and strain. Take 1-4 ounces per day. Grain (ground): Used as flour. Malt (extract): 30-60 grams. Sprouts: 3-12 grams.

Basil (baz el)
(*Ocymum basilicum*)

Synonyms/Related Species: Basil Bush (*ocymum minumum*), Chinese Basil (*ocymum gratissimum*), Common Basil, Fever Plant (*ocymum viride*), Garden Basil, Indian Basil (*ocymum canum*), Japanese Basil (*ocymum crispum*), Java Basil (*ocymum teniflorum*), St. Josephwort, and Sweet Basil.

Family/Class: Labiatae (mint).

Habitat: Africa, Arabia, China, Egypt, England, France, Greece, India, Japan, Java, Malaysia, North America, Persia, and Scotland.

Flavor: Pungent.

Parts Used: Aerial.

Properties: Alterative, analgesic, anesthetic (local), antibiotic, antioxidant, antiphlogistic, antispasmodic, aromatic, carminative, diaphoretic, diuretic, nervine, parasiticide, stimulant, and stomachic.

Constituents: Caffeic acid, estragole, eugenol (eugenic acid), flavonoids, linalool, minerals (calcium, iron, magnesium, phosphorous, potassium), phosphoric acid, safrol, tannic acid, vitamins (A, B_{12}, C, D, E, M (folic acid), and volatile oil.
Historical Uses: Acne, colds, constipation, enteritis, fever (ephemeral, rheumatic), flatulence, flavoring agent, headache, indigestion, infection (bacterial), inflammation, influenza, insect bites or stings, insomnia, intestinal problems, kidney problems, menstrual problems, motion sickness, muscle and joint pain, nausea, nervous conditions, pain, parasites (ringworm), perfume, respiratory conditions, rheumatism, spasmodic conditions, urinary problems, vomiting, and whooping cough.
Discussion: May aid digestion; calm the nervous system; clear and open bronchial passages; enhance respiratory system and stomach functions; induce sleep; inhibit oxidation and inhibit or destroy developement and growth of bacteria and other microorganisms; promote perspiration and urine flow; reestablish healthy system functions; stimulate appetite, the immune system, menstruation, and peristalsis.
Cautions/Contraindications: Avoid use if pregnant or breast-feeding, or if you have liver disease.
Adverse Reactions: Nausea and/or vomiting.
Herb/Drug Interactions: This herb could cause an interaction (possibly severe) when taken with the following drugs: None known.
Preparations/Dosage: Crude Herb: 3-9 grams. Infusion: 1-1½ cups per day. Tincture: 10-15 drops (0.666-1 cc.) one to three times per day.
Isolation: Safrol: Average dose of 20-30 drops (1.333-2 cc.) for use as an analgesic.

Bay (bā)

(*Laurus nobilis*)

Synonyms/Related Species: Bay Laurel, Daphne, Grecian Laural, Green Bay, Indian Bay, Laurel, Laurier, Laurus, Lorier, Noble Laurel, Roman Laurel, Sweet Bay, and True Laurel.
Family/Class: Lauraceae (laurel).
Habitat: Britain, Europe, and the Mediterranean.
Flavor: Pungent.
Parts Used: Fruit, leaves.
Properties: Abortifacient, analgesic, anesthetic (local), antiperiodic, antiphlogistic, antispasmodic, aromatic, astringent, carminative, counterirritant, diaphoretic, diuretic, emmenagogue, emetic, hemostatic, hypotensive, insect repellent, malariacidal, narcotic, parasiticide, stimulant, stomachic, and vasodilator.
Constituents: Alkaloids, eucalyptol (cineol), eugenol (eugenic acid), fatty acids (arachidonic, linoleic, linolenic, oleic, palmitic, stearic), fixed oils (olein, palmitin, stearin), geraniol (rhodinol), lauric acid, pinene, reticuline, sesquiterpene lactones, tannic acid, and volatile oil.
Historical Uses: Ague, amenorrhea, appetite loss, arthritis, asthma, bleeding, bronchitis, bruises, cockroaches, colds, colic, congestion (uterine, vaginal), cough, cramps, depression (mild/moderate), diarrhea, diphtheria, dizziness, dysentery, dysmenorrhea, earache, fainting, fever (ephemeral, intermittent, rheumatic), flatulence, flavoring agent, fleas, gastroenteritis, gastrointestinal problems, headache, hysteria, hypertension (mild/moderate), indigestion, infection, inflammation, insanity, insect bites or stings, leukorrhea, liver problems, malaria, meningitis, menstrual problems, moths, muscle and joint pain, nausea, nervous conditions,

neuralgia, pain, parasites (lice and their nits, malarial plasmodia), poisoning (food), poison ivy/oak, pruritus, rheumatism, shortness of breath, skin problems, sores, sore throat, spasmodic conditions, sprain, ulcer (duodenal, gastric, peptic, syriac), urethritis, vaginitis, and wounds (minor).

Discussion: May aid digestion; cause blood vessel dilatation; clear and open bronchial passages; enhance intestinal system and stomach functions; induce abortion; promote perspiration and urine flow; reduce blood pressure levels; stimulate menstruation and uterine contractions.

Cautions/Contraindications: Avoid use if pregnant or breast-feeding. May cause dermatitis in susceptible individuals.

Adverse Reactions: Liver damge (often characterized by jaundice), nausea, stupor, and/or vomiting.

Herb/Drug Interactions: This herb could cause an interaction (possibly severe) when taken with the following drugs: Hypotensive drugs.

Preparations/Dosage: Crude herb: 3-6 grams. Infusion: ½-1 cup per day. Oil of Bay (external uses only): Heat bay berries and leaves in a small amount of olive oil. Tincture: 5-10 drops (0.333-0.666 cc.) one to three times per day.

Isolation: Eucalyptol: 5 drops (0.333 cc.) in atomization or inhalation therapy for use in respiratory conditions.

Bayberry (bā ber ē)
(*Myrica cerifera*)

Synonyms/Related Species: Baiberie, California Bayberry (*myrica californica*), Candleberry, Myrica, Myrikē, Pacific Wax Myrtle, Tallow Shrub, Wachsgagle, Waxberry, Wax Myrtle, and Weax Mirtille.

Family/Class: Myricaceae (bayberry).

Habitat: North America.

Flavor: Pungent.

Parts Used: Bark (root), berries (wax), leaves.

Properties: Antibiotic, antifungal, antiphlogistic, antiscorbutic, antispasmodic, aromatic, astringent, carminative, depurative, diaphoretic, emetic, emmenagogue, expectorant, hemostatic, narcotic, parasiticide, sedative, stimulant, tonic, and vasodilator.

Constituents: Albumin (albumen), fatty acids (oleic, palmitic, stearic), fixed oils (olein, palmitin, stearin), gallic acid, gum, inulin (starch), lignin, myristin (myristic acid), tannic acid, vitamin C, volatile oil, and wax.

Historical Uses: Abscess, acne, arthritis, bleeding, bronchitis, bruises, canker sores, chills, cholera, colds, colitis, congestion (uterine, vaginal), constipation, cough, cramps, cystitis, diarrhea, digestive complaints, dysentery, fever (ephemeral, scarlet), flatulence, flavoring agent, gangrene, gargle/mouth rinse, gastrointestinal problems, glandular problems, goiter, hemorrhage (metrorrhagia), hemorrhoids, indigestion, infection (bacterial, fungal), inflammation, influenza, insufficiency (circulatory, venous), jaundice, lesions (tubercle), leukorrhea, liver problems, lochia, menorrhagia, menstrual problems, mucus, perfume, parasites (ringworm), periodontal disease, prolapse (rectal, uterine), respiratory conditions, scarletina, scrofula, scurvy, sexually transmitted diseases (STDs), sinusitis, sore throat, spasmodic conditions, stomatitis, syphilis, tuberculosis, ulcer (duodenal, fistula, gastric, peptic, stasis, syphilitic, tuberculous, varicose), vaginitis, varicose veins, and wounds (minor).

Discussion: May aid digestion; cause blood vessel dilatation; cleanse the whole system; clear and open bronchial passages; enhance circulatory system, liver, lung, and spleen functions; increase blood flow to lymph and mucous membrane tissues; inhibit or destroy development and growth of bacteria and other microorganisms; promote perspiration and adrenal rejuvenation; purify the blood; restore normal tone to tissues; stimulate the immune system; stimulate menstruation and peristalsis.
Cautions/Contraindications: Avoid use if pregnant or breast-feeding, or if you have colitis, colon cancer, congestive heart failure, gastrointestinal problems, hypertension, kidney disease, stomach cancer, or those on a sodium restricted diet. Individuals who must monitor their potassium and/or sodium balance should exercise caution when using this herb as bayberry alters the way the body utilizes potassium and sodium. May cause potassium and sodium retention.
Adverse Reactions: Coma, convulsions, hematuria (blood in the urine), nausea, stupor, and/or vomiting.
Herb/Drug Interactions: This herb could cause an interaction (possibly severe) when taken with the following drugs: None known.
Preparations/Dosage: Crude Herb: 3-9 grams. Bark (powdered): Average dose in substance 20-30 grains (1.333-2 gm.). Decoction (bark or leaves): 1-2 cups per day. Extract: 1-10 drops (0.066-0.666 cc.) one to two times per day. Tincture: 10-15 drops (0.666-1 cc.) one to three times per day. Wax (berries): Boil berries in water for 15-20 minutes. Let water cool and skim wax off surface.
Isolation: Myricin: Average dose of 1-3 grains (0.066-0.2 gm.) for use as an antisyphilitic.
Did You Know? It takes approximately four pounds of bayberries to make one pound of wax.

Bearberry (ber·ber ē)
(*Arctostaphylos uva-ursi*)

Synonyms/Related Species: Alpine Bearberry (*arctostaphylos rubra*), Arberry, Arbutus Uva-Ursi, Bearsgrapes, Black Bearberry (*arctostaphylos alpina*), Common Bearberry, Coralillo, Creeping Manzanita, Greenleaf Manzanita (*arctostaphylos patula*), Hog Cranberry, Kinnikinnik, Mansaneta, Mealberry, Mountain Box, Mountain Cranberry, Redberry Leaves, Sagackhomi, Sandberry, Upland Cranberry, Uva-Ursi, and White-Leaved Manzanita (*arctostaphylos manzanita*).
Family/Class: Ericaceae (heath).
Habitat: The Alpine zone, the Altai Mountains, Asia, Britain, Europe, the Himalayas, Ireland, North America, Scandinavia, Scotland, and Siberia.
Flavor: Bitter.
Parts Used: Leaves.
Properties: Analgesic, antibiotic, antifungal, antilithic, antiphlogistic, antispasmodic, astringent, depurative, diuretic, hemostatic, lithotriptic, oxytocic, stimulant, tonic, urinary antiseptic, and vasoconstrictor.
Constituents: Allantoin, arbutin, flavonoids, gallic acid, malic acid, tannic acid, ursone (ursolic acid), and volatile oil.
Historical Uses: Abscess, acne, alkaline urine, arthritis, bleeding, bronchitis, burns (minor), calculus, candida, canker sores, cramps, cystitis, diabetes, diarrhea, digestive complaints, dysentery, dysmenorrhea, edema, enuresis (urinary incontinence), escherichia coli (e-coli), fever (ephemeral, herpetic, rheumatic), gallstones, gastritis, gleet, gonorrhea, gout, hematuria (blood in

the urine), hemorrhage, hemorrhoids, herbal tobacco, herpes, hives, indigestion, infection (bacterial, bladder, fungal, kidney, sexually transmitted, urinary tract), inflammation, insufficiency (pancreatic), irritable bowel syndrome (IBS), kidney stones, lithemia, liver problems, lumbago, menopausal/menstrual problems, menorrhagia, moniliasis, mucus, muscle and joint pain, nephritis, pain, pimples, prostatitis, pyelitis, rash, rheumatism, sexually transmitted diseases (STDs), skin problems, spasmodic conditions, spleen problems, syphilis, ulcer (syphilitic), urethritis, uterine problems, weight loss, and wounds (minor).
Discussion: May constrict the blood vessels; dissolve calculi; enhance cardiovascular system, intestinal system, liver, and urinary system functions; inhibit or destroy developement and growth of bacteria and other microorganisms; purify the urinary system; prevent the development of calculus or stones; promote urine flow; reduce excessive lithic acid (uric acid) and urate levels in the blood, tophi, and urine, and the frequency of nighttime urination; restore normal tone to tissues; stimulate uterine contractions; strengthen the urinary system.
Cautions/Contraindications: Avoid use if pregnant or breast-feeding, or if you have chronic kidney disease, ulcer (duodenal, peptic), or if you have gastric sensitivity. Do not adminiter to children under 12 years of age. Do not administer simultaneously with food or medications that increase lithic acid levels. May interfere with the absorption of atropine (when taken by mouth), codeine, ephedrine, pseudoephedrine, and theophylline drugs. Use for no longer than one week.
Adverse Reactions: Aggravation of acid reflux disease, liver damage (often characterized by jaundice), mucous membrane problems, nausea, respiratory distress, tinnitus, and/or vomiting.
Herb/Drug Interactions: This herb could cause an interaction (possibly severe) when taken with the following drugs: Autonomic drugs, Diuretic drugs, Opiate Agonists/Narcotic drugs, and Theophylline drugs.
Preparations/Dosage: Crude herb: 3-9 grams. Extract (powdered): Average dose in substance 5-15 grains (0.333-1 gm.). Infusion: 1-3 cups per day. Tincture: 10-30 drops (0.666-2 cc.) one to three times per day.
Isolation: Arbutin: Average dose of 5-15 grains (0.333-1 gm.) for use as a diuretic and urinary antiseptic.

Bedstraw (bed strô)
(*Galium aperine*)

Synonyms/Related Species: American Bedstraw (*galium tinctorum*), Barweed, Catchweed, Cheese Rennet, Cheese Renning, Cleavers (*galium aparine*), Cleaverwort, Clivers, Coachweed, Curdwort, Goosebill, Goose Grass, Gosling Weed, Grip Grass, Hayriffe, Hayruff, Heath Bedstraw (*galium saxatile*), Hedge Bedstraw (*galium molugo*), Hedge-Burs, Hedgeheriff, Lady's Bedstraw (*galium verum*), Maid's Hair, Mutton Chops, Northern Bedstraw (*galium boreale*), Our Lady's Bedstraw, Petit Muguet, Petty Mugget, Rough Marsh Bedstraw (*galium uliginosum*), Small Bedstraw (*galium trifidum*), Sweet-Scented Bedstraw (*galium triflorum*), Water Bedstraw (*galium palustre*), Yellow Bedstraw, Yellow Cleavers, and Yellow Galium.
Family/Class: Rubiaceae (madder).
Habitat: Alaska, the Alpine and Subalpine zones, Asia, England, Europe, France, Iran, Lapland, North America, Russia, Syria, and the Yukon Territory.
Flavor: Pungent/ bitter.
Parts Used: Leaves, seeds.

Properties: Alterative, anticarcinogen, antiphlogistic, antiscorbutic, antispasmodic, astringent, carminative, depurative, diaphoretic, diuretic, expectorant, hemostatic, laxative, lithotriptic, nervine, tonic, and vulnerary.
Constituents: Anthracene, anthraquinone, asperuloside, caffeic acid, chlorogenic acid, chlorophyll, citric acid, flavonoids, glycosides, inulin (starch), rutin, scandoside, tannic acid, and vitamin C.
Historical Uses: Arthritis, bleeding, blisters, burns (minor), calculus, cancer, colds, cystitis, dandruff, diarrhea, dysphasia, dysuria (painful/difficult urination), earache, edema, eczema, epilepsy, fever, freckles, glandular problems, glandular swelling, gleet, gonorrhea, hair rinse, hepatitis, infection (sexually transmitted, urinary tract), infertility, inflammation, insect bites or stings, kidney stones, leprosy, lesions (tubercle), liver problems, mood swings, mucus, nosebleed, poison ivy/oak, psoriasis, rash, respiratory conditions, scrofula, scurvy, sexually transmitted diseases (STDs), skin problems, sores, spasmodic conditions, stretch marks, substitute for coffee (seeds), sunburn, tonsillitis, tuberculosis, tumors, ulcer (duodenal, fistula, gastric, peptic, tuberculous), urethritis, urodialysis (suppression of urine), weight loss, and wounds (minor).
Discussion: May aid digestion; calm the nervous system; clear and open bronchial passages; decrease the effect of carcinogens; dissolve calculi; enhance bladder and gallbladder functions; increase metabolic function; prevent hemorrhage in persons with hypertension; promote bowel evacuation, perspiration, and urine flow; purify the blood; reduce capillary fragility and blood pressure levels; reestablish healthy system functions; restore normal tone to tissues; serve as a weight loss aid; speed healing; stimulate the glandular system and peristalsis.
Cautions/Contraindications: Avoid use if pregnant or breast-feeding, or if you have a diabetes or poor circulation.
Adverse Reactions: Diarrhea, mucous membrane problems, nausea, and/or vomiting.
Herb/Drug Interactions: This herb could cause an interaction (possibly severe) when taken with the following drugs: Diuretic drugs.
Preparations/Dosage: Crude Herb: 3-9 grams. Extract: 5-10 drops (0.333-0.666 cc.) one to two times per day. Infusion: ½-1 cup per day. Juice: Mix ½-1 teaspoon juice in 1 cup of hot water per day. Seeds (dried/roasted): Used as a substitute for coffee. Tincture: 15-30 drops (1-2 cc.) one to three times per day.

Beet (bēt)

(*Beta vulgaris*)

Synonyms/Related Species: Beta, Bete, Chard, Garden Beet, Red Beetroot, Sea Beet (*beta maritima*), Spinach Beet, Sugar Beet, and White Beet.
Family/Class: Chenopodiaceae (goosefoot).
Habitat: Africa, Asia, Britain, England, Europe, France, Germany, India, North America, Russia, and Turkey.
Flavor: Bitter/bland.
Parts Used: Leaves (lower), root.
Properties: Anticarcinogen, anti-inflammatory, emmenagogue, hemostatic, and nutritive
Constituents: Adipic acid, amino acids (carnitine, glutamine), betaine (lycine), betanin, carbohydrates, citric acid, disaccharide, fiber, glutaric acid, gum, inulin (starch), ketose, malic acid, minerals (calcium, iron, magnesium, phosphorous, potassium, sodium, sulfur),

monosaccharides, oxaluric acid, pectic acid, pectin, phosphoric acid, polysaccharides, prolactin, protein, saponins, tartaric acid, and vitamins (A, B_2 (riboflavin), B3 (niacin).
Historical Uses: Alopecia, amenorrhea, beverage (root), bleeding, blisters, cancer (colon, lung), chronic fatigue syndrome (CFS), dandruff, dietary supplementation, Epstein Barr Virus (EBV), erysipelas, fibromyalgia, food source, headache, inflammation, jaundice, liver problems, malnutrition, mononucleosis (infectious), nosebleed, pruritus, skin problems, sores, substitute for spinach (leaves), tinnitus, and toothache.
Discussion: May assist in regenerating a key cellular antioxidant enzyme called methionine reductase, which prevents the build-up of homocysteine in the body; decrease the effect of carcinogens; inhibit fatty deposits in the liver; provide dietary supplementation; serve as a nutritional adjuvant to therapeutic programs; stimulate menstruation; stop or slow abnormal cell growth.
Cautions/Contraindications: Avoid use if pregnant or breast-feeding.
Adverse Reactions: Diarrhea (possibly bloody), edema, gastrointestinal cramps (severe), hypocalcemia (blood calcium levels that are below normal) hematuria (blood in the urine), nausea, and/or vomiting.
Herb/Drug Interactions: This herb could cause an interaction (possibly severe) when taken with the following drugs: None known.
Preparations/Dosage: Root: Baked, boiled, pickled, plain, or stewed. Juice (fresh): 1 cup per day. Leaves: Boiled and eaten as a vegetable.
Isolation: Betaine: Average dose of 2-4 grains (0.13-0.26 gm.) for use as an emmenagogue.

Belladonna (bel e·don e)
(*Atropa belladonna*)

Synonyms/Related Species: Atropos, Black Cherry, Deadly Nightshade, Devil's Cherries, Devil's Herb, Deuil, Divale, Dwayberry, Dwayle, Fair Lady, Great Morel, Naughty Man's Cherries, Poison Black Cherry, and Sleeping Nightshade.
Family/Class: Solanaceae (nightshade).
Habitat: Africa, Algeria, Asia, the Balkans, Britain, Denmark, England, Europe, France, Iran, Ireland, Italy, North America, and Sweden.
Flavor: Bitter.
Parts Used: Leaves, root.
Properties: Anticarcinogen, antiphlogistic, antispasmodic, diuretic, hypnotic, mydriatic, narcotic, sedative, and stimulant.
Constituents: Alkaloids, atropamine, atropine, atroscine, belladonnine, coumarin, flavonoids, hyoscyamine, inulin (starch), scopolamine, scopoleine, scopoline, solanine, tannic acid, and tropine.
Historical Uses: Arrhythmia, asthma, bladder problems, bronchitis, bunions, cardiovascular conditions, cancer, cerebrospinal hyperemia, colic, colitis, constipation, corns, cough, delirium tremens (DTs), enuresis (urinary incontinence), ephidrosis (excessive perspiration), eye problems, fever (ephemeral, enteric, rheumatic), gout, hysteria, infection, inflammation, insomnia, iritis, kidney problems, liver problems, mania, muscle and joint pain, nervous conditions, neuralgia, pain, pneumonia, poisoning (calabar bean, chloroform, opium), rheumatism, sciatica, sore throat, spasmodic conditions, sprain, typhoid, ulcer (bouveret, gastric), and whooping cough.

Discussion: May decrease the effect of carcinogens; enhance liver function; increase the frequency of the heart's action; lessen the vascularity of the iris; produce pupil dilatation; promote urine flow; reduce the frequency of nighttime urination; serve as an adjuvant to alcoholism treatment programs to assist in easing delirium tremens (DTs), and serve as an antidote for calabar bean, chloroform, and opium poisoning; stimulate the cardiovascular and respiratory systems, and stimulate the sympathetic nerves and depress the cerebrospinal nerves.

Cautions/Contraindications: Avoid use if pregnant or breast-feeding. Avoid handling or collecting the plant if you have any open wounds on the hands. Do not confuse this plant with Chinese sumach (*ailanthus altissima*), American nightshade (*phytolacca americana*), or Japanese belladonna (*scopolia carniolica*). Prolonged use may lead to a tolerance to the accumulation of tropine-alkaloids in the parasympathetic system; thus more of the herb is required to achieve the same effects. Not for long-term use. Use with professional guidance/supervision.

Adverse Reactions: Atropinism (poisoning due to the misuse of atropine), bradycardia, cardiac failure, compulsion to talk, convulsions, delirium, diarrhea (possibly bloody), dryness (mouth), exhaustion, gastrointestinal cramps (severe), hallucinations, laryngitis, manic attacks, nausea, paralysis, pupil dilatation, reduced perspiration, restlessness, stupor, tachycardia, tremors, vomiting, and/or possible death.

Herb/Drug Interactions: This herb could cause an interaction (possibly severe) when taken with the following drugs: Autonomic drugs.

Preparations/Dosage: Crude Herb: 1-3 grams. Extract (leaves): 1-3 drops (0.06-0.2 cc.) per day. Extract (root): ¼-1 drop (0.03-0.06 cc.) per day. Extract (solid/leaf): Average dose in substance ¼ grain (0.015 gm.). Infusion: 1-2 teaspoons one to two times per day. Juice: 1-5 drops (0.066-0.333 cc.) in water per day. Leaves (powdered): Average dose in substance 1-2 grains (0.066-0.133 gm.). Root (powdered): Average dose in substance 1-5 grains (0.066-0.3 gm.). Tincture (leaf): 5-10 drops (0.333-0.666 cc.).

Isolation: Atropine: Soluble in alcohol and sparingly so in water. Average dose of $^{1}/_{150}$ grain (0.4 mg.) for use as a mydriatic and narcotic. Atropine sulfate: Soluble in water. Average dose of $^{1}/_{120}$ grain (0.5 mg.) for use as a mydriatic and narcotic. Scopolamine hydrobromide: Subcutaneous dose $^{1}/_{120}$ grain (0.5 mg.) for use as a sedative, or in a 0.1-0.3% solution used locally as a mydriatic.

Betel (bēt ’l)
(*Piper betle*)

Synonyms/Related Species: Chavica Betel, Vettila, and Vettilai.

Family/Class: Piperaceae (pepper).

Habitat: Africa, Asia, India, Java, Madagascar, and Malaysia.

Flavor: Bitter.

Parts Used: Fruit, leaves, oil, root.

Properties: Anesthetic (local), antibiotic, antigalactic, antilithic, antioxidant, antiperiodic, antiseptic, carminative, counterirritant, diuretic, expectorant, lithotriptic, malariacidal, sialogogue, stimulant, and tonic.

Constituents: Cadinene, carbolic acid (phenol), chavibetol, chavicine, chavicol, eugenol (eugenic acid), inulin (starch), monosaccharides, piperazine, piperine, tannic acid, and volatile oil.

Historical Uses: Abscess, ague, colds, cough, digestive complaints, diphtheria, ear infection, fever (ephemeral, intermittent), flatulence, gallstones, gargle/mouth rinse, gastrointestinal problems, gout, indigestion, kidney stones, lithemia, malaria, parasites (malarial plasmodia), respiratory conditions, rheumatism, sexually transmitted diseases (STDs), syphilis, ulcer (syphilitic, syriac), and urinary calculus.
Discussion: May aid digestion; clear and open bronchial passages; diminish or suppress lactation; dissolve calculi; inhibit oxidation; prevent the development of calculus or stones; promote saliva secretion; reduce excessive lithic acid (uric acid) and urate levels in the blood, tophi, and urine; restore normal tone to tissues.
Cautions/Contraindications: Avoid use if pregnant or breast-feeding. Do not confuse this plant with areca nut (*areca catechu*).
Adverse Reactions: Nausea, salivation (increased), and/or vomiting.
Herb/Drug Interactions: This herb could cause an interaction (possibly severe) when taken with the following drugs: None known.
Preparations/Dosage: Betel Oil: 1-2 drops (0.06-0.1 cc.) in water or on a sugarcube. Juice (4 leaves): ¼-½ teaspoon in water per day. Leaf (fresh): Chew a small amount of fresh betel leaf until masticated (similar to chewing tobacco). Juice is swallowed and the remaining plant residue is then discarded (one "chew" can last several hours and is replaced by a fresh amount of leaf).
Isolation: Piperine: Average dose of 1-5 grains (0.066-0.333 gm.) for use as an antiperiodic. Piperazine hydrochlorate: Average dose in 2% solution, 5 grains (0.33 gm.), administered hypodermically; orally (by mouth), 8 grains (0.5 gm.) for use as a diuretic and antisyphilitic.

Bethroot (beth·root)
(*Trillium pendulum*)

Synonyms/Related Species: Coughroot, Cuckoo Pint, Giant Trillium (*trillium chloropetalum*), Giant Wakerobin, Ground Lily, Indian Balm, Indian Shamrock, Jew's Harp Plant, Lamb's Quarters, Milk Ipecac, Nightshade, Pariswort, Rattlesnake Root, Three-Leaved Wakerobin (*trillium erectum*), Western Trillium (*trillium ovatum*), and Western Wakerobin.
Family/Class: Liliaceae (lily).
Habitat: Asia, Europe, North America, and the Subalpine zone.
Flavor: Pungent/bitter.
Parts Used: Leaves, root.
Properties: Alterative, antibiotic, antispasmodic, aphrodisiac, astringent, cardiant, counterirritant, diaphoretic, emmenagogue, expectorant, febrifuge, hemostatic, oxytocic, sialogogue, and tonic.
Constituents: Aglycone (genin), fatty acids (oleic, palmitic, stearic), fixed oils (olein, palmitin, stearin), glycosides, gum, inulin (starch), resin, saponins, tannic acid, trilliin, and volatile oil.
Historical Uses: Abscess, amenorrhea, arrhythmia, bleeding, bronchitis, colds, congestion (lung, uterine, vaginal), cough, diarrhea, dysentery, fever (ephemeral), gangrene, hemorrhage (metrorrhagia), hemorrhoids, infection (bacterial), insect bites or stings, insufficiency (venous), leukorrhea, menorrhagia, menstrual problems, mucus, nosebleed, pain, respiratory conditions, skin problems, sore throat, spasmodic conditions, toothache, tumors, ulcer (duodenal, gastric, peptic, stasis, varicose), uterine problems, vaginitis, varicose veins, and wounds (minor).

Discussion: May arouse sexual impulses; clear and open bronchial passages; inhibit or destroy development and growth of bacteria and other microorganisms; promote perspiration and saliva secretion; reestablish healthy system functions; restore normal tone to tissues; stimulate the cardiovascular system, menstruation, and uterine contractions.
Cautions/Contraindications: Avoid use if pregnant or breast-feeding. May cause dermatitis in susceptible individuals.
Adverse Reactions: Diarrhea (possibly bloody), gastrointestinal cramps (severe), nausea, salivation (increased), and/or vomiting.
Herb/Drug Interactions: This herb could cause an interaction (possibly severe) when taken with the following drugs: None known.
Preparations/Dosage: Crude Herb: 3-6 grams. Decoction (root): 1-2 cups per day. Extract: 5-10 drops (0.333-0.666 cc.) one to two times per day. Root (powdered): Average dose in substance 15-30 grains (0.98-2 gm.). Tincture: 10-15 drops (0.666-1 cc.) one to three times per day.
Isolation: Trilliin: Average dose of 2-4 grains (0.13-0.26 gm.) for use as an astringent, expectorant, and tonic.

Betony (bet e·nē)
(*Stachys betonica*)

Synonyms/Related Species: Bishopswort, California Hedge-Nettle (*stachys bullata*), Clown's Woundwort, European Wood Betony, Field Stachys (*stachys arvensis*), Hedge Stachys (*stachys sylvatica*), Hedge Woundwort, Lousewort, Marsh Stachys (*stachys palustris*), Purple Betony, Swamp Hedge-Nettle, and True Woundwort (*stachys germanica*).
Family/Class: Labiatae (mint).
Habitat: England, Europe, North America, Portugal, Spain, and the Yukon Territory.
Flavor: Bitter.
Parts Used: Leaves.
Properties: Alterative, antibiotic, antifungal, antiphlogistic, antispasmodic, aromatic, astringent, carminative, depurative, diaphoretic, diuretic, emetic, emmenagogue, expectorant, hemostatic, hypoglycemic, hypotensive, laxative, lithotriptic, nervine, sedative, stimulant, tonic, and vulnerary.
Constituents: Alkaloids, betaine (lycine), caffeic acid, cholorgenic acid, flavonoids, glycosides, minerals (magnesium, manganese, phosphorous), palustrine, saponins, stachydrine, stachyose, tannic acid, and volatile oil.
Historical Uses: Abdominal pain, abscess, amenorrhea, anxiety, appetite loss, asthma, bladder problems, bleeding, bronchitis, calculus, candida, colds, colic, convulsions, cough, cramps, delirium, diarrhea, digestive complaints, dizziness, dysentery, earache, epilepsy, fainting, febrile diseases, fever (ephemeral, rheumatic), flatulence, gallbladder problems, gallstones, gargle/mouth rinse, gastritis, gastrointestinal problems, gout, headache, hematuria (blood in the urine), hemoptysis, hyperactivity, hyperglycemia, hypertension (mild/moderate), hysteria, indigestion, infection (bacterial, fungal), inflammation, influenza, insanity, insomnia, insufficiency (venous), irritable bowel syndrome (IBS), jaundice, kidney stones, liver problems, lung problems, menstrual problems, migraine, moniliasis, mucus, muscle and joint pain, nervous conditions, neuralgia, neurasthenia, night sweats, pain, palsy, pharyngitis, respiratory conditions, rheumatism, skin problems, sores, sore throat, spasmodic conditions, spleen problems, sprain,

stomachache, stomatitis, ulcer (duodenal, gastric, peptic, stasis, varicose), varicose veins, and wounds (minor).

Discussion: May aid digestion; calm the nervous system; cause blood vessel dilatation; clear and open bronchial passages; dissolve calculi; enhance cardiovascular system and liver functions; enhance the circulatory system, heart, liver; inhibit or destroy developement and growth of bacteria and other microorganisms; promote perspiration and urine flow; purify the blood; reduce blood sugar levels and blood pressure levels; reestablish healthy system functions; restore normal tone to tissues; speed healing; stimulate appetite and menstruation.

Cautions/Contraindications: Avoid use if pregnant or breast-feeding.

Adverse Reactions: Diarrhea (severe/possibly bloody), gastrointestinal cramps (severe), impaired motor control, lethargy, nausea, staggering, and/or vomiting.

Herb/Drug Interactions: This herb could cause an interaction (possibly severe) when taken with the following drugs: Antidiabetic drugs and Hypotensive drugs.

Preparations/Dosage: Crude Herb: 3-6 grams. Decoction: ½ cup per day. Infusion: 1-2 cups per day. Tincture: 10-30 drops (0.666-2 cc.) one to three times per day.

Isolation: Betaine: 2-4 grains (0.13-0.26 gm.) for use as an emmenagogue.

Bindweed (bīnd wēd)
(*Convolvulus arvensis*)

Synonyms/Related Species: Bearbind, Conquerer Root, Devil's Vine, Field Convolvulus, Greater Bindweed (*convolvulus sepium*), Heavenly Blue, Hedge Bindweed, Hedge Lily, Hooded Bindweed, Ipomea Jalapa, Ipomoea Purga, Jalap, Jalap Bindweed (*convolvulus jalapa*), Morning Glory (*convolvulus purpureus*), Morning Glory Root, Old Man's Nightcap, Orizaba Jalap Root, Pearl Gates, Purga, Scammony, Sea Bindweed (*convolvulus soldanella*), Syrian Bindweed (*convolvulus scammonia*), Tuberous-Rooted Bindweed (*convolvulus batatas*), Vona-Nox, Wild Morning Glory (*convolvulus arvensis*), and Xalapa.

Family/Class: Convolvulaceae (morning glory).

Habitat: Asia, Chile, China, England, Europe, India, Mexico, North America, Persia, Portugal, Scotland, Spain, South America, and Syria.

Flavor: Bitter/pungent.

Parts Used: Gum resin, root.

Properties: Antiphlogistic, carminative, diuretic, emetic, hallucinogen, laxative, narcotic, and parasiticide.

Constituents: Acetic acid, alkaloids, cinnamic acid, convolvulin, cyanin, ergoline, fatty acids (pelargonic, propiolic), glycosides, gum, hydrocyanic acid, inulin (starch), isobutyric acid, jalapin, lysergic acid, monosaccharides, nitrates, pharbitin, rhamnose, scopoletin, tannic acid, valerianic acid, and volatile oil.

Historical Uses: Arthritis, colic, conjunctivitis, constipation, edema, fever (ephemeral, rheumatic), flatulence, gastrointestinal problems, headache, indigestion, inflammation, insomnia, jaundice, liver problems, mucus, muscle and joint pain, pain, parasites (ringworm), rheumatism, skin problems, and urinary tract infection.

Discussion: May aid digestion; enhance intestinal system, kidney, and lung functions; promote bowel evacuation and urine flow; stimulate peristalsis.

Cautions/Contraindications: Avoid use if pregnant or breast-feeding, or if you have alimentary canal inflammation or intestinal irritation. The seeds contain hydrocyanic acid and are extremely poisonous.
Adverse Reactions: Ataxia, coma, confusion, convulsions, diarrhea, gastrointestinal cramps, hallucinations, hydrocyanism (hydrocyanic acid poisoning), nausea, stupor, a variety of psychotropic effects, visual disturbances, vomiting, and/or possible death.
Herb/Drug Interactions: This herb could cause an interaction (possibly severe) when taken with the following drugs: None known.
Preparations/Dosage: Crude Herb: 3-6 grams. Decoction (root): 1 cup per day. Gum resin (powdered): Average dose in substance 2-5 grains (0.13-0.324 gm.). Juice: ¼-½ teaspoon. Root (powdered): Average dose in substance 3-12 grains (0.2-0.78 gm.). Tincture: 10-15 drops (0.666-1 cc.) one to three times per day.
Isolation: Jalapin: Average dose of 1-3 grains (0.066-0.2 gm.) for use as a laxative.

Birch (bûrch)
(*Betula alba*)

Synonyms/Related Species: Beorc, Bereza, Berke, Bhurga, Black Birch (*betula lenta*), Bog Birch, Bouleau, Canoe Birch, Cherry Birch (*betula benta*), Common Birch, Dwarf Birch (*betula nana*), European Birch (*betula alnus*), Lady Birch, Lady of the Woods, Mountain Birch, Paper Birch (*betula papyrifera*), Scrub Birch, Silver Birch, Spice Birch, Swamp Birch (*betula pumila*), Sweet Birch, Water Birch (*betula occidentalis*), White Birch, and Yellow Birch.
Family/Class: Betulaceae (birch).
Habitat: Alaska, the Alpine and Subalpine zones, Asia, Europe, Iceland, North America, Siberia, Sicily, and the Yukon Territory.
Flavor: Bitter/pungent.
Parts Used: Bark (inner), buds, leaves (fresh), oil, sap.
Properties: Abortifacient, analgesic, antibiotic, anticarcinogen, antiphlogistic, antispasmodic, antiviral, aromatic, astringent, counterirritant, depurative, diaphoretic, diuretic, hemostatic, insect repellent, laxative, lithotriptic, sedative, and stimulant.
Constituents: Betulin, caffeic acid, creosol, fatty acids (oleic, palmitic, stearic), fixed oils (olein, palmitin, stearin), flavonoids, fluoride, guaiacol, glycosides, methyl salicylate, minerals (calcium, chlorine, copper, iron, magnesium, phosphorous, potassium, silicon, sodium), myricetin, phosphoric acid, proanthocyanidins, quercetin, resins, saponins, silicic acid, tannic acid, vitamins (A, B_1 (thiamine), B_2 (riboflavin), C (ascorbic acid), E (alpha-tocopheral), and volatile oil.
Historical Uses: Abscess, acne, alopecia, arthritis, beverage (sap), bleeding, calculus, cancer (melanoma), canker sores, cellulite, cholera, dandruff, dentifrice, diarrhea, dysentery, eczema, edema, fever (ephemeral, rheumatic), gallstones, gargle/mouth rinse, gout, gnats, headache, hypercholesteremia, infection (bacterial, bladder, viral), inflammation, insomnia, kidney stones, muscle and joint pain, pain, periodontal disease, premenstrual syndrome (PMS), psoriasis, rash, rheumatism, skin problems, sores, spasmodic conditions, substitute for wintergreen oil (oil), urinary problems, warts (digitate, filiform, fugitive, glabra, mother, plana juvenilis, plantar, seborrhoeic, vulgaris), and wounds (minor).
Discussion: May decrease the effect of carcinogens; dissolve calculi; induce abortion; inhibit or destroy developement and growth of bacteria and other microorganisms; promote bowel

evacuation, perspiration, and urine flow; purify the blood; reduce cholesterol levels; stimulate hair growth and peristalsis.
Cautions/Contraindications: Avoid use if pregnant or breast-feeding, or if you have insufficiency (cardiac, kidney). May cause dermatitis in susceptible individuals.
Adverse Reactions: Nausea and/or vomiting.
Herb/Drug Interactions: This herb could cause an interaction (possibly severe) when taken with the following drugs: None known.
Preparations/Dosage: Crude Herb: 3-9 grams. Decoction (bark or buds): ½-¾ cup per day. Extract (leaves): 5-10 drops (0.333-0.666 cc.) one to two times per day. Extract (powdered): Average dose in substance 20-30 grains (1.333-2 gm.). Infusion (buds or leaves): ½-1 cup per day. Oil (fixed oil) of White Birch (*oleum betulae papyrifera*): External Uses only. Oil (volatile oil) of Black Birch Bark (*oleum betulae lenta volatile*): 1-5 drops (0.066-0.333 cc.) in water or on a sugarcube. Juice: 1 teaspoon in water as needed. Tincture: 10-15 drops (0.666-1 cc.) one to three times per day.
Isolation: Creosol: Average dose of ½-2 drops (0.025-0.1 cc.) for use as an antimicrobic.
Did You Know? The trunk of the birch tree is tapped similar to that of a maple tree for the extraction of the sugary sap. Birch trees yield approximately 5-10 gallons of sap per day, and one tree can yield an average of sixteen gallons of sap in a single season.

Birthwort (bûrth wûrt)
(*Aristolochia clematitis*)

Synonyms/Related Species: Brazilian Snakeroot (*aristolochia cymbifera*), California Dutchman's Pipe (*aristolochia californica*), Indian Birthwort (*aristolochia indica*), Jarra, Jarrinha, Long-Rooted Birthwort (*aristolochia longa*), Mexican Snakeroot (*aristolochia foetida*), Milhommen, Serpentaria, Texas Snakeroot (*aristolochia reticulata*), Upright Birthwort, and Virginia Snakeroot (*aristolochia serpentaria*).
Family/Class: Aristolochiaceae (birthwort).
Habitat: Arabia, Asia, Brazil, the Causasus, Egypt, England, Europe, India, Japan, Mexico, North America, and South America.
Flavor: Pungent.
Parts Used: Root.
Properties: Antiphlogistic, aphrodisiac, aromatic, astringent, diaphoretic, diuretic, emmenagogue, emetic, oxytocic, stimulant, and tonic.
Constituents: Albumin (albumen), alkaloids, aristolic acid, aristolochine, aristolochic acid, gum, inulin (starch), lignin, minerals (iron, silicon), resin, silicic acid, and tannic acid
Historical Uses: Allergy, amenorrhea, appetite loss, arthritis, colds, colic, gallbladder problems, fever (ephemeral, enteric, rheumatic), gargle/mouth rinse, gastrointestinal problems, gout, indigestion, infection, inflammation, menstrual problems, muscle and joint pain, neuralgia, pneumonia, pruritus, respiratory conditions, rheumatism, skin problems, small pox, snakebite, typhoid, ulcer (bouveret, duodenal, gastric, peptic, stasis), and wounds (minor).
Discussion: May arouse sexual impulses; promote perspiration and urine flow; restore normal tone to tissues; serve as an adjuvant to quinine and as a hormonal-based aid for sterility problems; stimulate appetite, the immune system, menstruation, and uterine contractions.
Cautions/Contraindications: Avoid use if pregnant or breast-feeding. Not for long-term use. Use with professional guidance/supervision.

Adverse Reactions: Coma, gastroenteritis (severe), hematuria (blood in the urine), nausea, respiratory failure, spasmodic conditions, vomiting, and/or possible death.
Herb/Drug Interactions: This herb could cause an interaction (possibly severe) when taken with the following drugs: None known.
Preparations/Dosage: Crude Herb: 3-6 grams. Decoction: ¼-½ cup per day. Extract (cold): ½ teaspoon. Root (powdered): Average dose in substance 15 grains (0.666-0.98 gm.).

Bistort (bis tôrt)
(*Polygonum bistorta*)

Synonyms/Related Species: Adderwort, Alpine Bistort (*polygonum viviparum*), Alpine Knotweed, American Bistort, Columbrina, Common Knotweed (*polygonum aviculare*), Common Smartweed, Dracunculus, Dragonwort, Easter Giant, Easter Ledges, Easter Mangiant, Fo-Ti (*Polygonum multiflorum*), Heart's Ease, Ivy Knotweed (*polygonum convolvulus*), Japanese Knotweed (*polygonum cuspidatum*), Knotweed, Lady's Thumb (*polygonum persicaria*), Mountain Knotweed (*polygonum douglasii*), Nine Joints, Ninety-Knot, Oderwort, Osterick, Passions, Patience Dock, Polysgony, Redlegs, Russian Knotgrass, Serpentaria, Serpentary Dragonwort, Snakeroot, Snakeweed, Sweet Dock, Twice-Writhen, Water Pepper (*polygonum hydropiper*), Water Smartweed (*polygonum amphibium*), Western Bistort (*polygonum bistortoides*), and Yard Knotweed (*polygonum arenastrum*).
Family/Class: Polygonaceae (buckwheat).
Habitat: Alaska, the Alpine and Subalpine zones, Asia, China, England, Europe, the Himalayas, Iceland, Ireland, Japan, North America, Russia, Scotland, and Siberia.
Flavor: Pungent.
Parts Used: Root.
Properties: Alterative, antibiotic, antiperiodic, antiphlogistic, astringent, counterirritant, depurative, diaphoretic, diuretic, emmenagogue, emetic, expectorant, hemostatic, hepatic, insect repellent, laxative, lithotriptic, malariacidal, nutritive, parasiticide, stimulant, tonic, and vulnerary.
Constituents: Avicularin, aviculin, bisulfate, catechins, coumarin, emodin, flavonoids, galactoside, gallic acid, gum, inulin (starch), lignin, minerals (silicon), mucilage, quercitol, rhamnazine, scopoletin, silicic acid, tannic acid, umbelliferone, vitamins (A, B_3 (niacin), B_x (para-aminobenzoic acid (PABA), B_1 (thiamine), B_2 (riboflavin), B_5 (pantothenic acid), B_6 (pyridoxine), B_{12}, C (ascorbic acid), choline, H (biotin), inositol, M (folic acid), and vitexin.
Historical Uses: Abscess, ague, alopecia, amenorrhea, anemia, angina, arteriosclerosis, arthritis, bleeding, bronchitis, bruises, calculus, cancer, canker sores, cardiovascular conditions, cholera, colds, colic, congestion (uterine, vaginal), constipation, cough, debility, diabetes, diarrhea, dietary supplementation, digestive complaints, diverticulitis, dizziness, dry skin, dysentery, dysuria (painful/difficult urination), earache, eczema, edema, enteritis, epilepsy, erectile dysfunction, fatigue, fever (ephemeral, intermittent, rheumatic, rocky mountain spotted), fleas, flies, fractures, gallstones, gangrene, gargle/mouth rinse, gastroenteritis, gastrointestinal problems, gout, headache, hematuria (blood in the urine), hemorrhage, hemorrhoids, hypoglycemia, infection (bacterial), infertility, inflammation, injury (tendon), insect bites or stings, insomnia, insufficiency (venous), irritable bowel syndrome (IBS), jaundice, kidney problems, kidney stones, laryngitis, lesions (tubercle), lethargy, leukorrhea, malaria, malnutrition, measles, memory/cognitive problems, menorrhagia, menstrual problems, mucus, muscle and joint pain, neurasthenia, nocturnal emission, nosebleed, organ transplantation, pain,

palsy, parasites (malarial plasmodia, scabies), periodontal disease, plague, pleurisy, poisony ivy/oak, polyps (nasal), pruritus, respiratory conditions, rheumatism, scrofula, skin problems, small pox, snakebite, sores, sore throat, sprain, sores, spermatorrhea, stomatitis, toothache, tuberculosis, tumors, ulcer (duodenal, fistula, gastric, peptic, tuberculous), urinary problems, uterine problems, vaginitis, vertigo, and wounds (minor).

Discussion: May aid digestion; clear and open bronchial passages; darken prematurely gray hair; dissolve calculi; enhance immune system, intestinal system, kidney, liver, nervous system, pancreatic, and spleen functions; improve memory and cognition; increase endurance, energy, fertility, libido, and stamina; inhibit or destroy development and growth of bacteria and other microorganisms; promote bowel evacuation, perspiration, and urine flow; protect the liver; provide dietary supplementation; purify the blood; reduce arterial plaque formation, blood pressure levels, cholesterol levels, triglyceride levels, and the emission of semen during sleep; reestablish healthy system functions; restore normal tone to tissues; serve as an adjuvant in organ transplantation to aid in their acceptance, and serve as a nutritional adjuvant to therapeutic programs; speed healing; stimulate menstruation and peristalsis; strengthen bones, ligaments, muscles, tendons, and the vascular system.

Cautions/Contraindications: Avoid use if pregnant or breast-feeding. May cause dermatitis in susceptible individuals.

Adverse Reactions: Diarrhea (severe), gastritis, hematuria (blood in the urine), mucous membrane problems, nausea, and/or vomiting.

Herb/Drug Interactions: This herb could cause an interaction (possibly severe) when taken with the following drugs: None known.

Preparations/Dosage: Crude Herb: 3-9 grams. Decoction: ¼-½ cup per day. Extract: 5-10 drops (0.333-0.666 cc.) one to two times per day. Infusion: ½-1 cup per day. Juice (fresh): External uses only. Diluted in water. Root (powdered): Average dose in substance 20-30 grains (1.333-2 gm.). Tincture: 10-20 drops (0.666-1.25 cc.) one to three times per day.

Bitterroot (bit'er·root)

(*Lewisia rediviva*)

Synonyms/Related Species: Alpine Lewisia (*lewisia pygmaea*) and Montana Root.

Family/Class: Portulacaceae (purslane).

Floral Emblem: Montana.

Habitat: The Alpine and Subalpine zones, and North America.

Flavor: Bitter/sweet.

Parts Used: Root.

Properties: Alterative, depurative, nutritive, and tonic.

Constituents: Bitter substance and inulin (starch).

Historical Uses: Angina, diabetes, dietary supplementation, malnutrition, pain, pleurisy, poison ivy/oak, rash, skin problems, sore throat, sores, and survival food.

Discussion: May enhance liver and spleen functions; provide dietary supplementation; purify the blood; reestablish healthy system functions; restore normal tone to tissues; serve as a nutritional adjuvant to therapeutic programs.

Cautions/Contraindications: Avoid use if pregnant or breast-feeding.

Adverse Reactions: Nausea and/or vomiting.

Herb/Drug Interactions: This herb could cause an interaction (possibly severe) when taken with the following drugs: None known.
Preparations/Dosage: Crude Herb: 6-12 grams. Decoction: ½-¾ cup per day. Root (crushed/leached): Boil or cook until root reaches a jelly-like or gruel-like consistency. Root (powdered): Average dose in substance 5-10 grains (0.324-0.666 gm.). Tincture: 10-20 drops (0.666-1.25 cc.) one to three times per day.

Bittersweet (bi terswēt)
(*Solanum dulcamara*)

Synonyms/Related Species: Amaradulcis, Bittersweet Herb, Bittersweet Nightshade, Black Nightshade (*solanum nigrum*), Blue Nightshade, Buffalo-Bur (*solanum rostratum*), Cut-Leaved Nightshade (*solanum triflorum*), Deadly Nightshade (*solanum americanum*), Dulcamara, Dulcis Amarus, European Bittersweet, Felonwood, Felonwort, Garden Nightshade, Nightshade, Nightshade Vine, Scarlet Berry, Staff Vine, and Woody Nightshade.
Family/Class: Solanaceae (nightshade).
Habitat: Africa, Algeria, Arabia, Asia, Australia, Brazil, Britain, China, England, Europe, the Fiji Islands, France, India, Japan, Madagascar, North America, and Peru.
Flavor: Bitter/sweet.
Parts Used: Bark (root and twig).
Properties: Alterative, antibiotic, antifungal, antiphlogistic, antispasmodic, antiviral, aphrodisiac, astringent, depurative, diaphoretic, diuretic, emetic, hemostatic, laxative, and narcotic.
Constituents: Alkaloids, dulcamarine, glycosides, gum, inulin (starch), monosaccharides, resin, saponins, and solanine.
Historical Uses: Abscess, acne, amenorrhea, anxiety, arthritis, asthma, bleeding, bronchitis, bruises, candida, colitis, corns, cough, eczema, fever (ephemeral, herpetic, rheumatic), glandular swelling, gout, herpes, hysteria, infection (bacterial, fungal, viral), inflammation, jaundice, lesions (tubercle), moniliasis, muscle and joint pain, pain, respiratory conditions, rheumatism, scrofula, sexually transmitted diseases (STDs), sinusitis, skin problems, spasmodic conditions, sprain, syphilis, tuberculosis, ulcer (duodenal, fistula, gastric, peptic, syphilitic, tuberculous), warts (digitate, filiform, fugitive, glabra, mother, plana juvenilis, plantar, seborrhoeic, vulgaris), and whooping cough.
Discussion: May arouse sexual impulses; purify the blood; enhance digestive system, glandular system, liver, lung, and stomach functions; inhibit or destroy development and growth of bacteria and other microorganisms; promote bowel evacuation, perspiration, and urine flow; reestablish healthy system functions; slow heart rate and respiration; stimulate peristalsis.
Cautions/Contraindications: Avoid use if pregnant or breast-feeding. Do not confuse this plant with belladonna (*atropa belladonna*). Not for long-term use. The berries and leaves are poisonous. Use with professional guidance/supervision.
Adverse Reactions: Arrhythmia, central nervous system paralysis, coma, convulsions, delirium, diarrhea, dizziness, headache, nausea, pupil dilatation, scratchy throat, stupor, vertigo, vomiting, and/or possible death.
Herb/Drug Interactions: This herb could cause an interaction (possibly severe) when taken with the following drugs: None known.

Preparations/Dosage: Crude Herb: 3-6 grams. Decoction: 1-3 tablespoons one to two times per day. Extract: 3-5 drops (0.2-0.333 cc.) one to two times per day. Tincture: 5-10 drops (0.333-0.666 cc.) one to three times per day.

Black-Eyed Susan (blak·īd soo zh̀)
(*Rudbeckia hirta*)

Synonyms/Related Species: Coneflower, Dormilón, Golden Glow, Green-Headed Coneflower, Lance-Leaved Coneflower, Tall Coneflower (*rudbeckia laciniata*), Thimbleweed, Western Rayless Coneflower (*rudbeckia occidentalis*), and Yellow Daisy.
Family/Class: Compositae (composite).
Floral Emblem: Maryland.
Habitat: Britain and North America.
Flavor: Bitter.
Parts Used: Flowers, leaves, root.
Properties: Diaphoretic, diuretic, emmenagogue, emetic, febrifuge, stimulant, and tonic.
Constituents: Betaine (lycine), fatty acids (arachidonic, linoleic, linolenic), inulin (starch), inuloid, monosaccharides, and sterols.
Historical Uses: Colds, congestive heart failure (CHF), cough, dysmenorrhea, earache, fever (ephemeral), gleet, gonorrhea, headache, infection (sexually transmitted, urinary tract), kidney problems, poison ivy/oak, sexually transmitted diseases (STDs), snakebite, sores, syphilis, toothache, ulcer (syphilitic), urethritis, and urinary problems.
Discussion: May promote perspiration and urine flow; restore normal tone to the tissues; stimulate menstruation and the immune system.
Cautions/Contraindications: Avoid use if pregnant or breast-feeding. May cause allergic reactions and dermatitis in susceptible individuals.
Adverse Reactions: Nausea and/or vomiting.
Herb/Drug Interactions: This herb could cause an interaction (possibly severe) when taken with the following drugs: None known.
Preparations/Dosage: Crude Herb: 3-6 grams. Decoction: ¼ cup per day. Infusion: ½-1 cup per day. Tincture: 5-20 drops (0.333-1.25 cc.) one to three times per day.
Isolation: Betaine: Average dose of 2-4 grains (0.13-0.26 gm.) for use as emmenagogue.

Bladderwrack (blad er·rak)
(*Fucus versiculosus*)

Synonyms/Related Species: Arame, Black-Wrack (*fucus serratus*), Black-Tang, Cutweed Fucus, Fuci, Gulf-Wrack (*fucus natans*), Knobbed-Wrack (*fucus nodosus*), Kombu, Long-Frond Brown Algae, Red-Wrack, Rock Lichen, Rockweed, Sea Vegetable, Sea-Wrack, and Vraic.
Family/Class: Fucaceae - Laminariaceae (brown algae).
Habitat: The Baltic Sea, England, Europe, France, the Mediterranean, the North Sea (formerly the German Ocean), Norway, Japan, the Strait of Gibraltar, Sweden, and the Atlantic and Pacific coasts of the United States.
Flavor: Salty.
Parts Used: Thallus.
Properties: Alterative, antibiotic, anticarcinogen, antiphlogistic, astringent, demulcent, diuretic, expectorant, hemostatic, laxative, nutritive, and vasodilator.

Constituents: Alginic acid, cellulose, fatty acids (arachidonic, linoleic, linolenic), fiber, fucosan, fucose, fucosterol, lethicin, minerals (aluminum, barium, bismuth, boron, bromine, calcium, chlorine, chromium, cobalt, copper, gallium, iodine, iron, lithium, magnesium, manganese, nickel, phosphorus, potassium, silicon, silver, sodium, strontium, sulfur, tin, titanium, vanadium, zinc, zirconium), mannitol (mannite), mucilage, polysaccharides, protein, silicic acid, vitamins (A, B_2 (riboflavin), C (ascorbic acid), E (alpha-tocopheral), K), and volatile oil.

Historical Uses: Acne, acquired immune deficiency syndrome (AIDS), alopecia, amenorrhea, anemia, arteriosclerosis, arteriostenosis, arthritis, asthma, benign breast disease, bleeding, bruises, bursitis, cancer (bone), cellulite, colds, colitis, constipation, cough, cramps, deficiency (iodine), diabetes, diarrhea, dietary supplementation, digestive complaints, dysmenorrhea, eczema, edema, fever (ephemeral, rheumatic), gallbladder problems, glandular problems, glandular swelling, goiter, gout, headache, heart disease, Hodgkin's disease, human immunodeficiency virus (HIV), hyperlipemia, hypothyroidism, indigestion, infection, inflammation, insufficiency (adrenal, pancreatic), kidney problems, lesions (tubercle), leukemia, liver problems, malnutrition, menopausal/menstrual problems, menorrhagia, mucus, muscle and joint pain, nephritis, nervous conditions, neuritis, orchitis (testicular inflammation), poisoning (heavy metal), prostate problems, psoriasis, respiratory conditions, rheumatism, scrofula, sexually transmitted diseases (STDs), skin problems, spleen problems, sprain, syphilis, tuberculosis, tumors, ulcer (duodenal, fistula, gastric, peptic, syphilitic, tuberculous), uterine problems, weight loss, and wrinkles.

Discussion: May alkalize blood chemistry; boost stamina; cause blood vessel dilatation; clear and open bronchial passages; decrease the effect of carcinogens; enhance glandular and pancreatic system functions; increase the body's ability to burn fat through exercise; improve lipid metabolism; reduce cholesterol levels; promote bowel evacuation, the excretion of heavy metals, and urine flow; protect against absorption of the radioactive substance strontium-90 and protect against heart disease; provide dietary supplementation; reduce blood pressure levels; reestablish healthy system functions; regulate body temperature; serve as a nutritional adjuvant to therapeutic programs; soften stools; soothe mucous membrane irritation; stimulate the immune system, metabolism, peristalsis, and the thyroid gland; supply all the minerals needed for proper functioning of the human body.

Cautions/Contraindications: Avoid use if pregnant or breast-feeding, or if you have cardiovascular conditions, hyperthyroidism, hypertension, a weak digestive system, or an iodine sensitivity. Avoid collecting bladderwrack close to shore as industrial pollutants may have contaminated it. Due to the high rate of iodine, limit bladderwrack consumption to once a week. May interfere with the effectiveness of certain thyroid medications.

Adverse Reactions: Abdominal pain, arrhythmia, diarrhea, edema, fever, hypertrophy (thyroid), iodism (iodine poisoning), nausea, priapism, thirst, and/or vomiting.

Herb/Drug Interactions: This herb could cause an interaction (possibly severe) when taken with the following drugs: Hypotensive drugs and Thyroid drugs.

Preparations/Dosage: Crude Herb: 3-12 grams. Decoction: ½-1 cup per day. Extract: 5-10 drops (0.333-0.666 cc.). Extract (powdered): 3-10 grains (0.2-0.666 gm.). Tincture: 15-30 drops (1-2 cc.). Weight Loss (pill form): 4 grains (0.25 gm.) of powdered extract per pill (may be combined with marshmallow and licorice). Take one pill three times per day before meals. Weight loss should be noticeable within one week.

Note: If thyroid function is normal, bladderwrack may not promote weight loss.

Isolation: Mannitol hexanitrate: Average dose of 15-60 mg. (¼-1 grain) for use as a vasodilator.

Blessed Thistle (bles id this el)
(*Cnicus benedictus*)

Synonyms/Related Species: Cardin, Carduus Benedictus, Holy Thistle, Spotted Thistle, and St. Benedict Thistle.
Family/Class: Compositae (composite).
Habitat: Asia, England, Europe, and North America.
Flavor: Sweet/bitter.
Parts Used: Aerial.
Properties: Alterative, antibiotic, anticarcinogen, antiperiodic, astringent, carminative, depurative, diaphoretic, diuretic, emmenagogue, emetic, febrifuge, hemostatic, malariacidal, stimulant, tonic, and vulnerary.
Constituents: Cnicin, minerals (calcium, iron, manganese, phosphorus, potassium), mucilage, sesquiterpenes, tannic acid, vitamins (B_1 (thiamine), B_2 (riboflavin), B_3 (niacin), B_5 (pantothenic acid), B_6 (pyridoxine), B_{12}, choline, B_x (para-aminobenzoic acid (PABA), H (biotin), inositol, M (folic acid), and volatile oil.
Historical Uses: Abscess, ague, amenorrhea, appetite loss, arthritis, bleeding, cancer, chilblains, congestion (uterine, vaginal), constipation, cramps, diarrhea, digestive complaints, dysmenorrhea, edema, fever (ephemeral, intermittent), flatulence, gallbladder problems, headache, hepatitis, hormonal imbalances, indigestion, infection (bacterial), insufficiency (circulatory), jaundice, kidney problems, leukorrhea, liver problems, malaria, memory/cognitive problems, menopausal/menstrual problems, menorrhagia, mucus, parasites (malarial plasmodia), plague, respiratory conditions, spleen problems, sores, thrombosis (blood clot), vaginitis, and wounds (minor).
Discussion: May aid digestion; balance the hormonal system; cleanse the blood and liver; decrease the effect of carcinogens; enhance cardiovascular, liver, lung, spleen, and stomach functions; improve memory and cognition; increase circulation; inhibit or destroy development and growth of bacteria and other microorganisms; promote perspiration and urine flow; protect against and help dissolve thrombus (blood clot); purify the blood; reestablish healthy system functions; speed healing; stimulate gastric secretions and menstruation.
Cautions/Contraindications: Avoid use if pregnant or breast-feeding, or if you have acidity (gastric) or an ulcer (gastric, peptic).
Adverse Reactions: Diarrhea, nausea, and/or vomiting.
Herb/Drug Interactions: This herb could cause an interaction (possibly severe) when taken with the following drugs: None known.
Preparations/Dosage: Crude Herb: 3-6 grams. Extract: 3-5 drops (0.2-0.333 cc.) one to two times per day. Infusion: 1-1½ cups per day. Leaves (powdered): Average dose in substance 15-30 grains (0.98-2 gm.). Tincture: 5-20 drops (0.333-1.25 cc.) one to three times per day.

Bloodroot (blud root)
(*Sanguinaria canadensis*)

Synonyms/Related Species: Coon root, Indian Paint, Indian Red Paint, Indian Plant, Paucoon, Pauson, Red Paint Root, Red Puccoon, Red Root, Sanguinaria, and Tetterwort.
Family/Class: Papaveraceae (poppy).
Habitat: North America.
Flavor: Bitter/pungent.
Parts Used: Root.

Properties: Alterative, analgesic, antibiotic, anticarcinogen, antifungal, antiphlogistic, diuretic, emetic, emmenagogue, expectorant, hypnotic, laxative, parasiticide, sedative, stimulant, and tonic.
Constituents: Alkaloids, berberine, chelerythrine, coptisine, inulin (starch), protopine, resin, and sanguinarine.
Historical Uses: Abscess, arrythmia, asthma, athlete's foot, bronchitis, burns (minor), cancer (skin), colds, cough, croup, eczema, emphysema, fever, gargle/mouth rinse, gleet, gonorrhea, infection (bacterial, fungal, sexually transmitted), inflammation, insomnia, jaundice, laryngitis, liver problems, lung problems, mucus, muscle and joint pain, nervous conditions, pain, parasites (ringworm, scabies), periodontal disease, pneumonia, respiratory conditions, sexually transmitted diseases (STDs), sinusitis, skin problems, sores, sore throat, urethritis, and warts (digitate, filiform, fugitive, glabra, mother, plana juvenilis, plantar, seborrhoeic, vulgaris).
Discussion: May clear and open bronchial passages; decrease the effect of carcinogens; enhance cardiovascular system, circulatory system, digestive system, intestinal system, liver, and respiratory system functions; induce sleep; inhibit or destroy development and growth of bacteria and other microorganisms; promote bowel evacuation and urine flow; reestablish healthy system functions; stimulate menstruation and peristalsis.
Cautions/Contraindications: Avoid use if pregnant or breast-feeding. Not for long-term use. Use with professional guidance/supervision.
Adverse Reactions: Burning sensation in the stomach, exhaustion (extreme), fainting, nausea, thirst, vertigo, visual disturbances, and/or vomiting.
Herb/Drug Interactions: This herb could cause an interaction (possibly severe) when taken with the following drugs: None known.
Preparations/Dosage: Crude Herb: 3-6 grams. Decoction: ⅛ cup per day. Extract: 1-3 drops (0.06-0.2 cc.) one to two times per day. Root (powdered): Average dose in substance 10-30 grains (0.666-2 gm.). Tincture: 1-10 drops (0.066-0.666 cc.) one to three times per day.
Isolation: Berberine: Average dose of 1-5 grains (0.066-0.333 gm.) for use as an antiperiodic and tonic. Protopine: Average dose of 40-100 grains (2.5-7 gm.) for use as an analgesic or hypnotic. Sanguinarine: Average dose of $^{1}/_{40}$-¼ grain (0.0016-0.016 gm.) for use as an expectorant and tonic. Sanguinarine (in fluid extract form): 1½ drops (0.1 cc.). Sanguinarine (in tincture form): 1-2 drops (0.06-0.1 cc.).

Blueberry (bloo ber ē)

(*Vaccinium myrtillus*)

Synonyms/Related Species: Airelle, Bilberry, Black Blueberry (*vaccinium globulare*), Black Huckleberry (*vaccinium membranaceum*), Black Whortleberry, Bleaberry, Bloberrie, Bog Blueberry (*vaccinium uliginosum*), Bollebar, Bulberry, Burren Myrtle, California Huckleberry (*vaccinium ovatum*), Dwarf Blueberry (*vaccinium cespitosum*), European Huckleberry, European Whortleberry, Evergreen Huckleberry (*vaccinium ovatum*), Farkleberry (*vaccinium arboreum*), Huckleberry (*vaccinium parviflorum*), Low Bilberry (*vaccinium myrtillus*), Mountain Huckleberry, North American Blueberry, Oval-Leaved Blueberry (*vaccinium ovalifolium*), Rocky Mountain Blueberry, and Western Blueberry.
Family/Class: Ericaceae (heath).
Habitat: Alaska, the Alpine and Subalpine zones, Asia, Barbary, Britain, Europe, North America, Scotland, Siberia, and the Yukon Territory.

Flavor: Sweet.
Parts Used: Berries, leaves.
Properties: Anthelmintic, antibiotic, antigalactic, antilithic, antioxidant, antiphlogistic, antiscorbutic, astringent, diuretic, hemostatic, hypoglycemic, laxative, lithotriptic, nutritive, tonic, and vermifuge.
Constituents: Anthocyanin, caffeic acid, carbohydrates, chlorogenic acid, citric acid, fatty acids (arachidonic, linoleic, linolenic), flavonoids, glycosides, hydroquinone, malic acid, minerals (calcium, iron, manganese, potassium, selenium, silicon, sodium), monosaccharides, myrtillin, nonacosane, oligomeric procyanidines, pectic acid, pectin, quercetin, quinic acid, silicic acid, tannic acid, ursone (ursolic acid), and vitamin (C (ascorbic acid).
Historical Uses: Anemia, appetite loss, arteriosclerosis, arteriostenosis, arthritis, bladder problems, bleeding, burns (minor), calculus, cataracts, chronic fatigue syndrome (CFS), cold extremities, colds, congestion (uterine, vaginal), constipation, cough, cystitis, diabetes, diabetic retinopathy, diarrhea, dietary supplementation, digestive complaints, dysentery, dysmenorrhea, eczema, edema, emaciation, enteritis, Epstein Barr Virus (EBV), fever (ephemeral, enteric, rheumatic), fibromyalgia, flatulence, gallstones, gargle/mouth rinse, glaucoma, glycosuria, gout, hematuria (blood in the urine), hemorrhoids, hyperglycemia, indigestion, infection (bacterial, urinary tract), inflammation, insufficiency (venous), kidney problems, kidney stones, leukoplakia, leukorrhea, light sensitivity (eye), lithemia, macular degeneration, malnutrition, mononucleosis (infectious), mucus, multiple sclerosis (MS), muscle and joint pain, nausea, nephritis, neuralgia, neuropathy, night blindness (eye), parasites (roundworms), periodontal disease, Raynaud's disease, respiratory conditions, retinitis, rheumatism, rheumatoid arthritis (RA), scurvy, skin problems, sore throat, stomatitis, substitute for bearberry, typhoid, ulcer (bouveret, peptic, stasis, varicose), urinary problems, vaginitis, varicose veins, visual disturbances, vomiting, and wounds (minor).
Discussion: May aid carbohydrate metabolism; diminish or suppress lactation; dissolve calculi; encourage insulin production; enhance cardiovascular, circulatory, liver, immune system, and intestinal system functions; increase circulation; inhibit oxidation and inhibit or destroy developement and growth of bacteria and other microorganisms; improve microcirculation to the eyes, night vision, vascular integrity, and visual acuity; prevent the development of calculus or stones; promote bowel evacuation and urine flow; protect tendons, ligaments, and cartilage from damage; provide dietary supplementation; reduce blood sugar levels, congestion (blood vessel), excessive lithic acid (uric acid) and urate levels in the blood, tophi, and urine, the formation and adherence of platelets to blood vessel walls, and triglyceride levels; restore normal tone to tissues and restore vision after a glare; serve as a nutritional adjuvant to therapeutic programs; speed healing; stimulate peristalsis and the formation of new capillaries; strengthen arteries, the blood-brain barrier, capillaries, veins, and vision.
Cautions/Contraindications: Avoid use if pregnant or breast-feeding, or if you have pre-existing nephritis or you are hypoglycemic.
Adverse Reactions: Edema, diarrhea, nausea, and/or vomiting.
Herb/Drug Interactions: This herb could cause an interaction (possibly severe) when taken with the following drugs: Antidiabetic drugs.
Preparations/Dosage: Crude Herb: 3-9 grams. Berries (powdered): Average dose in substance 15-60 grains (1-4 gm.). Berries (fresh): May be ingested freely. Decoction (berries): 1-2 cups per day. Extract: 5-15 drops (0.333-1 cc.) one to two times per day. Infusion (leaves): 1-2 cups per day. Juice (fresh): 1 cup per day. Syrup: 60 grams mixed in one liter of water. Tincture: 10-30 drops (0.666-2 cc.) one to three times per day.

Blue Flag (bloo flag)
(*Iris versicolor*)

Synonyms/Related Species: American Blue Flag, Dragon Flower, Flag Lily, Fleur de Lis, Iris, Jacob's Sword, Lirio, Liver Lily, Orris Root (*iris florentina*), Poison Flag, Rocky Mountain Iris, Snake Lily, Water Flag, Western Blue Flag (*iris missouriensis*), White Flag Root, Wild Iris, Yellow Flag, and Yellow Iris.

Family/Class: Iridaceae (iris).

Floral Emblem: Tennessee.

Habitat: Europe and North America.

Flavor: Pungent.

Parts Used: Root.

Properties: Alterative, antibiotic, antiphlogistic, depurative, diaphoretic, diuretic, emetic, expectorant, laxative, sialogogue, and stimulant.

Constituents: Flavonoids, glycosides, gum, inulin (starch), iridin, phthalic acid, resin, salicylic acid, sterols, tannic acid, volatile oil, and xanthones.

Historical Uses: Abscess, acne, asthma, burns (minor), chills, colds, constipation, diarrhea, digestive complaints, eczema, edema, enteritis, fever (ephemeral, herpetic, rheumatic, septic), flatulence, gallbladder problems, gastritis, gastrointestinal problems, glandular problems, gleet, gonorrhea, goiter, hepatitis, herpes, indigestion, infection (bacterial, sexually transmitted), inflammation, irritable bowel syndrome (IBS), jaundice, kidney problems, lesions (tubercle), liver problems, migraine, mucus, muscle and joint pain, nausea, poisoning (blood), psoriasis, respiratory conditions, rheumatism, scrofula, sexually transmitted diseases (STDs), sinusitis, skin problems, sores, syphilis, toothache, tuberculosis, tumors, ulcer (duodenal, fistula, gastric, peptic, syphilitic, tuberculous), urethritis, urinary problems, vomiting, and weight loss.

Discussion: May clear and open bronchial passages; enhance gallbladder and liver functions; inhibit or destroy development and growth of bacteria and other microorganisms; promote bowel evacuation, perspiration, saliva secretion, and urine flow; purify the blood; reestablish healthy system functions; stimulate bile flow, gastric secretions, the glandular system, pancreatic enzymes, and peristalsis.

Cautions/Contraindications: Avoid use if pregnant or breast-feeding. Do not confuse this plant with calamus (*acorus calamus*). May cause dermatitis in susceptible individuals. Not for long-term use. Use with professional guidance/supervision.

Adverse Reactions: Diarrhea (severe), eye inflammation, gastrointestinal problems, headache, mouth and throat irritation, nausea, salivation (increased), stomach cramps (severe), and/or vomiting.

Herb/Drug Interactions: This herb could cause an interaction (possibly severe) when taken with the following drugs: None known.

Preparations/Dosage: Crude Herb: 3-6 grams. Extract (solid): 10-15 grains (0.666-0.98 gm.). Infusion: 2-3 tablespoons one to three times per day. Root (powdered): Average dose in substance 5-15 grains (0.324-1 gm.). Tincture: 5-10 drops (0.333-0.666 cc.) one to three times per day.

Boldo (bol do)
(*Peumus boldus*)

Synonyms/Related Species: Baldu.
Family/Class: Umbelliferae (parsley).
Habitat: Chile, the Mediterranean, and Peru.
Flavor: Bitter.
Parts Used: Leaves.
Properties: Alterative, antibiotic, antilithic, antiperiodic, antiphlogistic, antispasmodic, aromatic, diuretic, hepatic, lithotriptic, malariacidal, stimulant, and tonic.
Constituents: Alkaloids, boldoin, eucalyptol (cineol), flavonoids, glycosides, terpenes, terpineol, and volatile oil.
Historical Uses: Ague, appetite loss, arthritis, asthma, bronchitis, calculus, congestion (uterine, vaginal), digestive complaints, diphtheria, fever (ephemeral, intermittent, rheumatic), gallbladder problems, gallstones, gastrointestinal problems, gleet, gonorrhea, gout, hemorrhoids, hepatitis, indigestion, infection (bacterial, sexually transmitted, urinary tract), inflammation, jaundice, kidney stones, leukorrhea, lithemia, liver problems, malaria, muscle and joint pain, parasites (malarial plasmodia), respiratory conditions, rheumatism, sexually transmitted diseases (STDs), spasmodic conditions, ulcer (duodenal, gastric, peptic, syriac), urethritis, vaginitis, and wounds (minor).
Discussion: May dissolve calculi; enhance gallbladder, kidney, liver, and spleen functions; inhibit or destroy development and growth of bacteria and other microorganisms; prevent the development of calculus or stones; promote urine flow; protect the liver; reduce excessive lithic acid (uric acid) and urate levels in the blood, tophi, and urine; reestablish healthy system functions; restore normal tone to tissues; stimulate appetite, bile flow, gastric secretions, and peristalsis.
Cautions/Contraindications: Avoid use if pregnant or breast-feeding, or if you have liver disease, or an obstruction (biliary). Not for long-term use. Use with professional guidance/supervision.
Adverse Reactions: Convulsions, depression, excitability, gastrointestinal cramps, hallucinations, nausea, paralysis, partial loss of motor skills, reflex exaggeration, respiratory failure, vomiting, and/or possible death.
Herb/Drug Interactions: This herb could cause an interaction (possibly severe) when taken with the following drugs: None known.
Preparations/Dosage: Crude Herb: 3-9 grams. Extract: 1-5 drops (0.066-0.333 cc.) one to two times per day. Infusion: 1 cup per day. Oil of Boldo (*oleum boldus*): 1-5 drops (0.066-0.333 cc.) in water or on a sugarcube. Tincture: 5-20 drops (0.333-1.25 cc.) one to three times per day.
Isolation: Eucalyptol: 5 drops (0.333 cc.) in atomization or used in inhalation therapy for respiratory conditions.

Boneset (bōn set)
(*Eupatorium perfoliatum*)

Synonyms/Related Species: Ague Weed, Crosswort, Feverwort, Indian Sage, Richweed, Sweating Plant, Teasel, Thoroughwort, Vegetable Antimony, White Snakeroot (*eupatorium rugosum*), and Wood Boneset.
Family/Class: Compositae (composite).

Habitat: The Appalachians and North America.
Flavor: Bitter.
Parts Used: Leaves.
Properties: Alterative, antibiotic, antiperiodic, antiphlogistic, astringent, depurative, diaphoretic, diuretic, emetic, expectorant, hypoglycemic, laxative, malariacidal, stimulant, stomachic, and tonic.
Constituents: Eufoliatin, eufoliatorin, flavonoids, gum, hebenolide, inulin (starch), minerals (calcium, magnesium, potassium), monosaccharides, polysaccharides, pyrrolizidines, quercetin, resin, rutin, sesquiterpene lactones, sterols, tannic acid, tremetol, vitamins (B_x (para-aminobenzoic acid (PABA), C (ascorbic acid), volatile oil, and wax.
Historical Uses: Ague, appetite loss, arthritis, bronchitis, chills, cholera, colds, cough, debility, diarrhea, digestive complaints, edema, fever (ephemeral, enteric, intermittent, rheumatic, yellow), fractures, hyperglycemia, indigestion, infection (bacterial), inflammation, influenza, jaundice, liver problems, malaria, measles, mucus, mumps, muscle and joint pain, pain, parasites (malarial plasmodia), pneumonia, respiratory conditions, rheumatism, sore throat, tumors, typhoid, and ulcer (bouveret).
Discussion: May cleanse the liver; clear and open bronchial passages; enhance the digestive system, liver, immune system, and respiratory system functions; inhibit or destroy development and growth of bacteria and other microorganisms; prevent hemorrhage in persons with hypertension; promote bowel evacuation, perspiration, and urine flow; reduce blood sugar levels and capillary fragility; reestablish healthy system functions; restore normal tone to tissues; stimulate appetite, peristalsis, and white blood cells.
Cautions/Contraindications: Avoid use if pregnant or breast-feeding, or if you have cancer, liver disease, or a history of alcoholism. May negate the bacteriostatic effects of sulfonamide drugs. Not for long-term use. Use with professional guidance/supervision.
Adverse Reactions: An acetone-like breath odor, appetite loss, coma, constipation, delirium, diarrhea, drooling, hemorrhage, increased respiration, hematuria (blood in the urine), liver damage (permanent), milk sickness, muscle stiffness and tremors, nausea, perspiration, sluggish behavior, stomach cramps, thirst, trembling, vomiting, and/or possible death.
Herb/Drug Interactions: This herb could cause an interaction (possibly severe) when taken with the following drugs: Antibiotic drugs and Hypoglycemic drugs.
Preparations/Dosage: Crude Herb: 3-6 grams. Extract: 5-10 drops (0.333-0.666 cc.) one to two times per day. Extract (powder): Average dose in substance 1-3 grains (0.066-0.2 gm.). Infusion: ½-2 cups per day. Leaves (powdered): Average dose in substance 5-15 grains (0.324-1 gm.). Tincture: 10-30 drops (0.666-2 cc.) one to three times per day.

Borage (bûr ij)
(*Borago officinalis*)

Synonyms/Related Species: Barrach, Bourage, Bugloss, Burage, Common Bugloss, Corago, and Euphrosinum.
Family/Class: Boraginaceae (borage).
Habitat: Europe, the Mediterranean, and North America.
Flavor: Bitter.
Parts Used: Flowers, leaves, seeds (oil).
Properties: Anticoagulant, antidepressant, antiphlogistic, astringent, demulcent, depurative, diaphoretic, diuretic, expectorant, hemostatic, hypotensive, laxative, parasiticide, tonic, and vasodilator.

Constituents: Alkaloids, amabiline, fatty acids (arachidonic, gammalinolenic acid (GLA), linoleic, linolenic, oleic, palmitic, stearic), fixed oils (olein, palmitin, stearin), minerals (calcium, potassium, silicon), mucilage, pyrrolizidine, silicic acid, supinin, tannic acid, vitamins (choline), and volatile oil.

Historical Uses: Acne, arthritis, bladder problems, bleeding, benign breast disease, bronchitis, cardiovascular conditions, cirrhosis, colds, conjunctivitis, cough, dehydration, depression (mild/moderate), digestive complaints, diphtheria, eczema, fever (ephemeral, rheumatic), gargle/mouth rinse, hypertension (mild/moderate), infection, inflammation, influenza, insomnia, jaundice, kidney problems, liver problems, lung problems, menopausal problems, mucus, multiple sclerosis (MS), muscle and joint pain, nervous conditions, pain, parasites (ringworm), periodontal disease, peritonitis, phlebitis, pleurisy, premenstrual syndrome (PMS), prostatitis, pruritus, psoriasis, rash, respiratory conditions, rheumatism, snakebite, sore throat, ulcer (duodenal, gastric, peptic), and wounds (minor).

Discussion: May aid digestion; cause blood vessel dilatation; clear and open bronchial passages; delay or reduce coagulation of the blood; enhance adrenal, kidney, and lung functions; minimize imbalances and abnormalities of essential fatty acids in prostaglandin production; prevent the deposition of fat in the liver; promote bowel evacuation, perspiration, and urine flow; purify the blood; reduce blood pressure levels, cholesterol levels, and heart rate; restore normal tone to tissues; soothe mucous membrane irritation; stimulate peristalsis.

Cautions/Contraindications: Avoid use if pregnant or breast-feeding. Some persons may experience bleeding or increased clotting time when using this herb with anticoagulant drugs or aspirin. Not for long-term use.

Adverse Reactions: Bleeding (possibly serious), coagulation problems, diarrhea, dizziness, headache, nausea, and/or vomiting.

Herb/Drug Interactions: This herb could cause an interaction (possibly severe) when taken with the following drugs: Anticoagulant drugs, Hypotensive drugs, Salicylates, and Subsalicylates.

Preparations/Dosage: Crude Herb: 3-9 grams. Extract: 5-10 drops (0.333-0.666 cc.) one to two times per day. Infusion: ½-1 cup per day. Seed Oil (*oleum borago*): 150-250 mg. Tincture: 10-15 drops (0.666-1 cc.) one to three times per day.

Bryony (brī e·nē)
(*Bryonia dioica*)

Synonyms/Related Species: Black-Berried White Bryony, Devil's Turnip, English Mandrake, European White Bryony (*bryonia alba*), Ladie's Seal, Navet du Diable, Red Bryony, Tamus, Tetterberry, Wild Bryony, Wild Hops, Wild Nep, Wild Vine, and Wood Vine.

Family/Class: Cucurbitaceae (gourd).

Habitat: England, Europe, Iran, and the United States.

Flavor: Bitter/pungent.

Parts Used: Root.

Properties: Analgesic, antiperiodic, antiphlogistic, antispasmotic, counterirritant, diuretic, emetic, laxative, lithotriptic, malariacidal, and stimulant.

Constituents: Brein, bryonin, cucurbitol, fatty acids (arachidonic, linoleic, linolenic), glycosides, gum, inulin (starch), lectins, monosaccharides, sterols, and triterpenes.

Historical Uses: Ague, arthritis, bronchitis, calculus, colds, connective tissue problems, constipation, cough, cramps, diabetes, edema, fever (ephemeral, intermittent, rheumatic), gallstones, gastrointestinal problems, glandular swelling, gout, infection, inflammation, influenza, kidney stones, lethargy, leprosy, liver problems, lumbago, malaria, metabolic problems, muscle and joint pain, pain, palsy, parasites (malarial plasmodia), pleurisy, pneumonia, respiratory conditions, rheumatism, sciatica, spasmodic conditions, sputum cruentum (bloody sputum), tumors, urinary problems, and whooping cough.
Discussion: May dissolve calculi; promote bowel evacuation and urine flow; stimulate the arterioles and peristalsis.
Cautions/Contraindications: Avoid use if pregnant or breast-feeding. May cause dermatitis in susceptible individuals. Not for long-term use. The berries are poisonous. Use with professional guidance/supervision.
Adverse Reactions: Diarrhea (bloody), dizziness, colic, gastrointestinal inflammation, kidney problems, lowered body temperature, mucous membrane problems, nausea, paralysis, respiratory distress, spasmodic conditions, vertigo, vomiting, and/or possible death.
Herb/Drug Interactions: This herb could cause an interaction (possibly severe) when taken with the following drugs: None known.
Preparations/Dosage: Crude Herb: 3-6 grams. Extract: 1-5 drops (0.066-0.333 cc.) one to two times per day. Extract (solid): Average dose in substance ¼-1 grain (0.015-0.066 gm.). Infusion: 1 teaspoon every two hours if necessary or as required. Root (powdered): Average dose in substance 20-60 grains (1.333-2 gm.). Tincture: 5-10 drops (0.333-0.666 cc.) one to three times per day.
Isolation: Bryonin: Average dose of $^{1}/_{6}$-2 grains (0.011-0.133 gm.) for use as a drastic laxative or vesicant.

Buchu (bu ku)

(*Barosma betulina*)

Synonyms/Related Species: Barosma, Bookoo, Bucku, Buku, Diosma Betulina, Long Buchu (*barosma serratifolia*), Oval Buchu (*barosma crenulata*), and Short Buchu.
Family/Class: Rutaceae (rue).
Habitat: Africa.
Flavor: Pungent.
Parts Used: Leaves.
Properties: Antibiotic, antifungal, antilithic, antiphlogistic, aromatic, astringent, carminative, diaphoretic, diuretic, hemostatic, lithotriptic, stimulant, stomachic, and tonic.
Constituents: Barosmin, diosphenol (barosma camphor), flavonoids, mucilage, resins, rutin, and volatile oil.
Historical Uses: Arthritis, bladder problems, bleeding, calculus, candida, cholera, congestion (uterine, vaginal), cystitis, diabetes, digestive complaints, dysuria (painful/difficult urination), edema, enuresis (urinary incontinence), fever (ephemeral, rheumatic), gallstones, gastritis, gout, indigestion, infection (bacterial, fungal, urinary tract), inflammation, irritable bowel syndrome (IBS), kidney problems, kidney stones, leukorrhea, lithemia, moniliasis, mucus, muscle and joint pain, nephritis, premenstrual syndrome (PMS), prostate problems, prostatitis, pyelitis, respiratory conditions, rheumatism, sexually transmitted diseases (STDs), urethritis, and vaginitis.
Discussion: May aid digestion; dissolve calculi; enhance lung, stomach, and urinary functions; inhibit or destroy development and growth of bacteria and other microorganisms; prevent the

development of calculus or stones, and hemorrhage in persons with hypertension; promote perspiration and urine flow; reduce capillary fragility, excessive lithic acid (uric acid) and urate levels in the blood, tophi, and urine, and the frequency of nighttime urination; restore normal tone to tissues; strengthen the urinary system.
Cautions/Contraindications: Avoid use if pregnant or breast-feeding, or if you have congestive heart failure, hypertension, or a pre-existing kidney problem. Increase consumption of foods high in potassium when taking buchu.
Adverse Reactions: Nausea and/or vomiting.
Herb/Drug Interactions: This herb could cause an interaction (possibly severe) when taken with the following drugs: Diuretic drugs.
Preparations/Dosage: Crude Herb: 3-6 grams. Extract: 5-10 drops (0.333-0.666 cc.) one to two times per day. Extract (solid): Average dose in substance 5-15 grains (0.324-1 gm.). Infusion: ¼-½ cup per day. Leaves (powdered): Average dose in substance 15-30 grains (0.98-2 gm.). Tincture: 10-15 drops (0.666-1 cc.) one to three times per day.
Isolation: Barosmin: Average dose of 2-3 grains (0.13-0.2 gm.) for use as a diuretic and tonic.

Buckbean (buk bēn)
(*Menyanthes trifoliata*)

Synonyms/Related Species: Bean Trefoil, Bocksbohne, Bogbean, Bog Myrtle, Boksboon, Brook Bean, Goat's Bean, Marsh Clover, Marsh Trefoil, Moon Flower, Scharbock, Scorbutus, Trefoil, Water Shamrock, and Water Trefoil.
Family/Class: Gentianaceae (gentian).
Habitat: Alaska, Asia, England, Europe, North America, and Scotland.
Flavor: Bitter.
Parts Used: Leaves.
Properties: Antiphlogistic, antiscorbutic, carminative, diuretic, hypotensive, laxative, sedative, sialogogue, stomachic, tonic, and vasodilator.
Constituents: Bitter principle, flavonoids, gentianin, glucoside, menyanthin, minerals (iodine, iron), rutin, saponins, vitamins (C (ascorbic acid), and volatile oil.
Historical Uses: Ague, anorexia, appetite loss, arthritis, constipation, debility, digestive complaints, edema, exhaustion, fever (ephemeral, herpetic, rheumatic), fibromyalgia, flatulence, glandular swelling, gout, headache, hemoptysis, herbal tobacco, herpes, hypertension (mild/moderate), indigestion, infection, inflammation, jaundice, liver problems, migraine, muscle and joint pain, nausea, rheumatism, rheumatoid arthritis (RA), scurvy, sexually transmitted diseases (STDs), skin problems, sores, ulcer (duodenal, gastric, peptic), and uterine problems.
Discussion: May aid digestion; cause blood vessel dilatation; enhance stomach function; prevent hemorrhage in persons with hypertension; promote bowel evacuation, saliva secretion, and urine flow; protect the liver; reduce blood pressure levels and capillary fragility; restore normal tone to tissues; stimulate appetite, bile flow, gastric secretions, and peristalsis.
Cautions/Contraindications: Avoid use if pregnant or breast-feeding or if you suffer from colitis or diarrhea.
Adverse Reactions: Colitis, diarrhea, dysentery, gastrointestinal problems, nausea, salivation (increased), and/or vomiting.
Herb/Drug Interactions: This herb could cause an interaction (possibly severe) when taken with the following drugs: Hypotensive drugs.

Preparations/Dosage: Crude Herb: 3-6 grams. Extract (cold): ½-1 cup per day. Infusion: ½-1 cup. Leaves (powdered): Average dose in substance 20-30 grains (1.333-2 gm.). Tincture: 5-20 drops (0.333-1.25 cc.).

Bugleweed (byoo gel·wēd)
(*Lycopus americanus*)

Synonyms/Related Species: Chinese Bugleweed (*lycopus lucidus*), Common Gipsyweed, Cut-Leaved Water Horehound, Egyptian's Herb, European Bugleweed (*lycopus europaeus*), Gipsy-Wort, Gypsywort, Sweet Bugleweed, Virginia Water Horehound (*lycopus virginicus*), Water Horehound, and Western Bugleweed.
Family/Class: Labiatae (mint).
Habitat: Asia, China, and North America.
Flavor: Bitter.
Parts Used: Aerial.
Properties: Antiphlogistic, astringent, cardiac depressant, diuretic, emmenagogue, hemostatic, narcotic, nervine, sedative, stimulant, and tonic.
Constituents: Bitter principle, caffeic acid, chlorogenic acid, ellagic acid, flavonoids, lycopin, tannic acid, and volatile oil.
Historical Uses: Amenorrhea, arrhythmia, appetite loss, asthma, bleeding, bruises, cardiovascular conditions, colds, cough, debility, diabetes, diarrhea, dysentery, fever, gastritis, gastrointestinal problems, hangover (caused by alcohol consumption), hemorrhoids, hemorrhage, hyperthyroidism, hypertrophy (thyroid), indigestion, inflammation, insomnia, insufficiency (circulatory), jaundice, lesions (tubercle), lung problems, menorrhagia, mucous membrane problems, nervous conditions, nosebleed, pain, premenstrual syndrome (PMS), respiratory conditions, scrofula, shortness of breath, sores, tremors, tuberculosis, ulcer (duodenal, fistula, gastric, peptic, tuberculous), urinary problems, and wounds (minor).
Discussion: May calm the nervous system; diminish or reduce functional activity of the heart; enhance circulatory system, respiratory system, and thyroid functions; promote urine flow; reduce iodine metabolism and thyroxine release in the thyroid and reduce the pulse rate; regulate the hormonal system; restore normal tone to tissues; speed healing; stimulate appetite and menstruation.
Cautions/Contraindications: Avoid use if pregnant or breast-feeding, or if you have hyporthyroidism or glandular swelling.
Adverse Reactions: Bradycardia, hypertrophy (thyroid), lethargy, nausea, stupor, and/or vomiting.
Herb/Drug Interactions: This herb could cause an interaction (possibly severe) when taken with the following drugs: Thyroid drugs.
Preparations/Dosage: Crude Herb: 3-9 grams. Extract: 10-30 drops (0.666-2 cc.) one to two times per day. Infusion: 1-2 cups per day.
Isolation: Lycopin: Average dose of 1-4 grains (0.066-0.26 gm.) for use as a stimulant and tonic.

Bupleurum (byoo'ploor·em')
(*Bupleurum falcatum*)

Synonyms/Related Species: Chinese Thoroughwax (*bupleurum chinensis*), and Thorough Wax.
Family/Class: Umbelliferae (parsley).
Habitat: Asia, China, and Europe.
Flavor: Pungent/bitter.
Parts Used: Root.
Properties: Alterative, analgesic, anticoagulant, antiphlogistic, antispasmodic, carminative, cytotoxic, diaphoretic, and febrifuge.
Constituents: Bupleurumol, fufural (furfurol), saponins, and sterols.
Historical Uses: Abdominal pain, anxiety, asthma, cancer (breast, colon, liver), cold extremities, colds, constipation, debility, deficiency (nutritional), diarrhea, digestive complaints, dizziness, fever, flatulence, hepatitis, hypoglycemia, hysteria, inflammation, influenza, liver problems, mood swings, nausea, nervous conditions, pain, prolapse (rectal, uterine), restlessness, spasmodic conditions, tumors, vertigo, and vomiting.
Discussion: May aid digestion; delay or reduce coagulation of the blood; enhance gallbladder, liver, and pericardium functions as well as enhancing cortisone levels in the blood and kidneys; induce cancer cells to destroy themselves; inhibit lipid peroxide formation in the cardiac muscle or liver and the vascularization of tumors; lower cholesterol and blood sugar levels; promote perspiration and clearance of the hepatitis B antigen from the blood; protect the blood vessels, heart, and liver from damage; reestablish healthy system functions; serve as an adjuvant to chemotherapy; strengthen the eyes and muscles; stimulate the immune system and peristalsis.
Cautions/Contraindications: Avoid use if pregnant or breast-feeding.
Adverse Reactions: Convulsions, diarrhea (possible bloody), gastrointestinal cramps (severe), hematuria (blood in the urine), nausea, paralysis, stupor, and/or vomiting.
Herb/Drug Interactions: This herb could cause an interaction (possibly severe) when taken with the following drugs: Anticoagulant drugs, Interferon drugs, Salicylates, and Subsalicylates.
Preparations/Dosage: Crude Herb: 3-12 grams. Infusion: 1 cup per day

Burdock (bûr dok)
(*Arctium lappa*)

Synonyms/Related Species: American Burdock, Bardana, Beggar's Buttons, Burr, Burrseed, Clot-Bur, Cockle Buttons, Cocklebur, Common Burdock (*arctium minus*), European Burdock, Fox's Clote, Gobo, Great Burrdock, Lappa, and Thorny Burr.
Family/Class: Compositae (composite).
Habitat: Asia, England, Europe, and North America.
Flavor: Root: sweet. Leaves/Seeds: bitter.
Parts Used: Leaves, root, seeds.
Properties: Alterative, analgesic, antibiotic, anticarcinogen, antifungal, antilithic, antiphlogistic, antiscorbutic, antispasmodic, aphrodisiac, aromatic, demulcent, depurative, diaphoretic, diuretic, expectorant, laxative, lithotriptic, nutritive, parasiticide, and stomachic.
Constituents: Arctigenin, arctiin, caffeic acid, carbohydrates, fatty acids (oleic, palmitic, stearic), fixed oils (olein, palmitin, stearin), inulin (starch), flavones, lappin, minerals (copper, iodine, iron, silicon, sulfur, zinc), monosaccharides, polysaccharides, polyacetylenes, protein, resin, sesquiterpene lactones, mucilage, resin, silicic acid, tannic acid, vitamins (A, B_1

(thiamine), B_2 (riboflavin), B_3 (niacin), B_5 (pantothenic acid), B_6 (pyridoxine), B_x (para-aminobenzoic acid (PABA), C (ascorbic acid), E (alpha-tocopheral), H (biotin), M (folic acid), and volatile oil.

Historical Uses: Abscess, acne, allergy (pollen), alopecia, anorexia, appetite loss, arthritis, asthma, bronchitis, bruises, burns (minor), bursitis, calculus, cancer, canker sores, chicken pox, colds, constipation, cough, cystitis, dandruff, diarrhea, dietary supplementation, digestive complaints, dry skin, dysuria (painful/difficult urination), eczema, edema, fever (ephemeral, hay, herpetic, rheumatic, scarlet), gallstones, gastrointestinal problems, glandular swelling, gleet, gonorrhea, gout, headache, hemorrhoids, herpes, infection (bacterial, bladder, fungal, sexually transmitted), inflammation, influenza, insect bites or stings, kidney problems, kidney stones, leprosy, lesions (tubercle), lithemia, liver problems, lumbago, lung problems, lupus, malnutrition, measles, mucus, muscle and joint pain, nervous conditions, pain, parasites (ringworm), pimples, pneumonia, poison ivy/oak, prolapse (rectal, uterine), pruritus, psoriasis, rheumatism, scarletina, sciatica, scrofula, scurvy, sexually transmitted diseases (STDs), sinusitis, skin problems, small pox, sores, sore throat, spasmodic conditions, styes, syphilis, tonsillitis, tuberculosis, tumors, ulcer (duodenal, fistula, gastric, peptic, syphilitic, tuberculous), urethritis, urinary problems, weight loss, and wounds (minor).

Discussion: May arouse sexual impulses; balance the hormonal system; clear and open bronchial passages; decrease the effect of carcinogens; dissolve calculi; enhance kidney, liver, lung, and stomach functions; inhibit or destroy developement and growth of bacteria and other microorganisms; neutralize carcinogens; prevent the development of calculus or stones; promote bowel evacuation, perspiration, and urine flow; provide dietary supplementation; purify the blood; reduce excessive lithic acid (uric acid) and urate levels in the blood, tophi, and urine; reestablish healthy system functions; serve as a nutritional adjuvant to therapeutic programs; speed healing; stimulate bile flow, the immune system, peristalsis, and uterine contractions; stop or slow abnormal cell growth.

Cautions/Contraindications: Avoid use if pregnant or breast-feeding, or if you have hypertension, or if you have an iodine sensitivity. May interfere with the effectiveness of certain thyroid medications. May negate the bacteriostatic effects of sulfonamide drugs.

Adverse Reactions: Abdominal pain, arrhythmia, diarrhea, fever, gastrointestinal problems, hypertrophy (thyroid), iodism (iodine poisoning), liver damage (often characterized by jaundice), nausea, priapism, thirst, and/or vomiting.

Herb/Drug Interactions: This herb could cause an interaction (possibly severe) when taken with the following drugs: Antibiotic drugs and Thyroid drugs.

Preparations/Dosage: Crude Herb: 3-9 grams. Decoction (root): ½-1 cup per day. Extract (crushed seeds): 10-30 drops (0.666-2 cc.) one to two times per day. Extract (root): 5-10 drops (0.333-0.666 cc.). Extract (solid): Average dose in substance 5-15 grains (0.324-1 gm.). Infusion (crushed seeds): 1-2 cups per day. Juice: Combine equal amounts of grated root and water. Squeeze out liquid. Take 1 cup per day. Leaves (young): Boiled and eaten as a vegetable or used in salads. Root (young/1st year): Peeled, boiled (in two changes of water), and eaten as a vegetable. Tincture (root): 10-20 drops (0.666-1.25 cc.) one to three times per day.

Burnet (bûr nit)
(*Sanguisorba officinalis*)

Synonyms/Related Species: Common Burnet, Garden Burnet, Great Burnet, Great Wild Burnet, and Pimpernel.
Family/Class: Rosaceae (rose).
Habitat: Asia, Britain, Europe, Germany, and North America.
Flavor: Bitter/sour.
Parts Used: Root.
Properties: Alterative, antibiotic, antifungal, antiphlogistic, antispasmodic, astringent, carminative, diaphoretic, diuretic, hemostatic, stomachic, tonic, and vulnerary.
Constituents: Flavonoids, glycosides, rutin, saponins, sterols, and tannic acid.
Historical Uses: Abscess, arrhythmia, bleeding, bronchitis, burns (minor), colitis, congestion (uterine, vaginal), diarrhea, digestive complaints, dizziness, dysentery, eczema, enteritis, fever (ephemeral, scarlet), flatulence, gargle/mouth rinse, gastritis, gastrointestinal problems, hemafecia (blood in the stool), hemorrhage (metrorrhagia), hemorrhoids, hot flashes, indigestion, infection (bacterial, fungal), inflammation, insufficiency (venous), leukorrhea, measles, melancholy, menopausal/menstrual problems, mucus, nausea, phlebitis, respiratory conditions, scarletina, sores, spasmodic conditions, ulcer (duodenal, gastric, peptic, stasis, varicose), vaginitis, varicose veins, and wounds (minor).
Discussion: May aid digestion; enhance colon, liver, and stomach functions; inhibit or destroy developement and growth of bacteria and other microorganisms; prevent hemorrhage in persons with hypertension; promote perspiration and urine flow; reduce capillary fragility; reestablish healthy system functions; restore normal tone to tissues; speed healing.
Cautions/Contraindications: Avoid use if pregnant or breast-feeding.
Adverse Reactions: Diarrhea (possibly bloody), gastrointestinal cramps (severe), nausea, and/or vomiting.
Herb/Drug Interactions: This herb could cause an interaction (possibly severe) when taken with the following drugs: None known.
Preparations/Dosage: Crude Herb: 3-12 grams. Extract (cold): ½-1 cup per day. Infusion: 1 cup per day. Root (powdered): Average dose ¼-½ teaspoon in water per day. Tincture: 5-20 drops (0.333-1.25 cc.) on to three times per day.

Cabbage (kab ij)
(*Brassica oleracea*)

Synonyms/Related Species: Caboche and Garden Cabbage.
Family/Class: Brassicaceae (mustard).
Habitat: England and the Mediterranean with wide cultivation.
Flavor: Bitter/bland.
Parts Used: Leaves.
Properties: Carminative.
Constituents: Alkyl nitrile, isothiocyanates, glycosides, goitrin, minerals (calcium, chlorine, iron, magnesium, manganese, phosphorous, sulfur), monosaccharides, mustard oil, phosphoric acid, rhodanides, and vitamins (A, B_6 (pyridoxine), C (ascorbic acid).
Historical Uses: Digestive complaints, flatulence, gastralgia, gastritis, indigestion, and ulcer (duodenal, gastric).
Discussion: May aid digestion; protect the stomach mucous membranes from hydrochloric acid.

Cautions/Contraindications: Avoid use if pregnant or breast-feeding. May interfere with iodide metabolism. May cause dermatitis in susceptible individuals.
Adverse Reactions: Diarrhea (possibly bloody), flatulence (excessive), gastritis, goiter, indigestion, irritable bowel syndrome (IBS), nausea, suppression (thyroid), and/or vomiting.
Herb/Drug Interactions: This herb could cause an interaction (possibly severe) when taken with the following drugs: None known.
Preparations/Dosage: Crude Herb: 3-6 grams. Extract: 30-60 drops (2-4 cc.) one to two times per day. Juice: 1 teaspoon in water one to two times per day. Leaves: Raw or boiled and eaten as a vegetable.

Cabbage, Skunk (kab ij, skungk)

(*Symplocarpus foetidus*)

Synonyms/Related Species: Collard, Meadow Cabbage, Polecatweed, Skunkweed, Swamp Cabbage, and Yellow Skunk Cabbage.
Family/Class: Araceae (arum).
Habitat: Alaska and North America.
Flavor: Pungent.
Parts Used: Root.
Properties: Abortifacient, antifungal, antiphlogistic, antispasmodic, depurative, diaphoretic, diuretic, emetic, expectorant, hemostatic, narcotic, nervine, sedative, and stimulant.
Constituents: Fatty acids (oleic, palmitic, stearic), fixed oils (olein, palmitin, stearin), inulin (starch), lime (calcium oxide), minerals (calcium, iron, manganese, silicon), silica (silicon dioxide), oxalic acid, enzymes, resin, volatile oil, and wax.
Historical Uses: Abscess, allergy (pollen), arthritis, asthma, bleeding, bronchitis, burns (minor), colds, constipation, convulsions, cough, cramps, edema, epilepsy, fever (ephemeral, hay, rheumatic), headache, hemorrhage, hysteria, infection (bacterial, fungal), inflammation, influenza, laryngitis, lung problems, mucus, muscle and joint pain, nervous conditions, pain, respiratory conditions, rheumatism, sores, sore throat, spasmodic conditions, and whooping cough.
Discussion: May calm the nervous system; clear and open bronchial passages; induce abortion; promote perspiration and urine flow; purify the blood; stimulate uterine contractions.
Cautions/Contraindications: Avoid use if pregnant or breast-feeding. May cause dermatitis in susceptible individuals.
Adverse Reactions: Diarrhea, headache, nausea, oxalism (oxalic acid or oxalate poisoning), stupor, vertigo, visual disturbances, and/or vomiting.
Herb/Drug Interactions: This herb could cause an interaction (possibly severe) when taken with the following drugs: None known.
Preparations/Dosage: Crude Herb: 1-3 grams. Extract: 1-5 drops (0.066-0.333 cc.) one to two times per day. Infusion: ½-1 cup per day. Root (powdered): Average dose in substance 10-20 grains (0.666-1.333 gm.). Tincture: 3-10 drops (0.2-0.666 cc.) one to three times per day.

Cacao (ke·kā ō)

(*Theobroma cacao*)

Synonyms/Related Species: Chocolate, Cocoa, and Theobroma.
Family/Class: Sterculiaceae (cacao).

Habitat: Ceylon, Java, Mexico, and other tropical regions.
Flavor: Bitter/sweet.
Parts Used: Seeds.
Properties: Analgesic, antiphlogistic, aphrodisiac, astringent, diuretic, hemostatic, stimulant, tonic, and vasodilator.
Constituents: Alkaloids, anthocyanidin, caffeine, fixed oils (oil of theobroma or cacao butter), minerals (magnesium), monomethylxanthine (heteroxanthine), mucilage, oxaluric acid, phenylethylamine, protein, serotonin, stigmasterol, tannic acid, theobromine, triglycerides, and tryptamine.
Historical Uses: Alopecia, asthma, bladder problems, bleeding, burns (minor), colds, cough, diarrhea, dry skin, edema, fever (ephemeral, rheumatic), flavoring agent, indigestion, infection, inflammation, influenza, kidney problems, liver problems, muscle and joint pain, periodontal disease, rheumatism, sore nipples, substitute for coffee, and toothache.
Discussion: May aid digestion; arouse sexual impulses; boost cardiovascular blood flow; cause blood vessel dilatation; clear and open the bronchial passages; inhibit tooth decay; promote urine flow; restore normal tone to tissues; soften skin; soothe nipple soreness.
Cautions/Contraindications: Avoid use if pregnant or breast-feeding, or if you have anxiety, diabetes, heart disease, hypercholesteremia, hypertension, and/or insomnia. May cause allergic reactions in susceptible individuals.
Adverse Reactions: Anxiety, digestive complaints, constipation, elevated blood pressure and blood sugar levels, headache, hyperactivity, indigestion, insomnia, migraine, nausea, racing pulse, and/or vomiting.
Herb/Drug Interactions: This herb could cause an interaction (possibly severe) when taken with the following drugs: None known.
Preparations/Dosage: Consumption of normal amounts of chocolate products by healthy individuals produces no known health hazards or side effects.
Did You Know? Cacao contains only 10-15 % as much caffeine as coffee. The harvested seeds of the cacao bean are crushed, roasted, and ground. The seeds are then initially processed into a liquid known as cacao liquor. The liquor is then further processed to remove its oil content or cacao butter. The final product, a combination of defatted cacao powder with a little cacao butter added back in, is known as chocolate.

Cactus, Mescal (kak tes, mes·kal)
(*Lophophora williamsii*)

Synonyms/Related Species: Devil's Root, Dumpling Cactus, Lophophora, Mescal, Pellote, Peyote, and Sacred Mushroom.
Family/Class: Cactaceae (cactus).
Habitat: Central America, Mexico, and Texas.
Flavor: Bitter.
Parts Used: Entire plant. Mescalin buttons (ripe and dried with hair tufts removed).
Properties: Antiphlogistic, antispasmodic, cardiant, emetic, hallucinogen, narcotic, and stimulant.
Constituents: Alkaloids, lophophorine, mezcaline (mescaline), and pellotine.
Historical Uses: Arthritis, asthma, bruises, colds, diarrhea, fever (ephemeral, enteric, rheumatic, scarlet), gastrointestinal problems, gleet, gonorrhea, gout, hysteria, infection (sexually transmitted), inflammation, influenza, insomnia, lesions (tubercle), muscle and joint pain, pain,

neuralgia, neurasthenia, pneumonia, rheumatism, scarletina, scrofula, sexually transmitted diseases (STDs), spasmodic conditions, syphilis, tuberculosis, typhoid, ulcer (bouveret, fistula, syphilitic, tuberculous), and urethritis.

Discussion: May induce sleep; stimulate the cardiovascular system, nervous system, and respiratory system.

Cautions/Contraindications: Avoid use if pregnant or breast-feeding, or if you have cardiovascular conditions. Frequent use of the buttons may lead to addiction. Initial use of the buttons produce pupil dilatation with possible nause and vomiting followed by partial anesthesia-like effects, hallucinations (auditory and visual), muscle relaxation, stupor, ataxia, and a loss of the sense of time. The hair tufts on the buttons contain arsenic and must be removed prior to use of the buttons. Not for long-term use. Use with extreme care and under the guidance/supervision of someone who is familiar with it.

Adverse Reactions: Arrhythmia, arsenism (chronic arsenic poisoning), breathing difficulty, cardiac failure, diarrhea (severe), mescalism (the habitual use of mescal buttons), respiratory failure, nausea, vomiting (projectile), and/or possible death.

Herb/Drug Interactions: This herb could cause an interaction (possibly severe) when taken with the following drugs: Cardiac drugs.

Preparations/Dosage: Crude Herb (powdered): Average dose in substance 7-15 grains (0.5-1 gm.). Extract: 10-15 drops (0.666-1 cc.) one to two times per day. Mescal (fermented juice): 1-2 cups per day. Mescalin Buttons (ceremonial use - produces cerebral excitement and induces visions): 215-230 grains (4-5 buttons). Tincture: 1-2 teaspoons once per day.

Isolation: Pellotine: Average dose of ⅓-1 grain (0.02-0.06 gm.) for use as a hypnotic. Pellotine hydrochloride: Soluble in water and slightly so in alcohol. Average dose of ¾-1½ grains (0.05-0.1 gm.) for use as a hypnotic.

Note: This plant is categorized as an illegal narcotic in the United States and neither historical, medicinal nor therapeutic usage is officially permitted without authorization. Some Native American tribes have received authorization to incorporate it into their traditional healing and religious ceremonies.

Cactus, Pricklypear (kak tes, prik lē·pâr)
(*Opuntia basilaris*)

Synonyms/Related Species: Beavertail Pricklypear, Brittle Pricklypear Cactus (*opuntia fragilis*), Mexican Pricklypear Cactus (*opuntia streptacantha*), Nagphani (*opuntia dillenii*), Plains Pricklypear Cactus (*opuntia polyacantha*), Prickly Indian Fig Tree (*opuntia ficus-indica*), and Pricklypear.

Family/Class: Cactaceae (cactus).

Habitat: Arizona, Australia, California, Canada, Colorado, Europe, India, the Mediterranean, Mexico, Nevada, New Mexico, Spain, and Utah.

Flavor: Fruit: sweet. Seeds/Stem: bland.

Parts Used: Fruit (seeds/spines removed), seeds, stems (spines removed).

Properties: Analgesic, anti-inflammatory, astringent, diuretic, hemostatic, hypoglycemic, laxative, nutritive, oxytocic, and vulnerary.

Constituents: Cactin and resins.

Historical Uses: Abscess, bleeding, burns (minor), diabetes, diarrhea, dietary supplementation, hypercholesteremia, hyperglycemia, infection, inflammation, malnutrition, moles (skin), muscle

and joint pain, pain, skin problems, sores, urethritis, warts (digitate, filiform, fugitive, glabra, mother, plana juvenilis, plantar, seborrhoeic, vulgaris), and wounds (minor).
Discussion: May promote bowel evacuation and urine flow; provide dietary supplementation; reduce blood sugar levels, cholesterol levels, and insulin usage; serve as a nutritional adjuvant to therapeutic programs; speed healing; stimulate peristalsis and uterine contractions.
Cautions/Contraindications: Avoid use if pregnant or breast-feeding.
Adverse Reactions: Diarrhea, nausea, and/or vomiting.
Herb/Drug Interactions: This herb could cause an interaction (possibly severe) when taken with the following drugs: Antidiabetic drugs.
Preparations/Dosage: Extract: 5-10 drops (0.333-0.666 cc.) one to two times per day. Fruit (peeled/fresh/dried): May be eaten freely. Juice (fruit): 1-2 teaspoons in water per day. Leaves (peeled): Cooked and eaten as a vegetable. Seeds (roasted/ground): Used as flour. Stems (peeled/fresh): Have a cucumber-like flavor and may be eaten freely. Tincture: 10-20 drops (0.666-1.25 cc.) one to three times per day.

Cactus, Saguaro (kak tes, se·gwä rō)
(*Carnegiea gigantea*)

Synonyms/Related Species: Giant Cactus and Sahuaro.
Family/Class: Cactaceae (cactus).
Floral Emblem: Arizona.
Habitat: The Sonoran Desert.
Flavor: Sweet/bland.
Parts Used: Fruit, seeds, stems (young).
Properties: Antiphlogistic, cardiant, diuretic, hallucinogen, hypnotic, nutritive, sedative, stimulant, and tonic.
Constituents: Alkaloids, cactin, carnegine, pectenine, and pellotine.
Historical Uses: Anemia, angina, anxiety, arrhythmia, bladder problems, beverage (fermented fruit), bronchitis, cardiovascular conditions, congestion (cerebral), cough, dietary supplementation, dysmenorrhea, dyspnea, edema, fever (ephemeral, rheumatic), goiter, headache, hemorrhage (pulmonary), hypersensitivity, hypotension, inflammation, insomnia, insufficiency (mitral vlave), jam/jelly (fruit), malnutrition, menstrual problems, mental disturbances, mucus membrane problems, myocarditis, neurologic conditions, pneumonia (interstitial), premenstrual syndrome (PMS), prostate problems, Raynaud's disease, rheumatism, shortness of breath, tachycardia, tinnitus, valvular disease, and visual disturbances.
Discussion: May enhance nervous system and respiratory system functions; promote urine flow; provide dietary supplementation; restore normal tone to tissues; serve as a nutritional adjuvant to therapeutic programs; stimulate cardiovascular system and vasomotor function.
Cautions/Contraindications: Avoid use if pregnant or breast-feeding.
Adverse Reactions: Arrhythmia, hallucinations, lethargy, nausea, respiratory problems, stupor, and/or vomiting.
Herb/Drug Interactions: This herb could cause an interaction (possibly severe) when taken with the following drugs: Cardiac drugs.
Preparations/Dosage: Extract: 5-10 drops (0.333-0.666 cc.) one to two times per day. Fruit (fresh/seeds removed): May be eaten freely or made into jam/jelly. Fruit (fermented/seeds removed): Used to make an intoxicating beverage. Seeds (roasted/ground): Used as flour. Stems

(young/peeled): May be eaten freely. Tincture: 10-20 drops (0.666-1.25 cc.) one to three times per day.

Calamus (kal e·mes)
(*Acorus calamus*)

Synonyms/Related Species: Bachh, Bastard Flag, Cinnamon Sedge, Culmus, Gladdon, Gramineus, Grass Myrtle, Kalamos, Myrtle Flag, Myrtle Sedge, Racha, Shih-Ch'ang Pu, Sweet Cane, Sweet Flag (*acorus americanus*), Sweet Garden Flag, Sweet Grass, Sweet Myrtle, Sweet Root, Sweet Rush, and Sweet Sedge.

Family/Class: Araceae (arum).

Habitat: Asia, Belgium, Ceylon, China, England, Europe, France, Germany, Hungary, India, Japan, Lithuania, Myanmar (formerly Burma), North America, Poland, Russia, Siberia, and Turkey.

Flavor: Bitter/pungent.

Parts Used: Root.

Properties: Anesthetic (local), antibiotic, antioxidant, antiperiodic, antiphlogistic, antispasmodic, aphrodisiac, aromatic, carminative, diaphoretic, emetic, emmenagogue, expectorant, hallucinogen, hypotensive, insect repellent, malariacidal, parasiticide, sedative, sialogogue, stimulant, stomachic, tonic, and vasodilator.

Constituents: Acorin, camphene, caryophyllin, eugenol (eugenic acid), glycosides, gum, inulin (starch), minerals (phosphorus, potassium, sulfur), monosaccharides, mucilage, pinene, resin, tannic acid, vitamins (choline), and volatile oil.

Historical Uses: Abdominal pain, addiction (cocaine, heroin, marijuana, morphine, nicotine), ague, amnesia, angina, anorexia, ants, anxiety, appetite loss, arrhythmia, asthma, bronchitis, cirrhosis, colds, colic, convulsions, cough, cramps, dentifrice, depression (mild/moderate), diarrhea, digestive complaints, diphtheria, dizziness, dysentery, epilepsy, fatigue, fever (ephemeral, enteric, intermittent, rheumatic), flatulence, flavoring agent, fleas, gastritis, gastrointestinal problems, headache, hypertension (mild/moderate), hysteria, indigestion, infection (bacterial), inflammation, insanity, insomnia, irritable bowel syndrome (IBS), liver problems, malaria, melancholy, memory/cognitive problems, mucus, muscle and joint pain, nausea, nervous conditions, pain, parasites (lice and their nits, malarial plasmodia, scabies), periodontal disease, plague, respiratory conditions, rheumatism, seizure conditions, skin problems, slurred speech, spasmodic conditions, stomachache, substitute for cinnamon/ginger/nutmeg, tinnitus, toothache, typhoid, ulcer (bouveret, duodenal, gastric, peptic), vertigo, and vomiting.

Discussion: May aid digestion; arouse sexual impulses; assist in cessation of marijuana and tobacco smoking; cause blood vessel dilatation; clear and open bronchial passages; ease nausea and vomiting, which occur during the first few days of drug withdrawal from cocaine, heroin, and morphine; enhance cardiovascular, liver, nervous system, spleen, and stomach functions; improve cognition, concentration, and memory; increase endurance, energy, and stamina; inhibit oxidation and inhibit or destroy developement and growth of bacteria and other microorganisms; prevent the deposition of fat in the liver; promote perspiration and saliva secretion; protect brain tissue; prevent the secretion of histamine; reduce blood pressure levels; restore normal tone to tissues; stimulate appetite and menstruation.

Cautions/Contraindications: Avoid use if pregnant or breast-feeding. Not for long-term use. Use with professional guidance/supervision.

Adverse Reactions: Drowsiness, hallucinations, liver damage (often characterized by jaundice), nausea, salivation (increased), and/or vomiting.
Herb/Drug Interactions: This herb could cause an interaction (possibly severe) when taken with the following drugs: Hypotensive drugs.
Preparations/Dosage: Crude Herb: 3-9 grams. Decoction: ½-1 cup per day. Extract: 5-10 drops (0.333-0.666 cc.) one to two times per day. Infusion: 1-2 cups per day. Oil: 2-3 drops (0.133-0.2 cc.) in water or on a sugar cube. Tincture: 10-30 drops (0.666-2 cc.) one to three times per day.
Note: Calamus may cause a temporary, harmless tingling and/or numbing of the mouth and tongue.

Calendula (ke·len joo·le)
(*Calendula officinalis*)

Synonyms/Related Species: Calendae, Calendula Marigold, Caltha, Common Marigold, Fiore d'ogni mese, Goldbloom, Golde, Golden Marigold, Golds, Holigold, Holligold, Kalendae, Marigold, Marygold, Marybud, Pot Calendula, Pot Marigold, and Ruddes.
Family/Class: Compositae (composite).
Habitat: Asia, Europe, Italy, Latin America, the Mediterranean, and the United States.
Flavor: Pungent/bitter.
Parts Used: Flower (petals), leaves.
Properties: Alterative, antibiotic, anticarcinogen, antifungal, antiperiodic, antiphlogistic, antispasmodic, antiviral, astringent, depurative, diaphoretic, diuretic, emmenagogue, hemostatic, malariacidal, stimulant, and vulnerary.
Constituents: Bitter principle, calendulin, coumarin, flavonoids, glycosides, minerals (phosphorus), mucilage, polysaccharides, resin, saponins, vitamins (A, C (ascorbic acid), and volatile oil.
Historical Uses: Abscess, acne, acquired immune deficiency syndrome (AIDS), ague, allergy (food), amenorrhea, anemia, bleeding, bronchitis, bruises, burns (minor), callouses, cancer (skin), chilblains, colds, colitis, conjunctivitis, constipation, convulsions, corns, cramps, diarrhea, dry skin, dysmenorrhea, ear infection, earache, eczema, fever (herpetic, intermittent), frostbite, gallbladder problems, gargle/mouth rinse, gastritis, gastrointestinal problems, headache, hemorrhoids, hepatitis, herpes, human immunodeficiency virus (HIV), indigestion, infection (bacterial, fungal, viral), inflammation, influenza, insect bites or stings, insufficiency (venous), jaundice, liver problems, malaria, mastitis, measles, mucous membranes, mucus, pain, parasites (malarial plasmodia), phlebitis, sexually transmitted diseases (STDs), shingles, skin problems, sore throat, spasmodic conditions, sprain, sunburn, and windburn, thrombophlebitis, toothache, tumors, ulcer (duodenal, gastric, stasis, varicose), urinary problems, varicose veins, vomiting, warts (digitate, filiform, fugitive, glabra, mother, plana juvenilis, plantar, seborrhoeic, vulgaris), wounds (minor), and wrinkles.
Discussion: May decrease the effect of carcinogens; enhance cardiovascular, circulatory, digestive, and respiratory system functions; inhibit or destroy developement and growth of bacteria and other microorganisms; promote perspiration and urine flow; purify the blood; reestablish healthy system functions; soothe and protect sensitive skin; speed healing; stimulate bile flow, collagen production, the immune system, menstruation, peristalsis, and the growth of healthy eye tissue.

Cautions/Contraindications: Avoid use if pregnant or breast-feeding. Do not confuse this plant with the common garden marigold (*tagetes spp.*). May increase the sedative effects of anxiety or insomnia drugs.
Adverse Reactions: Diarrhea (possibly bloody), gastrointestinal cramps (severe), nausea, and/or vomiting.
Herb/Drug Interactions: This herb could cause an interaction (possibly severe) when taken with the following drugs: Anxiolytic drugs.
Preparations/Dosage: Crude Herb: 3-6 grams. Extract: 3-5 drops (0.2-0.333 cc.) one to two times per day. Infusion: 1-2 tablespoons every one to two hours. Juice: 1 teaspoon in water 0ne to two times per day. Tincture: 5-20 drops (0.333-1.25 cc.) one to three times per day.

Camphor Tree (kam fer trē)
(*Cinnamomum camphora*)

Synonyms/Related Species: Camfora, Camphor, Cemphire, Gum Camphor, Kāfūr, Kāpūr, Karpurah, and Laurel Camphor.
Family/Class: Lauraceae (laurel).
Habitat: Argentina, Asia, Borneo, California, the Canary Islands, Ceylon, China, Egypt, Florida, India, Japan, Madagascar, Sumatra, and Vietnam.
Flavor: Pungent/bitter.
Parts Used: Crystallized compound (camphor), leaves.
Properties: Analgesic, antibiotic, antiphlogistic, antispasmodic, aromatic, counterirritant, diaphoretic, insect repellent, narcotic, parasiticide, sedative, and stimulant.
Constituents: Borneol, camphor, and volatile oil.
Historical Uses: Abdominal pain, arthritis, asthma, bronchitis, bruises, chilblains, chills, cholera, colds, colic, coma, cough, delirium, depression (mild/moderate), diarrhea, digestive complaints, dizziness, embalming (asia), exhaustion, fainting, fever (ephemeral, enteric, rheumatic), flatulence, gastrointestinal problems, hysteria, infection (bacterial), inflammation, lung problems, moths, muscle and joint pain, nervous conditions, neuralgia, pain, parasites (ringworm, scabies), pneumonia, pruritus, respiratory conditions, rheumatism, spasmodic conditions, sprain, typhoid, and ulcer (bouveret).
Discussion: May clear and open the bronchial passages; enhance cardiovascular system, liver, and respiratory system functions; inhibit or destroy development and growth of bacteria and other microorganisms; promote perspiration; serve as a smelling salt; stimulate the circulatory system.
Cautions/Contraindications: Avoid use if pregnant or breast-feeding, or if you have cardiovascular conditions, hypertension, or hypotension. May cause dermatitis in susceptible individuals. Use only the natural herb for external and internal administration, as the chemically prepared camphor is contaminated with other chemicals and can be highly poisonous.
Adverse Reactions: Arrhythmia, convulsions, delirium, nausea, paralysis, respiratory distress, spasmodic conditions, vomiting, and/or possible death.
Herb/Drug Interactions: This herb could cause an interaction (possibly severe) when taken with the following drugs: None known.
Preparations/Dosage: Crude Herb (leaves): 3-12 grams. Camphor Water (*aqua camphorae*): 1-2 ounces per day. Extract: 50-100 mg. per day. Infusion (leaves): 1 teaspoon per day. Oil of Camphor (*oleum camphorae*): 1-3 drops in water or on a sugarcube. Spirit of Camphor (*spiritus*

camphorae): A 10% alcoholic solution of camphor. Take 5-20 drops (0.333-1.25 cc.) per day. Tincture: 3-5 drops (0.2-0.333 cc.) one to three times per day. The external use of the gum resin/oil should consist of no more than 1-2 drops and should be diluted with a good quality vegetable oil prior to use.

Isolation: Camphor: Average dose of 2 grains (0.12 gm.) for use as a powerful irritant and stimulant, diaphoretic and narcotic. Camphor is toxic in overdoses and sedative in small doses.

Canadian Hemp (ke·nā dē·en hemp)
(*Apocynum cannabinum*)

Synonyms/Related Species: Bitterroot, Black Indian Hemp, Canada Hemp, Catchfly, Dogbane, Hemp, Hemp Dogbane (*apocynum androsaemifolium*), Honeybloom, Indian Physic, Milk Ipecac, Milkweed, Mountain Hemp, Rheumatism Weed, Spreading Dogbane, Wallflower, Wandering Milkweed, Western Wallflower, and Wild Ipecac.

Family/Class: Apocynaceae (dogbane).

Habitat: Alaska, Germany, North America, Russia, and the Subalpine zone.

Flavor: Bitter/pungent.

Parts Used: Root.

Properties: Antiphlogistic, aphrodisiac, cardiant, counterirritant, diaphoretic, diuretic, emetic, expectorant, laxative, lithotriptic, stimulant, tonic, and vasoconstrictor.

Constituents: Apocynein, apocynin, bitter principle, fatty acids (arachidonic, linoleic, linolenic), glycosides, inulin (starch), resin, saponins, sterols, strophanthidin, strophanthin, tannic acid, and volatile oil.

Historical Uses: Addiction (alcohol), alopecia, arrhythmia, arthritis, asthma, calculus, cardiovascular conditions, cirrhosis, constipation, cough, cramps, digestive complaints, edema, fever (ephemeral, rheumatic), gallstones, headache, indigestion, inflammation, kidney stones, liver problems, muscle and joint pain, pleurisy, pneumonia, rheumatism, sexually transmitted diseases (STDs), syphilis, ulcer (syphilitic), and warts (digitate, filiform, fugitive, glabra, mother, plana juvenilis, plantar, seborrhoeic, vulgaris).

Discussion: May aid in alcohol withdrawal symptoms; arouse sexual impulses; cause blood vessel constriction; clear and open bronchial passages; constrict the blood vessels; depress the pulse rate; dissolve calculi; elevate blood pressure levels; increase systolic contraction, lengthen diastolic contraction, and cardiac tissue contraction strength; promote bowel evacuation, perspiration, and urine flow; restore normal tone to tissues; stimulate the cardiovascular system, hair growth, and peristalsis.

Cautions/Contraindications: Avoid use if pregnant or breast-feeding. Do not confuse this herb with marijuana (*cannabis sativa*) or jaborandi (*pilocarpus spp.*). The leaves are poisonous. Not for long-term use. Use with professional guidance/supervision.

Adverse Reactions: Arrhythmia, cardiac failure, diarrhea (possibly bloody), fluctuations in blood pressure levels (possibly severe), gastrointestinal cramps (severe), hematuria (blood in the urine), mucous membrane problems, nausea, respiratory distress, vomiting (possibly violent), and/or possible death.

Herb/Drug Interactions: This herb could cause an interaction (possibly severe) when taken with the following drugs: Cardiac drugs.

Herb/Herb Interactions: Do not use with Foxglove (*digitalis spp.*) or Strophanthus (*strophanthus spp.*).

Preparations/Dosage: Crude Herb: 1-3 grams. Extract: 1-3 drops (0.06-0.2 cc.) one to two times per day. Infusion: ½-1 teaspoon one to five times per day. Root (powdered): Average dose in substance 1 grain (0.066 gm.). Tincture: 2-5 drops (0.133-0.333 cc.) one to three times per day.
Isolation: Apocynin: Average dose of ¼-½ grain (0.016-0.033 gm.) for use as a tonic.

Caraway (kar e·wā)
(*Carum carvi*)

Synonyms/Related Species: Alcaravea, Carui, Carum, Karawiyā', Karawya, Karon, and Kuemmel.
Family/Class: Umbelliferae (parsley).
Habitat: Africa, Asia, Austria, the Caucasus, England, Europe, Finland, France, Germany, the Himalayas, Holland, India, Mongolia, Morocco, North America, Norway, Persia, Russia, Siberia, Spain, and Turkey.
Flavor: Pungent.
Parts Used: Seeds.
Properties: Analgesic, antibiotic, antiphlogistic, antispasmodic, aromatic, carminative, emmenagogue, expectorant, parasiticide, sedative, stimulant, stomachic, and tonic.
Constituents: Carvacrol, carvene (limonene), carvol, coumarin, fatty acids (arachidonic, linoleic, linolenic, oleic, palmitic, petroselinic, stearic), fixed oils (olein, palmitin, stearin), minerals (calcium, cobalt, copper, iodine, iron, lead, magnesium, phosphorous, potassium, silicon, zinc), phosphoric acid, polysaccharides, protein, resin, silicic acid, tannic acid, vitamins (B_1 (thiamine), B_2 (riboflavin), B_3 (niacin), B_5 (pantothenic acid), B_6 (pyridoxine), B_{12}, B_x (para-aminobenzoic acid (PABA), choline, H (biotin), inositol, M (folic acid), and volatile oil.
Historical Uses: Appetite loss, bronchitis, colds, colic, cough, cramps, digestive complaints, dysmenorrhea, fever, flatulence, flavoring agent, gallbladder problems, gargle/mouth rinse, gastritis, gastrointestinal problems, indigestion, infection (bacterial), inflammation, irritable bowel syndrome (IBS), liver problems, mucus, nausea, nervous conditions, pain, parasites (scabies), spasmodic conditions, and toothache.
Discussion: May aid digestion; clear and open bronchial passages; enhance colon, lung, and stomach functions; inhibit or destroy development and growth of bacteria and other microorganisms; promote urine flow; restore normal tone to tissues; stimulate menstruation.
Cautions/Contraindications: Avoid use if pregnant or breast-feeding, or if you have an iodine sensitivity. May interfere with the effectiveness of certain thyroid medications.
Adverse Reactions: Abdominal pain, arrhythmia, diarrhea, fever, hematuria (blood in the urine), hypertrophy (thyroid), iodism (iodine poisoning), liver damage (often characterized by jaundice), nausea, priapism, thirst, and/or vomiting.
Herb/Drug Interactions: This herb could cause an interaction (possibly severe) when taken with the following drugs: Thyroid drugs.
Preparations/Dosage: Crude Herb: 3-9 grams. Caraway Water: 1 drachm (4 cc.). Decoction: ½-1 cup per day. Infusion: 1-2 cups per day. Oil of Caraway (*oleum cari*): 1-10 drops (0.066-0.666 cc.) in water or on a sugarcube one to two times per day. Seed (powdered): Average dose ¼-½ teaspoon one to three times per day. Tincture: 5-20 drops (0.333-1.25 cc.) one to three times per day.

Cardamom (kär de·mem)
(*Elettaria cardamomum*)

Synonyms/Related Species: Aleppy Cardamum, Capalaga, Ceylon Wild Cardamom (*elettaria major*), Ebil, Elattari, Gujatatti Elachi, Ilachi, Kakelah Seghar, and Malabar Cardamom.
Family/Class: Zingiberaceae (ginger).
Habitat: Asia, Ceylon, China, Guatamala, India, Japan, and Sri Lanka.
Flavor: Pungent.
Parts Used: Seeds (ripe).
Properties: Antibiotic, antifungal, antiperiodic, antiphlogistic, antispasmodic, antiviral, aromatic, carminative, expectorant, laxative, malariacidal, stimulant, stomachic, and tonic.
Constituents: Eucalyptol (cineol), fatty acids (oleic, palmitic, stearic), fiber, fixed oils (olein, palmitin, stearin), gum, inulin (starch), linalool, minerals (potassium), mucilage, resin, terpineol, and volatile oil.
Historical Uses: Ague, appetite loss, asthma, bronchitis, colds, colic, congestion (uterine, vaginal), cough, diarrhea, diphtheria, enuresis (urinary incontinence), fever (ephemeral, intermittent), flatulence, flavoring agent, gallbladder problems, gastralgia, gastrointestinal problems, headache, indigestion, infection (bacterial, fungal, viral), inflammation, lesions (tubercle), leukorrhea, liver problems, malaria, mucus, parasites (malarial plasmodia), scrofula, spasmodic conditions, spermatorrhea, tuberculosis, ulcer (duodenal, fistula, gastric, peptic, syriac, tuberculous), urethritis, vaginitis, and wounds (minor).
Discussion: May aid digestion; clear and open bronchial passages; enhance kidney, lung, spleen, and stomach functions; inhibit development or destroy growth of bacteria and other microorganisms; promote bowel evacuation; stimulate peristalsis.
Cautions/Contraindications: Avoid use if pregnant or breast-feeding. May increase the effectiveness of streptomycin.
Adverse Reactions: Diarrhea, nausea, and/or vomiting.
Herb/Drug Interactions: This herb could cause an interaction (possibly severe) when taken with the following drugs: Antibiotic drugs.
Preparations/Dosage: Crude Herb: 3-6 grams. Extract: 3-5 drops (0.2-0.333 cc.). Infusion: 1 ounce (30 cc.). Seeds (powdered): 15-30 grains (0.98-2 gm.). Tincture: 5-20 drops (0.333-1.25 cc.).
Isolation: Eucalyptol: 5 drops (0.3 cc.) in atomization or inhalation therapy for use in respiratory conditions.

Caroba (kah·ro bah)
(*Jacaranda procera*)

Synonyms/Related Species: Bignonia Caroba and Tupi.
Family/Class: Bignoniaceae (bignonia).
Habitat: South America and the tropical regions of North America.
Flavor: Bitter.
Parts Used: Leaves.
Properties: Antiphlogistic and antispasmodic.
Constituents: Alkaloids and carobine.

Historical Uses: Arthritis, epilepsy, fever (ephemeral, rheumatic), gleet, gonorrhea, gout, infection (sexually transmitted), inflammation, muscle and joint pain, pain, rheumatism, sexually transmitted diseases (STDs), skin problems, syphilis, ulcer (syphilitic), and urethritis.
Discussion: May reduce tissue inflammation.
Cautions/Contraindications: Avoid use if pregnant or breast-feeding. Do not confuse this herb with carob tree (*ceratonia siliqua*).
Adverse Reactions: Diarrhea, nausea, and/or vomiting.
Herb/Drug Interactions: This herb could cause an interaction (possibly severe) when taken with the following drugs: None known.
Preparations/Dosage: Extract: 5-8 drops (0.333-0.5 cc.). Leaves (powdered): 15-60 grains (0.98-4 gm.). Tincture: 10-15 drops (0.666-1 cc.).

Cascara Sagrada (kās·kâr e se·grā de)
(*Rhamnus purshianus*)

Synonyms/Related Species: Alder-Buckthorn (*rhamnus frangula*), Alder-Leaved Buckthorn (*rhamnus alnifolia*), Alder Dogwood, Arrow Wood, Bearwood, Black Alder, Black Alder Dogwood, Bird Cherry, Black Alder Tree, Black Dogwood, Buckthorn (*rhamnus cathartica*), California Buckthorn, Cáscara Bark, Cáscara Buckthorn, Chittem Bark, Chitum, Coffeeberry (*rhamnus californica*), Common Buckthorn, Dogwood Bark, European Black Alder, European Buckthorn, Frangula Bark, Hartshorn, Purging Buckthorn, Purshiana Bark, Sacred Bark, Sagrada Bark, Waythorn, and Yellow Bark.
Family/Class: Rhamnaceae (buckthorn).
Habitat: Africa, Asia, the Caucasus, England, Europe, North America, and Scotland.
Flavor: Bitter.
Parts Used: Bark (harvested from 3-4 year old branches and aged for one year).
Properties: Alterative, antiphlogistic, astringent, depurative, diaphoretic, diuretic, emetic, hemostatic, hypotensive, laxative, lithotriptic, nervine, stimulant, tonic, and vasodilator.
Constituents: Alkaloids, aloin, anthraquinones, bitter principle, emodin, enzymes, frangulin, glycosides, gum, inulin (starch), malic acid, minerals (aluminum, calcium, lead, manganese, potassium, strontium, tin), monosaccharides, rhamnin, resins, saponins, tannic acid, vitamins (B_1 (thiamine), B_2 (riboflavin), B_3 (niacin), B_5 (pantothenic acid), B_6 (pyridoxine), B_{12}, B_x (para-aminobenzoic acid (PABA), choline, H (biotin), inositol, M (folic acid), and volatile oil.
Historical Uses: Appendicitis, appetite loss, arthritis, bleeding, burns (minor), calculus, colds, colic, colitis, congestive heart failure (CHF), constipation, cough, croup, diarrhea, digestive complaints, dysentery, dysmenorrhea, edema, fever (ephemeral, rheumatic), flatulence, gallbladder problems, gallstones, gastrointestinal problems, gleet, gonorrhea, gout, hemorrhoids, hypertension (mild/moderate), indigestion, infection (sexually transmitted), inflammation, influenza, insomnia, jaundice, kidney problems, kidney stones, liver problems, mania, mucus, muscle and joint pain, nausea, nervous conditions, poisoning (lead), poison ivy/oak, pruritus, rash, respiratory conditions, rheumatism, sciatica, sexually transmitted diseases (STDs), skin problems, sores, spleen problems, surgery (postrectoanal), toothache, urethritis, warts (digitate, filiform, fugitive, glabra, mother, plana juvenilis, plantar, seborrhoeic, vulgaris), weight loss, and wounds (minor).
Discussion: May calm the nervous system; cause blood vessel dilatation; cleanse the whole system; dissolve calculi; enhance gastrointestinal, liver, muscles, pancreatic, spleen, and stomach

functions; promote bowel evacuation, perspiration, and urine flow; reduce tissue inflammation; reestablish healthy system functions; restore normal tone to tissues; stimulate bile flow and peristalsis.
Cautions/Contraindications: Avoid use if pregnant or breast-feeding, or if you have abdominal pain of unknown origin, appendicitis, colitis, Crohn's disease, enteritis, a chronic gastrointestinal problem, irritable bowel syndrome (IBS), obstruction (intestinal), or ulcer (duodenal, peptic). Berries are poisonous. Do not administer to children under 12 years old. May cause a temporary discoloration of the stools. May cause laxative dependence. Not for long-term use. Use for no longer than one to two weeks.
Adverse Reactions: Arrhythmia, bone deterioration, cholera, diarrhea (possibly bloody), dizziness, edema, electrolyte and potassium loss, exhaustion (extreme), gastrointestinal cramps (severe), hematuria (blood in the urine), nausea, and/or vomiting.
Herb/Drug Interactions: This herb could cause an interaction (possibly severe) when taken with the following drugs: Cardiac drugs, Corticosteroids, Diuretic drugs, Hypotensive drugs, and Laxatives.
Herb/Herb Interactions: Licorice root.
Preparations/Dosage: Bark (powdered): ¼-½ teaspoon. Decoction: ¼-½ cup per day. Extract: 5-10 drops (0.333-0.666 cc.) one to two times per day. Extract (powdered): Average dose in substance 2-10 grains (0.133-0.666 gm.). Infusion: 1 cup per day. Syrup: ½-2 drachms (4-8 cc.). Tincture: 5-15 drops (0.333-1 cc.) one to three times per day. To render the bark safe for use and reduce the strong emetic effect it should be aged for one year or heated above 212° F. (100° C.).
Isolation: Rhamnin: Average dose of 2-6 grains (0.133-0.4 gm.) for use as a laxative.

Cashew (kash oo)
(Anacardium occidentale)

Synonyms/Related Species: Cajueiro, East Indian Almond, and Jambu.
Family/Class: Anacardiaceae (cashew).
Habitat: Africa, Brazil, the Caribbean, Central America, India, Mozambique, and the United States.
Flavor: Bitter/sweet.
Parts Used: Kernel (roasted), oil.
Properties: Antibiotic, astringent, caustic, counterirritant, diuretic, hemostatic, hypoglycemic, insect repellent, parasiticide, and vesicant.
Constituents: Anacardic acid, anacardol, cardol, fatty acids (arachidonic, linoleic, linolenic, oleic, palmitic, stearic), fixed oils (olein, palmitin, stearin), gum, inulin (starch), minerals (iron, magnesium), protein, and vitamins (B_3 (niacin).
Historical Uses: Ants, bleeding, diabetes, corns, elephantiasis, gastrointestinal problems, hyperglycemia, infection (bacterial), moths, parasites (ringworm), snakebite, ulcer (duodenal, gastric, peptic), vaginitis, and warts (digitate, filiform, fugitive, glabra, mother, plana juvenilis, plantar, seborrhoeic, vulgaris).
Discussion: May inhibit development or destroy growth of bacteria and other microorganisms; promote urine flow; protect the kidneys; reduce blood sugar levels.
Cautions/Contraindications: Avoid use if pregnant or breast-feeding. Cashews must be roasted prior to eating them, as raw cashews can be toxic. If you experience sensitivity to poison ivy, you may experience sensitivity to cashew. May cause allergic reactions and contact dermatitis

(possibly severe) in susceptible individuals. Roasting the nut in the shell or heating the oil prior to use will render the oil less caustic. Cahew nuts with black spots should be avoided, as these spots are an indication of contamination or a sign that the nuts have been improperly prepared.
Adverse Reactions: Blistering of the mouth and throat, nausea, respiratory distress, and/or vomiting.
Herb/Drug Interactions: This herb could cause an interaction (possibly severe) when taken with the following drugs: Antidiabetic drugs.
Preparations/Dosage: Cashew kernels (roasted): A handful may be eaten daily. Oil: Use as a wash on floors/windowsills to repel ants and moths. Oil of Cashew (*oleum anacardeum*): External uses only. 1-2 drops (0.06-0.1 cc.) Diluted.

Castor Oil Plant (kas ter·oil plant)
(*Ricinus communis*)

Synonyms/Related Species: Bofareira, Bronze King (*ricinus africanus*), Eranda, Kiki, Mexico Seed, Oil Plant, and Palma Christi.
Family/Class: Euphorbiacea (spurge).
Habitat: Africa, Algeria, Calcutta, Egypt, England, Europe, France, Greece, India, the Mediterranean, and North America.
Flavor: Bitter/sweet.
Parts Used: Seed oil.
Properties: Anticarcinogen, antiphlogistic, antiviral, demulcent, hemagglutinin, insect repellent, laxative, narcotic, and parasiticide.
Constituents: Alkaloids, chelidonic acid, chelidonine, enzymes, fatty acids (arachidonic, linoleic, linolenic, oleic, palmitic, stearic), fixed oils (olein, palmitin, stearin), lectins, protein, ricin, ricinine, ricinoleic acid (ricinolic acid), saponins, triglycerides, vitamin A, and volatile oil.
Historical Uses: Abscess, aquired immune deficiency syndrome (AIDS), alopecia, bruises, bunions, cancer, colic, constipation, corns, cysts, dandruff, diarrhea, dysentery, ear infection, enteritis, epilepsy, fever, flies, gastrointestinal problems, headache, hemorrhoids, infection (bacterial, viral), inflammation, insomnia, leprosy, liver problems, migraine, muscle and joint pain, nervous conditions, pain, paralysis, parasites (ringworm), pimples, poisoning (food), pruritus, skin problems, sores, tumors, warts (digitate, filiform, fugitive, glabra, mother, plana juvenilis, plantar, seborrhoeic, vulgaris), and wounds (minor).
Discussion: May cause agglutination of red blood corpuscles; decrease the effect of carcinogens; enhance liver and spleen functions; promote bowel evacuation and lymph node drainage; soothe mucous membrane irritation; stimulate the immune system and peristalsis.
Cautions/Contraindications: Avoid use if pregnant or breast-feeding, or if you have abdominal pain of unknown origin, appendicitis, inflammatory intestinal disease, or an obstruction (intestinal). Do not administer to children under 12 years old. Do not use for longer than 10-15 days consecutively. Ingestion of the seed is poisonous and can be fatal. Use only seed oil that has been "cold drawn" as the use of heat to express the oil will allow the poisonous principles found in the seeds to dissolve into and mix with the oil.
Adverse Reactions: Burning of the mouth and throat, debility, diarrhea (possibly bloody), circulatory collapse, electrolyte loss, gastroenteritis, gastrointestinal cramps (severe), shock (hypovolemic), hematuria (blood in the urine), liver damage (often characterized by jaundice), nausea, permanent internal organ damage, vision disturbances, vomiting, and/or possible death.

Herb/Drug Interactions: This herb could cause an interaction (possibly severe) when taken with the following drugs: Laxatives.
Preparations/Dosage: Seed Oil (*oleum ricini*): 1-4 teaspoons (may be mixed with cinnamon or peppermint water, coffee (brewed), or vegetable glycerin) once or twice per day.
Isolation: Chelidonine sulfate: Average dose of 1½-3 grains (0.09-0.2 gm.) for use as a mild narcotic. Chelidonine tannate: Average dose in substnace 3 grains (0.2 gm.) for use as a mild narcotic.

Catalpa (kah·tal pah)
(*Catalpa bignonioides*)

Synonyms/Related Species: Kutuhlpa.
Family/Class: Bignoniaceae (bignonia).
Habitat: Asia, China, Japan, and North America.
Flavor: Bitter.
Parts Used: Seeds.
Properties: Aromatic, bronchodilator, and carminative.
Constituents: Catalpin and catalposide.
Historical Uses: Asthma, digestive complaints, flatulence, indigestion, and respiratory conditions.
Discussion: May aid digestion; dilate or expand the air passages of the lungs.
Cautions/Contraindications: Avoid use if pregnant or breast-feeding. May cause dermatitis in susceptible individuals.
Adverse Reactions: Diarrhea, slowed pulse rate, nausea, and/or vomiting.
Herb/Drug Interactions: This herb could cause an interaction (possibly severe) when taken with the following drugs: Bronchodilator drugs.
Preparations/Dosage: Crude Herb (powdered): 3-6 grams. Tincture: 2 drachms (8 cc.) one to three times per day.

Catha (kath a)
(*Catha edulis*)

Synonyms/Related Species: Flower of Paradise, Kat, Khat Plant, and Qat.
Family/Class: Celastraceae (staff-tree).
Habitat: Asia, Africa, Arabia, Australia, and North America.
Flavor: Bitter/sweet.
Parts Used: Leaves, twigs.
Properties: Stimulant and tonic.
Constituents: Alkaloids, flavonoids, katine, norpseudoephedrine, protein, sterols, tannic acid, triterpenes, vitamins (choline), and volatile oil.
Historical Uses: Cirrhosis, diphtheria, exhaustion, fatigue, liver problems, and weight loss.
Discussion: May enhance adrenal, brain, kidney, nervous system, and spinal cord functions; prevent the deposition of fat in the liver; restore normal tone to tissues.
Cautions/Contraindications: Avoid use if pregnant or breast-feeding. Catha is highly addictive and causes dependence. Withdrawal symptoms may include anorexia, apathy, depression, inter-

family problems, irritability, mood swings, and a tendency to become withdrawn. Use with professional guidance/supervision.
Adverse Reactions: Cancer (esophageal) increased risk, constipation, elevated blood pressure levels, gastrointestinal problems, labored respiration, lesions, nausea, paralysis, periodontal disease, and/or vomiting.
Herb/Drug Interactions: This herb could cause an interaction (possibly severe) when taken with the following drugs: None known.
Preparations/Dosage: Leaf (fresh): Chew a small amount of fresh catha leaf until masticated (similar to chewing tobacco). Juice is swallowed and the remaining plant residue is then discarded (one "chew" can last several hours and is replaced by a fresh amount of leaf). Infusion (leaves/twigs): ½-1 cup per day.

Catnip (kat nip)
(*Nepeta cataria*)

Synonyms/Related Species: Catswort, Field Balm, and Nip.
Family/Class: Labiatae (mint).
Habitat: Asia, Europe, and North America.
Flavor: Bitter/pungent.
Parts Used: Aerial.
Properties: Analgesic, antibiotic, antiphlogistic, antispasmodic, aromatic, astringent, carminative, diaphoretic, diuretic, emmenagogue, hemostatic, lithotriptic, nervine, sedative, stimulant, stomachic, tonic, tranquilizer, and vermin repellent.
Constituents: Bitter principle, camphor, caryophyllin, carvacrol, nepetalactone, nerol, minerals (magnesium, manganese, phosphorus, sodium, sulfur), pulegone, tannic acid, thymol, vitamins (A, B_1 (thiamine), B_2 (riboflavin), B_3 (niacin), B_5 (pantothenic acid), B_6 (pyridoxine), B_{12}, B_x (para-aminobenzoic acid (PABA), C (ascorbic acid), choline, H (biotin), inositol, M (folic acid), and volatile oil.
Historical Uses: Acne, addiction (drug, nicotine), amenorrhea, anemia, asthma, bladder problems, bleeding, bronchitis, calculus, chills, colds, colic, convulsions, cough, cramps, diarrhea, digestive complaints, dysmenorrhea, epilepsy, fatigue, fever (ephemeral, scarlet), flatulence, gallstones, headache, hemorrhoids, hiccups, hives, hyperactivity, hypoglycemia, hysteria, indigestion, infection (bacterial), infertility, inflammation, influenza, insanity, insomnia, insufficiency (circulatory), kidney stones, laryngitis, measles, mucus, nausea, nervous conditions, pain, pneumonia, restlessness, scarletina, shock, skin problems, small pox, sores, sore throat, spasmodic conditions, toothache, vermin, and vomiting.
Discussion: May aid digestion; calm the nervous system; dissolve calculi; ease drug and nicotine withdrawal symptoms; enhance circulatory system, gallbladder, nervous system, and stomach functions; induce sleep; inhibit or destroy development and growth of bacteria and other microorganisms; promote perspiration and urine flow; reduce chicken pox and measles eruptions; restore normal tone to tissues; serve as an adjuvant to ease drug withdrawal symptoms; stimulate gastric secretions and menstruation.
Cautions/Contraindications: Avoid use if pregnant or breast-feeding, or if you have acidity (gastric) or an ulcer (gastric, peptic).
Adverse Reactions: Edema, menorrhagia, nausea, and/or vomiting.
Herb/Drug Interactions: This herb could cause an interaction (possibly severe) when taken with the following drugs: None known.

Preparations/Dosage: Crude Herb: 3-6 grams. Infusion: 1-2 cups per day. Tincture: 10-30 drops (0.666-2 cc.) one to three times per day.

Cat's Claw (kats klô)
(*Uncaria guianensis*)

Synonyms/Related Species: Uña de gato.
Family/Class: Rubiaceae (madder).
Habitat: The Peruvian Rain Forest.
Flavor: Bitter.
Parts Used: Bark (inner).
Properties: Antibiotic, anticarcinogen, anticoagulant, antifertilizin, antioxidant, antiphlogistic, antiviral, astringent, cytostatic, depurative, hemostatic, hypotensive, tonic, and vasodilator.
Constituents: Alkaloids, anthocyanidin, sterols, tannic acid, and triterpenes.
Historical Uses: Acquired immune deficiency syndrome (AIDS), allergy, arthritis, asthma, autoimmune disease, bleeding, bursitis, cancer (breast, melanoma, squamous cell carcinoma), cardiovascular conditions, chronic fatigue syndrome (CFS), colds, colitis, Crohn's disease, digestive complaints, Epstein Barr Virus (EBV), fever (ephemeral, herpetic, rheumatic), fibromyalgia, gastritis, gastrointestinal problems, headache, herpes, Hodgkin's disease, human immunodeficiency virus (HIV), hypertension (mild/moderate), infection (bacterial), inflammation, influenza, irritable bowel syndrome (IBS), leukemia, Lyme disease, mononucleosis (infectious), rheumatism, sexually transmitted diseases (STDs), sinusitis, tumors (Kaposi's sarcoma), ulcer (peptic), and viral infection.
Discussion: May assist the body to produce T-cells and white blood cells in normal numbers; cause blood vessel dilatation and remission of Kaposi's sarcoma; cleanse the intestinal tract; decrease the effect of carcinogens; delay or reduce coagulation of the blood; diminish chemical sensitivities; enhance liver function; increase the body's white blood cell count when needed, and reduce it when count is too high; inhibit HIV cell growth, oxidation, and inhibit development or destroy growth of bacteria and other microorganisms; neutralize fertilizin (fertilization); reduce blood pressure levels; restore normal tone to tissues; stop or slow abnormal cell growth; offset the negative effects of AZT, chemotherapy, and radiation therapy; stimulate the immune system.
Cautions/Contraindications: Avoid use if pregnant or breast-feeding, or if you are diabetic, or if you have a coagulation problem. Some persons may experience bleeding or increased clotting time when using this herb with anticoagulant drugs or aspirin.
Adverse Reactions: Bleeding (possibly serious), coagulation problems, nausea, and/or vomiting.
Herb/Drug Interactions: This herb could cause an interaction (possibly severe) when taken with the following drugs: Antidiabetic drugs, Anticoagulant drugs, Hypotensive drugs, Salicylates, and Subsalicylates
Preparations/Dosage: Crude Herb: 3-6 grams. Decoction: ½-1 cup per day.

Cattail (kat tāl)
(*Typha latifolia*)

Synonyms/Related Species: Narrow-Leaf Cattail (*typha angustifolia*), Typha, Typhē.
Family/Class: Typhaceae (cattail).
Habitat: Britain, Europe, and North America.
Flavor: Bitter/sweet.
Parts Used: Flowers, pollen, root.
Properties: Anesthetic (local), antiphlogistic, antispasmodic, astringent, carminative, diaphoretic, diuretic, emetic, emmenagogue, hemostatic, lithotriptic, nervine, nutritive, stimulant, stomachic, tonic, vermin repellent, and vulnerary.
Constituents: Fatty acids (oleic, palmitic, stearic), fixed oils (olein, palmitin, stearin), sitosterol, tannic acid, and volatile oil.
Historical Uses: Abdominal pain, amenorrhea, angina, arthritis, bleeding, burns (minor), calculus, colds, cough, cystitis, dietary supplementation, digestive complaints, diarrhea, dry skin, dysentery, dysmenorrhea, fever (ephemeral, enteric, yellow), flatulence, gallstones, gleet, gonorrhea, headache, hemafecia (blood in the stool), hematemesis (vomiting of blood), hematuria (blood in the urine), hemorrhoids, hysteria, indigestion, infection (sexually transmitted), inflammation, insomnia, kidney stones, malnutrition, menorrhagia, menstrual problems, muscle strain, nervous conditions, nosebleed, pain, sciatica, sexually transmitted diseases (STDs), sores, spasmodic conditions, sprain, sputum cruentum (bloody sputum), substitute for procaine hydrochloride, synovitis, toothache, tumors, typhoid, ulcer (bouveret, duodenal, gastric, peptic), urethritis, vermin, and wounds (minor).
Discussion: May aid digestion; calm the nervous system; dissolve calculi; enhance stomach function; increase circulation; promote perspiration and urine flow; provide dietary supplementation; restore normal tone to tissues; serve as a nutritional adjuvant to therapeutic programs; speed healing; stimulate menstruation.
Cautions/Contraindications: Avoid use if pregnant or breast-feeding.
Adverse Reactions: Nausea and/or vomiting.
Herb/Drug Interactions: This herb could cause an interaction (possibly severe) when taken with the following drugs: None known.
Preparations/Dosage: Flower Pollen: Used as a flavoring or thickening agent for gravies, soups, etc., or it can be sifted and mixed with equal parts of whole-wheat flour for use in baking. Flower Down: Apply topically as a dressing for burns (minor), chafing, scalds, sores, and wounds. Flower Stalk (young): Peeled, boiled (about 15-20 minutes), and eaten as a vegetable. The young stalks have a corn-like flavor when boiled. Root/Shoots (young): Boiled and eaten as a vegetable or dried, roasted, and ground into flour for use in baking. Root Juice: Acts as an anesthetic to help relieve discomfort and pain when applied topically.
Did You Know? The actions and uses of cattail root juice are *very* similar to those of procaine hydrochloride (used as a base in the anesthetic drug known as Novocain®). However, due to the high incidence of allergic reactions, the use of Novocain® has declined and has since been replaced by Lidocain®.

Cayenne (kī·en)
(*Capsicum annuum*)

Synonyms/Related Species: African Pepper, Bird Pepper, Capsicum (*capsicum frutescens*), Cayenne Pepper, Chillies, Chili Pepper, Cockspur Pepper, Goat's Pod, Grains of Paradise, Hot

Pepper, Hungarian Pepper, Kynnha, Paprika, Pod Pepper, Red Pepper, Spanish Pepper, Sweet Pepper, and Zanzibar Pepper.

Family/Class: Solanaceae (nightshade).

Habitat: Central America, Europe, India, Mexico, and Zanzibar.

Flavor: Pungent.

Parts Used: Fruitpods (ripe/dried with seeds removed)

Properties: Antibiotic, anticarcinogen, antiperiodic, antiphlogistic, antispasmodic, astringent, carminative, counterirritant, depurative, expectorant, hemostatic, hypertensive, hypotensive, malariacidal, nutritive, sialagogue, stimulant, vasoconstrictor, and vasodilator.

Constituents: Alkaloid, capsaicin, capsanthin, capsicol, esters, fatty acids (oleic, palmitic, stearic), fixed oils (olein, palmitin, stearin), flavonoids, minerals (calcium, iron, magnesium, phosphorus, potassium, sulfur), saponins, and vitamins (A, B_1 (thiamine), B_2 (riboflavin), B_3 (niacin), B_5 (pantothenic acid), B_6 (pyridoxine), B_{12}, B_x (para-aminobenzoic acid (PABA), C (ascorbic acid), choline, H (biotin), inositol, M (folic acid).

Historical Uses: Addiction (alcohol), ague, allergy (pollen), appetite loss, arteriosclerosis, arthritis, asthma, bleeding, bronchitis, bruises, burns (minor), cancer (lung), cellulite, chilblains, chills, colds, conjunctivitis, convulsions, cough, cramps, diabetes, diarrhea, dietary supplementation, diphtheria, digestive complaints, dysentery, fatigue, fever (ephemeral, hay, intermittent, rheumatic, yellow), flatulence, flavoring agent, frostbite, gargle/mouth rinse, gastrointestinal problems, hangover (caused by alcohol consumption), heart disease, hemorrhage, hepatitis, hypertension (mild/moderate), hypotension, indigestion, infection (bacterial), inflammation, influenza, insect bites or stings, insufficiency (pancreatic, venous), jaundice, kidney problems, laryngitis, liver problems, lumbago, malaria, malnutrition, memory/cognitive problems, migraine, motion sickness, mucus, muscle and joint pain, nausea, nerve damage (caused by diabetes or herpes), neuralgia, pain, palsy, paralysis, parasites (malarial plasmodia), Parkinson's disease, periodontal disease, pleurisy, poisoning (food), respiratory conditions, rheumatism, sexually transmitted diseases (STDs), shingles, shock, sinusitis, snakebite, sore throat, spasmodic conditions, spleen problems, sprain, stroke (apoplectic, heat), sunburn, tetanus, toothache, tonsillitis, trismus (lockjaw), tumors, ulcer (stasis, syriac, varicose), varicose veins, weight loss, and wounds (minor).

Discussion: May aid digestion; balance blood pressure levels; cause blood vessel constriction or dilatation; clear and open bronchial passages; decrease the effect of carcinogens; enhance cardiovascular, pancreatic, and kidney functions; increase male potency; inhibit development or destroy growth of bacteria and other microorganisms; promote saliva flow; protect against heart disease and stroke (apoplectic); reduce the carcinogenic effect of air pollution as well as the formation of tobacco induced cancer (lung); promote perspiration; protect the intestines and stomach lining against damage caused from aspirin; provide dietary supplementation; purify the blood; reduce pain sensitivity; serve as a nutritional adjuvant to therapeutic programs; stimulate appetite, female orgasm, gastric secretions, and metabolism.

Cautions/Contraindications: Avoid use if pregnant or breast-feeding, or if you have gastritis or ulcer (duodenal, gastric, peptic). Do not apply to broken skin. May increase the side effects of liver drugs.

Adverse Reactions: Colic, diarrhea (severe/possibly bloody), gastroenteritis, gastrointestinal cramps (severe), hematuria (blood in the urine), liver damage (often characterized by jaundice), mucous membrane problems, nausea, salivation (increased), skin blistering, ulcer formation, and/or vomiting.

Herb/Drug Interactions: This herb could cause an interaction (possibly severe) when taken with the following drugs: Hepatic drugs, Hypotensive drugs, Salicylates, and Subsalicylates.
Preparations/Dosage: Crude Herb: 1-3 grams. Decoction: ¼-1 tablespoon per day. External Uses: Apply as a poultice, leaving on the skin for no longer than 5-10 minutes (leaving cayenne on the skin for longer periods of time may result in skin blistering and ulceration). Fruitpod (powdered): Average dose in substance 1-5 grains (0.066-0.324 gm.). Infusion: ½ fl. ounce per day. Pills (1-10 grains/0.066-0.666 gm. per pill). Take one pill daily. Tincture: 10-15 drops (0.666-1 cc.) one to three times per day.

Celandine (sel en·dīn)
(*Chelidonium majus*)

Synonyms/Related Species: Celidoine, Chelidon, Common Celandine, Garden Celandine, Great Celandine, Tetterwort, and True Celandine.
Family/Class: Papaveraceae (poppy).
Habitat: Asia and Europe.
Flavor: Bitter/pungent.
Parts Used: Root, tops.
Properties: Alterative, analgesic, antibiotic, anticarcinogen, anti-inflammatory, antispasmodic, cardiant, caustic, counterirritant, depurative, diaphoretic, diuretic, expectorant, hypnotic, hypotensive, laxative, narcotic, parasiticide, sedative, stimulant, vasodilator, and vulnerary.
Constituents: Alkaloids, berberine, bitter principle, caffeic acid, chelerythrine, chelidonine, cryptopine, histamine, homochelidonine A and B, protopine, sanguinarine, saponins, sparteine, tannic acid, and vitamins (A, C (ascorbic acid), choline).
Historical Uses: Angina, anaphylaxis, appetite loss, arteriosclerosis, arthritis, asthma, benign breast disease, bronchitis, cancer (stomach), calluses, cholecystitis, cirrhosis, colds, corns, cramps, diphtheria, eczema, edema, fever (ephemeral, herpetic, rheumatic), gallbladder problems, gallstones, gastroenteritis, gastrointestinal problems, gout, hemorrhoids, hepatitis, herpes, hypertension (mild/moderate), infection (bacterial), inflammation, jaundice, liver problems, Menier's disease, menstrual problems, mucus, muscle and joint pain, neurologic conditions, pain, parasites (ringworm, scabies), peripheral vascular disease, pneumonia, polyps (intestinal), psoriasis, rash, respiratory conditions, rheumatism, rheumatoid arthritis (RA), sexually transmitted diseases (STDs), skin problems, spasmodic conditions, toothache, ulcer (indolent), warts (digitate, filiform, fugitive, glabra, mother, plana juvenilis, plantar, seborrhoeic, vulgaris), and whooping cough.
Discussion: May cause blood vessel dilatation; clear and open bronchial passages; decrease the effect of carcinogens; enhance gallbladder, liver, pancreas, and stomach functions; inhibit or destroy development and growth of bacteria and other microorganisms; prevent the deposition of fat in the liver; promote bowel evacuation, perspiration, and urine flow; purify the liver; reduce blood pressure levels; reestablish healthy system functions; speed healing; stimulate gastric secretions, the cardiovascular system, and peristalsis.
Cautions/Contraindications: Avoid use if pregnant or breast-feeding. Not for long-term use. Wear gloves when handling the crushed plant as skin poisoning may occur.
Adverse Reactions: Arrhythmia, burning of the mouth and throat, congestion (liver, lung), diarrhea (possibly bloody), dizziness, dry mouth, gastrointestinal cramps (severe), hematuria (blood in the urine), nausea, stupor, and/or vomiting.

Herb/Drug Interactions: This herb could cause an interaction (possibly severe) when taken with the following drugs: Cardiac drugs, Diuretic drugs, and Hypotensive drugs.
Herb/Herb Interactions: Do not use this herb with Foxglove (*digitalis spp.*).
Preparations/Dosage: Crude Herb: 3-6 grams. Crude Herb (powdered): Average dose in substance 15-60 grains (0.98-4 gm.). Decoction: ½ cup per day. Extract: 5-10 drops (0.333-0.666 cc.) one to two times per day. Infusion: ½-1 cup per day. Juice: 5-10 drops (0.333-0.666 cc.) in sweetened water. Tincture: 10-15 drops (0.666-1 cc.) one to three times per day. External Uses: Corns/Warts: Mix the juice with vinegar and dab (avoid letting the juice come in contact with other skin) on corns or warts two to three times per day.
Isolation: Chelidonine sulfate: Average dose of 1½-3 grains (0.09-0.2 gm.) for use as a mild narcotic. Chelidonine tannate: Average dose of 3 grains (0.2 gm.) for use as a mild narcotic. Cryptopine: Average dose of ⅛ grain (0.008 gm) for use as an analgesic and hypnotic. Histamine phosphate: Used in a 1:1000 solution in an average dose of 5 drops (0.3 cc.) administered intravenously or subcutaneously, for use as a powerful vasodilator, or for use as a stimulant. Protopine: Average dose of 40-100 grains (2.5-7 gm.) for use as an analgesic and hypnotic. Sanguinarine: Average dose of $^{1}/_{40}$-¼ grain (0.0016-0.016 gm.) for use as an expectorant and tonic. Sparteine sulfate: Average dose of ½ grain (30 mg.) for use as a cardiant, diuretic, and stimulant. Sparteine's action is similar to that of digitalis.

Celery (sel er·ē)

(*Apium graveolens*)

Synonyms/Related Species: Marsh Parsley, Seleri, Sellari, Smallage, and Wild Celery.
Family/Class: Umbelliferae (parsley).
Habitat: Africa, Argentina, Asia, Britain, England, Europe, India, Lapland, North America, Russia, and South America.
Flavor: Pungent (slightly).
Parts Used: Leaves, root, seeds (ripe), stalks.
Properties: Abortifacient, anticarcinogen, antilithic, antiphlogistic, antispasmodic, carminative, depurative, diuretic, emmenagogue, hypoglycemic, hypotensive, lithotriptic, nervine, sedative, stimulant, tonic, and vasodilator.
Constituents: Apiol, apiolin, bergapten, carvene (limonene), coumarins, fatty acids (oleic, palmitic, stearic), fixed oils (olein, palmitin, stearin), flavonoids, minerals (calcium, iron, magnesium, phosphorus, potassium, silicon, sodium, sulfur), phthalides, psoralens, quercitrin, resin, silicic acid, and vitamins (A, B, C (ascorbic acid).
Historical Uses: Amenorrhea, anxiety, appetite loss, arthritis, bladder problems, calculus, cancer, colds, congestive heart failure (CHF), diabetes, dysmenorrhea, dysuria (painful/difficult urination), edema, erectile dysfunction, exhaustion, fever (ephemeral, rheumatic), flatulence, flavoring agent, frigidity, gallstones, gout, headache, hyperglycemia, hypertension (mild/moderate), hysteria, indigestion, inflammation, influenza, insomnia, kidney problems, kidney stones, lithemia, liver problems, lumbago, malnutrition, mucus, muscle and joint pain, nephritis, nervous conditions, neuralgia, premenstrual syndrome (PMS), psoriasis, respiratory conditions, rheumatism, spasmodic conditions, spleen problems, vomiting, and weight loss.
Discussion: May aid digestion; calm the nervous system; cause blood vessel dilatation; decrease the effect of carcinogens; dissolve calculi; induce abortion; promote urine flow; reduce blood pressure levels, blood sugar levels, and excessive lithic acid (uric acid) and urate levels in the

blood, tophi, and urine; restore normal tone to tissues; prevent the development of calculus or stones; purify the blood; stimulate menstruation and uterine contractions.
Cautions/Contraindications: Avoid use if pregnant or breast-feeding, or if you have an acute kidney problem. May cause potassium depletion. May cause dermatitis in susceptible individuals.
Adverse Reactions: Edema.
Herb/Drug Interactions: This herb could cause an interaction (possibly severe) when taken with the following drugs: Antidiabetic drugs, Diuretic drugs, and Hypotensive drugs.
Preparations/Dosage: Crude Herb: 3-9 grams. Decoction (leaves and/or seeds): ½-1 cup per day. Extract: 3-5 drops (0.2-0.333 cc.) one to two times per day. Juice: 1-2 tablespoons (combine with carrot and apple juice for a tasty beverage) per day. Oil (*apii oleum*): 6-8 drops in water one to two times per day. Seed (*apii fructus*): Average dose in substance 15-30 grains (0.98-2 gm.). Stalks: Cooked or raw as a vegetable.
Isolation: Apiol: 3-5 drops (0.18-0.333 cc.) for use in menstrual problems. Apiolin: Average dose of 3 drops (0.18 cc.) for use as an emmenagogue.

Centaury (sen tô·rē)
(*Erythraea centaurium*)

Synonyms/Related Species: Algerian Centaury (*erythraea acaulis*), American Centaury, Bitterbloom, Bitter Clover, Bitter Herb, Broad-Leaved Centaury (*erythraea latifolia*), California Centaury (*erythraea venustum*), Canchalagua, Centaury Gentian, Century, Chilian Centaury (*erythraea chilensis*), Christ's Ladder, Common Centaury, Desert Centaury, Dwarf Centaury (*erythraea pulchella*), Dwarf Tufted Centaury (*erythraea littoralis*), European Centaury (*erythraea centaurium*), Filwort, Great Basin Centaury (*erythraea exaltatum*), Kentaureion, Kentauros, Lesser Centaury, Red Centaury, Rose Pink, and Wild Succory.
Family/Class: Gentianaceae (gentian).
Habitat: Africa, Britain, Engand, Europe, the Mediterranean, North America, and Scandinavia.
Flavor: Bitter.
Parts Used: Aerial
Properties: Alterative, antibiotic, antioxidant, antiperiodic, antiphlogistic, aromatic, depurative, diuretic, emmenagogue, hypotensive, laxative, lithotriptic, malariacidal, parasiticide, sialogogue, stimulant, stomachic, tonic, vasodilator, and vulnerary.
Constituents: Alkaloids, bitter principle, gentiopicrin, sweroside, valerianic acid, and wax.
Historical Uses: Age spots, ague, amenorrhea, anemia, appetite loss, calculus, diabetes, digestive complaints, eczema, enuresis (urinary incontinence), freckles, gallbladder problems, gastritis, gastrointestinal problems, fever (intermittent, rheumatic), flatulence, gout, hypertension (mild/moderate), indigestion, infection (bacterial), inflammation, irritable bowel syndrome (IBS), jaundice, kidney stones, malaria, melancholy, muscle and joint pain, nausea, parasites (lice and their nits, malarial plasmodia), rheumatism, skin problems, sores, ulcer (peptic), and wounds (minor).
Discussion: May aid digestion; cause blood vessel dilatation; dissolve calculi; enhance cardiovascular system, digestive system, liver, nervous system, reproductive system, stomach, and urinary system functions; increase production of hydrochloric acid, pepsin, and other digestive enzymes; inhibit oxidation and inhibit or destroy development and growth of bacteria and other microorganisms; promote bowel evacuation and saliva secretion; purify the blood;

reduce blood pressure levels and the frequency of nighttime urination; reestablish healthy system functions; restore normal tone to tissues; speed healing; stimulate appetite, gastric secretions, and peristalsis.
Cautions/Contraindications: Avoid use if pregnant or breast-feeding, or if you have ulcer (duodenal, gastric).
Adverse Reactions: Nausea, salivation (increased), and/or vomiting.
Herb/Drug Interactions: This herb could cause an interaction (possibly severe) when taken with the following drugs: Hypotensive drugs.
Preparations/Dosage: Crude Herb: 3-9 grams. Extract: 3-5 drops (0.2-0.333 cc.) one to two times per day. Infusion: 1 teaspoon per day. Tincture: 10-15 drops (0.666-1 cc.).

Chamomile, German (kam e·mīl, jûr men)
(*Matricaria chamomilla*)

Synonyms/Related Species: Camomile, Hungarian Chamomile, Mayweed (*matricaria inodora*), Pinheads, Single Chamomile.
Family/Class: Compositae (composite).
Habitat: Asia, Europe, Hungary, and North America.
Flavor: Bitter/pungent.
Parts Used: Flowers.
Properties: Analgesic, antibiotic, anticarcinogen, anticoagulant, antifungal, antihistamine, antioxidant, antiphlogistic, antispasmodic, aromatic, carminative, counterirritant, diaphoretic, hemostatic, emmenagogue, nervine, sedative, and tonic.
Constituents: Aglycones, azulene, bitter principle, coumarin, flavonoids, glycosides, minerals (calcium, potassium), mucilage, quercetin, rutin, tannic acid, umbelliferone, vitamins (choline), and volatile oil.
Historical Uses: Acne, allergy, anxiety, appetite loss, arteriosclerosis, asthma, attention deficit disorder (ADD), bronchitis, bruises, burns (minor), cancer (endometrial), cirrhosis, colds, colic, conjunctivitis, constipation, corns, cramps, dandruff, diarrhea, digestive complaints, diphtheria, diverticulitis, eczema, edema, eyewash, fever (ephemeral, enteric, rheumatic), flatulence, flavoring agent, gallbladder problems, gangrene, gastritis, gastrointestinal problems, gout, hair rinse (blonde to light brown hair), headache, hemorrhage, hemorrhoids, hives, hyperactivity, hysteria, indigestion, infection (bacterial, fungal), inflammation, influenza, insomnia, irritable bowel syndrome (IBS), jaundice, kidney problems, liver problems, menstrual problems, lumbago, lupus, migraine, mucous membranes, mucus, muscle and joint pain, nausea, nervous conditions, neuralgia, pain, periodontal disease, premenstrual syndrome (PMS), pruritus, psoriasis, rash, restlessness, respiratory conditions, rheumatism, sciatica, shampoo, skin problems, sore nipples, sores, spasmodic conditions, substitute for pineapple weed (*matricaria discoidea*) and roman chamomile (*anthemis nobilis*), toothache, typhoid, ulcer (bouveret, duodenal, gastric, peptic), and wounds (minor).
Discussion: May aid digestion; calm the nervous system; counteract the effect of histamine; decrease the effect of carcinogens; delay or reduce coagulation of the blood; enhance stomach, liver, and lung functions; induce sleep; inhibit oxidation and inhibit or destroy developement and growth of bacteria and other microorganisms; prevent the deposition of fat in the liver and hemorrhage in persons with hypertension; promote perspiration; reduce capillary fragility; restore normal tone to tissues; soothe nipple soreness; stimulate menstruation.

Cautions/Contraindications: Avoid use if pregnant or breast-feeding, or if you are allergic to ragweed or pollen. Individuals with ragweed sensitivity may experience allergic symptoms when using german chamomile. May cause allergic reactions (possibly severe) and dermatitis in susceptible individuals. Some persons may experience bleeding or increased clotting time when using this herb with anticoagulant drugs or aspirin.
Adverse Reactions: Bleeding (possibly serious), coagulation problems, nausea, and/or vomiting.
Herb/Drug Interactions: This herb could cause an interaction (possibly severe) when taken with the following drugs: Anticoagulant drugs, Salicylates, and Subsalicylates.
Preparations/Dosage: Crude Herb: 3-12 grams. Extract: 5-10 drops (0.333-0.666 cc.) one to two times per day. Infusion: ½-2 cups per day. Tincture: 10-30 drops (0.666-2 cc.) one to three times per day.

Chamomile, Roman (kam e·mīl, rō men)
(Anthemis nobilis)

Synonyms/Related Species: Common Chamomile, Corn Chamomile (*anthemis arvensis*), Dog Chamomile, English Chamomile, Ground Apple, Kamai Melon, Little Apple, Low Chamomile, Manzanilla, Maythen, Scotch Chamomile, Stinking Chamomile (*anthemis cotula*), Stinking Mayweed, True Chamomile, Whig Plant, and Wild Chamomile.
Family/Class: Compositae (composite).
Habitat: Africa, Argentina, Belgium, England, Europe, France, Italy, North America, Poland, Saxony, and Spain.
Flavor: Bitter.
Parts Used: Flowers.
Properties: Analgesic, antibiotic, antifungal, antiphlogistic, antispasmodic, aromatic, carminative, diuretic, diaphoretic, emmenagogue, lithotriptic, nervine, sedative, stomachic, and tonic.
Constituents: Azulene, caffeic acid, ferulic acid, flavonoids, glycosides, calcium, iron, magnesium, manganese, potassium, zinc, monosaccharides, mucilage, nobilin, resin, sesquiterpene lactones, tannic acid, vitamins (A, choline), and volatile oil.
Historical Uses: Abscess, acne, anxiety, appetite loss, asthma, bladder problems, bronchitis, burns (minor), calculus, cirrhosis, colds, colic, colitis, conjunctivitis, constipation, cough, cramps, diarrhea, digestive complaints, diphtheria, dysmenorrhea, earache, eczema, fever (ephemeral, enteric, rheumatic), flatulence, gallstones, gargle/mouth rinse, gastritis, gastrointestinal problems, gout, hair rinse (blonde to light brown hair), headache, hyperactivity, hysteria, indigestion, infection (bacterial, fungal), inflammation, influenza, insomnia, irritable bowel syndrome (IBS), jaundice, kidney problems, kidney stones, measles, menstrual problems, migraine, mucus, muscle and joint pain, nausea, nervous conditions, nipple soreness, pain, periodontal disease, pneumonia, pruritus, restlessness, rheumatism, sciatica, shampoo, skin problems, sore nipples, sore throat, spasmodic conditions, substitute for pineapple weed (*matricaria discoidea*) and german chamomile (*matricaria chamomilla*), toothache, tumors, typhoid, ulcer (bouveret, peptic), and wounds (minor).
Discussion: May aid digestion; calm the nervous system; dissolve calculi; ease drug or nicotine withdrawal symptoms; enhance immune system and stomach functions; induce sleep; increase mental alertness and production of the hormone thyroxine; inhibit or destroy developement and growth of bacteria and other microorganisms; prevent the deposition of fat in the liver; promote

perspiration and urine flow; rejuvenate hair and skin texture; restore normal tone to tissues; soothe nipple soreness; stimulate menstruation.

Cautions/Contraindications: Avoid use if pregnant or breast-feeding, or if you are allergic to ragweed or pollen. May cause allergic reactions (possibly severe) and dermatitis in susceptible individuals. Some persons may experience bleeding or increased clotting time when using this herb with anticoagulant drugs or aspirin.

Adverse Reactions: Bleeding (possibly serious), coagulation problems, nausea, and/or vomiting.

Herb/Drug Interactions: This herb could cause an interaction (possibly severe) when taken with the following drugs: Anticoagulant drugs, Salicylates, and Subsalicylates.

Preparations/Dosage: Crude Herb: 6-9 grams. Extract: 5-8 drops (0.333-0.5 cc.) one to two times per day. Extract (powdered): Average dose in substance 10-15 grains (0.666-0.98 gm.). Infusion: 1-2 cups per day. Oil of Chamomile (*oleum chamomilla*): ½-3 drops (0.03-0.2 cc.) in water or on a sugarcube. Tincture: 10-20 drops (0.666-1.25 cc.) one to three times per day.

Chaparral (chap e·ral)
(*Larrea divaricata*)

Synonyms/Related Species: Chapar′ro Amargo′so, Creosote Bush (*larrea tridentate*), Dwarf Oak, Evergreen Oak, Gobernadora, Greasewood, Hediondilla, Larrea, and Stinkweed.

Family/Class: Zygophyllaceae (caltrop).

Habitat: Mexico, North America.

Flavor: Bitter/pungent.

Parts Used: Leaves.

Properties: Alterative, analgesic, antibiotic, anticarcinogen, antioxidant, antiphlogistic, antiviral, depurative, diuretic, expectorant, hyperglycemic, laxative, tonic, and vasodepressor.

Constituents: Minerals (aluminum, barium, chlorine, potassium, silicon, sodium, sulfur, tin), nordihydroguaiaretic acid (NGDA), protein, and silicic acid.

Historical Uses: Abscess, acne, allergy (pollen), amenorrhea, arthritis, asthma, bronchitis, bruises, burns (minor), bursitis, cancer, carpal tunnel syndrome, cataracts, cavities, chicken pox, colds, cough, cramps, dandruff, deodorant, diarrhea, digestive complaints, dysmenorrhea, dysentery, eczema, fever (ephemeral, hay, rheumatic), gargle/mouth rinse, gastrointestinal problems, hemorrhoids, hepatitis, human immunodeficiency virus (HIV), infection (bacterial, kidney, urinary tract, viral), inflammation, influenza, insect bites or stings, insufficiency (circulatory), lesions (tubercle), leukemia, menstrual problems, mucus, muscle and joint pain, nausea, neuritis, pain, periodontal disease, pimples, prolapse (rectal, uterine), prostate problems, psoriasis, rash, respiratory conditions, rheumatism, sciatica, scrofula, sexually transmitted diseases (STDs), skin problems, snakebite, sores, tuberculosis, tumors, ulcer (fistula, tuberculous), warts (digitate, filiform, fugitive, glabra, mother, plana juvenilis, plantar, seborrhoeic, vulgaris), weight loss, and wounds (minor).

Discussion: May cause vasomotor depression; cleanse the system of LSD residue; clear and open bronchial passages; decrease the effect of carcinogens; enhance kidney, liver, and lung functions; increase adrenal gland ascorbic acid levels; inhibit oxidation and inhibit or destroy developement and growth of bacteria and other microorganisms; promote bowel evacuation and urine flow; purify the blood; reestablish healthy system functions; restore normal tone to tissues; serve as an adjuvant to cancer therapies; stimulate hair growth and peristalsis; stop or slow abnormal cell growth.

Cautions/Contraindications: Avoid use if pregnant or breast-feeding, or if you have kidney or liver disease, or a glandular problem. May cause allergic reactions, photosensitivity, or photodermatosis in susceptible individuals. Not for long-term use.
Adverse Reactions: Aggressive behavior, edema, growth reduction, hypersensitivity, liver damage (often characterized by jaundice), irritability, nausea, skin problems, testicular shrinkage, and/or vomiting.
Herb/Drug Interactions: This herb could cause an interaction (possibly severe) when taken with the following drugs: None known.
Preparations/Dosage: Crude Herb: 3-6 grams. Extract: 30-60 drops (2-4 cc.) one to two times per day. Infusion: ½-1 cup per day. Tincture: 10-15 drops (0.666-1 cc.) one to three times per day.
Did You Know? Despite its name of creosote bush, this plant contains no creosote.

Chaste Tree (chāst trē)

(*Vitex agnus castus*)

Synonyms/Related Species: Monk's Pepper and Vitex.
Family/Class: Verbenaceae (verbena).
Habitat: Asia and the Mediterranean.
Flavor: Pungent/bitter.
Parts Used: Fruit.
Properties: Analgesic, anaphrodisiac, anticarcinogen, antiperiodic, antiphlogistic, aphrodisiac, emmenagogue, malariacidal, tonic, and vulnerary.
Constituents: Androstenedione (androgenic steroid), aucubin, bitter principle, eucalyptol (cineol), fatty acids (oleic, palmitic, stearic), fixed oils (olein, palmitin, stearin), flavonoids, glycosides, saponins, and volatile oil.
Historical Uses: Acne, ague, amenorrhea, asthma, benign breast disease, bronchitis, cancer (prostate), canker sores, congestion (uterine, vaginal), constipation, cystitis, cysts (ovarian), diphtheria, dysmenorrhea, edema, endometriosis, fever (intermittent), fibroids (uterine), hormonal imbalances, hot flashes, infertility, inflammation, leukorrhea, malaria, menopausal/menstrual problems, menorrhagia, muscle and joint pain, pain, paralysis, parasites (malarial plasmodia), premenstrual syndrome (PMS), ulcer (duodenal, gastric, peptic, syriac), urethritis, vaginitis, and wounds (minor).
Discussion: May arouse sexual impulses; cause decreased sperm production in males; decrease the effect of carcinogens; enhance circulatory system, female reproductive system, liver, and spleen functions; facilitate hormonal health; increase estrogen and progesterone levels; lessen sexual desire; maintain female emotional balance before and during the menstrual cycle; rebalance the system after birth control pills have been stopped; reduce testosterone production; regulate ovulation; restore normal tone to tissues; speed healing; stimulate menstruation, pituitary gland function, progesterone production, uterine lining growth, and the release of multiple eggs from the ovaries, which could result in multiple births; suppress an overactive libido; may cause atrophy (testicular). Chaste berry has a reputation as both an aphrodisiac and an anaphrodisiac, as it will usually enable what is appropriate to occur.
Cautions/Contraindications: Avoid use if pregnant or breast-feeding, or if you have anemia, debility, an estrogen dependant cancer, or if you have a history of estrogen dependant cancers. May cause decreased sperm production in males.

Adverse Reactions: Diarrhea (possibly bloody), gastrointestinal cramps (severe), menorrhagia, nausea, rash, and/or vomiting.
Herb/Drug Interactions: This herb could cause an interaction (possibly severe) when taken with the following drugs: Antipsychotic drugs, Hormones and Synthetic Substitutes (i.e. conjugated estrogens, contraceptives (oral, etc.), and other hormonal replacement therapy (HRT), and Smoking Cessation aids.
Preparations/Dosage: Crude Herb: 3-6 grams. Infusion: 1 cup per day. Tincture (berries): 10-30 drops (0.666-2 cc.) one to three times per day.
Isolation: Eucalyptol: 5 drops (0.3 cc.) in atomization or inhalation therapy for use in respiratory conditions.

Cherry, Antilles (cher ē, an·til ēz)
(*Malpighia punicifolia*)

Synonyms/Related Species: Acerola, Barbados Cherry, and Sour Cherry.
Family/Class: Malpighiaceae (malpighia).
Habitat: India.
Flavor: Sour.
Parts Used: Fruit.
Properties: Anticarcinogen, antihistamine, antioxidant, antispasmodic, and antiviral.
Constituents: Anthocyanidins, hydrocyanic acid, inulin (starch), minerals (magnesium, niacin, pantothenic acid, potassium), and vitamins (A, B_1 (thiamine), B_{12}, C (ascorbic acid).
Historical Uses: Allergy, angina, atherosclerosis, bronchitis, cancer, colds, glaucoma, herpes, infection (viral), infertility, influenza, nervous conditions, Parkinson's disease, sexually transmitted diseases (STDs), and wrinkles.
Discussion: May counteract the effect of histamine; decrease the effect of carcinogens; enhance adrenal and liver functions; inhibit oxidation; intensify the cell protective effects of vitamin C, and replaces vitamin C depletion during corticosteroid treatments; maintain collagen formation; protect the body from the effects of heavy metal exposure or pollutants.
Cautions/Contraindications: Avoid use if pregnant or breast-feeding, or if you have hemochromatosis, or immediately after any cancer surgery and for the two-three weeks that follow. Drink six to eight glasses of water daily when taking acerola. May result in the formation of kidney stones in those individuals with an excessive amount of oxalic acid in the urine.
Adverse Reactions: Diarrhea, flatulence, nausea, and/or vomiting.
Herb/Drug Interactions: This herb could cause an interaction (possibly severe) when taken with the following drugs: None known.
Preparations/Dosage: Crude Herb: 1.5-2 grams.
Isolation: Hydrocyanic acid (*acidum hydrocyanicum dilutum*): Used in a 2% solution, average dose of 1-5 drops (0.066-0.333 cc.) for use as an antispasmodic.

Cherry, Wild (cher ē, wīld)
(*Prunus serotina*)

Synonyms/Related Species: Bitter Cherry (*prunus emarginata*), Black Cherry, Black Choke, Cerasus Tree, Chokecherry (*prunus virginiana*), Holly-Leaf Cherry (*prunus ilicifolia*), Kerasos Tree, Pin Cherry (*prunus pensylvanica*), Rum Cherry, Sour Cherry (*prunus cerasus*), Virginian Prune, Western Chokecherry, Wild Black Cherry, and Wilde Cheri.
Family/Class: Rosaceae (rose).
Habitat: Europe and North America.
Flavor: Bark: pungent. Fruit Pulp: bitter.
Parts Used: Bark (inner), fruit pulp (pit/stone removed).
Properties: Antiperiodic, antiphlogistic, aromatic, astringent, carminative, demulcent, diuretic, expectorant, hemostatic, hypotensive, malariacidal, narcotic, sedative, stimulant, stomachic, tonic, and vasodilator.
Constituents: Amygdaline, gallic acid, hydrocyanic acid, inulin (starch), lignin, minerals (calcium, iron, potassium), prunin, resin, tannic acid, and volatile oil.
Historical Uses: Ague, appetite loss, arrhythmia, asthma, bleeding, bronchitis, chills, colds, colitis, constipation, convalescence, cough, cystitis, diarrhea, digestive complaints, dysentery, enema, fever (intermittent), gallbladder problems, gastritis, gastrointestinal problems, gout, hemorrhage, hemorrhoids, hypertension (mild/moderate), indigestion, infection (urinary tract), inflammation, influenza, insomnia, irritability, lesions (tubercle), lung problems, malaria, mucus, nervous conditions, night sweats, parasites (malarial plasmodia), pneumonia, respiratory conditions, scrofula, sore throat, tuberculosis, ulcer (duodenal, fistula, gastric, peptic, tuberculous), and whooping cough.
Discussion: May aid digestion; cause blood vessel dilatation; clear and open bronchial passages; enhance bladder, lung, pancreatic, spleen, and stomach functions; promote urine flow; reduce blood pressure levels; restore normal tone to tissues; soothe mucous membrane irritation; stimulate appetite.
Cautions/Contraindications: Avoid use if pregnant or breast-feeding. The leaves and fruit pits contain hydrocyanic acid and are extremely poisonous.
Adverse Reactions: Hydrocyanism (hydrocyanic acid poisoning), nausea, and/or vomiting.
Herb/Drug Interactions: This herb could cause an interaction (possibly severe) when taken with the following drugs: Hypotensive drugs.
Preparations/Dosage: Crude Herb: 3-9 grams. Decoction: ½ cup per day. Fruit (pulp): Jam/Jelly. Infusion: 1-2 cups per day. Syrup: ½-1 tablespoon per day in water. Tincture: 5-30 drops (0.33-2 cc.) one to three times per day.
Isolation: Prunin: Average dose of 2-3 grains (0.132-0.195 gm.) for use as a nervine, and in thoracic (chest) conditions.
Note: Extract wild cherry bark in cold water as high temperatures cause a deterioration of its constituents.

Chestnut, Horse (ches nut, hôrs)
(*Aesculus hippocastanum*)

Synonyms/Related Species: Buckeye, California Buckeye (*aesculus californica*), Dwarf Horse Chestnut (*aesculus parviflora*), European Horse Chestnut, Red Buckeye (*aesculus pavia*), Red Horse Chestnut (*aesculus rubicunda*), Spanish Chestnut, and Yellow Buckeye (*aesculus flava*).

Family/Class: Sapindaceae (soapberry).
Habitat: Asia, Bulgaria, the Caucasus, Denmark, England, Europe, Greece, the Himalayas, Iran, North America, Russia, and Scandinavia.
Flavor: Bitter.
Parts Used: Bark (branch), fruit, nut (oil and seeds).
Properties: Anticoagulant, antioxidant, antiperiodic, antiphlogistic, astringent, expectorant, hemolytic, hemostatic, malariacidal, narcotic, nutritive, and tonic.
Constituents: Aescin, aesculin, argyroscin, carbohydrates, coumarin, fatty acids (arachidonic, linoleic, linolenic, oleic, palmitic, stearic), fixed oils (olein, palmitin, stearin), flavonoids, fraxin, inulin (starch), monosaccharides, oligomeric proanthocyanidins, oligosaccharides, polysaccharides, protein, quercetin, resin, rutin, saponins, scopolin, sterols, and tannic acid.
Historical Uses: Ague, arthritis, bleeding, bronchitis, bruises, burns (minor), cellulite, colds, congestion (lung), cough, cramps, dietary supplementation, eczema, edema, enteritis, fever (ephemeral, intermittent, rheumatic), gastritis, glandular problems, hemorrhoids, hypertrophy (benign prostatic), infection, inflammation, insufficiency (venous), lochia, lymphedema, malaria, malnutrition, mucus, muscle and joint pain, neuralgia, pain, parasites (malarial plasmodia), phlebitis, pruritus, respiratory conditions, rheumatism, spasmodic conditions, spider veins, sores, sprain, sunscreen, thrombophlebitis, trauma (brain), tumors, ulcer (duodenal, gastric, peptic, stasis, varicose), varicose veins, wounds (minor), wrinkles.
Discussion: May cause hemolysis; clear and open bronchial passages; delay or reduce coagulation of the blood; enhance intestinal system function; inhibit oxidation; prevent hemorrhage in persons with hypertension; provide dietary supplementation; reduce capillary fragility; restore normal tone to tissues; serve as a nutritional adjuvant to therapeutic programs and as a postoperative tissue swelling adjuvant to help stabilize patients who have brain trauma; strengthen the contractile fibers and vein walls.
Cautions/Contraindications: Avoid use if pregnant or breast-feeding. Do not administer to children. Do not confuse this plant with chestnut (*castanea sativa*). Some persons may experience bleeding or increased clotting time when using this herb with anticoagulant drugs or aspirin. Not for long-term use. Use with professional guidance/supervision.
Adverse Reactions: Anaphylaxis, bleeding (possibly serious), coagulation problems, confusion, diarrhea, dizziness, fainting, flushing, headache, hematuria (blood in the urine), hemolysis, increased body temperature, gastrointestinal problems, nausea, pupil dilatation, paralysis, stupor, thirst (excessive), visual disturbances, and/or vomiting.
Herb/Drug Interactions: This herb could cause an interaction (possibly severe) when taken with the following drugs: Anticoagulant drugs, Salicylates, and Subsalicylates.
Preparations/Dosage: Bark (powdered): Average dose in substance ¼-½ teaspoon. Extract (fruit): 1-3 drops (0.06-0.2 cc.) one to two times per day. Extract (bark): 1/16 ounce per day. Infusion (bark): ¼-½ tablespoons per day. Tincture (fruit): 3-5 drops (0.2-0.333 cc.) one to three times per day. External uses: Oil (nut): Combine a small amount of horse chestnut oil with other herbal oils to make a linament or ointment.
Isolation: Aescin: Average dose of 30-150 mg. applied topically or administered intramuscularly, for use as an analgesic and antiperiodic. Adverse reactions that may occur upon intramuscular injection (I.M) include anaphylaxis, gastrointestinal mucous membrane problems, limited kidney function, and skin rash.
To Neutralize Toxic Principles Before Use: Fruit (green fruit capsule): Cut-up or pulverize, leach in water (numerous times), strain and preroast before use. Bark: Leach in water (numerous

times) before use. Seeds: Crush or grind and leach in water (numerous times), strain and boil for 30 minutes before use.

Chestnut, Sweet (ches nut, swēt)
(*Castanea sativa*)

Synonyms/Related Species: American Chestnut, Chastaigne, Chesten-Nut, Eubœan Nut, Great Chestnut, Hēdys Kastaneia, Husked Nut, Jupiter's Nut, Sardian Nut, Spanish Chestnut, Suavis Castanea, and Swete Chesteine.
Family/Class: Fagaceae (beech).
Habitat: Asia, England, Europe, France, Greece, Italy, North America, and Spain.
Flavor: Sweet.
Parts Used: Nut (roasted).
Properties: Anticoagulant, antioxidant, antiphlogistic, astringent, expectorant, hemolytic, hemostatic, and tonic.
Constituents: Flavonoids, glycosides, minerals (magnesium, sulfur), myricetin, quercitrin, rutin, tannic acid, and volatile oil.
Historical Uses: Ague, arthritis, bleeding, bronchitis, bruising, colds, cough, diarrhea, eczema, fever (ephemeral, rheumatic), food source (nuts), gargle/mouth rinse, inflammation, insufficiency (circulatory, venous), mucus, muscle and joint pain, pain, phlebitis, psoriasis, respiratory conditions, rheumatism, skin problems, sore throat, sprain, thrombosis (blood clot), trauma (postoperative), ulcer (stasis, varicose), varicose veins, and whooping cough.
Discussion: May cause hemolysis; clear and open bronchial passages; delay or reduce coagulation of the blood; enhance intestinal system function; prevent sunburn and hemorrhage in persons with hypertension; increase capillary and red cell resistance; inhibit oxidation; reduce capillary fragility and reduce the effects of postoperative tissue trauma; restore normal tone to tissues; strengthen contractile fibers, and the vascular system.
Cautions/Contraindications: Avoid use if pregnant or breast-feeding. Do not administer to children. Do not confuse this plant with horse chestnut (*aesculus hippocastanum*). Some persons may experience bleeding or increased clotting time when using this herb with anticoagulant drugs or aspirin. The outer husks are poisonous.
Adverse Reactions: Anaphylaxis, bleeding (possibly serious), coagulation problems, diarrhea, facial reddening, dizziness, elevated body temperature, gastrointestinal problems, fainting, pupil dilatation, hematuria (blood in the urine), nausea, thirst (excessive), visual disturbances, and/or vomiting.
Herb/Drug Interactions: This herb could cause an interaction (possibly severe) when taken with the following drugs: Anticoagulant drugs, Salicylates, and Subsalicylates.
Preparations/Dosage: Crude Herb: 1-3 grams. Nuts (roasted): Handful per day.

Chickweed (chik wēd)
(*Stellaria media*)

Synonyms/Related Species: Adder's Mouth, Augentrosgräs, Common Chickweed, Common Starwort, Indian Chickweed, Long-Leaved Starwort (*stellaria longifolia*), Long-Stalked Chickweed, Long-Stalked Starwort (*stellaria longpipes*), Northern Starwort (*stellaria calycantha*), Passerina, Satin Flower, Star Chickweed, Starweed, Starwort, Stellaire, Stitchwort,

Thick-Leaved Starwort (*stellaria crassifolia*), Tongue-Grass, Umbellate Starwort (*stellaria umbellata*), and Winterweed.
Family/Class: Caryophyllaceae (pink).
Habitat: Worldwide.
Flavor: Bitter/sweet.
Parts Used: Aerial.
Properties: Alterative, antibiotic, anticarcinogen, antiphlogistic, antiscorbutic, carminative, demulcent, depurative, diuretic, expectorant, hemostatic, laxative, nutritive, and vulnerary.
Constituents: Alkaloids, carboxylic acids, coumarins, flavonoids, minerals (calcium, copper, iron, magnesium, manganese, phosphorus, potassium, zinc), mucilage, lecithin, rutin, saponins, triterpenoids, and vitamins (B_1 (thiamine), B_2 (riboflavin), B_3 (niacin), B_5 (pantothenic acid), B_6 (pyridoxine), B_{12}, B_x (para-aminobenzoic acid (PABA), C (ascorbic acid), D, H (biotin), M (folic acid).
Historical Uses: Abscess, acne, allergy (pollen), appetite problems, arteriosclerosis, asthma, auditory problems, bleeding, bronchitis, bruises, burns (minor), bursitis, cancer (testicular), colds, colitis, conjunctivitis, constipation, convulsions, cough, cramps, diabetes, dietary supplementation, edema, eczema, erectile dysfunction, fever (ephemeral, hay, rheumatic, septic), gout, hemorrhoids, hives, indigestion, infection (bacterial), inflammation, laryngitis, malnutrition, mucus, muscle and joint pain, pain, peritonitis, pleurisy, poisoning (blood), pruritus, psoriasis, rash, respiratory conditions, rheumatism, scurvy, skin problems, sores, sore throat, substitute for spinach (young leaves), ulcer (duodenal, gastric, indolent, peptic, stasis), weight loss, and wounds (minor).
Discussion: May aid digestion; balance the thyroid; clear and open bronchial passages; decrease the effect of carcinogens; dissolve plaque from the blood vessels; inhibit or destroy development and growth of bacteria and other microorganisms; prevent hemorrhage in persons with hypertension; promote bowel evacuation and urine flow; provide dietary supplementation; purify the blood; reduce capillary fragility; reestablish healthy system functions; purify the blood; serve as a nutritional adjuvant to therapeutic programs; soften and soothe skin; speed healing; stimulate peristalsis.
Cautions/Contraindications: Avoid use if pregnant or breast-feeding.
Adverse Reactions: Nausea and/or vomiting.
Herb/Drug Interactions: This herb could cause an interaction (possibly severe) when taken with the following drugs: None known.
Preparations/Dosage: Crude Herb: 3-12 grams. Decoction: 1 cup per day. Infusion: ½-1 cup per day. Juice: 1 teaspoon -1 tablespoon in water per day. Leaves (young): Cooked as a vegetable or eaten raw in a salad. Green Drink: To prepare a healthy, refreshing green drink, place a handful of fresh chickweed herb into a blender with pineapple juice, blend and strain. External Uses: Indolent ulcer: Apply fresh, bruised leaves as a poultice. Pruritus (itching): Prepare a strong infusion of the fresh plant and add to bath water.

Chicory (chik e·rē)
(*Cichorium intybus*)

Synonyms/Related Species: Blue Sailors, Cichorium, Cicoree, Endive, Hendibeh, Kichora, Succory, Wild Chicory, and Wild Succory.
Family/Class: Compositae (composite).

Habitat: Africa, Australia, England, Europe, Iran, Ireland, New Zealand, North America, and Scotland.
Flavor: Bitter.
Parts Used: Leaves, root.
Properties: Alterative, antibiotic, anticarcinogen, antilithic, antioxidant, antiphlogistic, carminative, depurative, diuretic, hepatic, hypoglycemic, hypotensive, laxative, lithotriptic, nutritive, tonic, and vasodilator.
Constituents: Bitter principle, caffeic acid, chlorogenic acid, coumarin, flavonoids, glycosides, inulin (starch), minerals (potassium), monosaccharides, sesquiterpene lactones, mucilage, tannic acid, tartaric acid, umbelliferone, and vitamins (A, B, C (ascorbic acid), D, K).
Historical Uses: Abscess, anemia, appetite loss, arteriosclerosis, arthritis, bladder problems, calculus, cancer (breast), conjunctivitis, constipation, dietary supplementation, digestive complaints, edema, fever (ephemeral, rheumatic), flatulence, gallbladder problems, gallstones, gastritis, gastrointestinal problems, gout, hepatitis, hyperglycemia, hypertension (mild/moderate), indigestion, infection (bacterial), infertility, inflammation, jaundice, kidney problems, kidney stones, lithemia, liver problems, malnutrition, skin problems, mastitis, mucus, muscle and joint pain, rheumatism, snakebite, spleen problems, substitute for coffee (root; ground/roasted), tachycardia, and weight loss.
Discussion: May aid digestion; cause blood vessel dilatation; decrease the effect of carcinogens; dissolve calculi; enhance digestive system, gallbladder, and liver functions; improve lipid profiles and cholesterol ratios; inhibit oxidation and inhibit or destroy developement and growth of bacteria and other microorganisms; prevent the development of calculus or stones; promote bowel evacuation, cholesterol and lipid excretion, and urine flow; protect the liver; provide dietary supplementation; reduce blood pressure levels, blood sugar levels, cholesterol levels, and excessive lithic acid (uric acid) and urate levels in the blood, tophi, and urine; purify the blood; reestablish healthy system functions; restore normal tone to tissues; serve as a nutritional adjuvant to therapeutic programs; slow pulse rate; stimulate peristalsis.
Cautions/Contraindications: Avoid use if pregnant or breast-feeding. May cause allergic reactions in susceptible individuals.
Adverse Reactions: Congestion (digestive organs), diarrhea, gastritis, indigestion, irritable bowel syndrome (IBS), nausea, visual disturbances, and/or vomiting.
Herb/Drug Interactions: This herb could cause an interaction (possibly severe) when taken with the following drugs: Antidiabetic drugs and Hypotensive drugs.
Preparations/Dosage: Crude Herb: 3-6 grams. Infusion: 1-2 cups per day. Decoction (root): ½-1 cup per day. Juice: 1 tablespoon in water per day. Leaves (young/blanched): Eaten raw in salads. Root (young): Cooked and eaten as a vegetable.

Chiretta (ki·ret ah)
(*Swertia chirata*)

Synonyms/Related Species: Andrographis, Indian Balmony, Indian Gentian, Kalmegh, King of Bitters, Kiryat, Swertia, and True Chiretta.
Family/Class: Gentianaceae (gentian).
Habitat: India and Nepal.
Flavor: Bitter.
Parts Used: Aerial.

Properties: Antibiotic, anticarcinogen, anticoagulant, antifertilizin, antifungal, antiphlogistic, antiviral, laxative, parasiticide, sedative, sialogogue, stimulant, and tonic.
Constituents: Chiratin, swerchirin, swertiamarin, and xanthones.
Historical Uses: Acquired immune deficiency syndrome (AIDS), appetite loss, arteriosclerosis, asthma, athlete's foot, cancer (breast, prostate, skin), cardiovascular conditions, colds, constipation, diabetes, diarrhea, digestive complaints, escherichia coli (e-coli), fatigue, fever (ephemeral, herpetic), gallbladder problems, gastritis, gastrointestinal problems, glandular problems, glandular swelling, gleet, gonorrhea, headache, hepatitis, herpes, hiccups, human immunodeficiency virus (HIV), indigestion, infection (bacterial, fungal, sexually transmitted, viral), inflammation, influenza, irritable bowel syndrome (IBS), leishmaniasis, liver problems, muscle and joint pain, nausea, pain, parasites (leishmania, lice and their nits, ringworm, scabies), respiratory conditions, sexually transmitted diseases (STDs), sore throat, tinea cruris (jock itch), tumors (non-Hodgkin's lymphoma), and urethritis.
Discussion: May aid digestion; balance blood sugar levels; decrease the effect of carcinogens; delay or reduce coagulation of the blood; enhance gallbladder function; inhibit development or destroy growth of bacteria and other microorganisms; maintain T cell counts; neutralize fertilizin (fertilization) in males/females; promote bowel evacuation and saliva secretion; restore normal tone to tissues; stimulate gastric secretions and peristalsis.
Cautions/Contraindications: Avoid use if pregnant or breast-feeding, or if you have acidity (gastric) or an ulcer (duodenal, gastric, peptic). Some persons may experience bleeding or increased clotting time when using this herb with anticoagulant drugs or aspirin.
Adverse Reactions: Anaphylaxis, arrhythmia, bleeding (possibly serious), coagulation problems, dizziness, nausea, salivation (increased), and/or vomiting.
Herb/Drug Interactions: This herb could cause an interaction (possibly severe) when taken with the following drugs: Anticoagulant drugs, Salicylates, and Subsalicylates.
Preparations/Dosage: Crude Herb (powdered): Average dose in substance 5-30 grains (0.324-2 gm.). Extract: 5-8 drops (0.333-0.5 cc.). Extract (solid): Average dose in substance 4-8 grains (0.26-0.5 gm.). Infusion: ½-1 cup per day. Tincture: 15-30 drops (1-2 cc.) one to three times per day.

Chive (chīv)

(*Allium schoenoprasum*)

Synonyms/Related Species: Ail Civitte, Cives, Petit Poureau, and Rush-Leek.
Family/Class: Liliaceae (lily).
Habitat: The Alps, Asia, China, England, Europe, France, Greece, India, Italy, the Mediterranean, North America, Siberia, and Sweden.
Flavor: Pungent.
Parts Used: Leaves (fresh).
Properties: Analgesic, antibiotic, antispasmodic, carminative, diuretic, expectorant, hypotensive, and vasodilator.
Constituents: Allicin, allyl, carbohydrates, flavonoids, fructosans, minerals (arsenic, calcium, iron, manganese, potassium, selenium, sodium, sulfur, zinc), polysaccharides, saponins, and vitamins (A, B_1 (thiamine), C (ascorbic acid), M (folic acid).

Historical Uses: Anemia, angina, cardiovascular conditions, colds, cough, depression (mild/moderate), digestive complaints, dyspnea, flatulence, flavoring agent, halitosis, heart disease, indigestion, infection (bacterial), mucus, nausea, pain, and spasmodic conditions.
Discussion: May aid digestion; cause blood vessel dilatation; clear and open bronchial passages; inhibit or destroy developement and growth of bacteria and other microorganisms; promote urine flow; protect against heart disease; reduce blood pressure levels and cholesterol levels; stimulate appetite and metabolism.
Cautions/Contraindications: Avoid use if pregnant or breast-feeding. Do not confuse chives with poisonous death camas (*zigadenus spp.*), which does not have that 'onion' smell. May cause dermatitis in susceptible individuals.
Adverse Reactions: Diarrhea (possibly bloody), edema, acid reflux (esophageal irritation caused by gastric acid), flatulence (excessive), indigestion, irritable bowel syndrome (IBS), nausea, and/or vomiting.
Herb/Drug Interactions: This herb could cause an interaction (possibly severe) when taken with the following drugs: Hypotensive drugs.
Preparations/Dosage: Crude Herb: 3-9 grams. Leaves: Chop up and sprinkle over food. Syrup (*syrupus allii*): 1-4 drachms (4-15 cc.).

Cinnamon, Cassia (sin e·men, kash e)
(*Cinnamomum cassia*)

Synonyms/Related Species: Bastard Cinnamon, Canton Cassia, Cassia, Chinese Cassia Buds, Chinese Cinnamon, False Cinnamon, Kasia, Qāsa', and Qesi'ah.
Family/Class: Lauraceae (laurel).
Habitat: Asia, Ceylon, China, Europe, Japan, Java, Mexico, Myanmar (formerly Burma), South America, Sumatra, and Vietnam.
Flavor: Pungent.
Parts Used: Bark.
Properties: Analgesic, anesthetic (local), antibiotic, antiemetic, antifungal, antigalactic, antimicrobic, antiphlogistic, antispasmodic, aromatic, astringent, carminative, counterirritant, demulcent, diaphoretic, emmenagogue, expectorant, hemostatic, parasiticide, stimulant, and stomachic.
Constituents: Cinnamic aldehyde, cinnamic acid, cinnamyl acetate, eugenic acid (eugenol), inulin (starch), monosaccharides, mucilage, orthocumaric aldehyde, phenylpropyl acetate, phellandrene, tannic acid, and volatile oil.
Historical Uses: Amenorrhea, angina, appetite loss, arthritis, bleeding, bronchitis, colds, colic, cough, cramps, diarrhea, digestive complaints, dysentery, dysmenorrhea, enuresis, erectile dysfunction, exhaustion, fever (ephemeral, rheumatic), flatulence, gastritis, gastrointestinal problems, hemorrhage (metrorrhagia), indigestion, infection (bacterial, fungal), inflammation, influenza, insufficiency (venous), irritable bowel syndrome (IBS), menopausal/menstrual problems, menorrhagia, mucus, muscle and joint pain, nausea, pain, parasites respiratory conditions, rheumatism, spasmodic conditions, substitute for ceylon cinnamon (*cinnamomum zeylanicum*), hernias (scrotal), ulcer (duodenal, gastric, peptic, stasis), wheezing, and vomiting.
Discussion: May aid digestion; clear and open bronchial passages; diminish or suppress lactation; enhance immune system, kidney, liver, stomach, and urinary system functions; increase circulation; inhibit or destroy developement and growth of bacteria and other

microorganisms; promote motility and perspiration; soothe mucous membrane irritation; stimulate menstruation.
Cautions/Contraindications: Avoid use if pregnant or breast-feeding, or if you have an allergy, high fever, hypertension, irritable bowel syndrome (IBS), a prostate problem, or suffer from emaciation, or if you have a blood coagulation problem. Cassia cinnamon is unrelated to the sennas (*cassia spp.*). Individuals who are allergic to balsam should avoid using cinnamon. May cause allergic reactions and dermatitis in susceptible individuals. Some persons may experience bleeding or increased clotting time when using this herb with anticoagulant drugs or aspirin. Not for long-term use.
Adverse Reactions: Bleeding (possibly serious), coagulation problems, hematuria (blood in the urine), nausea, respiratory distress, and/or vomiting.
Herb/Drug Interactions: This herb could cause an interaction (possibly severe) when taken with the following drugs: Anticoagulant drugs, Salicylates, and Subsalicylates.
Preparations/Dosage: Crude Herb: 3-9 grams. Bark (powdered): Average dose in substance 10-20 grains (0.666-1.333 gm.). Oil of Cinnamon (*oleum cinnamomum*): 1-3 drops (0.06-0.2 cc.) in water or on a sugarcube.
Isolation: Cinnamic aldehyde: Average dose of ½-2 drops (0.025-0.1 cc.) for use as an anesthetic and antimicrobic.
Note: Cassia cinnamon has a much stronger flavor than Ceylon cinnamon.

Cinnamon, Ceylon (sin e·men, sā·län)
(*Cinnamomum zeylanicum*)

Synonyms/Related Species: Amboyna Cinnamon (*cinnamomum culiawan*), Cinnamon Bark, Saigon Cinnamon (*cinnamomum saigonicum*), Kinnamōmon, and Qinnāmōn.
Family/Class: Lauraceae (laurel).
Habitat: Asia, Brazil, Ceylon, China, India, Jamaica, Java, Malabar, Mauritius, Saigon, Sri Lanka, and Sumatra.
Flavor: Pungent/sweet.
Parts Used: Bark.
Properties: Analgesic, antibiotic, anticarcinogen, antifungal, antiphlogistic, antiviral, aromatic, astringent, carminative, diaphoretic, expectorant, hemostatic, laxative, stimulant, stomachic, and vasodilator.
Constituents: Cinnamate, cinnamic aldehyde, cinnamic acid, coumarin, eugenic acid (eugenol), gum, inulin (starch), mannitol (mannite), minerals (calcium), monosaccharides, mucilage, resin, tannic acid, and volatile oil.
Historical Uses: Appetite loss, arthritis, bleeding, bronchitis, cancer (liver), candida, cardiovascular conditions, chills, colds, cough, cramps, diarrhea, digestive complaints, diarrhea, escherichia coli (e-coli), fever (ephemeral, rheumatic), fibroids, flatulence, flavoring agent, hemorrhage (metrorrhagia), indigestion, infection (bacterial, fungal, urinary tract, viral), inflammation, influenza, lesions (tubercle), menstrual problems, moniliasis, muscle and joint pain, nausea, pain, periodontal disease, rheumatism, scrofula, spasmodic conditions, tuberculosis, ulcer (fistula, peptic, tuberculous), vomiting, and wounds (minor).
Discussion: May aid digestion; cause blood vessel dilatation; clear and open bronchial passages; decrease the effect of carcinogens; enhance liver, spleen, stomach, and urinary system functions; increase circulation; inhibit or destroy developement and growth of bacteria and other

microorganisms; promote bowel evacuation, motility, and perspiration; serve as an adjuvant to HIV (human immunodeficiency virus) or AIDS (acquired immune deficiency syndrome) therapies; stimulate all vital body functions.

Cautions/Contraindications: Avoid use if pregnant or breast-feeding, or if you have an allergy, high fever, hypertension, irritable bowel syndrome (IBS), or a prostate problem. Individuals who are allergic to balsam should avoid using cinnamon. May cause allergic reactions and dermatitis in susceptible individuals.

Adverse Reactions: Hematuria (blood in the urine), nausea, respiratory distress, and/or vomiting.

Herb/Drug Interactions: This herb could cause an interaction (possibly severe) when taken with the following drugs: None known.

Preparations/Dosage: Crude Herb: 3-6 grams. Bark (powdered): Average dose in substance 3-6 grains (0.2-0.4 gm.). Cinnamon Water (*aqua cinnamomum*): 1-2 ounces per day. Extract: 5-10 drops (0.333-0.666 cc.) one to two times per day. Oil of Cinnamon (oleum cinnamomum): 1½ drops (0.1 cc.) in water or on a sugarcube. Tincture: 10-15 drops (0.666-1 cc.) one to three times per day.

Isolation: Cinnamic aldehyde: Average dose of ½-2 drops (0.025-0.1 cc.) for use as an anesthetic and antimicrobic. Mannitol hexanitrate: Average dose of 15-60 mg. for use as a vasodilator.

Cinnamon, White (sin e·men, hwīt)
(*Canella alba*)

Synonyms/Related Species: American Canella (*canella winterana*), Canella Cinnamon, Jamaica Canella (*canella macranthum*), Malambo Bark (*canella axillaries*), White Wood, and Wild Cinnamon (*canella inners*).

Family/Class: Canellaceae (canella).

Habitat: The Bahamas, Brazil, the Caribbean, Florida, India, and Jamaica.

Flavor: Pungent.

Parts Used: Bark (cork layer removed).

Properties: Antiperiodic, antiphlogistic, antiscorbutic, aromatic, carminative, laxative, malariacidal, stimulant, stomachic, tonic, and vasodilator.

Constituents: Albumin (albumen), bitter principle, eucalyptol (cineol), eugenic acid (eugenol), gum, inulin (starch), mannitol (mannite), resin, terpenes, vitamins (C (ascorbic acid), and volatile oil.

Historical Uses: Ague, asthma, bronchitis, colic, dermatitis, diarrhea, digestive complaints, diphtheria, fever (ephemeral, intermittent), flatulence, flavoring agent, gastritis, gastrointestinal problems, indigestion, insufficiency (venous), malaria, parasites (malarial plasmodia), rash, respiratory conditions, scurvy, skin problems, toothache, ulcer (duodenal, gastric, peptic, stasis, syriac), urethritis, and wounds (minor).

Discussion: May aid digestion; cause blood vessel dilatation; enhance stomach functions; increase circulation; promote bowel evacuation; restore normal tone to tissues; stimulate peristalsis.

Cautions/Contraindications: Avoid use if pregnant or breast-feeding, or if you have an allergy, high fever, hypertension, irritable bowel syndrome (IBS), or a prostate problem. Individuals

who are allergic to balsam should avoid using cinnamon. May cause allergic reactions and dermatitis in susceptible individuals.
Adverse Reactions: Hematuria (blood in the urine), nausea, respiratory distress, and/or vomiting.
Herb/Drug Interactions: This herb could cause an interaction (possibly severe) when taken with the following drugs: None known.
Preparations/Dosage: Bark (powdered): Average dose in substance 10-40 grains (0.666-2.666 gm.).
Isolation: Eucalyptol: 5 drops (0.3 cc.) in atomization or inhalation therapy for use in respiratory conditions. Mannitol hexanitrate: Average dose of 15-60 mg. for use as a vasodilator.

Cinquefoil (sink fo'il)
(*Potentilla canadensis*)

Synonyms/Related Species: Arctic Cinquefoil (*potentilla hyparctica*), Biscuits, Bloodroot, Bush Cinquefoil, Crampweed, Earthbank, English Sarsaparilla, European Cinquefoil (*potentilla tormentilla*), Ewe Daisy, Five Finger Blossom, Five Fingered Grass, Five Fingers, Five-Leaf Grass (*potentilla reptans*), Goose Tansy, Goosewort, Graceful Cinquefoil (*potentilla gracilis*), Marsh Cinquefoil (*potentilla palustris*), Moor Grass, One-Flowered Cinquefoil (*potentilla uniflora*), Potentilla, Prince's Feather, Quinquefolium, Septfoil, Shepherd's Knapperty, Shepherd's Knot, Shrubby Cinquefoil (*potentilla fruticosa*), Silver Cinquefoil, Silverweed (*potentilla anserine*), Snow Cinquefoil (*potentilla nivea*), Sticky Cinquefoil (*potentilla glandulosa*), Sunkfield, Synkefoyle, Thormantle, Tormentilla, Trailing Tansy, Turmentill, Upright Septfoil (*potentilla erecta*), Villous Cinquefoil (*potentilla villosa*), and Wild Agrimony.
Family/Class: Rosaceae (rose).
Habitat: The Alpine zone, Europe, and North America.
Flavor: Bitter/sweet.
Parts Used: Flowers, leaves, root (excluding shrubby cinquefoil *potentilla fruticosa*), stems.
Properties: Analgesic, anticarcinogen, antiperiodic, antiphlogistic, antiscorbutic, antispasmodic, aromatic, astringent, carminative, diuretic, hemostatic, malariacidal, stimulant, tonic, and vulnerary.
Constituents: Coumarin, ellagic acid, minerals (potassium), organic acid, phloroglucin, protocatechuic acid, quercetin, resin, scopoletin, tannic acid, umbelliferone, and vitamin C (ascorbic acid).
Historical Uses: Acidity (gastric), age spots, ague, arthritis, bleeding, blisters, bruises, calculus, cancer, canker sores, cholera, colic, congestion (uterine, vaginal), cough, cramps, diarrhea, digestive complaints, dysentery, dysmenorrhea, enteritis, eyewash, fainting, fever (ephemeral, intermittent), flatulence, freckles, gargle/mouth rinse, gastritis, gastrointestinal problems, gleet, gonorrhea, gout, headache, hemorrhage (metrorrhagia), hemorrhoids, indigestion, infection (sexually transmitted), inflammation, insect bites or stings, irritable bowel syndrome (IBS), jaundice, laryngitis, leukorrhea, liver problems, malaria, menorrhagia, muscle and joint pain, nosebleed, pain, parasites (malarial plasmodia), periodontal disease, pimples, poison ivy/oak, premenstrual syndrome (PMS), sciatica, scurvy, sexually transmitted diseases (STDs), shingles, skin problems, small pox, snakebite, sores, sore throat, spasmodic conditions, stomach cramps, sunburn, tetanus, tonsillitis, toothache, trismus (lockjaw), ulcer (duodenal, gastric, peptic, stasis),

urethritis, vaginitis, warts (digitate, filiform, fugitive, glabra, mother, plana juvenilis, plantar, seborrhoeic, vulgaris), whooping cough, windburn, and wounds (minor).
Discussion: May aid digestion; decrease the effect of carcinogens; promote urine flow; restore normal tone to tissues; speed healing; stimulate uterine contractions.
Cautions/Contraindications: Avoid use if pregnant or breast-feeding.
Adverse Reactions: Gastrointestinal irritation hematuria (blood in the urine), nausea, and/or vomiting.
Herb/Drug Interactions: This herb could cause an interaction (possibly severe) when taken with the following drugs: None known.
Preparations/Dosage: Crude Herb: 3-6 grams. Decoction: ½-1 cup per day. Extract: 5-10 drops (0.333-0.666 cc.). Infusion: 1-2 cups per day. Juice: 2-4 ounces in water per day. Root (powdered): Average dose in substance ¼-½ teaspoon. Tincture: 10-30 drops (0.666-2 cc.) one to three times per day.

Clove (klōv)
(*Syzygium aromaticum*)

Synonyms/Related Species: Clavus, Clove Tree, and Clowe.
Family/Class: Myrtaceae (myrtle).
Habitat: Brazil, India, Indonesia, Jamaica, Madagascar, the Molucca Islands, the Philippines, Sri Lanka, Sumatra, and Tanzania.
Flavor: Pungent.
Parts Used: Flowerbuds (dried).
Properties: Analgesic, anesthetic (local), antibiotic, anticarcinogen, antiemetic, antifungal, antioxidant, antiphlogistic, antiseptic, antispasmodic, antiviral, aphrodisiac, aromatic, carminative, expectorant, and parasiticide.
Constituents: Caryophyllin, eugenol (eugenic acid), flavonoids, gum, minerals (calcium, magnesium, phosphorus, potassium, sodium), resin, tannic acid, triterpenes, vitamins (A, B_1 (thiamine), B_2 (riboflavin), B_3 (niacin), B_5 (pantothenic acid), B_6 (pyridoxine), B_{12}, B_x (para-aminobenzoic acid (PABA), C (ascorbic acid), H (biotin), M (folic acid), volatile oil, and wax.
Historical Uses: Athlete's foot, bronchitis, cancer (stomach), colds, colitis, cough, cystitis, chronic fatigue syndrome (CFS), flavoring agent, diarrhea, digestive complaints, dizziness, dysentery, earache, epilepsy, Epstein Barr Virus (EBV), erectile dysfunction, fever (ephemeral, herpetic), fibromyalgia, flatulence, halitosis, herpes, hiccups, hypotension, indigestion, infection (bacterial, fungal, viral), infertility, inflammation, kidney problems, mononucleosis (infectious), mucus, muscle and joint pain, nausea, pain, palsy (Bell's), parasites (ringworm), periodontal disease, poisoning (food), respiratory conditions, sexually transmitted diseases (STDs), skin problems, spasmodic conditions, toothache, tumors, ulcer (peptic, stasis), urinary problems, vomiting, warts (digitate, filiform, fugitive, glabra, mother, plana juvenilis, plantar, seborrhoeic, vulgaris), and wounds (minor).
Discussion: May aid digestion; arouse sexual impulses; clear and open bronchial passages; decrease the effect of carcinogens; increase circulation; inhibit oxidation and inhibit or destroy developement and growth of bacteria and other microorganisms; protect against cancer (stomach); stimulate the libido.

Cautions/Contraindications: Avoid use if pregnant or breast-feeding, or if you have a history of cancer. May increase the effectiveness of antiviral drugs. Do not administer to children under 12 years old. May cause dermatitis in susceptible individuals.
Adverse Reactions: Edema, gastrointestinal problems, mucous membrane irritation, nausea, and/or vomiting.
Herb/Drug Interactions: This herb could cause an interaction (possibly severe) when taken with the following drugs: Antiviral drugs.
Preparations/Dosage: Crude Herb: 2-5 grams. Flowerbuds (powdered): Average dose in substance 5-10 grains (0.324-0.666 gm.). Infusion: ¼-½ cup per day. Oil of Cloves (*oleum caryophylli*): 2-5 drops (0.133-0.333 cc.) in water, on a sugarcube, or dropped directly into an aching tooth cavity. Tincture: 5-30 drops (0.333-2 cc.) one to three times per day.

Coconut (kō ke·nut)
(*Cocos nucifera*)

Synonyms/Related Species: Coco Palm.
Family/Class: Palmaceae (palm).
Habitat: Hawaii, Java, and other tropical regions.
Flavor: Sweet.
Parts Used: Milk, nutmeat, oil.
Properties: Astringent, humectant, and nutritive.
Constituents: Chloride, fatty acids (oleic, palmitic, stearic), fixed oils (olein, palmitin, stearin), minerals (chlorine, magnesium, sodium, sulfur), monosaccharides, and tannic acid.
Historical Uses: Bleeding, burns (minor), dietary supplementation, flavoring agent (milk, nutmeat), malnutrition, toothache, ulcer (duodenal, gastric, peptic, stasis), and wounds (minor).
Discussion: May provide dietary supplementation; serve as a nutritional adjuvant to therapeutic programs; soften and soothe the skin.
Cautions/Contraindications: Avoid use if pregnant or breast-feeding.
Adverse Reactions: Diarrhea, edema, nausea, and/or vomiting.
Herb/Drug Interactions: This herb could cause an interaction (possibly severe) when taken with the following drugs: None known.
Preparations/Dosage: Milk and/or Nutmeat (fresh/dried): May be ingested freely. Oil: External/topical use. Sap: Used to make a dark, coarse, crude sugar known as jaggery or palm sugar, and also a beverage known as palm wine or toddy.

Codonopsis (kod·o·nop·ses)
(*Codonopsis tangsheng*)

Synonyms/Related Species: Poor Man's Ginseng and Tangshen.
Family/Class: Campanulaceae (bellflower).
Habitat: Asia with cultivation worldwide.
Flavor: Bitter/sweet.
Parts Used: Root.
Properties: Alterative, analgesic, antacid, anticarcinogen, antidepressant, antiphlogistic, antispasmodic, carminative, demulcent, expectorant, hemostatic, hypoglycemic, hypotensive, stimulant, stomachic, tonic, and vasodilator.

Constituents: Aglycone (genin), fatty acids (arachidonic, linoleic, linolenic, oleic, palmitic, stearic), fixed oils (olein, palmitin, stearin), gum, inulin (starch), minerals (calcium, copper, iron, magnesium, manganese, phosphorus, potassium, silicon, sodium, sulfur, tin, zinc), monosaccharides, pectic acid, pectin, polysaccharides, resin, saponins, silicic acid, sterols, vitamins (A, B_1 (thiamine), B_2 (riboflavin), B_3 (niacin), B_{12}, choline, E (alpha-tocopheral), and volatile oil.

Historical Uses: Acidity (gastric), age spots, anemia, anxiety, appetite loss, arthritis, asthma, auditory problems, bleeding, bronchitis, cancer, cardiovascular conditions, chronic fatigue syndrome (CFS), cirrhosis, colds, constipation, cough, cramps, croup, Cushing's disease, cystitis, debility, depression (mild/moderate), diarrhea, diabetes, digestive complaints, diminished sex drive, diphtheria, edema, Epstein Barr Virus (EBV), erectile dysfunction, exhaustion, fatigue, fever (ephemeral, rheumatic), fibromyalgia, flatulence, headache, hemorrhage, hyperglycemia, hypertension (mild/moderate), indigestion, infection, infertility, inflammation, influenza, lochia, lupus, Lyme disease, memory/cognitive problems, menopausal/menstrual problems, mononucleosis (infectious), mucus, muscle and joint pain, nausea, nervous conditions, pain, respiratory conditions, rheumatism, shock, shortness of breath, sores, spasmodic conditions, substitute for ginseng (*panax ginseng*), thirst, ulcer (peptic), urinary problems, visual disturbances, and vomiting.

Discussion: May aid digestion; balance blood pressure levels; cause blood vessel dilatation; clear and open bronchial passages; decrease the effect of carcinogens; enhance cardiovascular system, circulatory system, glandular system, hormonal system, nervous system, reproductive system, spleen, and stomach functions; improve memory, cognition, and sexual performance; increase body fluids, endurance, energy, longevity, lung capacity, mental acuity, red and white blood cell counts, resistance to illness, stamina, and vitality; neutralize acidity; offset the negative effects of chemotherapy and radiation therapy; prevent the deposition of fat in the liver; reduce blood pressure levels, blood sugar levels, cholesterol levels, and pepsin secretions in the stomach; reestablish healthy system functions; restore normal tone to tissues; slow the aging process; soothe mucous membrane irritation; stimulate the immune system; strengthen auditory function, the bones, ligaments, tendons, and vision.

Cautions/Contraindications: Avoid use if pregnant or breast-feeding, or if you have been diagnosed with acute inflammatory disease, or if your stomach does not produce enough acid to digest food properly. May cause insomnia when consumed with beverages or foods containing caffeine. Some persons may experience bleeding or increased clotting time when using this herb with anticoagulant drugs or aspirin.

Adverse Reactions: Bleeding (possibly serious), breast tenderness, coagulation problems, diarrhea (possibly bloody), dizziness, edema, elevated blood pressure levels, fever, gastrointestinal cramps (severe), hematuria (blood in the urine), hemorrhage, menstrual problems, nausea, skin rash, sleep disturbances, and/or vomiting.

Herb/Drug Interactions: This herb could cause an interaction (possibly severe) when taken with the following drugs: Antidiabetic drugs, Anticoagulant drugs, Corticosteroids, Hypotensive drugs, Monoamine Oxidase Inhibitor (MAOI) drugs, Salicylates, and Subsalicylates.

Preparations/Dosage: Crude Herb: 6-12 grams. Decoction: ½-1 cup per day. Tincture: 15-30 drops (1-2 cc.) one to three times per day.

<u>Note</u>: Codonopsis is milder in action and safer than ginseng, and can be administered for a longer period of time.

Coffee (kôf ē)
(*Coffea arabica*)

Synonyms/Related Species: Caffea, Coffee Shrub, and Qahveh.
Family/Class: Rubiaceae (madder).
Habitat: Africa, Arabia, Asia, and Columbia.
Flavor: Bitter.
Parts Used: Leaves, seeds (dried).
Properties: Antiphlogistic, antispasmodic, aromatic, astringent, diuretic, hemostatic, hypotensive, stimulant, and vasodilator.
Constituents: Alkaloids, caffeic acid, caffeine, carbohydrates, chlorogenic acid, fats, ferulic acid, gum, minerals (magnesium), monosaccharides, protein, tannic acid, theobromine, theophylline, trigonelline, and wax.
Historical Uses: Asthma, bleeding, cardiac conditions, colds, congestive heart failure, constipation, diarrhea, dysmenorrhea, edema, fatigue, fever, flavoring agent, headache, hypertension (mild/moderate), inflammation, influenza, jet lag, menstrual problems, migraine, mucus, muscle and joint pain, pain, poisoning (opium), rheumatism, weight loss, whooping cough, and wounds (minor).
Discussion: May adjust the circadian rhythm, thus helping to minimize jet lag, which occurs after flying across time-zones; cause blood vessel dilatation; clear and open bronchial passages; ease alcohol, morphine, and opium withdrawal symptoms; increase energy, endurance, and stamina; promote urine flow; reduce blood pressure levels and fertility in women; serve as an antidote to opium poisoning; stimulate the cardiovascular system, the nervous system, gastric secretions, and metabolism.
Cautions/Contraindications: Avoid use if pregnant or breast-feeding, or if you have anemia, anxiety/panic attacks, chronic digestive complaints, fertility problems, a sensitive cardiovascular system, convulsions, diabetes, hypercholesteremia, hyperthyroidism, kidney disease, menorrhagia, or ulcer (gastric, peptic), or if you have a history of cancer, heart disease, or stroke (apoplectic). Counteracts the sedative effects of antihistamines. Interferes with iron absorption. May interfere with the absorption of other medications. Symptoms of caffeine withdrawal consist of but are not limited to gastrointestinal upset, headache, insomnia, irritability, jitters, or trembling.
Adverse Reactions: Acidity (gastric), addictions, anxiety, appetite loss, arrhythmia, benign breast disease, confusion, constipation, diarrhea, dizziness, gastritis, gastrointestinal problems, headache, heart attack (increased risk), elevated blood pressure and cholesterol levels, indigestion, insomnia, irritable bowel syndrome (IBS), migraine, nausea, nervous conditions, premenstrual syndrome (PMS), respiratory conditions, restlessness, spasmodic conditions, tinnitus, trembling, and/or vomiting.
Herb/Drug Interactions: This herb could cause an interaction (possibly severe) when taken with the following drugs: Antihistamine drugs, Caffeine, Hypotensive drugs, and other Medications/Products containing caffeine.
Herb/Herb Interactions: Do not use with other herbs containing high amounts of caffeine such as Maté (*ilex paraguayiensis*), Guarana (*paullinia cupana*), and Cola Nut (*Cola acuminata*).
Preparations/Dosage: Crude Herb (ground): 3-9 grams.
Isolation: Caffeine: Soluble in alcohol and water. Average dose of 1-3 grains (0.06-0.2 gm.) for use as a diuretic, nervine, and stimulant, and in poisoning (opium). Theobromine calcium gluconate: Average dose of 0.32-0.65 gm. for use in hypertension. Theobromine salicylate:

Soluble (sparingly) in water. Average dose of 15 grains (1 gm.) for use as a diuretic. Theobromine sodiosalicylate: Used in a 5% solution, average dose of 15 drops (1cc.) for use as a diuretic. Theobromine and sodium acetate: Average dose of 15-45 grains (1-3 gm.) for use as a powerful diuretic (powerful). Theophylline and sodium acetate: Average dose of 2-5 grains (0.12-0.3 gm.) for use as a diuretic.

Cohosh, Black (kō hosh, blak)
(*Cimicifuga racemosa*)

Synonyms/Related Species: Black Snakeroot, Bugbane, Bugwort, Rattle Root, Rattleweed, Richweed, Squawroot, Tall Bugbane, and Western Bugbane (*cimicifuga elata*).
Family/Class: Ranunculaceae (buttercup).
Habitat: Europe and North America.
Flavor: Bitter/pungent.
Parts Used: Root.
Properties: Alterative, anticarcinogen, antiperiodic, antiphlogistic, antispasmodic, astringent, cardiant, depurative, diaphoretic, diuretic, emetic, emmenagogue, expectorant, hemostatic, hypoglycemic, hypotensive, lithotriptic, malariacidal, narcotic, oxytocic, sedative, stimulant, tonic, vasodilator, and vesicant.
Constituents: Bitter principle, cimicifugin, fatty acids (oleic, palmitic, stearic), ferulic acid, fixed oils (olein, palmitin, stearin), glycosides, gum, inulin (starch), minerals (calcium, iron, magnesium, phosphorus, potassium, silicon), monosaccharides, phytoestrogen, protoanemonin, resin, salycilates, saponins, tannic acid, vitamins (A, B_1 (thiamine), B_2 (riboflavin), B_3 (niacin), B_5 (pantothenic acid), B_6 (pyridoxine), B_{12}, B_x (para-aminobenzoic acid (PABA), choline, H (biotin), inositol, M (folic acid), volatile oil, and wax.
Historical Uses: Ague, amenorrhea, arrhythmia, arthritis, asthma, bladder problems, bleeding, bronchitis, calculus, cancer (prostate), cholera, chorea, colds, convulsions, cough, cramps, diabetes, diarrhea, digestive complaints, dryness (vaginal), dysmenorrhea, edema, epilepsy, fatigue, fever (ephemeral, enteric, intermittent, rheumatic, yellow), gallstones, gastrointestinal problems, glandular problems, headache, hemorrhage, hormonal imbalances, hot flashes, hyperglycemia, hypertension (mild/moderate), hysteria, indigestion, inflammation, influenza, insect bites or stings, insomnia, insufficiency (circulatory), kidney stones, lesions (tubercle), liver problems, lung problems, lumbago, malaria, measles, meningitis, menopausal/menstrual problems, mood swings, mucus, muscle and joint pain, nervous conditions, neuralgia, pain, parasites (malarial plasmodia), premenstrual syndrome (PMS), prolapse (uterine), rapid pulse rate, rash, rheumatism, scrofula, sexually transmitted diseases (STDs), shortness of breath, skin problems, small pox, snakebite, sores, spasmodic conditions, syphilis, tinnitus, tuberculosis, typhoid, ulcer (bouveret, fistula, syphilitic, tuberculous), uterine problems, and whooping cough.
Discussion: May balance the hormonal system; cause blood vessel dilatation; clear and open bronchial passages; decrease the effect of carcinogens; dissolve calculi; enhance digestive system, kidney, liver, nervous system, respiratory system, and spleen functions; increase circulation and the proliferation of vaginal tissue; promote perspiration and urine flow; purify the blood; reduce blood sugar levels and blood pressure levels; reestablish healthy system functions; restore normal tone to tissues; soothe mucous membrane irritation; stimulate the cardiovascular system, menstruation, and uterine contractions.

Cautions/Contraindications: Avoid use if pregnant or breast-feeding, or if you have an estrogen dependent cancer, or if you have a history of estrogen dependant cancers, or if you have heart disease. Estrogen containing substances may contribute to abnormal blood coagulation, migraine, and could promote the developement of certain types of estrogen dependant cancers. Not for long-term use.
Adverse Reactions: Blistering of the mouth and throat, blurred vision, convulsions, diarrhea (possibly bloody), dizziness, fainting, gastrointestinal cramps (severe), headache, hematuria (blood in the urine), kidney failure, nausea, salivation, vomiting, and/or possible death.
Herb/Drug Interactions: This herb could cause an interaction (possibly severe) when taken with the following drugs: Antidiabetic drugs, Hormones and Synthetic Substitutes (i.e. conjugated estrogens, contraceptives (oral, etc.), and other hormonal replacement therapy (HRT), Hypotensive drugs, and Sedative drugs.
Preparations/Dosage: Crude Herb: 3-9 grams. Decoction: 1-3 tablespoons one to four times per day. Extract: 5-10 drops (0.333-0.666 cc.) one to two times per day. Extract (powdered): Average dose in substance 4 grains (0.25 gm.). Tincture: 10-30 drops (0.666-2 cc.) one to three times per day.
Isolation: Cimicifugin: Average dose of 1-3 grains (0.06-0.19 gm.) used as an antispasmodic, diaphoretic, and narcotic.

Cohosh, Blue (kō hosh, bloo)
(*Caulophyllum thalictroids*)

Synonyms/Related Species: Beechdrops, Blueberry Root, Blue Ginseng, Papoose Root, Squaw Root, and Yellow Ginseng.
Family/Class: Berberidaceae (barberry).
Habitat: North America.
Flavor: Sweet/bitter/pungent.
Parts Used: Root.
Properties: Antibiotic, antiphlogistic, antispasmodic, cardiac depressant, diaphoretic, diuretic, emmenagogue, expectorant, oxytocic, and vesicant.
Constituents: Alkaloids, anagyrines, caulophylline, glycosides, gum, inulin (starch), minerals (calcium, iron, magnesium, phosphorus, potassium, silicon, sodium), resin, silicic acid, and vitamins (B_1 (thiamine), B_2 (riboflavin), B_3 (niacin), B_5 (pantothenic acid), B_6 (pyridoxine), B_{12}, B_x (para-aminobenzoic acid (PABA), E (alpha-tocopheral), H (biotin), M (folic acid).
Historical Uses: Ague, amenorrhea, anxiety, arrhythmia, arthritis, asthma, benign breast disease, bronchitis, coffee substitute, colds, colic, congestion (uterine, vaginal), convulsions, cough, cramps, debility, dehydration, diabetes, dysmenorrhea, edema, epilepsy, fatigue, fever (ephemeral, rheumatic), hiccups, hysteria, infection (bacterial, bladder, kidney), inflammation, insect bites or stings, insomnia, leukorrhea, meningitis, menstrual problems, mucus, muscle and joint pain, nausea, nervous conditions, neuralgia, respiratory conditions, restlessness, rheumatism, sore throat, spasmodic conditions, urinary problems, uterine problems, vaginitis, and whooping cough.
Discussion: May clear and open bronchial passages; diminish or reduce functional activity of the heart; enhance liver function; inhibit ovulation and inhibit development or destroy growth of bacteria and other microorganisms; promote perspiration and urine flow; serve as a contraceptive (female); stimulate menstruation and uterine contractions.

Cautions/Contraindications: Avoid use if pregnant or breast-feeding, or if you have diabetes, glaucoma, heart disease, hypertension, or a history heart attack or stroke (apoplectic). Berries are poisonous. Blue cohosh should be combined with other herbs and not used alone. May cause dermatitis in susceptible individuals. Not for long-term use. Use with professional guidance/supervision.
Adverse Reactions: Blistering of the mouth and throat, blurred vision, convulsions, cardiac failure, diarrhea, dizziness, edema, fainting, gastrointestinal cramps (severe), headache, hematuria (blood in the urine), hypotension, kidney failure, nausea, salivation, vomiting, and/or possible death.
Herb/Drug Interactions: This herb could cause an interaction (possibly severe) when taken with the following drugs: None known.
Preparations/Dosage: Crude Herb: 3-6 grams. Decoction: ¼-½ tablespoon per day. Extract: 3-5 drops (0.2-0.333 cc.) one to two times per day. Extract (solid): Average dose in substance 5-10 grains (0.324-0.666 gm.). Infusion: 1-2 tablespoons one to two times per day. Tincture: 5-10 drops (0.333-0.666 cc.) one to three times per day.

Cola Nut (kō le nut)
(*Cola acuminata*)

Synonyms/Related Species: Bissy Nut, Caffeine Nut, Guru Nut, and Kola Nut.
Family/Class: Sterculiaceae (cacao).
Habitat: Africa, Angola, India, Sierra Leone, South America, Togo, and other tropical regions.
Flavor: Bitter.
Parts Used: Seeds.
Properties: Aphrodisiac, astringent, cardiant, diuretic, emmenagogue, hemostatic, hypotensive, nervine, stimulant, tonic, and vasodilator.
Constituents: Alkaloids, betaine (lycine), caffeine, catechins, fats, glycosides, inulin (starch), monosaccharides, oligomeric proanthocyanidins, protein, tannic acid, theobromine, and theophylline.
Historical Uses: Amenorrhea, anorexia, asthma, bleeding, congestive heart failure (CHF), debility, depression (mild/moderate), diarrhea, edema, fatigue, flavoring agent, headache, hypertension (mild/moderate), inflammation, migraine, muscle and joint pain, nervous conditions, neuralgia, pain, poisoning (opium), rheumatism, and wounds (minor).
Discussion: May arouse sexual impulses; calm the nervous system; cause blood vessel dilatation; enhance glandular system, kidney, and liver functions; increase endurance, motility, and stamina; promote urine flow; reduce blood pressure levels; restore normal tone to tissues; stimulate the cardiovascular system, gastric secretions, and menstruation; suppress hunger and thirst.
Cautions/Contraindications: Avoid use if pregnant or breast-feeding, or if you have ulcer (duodenal, gastric, peptic).
Adverse Reactions: Arrhythmia, cardiac failure, excitability, insomnia, nausea, nervousness, restlessness, tachycardia, vomiting, and/or possible death.
Herb/Drug Interactions: This herb could cause an interaction (possibly severe) when taken with the following drugs: Caffeine, Hypotensive drugs, and other Medications/Products containing caffeine.

Herb/Herb Interactions: Do not use with other herbs containing high amounts of caffeine such as Maté (*ilex paraguayiensis*), Guarana (*paullinia cupana*), and Coffee (*coffea arabica*).
Preparations/Dosage: Capsules: 1-2 capsules. Crude herb: 1-6 grams. Extract: 20-30 drops (1.25-2 cc.). Extract (solid): 2-8 grains (0.133-0.5 gm.). Infusion: 1 cup. Tincture: 30-60 drops (2-4 cc.).
Isolation: Betaine: Average dose of 2-4 grains (0.13-0.26 gm.) for use as an emmenagogue. Caffeine: Soluble in alcohol and water. Average dose of 1-3 grains (0.06-0.2 gm.) for use as a diuretic, nervine, and stimulant, and in poisoning (opium). Theobromine calcium gluconate: Average dose of 0.32-0.65 gm. for use in hypertension. Theobromine salicylate: Soluble (sparingly) in water. Average dose of 15 grains (1 gm.) for use as a diuretic. Theobromine sodiosalicylate: Used in a 5% solution, average dose of 15 drops (1cc.) for use as a diuretic. Theobromine and sodium acetate: Average dose of 15-45 grains (1-3 gm.) for use as a powerful diuretic. Theophylline and sodium acetate: Average dose of 2-5 grains (0.12-0.3 gm.) for use as a diuretic.

Coltsfoot (kōlts foot)
(*Petasites frigidus*)

Synonyms/Related Species: Arctic Coltsfoot (*petasites nivalis*), Arrow-Leaved Coltsfoot (*petasites sagittatus*), British Tobacco, Bullsfoot, Butterbur (*petasites hybridus*), Chinese Coltsfoot (*petasites japonicus*), Coughwort, Donnhove, Fieldhove, Palmate-Leaved Coltsfoot, Sweet Coltsfoot, Umbrella Leaves, Umbrella Plant, and Western Coltsfoot.
Family/Class: Compositae (composite).
Habitat: Alaska, the Alpine and Subalpine zones, Asia, China, England, Europe, Germany, India, North America, and Sweden.
Flavor: Bitter.
Parts Used: Flowers, leaves.
Properties: Abortifacient, antiphlogistic, antispasmodic, astringent, cardiant, demulcent, diaphoretic, diuretic, expectorant, hemostatic, parasiticide, stimulant, and tonic.
Constituents: Alkaloids, arabinose, bitter principle, flavones, flavonoids, galactose, glycosides, inulin (starch), minerals (calcium, copper, iron, manganese, potassium, sulfur, zinc), monosaccharides, mucilage, pectic acid, pectin, polysaccharides, quercetin, resin, rutin, saponins, senecionine, sterols, tannic acid, triterpenes, vitamins (A, B6 (pyridoxine), B_{12}, C (ascorbic acid), and volatile oil.
Historical Uses: Abscess, appetite loss, arthritis, asthma, bleeding, bronchitis, burns (minor), calculus, cardiovascular conditions, chills, colds, cough, cystitis, diarrhea, dysmenorrhea, emphysema, erysipelas, fever (ephemeral, rheumatic), gallbladder problems, gastritis, gastrocardiac syndrome, gastroduodenitis, gastrointestinal problems, headache, herbal tobacco (leaves), infection (bacterial), inflammation, influenza, insect bites or stings, insomnia, insufficiency (pancreatic), laryngitis, lesions (tubercle), liver problems, lung problems, migraine, mucus, muscle and joint pain, nervous conditions, neuralgia, parasites (scabies), phlebitis, plague, pleurisy, pneumonia, respiratory conditions, rheumatism, scrofula, shortness of breath, silicatosis, skin problems, sores, sore throat, spasmodic conditions, tonsillitis, tracheitis, tuberculosis, ulcer (fistula, peptic, stasis, tuberculous), urinary problems, wheezing, whooping cough, and wounds (minor).

Discussion: May clear and open bronchial passages; enhance lung and pancreatic functions; induce abortion; prevent hemorrhage in persons with hypertension; promote perspiration and urine flow; reduce capillary fragility and tissue inflammation; restore normal tone to tissues; soothe mucous membrane irritation; stimulate appetite and the cardiovascular system.
Cautions/Contraindications: Avoid use if pregnant or breast-feeding, or if you have hypertension, or if you have a history of alcoholism or liver disease. Not for long-term use.
Adverse Reactions: Arrhythmia, diarrhea (possibly bloody), gastrointestinal cramps (severe), hematuria (blood in the urine), liver damage (often characterized by jaundice), nausea, and/or vomiting.
Herb/Drug Interactions: This herb could cause an interaction (possibly severe) when taken with the following drugs: None known.
Preparations/Dosage: Crude Herb: 3-9 grams. Infusion (flowers or leaves): 1 cup per day. Juice: 1-2 tablespoons in water per day. Tincture: 10-20 drops (0.666-1.25 cc.) one to three times per day.

Columbine (käl em·bīn)

(*Aquilegia canadensis*)

Synonyms/Related Species: Aquila, Blue Columbine, Colorado Columbine, Columba, Columbina, Crimson Columbine, Culverwort, Red Columbine (*aquilegia formosa*), Rocky Mountain Columbine, Wild Columbine (*aquilegia vulgaris*), and Yellow Columbine (*aquilegia flavescens*).
Family/Class: Ranunculaceae (buttercup).
Floral Emblem: Colorado.
Habitat: Europe and North America.
Flavor: Bitter/pungent.
Parts Used: Leaves, root, seeds.
Properties: Antiphlogistic, astringent, diaphoretic, diuretic, emetic, hemostatic, lithotriptic, oxytocic, parasiticide, stimulant, and vesicant.
Constituents: Alkaloids, protoanemonin, and volatile oil.
Historical Uses: Arthritis, bleeding, canker sores, cardiovascular conditions, cough, diarrhea, dizziness, fever (ephemeral, rheumatic), gallstones, hemorrhage (metrorrhagia), inflammation, insect bites or stings, jaundice, kidney problems, kidney stones, liver problems, muscle and joint pain, parasites (lice and their nits), rheumatism, sexually transmitted diseases (STDs), sores, sore throat, stomachache, and urinary calculus.
Discussion: May dissolve calculi; increase stamina; promote perspiration and urine flow; stimulate uterine contractions.
Cautions/Contraindications: Avoid use if pregnant or breast-feeding. Not for long-term use.
Adverse Reactions: Blistering of the mouth and throat, convulsions, diarrhea (severe), dizziness, fainting, hematuria (blood in the urine), kidney failure, nausea, salivation, stomach pain, vomiting, and/or possible death.
Herb/Drug Interactions: This herb could cause an interaction (possibly severe) when taken with the following drugs: None known.
Preparations/Dosage: Crude Herb: 3-6 grams. Infusion: 1-2 tablespoons one to two times per day. Tincture: 5-10 drops (0.333-0.666 cc.) one to three times per day.

Did You Know? *Aquilegia formosa* and *aquilegia flavescens* crossbreed, producing hybrid flowers that are both pink and yellow.

Comfrey (kum frē)
(*Symphytum officinale*)

Synonyms/Related Species: Black Root, Blackwort, Boneset, Bruisewort, Common Comfrey, Confirie, Consound Root, English Comfrey (*symphytum tuberosum*), Gum Plant, Healing Herb, Knitbone, Prickly Comfrey (*symphytum asperimum*), Russian Comfrey (*symphytum uplandicum*), Salsify, Slippery Root, Wallwort, and Yalluc.
Family/Class: Boraginaceae (borage).
Habitat: Asia, England, Europe, North America, Russia, and Scotland.
Flavor: Bitter/sweet.
Parts Used: Leaves, root.
Properties: Alterative, analgesic, anticarcinogen, antioxidant, antiphlogistic, astringent, carminative, demulcent, depurative, diuretic, expectorant, hemostatic, laxative, lithotriptic, nutritive, stimulant, stomachic, tonic, and vulnerary.
Constituents: Alkaloids, allantoin, amino acids (lysine), chlorophyll, inulin (starch), minerals (calcium, copper, iron, magnesium, phosphorus, potassium, silicon, sulfur, zinc), monosaccharides, mucilage, protein, pyrrolizidine, resin, saponins, silicic acid, tannic acid, triterpenes, vitamins (A, B_{12}, C (ascorbic acid), choline, E (alpha-tocopheral), and volatile oil.
Historical Uses: Abscess, acne, allergy (pollen), anemia, arthritis, asthma, athlete's foot, benign breast disease, bladder problems, bleeding, broken bones, bronchitis, bruises, burns (minor), bursitis, calculus, cancer, candida, cirrhosis, colds, colitis, congestion (uterine, vaginal), cough, cramps, dandruff, diabetes, diarrhea, dietary supplementation, digestive complaints, diphtheria, dysentery, eczema, emaciation, emphysema, fatigue, fever (ephemeral, hay, herpetic, rheumatic), flatulence, fractures, gallstones, gallbladder problems, gangrene, gargle/mouth rinse, gastritis, gastrointestinal problems, gout, hematuria, hemorrhage, hemorrhoids, herpes, hernias (hiatal), infection (bacterial), inflammation, injury (blunt-force), insect bites or stings, insufficiency (pancreatic), kidney problems, kidney stones, laryngitis, lesions (tubercle), leukemia, leukorrhea, liver problems, lung problems, malnutrition, menorrhagia, menstrual problems, mucous membrane problems, moniliasis, mucus, muscle and joint pain, pain, periodontal disease, pleurisy, pneumonia, psoriasis, respiratory conditions, rheumatism, scrofula, sexually transmitted diseases (STDs), sinusitis, skin problems, skin tags, sores, sore throat, sprain, substitute for spinach (young leaves), tonsillitis, trauma, tuberculosis, tumors, ulcer (duodenal, fistula, gastric, indolent, tuberculous), vaginitis, warts (digitate, filiform, fugitive, glabra, mother, plana juvenilis, plantar, seborrhoeic, vulgaris), and wounds (minor).
Discussion: May aid digestion; balance blood sugar levels; clear and open bronchial passages; decrease the effect of carcinogens; dissolve calculi; enhance digestive system, kidney, lung, and pancreatic system functions; increase circulation; inhibit oxidation; prevent the deposition of fat in the liver; promote bone growth, bowel evacuation, pepsin secretions, and urine flow; provide dietary supplementation; purify the blood; reestablish healthy system functions; restore normal tone to tissues; serve as a nutritional adjuvant to therapeutic programs; soothe mucous membrane irritation; speed healing; stimulate peristalsis and the proliferation of cells; strengthen epithelial cells and the skeletal system.

Cautions/Contraindications: Avoid use if pregnant or breast-feeding, or if you have a history of alcoholism, cancer, or liver disease, or if you are on a potassium restricted diet. Do not allow comfrey to come in contact with unaffected skin during external uses. Do not use on deep or gaping wounds and do not use for longer than 4 weeks at a time. Due to the speediness of this wound healer, make sure that all dirt and debris has been cleansed from the wound site prior to the application of comfrey. Do not confuse this plant with boneset (*eupatorium perfoliatum*). Do not confuse comfrey leaves with those of first year foxglove (*digitalis purpurea*) leaves. Due to recent controversy suggesting that prolonged internal use (2-3 months) of comfrey root may cause liver problems in some individuals, it may be advisable to refrain from using the herb for no more than 2 weeks at a time. External use recommended. Not for long-term use. Use with professional guidance/supervision.
Adverse Reactions: Diarrhea (severe/possibly bloody), gastrointestinal cramps (severe), hepatic veno-occlusive disease (HVOD), nausea, and/or vomiting.
Herb/Drug Interactions: This herb could cause an interaction (possibly severe) when taken with the following drugs: Antibiotic drugs, Corticosteroids, HMG-CoA Reductase Inhibitor drugs, Hypertensive drugs, and Hypotensive drugs.
Preparations/Dosage: Crude Herb (root): 6-12 grams. Crude Herb (leaves): 3-9 grams. Decoction: ¼ cup per day. Extract: 3-5 drops (0.2-0.333 cc.) one to two times per day. Infusion: ½-1 cup per day. Tincture (root): 5-10 drops (0.333-0.666 cc.) one to three times per day. Tincture (leaves): 10-15 drops (0.666-1 cc.) one to three times per day.

Condurango (kon·du·rang go)
(*Equatoria Garciana*)

Synonyms/Related Species: Condor Vine, Cundurangu, Eagle Vine, Gonolobus Condurango, and Marsdenia Condurango.
Family/Class: Asclepiadaceae (milkweed).
Habitat: Bolivia, Ceylon, the Andes Mountains of South America (generally on the Western exposure at altitudes of 4,000-5,000 feet), Ecuador, India, Java, and Peru.
Flavor: Bitter.
Parts Used: Bark.
Properties: Alterative, carminative, diuretic, emmenagogue, nervine, stimulant, stomachic, and tonic.
Constituents: Bitter principle, condurangin, glycosides, inulin (starch), monosaccharides, sterols, tannic acid, and volatile oil.
Historical Uses: Anxiety, appetite loss, cancer (early stages), digestive complaints, emaciation, flatulence, gastrointestinal problems, hyperacididty, indigestion, mucus, nervous conditions, sexually transmitted diseases (STDs), syphilis, and ulcer (gastric, syphilitic).
Discussion: May aid digestion; calm the nervous system and relax the nerves of the stomach; enhance functional activity of the stomach; increase circulation; promote urine flow; reestablish healthy system functions; restore normal tone to tissues; stimulate appetite and menstruation.
Cautions/Contraindications: Avoid use if pregnant or breast-feeding.
Adverse Reactions: Convulsions, nausea, paralysis, vertigo, visual disturbances, and/or vomiting.
Herb/Drug Interactions: This herb could cause an interaction (possibly severe) when taken with the following drugs: None known.

Preparations/Dosage: Crude Herb: 3-6 grams. Extract: 20-30 drops (1.25-2 cc.) one to two times per day. Infusion: 1 cup per day. Tincture: 15-30 drops (1-2 cc.) one to three times per day.
Did You Know? Peruvian Bark (*cinchona officinalis*), which contains the important constituent quinine, and Condurangu both originate in the same region and flourish only under identical climactic conditions.

Copaiba (kō·pā be)
(*Copaifera langsdorffii*)

Synonyms/Related Species: Balsam Copaiba (*copaifera officinalis*), Cupaiba, and South American Balsam.
Family/Class: Leguminosae (legume).
Habitat: Africa, India, and South America.
Flavor: Bitter/pungent.
Parts Used: Oleoresin.
Properties: Antibiotic, anticarcinogen, antiseptic, aromatic, carminative, diuretic, expectorant, laxative, and stimulant.
Constituents: Caryophyllin, resene, and volatile oil.
Historical Uses: Arthritis, bronchitis, cancer (basal cell carcinoma, skin), chilblains, colds, congestion (uterine, vaginal), cystitis, dandruff, diarrhea, eczema, edema, fever (ephemeral, herpetic), flatulence, gleet, gonorrhea, hemorrhoids, herpes, infection (bacterial, sexually transmitted, urinary tract), inflammation, leukorrhea, mucus, psoriasis, respiratory conditions, sexually transmitted diseases (STDs), skin problem, syphilis, ulcer (syphilitic), urethritis, and vaginitis.
Discussion: May aid digestion; clear and open bronchial passages; decrease the effect of carcinogens; inhibit development or destroy growth of bacteria and other microorganisms; promote bowel evacuation and urine flow; stimulate peristalsis.
Cautions/Contraindications: Avoid use if pregnant or breast-feeding, or if you are allergic to balsam. External uses only. May cause allergic reactions and dermatitis in susceptible individuals.
Adverse Reactions: Chills, cholera, fever, groin pain, hematuria (blood in the urine), insomnia, measle-like skin eruptions, mucous membrane problems, nausea, tremors, and/or vomiting.
Herb/Drug Interactions: This herb could cause an interaction (possibly severe) when taken with the following drugs: None known.
Preparations/Dosage: Oil of Copaiba (*oleum copaifera*): 5-20 drops (0.333-1.25 cc.) in water, on a sugarcube, or in capsule or pill form. Oleoresin (powdered): Average dose in substance 15-20 grains (0.98-1.333 gm.) used externally. Do not apply the resin in its raw form; dilute it with a good quality vegetable oil prior to application.

Coptis (kop tis)
(*Coptis trifolia*)

Synonyms/Related Species: Canker Root, Chinese Coptis (*coptis chinensis*), Chuen Lien, Goldthread, Hwang Lien, Indian Coptis, Japanese Coptis (*coptis anemonœfolia*), Mahmira,

Mishmi Bitter, Mouthroot, Mu Lien, Oregon Goldthread (*coptis laciniata*), Vegetable Gold, and Yellow Root.
Family/Class: Ranunculaceae (buttercup).
Habitat: Asia, Greenland, Iceland, India (Mishmi Mountains), North America, and Siberia.
Flavor: Bitter.
Parts Used: Root.
Properties: Antibiotic, anticarcinogen, antifungal, antiphlogistic, astringent, hypoglycemic, parasiticide, sedative, stimulant, tonic, and vesicant.
Constituents: Albumin (albumen), alkaloids, berberine, coptine, fatty acids (oleic, palmitic, stearic), fixed oils (olein, palmitin, stearin), lignin, monosaccharides, and protoanemonin.
Historical Uses: Appetite loss, arteriosclerosis, cancer (basal cell carcinoma), candida, canker sores, conjunctivitis, cravings (alcohol), digestive complaints, eyewash, fever (ephemeral, herpetic), gargle/mouth rinse, giardiasis, herpes, hyperglycemia, indigestion, infection (bacterial, fungal, urinary tract), inflammation, lesions (tubercle), moniliasis, osteomyelitis, parasites (trichomonas), periodontal disease, scrofula, sexually transmitted diseases (STDs), skin problems, sore throat, tuberculosis, and ulcer (fistula, tuberculous).
Discussion: May decrease the effect of carcinogens; destroy the craving for alcoholic beverages; inhibit abnormal cell growth and inhibit development or destroy growth of bacteria and other microorganisms; reduce blood sugar levels and cholesterol levels; restore normal tone to tissues; stimulate appetite.
Cautions/Contraindications: Avoid use if pregnant or breast-feeding, or if you have diabetes, diarrhea, indigestion, or Raynaud's disease. May interfere with the absorption of tetracycline antibiotics.
Adverse Reactions: Blistering of the mouth and throat, convulsions, dizziness, drowsiness, fainting, hypotension, hematuria (blood in the urine), kidney failure, salivation, vomiting, and/or possible death.
Herb/Drug Interactions: This herb could cause an interaction (possibly severe) when taken with the following drugs: Antibiotic drugs and Antidiabetic drugs.
Preparations/Dosage: Crude Herb: 1-3 grams. Decoction: 1 tablespoon one to two times per day. Extract: 3-5 drops (0.2-0.333 cc.) one to two times per day. Indian Coptis (*coptis teeta*) Root (powdered): Average dose in substance 5-10 grains (0.333-0.666 gm.). Goldthread (*coptis trifolia*) Root (powdered): Average dose in substance 10-20 grains (0.666-1.333 gm.). Tincture (root): 5-10 drops (0.333-0.666 cc.) one to three times per day.

Coriander (kôr ē·an der)

(*Coriandrum sativum*)

Synonyms/Related Species: Chinese Parsley, Cilantro, Goid, Koriandron, and Koros.
Family/Class: Umbelliferae (parsley).
Habitat: Africa, Asia, Britain, Egypt, England, Europe, Germany, India, the Mediterranean, North America, Russia, and South America.
Flavor: Pungent.
Parts Used: Leaves, seeds.
Properties: Alterative, antibiotic, antifungal, antioxidant, antiphlogistic, antispasmodic, aphrodisiac, aromatic, carminative, diaphoretic, diuretic, hypoglycemic, larvacide, stimulant, stomachic, and narcotic.

Constituents: Alkaloid, borneol, camphor, carvene (limonene), coumarin, fatty acids (arachidonic, linoleic, linolenic, oleic, palmitic, petroselinic, stearic), fixed oils (olein, palmitin, stearin), geraniol (rhodinol), linalool, malic acid, scopoline, umbelliferone, vitamins (C (ascorbic acid), and volatile oil.

Historical Uses: Allergy, appetite loss, arthritis, bladder problems, cancer (colon, stomach), chest pain, cough, diabetes, diarrhea, digestive complaints, dysentery, eyewash, fever (ephemeral, rheumatic), flatulence, flavoring agent, halitosis, headache, hemorrhoids, hyperglycemia, indigestion, infection (bacterial, fungal, urinary tract), inflammation, leprosy, measles, muscle and joint pain, nausea, preservative (meat), perfume, rash, rheumatism, spasmodic conditions, toothache, and wounds (minor).

Discussion: May aid digestion; arouse sexual impulses; destroy insect larvae that infest meat; enhance stomach and urinary system function; inhibit oxidation and inhibit or destroy developement and growth of bacteria and other microorganisms; promote perspiration and urine flow; protect against cancer (colon, stomach); reduce blood sugar and cholesterol levels; reestablish healthy system functions; stimulate appetite and gastric secretions.

Cautions/Contraindications: Avoid use if pregnant or breast-feeding. May cause allergic reactions in susceptible individuals.

Adverse Reactions: Diarrhea, hypersensitivity, stupor, nausea, and/or vomiting.

Herb/Drug Interactions: This herb could cause an interaction (possibly severe) when taken with the following drugs: Antidiabetic drugs.

Preparations/Dosage: Crude Herb: 3-9 grams. Infusion (crushed seeds): 1 cup per day. Leaves (fresh): Flavoring agent in baking/cooking or as a garnish. Leaves (powdered): Average dose in substance 20-60 grains (1.333-4 gm.). Oil of Coriander (*oleum coriandri*): 2-5 drops (0.133-0.333 cc.) in water or on a sugarcube. Seeds (powdered): Average dose in substance 10-60 grains (0.666-4 gm.). Tincture: 5-30 drops (0.333-2 cc.) one to three times per day.

Corn (kôrn)

(*Zea mays*)

Synonyms/Related Species: Cornsilk, Indian Corn, Maize, Yumixu, and Zea.

Family/Class: Graminaceae (grass).

Habitat: Africa, Australia, France, India, North America, South America, and other regions worldwide.

Flavor: Sweet/bland.

Parts Used: Kernels/seed, silk, stigmas.

Properties: Alterative, analgesic, antibiotic, antiemetic, antiphlogistic, antiseptic, demulcent, diuretic, hypotensive, lithotriptic, nutritive, stimulant, and vasodilator.

Constituents: Alkaloids, allantoin, anthocyanins, bitter principle, carbohydrates, cellulose, cryptoxanthin, fatty acids (oleic, palmitic, stearic), fixed oils (olein, palmitin, stearin), flavonoids, gluten, hordenine, inulin (starch), maisin, maizenic acid, menthol, minerals (magnesium, phosphorous, potassium, silicon, sodium, sulfur), monosaccharides, phosphoric acid, resin, saponins, silicic acid, sterols, tannic acid, terpineol, thymol, vitamins (B, B_3 (niacin), B_x (para-aminobenzoic acid (PABA), C (ascorbic acid), K), volatile oil, and zeaxanthin.

Historical Uses: Arteriosclerosis, baking (corn meal and corn starch), bladder problems, bronchitis, calculus, cardiovascular conditions, carpal tunnel syndrome, cholesterol, colds, convalescence, cough, cystitis, diarrhea, edema, enuresis (urinary incontinence), fever (ephemeral, rheumatic, enteric), food source, gallstones, gleet, gonorrhea, hypertension (mild/moderate), infection (bacterial, sexually transmitted, urinary tract), inflammation, jaundice, kidney problems, kidney stones, leukorrhea, liver problems, nausea, neuralgia, pain, premenstrual syndrome (PMS), prostate problems, prostatitis, rheumatism, sexually transmitted diseases (STDs), skin problems, stomatitis, ulcer (duodenal, gastric, peptic), urethritis, vomiting, and weight loss.

Discussion: May cause blood vessel dilatation; dissolve calculi; enhance cardiovascular system, intestinal system, liver, and urinary system functions; increase blood pressure levels; inhibit or destroy development and growth of bacteria and other microorganisms; promote urine flow; reduce blood pressure levels, electrolyte/potassium loss, and the frequency of nighttime urination; reestablish healthy system functions; soothe mucous membrane irritation; strengthen the urinary system.

Cautions/Contraindications: Avoid use if pregnant or breast-feeding. Atrial fibrillation, excessive potassium levels, and muscle twitches may occur with the use of hypertension drugs. May negate the bacteriostatic effects of sulfonamide drugs.

Adverse Reactions: Edema, nausea, and/or vomiting.

Herb/Drug Interactions: This herb could cause an interaction (possibly severe) when taken with the following drugs: Antibiotic drugs and Hypotensive drugs.

Preparations/Dosage: Crude Hherb (stigma): 3-9 grams. Crude Herb (silk): 6-15 grams. Extract (silk or stigma): 5-10 drops (0.333-0.666 cc.). Infusion (stigma): 1-2 cups per day. Infusion (silk): 1-2 tablespoons one to two times per day. Kernels: Dried and ground into meal, powdered and used as flour, or boil raw kernels as a vegetable. Syrup (stigma): ½-1 tablespoon in water one to two times per day. Tincture: 10-30 drops (0.666-2 cc.) one to three times per day.

Isolation: Maizenic acid: Average dose of ⅛ grain (0.008 gm.) for use as a diuretic. Menthol: Average dose of ½-2 grains (0.033-0.133 gm.) applied topically, for use as an analgesic. Thymol: Average dose of ½-2 grains (0.033-0.133 gm.) for use as an anthelmintic and antimicrobic, or in a 1:1000 solution, applied topically, for use as an antirheumatic and antiseptic.

Cornflower (kôrn flou er)

(*Centaurea cyanus*)

Synonyms/Related Species: Bachelor's Buttons, Bluebonnet, Blue Centaury, Bluet, Centauren, and Cyani.

Family/Class: Compositae (composite).

Floral Emblem: Texas.

Habitat: Europe, the Middle East, and North America.

Flavor: Bitter.

Parts Used: Flowers.

Properties: Antibiotic, antifungal, antiphlogistic, diuretic, emmenagogue, expectorant, hypotensive, laxative, lithotriptic, nervine, stimulant, tonic, and vasodilator.

Constituents: Anthocyanin, anthocyanidin, bitter principle, cyanin (coumarin glycoside), flavonoids, minerals (potassium, silicon), resin, saponins, silicic acid, tannic acid, vitamins (B, B_x (para-aminobenzoic acid (PABA), C (ascorbic acid), K), and volatile oil.

Historical Uses: Arteriosclerosis, bladder problems, bruises, calculus, candida, canker sores, cardiovascular conditions, cholesterol, colds, congestion (liver), conjunctivitis, cough, cystitis, dermatitis, eczema, edema, enuresis (urinary incontinence), eyewash, eye problems, fever (ephemeral), gallstones, gleet, gonorrhea, hypertension (mild/moderate), indigestion, infection (bacterial, fungal, sexually transmitted), inflammation, insect bites or stings, jaundice, kidney problems, kidney stones, menstrual problems, moniliasis, mucus, mumps, nervous conditions, paralysis (temporary), plague, potpourri, prostate problems, prostatitis, sexually transmitted diseases (STDs), snakebite, sores, toothache, ulcer (dendritic, duodenal, gastric, peptic), urethritis, urinary problems, and weight loss.

Discussion: May calm the nervous system; cause blood vessel dilatation; clear and open bronchial passages; dissolve calculi; enhance gallbladder, liver, and urinary system functions; inhibit development or destroy growth of bacteria and other microorganisms; promote bowel evacuation and urine flow; reduce blood pressure levels and the frequency of nighttime urination; stimulate menstruation and peristalsis; strengthen the urinary system.

Cautions/Contraindications: Avoid use if pregnant or breast-feeding. May negate the bacteriostatic effects of sulfonamide drugs.

Adverse Reactions: Diarrhea (possibly bloody), gastrointestinal cramps (severe), hematuria (blood in the urine), nausea, and/or vomiting.

Herb/Drug Interactions: This herb could cause an interaction (possibly severe) when taken with the following drugs: Antibiotic drugs and Hypotensive drugs.

Preparations/Dosage: Crude Herb: 1-3 grams. Infusion: 1-3 cups per day.

Corydalis (ke·rid e·lis)

(*Corydalis tuberosa*)

Synonyms/Related Species: Chinese Corydalis (*corydalis yanhusuo*), Early Fumitory (*corydalis cava*), Golden Corydalis (*corydalis aurea*), Golden Smoke, Korydallis, Pink Corydalis (*corydalis sempervirens*), and Turkey Corn.

Family/Class: Fumariaceae (fumitory).

Habitat: Alaska, Asia, Europe, North America, and the Yukon Territory.

Flavor: Bitter/pungent.

Parts Used: Root.

Properties: Alterative, analgesic, antiphlogistic, antispasmodic, diuretic, emmenagogue, hallucinogen, hypnotic, hypotensive, narcotic, sedative, tonic, tranquilizer, and vasodilator.

Constituents: Alkaloids, bitter principle, bulbocapnine, canadine, corybulbine, corycavine, corydaline, corydine, fumarine (protopine), fumaric acid, inulin (starch), isoquinoline, resin, and tetrahydropalmatine.

Historical Uses: Abdominal pain, angina, anxiety, arthritis, cataracts, chorea, convulsions, depression (mild/moderate), dysentery, dysmenorrhea, fever (ephemeral, rheumatic), flatulence, headache, hypertension (mild/moderate), hysteria, inflammation, insomnia, lesions (tubercle), melancholy, Meniere's disease, menstrual problems, muscle and joint pain, pain, palsy, Parkinson's disease, neurosis, nerve damage, nervous conditions, restless leg syndrome, rheumatism, scrofula, sexually transmitted diseases (STDs), skin problems, spasmodic conditions, syphilis, tuberculosis, tremors, ulcer (fistula, syphilitic, tuberculous), and urinary problems.

Discussion: May cause blood vessel dilatation; enhance cardiovascular system, liver, and lung functions; induce sleep; inhibit motor activities; promote urine flow; reduce blood pressure

levels; reestablish healthy system functions; restore normal tone to tissues; stimulate menstruation and peristalsis.
Cautions/Contraindications: Avoid use if pregnant or breast-feeding. Avoid single use of this herb. Combine it with skullcap or valerian. Not for long-term use. Use with professional guidance/supervision.
Adverse Reactions: Drowsiness, hallucinations, hysteria, muscle tremors, nausea, nervousness, stupor, and/or vomiting.
Herb/Drug Interactions: This herb could cause an interaction (possibly severe) when taken with the following drugs: Anxiolytic drugs and Hypotensive drugs.
Preparations/Dosage: Crude Herb: 3-12 grams. Decoction: ½-1 cup per day. Tincture: 5-20 drops (0.333-1.25 cc.).
Isolation: Corydaline: Average dose of 1-5 grains (0.066-0.333 gm.) for use as a diuretic and tonic. Protopine: Average dose of 40-100 grains (2.5-7 gm.) for use as an analgesic and hypnotic.

Costmary (kost mâr ē)
(*Chrysanthemum balsamita*)

Synonyms/Related Species: Balsam Herb, Coursemary, Herbe Sainte-Marie, and Mace.
Family/Class: Compositae (composite).
Habitat: Asia, England, and Europe.
Flavor: Pungent.
Parts Used: Leaves.
Properties: Alterative, antibiotic, antiphlogistic, aromatic, astringent, carminative, diaphoretic, diuretic, emmenagogue, laxative, stomachic, toxic, and vermin repellent.
Constituents: Tanacetin, tannic acid, and volatile oil.
Historical Uses: Blisters, bruises, burns (minor), colds, debility, dysentery, fever (ephemeral, rheumatic), flatulence, flavoring agent, gout, hair rinse, headache, indigestion, infection (bacterial), inflammation, influenza, insufficiency (venous), malnutrition, mucus, muscle and joint pain, potpourri, pruritus, respiratory conditions, rheumatism, sciatica, shingles, skin problem, sores, ulcer (duodenal, gastric, peptic, stasis, varicose), varicose veins, and vermin.
Discussion: May aid digestion; enhance liver, lung, nervous system, and stomach functions; inhibit or destroy development and growth of bacteria and other microorganisms; promote bowel evacuation, perspiration, and urine flow; purify the blood; reestablish healthy system functions; stimulate menstruation and peristalsis.
Cautions/Contraindications: Avoid use if pregnant or breast-feeding. Not for long-term use. Use with professional guidance/supervision.
Adverse Reactions: Abdominal pain, convulsions, nausea, respiratory distress, and/or vomiting.
Herb/Drug Interactions: This herb could cause an interaction (possibly severe) when taken with the following drugs: None known.
Preparations/Dosage: Crude Herb: 1-3 grams. Leaves (powdered): Average dose in substance ¼-½ teaspoon. Oil: 1-3 drops (0.066-0.2 cc.) in water or on a sugarcube. Tincture: 10-30 drops (0.666-2 cc.) one to three times per day.

Cotton (kot n)

(*Gossypium herbaceum*)

Synonyms/Related Species: Gossypii, Qutun, and Sea Island Cotton (*gossypium barbadense*).
Family/Class: Malvaceae (mallow).
Habitat: Africa, Asia, the Bahamas, Egypt, Europe, India, the Mediterranean, Persia, and the United States.
Flavor: Sweet/sour.
Parts Used: Bark (root), seeds.
Properties: Abortifacient, antiperiodic, antiphlogistic, demulcent, emmenagogue, hemostatic, malariacidal, oxytocic, stimulant, and tonic.
Constituents: Betaine (lycine), chlorophyll, fatty acids (oleic, palmitic, stearic), fixed oils (olein, palmitin, stearin), gossypiin, gossypol, gum, monosaccharides, mucilage, protein, resin, salicylic acid, sesquiterpenes, tannic acid, vitamins (E (alpha-tocopheral), and volatile oil.
Historical Uses: Ague, amenorrhea, contraceptive (male), cough, diarrhea, dysentery, dysmenorrhea, erectile dysfunction, fever (intermittent), food source (seeds), frigidity, headache, hemorrhage (metrorrhagia), inflammation, malaria, menorrhagia, menstrual problems, nausea, parasites (malarial plasmodia), urethritis, weight loss.
Discussion: May depress the appetite; enhance kidney and liver functions; induce abortion; restore normal tone to tissues; serve as a short-term male contraceptive (oil); soothe mucous membrane irritation; stimulate menstruation and uterine contractions.
Cautions/Contraindications: Avoid use if pregnant or breast-feeding. Not for long-term use. Use with professional guidance/supervision.
Adverse Reactions: Nausea and/or vomiting.
Herb/Drug Interactions: This herb could cause an interaction (possibly severe) when taken with the following drugs: None known.
Preparations/Dosage: Crude Herb: 3-6 grams. Decoction (bark): ½-2 ounces per day. Extract (solid): Average dose in substance 15-20 grains (0.98-1.333 gm.). Extract (bark): 5-10 drops (0.333-0.666 cc.) one to two times per day. Tincture: 10-15 drops (0.666-1 cc.) one to three times per day.
Isolation: Betaine: Average dose of 2-4 grains (0.13-0.26 gm.) for use as an emmenagogue. Gossypiin: Average dose of 1-5 grains (0.066-0.333 gm.) for use as an emmenagogue and diuretic.

Couchgrass (kouch gras)

(*Agropyron* (*triticum*) *repens*)

Synonyms/Related Species: Agrospuros, Broad-Glumed Wheatgrass (*agropyron spicatum*), Civice, Crested Wheatgrass (*agropyron cristatum*), Cutch, Dog-Grass, Durfa Grass, Quackgrass, Scotch Quelch, Slender Wheatgrass (*agropyron trachycaulum*), Triticum, Twitch Grass, Violet Wheatgrass (*agropyron violaceum*), Wheatgrass, and Witchgrass.
Family/Class: Graminaceae (grass).
Habitat: Asia, Australia, Britain, Europe, Germany, Greenland, the Mediterranean, North America, Russia, and South America.
Flavor: Sweet.
Parts Used: Root.
Properties: Antibiotic, antioxidant, antiphlogistic, astringent, demulcent, depurative, diaphoretic, diuretic, hemostatic, lithotriptic, nutritive, sedative, tonic, and vasodilator.

Constituents: Amino acids (glutathione, methionine), carbohydrates, fatty acids (oleic, palmitic, stearic), fixed oils (olein, palmitin, stearin), glutelin, gluten, glutin, glycosides, gum, lactic acid, mannitol (mannite), minerals (calcium, iron, magnesium, manganese, phosphorus, potassium, silicon, sodium, sulfur), monosaccharides, mucilage, reductase, saponins, silicic acid, triticin, vitamins (A, B_1 (thiamine), B_2 (riboflavin), B_3 (niacin), B_5 (pantothenic acid), B_6 (pyridoxine), B_{12}, B_x (para-aminobenzoic acid (PABA), C (ascorbic acid), choline, E (alpha-tocopheral), H (biotin), inositol, M (folic acid), and volatile oil.

Historical Uses: Arrhythmia, bladder problems, bleeding, bronchitis, calculus, colds, constipation, cough, cystitis, diabetes, diarrhea, dietary supplementation, dysuria (painful/difficult urination), edema, enuresis (urinary incontinence), eye problems, fever (ephemeral, rheumatic), gallbladder problems, gallstones, gastrointestinal problems, gleet, gonorrhea, gout, hypercholesteremia, infection (bacterial, sexually transmitted), inflammation, insomnia, irritability, jaundice, kidney problems, kidney stones, laryngitis, lumbago, lung problems, liver problems, malnutrition, menopausal/menstrual problems, mood swings, mucus, muscle and joint pain, nephritis, night sweats, plantar fasciitis (foot pad inflammation), pyelitis, prostate problems, prostatitis, respiratory conditions, rheumatism, sexually transmitted diseases (STDs), skin problems, sore throat, syphilis, ulcer (syphilitic), urethritis, and urinary problems.

Discussion: May cause blood vessel dilatation; cleanse the whole system; dissolve calculi; enhance cardiovascular system, gallbladder, liver, respiratory system, and urinary system functions; inhibit or destroy development and growth of bacteria and other microorganisms; prevent kidney stones; promote perspiration and urine flow; provide dietary supplementation; purify the blood; reduce cholesterol levels and reduce the frequency of nighttime urination; restore normal tone to tissues; serve as a nutritional adjuvant to therapeutic programs; soothe mucous membrane irritation; strengthen the urinary system.

Cautions/Contraindications: Avoid use if pregnant or breast-feeding, or if you have edema, heart disease, constipation, kidney problems, or an obstruction (intestinal).

Adverse Reactions: Diarrhea (possibly bloody), edema, gastrointestinal cramps (severe), hematuria (blood in the urine), nausea, and/or vomiting.

Herb/Drug Interactions: This herb could cause an interaction (possibly severe) when taken with the following drugs: None known.

Preparations/Dosage: Crude Herb: 3-9 grams. Decoction: ½-1 cup per day. Extract: 5-10 drops (0.333-0.666 cc.) one to two times per day. Infusion: 1-2 cups per day. Juice: 1-2 tablespoons in water one to two times per day. Tincture: 10-20 drops (0.666-1.25 cc.) one to three times per day.

Isolation: Mannitol hexanitrate: Average dose of 15-60 mg. for use as a vasodilator.

Cow Parsnip (kou pärs nip)

(*Heracleum maximum*)

Synonyms/Related Species: American Masterwort, Cow Cabbage, Hogweed, Keck, Masterwort (*heracleum lanatum*), and Woolly Masterwort (*heracleum sphondylium*).

Family/Class: Umbelliferae (parsley).

Habitat: Alaska, North America, and the Subalpine zone.

Flavor: Bitter.

Parts Used: Flowers, root, leaves, seeds (ripe/unripe), stems

Properties: Analgesic, antiphlogistic, antispasmodic, carminative, counterirritant, emmenagogue, expectorant, hypotensive, insect repellant, laxative, sedative, stimulant, vasomotor depressant, and vasodilator.
Constituents: Coumarins, saponins, and volatile oil.
Historical Uses: Abdominal pain, abscess, amenorrhea, asthma, bruises, cholera, colds, colic, colitis, convulsions, cramps, dandruff, diarrhea, digestive complaints, dysmenorrhea, epilepsy, eye problems, fainting, fever (ephemeral, intermittent, rheumatic), flatulence, flies (flowers), gastritis, gastrointestinal problems, headache, hernias (hiatal), hypertension (mild/moderate), indigestion, infection (bacterial), inflammation, influenza, irritable bowel syndrome (IBS), lesions (tubercle), menstrual problems, mosquitos (flowers), mucus, muscle and joint pain, nausea, nervous conditions, neuralgia, pain, palsy, periodontal disease, rheumatism, sciatica, scrofula, sexually transmitted diseases (STDs), sores, sore throat, spasmodic conditions, syphilis, toothache, tuberculosis, ulcer (fistula, syphilitic, tuberculous), warts (digitate, filiform, fugitive, glabra, mother, plana juvenilis, plantar, seborrhoeic, vulgaris), and wounds (minor).
Discussion: May aid digestion; cause blood vessel dilatation and vasomotor depression; clear and open bronchial passages; promote bowel evacuation; reduce blood pressure levels; soothe mucus membrane irritation; stimulate menstruation and peristalsis.
Cautions/Contraindications: Avoid use if pregnant or breast-feeding. May cause photosensitivity or photodermatosis in susceptible individuals. Do not confuse this herb with poison hemlock (*conium maculatum*).
Adverse Reactions: Diarrhea (possibly bloody), gastrointestinal cramps (severe), hematuria (blood in the urine), menorrhagia, mouth and throat irritation, nausea, and/or vomiting.
Herb/Drug Interactions: This herb could cause an interaction (possibly severe) when taken with the following drugs: Hypotensive drugs.
Preparations/Dosage: Crude Herb: 1-3 grams. Leaves (young): Eaten in salads. Seeds: Use as a flavoring agent or sprinkle sparingly over salads. Stems (young): Peeled or cooked and eaten as a vegetable.

Cramp Bark (kramp bärk)
(*Viburnum opulus*)

Synonyms/Related Species: American Bush Cranberry, American Sloe, Black Haw (*viburnum prunifolium*), Cranberry Tree, European Cranberry, Genuine Cramp Bark, Guelder Rose, Highbush Cranberry (*viburnum edule*), May Rose, Pembina, Red Elder, Rose Elder, Snowball Bush, Squashberry, Squaw Bush, Stagbush, Sweet Viburnum, Water Elder, Whitsun Rose, and Wild Guelder Rose.
Family/Class: Caprifoliaceae (honeysuckle).
Habitat: Alaska, the Alpine and Subalpine zones, England, and North America.
Flavor: Bitter.
Parts Used: Bark (root/stem), berry (seed removed).
Properties: Analgesic, antiperiodic, antiphlogistic, antiscorbutic, antispasmodic, astringent, diuretic, hemostatic, hypotensive, lithotriptic, malariacidal, nervine, sedative, stimulant, tonic, urinary antiseptic, and vasodilator.
Constituents: Alkaloids, arbutin, caffeic acid, catechins, chlorogenic acid, coumarins, flavonoids, hydroquinone, minerals (calcium, magnesium, potassium), resin, salicin, salicylic acid, saponins, scopoletin, scoplin, sterols, tannic acid, ursone (ursolic acid), valerianic acid, viburnine, vitamins (C (ascorbic acid), K), and volatile oil.

Historical Uses: Ague, allergy (pollen), amenorrhea, arrhythmia, arthritis, asthma, bleeding, calculus, cardiac insufficicency, colds, colic, constipation, convulsions, cough, cramps, diarrhea, dysentery, dysmenorrhea, eczema, epilepsy, fainting, fever (ephemeral, hay, intermittent, rheumatic), gallstones, gargle/mouth rinse, headache, hemorrhage (metrorrhagia), hiccups, hypertension (mild/moderate), hysteria, indigestion, infection, inflammation, jaundice, kidney stones, lung problems, malaria, menopausal/menstrual problems, menorrhagia, mood swings, muscle and joint pain, nervous conditions, neuralgia, ovarian problems, pain, parasites (malarial plasmodia), premenstrual syndrome (PMS), rheumatism, scurvy, spasmodic conditions, skin problems, tetanus, trismus (lockjaw), ulcer (duodenal, gastric, peptic), urinary problems, and uterine problems.

Discussion: May calm the nervous system; cause blood vessel dilatation; dissolve calculi; enhance cardiovascular system, intestinal system, liver, and lung functions; increase circulation; promote urine flow; regulate pulse rate; reduce blood pressure levels; relieve voluntary and involuntary muscular spasm; restore sympathetic and parasympathetic balance, and restore normal tone to tissues; stimulate uterine contractions.

Cautions/Contraindications: Avoid use if pregnant or breast-feeding, or if you have a kidney problem. Due to the high salicin content and the possibility of Reye's syndrome, do not administer to children suffering from fever, chicken pox, influenza, or other infection (viral). Persons with aspirin sensitivities should not take cramp bark. Some persons may experience bleeding or increased clotting time when using this herb with anticoagulant drugs or aspirin.

Adverse Reactions: Bleeding (possibly serious), coagulation problems, diarrhea (possibly bloody), gastrointestinal cramps (severe), nausea, tinnitus, and/or vomiting.

Herb/Drug Interactions: This herb could cause an interaction (possibly severe) when taken with the following drugs: Anticoagulant drugs, Hypotensive drugs, Salicylates, and Subsalicylates.

Preparations/Dosage: Crude Herb: 3-9 grams. Berries (seed removed): Eaten fresh, lightly cooked, or used for jam/jelly. Decoction: ½-1 cup per day. Extract: 5-10 drops (0.333-0.666 cc.) one to two times per day. Tincture: 10-15 drops (0.666-1 cc.) one to three times per day.

Isolation: Arbutin: Average dose of 5-15 grains (0.3-1 gm.) used as a diuretic and urinary antiseptic. Salicin: Average dose of 5-30 grains (0.333-2 gm.) for use as an analgesic, antiperiodic, and febrifuge. Salicin's action is similar to that of quinine. Viburnine: Average dose of 1-3 grains (0.066-0.2 gm.) for use as an antispasmodic.

Cranesbill (krānz bil)

(*Geranium maculatum*)

Synonyms/Related Species: American Cranesbill, Bicknell's Geranium (*geranium bicknellii*), Carolina Geranium (*geranium carolinianum*), Cranesbill Geranium (*geranium viscosissimum*), Crowfoot, Dove's Foot, Geranion, Pineywoods Geranium (*geranium caespitosum*), Redstem Storksbill, Richardson's Geranium (*geranium richardsonii*), Spotted Cranesbill, Sticky Purple Geranium, Storksbill, Western Purple Cranesbill (*geranium atropurpureum*), White Geranium, Wild Alum Root, and Wild Geranium.

Family/Class: Geraniaceae (geranium).

Habitat: Africa, Asia, England, Europe, Japan, North America, South America, and the Yukon Territory.

Flavor: Sweet/sour/bitter.

Parts Used: Leaves, root.
Properties: Antibiotic, antiviral, astringent, coagulant, hemostatic, tonic, and vulnerary.
Constituents: Flavonoids, gallic acid, geraniin, geraniol (rhodinol), gum, inulin (starch), monosaccharides, pectic acid, pectin, quercetin, resin, rutin, and tannic acid.
Historical Uses: Acne, bleeding, burns (minor), canker sores, cholera, colitis, congestion (uterine, vaginal), conjunctivitis, diabetes, diarrhea, digestive complaints, dysentery, edema, enteritis, fever (ephemeral, enteric), gargle/mouth rinse, gastritis, gastrointestinal problems, gleet, gout, headache, hematuria, hemorrhage (metrorrhagia), hemorrhoids, infection (bacterial, viral), inflammation, leukorrhea, lochia, menorrhagia, mucus, oily skin, periodontal disease, rash, sores, sore throat, stomatitis, tonsillitis, typhoid, ulcer (bouveret, duodenal, gastric, indolent, peptic), vaginitis, vomiting, and wounds (minor).
Discussion: May enhance cardiovascular system, intestinal system, liver, and stomach functions; increase coagulation; inhibit or destroy development and growth of bacteria and other microorganisms; prevent hemorrhage in persons with hypertension; reduce capillary fragility; restore normal tone to tissues; speed healing.
Cautions/Contraindications: Avoid use if pregnant or breast-feeding. Do not confuse this herb with poisonous monkshood (*aconitum spp.*).
Adverse Reactions: Gastritis, hematuria (blood in the urine), nausea, and/or vomiting.
Herb/Drug Interactions: This herb could cause an interaction (possibly severe) when taken with the following drugs: None known.
Preparations/Dosage: Crude Herb: 3-9 grams. Decoction (root): ½-1 cup per day. Extract: 5-30 drops (0.333-2 cc.) one to two times per day. Infusion: 1-2 cups per day. Root (powdered): Average dose in substance 15-30 grains (0.98-2 gm.). Tincture: 5-30 drops (0.333-2 cc.) one to three times per day.
Isolation: Geraniin: Average dose of 1-3 grains (0.066-0.199 gm.) for use as an astringent.

Croton (krōt n)
(*Croton tiglium*)

Synonyms/Related Species: Bahama Cascarilla, California Croton (*croton californicus*), Cāscara, Cáscara Bark, Cascarilla (*croton eluteria*), False Quinquina, Klotzsch, Krotōn, Mexican Copalchi Bark (*croton niveus*), Sweet Bark, Sweetwood Bark, Texas Croton (*croton texensis*), Tiglii, West Indian Cascarilla, and West Indian Wild Rosemary (*croton cascarilla*).
Family/Class: Euphorbiacea (spurge).
Habitat: Asia, the Bahamas, India, Mexico, and North America.
Flavor: Pungent.
Parts Used: Bark (dried/from cascarilla), Seed Oil (from ripened seeds).
Properties: Antiperiodic, antiphlogistic, aromatic, carminative, caustic, counterirritant, diuretic, emetic, emmenagogue, expectorant, laxative, malariacidal, narcotic, stomachic, and tonic.
Constituents: Acetic acid, albumin (albumen), alkaloids, betaine (lycine), carvene (limonene), cascarillin, crotonallin, crotonarin, crotonglobulin, cymene, diterpenes, eugenol (eugenic acid), fatty acids (crotonic, oleic, palmitic, stearic, tiglic), fixed oils (olein, palmitin, stearin), formic acid, gum, isobutyric acid, lauric acid, lignin, minerals (calcium), myristin (myristic acid), resin, phorbol ester, resin, tannic acid, valerianic acid, volatile oil, and wax.
Historical Uses: Abdominal pain, ague, arthritis, bronchitis, colds, colic, constipation, convalescence, digestive complaints, dysentery, fever (ephemeral, intermittent, rheumatic),

flatulence, gallbladder problems, gastritis, gastrointestinal problems, gleet, gonorrhea, gout, headache, hemorrhoids, indigestion, infection (sexually transmitted), inflammation, malaria, muscle and joint pain, neuralgia, obstruction (intestinal), parasites (malarial plasmodia), poisoning (lead), rheumatism, sexually transmitted disease (STDs), sores, syphilis, ulcer (syphilitic), urethritis, and warts (filiform, fugitive, glabra, mother, plana juvenilis, plantar, seborrhoeic).

Discussion: May affect prostaglandin metabolism; aid digestion, clear and open bronchial passages; promote bowel evacuation and urine flow; restore normal tone to tissues; stimulate menstruation and peristalsis.

Cautions/Contraindications: Avoid use if pregnant or breast-feeding. Do not administer to children. May cause dermatitis in susceptible individuals. Not for long-term use. Use with professional guidance/supervision.

Adverse Reactions: Blistering (severe), crotonism (poisoning by croton oil), diarrhea (severe), gastrointestinal cramps (severe), giddiness, intoxication-like symptoms, nausea, stupor, and/or vomiting.

Herb/Drug Interactions: This herb could cause an interaction (possibly severe) when taken with the following drugs: None known.

Preparations/Dosage: Cascarilla Bark (powdered): Average dose in substance 20-30 grains (1.3-1.85 gm.) for use as a stomachic. Croton Oil (*oleum tiglii* or *oleum crotonis*): internal uses: place no more than ¼-½ drop (0.0165-0.03 cc.) of the seed oil on a sugar cube (results should be readily noticeable) for use as a drastic laxative; external uses (extremely diluted): for use as a vesicant. Infusion (bark): ½-1 cup per day. Tincture (bark): 5-20 drops (0.333-1.25 cc.) one to three times per day.

Isolation: Betaine: Average dose of 2-4 grains (0.13-0.26 gm.) for use as an emmenagogue.

Cubeb (kyoo beb)
(*Piper cubeba*)

Synonyms/Related Species: Java Pepper, Kabā'ba, and Tailed Pepper.

Family/Class: Piperaceae (pepper).

Habitat: Arabia, India, Indonesia, Java, Malaysia, Penang, New Guinea, Sri Lanka, and Sumatra.

Flavor: Pungent.

Parts Used: Fruit (dried/unripe).

Properties: Antibiotic, antilithic, antiperiodic, antiphlogistic, aromatic, carminative, counterirritant, diuretic, expectorant, hepatic, laxative, malariacidal, stimulant, stomachic, and vermifuge.

Constituents: Bitter principle, cubebic acid, cubebene, cubebin, fatty acids (oleic, palmitic, stearic), fixed oils (olein, palmitin, stearin), lignin, piperazine, piperine, resin, and volatile oil.

Historical Uses: Abscess, allergy (pollen), arthritis, asthma, bronchitis, calculus, colds, congestion (uterine, vaginal), cough, cystitis, digestive complaints, fever (ephemeral, hay, intermittent, rheumatic), gallstones, gleet, gonorrhea, gout, hemorrhoids, indigestion, infection (bacterial, sexually transmitted, urinary tract), inflammation, kidney stones, leukorrhea, lithemia, malaria, mucus, muscle and joint pain, parasites (malarial plasmodia), prostate problems, respiratory conditions, rheumatism, sexually transmitted diseases (STDs), sprain, syphilis, ulcer (syphilitic), urethritis, and vaginitis.

Discussion: May aid digestion; clear and open bronchial passages; enhance lung, kidney, and stomach functions; increase absorption of nutrients and other herbs; inhibit or destroy development and growth of bacteria and other microorganisms; prevent the development of calculus and stones; promote bowel evacuation and urine flow; protect the liver; reduce excessive levels of lithic acid (uric acid) and urates in the blood, tophi, and urine.
Cautions/Contraindications: Avoid use if pregnant or breast-feeding, or if you have acidity (gastric) or insufficiency (gastric).
Adverse Reactions: Bladder problems, diarrhea, nausea, skin rash, and/or vomiting.
Herb/Drug Interactions: This herb could cause an interaction (possibly severe) when taken with the following drugs: None known.
Preparations/Dosage: Crude Herb: 3-6 grams. Infusion: ½ cup per day. Oil of Cubeb (*oleum cubebae*): 5-15 drops (0.3-1 cc.) in water or on a sugarcube. Oleoresin: Average dose in substance 8 grains (0.5 gm.). Fruit (powdered): Average dose in substance ½-1 teaspoon per day.
Isolation: Piperazine hydrochlorate: Dose in 2% solution, 5 grains (0.33 gm.), administered hypodermically; or orally (by mouth), 8 grains (0.5 gm.) for use as an antilithic, antisyphilitic, and diuretic. Piperine: Soluble (slightly) in water. Average dose of 1-5 grains (0.06-0.33 gm.) for use as an antiperiodic.

Culver's Root (kul verz root)
(*Veronica virginicum*)

Synonyms/Related Species: Alpine Speedwell (*veronica wormskjoldii*), American Brooklime, American Speedwell (*veronica americana*), Arctic Speedwell (*veronica alpina*), Beaumont Root, Black Root, Brooklime, Common Speedwell (*veronica officinalis*), Culver's Physic, European Speedwell, Hini, Leptandra, Oxadoddy, Persian Self-Heal (*veronica persica*), Physic Root, Purple Leptandra, Speedwell, Tall Speedwell, Thyme-Leaved Speedwell (*veronica serpyllifolia*), Veronica, and Whorlywort.
Family/Class: Scrophulariaceae (figwort).
Habitat: Alaska, the Alpine and Subalpine zones, Europe, the United States, and the Yukon Territory.
Flavor: Bitter/pungent.
Parts Used: Leaves, root.
Properties: Alterative, antiperiodic, antiphlogistic, antispasmodic, carminative, cholagogue, depurative, diaphoretic, diuretic, emetic, expectorant, laxative, lithotriptic, malariacidal, sedative, tonic, and vasodilator.
Constituents: Cinnamic acid, dextrose, glycosides, gum, mannitol (mannite), minerals (magnesium, potassium), resin, saponins, sterols, tannic acid, vitamins (C (ascorbic acid), and volatile oil.
Historical Uses: Abdominal pain, ague, asthma, bronchitis, cholera, colitis, constipation, cough, depression (mild/moderate), diarrhea, digestive complaints, dizziness, dysentery, edema, enteritis, fever (ephemeral, intermittent), gallbladder problems, gallstones, gout, headache, hepatitis, indigestion, inflammation, jaundice, kidney stones, leprosy, lesions (tubercle), liver problems, lung problems, malaria, muscle and joint pain, parasites (malarial plasmodia), poisoning (food), respiratory conditions, rheumatism, scrofula, scurvy, sexually transmitted diseases (STDs), spasmodic conditions, syphilis, tuberculosis, ulcer (fistula, syphilitic, tuberculous), and urinary calculus.

Discussion: May aid digestion; cause blood vessel dilatation; clear and open bronchial passages; dissolve calculi; enhance liver function; increase the flow of bile; promote bowel evacuation, perspiration, and urine flow; purify the blood; reestablish healthy system functions; restore normal tone to tissues; stimulate peristalsis.
Cautions/Contraindications: Avoid use if pregnant or breast-feeding.
Adverse Reactions: Diarrhea (possibly bloody), gastrointestinal cramps (severe), nausea, and/or vomiting.
Herb/Drug Interactions: This herb could cause an interaction (possibly severe) when taken with the following drugs: None known.
Preparations/Dosage: Crude Herb: 1-3 grams. Extract: 5-15 drops (0.333-1 cc.) one to two times per day. Extract (powdered): Average dose in substance 4 grains (0.25 gm.). Infusion: 1-2 cups per day. Juice: 2 teaspoons in water one to two times per day. Resin (powdered): Average dose in substance 2-4 grains (0.133-0.26 gm.). Root (powdered): Average dose in substance 15-30 grains (0.98-2 gm.). Tincture: 10-30 drops (0.666-2 cc.) one to three times per day.
Isolation: Leptandrin: Average dose of ¼-2 grains (0.015-0.133 gm.) for use as a cholagogue, laxative, and tonic. Mannitol hexanitrate: Average dose of 15-60 mg. for use as a vasodilator.

Cumin (kum in)
(*Cumimum cyminum*)

Synonyms/Related Species: Kammōn and Kyminon.
Family/Class: Umbelliferae (parsley).
Habitat: Asia, Egypt, India, Iran, the Mediterranean, Pakistan, South America, and the United States.
Flavor: Pungent.
Parts Used: Fruit/seed.
Properties: Abortifacient, analgesic, antibiotic, anticarcinogen, anticoagulant, antifertilizin, antiphlogistic, antiscorbutic, antispasmodic, aphrodisiac, aromatic, carminative, diaphoretic, diuretic, emmenagogue, insect repellent, laxative, stimulant, stomachic, and tonic.
Constituents: Amino acids (alanine, arginine, asparagine, glutamic, glycine, leucine, lysine, methionine, phenylalanine, threonine, tryptophan, tyrosine), carvene (limonene), cuminic acid, cymene, fatty acids (arachidonic, linoleic, linolenic, oleic, palmitic, stearic), fixed oils (olein, palmitin, stearin), gum, lipase, minerals (iron, potassium), monosaccharides, mucilage, pinene, quinone, resin, sterols, tannic acid, terpenes, vitamins (C (ascorbic acid), and volatile oil.
Historical Uses: Abscess, allergy, arthritis, asthma, bronchitis, bruises, calluses, cancer, colds, colic, corns, cough, diarrhea, digestive complaints, dysentery, emphysema, eye soreness, fever (ephemeral, rheumatic), flatulence, flavoring agent, gastrointestinal problems, headache, hemorrhoids, hydrophobia (rabies in humans), indigestion, infection (bacterial), inflammation, influenza, irritable bowel syndrome (IBS), jaundice, liver problems, moths, muscle and joint pain, orchitis, pain, paralysis, respiratory conditions, rheumatism, sclerosis, scurvy, skin problems, snakebite, spasmodic conditions, tumors, warts (digitate, filiform, fugitive, glabra, mother, plana juvenilis, plantar, seborrhoeic, vulgaris), and wounds (minor).
Discussion: May aid digestion; arouse sexual impulses; decrease the effect of carcinogens; delay or reduce coagulation of the blood; enhance liver, spleen, and stomach functions; increase circulation; induce abortion; inhibit or destroy development and growth of bacteria and other microorganisms; neutralize fertilizin (fertilization); promote bowel evacuation, perspiration, and

urine flow; restore normal tone to tissues; stimulate menstruation, peristalsis, and uterine contractions.
Cautions/Contraindications: Avoid use if pregnant or breast-feeding. Some persons may experience bleeding or increased clotting time when using this herb with anticoagulant drugs or aspirin.
Adverse Reactions: Bleeding (possibly serious), coagulation problems, diarrhea, nausea, and/or vomiting.
Herb/Drug Interactions: This herb could cause an interaction (possibly severe) when taken with the following drugs: Anticoagulant drugs, Salicylates, and Subsalicylates.
Preparations/Dosage: Crude Herb: 3-9 grams. Fruit/Seeds: used in cooking as a flavoring agent. Infusion: 1-3 cups per day.

Currant (kûr ent)
(*Ribes americanum*)

Synonyms/Related Species: Black Currant (*ribes nigrum*), Bristly Black Currant (*ribes lacustre*), Coraunt, Garden Currant, Garnetberry, Golden Currant (*ribes aureum*), Gooseberry, Mountain Gooseberry (*ribes montigenum*), Mountain Prickly Currant, Northern Black Currant (*ribes hudsonianum*), Northern Gooseberry (*ribes oxyacanthoides*), Quinsy Berry, Raisin Tree, Red Currant (*ribes rubrum*), Ribes, Skunk Currant (*ribes glandulosum*), Squaw Currant, Squinancy Berries, Sticky Currant (*ribes viscosissimum*), Trailing Black Currant (*ribes laxiflorum*), Wax Currant (*ribes cereum*), White-Stemmed Gooseberry (*ribes inerme*), and Wineberry.
Family/Class: Saxifragaceae (saxifrage).
Habitat: Alaska, the Alpine zone, Europe, the Himalayas, New Foundland, North America, Siberia, and the Yukon Territory.
Flavor: Bitter/sweet.
Parts Used: Fruit, leaves.
Properties: Antiphlogistic, antiscorbutic, depurative, diaphoretic, diuretic, hemostatic, laxative, lithotriptic, nutritive, sialogogue, stomachic, and tonic.
Constituents: Citric acid, fatty acids (arachidonic, linoleic, linolenic, oleic, omega 3 and omega 6, palmitic, stearic), fixed oils (olein, palmitin, stearin), flavonoids, malic acid, minerals (copper, iron), monosaccharides, tannic acid, and vitamin C (ascorbic acid).
Historical Uses: Addiction (alcohol), alopecia, anemia, appetite loss, arteriosclerosis, arthritis, asthma, blisters, bronchitis, burns (minor), calculus, colds, colic, constipation, cough, diabetes, diarrhea, dietary supplementation, dysentery, edema, eye problems, fever (ephemeral, rheumatic), gallstones, gargle/mouth rinse, gout, heart disease, hemorrhage, hemorrhoids, inflammation, jam/jelly, jaundice, kidney problems, kidney stones, laryngitis, malnutrition, mucus, muscle and joint pain, nausea, periodontal disease, premenstrual syndrome (PMS), respiratory conditions, rheumatism, scurvy, skin problems, sore throat, thirst, visual disturbances, whooping cough.
Discussion: May cleanse the whole system; dissolve calculi; enhance cardiovascular, kidney, nervous system, and stomach functions; prevent cell degeneration; promote bowel evacuation, saliva secretion, and urine flow; protect from arsenic damage and protect against arterial damage, elevated cholesterol levels, and heart disease; provide dietary supplementation; quench thirst; restore normal tone to tissues; serve as a nutritional adjuvant to therapeutic programs; stimulate

appetite and peristalsis; strengthen the brain cells and nerves; useful as a substitute for alcohol craving (juice thinned with water).
Cautions/Contraindications: Avoid use if pregnant or breast-feeding. May cause allergic reactions in susceptible individuals.
Adverse Reactions: Diarrhea, nausea, salivation (increased), and/or vomiting.
Herb/Drug Interactions: This herb could cause an interaction (possibly severe) when taken with the following drugs: None known.
Preparations/Dosage: Crude Herb: 3-15 grams. Infusion (fruit and/or leaves): 1-1½ cups per day. Juice (fruit): 1-3 tablespoons in water per day.

Custard Apple (kus'terd ap'l)
(*Annona reticulata*)

Synonyms/Related Species: Cherimoya (*annona cherimola*), Papaw, Soursop (*annona muricata*), Sugar Apple, and Sweetsop (*annona squamosa*).
Family/Class: Annonaceae (custard apple).
Habitat: Africa, Asia, and India.
Flavor: Sweet.
Parts Used: Fruit.
Properties: Antiphlogistic, laxative, and narcotic.
Constituents: Alkaloids, asiminine, fatty acids (oleic, palmitic, stearic), and fixed oils (olein, palmitin, stearin), resin.
Historical Uses: Boils, fever (scarlet), inflammation, skin problems, and ulcer (duodenal, gastric, peptic).
Discussion: May promote bowel evacuation; stimulate peristalsis.
Cautions/Contraindications: Avoid use if pregnant or breast-feeding. Do not confuse this plant with papaya also called papaw (*carica papaya*).
Adverse Reactions: Diarrhea, nausea, stupor, and/or vomiting.
Herb/Drug Interactions: This herb could cause an interaction (possibly severe) when taken with the following drugs: None known.
Preparations/Dosage: Fruit (fresh): May be ingested freely.

Cypress (si pres)
(*Cupressus sempervirens*)

Synonyms/Related Species: Cipres and Kyparissos.
Family/Class: Cupressaceae (cypress).
Habitat: Asia, Europe, the Mediterranean, North America, and Turkey.
Flavor: Bitter.
Parts Used: Oil (from leaves and young branches).
Properties: Antibiotic, antihidrotic, antiphlogistic, antispasmodic, aromatic, astringent, counterirritant, diaphoretic, expectorant, insect repellent, narcotic, sedative, stimulant, tonic, vasoconstrictor, and vulnerary.
Constituents: Camphene, camphor, cupressin, cymene, pinene, sabinol, terpin, and volatile oil.
Historical Uses: Amenorrhea, anxiety, arthritis, asthma, bronchitis, cellulite, chilblains, chills, colds, cough, cystitis, dandruff, diarrhea, dysmenorrhea, edema, enuresis (urinary incontinence), ephidrosis, fever (ephemeral, rheumatic), fleas, hemorrhoids, hormonal imbalances, infection

(bacterial), inflammation, influenza, insufficiency (venous), laryngitis, menopausal/menstrual problems, menorrhagia, mucus, muscle and joint pain, nosebleed, periodontal disease, respiratory conditions, rheumatism, skin problems, spasmodic conditions, ulcer (stasis, varicose), varicose veins, whooping cough, and wounds (minor).
Discussion: May cause blood vessel constriction; clear and open bronchial passages; inhibit or destroy development and growth of bacteria and other microorganisms; promote perspiration; reduce urine flow and reduce the frequency of nighttime urination; restore normal tone to tissues; speed healing; strengthen the urinary system.
Cautions/Contraindications: Avoid use if pregnant or breast-feeding. Not for long-term use. Use with professional guidance/supervision.
Adverse Reactions: Hematuria (blood in the urine), nausea, and/or vomiting.
Herb/Drug Interactions: This herb could cause an interaction (possibly severe) when taken with the following drugs: None known.
Preparations/Dosage: Cypress Oil (*oleum cupressus*): for external/topical uses.
Isolation: Camphor: Average dose of 2 grains (0.12 gm.) for use as a powerful irritant and stimulant, diaphoretic and narcotic. Camphor is toxic in overdoses and sedative in small doses. Terpin hydrate: Average dose of 5 grains (0.33 gm.) for use in chronic cough.

Daisy (dā zē)

(*Bellis perennis*)

Synonyms/Related Species: Bairnwort, Belidis, Bellus, Bruisewort, Common Daisy, Day's Eye, English Daisy, and Wild Daisy.
Family/Class: Compositae (composite).
Habitat: Asia, Britain, England, Europe, Ireland, the Mediterranean, Moscow, North America, Portugal, Scandinavia, and Scotland.
Flavor: Bitter/pungent.
Parts Used: Flowers, leaves.
Properties: Analgesic, antibiotic, antifungal, antiphlogistic, antiscorbutic, antispasmodic, astringent, carminative, demulcent, expectorant, hemostatic, laxative, and tonic.
Constituents: Bitter principle, flavonoids, mucilage, polygalin (polygalic acid), saponins, tannic acid, vitamin C (ascorbic acid), and volatile oil.
Historical Uses: Arthritis, bleeding, bronchitis, bruises, burns (minor), canker sores, colds, colic, cough, diarrhea, digestive complaints, fever (ephemeral, rheumatic), flatulence, gargle/mouth rinse, gastrointestinal problems, gout, indigestion, infection (bacterial, fungal), inflammation, kidney problems, liver problems, mucus, muscle and joint pain, pain, respiratory conditions, rheumatism, scurvy, skin problems, sore throat, sores, spasmodic conditions, and wounds (minor).
Discussion: May aid digestion; clear and open bronchial passages; inhibit or destroy developement and growth of bacteria and other microorganisms; promote bowel evacuation; restore normal tone to tissues; soothe mucous membrane irritation; stimulate peristalsis.
Cautions/Contraindications: Avoid use if pregnant or breast-feeding. May cause allergic reactions and dermatitis in susceptible individuals.
Adverse Reactions: Diarrhea (possibly bloody), gastrointestinal cramps (severe), hematuria (blood in the urine), nausea, and/or vomiting.

Herb/Drug Interactions: This herb could cause an interaction (possibly severe) when taken with the following drugs: None known.
Preparations/Dosage: Crude Herb: 3-6 grams. Infusion (flowers and/or leaves): 1 cup per day. Juice: 1 teaspoon to 1 tablespoon in water one to two times per day.

Daisy, False (dā zē, fôls)
(*Eclipta prostrada*)

Synonyms/Related Species: Eclipta.
Family/Class: Compositae (composite).
Habitat: Asia, India, and North America.
Flavor: Sweet/sour.
Parts Used: Entire plant.
Properties: Alterative, antibiotic, antifungal, anti-inflammatory, antiviral, astringent, hemostatic, stimulant, and tonic.
Constituents: Saponins, tannic acid, and vitamin A.
Historical Uses: Bleeding, candida, cirrhosis, dizziness, eczema, hair conditioner, hemoptysis (spitting up of blood), hemorrhage, hepatitis, infection (bacterial, fungal, viral), inflammation, migraine, moniliasis, neurosis, sinusitis, snakebite, tinnitus, vertigo, visual disturbances, and vomiting.
Discussion: May enhance kidney and liver functions; inhibit or destroy developement and growth of bacteria and other microorganisms; stimulate hair growth and the immune system.
Cautions/Contraindications: Avoid use if pregnant or breast-feeding. May cause allergic reactions in susceptible individuals.
Adverse Reactions: Diarrhea (possibly bloody), gastrointestinal cramps (severe), hematuria (blood in the urine), nausea, and/or vomiting.
Herb/Drug Interactions: This herb could cause an interaction (possibly severe) when taken with the following drugs: None known.
Preparations/Dosage: Crude Herb: 6-12 grams. Infusion: ½-1 cup per day. Hair Conditioner: Heat leaf juice with coconut oil and apply topically.

Daisy, Ox-Eye (dā zē, oks ·ī)
(*Leucanthemum vulgare*)

Synonyms/Related Species: Big Daisy, Bull Daisy, Butter Daisy, Dog Daisy, Dun Daisy, Field Daisy, Golden Daisy, Gowan, Great Ox-Eye, Horse Daisy, Marguerite, Maudlin Daisy, Mid-Summer Daisy, Moon Daisy, Moon Flower, Moon Penny, White Daisy, and White Weed.
Family/Class: Compositae (composite).
Habitat: Asia, Europe, North America, and Russia.
Flavor: Bitter.
Parts Used: Flowers, leaves.
Properties: Antifungal, antiphlogistic, antispasmodic, astringent, counterirritant, diaphoretic, diuretic, expectorant, hemostatic, insect repellent, and tonic.
Constituents: Bitter principles, flavonoids, mucilage, saponins, tannic acid, and volatile oil.
Historical Uses: Arthritis asthma, bleeding, bruises, candida, colds, cough, dandruff, diarrhea, dizziness, edema, excitability, fever (ephemeral, rheumatic), fleas, infection (fungal),

inflammation, menstrual problems, moniliasis, mucus, muscle and joint pain, nervous conditions, night sweats, respiratory conditions, rheumatism, spasmodic conditions, ulcer (duodenal, gastric, peptic), urinary problems, warts (digitate, filiform, fugitive, glabra, mother, plana juvenilis, plantar, seborrhoeic, vulgaris), whooping cough, and wounds (minor).

Discussion: May clear and open bronchial passages; enhance kidney and liver functions; promote perspiration and urine flow; restore normal tone to tissues.

Cautions/Contraindications: Avoid use if pregnant or breast-feeding or if you are allergic to chamomile. May cause allergic reactions or dermatitis in susceptible individuals.

Adverse Reactions: Diarrhea (possibly bloody), gastrointestinal cramps (severe), nausea, and/or vomiting.

Herb/Drug Interactions: This herb could cause an interaction (possibly severe) when taken with the following drugs: None known.

Preparations/Dosage: Crude Herb: 3-6 grams. Extract: 5-10 drops (0.333-0.666 cc.) one to two times per day. Infusion: 1-2 cups per day. Leaves (young): Eaten in salads. Tincture: 10-20 drops (0.666-1.25 cc.) one to three times per day.

Damiana (dam ē·an e)
(*Turnera diffusa*)

Synonyms/Related Species: Brazilian Damiana (*turnera opifera*) and Mexican Damiana (*turnera aphrodisiaca*).

Family/Class: Turneraceae (damiana).

Habitat: Africa, California, Central America, India, Mexico, South America, and Texas.

Flavor: Bitter.

Parts Used: Leaves.

Properties: Antibiotic, antidepressant, antiperiodic, antiphlogistic, aphrodisiac, aromatic, carminative, diuretic, emmenagogue, expectorant, hypoglycemic, laxative, malariacidal, nervine, stimulant, tonic, and urinary antiseptic.

Constituents: Alkaloids, arbutin, bitter principle, cadinene, eucalyptol (cineol), flavonoids, glycosides, gum, inulin (starch), pinene, resin, tannic acid, thymol, and volatile oil.

Historical Uses: Acne, ague, amenorrhea, anxiety, asthma, bronchitis, colds, congestion (uterine, vaginal), constipation, cough, cystitis, debility, depression (mild/moderate), digestive complaints, diminished sex drive, diphtheria, dysmenorrhea, eczema, emphysema, enuresis (urinary incontinence), erectile dysfunction, exhaustion, fever (ephemeral, intermittent), flatulence, frigidity, headache, hormonal imbalances, hot flashes, hyperglycemia, indigestion, infection (bacterial, urinary tract), infertility, inflammation, lethargy, leukorrhea, malaria, menopausal/menstrual problems, mucus, nervous conditions, parasites (malarial plasmodia), Parkinson's disease, prostate problems, respiratory conditions, trauma (sexual), ulcer (duodenal, gastric, peptic, syriac), urethritis, vaginitis, and wounds (minor).

Discussion: May aid digestion; arouse sexual impulses; balance the female hormonal system; calm the nervous system; clear and open bronchila passages; enhance circulatory and urinary system functions; increase sperm count; inhibit or destroy development and growth of bacteria and other microorganisms; promote bowel evacuation and urine flow; reduce blood sugar levels and the frequency of nighttime urination; restore normal tone to tissues; serve as an adjuvant to depression therapies; stimulate the genitourinary tract, menstruation, metabolism, and peristalsis; strengthen the nervous system, reproductive system, and urinary system.

Cautions/Contraindications: Avoid use if pregnant or breast-feeding, or if you have kidney, liver, or urinary tract disease. May interfere with iron absorption and prescription drugs.
Adverse Reactions: Headache, insomnia, nausea, and/or vomiting.
Herb/Drug Interactions: This herb could cause an interaction (possibly severe) when taken with the following drugs: Antidiabetic drugs.
Preparations/Dosage: Crude Herb: 3-6 grams. Extract: 5-10 drops (0.333-0.666 cc.) one to two times per day. Extract (solid): Average dose in substance 5-10 grains (0.324-0.666 gm.). Infusion: 1-2 cups per day. Leaves (powdered): Average dose in substance 3-5 grains (0.2-0.324 gm.). Tincture: 15-30 drops (1-2 cc.) one to three times per day.
Isolation: Arbutin: Average dose of 5-15 grains (0.3-1 gm.) used as a diuretic and urinary antiseptic. Eucalyptol: 5 drops (0.3 cc.) in atomization or inhalation therapy for use in respiratory conditions.

Dandelion (dan de·lī en)
(*Taraxacum officinale*)

Synonyms/Related Species: Atirasa, Blow Ball, Cankerwort, Common Dandelion, Dent de Lion, Horned Dandelion (*taraxacum ceratophorum*), Leontodon, and Lion's Tooth.
Family/Class: Compositae (composite).
Habitat: Alaska, Europe, Greece, and North America.
Flavor: Bitter.
Parts Used: Leaves, latex (from leaves and stem), root.
Properties: Alterative, anticarcinogen, antifungal, antioxidant, antiphlogistic, antiscorbutic, cholagogue, depurative, diuretic, hepatic, hypoglycemic, hypotensive, laxative, lithotriptic, nutritive, sialogogue, stimulant, stomachic, tonic, and vasodilator.
Constituents: Bitter principle, enzymes, fats, flavonoids, gluten, gum, inulin (starch), lactupicrin, levulin, mannitol (mannite), minerals (calcium, cobalt, copper, iron, magnesium, nickel, phosphorus, potassium, sodium, tin, zinc), monosaccharides, mucilage, pectic acid, pectin, polysaccharides, protein, resin, sterols, tannic acid, taraxacerin, taraxacin, triterpenes, and vitamins (A, B_1 (thiamine), B_2 (riboflavin), B_3 (niacin), C (ascorbic acid), choline, D, E (alpha-tocopheral), inositol).
Historical Uses: Abscess, acne, age spots, allergy, anemia, appetite loss, arthritis, asthma, bladder problems, blisters, bronchitis, calculus, cancer (breast), candida, cirrhosis, colds, constipation, corns, cramps, cystitis, dermatitis, diabetes, dietary supplementation, digestive complaints, diphtheria, dry skin, dysmenorrhea, dysuria (painful/difficult urination), eczema, edema, fatigue, fever (ephemeral, rheumatic), flatulence, gallstones, gastritis, gout, headache, hemorrhoids, hepatitis, hyperglycemia, hypertension (mild/moderate), hypotension, indigestion, infection (bacterial, fungal, urinary tract), inflammation, insomnia, irritable bowel syndrome (IBS), jaundice, kidney problems, kidney stones, liver problems, malnutrition, mastitis, memory/cognitive problems, menstrual problems, moniliasis, muscle and joint pain, nephritis, nervous conditions, osteoporosis, premenstrual syndrome (PMS), pruritus, psoriasis, rheumatism, salad (young leaves), scurvy, skin problems, snakebite, spleen problem, stomachache, tumors, ulcer (duodenal, gastric, peptic), warts (digitate, filiform, fugitive, glabra, mother, plana juvenilis, plantar, seborrhoeic, vulgaris), and weight loss.
Discussion: May aid digestion; cause blood vessel dilatation; decrease the effect of carcinogens; dissolve calculi; enhance gallbladder, pancreatic, kidney, liver, spleen, stomach, and urinary

system functions; increase circulation and endurance; inhibit oxidation; prevent the deposition of fat in the liver; promote bile flow, bowel evacuation, saliva secretion, and urine flow; protect the liver and protect against cancer (breast); provide dietary supplementation; purify the blood; reduce blood pressure levels, blood sugar levels, and cholesterol levels; reestablish healthy system functions; restore normal tone to tissues; serve as a nutritional adjuvant to therapeutic programs; stimulate appetite, gastric secretions, metabolism, and peristalsis; stop or slow abnormal cell growth; strengthen tooth enamel and the vascular system.

Cautions/Contraindications: Avoid use if pregnant or breast-feeding, or if you have a biliary problem. May reduce the effectiveness of antibiotic, blood sugar, or insulin drugs. Individuals with known sensitivity to chamomile or yarrow should avoid using dandelion. Consume foods high in potassium as dandelion may cause potassium depletion. May cause allergic reactions and dermatitis in susceptible individuals.

Adverse Reactions: Diarrhea, edema, nausea, salivation (increased), and/or vomiting.

Herb/Drug Interactions: This herb could cause an interaction (possibly severe) when taken with the following drugs: Antibiotic drugs, Antidiabetic drugs, Diuretic drugs, and Hypotensive drugs.

Preparations/Dosage: Crude Herb: 3-9 grams. Decoction: ¼-½ cup per day. Extract: 5-10 drops (0.333-0.666 cc.) one to two times per day. Extract (solid): Average dose in substance 5-15 grains (0.324-1 gm.). Infusion: ½-1 cup per day. Juice: 1-2 teaspoons in water per day. Tincture: 10-20 drops (0.666-1.25 cc.) one to three times per day. External Uses: Latex: Apply latex directly to corn or wart twice daily and cover with a bandaid. Repeat application for 3-5 days or until corn or wart is gone.

Isolation: Mannitol hexanitrate: Average dose of 15-60 mg. for use as a vasodilator. Taraxacerin or Taraxacin: Soluble in alcohol and water. Average dose of 2-4 grains (0.133-0.26 gm.) for use as a simple bitter.

Devil's Claw (dev'elz klô)

(*Harpagophytum procumbens*)

Synonyms/Related Species: Grapple Plant and Wood Spider.

Family/Class: Pedaliaceae (pedalium).

Habitat: Africa, the Kalahari, and the Savannas.

Flavor: Bitter.

Parts Used: Root.

Properties: Analgesic, anticoagulant, antiperiodic, antiphlogistic, cardiant, depurative, diuretic, hepatic, hypoglycemic, laxative, lithotriptic, malariacidal, stimulant, and stomachic.

Constituents: Chlorogenic acid, gum, flavonoids, glycosides, minerals (aluminum, barium, chlorine, potassium, silicon, sodium, sulfur, tin), monosaccharides, protein, resin, silicic acid, stachyose, sterols, and ursone (ursolic acid).

Historical Uses: Ague, appetite loss, arteriosclerosis, arthritis, calculus, cardiac conditions, carpal tunnel syndrome, diabetes, emaciation, fever (ephemeral, intermittent, rheumatic), gallbladder problems, gastrointestinal problems, gout, headache, hypercholesteremia, hyperglycemia, hyperlipoidemia, indigestion, inflammation, insufficiency (venous), kidney stones, liver problems, malaria, muscle and joint pain, neuralgia, pain, parasites (malarial plasmodia), rheumatism, sciatica, skin problems, tendinitis, and weight loss.

Discussion: May cleanse the whole system; delay or reduce coagulation of the blood; dissolve calculi; enhance liver and stomach functions; increase circulation; promote bowel evacuation and

urine flow; protect the liver; reduce blood sugar levels, cholesterol levels, and lipid levels; stimulate appetite, the cardiovascular system, gallbladder function, the glandular system, peristalsis, and uterine contractions.
Cautions/Contraindications: Avoid use if pregnant or breast-feeding, or if you have a cardiovascular condition, gallstones, an insufficiency (gastric), or ulcer. Some persons may experience bleeding or increased clotting time when using this herb with anticoagulant drugs or aspirin.
Adverse Reactions: Arrhythmia, bleeding (possibly serious), blood pressure fluctuactions, coagulation problems, diarrhea (severe), edema, headache, nausea, tinnitus, and/or vomiting.
Herb/Drug Interactions: This herb could cause an interaction (possibly severe) when taken with the following drugs: Antibiotic drugs, Anticoagulant drugs, Antidiabetic drugs, Salicylates, and Subsalicylates.
Preparations/Dosage: Crude Herb: 3-9 grams. Decoction: ½-1 cup per day. Infusion: 1-3 cups per day. Root (powdered): Average dose in substance ½-1 teaspoon. Tincture: 10-30 drops (0.666-2 cc.) one to three times per day.
Isolation: Barium arsenate: Average dose of $^{1}/_{16}$-¼ grain (0.004-0.016 gm.) for use in emaciation and skin problems. Barium chloride: Average dose of ⅓-1⅔ grains (20-100 mg.) for use as a cardiant.

Devil's Club (dev elz klub)
(*Oplopanax horridum*)

Synonyms/Related Species: Chinese Devil's Club (*oplopanax elatus*), Japanese Devil's Club (*oplopanax japonicus*), and Prickly Porcupine Ginseng.
Family/Class: Araliaceae (ginseng).
Habitat: Alaska, Asia, China, Japan, Korea, and North America.
Flavor: Bitter.
Parts Used: Bark (inner/root), root, stems (outer bark and spines removed).
Properties: Alterative, analgesic, antibiotic, antidiabetic, antifungal, antigalactic, antiphlogistic, antiviral, carminative, depurative, diaphoretic, emetic, hypoglycemic, laxative, parasiticide, stomachic, and tonic.
Constituents: Cadinene and saponin.
Historical Uses: Abscess, amenorrhea, appetite loss, arthritis, bronchitis, bruises, calculus, cancer, colds, constipation, cough, dandruff, diabetes, emaciation, fever (ephemeral, rheumatic), flatulence, fractures, gallstones, hyperglycemia, indigestion, infection (bacterial, fungal, viral), inflammation, influenza, insect bites or stings, lesions (tubercle), muscle and joint pain, pain, parasites (lice and their nits), pneumonia, rheumatism, scrofula, sores, stomachache, toothache, tuberculosis, ulcer (duodenal, fistula, gastric, peptic, stasis, tuberculous), weight loss, and wounds (minor).
Discussion: May aid digestion; curb sugar cravings; diminish or suppress lactation; enhance pancreatic, spleen, and stomach functions; inhibit or destroy development and growth of bacteria and other microorganisms; prevent the development of diabetes; promote bowel evacuation and perspiration; purify the blood; reduce blood sugar levels; reestablish healthy system functions; regulate menstrual flow following childbirth; restore normal tone to tissues; serve as a source of natural insulin.

Cautions/Contraindications: Avoid use if pregnant or breast-feeding. Berries are poisonous. May cause an allergic reaction in susceptible individuals. Not for long-term use.
Adverse Reactions: Diarrhea (severe/possibly bloody), gastrointestinal pain (severe), hematuria (blood in the urine), nausea, and/or vomiting.
Herb/Drug Interactions: This herb could cause an interaction (possibly severe) when taken with the following drugs: Antidiabetic drugs.
Preparations/Dosage: Crude Herb: 3-9 grams. Decoction: ½ cup per day. Infusion: ½-1 cup per day.

Dill (dil)
(*Anethum graveolens*)
Synonyms/Related Species: Anethon and Garden Dill.
Family/Class: Umbelliferae (parsley).
Habitat: The Mediterranean, North America, and Russia.
Flavor: Pungent.
Parts Used: Leaves, seed.
Properties: Anesthetic (local), antibiotic, antiphlogistic, antiscorbutic, antispasmodic, aromatic, astringent, carminative, diuretic, emmenagogue, sedative, stimulant, and stomachic.
Constituents: Anethene, bergapten, carvol, carvene (limonene), esculin, eugenol (eugenic acid), fatty acids (oleic, palmitic, stearic), fixed oils (olein, palmitin, stearin), flavonoids, glycosides, myristicine, phellandrene, pinene, protein, triterpenes, umbelliferone, vitamins (C (ascorbic acid), and volatile oil.
Historical Uses: Abdominal pain, appetite loss, bronchitis, colds, colic, cough, diarrhea, digestive complaints, edema, escherichia coli (e-coli), fever, flatulence, flavoring agent, gallbladder problems, gastralgia, gastrointestinal problems, halitosis, hemorrhoids, hiccups, indigestion, infection (bacterial), inflammation, influenza, insomnia, jaundice, kidney problems, liver problems, scurvy, spasmodic conditions, ulcer (duodenal, gastric, peptic), urinary problems, and urinary tract infection.
Discussion: May aid digestion; enhance liver, spleen, and stomach functions; inhibit or destroy developement and growth of bacteria and other microorganisms; promote urine flow; stimulate appetite and menstruation.
Cautions/Contraindications: Avoid use if pregnant or breast-feeding. Do not confuse this plant with poisonous members of the parsley family. May cause photosensitivity or photodermatosis in susceptible individuals.
Adverse Reactions: None known.
Herb/Drug Interactions: This herb could cause an interaction (possibly severe) when taken with the following drugs: None known.
Preparations/Dosage: Crude Herb: 3-9 grams. Dillseed Water (*aqua anethi*): ½ oz. (15 cc.) per day. Extract: 10-15 drops (0.666-1 cc.) one to two times per day. Infusion (seeds/bruised): ½-1 cup per day. Oil of Dill Seed (*oleum anethi*): 2-5 drops (0.133-0.333 cc.) in water or on a sugarcube.
Isolation: Esculin: Average dose of 10-15 grains (0.66-1 gm.) for use as a febrifuge.

Dita (dē te)

(*Alstonia scholaris*)

Synonyms/Related Species: Alstonia Bark, Australia Fever Bush, Australian Quinine (*alstonia constricta*), Chatim, Devil's Bit, Fever Bark, Java Dita Bark (*alstonia spectabilis*), Pale Mara, and Poele.
Family/Class: Apocynaceae (dogbane).
Habitat: Asia, Australia, India, Java, the Philippines, and Wales.
Flavor: Bitter.
Parts Used: Bark, seeds.
Properties: Antiperiodic, antiphlogistic, antispasmodic, aphrodisiac, astringent, bitter, hemostatic, malariacidal, stimulant, and tonic.
Constituents: Alkaloids, alstonamine, alstonine, chlorogenic acid, ditamine, ditaine, echitenine, fatty substance, glycosides, porphyrine, porphyrosine, resin, and tannic acid.
Historical Uses: Ague, bleeding, diarrhea, dysentery, dysmenorrhea, fever (intermittent, rheumatic), gastrointestinal problems, inflammation, malaria, muscle and joint pain, parasites (malarial plasmodia), rheumatism, spasmodic conditions, and substitute for quinine.
Discussion: May arouse sexual impulses; delay orgasm during coitus; help retain erection; restore normal tone to tissues; stimulate uterine contractions.
Cautions/Contraindications: Avoid use if pregnant or breast-feeding. Not for long-term use.
Adverse Reactions: Diarrhea, nausea, and/or vomiting.
Herb/Drug Interactions: This herb could cause an interaction (possibly severe) when taken with the following drugs: None known.
Preparations/Dosage: Bark (powdered): Average dose in substance 2-4 grains (0.133-0.26 gm.). Decoction: ⅛-¼ cup per day. Extract: 5-10 drops (0.333-0.666 cc.). Tincture: 10-15 drops (0.666-1 cc.). Aphrodisiac Uses (seeds/crushed): Initial Use: Soak 2 grams of seeds in 2 ounces of water overnight. Strain off the liquid the following day and drink. Increase the dosage a little at a time as needed.
Note: The aphrodisiac use of dita seeds may include a temporary, unharmful physical effect in the form of a tingling sensation in the genitourinary tract.

Dock (däk)

(*Rumex crispus*)

Synonyms/Related Species: Bitter Dock, Broad-Leaved Dock, Butter Dock, Canaigre, Common Wayside Dock, Curled Dock, Desert Dock (*rumex hymenosepalus*), Desert Rhubarb, Golden Dock (*rumex maritimus*), Great Water Dock (*rumex hydrolapathum*), Herb Patience, Monk's Rhubarb, Narrow Dock, Passion's Dock, Patience Dock (*rumex alpinus*), Red Dock, Round-Leaved Dock (*rumex obtusifolius*), Rumex, Sharp-Pointed Dock (*rumex acetus*), Sour Dock, Water Dock, Western Dock (*rumex aquaticus*), Willow Dock (*rumex salicifolius*), and Yellow Dock.
Family/Class: Polygonaceae (buckwheat)
Habitat: Africa, Europe, North America, the Subalpine zone, and the Yukon Territory.
Flavor: Bitter.
Parts Used: Root.
Properties: Alterative, antibiotic, anticarcinogen, antiphlogistic, antiscorbutic, astringent, carminative, cholagogue, depurative, hemostatic, laxative, and tonic.

Constituents: Aglycone (genin), chrysophanic acid (rumicin), emodin, flavonoids, glycoside, lapodin, minerals (calcium, iron, manganese, nickel, potassium), monosaccharides, oxalic acid, quercetin, tannic acid, and vitamins A and C (ascorbic acid).
Historical Uses: Acne, amenorrhea, anemia, bladder problems, bleeding, blisters, bronchitis, burns (minor), cancer (intestinal), chicken pox, constipation, cough, diarrhea, digestive complaints, diverticulitis, ear infection, eczema, edema, fatigue, fever (ephemeral, herpetic, rheumatic, scarlet), gallbladder problems, gastrointestinal problems, glandular problems, headache, hemorrhage, hemorrhoids, hepatitis, herpes, indigestion, infection (bacterial), inflammation, insufficiency (venous), jaundice, laryngitis, leprosy, lesions (tubercle), leukemia, liver problems, mucus, muscle and joint pain, poison ivy/oak, poisoning (arsenic), pruritus, psoriasis, rash, respiratory conditions, rheumatism, scarletina, scrofula, scurvy, sexually transmitted diseases (STDs), skin problems, sores, spleen problems, syphilis, tuberculosis, tumors, ulcer (duodenal, fistula, gastric, peptic, syphilitic, tuberculous), urticaria, and wounds (minor).
Discussion: May aid digestion; decrease the effect of carcinogens; enhance digestive system, intestinal system, liver, and lymphatic system functions; improve iron absorption; increase circulation; inhibit or destroy development and growth of bacteria and other microorganisms; promote bile flow and bowel evacuation; purify the blood; reestablish healthy system functions; restore normal tone to tissues; serve as an antidote for arsenic poisoning; stimulate peristalsis; strengthen the vascular system.
Cautions/Contraindications: Avoid use if pregnant or breast-feeding, or if you have acidity (gastric), diarrhea, irritable bowel syndrome (IBS), a kidney problem, or have a history of kidney stones. May cause dermatitis in susceptible individuals.
Adverse Reactions: Diarrhea (possibly severe), flatulence, gastrointestinal cramps, laxative dependency, mucous membrane problems, hematuria (blood in the urine), nausea, oxalism (oxalic acid or oxalate poisoning), and/or vomiting.
Herb/Drug Interactions: This herb could cause an interaction (possibly severe) when taken with the following drugs: None known.
Preparations/Dosage: Crude Herb: 3-9 grams. Extract (powdered): Average dose in pill form 1-4 grains (0.066-0.26 gm.). Infusion: 1-2 cups per day. Tincture: 15-30 drops (1-2 cc.) one to three times per day.
Isolation: Chrysopahanic acid: Average dose of 1-10 grains (0.065-0.666 gm.) for use in skin problems. Oxalic acid: Average dose of ½-¾ grain (0.0333-0.048) for use in amenorrhea.

Dodder (dod er)
(*Cuscuta americana*)

Synonyms/Related Species: Beggarweed, Chaparral Dodder (*cuscuta californica*), Chinese Dodder (*cuscuta chinensis*), Compact Dodder (*cuscuta compacta*), Devil's Guts, European Dodder (*cuscuta epithymum*), Lesser Dodder, Love-Vine, Scaldweed, and Strangle Tare.
Family/Class: Convolvulaceae (morning glory).
Habitat: Africa, Asia, Europe, and the United States.
Flavor: Pungent.
Parts Used: Entire plant.
Properties: Antifertilizin, antiphlogistic, aphrodisiac, astringent, demulcent, diuretic, hemostatic, hepatic, laxative, ophthalmic, tonic, and vulnerary.
Constituents: Cuscitin, saponins, and tannic acid.

Historical Uses: Arrhythmia, arthritis, bleeding, constipation, contraceptive, diarrhea, diuria (frequent daytime urination), dizziness, enuresis (urinary incontinence), erectile dysfunction, eye problems, fainting, fever (ephemeral, rheumatic), glandular problems, glandular swelling, infection (urinary tract), inflammation, insect bites or stings, jaundice, lesions (tubercle), liver problems, melancholy, muscle and joint pain, nocturnal emission, nosebleed, premature ejaculation, prostatitis, rheumatism, rheumatoid arthritis (RA), sciatica, scrofula, spermatorrhea, spleen problems, tinnitus, tuberculosis, tumors, ulcer (fistula, tuberculous), and urinary problems.

Discussion: May arouse sexual impulses; enhance digestive system, kidney, liver, and urinary system functions; improve vision; increase circulation and sperm count; neutralize fertilizin (fertilization), promote urine flow; protect the liver; reduce the persistent urge to urinate, the frequency of nighttime urination, and the emission of semen during sleep; restore normal tone to tissues; soothe mucous membrane irritation; speed healing; strengthen bones, ligaments, and the urinary system.

Cautions/Contraindications: Avoid use if pregnant or breast-feeding. Care should be used when collecting as parasitic plants have a tendency to accumulate toxins from their hosts.

Adverse Reactions: Diarrhea (possibly bloody), gastrointestinal cramps (severe), hematuria (blood in the urine), nausea, and/or vomiting.

Herb/Drug Interactions: This herb could cause an interaction (possibly severe) when taken with the following drugs: None known.

Preparations/Dosage: Crude Herb: 3-12 grams. Infusion: ½-1 cup per day. Juice: ½-1 teaspoon in water per day.

Dogwood (dôg wood)
(*Cornus florida*)

Synonyms/Related Species: Akenia (*cornus mascula*), American Boxwood, American Dogwood, Bitter Redberry, Boxwood, Budwood, Bunchberry (*cornus canadensis*), Common Dogwood, Cornel, Cornouille, Dog-Tree, Dwarf Dogwood (*cornus suecica*), European Dogwood (*cornus stolonifera*), Florida Cornel, Kizziljiek, New England Boxwood, Red-Osier Dogwood (*cornus sericea*), Redwood, Round-Leaved Dogwood (*cornus circinata*), Silky Cornel, Swamp Dogwood, and Virginia Dogwood.

Family/Class: Cornaceae (dogwood).

Floral Emblem: North Carolina and Virginia.

Habitat: Alaska, Greece, North America, Scotland, Turkey, and the Yukon Territory.

Flavor: Bitter.

Parts Used: Bark (root).

Properties: Antibiotic, antiperiodic, antiphlogistic, antispasmodic, astringent, depurative, emetic, hemostatic, laxative, malariacidal, parasiticide, sedative, stimulant, and tonic.

Constituents: Cornin, gallic acid, gum, lignin, lime (calcium oxide), minerals (calcium, iron, magnesium, potassium), resin, saponins, tannic acid, volatile oil, and wax.

Historical Uses: Ague, anthrax (ulcerations), appetite loss, bleeding, cholera, colds, cough, dandruff, diarrhea, digestive complaints, dysmenorrhea, exhaustion, eyewash, fatigue, fever (ephemeral, enteric, intermittent, rheumatic), herbal tobacco (inner bark), infection (bacterial), inflammation, insomnia, liver problems, lochia, malaria, migraine, muscle and joint pain, nervous conditions, neuralgia, ovarian pain, parasites (malarial plasmodia), rash, rheumatism,

sinusitis, skin problems, sore eyes, spasmodic conditions, substitute for peruvian bark and quinine, toothache, typhoid, ulcer (bouveret, duodenal, gastric, peptic), and wounds (minor).
Discussion: May enhance cardiovascular system function; inhibit or destroy development and growth of bacteria and other microorganisms; promote bowel evacuation; purify the blood; restore normal tone to tissues; stimulate appetite, peristalsis, and uterine contractions.
Cautions/Contraindications: Avoid use if pregnant or breast-feeding. Do not confuse these species with Dogwood, Jamaican (*pisicia erythrina*). May cause dermatitis in susceptible individuals.
Adverse Reactions: Diarrhea (possibly bloody), gastrointestinal cramps (severe), hematuria (blood in the urine), nausea, and/or vomiting.
Herb/Drug Interactions: This herb could cause an interaction (possibly severe) when taken with the following drugs: Antimalarial drugs.
Preparations/Dosage: Crude Herb: 1-3 grams. Infusion: ½ cup per day. Tincture: 10-30 drops (0.666-2 cc.) one to three times per day.
Isolation: Cornin: Average dose of 2-4 grains (0.133-0.266 gm.) for use as an antiperiodic and tonic.

Dogwood, Jamaican (dôg wood, je·mā ken)
(*Piscidia erythrina*)

Synonyms/Related Species: Fish Poison Tree and Piscis Caedere Tree.
Family/Class: Leguminosea (legume).
Habitat: Central America, India, and South America.
Flavor: Bitter/pungent.
Parts Used: Bark.
Properties: Analgesic, antispasmodic, diaphoretic, insecticide, narcotic, parasiticide, scabicide, and sedative.
Constituents: Bitter principle, fatty substance, flavonoids, piscidin, resin, rotenone, and tannic acid.
Historical Uses: Anxiety, asthma, dysmenorrhea, fear, hysteria, insects, insomnia, nervous conditions, neuralgia, pain, parasites (scabies and their nits), spasmodic conditions, toothache, and whooping cough.
Discussion: May destroy insects and scabies and their nits; promote perspiration.
Cautions/Contraindications: Avoid use if pregnant or breast-feeding.
Adverse Reactions: Nausea, pupil dilatation, stupor, and/or vomiting.
Herb/Drug Interactions: This herb could cause an interaction (possibly severe) when taken with the following drugs: None known.
Preparations/Dosage: Crude Herb: 3-6 grams. Extract (solid): Average dose in substance 1-5 grains (0.066-0.324 gm.). Tincture: 5-30 drops (0.333-2 cc.) one to three times per day.
Did You Know? Some natives still use Jamaican dogwood for fishing. They place the leaves (bruised), bark, and/or young branches into a basket and drag it through the water to stupefy fish; the fish are then plucked from the water surface.

Duckweed (duk wēd)
(*Lemna minor*)

Synonyms/Related Species: Common Duckweed, Ivy-Leaved Duckweed (*lemna trisulca*), and Large Duckweed.
Family/Class: Lemnaceae (duckweed).
Habitat: Worldwide.
Flavor: Bitter/pungent.
Parts Used: Entire plant.
Properties: Alterative, antiphlogistic, cardiant, diaphoretic, and diuretic.
Constituents: Fatty acids (arachidonic, linoleic, linolenic), flavonoids, glycosides, monosaccharides, polysaccharides, and saponins.
Historical Uses: Congestive heart failure (CHF), edema, fever (ephemeral, rheumatic), infection (urinary tract), inflammation, influenza, insect bites or stings, jaundice, liver problems, measles, muscle and joint pain, rash, respiratory conditions, rheumatism, and skin problems.
Discussion: May enhance lung function; promote perspiration and urine flow; reestablish healthy system functions; stimulate the cardiovascular system.
Cautions/Contraindications: Avoid use if pregnant or breast-feeding. Harvest duckweed from fresh water as it may accumulate heavy metals and toxins from polluted water.
Adverse Reactions: Arrhythmia, diarrhea (possibly bloody), gastrointestinal cramps (severe), hematuria (blood in the urine), nausea, and/or vomiting.
Herb/Drug Interactions: This herb could cause an interaction (possibly severe) when taken with the following drugs: None known.
Preparations/Dosage: Crude Herb: 3-9 grams. Infusion: 1-3 cups per day.

Dusty Miller (dus tē mil er)
(*Cineraria maritima*)

Synonyms/Related Species: Cinerarius and Senecio Maritima.
Family/Class: Compositae (composite).
Habitat: The Mediterranean and North America.
Parts Used: Leaf juice (sterilized).
Properties: Ophthalmic.
Constituents: Alkaloids, retrorsine, jacobine, senecifolin, and senecionine.
Historical Uses: Cataracts, conjunctivitis, eye problems, eye drops, eyewash, and visual disturbances.
Discussion: May enhance eye function; strengthen the vision.
Cautions/Contraindications: External uses only.
Adverse Reactions: Liver damgage (often characterized by jaundice).
Herb/Drug Interactions: This herb could cause an interaction (possibly severe) when taken with the following drugs: None known.
Preparations/Dosage: See "Forms of Herbal Preparation" for information on preparing eye drops.

Elder (el der)
(*Sambucus canadensis*)

Synonyms/Related Species: American Elder, Asian Elderberry (*sambucus latipinna*), Black Elderberry (*sambucus racemosa*), Blue Elderberry (*sambucus cerulea*), Common Elder, Danewort, Dwarf Elder (*sambucus ebulus*), Ellanwood, European Elder (*sambucus nigra*), German Elder, Mexican Elderberry (*sambucus mexicana*), Nature's Remedy Chest, Red Elder, Rob Elder, Sweet Elder, Walewort, and Wild Elder.

Family/Class: Caprifoliaceae (honeysuckle).

Habitat: Asia, Britain, Europe, Germany, Mexico, North America, and the Subalpine zone.

Flavor: Bitter.

Parts Used: Bark (inner/aged one year), berries (ripe/black), flowers.

Properties: Alterative, antibiotic, anticarcinogen, antifungal, antiphlogistic, antispasmodic, antiviral, carminative, cholagogue, demulcent, depurative, diaphoretic, diuretic, emetic, expectorant, hepatic, laxative, narcotic, nervine, oxytocic, sedative, and stimulant.

Constituents: Agglutinin, albumin (albumen), alkaloids, alkane, amino acids (tyrosine), caffeic acid, chlorogenic acid, chlorophyll, coniine, fatty acids (arachidonic, linoleic, linolenic, oleic, palmitic, stearic), fixed oils (olein, palmitin, stearin), flavonoids, glycosides, gum, hydrocyanic acid, inulin (starch), invertin (sucrase), lectin, lignin, lime (calcium oxide), minerals (calcium, potassium), monosaccharides, mucilage, pectic acid, pectin, phenolic acids, quercitin, resin, rutin, sambucin, saponins, sterols, tannic acid, ursone (ursolic acid), viburnic acid, vitamins (A, C (ascorbic acid), and volatile oil, wax.

Historical Uses: Acne, allergy (pollen), arthritis, asthma, bronchitis, bruises, burns (minor), cancer, chilblains, colds, conjunctivitis, constipation, convulsions, cough, digestive complaints, dry skin, dysmenorrhea, ear infection, edema, epilepsy, eyestrain, fever (ephemeral, hay, herpetic, rheumatic), gargle/mouth rinse, gout, headache, hemorrhoids, herpes, human immunodeficiency virus (HIV), indigestion, infection (bacterial, fungal, viral), inflammation, influenza, jam/jelly (berry), laryngitis, lumbago, meningitis, mucus, muscle and joint pain, nervous conditions, neuralgia, pain, pneumonia, rash, respiratory conditions, rheumatism, scalds, sciatica, sexually transmitted diseases (STDs), sinusitis, skin problems, sores, sore throat, spasmodic conditions, sprain, stomachache, syphilis, tonsillitis, tumors, ulcer (duodenal, gastric, peptic, syphilitic), wounds (minor), and wrinkles.

Discussion: May aid digestion; calm the nervous system; cause agglutination (clumping) of bacteria, red blood corpuscles, or other cells; cleanse the whole system; clear and open bronchial passages; decrease the effect of carcinogens; enhance colon, liver, lung, and stomach functions; increase circulation; inhibit or destroy development and growth of bacteria and other microorganisms; prevent hemorrhage in persons with hypertension; promote bile flow, bowel evacuation, perspiration, and urine flow; protect the liver; purify the blood; reduce capillary fragility; reestablish healthy system functions; serve as a safe alternative to influenza A and B treatments; soothe mucous membrane irritation; stimulate the immune system, peristalsis, and uterine contractions.

Cautions/Contraindications: Avoid use if pregnant or breast-feeding. Bark must be aged for one year to avoid possible hydrocyanic acid poisoning. Berries of Dwarf elder and Red elder are poisonous. The stems contain hydrocyanic acid and are extremely poisonous. Use only the ripened bluish or purplish-black berries of Blue or Black elder, and lightly cook them prior to ingestion to prevent diarrhea, gastrointestinal problems, and vomiting.

Adverse Reactions: Cardiac failure, diarrhea (severe/possibly bloody), gastroenteritis (severe), hematuria (blood in the urine), hydrocyanism (hydrocyanic acid poisoning), nausea, respiratory distress, stupor, and/or vomiting.
Herb/Drug Interactions: This herb could cause an interaction (possibly severe) when taken with the following drugs: None known.
Preparations/Dosage: Crude Herb: 3-6 grams. Decoction (bark): ½-1 cup per day. Elderflower Water (*aqua sambuci*): 10 pounds elder flowers distilled in 1 gallon of water. The water is ready for use when the initial unpleasant odor turns agreeably aromatic. Infusion (berries): 1-2 tablespoons per day. Infusion (flowers and/or leaves): 1-2 cups per day. Juice (berries): 1-2 tablespoons in water per day. Syrup (berries): 1-2 tablespoons in water per day. Tincture (flowers): 15-30 drops (1-2 cc.) one to three times per day.

Elecampane (el i·kam·pān)
(*Inula helenium*)

Synonyms/Related Species: Alantwurzel, Aunée, Elf Dock, Enula, Helenion, Horse Elder, Horseheal, Inulo, Marchalan, Scabwort, Velvet Dock, and Yellow Starwort.
Family/Class: Compositae (composite).
Habitat: Asia, England, Europe, Germany, Scotland, and the United States.
Flavor: Bitter/pungent.
Parts Used: Flowers, root.
Properties: Alterative, antibiotic, antiemetic, antifungal, antiphlogistic, astringent, carminative, diaphoretic, diuretic, emmenagogue, expectorant, hemostatic, hepatic, parasiticide, sedative, stimulant, stomachic, and tonic.
Constituents: Alantic acid, azulene, inulain, inulin (starch), inulol (alantol), minerals (calcium, potassium, sodium), mucilage, pectic acid, pectin, polysaccharide, resin, sterols, and volatile oil.
Historical Uses: Amenorrhea, anemia, appetite loss, asthma, bladder problems, bleeding, bronchitis, candida, colds, colic, convulsions, cough, cramps, digestive complaints, diphtheria, edema, emaciation, emphysema, fever (ephemeral, herpetic), flatulence, gargle/mouth rinse, gastritis, gastrointestinal problems, gout, herpes, hiccups, indigestion, infection (bacterial, fungal), inflammation, insufficiency (pancreatic), irritable bowel syndrome (IBS), lesions (tubercle), melancholy, menopausal/menstrual problems, moniliasis, mucus, muscle and joint pain, nausea, neuralgia, night sweats, parasites (scabies), periodontal disease, pneumonia, rash, respiratory conditions, sciatica, scrofula, sexually transmitted diseases (STDs), shortness of breath, skin problems, snakebite, tuberculosis, ulcer (fistula, syriac, tuberculous), vomiting, wheezing, and whooping cough.
Discussion: May aid digestion and assimilation; clear and open bronchial passages; enhance lung, pancreatic, spleen, stomach, and urinary functions; inhibit or destroy developement and growth of bacteria and other microorganisms; neutralize poisons and toxins; promote perspiration and urine flow; reestablish healthy system functions; restore normal tone to tissues; serve as a source of natural insulin; stimulate appetite, menstruation and peristalsis.
Cautions/Contraindications: Avoid use if pregnant or breast-feeding.
Adverse Reactions: Diarrhea, edema, elevated blood sugar levels, gastrointestinal cramps, mucous membrane problems, nausea, and/or vomiting.
Herb/Drug Interactions: This herb could cause an interaction (possibly severe) when taken with the following drugs: None known.

Preparations/Dosage: Crude Herb: 3-9 grams. Decoction (root): ½-1 cup per day. Infusion (flowers): 1-2 cups per day. Root (powdered): Average dose in substance 15-30 grains (0.98-2 gm.). Tincture: 10-30 drops (0.666-2 cc.) one to three times per day.
Isolation: Inulol (alantol): Average dose of $^{1}/_{6}$-½ drop (0.011-0.032 cc) for use as an expectorant and stimulant in bronchitis, emaciation, and tuberculosis (pulmonary).

Ephedra (e·fed ra)
(*Ephedra nevadensis*)

Synonyms/Related Species: American Ephedra, Brigham Young Weed, Desert Herb, Desert Tea, Epitonin, Green Ephedra (*ephedra viridis*), Ma-Huang (*ephedra sinica*), Mormon Tea, Squaw Tea, and Teamster's Tea.
Family/Class: Ephedraceae (ephedra).
Habitat: Asia, China, Europe, Japan, Mongolia, Siberia, and the United States.
Flavor: Bitter/pungent/sweet.
Parts Used: Leaves, root, stems/twigs.
Properties: Antiphlogistic, antispasmodic, astringent, depurative, diaphoretic, diuretic, expectorant, hemostatic, hypertensive, mydriatic, stimulant, tonic, and vasoconstrictor
Constituents: Alkaloids, ephedrine, minerals (cobalt, copper, nickel, strontium), pseudoephedrine, saponins, tannic acid, vitamins (B_{12}), and volatile oil.
Historical Uses: Abscess, Addison's disease, allergy (pollen), amenorrhea, arrhythmia, arthritis, asthma, bladder problems, bleeding, bronchitis, bursitis, chills, colds, cough, depression (mild/moderate), diarrhea, diphtheria, edema, emphysema, epilepsy, fever (ephemeral, hay, rheumatic, scarlet), gallbladder problems, gastrointestinal problems, gleet, gonorrhea, gout, headache, hemorrhage, hives, hypotension, infection (bacterial, sexually transmitted, urinary tract), inflammation, influenza, kidney problems, lung problems, menstrual problems, mucus, muscle and joint pain, night sweats, nosebleed, pneumonia, rash, respiratory conditions, rheumatism, scarletina, sexually transmitted diseases (STDs), sinusitis, skin problems, sores, spasmodic conditions, syphilis, ulcer (syphilitic, syriac), urethritis, wheezing, and whooping cough.
Discussion: May cause blood vessel constriction and pupil dilatation; clear and open the bronchial passages; elevate blood pressure levels; enhance glandular system and lung functions; promote perspiration and urine flow; purify the blood; restore normal tone to tissues; slow and strengthen the heart rate; stimulate the nervous system.
Cautions/Contraindications: Avoid use if pregnant or breast-feeding, or if you have anorexia, anxiety, arteriosclerosis, bulimia, diabetes, glaucoma, a cardiovascular condition, high fever, history of kidney stones, hypertension, hyperthyroidism, hypertrophy (benign prostatic), insomnia, an insufficiency (adrenal), lupus, a nervous condition, restlessness, or if you have heart, liver, or kidney disease. Be sure to drink at least six to eight glasses of water daily when taking ephedra. Do not administer to children. Do not exceed representative dosage. Competitive athletes should be cautious concerning the use of ephedra as the United States Olympic Committee has listed it as a banned substance. May decrease the effectiveness of corticosteroid drugs. May increase the effects of monoamine oxidase inhibitor (MAOI) drugs. Overuse of ephedra combined with vigorous exercise and inadequate water intake may cause the formation of kidney stones. Not for long-term use. Use under professional guidance/supervision.

Adverse Reactions: Arrhythmia, asphyxiation, cardiac failure, diarrhea (possibly bloody), ephidrosis (excessive perspiration), gastrointestinal cramps (severe), headache, hematuria (blood in the urine), hemorrhage (cerebral), hypertension, insomnia, irritability, kidney failure, nausea, nephritis, nervousness, pupil dilatation, restlessness, spasmodic conditions, tachycardia, trembling, vomiting, and/or possible death.
Herb/Drug Interactions: This herb could cause an interaction (possibly severe) when taken with the following drugs: Antidepressant drugs, Autonomic drugs, Beta-Adrenergic Blocking drugs, Bronchodilator drugs, Caffeine or caffeine containing products, Cardiac drugs, Corticosteroids, other Medications/Products containing ephedra, phenylpropanolamine, or pseudoephedrine, Monoamine Oxidase (MAOIs) Inhibitors, and Phenylpropanolamine drugs.
Preparations/Dosage: External uses are recommended. Crude Herb (leaves and/or stems): 3-6 grams. Crude Herb (root): 6-9 grams. Decoction: ½ cup per day. Infusion: 1 cup per day.
Isolation: Ephedrine (hydrochloride or sulfate): Average dose of ⅜ grain (25 mg.) for use in Addison's disease, asthma, circulatory problems, hypotension, hemorrhage, and as a mydriatic. Ephedrine's chemical structure and physiologic action is similar to that of epinephrine. Pseudoephedrine: ¾ grain (0.05 gm.) for use as a bronchial stimulant and as a mydriatic. Strontium bromide: 10-60 grains (0.666-4 gm.) for use as an antiepileptic, antinephritic, and tonic. Strontium salicylate: Soluble in forty parts water, and freely in alcohol. Average dose in capsule 5-15 grains (0.3-1 gm.) for use in gout, intestinal problems, and rheumatic conditions.

Epimedium (ep e·mē·dē·um)

(*Epimedium grandiflorum*)

Synonyms/Related Species: Goatwort, Horny Goatweed, and Lusty Goatherb.
Family/Class: Berberidaceae (barberry).
Habitat: Asia and North America.
Flavor: Pungent.
Parts Used: Leaves.
Properties: Antibiotic, antiphlogistic, aphrodisiac, diaphoretic, diuretic, expectorant, hypertensive, parasiticide, stomachic, teniacide, teniafuge, tonic, vasoconstrictor, vermifuge, and vulnerary.
Constituents: Benzene, fatty acids (arachidonic, linoleic, linolenic, oleic, palmitic, stearic), fixed oils (olein, palmitin, stearin), glycosides, sterols, tannic acid, and vitamin E (alpha-tocopheral).
Historical Uses: Acquired immune deficiency syndrome (AIDS), arthritis, asthma, bronchitis, cancer, colds, cramps, diarrhea, diminished sex drive, diuria (frequent daytime urination), dizziness, enuresis (urinary incontinence), erectile dysfunction, extremity numbness, fever (ephemeral, rheumatic), forgetfulness, frigidity, gleet, gonorrhea, human immunodeficiency virus (HIV), hypothyroidism, infection (bacterial, sexually transmitted), inflammation, influenza, kidney problems, leukemia, menstrual problems, mucus, muscle and joint pain, orchitis, parasites (crabs and their nits, lice and their nits, tapeworm), prostate problems, respiratory conditions, rheumatism, sexually transmitted diseases (STDs), spasmodic conditions, spermatorrhea, and urethritis.
Discussion: May arouse sexual impulses; clear and open bronchial passages; dilate the blood vessels; enhance adrenal, liver, kidney, and stomach functions; inhibit or destroy development and growth of bacteria and other microorganisms; promote bone formation, perspiration, and

urine flow; reduce blood pressure levels and the persistent urge to urinate; restore normal tone to tissues; speed healing; stimulate androgen hormone production, sperm production, and sexual activity in males and females; strengthen the urinary system.
Cautions/Contraindications: Avoid use if pregnant or breast-feeding, or if you have emaciation, a hypersexual condition, hypertension, a prostate problem, or wet dreams. Not for long-term use.
Adverse Reactions: Dizziness, dry mouth, exaggerated reflexes, excessive thirst, nausea, nosebleed, respiratory distress, spasmodic conditions, and/or vomiting.
Herb/Drug Interactions: This herb could cause an interaction (possibly severe) when taken with the following drugs: Hypertensive drugs.
Preparations/Dosage: Crude Herb: 3-12 grams. Infusion: 1-2 cups per day.

Eucalyptus (yoo ke·lip tes)
(*Eucalyptus globulus*)

Synonyms/Related Species: Blue Gum Tree, Citron-Scented Gum (*eucalyptus citriodora*), Fever Tree, Gully Ash (*eucalyptus smithii*), Gum Tree, Lemon-Scented Iron Bark (*eucalyptus staigeriana*), Malee Box, Paddy River Box (*eucalyptus macarthurii*), Peppermint Gum (*eucalyptus dives*), Red Gum (*eucalyptus nostrata*), Silver Malee Scrub (*eucalyptus polybractea*), Stringy Bark Tree, Tasmanian Blue Gum Tree, and White Top Peppermint (*eucalyptus radiata*).
Family/Class: Myrtaceae (myrtle).
Habitat: Africa, Australia, Europe, India, and Tasmania.
Flavor: Pungent.
Parts Used: Leaves.
Properties: Antibiotic, anticarcinogen, antifungal, antilithic, antiperiodic, antiphlogistic, antispasmodic, antiviral, aromatic, astringent, counterirritant, diuretic, expectorant, insect repellent, lithotriptic, malariacidal, parasiticide, stimulant, and tonic.
Constituents: Bitter principles, caffeic acid, camphene, carvene (limonene), citronellol, ellagic acid, eucalyptene, eucalyptol (cineol), ferulic acid, gallic acid, geraniol (rhodinol), pinene, piperitol, piperitone, resin, rutin, sesquiterpenes, tannic acid, and volatile oil.
Historical Uses: Abscess, ague, arthritis, asthma, bleeding, bronchitis, burns (minor), calculus, cancer, cockroaches, colds, congestion (uterine, vaginal), cough, croup, diphtheria, edema, emphysema, fever (ephemeral, enteric, intermittent, rheumatic, scarlet), fleas, gallstones, gangrene, gargle/mouth rinse, gleet, gonorrhea, gout, hemorrhoids, indigestion, infection (bacterial, fungal, sexually transmitted, viral), inflammation, influenza, kidney stones, laryngitis, lesions (tubercle), leukorrhea, lithemia, lochia, lung problems, malaria, measles, mosquitos, mucus, muscle and joint pain, nausea, neuralgia, paralysis, parasites (lice and their nits, malarial plasmodia), periodontal disease, pneumonia, prolapse (rectal, uterine), respiratory conditions, rheumatism, scarletina, scrofula, sexually transmitted diseases (STDs), sinusitis, skin problems, sores, sore throat, spasmodic conditions, tuberculosis, typhoid, ulcer (bouveret, duodenal, fistula, gastric, peptic, syriac, tuberculous), urethritis, vaginitis, whooping cough, and wounds (minor).
Discussion: May clear and open bronchial passages; decrease the effect of carcinogens; dissolve calculi; enhance kidney and lung functions; inhibit or destroy development and growth of bacteria and other microorganisms; prevent the development of calculus or stones, and hemorrhage in persons with hypertension; promote urine flow; reduce capillary fragility and

excessive lithic acid (uric acid) and urate levels in the blood, tophi, and urine; restore normal tone to tissues; stimulate the cardiovascular system.
Cautions/Contraindications: Avoid use if pregnant or breast-feeding, or if you have a biliary problem, gastrointestinal inflammation, or liver disease. Do not apply eucalyptus oil to the faces of small children as this can lead to asphyxiation or an asthma-like attack. May cause allergic reactions and dermatitis in susceptible individuals.
Adverse Reactions: Asthma-like attack, circulatory collapse, diarrhea, hypotension, intestinal cramps, hematuria (blood in the urine), nausea, respiratory distress, spasmodic conditions, and/or vomiting.
Herb/Drug Interactions: This herb could cause an interaction (possibly severe) when taken with the following drugs: None known.
Preparations/Dosage: Crude Herb: 3-12 grams. Extract: 10-15 drops (0.666-1 cc.) one to two times per day. Infusion: ½ cup per day. Eucalyptus Oil (aqueous distillation of fresh leaves): Boil leaves in water and condense the vapor to recover the oil (the oil should be colourless or straw-colored when properly prepared). Combine oil with equal parts of water and slippery elm. Take 5-10 drops (0.333-0.666 cc.). External Uses: Leaves: May be applied directly to the affected part in the form of a poultice. Oil of Eucalyptus Oil (*oleum eucalypti*): 2-5 drops (0.133-0.333 cc.) in water, on a sugarcube, or diluted and applied to the throat and chest areas. Inhalation Therapy: Aqueous tincture (diluted) may be inhaled in the form of spray; if the oil is to be employed, it may be dropped on some cotton, from which the vapor may be inhaled. Respiratory Conditions: Eucalyptus leaves made up into cigars or cigarettes and smoked may afford relief in respiratory conditions.
Isolation: Eucalyptol: 5 drops (0.3 cc.) in atomization or inhalation therapy for use in respiratory conditions.
Did You Know? Eucalyptus trees help control and regulate areas that have a high water table.

Evening Primrose (ēv ning prim rōz)

(*Oenothera biennis*)

Synonyms/Related Species: Belle de Nuit, Cabish, Common Evening Primrose, Cut-Leaved Evening Primrose (*oenothera coronopifolia*), Fever Plant, Field Primrose, German Ranpion, Gumbo Primrose, Hooker's Evening Primrose (*oenothera hookeri*), L'herbe aux ânes, Large Ranpion, Moon Rose, Night-Willow Herb, Primrose, Rockrose, Sandlily, Stemless Yellow Evening Primrose (*oenothera flava*), Tall Evening Primrose (*oenothera elata*), Tree Primrose, White Evening Primrose (*oenothera cespitosa*), and Wild Evening Primrose (*oenothera odorata*).
Family/Class: Primulaceae (primrose).
Habitat: Asia, Britain, England, Europe, France, India, Italy, North America, and the Subalpine zone.
Flavor: Sweet.
Parts Used: Bark (stem), leaves, seeds (oil).
Properties: Anticarcinogen, anticoagulant, antiphlogistic, antispasmodic, astringent, diuretic, erythropoietic, hemostatic, hypotensive, laxative, sedative, stimulant, and vasodilator.
Constituents: Fatty acids (arachidonic, gammalinolenic acid (GLA), linoleic, linolenic, oleic, palmitic, stearic), fixed oils (olein, palmitin, stearin), minerals (magnesium, potassium), mucilage, primulite, primulaverin, primverase, and primverin.

Historical Uses: Abscess, acne, addiction (alcohol), allergy, alopecia, angina, anorexia, anxiety, arthritis, asthma, benign breast disease, bleeding, bruises, cancer (liver), cardiovascular conditions, cirrhosis, cold extremities, colds, conjunctivitis, constipation, cough, cramps, cystic fibrosis, dandruff, deficiency conditions, degenerative conditions (mental), depression (mild/moderate), dermatitis, diabetes, diabetic retinopathy, diarrhea, dry skin, dryness conditions, dysmenorrhea, eczema, fatty acid problems, fever (ephemeral, rheumatic), gastrointestinal problems, glaucoma, hangover (caused by alcohol consumption), headache, hemorrhoids, hyperactivity, hypertension (mild/moderate), infection (bacterial), infertility, inflammation, insufficiency (circulatory), lesions, lethargy, liver problems, menopausal/menstrual problems, migraine, mucus, multiple sclerosis (MS), muscle and joint pain, nervous conditions, neuralgia, neurotic conditions, osteoarthritis (OA), Parkinson's disease, poisoning (lithium), premenstrual syndrome (PMS), prostatitis, psoriasis, rash, Raynaud's syndrome, respiratory conditions, rheumatism, rheumatoid arthritis (RA), schizophrenia, sinusitis, Sjögren's syndrome, skin problems, sores, spasmodic conditions, thrombosis, tremors, ulcer (duodenal, gastric, peptic), weight loss, whooping cough, and wounds (minor).
Discussion: May aid in the formation of healthy red blood cells; cause blood vessel dilatation; decrease the effect of carcinogens; delay or reduce coagulation of the blood; ease alcohol withdrawal symptoms and post-drinking depression; enhance cardiovascular system, circulatory system, kidney, liver, and nervous system functions; increase mobility; minimize imbalances and abnormalities of essential fatty acids in prostaglandin production; promote perspiration and urine flow; reduce blood pressure levels, cholesterol levels, and heart rate; stimulate immune system and the vagus nerve; stop or slow abnormal cell growth; strengthen blood vessel walls.
Cautions/Contraindications: Avoid use if pregnant or breast-feeding, or if you have a history of seizure conditions. Common, temporary side effects upon initial use may include headache and mild skin rash. Taking primrose oil with food may help alleviate headache, and taking primrose simultaneously with vitamin E will prevent oxidation inside the body. May cause dermatitis in susceptible individuals. Some persons may experience bleeding or increased clotting time when using this herb with anticoagulant drugs or aspirin.
Adverse Reactions: Bleeding (possibly serious), coagulation problems, nausea, and/or vomiting.
Herb/Drug Interactions: This herb could cause an interaction (possibly severe) when taken with the following drugs: Anticoagulant drugs, Anticonvulsive/Antiseizure drugs, Hypotensive drugs, Salicylates, and Subsalicylates.
Preparations/Dosage: Crude Herb: 3-6 grams. Bark and/or leaves (powdered): Average dose in substance 5-30 grains (0.324-2 gm.). Decoction: ½-1 cup per day. Infusion: 1 cup per day. Seed Oil (*oleum oenothera*): Average dose in substance 150-250 mg. (capsule form) per day. Tincture: 5-30 drops (0.333-2 cc.) one to three times per day.
Did You Know? The primrose family produces an astonishing number of hybrid species.

Eyebright (ī brīt)

(*Euphrasia officinalis*)

Synonyms/Related Species: Augentröst, Casse-Lunette, Euphrasia, North American Eyebright (*euphrasia mollis*), and Red Eyebright.
Family/Class: Scrophulariaceae (figwort).
Habitat: Alaska, Asia, Britain, Europe, France, Germany, and North America.
Flavor: Bitter.

Parts Used: Aerial.
Properties: Antibiotic, antiphlogistic, astringent, depurative, expectorant, hemostatic, tonic, and vasodilator.
Constituents: Alkaloids, caffeic acid, ferulic acid, flavonoids, gallic acid, glycosides, lignin, mannitol (mannite), minerals (copper, iodine, iron, potassium, silicon, sulfur, zinc), monosaccharides, resin, saponins, silicic acid, sterol, tannic acid, vitamins (A, B_1 (thiamine), B_2 (riboflavin), B_3 (niacin), B_5 (pantothenic acid), B_6 (pyridoxine), B_{12}, B_x (para-aminobenzoic acid (PABA), C (ascorbic acid), choline, D, E (alpha-tocopheral), H (biotin), inositol, M (folic acid), and volatile oil.
Historical Uses: Allergy (pollen), bleeding, bruises, canker sores, cataracts, cirrhosis, colds, conjunctivitis, cough, diabetes, digestive complaints, diphtheria, ear infection, earache, eyewash, eyestrain, fever (ephemeral, hay), gargle/mouth rinse, glaucoma, headache, infection (bacterial), inflammation, laryngitis, light sensitivity (eye), measles, memory/cognitive problems, mucus, respiratory conditions, sinusitis, sore throat, styes, ulcer (duodenal, gastric, peptic).
Discussion: May cause blood vessel dilatation; clear and open bronchial passages; constrict nasal and conjunctival membranes; enhance liver and lung functions; improve memory and cognition; inhibit or destroy development and growth of bacteria and other microorganisms; prevent the deposition of fat in the liver; purify the blood; restore normal tone to tissues; strengthen vision.
Cautions/Contraindications: Avoid use if pregnant or breast-feeding, or if you have an iodine sensitivity. May interfere with the effectiveness of certain thyroid medications. Use with professional guidance/supervision.
Adverse Reactions: Abdominal pain, arrhythmia, diarrhea (possibly bloody), fever, gastrointestinal cramps (severe), hematuria (blood in the urine), hypertrophy (thyroid), iodism (iodine poisoning), nausea, priapism, thirst, and/or vomiting.
Herb/Drug Interactions: This herb could cause an interaction (possibly severe) when taken with the following drugs: Thyroid drugs.
Preparations/Dosage: Crude Herb: 1-5 grams. Extract: 10-15 drops (0.666-1 cc.) one to two times per day. Infusion (leaves): 1-2 cups per day. Tincture: 15-30 drops (1-2 cc.) one to three times per day. External Uses: Compress: Place one teaspoon of dried eyebright in one pint of distilled or purified water and boil for l0 minutes, let cool to luke-warm. Moisten a piece of cotton, gauze, or muslin in the warm liquid and wring out so it no longer drips. Place over the eyes and leave on for 10-l5 minutes. Repeat several times a day.
Isolation: Mannitol hexanitrate: Average dose of 15-60 mg. for use as a vasodilator.

Fennel (fen el)
(*Foeniculum vulgare*)

Synonyms/Related Species: Bitter Fennel, Common Fennel, Large Fennel, Mahdurika, Sweet Fennel, and Wild Fennel (*foeniculum officinale*).
Family/Class: Umbelliferae (parsley).
Habitat: Argentina, Asia, Europe, Germany, India, Iran, the Mediterranean, and North America.
Flavor: Pungent/sweet.
Parts Used: Leaves, root, seed.
Properties: Anthelmintic, antibiotic, antilithic, antiphlogistic, antispasmodic, aromatic, carminative, diuretic, emmenagogue, expectorant, insect repellent, laxative, lithotriptic, sedative, stimulant, stomachic, and vermifuge.

Constituents: Anethene, anisic acid, bergapten, camphene, carvene (limonene), carvol, coumarin, dextro-fenchone, dipentene, fatty acids (oleic, palmitic, stearic), fixed oils (olein, palmitin, stearin), flavonoids, minerals (calcium, potassium, sodium, sulfur), phellandrene, phytoestrogen, pinene, scoparin, stigmasterol, umbelliferone, and volatile oil.
Historical Uses: Amenorrhea, appetite loss, asthma, bronchitis, calculus, colds, colic, colitis, congestion (lung), convulsions, cough, cramps, digestive complaints, dysentery, emphysema, eye problems, fever (ephemeral, rheumatic), flatulence, flavoring agent (leaves, seeds), fleas (powdered plant), gallbladder problems, gallstones, gargle/mouth rinse, gastritis, gastrointestinal problems, gout, halitosis, headache, hyperactivity, indigestion, infection (bacterial), inflammation, insect bites or stings, insomnia, irritable bowel syndrome (IBS), jaundice, kidney problems, kidney stones, laryngitis, lithemia, liver problems, menopausal/menstrual problems, migraine, mucus, muscle and joint pain, nervous conditions, orchitis, parasites (pinworm), poisoning (food), pruritus, respiratory conditions, rheumatism, sinusitis, skin problems, snakebite, spasmodic conditions, spleen problems, and weight loss.
Discussion: May aid digestion; clear and open bronchial passages; dissolve calculi; enhance stomach function; inhibit or destroy development and growth of bacteria and other microorganisms; offset the negative effects of chemotherapy and radiation therapy; prevent the development of calculus or stones; promote bowel evacuation and urine flow; reduce excessive lithic acid (uric acid) and urate levels in the blood, tophi, and urine; stimulate menstruation and peristalsis.
Cautions/Contraindications: Avoid use if pregnant or breast-feeding, or if you have an estrogen dependant cancer, or a history of estrogen dependant cancers. Do not administer to small children. Do not confuse this plant with poison hemlock (*conium maculatum*). Estrogen containing substances may contribute to abnormal blood clotting, migraine, and could promote the developement of certain types of estrogen dependant cancers. May cause allergic reactions and dermatitis in susceptible individuals. Not for long-term use.
Adverse Reactions: Edema, nausea, seizure conditions, and/or vomiting.
Herb/Drug Interactions: Hormones and Synthetic Substitutes (i.e. conjugated estrogens, contraceptives (oral, etc.), and other hormonal replacement therapy (HRT).
Preparations/Dosage: Crude Herb: 3-9 grams. Decoction (root and/or seeds): ½-1 cup per day. Extract: 5-10 drops (0.333-0.666 cc.). Fennel Water (*aqua foeniculi*): 30-90 drops (2-5 cc.) per day. Infusion (leaves and/or seeds): 1 cup per day. Tincture: 10-30 drops (0.666-2 cc.) one to three times per day.
Isolation: Anisic acid: Average dose of 5-10 grains (0.333-0.666 gm.) for use as an antibiotic and antirheumatic.

Fenugreek (fen yoo·grēk)
(*Trigonella foenum-graecum*)

Synonyms/Related Species: Bird's Foot, Greek Hayseed, and Helba.
Family/Class: Leguminosae (legume).
Habitat: Africa, Asia, Egypt, England, India, the Mediterranean, and Morocco.
Flavor: Bitter.
Parts Used: Seeds.

Properties: Alterative, antibiotic, anticoagulant, antiphlogistic, aphrodisiac, carminative, demulcent, depurative, emmenagogue, expectorant, hypoglycemic, hypotensive, laxative, lithotriptic, nutritive, stimulant, tonic, and vulnerary.
Constituents: Albumin (albumen), betaine (lycine), fatty acids (oleic, palmitic, stearic), fixed oils (olein, palmitin, stearin), flavonoids, lecithin, minerals (iron), mucilage, phosphates, phytoestrogen, protein, saponins, sterols, trigonelline, trimethylamine, vitamins (A, B_1 (thiamine), B_2 (riboflavin), B_3 (niacin), choline, D), and volatile oil.
Historical Uses: Abscess, allergy, anemia, appetite loss, arthritis, bronchitis, bruises, calculus, cirrhosis, colds, cough, debility, diabetes, dietary supplementation, digestive complaints, diphtheria, eczema, edema, emphysema, fever (ephemeral, septic), flatulence, gallstones, gargle/mouth rinse, glandular swelling, gout, halitosis, headache, hemorrhoids, hypercholesteremia, hyperglycemia, indigestion, infection (bacterial), inflammation, kidney stones, lesions (tubercle), liver problems, malnutrition, migraine, mucus, nervous conditions, neuralgia, neurasthenia, osteomyelitis, poisoning (blood), respiratory conditions, rickets, sciatica, scrofula, skin problems, sores, sore throat, tuberculosis, tumors, ulcer (duodenal, fistula, gastric, peptic, tuberculous), uterine problems, and wounds (minor).
Discussion: May aid digestion; arouse sexual impulses; cleanse the glandular system; clear and open bronchial passages; delay or reduce coagulation of the blood; dissolve calculi; enhance kidney and liver functions; inhibit or destroy development and growth of bacteria and other microorganisms; prevent the deposition of fat in the liver; promote bowel evacuation; provide dietary supplementation; reduce blood sugar levels and cholesterol levels; reestablish healthy system functions; regulate insulin levels; restore normal tone to tissues; serve as a nutritional adjuvant to therapeutic programs; soothe mucous membrane irritation; speed healing; stimulate menstruation and peristalsis. For diabetes, gout, and neurasthenia, the seeds can be taken simultaneously with insulin.
Cautions/Contraindications: Avoid use if pregnant or breast-feeding, or if you have an estrogen dependant cancer, or if you have a history of estrogen dependant cancers, or if you are taking anticoagulant drugs. Estrogen containing substances may contribute to abnormal blood clotting, migraine, and could promote the developement of certain types of estrogen dependant cancers.
Adverse Reactions: Diarrhea (possibly bloody), gastrointestinal cramps (severe), hematuria (blood in the urine), nausea, and/or vomiting.
Herb/Drug Interactions: Anticoagulant drugs, Antidiabetic drugs, Hormones and Synthetic Substitutes (i.e. conjugated estrogens, contraceptives (oral, etc.), and other hormonal replacement therapy (HRT), Salicylates, and Subsalicylates.
Preparations/Dosage: Crude Herb: 3-9 grams. Decoction: 1-2 cups per day. Tincture: 10-30 drops (0.666-2 cc.) one to three times per day.
Isolation: Trimethylamine hydrochlorate: Average dose of 1-3 grains (0.066-0.2 gm.) for use in gout and rheumatism.

Fern, Maidenhair (fûrn, mād n·hâr)
(*Adiantum aleuticum*)

Synonyms/Related Species: California Maidenhair Fern (*adiantum jordani*), Five-Finger Fern (*adiantum pedatum*), Hair of Venus, Lady Fern, Maiden Fern, Maidenhair, Rock Fern, True Maidenhair, and Venus Maidenhair Fern (*adiantum capillus-venerus*).

Family/Class: Aspleniaceae (spleenwort).
Habitat: The Alpine zone, Britain, China, Europe, India, Ireland, North America, the Philippines, and the Yukon Territory.
Flavor: Bitter.
Parts Used: Fronds, root.
Properties: Analgesic, antiphlogistic, aromatic, astringent, demulcent, depurative, and diuretic, emmenagogue, expectorant, hemostatic, hypoglycemic, lithotriptic, stimulant, tonic.
Constituents: Cinnamic acid, flavonoids, mucilage, proanthocyanidins, tannic acid, and volatile oil.
Historical Uses: Alopecia, amenorrhea, asthma, bleeding, bronchitis, calculus, colds, colic, cough, dysmenorrhea, fever, gallstones, gout, hemorrhage, hyperglycemia, impetigo, infection, inflammation, influenza, insect bites or stings, jaundice, kidney stones, laryngitis, liver problems, menstrual problems, mucus, pain, pleurisy, respiratory conditions, sore throat, whooping cough, and wounds (minor).
Discussion: May clear and open bronchial passages; dissolve calculi; promote urine flow; purify the blood; reduce glucose levels in the blood; restore normal tone to tissues as well as hair color due to premature graying; soothe mucous membrane irritation; stimulate menstruation.
Cautions/Contraindications: Avoid use if pregnant or breast-feeding. Do not confuse with bracken leaf fronds (*pteridium aquilinum*).
Adverse Reactions: Nausea and/or vomiting.
Herb/Drug Interactions: This herb could cause an interaction (possibly severe) when taken with the following drugs: None known.
Preparations/Dosage: Crude Herb: 3-9 grams. Infusion: 1-2 cups per day. Tincture: 10-30 drops (0.666-2 cc.) one to three times per day.

Fern, Male (fûrn, māl)

(*Aspidium (Dryopteris) filix-mas*)

Synonyms/Related Species: American Aspidium, Aspidium, Bear's Paw Root, Chinese Woodfern (*aspidium* (*dryopteris*) *crassirhizoma*), Coastal Woodfern (*aspidium* (*dryopteris*) *arguta*), Knotty Brake, Male Shield Fern, Marginal Fern (*aspidium (dryopteris) marginalis*), Mountain Woodfern (*aspidium (dryopteris) expansa*), Narrow Spiny Woodfern (*aspidium (dryopteris) spinulosa*), Shield Fern, Sweet Brake, and Woodfern.
Family/Class: Dryopteridaceae (woodfern).
Habitat: Africa, Asia, Europe, India, North, South America, the Subalpine zone, and the Yukon Territory.
Flavor: Bitter/sweet.
Parts Used: Root.
Properties: Alterative, anthelmintic, antibiotic, antiphlogistic, antiviral, astringent, hemostatic, parasiticide, teniacide, and teniafuge.
Constituents: Albaspidin, albumin (albumen), aspidin, aspidinol, filicic acid, filicon, filixic acid, fatty acids (oleic, palmitic, stearic), fixed oils (olein, palmitin, stearin), flavaspidic acid, flavonoids, gum, lignin, monosaccharides, pectic acid, pectin, resin, and tannic acid.
Historical Uses: Abscess, ancylostomiasis, bleeding, earache, fever (ephemeral, rheumatic), glandular swelling, hemorrhage (metrorrhagia), infection (bacterial, viral), inflammation, influenza, insomnia, mumps, muscle and joint pain, neuralgia, parasites (hookworm, liver flukes,

roundworm, tapeworm), poisoning (plant, shellfish), rheumatism, rickets, sciatica, sores, toothache, and weight loss.

Discussion: May enhance colon, liver, and stomach functions; inhibit development or destroy growth of bacteria and other microorganisms; reestablish healthy system functions; serve as an antidote to neutralize plant and shellfish poisoning.

Cautions/Contraindications: Avoid use if pregnant or breast-feeding, or if you have anemia, a cardiovascular condition, debility, diabetes, a liver or kidney problem, or ulcer (duodenal, peptic). Do not consume alcoholic beverages while taking male fern. May cause allergic reactions in susceptible individuals. Not for long-term use. Use with professional guidance/supervision.

Adverse Reactions: Albuminuria, bilirubinuria, blindness, cardiac failure, convulsions, coma, cramping, diarrhea, dyspnea, headache, loss of reflexes, nausea, optic neuritis, respiratory failure, visual disturbances, vomiting, and/or possible death.

Herb/Drug Interactions: This herb could cause an interaction (possibly severe) when taken with the following drugs: None known.

Preparations/Dosage: Crude Herb: 3-6 grams. Decoction: ¼-½ cup per day. Root (powdered): Average dose in substance 60 grains-15 grams (1-4 drachms).

Isolation: Filicic acid: Average dose of 8-15 grains (0.5-1 gm.) for use as an anthelmintic. Filicon: Average dose of 2 grains (0.133 gm.) for use as a teniacide and teniafuge for tapeworm.

Fern, Polypody (fûrn, päl i·pō dē)

(Polypodium vulgare)

Synonyms/Related Species: Anapsos (*polypodium leucotomos*), Bracken, California Polypody (*polypodium californicum*), Common Polypody, Female Fern, Fern Brake, Licorice Fern (*polypodium glycyrrhiza*), Oak Fern, Polypody of the Oak, Rock Brake, Rock Polypody, Smooth Cliff Brake, Stone Brake, Wall Fern, and Western Polypody (*polypodium hesperium*).

Family/Class: Polypodiaceae (polypody).

Habitat: Alaska, Asia, Central America, Europe, and North America.

Flavor: Bitter/sweet.

Parts Used: Root.

Properties: Alterative, antiphlogistic, antiscorbutic, astringent, carminative, demulcent, diuretic, expectorant, hemostatic, laxative, teniacide, teniafuge, tonic, and vulnerary.

Constituents: Bitter principle, inulin (starch), monosaccharides, mucilage, osladin, resin, vitamins (C (ascorbic acid), and volatile oil.

Historical Uses: Ague, appetite loss, arthritis, bleeding, cancer (skin), colds, colic, cough, edema, fever (ephemeral, rheumatic), indigestion, inflammation, jaundice, laryngitis, liver problems, melancholy, mucus, multiple sclerosis (MS), muscle and joint pain, pain, parasites (tapeworm), polyps, psoriasis, respiratory conditions, rheumatism, scurvy, skin problems, sore throat, and whooping cough.

Discussion: May clear and open bronchial passages; enhance kidney and liver functions; prevent cancer (skin); promote bowel evacuation and urine flow; protect against ultraviolet solar radiation; reestablish healthy system functions; restore normal tone to tissues; serve as an immune suppressant adjuvant in muscular sclerosis therapies, and serve as an oral (ingested) sunscreen; soothe mucous membrane irritation; speed healing; stimulate the immune system and peristalsis.

Cautions/Contraindications: Avoid use if pregnant or breast-feeding. May cause allergic reactions in susceptible individuals. Not for long-term use.
Adverse Reactions: Nausea and/or vomiting.
Herb/Drug Interactions: This herb could cause an interaction (possibly severe) when taken with the following drugs: None known.
Preparations/Dosage: Crude Herb: 3-9 grams. Decoction: ½-1 cup per day. Root (powdered): Average dose in substance 60 grains-15 grams (1-4 drachms).

Fern, Royal (fûrn, roi el)
(*Osmunda regalis*)

Synonyms/Related Species: Bog Onion, Buckthorn Brake, Cinnamon Fern (*osmunda cinnamomea*), Flowering Fern, King's Fern, Royal Flowering Fern, and Water Fern.
Family/Class: Polypodiaceae (polypody).
Habitat: Africa, Asia, Britain, England, Europe, Ireland, New Foundland, North America, Scotland, and South America.
Flavor: Bitter.
Parts Used: Root.
Properties: Astringent, demulcent, hemostatic, and tonic.
Constituents: Bitter principle, minerals (calcium, lime (calcium oxide), and mucilage.
Historical Uses: Bleeding, bruises, convalescence, cough, hemorrhage (metrorrhagia), jaundice, liver problems, lumbago, menorrhagia, nosebleed, sprain, whooping cough, and wounds (minor).
Discussion: May restore normal tone to tissues; soothe mucous membrane irritation.
Cautions/Contraindications: Avoid use if pregnant or breast-feeding.
Adverse Reactions: Nausea and/or vomiting.
Herb/Drug Interactions: This herb could cause an interaction (possibly severe) when taken with the following drugs: None known.
Preparations/Dosage: Crude Herb: 3-6 grams. Infusion: 1-2 cups per day. Tincture: 10-30 drops (0.666-2 cc.) one to three times per day.

Feverfew (fē ver·fyoo)
(*Tanacetum parthenium*)

Synonyms/Related Species: Bachelor's Buttons, Common Feverfew, Featherfew, Feverfuge, Flirtwort, Mid-Summer Daisy, and Sweet Feverfew (*tanacetum suaveolens*).
Family/Class: Compositae (composite).
Habitat: Australia, Europe, and North America.
Flavor: Bitter.
Parts Used: Flowers, leaves.
Properties: Abortifacient, analgesic, antibiotic, anticoagulant, antihistamine, antiperiodic, antiphlogistic, aromatic, carminative, depurative, diaphoretic, emmenagogue, expectorant, laxative, malariacidal, sedative, stimulant, tonic, and vasodilator.
Constituents: Borneol, camphene, flavonoids, linalool, minerals (iron, manganese, phosphorus, potassium, selenium, silicon, sodium, zinc), pyrethrine, pyrethron, sesquiterpene lactones, silicic acid, tannic acid, terpene, vitamins (A, B_3 (niacin), C (ascorbic acid), and volatile oil.

Historical Uses: Ague, allergy, amenorrhea, appetite loss, arthritis, asthma, bronchitis, chills, colds, colic, cough, depression (mild/moderate), diarrhea, digestive complaints, dizziness, dysmenorrhea, earache, edema, fever (ephemeral, intermittent, rheumatic), flatulence, gargle/mouth rinse, headache, hot flashes, hysteria, indigestion, infection (bacterial), inflammation, influenza, insect bites or stings, insomnia, malaria, menopausal/menstrual problems, migraine, melancholy, mucus, muscle and joint pain, nausea, nervous conditions, pain, parasites (malarial plasmodia), premenstrual syndrome (PMS), respiratory conditions, rheumatism, rheumatoid arthritis (RA), sinusitis, spasmodic conditions, tinnitus, toothache, vertigo, vomiting, wheezing, and wounds (minor).
Discussion: May aid digestion; clear and open bronchial passages; counteract the effect of histamine; decrease the frequency and severity of headaches; delay or reduce coagulation of the blood; dilate blood vessels; induce abortion; inhibit or destroy development and growth of bacteria and other microorganisms, inhibit the release of serotonin, and inhibit the secretion of granular contents from platelets and neutrophils in the blood; promote bowel evacuation and perspiration; purify the blood; restore normal tone to tissues; serve as an adjuvant in alcohol d.t.'s and opium addiction therapies; stimulate appetite, menstruation, peristalsis, and uterine contractions.
Cautions/Contraindications: Avoid use if pregnant or breast-feeding, or if you have a coagulation problem. May cause allergic reactions in susceptible individuals. Some persons may experience bleeding or increased clotting time when using this herb with anticoagulant drugs or aspirin.
Adverse Reactions: Bleeding (possibly serious), coagulation problems, edema, mouth and throat irritation, nausea, and/or vomiting.
Herb/Drug Interactions: This herb could cause an interaction (possibly severe) when taken with the following drugs: Anticoagulant drugs, Salicylates, and Subsalicylates.
Preparations/Dosage: Crude Herb: 3-9 grams. Flowers (powdered): Average dose in substance ½-1 drachm (2-4 cc.). Infusion: 1-2 cups per day. Leaves (freeze dried): Average dose in substance 50-100 mg. (¾-2 grains). Tincture: 10-30 drops (0.666-2 cc.) one to three times per day. Tincture: 15-40 drops (1-3 cc.) as often as needed for alcoholic delirium tremens (DTs).

Figwort (fig·wûrt)
(*Scrophularia nodosa*)

Synonyms/Related Species: Balm-Leaved Figwort (*scrophularia scorodoma*), Bishop's Leaves, Brownwort, California Figwort (*scrophularia californica*), Carpenter's Square, Chinese Figwort (*scrophularia ningpoensis*), Deilen-Ddu, Heal-All, Herbe du Siege, Kernelwort, Knotted Figwort, Knotty-Rooted Figwort, Rose Noble, Scrofula Plant, Water Figwort (*scrophularia aquatica*), and Yellow Figwort (*scrophularia vernalis*).
Family/Class: Scrophulariaceae (figwort).
Habitat: Asia, Britain, Europe, France, Ireland, and North America.
Flavor: Bitter/pungent.
Parts Used: Leaves.
Properties: Alterative, analgesic, antibiotic, antifungal, anti-inflammatory, demulcent, depurative, diuretic, emmenagogue, hemostatic, hypotensive, laxative, parasiticide, sedative, stimulant, tonic, and vasodilator.

Constituents: Acetic acid, caffeic acid, chlorogenic acid, ferulic acid, flavonoids, glycosides, hesperidin, propionic acid, and saponins.
Historical Uses: Abscess, acne, amenorrhea, anemia, anxiety, arrhythmia, athlete's foot, benign breast disease, bruises, burns (minor), canker sores, constipation, cramps, diabetes, digestive complaints, dizziness, eczema, edema, emaciation, gangrene, glandular problems, glandular swelling, goiter, heart disease, hemorrhage, hemorrhoids, hives, hypertension (mild/moderate), infection (bacterial, fungal), inflammation, insomnia, impetigo, insufficiency (venous), kidney problems, lesions (tubercle), liver problems, lochia, menstrual problems, night sweats, pain, parasites (ringworm, scabies), pruritus, psoriasis, rash, restlessness, scrofula, skin problems, sore throat, sores, sprain, thirst, tonsillitis, tuberculosis, tumors, ulcer (duodenal, fistula, gastric, peptic, stasis, tuberculous, varicose), varicose veins, and wounds (minor).
Discussion: May aid in clotting of blood; cause blood vessel dilatation; cleanse the whole system; enhance kidney, lung, and glandular system functions; inhibit or destroy developement and growth of bacteria and other microorganisms; promote bowel evacuation and urine flow; protect against heart disease; purify the blood; reduce blood pressure levels; reestablish healthy system functions; soothe mucous membrane irritation; stimulate the cardiovascular system, menstruation, and peristalsis.
Cautions/Contraindications: Avoid use if pregnant or breast-feeding, or if you have tachycardia.
Adverse Reactions: Diarrhea (possibly bloody), gastrointestinal cramps (severe), hematuria (blood in the urine), nausea, and/or vomiting.
Herb/Drug Interactions: This herb could cause an interaction (possibly severe) when taken with the following drugs: Hypotensive drugs.
Preparations/Dosage: Crude Herb: 9-15 grams. Decoction: ½-1 cup per day. Infusion: 1-2 cups per day. Tincture: 15-30 drops (1-2 cc.) one to three times per day.

Fir (fûr)
(*Abies balsamea*)

Synonyms/Related Species: Alpine Fir (*abies lasiocarpa*), Balm of Gilead Fir, Balsam Fir, Canada Balsam, Föhre, Fyrh, Grand Fir (*abies grandis*), Montana Grand Fir, Subalpine Fir (*abies bifolia*), and White Fir (*abies concolor*).
Family/Class: Pinaceae (pine).
Habitat: Alaska, the Alpine and Subalpine zones, North America, and the Yukon Territory.
Flavor: Bitter.
Parts Used: Bark, leaves/needles, oleoresin.
Properties: Antibiotic, antiphlogistic, carminative, diaphoretic, diuretic, expectorant, laxative, sedative, and stimulant.
Constituents: Borneol, camphene, carvene (limonene), coniferin, myrcene, pinene, santene, terpene, and vitamin C (ascorbic acid).
Historical Uses: Abscess, alopecia, arthritis, bronchitis, burns (minor), canker sores, colds, conjunctivitis, cough, dandruff, digestive complaints, edema, eye problems, fever (ephemeral, rheumatic), gargle/mouth rinse, gonorrhea, headache, infection (bacterial), inflammation, kidney problems, lesions (tubercle), liver problems, mucus, muscle and joint pain, neuralgia, pain, respiratory conditions, rheumatism, scrofula, sexually transmitted diseases (STDs), sores, sore throat, substitute for balm of gilead (resin), toothache, tuberculosis, ulcer (duodenal, fistula, gastric, peptic, tuberculous), and wounds (minor).

Discussion: May aid digestion; clear and open bronchial passages; inhibit or destroy development and growth of bacteria and other microorganisms; promote bowel evacuation, perspiration, and urine flow; stimulate uterine contractions.
Cautions/Contraindications: Avoid use if pregnant or breast-feeding, or if you have asthma, cardiovascular conditions, or whooping cough.
Adverse Reactions: Nausea and/or vomiting.
Herb/Drug Interactions: This herb could cause an interaction (possibly severe) when taken with the following drugs: None known.
Preparations/Dosage: Crude Herb: 1-3 grams. Decoction: ¼-½ cup per day. Infusion (needles): ½-1 cup per day. Oleoresin: Average dose in substance 5 grains (0.3 gm.).

Flax (flaks)

(*Linum usitatissimum*)

Synonyms/Related Species: Common Flax, Dwarf Flax, Fairy Flax, King's Flax (*linum kingii*), Linseed Oil, Mill Mountain, Mountain Flax (*linum catharticum*), Prairie Flax, Purging Flax (*linum perenne*), Western Blue Flax (*linum lewisii*), Wild Blue Flax, Winterlien, and Yellow Flax (*linum rigidum*).
Family/Class: Linaceae (flax).
Habitat: Alaska, Egypt, England, Europe, and North America.
Flavor: Sweet.
Parts Used: Seeds (ripe).
Properties: Anticarcinogenic, antiphlogistic, analgesic, demulcent, hypoglycemic, laxative, lithotriptic, and stimulant.
Constituents: Alkaloids, fatty acids (arachidonic, linoleic, linolenic, oleic, omega 3 and omega 6, palmitic, stearic), fixed oils (olein, palmitin, stearin), glycosides, gum, lignin, linamarin, minerals (calcium, potassium), mucilage, nitrates, protein, tannic acid, and wax.
Historical Uses: Alopecia, bladder infection, bronchitis, bruises, burns (minor), calculus, colds, constipation, cough, digestive complaints, diverticulitis, dry skin, enteritis, fever (ephemeral, rheumatic), flatulence, gallstones, gastritis, gastrointestinal problems, goiter, headache, hyperglycemia, indigestion, inflammation, irritable bowel syndrome (IBS), jaundice, kidney stones, liver problems, mucous membranes, mucus, nausea, pain, pleurisy, pneumonia, respiratory conditions, rheumatism, ulcer (duodenal, gastric, peptic), urinary problems, and wounds (minor).
Discussion: May dissolve calculi; enhance cardiovascular system, digestive system, hormonal system, and nervous system functions; increase bulk in the intestines; promote bowel evacuation; reduce blood sugar levels, cholesterol levels, and colon damage caused by cathartic (laxative) abuse; soften the skin; soothe mucous membrane irritation; stimulate peristalsis.
Cautions/Contraindications: Avoid use if pregnant or breast-feeding, or if you have an esophageal or gastrointestinal stricture, esophagitis, gastroenteritis, or obstruction (intestinal). Do not use unripe/immature seeds, the green parts of the herb, or the root as they contain cyanide-like compounds and can cause poisoning. Increase fluid intake when using flaxseed. May interfere with the absorption of other drugs.
Adverse Reactions: Abdominal pain, cardiac failure, convulsions, debility, diarrhea (severe), enteritis (severe), excitement, hydrocyanism (poisoning by hydrocyanic acid), nausea, obstruction (intestinal), respiratory distress, paralysis, staggering, vomiting, and/or possible death.

Herb/Drug Interactions: This herb could cause an interaction (possibly severe) when taken with the following drugs: Antidiabetic drugs.
Preparations/Dosage: Crude Herb: 9-15 grams. Decoction: ¼-½ cup per day. Linseed Oil: To help eliminate gallstones, take 1½-2 tablespoons of oil and lie down on your left side for approximately 45 minutes (the stones should pass into the intestines for elimination). Seeds (ripe/whole): Take 1-2 tablespoons and wash them down with plenty of water.

Foxglove (foks gluv)
(*Digitalis purpurea*)

Synonyms/Related Species: American Foxglove, Balkan Foxglove (*digitalis lanata*), Dead Men's Bells, Digitalis, Fairy's Fingers, Lion's Mouth, and Purple Foxglove.
Family/Class: Scrophulariaceae (figwort).
Habitat: The Balkans, Britain, Europe, and the United States.
Flavor: Bitter/pungent.
Parts Used: Leaves.
Properties: Cardiant, diuretic, hemostatic, hypertensive, hypotensive, stimulant, tonic, vasoconstrictor, and vasodilator.
Constituents: Anthraquinone, digitalein, digitalin, digitalis, digitin, digitogenin, digitonin, digitophyllin, digtoxin, digitoxose, gitalin, gitonin, gitoxigenin, glycosides, gum, inulin (starch), lanatoside, monosaccharides, saponins, and volatile oil.
Historical Uses: Abscess, cardiovascular conditions, congestive heart failure (CHF), delirium, edema, epilepsy, headache, hemorrhage, hypertension (mild/moderate), hypotension, infection (bacterial), inflammation, mania, paralysis, ulcer (duodenal, gastric, peptic), and wounds (minor).
Discussion: May elevate blood pressure levels in hypotensive persons and reduce blood pressure levels in hypertensive persons; increase systole, lengthening of diastole, and contraction of the arterioles; lower the hearts oxygen requirement; promote urine flow; restore normal tone to tissues; stimulate the cardiovascular system.
Cautions/Contraindications: Avoid use if pregnant or breast-feeding. Do not confuse the first year leaf growth (rosette) of foxglove with comfrey (*symphytum officinalis*) as this mistake has lead to fatalities. Harvest leaves from 2 year old plants as they are in their most active state. May increase the side effects of antibiotic and corticosteroid drugs. Monitor potassium levels when using this plant. May cause dermatitis, headache, and nausea upon harvesting in susceptible individuals. Not for long-term use. This herb is *extremely* potent and is strongly recommended for use under professional guidance/supervision.
Adverse Reactions: Arrhythmia, asphyxiation, bradycardia, cardiac failure, cerebral disturbances (i.e. seeing all objects as blue), confusion, convulsions, depression, diarrhea, gastrointestinal problems, gynecomastia, hallucinations, headache, hypotension, mouth inflammation, nausea, psychosis, stupor, tachycardia, tremors, visual disturbances, vomiting, and/or possible death.
Herb/Drug Interactions: This herb could cause an interaction (possibly severe) when taken with the following drugs: Antibiotic drugs, Anticoagulant drugs, Antidepressant drugs, Cardiac drugs, Diuretic drugs, Corticosteroids, Hypotensive drugs, Potassium Chloride, and Selective Serotonin Reuptake Inhibitor (SSRI) drugs.
Herb/Herb Interactions: Do not use this herb with senna (*cassia spp.*).

Preparations/Dosage: Crude Herb: 1-3 grams. Extract: 1-3 drops (0.06-0.2 cc.) one to two times per day. Extract (solid): Average dose in substance ⅛ grain (0.008 gm.). Infusion: ⅛-¼ cup per day. Leaves (powdered): Average dose in substance 1½ grains (0.1 gm.). Tincture: 5-10 drops (0.333-0.666 cc.) one to three times per day.
Isolation: Digitalein: Soluble in alcohol and water. Average dose of $^{1}/_{64}$-$^{1}/_{32}$ grain (0.001-0.002 gm) for use as a cardiac tonic and diuretic. Digitalis: Average dose of 1½ grains (0.1 gm.) for use as a cardiant, diuretic, and stimulant. Digitoxin: $^{1}/_{250}$-$^{1}/_{125}$ grain (0.00025-0.0005 gm) for use as a cardiant.
Did You Know? A single foxglove plant produces an incredible number of seeds (from one to two million), thus ensuring its propagation.

Frankincense (frangk in·sens)
(*Boswellia carteri*)

Synonyms/Related Species: Boswellia, Francencens, Libanos, Olibanum, Ru Xiang, Salai Guggul, Shallaki, and True Frankincense.
Family/Class: Burseraceae (resiniferous).
Habitat: Africa, Arabia, and Somalia.
Flavor: Pungent/bitter.
Parts Used: Gum resin.
Properties: Antibiotic, anticarcinogen, antiphlogistic, antispasmodic, carminative, cytotoxic, counterirritant, emmenagogue, nervine, stimulant, and vesicant.
Constituents: Arabic acid (arabin), bassorin (bassora gum), boswellinic acid, dipentene, phellandrene, pinene, resin, and volatile oil.
Historical Uses: Abscess, arthritis, asthma, bronchitis, bruises, cancer, chilblains, colitis, Crohn's disease, diarrhea, dysentery, dysmenorrhea, edema, fever (ephemeral, rheumatic), incense, infection (bacterial), inflammation, laryngitis, leprosy, leukemia, lung problems, muscle and joint pain, osteoarthritis (OA), pain, perfume, psoriasis, rheumatism, rheumatoid arthritis (RA), sores, spasmodic conditions, substitute for balsam of peru or balsam of tolu, and tumors.
Discussion: May aid digestion; calm the nervous system; decrease the effect of carcinogens; enhance cardiovascular system, liver, and spleen functions; induce cancer cells to destroy themselves; inhibit or destroy development and growth of bacteria and other microorganisms; serve as an alternative to non-steroidal anti-inflammatory drugs (NSAIDs) and steroids; stimulate menstruation.
Cautions/Contraindications: Avoid use if pregnant or breast-feeding.
Adverse Reactions: Blistering of the skin, menorrhagia, nausea, and/or vomiting.
Herb/Drug Interactions: This herb could cause an interaction (possibly severe) when taken with the following drugs: None known.
Preparations/Dosage: External Use Only. Gum resin: 3-6 grams.

Fringe Tree (frinj trē)
(*Chionanthus virginicus*)

Synonyms/Related Species: Chionanthus, Gray Beard Tree, Old Man's Beard, Poison Ash, Snowdrop Tree, and White Fringe.
Family/Class: Oleaceae (olive).

Habitat: Asia and North America.
Flavor: Bitter.
Parts Used: Bark (root).
Properties: Alterative, antiperiodic, antiphlogistic, diuretic, hepatic, laxative, lithotriptic, malariacidal, narcotic, sedative, and tonic.
Constituents: Chionanthin, lignin, glucoside, phyllirine, and saponins.
Historical Uses: Ague, calculus, cirrhosis, fever (ephemeral, enteric, intermittent), gallbladder problems, gallstones, glandular problems, gout, hepatitis, indigestion, inflammation, insomnia, jaundice, kidney stones, liver problems, malaria, pain, parasites (malarial plasmodia), skin problems, typhoid, ulcer (bouveret), and wounds (minor).
Discussion: May correct excessive discharge of mucus into the gastrointestinal tract; dissolve calculi; enhance gallbladder, liver, and spleen functions; promote digestion of fats, bowel evacuation, and urine flow; protect the liver; reestablish healthy system functions; restore normal tone to tissues; stimulate peristalsis.
Cautions/Contraindications: Avoid use if pregnant or breast-feeding.
Adverse Reactions: Diarrhea (possibly bloody), gastrointestinal cramps (severe), nausea, stupor, and/or vomiting.
Herb/Drug Interactions: This herb could cause an interaction (possibly severe) when taken with the following drugs: None known.
Preparations/Dosage: Crude Herb: 3-6 grams. Decoction: ½-1 cup per day. Extract: 3-5 drops (0.2-0.333 cc.) one to two times per day. Tincture: 5-10 drops (0.333-0.666 cc.) one to three times per day.
Isolation: Chionanthin: Average dose of 1-3 grains (0.065-0.19 gm.) for use as a laxative, sedative, and tonic.

Fritillary (frit e·ler ē)
(*Fritillaria thunbergii*)

Synonyms/Related Species: Chequered Daffodil, Common Fritillary (*fritillaria meleagris*), Ginny Flower, Guinea-Hen Flower, Lazarus Bell, Leopard Lily, Mission Bells, Narcissus Caparonius, Pheasant Lily, Purple Fritillary (*fritillaria atropurpurea*), Snake's Head Fritillary, Turkey Hen, and Yellow Bells (*fritillaria pudica*).
Family/Class: Liliaceae (lily).
Habitat: The Alpine zone, Britain, England, and North America.
Flavor: Bitter.
Parts Used: Bulb.
Properties: Anticarcinogen, antiphlogistic, antisialic, expectorant, hypotensive, and tonic.
Constituents: Alkaloids, fritillarine, and verticine.
Historical Uses: Abscess, asthma, bronchitis, cancer (lung), colds, cough, fever (ephemeral), glandular swelling, inflammation, influenza, laryngitis, lesions (tubercle), lupus, pneumonia, respiratory conditions, scrofula, tuberculosis, and ulcer (fistula, tuberculous).
Discussion: May clear and open bronchial passages; decrease the effect of carcinogens; increase blood sugar levels; reduce heart rate, blood pressure levels, and saliva secretion; restore normal tone to tissues; stimulate uterine contractions.

Cautions/Contraindications: Avoid use if pregnant or breast-feeding, or if you have hyperglycemia or a weak digestive system. Unprocessed fritillaria should never be taken internally.
Adverse Reactions: Depression of cardiovascular, circulatory, and respiratory functional activity, nausea, vomiting, and possible death.
Herb/Drug Interactions: This herb could cause an interaction (possibly severe) when taken with the following drugs: None known.
Preparations/Dosage: Crude Herb: 1-3 grams. Infusion: ¼-½ cup per day.

Fumitory (fyoo me·tôr ē)
(*Fumaria officinalis*)

Synonyms/Related Species: American Fumitory (*fumaria indica*), Bladdered Fumitory (*fumaria vesicaria*), Climbing Fumitory (*fumaria claviculata*), Earth Smoke, Glaucus Fumitory (*fumaria sempervirens*), Great-Flowered Fumitory (*fumaria mobilis*), Hedge Fumitory, Lyre Flower (*fumaria spectabilis*), Naked-Stalked Fumitory (*fumaria cucullaria*), Narrow-Leaved Fumitory (*fumaria spicula*), Ramping Fumitory (*fumaria capreolata*), Siberian Fumitory (*fumaria sibirica*), Small-Flowered Fumitory (*fumaria parviflora*), Smoke of the Earth, Spongy-Flowered Fumitory (*fumaria fungosa*), White-Flowered Fumitory (*fumaria capnoides*), and Yellow Fumitory (*fumaria lutea*).
Family/Class: Fumariaceae (fumitory).
Habitat: Africa, Asia, Australia, Barbary, Britain, Europe, France, Italy, Japan, North America, Portugal, Siberia, and Spain.
Flavor: Bitter.
Parts Used: Leaves.
Properties: Alterative, antiphlogistic, antiscorbutic, depurative, diaphoretic, diuretic, hepatic, laxative, lithotriptic, parasiticide, stomachic, and tonic.
Constituents: Alkaloids, bitter principle, bulbocapnine, canadine, corydaline, fumaric acid, fumarine (protopine), mucilage, resin, and vitamin C (ascorbic acid).
Historical Uses: Acne, calculus, conjunctivitis, constipation, depression (mild/moderate), eczema, fever (ephemeral, rheumatic), gallbladder problems, gallstones, gargle/mouth rinse, gout, inflammation, jaundice, leprosy, liver problems, melancholy, muscle and joint pain, pimples, plague, parasites (scabies), psoriasis, rheumatism, scurvy, skin problems, sores, tumors, and wounds (minor).
Discussion: May dissolve calculi; enhance stomach function; promote bowel evacuation, perspiration, and urine flow; purify the blood; reestablish healthy system functions; restore normal tone to tissues; stimulate peristalsis.
Cautions/Contraindications: Avoid use if pregnant or breast-feeding.
Adverse Reactions: Diarrhea, flatulence, gastrointestinal cramps, nausea, and/or vomiting.
Herb/Drug Interactions: This herb could cause an interaction (possibly severe) when taken with the following drugs: None known.
Preparations/Dosage: Crude Herb: 3-9 grams. Infusion: 1-2 cups per day. Juice: 1-2 ounces in water per day. Tincture: 5-15 drops (0.333-1 cc.) one to three times per day.
Isolation: Corydaline: Average dose of 1-5 grains (0.066-0.333 gm.) for use as a diuretic and tonic. Fumarine (protopine): 40-100 grains (2.5-7 gm.) for use as an analgesic and hypnotic.

Fungi, Cordyceps (fun je, kôr di·seps)

(*Cordyceps sinensis*)

Synonyms/Related Species: Caterpillar Fungus, Clubhead Fungus (*cordyceps ophioglossoides*), Cordiceps, Deer Fungus, Dong Chong, Gray Cordyceps (*cordyceps hawkesii*), Jinbangbang Chongcao (*cordyceps shanxiensis*), Kordylēceps, Summer Plant, Winterworm, and Xiangbang Chongcao (*cordyceps barnesii*).
Family/Class: Ascomycetes (sac fungi).
Habitat: Asia, China, Europe, and North America.
Flavor: Sweet/pungent.
Parts Used: Fruiting body.
Properties: Antibiotic, anticarcinogen, anticoagulant, aphrodisiac, erythropoietic, hemostatic, hypnotic, nutritive, sedative, tonic, and vasodilator.
Constituents: Adenine, adenosine, alkaloids, amino acids (glutamic, tryptophan, tyrosine), carbohydrates, ergosterol, fatty acids (arachidonic, linoleic, linolenic, oleic, palmitic, stearic), fiber, fixed oils (olein, palmitin, stearin), mannitol (mannite), monosaccharides, ophiocordin, polysaccharides, protein, saponins, sitosterol, triterpenoids, uracil, and uridin.
Historical Uses: Amenorrhea, anemia, arrhythmia, asthma, bleeding, cancer (lung), chronic fatigue syndrome (CFS), cough, debility, dietary supplementation, diminished sex drive, emaciation, Epstein Barr Virus (EBV), erectile dysfunction, exhaustion, fibromyalgia, hemorrhage (metrorrhagia), hepatitis, hypercholesteremia, hyperlipoidemia, hypoglycemia, infection (bacterial), insomnia, insufficiency (adrenal, immune), kidney problems, liver problems, malnutrition, menorrhagia, menstrual problems, mononucleosis (infectious), mucus, muscle and joint pain, nephritis, neurasthenia, rickets, tinnitus, and tumors.
Discussion: May arouse sexual impulses; cause blood vessel dilatation; clear and open bronchial passages; decrease the effect of carcinogens; delay or reduce coagulation of the blood; enhance cardiovascular system, immune system, kidney, and liver functions; have an antiaging effect; increase athletic performance, endurance, energy, red blood cells, and sperm production; inhibit or destroy development and growth of bacteria and other microorganisms; provide dietary supplementation; reduce cholesterol levels and triglyceride levels; restore normal tone to tissues; serve as a nutritional adjuvant to therapeutic programs and as an antidote for opium addiction; stimulate circulation, the endocrine system, and the immune system; stop or slow abnormal cell growth.
Cautions/Contraindications: Avoid use if pregnant or breast-feeding, or if you have an estrogen dependant cancer, or a history of estrogen dependant cancers, or if you have heart disease, hypertension, or multiple sclerosis (MS), or if you are on long-term aspirin therapy, or if you are using an asthma inhaler, or or if you have a known allergy (mold). May increase the effects of epinephrine drugs. Some persons may experience bleeding or increased clotting time when using this herb with anticoagulant drugs or aspirin.
Adverse Reactions: Bleeding (possibly serious), coagulation problems, nausea, and/or vomiting.
Herb/Drug Interactions: This herb could cause an interaction (possibly severe) when taken with the following drugs: Anticoagulant drugs, Bronchodilator drugs, Immune Suppressive drugs, Monoamine oxidase inhibitors (MAOIs), Salicylates, and Subsalicylates.
Preparations/Dosage: Crude Herb: 3-40 grams. Decoction: ½-1 cup per day. Infusion: 1-3 cups per day.
Isolation: Mannitol hexanitrate: Average dose of 15-60 mg. for use as a vasodilator.

Fungi, Corn Smut (fun je, kôrn smut)
(*Ustilago maydis*)

Synonyms/Related Species: Blasted Corn, Burnt Corn, Smut (*ustilago zeae*), and Ustulatus.
Family/Class: Basidiomycetes (club fungi).
Habitat: Worldwide.
Flavor: Sweet/bland.
Parts Used: Fruiting body.
Properties: Abortifacient, antibiotic, antifungal, antitumor, carminative, emmenagogue, hemostatic, laxative, nutritive, oxytocic, stimulant, and tonic.
Constituents: Alkaloids, ustilagic acid, and ustilagine.
Historical Uses: Alopecia, amenorrhea, bleeding, candida, catarrh, congestion (uterine, vaginal), constipation, dandruff, dietary supplementation, digestive complaints, dysmenorrhea, flatulence, food source, gleet, gonorrhea, hemorrhage (metrorrhagia), hepatitis, hives, infection (fungal, sexually transmitted), leukorrhea, liver problems, lochia, malnutrition, menstrual problems, moniliasis, psoriasis, rash, sexually transmitted diseases (STDs), skin problems, tumors, ulcer (duodenal, gastric, peptic), urethritis, and vaginitis.
Discussion: May aid digestion; enhance gastrointestinal and liver functions; induce abortion; promote bowel evacuation; provide dietary supplementation; restore normal tone to tissues; serve as a nutritional adjuvant to therapeutic programs; stimulate menstruation, peristalsis, and uterine contractions.
Cautions/Contraindications: Avoid use if pregnant or breast-feeding.
Adverse Reactions: Diarrhea, nausea, and/or vomiting.
Herb/Drug Interactions: This herb could cause an interaction (possibly severe) when taken with the following drugs: None known.
Preparations/Dosage: Crude Herb: 3-9 grams. Extract: 15-60 drops (1-4 cc.). Tincture: 5-30 drops (0.333-2 cc.).
Note: Corn smut is safer and much weaker in action than ergot (*claviceps purpurea*).

Fungi, Ergot (fun je, ur get)
(*Claviceps purpurea*)

Synonyms/Related Species: Argot, Clavus, Cockspur Rye, Er gota, Holy Fire, Hornseed, Mother of Rye, Mutterkorn, Smut Rye, Spurred Rye, St. Anthony's Fire, St. Martial's Fire, and Wombgrain.
Family/Class: Ascomycetes (sac fungi).
Habitat: Worldwide.
Flavor: Sweet/bitter.
Parts Used: Sclerotium (dried).
Properties: Abortifacient, emmenagogue, hemostatic, oxytocic, stimulant, and vasoconstrictor.
Constituents: Alkaloids, clavicepsin, ergochrysin, ergoclavine, ergocristine, ergomonamine, ergonovine, ergosine, ergostenol, ergosterol, ergotamine, ergothioneine, ergothionone, ergotinine, ergototoxine, lysergic acid, and lysergic acid diethylamide (LSD).
Historical Uses: Auditory problems, bleeding, cough, deep vein thrombosis (DVT), diabetes, dizziness, dysmenorrhea, ear infection, epilepsy, headache, hemorrhage (metrorrhagia), lochia, menopausal/menstrual problems, migraine, motion sickness, nervous conditions, night sweats, tinnitus, and whooping cough.

Discussion: May cause blood vessel constriction; induce abortion; regulate the autonomic nervous system; stimulate menstruation and uterine contractions.
Cautions/Contraindications: Avoid use if pregnant or breast-feeding, or if you have hyperthyroidism, a liver problem, or poisoning (blood). May increase absorption of epinephrine and norepinephrine and may inhibit absorption of these amines after nerve stimulation therapy. Not for long-term use. Use with professional guidance/supervision.
Adverse Reactions: Burning sensations in the hands and feet, ergotism (chronic poisoning by ergot), cardiac failure, congestion (cerebrospinal), coma, confusion, convulsions, cramps, diarrhea, dry gangrene, hallucinations, loss of consciousness, nausea, respiratory failure, spasmodic conditions, tachycardia, thirst (excessive), vomiting, and/or possible death.
Herb/Drug Interactions: This herb could cause an interaction (possibly severe) when taken with the following drugs: Bronchodilator drugs.
Preparations/Dosage: Crude Herb (dried): Average dose in substance 150-450 mg.
Isolation: Ergonovine: Average dose of 0.2-0.4 mg ($^1/_{300}$-$^1/_{150}$ grain), administered orally (by mouth), or average dose of 0.2 mg ($^1/_{300}$ grain), administered intravenously, for use as an oxytocic. Ergotamine: Average dose of 0.12-0.25 mg ($^1/_{500}$-$^1/_{250}$ grain), administered intravenously, for use as an oxytocic. Ergotamine tartrate: Average dose of $^1/_{200}$ grain (0.5 mg.) for use as a hypertensive and stimulant in hemorrhage (postpartum) and migraine.

Galangal (ge·lang gel)
(*Alpinia officinarum*)

Synonyms/Related Species: Catarrh Root, China Root, Chinese Galangal, Chinese Ginger, Colic Root, East India Catarrh Root, East Indian Root, Gargaut, Greater Galangal (*alpinia galanga*), Khalanjān, Ko-Liang-Kiang, and Lesser Galangal.
Family/Class: Zingiberaceae (ginger).
Habitat: Arabia, Asia, China, Greece, India, Indonesia, Iran, Java, and Thailand.
Flavor: Pungent.
Parts Used: Root.
Properties: Antibiotic, anticarcinogen, antiemetic, antiperiodic, antiphlogistic, antispasmodic, aphrodisiac, aromatic, carminative, counterirritant, diaphoretic, diuretic, emmenagogue, expectorant, malariacidal, parasiticide, stimulant, and tonic.
Constituents: Eucalyptol (cineol), flavonoids, gingerol, inulin (starch), kaempferide, resin, sesquiterpenes, tannic acid, and volatile oil.
Historical Uses: Ague, allergy, amenorrhea, appetite loss, arrhythmia, arteriosclerosis, arthritis, asthma, benign breast disease, bursitis, bronchitis, cancer, cellulite, chilblains, chills, colds, colic, colitis, congestion (uterine, vaginal), cough, cramps, diarrhea, digestive complaints, diphtheria, edema, enteritis, erectile dysfunction, fever (ephemeral, hankow, intermittent), flatulence, flavoring agent, gallbladder problems, gastritis, gastrointestinal problems, glandular problems, headache, hypercholesteremia, indigestion, infection (bacterial), inflammation, influenza, leukorrhea, liver problems, lymphedema, malaria, nausea, motion sickness, mucus, muscle and joint pain, nausea, nervous conditions, neuralgia, pain, parasites (anisakid, malarial plasmodia, schistosoma), periodontal disease, respiratory conditions, schistosomiasis, seizure conditions, sinusitis, sore throat, spasmodic conditions, sprain, strep throat, toothache, ulcer (duodenal, gastric, peptic, syriac), urethritis, vaginitis, vomiting, whooping cough, and wounds (minor).

Discussion: May aid digestion; arouse sexual impulses; assist in the assimilation of other herbs; clear and open bronchial passages; decrease the effect of carcinogens; enhance cardiovascular system, kidney, liver, lung, respiratory system, and spleen functions; increase circulation; inhibit or destroy development and growth of bacteria and other microorganisms; promote perspiration and urine flow; restore normal tone to tissues; stimulate appetite and menstruation.
Cautions/Contraindications: Avoid use if pregnant or breast-feeding, or if you have a coagulation problem or gallstones. Individuals undergoing elective surgery should avoid the use of Galangal for two to three weeks prior to the surgery. May interfere with vitamin and iron absorption. Some persons may experience bleeding or increased clotting time when using this herb with anticoagulant drugs or aspirin.
Adverse Reactions: Bleeding (possibly serious), coagulation problems, nausea, and/or vomiting.
Herb/Drug Interactions: This herb could cause an interaction (possibly severe) when taken with the following drugs: Anticoagulant drugs, Anxiolytic drugs, Salicylates, and Subsalicylates.
Preparations/Dosage: Crude Herb: 3-6 grams. Infusion: 1-2 cups per day. Root (powdered): Average dose of 15-30 grains (0.98-2 gm.). Tincture: 5-20 drops (0.333-1.25 cc.) one to three times per day.
Isolation: Eucalyptol: 5 drops (0.3 cc.) in atomization or inhalation therapy for use in respiratory conditions.

Gamboge (gam·bōj)
(Garcinia hanburyi)

Synonyms/Related Species: Camboge, Gummi Gutta, Gutta Cambogia, and Indian Gamboge (*garcinia morella*).
Family/Class: Hypericaceae (st. johnswort).
Habitat: Cambodia, Ceylon, China, India, Siam, and Sri Lanka.
Flavor: Pungent.
Parts Used: Gum resin.
Properties: Alterative, anti-inflammatory carminative, hypotensive, laxative, teniacide, teniafuge, and vasodilator.
Constituents: Gambogic acid, mucilage, and xanthones.
Historical Uses: Congestion (cerebral), constipation, diarrhea, digestive complaints, edema, hypertension (mild/moderate), inflammation, parasites (tapeworm), tumors, and weight loss.
Discussion: May aid digestion; cause blood vessel dilatation; enhance liver and spleen functions; promote bowel evacuation; reduce blood pressure levels; reestablish healthy system functions; stimulate metabolism and peristalsis.
Cautions/Contraindications: Avoid use if pregnant or breast-feeding. Do not administer this plant singly; combine it with other herbs such as licorice and ginger. Not for long-term use. Use with professional guidance/supervision.
Adverse Reactions: Abdominal pain (severe), diarrhea (severe), nausea, respiratory distress, vomiting, and/or possible death.
Herb/Drug Interactions: This herb could cause an interaction (possibly severe) when taken with the following drugs: Hypotensive drugs.
Preparations/Dosage: Gum resin: Average dose in substance ½-5 grains (0.133-0.324 gm.).

Garlic (gär lik)
(*Allium sativum*)

Synonyms/Related Species: Artichoke Garlic, Bear's Garlic, Broad-Leaved Garlic, Common Garlic, Crow Garlic (*allium oleraceum*), Field Garlic (*allium vineale*), Poor Man's Treacle, Ramsons Garlic (*allium ursinum*), Rustic's Treacle, Serpent Garlic, Silver Skin Garlic, Stinking Rose, and Wild Wood Garlic.
Family/Class: Liliaceae (lily).
Habitat: The Alps, Asia, China, England, Europe, France, Greece, India, Italy, the Mediterranean, North America, Siberia, and Sweden.
Flavor: Pungent.
Parts Used: Bulb.
Properties: Alterative, anthelmintic, antibiotic, anticarcinogen, anticoagulant, antifungal, antiphlogistic, antiviral, carminative, counterirritant, depurative, diaphoretic, diuretic, expectorant, hypoglycemic, hypolipidemic, hypotensive, laxative, parasiticide, stimulant, teniacide, teniafuge, tonic, vasodilator, vermifuge, and vulnerary.
Constituents: Allicin, allyl, carbohydrates, flavonoids, minerals (calcium, copper, iron, manganese, potassium, selenium, sodium, sulfur, zinc), monosaccharides, polysaccharides, protein, saponins, vitamins (A, B_1 (thiamine), C (ascorbic acid), and volatile oil.
Historical Uses: Acquired immune deficiency syndrome (AIDS), allergy, anemia, angina, arteriosclerosis, arthritis, asthma, athlete's foot, auditory problems, bronchitis, calluses, cancer (bladder, breast, colon, skin, stomach), candida, cardiovascular conditions, cholera, colds, colic, colitis, congestion (uterine, vaginal), corns, cough, cramps, debility, depression (mild/moderate), diabetes, diarrhea, digestive complaints, diphtheria, dizziness, dysentery, ear infection, earache, emaciation, emphysema, epilepsy, fever (ephemeral, enteric, herpetic, rheumatic), flatulence, gallbladder problems, gangrene, gastritis, gastrointestinal problems, headache, hepatitis, herpes, high triglyceride levels, human immunodeficiency virus (HIV), hydrophobia (rabies in humans), hypercholesteremia, hyperglycemia, hyperlipoidemia, hypertension (mild/moderate), hysteria, indigestion, infection (bacterial, bladder, fungal, viral), inflammation, influenza, insect bites or stings, insomnia, insufficiency (circulatory), irritable bowel syndrome (IBS), leprosy, lesions (tubercle), leukorrhea, Lyme disease, meningitis, menstrual problems, moniliasis, mucus, muscle and joint pain, neuralgia, otitis, parasites (pinworm, ringworm, tapeworm), poisoning (food, heavy metal), prostate problems, respiratory conditions, rheumatism, sciatica, scorpion stings, scrofula, septicimia, sexually transmitted diseases (STDs), sinusitis, skin problems, sore throat, strep throat, stomachache, thrombosis (blood clot), toothache, tuberculosis, tumors, typhoid, ulcer (bouveret, duodenal, fistula, gastric, peptic, syriac, tuberculous), urinary problems, vaginitis, warts (digitate, filiform, fugitive, glabra, mother, plana juvenilis, plantar, seborrhoeic, vulgaris), whooping cough, and wounds (minor).
Discussion: May aid digestion; cause blood vessel dilatation; clear and open bronchial passages; decrease the effect of carcinogens; delay or reduce coagulation of the blood; enhance cardiovascular, circulatory, digestive, and respiratory system functions as well as fibrinolytic activity; inhibit or destroy development and growth of bacteria and other microorganisms; offset the negative effects of chemotherapy and radiation therapy; promote bowel evacuation, perspiration, the excretion of heavy metals, and urine flow; purify the blood and lymphatic system; reduce prescription drug insulin doses; prolong bleeding and clotting time; prevent age-related vascular changes; reduce blood pressure levels, blood sugar levels, cholesterol levels, and triglyceride levels; reestablish healthy system functions; restore normal tone to tissues; serve as

an adjuvant to antibiotic resistant bacteria; speed healing; stimulate cell growth, hair growth, the immune system, metabolism, and peristalsis; stop or slow abnormal cell growth.

Cautions/Contraindications: Avoid use if pregnant or breast-feeding, or if you have a coagulation problem, gastroenteritis, or if you have a sensitive stomach. Individuals undergoing elective surgery should avoid the use of garlic for two to three weeks prior to the surgery. May cause allergic reactions and dermatitis in susceptible individuals. Some persons may experience bleeding or increased clotting time when using this herb with anticoagulant drugs or aspirin. Use extreme caution when administering garlic preparations internally to children as poisoning has occurred.

Adverse Reactions: Bleeding (possibly serious), coagulation problems, diarrhea (possibly bloody), edema, acid reflux (esophageal irritation caused by gastric acid), flatulence (excessive), hematuria (blood in the urine), indigestion, irritable bowel syndrome (IBS), nausea, and/or vomiting.

Herb/Drug Interactions: This herb could cause an interaction (possibly severe) when taken with the following drugs: Anticoagulant drugs, Antidiabetic drugs, Hypotensive drugs, Salicylates, and Subsalicylates.

Preparations/Dosage: Crude Herb: 3-6 grams. Clove (grated or whole): Eat 1 whole clove or 1 grated clove mixed with honey once per day. Juice: 10-30 (0.666-2 cc.) drops per day in water. Syrup (*syrupus allii*): 1-4 drachms (4-15 cc.). Tincture: 5-30 drops (0.333-2 cc.) one to three times per day.

Isolation: Allyl tribromide: Average dose of 5 drops (0.333 gm.) for use as an analgesic and antispasmodic.

Did You Know? More than 2000 studies both clinical and scientific have been conducted to evaluate the therapeutic uses of garlic.

Gentian (jen shen)

(*Gentiana lutea*)

Synonyms/Related Species: American Gentian, Arctic Gentian (*gentiana algida*), Bitterroot, Bitterwort, Blue Bells, Blue Gentian (*gentiana catesbaei*), Chinese Gentian Root, Five-Flowered Gentian, Fringed Gentian (*gentiana crinita*), Glaucous Gentian (*gentiana glauca*), Marsh Gentian (*gentiana ochroleuca*), Moss Gentian (*gentiana prostrata*), Mountain Bog Gentian (*gentiana calycosa*), Pale Gentian, Pleated Gentian (*gentiana affinis*), Quinqueflora, Southern Gentian, Stiff Gentian (*gentiana quinquefolia*), Wild Gentian, and Yellow Gentian.

Family/Class: Gentianaceae (gentian).

Habitat: Alaska, the Alpine and Subalpine zones, Europe, North America, Portugal, the Pyrenees, Spain, Switzerland, and the Yukon Territory.

Flavor: Bitter.

Parts Used: Root.

Properties: Antacid, antibiotic, antioxidant, antiperiodic, antiphlogistic, depurative, emmenagogue, lithotriptic, malariacidal, sialogogue, stomachic, and tonic.

Constituents: Alkaloids, bitter principle, gentianin (gentiotannic acid), gentianose, gentiopicrin, minerals (iron, lead, manganese, silicon, sulfur, zinc), monosaccharides, silicic acid, vitamins (B_1 (thiamine), B_2 (riboflavin), B_3 (niacin), B_5 (pantothenic acid), B_6 (pyridoxine), B_{12}, choline, B_x (para-aminobenzoic acid (PABA), H (biotin), inositol, M (folic acid), and volatile oil.

Historical Uses: Acidity (gastric), ague, amenorrhea, anemia, anorexia, appetite loss, bruises, calculus, cataracts, chills, constipation, cramps, debility, diabetes, diabetic retinopathy, diarrhea,

digestive complaints, emaciation, exhaustion, fainting, fever (ephemeral, intermittent, rheumatic), flatulence, gallstones, gastritis, gastrointestinal problems, gout, hepatitis, herbal tobacco, hysteria, indigestion, infection (bacterial), inflammation, irritable bowel syndrome (IBS), jaundice, kidney stones, lesions (tubercle), liver problems, malaria, muscle and joint pain, nausea, parasites (malarial plasmodia), pelvic inflammatiory disease (PID), rheumatism, scrofula, sexually transmitted diseases (STDs), sprain, tuberculosis, ulcer (fistula, tuberculous), vomiting, and wounds (minor).
Discussion: May dissolve calculi; enhance gallbladder, kidney, liver, pancreatic, spleen, and stomach functions; increase circulation and white blood cell count; inhibit oxidation and inhibit or destroy development and growth of bacteria and other microorganisms; neutralize acidity; promote saliva secretion; purify the blood; restore normal tone to tissues; stimulate appetite, gastric secretions, and menstruation.
Cautions/Contraindications: Avoid use if pregnant or breast-feeding, or if you have acidity (gastric), chronic gastrointestinal problems, ulcer (duodenal, gastric, peptic), or hypertension.
Adverse Reactions: Menorrhagia, nausea, salivation (increased), and/or vomiting.
Herb/Drug Interactions: This herb could cause an interaction (possibly severe) when taken with the following drugs: None known.
Preparations/Dosage: Crude Herb: 3-6 grams. Decoction: ½-1 cup per day. Tincture: 5-15 drops (0.333-1 cc.).

Ginger (jin jer)
(*Zingiber officinale*)

Synonyms/Related Species: African Ginger, Ardrakam, Black Ginger, East Indian Ginger, Gan Jiang, Jamaican Ginger, Sunthi, White Ginger, and Zingiber.
Family/Class: Zingiberaceae (ginger).
Habitat: Africa, Asia, India, Jamaica, and North America.
Flavor: Pungent.
Parts Used: Root.
Properties: Anthelmintic, anticarcinogen, anticoagulant, antioxidant, antiperiodic, antiphlogistic, antispasmodic, aromatic, astringent, carminative, cholagogue, counterirritant, diaphoretic, diuretic, emmenagogue, expectorant, hemostatic, malariacidal, parasiticide, sialogogue, stimulant, tonic, and vermifuge.
Constituents: Borneol, citral (geranial), curcumen, eucalyptol (cineol), fats, gingerin, gingerol, inulin (starch), linalool, minerals (calcium, iron, magnesium, phosphorus, sodium), neral, protein, resin, vitamins (A, B_1 (thiamine), B_2 (riboflavin), B_3 (niacin), B_5 (pantothenic acid), B_6 (pyridoxine), B_{12}, B_x (para-aminobenzoic acid (PABA), C (ascorbic acid), H (biotin), M (folic acid), volatile oil, and zingiberene.
Historical Uses: Ague, allergy, amenorrhea, arrhythmia, arteriosclerosis, arthritis, asthma, benign breast disease, bleeding, bursitis, bronchitis, cancer, cellulite, chilblains, chills, cholera, colds, colic, colitis, congestion (uterine, vaginal), constipation, cough, cramps, diarrhea, digestive complaints, diphtheria, dizziness, edema, fever (ephemeral, hankow, intermittent), flatulence, gastritis, gastrointestinal problems, headache, hypercholesteremia, indigestion, inflammation, influenza, leukorrhea, lymphedema, irritable bowel syndrome (IBS), malaria, migraine, motion sickness, mucus, muscle and joint pain, nausea, nervous conditions, neuralgia, pain, parasites and worm (anisakid worm, malarial plasmodia, roundworm, schistosoma), respiratory conditions, schistosomiasis, seizure conditions, sinusitis, sore throat, spasmodic

conditions, sprain, strep throat, substitute for wild ginger (*asarum spp.*), toothache, ulcer (duodenal, gastric, peptic, syriac), urethritis, vaginitis, vertigo, vomiting, whooping cough, and wounds (minor).

Discussion: May aid digestion; assist in the absorption of other nutrients; clear and open bronchial passages; decrease the effect of carcinogens; delay or reduce coagulation of the blood; enhance cardiovascular system, kidney, liver, lung, and spleen functions; increase circulation; inhibit oxidation; promote bile flow, perspiration, and saliva secretion; restore normal tone to tissues; stimulate appetite, gastric secretions, menstruation, and peristalsis.

Cautions/Contraindications: Avoid use if pregnant or breast-feeding, or if you have a coagulation problem, gallstones, or an intestinal problem. Individuals undergoing elective surgery should avoid the use of ginger for two to three weeks prior to the surgery. May interfere with vitamin and iron absorption. Some persons may experience bleeding or increased clotting time when using this herb with anticoagulant drugs or aspirin.

Adverse Reactions: Bleeding (possibly serious), coagulation problems, edema, ephidrosis, gastric irritation, menorrhagia, nausea, salivation (increased), and/or vomiting.

Herb/Drug Interactions: This herb could cause an interaction (possibly severe) when taken with the following drugs: Anesthetic drugs (major), Anticoagulant drugs, Antineoplastic drugs, Anxiolytic drugs, Salicylates, and Subsalicylates.

Preparations/Dosage: Crude Herb: 3-6 grams. Root (powdered): Average dose in substance 5-15 grains (0.3-1 gm.). Extract: 5-15 drops (0.333-1 cc.) one to two times per day. Infusion: 1-3 cups per day. Tincture: 10-15 drops (0.666-1 cc.) one to three times per day.

Isolation: Eucalyptol: 5 drops (0.3 cc.) in atomization or inhalation therapy for use in respiratory conditions. Gingerin: Average dose of 1 drop (0.06 cc.) for use as a carminative and stimulant.

Did You Know? White ginger and black ginger come from the same plant. When the outer covering of the root is scraped off it is called white ginger, and when the outer root cover is left on it is called black ginger.

Ginger, Wild (jin jer, wīld)

(*Asarum canadense*)

Synonyms/Related Species: Asarabacca (*asarum europaeum*), Asarum (*asarum caudatum*), Canada Snakeroot, European Snakeroot, Hazelwort, Indian Ginger, Long-Tailed Wild Ginger, Public House Plant, Vermont Snakeroot, and Wild Nard.

Family/Class: Aristolochiaceae (birthwort).

Habitat: Europe, North America, and Siberia.

Flavor: Pungent.

Parts Used: Root.

Properties: Abortifacient, analgesic, antibiotic, antifungal, antispasmodic, diaphoretic, diuretic, emetic, expectorant, laxative, and stimulant.

Constituents: Aristolochic acid, caffeic acid, chlorogenic acid, flavonoids, and volatile oil.

Historical Uses: Abscess, ague, angina, bronchitis, colic, colds, constipation, cough, cramps, dehydration, edema, eye inflammation, headache, indigestion, infection (bacterial, fungal), inflammation, jaundice, liver problems, migraine, mucus, pain, perfume (root oil), pneumonia, respiratory conditions, spasmodic conditions, substitute for ginger (*zingiber spp.*), and toothache.

Discussion: May clear and open bronchial passages; increase circulation; induce abortion; inhibit or destroy development and growth of bacteria and other microorganisms; promote bowel evacuation, perspiration, and urine flow; stimulate menstruation, peristalsis, and uterine contractions.

Cautions/Contraindications: Avoid use if pregnant or breast-feeding, or if you have a coagulation problem, gallstones, or an intestinal problem. Individuals undergoing elective surgery should avoid the use of ginger for two to three weeks prior to the surgery. May interfere with vitamin and iron absorption. Some persons may experience bleeding or increased clotting time when using this herb with anticoagulant drugs or aspirin.

Adverse Reactions: Bleeding (possibly serious), coagulation problems, edema, ephidrosis, gastric irritation, menorrhagia, nausea, salivation (increased), and/or vomiting.

Herb/Drug Interactions: This herb could cause an interaction (possibly severe) when taken with the following drugs: Anesthetic drugs (major), Anticoagulant drugs, Antineoplastic drugs, Anxiolytic drugs, Salicylates, and Subsalicylates.

Preparations/Dosage: Crude Herb: 3-6 grams. Decoction: 1-2 tablespoons one to three times per day or as needed. Root (powdered): Average dose in substance 5-20 grains (0.324-1.333 gm.). Tincture: 2-5 drops (0.133-0.333 cc.) one to three times per day.

Ginkgo (gin kō)
(*Ginkgo biloba*)

Synonyms/Related Species: Bai guo ye, Jingko, and Maidenhair Tree.

Family/Class: Ginkgoaceae (ginkgo).

Habitat: Asia, Japan, and the United States.

Flavor: Bitter.

Parts Used: Leaves.

Properties: Anticarcinogen, anticoagulant, astringent, antioxidant, depurative, expectorant, hemostatic, sedative, toxic, and vasodilator.

Constituents: Acetic acid, amino acids (alanine, arginine, cysteine, valine), arabinose, carbohydrates, disaccaharide, fatty acids (arachidonic, linoleic, linolenic, oleic, palmitic, stearic), fiber, fixed oils (olein, palmitin, stearin), flavonoids, ginkgetin, ginkolide, lignin, minerals (calcium, copper, iron, magnesium, manganese, zinc), monosaccharides, proanthocyanidins, quercetin, resin, sesquiterpenes, tannic acid, valerianic acid, vitamins (A, B, B_1 (thiamine), C (ascorbic acid), and volatile oil.

Historical Uses: Allergy, Alzheimer's disease, anxiety, arteriosclerosis, arteriostenosis, arthritis, asthma, attention deficit disorder (ADD), auditory problems, bleeding, bronchitis, cancer, cardiovascular conditions, cataracts, cellulite, colds, congestion (uterine, vaginal), cough, cramps, depression (mild/moderate), diabetes, diabetic retinopathy, dizziness, diminished sex drive, dizziness, ear problems, edema, erectile dysfunction, eye problems, floaters, glaucoma, headache, hormonal imbalances, inflammation, injury (skull), insufficiency (circulatory, venous), intermittent claudication, lesions (tubercle), leukorrhea, lung problems, macular degeneration, memory/cognitive problems, migraine, seizure conditions, mood swings, mucus, multiple sclerosis (MS), neurologic conditions, ocular nerve damage, Parkinson's disease, phlebitis, Raynaud's disease, respiratory conditions, scrofula, shock (toxic shock syndrome), spermatorrhea, tinnitus, tuberculosis, ulcer (fistula, stasis, tuberculous, varicose), vaginitis, varicose veins, vertigo, visual disturbances, and wheezing.

Discussion: May cause blood vessel dilatation; clear and open bronchial passages; decrease the effect of carcinogens; delay or reduce coagulation of the blood; enhance kidney and lung functions; increase cerebral circulation; improve cognition, concentration, glucose utilization, memory, mental acuity, mood, and sociability; inhibit oxidation; offset the negative effects of chemotherapy and radiation therapy as well as the sexual dysfunction side effects that sometimes occur with the use of selective serotonin reuptake inhibitor (SSRI) drugs; prevent free radical damage; promote the transmission of nerve impulses; purify the blood; regulate urine flow; stop or slow abnormal cell growth; strengthen erections and the vascular system.

Cautions/Contraindications: Avoid use if pregnant or breast-feeding, or if you have a coagulation problem, have a history of stroke (apoplectic), have depression (severe), or hypersensitivity. Individuals undergoing elective surgery should avoid the use of ginkgo for two to three weeks prior to the surgery. May cause allergic reactions and dermatitis in susceptible individuals. Some persons may experience bleeding or increased clotting time when using this herb with anticoagulant drugs or aspirin. Not for long-term use.

Adverse Reactions: Bleeding (possibly serious), coagulation problems, diarrhea, fever, gastrointestinal cramps, headache, hypotension, irritability, nausea, restlessness, tremors, and/or vomiting.

Herb/Drug Interactions: This herb could cause an interaction (possibly severe) when taken with the following drugs: Anticoagulant drugs, Antidepressant drugs, Diuretic drugs, Immune Suppressive drugs, Monoamine Oxidase Inhibitor (MAOI) drugs, Salicylates, Selective Serotonin Reuptake Inhibitor (SSRI) drugs, and Subsalicylates.

Preparations/Dosage: Crude Herb: 3-6 grams.

Did You Know? Ginkgo trees are one of the oldest living tree species. They are resistant to fungi, insects, pollution, and radiation, and can live for as long as one thousand years.

Ginseng (jin seŋ)

(Panax ginseng)

Synonyms/Related Species: American Ginseng (*panax quinquifolium*), Asiatic Ginseng (*panax schinseng*), Chinese Ginseng, Chinese Seng, Dwarf Ginseng (*panax trifolius*), Five Fingers, Five-Leaf Ginseng, Garantoquen, Gintz'æn, Jen Shen, Jin-Chen, Korean Ginseng, Life of Man, Man Root, Ninsin, Oriental Ginseng, Panakos, Red Berry, Red Ginseng, Renshen, Schinseng, Seng, True Ginseng, and Wonder of the World.

Family/Class: Araliaceae (ginseng).

Habitat: China, Japan, Korea, and North America.

Flavor: Sweet/bitter.

Parts Used: Root.

Properties: Alterative, analgesic, anticarcinogen, anticoagulant, antidepressant, antiphlogistic, antispasmodic, carminative, demulcent, hemostatic, hypoglycemic, nutritive, stimulant, stomachic, and tonic.

Constituents: Aglycone (genin), fatty acids (arachidonic, linoleic, linolenic), gum, inulin (starch), minerals (calcium, copper, germanium, iron, magnesium, manganese, phosphorus, potassium, silicon, sodium, sulfur, tin, vanadium, zinc), monosaccharides, panaquilon (panacon), pectic acid, pectin, polysaccharides, resin, silicic acid, sterols, triterpenic saponosides (ginsengosides), vitamins (A, B_1 (thiamine), B_2 (riboflavin), B_3 (niacin), B_{12}, choline, E (alpha-tocopheral), and volatile oil.

Historical Uses: Age spots, anemia, anxiety, appetite loss, arthritis, arteriosclerosis, auditory problems, bipolar/manic depressive condition, bleeding, bronchitis, cancer (lung, stomach), cardiovascular conditions, chronic fatigue syndrome (CFS), cirrhosis, colds, constipation, cough, cramps, croup, Cushing's disease, cystitis, debility, depression (mild/moderate), diabetes, dietary supplementation, digestive complaints, diminished sex drive, diphtheria, edema, Epstein Barr Virus (EBV), erectile dysfunction, fatigue, febrile diseases, fever (ephemeral, rheumatic), fibromyalgia, hangover (caused by alcohol consumption), headache, heart disease, hemorrhage, hyperglycemia, infertility, inflammation, influenza, irritability, liver problems, lochia, Lyme disease, malnutrition, memory/cognitive problems, menopausal/menstrual problems, mononucleosis (infectious), muscle and joint pain, nausea, nervous conditions, pain, respiratory conditions, rheumatism, shock, sores, spasmodic conditions, thirst, ulcer (duodenal, gastric, peptic), urinary problems, visual disturbances, and vomiting.

Discussion: May aid digestion; balance blood pressure levels; decrease the effect of carcinogens; delay or reduce coagulation of the blood; enhance cardiovascular system, circulatory system, digestive system, glandular system, hormonal system, nervous system, reproductive system, respiratory system functions; improve memory, cognition, and sexual performance; increase body fluids, energy, longevity, lung capacity, mental acuity, resistance to illness, stamina, and vitality; offset the negative effects of chemotherapy and radiation therapy; prevent the deposition of fat in the liver; protect against heart disease; provide dietary supplementation; reduce blood sugar levels and cholesterol levels; reestablish healthy system functions; serve as a nutritional adjuvant to therapeutic programs; slow the aging process; soothe mucous membrane irritation; stimulate the immune system; strengthen auditory function, the bones, ligaments, tendons, and vision.

Cautions/Contraindications: Avoid use if pregnant or breast-feeding, or if you have been diagnosed with acute inflammatory disease, or if your stomach does not produce enough acid to digest food properly, or if you have arrythmias, asthma, benign breast disease, coagulation problem, emphysema, fever, hypertension, or insomnia. May cause insomnia when consumed with beverages or foods containing caffeine. Some persons may experience bleeding or increased clotting time when using this herb with anticoagulant drugs or aspirin.

Adverse Reactions: Bleeding (possibly serious), breast tenderness, coagulation problems, dizziness, edema, elevated blood pressure levels, fever, hemorrhage, menstrual problems, nausea, nervousness, rash, sleep disturbances, and/or vomiting.

Herb/Drug Interactions: This herb could cause an interaction (possibly severe) when taken with the following drugs: Anticoagulant drugs, Antidiabetic drugs, Corticosteroids, Influenza vaccine, Monoamine Oxidase Inhibitor (MAOI) drugs, Salicylates, and Subsalicylates.

Preparations/Dosage: Crude Herb: 3-9 grams. Decoction: ½-1 cup per day. Infusion: 1-3 cups per day. Tincture: 10-30 drops (0.666-2 cc.) one to three times per day.

Ginseng, Siberian (jin seŋ, sī·bir ē·en)

(*Eleutherococcus senticosus*)

Synonyms/Related Species: Devil's Shrub, Eleuthero, and Si-Wu-Jia.
Family/Class: Araliaceae (ginseng).
Habitat: Asia, Japan, and Siberia.
Flavor: Sweet/pungent.
Parts Used: Bark (root).
Properties: Alterative, anticarcinogen, anticoagulant, antiphlogistic, antispasmodic, aromatic, depurative, hemostatic, tonic, and vasodilator.

Constituents: Acrylic acid, coumarin, eleutheroside, glycosides, inulin (starch), lignin, polysaccharides, resin, saponins, sesamine, syringin, triterpenes, vitamins (A, B_1 (thiamine), B_2 (riboflavin), B_{12}, E (alpha-tocopheral), and volatile oil.

Historical Uses: Acne, acquired immune deficiency syndrome (AIDS), age spots, anxiety, appetite loss, arthritis, asthma, athletes, attention deficit disorder (ADD), autoimmune disease, bleeding, bronchitis, cancer (carcinoma, ovarian), cardiovascular conditions, chronic fatigue syndrome (CFS), colds, constipation, cough, debility, depression (mild/moderate), diabetes, digestive complaints, diminished sex drive, environmental stress sensitivity (i.e. drafts, noise, weather changes), Epstein Barr Virus (EBV), erectile dysfunction, fatigue, fever (ephemeral, rheumatic), fibromyalgia, glandular problems, heart disease, Hodgkin's disease, human immunodeficiency virus (HIV), hypercholesteremia, hypoglycemia, infection (viral), inflammation, influenza, insomnia, lesions (tubercle), leukemia, lupus, lung problems, Lyme disease, memory/cognitive problems, Meniere's disease, migraine, mononucleosis (infectious), mumps, muscle and joint pain, Parkinson's disease, prostate problems, respiratory conditions, rheumatism, scrofula, skin problems, spasmodic conditions, substitute for ginseng (*panax ginseng*), tuberculosis, tumors (Kaposi's sarcoma, multiple myeloma), ulcer (fistula, tuberculous), and urinary problems.

Discussion: May allow for harder athletic workouts in a shorter period of time and prevent that rundown feeling after heavy training; balance blood sugar levels and hormonal production; cause blood vessel dilatation; cleanse the liver; delay or reduce coagulation of the blood; dispose of lactic acid in the body; decrease the effect of carcinogens; enhance cardiovascular system, glandular system, lung, and nervous system functions; improve cognition, concentration, and memory; increase athletic performance, energy, muscular activity, sex drive, stamina, and oxygen consumption as well as resistance to external environmental factors, illness, and stress; offset the negative effects of chemotherapy and radiation therapy; quicken the reflexes; protect against heart disease; reduce cholesterol levels and post influenza virus vaccination reactions; reestablish healthy system functions; restore normal tone to tissues; serve as an adjuvant in patient rehabilitation; speed healing; stimulate appetite, the immune system, natural killer (NK) cell activity, T-cell activity, and testosterone production.

Cautions/Contraindications: Avoid use if pregnant or breast-feeding, or if you have hypertension, lupus, myasthenia gravis, a prostate problem, rheumatoid arthritis (RA), coagulation problem, or Sjögren's syndrome. May cause insomnia if taken close to bedtime. May increase the sleep-inducing effect of barbiturates. Some persons may experience bleeding or increased clotting time when using this herb with anticoagulant drugs or aspirin.

Adverse Reactions: Bleeding (possibly serious), coagulation problems, diarhea (possibly bloody), gastrointestinal cramps (severe), hematuria (blood in the urine), nausea, and/or vomiting.

Herb/Drug Interactions: This herb could cause an interaction (possibly severe) when taken with the following drugs: Anticoagulant drugs, Antineoplastic drugs, Cardiac Drugs, Influenza vaccine, Monoamine Oxidase Inhibitor (MAOI) drugs, Opiate Agonists/Narcotic drugs, Salicylates, and Subsalicylates.

Preparations/Dosage: Crude Herb: 3-12 grams. Decoction: ½-1 cup per day. Infusion: 1-3 cups per day. Tincture: 10-30 drops (0.666-2 cc.) one to three times per day.

Ginseng, Tienchi (jin seŋ, tin·chē)
(*Panax pseudoginseng*)

Synonyms/Related Species: San-qi, Tian-qi, and Tienchi Root.
Family/Class: Araliaceae (ginseng).
Habitat: Cultivated in China.
Flavor: Sweet/bitter.
Parts Used: Root.
Properties: Astringent, emmenagogue, hemostatic, hypoglycemic, hypotensive, stimulant, stomachic, tonic, vasodilator, and vulnerary.
Constituents: Arasopanin and volatile oil.
Historical Uses: Angina, bleeding, bruises, diabetic retinopathy, fatigue, fractures, hemorrhage (metrorrhagia), hyperglycemia, hypertension (mild/moderate), inflammation, neuritis (optic), pain, skin tumors, sprain, thrombosis (blood clot), trauma (postoperative), tumors, and wounds (minor and surgical).
Discussion: May cause blood vessel dilatation; enhance cardiovascular system, colon, liver, and stomach functions; heal capillaries and membranes at the back of the eye; improve athletic performance and heart muscle function; increase stamina; reduce blood pressure levels, blood sugar levels, and the effects of postoperative tissue trauma; restore normal tone to tissues; speed healing; stimulate menstruation and metabolism.
Cautions/Contraindications: Avoid use if pregnant or breast-feeding, or if you have been diagnosed with acute inflammatory disease, or if your stomach does not produce enough acid to digest food properly. Some persons may experience bleeding or increased clotting time when using this herb with anticoagulant drugs or aspirin.
Adverse Reactions: Bleeding (possibly serious), breast tenderness, coagulation problems, dizziness, edema, elevated blood pressure levels, fever, hemorrhage, menstrual problems, nausea, rash, sleep disturbances, and/or vomiting.
Herb/Drug Interactions: This herb could cause an interaction (possibly severe) when taken with the following drugs: Anticoagulant drugs, Antidiabetic drugs, Hypotensive drugs, Monoamine Oxidase Inhibitor (MAOI) drugs, Salicylates, and Subsalicylates.
Preparations/Dosage: Crude Herb: 1-3 grams. Decoction: ¼-½ cup per day. Infusion: ½-2 cups per day. Tincture: 5-10 drops (0.333-0.666 cc.) one to three times per day.

Globemallow (glōb·mal ō)
(*Sphaeralcea angustifolia*)

Synonyms/Related Species: Copper Globemallow, Scarlet Globemallow (*sphaeralcea coccinea*), and White-Stemmed Globemallow (*sphaeralcea munroana*).
Family/Class: Malvaceae (mallow).
Habitat: North America.
Flavor: Bitter.
Parts Used: Flower, leaves, root.
Properties: Antifertilizin, antiphlogistic, astringent, demulcent, hemostatic, laxative, and stimulant.
Constituents: Mucilage and tannic acid.
Historical Uses: Acne, appetite loss, arthritis, bleeding, blisters, bruises, colds, constipation, cough, dandruff, diarrhea, eyewash, fever (ephemeral, rheumatic), fractures, gastrointestinal

problems, hair rinse, headache, hemafecia (blood in the stool), inflammation, influenza, laryngitis, muscle and joint pain, nausea, rash, rheumatism, skin problems, snakebite, sores, sore throat, and wounds (minor).
Discussion: May neutralize fertilizin (fertilization); promote bowel evacuation; soothe mucous membrane irritation; speed healing; stimulate appetite and peristalsis.
Cautions/Contraindications: Avoid use if pregnant or breast-feeding.
Adverse Reactions: Diarrhea, nausea, and/or vomiting.
Herb/Drug Interactions: This herb could cause an interaction (possibly severe) when taken with the following drugs: None known.
Preparations/Dosage: External uses only.

Goat's Rue (gōts roo)
(*Galega officinalis*)

Synonyms/Related Species: American Goat's Rue (*galega virginiana*), European Goat Rue, French Lilac, Galega, Herba Ruta Caprariae, Italian Fitch, and Pestilenzkraut.
Family/Class: Leguminosae (legume).
Habitat: Asia, Britain, Europe, Germany, and North America.
Flavor: Bitter.
Parts Used: Flowering tops, leaves.
Properties: Antibiotic, diaphoretic, diuretic, expectorant, febrifuge, hypoglycemic, and laxative.
Constituents: Alkaloids, flavonoids, galegine, tannic acid, and vasicine (peganine).
Historical Uses: Abscess, asthma, bronchitis, dislocations, fever (ephemeral), footbath, hyperglycemia, infection (bacterial), muscle strain, plague, respiratory conditions, and sprain.
Discussion: May clear and open bronchial passages; inhibit or destroy development and growth of bacteria and other microorganisms; promote bowel evacuation, perspiration, and urine flow; reduce blood sugar levels; stimulate peristalsis.
Cautions/Contraindications: Avoid use if pregnant or breast-feeding. Use with professional guidance/supervision.
Adverse Reactions: Asphyxiation, paralysis, salivation, spasmodic conditions, and possible death.
Herb/Drug Interactions: This herb could cause an interaction (possibly severe) when taken with the following drugs: Antidiabetic drugs.
Preparations/Dosage: Crude Herb: 1-2 grams. Infusion: 1 cup per day. Tincture: 5-20 drops (0.333-1.25 cc.) one to three times per day.

Goldenrod (gōl den·rod)
(*Solidago canadensis*)

Synonyms/Related Species: Aaron's Rod, Anise-Scented Goldenrod (*solidago odora*), Blue Mountain Tea, Bohea Tea, Canada Goldenrod, European Goldenrod (*solidago virgaurea*), Giant Goldenrod (*solidago gigantea*), Goldruthe, Gray Goldenrod (*solidago nemoralis*), Missouri Goldenrod (*solidago missouriensis*), Northern Goldenrod (*solidago multiradiata*), Smooth Goldenrod, Solidago, Spike-Like Goldenrod (*solidago simplex*), Sweet Goldenrod, Wound Weed, and Woundwort.
Family/Class: Compositae (composite).

Floral Emblem: Kentucky and Nebraska.
Habitat: Alaska, the Alpine zone, Asia, Britain, Europe, and North America.
Flavor: Bitter.
Parts Used: Flowers, leaves.
Properties: Analgesic, antibiotic, antifungal, antiphlogistic, antispasmodic, aromatic, astringent, carminative, diaphoretic, diuretic, expectorant, hemostatic, laxative, lithotriptic, sedative, stimulant, tonic, and vulnerary.
Constituents: Cadinene, caffeic acid, chlorogenic acid, flavonoids, polysaccharides, rutin, saponins, tannic acid, vitamin A, and volatile oil.
Historical Uses: Abscess, allergy, alopecia, amenorrhea, angina, arthritis, asthma, bleeding, bronchitis, burns (minor), calculus, colds, cough, cramps, cystitis, diabetes, diarrhea, diphtheria, dysentery, dysmenorrhea, eczema, edema, fever (ephemeral, rheumatic), flatulence, gallstones, gout, headache, hemorrhage, hemorrhoids, infection (bacterial, fungal, urinary tract), inflammation, influenza, insect bites or stings, kidney stones, lesions (tubercle), menorrhagia, menstrual problems, mucus, muscle and joint pain, nephritis, pain, prostate problems, respiratory conditions, rheumatism, scrofula, sores, sore throat, spasmodic conditions, toothache, tuberculosis, tumors, urethritis, ulcer (duodenal, fistula, gastric, peptic, syriac, tuberculous), whooping cough, and wounds (minor).
Discussion: May aid digestion; clear and open bronchial passages; dissolve calculi; inhibit or destroy development and growth of bacteria and other microorganisms; prevent hemorrhage in persons with hypertension; promote bowel evacuation, perspiration, and urine flow; reduce capillary fragility; restore normal tone to tissues; speed healing; stimulate peristalsis.
Cautions/Contraindications: Avoid use if pregnant or breast-feeding, or if you have cardiovascular conditions, edema, or a kidney problem. May cause allergic reactions and dermatitis in susceptible individuals.
Adverse Reactions: Diarrhea (possibly bloody), gastrointestinal cramps (severe), hematuria (blood in the urine), nausea, and/or vomiting.
Herb/Drug Interactions: This herb could cause an interaction (possibly severe) when taken with the following drugs: None known.
Preparations/Dosage: Crude Herb: 3-6 grams. Flowering tops and/or Leaves (powdered): ½-1 teaspoon in honey one to two times per day. Infusion: 1-2 cups per day. Tincture: 10-30 drops (0.666-2 cc.) one to three times per day.

Goldenseal (gōl den·sēl)
(*Hydrastis canadensis*)

Synonyms/Related Species: Eye Balm, Ground Raspberry, Hydrastis, Indian Dye, Indian Paint, Indian Plant, Jaundice Root, Orangeroot, Puccoon Root, Turmeric Root, Warnera, Wild Curcuma, Yellow Puccoon, and Yellow Root.
Family/Class: Ranunculaceae (buttercup).
Habitat: North America.
Flavor: Bitter.
Parts Used: Root.
Properties: Alterative, antibiotic, anticarcinogen, antifungal, antiperiodic, antiphlogistic, antiviral, astringent, bitter, demulcent, depurative, diuretic, hemostatic, hypertensive, laxative, malariacidal, oxytocic, parasiticide, tonic, vasoconstrictor, and vesicant.

Constituents: Albumin (albumen), alkaloids, berberine, canadine, chologenic acid, fatty acids (arachidonic, linoleic, linolenic, oleic, palmitic, stearic), fixed oils (olein, palmitin, stearin), hydrastine, inulin (starch), minerals (calcium, copper, iron, manganese, phosphorus, potassium, sodium, zinc), lignin, monosaccharides, protoanemonin, resin, tannic acid, vitamins (A, B_1 (thiamine), B_2 (riboflavin), B_3 (niacin), B_5 (pantothenic acid), B_6 (pyridoxine), B_{12}, B_x (para-aminobenzoic acid (PABA), choline, C (ascorbic acid), E (alpha-tocopheral), H (biotin), inositol, M (folic acid), and volatile oil.

Historical Uses: Ague, allergy (pollen), asthma, bleeding, bronchitis, burns (minor), cancer (carcinoma, cervical, oral), candida, canker sores, chicken pox, cirrhosis, colds, colitis, congestion (uterine, vaginal), conjunctivitis, constipation, cough, diarrhea, digestive complaints, diphtheria, dysentery, earache, eczema, eyewash, fever (ephemeral, enteric, hay, herpetic, intermittent, scarlet), flatulence, gallbladder problems, gargle/mouth rinse, gastritis, gastroenteritis, gastrointestinal problems, gleet, gonorrhea, hemorrhage (metrorrhagia), hemorrhoids, hepatitis, herpes, hypoglycemia, impetigo, indigestion, infection (bacterial, bladder, fungal, sexually transmitted, viral), infertility, inflammation, influenza, insufficiency (circulatory, pancreatic), irritable bowel syndrome (IBS), kidney problems, laryngitis, leukorrhea, liver problems, lochia, malaria, measles, meningitis, menorrhagia, menstrual problems, moniliasis, mucous membranes, nausea, nephritis, nervous condition, night sweats, parasites (malarial plasmodia, ringworm), periodontal disease, prostate problems, psoriasis, respiratory conditions, rhinitis, scarletina, sexually transmitted diseases (STDs), sinusitis, skin problems, small pox, sore throat, sores, syphilis, tonsillitis, tumors (brain), typhoid, ulcer (bouveret, duodenal, gastric, peptic, syphilitic, syriac), urethritis, uterine problems, vaginitis, weight loss, and wounds (minor).

Discussion: May cause blood vessel constriction; cleanse the whole system; decrease the effect of carcinogens; enhance cardiovascular system, colon, digestive system, glandular system, liver, and pancreatic functions; increase blood pressure levels, circulation, and white blood cell activity; inhibit or destroy developement and growth of bacteria and other microorganisms; offset the negative effects of chemotherapy and radiation therapy; promote bowel evacuation and urine flow; reestablish healthy system functions; restore normal tone to tissues; soothe mucous membrane irritation; stimulate the immune system, peristalsis, and uterine contractions.

Cautions/Contraindications: Avoid use if pregnant or breast-feeding, or if you have chronic indigestion, diabetes, diarrhea, glaucoma, heart disease, a history of stroke (apoplectic), hypertension, or Raynaud's disease. May reduce absorption of antibiotic drugs. Some persons may experience bleeding or increased clotting time when using this herb with anticoagulant drugs or aspirin. Not for long-term use. Use with professional guidance/supervision.

Adverse Reactions: Bleeding (possibly serious), blistering of the mouth and throat, bradycardia, coagulation problems, constipation, convulsions, delirium, diarrhea, dizziness, edema, excitability, fainting, hallucinations, hematuria (blood in the urine), kidney failure, liver damage (often characterized by jaundice), mucous membrane problems, nausea, paralysis, respiratory failure, salivation, spasmodic conditions, stomach pain, vomiting, and possible death.

Herb/Drug Interactions: This herb could cause an interaction (possibly severe) when taken with the following drugs: Antibiotic drugs, Anticoagulant drugs, Salicylates, and Subsalicylates.

Preparations/Dosage: Crude Herb: 3-6 grams. Extract: 8-30 drops (0.5-2 cc.) one to two times per day. Extract (powdered): Average dose in substance 8 grains (0.5 gm.). Fluidglycerite: 30-60 drops (2-4 cc.) one to three times per day. Infusion: 1-2 teaspoons one to two times per day. Root (powdered): Average dose in substance 10 grains (0.666 gm.). Tincture: 30-90 drops (2-5 cc.) one to three times per day. Eye Rinse: Combine 1 teaspoon powdered root, 1 teaspoon boric acid, and 1 pint boiling water. Stir well and let cool. Strain. To strained liquid add ½ cup water.

Gotu Kola (got·ū kō lā)
(*Hydrocotyle asiatica*)

Synonyms/Related Species: Brahmi, Centella, Common Pennywort (*hydrocotyle vulgaris*), European Hydrocotyle, Fo-Ti-Tieng, Hydrocotyle, Indian Pennywort, Ji Xue Cao, Mandukaparni, Marsh Penny, Thick-Leaved Pennywort, White Rot, and Whorled Marsh Pennywort.
Family/Class: Umbelliferae (parsley).
Habitat: Africa, Asia, Australia, Ceylon, Columbia, Europe, India, Indonisia, Madagascar, North America, South America, South Sea Islands, and Sri Lanka.
Flavor: Bitter/pungent.
Parts Used: Leaves.
Properties: Alterative, antibiotic, antidepressant, antiphlogistic, antispasmodic, depurative, diuretic, hypotensive, narcotic, nervine, sedative, stimulant, tonic, and vasodilator.
Constituents: Minerals (magnesium), saponins, tannic acid, triterpene acids, vellarin, vitamins (A, B, B_2 (riboflavin), E (alpha-tocopheral), K), and volatile oil.
Historical Uses: Aging, Alzheimer's disease, asthma, blisters, bruises, burns (minor), cellulitis, cervicitis, cirrhosis, colds, cough, dehydration, depression (mild/moderate), dermatitis, diarrhea, digestive complaints, dysentery, edema, epilepsy, exhaustion, eye problems, fatigue, fever (ephemeral, rheumatic), gastritis, gastrointestinal problems, hepatitis, hypertension (mild/moderate), hysteria, indigestion, infection (bacterial, urinary tract), inflammation, insomnia, insufficiency (venous), leprosy, lesions (surgical, tubercle), liver problems, lupus, memory/cognitive problems, mental disturbances, measles, menopausal problems, muscle and joint pain, nervous conditions, periodontal disease, phlebitis, pruritus, psoriasis, respiratory conditions, rheumatism, scars, scleroderma, sclerosis, scrofula, sexually transmitted diseases (STDs), shortness of breath, sinusitis, skin problems, sore throat, spasmodic conditions, syphilis, tonsillitis, thyroid, tuberculosis, tumors, ulcer (duodenal, fistula, gastric, peptic, stasis, syphilitic, tuberculous, varicose), vaginitis, varicose veins, and wounds (minor).
Discussion: May calm the nervous system; cause blood vessel dilatation; enhance cardiovascular system, liver, and respiratory system functions; improve memory and cognition; increase circulation, energy, and longevity; inhibit or destroy development and growth of bacteria and other microorganisms; promote hair growth and urine flow; purify the blood; reduce blood pressure levels and post-operative scarring; reestablish healthy system functions; restore normal tone to tissues; speed healing; stimulate the immune system and skin cell regeneration; strengthen the connective tissues, hair, nerves, skin, nails, and vascular system.
Cautions/Contraindications: Avoid use if pregnant or breast-feeding, or if you have cancer or hypercholesteremia. Do not confuse gotu kola with cola nut (also spelled kola). Cola nut contains caffeine and is not the same plant, nor is it remotely related to gotu kola. May cause dermatitis in susceptible individuals.
Adverse Reactions: Diarrhea (possibly bloody), gastrointestinal cramps (severe), headache, hematuria (blood in the urine), nausea, stupor, vertigo, and/or vomiting.

Herb/Drug Interactions: This herb could cause an interaction (possibly severe) when taken with the following drugs: Antidiabetic drugs, Hypotensive drugs, Sedative drugs, and Tranquilizer drugs.
Preparations/Dosage: Crude Herb: 3-15 grams. Infusion: 1-3 cups per day.

Goutweed (gout·wēd)
(*Aegopodium podagraria*)

Synonyms/Related Species: Achweed, Ashweed, Bishop's Elder, Bishopsweed, Bishopwort, Bullwort, Cumin-Royal, Eltroot, English Masterwort, Goatweed, Gout Herb, Goutwort, Ground Elder, Herb Gerarde, Herb William, Jack-Jump-About, Pigweed, Podagra, Weyl Ash, White Ash, and Wild Masterwort.
Family/Class: Umbelliferae (parsley).
Habitat: The Alpine zone, Asia, Europe, and Russia.
Flavor: Pungent.
Parts Used: Aerial.
Properties: Antiphlogistic, antiscorbutic, diuretic, lithotriptic, and sedative.
Constituents: Caffeic acid, chlorogenic acid, flavonol glycosides, vitamins (C (ascorbic acid), and volatile oil.
Historical Uses: Bladder problems, fever (ephemeral, rheumatic), gallstones, gastrointestinal problems, gout, hemorrhoids, inflammation, kidney problems, kidney stones, muscle and joint pain, rheumatism, sciatica, and scurvy.
Discussion: May dissolve calculi; promote urine flow; reduce tissue inflammation.
Cautions/Contraindications: Avoid use if pregnant or breast-feeding.
Adverse Reactions: Nausea and/or vomiting.
Herb/Drug Interactions: This herb could cause an interaction (possibly severe) when taken with the following drugs: None known.
Preparations/Dosage: Crude Herb: 3-6 grams. Infusion: 1-2 cups per day. Leaves (young): Boiled and eaten as a vegetable.

Grape (grāp)
(*Vitis vinifera*)

Synonyms/Related Species: Asian Grape (*vitis carnosa*), East Indian Grape Vine (*vitis latifolia*), and Wild Grape.
Family/Class: Vitaceae (grape).
Habitat: Asia, Europe, France, India, and the United States.
Flavor: Sweet/sour.
Parts Used: Fruit, leaves.
Properties: Analgesic, anticarcinogen, anticoagulant, antidepressant, antihistamine, antioxidant, antiphlogistic, antiviral, depurative, diuretic, hypotensive, nutritive, tonic, and vasodilator.
Constituents: Carbohydrates, catechins, citric acid, dextrose, flavones, flavonoids, minerals (iron, magnesium, potassium), malic acid, monosaccharides, oligomeric proanthocyanidins (OPCs), oxalic acid, pectic acid, pectin, quercetin, resveratrol, succinic acid, tannic acid, tartaric acid, and vitamins (A, B, C (ascorbic acid), E (alpha-tocopheral).

Historical Uses: Allergy, Alzheimer's disease, arrhythmia, arteriosclerosis, arthritis, asthma, attention deficit disorder (ADD), cancer (bladder, breast, colon, ovarian, prostate), canker sores, cardiovascular disease, cataracts, Celiac disease, chronic fatigue syndrome (CFS), coronary artery disease (CAD), cough, degenerative conditions, diabetic retinopathy, dietary supplementation, eczema, edema, emphysema, Epstein Barr Virus (EBV), fever (ephemeral, herpetic, rheumatic), fibromyalgia, glandular problems, gout, headache, heart disease, herpes, hives, human immunodeficiency virus (HIV), hypertension (mild/moderate), infection (viral), inflammation, injury (connective tissue), insufficiency (circulatory, venous), leukemia, lymphedema, macular degeneration, malnutrition, migraine, mononucleosis (infectious), muscle and joint pain, night sweats, nosebleed, pain, Parkinson's disease, polio, prostatitis, respiratory viruses, rheumatism, senility, sexually transmitted diseases (STDs), stroke (apoplectic), tendinitis, thirst, ulcer (stasis, varicose), urinary problems, varicose veins, wrinkles, and wounds (minor).
Discussion: May cause blood vessel dilatation; cleanse the whole system; counteract the effect of histamine; decrease the effect of carcinogens; delay or reduce coagulation of the blood; enhance cardiovascular system, kidney, and liver functions; increase collagen production, the effectiveness of cancer therapy drugs, and vitamin C levels; inhibit oxidation; offset the negative effects of chemotherapy and radiation therapy; promote urine flow; protect the skin from ultraviolet damage and protect against heart disease; provide dietary supplementation; reduce arterial plaque formation; repair nervous system damage; restore normal tone to tissues; serve as a nutritional adjuvant to therapeutic programs; speed healing; stimulate the immune system; stop or slow abnormal cell growth; strengthen blood vessels, capillaries, and the connective tissues.
Cautions/Contraindications: Avoid use if pregnant or breast-feeding, or if you have anemia. May interfere with iron absorption. Some persons may experience bleeding or increased clotting time when using this herb with anticoagulant drugs or aspirin
Adverse Reactions: Bleeding (possibly serious), coagulation problems, nausea, oxalism (oxalic acid or oxalate poisoning), and/or vomiting.
Herb/Drug Interactions: This herb could cause an interaction (possibly severe) when taken with the following drugs: Antibiotic drugs, Anticoagulant drugs, Antineoplastic drugs, Calcium Channel Blocker drugs, Hypotensive drugs, Immune Suppressive drugs, Salicylates, and Subsalicylates.
Preparations/Dosage: Crude Herb: 3-9 grams. Fresh fruit or juice may be ingested freely.

Grapefruit (grāp froot)
(Citrus paradisi)

Synonyms/Related Species: Pomelo.
Family/Class: Rutaceae (rue).
Habitat: Tropical and subtropical regions worldwide.
Flavor: Sour/sweet.
Parts Used: Fruit.
Properties: Antibiotic, anticarcinogen, antifungal, antioxidant, antiscorbutic, aromatic, and nutritive.
Constituents: Carbohydrates, carvene (limonene), coumarin, fiber, flavonoids, glycosides, lycopene, naringin, minerals (potassium), protein, terpene, vitamins (A, B_3 (niacin), C (ascorbic acid), and volatile oil.

Historical Uses: Beverage, cancer (prostate), candida, dietary supplementation, ear infection, escherichia coli (e-coli), fever (ephemeral, herpetic), herpes, infection (bacterial, fungal), influenza, leukorrhea, malnutrition, moniliasis, parasites, salmonella, scurvy, sexually transmitted diseases (STDs), sinusitis, tumors, vaginitis, and weight loss.
Discussion: May decrease the effect of carcinogens; inhibit oxidation and inhibit or destroy development and growth of bacteria and other microorganisms; provide dietary supplementation and needed nutrients with very few calories; reduce arterial plaque formation; serve as a nutritional adjuvant to therapeutic programs; strengthen blood vessels, capillaries, and connective tissues.
Cautions/Contraindications: Avoid use if pregnant or breast-feeding. Avoid direct contact with skin or mucosal surfaces. May increase the absorption of prescription drugs. Allergic reactions may occur in young children when first introducing them to citrus juices.
Adverse Reactions: Mucous membrane irritation.
Herb/Drug Interactions: This herb could cause an interaction (possibly severe) when taken with the following drugs: HMG-CoA Reductase Inhibitors, Hormones and Synthetic Substitutes (i.e. conjugated estrogens, contraceptives (oral, etc.), and other hormonal replacement therapy (HRT).
Preparations/Dosage: Fresh fruit pulp or juice may be ingested freely.

Gromwell (grom wel)
(*Lithospermum arnebia*)

Synonyms/Related Species: European Puccoon (*lithospermum officinale*), Lemonweed, Narrow-Leaved Puccoon, Stoneseed, Western Puccoon, Yellow Gromwell (*lithospermum incisum*), and Yellow Puccoon (*lithospermum ruderale*).
Family/Class: Boraginaceae (borage).
Habitat: Europe and North America.
Flavor: Bitter/sweet.
Parts Used: Entire plant.
Properties: Alterative, anticarcinogen, antiphlogistic, astringent, demulcent, depurative, hemostatic, hepatotoxic, laxative, and lithotriptic.
Constituents: Alkaloids and saponins.
Historical Uses: Bleeding, calculus, cancer (skin), congestion (uterine, vaginal), contraceptive (female), dermatitis, diarrhea, fever (ephemeral, herpetic, rheumatic), gallstones, hemorrhoids, herpes, inflammation, kidney problems, kidney stones, leukorrhea, muscle and joint pain, poison ivy/oak, rash, rheumatism, sexually transmitted diseases (STDs), and vaginitis.
Discussion: May cleanse the intestinal system; decrease the effect of carcinogens; dissolve calculi; promote bowel evacuation; soothe mucous membrane irritation; stimulate peristalsis; may induce a temporary sterility.
Cautions/Contraindications: Avoid use if pregnant or breast-feeding.
Adverse Reactions: Diarrhea (possibly bloody), gastrointestinal cramps (severe), hematuria (blood in the urine), liver damage (often characterized by jaundice), nausea, and/or vomiting.
Herb/Drug Interactions: This herb could cause an interaction (possibly severe) when taken with the following drugs: None known.
Preparations/Dosage: Crude Herb: 3-6 grams. External uses are recommended.

Groundsel (ground s'l)
(*Senecio vulgaris*)

Synonyms/Related Species: Alpine Meadow Groundsel (*senecio cymbalarioides*), Arrow-Leaved Groundsel (*senecio triangularis*), Balsam Groundsel (*senecio pauperculus*), Black-Tipped Groundsel (*senecio lugens*), Butterweed Groundsel (*senecio serra*), Canadian Groundsel, Cocash Weed, Common Groundsel, Coughweed, Dwarf Mountain Groundsel (*senecio conterminus*), European Ragwort (*senecio jacobaea*), False Valerian, Golden Senacio, Golden Groundsel (*senecio aureus*), Golden Ragwort, Ground Glutton, Grundswelgan, Groundsill, Gundœswelgiœ, Hoary Groundsel (*senecio erucifolius*), Life Root, Mountain Groundsel (*senecio sylvatica*), Ragwort, Rayless Alpine Groundsel (*senecio pauciflorus*), Rock Groundsel (*senecio fremontii*), Rocky Mountain Groundsel (*senecio streptanthifolius*), Senex, Sention, Simson, Squaw-Weed, Stinking Groundsel, Streambank Groundsel (*senecio pseudaureus*), Tansy Ragwort, Threadleaf Groundsel (*senecio flaccidus*), Viscid Groundsel (*senecio viscosus*), Western Groundsel (*senecio integerrimus*), and Wolly Groundsel (*senecio canus*).
Family/Class: Compositae (composite).
Habitat: The Alpine to Subalpine zones, Asia, Britain, the Channel Islands, England, Europe, Ireland, Norfolk, North America, Russia, Scotland, and Siberia.
Flavor: Bitter/pungent.
Parts Used: Leaves, root.
Properties: Abortifacient, antiphlogistic, antiscorbutic, astringent, carminative, demulcent, diaphoretic, diuretic, emetic, emmenagogue, expectorant, hemostatic, laxative, lithotriptic, oxytocic, stimulant, tonic, toxic, and vulnerary.
Constituents: Alkaloids, flavonoids, mucilage, quercetin, resin, saponins, senecifolin, senecionine, sesquiterpenes, tannic acid, and vitamin C (ascorbic acid).
Historical Uses: Acne, amenorrhea, arthritis, bleeding, calculus, cardiovascular conditions, colds, colic, congestion (uterine, vaginal), debility, diarrhea, digestive complaints, dry skin, dysmenorrhea, epilepsy, fever (ephemeral, rheumatic), flatulence, gallstones, gargle/mouth rinse, gout, headache, indigestion, infection, inflammation, insect bites or stings, kidney problems, kidney stones, jaundice, lesions (tubercle), leukemia, leukorrhea, liver problems, lung problems, menstrual problems, menorrhagia, mucus, muscle and joint pain, pimples, respiratory conditions, rheumatism, rheumatoid arthritis (RA), sciatica, scrofula, sores, sore throat, scurvy, skin problems, tuberculosis, ulcer (duodenal, fistula, gastric, peptic, tuberculous), vaginitis, and wounds (minor).
Discussion: May aid digestion; clear and open bronchial passages; dissolve calculi; enhance urinary system function; induce abortion; promote bowel evacuation, perspiration, and urine flow; reduce tissue inflammation; restore normal tone to tissues; speed healing; stimulate menstruation, peristalsis, and uterine contractions.
Cautions/Contraindications: Avoid use if pregnant or breast-feeding.
Adverse Reactions: Elevated blood pressure levels, nausea, necrosis of the liver, and/or vomiting.
Herb/Drug Interactions: This herb could cause an interaction (possibly severe) when taken with the following drugs: None known.
Preparations/Dosage: Crude Herb: 3-6 grams. Extract (solid): Average dose in substance 5-10 grains (0.333-0.666 gm.). Infusion: 1-3 cups per day. Juice: ½-1 drachm (1.85-4 cc.) used externally as a wash. Root (powdered): Average dose in substance 30-60 grains (2-4 gm.).

Guaiacum (gwī e·kem)

(*Guaiacum sanctum*)

Synonyms/Related Species: Guayacán, Lignum Vitae (*guaiacum officinale*), and Pockwood.
Family/Class: Zygophyllaceae (caltrop).
Habitat: Central America, India, and South America.
Flavor: Bitter.
Parts Used: Resin.
Properties: Anesthetic (local), antibiotic, antifungal, antiphlogistic, antispasmodic, aromatic, diaphoretic, diuretic, laxative, and stimulant.
Constituents: Aglycone (genin), guaiacetin, guaiacin, guaiacol, lignin, resin, saponins, vanillin (methyl pyrocatechinic acid), and volatile oil.
Historical Uses: Arthritis, bronchitis, fever (ephemeral, rheumatic, enteric), gargle/mouth rinse, gout, infection (bacterial, fungal), inflammation, lesions (tubercle), muscle and joint pain, night sweats, pain, pneumonia, respiratory conditions, rheumatism, rheumatoid arthritis (RA), scrofula, sexually transmitted diseases (STDs), skin problems, spasmodic conditions, syphilis, tonsillitis, tuberculosis, and ulcer (fistula, syphilitic, tuberculous).
Discussion: May enhance bladder, colon, and lung functions; increase circulation; inhibit or destroy developement and growth of bacteria and other microorganisms; promote bowel evacuation, perspiration, and urine flow; stimulate gastric secretions and peristalsis.
Cautions/Contraindications: Avoid use if pregnant or breast-feeding, or if you have ulcer (gastric, peptic). May cause dermatitis in susceptible individuals.
Adverse Reactions: Diarrhea (possibly bloody), gastroenteritis (severe), hematuria (blood in the urine), nausea, and/or vomiting.
Herb/Drug Interactions: This herb could cause an interaction (possibly severe) when taken with the following drugs: None known.
Preparations/Dosage: Resin: Average dose in substance 2-5 grains (0.133-0.324 gm.). Tincture: 10-15 drops (0.666-1 cc.) one to three times per day.
Isolation: Guaiacol carbonate: Average dose of 15 grains (1 gm.) for use in fever (enteric) and tuberculosis. Guaiacamphol (the camphoric acid ester of guaiacol): Average dose of 3-15 grains (0.19-1 gm.) for use in night sweats due to emaciation.

Guarana (gwä rä·nä)

(*Paullinia cupana*)

Synonyms/Related Species: Brazilian Cocoa, Paullinia, Uabano, and Uaranzeiro.
Family/Class: Sapindaceae (soapberry).
Habitat: South America.
Flavor: Bitter.
Parts Used: Seeds.
Properties: Analgesic, anticoagulant, aphrodisiac, astringent, cardiant, diuretic, febrifuge, hypotensive, narcotic, nervine, stimulant, tonic, and vasodilator.
Constituents: Alkaloids, caffeine, fatty acids (oleic, palmitic, stearic), fixed oils (olein, palmitin, stearin), guaranine, inulin (starch), lipids, oligomeric proanthocyanidins, protein, saponins, tannic acid, theobromine, and theophylline.
Historical Uses: Arthritis, congestion (uterine, vaginal), depression (mild/moderate), diarrhea, edema, exhaustion, fatigue, fever (ephemeral), gastrointestinal problems, headache,

hypertension, leukorrhea, menstrual problems, migraine, muscle and joint pain, pain, poisoning (opium), premenstrual syndrome (PMS), rheumatism, vaginitis, and weight loss.

Discussion: May arouse sexual impulses; calm the nervous system; delay or reduce coagulation of the blood; enhance adrenal and kidney functions; increase endurance, energy, and gastric secretions; promote urine flow; restore normal tone to tissues; serve as an antidote to opium poisoning; stimulate the cardiovascular system.

Cautions/Contraindications: Avoid use if pregnant or breast-feeding, or if you have anxiety, depression (severe), hyperthyroidism, a kidney problem, a sensitive cardiovascular system, or a spasmodic condition, or if you have ulcer (gastric, peptic), or if you consume large amounts of caffeine containing products. May increase the side effects of ephedrine, pseudoephedrine, theophylline, and medications containing ephedra. Some persons may experience bleeding or increased clotting time when using this herb with anticoagulant drugs or aspirin. Not for long-term use.

Adverse Reactions: Agitation, arrhythmia, bleeding (possibly serious), blood sugar fluctuations, coagulation problems, diarrhea (possibly bloody), elevated blood pressure levels, gastrointestinal cramps (severe), habituation, hematuria (blood in the urine), insomnia, irritability, jitters/shakes, nausea, nervousness, stupor, and/or vomiting.

Herb/Drug Interactions: This herb could cause an interaction (possibly severe) when taken with the following drugs: Antibiotic drugs, Anticoagulant drugs, Autonomic drugs, Caffeine, H-2 Blocker drugs, Salicylates, Subsalicylates, Theophylline drugs, and other Medications/Products containing caffeine, ephedra, or pseudoephedrine.

Preparations/Dosage: Dried Paste (prepared from seeds): Average dose in substance 60 grains-7 grams. Seeds (powdered): Average dose in substance 10 grains (0.666 gm.). Tincture: 5-30 drops (0.333-2 cc.) one to three times per day.

Isolation: Caffeine: Soluble in alcohol and water. Average dose of 1-3 grains (0.06-0.2 gm.) for use as a diuretic, nervine, and stimulant, and in poisoning (opium). Guaranine: Average dose of 1-3 grains (0.066-0.199 gm.) for use as a diuretic, nervine, and stimulant, and in poisoning (opium). Guaranine's action is similar to that of caffeine. Theobromine calcium gluconate: Average dose of 0.32-0.65 gm. for use in hypertension. Theobromine salicylate: Soluble (sparingly) in water. Average dose of 15 grains (1 gm.) for use as a diuretic. Theobromine sodiosalicylate: Used in a 5% solution, average dose of 15 drops (1cc.) for use as a diuretic. Theobromine and sodium acetate: Average dose of 15-45 grains (1-3 gm.) for use as a powerful diuretic. Theophylline and sodium acetate: Average dose of 2-5 grains (0.12-0.3 gm.) for use as a diuretic.

<u>Note</u>: It may be of benefit to use vitamin supplementation to replace lost B vitamins and help calm the nerves when using guarana.

Did You Know? Guarana contains three times the caffeine content of coffee, which makes this herb the highest known source of caffeine, and its effects are similar to that of *heavy* coffee drinking.

Gumweed (gum·wēd)

(*Grindelia robusta*)

Synonyms/Related Species: August Flower, Curly-Cup Gumweed (*grindelia squarrosa*), Great Valley Gumweed, Grindelia (*grindelia camporum*), Gum Plant, Hardy Grindelia, Resinweed, Rosinweed, Scaly Grindelia, Subalpine Gumweed (*grindelia subalpina*), and Tarweed.

Family/Class: Compositae (composite).
Habitat: North America and the Subalpine zone
Flavor: Bitter/pungent.
Parts Used: Flowering tops, leaves.
Properties: Abortifacient, antibiotic, antiperiodic, antiphlogistic, antispasmodic, cardiac depressant, demulcent, diuretic, expectorant, hypotensive, malariacidal, sedative, stimulant, tonic, and vasodilator.
Constituents: Alkaloids, borneol, grindeline, grindelol, minerals (arsenic, cadmium, lead, selenium, tin, zinc), levulin, monosaccharides, resin, saponins, tannic acid, and volatile oil.
Historical Uses: Abscess, ague, allergy (pollen), asthma, blisters, bronchitis, burns (minor), chewing gum (young flowers), colds, colic, congestion (spleen), cough, cystitis, dermatitis, digestive complaints, dysmenorrhea, eczema, edema, emphysema, fever (ephemeral, hay, intermittent, rheumatic), gleet, gonorrhea, hypertension (mild/moderate), impetigo, indigestion, infection (bacterial, bladder, sexually transmitted, urinary tract), inflammation, influenza, insect bites or stings, kidney problems, lesions (tubercle), liver problems, malaria, measles, menorrhagia, mucus, nervous conditions, pain, parasites (malarial plasmodia), pneumonia, poison ivy/oak, psoriasis, rash, respiratory conditions, rheumatism, scrofula, sexually transmitted diseases (STDs), skin problems, small pox, snow blindness, sores, spasmodic conditions, syphilis, tachycardia, tuberculosis, ulcer (fistula, syphilitic, tuberculous), urethritis, urinary problems, uterine problem, vaginitis, whooping cough, and wounds (minor).
Discussion: May cause blood vessel dilatation; clear and open bronchial passages; diminish or reduce functional activity of the heart; enhance spleen function; induce abortion; inhibit or destroy development and growth of bacteria and other microorganisms; promote urine flow; relax the smooth muscles; reduce blood pressure levels; restore normal tone to tissues; soothe mucous membrane irritation; stimulate uterine contractions.
Cautions/Contraindications: Avoid use if pregnant or breast-feeding, or if you have cardiovascular conditions. This herb has a tendency to absorb selenium from the soil and using large amounts of the herb may result in poisoning. Not for long-term use.
Adverse Reactions: Bradycardia, diarrhea (possibly bloody), drowsiness, elevated blood pressure levels, gastrointestinal cramps (severe), hematuria (blood in the urine), nausea, and/or vomiting.
Herb/Drug Interactions: This herb could cause an interaction (possibly severe) when taken with the following drugs: Hypotensive drugs.
Preparations/Dosage: Crude Herb: 3-6 grams. Extract (powdered): Average dose in substance 5-15 grains (0.324-1 gm.). Flowering tops/Leaves (powdered): Average dose in substance 30-40 grains (2-2.666 gm.). Infusion: 1 cup per day. Tincture: 5-20 drops (0.333-1.25 cc.) one to three times per day.

Harmel (har mel)

(*Peganum harmala*)

Synonyms/Related Species: African Rue and Syrian Rue.
Family/Class: Zygophyllaceae (caltrop).
Habitat: Africa, Asia, the Mediterranean, Syria, Turkey, and the United States.
Flavor: Bitter.
Parts Used: Root, seed (oil).

Properties: Abortifacient, antibiotic, antifungal, antiperiodic, antiphlogistic, antispasmodic, aphrodisiac, emetic, hallucinogen, laxative, malariacidal, narcotic, parasiticide, and stimulant.
Constituents: Alkaloids, harmaline, harmine, harmol, and volatile oil.
Historical Uses: Ague, angina, asthma, bronchitis, colic, cough, croup, encephalitis lethargica, fever (ephemeral, intermittent, rheumatic), flatulence, gallstones, hysteria, infection (bacterial, fungal), inflammation, malaria, menstrual problems, muscle and joint pain, paralysis (cerebral), parasites (malarial plasmodia), parkinsonism, respiratory conditions, rheumatism, spasmodic conditions, and uterine problems.
Discussion: May arouse sexual impulses; induce abortion; inhibit development or destroy growth of bacteria and other microorganisms; promote bowel evacuation; stimulate uterine contractions.
Cautions/Contraindications: Avoid use if pregnant or breast-feeding. Harmel is a monoamine oxidase inhibitor (MAOI) herb. The combined use of harmel with sedative, tranquilizer, antihistamine, narcotic, migraine, anxiety, nitroglycerin, or tricyclic antidepressant drugs will cause hypertensive crisis. The combined use of harmel with amphetamines, cocaine, LSD, alcohol (including wine) avocados, unripe bananas, and dairy products (including aged cheese) will cause hypotensive crisis. It is recommended that no other drugs be used in combination with or within a ten-hour period of the use of harmel.
Adverse Reactions: Cardiac failure, confusion, debility, delirium, depression, diarrhea (severe), dizziness, exhaustion (extreme), fainting, gastrointestinal pain, hallucinations, hematuria (blood in the urine), hypertensive crisis (severe rise in blood pressure levels), hypotensive crisis (arrythmias, breathing difficulty, chills, severe drop in blood pressure levels), insomnia, liver damage (often characterized by jaundice), nausea, paralysis, respiratory failure, spasmodic conditions, tremors, vertigo, vomiting, and/or possible death.
Herb/Drug Interactions: This herb could cause an interaction (possibly severe) when taken with the following drugs: Amphetamine drugs, Antidepressant drugs, Antihistamine drugs, Anxiolytic drugs, Cardiac drugs, Migraine drugs, Monamine Oxidase Inhibitors (MAOIs), Opiate Agonists/Narcotic drugs, Sedative drugs, and Tranquilizer drugs.
Preparations/Dosage: Crude Herb: 1-2 grams. Root (powdered): Average dose in substance 10-15 grains (0.666-0.98 gm.). Decoction: ¼ cup per day. Extract (cold): ½ cup per day. Tincture: 5-10 drops (0.333-0.666 cc.) one to three times per day.
Isolation: Harmine: Average dose of ⅓-⅔ grain (0.02-0.04 gm.) administered intramuscularly or subcutaneously, for use in paralysis (cerebral) and parkinsonism.

Hawthorn (hô thôrn)
(*Crataegus oxyacantha*)

Synonyms/Related Species: Black Hawthorn (*crataegus douglasii*), Crataegus, English Hawthorn, Hagedorn (*crataegus laevigata*), Hedgethorn, Jerusalem Hawthorn (*crataegus aronia*), May Blossom, May Tree, Pixie Pears, Red Hawthorn (*crataegus columbiana*), River Hawthorn (*crataegus rivularis*), Shan Zha (*crataegus pinnatifida*), Thorn-Apple Tree, and Whitehorn.
Family/Class: Rosaceae (rose).
Floral Emblem: Missouri.
Habitat: Alaska, the Alpine and Subalpine zone, Africa, Asia, China, England, Europe, Germany, Jerusalem, and North America.

Flavor: Sweet/sour.
Parts Used: Berries, flowers.
Properties: Antibiotic, anticarcinogen, antiphlogistic, antispasmodic, astringent, cardiant, carminative, diuretic, emmenagogue, hemostatic, hypotensive, sedative, tonic, and vasodilator.
Constituents: Citric acid, crataegin, flavonoids, glycosides, minerals (aluminum, beryllium, iron, nickel, phosphorus, silicon, sodium, sulfur, tin, zinc), phenolic acids, proanthocyanidins, rutin, saponins, silicic acid, tartaric acid, tannic acid, and vitamins (B_1 (thiamine), B_2 (riboflavin), B_3 (niacin), B_5 (pantothenic acid), B_6 (pyridoxine), B_{12}, B_x (para-aminobenzoic acid (PABA), C (ascorbic acid), choline, H (biotin), inositol, M (folic acid).
Historical Uses: Alzheimer's disease, angina, anxiety, appetite loss, arrhythmia, arteriosclerosis, arthritis, attention deficit disorder (ADD), bleeding, bradycardia, cancer (larynx), cardiovascular conditions, cardiomyopathy, cellulite, chest pressure/tightness, constipation, coronary artery disease, diabetes, diabetic retinopathy, diarrhea, dysentery, edema, fever (ephemeral, rheumatic), fractures, gastritis, glaucoma, halitosis, hypertension (mild/moderate), hypertrophy (heart), hypoglycemia, indigestion, infection (bacterial), inflammation, insomnia, insufficiency (valvular, venous), irritable bowel syndrome (IBS), kidney problems, leukemia, lupus, memory/cognitive problems, muscle and joint pain, myocarditis, nervous conditions, neurosis, osteoporosis, restlessness, rheumatism, sore throat, spasmodic conditions, stroke (apoplectic), tachycardia, ulcer (stasis, varicose), and varicose veins.
Discussion: May aid digestion; cause blood vessel dilatation; decrease the effect of carcinogens; enhance cardiovascular system, liver, spleen, and stomach functions; improve memory and cognition; increase circulation, collagen production, and the pumping force of the heart; inhibit or destroy development and growth of bacteria and other microorganisms; normalize blood pressure levels; prevent congestive heart failure (CHF); prevent hemorrhage in persons with hypertension; promote urine flow; protect against heart disease; reduce arterial plaque formation and capillary fragility; speed recovery from heart attack; stimulate the cardiovascular system; strengthen the bones, cartilage, ligaments, and vascular system.
Cautions/Contraindications: Avoid use if pregnant or breast-feeding, or if you have congestive heart failure. May intensify the actions of other herbs. Not for long-term use.
Adverse Reactions: Arrhythmia, diarrhea (possibly bloody), dizziness, drop in blood pressure levels (dramatic), edema, fainting, gastrointestinal cramps (severe), hematuria (blood in the urine), nausea, and/or vomiting.
Herb/Drug Interactions: This herb could cause an interaction (possibly severe) when taken with the following drugs: Cardiac drugs and Hypotensive drugs.
Herb/Herb Interactions: Foxglove.
Preparations/Dosage: Crude Herb (berry): 3-9 grams. Decoction (berry): 1-1½ cups. Extract (berry): 10-15 drops (0.666-1 cc.). Infusion (flower): 1-1½ cups. Tincture: 15-30 drops (1-2 cc.).
Did You Know? Ancient cultures used the thorns of hawthorn like acupuncture needles. They combined this early form of acupuncture with moxibustion. The thorns were inserted into joints with arthritic pain and allowed to burn down onto those areas of discomfort.

Hellebore, Black (hel e·bôr, blak)

(*Helleborus niger*)

Synonyms/Related Species: Bearsfoot Hellebore (*helleborus foetidus*), Christe Herb, Christmas Rose, Eleinbora, Green Hellebore (*helleborus viridis*), Melampode, and Stinking Hellebore.

Family/Class: Ranunculaceae (buttercup).
Habitat: Asia, England, Europe, Germany, Greece, and North America.
Flavor: Bitter/sweet.
Parts Used: Root.
Properties: Abortifacient, alterative, cardiant, counterirritant, diaphoretic, emmenagogue, emetic, expectorant, febrifuge, laxative, mydriatic, narcotic, nervine, and stimulant.
Constituents: Alkaloids, glycosides, helleborein, helleborin, hellebrin, inulin (starch), protoanemonin, resin, and saponins.
Historical Uses: Amenorrhea, ascites, cardiovascular conditions, colds, depression (mild/moderate), edema, epilepsy, fever (ephemeral), hysteria, mania, mucus, nausea, nervous conditions, and skin problems.
Discussion: May calm the nervous system; cause pupil dilatation; clear and open bronchial passages; induce abortion; promote bowel evacuation and perspiration; reestablish healthy system functions; stimulate the cardiovascular system, menstruation, peristalsis, and uterine contractions.
Cautions/Contraindications: Avoid use if pregnant or breast-feeding. Do not confuse this plant with baneberry (*actaea spicata*). May cause dermatitis in susceptible individuals. Not for long-term use. Use with professional guidance/supervision.
Adverse Reactions: Arrhythmia, asphyxiation, cardiac failure, convulsions, diarrhea, dizziness, fainting, hematuria (blood in the urine), kidney failure, mucous membrane problems, nausea, pupil dilatation, salivation, scratchy throat, shortness of breath, stomach pain, stupor, vomiting, and/or possible death.
Herb/Drug Interactions: This herb could cause an interaction (possibly severe) when taken with the following drugs: Cardiac drugs.
Herb/Herb Interactions: Foxglove.
Preparations/Dosage: Crude Herb: 1-3 grams. Decoction: ⅛-¼ cup per day. Extract: (powdered): Average dose in substance ½-5 grains (0.033-0.33 gm.). Extract (solid): Average dose in substance 1-2 grains (0.066-0.133 gm.). Root (powdered): Average dose in substance 10-20 grains (0.666-1.333 gm.). Tincture: 5-15 drops (0.333-1 cc.) one to three times per day.
Isolation: Helleborein: Average dose of $^{1}/_{20}$-$^{1}/_{10}$ grain (0.0033-0.0066 gm.) for use as a cardiant, diuretic, mydriatic, and stimulant. Helleborein's action is similar to that of digitalis.

Hellebore, False (hel e·bôr, fôls)

(*Adonis vernalis*)

Synonyms/Related Species: Adonis, Asian Hellebore (*adonis amurensis*), Bird's Eye, Pheasant's Eye (*adonis autumnalis*), Red Chamomile (*adonis aestivalis*), Red Mathes, Rose-a-Rubie, and Sweet Vernal.
Family/Class: Ranunculaceae (buttercup).
Habitat: Africa, Asia, England, and Europe.
Flavor: Bitter.
Parts Used: Root.
Properties: Abortifacient, cardiant, caustic, diuretic, insecticide, narcotic, stimulant, tonic, and vesicant.
Constituents: Adonidin, adonin, adonitol (adonit), glycosides, and monosaccharide.

Historical Uses: Corns, insects (beetles, caterpillars, currant worm, cutworm, grasshoppers, grubs), urinary problems, and warts (digitate, filiform, fugitive, glabra, mother, plana juvenilis, plantar, seborrhoeic, vulgaris).
Discussion: May cause blisters or blistering; induce abortion; promote urine flow; restore normal tone to tissues; stimulate the cardiovascular system.
Cautions/Contraindications: Avoid use if pregnant or breast-feeding. May cause dermatitis in susceptible individuals. Not for long-term use. Use with professional guidance/supervision. Wear gloves when harvesting. Wear gloves and protective clothing when using as an insecticide.
Adverse Reactions: Arrhythmia, diarrhea, mouth, skin, and throat blistering; nausea, and/or vomiting.
Herb/Drug Interactions: This herb could cause an interaction (possibly severe) when taken with the following drugs: Cardiac drugs.
Herb/Herb Interactions: Do not use with Foxglove (*digitalis spp*.).
Preparations/Dosage: Crude Herb: 1-3 grams. Extract: 1-2 drops (0.06-0.1 cc.) one to two times per day. Corns and Warts: Dab extract or strong infusion directly onto affected area once daily. Cover with bandaid. Repeat as needed or until wart is gone. Insecticide: Mix equal amounts of powdered root with flour or hydrated lime and use as a dust, or mix one ounce powdered root to two gallons of water and use as a spray to destroy insects on fruits and vegetables. Make sure to wash fruit and vegetables well before eating.
Isolation: Adonidin: Average dose of ⅛-¼ grain (0.0075-0.015 gm.) for use as a cardiant, diuretic, and stimulant. Adonidin's action is similar to that of digitalis.

Hellebore, White (hel e·bôr, hwīt)
(*Veratrum viride*)

Synonyms/Related Species: American White Hellebore, California Hellebore (*veratrum californicum*), Cebadilla, Cevadilla, Corn Lily, German White Hellebore (*veratrum album*), Green Hellebore, Indian Hellebore, Mexican White Hellebore (*veratrum officinale*), Sabadilla (*veratrum sabadilla*), Swamp Hellebore, and Weisze Nieszwurzel.
Family/Class: Liliaceae (lily).
Habitat: Alaska, Europe, Germany, Guatamala, Italy, Lapland, North America, the Subalpine zone, and Venezuala.
Flavor: Bitter.
Parts Used: Root.
Properties: Abortifacient, analgesic, antiphlogistic, antispasmodic, cardiac depressant, counterirritant, diaphoretic, diuretic, emetic, emmenagogue, expectorant, hypotensive, laxative, narcotic, parasiticide, sedative, stimulant, stomachic, taenicide, tonic, and vasodilator.
Constituents: Alkaloids, cevadine (sabadine), cevine (sabadinine), fatty acids (arachidonic, linoleic, linolenic), inulin (starch), minerals (silicon), jervine, phosphates, resin, rubijervine, silicic acid, veratralbine, veratridine, veratrine, and veratroidine.
Historical Uses: Abscess, amenorrhea, arrhythmia, arteriosclerosis, ascites, bronchitis, bruises, cardiovascular conditions, cough, cramps, cystitis, dandruff, dehydration, epilepsy, fever (ephemeral, rheumatic), fractures, gout, headache, hepatitis, hypertension (mild/moderate), infection (bacterial), inflammation, insanity, insomnia, mania, menstrual problems, muscle and joint pain, nephritis, neuralgia, pain, parasites (lice and their nits, scabies, tapeworm), peritonitis,

pleurisy, pneumonia, pruritus, rash, respiratory conditions, rheumatism, sinusitis, skin problems, sore throat, spasmodic conditions, sprain, and tonsillitis.
Discussion: May cause blood vessel dilatation, motor depression, and vasomotor depression; clear and open bronchial passages; diminish or reduce functional activity of the heart; enhance stomach function; induce abortion; prolong the contractions of the heart; promote bowel evacuation, perspiration, and urine flow; protect against stroke (apoplectic); reduce blood pressure levels and pulse rate; restore normal tone to tissues; slow respiration; stimulate menstruation, the nerves, and peristalsis.
Cautions/Contraindications: Avoid use if pregnant or breast-feeding, or if you have a potassium deficiency. May cause dermatitis in susceptible individuals. Not for long-term use. Use with professional guidance/supervision.
Adverse Reactions: Arrhythmia, asphyxiation, bradycardia, burning sensation in the mouth and throat, cardiac failure, confusion, convulsions, depression, diarrhea, dizziness, exhaustion (extreme), frothing at the mouth, gastrointestinal cramps (severe), gynecomastia, hallucinations, heart failure, hypotension, lowered body temperature, mucous membrane problems, limited urine flow, monoplegia, muscle cramps, nausea, pallor, paralysis, psychosis, reduced blood pressure levels, salivation, shivering, shock, slowed pulse rate, sneezing, stomach pain, stupor, swallowing difficulty, tetanus, thirst, trismus (lockjaw), vertigo, visual disturbances, vomiting, and/or possible death.
Herb/Drug Interactions: This herb could cause an interaction (possibly severe) when taken with the following drugs: Calcium Carbonate, Cardiac drugs, Gluco-Corticoid drugs, Hypotensive drugs, and Laxative drugs.
Preparations/Dosage: Crude Herb: 1-3 grams. Extract: 1-3 drops (0.06-0.2 cc.) one to two times per day. Extract (powdered): Average dose in substance 1-2 grains (0.066-0.133 gm.). Root (powdered): Average dose in substance 1-2 grains (0.066-0.133 gm.). Tincture: 3-5 drops (0.2-0.333 cc.) one to three times per day.
Isolation: Veratrine: Average dose of $^{1}/_{30}$ grain (0.002 gm.) for use as a cardiac depressant, irritant, and stimulant.

Hemlock, Mountain (hem läk, moun ten)
(*Tsuga mertensiana*)

Synonyms/Related Species: Canada Pitch Tree, Hemlock Spruce (*tsuga canadensis*), Hymlik, Pacific Hemlock, Pinus Bark, Tanner's Bark, Weeping Spruce, West Coast Hemlock, and Western Hemlock (*tsuga heterophylla*).
Family/Class: Pinaceae (pine).
Habitat: Alaska, Asia, North America, and the Subalpine zone.
Flavor: Bitter.
Parts Used: Bark, branches, needles.
Properties: Abortifacient, antiphlogistic, astringent, counterirritant, diaphoretic, diuretic, emetic, hemostatic, laxative, parasiticide, and stimulant.
Constituents: Resin, tannic acid, and volatile oil.
Historical Uses: Abscess, appetite loss, arthritis, bleeding, bruises, burns (minor), colds, conjunctivitis, cough, diarrhea, dry skin, fever (ephemeral, rheumatic), gallbladder problems, gargle/mouth rinse, infection (bacterial), inflammation, influenza, kidney problems, lesions (tubercle), moles, muscle and joint pain, pain, parasites (lice and their nits), phlebitis, rheumatism, scrofula, sexually transmitted diseases (STDs), sore throat, sores, syphilis,

toothache, tuberculosis, ulcer (duodenal, fistula, gastric, peptic, syphilitic, tuberculous), urinary problems, warts (digitate, filiform, fugitive, glabra, mother, plana juvenilis, plantar, seborrhoeic, vulgaris), and wounds (minor).
Discussion: May induce abortion; promote bowel evacuation, perspiration, and urine flow; stimulate appetite and peristalsis.
Cautions/Contraindications: Avoid use if pregnant or breast-feeding. Not for long-term use.
Adverse Reactions: Gastrointestinal problems, nausea, and/or vomiting.
Herb/Drug Interactions: This herb could cause an interaction (possibly severe) when taken with the following drugs: None known.
Preparations/Dosage: Crude Herb: 3-6 grams. Decoction: ¼-½ cup per day. Infusion: 1 cup per day.

Hemlock, Poison (hem läk, poi zen)
(*Conium maculatum*)

Synonyms/Related Species: Beaver Poison, California Fern, Fool's Parsley, Herb Bennet, Musquash Root, Poison Parsley, and Spotted Cowbane.
Family/Class: Umbelliferae (parsley).
Habitat: Africa, Asia, England, Europe, North America, and South America.
Flavor: Bitter.
Parts Used: Leaves, seeds.
Properties: Analgesic, anti-inflammatory, antispasmodic, mydriatic, narcotic, and sedative.
Constituents: Alkaloids, atropine, conhydrine, coniine (propylpiperidine), fatty acids (oleic, palmitic, stearic), fixed oils (olein, palmitin, stearin), and mucilage.
Historical Uses: Asthma, bronchitis, cancer, cerebrospinal hyperemia, colic, constipation, cough, cramps, enuresis (urinary incontinence), epilepsy, excitability, inflammation, mania, nervous conditions, iritis, pain, poisoning (strychnine), spasmodic conditions, tetanus, trismus (lockjaw), tumors, ulcer (duodenal, gastric, peptic), and whooping cough.
Discussion: May increase the frequency of the heart's action; lessen the vascularity of the iris; produce pupil dilatation; reduce the frequency of nighttime urination; serve as an antidote to strychnine poisoning; stimulate the sympathetic and depress the cerebrospinal nerves; strengthen respiration.
Cautions/Contraindications: Avoid use if pregnant or breast-feeding. Do not confuse this plant with parsley (*petrosellinum sativum*), cow parsnip (*heracleum lanatum*), fennel (*foeniculum vulgare*), wild chervil (*anthriscus sylvestris*), or fool's parsley (*aethusa cynapium*). Prolonged use may lead to a tolerance to the accumulation of tropine-alkaloids in the parasympathetic system; thus more of the herb is required to achieve the same effects. Not for long-term use. Use with professional guidance/supervision.
Adverse Reactions: Arrhythmia, asphyxiation, atropinism (poisoning due to the misuse of atropine), bradycardia, clenching of the teeth, convulsions, difficulty swallowing, foaming at the mouth, loss of consciousness, impaired speech, nausea, nervousness, paralysis, stupor, twitching, visual disturbances, vomiting, and/or possible death.
Herb/Drug Interactions: This herb could cause an interaction (possibly severe) when taken with the following drugs: None known.
Preparations/Dosage: Crude Herb: 1-3 grams. Extract (leaves): 5-10 drops (0.333-0.666 cc.) one to two times per day. Extract (seed): 2-5 drops (0.133-0.333 cc.) one to two times per day. Extract (solid): Average dose in substance 2-6 grains (0.133-0.4 gm.). Juice (leaves): 1-2

drachms (4-8 cc.) in eight to ten ounces of water per day. Leaves (powdered): Average dose in substance 1-3 grains (0.066-0.2 gm.).
Isolation: Atropine: Soluble in alcohol and sparingly so in water. Average dose of $^{1}/_{150}$ grain (0.4 mg.) for use as a mydriatic and narcotic. Atropine sulfate: Soluble in water. Average dose of $^{1}/_{120}$ grain (0.5 mg.) for use as a mydriatic and narcotic.

Hemlock, Water (hem läk, wô ter)
(*Cicuta virosa*)

Synonyms/Related Species: American Cowbane (*cicuta maculata*), Bulbous Water Hemlock (*cicuta bulbifera*), Cowbane, Douglas' Water Hemlock (*cicuta douglasii*), Spotted Water Hemlock, and Western Water Hemlock.
Family/Class: Umbelliferae (parsley).
Habitat: Alaska, Europe, North America, the Subalpine zone, and the Yukon Territory.
Flavor: Pungent.
Parts Used: Root.
Properties: Analgesic, astringent, emetic, laxative, sialagogue, and tonic.
Constituents: Alkaloids, cicutine, and cicutoxin.
Historical Uses: Arthritis, diarrhea, muscle and joint pain, rheumatism, and sores.
Discussion: May promote bowel evacuation and saliva secretion.
Cautions/Contraindications: Avoid use if pregnant or breast-feeding. Do not confuse this plant with parsley (*petrosellinum sativum*), cow parsnip (*heracleum lanatum*), fennel (*foeniculum vulgare*), wild chervil (*anthriscus sylvestris*), or fool's parsley (*aethusa cynapium*). Not for long-term use. Use with professional guidance/supervision.
Adverse Reactions: Arrhythmia, asphyxiation, bradycardia, clenching of the teeth, convulsions (violent), diarrhea (severe), difficulty swallowing, foaming at the mouth, gastrointestinal cramps (severe), hematuria (blood in the urine), loss of consciousness, impaired speech, nausea, nervousness, paralysis, salivation (increased), stupor, tremors, twitching, visual disturbances, vomiting, and/or possible death.
Herb/Drug Interactions: This herb could cause an interaction (possibly severe) when taken with the following drugs: None known.
Preparations/Dosage: External Uses only.

Henbane (hen bān)
(*Hyoscyamus niger*)

Synonyms/Related Species: Common Henbane, Devil's Eye, Egyptian Henbane (*hyoscyamus muticus*), Fetid Nightshade, Insane Root, Jupiter's Bean, Jusquiame, Poison Tobacco, Russian Henbane (*hyoscyamus albus*), Sakran, Stinking Nightshade, Swine Bean, and Wild Hyoscyamus.
Family/Class: Solanaceae (nightshade).
Habitat: Africa, Asia, Australia, Egypt, England, Europe, Germany, India, Ireland, the Mediterranean, North America, Russia, Scotland, Siberia, and Wales.
Flavor: Bitter.
Parts Used: Flowering tops, leaves.
Properties: Analgesic, antiphlogistic, antispasmodic, diuretic, hypnotic, mydriatic, narcotic, parasiticide, and sedative.

Constituents: Albumin (albumen), alkaloids, atropine, esters, fatty acids (oleic, palmitic, stearic), fixed oils (olein, palmitin, stearin), flavonoids, hyoscyamine, minerals (calcium, potassium), mucilage, rutin, saponins, scopolamine (hyoscine), solanine, tannic acid, vitamins (choline), and volatile oil.

Historical Uses: Arrhythmia, asthma, bladder problems, cerebrospinal hyperemia, chilblains, cirrhosis, colic, colitis, constipation, convulsions, cough, delirium, delirium tremens (DTs), diphtheria, earache, edema, enuresis (urinary incontinence), ephidrosis (excessive perspiration), epilepsy, fever, gargle/mouth rinse, glaucoma, gleet, gonorrhea, gout, headache, hysteria, infection (sexually transmitted, urinary tract), inflammation, insomnia, iritis, liver problems, mania, muscle and joint pain, muscle tremors, nervous conditions, pain, parasites (lice and their nits), prostate problems, sciatica, sexually transmitted diseases (STDs), spasmodic conditions, tachycardia, toothache, ulcer (duodenal, gastric, peptic), urethritis, vaginitis, and whooping cough.

Discussion: May depress the cerebrospinal nerves; increase the frequency of the heart's action; induce sleep; lessen the vascularity of the iris; minimize the formation of scar tissue; prevent the deposition of fat in the liver and hemorrhage in persons with hypertension; produce pupil dilatation; promote urine flow; reduce capillary fragility and the frequency of nighttime urination; relax the smooth muscles; serve as an adjuvant to alcoholism treatment programs to assist in easing delirium tremens (DTs); stimulate the cardiovascular system and sympathetic nervous system; strengthen the respiratory system.

Cautions/Contraindications: Avoid use if pregnant or breast-feeding. Due to the high toxicity of this plant, external uses are recommended. Not for long-term use. Prolonged use may lead to a tolerance to the accumulation of tropine-alkaloids in the parasympathetic system; thus more of the herb is required to achieve the same effects. Use with professional guidance/supervision.

Adverse Reactions: Arrhythmia, asphyxiation, atropinism (atropine poisoning), convulsions, decreased perspiration, delirium, diarrhea (possibly bloody), dizziness, dryness (mouth), dysuria (painful/difficult urination), excitability, fainting, flushing, gastrointestinal cramps (severe), giddiness, hematuria (blood in the urine), pupil dilatation, hallucinations, mania, reduced peristalsis, respiratory collapse, restlessness, rheumatic conditions, stupor, visual disturbances, and/or possible death.

Herb/Drug Interactions: This herb could cause an interaction (possibly severe) when taken with the following drugs: Anesthetic drugs, Antibiotic drugs, Antidepressant drugs, Antihistamine drugs, and Cardiac drugs.

Preparations/Dosage: Crude Herb: 1-3 grams. Extract: 1-3 drops (0.06-0.2 cc.) one to two times per day. Extract (solid): Average dose in substance 2-8 grains (0.133-0.5 gm.). Leaves (powdered): Average dose in substance 2-10 grains (0.133-0.666 gm.). Tincture: 2-5 drops (0.133-0.333 cc.) one to three times per day.

Isolation: Atropine: Soluble in alcohol and sparingly so in water. Average dose of $^{1}/_{150}$ grain (0.4 mg.) for use as a mydriatic and narcotic. Atropine sulfate: Soluble in water. Average dose of $^{1}/_{120}$ grain (0.5 mg.) for use as mydriatic and narcotic. Scopolamine hydrobromide: Average dose of $^{1}/_{120}$ grain (0.5 mg.) administered subcutaneously, for use as a mydriatic and sedative, or used locally in a 0.1-0.3% solution.

Henna (hen e)
(*Lawsonia inermis*)

Synonyms/Related Species: Alcanna, Al-Khanna, Egyptian Privet, Hinnā', Jamaica Mignonette, Mehndi, Mignonette Tree, Smooth Lawsonia, and Reseda.
Family/Class: Lythraceae (loosestrife).
Habitat: Africa, Arabia, Asia, Egypt, India, Iran, Persia, and Syria.
Flavor: Bitter/pungent.
Parts Used: Leaves.
Properties: Astringent and emmenogogue.
Constituents: Hennotannic acid.
Historical Uses: Amenorrhea, gargle/mouth rinse, hair dye, headache, jaundice, liver problems, skin dye, skin problems, and small pox.
Discussion: May stimulate menstruation and uterine contractions.
Cautions/Contraindications: Avoid internal use if pregnant or breast-feeding.
Adverse Reactions: Gastrointestinal problems, nausea, and/or vomiting.
Herb/Drug Interactions: This herb could cause an interaction (possibly severe) when taken with the following drugs: None known.
Preparation/Dosage: Crude Herb (dried/powdered): 3-6 grams. Decoction: ¼-½ cup per day.

Herbal Ash

Synonyms/Related Species: Vegetable Ash.
Description: Herbal ash is made from the organic materials of nonpoisonous herbs and plants, wood (shavings), or vegetables. Once ingested, the ash binds with certain chemicals in the digestive tract, and prevents them from being absorbed into your system.
Parts Used: Ash.
Properties: Absorbent.
Historical Uses: Diarrhea, digestive complaints, flatulence, gastritis, gastrointestinal problems, halitosis, indigestion, irritable bowel syndrome (IBS), poisoning (non-caustic), ulcer (gastric).
Discussion: May lower cholesterol levels; protect against heart disease; relieve flatulence and indigestion; rid the body of toxins; serve as an antidote to non-caustic poisons.
Cautions/Contraindications: Avoid use if pregnant or breast-feeding, or if you have an obstruction (intestinal). Do not use herbal ash at the same time as syrup of ipecac (ash can be used after ipecac has done its job). May interfere with the absorption of various nutrients and medications (take it at least two hours before or after other products). Taking ash with milk or other dairy products may reduce its effectiveness. Do not ingest more than 4,000 mg. in any 24-hour period. Not for long-term use.
Adverse Reactions: Black stools, constipation, diarrhea, gastrointestinal problems, nausea, and/or vomiting.
Herb/Drug Interactions: This herb could cause an interaction (possibly severe) when taken with the following drugs: None known.
Preparation/Dosage: Ash (powdered): Mix 1 to 2 tablespoons of the ash powder in a tall glass of water and drink it through a straw to lessen teeth staining (immediately brush your teeth and rinse if your teeth or tongue do become stained). Diarrhea: Mix 2-3 tablespoons of powder in a tall glass of cool water and drink (through a straw) after every loose stool; or put 520 mg. in a capsule and take every 30-60 minutes or as needed until symptoms abate.

Bloating/Flatulence/Gas: Mix 2 tablespoons of powder into a large glass of water ½ hour before a meal. Sip through a straw; or put 500 mg in a capsule and take after meals or every one to two hours as needed until symptoms abate. See "Forms of Herbal Preparation" section.

Honeysuckle (hun ē·suk el)
(*Lonicera periclymenum*)

Synonyms/Related Species: Asian Honeysuckle (*lonicera xylosteum*), Black Twinberry, Bracted Honeysuckle (*lonicera involucrata*), Bush Honeysuckle (*lonicera diervilla*), Capri-Foglio, Dutch Honeysuckle, English Wild Honeysuckle, European Fly Honeysuckle (*lonicera xylosteum*), Garden Honeysuckle, Geisblatt, Goat's Leaf, Italian Honeysuckle (*lonicera caprifolium*), Japanese Honeysuckle (*lonicera japonica*), Orange Honeysuckle (*lonicera ciliosa*), Ornamental Flower, Red Twinberry, Siberian Honeysuckle (*lonicera tartarica*), Twinberry Honeysuckle, Twining Honeysuckle (*lonicera dioica*), Utah Honeysuckle (*lonicera utahensis*), Western Trumpet Honeysuckle (*lonicera ciliosa*), and Woodbine (*lonicera periclymenum*).
Family/Class: Caprifoliaceae (honeysuckle).
Habitat: Asia, China, Europe, France, Germany, Italy, Japan, the Mediterranean, North America, and Siberia.
Flavor: Bitter.
Parts Used: Flowers.
Properties: Alterative, antibiotic, anticarcinogen, antiphlogistic, antiviral, diaphoretic, diuretic, emetic, expectorant, and laxative.
Constituents: Mucilage, salicylic acid, saponins, and tannic acid.
Historical Uses: Abscess, alopecia, arthritis, asthma, bruises, burns (minor), cancer (breast), canker sores, colds, conjunctivitis, Crohn's disease, dandruff, diarrhea, digestive complaints, dysuria (painful/difficult urination), epilepsy, eye problems, fever (ephemeral, rheumatic), fractures, gastrointestinal problems, gleet, gonorrhea, headache, hypercholesteremia, infection (bacterial, sexually transmitted, urinary tract, viral), inflammation, influenza, insomnia, keratitis (cornea inflammation), lesions (tubercle), lung problems, mastitis, muscle and joint pain, perfume, poison ivy/oak, rash, respiratory conditions, rheumatism, scrofula, sexually transmitted diseases (STDs), skin problems, sore throat, sores, tuberculosis, tumors, ulcer (fistula, tuberculous), urethritis, uterine problems, and wounds (minor).
Discussion: May clear and open bronchial passages; decrease the effect of carcinogens; enhance liver function; inhibit development or destroy growth of bacteria and other microorganisms; promote bowel evacuation, perspiration, and urine flow; reduce cholesterol levels; reestablish healthy system functions; stimulate peristalsis.
Cautions/Contraindications: Avoid use if pregnant or breast-feeding. Berries are toxic. Not for long-term use. Use with professional guidance/supervision.
Adverse Reactions: Diarrhea (possibly bloody), gastrointestinal cramps (severe), hematuria (blood in the urine), kidney problems, nausea, urinary tract infection, and/or vomiting.
Herb/Drug Interactions: This herb could cause an interaction (possibly severe) when taken with the following drugs: None known.
Preparations/Dosage: Crude Herb: 3-12 grams. Infusion: ½-1 cup per day.

Hop (hop)
(*Humulus lupulus*)

Synonyms/Related Species: American Hop (*humulus americanus*), Hop Vine, Lupulus, and Zarsa.
Family/Class: Urticacea (nettle).
Habitat: Asia, Australia, the Canary Islands, China, England, Europe, France, Germany, the Netherlands, Russia, Scotland, Sweden, and the United States.
Flavor: Bitter.
Parts Used: Strobiles/leafy cone-like catkins (ripe/dried).
Properties: Analgesic, antibiotic, antiphlogistic, aromatic, astringent, depurative, diuretic, hemostatic, hypnotic, hypotensive, lithotriptic, nervine, sedative, stimulant, stomachic, tonic, and vasodilator.
Constituents: Asparagin, caffeic acid, chlorogenic acid, ferulic acid, flavonoids, fluorine, humulin, humulon, minerals (chlorine, copper, iodine, iron, lead, magnesium, manganese, sodium, zinc), lupulin, lupulon, phloroglucin (phloroglucinol), phytoestrogen, proanthocyanidines, resin, tannic acid, vitamins (B_1 (thiamine), B_2 (riboflavin), B_3 (niacin), B_5 (pantothenic acid), B_6 (pyridoxine), B_{12}, B_x (para-aminobenzoic acid (PABA), choline, H (biotin), inositol, M (folic acid), and volatile oil.
Historical Uses: Abcesses, abdominal pain, abscess, anxiety, appetite loss, arthritis, belching, bleeding, bronchitis, bruises, calculus, cirrhosis, colds, colitis, cramps, delirium, diarrhea, digestive complaints, diphtheria, dizziness, dysentery, earache, eczema, edema, fever (ephemeral, rheumatic), flatulence, flavoring agent, gallstones, gastrointestinal problems, gleet, gonorrhea, headache, hyperactivity, hyperexcitability, hypertension (mild/moderate), hysteria, indigestion, infection (bacterial, sexually transmitted), inflammation, influenza, insomnia, irritability, jaundice, kidney stones, lesions (tubercle), mastitis, menopausal/menstrual problems, mood swings, nausea, nervous conditions, neuralgia, overactive libido, pain, pleurisy, pneumonia, pruritus, restlessness, rheumatism, sexually transmitted diseases (STDs), skin problems, sores, sore throat, spasmodic conditions, toothache, tuberculosis, tumors, ulcer (duodenal, gastric, peptic), urethritis, uterine problems, and whooping cough.
Discussion: May balance the hormonal system; calm the nervous system; cause blood vessel dilatation; dissolve calculi; enhance liver, spleen, and stomach functions; induce sleep; inhibit development or destroy growth of bacteria and other microorganisms; prevent the deposition of fat in the liver; promote urine flow; prevent the deposition of fat in the liver; purify the blood; reduce blood pressure levels and hypersexual problems; restore normal tone to tissues; soften skin; stimulate appetite, gastric secretions, and peristalsis.
Cautions/Contraindications: Avoid use if pregnant or breast-feeding, or if you have an estrogen dependant cancer, or if you have a history of estrogen dependant cancers, or if you have erectile dysfunction, gynecomastia, or depression. Due to the high estrogen potency of hops, do not administer to children of either sex who have not reached puberty. Estrogen containing substances may contribute to abnormal blood clotting, migraine, and could promote the developement of certain types of estrogen dependant cancers. Excessive handling of the fresh plant may cause cessation of menstruation in women. Individuals undergoing elective surgery should avoid the use of hops for two to three weeks prior to the surgery. May cause allergic reactions and dermatitis in susceptible individuals.
Adverse Reactions: Nausea and/or vomiting.

Herb/Drug Interactions: This herb could cause an interaction (possibly severe) when taken with the following drugs: Anxiolytic drugs, Hormones and Synthetic Substitutes (i.e. conjugated estrogens, contraceptives (oral, etc.), and other hormonal replacement therapy (HRT).
Preparations/Dosage: Crude Herb: 3-6 grams. Infusion: ½-1 cup per day. Tincture: 5-20 drops (0.333-1.25 cc.) one to three times per day.
Isolation: Asparagin: Soluble in hot water, but insoluble in alcohol and ether. Average dose of 1-2 grains (0.066-0.133 gm.) for use as a diuretic. Lupulin: Average dose of 5-10 grains (0.333-0.666 gm.) for use as a sedative and stomachic.

Horehound (hôr hound)
(*Marrubium vulgare*)

Synonyms/Related Species: Houndsbane, Marrubio, and White Horehound.
Family/Class: Labiatae (mint).
Habitat: Africa, Asia, Australia, Europe, the Mediterranean, and the United States.
Flavor: Bitter/pungent.
Parts Used: Aerial.
Properties: Antibiotic, antiperiodic, antiphlogistic, antispasmodic, aromatic, carminative, diaphoretic, diuretic, expectorant, laxative, malariacidal, stimulant, and tonic.
Constituents: Caffeic acid, camphene, chlorogenic acid, cymene, diterpenes, fatty acids (arachidonic, linoleic, linolenic), flavones, flavonoids, marrubin, minerals (iron, potassium, sulfur), resin, tannic acid, and vitamins (A, B_1 (thiamine), B_2 (riboflavin), B_3 (niacin), B_5 (pantothenic acid), B_6 (pyridoxine), B_{12}, B_x (para-aminobenzoic acid (PABA), C (ascorbic acid), E (alpha-tocopheral), H (biotin), M (folic acid), volatile oil.
Historical Uses: Ague, amenorrhea, appetite loss, arrhythmia, asthma, beverage, bronchitis, colds, cough, croup, diarrhea, digestive complaints, dysmenorrhea, eczema, earache, fever (ephemeral, enteric, herpetic, intermittent), flatulence, gallbladder problems, gastritis, gastrointestinal problems, hepatitis, herpes, hysteria, indigestion, infection (bacterial), inflammation, irritable bowel syndrome (IBS), jaundice, laryngitis, lesions (tubercle), liver problems, lung problems, malaria, menstrual problems, mucus, parasites (malarial plasmodia), pruritus, respiratory conditions, scrofula, sexually transmitted diseases (STDs), shingles, sinusitis, skin problems, sore throat, spasmodic conditions, tuberculosis, typhoid, ulcer (bouveret, duodenal, fistula, tuberculous), whooping cough, and wounds (minor).
Discussion: May aid digestion; balance blood pressure levels; clear and open bronchial passages; enhance liver, lung, nervous system, and spleen functions; inhibit or destroy development and growth of bacteria and other microorganisms; promote bowel evacuation, perspiration, and urine flow; restore normal tone to tissues; speed healing; stimulate appetite, gastric secretions, and peristalsis.
Cautions/Contraindications: Avoid use if pregnant or breast-feeding, or if you have a cardiovascular condition or ulcer (gastric, peptic). May cause dermatitis in susceptible individuals.
Adverse Reactions: Arterial tension, diarrhea, increased menstrual flow, nausea, and/or vomiting.
Herb/Drug Interactions: This herb could cause an interaction (possibly severe) when taken with the following drugs: None known.
Preparations/Dosage: Crude Herb: 3-9 grams. Extract: 3-5 drops (0.2-0.333 cc.) one to two times per day. Extract (solid): Average dose in substance 5-15 grains (0.333-1 gm.). Infusion:

1-2 cups per day. Juice: 1 teaspoon in water one to two times per day. Syrup: ½-1 teaspoon in water one to three times per day. Tincture: 5-30 drops (0.333-2 cc.) one to three times per day.

Horsemint (hôrs mint)
(*Monarda punctata*)

Synonyms/Related Species: American Horsemint, Bee Balm (*monarda didyama*), Blue Balm, High Balm, Mintleaf Bee Balm, Mountain Balm, Mountain Mint (*monarda sylvestris*), Oregana de la Sierra, Oswego Tea, Scarlet Monarda, Spotted Monarda, Wild Bergamot (*monarda fistulosa*), Wild Oregano (*monarda pectinata*), and Woodland Mint.
Family/Class: Labiatae (mint).
Habitat: Europe and North America.
Flavor: Pungent/bitter.
Parts Used: Flowers, leaves.
Properties: Alterative, analgesic, antibiotic, antifungal, antiphlogistic, antiscorbutic, antispasmodic, aromatic, cardiant, carminative, counterirritant, diaphoretic, diuretic, emmenagogue, expectorant, hemostatic, insect repellent, parasiticide, sedative, stimulant, stomachic, and tonic.
Constituents: Carvacrol, carvene (limonene), carvol, cymene, flavonoids, hydrocarbon, hydroquinone, linalool, menthol, monardin, resin, tannic acid, thymol, vitamins (C (ascorbic acid), and volatile oil.
Historical Uses: Abdominal pain, acne, alkaline urine, amenorrhea, angina, arthritis, beverage, bleeding, bronchitis, candida, chills, colds, colic, conjunctivitis, convulsions, cough, diarrhea, digestive complaints, dysuria (painful/difficult urination), edema, fever (ephemeral, rheumatic), flatulence, flies, gargle/mouth rinse, gastritis, gastrointestinal problems, headache, insect bites or stings, indigestion, infection (bacterial, fungal), inflammation, influenza, jaundice, kidney problems, lung problems, menopausal/menstrual problems, moniliasis, mucus, muscle and joint pain, nausea, nervous conditions, neuralgia, pain, parasites (scabies), perfume, pneumonia, poisoning (narcotic), potpourri, pruritus, respiratory conditions, rheumatism, scurvy, skin problems, sore throat, spasmodic conditions, styes, tinnitus, toothache, urinary problems, vomiting, and wounds (minor).
Discussion: May aid digestion; clear and open bronchial passages; enhance liver, respiratory system, and stomach functions; inhibit development or destroy growth of bacteria and other microorganisms; promote perspiration and urine flow; reestablish healthy system functions; restore normal tone to tissues; stimulate appetite, the cardiovascular system, and menstruation.
Cautions/Contraindications: Avoid use if pregnant or breast-feeding. Do not confuse this plant with bergamot orange (*citrus bergamia*). May cause dermatitis in susceptible individuals.
Adverse Reactions: Nausea, skin problems, and/or vomiting.
Herb/Drug Interactions: This herb could cause an interaction (possibly severe) when taken with the following drugs: None known.
Preparations/Dosage: Crude Herb: ½-6 grams. Infusion: 1-2 cups per day. Oil of Horsemint: Heat leaves in olive oil. Let cool and strain. Take 2-8 drops (0.133-0.5 cc.) in water per day. Tincture: 10-30 drops (0.666-2 cc.) one to three times per day.
Isolation: Menthol: Average dose of ½-2 grains (0.033-0.133 gm.) applied topically, for use as an analgesic.

Horseradish (hôrs ·rad ish)
(*Cochlearia armoracia*)

Synonyms/Related Species: Armoracia, Great Raifort, Hungarian Horseradish (*cochlearia macrocarpa*), Mountain Radish, and Red Cole.
Family/Class: Brassicaceae (mustard).
Habitat: Asia, Britain, Denmark, Europe, Finland, Germany, Greece, Hungary, the Mediterranean, North America, Poland, Russia, and Sicily.
Flavor: Pungent.
Parts Used: Root (fresh/dried).
Properties: Antibiotic, anticarcinogen, antifungal, antiphlogistic, antiscorbutic, antispasmodic, carcinostatic, carminative, counterirritant, diuretic, emetic, expectorant, laxative, sialogogue, and stimulant.
Constituents: Albumin (albumen), asparagin, flavones, glycosides, gum, inulin (starch), isothiocyanate, minerals (calcium, iron, phosphorus, potassium, sodium, sulfur), monosaccharides, myrosin, resin, sinalbin, sinigrin, vitamins (A, B_1 (thiamine), B_2 (riboflavin), B_3 (niacin), B_5 (pantothenic acid), B_6 (pyridoxine), B_{12}, B_x (para-aminobenzoic acid (PABA), C (ascorbic acid), H (biotin), inositol, M (folic acid), and volatile oil.
Historical Uses: Appetite loss, arthritis, asthma, bronchitis, bruises, chilblains, circulation, colds, congestion (cerebral, lung), cough, cystitis, edema, fever (ephemeral, rheumatic), freckles, gallbladder problems, gout, infection (bacterial, bladder, fungal, urinary tract), inflammation, influenza, jaundice, kidney problems, laryngitis, liver problems, lung problems, mucus, muscle and joint pain, neuralgia, palsy, respiratory conditions, rheumatism, sciatica, scurvy, sinusitis, spasmodic conditions, tumors, whooping cough, and wounds (minor).
Discussion: May aid digestion; clear and open bronchial passages; decrease the effect of carcinogens; enhance nervous system function; increase circulation; inhibit or destroy development and growth of bacteria and other microorganisms; promote bowel evacuation, saliva secretion, and urine flow; stimulate peristalsis.
Cautions/Contraindications: Avoid use if pregnant or breast-feeding, or if you have hypothyroidism, ulcer (duodenal, gastric, peptic), or kidney disease. Do not administer to children under 12 years old. May interfere with iodide metabolism. May cause dermatitis in susceptible individuals.
Adverse Reactions: Diarrhea (possibly bloody), digestive complaints, edema, gastritis, gastrointestinal problems, goiter, indigestion, irritable bowel syndrome (IBS), nausea, salivation (increased), suppression (thyroid), and/or vomiting.
Herb/Drug Interactions: This herb could cause an interaction (possibly severe) when taken with the following drugs: Thyroid drugs.
Preparations/Dosage: Crude Herb: 3-6 grams. Extract: 3-8 drops (0.2-0.5 cc.) one to two times per day. Root: ⅛-¼ teaspoon per day. Juice: ½-1 tablespoon in glycerin or water one to two times per day. Root (powdered): Average dose in substance 10-20 grains (0.666-1.333 gm.). Tincture: 10-15 drops (0.666-1 cc.) one to three times per day.
Isolation: Asparagin: Soluble in hot water, but insoluble in alcohol and ether. Average dose of 1-2 grains (0.066-0.133 gm.) for use as a diuretic.

Horsetail (hôrs ·tāl)
(*Equisetum arvense*)

Synonyms/Related Species: Bottlebrush, Common Horsetail, Common Scouring Rush (*equisetum hyemale*), Corn Horsetail, Dutch Rushes, Dwarf Scouring Rush (*equisetum scirpoides*), Field Horsetail, Giant Pacific Horsetail (*equisetum telmateia*), Great Horsetail (*equisetum maximum*), Horse Willow, Jointed Rush, Marsh Horsetail (*equisetum palustre*), Meadow Horsetail (*equisetum pratense*), Northern Scouring Rush (*equisetum variegatum*), Paddock Pipes, Pewterwort, Queue de Cheval, River Horsetail, Scouring Rush, Shave Grass, Smooth Scouring Rush (*equisetum laevigatum*), Swamp Horsetail (*equisetum fluviatile*), Toadpipe, and Woodland Horsetail (*equisetum sylvaticum*).
Family/Class: Equisetaceae (horsetail).
Habitat: Alaska, the Alpine and Subalpine zones, Asia, Greenland, Japan, Europe, the Himalayas, Iran, North America, Turkey, and the Yukon Territory.
Flavor: Bitter.
Parts Used: Shoots.
Properties: Alterative, antiphlogistic, astringent, depurative, diaphoretic, diuretic, emmenagogue, hemostatic, laxative, lithotriptic, and tonic.
Constituents: Aconitic acid, alkaloids, caffeic acid, chlorogenic acid, inulin (starch), luteolin, minerals (calcium, cobalt, copper, iodine, iron, magnesium, manganese, potassium, selenium, silicon, sodium, sulfur), monosaccharides, nicotine, quercetin, resin, saponins, silicic acid, tannic acid, tartaric acid, vitamins (B_1 (thiamine), B_2 (riboflavin), B_3 (niacin), B_5 (pantothenic acid), B_6 (pyridoxine), B_{12}, B_x (para-aminobenzoic acid (PABA), H (biotin), E (alpha-tocopheral), M (folic acid), and volatile oil.
Historical Uses: Alopecia, anemia, arteriosclerosis, arthritis, bleeding, burns (minor), bursitis, calculus, canker sores, cellulite, chilblains, conjunctivitis, convulsions, cramps, cystitis, diarrhea, diuria (frequent daytime urination), dysentery, edema, emphysema, enterorrhagia, enuresis (urinary incontinence), eyewash, fever (ephemeral, rheumatic), flatulence, fractures, frostbite, gallstones, gargle/mouth rinse, glandular problems, gout, hemorrhage (metrorrhagia), hemorrhoids, hypertrophy (benign prostatic), indigestion, infection (bladder, urinary tract), inflammation, injury (tooth), insufficiency (circulatory), jaundice, kidney problems, kidney stones, lesions (tubercle), liver problems, lung problems, menorrhagia, mucus, muscle and joint pain, nervous conditions, nosebleed, osteoporosis, pruritus, rash, rheumatism, rheumatoid arthritis (RA), scrofula, skin problems, sores, tuberculosis, tumors, urinary problems, ulcer (duodenal, fistula, gastric, peptic, tuberculous), and wounds (minor).
Discussion: May cleanse the whole system; dissolve calculi; encourage calcium absorption; enhance urinary system function; increase circulation and acidity (urine); promote bowel evacuation, perspiration, and urine flow; reduce the persistent urge to urinate and the frequency of nighttime urination; reestablish healthy system functions; restore normal tone to tissues; speed healing; stimulate menstruation, metabolism, and peristalsis; strengthen the bones, connective tissues, hair, nails, skin, and the urinary system.
Cautions/Contraindications: Avoid use if pregnant or breast-feeding, or if you have cardiovascular conditions, a history of kidney stones, hypertension, cancer (prostate), edema, or an iodine sensitivity, or if you eat a cholesterol rich diet. Increase fluid intake when using horsetail. May interfere with the effectiveness of certain thyroid medications. Vitamin B_1 supplementation is highly recommended while using this herb as horsetail may have a

destructive effect on thiamine. May negate the bacteriostatic effects of sulfonamide drugs. May cause dermatitis in susceptible individuals. Not for long-term use.
Adverse Reactions: Arrhythmia, cardiac damage, cold extremities, debility, diarrhea (possibly bloody), edema, fever, gastrointestinal cramps (severe), hypertrophy (thyroid), iodism (iodine poisoning), hematuria (blood in the urine), nausea, priapism, thirst, weight loss, and/or vomiting.
Herb/Drug Interactions: This herb could cause an interaction (possibly severe) when taken with the following drugs: Antibiotic drugs, Diuretic drugs, and Thyroid drugs.
Preparations/Dosage: Crude Herb: 3-6 grams. Extract: 5-8 drops (0.333-0.5 cc.) one to two times per day. Infusion: 1-2 cups per day. Tincture: 5-30 drops (0.3-2 cc.) one to three times per day.

Hound's Tongue (houndz tung)
(*Cynoglossum officinale*)

Synonyms/Related Species: Common Hound's Tongue, Dog's Tongue, Dog-Bur, European Hound's Tongue, Gypsy Flower, Pacific Hound's Tongue (*cynoglossum grande*), Virginia Mouse Ear (*cynoglossum morrisoni*), and Woolmat.
Family/Class: Boraginaceae (borage).
Habitat: Europe, Germany, North America, and Switzerland.
Flavor: Bitter.
Parts Used: Leaves, root.
Properties: Analgesic, anti-inflammatory, astringent, demulcent, expectorant, hemostatic, hepatotoxic, and vulnerary.
Constituents: Allantoin, alkaloids, tannic acid, and volatile oil.
Historical Uses: Bleeding, bronchitis, burns (minor), colds, cough, diarrhea, dysentery, gastrointestinal problems, gleet, gonorrhea, hemorrhoids, infection (sexually transmitted), inflammation, insect bites or stings, lung problems, mucus, pain, rash, respiratory conditions, scalds, sexually transmitted diseases (STDs), sore throat, substitute for comfrey, ulcer (duodenal, gastric, peptic), urethritis, and wounds (minor).
Discussion: May cause nervous system depression; clear and open bronchial passages; enhance digestive system function; soothe mucous membrane irritation; speed healing.
Cautions/Contraindications: Avoid use if pregnant or breast-feeding. May cause dermatitis in susceptible individuals. Not recommended for long-term use.
Adverse Reactions: Liver damage (often characterized by jaundice), nausea, and/or vomiting.
Herb/Drug Interactions: This herb could cause an interaction (possibly severe) when taken with the following drugs: None known.
Preparations/Dosage: External uses are recommended. Crude Herb: 3-6 grams. Infusion: 1 cup per day.

Houseleek (hous lēk)
(*Sempervivum tectorum*)

Synonyms/Related Species: Aaron's Rod, Ayegreen, Bullock's Eye, Donnersbart, Jupiter's Beard, Sengreen, Thor's Beard, and Thunder Plant.
Family/Class: Crassulaceae (orpine).
Habitat: Africa, Asia, Europe, France, Germany, and Greece.

Flavor: Bitter.
Parts Used: Leaves.
Properties: Antiphlogistic, astringent, caustic, diuretic, emetic, hemostatic, laxative, and parasiticide.
Constituents: Bitter substances, lime (calcium oxide), malic acid, minerals (calcium), monosaccharides, mucilage, succinic acid, and tannic acid.
Historical Uses: Bleeding, bruises, burns (minor), canker sores, corns, diarrhea, dysentery, earache, erysipelas, eye soreness, fever, gargle/mouth rinse, headache, inflammation, insect bites or stings, insomnia, neuralgia, nosebleed, parasites (ringworm), pruritus, shingles, skin problems, stomatitis, ulcer (duodenal, gastric, peptic, tuberculous), and warts (digitate, filiform, fugitive, glabra, mother, plana juvenilis, plantar, seborrhoeic, vulgaris).
Discussion: May induce sleep; promote bowel evacuation and urine flow; serve as an antidote to neutralize the sting from nettles; stimulate peristalsis.
Cautions/Contraindications: Avoid use if pregnant or breast-feeding. Not for long-term use.
Adverse Reactions: Nausea and/or vomiting.
Herb/Drug Interactions: This herb could cause an interaction (possibly severe) when taken with the following drugs: None known.
Preparations/Dosage: Crude Herb: 3-6 grams. Infusion: 1 cup per day. Corns/Warts: Apply 2-10 drops (0.133-0.666 cc.) of the juice directly on corn or wart one to two times per day. Repeat as needed until wart or corn is gone. Leaves: Place fresh leaf directly on corn or wart. Cover with bandaid to keep in place. Replace leaf daily until corn or wart is gone. Tincture: 5-20 drops (0.333-1.25 cc.) one to three times per day.

Hydrangea (hī·drān jē·ē)
(*Hydrangea aborescens*)

Synonyms/Related Species: Common Hydrangea, Garden Hydrangea (*hydrangea hortensis*), Oak-Leaved Hydrangea (*hydrangea quercifolia*), Seven Barks, and Wild Hydrangea.
Family/Class: Saxifragaceae (saxifrage).
Habitat: Asia, China, Japan, and the United States.
Flavor: Bitter.
Parts Used: Root.
Properties: Antiphlogistic, astringent, carminative, diuretic, hemostatic, laxative, lithotriptic, sedative, sialagogue, stimulant, and tonic.
Constituents: Albumin (albumen), fatty acids (oleic, palmitic, stearic), fixed oils (olein, palmitin, stearin), flavonoids, glycosides, gum, hydrangin, inulin (starch), minerals (calcium, iron, lime (calcium oxide), phosphorus, potassium, magnesium, sodium, sulfur), monosaccharides, resin, rutin, saponins, and volatile oil.
Historical Uses: Arteriosclerosis, arthritis, bladder problems, bleeding, calculus, cystitis, edema, fever (ephemeral, rheumatic), gallstones, gleet, gonorrhea, gout, hypertrophy (benign prostatic), indigestion, infection (sexually transmitted, urinary tract), inflammation, kidney stones, muscle and joint pain, rheumatism, sexually transmitted diseases (STDs), substitute for cortisone, urethritis, and vaginitis.
Discussion: May aid digestion; dissolve calculi; prevent hemorrhage in persons with hypertension; promote bowel evacuation, saliva secretion, and urine flow; reduce capillary fragility; restore normal tone to tissues; stimulate peristalsis.

Cautions/Contraindications: Avoid use if pregnant or breast-feeding.
Adverse Reactions: Chest tightness, diarrhea (possibly bloody), dizziness, edema, gastrointestinal cramps (severe), hematuria (blood in the urine), nausea, salivation (increased), vertigo, and/or vomiting.
Herb/Drug Interactions: This herb could cause an interaction (possibly severe) when taken with the following drugs: None known.
Preparations/Dosage: Crude Herb: 3-6 grams. Extract: 3-5 drops (0.2-0.333 cc.) one to two times per day. Infusion: 1 cup per day. Root (powdered): Average dose in substance 15-30 grains (0.324-2 gm.). Tincture: 5-20 drops (0.333-1.25 cc.) one to three times per day.

Iboga (i·bō ge)
(*Tabernanthe iboga*)

Synonyms/Related Species: None known.
Family/Class: Apocynaceae (dogbane).
Habitat: Africa (primarily the Congo region).
Flavor: Bitter.
Parts Used: Bark (root), root.
Properties: Anesthetic, aphrodisiac, diuretic, hallucinogen, hypertensive, narcotic, sialagogue, stimulant, and vasoconstrictor.
Constituents: Alkaloid, glycosides, ibogaine, and indole.
Historical Uses: Addiction (heroin), appetite loss, erectile dysfunction, frigidity, neurasthenia, pain, sexually transmitted diseases (STDs), syphilis, and ulcer (syphilitic).
Discussion: May arouse sexual impulses; cause blood vessel constriction; elevate body temperature and blood pressure levels; inhibit cholinesterase; promote saliva secretion and urine flow; serve as an adjuvant to the treatment (and possible cure) of heroin addiction as well as other drug rehabilitation therapies; stimulate appetite, digestion, and the central nervous system.
Cautions/Contraindications: Avoid use if pregnant or breast-feeding, or if you have hypertension or are in fragile health. Iboga is a monoamine oxidase inhibitor (MAOI) herb. The combined use of iboga with sedative, tranquilizer, antihistamine, narcotic, or tricyclic antidepressant drugs will cause hypertensive crisis. The combined use of iboga with amphetamines, cocaine, LSD, alcohol (including wine) avocados, unripe bananas, and dairy products (including aged cheese) will cause hypotensive crisis. It is recommended that no other drugs be used in combination with or within a ten-hour period of the use of iboga. Do not use niando (*alchornea floribunda*) while taking iboga. Physical effects upon initial use of iboga include ataxia, changes in perception, circulatory disturbances (chills/hot flashes), dizziness, heightened empathy, nausea, and vivid visual imagery occurring behind closed eyes.
Adverse Reactions: Anxiety, apprehension, confusion, convulsions, debility, dizziness, fainting, gastrointestinal problems, hallucinations (possibly frightening), hypertensive crisis (severe rise in blood pressure levels), hypotensive crisis (arrythmias, breathing difficulty, chills, severe drop in blood pressure levels), liver damage (often characterized by jaundice), nausea, paralysis, respiratory failure, salivation (excessive), vomiting, and/or possible death.
Herb/Drug Interactions: This herb could cause an interaction (possibly severe) when taken with the following drugs: Amphetamine drugs, Antidepressant drugs, Antihistamine drugs, Anxiolytic drugs, Cardiac drugs, Migraine drugs, Monamine Oxidase Inhibitors (MAOIs), Opiate Agonists/Narcotic drugs, Sedative drugs, and Tranquilizer drugs.

Preparations/Dosage: Bark (root/powdered): Beginners should start with 200-300 mg. Persons already experienced in using iboga can take up to 1 gram. Decoction (root): ¼-½ cup per day. Note: Fasting for 16-18 hours prior to taking iboga will help to offset any nausea. Also taking 2-3 motion sickness pills one hour prior to ingesting iboga will help to eliminate nausea.

Impatiens (im·pā shē·enz)
(*Impatiens biflora*)

Synonyms/Related Species: Common Balsam-Weed (*impatiens balsamina*), Himalayan Impatiens (*impatiens roylei*), Horned Balsam (*impatiens cornuta*), European Impatiens (*impatiens noli-me-tangere*), Jewelweed (*impatiens aurea*), Silverweed, Slipperweed, Snapweed, Speckled Jewels (*impatiens biflora*), Spotted Touch-Me-Not, Swallow-Leaf, Touch-Me-Not, Western Jewelweed, Wild Balsam, Wild Celandine, Wild Lady's Slipper, and Zanzibar Impatiens (*impatiens sultani*).
Family/Class: Balsaminaceae (balsam).
Habitat: Alaska, Africa, Asia, Ceylon, China, England, Europe, the Himalayas, India, Japan, North America, and Zanzibar.
Flavor: Pungent.
Parts Used: Arial.
Properties: Carminative, demulcent, diuretic, emetic, laxative, and nervine.
Constituents: Alkaloids, mucilage, and tannic acid.
Historical Uses: Digestive complaints, hemorrhoids, inflammation, insect bites or stings, nervous conditions, rash, and skin problems.
Discussion: May aid digestion; calm the nervous system; promote bowel evacuation and urine flow; soothe mucous membrane irritation; stimulate peristalsis.
Cautions/Contraindications: Avoid use if pregnant or breast-feeding.
Adverse Reactions: Diarrhea (severe), gastrointestinal cramps (severe), mucous membrane problems, nausea, and/or vomiting.
Herb/Drug Interactions: This herb could cause an interaction (possibly severe) when taken with the following drugs: None known.
Preparations/Dosage: External uses only.

Indigo (in de·gō)
(*Baptisia tinctoria*)

Synonyms/Related Species: Baptisis Indikon, Horse-Fly Weed, Indian Dye, Rattlebush, and Wild Indigo.
Family/Class: Leguminosae (legume).
Habitat: India and North America.
Flavor: Pungent.
Parts Used: Bark (root), leaves.
Properties: Alterative, antibiotic, anticarcinogen, antiperiodic, antiphlogistic, antiviral, astringent, cardiac depressant, depurative, emmenagogue, emetic, hemostatic, laxative, malariacidal, and stimulant.
Constituents: Albumin (albumen), alkaloids, anagyrine, baptin, baptisin, coumarin, glycosides, gum, indican, indiglucin, indigogen, inulin (starch), polysaccharides, resin, and scopoletine.

Historical Uses: Abscess, ague, amenorrhea, angina, arthritis, bleeding, cancer, canker sores, colds, congestion (uterine, vaginal), diphtheria, dysentery, ear infection, erysipelas, fever (ephemeral, enteric, herpetic, intermittent, scarlet, septic, typhus), glandular problems, glandular swelling, herpes, infection (bacterial, viral), inflammation, influenza, laryngitis, lesions (tubercle), leukorrhea, lymphadenitis, malaria, meningitis, parasites (malarial plasmodia), periodontal disease, pharyngitis, pneumonia, poisoning (blood, sepsis), respiratory conditions, scarletina, scrofula, sexually transmitted diseases (STDs), stomatitis, sore nipples, sore throat, sores, tonsillitis, tuberculosis, tumors, typhoid, typhus, ulcer (bouveret, duodenal, fistula, gastric, peptic, syriac, tuberculous, veneroid), vaginitis, and wounds (minor).
Discussion: May decrease the effect of carcinogens; diminish or reduce functional activity of the heart; enhance liver function; cleanse the lymphatic system; inhibit or destroy development and growth of bacteria and other microorganisms; promote bowel evacuation; raise blood leukocyte count; reestablish healthy system functions; soothe nipple soreness; stimulate the immune system, menstruation, and peristalsis.
Cautions/Contraindications: Avoid use if pregnant or breast-feeding.
Adverse Reactions: Diarrhea, nausea, and/or vomiting.
Herb/Drug Interactions: This herb could cause an interaction (possibly severe) when taken with the following drugs: None known.
Preparations/Dosage: Crude Herb: ½-6 grams. Decoction: ½-1 tablespoon one to two times per day. Tincture: 2-5 drops (0.133-0.333 cc.) one to three times per day.

Ipecacuanha (ip e·kak yoo·ä ne)
(*Cephaelis ipecacuanha*)

Synonyms/Related Species: Brazilian Ipecacuanha, Cartagena Ipecacuanha, Indian Ipecacuanha (*psychotria ipecacuanha*), Matto Grosso Ipecacuanha, Rio Ipecacuanha, and White Ipecacuanha.
Family/Class: Rubiaceae (madder).
Habitat: Bolivia, Brazil, Columbia, India, Malaysia, New Grenada, and Peru.
Flavor: Bitter.
Parts Used: Root.
Properties: Antiprotozoan, antispasmodic, counterirritant, diaphoretic, emetic, expectorant, laxative, parasiticide, and stimulant.
Constituents: Alkaloids, cephaeline, emetine, inulin (starch), ipecacuanhin, monosaccharides, psychotrine, saponins, resin, vitamins (choline), and volatile oil.
Historical Uses: Asthma, bronchitis, cholera, cirrhosis, cough, croup, diarrhea, diphtheria, dysentery, hemorrhage (typhoid), hepatitis, laryngitis, liver problems, mucus, parasites (amebas), poisoning (non-caustic organic), pyorrhea, respiratory conditions, and spasmodic conditions.
Discussion: May clear and open bronchial passages; enhance liver and lung functions; prevent the deposition of fat in the liver; promote bowel evacuation and perspiration; reduce both the rate of growth and the rate of reproduction of protozoa; stimulate peristalsis.
Cautions/Contraindications: Avoid use if pregnant or breast-feeding. May cause allergic reactions and dermatitis in susceptible individuals. Not for long-term use. Use with professional guidance/supervision.
Adverse Reactions: Arrhythmia, bronchitis (severe), cardiac failure, coma, convulsions, diarrhea (possibly bloody), gastroenteritis (severe), hematuria (blood in the urine), hypotension,

mucous membrane erosion, nausea, respiratory problems, shock, tachycardia, vomiting, and/or possible death.
Herb/Drug Interactions: This herb could cause an interaction (possibly severe) when taken with the following drugs: None known.
Preparations/Dosage: Crude Herb (powdered): Average dose in substance 5-30 grains (0.324-2 gm.). Emetic: Average dose in substance 7½ grains (0.5 gm.). Expectorant: Average dose in substance $^{1}/_{6}$-1 grain (0.011-0.066 gm.). Extract (emetic): 8 drops (0.5 cc.). Syrup: ½-2 drachms (1.85-8 cc.).
Isolation: Emetine bismuth iodide: Containing from 17-23% of anhydrous emetine and from 15-20% percent of bismuth, used in 3-grain (0.2 gm.) doses for dysentery. Emetine hydrochloride: Average dose of ⅓ grain (0.02 gm.), administered hypodermically, for use in dysentery.

Ivy, American (ī vē, e·mer e·ken)
(*Parthenocissus quinquefolia*)

Synonyms/Related Species: American Woodbine, Creeper, False Grapes, Five Leaves, Virginia Creeper, Wild Woodvine, Wodebinde, Woodbine, Woodvine, Woody Climber, and Wudubinde.
Family/Class: Vitaceae (grape).
Habitat: North America.
Flavor: Bitter.
Parts Used: Bark, leaves, gum/resin, twigs.
Properties: Antiphlogistic, antispasmodic, astringent, diaphoretic, emetic, emmenagogue, expectorant, hemostatic, laxative, parasiticide, stimulant, and tonic.
Constituents: Ampelopsin, glycollic acid, gum, hederagenin, hederin, minerals (calcium potassium, sodium), oxalic acid, pyrocatachin, resin, tannic acid, and tartaric acid.
Historical Uses: Bleeding, bunions, colds, corns, cough, digestive complaints, edema, fever (ephemeral, rheumatic), glandular swelling, headache, inflammation, migraine, parasites (lice and their nits), respiratory conditions, rheumatism, spasmodic conditions, spleen problems, toothache, and ulcer (indolent).
Discussion: May clear and open bronchial passages; promote bowel evacuation and perspiration; restore normal tone to tissues; stimulate menstruation and peristalsis.
Cautions/Contraindications: Avoid use if pregnant or breast-feeding. Berries are poisonous.
Adverse Reactions: Breathing difficulties, edema, excitement, fever, coma, convulsions, diarrhea, nausea, oxalism (oxalic acid or oxalate poisoning), and/or vomiting.
Herb/Drug Interactions: This herb could cause an interaction (possibly severe) when taken with the following drugs: None known.
Preparations/Dosage: Crude Herb (bark/leaves/twigs): 3-6 grams. Decoction: ½-1 cup per day. Extract (bark/twigs): 3-5 drops (0.2-0.333 cc.) one to two times per day. Infusion: 1-2 cups per day. Gum/resin: Average dose in substance 2-4 grains (0.13-0.26 gm.). Tincture: 5-15 drops (0.333-1 cc.) one to three times per day.

Ivy, Ground (ī vē, ground)
(*Glechoma* (*Nepeta*) *hederacea*)

Synonyms/Related Species: Ale-Hoof, Cat's Paw, Creeping Charlie, False Catmint, Gill-Over-The-Ground, Haymaids, Hedge Maids, Turnhoof, and Variegated Ground Ivy.

Family/Class: Labiatae (mint family).
Habitat: Europe and North America.
Flavor: Bitter.
Parts Used: Flowering tops, leaves.
Properties: Antiphlogistic, aromatic, astringent, carminative, depurative, diaphoretic, diuretic, emmenagogue, lithotriptic, nervine, stimulant, and tonic.
Constituents: Bitter principle, camphor, caryophyllin, carvacrol, minerals (magnesium, manganese, phosphorus, sodium, sulfur), nepetalactone, nerol, pulegone, tannic acid, thymol, and volatile oil.
Historical Uses: Abscess, appetite loss, asthma, bronchitis, bruises, calculus, colds, cough, diarrhea, enteritis, fever (ephemeral, rheumatic), gallstones, gout, headache, hemorrhoids, hysteria, indigestion, inflammation, jaundice, kidney problems, kidney stones, liver problems, lung problems, mucus, muscle and joint pain, nervous conditions, neurasthenia, poisoning (lead), respiratory conditions, rheumatism, sciatica, sore throat, tinnitus, and urinary problems.
Discussion: May aid digestion; dissolve calculi; promote perspiration and urine flow; purify the blood; restore normal tone to tissues; serve as an antidote to lead poisoning; stimulate gastric secretions and menstruation.
Cautions/Contraindications: Avoid use if pregnant or breast-feeding, or if you have ulcer (peptic, gastric).
Adverse Reactions: Insomnia, mouth and throat irritation, nausea, respiratory distress, and/or vomiting.
Herb/Drug Interactions: This herb could cause an interaction (possibly severe) when taken with the following drugs: None known.
Preparations/Dosage: Crude Herb: 3-6 grams. Infusion: ½-1 cup per day. Juice: ½-1 teaspoon in water one to two times per day. Tincture: 5-20 drops (0.333-1.25 cc.) one to three times per day.

Ivy, Poison (ī vē, poi zen)
(*Toxicodendron radicans*)

Synonyms/Related Species: Leaves of Three and Poison Vine.
Family/Class: Anacardiaceae (cashew).
Habitat: Asia, British Columbia, Europe, Germany, and North America.
Flavor: Pungent/bitter.
Parts Used: Leaves.
Properties: Antiphlogistic, counterirritant, narcotic, parasiticide, and stimulant.
Constituents: Toxicodendrin, toxicodendrol, and urushiol.
Historical Uses: Arthritis, eczema, edema, fever (ephemeral, herpetic, rheumatic), herpes, infection, inflammation, muscle and joint pain, palsy, paralysis, parasites (ringworm), rash, rheumatism, sexually transmitted diseases (STDs), skin problems, and warts (digitate, filiform, fugitive, glabra, mother, plana juvenilis, plantar, seborrhoeic, vulgaris).
Discussion: May enhance liver function; stimulate the immune system.
Cautions/Contraindications: Avoid use if pregnant or breast-feeding. Berries and root are poisonous. Keep away from eyes and mucous membranes. May cause contact dermatitis (possibly severe) in susceptible individuals. Use protective clothing and gloves when harvesting.

Adverse Reactions: Conjunctivitis, corneal inflammation, delirium, diarrhea, difficulty swallowing, drowsiness, fainting, fever, gastric irritation, hematuria (blood in the urine), infection, intestinal cramps, itching (possibly severe), respiratory distress, skin and mucous membrane eruptions (severe), nausea, stupor, vertigo, and/or vomiting.
Herb/Drug Interactions: This herb could cause an interaction (possibly severe) when taken with the following drugs: None known.
Preparations/Dosage: External uses recommended. Great care must be taken when using poison ivy preparations externally, and internal use or ingestion of toxicodendron preparations is recommended *only* for those persons who have long used and are experienced with its uses in this way. Topical Use: Cover unaffected areas of skin and apply (wearing gloves) in extremely small-diluted amounts. May cause skin irritation, redness, and inflammation upon application. Thoroughly wash affected area afterwards with a soapy solution to remove any resinous residue. Keep away from eyes and mucous membranes. Internal Use: Initially, those persons who are not used to ingesting poison ivy should begin with *extremely* small-diluted amounts, as the ingestion of large amounts can cause severe adverse effects resulting in possible death due to asphyxiation. Tincture 1:4 (a dose of 25%): 1-5 drops (0.066-0.333 cc.) once per day.
Prevention: Remove affected clothing and place in plastic bag until they can be washed in hot soapy water (wear gloves when removing clothing from bag as contact with the toxic oil can cause severe skin reactions). Washing skin thoroughly within 10 minutes of exposure with hot soapy water may help to remove the toxic (urushiol) oil and prevent skin reactions.
First Aid for Dermatitis: Mild to Moderate Cases: Cold soaks in the bathtub for 20 minutes several times daily may help relieve inflammation. Corticosteroid or Corticosterone creams applied topically (avoid genital area) can help to relieve itching and inflammation. Oral (systemic) corticosteroids can also help relieve discomforts. Severe Cases or affected areas involving the anal or genital area require immediate medical attention.
Did You Know? The toxic oil urushiol can remain active on surfaces for as long as 5 years, and this oil is so potent that as little as a billionth of a gram (nanogram) can cause a rash.

Jack-in-the-Pulpit (jak in·the·pool pit)
(*Arum triphyllum*)

Synonyms/Related Species: American Arum, Asian Arum (*arum dioscorides*), Cuckoo Pint (*arum maculatum*), Cypress Powder, Devil's Ear, Dragon Arum (*arum dracontium*), Dragon Root, Indian Turnip (*arum indicum*), Italian Arum (*arum italicum*), Manguri, Memory Root, Pepper Turnip, Wake Robin, and Wild Turnip.
Family/Class: Araceae (arum).
Habitat: Asia, Europe, France, Hawaii, India, Italy, the Mediterranean, the Pacific Islands, North America, and South America.
Flavor: Pungent.
Parts Used: Root.
Properties: Antiphlogistic, diaphoretic, expectorant, laxative, parasiticide, and stomachic.
Constituents: Albumin (albumen), alkaloids, glycosides, gum, inulin (starch), lignin, mannan, minerals (calcium, potassium), monosaccharides, mucilage, saponins, oxalic acid, and oxalates.
Historical Uses: Amenorrhea, asthma, bronchitis, colds, croup, fever (ephemeral, rheumatic), flatulence, gargle/mouth rinse, inflammation, laryngitis, muscle and joint pain, pain, parasites

(ringworm), respiratory conditions, rheumatism, sore throat, sores, stomatitis, tonsillitis, and whooping cough.
Discussion: May clear and open bronchial passages; enhance stomach function; promote bowel evacuation and perspiration; stimulate peristalsis.
Cautions/Contraindications: Avoid use if pregnant or breast-feeding. Not for long-term use. Use with professional guidance/supervision.
Adverse Reactions: Breathing difficulties, coagulation problems, diarrhea (possibly bloody), gastroenteritis, gastrointestinal cramps (severe), hematuria (blood in the urine), mouth/throat burning, mucous membrane problems, oxalism (oxalic acid or oxalate poisoning), respiratory failure, and/or possible death.
Herb/Drug Interactions: This herb could cause an interaction (possibly severe) when taken with the following drugs: Anticoagulant drugs, Salicylates, and Subsalicylates.
Preparations/Dosage: Root (dried/powdered): Average dose in substance 5-10 grains (0.324-0.666 gm.). Infusion: ¼-½ cup per day.

Jambul (jam bul)
(*Syzygium jambolanum*)

Synonyms/Related Species: Java Plum, Rose Apple, and Syzygy.
Family/Class: Myrtaceae (myrtle).
Habitat: Asia, the Antilles, Australia, and India.
Flavor: Bitter.
Parts Used: Seeds.
Properties: Anticarcinogen, anti-inflammatory, antispasmodic, aphrodisiac, astringent, carminative, diuretic, hemostatic, stomachic, and tonic.
Constituents: Albumin (albumen), antimellin, bergenin, chlorophyll, ellagic acid, eugenin, fatty acids (arachidonic, linoleic, linolenic, oleic, palmitic, stearic), fixed oils (olein, palmitin, stearin), flavonoids, gallic acid, glycosides, myristin (myristic acid), quercetin, resin, sterols, tannic acid, triterpenes, and volatile oil.
Historical Uses: Arteriosclerosis, asthma, bleeding, bronchitis, cancer, constipation, contraceptive (male), depression (mild/moderate), diabetes, diarrhea, digestive complaints, dysentery, exhaustion, flatulence, glycosuria, hypertrophy (spleen), inflammation, insufficiency (pancreatic), nervous conditions, spasmodic conditions, and ulcer (duodenal, gastric, peptic).
Discussion: May aid digestion; arouse sexual impulses; decrease the effect of carcinogens; enhance pancreatic, spleen, and stomach functions; offset the negative effects of chemotherapy and radiation therapy; prevent the formation of cataracts; promote urine flow; reduce blood sugar levels and free radicals; restore normal tone to tissues.
Cautions/Contraindications: Avoid use if pregnant or breast-feeding.
Adverse Reactions: Nausea and/or vomiting.
Herb/Drug Interactions: This herb could cause an interaction (possibly severe) when taken with the following drugs: None known.
Preparations/Dosage: Crude Herb: 1-2 grams (approximately 25-30 seeds). Extract: 1-5 drops (0.066-0.333 cc.) one to two times per day. Seeds (powdered): Average dose in substance 5-30 grains (0.3-2 gm.) one to three times per day. Tincture: 5-30 drops (0.333-2 cc.) one to three times per day.

Jasmine (jaz min)
(*Jasminum officinale*)

Synonyms/Related Species: Arabian Jasmine (*jasminum sambac*), Carolina Jasmine (*jasminum nitidum*), Catalonian Jasmine, Chameli, Chinese Jasmine (*jasminum nudiflorum*), Common White Jasmine, European Jasmine (*jasminum fruticans*), Habbez-Zelim (*jasminum floribundum*), Indian Jasmine (*jasminum angustifolium*), Italian Yellow-Flowered Jasmine (*jasminum humile*), Sien-Hing-Hwa, Spanish Jasmine (*jasminum grandiflorum*), True Yellow Jasmine (*jasminum odoratissimum*), White Jasmine, Yasmin, Yellow Jasmine, and Zambak Jasmine.
Family/Class: Oleaceae (olive).
Habitat: Algeria, Asia, Britain, the Canary Islands, Catalonia, Europe, India, the Mediterranean, Persia, Turkey, and other subtropical and tropical regions.
Flavor: Bitter.
Parts Used: Flowers.
Properties: Antigalactic, aphrodisiac, aromatic, depurative, nervine, parasiticide, teniacide, and teniafuge.
Constituents: Benzyl, indole, jasminiflorin, jasminin, jasmone, linalool, linalyl acetate, methyl anthranilate (methyl orthoaminobenzoate), monosaccharides, and volatile oil.
Historical Uses: Cough, eye problems, frigidity, laryngitis, mastitis, parasites (ringworm, tapeworm), perfume, potpourri, and snakebite.
Discussion: May arouse sexual impulses; calm the nervous system; diminish or suppress lactation; purify the blood.
Cautions/Contraindications: Avoid use if pregnant or breast-feeding. Do not confuse this herb with jessamine (*gelsemium sempervirens*).
Adverse Reactions: Clammy skin, coma, convulsions (violent), labored breathing, muscle rigidity, nausea, pupil dilatation, slow pulse rate, and/or vomiting.
Herb/Drug Interactions: This herb could cause an interaction (possibly severe) when taken with the following drugs: None known.
Preparations/Dosage: Crude Herb: 3-6 grams. Infusion: 1 cup per day.
Did You Know? It takes approximately 3 pounds of jasmine flowers to perfume 1 pound of lard.

Jequirity (ji·kwir e·tē)
(*Abrus precatorius*)

Synonyms/Related Species: Crab's Eyes, Goonteh, Gunga, Indian Licorice, Jumble-Beads, Prayer Beads, Rati, Rosary Pea, and Wild Licorice.
Family/Class: Leguminosae (legume).
Habitat: India and the Unites States (primarily Florida).
Flavor: Sweet.
Parts Used: Root, seeds.
Properties: Abortifacient, counterirritant, and ophthalmic.
Constituents: Alkaloid, abrin (jequeritin), and glycyrrhizin.
Historical Uses: Conjunctivitis, eye problems, inflammation, substitute for licorice, and trachoma.
Discussion: May cause eye irritation; increase circulation; induce abortion; stimulate uterine contractions.

Cautions/Contraindications: Avoid use if pregnant or breast-feeding. External uses only. Ingestion of the seeds is poisonous and may result in death. Poisoning has been recorded in adults following the ingestion of ½-1 seed. Death in children following the ingestion of one seed has been recorded from the colorful seeds being strung on necklaces and giving to children to wear. Not for long-term use. Symptoms of poisoning may not appear for several hours or days after ingestion due to the erratic absorption of the toxins inside of the hard seed coat. Due to its extreme potency this herb is recommended for professional use.
Adverse Reactions: Arrhythmia, blindness, hematuria (blood in the urine), convulsions, destruction of red blood cells, diarrhea, mouth burns (minor), nausea, vomiting, and/or possible death.
Herb/Drug Interactions: This herb could cause an interaction (possibly severe) when taken with the following drugs: None known.
Preparations/Dosage: External uses only. See "Forms of Herbal Preparation" for eye drops.

Jessamine (jes'e·min)
(*Gelsemium sempervirens*)

Synonyms/Related Species: Carolina Jessamine (*gelsemium nitidum*), False Jasmine, Gelsemium, Myanmar Gelsemium (*gelsemium elegans*), Wild Jessamine, Wild Woodbine, Woodbine, and Yellow Jessamine.
Family/Class: Loganiaceae (logania).
Habitat: Guatemala, Myanmar (formerly Burma), and North America.
Flavor: Bitter.
Parts Used: Root.
Properties: Antiphlogistic, antispasmodic, aromatic, cardiant, bronchodilator, diaphoretic, hypotensive, mydriatic, nervine, sedative, and vasodilatory.
Constituents: Alkaloids, coumarin, fatty acids (oleic, palmitic, stearic), fixed oils (olein, palmitin, stearin), gelsemicine, gelsemine, gelseminine, inulin (starch), minerals (calcium, iron, lime (calcium oxide), magnesium, potassium, silicon, sodium), resin, sempervirine, silicic acid, and volatile oil.
Historical Uses: Asthma, bronchitis, cardiovascular conditions, chorea, convulsions, cough, croup, cysts (ovarian), delirium tremens (DTs), digestive complaints, dysmenorrhea, dysuria (painful/difficult urination), endometriosis, epilepsy, fever (ephemeral, enteric, rheumatic, typhoid), fibroids (uterine), gastritis, gastrointestinal problems, glandular problems, glandular swelling, headache, hysteria, indigestion, inflammation, insomnia, irritable bowel syndrome (IBS), muscle and joint pain, nervousness, neuralgia, pain, pleurisy, pneumonia, respiratory conditions, rheumatism, sciatica, spasmodic conditions, typhoid, ulcer (bouveret), and whooping cough.
Discussion: May cause motor depression; dilate or expand the air passages of the lungs; serve as an adjuvant to alcoholism treatment programs to assist in easing delirium tremens (DTs); soothe the nerves; stimulate the cardiovascular system and respiratory system.
Cautions/Contraindications: Avoid use if pregnant or breast-feeding. Do not confuse this herb with jasmine (*jasminum officinale*). Not for long-term use. Use with professional guidance/supervision.
Adverse Reactions: Arrhythmia, breathing and swallowing difficulties, cardiac failure, coma, cyanosis (a bluish discoloration of the skin and the whites of the eyes), depression, diarrhea

(severe), dizziness, dryness (mouth), enteritis (severe), eyelid heaviness, fainting, headache, inhibition of eyeball movement, limb trembling, loss of speech, muscle stiffness, paralysis, perspiration, pupil dilatation, spasmodic conditions, visual disturbances, vomiting, and/or possible death.
Herb/Drug Interactions: This herb could cause an interaction (possibly severe) when taken with the following drugs: None known.
Preparations/Dosage: Crude Herb: ½-1 gram. Infusion: ⅛-¼ cup per day.

Jimson Weed (jim sen wēd)
(*Datura stramonium*)

Synonyms/Related Species: Angel's Trumpet (*datura suaveolens*), Apple of Peru, Chinese Datura (*datura ferox*), Datura, Devil's Apple, Devil's Trumpet (*datura metel*), D'hustúra, Gabriel's Trumpet, Hairy Thorn Apple, Indian Datura (*datura fastuosa*), Jamestown Weed, Jimpson Weed, Mad-Apple, Mexican Datura (*datura quercifolia*), Peru-Apple, Stinkweed, Stinkwort, Stramonium, Tatorea, The Little Smoke, Thorn Apple, Tree Datura (*datura arborea*), Unmata, and Yerba del Diable.
Family/Class: Solanaceae (nightshade).
Habitat: Africa, Asia, the Caspian, Central America, Europe, Hawaii, India, Mexico, Peru, Russia, Siberia, and South America.
Flavor: Bitter.
Parts Used: Leaves, seed.
Properties: Analgesic, anticarcinogen, anticholinergic, antispasmodic, diuretic, hallucinogen, hypnotic, mydriatic, narcotic, parasiticide, and sedative.
Constituents: Alkaloids, atropine, belladonnine, coumarin, daturine, fatty acids (oleic, palmitic, stearic), fixed oils (olein, palmitin, stearin), flavonoids, gum, hyoscyamine, inulin (starch), malic acid, protein, resin, saponins, scopolamine (hyoscine), scopoleine, solanine, tannic acid, umbelliferone, vitamins (choline), and volatile oil.
Historical Uses: Abscess, arrhythmia, arthritis, asthma, bladder problems, bronchitis, cancer, cerebrospinal hyperemia, cirrhosis, colic, colitis, constipation, convulsions, cough, cramps, delirium, diphtheria, edema, enuresis (urinary incontinence), ephidrosis (excessive perspiration), glaucoma, hemorrhoids, herbal tobacco, hysteria, indigestion, infection (bacterial), influenza, insomnia, iritis, motion sickness, muscle and joint pain, nervous conditions, pain, parasites (ringworm), Parkinson's disease, prostate problems, prostatitis, respiratory conditions, rheumatism, sciatica, sinusitis, spasmodic conditions, tachycardia, ulcer (gastric), and whooping cough.
Discussion: May block the passage of impulses through the parasympathetic nerves; clear and open the bronchial passages; decrease the effect of carcinogens; increase the frequency of the heart's action; induce sleep; lessen the vascularity of the iris; prevent the deposition of fat in the liver; produce pupil dilatation; promote urine flow; reduce the frequency of nighttime urination; stimulate the sympathetic and depress the cerebrospinal nerves; strengthen the respiratory system.
Cautions/Contraindications: Avoid use if pregnant or breast-feeding, or if you have arrhythmia, edema, glaucoma, hypertrophy (benign prostatic), paralytic ileus, pyloristenosis, or tachycardia. External uses only. May cause dermatitis in susceptible individuals. Prolonged use may lead to a tolerance to the accumulation of tropine-alkaloids in the parasympathetic system;

thus more of the herb is required to achieve the same effects. Not for long-term use. Use with professional guidance/supervision.

Adverse Reactions: Arrhythmia, asphyxiation, cardiac damage, coma, compulsive speech, constipation, convulsions, decreased perspiration, delirium, diarrhea (possibly bloody), dry mouth and throat, excessive thirst, flushing, gastrointestinal cramps (severe), hallucinations, headache, hematuria (blood in the urine), hypertension, increased body temperature, mania, mental disturbances, nausea, pupil dilatation, restlessness, seizure conditions, stupor, tachycardia, urinary problems, visual disturbances, vomiting, and/or possible death.

Herb/Drug Interactions: This herb could cause an interaction (possibly severe) when taken with the following drugs: Antidepressant drugs.

Preparations/Dosage: Crude Herb: 3-6 grams. Extract (leaves): 1-3 drops (0.06-0.2 cc.) one to two times per day. Extract (seeds): 1-2 drops (0.06-0.1 cc.) one to two times per day. Extract (powdered): Average dose in substance $^1/_6$ grain (0.011 gm.). Extract (solid): Average dose in substance ¼-1 grain (0.015-0.066 gm.). Leaves (powdered): Average dose in substance $^1/_{10}$-5 grains (0.006-0.3 gm.). Tincture (leaves): 5-15 drops (0.333-1 cc.) one to three times per day. Respiratory Conditions (leaves): 2 grams per therapeutic session (no more than 1 ounce per week) smoked for respiratory conditions. Smoke therapy sessions occurring too frequently may cause fainting and severe headaches.

Isolation: Atropine: Soluble in alcohol and sparingly so in water. Average dose of $^1/_{150}$ grain (0.4 mg.) for use as a mydriatic and narcotic. Atropine sulfate: Soluble in water. Average dose of $^1/_{120}$ grain (0.5 mg.) for use as a mydriatic and narcotic.

Jujube (ju jūb)
(*Zizyphus vulgaris*)

Synonyms/Related Species: African Jujube (*zizyphus lotos*), Brustbeeren, Chinese Dates (*zizyphus agrestis*), Common Jujube, Ethiopian Jujube (*zizyphus spina christi*), Graythorn, Gray Lotebush (*zizyphus obtusifolia*), Indian Jujube (*zizyphus œnoplia*), Nabka (*zizyphus napeca*), Seedra, Senegal Jujube (*zizyphus barelei*), and Zyzyphus.

Family/Class: Rhamnaceae (buckthorn).

Habitat: Africa, Arabia, Asia, China, Europe, India, Italy, the Middle East, North America, Senegal, and Syria.

Flavor: Fruit: sweet. Root: bitter.

Parts Used: Fruit (fresh/dried with pit/stone removed), root.

Properties: Antiphlogistic, antiscorbutic, astringent, demulcent, expectorant, hemostatic, hypotensive, nervine, nutritive, sedative, stimulant, tonic, vasodilator, and vulnerary.

Constituents: Aglycone (genin), alkaloids, coumarin, disaccharide, flavonoids, galactose, malic acid, monosaccharides, mucilage, naringin, saponins, tannic acid, tartaric acid, triterpene, and vitamin C (ascorbic acid).

Historical Uses: Allergy, anxiety, appetite loss, arrhythmia, bleeding, culinary (fruit), dietary supplementation, diarrhea, dizziness, emaciation, ephidrosis (excessive perspiration), exhaustion, fatigue, fever (ephemeral, rheumatic), gleet, gonorrhea, hypertension (mild/moderate), infection (sexually transmitted), inflammation, insomnia, malnutrition, memory/cognitive problems, muscle and joint pain, nervous conditions, rheumatism, scurvy, sexually transmitted diseases (STDs), ulcer (duodenal, gastric, peptic), urethritis, and vaginitis.

Discussion: May calm the nervous system; cause blood vessel dilatation; clear and open bronchial passages; enhance pancreatic, spleen, and stomach functions; increase energy; improve muscle strength; provide dietary supplementation; reduce blood pressure levels; restore normal tone to tissues; serve as a nutritional adjuvant to therapeutic programs; soothe mucous membrane irritation; speed healing; stimulate appetite.
Cautions/Contraindications: Avoid use if pregnant or breast-feeding.
Adverse Reactions: Diarrhea (possibly bloody), gastrointestinal cramps (severe), hematuria (blood in the urine), nausea, and/or vomiting.
Herb/Drug Interactions: This herb could cause an interaction (possibly severe) when taken with the following drugs: Hypotensive drugs.
Preparations/Dosage: Crude Herb (fruit): 3-15 grams. Crude Herb (root): 3-6 grams. Fruit (fresh or dried): Ingest one handful daily or use fruit in baking or cooking. Infusion (root): ½-1 cup per day.

Juniper (ju ne·per)

(Juniperus communis)

Synonyms/Related Species: American Juniper (*juniperus virginiana*), California Juniper (*juniperus californica*), Common Juniper, Creeping Juniper, Ground Juniper (*juniperus horizontalis*), Oneseed Juniper (*juniperus monosperma*), Pencil Cedar, Prickly Juniper (*juniperus oxycedrus*), Red Cedar, and Rocky Mountain Juniper (*juniperus scopulorum*).
Family/Class: Cupressaceae (cedar).
Habitat: Alaska, the Alpine and Subalpine zones, Africa, Asia, Bermuda, Europe, France, North America, and the Yukon Territory.
Flavor: Pungent.
Parts Used: Berry.
Properties: Abortifacient, antibiotic, antifungal, antilithic, antiperiodic, antiphlogistic, antiscorbutic, aromatic, carminative, counterirritant, depurative, diaphoretic, diuretic, emmenagogue, hemostatic, hypotensive, lithotriptic, malariacidal, stimulant, and vasodilator.
Constituents: Camphene, carvene (limonene), caryophyllin, coniferin, cymene, diterpene, eucalyptol (cineol), flavonoids, glycosides, lignin, minerals (cobalt, copper, sulfur, tin), monosaccharides, myrcene, pinene, resin, sabinene, tannic acid, terpinene, thujone, vitamins (C (ascorbic acid), volatile oil, and wax.
Historical Uses: Abscess, ague, allergy (food, pollen), alopecia, amenorrhea, appetite loss, arthritis, asthma, bladder problems, bleeding, bronchitis, bruises, calculus, colds, colic, congestion (uterine, vaginal), convulsions, cough, cramps, cystitis, diabetes, diarrhea, digestive complaints, diphtheria, dysuria (painful/difficult urination), edema, enuresis (urinary incontinence), erectile dysfunction, fever (ephemeral, enteric, hay, intermittent, rheumatic), flatulence, flavoring agent, gallstones, gargle/mouth rinse, gastritis, gastrointestinal problems, gleet, gonorrhea, gout, halitosis, hemorrhoids, hypertension (mild/moderate), hypoglycemia, incense, indigestion, infection (bacterial, fungal, sexually transmitted, urinary tract), inflammation, insect bites or stings, insufficiency (pancreatic), irritable bowel syndrome (IBS), kidney problems, kidney stones, leprosy, lesions (tubercle), leukorrhea, lithemia, malaria, memory/cognitive problems, mucus, muscle and joint pain, nephritis, nervous conditions, neuralgia, pain, palsy, parasites (malarial plasmodia), periodontal disease, plague, potpourri, pruritus, psoriasis, respiratory conditions, rheumatism, sciatica, scrofula, scurvy, sexually

transmitted diseases (STDs), shortness of breath, snakebite, sore throat, sores, skin problems, tuberculosis, typhoid, ulcer (bouveret, duodenal, fistula, syriac, tuberculous), urethritis, vaginitis, and wounds (minor).

Discussion: May aid digestion; cause blood vessel dilatation; clear and open the bronchial passages; dissolve calculi; enhance adrenal, kidney, pancreatic, stomach, and urinary functions; improve memory and cognition; induce abortion; inhibit or destroy development and growth of bacteria and other microorganisms; prevent the development of calculus or stones; promote perspiration and urine flow; purify the blood; reduce blood pressure levels, excessive lithic acid (uric acid) and urate levels in the blood, tophi, and urine, and the frequency of nighttime urination; serve as an adjuvant to diabetic insulin therapies; stimulate gastric acid secretions, kidney nephrons, menstruation, and uterine contractions; strengthen the brain, optic nerves, and the urinary system.

Cautions/Contraindications: Avoid use if pregnant or breast-feeding, or if you have acidity (gastric), a fever, indigestion, kidney problems, or ulcer (gastric, peptic). Long-term use may cause sterility (permanent). May cause allergic reactions and dermatitis in susceptible individuals. Not for long-term use. Use only the ripened (bluish) berries.

Adverse Reactions: Convulsions, diarrhea, digestive tract and urinary tract irritation, diuresis (increased urination), hematuria (blood in the urine), personality changes, nausea, and/or vomiting.

Herb/Drug Interactions: This herb could cause an interaction (possibly severe) when taken with the following drugs: Diuretic drugs and Hypotensive drugs.

Preparations/Dosage: Crude Herb: 3-6 grams. Berries (powdered): Average dose in substance 2-10 grains (0.133-0.666 gm.). Berries (dried): A small handful (8-12) may be ingested daily. Extract (solid): Average dose in substance 5-15 grains (0.324-1 gm.). Infusion: ½-1 cup per day. Oil of Juniper (*oleum juniperi*): 3-5 drops (0.19-0.33 cc.) in water or on a sugarcube. Syrup: 1 tablespoon in water one to two times per day. Tincture: 10-30 drops (0.666-2 cc.) one to three times per day. External Uses: Oil of Juniper (*oleum juniperi*): Dilute with a good quality vegetable oil and apply topically or put 1-2 drops on a cloth and inhale for respiratory conditions.

Isolation: Eucalyptol: 5 drops (0.3 cc.) in atomization or inhalation therapy for use in respiratory conditions.

Did You Know? Traditionally, juniper berries were the primary flavoring agent in gin.

Kava (kä vä)
(*Piper methysticum*)

Synonyms/Related Species: Ava Pepper, Intoxicating Pepper, Khava, and Waka.

Family/Class: Piperaceae (pepper).

Habitat: Australia, Hawaii, and the South Sea Islands.

Flavor: Pungent.

Parts Used: Root.

Properties: Analgesic, anesthetic (local), antibiotic, antifungal, antilithic, antiperiodic, antiphlogistic, antispasmodic, aphrodisiac, cardiant, depressant, diaphoretic, diuretic, malariacidal, sedative, stimulant, tonic, and vermifuge.

Constituents: Alkaloids, glycosides, inulin (starch), kavaine, kawahin, kawin, piperazine, piperine, resin, and volatile oil.

Historical Uses: Ague, anxiety, bladder problems, bronchitis, bruises, calculus, congestion (uterine, vaginal), convulsions, cystitis, depression (mild/moderate), diminished sex drive, emaciation, enuresis (urinary incontinence), escherichia coli (e-coli), fatigue, fever (ephemeral, intermittent, rheumatic), gallstones, genitourinary problems, gleet, gonorrhea, gout, headache, infection (bacterial, fungal, sexually transmitted, urinary tract), inflammation, insomnia, kidney stones, leukorrhea, lithemia, malaria, memory/cognitive problems, nervous conditions, pain, parasites (malarial plasmodia), prostate problems, respiratory conditions, restlessness, rheumatism, sexually transmitted diseases (STDs), social phobia, spasmodic conditions, syphilis, toothache, ulcer (syphilitic), urethritis, vaginitis, and wounds (minor).
Discussion: May arouse sexual impulses; cause motor depression; diminish or reduce functional activity of the respiratory system; enhance mental acuity, sensory perception, and sociability; improve memory and cognition; inhibit development or destroy growth of bacteria and other microorganisms; prevent the development of calculus and stones; promote perspiration and urine flow; reduce excessive levels of lithic acid (uric acid) and urates in the blood, tophi, and urine, and the frequency of nighttime urination; restore normal tone to tissues; serve as an adjuvant to anxiety therapies; stimulate the cardiovascular system.
Cautions/Contraindications: Avoid use if pregnant or breast-feeding, or if you have Parkinson's disease, or depression (severe). Do not drive or operate machinery when taking kava. Do not consume alcohol while taking kava. May increase the danger of suicide. Side effects upon administration may include allergic reactions, equilibrium disturbances, fatigue, gastrointestinal problems, and/or pupil dilatation. Not for long-term use.
Adverse Reactions: Alteration of red and white blood cell counts, bloodshot eyes, diarrhea, diminished or reduced functional activity of the heart, drowsiness, emaciation, euphoria, eye damage, jaundice, lesions, liver damage (often characterized by jaundice), nausea, paralysis, rash, respiratory failure, skin problems, skin pigmentation, spinal cord damage, stimulation then depression of the respiratory system, and/or vomiting.
Herb/Drug Interactions: This herb could cause an interaction (possibly severe) when taken with the following drugs: Antidepressant drugs, Anxiolytic drugs, and Sedative drugs.
Preparations/Dosage: Crude Herb: 3-6 grams. Capsules (containing 5 grains or 0.3 gm. each): 2-3 per day. Decoction: ½-1 cup per day. Root (powdered): Average dose in substance 60 grains (1 drachm). Extract (solid): Average dose in substance 1-15 grains (0.066-1 gm.). Tincture: 5-20 drops (0.333- 1.25 cc.) one to three times per day. Ceremonial Use: For maximum effect mix one ounce of the chewed* root with ten ounces of coconut milk, two tablespoons of olive oil, and one tablespoon of lecithin. Blend all together thoroughly until the emulsion takes on a milky appearance. Makes enough for one to two persons. *Chewing the root mixes it with saliva, which helps to further release the powerful constituents.
Isolation: Piperazine hydrochlorate: Dose in 2% solution, 5 grains (0.33 gm.), administered hypodermically; or orally (by mouth), 8 grains (0.5 gm.) for use as an antilithic, antisyphilitic, and diuretic. Piperine: Soluble (slightly) in water. Average dose of 1-5 grains (0.06-0.33 gm.) for use as an antiperiodic.
Did You Know? Kava root can reach a thickness of three to five inches in as little as two to five years. Within six to eight years the root can reach weights of 15-20 pounds, and after twenty years can weigh as much as 85-100 pounds.

Kelp (kelp)
(*Laminaria digitata*)

Synonyms/Related Species: Brown Algae, Culp, Deep-Sea Tangle (*laminaria cloustoni*), Hijiki, Kombu, Long-Frond Brown Algae, Marine Seaweed, Sea-Girdles, Sea Vegetable, Tangle, and Wakame.
Family/Class: Fucaceae - Laminariaceae (brown algae).
Habitat: The Baltic Sea, England, Europe, France, the Mediterranean, the North Sea (formerly the German Ocean), Norway, Japan, the Strait of Gibraltar, Sweden, and the Atlantic and Pacific coasts of the United States.
Flavor: Salty.
Parts Used: Thallus.
Properties: Alterative, antibiotic, anticarcinogen, antiphlogistic, astringent, demulcent, diuretic, expectorant, hemostatic, laxative, nutritive, and vasodilator.
Constituents: Alginic acid, cellulose, fatty acids (arachidonic, linoleic, linolenic), fiber, fucosan, fucose, fucosterol, lethicin, mannitol (mannite), minerals (aluminum, barium, bismuth, boron, bromine, calcium, chlorine, chromium, cobalt, copper, gallium, iodine, iron, lithium, magnesium, manganese, nickel, phosphorus, potassium, silicon, silver, sodium, strontium, sulfur, tin, titanium, vanadium, zinc, zirconium), mucilage, polysaccharides, protein, silicic acid, vitamins (A, B_1 (thiamine), B_2 (riboflavin), C (ascorbic acid), E (alpha-tocopheral), K), and volatile oil.
Historical Uses: Acne, acquired immune deficiency syndrome (AIDS), alopecia, amenorrhea, anemia, arteriosclerosis, arteriostenosis, arthritis, asthma, benign breast disease, bleeding, bruises, bursitis, cancer (bone), cellulite, colds, colitis, constipation, cough, cramps, deficiency (iodine), diabetes, diarrhea, dietary supplementation, digestive complaints, dysmenorrhea, eczema, edema, fever (ephemeral, rheumatic), gallbladder problems, glandular problems, glandular swelling, goiter, gout, headache, heart disease, Hodgkin's disease, human immunodeficiency virus (HIV), hyperlipemia, hypothyroidism, indigestion, infection, inflammation, insufficiency (adrenal, pancreatic), kidney problems, lesions (tubercle), leukemia, liver problems, malnutrition, menopausal/menstrual problems, menorrhagia, mucus, muscle and joint pain, nephritis, nervous conditions, neuritis, orchitis (testicular swelling), poisoning (heavy metal), prostate problems, psoriasis, respiratory conditions, rheumatism, scrofula, sexually transmitted diseases (STDs), skin problems, spleen problems, sprain, syphilis, tuberculosis, tumors, ulcer (duodenal, fistula, gastric, peptic, syphilitic, tuberculous), uterine problems, weight loss, and wrinkles.
Discussion: May alkalize blood chemistry; boost stamina; cause blood vessel dilatation; clear and open bronchial passages; decrease the effect of carcinogens; enhance glandular system and pancreatic system functions; increase the body's ability to burn fat through exercise; improve lipid metabolism; reduce cholesterol levels; promote bowel evacuation, the excretion of heavy metals, and urine flow; protect against absorption of the radioactive substance strontium-90 and protect against heart disease; provide dietary supplementation; reestablish healthy system functions; regulate body temperature; serve as a nutritional adjuvant to therapeutic programs; soften stools; soothe mucous membrane irritation; stimulate the immune system, metabolism, peristalsis, and the thyroid gland; supply all the minerals needed for proper functioning of the human body.
Cautions/Contraindications: Avoid use if pregnant or breast-feeding, or if you have cardiovascular conditions, hyperthyroidism, hypertension, a weak digestive system, or an iodine sensitivity. Avoid harvesting kelp close to shore as industrial pollutants may have contaminated

it. Due to the high rate of iodine, limit kelp consumption to once a week. May interfere with the effectiveness of certain thyroid medications.
Adverse Reactions: Abdominal pain, arrhythmia, diarrhea, edema, fever, hypertrophy (thyroid), iodism (iodine poisoning), nausea, priapism, thirst, and/or vomiting.
Herb/Drug Interactions: This herb could cause an interaction (possibly severe) when taken with the following drugs: Thyroid drugs.
Preparations/Dosage: Crude Herb: 3-12 grams. Decoction: ½-1 cup per day. Extract: 5-10 drops (0.333-0.666 cc.) one to two times per day. Extract (powdered): Average dose in substance 3-10 grains (0.2-0.666 gm.). Tincture: 15-30 drops (1-2 cc.) one to three times per day. Weight Loss* (pill form): 4 grains (0.25 gm.) of powdered extract per pill (may be combined with marshmallow and licorice). Take one pill three times per day before meals. Weight loss should be noticeable within one week.
*If thyroid is functioning normally, kelp may not promote weight loss.
Isolation: Mannitol hexanitrate: Average dose of 15-60 mg. for use as a vasodilator.

Khella (kel lä)
(*Ammi visnaga*)

Synonyms/Related Species: Bishop's Weed and Indian Khella (*ammi majus*).
Family/Class: Umbelliferae (parsley).
Habitat: Argentina, Chile, India, the Mediterranean, and North America.
Flavor: Pungent.
Parts Used: Seeds.
Properties: Antifertilizin, antispasmodic, astringent, expectorant, hemostatic, lithotriptic, sedative, and vasodilator.
Constituents: Flavonoids, khellidine, khellin, khellinine, psoralen, quercetin, and volatile oil.
Historical Uses: Abdominal pain, angina, arteriosclerosis, asthma, bleeding, bronchitis, calculus, cardiovascular conditions, contraceptive (female), diarrhea, dysmenorrhea, gallstones, gastrointestinal problems, kidney stones, psoriasis, respiratory conditions, spasmodic conditions, tachycardia, ulcer (duodenal, gastric, peptic), vitiligo, and whooping cough.
Discussion: May cause blood vessel dilatation; clear and open bronchial passages; dissolve calculi; enhance bladder, cardiovascular system, gallbladder, liver, and lung functions; increase circulation; inhibit postcoital implantation activity (ground seeds); neutralize fertilizin (fertilization); normalize electrocardiogram results; reduce arterial plaque formation; stimulate skin repigmentation in natural sunlight.
Cautions/Contraindications: Avoid use if pregnant or breast-feeding, or if you are taking anticoagulant drugs, or if exposure to strong sunlight is unavoidable. Do not use sun tanning beds or lamps while taking khella as skin sensitivity to ultraviolet light may occur in some individuals. Use a sunblock when outdoors as khella increases the sensitivity of pigment forming cells. Not for long-term use. Use with professional guidance/supervision.
Adverse Reactions: Appetite loss, dizziness, elevated liver enzyme levels in the blood plasma, headache, insomnia, nausea, and/or vomiting.
Herb/Drug Interactions: This herb could cause an interaction (possibly severe) when taken with the following drugs: None known.
Preparations/Dosage: Crude Herb: 3-9 grams. Decoction: ½-1 cup per day. Tincture: 5-30 drops (0.333-2 cc.) one to three times per day.

Kudzu (kood zoo)
(*Pueraria thunbergiana*)

Synonyms/Related Species: Bidari Kand, Gaogen, Koken, Kuzu Root, and Pueraria Root.
Family/Class: Leguminosae (legume).
Habitat: Asia, Japan, and the United States.
Flavor: Sweet/pungent.
Parts Used: Root.
Properties: Abortifacient, anticarcinogen, antifertilizin, antiphlogistic, antispasmodic, antiviral, carminative, demulcent, diaphoretic, hypotensive, nutritive, tonic, and vasodilator.
Constituents: Inulin (starch), flavones, minerals (calcium), and phytoestrogen.
Historical Uses: Addiction (alcohol), angina, auditory problems, benign breast disease, cancer (breast, uterine), cardiovascular conditions, colds, contraceptive (female), diabetes, diarrhea, dietary supplementation, edema, fever (ephemeral, herpetic), flavoring agent, gastrointestinal problems, glaucoma, headache, herpes, hypertension (mild/moderate), hypoglycemia, infection (viral), inflammation, influenza, Lyme disease, malnutrition, muscle and joint pain, neurological condition, pain, palsy (Bell's), sexually transmitted diseases (STDs), spasmodic conditions, and substitute for arrowroot.
Discussion: May aid digestion; cause blood vessel dilatation; curb alcohol consumption; decrease the effect of carcinogens; enhance lung and stomach functions; increase circulation; induce abortion; inhibit postcoital implantation activity; neutralize fertilizin (fertilization); promote perspiration; provide dietary supplementation; reduce blood pressure levels; replenish body fluids; restore normal tone to tissues; serve as a nutritional adjuvant to therapeutic programs, and as a thickening agent for soup, gravy, or beverage (starch); soothe mucous membrane irritation; stimulate uterine contractions.
Cautions/Contraindications: Avoid use if pregnant or breast-feeding, or if you have an estrogen dependant cancer, or if you have a history of estrogen dependant cancers. Estrogen containing substances may contribute to abnormal blood clotting, migraine, and could promote the developement of certain types of estrogen dependant cancers.
Adverse Reactions: Nausea and/or vomiting.
Herb/Drug Interactions: This herb could cause an interaction (possibly severe) when taken with the following drugs: Antibiotic drugs, Hormones and Synthetic Substitutes (i.e. conjugated estrogens, contraceptives (oral, etc.), and other hormonal replacement therapy (HRT).
Preparations/Dosage: Crude Herb: 3-12 grams. Thickening Agent (root starch/powdered): Dissolve 1-2 tablespoons in two to four tablespoons cold water. Shake well.

Lady's Mantle (lā dēz man tel)
(*Alchemilla vulgaris*)

Synonyms/Related Species: Alkemelych, Bear's Foot, Common Lady's Mantle, Field Lady's Mantle (*alchemilla arvensis*), Frauenmantle, Leontopodium, Lion's Foot, Mountain Lady's Mantle (*alchemilla alpine*), Nine Hooks, Parsley Piert, Pied-de-Lion, Silver Lady's Mantle, and Stellaria.
Family/Class: Rosaceae (rose).
Habitat: Africa, Alaska, the Alpine and Subalpine zones, Asia, Britain, Europe, Greenland, the Himalayas, Iceland, the Mediterranean, North America, Siberia, and Sweden.
Flavor: Bitter.

Parts Used: Leaves.
Properties: Antiphlogistic, astringent, hemostatic, lithotriptic, tonic, and vulnerary.
Constituents: Bitter principles, flavonoids, glycosides, salicylic acid, and tannic acid.
Historical Uses: Abdominal pain, appetite loss, bleeding, bruises, calculus, congestion (uterine, vaginal), diarrhea, dysmenorrhea, eczema, enteritis, fever (ephemeral, rheumatic), flatulence, gallstones, gargle/mouth rinse, gastrointestinal problems, inflammation, kidney stones, leukorrhea, menopausal/menstrual problems, menorrhagia, muscle and joint pain, rash, rheumatism, sores, tumors, ulcer (duodenal, gastric, peptic), urinary problems, vaginitis, vomiting, and wounds (minor).
Discussion: May disolve calculi; enhance kidney and spleen functions; restore normal tone to tissues; speed healing.
Cautions/Contraindications: Avoid use if pregnant or breast-feeding.
Adverse Reactions: Nausea and/or vomiting.
Herb/Drug Interactions: This herb could cause an interaction (possibly severe) when taken with the following drugs: None known.
Preparations/Dosage: Crude Herb: 3-6 grams. Decoction: ½-1 cup per day. Infusion: 1-1½ cups per day. Tincture: 10-30 drops (0.666-2 cc.) one to three times per day.

Lady's Slipper (lā dēz slip er)
(*Cypripedium calceolus*)

Synonyms/Related Species: American Valerian (*cypripedium pubescens*), Bleeding Heart, Cypripedium, Moccasin Flower, Mountain Lady's Slipper (*cypripedium montanum*), Nerve Root, Noah's Ark, Showy Lady-Slipper, Slipper Root, Sparrow's Egg Lady's Slipper (*cypripedium passerinum*), Venus Shoe, Yellow Lady's Slipper (*cypripedium parviflorum*), and Yellow Moccasin Flower.
Family/Class: Orchidaceae (orchid).
Floral Emblem: Minnesota.
Habitat: Alaska, Europe, and North America.
Flavor: Bitter.
Parts Used: Root.
Properties: Antispasmodic, astringent, carminative, diaphoretic, febrifuge, hemostatic, nervine, sedative, and tonic.
Constituents: Cypripedin, gallic acid, phenanthrene, resin, tannic acid, vitamins (B_1 (thiamine), B_2 (riboflavin), B_3 (niacin), B_5 (pantothenic acid), B_6 (pyridoxine), B_{12}, B_x (para-aminobenzoic acid (PABA), H (biotin), inositol, M (folic acid), and volatile oil.
Historical Uses: Abdominal pain, anxiety, arrhythmia, bleeding, chorea, colic, cramps, cystic fibrosis, depression (mild/moderate), diarrhea, digestive complaints, epilepsy, exhaustion, fever (ephemeral, enteric), gastritis, gastrointestinal problems, headache, hysteria, indigestion, insomnia, irritable bowel syndrome (IBS), menorrhagia, menstrual problems, nervous conditions, neuralgia, neurosis, pruritus, restlessness, spasmodic conditions, tremors, typhoid, and ulcer (bouveret).
Discussion: May aid digestion; calm the nervous system; enhance cardiovascular and liver functions; normalize breathing and saliva flow; promote perspiration; restore normal tone to tissues.

Cautions/Contraindications: Avoid use if pregnant or breast-feeding. May cause dermatitis susceptible individuals. Not for long-term use. Use with professional guidance/supervision.
Adverse Reactions: Confusion, headache, nausea, and/or vomiting.
Herb/Drug Interactions: This herb could cause an interaction (possibly severe) when taken with the following drugs: None known.
Preparations/Dosage: Crude Herb: 3-6 grams. Decoction: 1 cup per day. Extract: 3-8 drops (0.2-0.5 cc.). Extract (solid): Average dose in substance 5-10 grains (0.324-0.666 gm.). Root (powdered): Average dose in substance 30-60 grains (2-4 gm.). Tincture: 10-30 drops (0.666-2 cc.) one to three times per day.
Isolation: Cypripedin: Average dose of ½-3 grains (0.032-0.19 gm.) for use as an antispasmodic, nervine, and sedative.

Lamb's Quarters (lamz kwôr terz)

(*Chenopodium album*)

Synonyms/Related Species: Baconweed, Dirtweed, Midden Myles, Mutton Tops, Pigweed, White Goosefoot and White Pigweed.
Family/Class: Chenopodiaceae (goosefoot).
Habitat: England, Europe, and North America.
Flavor: Sweet/sour.
Parts Used: Leaves, seeds.
Properties: Anthelmintic, antiscorbutic, antispasmodic, emmenagogue, nutritive, and vermifuge.
Constituents: Minerals (calcium, iron, phosphorus), oxalic acid, and vitamins (A, B_2 (riboflavin), B_3 (niacin), C (ascorbic acid).
Historical Uses: Ancylostomiasis, colic, conjunctivitis, dietary supplementation, eyewash, food source, headache, hysteria, malnutrition, menopausal/menstrual problems, nervous conditions, parasites (hookworm, roundworm), scurvy, sores, spasmodic conditions, stroke (apoplectic, heat), substitute for spinach (leaves), vertigo, and wounds (minor).
Discussion: May provide dietary supplementation; relieve heat from over exposure to sun; serve as a nutritional adjuvant to therapeutic programs; stimulate menstruation.
Cautions/Contraindications: Avoid use if pregnant or breast-feeding. Not for long-term use.
Adverse Reactions: Oxalism, nausea, and/or vomiting.
Herb/Drug Interactions: This herb could cause an interaction (possibly severe) when taken with the following drugs: None known.
Preparations/Dosage: Crude Herb (leaves): 3-6 grams. Leaves (fresh): Boiled and eaten as a vegetable. Seeds (dried/ground): Used as flour in baking. The flour resembles in clor and tastes like buckwheat. Seeds are equally nutritious when eaten raw.
Did You Know? Each plant produces over 70,000 seeds, thus ensuring its propagation.

Larch (lärch)

(*Larix decidua*)

Synonyms/Related Species: American Larch (*larix americana*), Black Larch, Common Larch, Eastern Larch (*larix laricina*), European Larch (*larix europaea*), Hackmatack, Larix, Meleze, Mountain Larch, Pinus Pendula, Subalpine Larch (*larix lyallii*), Tamarack, Venice Turpentine, and Western Larch (*larix occidentalis*).
Family/Class: Pinaceae (pine).

Alaska, the Alpine and Subalpine zones, Europe, North America, and the Yukon y.

r: Bitter.

.s Used: Bark (inner), leaves, resin (turpentine).

operties: Alterative, antibiotic, anticarcinogen, antifungal, antiphlogistic, antiviral, astringent, .iuretic, expectorant, laxative, stimulant, teniacide, teniafuge, tonic, and vulnerary.

Constituents: Fiber, laricinolic acid, larinolic acid, larixin (laricic acid), pinene, polysaccharide, tannic acid, and volatile oil.

Historical Uses: Amenorrhea, appetite loss, arthritis, bronchitis, bruises, burns (minor), cancer (colon), candida, colds, cough, cystitis, diarrhea, dysentery, eczema, fever (ephemeral, rheumatic), gangrene, gastrointestinal problems, hemoptysis, hemorrhage, hemorrhoids, infection (bacterial, fungal, viral), inflammation, influenza, jaundice, lesions (tubercle), menorrhagia, moniliasis, mucus, muscle and joint pain, nausea, neuralgia, parasites (tapeworm), poisoning (cyanide, opium), psoriasis, respiratory conditions, rheumatism, scrofula, skin problems, sore throat, sores, tuberculosis, tumors, ulcer (duodenal, fistula, gastric, peptic, tuberculous), and wounds (minor).

Discussion: May aid digestion; cleanse the intestinal system; decrease the effect of carcinogens; increase white blood cell counts and the growth of friendly bacteria in the colon; inhibit development and growth of microorganisms; promote bowel evacuation and urine flow; reduce cholesterol levels as well as the generation and absorption of fecal ammonia; reestablish healthy system functions; restore normal tone to tissues; serve as an antidote for cyanide or opium poisoning; speed healing; stimulate appetite, the immune system, and peristalsis.

Cautions/Contraindications: Avoid use if pregnant or breast-feeding. May cause dermatitis in susceptible individuals.

Adverse Reactions: Hematuria (blood in the urine), inflammation of the airway passages, nausea, and/or vomiting.

Herb/Drug Interactions: This herb could cause an interaction (possibly severe) when taken with the following drugs: None known.

Preparations/Dosage: Crude Herb: 3-6 grams. Decoction (bark): ¼-½ cup per day. Infusion (leaves): ½-1 cup per day. Venice Turpentine (resin/diluted): 5-8 drops (0.333-0.5 cc.) mixed with honey per day. Tincture: 10-30 drops (0.66-2 cc.) one to three times per day. External Uses: Compress: Soak cloth in hot water, wring out and moisten with a small amount of resin. Apply to affected area for 20-30 minutes once per day. Resin (diluted): Apply small amounts to affected area.

Larkspur (lärk spûr)

(*Delphinium consolida*)

Synonyms/Related Species: Arizona Larkspur (*delphinium amabile*), Branching Larkspur, Delphinium, European Larkspur (*delphinium ajacis*), Field Larkspur, Knight's Spur, Lousewort, Low Larkspur (*delphinium bicolor*), Mountain Larkspur (*delphinium occidentale*), Nelson's Larkspur (*delphinium nuttallianum*), Scarlet Larkspur, Staggerweed, Stavesacre (*delphinium staphisagria*), Subalpine Larkspur (*delphinium barbeyi*), Tall Larkspur, and Western Larkspur (*delphinium glaucum*).

Family/Class: Ranunculacea (buttercup).

Habitat: Alaska, the Alpine and Subalpine zones, Asia, Europe, France, Greece, Italy, and North America.

Flavor: Bitter/pungent.
Parts Used: Seeds (dried/ripe).
Properties: Antiphlogistic, diuretic, emmenagogue, laxative, narcotic, parasiticide, and sedative.
Constituents: Aconitine, ajacine, ajaconine, alkaloids, delphinine (delphine), delphinoidine, delphisine, protoanemonin, and staphisagrine.
Historical Uses: Asthma, edema, fever (ephemeral, rheumatic), hemorrhoids, inflammation, muscle and joint pain, neuralgia, pain, paralysis, parasites (crabs and their nits, lice and their nits, ringworm, scabies), and rheumatism.
Discussion: May promote bowel evacuation and urine flow; stimulate menstruation and peristalsis.
Cautions/Contraindications: Avoid use if pregnant or breast-feeding. Do not apply to skin that is irritated, raw, or has open sores. May cause dermatitis in susceptible individuals. May cause numbness and prickling of the fingers when harvesting. Not for long-term use. Use with professional guidance/supervision.
Adverse Reactions: Arrhythmia, asphyxiation, confusion, convulsions, depression, diarrhea, gastrointestinal problems, kidney damage, kidney failure, labored breathing, lethargy, nausea, nervousness, numbness and tingling of the mouth and throat, salivation, staggering, stomach and muscle cramps (severe), stupor, visual disturbances, vomiting, and/or possible death.
Herb/Drug Interactions: This herb could cause an interaction (possibly severe) when taken with the following drugs: None known.
Preparations/Dosage: External uses only: Seeds (powdered): 2-3 grains (0.133-0.2 gm.). Tincture: 1-10 drops (0.066-0.66 cc.) diluted in water.
Isolation: Delphinine: Average dose of $^{1}/_{64}$-¾ grain (0.001- 0.05 gm.) for external use as an analgesic.

Laurel, California (lôr el, kal e·fôrn ye)

(*Umbellularia californica*)

Synonyms/Related Species: California Bay, California Pepper Tree, California Spice-Tree, Pepperwood Tree, and Spice-Tree.
Family/Class: Lauraceae (laurel).
Habitat: The United States.
Flavor: Bitter.
Parts Used: Leaves.
Properties: Analgesic, antiphlogistic, counterirritant, expectorant, insect repellent, nutritive, parasiticide, and stimulant.
Constituents: Fatty acids (oleic, palmitic, stearic), fixed oils (olein, palmitin, stearin), safrol, umbellulone, and volatile oil.
Historical Uses: Abdominal pain, colds, colic, congestion (lung), diarrhea, dietary supplementation, dysmenorrhea, fainting, fever (ephemeral, rheumatic), fleas, gastroenteritis, headache, inflammation, malnutrition, meningitis, mucus, muscle and joint pain, neuralgia, pain, parasites (lice and their nits), poison ivy/oak, respiratory conditions, rheumatism, sore throat, sores, stomachache, and substitute for bay leaves.
Discussion: May clear and open bronchial passages; induce localized irritation; provide dietary supplementation; repel insects; serve as a nutritional adjuvant to therapeutic programs.
Cautions/Contraindications: Avoid use if pregnant or breast-feeding. Not for long-term use.

Adverse Reactions: Headache, liver damage (often characterized by jaundice), nausea, and/or vomiting.
Herb/Drug Interactions: This herb could cause an interaction (possibly severe) when taken with the following drugs: None known.
Preparations/Dosage: Crude Herb: 3-6 grams. Infusion: ½ cup per day. Leaves (powdered): Average dose in substance 10-15 grains (0.666-0.98 gm.). Tincture: 10-30 drops (0.66-2 cc.) one to three times per day.
Isolation: Safrol: Average dose of 20-30 drops (1.333-2 cc.) for use as an analgesic.

Laurel, Mountain (lôr'el, moun'ten)
(*Kalmia latifolia*)

Synonyms/Related Species: Bog Laurel (*kalmia polifolia*), Broad-Leaved Laurel, Calicobush, Cistus Chamaerhodendros, Glossy Bog Laurel (*kalmia polifolia*), Kalmia, Lambkill, Mountain Ivy, Narrow-Leaved Laurel, Purple Laurel, Rose Laurel, Sheep Laurel (*kalmia angustifolia*), Small Bog Laurel (*kalmia microphylla*), Spoonwood, and Swamp Laurel (*kalmia glauca*).
Family/Class: Ericaceae (heath).
Floral Emblem: Connecticut and Pennsylvania.
Habitat: Alaska, the Alpine and Subalpine zones, the Appalachians, and North America.
Flavor: Bitter.
Parts Used: Leaves.
Properties: Antiphlogistic, aromatic, astringent, demulcent, diuretic, emetic, hemostatic, hypnotic, lachrymator, narcotic, sedative, sialagogue, and urinary antiseptic.
Constituents: Alkaloids, andromedotoxin, arbutin, albumin (albumen), bitter principle, chlorophyll, glycosides, gum, minerals (calcium, iron), monosaccharides, tannic acid, and wax.
Historical Uses: Bleeding, diarrhea, fever (ephemeral, rheumatic), hemorrhage, inflammation, insomnia, jaundice, liver problems, muscle and joint pain, neuralgia, pain, rheumatism, sexually transmitted diseases (STDs), skin problems, syphilis, and ulcer (syphilitic).
Discussion: May inhibit the respiratory center; induce sleep; promote saliva excretion; soothe mucous membrane irritation.
Cautions/Contraindications: Avoid use if pregnant or breast-feeding. Not for long-term use. Use with professional guidance/supervision.
Adverse Reactions: Convulsions, diarrhea, salivation (excessive), eye irritation and tearing, headache, nausea, paralysis, respiratory distress, stupor, vomiting, and/or possible death.
Herb/Drug Interactions: This herb could cause an interaction (possibly severe) when taken with the following drugs: None known.
Preparations/Dosage: Crude Herb: 1-3 grams. Infusion: ½ tablespoon one to three times per day. Leaves (powdered): Average dose in substance 5-10 grains (0.324-0.666 gm.). Tincture: 2-5 drops (0.2-0.333 cc.) one to three times per day.
Isolation: Arbutin: Average dose of 5-15 grains (0.3-1 gm.) used as a diuretic and urinary antiseptic.

Lavender (lav en·der)
(*Lavandula officinalis*)

Synonyms/Related Species: Dwarf Lavender, English Lavender (*lavendula vera*), French Lavender (*lavendula stoechas*), Garden Lavender, Narrow-Leaved Lavender, Spike Lavender (*lavendula spica*), True Lavender, and White Lavender.
Family/Class: Labiatae (mint).
Habitat: The Alps, Arabia, England, Europe, France, Italy, the Mediterranean, Norway, Portugal, and Spain.
Flavor: Pungent/bitter.
Parts Used: Flower, leaves.
Properties: Antibiotic, antidepressant, antifungal, antihistamine, antiperiodic, antiphlogistic, antispasmodic, aromatic, carminative, counterirritant, diuretic, expectorant, insect repellent, malariacidal, nervine, sedative, stimulant, stomachic, tonic, and vermifuge.
Constituents: Borneol, cadinene, caffeic acid, camphor, carvene (limonene), coumarin, eucalyptol (cineol), flavonoids, geraniol (rhodinol), linalool, linalyl acetate, pinene, tannic acid, umbelliferone, and volatile oil.
Historical Uses: Acne, ague, allergy, anxiety, asthma, bronchitis, burns (minor), candida, colds, congestion (uterine, vaginal), cough, debility, depression (mild/moderate), digestive complaints, diphtheria, dizziness, eczema, exhaustion, fainting, fatigue, fever (ephemeral, enteric, intermittent), flatulence, gastrointestinal problems, headache, hysteria, indigestion, infection (bacterial, fungal), inflammation, insect bites or stings, insomnia, insufficiency (circulatory), irritable bowel syndrome (IBS), laryngitis, leukorrhea, malaria, memory/cognitive problems, migraine, moniliasis, moths, mucus, muscle and joint pain, nausea, nervous conditions, parasites (malarial plasmodia), perfume, pneumonia, potpourri, psoriasis, respiratory conditions, sachets, sore throat, spasmodic conditions, strep throat, toothache, typhoid, ulcer (bouveret, duodenal, gastric, peptic, syriac), urethritis, vaginitis, vomiting, and wounds (minor).
Discussion: May aid digestion; calm the nervous system; clear and open bronchial passages; counteract the effect of histamine; enhance nervous system and stomach functions; improve memory and cognition; increase pain threshold; inhibit or destroy development and growth of bacteria and other microorganisms; promote urine flow; restore normal tone to tissues; stimulate peristalsis.
Cautions/Contraindications: Avoid use if pregnant or breast-feeding, or if you have gallstones or an obstruction (biliary).
Adverse Reactions: Headache, nausea, respiratory passage irritation, and/or vomiting.
Herb/Drug Interactions: This herb could cause an interaction (possibly severe) when taken with the following drugs: None known.
Preparations/Dosage: Crude Herb: 3-9 grams. Infusion (flowers and/or leaves): ½-1 cup per day. Oil of Lavender Flowers (*oleum lavandulae florum*): 1-3 drops (0.06-0.2 cc.) in water or on a sugarcube. Tincture: 10-30 drops (0.666-2 cc.) one to three times per day.
Isolation: Eucalyptol: 5 drops (0.3 cc.) in atomization or inhalation therapy for use in respiratory conditions.
Did You Know? Sixty pounds of lavender flowers will yield approximately sixteen ounces of oil.

Lemon (lem en)
(*Citrus limonum*)

Synonyms/Related Species: Common Lemon, Java Lemon (*citrus javanica*), Laimūn, Limon, Neemoo, Pearl Lemon (*citrus margarita*), and Sweet Lemon (*citrus lumia*).
Family/Class: Rutaceae (rue).
Habitat: Asia, India, Italy, Java, the Mediterranean, and the United States (primarily California and Florida).
Flavor: Sour.
Parts Used: Fruit (pulp), peel/rind.
Properties: Anticarcinogen, antioxidant, antiperiodic, antiphlogistic, antiscorbutic, aromatic, astringent, carminative, counterirritant, diaphoretic, diuretic, hemostatic, malariacidal, stimulant, and tonic.
Constituents: Carvene (limonene), citral (geranial), citric acid, citrin, citronellal, coumarin, fiber, flavonoids, geraniol (rhodinol), gum, hesperidin, linalyl acetate, methyl anthranilate (methyl orthoaminobenzoate), monosaccharides, nutritive, resin, rutin, terpene, vitamin C (ascorbic acid), and volatile oil.
Historical Uses: Ague, appetite loss, arrhythmia, arthritis, beverage (juice), bleeding, cancer, colds, confectionary, dietary supplementation, fever (ephemeral, enteric, intermittent, rheumatic), flavoring agent, gargle/mouth rinse, hemorrhage, hepatitis, hiccups, indigestion, inflammation, influenza, jaundice, kidney stones, malaria, malnutrition, muscle and joint pain, nausea, parasites (malarial plasmodia), poisoning (narcotic), pruritus, rheumatism, scurvy, substitute for quinine, sunburn, thirst, tumors, typhoid, ulcer (bouveret), wounds (minor).
Discussion: May aid digestion; decrease the effect of carcinogens; inhibit oxidation; prevent hemorrhage in persons with hypertension; promote perspiration and urine flow; provide dietary supplementation; reduce capillary fragility and cholesterol levels; restore normal tone to tissues; serve as a nutritional adjuvant to therapeutic programs; stimulate appetite and gastric secretions; strengthen blood vessels, capillaries, and connective tissues.
Cautions/Contraindications: Avoid use if pregnant or breast-feeding, or if you have ulcer (peptic, gastric). Allergic reactions may occur in young children when first introducing them to citrus juices.
Adverse Reactions: Mouth and throat irritation, nausea, and/or vomiting.
Herb/Drug Interactions: This herb could cause an interaction (possibly severe) when taken with the following drugs: Antimalarial drugs.
Preparations/Dosage: Crude Herb (peel): 3-9 grams. Fruit (pulp): May be ingested freely. Juice (fresh): 4-6 ounces straight or diluted with water. Oil of Lemon (*oleum limonis*): 3-5 drops (0.2-0.333 cc.) in water or on a sugarcube. Tincture: 5-30 drops (0.333-2 cc.) one to three times per day.

Lemon Balm (lem en bäm)
(*Melissa officinalis*)

Synonyms/Related Species: Balm, Balm Mint, Bee Balm, Blue Balm, Garden Balm, Honey Plant, Melissa, Sweet Balm, and Sweet Mary.
Family/Class: Labiatae (mint).
Habitat: Asia, the Mediterranean, and the United States.

Flavor: Sour/pungent.
Parts Used: Flowering tops, leaves.
Properties: Analgesic, anesthetic (local), antibiotic, antihistamine, antispasmodic, antiviral, carminative, diaphoretic, emmenagogue, febrifuge, hypotensive, nervine, sedative, stimulant, stomachic, and vasodilator.
Constituents: Acids, caffeic acid, citral (geranial), citronellal, eugenol (eugenic acid), flavonoids, geraniol (rhodinol), glycosides, linalool, tannic acid, ursone (ursolic acid), and volatile oil.
Historical Uses: Amenorrhea, anxiety, arrhythmia, arthritis, asthma, attention deficit disorder (ADD), bronchitis, cardiovascular conditions, colds, colic, cramps, debility, depression (mild/moderate), digestive complaints, dizziness, dysmenorrhea, fainting, fatigue, fever (ephemeral, herpetic), flatulence, gastrointestinal problems, gout, headache, herpes, hypertension (mild/moderate), hyperthyroidism, hysteria, indigestion, infection (bacterial, viral), influenza, irritable bowel syndrome (IBS), insect bites or stings, insomnia, mastitis, melancholy, menopausal/menstrual problems, migraine, mumps, mucus, muscle and joint pain, nausea, nervous conditions, neuralgia, pain, respiratory conditions, sachets, sexually transmitted diseases (STDs), skin problems, sores, spasmodic conditions, toothache, tumors, vomiting, and wounds (minor).
Discussion: May aid digestion; calm the nervous system; cause blood vessel dilatation; counteract the effect of histamine; enhance liver, lung, and stomach functions; inhibit development or destroy growth of bacteria and other microorganisms; promote perspiration; reduce blood pressure levels; stimulate menstruation.
Cautions/Contraindications: Avoid use if pregnant or breast-feeding, or if you have glaucoma or a thyroid problem. May increase the sedative effect of barbiturates. May interfere with thyroid medications.
Adverse Reactions: Diarrhea, nausea, and/or vomiting.
Herb/Drug Interactions: This herb could cause an interaction (possibly severe) when taken with the following drugs: Amphetamine drugs, Anxiolytic drugs, Hypotensive drugs, and Thyroid Drugs.
Preparations/Dosage: Crude Herb: 1-6 grams. Infusion: 1 cup per day. Leaves/Flowering Tops (powdered): Average dose in substance 10-20 grains (0.666-1.333 gm.). Tincture: 10-30 drops (0.666-2 cc.) one to three times per day.

Lemon Grass (le men·gräs)

(*Andropogon nardus*)

Synonyms/Related Species: Citronella, Cus-Cus, Indian Grass, Khus-Khus (*andropogon zizanioides*), and Vetiver.
Family/Class: Graminaceae (grass).
Habitat: Asia, Australia, Central America, India, and South America.
Flavor: Sour.
Parts Used: Leaves (from lemon grass), root (from khus-khus).
Properties: Aromatic, astringent, carminative, febrifuge, hemostatic, hypotensive, insect repellent, nervine, sedative, stimulant, tonic, and vasodilator.
Constituents: Citral (geranial), citronellal, citronellol, geraniol (rhodinol), myrcene, terpenes, vitamins (A, C (ascorbic acid), and volatile oil.

Historical Uses: Abscess, amenorrhea, bladder problems, bleeding, colds, colic, cramps, digestive complaints, dizziness, fever (ephemeral), flatulence, flavoring agent, headache, hypertension (mild/moderate), indigestion, infection (bacterial), influenza, insect bites or stings, kidney problems, liver problems, mosquitos, mucous membrane problems, nausea, nervous conditions, potpourri, sachets, spleen problems, and vomiting.
Discussion: May aid digestion; calm the nervous system; cause blood vessel dilatation; reduce blood pressure levels; restore normal tone to tissues; stimulate menstruation.
Cautions/Contraindications: Avoid use if pregnant or breast-feeding. Do not confuse this plant with lemon verbena (*aloysia triphylla*).
Adverse Reactions: Mucous membrane irritation, nausea, and/or vomiting.
Herb/Drug Interactions: This herb could cause an interaction (possibly severe) when taken with the following drugs: Hypotensive drugs.
Preparations/Dosage: External uses only.

Lemon Verbena (le men ver·bē ne)
(*Aloysia triphylla*)

Synonyms/Related Species: Herb Louisa, Verbena, and Verveine.
Family/Class: Verbenaceae (verbena).
Habitat: Algeria, Europe, Israel, Morocco, and South America.
Flavor: Sour/bitter.
Parts Used: Leaves.
Properties: Antispasmatic, carminative, febrifuge, sedative, and stomachic.
Constituents: Flavones, flavonoids, geraniol (rhodinol), glycosides, monosaccharides, and volatile oil.
Historical Uses: Chills, colic, constipation, digestive complaints, fever (ephemeral), flatulence, gastrointestinal problems, hemorrhoids, indigestion, insomnia, insufficiency (circulatory, venous), skin problems, spasmodic conditions, ulcer (stasis, varicose), and varicose veins.
Discussion: May aid digestion; enhance stomach function.
Cautions/Contraindications: Avoid use if pregnant or breast-feeding. Do not confuse this plant with lemon grass (*andropogon nardus*).
Adverse Reactions: Mucous membrane irritation, nausea, and/or vomiting.
Herb/Drug Interactions: This herb could cause an interaction (possibly severe) when taken with the following drugs: None known.
Preparations/Dosage: Decoction (leaves): 3-4 tablespoons one to two times per day. Leaves (powdered): Average dose in substance 5-15 grains (0.324-1 gm.). Leaves (fresh): Fruits, salads, jellies, custards, and as a garnish in hot or iced drinks (i.e. iced or hot tea).

Lettuce (let is)
(*Lactuca sativa*)

Synonyms/Related Species: Acrid Lettuce, Bitter Lettuce, Blue Lettuce (*lactuca tatarica*), Garden Lettuce, Horseweed Lettuce (*lactuca canadensis*), Lactuca, Poison Lettuce, Prickly Lettuce (*lactuca serriola*), Strong-Scented Lettuce, Tall Blue Lettuce (*lactuca biennis*), and Wild Lettuce (*lactuca virosa*).
Family/Class: Compositae (composite).

Habitat: Austria, Britain, Europe, France, Germany, North America, Scotland, and the Yukon Territory.
Flavor: Bitter.
Parts Used: Leaves, Juice (dried).
Properties: Analgesic, antifungal, antispasmodic, astringent, carminative, diuretic, hemostatic, hypnotic, narcotic, sedative, and vasodilator.
Constituents: Caoutchouc, iron, lactucarium, lactucerin, lactucic acid, lactupicrin, lactucin, mannitol (mannite), nitrates, sesquiterpene lactones, triterpenes, vitamins (A, B_1 (thiamine), B_2 (riboflavin), C (ascorbic acid), and volatile oil.
Historical Uses: Angina, anxiety, arteriosclerosis, asthma, bleeding, bronchitis, candida, colic, cough, cramps, diarrhea, digestive complaints, dry skin, edema, gastritis, herbal tobacco, indigestion, infection (fungal, urinary tract), insomnia, irritable bowel syndrome (IBS), moniliasis, muscle and joint pain, nausea, nervous conditions, pain, poison ivy/oak, respiratory conditions, restlessness, spasmodic conditions, sunburn, and whooping cough.
Discussion: May aid digestion; cause blood vessel dilatation; induce sleep; promote urine flow.
Cautions/Contraindications: Avoid use if pregnant or breast-feeding. May cause dermatitis in susceptible individuals. Not for long-term use. Use with professional guidance/supervision.
Adverse Reactions: Accelerated respiration, dilated pupils, dizziness, dyspnea, emphysema, excitability, headache, lactucism (poisoning by lactuca), lung tissue damage, nausea, perspiration, tachycardia, tinnitus, visual disturbances, and/or vomiting.
Herb/Drug Interactions: This herb could cause an interaction (possibly severe) when taken with the following drugs: None known.
Preparations/Dosage: Extract (solid): Average dose in substance 1-5 grains (0.066-0.333 gm.). Infusion (leaves): ½-2 cups per day. Leaves: Boiled and eaten as a vegetable. Juice (dried/powdered): Average dose in substance 10-20 grains (0.666-1.333 gm.). Syrup: ½-1 teaspoon in water. Tincture: 5-30 drops (0.333-2 cc.) one to three times per day. Herbal Smoke: Leaves and/or Root: 1 ounce smoked in a waterpipe. Juice (dried): ½-1 gram (pea-sized ball) smoked in a waterpipe or put it on the end of a pin, and holding it over a flame, inhale the smoke. Juice No Heat Extraction: Cut the flower heads off the plant, gather the milky-colored juice that drains out, and let it air dry. Repeat this process over a two-week period by cutting a little off the top each time. Juice Heat Extraction: Heat (do not boil) the leaves in water for eight hours. Strain the liquid into a bowl. Place a heat lamp over the bowl of liquid, and using a fan, drive the water out of the extraction. The result will be a blackish gummy resin. Scrape the gummy resin from the bottom of the bowl, roll it into small pea-sized balls, and put them in a plastic bag to prevent them from drying out.
Isolation: Lactucarium: Average dose of 8-15 grains (0.5-1 gm.) for use as a mild hypnotic and sedative. Lactucin: Average dose of 1-5 grains (0.066-0.333 gm) for use as a sedative. Mannitol hexanitrate: Average dose of 15-60 mg. for use as a vasodilator.

Lichen, Icelandmoss (lī ken, īs lend môs)
(*Cetraria ericetorum*)

Synonyms/Related Species: Iceland Lichen.
Family/Class: Lichenes (leaf lichen).
Habitat: The Alpine zone, the Arctic, Boreal, and Britain.
Flavor: Sweet.

Parts Used: Thallus.
Properties: Antibiotic, antiemetic, antiphlogistic, demulcent, expectorant, nutritive, stimulant, and tonic.
Constituents: Cetrarin (cetraric acid), fatty acids (arachidonic, linoleic, linolenic), fumaric acid, lichenin, minerals (calcium, iodine, phosphorus, potassium, sodium, sulfur), monosaccharides, mucilage, oxalic acid, polysaccharides, usnic acid, and vitamins (A, D, E (alpha-tocopheral), K).
Historical Uses: Abscess, anemia, appetite loss, bladder problems, bronchitis, cardiovascular conditions, colds, cough, diarrhea, dietary supplementation, digestive complaints, dysentery, emaciation, fever, gastritis, gastroenteritis, indigestion, infection (bacterial), inflammation, kidney problems, laryngitis, lesions (tubercle), lung problems, malnutrition, mucous membrane irritation, mucus, nausea, respiratory conditions, scrofula, sore throat, survival food, tuberculosis, ulcer (fistula, tuberculous), vomiting, and wounds (minor).
Discussion: May clear and open bronchial passages; enhance lung and stomach functions; inhibit or destroy development and growth of bacteria and other microorganisms; provide dietary supplementation; restore normal tone to tissues; serve as a nutritional adjuvant to therapeutic programs; soothe mucous membrane irritation; stimulate appetite, gastric secretions, and peristalsis.
Cautions/Contraindications: Avoid use if pregnant or breast-feeding, or if you have an iodine sensitivity. May interfere with the effectiveness of certain thyroid medications.
Adverse Reactions: Abdominal pain, arrhythmia, diarrhea, edema, fever, hypertrophy (thyroid), iodism (iodine poisoning), nausea, oxalism (oxalic acid or oxalate poisoning), priapism, thirst, and/or vomiting.
Herb/Drug Interactions: This herb could cause an interaction (possibly severe) when taken with the following drugs: Thyroid drugs.
Preparations/Dosage: Crude Herb: 6-12 grams. Decoction: 1-2 cups per day.
Isolation: Cetrarin: Average dose of 1½-3 grains (0.099-0.2 gm.) for use as a stimulant.

Lichen, Usnea (lī ken, us nē·ah)
(*Usnea hirta*)

Synonyms/Related Species: Beard Moss, Bristly Moss, Large Usnea (*usnea barbata*), Old Man's Beard, Pitted Beard (*usnea cavernosa*), Powdered Beard (*usnea lapponica*), Rough Moss, Sugary Beard, and Usnea.
Family/Class: Lichenes (hair lichen).
Habitat: North America.
Flavor: Bitter/sweet.
Parts Used: Lichen.
Properties: Alterative, antibiotic, antifungal, demulcent, parasiticide, stimulant, and vermifuge.
Constituents: Barbatic acid, cetraric acid (cetrarin), diffractaic acid, evernic acid, lobaric acid, mucilage, stictininc acid, thamnolic acid, and usnic acid.
Historical Uses: Bronchitis, gastrointestinal problems, impetigo, infection (bacterial, bladder, fungal, urinary tract, viral), inflammation, lesions (tubercle), parasites (trichomonas), pleurisy, respiratory conditions, scrofula, tuberculosis, ulcer (fistula, tuberculous), urinary problems, and wounds (minor).
Discussion: May enhance lung function; inhibit development or destroy growth of bacteria and other microorganisms; reduce both the rate of growth and the rate of reproduction of

trichomonas; reestablish healthy system functions; soothe mucous membrane irritation; stimulate gastric secretions and peristalsis.
Cautions/Contraindications: Avoid use if pregnant or breast-feeding.
Adverse Reactions: Nausea and/or vomiting.
Herb/Drug Interactions: This herb could cause an interaction (possibly severe) when taken with the following drugs: None known.
Preparations/Dosage: Crude Herb: 3-6 grams. Tincture: 5-15 drops (0.333-1 cc.) one to three times per day.
Isolation: Cetrarin: Average dose of 1½-3 grains (0.099-0.2 gm.) for use as a stimulant.

Licorice (lik e·ris)
(*Glycyrrhiza lepidota*)

Synonyms/Related Species: American Licorice, Asiatic Licorice (*glycyrrhiza uralensis*), European Licorice (*glycyrrhiza glabra*), Glukosriza, Hungarian Licorice (*glycyrrhiza echinata*), Lacrisse, Lakriz, Liquorice, Lycorys, Madhukam, Persian Licorice, Regolizia, Russian Licorice (*Glycyrrhiza glandulifera*), Spanish Licorice, Sweet Root, Sweet Wood, and Wild Licorice.
Family/Class: Leguminosae (legume).
Habitat: Asia, China, England, Europe, France, Germany, Greece, Hungary, India, Italy, North America, Persia, Russia, Spain, and Syria.
Flavor: Sweet.
Parts Used: Root.
Properties: Alterative, anesthetic (local), antibiotic, anticarcinogen, anticoagulant, antifungal, antiphlogistic, antispasmodic, antiviral, demulcent, depurative, expectorant, hepatic, laxative, sedative, stimulant, and tonic.
Constituents: Aglycone (genin), amino acids (asparagine), anethol, coumarin, estragole, eugenol (eugenic acid), fenchone, flavonoids, glycyrrhizin (glycyrrhizic acid), gum, inulin (starch), lecithin, linalool, minerals (chromium, iodine, manganese, phosphorus, zinc), monosaccharides, phytoestrogen, polysaccharides, protein, resin, saponins, sterols, tannic acid, triterpenes, umbelliferone, vitamins (B_1 (thiamine), B_2 (riboflavin), B_3 (niacin), B_5 (pantothenic acid), B_6 (pyridoxine), B_{12}, B_x (para-aminobenzoic acid (PABA), E (alpha-tocopheral), H (biotin), M (folic acid), volatile oil, and wax.
Historical Uses: Acquired immune deficiency syndrome (AIDS), Addison's disease, age spots, arteriosclerosis, arthritis, asthma, bladder problems, bronchitis, allergy, cancer, candida, canker sores, Celiac disease, chronic fatigue syndrome (CFS), cirrhosis, colds, colic, constipation, cough, Crohn's disease, Cushing's disease, debility, digestive complaints, dysmenorrhea, eczema, emphysema, enteritis, Epstein Barr Virus (EBV), fever (ephemeral, herpetic), fibromyalgia, flavoring agent, gastritis, gastrointestinal problems, glandular problems, glandular swelling, gleet, gonorrhea, hemorrhoids, hepatitis, herpes, human immunodeficiency virus (HIV), hypoglycemia, indigestion, infection (bacterial, fungal, sexually transmitted, viral), inflammation, influenza, irritable bowel syndrome (IBS), laryngitis, liver problems, lung problems, lupus, Lyme disease, measles, Meniere's disease, menopausal/menstrual problems, moniliasis, mononucleosis (infectious), mucus, muscle and joint pain, Newcastle disease, palsy (Bell's), psoriasis, rash, respiratory conditions, rheumatoid arthritis (RA), sexually transmitted diseases (STDs), skin problems, sore throat, spasmodic conditions, ulcer (duodenal, gastric, peptic), urethritis, and vitiligo.

Discussion: May balance blood sugar levels; clear and open bronchial passages; decrease the effect of carcinogens; delay or reduce coagulation of the blood; enhance cardiovascular system, digestive system, glandular system, hormonal system, liver, lung, and spleen functions; facilitate the effects of other herbs; increase circulation; inhibit development or destroy growth of bacteria and other microorganisms, and inhibit production of toxic free radicals; prevent the hepatitis B and the HIV virus from spreading; promote bowel evacuation; protect the liver; purify the blood; reduce drug withdrawal symptoms, gastrointestinal irritation caused by the use of nonsteroidal anti-inflammatory drugs (NSAIDs), and testosterone levels in males; reestablish healthy system functions; restore normal tone to tissues; serve as an adjuvant to prednisolone therapy; soothe mucous membrane irritation; stimulate the immune system and peristalsis; stop or slow the progression of palsy to paralysis.
Cautions/Contraindications: Avoid use if pregnant or breast-feeding, or if you have an estrogen dependant cancer, or if you have a history of estrogen dependant cancers, or if you have benign breast disease, cirrhosis, diabetes, edema, erectile dysfunction, coagulation problem, glaucoma, heart disease, hepatitis, hypertension, hypothyroidism, infertility, kidney problems, liver problems, stroke (apoplectic), or an iodine sensitivity. Estrogen containing substances may contribute to abnormal blood clotting, migraine, and could promote the developement of certain types of estrogen dependant cancers. May increase the effectiveness of antibiotic and interferon drugs. May increase the side effects of corticosteroid drugs. Include potassium rich fruits and vegetables in your diet when taking licorice. May interfere with the effectiveness of certain thyroid medications. Some persons may experience bleeding or increased clotting time when using this herb with anticoagulant drugs or aspirin. Not for long-term use.
Adverse Reactions: Abdominal pain, arrhythmia, bleeding (possibly serious), coagulation problems, diarrhea, digestive complaints, edema, electrolyte imbalance, fever, gastritis, gastrointestinal problems, headache, hormonal imbalances, hypertension, hypertrophy (thyroid), indigestion, iodism (iodine poisoning), irritable bowel syndrome (IBS), lethargy, migraine, nausea, potassium loss, priapism, thirst, and/or vomiting.
Herb/Drug Interactions: This herb could cause an interaction (possibly severe) when taken with the following drugs: Antibiotic drugs, Anticoagulant drugs, Antimanic drugs, Calcium Carbonate, Corticosteroids, Cortisone, Cardiac drugs, Diuretic drugs, Hormones and Synthetic Substitutes (i.e. conjugated estrogens, contraceptives (oral, etc.), and other hormonal replacement therapy (HRT), Interferon drugs, Nonsteroidal Anti-inflammatory drugs (NSAIDs), Salicylates, Subsalicylates, and Thyroid drugs.
Preparations/Dosage: Crude Herb: 1-9 grams. Decoction: 1-2 cups per day. Extract (solid): Average dose in substance 60 grains (4 gm.). Root (powdered): Average dose in substance 30-60 grains (2-4 gm.). Tincture: 10-30 drops (0.666-2 cc.) one to three times per day.
Did You Know? Small amounts of licorice root are often added to formulas to mask the bitter taste of other herbs and help offset any adverse reactions.

Lilac (lī lek)

(*Syringa vulgaris*)

Synonyms/Related Species: Arabian Lilac, Common Lilac, Laylak, Mauve Lilac, Nīlak, Persian Lilac, Purple Lilac, and White Lilac.
Family/Class: Oleaceae (olive).
Floral Emblem: New Hampshire.

Habitat: Arabia, Europe, North America, and Persia.
Flavor: Bitter.
Parts Used: Leaves.
Properties: Antiperiodic, aromatic, febrifuge, malariacidal, tonic, and vermifuge.
Constituents: Saponins and syringin (lilacin, ligustrin).
Historical Uses: Ague, fever (ephemeral, intermittent), malaria, and parasites (malarial plasmodia).
Discussion: May restore normal tone to tissues.
Cautions/Contraindications: Avoid use if pregnant or breast-feeding.
Adverse Reactions: Diarrhea (possibly bloody), gastrointestinal cramps (severe), hematuria (blood in the urine), nausea, and/or vomiting.
Herb/Drug Interactions: This herb could cause an interaction (possibly severe) when taken with the following drugs: None known.
Preparations/Dosage: Crude Herb: 1-3 grams. Infusion: ¼-½ cup per day.

Lily, Glacier (lil'e, gla'sher)
(*Erythronium grandiflorum*)

Synonyms/Related Species: Adder's Tongue (*erythronium americanum*), Avalanche Lily, California Lily (*erythronium californicum*), Dogtooth Violet, Fawn Lily, Giant Lily (*erythronium giganteum*), Snow Lily, Trout Lily, Yellow Fawn Lily, and Yellow Snowdrop.
Family/Class: Liliaceae (lily).
Habitat: The Alpine zone and North America.
Flavor: Bitter/sweet.
Parts Used: Bulb, leaves.
Properties: Anti-inflammatory, antiscorbutic, astringent, demulcent, emetic, expectorant, hemostatic, and tonic.
Constituents: Mucilage, tuliposides, and vitamin C (ascorbic acid).
Historical Uses: Boils, colds, edema, glandular swelling, hemoptysis, hiccups, inflammation, lesions (tubercle), mucus, respiratory conditions, scrofula, skin problems, tuberculosis, tumors, and ulcer (fistula, tuberculous).
Discussion: May clear and open bronchial passages; restore normal tone to tissues; soothe mucous membrane irritation.
Cautions/Contraindications: Avoid use if pregnant or breast-feeding.
Adverse Reactions: Nausea and/or vomiting.
Herb/Drug Interactions: This herb could cause an interaction (possibly severe) when taken with the following drugs: None known.
Preparation/Dosage: Crude Herb: 3-6 grams. Bulbs and/or Leaves: May be cooked and eaten as a vegetable. Infusion: ½-1 cup per day. Juice: 1-2 tablespoons in water or cider one to two times per day.

Lily, Japanese (lil'ē, jap'e·nez')
(*Ophiopogon japonicus*)

Synonyms/Related Species: Creeping Lily Root, Dwarf Daylily, Dwarf Lilyturf, Ophiopogon, and Japanese Lily Turf.

Family/Class: Liliaceae (lily).
Habitat: Japan and North America.
Flavor: Sweet/bitter.
Parts Used: Bulb.
Properties: Demulcent, expectorant, febrifuge, hemostatic, nutritive, and tonic.
Constituents: Monosaccharide, mucilage, saponins, and stigmasterol.
Historical Uses: Anxiety, arrhythmia, asthma, bleeding, colds, constipation, cough, dandruff, dry skin, eczema, fever (ephemeral), hemoptysis, insomnia, lesions (tubercle), mucus, nausea, psoriasis, respiratory conditions, scrofula, thirst, tuberculosis, and ulcer (fistula, tuberculous).
Discussion: May clear and open bronchial passages; counteract fever; enhance cardiovascular, lung, and stomach functions; restore normal tone to tissues; soothe mucous membrane irritation.
Cautions/Contraindications: Avoid use if pregnant or breast-feeding, or if you have diarrhea.
Adverse Reactions: Diarrhea (possibly bloody), gastrointestinal cramps (severe), hematuria (blood in the urine), nausea, and/or vomiting.
Herb/Drug Interactions: This herb could cause an interaction (possibly severe) when taken with the following drugs: None known.
Preparation/Dosage: Crude Herb: 6-12 grams. Decoction: 1-2 cups per day.

Lily, Mariposa (lil ē, mar e·pō ze)
(*Calochortus apiculatus*)

Synonyms/Related Species: Butterfly Tulip, Elegant Mariposa Lily (*calochortus elegans*), Gunnison's Mariposa Lily (*calochortus gunnisonii*), Mariposa Tulip, Nuttall's Mariposa Lily (*calochortus nuttallii*), Sego Lily, Sígo, and Three-Spot Mariposa Lily.
Family/Class: Liliaceae (lily).
Floral Emblem: Utah.
Habitat: North America.
Flavor: Sweet.
Parts Used: Bulb.
Properties: Antimitotic, antiphlogistic, demulcent, expectorant, laxative, nutritive, sedative, and tonic.
Constituents: Alkaloid, colchicine, inulin (starch), and protein.
Historical Uses: Bruises, colds, cough, dietary supplementation, emaciation, fever, gastrointestinal problems, gout, inflammation, insect bites or stings, insomnia, irritability, lesions (tubercle), lung inflammation, malnutrition, mucus, pharyngitis, respiratory conditions, restlessness, rheumatism, salads (raw flower petals), scrofula, sores, sore throat, tonsillitis, tuberculosis, ulcer (fistula, tuberculous), and wounds (minor).
Discussion: May clear and open bronchial passages; inhibit mitosis (the division of active somatic and germ cells); promote bowel evacuation; provide dietary supplementation; restore normal tone to tissues; serve as a nutritional adjuvant to therapeutic programs; soothe mucous membrane irritation; stimulate peristalsis.
Cautions/Contraindications: Avoid use if pregnant or breast-feeding.
Adverse Reactions: Nausea and/or vomiting.
Herb/Drug Interactions: This herb could cause an interaction (possibly severe) when taken with the following drugs: Colchicine drugs.

Preparations/Dosage: Crude Herb: 3-9 grams. Bulb: Boiled and eaten as a vegetable. Decoction: ½-2 cups per day.
Isolation: Colchicine: Average dose of $^{1}/_{120}$-$^{1}/_{60}$ grain (0.5-1 mg.) for use in gout.

Lily, White Water (lil ē, hwīt wah ter)
(*Nymphaea odorata*)

Synonyms/Related Species: American White Water Lily, Cow Cabbage, Egyptian White Water Lily (*nymphaea caerulea*), Fragrant Water Lily, Large White Water Lily, Pond Lily, Sweet Scented Pond Lily, Sweet Water Lily, Water Cabbage, Water Lily, and White Water Lily (*nymphaea alba*).
Family/Class: Nymphaeaceae (water lily).
Habitat: Africa, Asia, Egypt, Europe, and North America.
Flavor: Bitter.
Parts Used: Root.
Properties: Alterative, analgesic, antibiotic, anticarcinogen, antifungal, antispasmodic, aromatic, astringent, demulcent, hemostatic, sedative, and tonic.
Constituents: Alkaloids, ammonia, fecula, gallic acid, glycosides, gum, inulin (starch), monosaccharides, mucilage, nupharine, nymphaline, resin, tannic acid, and tartaric acid.
Historical Uses: Boils, bleeding, bronchitis, bruises, burns (minor), cancer (uterine), candida, canker sores, congestion (uterine, vaginal), diarrhea, dysentery, eyewash, fibroids (uterine), gargle/mouth rinse, gleet, gonorrhea, infection (bacterial, sexually transmitted), inflammation, lesions (tubercle), leukorrhea, moniliasis, pain, pruritus, rash, scrofula, sexually transmitted diseases (STDs), skin problems, sore throat, sores, spasmodic conditions, toothache, tuberculosis, tumors, ulcer (duodenal, fistula, gastric, peptic, tuberculous), urethritis, vaginitis, and wounds (minor).
Discussion: May decrease the effect of carcinogens; enhance kidney and spleen functions; inhibit or destroy development and growth of bacteria and other microorganisms; reduce male libido; reestablish healthy system functions; restore normal tone to tissues; soothe mucous membrane irritation.
Cautions/Contraindications: Avoid use if pregnant or breast-feeding. Do not confuse this herb with poisonous water lily (*nymphaea tuberosa*), which is distinguished by its tuberous root and nearly odor free flowers.
Adverse Reactions: Nausea and/or vomiting.
Herb/Drug Interactions: This herb could cause an interaction (possibly severe) when taken with the following drugs: None known.
Preparations/Dosage: Crude Herb: 3-9 grams. Infusion: ½-1 cup per day. Root (powdered): Average dose in substance 30 grains (½ drachm).

Lily, Wood (lil ē, wood)
(*Lilium montanum*)

Synonyms/Related Species: Columbia Lily (*lilium columbianum*), Golden-Rayed Lily (*lilium auratum*), Madonna Lily (*lilium candidum*), Meadow Lily (*lilium candidum*), North American Tiger Lily, Tiger Lily (*lilium tigrinum*), Turk's Cap (*lilium martagon*), Western Wood Lily

(*lilium umbellatum*), White Lily, Wood Lily Root (*lilium umbellatum*), and Yellow Martagon (*lilium pomponium*).
Family/Class: Liliaceae (lily).
Floral Emblem: Saskatchewan.
Habitat: Asia, China, Columbia, England, Japan, the Mediterranean, North America, Palestine, Siberia, and Syria.
Flavor: Bulb: Bitter/sweet.
Parts Used: Bulb.
Properties: Antimitotic, antiphlogistic, antispasmodic, astringent, demulcent, expectorant, laxative, nervine, nutritive, sedative, and tonic.
Constituents: Alkaloids, colchicine, inulin (starch), mucilage, and protein.
Historical Uses: Bruises, burns (minor), colds, corns, cough, dietary supplementation, edema, emaciation, epilepsy, fever, gastrointestinal problems, gout, insect bites or stings, inflammation, insomnia, lesions (tubercle), malnutrition, mucus, respiratory conditions, restlessness, rheumatism, scalds, scrofula, sores, sore throat, spasmodic conditions, tuberculosis, tumors, ulcer (duodenal, fistula, gastric, peptic, tuberculous), and wounds (minor).
Discussion: May clear and open bronchial passages; enhance cardiovascular system and lung functions; inhibit mitosis (the division of active somatic and germ cells); promote bowel evacuation; provide dietary supplementation; restore normal tone to tissues; serve as a nutritional adjuvant to therapeutic programs; soothe mucous membrane irritation; stimulate peristalsis.
Cautions/Contraindications: Avoid use if pregnant or breast-feeding.
Adverse Reactions: Nausea and/or vomiting.
Herb/Drug Interactions: This herb could cause an interaction (possibly severe) when taken with the following drugs: Colchicine drugs.
Preparations/Dosage: Crude Herb: 3-12 grams. Bulb: May be cooked and eaten as a vegetable or eaten fresh. Infusion: 1 cup per day. Tincture: 1-10 drops (0.066-0.666 cc.).
Isolation: Colchicine: Average dose of $^{1}/_{120}$-$^{1}/_{60}$ grain (0.5-1 mg.) for use in gout.

Lily, Yellow Pond (lil ē, yel o pond)
(*Nuphar lutea*)

Synonyms/Related Species: European Yellow Pond Lily (*nuphar advena*), Frog-Lily, North America Yellow Pond Lily, Rocky Mountain Yellow Pond Lily (*nuphar polysepalum*), Spatterdock (*nuphar luteum*), and Yellow Cow Lily (*nuphar variegatum*).
Family/Class: Nymphaeaceae (water lily).
Habitat: Alaska, Africa, Asia, Europe, North America, and the Subalpine zone.
Flavor: Bitter.
Parts Used: Root.
Properties: Alterative, analgesic, antibiotic, anticarcinogen, antifungal, antispasmodic, aromatic, astringent, demulcent, depurative, hemostatic, sedative, and tonic.
Constituents: Alkaloids, ammonia, fecula, gallic acid, glycosides, gum, inulin (starch), monosaccharides, mucilage, nupharine, nymphaline, resin, tannic acid, and tartaric acid.
Historical Uses: Boils, bleeding, bronchitis, bruises, burns (minor), cancer (uterine), candida, canker sores, cardiovascular conditions, congestion (uterine, vaginal), diarrhea, dysentery, dysmenorrhea, eyewash, fibroids (uterine), gargle/mouth rinse, gastrointestinal problems, gleet, gonorrhea, hemorrhage, infection (bacterial, sexually transmitted), inflammation, lesions

(tubercle), leukorrhea, lung problems, moniliasis, nocturnal emission, pain, pruritus, rash, scrofula, sexually transmitted diseases (STDs), skin problems, sore throat, sores, spasmodic conditions, spermatorrhea, substitute for white pond lily (*nymphaea odorata*), toothache, tuberculosis, tumors, ulcer (duodenal, fistula, gastric, peptic, tuberculous), urethritis, vaginitis, and wounds (minor).

Discussion: May decrease the effect of carcinogens; enhance liver, spleen, and stomach functions; inhibit or destroy development and growth of bacteria and other microorganisms; purify the blood; reduce male libido and the emission of semen during sleep; reestablish healthy system functions; restore normal tone to tissues; soothe mucous membrane irritation; strengthen the reproductive system.

Cautions/Contraindications: Avoid use if pregnant or breast-feeding. Do not confuse this plant with poisonous water lily (nymphaea tuberosa), which is distinguished by its tuberous root and nearly odor free flowers.

Adverse Reactions: Diarrhea (severe), nausea, and vomiting.

Herb/Drug Interactions: This herb could cause an interaction (possibly severe) when taken with the following drugs: None known.

Preparations/Dosage: Crude Herb: 3-6 grams. Infusion: ½-1 cup per day. Root (powdered): Average dose in substance 30 grains (½ drachm).

Lily of the Valley (lil ē uv the val ē)
(*Convallaria majalis*)

Synonyms/Related Species: Convallaria, Jacob's Ladder, May Bells, May Lily, Muguet, North American Lily of the Valley (*convallaria montana*), and Our Lady's Tears.

Family/Class: Liliaceae (lily).

Habitat: Asia, England, Europe, and North America.

Flavor: Bitter/sweet.

Parts Used: Flowers, root.

Properties: Antiphlogistic, antispasmodic, cardiant, diuretic, emetic, laxative, lithotriptic, and tonic.

Constituents: Alkaloids, asparagin, convallamarin, convallaretin, convallarin, convallatoxin, glycosides, mucilage, and saponins.

Historical Uses: Arrhythmia, asthma, cardiovascular conditions, conjunctivitis, edema, epilepsy, fever (ephemeral, rheumatic), gallstones, gout, infection (urinary tract), inflammation, insufficiency (mitral valve, venous), kidney stones, leprosy, muscle and joint pain, nervous conditions, neurasthenia, rheumatism, spasmodic conditions, stroke (apoplectic), and urinary calculus.

Discussion: May dissolve calculi; enhance kidney function; increase circulation; promote bowel evacuation and urine flow; restore normal tone to tissues; serve as a substitute for foxglove (*digitalis purpurea*) in cardiac problems; stimulate the cardiovascular system and peristalsis.

Cautions/Contraindications: Avoid use if pregnant or breast-feeding. May cause dermatitis in susceptible individuals. Not for long-term use. Use with professional guidance/supervision.

Adverse Reactions: Arrhythmia, cardiac failure, elevated blood pressure levels, gastrointestinal cramps (severe), hematuria (blood in the urine), insufficiency (circulatory), respiratory distress, color perception problems, coma, headache, nausea, stupor, vomiting, and/or possible death.

Herb/Drug Interactions: This herb could cause an interaction (possibly severe) when taken with the following drugs: Calcium Carbonate, Cardiac drugs, and Laxatives.
Preparations/Dosage: Crude Herb: 1-3 grams. Decoction: ⅛-½ cup per day. Extract (leaves): ½-1 drop (0.03-0.06 cc.). Extract (flowers): 1 drop (0.06 cc.). Root (powdered): Average dose in substance ½ grain (30 mg.). Tincture: 1-3 drops (0.06-0.2 cc.) one to three times per day.
Isolation: Asparagin: Soluble in hot water, but insoluble in alcohol and ether. Average dose of 1-2 grains (0.066-0.133 gm.) for use as a diuretic. Convallamarin: Average dose of $^1/_5$-1 grain (0.013-0.065 gm.) for use as a cardiant, diuretic, and emetic.
Note: Lily of the Valley's actions are similar to that of foxglove (*digitalis*), but to a lesser degree.

Linden (lin den)

(*Tilia americana*)

Synonyms/Related Species: American Linden Basswood, Basswood, European Linden (*tilia europaea*), Italian Limetta, Limettae Fructus, Linn Flowers, Spoonwood, Tilden Flower, and Wycopy.
Family/Class: Tiliaceae (linden).
Habitat: Asia, Central America, Britain, Europe, India, North America, the Pyrenees, and Sweden.
Flavor: Sour.
Parts Used: Flowers, leaves.
Properties: Analgesic, antibiotic, anticarcinogen, antiscorbutic, antispasmodic, antioxidant, aromatic, astringent, demulcent, diaphoretic, diuretic, expectorant, febrifuge, hemostatic, hypotensive, lithotriptic, nervine, nutritive, sedative, stimulant, stomachic, and vasodilator.
Constituents: Carvene (limonene), chlorophyll, citral (geranial), citric acid, coumarin, fiber, flavonoids, gum, hesperidin, minerals (manganese), monosaccharides, mucilage, quercetin, pinene, resin, saponins, tannic acid, terpenes, tiliadin, vitamin C (ascorbic acid), and volatile oil.
Historical Uses: Appetite loss, arrhythmia, arteriosclerosis, beverage, bladder problems, bleeding, burns (minor), calculus, cancer, chills, colds, cough, diarrhea, dietary supplementation, ear infection, epilepsy, fever (ephemeral), flavoring agent, gallstones, gargle/mouth rinse, gastrointestinal problems, gout, halitosis, headache, hyperactivity, hypertension (mild/moderate), hysteria, indigestion, influenza, insomnia, irritability, kidney stones, laryngitis, malnutrition, menstrual problems, migraine, mucus, nervous conditions, night sweats, pain, respiratory conditions, scurvy, skin problems, sore throat, sores, spasmodic conditions, tumors, vomiting, and wounds (minor).
Discussion: May calm the nervous system; cause blood vessel dilatation; clear and open bronchial passages; decrease the effect of carcinogens; destroy harmful free radicals; dissolve calculi; enhance liver and stomach functions; inhibit oxidation; promote perspiration and urine flow; provide dietary supplementation; reduce blood pressure levels and cholesterol levels; serve as a nutritional adjuvant to therapeutic programs; soothe mucous membrane irritation; stimulate peristalsis; strengthen blood vessels, capillaries, and connective tissues.
Cautions/Contraindications: Avoid use if pregnant or breast-feeding. Allergic reactions may occur in young children when first introducing them to citrus juices.
Adverse Reactions: Diarrhea (possibly bloody), drowsiness, gastrointestinal cramps (severe), heart damage, hematuria (blood in the urine), mucous membrane irritation, nausea, and/or vomiting.

Herb/Drug Interactions: This herb could cause an interaction (possibly severe) when taken with the following drugs: Hypotensive drugs.
Preparations/Dosage: Crude Herb: 3-9 grams. Infusion (flowers): 1-2 cups per day. Tincture: 15-30 drops (1-2 cc.) one to three times per day.

Liquidambar (lik wid·am ber)
(*Liquidambar orientalis*)

Synonyms/Related Species: American Sweet Gum, Balsam Styracis, Copalm Balsam, European Styrax (*styrax officinale*), Gum Benzoin, Gum Tree, Java Storax (*liquidambar altingia*), Red Gum, Rosemalles, Siam Benzoin (*liquidambar formosana*), Star-Leaved Gum, Storax, Styrax, Sumatra Benzoin (*styrax benzoinx*), Sweet Gum Tree, White Gum, and Yagh.
Family/Class: Hamamelidaceae (witch hazel).
Habitat: Asia, China, Java, Myanmar (formerly Burma), North America, Sumatra, Syria, and Thailand.
Flavor: Pungent.
Parts Used: Bark (inner), resinous balsam.
Properties: Antiobiotic, anti-inflammatory, aromatic, astringent, carminative, counterirritant, diaphoretic, diuretic, emmenagogue, expectorant, hemostatic, parasiticide, and stimulant.
Constituents: Benzoin, benzyl, bitumen, cinnamic acid, storax (styrax), styracin, styracitol, styrene (styrol), and vanillin (methyl pyrocatechinic acid).
Historical Uses: Asthma, bleeding, bronchitis, bruises, colds, congestion (uterine, vaginal), cough, cystitis, diarrhea, diphtheria, dysentery, gleet, gonorrhea, hemorrhage (metrorrhagia), hemorrhoids, infection (bacterial, sexually transmitted), inflammation, laryngitis, leukorrhea, mucus, muscle and joint pain, nervous conditions, parasites (ringworm, scabies and their nits), pruritus, respiratory conditions, sexually transmitted diseases (STDs), skin problems, sores, substitute for copaiba and tea tree oil, ulcer (duodenal, syriac), urethritis, urinary problems, vaginitis, and wounds (minor).
Discussion: May aid digestion; clear and open bronchial passages; enhance cardiovascular system and spleen functions; increase circulation; inhibit or destroy development and growth of bacteria and other microorganisms; promote perspiration and urine flow; stimulate gastric secretions, menstruation, and mucous membranes.
Cautions/Contraindications: Avoid use if pregnant or breast-feeding, or if you have an ulcer (gastric, peptic). May cause dermatitis in susceptible individuals.
Adverse Reactions: Diarrhea, hematuria (blood in the urine), nausea, and/or vomiting.
Herb/Drug Interactions: This herb could cause an interaction (possibly severe) when taken with the following drugs: None known.
Preparations/Dosage: Crude Herb (bark): 1-3 grams. Crude Herb (resin/powdered): Average dose in substance 10-20 grains (0.666-1.333 gm.). Decoction: ¼-1 cup per day. Tincture: 10-30 drops (0.666-2 cc.) one to three times per day.
Did You Know? One liquidambar tree will yield approximately three pounds of benzoin annually for up to ten years.

Lobelia (lō·bēl ·ye)
(*Lobelia inflata*)

Synonyms/Related Species: Asthma Weed, Blue Lobelia (*lobelia syphilitica*), British Lobelia (*lobelia dortmanna*), Cardinal Flower (*lobelia cardinalis*), Emetic Root, Gagroot, Indian Tobacco (*lobelia kalmit*), Pukeweed, Red Lobelia, Vomitroot, and Wild Tobacco.
Family/Class: Campanulaceae (bellflower).
Habitat: Britain, England, and North America.
Flavor: Bitter.
Parts Used: Bark, flowering tops, leaves, seeds.
Properties: Alterative, analgesic, anticarcinogen, antiphlogistic, antispasmodic, diaphoretic, diuretic, emetic, expectorant, laxative, narcotic, nervine, parasiticide, sedative, and stimulant.
Constituents: Alkaloids, chlorophyll, fatty acids (oleic, palmitic, stearic), fixed oils (olein, palmitin, stearin), gum, lignin, lobelanidine, lobelidine, lobeline, lobelanine, lobinine, minerals (cobalt, copper, iron, lead, potassium, selenium, sodium, sulfur), and resin.
Historical Uses: Abscess, addiction (nicotine), allergy (pollen), angina, arrhythmia, arthritis, asthma, bronchitis, bruises, bursitis, cancer, canker sores, cardiovascular conditions, chorea, colds, colic, constipation, convulsions, cough, cramps, croup, diarrhea, digestive complaints, diphtheria, dysentery, ear infection, earache, eczema, edema, emphysema, epilepsy, erysipelas, eye problems, fever (ephemeral, hay, rheumatic, scarlet, septic), gleet, gonorrhea, headache, hepatitis, herbal tobacco, hydrophobia (rabies in humans), hyperactivity, hypoglycemia, infection (bacterial, sexually transmitted), inflammation, insect bites or stings, insomnia, insufficiency (circulatory), laryngitis, liver problems, lung problems, meningitis, menopausal/menstrual problems, migraine, mucus, muscle and joint pain, muscle strain, nephritis, nervous conditions, pain, palsy, parasites (ringworm), peritonitis, pleurisy, pneumonia, poisoning (blood, food), poison ivy/oak, pruritus, respiratory conditions, rheumatism, scarletina, seizure conditions, sexually transmitted diseases (STDs), shock, skin problems, spasmodic conditions, sprain, syphilis, tetanus, tinnitus, tonsillitis, toothache, trismus (lockjaw), tumors, ulcer (syphilitic, syriac), urethritis, urinary problems, weight loss, whooping cough, and wounds (minor).
Discussion: May calm the nervous system; clear and open bronchial passages; decrease the effect of carcinogens and functional activity of the spinal cord; increase circulation; promote bowel evacuation, perspiration, and urine flow; reduce nicotine withdrawal symptoms; reestablish healthy system functions; stimulate peristalsis, the respiratory center, and the vagus nerve.
Cautions/Contraindications: Avoid use if pregnant or breast-feeding. May cause relaxation and/or sleepiness in some individuals. Not for long-term use. Use with professional guidance/supervision.
Adverse Reactions: Anxiety, arrhythmia, bradycardia, breathing difficulties, chills, cold sweats, coma, convulsions, depression, diarrhea, dizziness, dryness (mouth), edema, exhaustion, headache, muscle twitches, nausea, paralysis, perspiration, reduced body temperature, stupor, tremors, urinary tract burning, vomiting, and/or possible death.
Herb/Drug Interactions: This herb could cause an interaction (possibly severe) when taken with the following drugs: None known.
Preparations/Dosage: Crude Herb: 3-6 grams. Bark (powdered): Average dose in substance 5-60 grains (0.3 gm.-1 drachm). Extract (solid): Average dose in substance 2-4 grains (0.133-0.26 gm.). Infusion: ¼-½ cup per day. Oil of Lobelia Seed: Mix 1 drop of seed oil with 10-20 grains (0.666-1.333 gm.) of ginger. Tincture: 5-15 drops (0.333-1 cc.) one to three times per day.

Isolation: Lobeline: Average dose of ¼-3 grains (0.015-0.2 gm.) for use as a stimulant, and as a powerful resuscitant in collapse, respiratory failure, and shock.

Lomatium (lo'ma·te·em)

(*Lomatium dissectum*)

Synonyms/Related Species: Biscuit Root (*lomatium montanum*), Bladder Parsnips, California Desert Parsley (*lomatium californicum*), Desert Parsley, Fern-Leaved Desert Parsley, Foothill Lomatium (*lomatium utriculatum*), Mountain Parsley, Nine-Leaved Desert Parsley (*lomatium triternatum*), Swale Desert Parsley (*lomatium ambiguum*), and Wild Desert Parsley.
Family/Class: Umbelliferae (parsley).
Habitat: North America.
Flavor: Bitter/sweet.
Parts Used: Root.
Properties: Antibiotic, antiviral, nutritive, sedative, and tonic.
Constituents: Tartaric acid, umbelliferone, and vitamins A and B.
Historical Uses: Abscess, acne, acquired immune deficiency syndrome (AIDS), anemia, anxiety, arthritis, asthma, bronchitis, bruises, burns, chronic fatigue syndrome (CFS), colds, congestion, conjunctivitis, cough, dandruff, debility, dizziness, fractures, gleet, gonorrhea, hay fever, headache, human immunodeficiency virus (HIV), infection (bacterial, sexually transmitted, urinary tract, viral), inflammation, influenza, insomnia, lung problems, memory/cognitive problems, mononucleosis, muscle and joint pain, pneumonia, respiratory conditions, restlessness, rheumatism, sexually transmitted diseases (STDs), sinusitis, skin problems, sore throat, sores, sprain, tuberculosis, urethritis, vaginitis, and wounds (minor).
Discussion: May stimulate appetite and the immune system; strengthen the cardiovascular system.
Cautions/Contraindications: Avoid use if pregnant or breast-feeding. May cause dermatitis in susceptible individuals.
Adverse Reactions: Gastrointestinal irritation, nausea, and/or vomiting.
Herb/Drug Interactions: None known.
Preparations/Dosage: Crude Herb: 3-6 grams. Infusion: ½-1 cup per day.

Longan (län'gen)

(*Euphoria longana*)

Synonyms/Related Species: Dragon's Eye and Lung Yen.
Family/Class: Sapindaceae (soapberry).
Habitat: Asia and India.
Flavor: Sweet.
Parts Used: Fruit (dried/fresh).
Properties: Nutritive, sedative, and tonic.
Constituents: Disaccharide, monosaccharides, saponins, tartaric acid, and vitamins A and B.
Historical Uses: Anemia, anxiety, arrhythmia, confectionary, dizziness, flavoring agent, hyperactivity, hypoglycemia, insomnia, memory/cognitive problems, and restlessness.
Discussion: May enhance heart, pancreas, and spleen functions; reduce the craving for sweets; nourish the blood; strengthen the heart muscle and the female reproductive organs.

Cautions/Contraindications: Avoid use if pregnant or breast-feeding.
Adverse Reactions: Diarrhea (possibly bloody), gastrointestinal cramps (severe), hematuria (blood in the urine), nausea, and/or vomiting.
Herb/Drug Interactions: This herb could cause an interaction (possibly severe) when taken with the following drugs: None known.
Preparations/Dosage: Crude Herb (dried/powdered): 3-12 grams. Fruit (fresh): Ingest small handful daily.

Loosestrife, Purple (loos strīf , pûr pel)
(*Lythrum salicaria*)

Synonyms/Related Species: Blooming Sally, Decodon, Flowering Sally, Hyssop Loosestrife (*lythrum hyssopifolia*), Long Purples, Lythrum, Mexican Salicaria (*lythrum apanxaloa*), Milk Willow Herb, Purple Willow Herb, Rainbow Weed, Sage Willow, Salicaria, Spiked Loosestrife, and Swamp Willow Herb (*lythrum verticillatum*).
Family/Class: Lythraceae (loosestrife).
Habitat: Asia, Australia, Britain, Europe, North America, and Russia.
Flavor: Sweet.
Parts Used: Aerial.
Properties: Antibiotic, astringent, demulcent, depurative, febrifuge, and hemostatic.
Constituents: Glycoside, mucilage, pectic acid, pectin, tannic acid, and volatile oil.
Historical Uses: Bleeding, candida, congestion (uterine, vaginal), constipation, diarrhea, dysentery, fever (ephemeral), gargle/mouth rinse, gastroenteritis, leukorrhea, liver problems, menorrhagia, nosebleed, rash, skin problems, sore throat, sores, vaginitis, and wounds (minor).
Discussion: May clear and open bronchial passages; enhance liver and spleen functions; inhibit or destroy development and growth of bacteria and other microorganisms; purify the blood; soothe mucous membrane irritation.
Cautions/Contraindications: Avoid use if pregnant or breast-feeding.
Adverse Reactions: Nausea and/or vomiting.
Herb/Drug Interactions: This herb could cause an interaction (possibly severe) when taken with the following drugs: None known.
Preparations/Dosage: Crude Herb: 3-6 grams. Crude Herb (powdered): Average dose in substance 30-60 grains (2-4 gm.). Infusion: 1 cup per day. Tincture: 10-15 drops (0.666-1 cc.) one to three times per day.

Loosestrife, Yellow (loos strīf , yel ō)
(*Lysimachia vulgaris*)

Synonyms/Related Species: Common Loosestrife, Creeping Jenny, Herb Willow, Lysimachia, Moneywort (*lysimachia nummularia*), Wandering Jenny, Willow Wort, Wood Loosestrife, Yellow Pimpernel, and Yellow Willow Herb.
Family/Class: Primulaceae (primrose).
Habitat: Asia and Europe.
Flavor: Bitter/pungent.
Parts Used: Aerial.
Properties: Antiscorbutic, astringent, demulcent, expectorant, febrifuge, and hemostatic.

Constituents: Mucilage, pectic acid, pectin, rutin, tannic acid, vitamin C (ascorbic acid), and volatile oil.
Historical Uses: Bleeding, bronchitis, colds, congestion (uterine, vaginal), cough, diarrhea, dysentery, eye problems, fever (ephemeral, enteric), leukorrhea, menorrhagia, mucus, nosebleed, respiratory conditions, scurvy, skin problems, sores, typhoid, ulcer (bouveret, duodenal, gastric, peptic), vaginitis, and wounds (minor).
Discussion: May clear and open bronchial passages; prevent hemorrhage in persons with hypertension; reduce capillary fragility; restore normal tone to tissues; soothe mucous membrane irritation.
Cautions/Contraindications: Avoid use if pregnant or breast-feeding.
Adverse Reactions: Nausea and/or vomiting.
Herb/Drug Interactions: This herb could cause an interaction (possibly severe) when taken with the following drugs: None known.
Preparations/Dosage: External uses only.

Lousewort (lous wûrt)
(*Pedicularis bracteosa*)

Synonyms/Related Species: Alpine Lousewort (*pedicularis sudetica*), Arctic Lousewort (*pedicularis langsdorfi*), Bracted Lousewort, Capitate Lousewort (*pedicularis capitata*), Chinese Lousewort (*pedicularis lasiophrys*), Coil-Beaked Lousewort (*pedicularis contorta*), Elephant's Head Lousewort (*pedicularis groenlandica*), Fernleaf, Feverweed, Indian Lousewort (*pedicularis pectinata*), Indian Warrior (*pedicularis densiflora*), Oeder's Lousewort (*pedicularis oederi*), Parrot's Beak, Parry's Lousewort (*pedicularis parryi*), Pediswyrt, Purple Lousewort (*pedicularis crenulata*), Sickletop Lousewort (*pedicularis racemosa*), and Woolly Lousewort (*pedicularis lanata*).
Family/Class: Scrophulariaceae (figwort).
Habitat: Alaska, the Alpine and Subalpine zones, the Arctic, Greenland, and North America.
Flavor: Bitter.
Properties: Antibiotic, antioxidant, antiphlogistic, aphrodisiac, astringent, diaphoretic, diuretic, emmenagogue, expectorant, laxative, narcotic, nervine, parasiticide, sedative, stomachic, tonic, and vulnerary.
Constituents: Alkaloids, delphinine (delphine), delphinoidine, delphisine, and glycosides.
Parts Used: Leaves.
Historical Uses: Abdominal pain, anxiety, asthma, colds, cough, edema, fever (ephemeral, rheumatic), headache, hemoptysis, hemorrhoids, hyperactivity, infection (bacterial), inflammation, mucus, muscle and joint pain, nervous conditions, neuralgia, pain, paralysis, parasites (crabs and their nits, lice and their nits, ringworm, scabies), respiratory conditions, rheumatism, and sores.
Discussion: May arouse sexual impulses; calm the nervous system; enhance stomach function; inhibit oxidation and inhibit or destroy development and growth of bacteria and other microorganisms; promote bowel evacuation, perspiration, and urine flow; relax the cerebrum and muscles; restore normal tone to tissues; speed healing; stimulate menstruation and peristalsis.
Cautions/Contraindications: Avoid use if pregnant or breast-feeding. May cause dermatitis in susceptible individuals. Not for long-term use. Use with professional guidance/supervision.
Adverse Reactions: Asphyxiation, diarrhea, gastrointestinal problems, lethargy, loss of motor control, nausea, stupor, vomiting, and/or possible death.

Herb/Drug Interactions: This herb could cause an interaction (possibly severe) when taken with the following drugs: None known.
Preparations/Dosage: Crude Herb: 3-6 grams. Infusion: 1-2 cups per day. Tincture: 1-2 drops (0.06-0.1 cc.) one to three times per day.
Isolation: Delphinine: $^{1}/_{64}$-¾ grain (0.001-0.05 gm.) for external use as an analgesic.

Lovage (luv āj)
(*Ligusticum officinale*)

Synonyms/Related Species: California Lovage, Canby's Lovage (*ligusticum canbyi*), Chinese Lovage (*ligusticum wallichi*), Chuchupate, Cornish Lovage, Coughroot, European Lovage, Fern-Leaved Lovage (*ligusticum filicinum*), Gray's Licorice Root (*ligusticum grayi*), Indian Parsley, Italian Lovage (*ligusticum scorticum*), Kishwoof, Lavose, Life Root, Ligusticum, Old English Lovage, Osha, Porter's Licorice Root (*ligusticum porteri*), and Sea Parsley.
Family/Class: Umbelliferae (parsley).
Habitat: The Balkans, Britain, Europe, Greece, the Mediterranean, and North America.
Flavor: Pungent/bitter.
Parts Used: Root.
Properties: Alterative, analgesic, anesthetic (local), antibiotic, antifungal, antiphlogistic, antispasmodic, antiviral, aromatic, carminative, depurative, diaphoretic, diuretic, emmenagogue, expectorant, hypotensive, lithotriptic, oxytocic, sedative, stimulant, stomachic, and vasodilator.
Constituents: Alkaloid, benzoic acid, bitter principle, bergapten, carvacrol, citronellal, coumarin, ferulic acid, fatty acids (angelic, oleic, palmitic, stearic), fixed oils (olein, palmitin, stearin), glycosides, inulin (starch), malic acid, monosaccharides, resin, saponins, sterols, terpineol, umbelliferone, and volatile oil.
Historical Uses: Abscess, angina, arthritis, asthma, bronchitis, calculus, candida, carpal tunnel syndrome, colds, colic, cough, cramps, cystitis, digestive complaints, dysmenorrhea, edema, eye problems, fever (ephemeral, herpetic, rheumatic), flatulence, gallstones, gastritis, gastrointestinal problems, gout, headache, herpes, hypertension (mild/moderate), incense, indigestion, infection (bacterial, fungal, viral), inflammation, influenza, irritable bowel syndrome (IBS), jaundice, kidney stones, menstrual problems, moniliasis, mucus, muscle and joint pain, nausea, pain, pleurisy, pruritus, respiratory conditions, rheumatism, sexually transmitted diseases (STDs), sinusitis, skin problems, sore throat, spasmodic conditions, stomachache, substitute for parsley, toothache, urinary problems, vomiting, and wounds (minor).
Discussion: May aid digestion; cause blood vessel dilatation; cleanse the whole system; clear and open bronchial passages; dissolve calculi; enhance lung, reproductive system, and stomach functions; improve cerebral blood flow; increase circulation; inhibit development or destroy growth of bacteria and other microorganisms; promote perspiration and urine flow; reduce blood pressure levels; reestablish healthy system functions; stimulate the immune system, menstruation, and uterine contractions.
Cautions/Contraindications: Avoid use if pregnant or breast-feeding, or if you have edema or a kidney problem.
Adverse Reactions: Diarrhea (possibly bloody), gastrointestinal cramps (severe), hematuria (blood in the urine), nausea, and/or vomiting.
Herb/Drug Interactions: This herb could cause an interaction (possibly severe) when taken with the following drugs: Hypotensive drugs.

Preparations/Dosage: Crude Herb: 3-9 grams. Decoction: ¼-½ cup per day. Infusion: 1-1½ cups. Root (powdered): Average dose in substance ¼-½ teaspoon one to two times per day. Tincture: 10-30 drops (0.666-2 cc.) one to three times per day.
Did You Know? Lovage roots can be stored for years without worry of decay as their oils render them resistant to microorganisms.

Lungwort (lung wûrt)
(*Pulmonaria officinalis*)

Synonyms/Related Species: Longwort, Maple Lungwort, Pulmonaria, and Spotted Lungwort.
Family/Class: Boraginaceae (borage).
Habitat: Europe and North America.
Flavor: Bitter/sweet.
Parts Used: Leaves.
Properties: Astringent, demulcent, diuretic, expectorant, hemostatic, stomachic, and tonic.
Constituents: Allantoin, caffeic acid, chlorogenic acid, flavonoids, minerals (iron, potassium, silicon), mucilage, quercetin, saponins, silicic acid, tannic acid, and volatile oil.
Historical Uses: Allergy (pollen), asthma, bleeding, bronchitis, bruises, burns (minor), colds, cough, croup, diarrhea, dysentery, fever (ephemeral, hay), gastrointestinal problems, glandular swelling, hemorrhoids, infection (urinary tract), inflammation, influenza, kidney problems, laryngitis, lesions (tubercle), lung problems, mucus, muscle and joint pain, night sweats, pain, respiratory conditions, scrofula, sinusitis, sore throat, tuberculosis, tumors, ulcer (fistula, tuberculous), whooping cough, and wounds (minor).
Discussion: May clear and open bronchial passages; enhance lung and stomachic functions; promote urine flow; restore normal tone to tissues; soothe mucous membrane irritation; stimulate gastric secretions.
Cautions/Contraindications: Avoid use if pregnant or breast-feeding, or if you have acidity (gastric) or an ulcer (gastric, peptic).
Adverse Reactions: Diarrhea (possibly bloody), gastrointestinal cramps (severe), hematuria (blood in the urine), nausea, and/or vomiting.
Herb/Drug Interactions: This herb could cause an interaction (possibly severe) when taken with the following drugs: None known.
Preparations/Dosage: Crude Herb: 3-9 grams. Infusion: 1-2 cups per day. Juice: 1 teaspoon mixed with honey one to two times per day. Tincture: 10-30 drops (0.666-2 cc.) one to three times per day.

Lycium (li cē·um)
(*Lycium pallidum*)

Synonyms/Related Species: Anderson's Lycium (*lycium andersonii*), Boxthorn, Chinese Lycium (*lycium chinensis*), Matrimony Vine (*lycium halimifolium*), Pale Wolfberry, and Wolfberry (*lycium barbarum*).
Family/Class: Solanaceae (nightshade).
Habitat: Asia, Europe, and North America.
Flavor: Sweet.
Parts Used: Berry, root.

Properties: Alterative, antiphlogistic, astringent, demulcent, depurative, emmenagogue, hemostatic, nutritive, and tonic.
Constituents: Alkaloids, betaine (lycine), cinnamic acid, esters, fatty acids (arachidonic, linoleic, linolenic), hyoscyamine, saponins, solanine, sterol, and vitamins (A, B_1 (thiamine), B_2 (riboflavin), C (ascorbic acid).
Historical Uses: Bleeding, bronchitis, chicken pox, congestion (uterine, vaginal), cough, dermatitis, diabetes, dietary supplementation, erectile dysfunction, fever (ephemeral, herpetic), hematuria (blood in the urine), herpes, inflammation, lesions (tubercle), leukorrhea, malnutrition, muscle and joint pain, night blindness, night sweats, nocturnal emission, nosebleed, poison ivy/oak, pruritus, rash, scrofula, sexually transmitted diseases (STDs), skin problems, thirst, toothache, tuberculosis, ulcer (fistula, tuberculous), vaginitis, visual disturbances, vomiting, wheezing, and whooping cough.
Discussion: May enhance kidney, liver, and lung functions; provide dietary supplementation; reestablish healthy system functions; purify the blood; reduce the emission of semen during sleep; restore normal tone to tissues; serve as a nutritional adjuvant to therapeutic programs; soothe mucous membrane irritation; stimulate menstruation and reproductive gland secretions; strengthen vision.
Cautions/Contraindications: Avoid use if pregnant or breast-feeding, or if you have an inflammatory condition, or experience indigestion, irritable bowel syndrome (IBS), or gastritis. Lycium contains alkaloids that have atropine-like actions, which can produce symptoms of poisoning similar to that of jimsonweed (*datura stramonium*).
Adverse Reactions: Diarrhea (possibly bloody), gastrointestinal cramps (severe), hematuria (blood in the urine), nausea, and/or vomiting.
Herb/Drug Interactions: This herb could cause an interaction (possibly severe) when taken with the following drugs: None known.
Preparations/Dosage: Crude Herb (berry or root): 3-12 grams. Infusion: ¼-1 cup per day.
Isolation: Betaine: Average dose of 2-4 grains (0.13-0.26 gm.) for use as an emmenagogue.

Maca (mak-ah)
(*Lepidium peruvianum*)

Synonyms/Related Species: Fertility Root, Health Root, Kechua Root, Life Root, Peruvian Ginseng, Quechua Root, Root of Life, and True Maca.
Family/Class: Brassicaceae (mustard).
Habitat: The Peruvian Andes.
Flavor: Sweet (butterscotch/malt-like).
Parts Used: Root.
Properties: Alterative, analgesic, antiphlogistic, aphrodisiac, expectorant, hypotensive, nutritive, tonic, and vasodilator.
Constituents: Alkaloids, carbohydrates, fatty acids (arachidonic, linoleic, linolenic), inulin (starch), isothiocyanates, minerals (calcium, copper, iodine, iron, magnesium, manganese, phosphorus, potassium, silica, sodium, zinc), monosaccharides, protein, sterols, saponins, tannic acid, and vitamins (A, B_1 (thiamine), B_2 (riboflavin), B_{12}, C (ascorbic acid), D, E (alpha-tocopheral).
Historical Uses: Addiction (various), amenorrhea, arthritis, atrophy (ovarian), benign breast disease, bronchitis, chronic fatigue syndrome (CFS), colds, convalescense, depression (mild/moderate), dietary supplementation, diminished sex drive, dryness conditions,

dysmenorrhea, Epstein Barr Virus (EBV), erectile dysfunction, fever (ephemeral, rheumatic), fibromyalgia, frigidity, hemorrhage (metrorrhagia), hormonal imbalances, hot flashes, hypertension (mild/moderate), infertility, inflammation, insomnia, malnutrition, memory/cognitive problems, menorrhagia, menopausal/menstrual problems, mood swings, mononucleosis (infectious), muscle and joint pain, osteoporosis, pain, perimenopause, premenstrual syndrome (PMS), respiratory conditions, rheumatism, and tumors.

Discussion: May arouse sexual impulses; boost energy levels, cause blood vessel dilatation; endurance, and stamina; clear and open bronchial passages; elevate mood; increase circulation, concentration, mental clarity, muscle tone, seminal volume, sexual desire, sperm production and motility; inhibit atrophy (ovarian) and tumor growth; normalize testosterone, progesterone, and estrogen hormones; promote multiple egg follicle maturation in females; provide dietary supplementation and nutritional support for the reproductive area; improve bone density; promote the growth of healthy bones, hair, and teeth; rebuild a weak immune system; reduce blood pressure levels; reestablish healthy system functions; regulate cholesterol levels and ovarian function; remineralize poorly nourished body systems; restore fertility and normal tone to tissues and organs; serve as a nutritional adjuvant to therapeutic programs and serve as a natural alternative to hormonal replacement therapy (HRT)*; stimulate the body to produce its own hormones.

Cautions/Contraindications: Avoid use if pregnant or breast-feeding, or if you have an estrogen dependant cancer, or if you have a history of estrogen dependant cancers, or if you are a male with a history of prostate cancer or have a high PSA level, or if you have an iodine sensitivity. Men using maca root on a regular basis should undergo periodic prostate specific antigen (PSA) tests. May interfere with the effectiveness of certain thyroid medications. May interfere with iodide metabolism. May cause allergic reactions and dermatitis in susceptible individuals.

Adverse Reactions: Diarrhea (possibly bloody), digestive complaints, edema, gastritis, gastrointestinal problems, goiter, hypertrophy (thyroid), indigestion, insufficiency (thyroid), irritable bowel syndrome (IBS), mucous membrane irritation, nausea, and/or vomiting.

Herb/Drug Interactions: This herb could cause an interaction (possibly severe) when taken with the following drugs: Hormones and Synthetic Substitutes (i.e. conjugated estrogens, contraceptives (oral, etc.), and other hormonal replacement therapy (HRT), Hypotensive drugs, and Thyroid drugs.)

Preparations/Dosage: Generally, maca root can be safely consumed (see cautions) up to three times a day, and can be prepared in a wide variety of methods including Huatia: Cook roots whole. Atunca: Boil and mash roots, then roll into balls and cook (in a fashion similar to meatballs). Powder: Put into capsule or tablet form.

Note: Maca root is nonaddictive and is basically classed as a food supplement in the same manner as spirulina, wheatgrass, and barley. Unlike guarana (*paullinia cupana*) and coffee (*coffea arabica*), maca root does not contain any caffeine; therefore it has no stimulant affect on the central nervous system.

Madder (mad er)
(*Rubia tinctoria*)

Synonyms/Related Species: Bengal Madder (*rubia cordifolia*), Dyer's Madder, Garance, Robbia, and Wild Madder (*rubia peregrina*).
Family/Class: Rubiaceae (madder).
Habitat: Africa, Asia, Britain, Europe, France, Holland, India, and the Mediterranean.
Flavor: Bitter.
Parts Used: Root (harvested when it is 3 years old).
Properties: Alterative, antiphlogistic, astringent, depurative, diuretic, emmenagogue, hemostatic, lithotriptic, and stimulant.
Constituents: Alizarin, monosaccharides, alizarinopurpurin, ruberythric acid, and tannic acid.
Historical Uses: Amenorrhea, appetite loss, bleeding, calculus, diarrhea, edema, fever, fractures, gallstones, gout, inflammation, jaundice, kidney stones, liver problems, menstrual problems, rickets, skin problems, spleen problems, and urinary problems.
Discussion: May dissolve calculi; enhance the cardiovascular system and liver functions; promote urine flow; purify the blood; reestablish healthy system functions; stimulate menstruation.
Cautions/Contraindications: Avoid use if pregnant or breast-feeding.
Adverse Reactions: Nausea and/or vomiting.
Herb/Drug Interactions: This herb could cause an interaction (possibly severe) when taken with the following drugs: None known.
Preparations/Dosage: Crude Herb: 3-9 grams. Infusion: 1-1½ cups per day. Root (powdered): Average dose in substance 30 grains (½ drachm).
Note: Ingestion of madder root will impart a temporary, harmless, rubescent (reddish) color to the bones and urine.

Magnolia (mag·nō lē·e)
(*Magnolia acuminata*)

Synonyms/Related Species: Beaver Tree, Blue Magnolia, Cucumber Tree, Holly Bay, Indian Bark, Laurel Magnolia (*magnolia grandiflora*), Red Bay, Swamp Laurel, Swamp Sassafras (*magnolia glauca*), Umbrella Magnolia (*magnolia tripetala*), Umbrella Tree, White Bay, and White Laurel (*magnolia virginiana*).
Family/Class: Magnoliaceae (magnolia).
Floral Emblem: Louisiana and Mississippi.
Habitat: England and North America.
Flavor: Bitter/pungent.
Parts Used: Bark (stem/root), flower buds.
Properties: Analgesic, anesthetic (local), antiemetic, antiperiodic, antiphlogistic, aromatic, astringent, carminative, diaphoretic, emmenagogue, expectorant, hemostatic, laxative, malariacidal, stimulant, stomachic, and tonic.
Constituents: Alkaloids, bitter principle, citral (geranial), estragole, eucalyptol (cineol), eugenol (eugenic acid), safrol, and volatile oil.
Historical Uses: Acidity (gastric), addiction (nicotine), ague, appetite loss, asthma, bleeding, bronchitis, chills, colds, colic, congestion (uterine, vaginal), cough, diarrhea, digestive complaints, diphtheria, dysentery, erysipelas, fever (ephemeral, intermittent, rheumatic),

flatulence, gastralgia, gastritis, gastrointestinal problems, headache, indigestion, inflammation, irritable bowel syndrome (IBS), leukorrhea, lung problems, malaria, mucus, muscle and joint pain, pain, parasites (malarial plasmodia), respiratory conditions, rheumatism, sinusitis, substitute for peruvian bark (*cinchona pubescens*), ulcer (duodenal, gastric, peptic, syriac), urethritis, vaginitis, vomiting, wheezing, and wounds (minor).
Discussion: May aid digestion; clear and open bronchial passages; enhance colon, lung, spleen, and stomach functions; promote bowel evacuation and perspiration; reduce nicotine withdrawal symptoms; restore normal tone to tissues; serve as an adjuvant to nicotine cessation therapies; stimulate appetite, menstruation, and peristalsis.
Cautions/Contraindications: Avoid use if pregnant or breast-feeding.
Adverse Reactions: Diarrhea, nausea, paralysis, and/or vomiting.
Herb/Drug Interactions: This herb could cause an interaction (possibly severe) when taken with the following drugs: None known.
Preparations/Dosage: Crude Herb (bark/buds): 3-6 grams. Bark (powdered): Average dose in substance 20-60 grains (2-4 gm.). Decoction (bark): ¼-½ cup per day. Infusion (buds): ½-1 cup per day. Tincture: 5-15 drops (0.333-1 cc.) one to three times per day.
Isolation: Eucalyptol: 5 drops (0.3 cc.) in atomization or inhalation therapy for use in respiratory conditions. Safrol: Average dose of 20-30 drops (1.333-2 cc.) for use as an analgesic.
Note: Magnolia bark can be used for a longer period of time and is a safer remedy than Peruvian bark.

Malabar (mal e·bär)
(*Adhatoda justicia*)

Synonyms/Related Species: Adhatoda, Adulsa Bakas, Arusa, Asian Malabar (*adhatoda vasica*), and Malabar Nut.
Family/Class: Acanthaceae (acanthus).
Habitat: Asia, India.
Flavor: Bitter.
Parts Used: Flowers, fruit, leaves, root.
Properties: Antibiotic, antispasmodic, expectorant, and febrifuge.
Constituents: Alkaloids, vasicine, and volatile oil.
Historical Uses: Abscess, asthma, bronchitis, colds, fever (ephemeral), infection (bacterial), lesions (tubercle), mucus, respiratory conditions, scrofula, spasmodic conditions, tuberculosis, and ulcer (fistula, tuberculous).
Discussion: May clear and open bronchial passages; inhibit or destroy development and growth of bacteria and other microorganisms.
Cautions/Contraindications: Avoid use if pregnant or breast-feeding.
Adverse Reactions: Alimentary canal irritation, diarrhea, excitability, gastrointestinal irritation, nausea, and/or vomiting.
Herb/Drug Interactions: This herb could cause an interaction (possibly severe) when taken with the following drugs: None known.
Preparations/Dosage: Crude Herb: 3-6 grams. Juice (fresh): 1-4 drachms (4-15 cc.). Tincture: 10-30 drops (0.666-2 cc.) one to three times per day.

Mallow (mal ō)
(*Malva sylvestris*)

Synonyms/Related Species: Blue Mallow, Cheeseflower (*malva parviflora*), Cheese Plant (*malva neglecta*), Chinese Malva (*malva verticillata*), Common Mallow, Country Mallow, Dwarf Mallow (*malva rotundifolia*), Little Mallow, and Malva.
Family/Class: Malvaceae (mallow).
Habitat: Asia, Britain, Egypt, England, Europe, and North America.
Flavor: Sweet.
Parts Used: Flowers, leaves.
Properties: Analgesic, antibiotic, antiphlogistic, astringent, demulcent, expectorant, and nutritive.
Constituents: Anthocyans, flavonoids, mucilage, and vitamin A.
Historical Uses: Abscess, acne, arthritis, asthma, bladder problems, bronchitis, colds, colitis, constipation, cough, dietary supplementation, dysmenorrhea, edema, emphysema, enteritis, fever (ephemeral, rheumatic), gastritis, hemoptysis, infection (bacterial), inflammation, laryngitis, lesions (tubercle), malnutrition, mastitis, neuropathy, osteoarthritis (OA), mucus, muscle and joint pain, pain, palsy (Bell's), rash, respiratory conditions, rheumatism, scrofula, seizure conditions, sore throat, sores, tonsillitis, tuberculosis, ulcer (fistula, tuberculous), vertigo, and wounds (minor).
Discussion: May increase circulation; provide dietary supplementation; serve as a nutritional adjuvant to therapeutic programs; stimulate the formation of healthy nerve tissue; strengthen the immune system.
Cautions/Contraindications: Avoid use if pregnant or breast-feeding. Do not confuse this plant with marshmallow (a*lthaea officinalis*).
Adverse Reactions: Nausea and/or vomiting.
Herb/Drug Interactions: This herb could cause an interaction (possibly severe) when taken with the following drugs: None known.
Preparations/Dosage: Crude Herb: 3-6 grams. Decoction: ½ cup per day. Infusion: ½-1 cup per day. Leaves: Boiled and eaten as a vegetable. Tincture: 10-30 drops (0.666-2 cc.) one to three times per day.

Mallow, Musk (mal ō, musk)
(*Hibiscus abelmoschus*)

Synonyms/Related Species: Chinese Hibiscus (*hibiscus rosa-sinensis*), Corkwood (*hibiscus tiliaceus*), Cuban Bast, Guinea Sorrel, Hibiscus, Indian Hibiscus (*hibiscus bancroftianus*), Jamaica Sorrel (*hibiscus sabdariffa*), Marsh Hibiscus (*hibiscus palustris*), Musk Seed, Okra (*hibiscus esculentus*), Rose of China, Syrian Mallow, Target-Leaved Hibiscus, Venice Mallow (*hibiscus trionum*), and Water Mallow.
Family/Class: Malvaceae (mallow).
Habitat: Africa, Asia, China, Egypt, India, Malaysia, and North America.
Flavor: Sour/sweet.
Parts Used: Flowers, leaves, root, seeds.

Properties: Alterative, antiphlogistic, antispasmodic, aphrodisiac, aromatic, astringent, carminative, demulcent, diaphoretic, diuretic, emmenagogue, nervine, and stimulant.
Constituents: Albumin (albumen), asparagin, fatty acids (oleic, palmitic, stearic), fixed oils (olein, palmitin, stearin), inulin (starch), monosaccharides, pectic acid, pectin, resin, mucilage, and volatile oil.
Historical Uses: Bleeding, colds, cough, diarrhea, digestive complaints, dysentery, fever, flatulence, gastrointestinal problems, gleet, gonorrhea, halitosis, infection (sexually transmitted), inflammation, influenza, pruritus, sexually transmitted diseases (STDs), skin problems, spasmodic conditions, stroke (heat), sunburn, and urethritis.
Discussion: May aid digestion; arouse sexual impulses; calm the nervous system; enhance liver and stomach functions; promote perspiration and urine flow; soothe mucous membrane irritation; stimulate menstruation and uterine contractions.
Cautions/Contraindications: Avoid use if pregnant or breast-feeding.
Adverse Reactions: Nausea and/or vomiting.
Herb/Drug Interactions: This herb could cause an interaction (possibly severe) when taken with the following drugs: None known.
Preparations/Dosage: Crude Herb (flowers): 3-6 grams. Decoction (root): ¼-½ cup per day. Infusion (flowers and/or seeds): ½-1 cup. Leaves: External uses only. Seeds: Chewed to sweeten the breath and relieve gastrointestinal problems.
Isolation: Asparagin: Soluble in hot water, but insoluble in alcohol and ether. Average dose of 1-2 grains (0.066-0.133 gm.) for use as a diuretic.
Note: Musk Mallow's actions are similar to that of mallow (*malva spp.*), but of a lesser degree.

Mandrake, American (man drāk, e·mer e·ken)

(*Podophyllum peltatum*)

Synonyms/Related Species: Duck's Foot, Ground Lemon, Hog Apple, Indian Apple, Indian Podophyllum (*podophyllum emodi*), May-Apple, Phyllon, Podos, Raccoon Berry, and Wild Lemon.
Family/Class: Berberidaceae (barberry).
Habitat: North America.
Flavor: Bitter.
Parts Used: Root, resin.
Properties: Alterative, analgesic, anticarcinogen, anticholinergic, antimitotic, antiphlogistic, aphrodisiac, astringent, cholagogue, counterirritant, emetic, hallucinogen, hemostatic, hepatic, laxative, lithotriptic, mydriatic, narcotic, sedative, sialagogue, stimulant, and tonic.
Constituents: Alkaloids, atropine, flavonols, glycosides, hyoscyamine, inulin (starch), lignin, monosaccharides, podophyllin, podophylloquercitin, and podophyllotoxin.
Historical Uses: Allergy (pollen), arthritis, asthma, bleeding, calculus, cancer, cerebrospinal hyperemia, colic, constipation, convulsions, cough, diarrhea, digestive complaints, edema, enuresis (urinary incontinence), fever (ephemeral, enteric, hay, rheumatic), gallstones, gastrointestinal problems, gout, headache, hemorrhoids, indigestion, infertility, inflammation, insomnia, iritis, jaundice, kidney stones, lesions (tubercle), liver problems, melancholy, muscle and joint pain, nervous conditions, pain, poisoning (lead), rheumatism, scrofula, sexually transmitted diseases (STDs), skin problems, sores, syphilis, tuberculosis, typhoid, ulcer (bouveret, fistula, gastric, syphilitic, tuberculous), uterine problems, venereal warts, vomiting,

warts (digitate, filiform, fugitive, glabra, mother, plana juvenilis, plantar, seborrhoeic, vulgaris), and whooping cough.

Discussion: May arouse sexual impulses; block the passage of impulses through the parasympathetic nerves; decrease the effects of carcinogens; dissolve calculi; enhance colon, digestive system, glandular system, and liver functions; increase the frequency of the heart's action; induce sleep; inhibit mitosis (the division of active somatic and germ cells); lessen the vascularity of the iris; produce pupil dilatation; promote bile flow, bowel evacuation, and saliva secretion; protect the liver; reestablish healthy system functions; reduce the frequency of nighttime urination; restore normal tone to tissues; stimulate the sympathetic and depress the cerebrospinal nerves, and peristalsis; strengthen the respiratory system.

Cautions/Contraindications: Avoid use if pregnant or breast-feeding. Do not confuse this herb with European mandrake (*mandragora officinalis*). May cause dermatitis in susceptible individuals. Prolonged use may lead to a tolerance to the accumulation of tropine-alkaloids in the parasympathetic system; thus more of the herb is required to achieve the same effects. Not for long-term use. Use with professional guidance/supervision.

Adverse Reactions: Arrhythmia, ataxia, atropinism (atropine poisoning), central nervous system depression, coma, decreased perspiration, delirium, diarrhea, dizziness, drowsiness, dryness (mouth), dysuria (painful/difficult urination), exhaustion, gastrointestinal cramps (severe), hallucinations, headache, insufficiency (circulatory), intestinal problems, lethargy, loss of consciousness, low blood cell count, mania, nausea, nephritis, pupil dilatation, reduced blood pressure levels, respiratory failure, restlessness, spasmodic conditions, stupor, tachycardia, vomiting of bile, weak pulse rate, and/or possible death.

Herb/Drug Interactions: This herb could cause an interaction (possibly severe) when taken with the following drugs: Autonomic drugs.

Preparations/Dosage: Crude Herb: 1-3 grams. Decoction: 1 teaspoon one to four times per day. Extract (solid): Average dose in substance 1-5 grains (0.066-0.324 gm.). Root (powdered): Average dose in substance 5-30 grains (0.324-2 gm.). Tincture (root): 1-5 drops (0.066-0.333 cc.) one to three times per day. Tincture (resin): 1-3 drops (0.06-0.2 cc.) one to three times per day.

Isolation: Atropine: Soluble in alcohol and sparingly so in water. Average dose of $^{1}/_{150}$ grain (0.4 mg.) for use as a mydriatic and narcotic. Atropine sulfate: Soluble in water. Average dose of $^{1}/_{120}$ grain (0.5 mg.) for use as a mydriatic and narcotic. Podophyllin: ⅛-½ grain (0.008-0.033 gm.) for use as a laxative.

Mandrake, European (man drāk, yoor e·pē en)

(*Mandragora officinalis*)

Synonyms/Related Species: Baaras, Circe's Plant, Devil's Apple, Dudaim, Love Apple, Mandragora, Oriental Mandrake, Satan's Apple, and True Mandrake.

Family/Class: Solanaceae (nightshade).

Habitat: Asia, England, Europe, and the Mediterranean.

Flavor: Bitter.

Parts Used: Root.

Properties: Alterative, analgesic, anticarcinogen, anesthetic, anticholinergic, antimitotic, antiphlogistic, aphrodisiac, astringent, emetic, hallucinogen, hemostatic, hepatic, hypnotic, laxative, lithotriptic, mydriatic, narcotic, sedative, sialagogue, stimulant, and tonic.

Constituents: Alkaloids, atropine, esters, glycosides, hyoscyamine, inulin (starch), lignin, mandragorine, monosaccharides, podophyllin, podophyllotoxin, podophylloquercetin, resin, saponins, scopolamine, and solanine.

Historical Uses: Allergy (pollen), arthritis, asthma, bleeding, calculus, cancer, cerebrospinal hyperemia, colic, constipation, convulsions, cough, delirium, delirium tremens (DTs), diarrhea, digestive complaints, edema, enuresis (urinary incontinence), fever (ephemeral, enteric, hay, rheumatic), gallstones, gout, headache, hemorrhoids, indigestion, infertility, inflammation, insomnia, iritis, jaundice, kidney stones, lesions (tubercle), liver problems, mania, melancholy, muscle and joint pain, nervous conditions, pain, poisoning (lead), rheumatism, scrofula, sexually transmitted diseases (STDs), skin problems, sores, syphilis, tuberculosis, typhoid, ulcer (bouveret, duodenal, fistula, gastric, peptic, syphilitic, tuberculous), uterine problems, vomiting, warts (digitate, filiform, fugitive, glabra, mother, plana juvenilis, plantar, seborrhoeic, venereal, vulgaris), and whooping cough.

Discussion: May arouse sexual impulses; block the passage of impulses through the parasympathetic nerves; decrease the effects of carcinogens; dissolve calculi; enhance digestive and glandular system functions; increase the frequency of the heart's action; induce sleep; inhibit mitosis (the division of active somatic and germ cells); lessen the vascularity of the iris; produce pupil dilatation; promote bowel evacuation and saliva secretion; protect the liver; reduce the frequency of nighttime urination; reestablish healthy system functions; restore normal tone to tissues; serve as an adjuvant to alcoholism treatment programs to assist in easing delirium tremens (DTs); stimulate the sympathetic and depress the cerebrospinal nerves, and peristalsis; strengthen the respiratory system.

Cautions/Contraindications: Avoid use if pregnant or breast-feeding. Do not confuse this herb with mandrake (*podophyllum peltatum*). May cause dermatitis in susceptible individuals. Prolonged use may lead to a tolerance to the accumulation of tropine-alkaloids in the parasympathetic system; thus more of the herb is required to achieve the same effects. Not for long-term use. Use with professional guidance/supervision.

Adverse Reactions: Arrhythmia, ataxia, atropinism (atropine poisoning), cardiac damage, coma, decreased perspiration, delirium, diarrhea (possibly bloody), dizziness, drowsiness, dryness (mouth), dysuria (painful/difficult urination), exhaustion, gastrointestinal cramps (severe), hallucinations, headache, lethargy, loss of consciousness, mania, nausea, nephritis, pupil dilatation, reduced peristalsis, respiratory failure, restlessness, spasmodic conditions, stupor, tachycardia, vomiting of bile, and/or possible death.

Herb/Drug Interactions: This herb could cause an interaction (possibly severe) when taken with the following drugs: Autonomic drugs.

Preparations/Dosage: Crude Herb (root): 1-2 grams. Decoction: 1 teaspoon one to four times per day. Extract: 1-2 drops (0.06-0.1 cc.) one to two times per day. Root (powdered): Average dose in substance 5-30 grains (0.324-2 gm.). Tincture: 2-5 drops (0.133-0.333 cc.). Ceremonial Uses: Place 1-2 grams of the powdered root into wine. Ceremonial Smoke: Dip herbal or tobacco cigarettes into mandrake extract or tincture and let them air dry.

Isolation: Atropine: Soluble in alcohol and sparingly so in water. Average dose of $^{1}/_{150}$ grain (0.4 mg.) for use as a mydriatic and narcotic. Atropine sulfate: Soluble in water. Average dose of $^{1}/_{120}$ grain (0.5 mg.) for use as a mydriatic and narcotic. Podophyllin: ⅛-½ grain (0.008-0.033 gm.) for use as a laxative.

Maple (mā p'l)
(*Acer saccharinum*)

Synonyms/Related Species: Bigleaf Maple (*acer macrophyllum*), Bird's Eye Maple, Black Maple (*acer nigrum*), Canyon Maple (*acer grandidentatum*), Common Maple (*acer campestre*), Curled Maple, Douglas Maple (*acer douglasii*), Great Maple (*acer pseudo-platanus*), Manitoba Maple (*acer negundo*), Norway Maple (*acer platanoids*), Red Maple (*acer rubrum*), Rocky Mountain Maple (*acer glabrum*), Sugar Maple, Swamp Maple, and Wasatch Maple.
Family/Class: Aceraceae (maple).
Habitat: Austria, Britain, Europe, Germany, India, Italy, Japan, Lithuania, North America, Norway, Poland, Savoy, Sweden, and Switzerland.
Flavor: Bark: bitter. Sap: sweet.
Parts Used: Bark (inner), sap.
Properties: Aromatic, astringent, hemostatic, tonic, and vulnerary.
Constituents: Allantoin, carbohydrates, minerals (calcium, iron, phosphorus, potassium, sodium), monosaccharides, tannic acid, triterpene saponins, and vitamins (B_6 (pyridoxine), chlorine).
Historical Uses: Bleeding, conjunctivitis, eye problems, eyewash, maple syrup (sap), and molasses (sap).
Discussion: May restore normal tone to tissues; speed healing.
Cautions/Contraindications: Avoid use if pregnant or breast-feeding.
Adverse Reactions: Diarrhea (possibly bloody), edema, flatulence, gastrointestinal cramps (severe), hematuria (blood in the urine), nausea, and/or vomiting.
Herb/Drug Interactions: This herb could cause an interaction (possibly severe) when taken with the following drugs: None known.
Preparations/Dosage: Crude Herb (bark): 3-6 grams. Decoction (bark): ¼-½ cup per day. Sap (processed): Maple syrup or molasses.

Marijuana (mar·e·hwan ah)
(*Cannabis sativa*)

Synonyms/Related Species: Asiatic Hemp, Bhang, Cannabis, Chanvre, Charas, Churrus, Common Hemp, Ganja, Grass, Guaza, Gunja, Haenep, Hanapa, Haschisch, Hemp, Hemp Plant, Indian Hemp (*cannabis indica*), Kannabis, Kif, Kunibu, Leaf of Delusion, Mary Jane, Nasha, Pot, Reefer, Sidhee, Subjee, Tekrouri, and Weed.
Family/Class: Cannabinaceae (hemp).
Habitat: Africa, Algeria, Asia, Calcutta, the Caucasus, China, England, Europe, India, Italy, North America, Persia, Russia, Siberia, Spain, Turkey, and other temperate regions worldwide.
Flavor: Bitter/sweet.
Parts Used: Flower tops, leaves, and seeds of the female plant.
Properties: Analgesic, anesthetic (local), antibiotic, anticarcinogen, antidepressant, antiperiodic, antiphlogistic, antispasmodic, convulsant, demulcent, euphoriant, expectorant, hypnotic, laxative, malariacidal, narcotic, nutritive, oxytocic, sedative, stimulant, and tranquilizer.
Constituents: Alkaloids, cannabene, cannabindon, cannabine, cannabinol, cannabitetanine, enzymes, flavonoids, glycosides, lipids, protein, tetrahydrocannabinol (THC), trigonelline, vitamins (choline, inositol), and volatile oil.

Historical Uses: Acquired immune deficiency syndrome (AIDS), addiction (alcohol), ague, anemia, angina, anxiety, appetite loss, asthma, bronchitis, cancer, cholera, cirrhosis, colds, constipation, convulsions, cough, cystitis, delirium tremens (DTs), depression (mild/moderate), dietary supplementation, diphtheria, ear problems, emaciation, emphysema, epilepsy, fever (ephemeral, intermittent, rheumatic), food source (seeds), gastrointestinal problems, glaucoma, gleet, gonorrhea, gout, headache, hysteria, infection (bacterial, sexually transmitted, urinary tract), inflammation, insomnia, liver problems, malaria, malnutrition, menopausal/menstrual problems, menorrhagia, migraine, mucus, muscle and joint pain, nausea, nervous conditions, neuralgia, neurasthenia, pain, parasites (malarial plasmodia), poisoning (strychnine), prolapse (rectal, uterine), respiratory conditions, rheumatism, sexually transmitted diseases (STDs), spasmodic conditions, tetanus, trismus (lockjaw), tumors, ulcer (duodenal, gastric, peptic), urethritis, vomiting, and whooping cough.

Discussion: May clear and open bronchial passages; create an abnormal or exaggerated sense of well-being; decrease the effect of carcinogens; enhance colon, spleen, and stomach functions; induce sleep; inhibit or destroy development and growth of bacteria and other microorganisms; offset the negative effects of chemotherapy, prescription drugs, and radiation therapy; prevent the deposition of fat in the liver; promote bowel evacuation; provide dietary supplementation; reduce alcohol and opiate addiction withdrawal symptoms as well as intraoccular eye pressure; serve as an adjuvant to alcoholism treatment programs to assist in easing delirium tremens (DTs), as a nutritional adjuvant to therapeutic programs, and as an adjuvant to aid psychotherapy; soothe mucous membrane irritation; stimulate appetite, peristalsis, and uterine contractions.

Cautions/Contraindications: Avoid use if pregnant or breast-feeding. Do not confuse this herb with Canadian hemp (*apocynum cannabinum*).

Adverse Reactions: Apathy, arrhythmia, concentration problems, confusion, convulsions, cough, chronic bronchitis or laryngitis, dizziness, erectile dysfunction, fainting, hallucinations, impairment of short-term memory and perception of time, increased tear flow, limb numbness, mood swings, nausea, panic, psychosis, and/or vomiting.

Herb/Drug Interactions: This herb could cause an interaction (possibly severe) when taken with the following drugs: None known.

Preparations/Dosage: Crude Herb (powdered): Average dose in substance 1-3 grains (0.066-0.2 gm.). Extract: 1-5 drops (0.066-0.333 cc.) one to two times per day. Extract (solid): Average dose in substance ¼-1 grain (0.015-0.066 gm.). Extract (powdered): Average dose in substance ½-20 grains (0.033-1.333 gm.). Hashish (smoking): Average dose ¼-1 grain (0.015-0.066 gm.). Infusion (leaves): 1-2 tablespoons one to four times per day. Infusion (seeds): ½-2 cups one to three times per day. Seeds (ground/powdered): Non-Intoxicating. Average dose in substance 9-30 grams for use as a food source. Tincture (tops/leaves): 2-10 drops (0.133-0.666 cc.) one to three times per day. Tincture (cannabinone/resin): 5-15 drops (0.333-1 cc.) one to three times per day.

<u>Note</u>: This plant is categorized as an illegal narcotic in the U.S. and neither historical medicinal nor therapeutic usage is officially permitted. It's use as an adjuvant to chronic conditions and pain is currently under investigation, and experimental human studies have been conducted with high success rates. At present, production is only permitted pharmaceutically for chronic conditions and pain usage in some states of the U.S.A. The production of certain varieties is also permitted for the extraction of hemp fibers used in cloth and cordage.

Marjoram (mär jer·em)
(*Origanum vulgare*)

Synonyms/Related Species: Delight of the Mountains, Knotted Marjoram (*origanum hortensis*), Mexican Oregano (*origanum mexicana*), Mexican Sage, Mountain Mint, Orosganos, Sweet Marjoram (*origanum marjorana*), Wild Marjoram, Winter Marjoram, and Wintersweet.
Family/Class: Labiatae (mint).
Habitat: Africa, Asia, England, Europe, Germany, Italy, the Mediterranean, Mexico, North America, and Spain.
Flavor: Bitter/pungent.
Parts Used: Leaves.
Properties: Analgesic, antibiotic, antifungal, antioxidant, antiphlogistic, antispasmodic, aromatic, carminative, diaphoretic, diuretic, emmenagogue, expectorant, nervine, stimulant, stomachic, tonic, urinary antiseptic, and vulnerary.
Constituents: Arbutin, caffeic acid, carvacrol, caryophyllin, chlorogenic acid, cymene, flavonoids, glycosides, linalool, myrcene, minerals (calcium, iron, magnesium, phosphorus, potassium, silicon, sodium, zinc), mucilage, phytoprogesterones, polysaccharides, silicic acid, tannic acid, terpenes, thymol, vitamins (A, B_1 (thiamine), B_2 (riboflavin), B_3 (niacin), B_{12}, C (ascorbic acid), E (alpha-tocopheral), and volatile oil.
Historical Uses: Abdominal pain, allergy (pollen), anemia (pernicious), arthritis, asthma, bronchitis, bruises, candida, colds, colic, convulsions, cough, cramps, depression (mild/moderate), diarrhea, digestive complaints, dizziness, dysmenorrhea, edema, enuresis (urinary incontinence), escherichia coli (e-coli), fever (ephemeral, hay, rheumatic), flatulence, flavoring agent, gallbladder problems, gastritis, gastrointestinal problems, giardia, gout, headache, indigestion, infection (bacterial, fungal, urinary tract), inflammation, influenza, insomnia, insufficiency (venous), lesions (tubercle), lung problems, measles, migraine, moniliasis, motion sickness, mucus, muscle and joint pain, nausea, nervous conditions, neuralgia, neurasthenia, pneumonia, poisoning (food, narcotic), potpourri, respiratory conditions, rheumatism, rheumatoid arthritis (RA), scrofula, sinusitis, spasmodic conditions, sprain, toothache, tuberculosis, ulcer (fistula, stasis, tuberculous, varicose), varicose veins, and whooping cough.
Discussion: May aid digestion; calm the nervous system; clear and open bronchial passages; enhance lung and stomach functions; increase red blood cell formation in persons with anemia; inhibit oxidation and inhibit development or destroy growth of bacteria and other microorganisms; promote perspiration and urine flow; reduce the frequency of nighttime urination; restore normal tone to tissues; serve as an antidote for narcotic poisons; speed healing; stimulate appetite and menstruation.
Cautions/Contraindications: Avoid use if pregnant or breast-feeding. Do not confuse oil of marjoram (*oleum majorana*) with oil of origanum (*oleum thymi*), which is extracted from thyme (*thymus vulgaris*). Not for long-term use.
Adverse Reactions: Diarrhea, edema, nausea, and/or vomiting.
Herb/Drug Interactions: This herb could cause an interaction (possibly severe) when taken with the following drugs: None known.
Preparations/Dosage: Crude Herb: 3-9 grams. Infusion: 1-2 cups per day. Juice: 1 tablespoon in water one to two times per day. Leaves (crushed/powdered): Flavoring agent in culinary. Tincture: 10-30 drops (0.666-2 cc.) one to three times per day.

Isolation: Arbutin: Average dose of 5-15 grains (0.3-1 gm.) for use as a diuretic and urinary antiseptic.

Marshmallow (märsh mal ō)
(*Althaea officinalis*)

Synonyms/Related Species: Althaea Rose, Cheeses, European Cheese Plant, Guimauve, Hollyhock (*althaea rosea*), Mallards, Mallow Rose, Mauls, Rose Mallow, Schloss Tea, Sweet Weed, and True Mallow.
Family/Class: Malvaceae (mallow).
Habitat: Asia, Denmark, Egypt, England, Europe, France, Greece, Scotland, and Syria.
Flavor: Sweet.
Parts Used: Flowers, leaves, root.
Properties: Antibiotic, antiphlogistic, alterative, astringent, demulcent, diuretic, expectorant, hemostatic, laxative, lithotriptic, nutritive, and vulnerary.
Constituents: Anthocyanidin, asparagin, cellulose, chlorophyll, inulin (starch), minerals (calcium, iodine, iron, sodium, zinc), monosaccharides, mucilage, pectic acid, pectin, polysaccharides, tannic acid, and vitamins (A, B_1 (thiamine), B_2 (riboflavin), B_3 (niacin), B_5 (pantothenic acid), B_6 (pyridoxine), B_{12}, B_x (para-aminobenzoic acid (PABA), H (biotin), M (folic acid).
Historical Uses: Abscess, allergy (pollen), asthma, benign breast disease, bladder problems, bleeding, bronchitis, bruises, burns (minor), calculus, colds, conjunctivitis, constipation, colitis, cough, Crohn's disease, cystitis, diabetes, diarrhea, dietary supplementation, dysentery, dysuria (painful/difficult urination), ear problems, eczema, edema, emaciation, emphysema, enteritis, enuresis (urinary incontinence), eyewash, fever (ephemeral, hay, septic), gallstones, gangrene, gargle/mouth rinse, gastritis, glandular problems, hemafecia (blood in the stool), hematuria (blood in the urine), indigestion, infection (bacterial), inflammation, influenza, insect bites or stings, irritations, kidney problems, kidney stones, laryngitis, lesions (tubercle), liver problems, lung problems, malnutrition, mastitis, mucus, muscle and joint pain, nausea, nephritis, pneumonia, poisoning (blood), psoriasis, rash, respiratory conditions, scrofula, skin problems, sore throat, sores, sprain, thirst, tonsillitis, toothache, tuberculosis, ulcer (duodenal, fistula, gastric, peptic, tuberculous), urethritis, urinary problems, whooping cough, and wounds (minor).
Discussion: May clear and open bronchial passages; dissolve calculi; enhance immune, respiratory, and urinary system functions; promote bowel evacuation and urine flow; provide dietary supplementation; reduce the frequency of nighttime urination; serve as a nutritional adjuvant to therapeutic programs; soothe mucous membrane irritation; speed healing; stimulate peristalsis.
Cautions/Contraindications: Avoid use if pregnant or breast-feeding, or if you have diabetes, an iodine sensitivity, or an obstruction (intestinal). Do not confuse this plant with mallow (*malva sylvestris*). May delay the absorption of other drugs when taken simultaneously. May interfere with the effectiveness of certain thyroid medications.
Adverse Reactions: Abdominal pain, arrhythmia, diarrhea, edema, fever, hypertrophy (thyroid), iodism (iodine poisoning), nausea, priapism, thirst, and/or vomiting.
Herb/Drug Interactions: This herb could cause an interaction (possibly severe) when taken with the following drugs: Thyroid drugs.

Preparations/Dosage: Crude Herb (flowers/leaves): 3-12 grams. Crude Herb (root): 3-9 grams. Decoction (root): 1 cup per day. Extract (cold): 1 cup per day. Infusion (flowers/leaves): 1-2 cups per day. Syrup (*syrupus mucilago althaea*): Mix with honey and take 1-2 tablespoons as needed for cough. Tincture: 15-40 drops (1-3 cc.) one to three times per day.
Isolation: Asparagin: Soluble in hot water, but insoluble in alcohol and ether. Average dose of 1-2 grains (0.066-0.133 gm.) for use as a diuretic.

Marsh Marigold (märsh mar e·gōld)
(*Caltha palustris*)

Synonyms/Related Species: American Cowslip, Bulbous Buttercup, Bull's Eye, Celery-Leaved Buttercup, Cowslip, Crowfoot, Crowfoot Buttercup, Cuckoo Buds, Marsh Crowfoot, Meadow Bouts, Mountain Marsh Marigold (*caltha leptosepala*), Palsywort, St. Anthony's Turnip, Water Crowfoot, Water Dragon, White Marsh Marigold (*caltha howellii*), and Yellow Marsh Marigold.
Family/Class: Ranunculaceae (buttercup).
Habitat: Alaska, the Alpine and Subalpine zones, and North America.
Parts Used: Entire plant (fresh).
Properties: Analgesic, anti-inflammatory, antispasmodic, counterirritant, diaphoretic, diuretic, emetic, expectorant, laxative, and vesicant.
Constituents: Alkaloids, protoanemonin, saponins, and triterpene lactones.
Historical Uses: Anemia, bronchitis, colds, constipation, cramps, inflammation, jaundice, liver problems, menstrual problems, muscle and joint pain, pain, paralysis, respiratory conditions, sinusitis, skin problems, sores, spasmodic conditions, warts (digitate, filiform, fugitive, glabra, mother, plana juvenilis, plantar, seborrhoeic, vulgaris), and wounds (minor).
Discussion: May clear and open bronchial passages; promote bowel evacuation, perspiration, and urine flow; raise blood sugar levels; reduce cholesterol levels and tissue inflammation; stimulate peristalsis.
Cautions/Contraindications: Avoid use if pregnant or breast-feeding. May cause dermatitis in susceptible individuals.
Adverse Reactions: Blistering of the skin, convulsions, diarrhea (possibly bloody), dizziness, fainting, gastrointestinal cramps (severe), hematuria (blood in the urine), liver damage (often characterized by jaundice), kidney failure, nausea, respiratory distress, salivation, vomiting, and/or possible death.
Herb/Drug Interactions: This herb could cause an interaction (possibly severe) when taken with the following drugs: None known.
Preparations/Dosage: External uses only.

Maté (mä tā)
(*Ilex paraguayiensis*)

Synonyms/Related Species: American Holly, Apalachin Maté (*ilex vomitoria*), Black Aldar, Black Drink Plant, Brazilian Holly, Brook Aldar, Dahoon Holly (*ilex dahoon*), Emetic Holly, English Holly (*ilex aquifolium*), False Aldar, Feverbush, Gón gouha, Houx Maté, Ilex Maté, Indian Black Drink, Jesuit's Tea, Paraguay Tea, Quechua Mati, Striped Aldar, White Holly (*ilex opaca*), Winterberry (*ilex verticillata*), Yaupon Holly (*ilex vomitoria*), and Yerba Maté.
Family/Class: Aquifoliaceae (holly).

Habitat: Asia, Central America, North America, and South America.
Flavor: Bitter.
Parts Used: Leaves.
Properties: Antiperiodic, astringent, depurative, diaphoretic, diuretic, emetic, hallucinogen, laxative, malariacidal, lithotriptic, parasiticide, stimulant, and tonic.
Constituents: Alkaloids, caffeic acid, caffeine, chlorogenic acid, flavonoids, glycosides, ilexanthine, minerals (magnesium, manganese, potassium), polyphenols, rutin, tannic acid, and theobromine.
Historical Uses: Arrhythmia, bladder problems, calculus, cardiovascular conditions, constipation, edema, fatigue, fever (ephemeral, intermittent), gallstones, infection (urinary tract), kidney stones, malaria, migraine, parasites (malarial plasmodia), poisoning (opium), substitute for coffee, and weight loss.
Discussion: May dissolve calculi; enhance nervous system function; increase endurance, energy, and stamina; maintain electrolyte balance; prevent hemorrhage in persons with hypertension; promote bowel evacuation, perspiration, and urine flow; reduce capillary fragility; restore normal tone to tissues; stimulate the immune system and peristalsis; purify the blood; serve as an antidote for opium poisoning; supress appetite.
Cautions/Contraindications: Avoid use if pregnant or breast-feeding, or if you have hyperactivity or ulcer (peptic). Berries are poisonous
Adverse Reactions: Aggravation of peptic ulcer, arrhythmia, cancer (esophageal, lung) increased risk, coma, diarrhea, drowsiness, gastrointestinal cramps, insomnia, nausea, nervousness, tachycardia, vomiting, and/or possible death.
Herb/Drug Interactions: This herb could cause an interaction (possibly severe) when taken with the following drugs: None known.
Preparations/Dosage: Crude Herb: 3-6 grams. Infusion: 1-2 cups per day.
Isolation: Caffeine: Soluble in alcohol and water. Average dose of 1-3 grains (0.06-0.2 gm.) for use as a diuretic, nervine, and stimulant, and in poisoning (opium). Theobromine calcium gluconate: Average dose of 0.32-0.65 gm. for use in hypertension. Theobromine salicylate: Soluble in water. Average dose of 15 grains (1 gm.) for use as a diuretic. Theobromine sodiosalicylate: Used in a 5% solution, average dose of 15 drops (1cc.) for use as a diuretic. Theobromine and sodium acetate: Average dose of 15-45 grains (1-3 gm.) for use as a powerful diuretic.

Matico (me·tē kō)

(*Piper angustifolium*)

Synonyms/Related Species: False Matico (*piper aduncum*), Long Pepper (*piper elongatum*), Moho-Moho, Pippali, Soldier's Herb, and Yerba Soldado.
Family/Class: Piperaceae (pepper).
Habitat: Central America, Europe, and South America.
Flavor: Pungent.
Parts Used: Leaves.
Properties: Analgesic, antibiotic, antilithic, antiperiodic, aphrodisiac, astringent, carminative, diuretic, expectorant, febrifuge, hemostatic, lithotriptic, malariacidal, stimulant, and tonic.
Constituents: Piperazine, piperine, resin, tannic acid, and volatile oil.

Historical Uses: Allergy (pollen), bleeding, bronchitis, asthma, calculus, colds, colic, cough, cystitis, diabetes, diarrhea, dysentery, fever (ephemeral, hay, intermittent), flavoring agent, gallstones, gargle/mouth rinse, gleet, gonorrhea, gout, headache, hemorrhage, hemorrhoids, indigestion, infection (bacterial, sexually transmitted), kidney stones, lithemia, malaria, mucus, muscle and joint pain, pain, parasites (malarial plasmodia), pharyngitis, prostate problems, respiratory conditions, rheumatism, sexually transmitted diseases (STDs), sores, syphilis, toothache, ulcer (duodenal, gastric, peptic, syphilitic), urethritis, urinary problems, and wounds (minor).
Discussion: May aid digestion; arouse sexual impulses; clear and open bronchial passages; dissolve calculi; enhance kidney, lung, spleen, and stomach functions; increase absorption of nutrients and other herbs; inhibit or destroy development and growth of bacteria and other microorganisms; prevent the development of calculus or stones; promote urine flow; protect the liver; reduce excessive lithic acid (uric acid) and urate levels in the blood, tophi, and urine; restore normal tone to tissues.
Cautions/Contraindications: Avoid use if pregnant or breast-feeding, or if you have acidity (gastric) or insufficiency (gastric).
Adverse Reactions: Bladder/kidney irritation, diarrhea, nausea, skin rash, and/or vomiting.
Herb/Drug Interactions: This herb could cause an interaction (possibly severe) when taken with the following drugs: None known.
Preparations/Dosage: Crude Herb: 3-6 grams. Infusion: 1-2 cups per day. Leaves (powdered): 30-60 grains (2-4 gm.). Tincture: 10-30 drops (0.666-2 cc.) one to three times per day.
Isolation: Piperazine hydrochlorate: Dose in 2% solution, 5 grains (0.33 gm.), administered hypodermically; or orally (by mouth), 8 grains (0.5 gm.) for use as an antilithic, antisyphilitic, and diuretic. Piperine: Soluble (slightly) in water. Average dose of 1-5 grains (0.06-0.33 gm.) for use as an antiperiodic.

Meadowsweet (med ō·swēt)

(*Spiraea ulmaria*)

Synonyms/Related Species: Birch-Leaved Spiraea (*spiraea betulifolia*), Bridewort, Chinese Spiraea (*spiraea fortunei*), Douglas's Spiraea (*spiraea douglasii*), Dropwort (*spiraea filipendula*), Goatsbeard (*spiraea hexapetala*), Lady of the Meadow, Meadow Wort, Nepal Spiraea (*spiraea bella*), Queen of the Meadow, Spiraea, Steeplebush (*spiraea tomentosa*), Subalpine Spiraea (*spiraea splendens*), White Meadowsweet (*spiraea prunifolia*), Wild Spiraea (*spiraea lucida*), and Willow-Leaved Spiraea (*spiraea salyciflora*).
Family/Class: Rosaceae (rose).
Habitat: Asia, China, England, Europe, Japan, Nepal, North America, and the Subalpine zone.
Flavor: Bitter.
Parts Used: Leaves.
Properties: Analgesic, antacid, antibiotic, antilithic, antiphlogistic, antispasmodic, aromatic, astringent, carminative, diaphoretic, diuretic, expectorant, hemostatic, lithotriptic, stimulant, and tonic.
Constituents: Flavonoids, gaultherin, glycosides, heliotropin, methyl salicylate, monosaccharides, mucilage, rutin, salicin, salicylic acid, tannic acid, vanillin (methyl pyrocatechinic acid), vitamins (C (ascorbic acid), and volatile oil.

Historical Uses: Acidity (gastric), arthritis, bladder problems, bleeding, calculus, colds, diarrhea, digestive complaints, eczema, edema, eye irritation, fever (ephemeral, rheumatic), flatulence, gallstones, gastritis, gastrointestinal problems, gout, indigestion, infection (bacterial, urinary tract), inflammation, influenza, irritable bowel syndrome (IBS), kidney problems, kidney stones, laryngitis, lithemia, mucus, muscle and joint pain, nausea, neuralgia, pain, pruritus, respiratory conditions, rheumatism, shortness of breath, spasmodic conditions, stomatitis, substitute for aspirin, wheezing, and wounds (minor).
Discussion: May aid digestion; clear and open bronchial passages; dissolve calculi; enhance bladder, colon, digestive system, and liver functions; inhibit or destroy development and growth of bacteria and other microorganisms; neutralize acidity; prevent the development of calculus or stones, and hemorrhage in persons with hypertension; promote perspiration and urine flow; reduce capillary fragility and excessive lithic acid (uric acid) and urate levels in the blood, tophi, and urine; restore normal tone to tissues; stimulate gastric secretions.
Cautions/Contraindications: Avoid use if pregnant or breast-feeding, or if you have an aspirin sensitivity, or if you have an ulcer (gastric, peptic). Some persons may experience bleeding or increased clotting time when using this herb with anticoagulant drugs or aspirin.
Adverse Reactions: Bleeding (possibly serious), coagulation problems, hematuria (blood in the urine), nausea, salicylism (salicylic acid poisoning), and/or vomiting.
Herb/Drug Interactions: This herb could cause an interaction (possibly severe) when taken with the following drugs: Anticoagulant drugs, Salicylates, and Subsalicylates.
Preparations/Dosage: Crude Herb: 3-9 grams. Infusion: 1 cup per day. Leaves (powdered): Average dose in substance ¼-½ teaspoon. Juice: 1 tablespoon per day in water. Tincture: 5-20 drops (0.333-1.25 cc.) one to three times per day.
Isolation: Salicin: Average dose of 5-30 grains (0.333-2 gm.) for use as an analgesic, antiperiodic, and febrifuge. Salicin's action is similar to that of quinine.

Melilot (mel e·lät)

(*Melilotus officinalis*)

Synonyms/Related Species: Bokhara Clover, Common Melilot, Common Sweet Clover, Corn Melilot (*melilotus arvensis*), Hay Flowers, King's Clover, Ribbed Melilot, Sweet Clover, Sweet Lucerne, Sweet Melilot, Sweet White Clover, White Melilot (*melilotus alba*), White Sweetclover, Wild Laburnum, Yellow Melilot, Yellow Sweetclover, and Zieger Kraut.
Family/Class: Leguminosae (legume).
Habitat: Asia, Australia, Europe, North America, and Switzerland.
Flavor: Pungent/bitter.
Parts Used: Flowering tops.
Properties: Alterative, analgesic, antibiotic, anticarcinogen, anticoagulant, antiphlogistic, antispasmodic, aromatic, astringent, carminative, demulcent, depurative, diuretic, expectorant, hemostatic, insect repellent, laxative, nutritive, sedative, and vulnerary.
Constituents: Coumaric acid, coumarilic acid, coumarin, flavonoids, fraxetin, melilotic acid, melilotin, quercetin, saponins, and umbelliferone.
Historical Uses: Abscess, acne, arthritis, asthma, bedbugs, benign breast disease, bleeding, bronchitis, bruises, cancer, colds, colic, colitis, cough, cramps, croup, degenerative conditions, depression (mild/moderate), diarrhea, dietary supplementation, dysmenorrhea, eczema, edema, fever (ephemeral, rheumatic), flatulence, gastralgia, glandular problems, gout, headache,

hemorrhoids, hepatitis, infection (bacterial), inflammation, insufficiency (venous), laryngitis, lesions (tubercle), lymphedema, malnutrition, mastitis, mononucleosis, mucus, muscle and joint pain, neuralgia, pain, psoriasis, lung problems, pruritus, respiratory conditions, rheumatism, sciatica, scrofula, skin problems, spasmodic conditions, thrombophlebitis, thrombosis (blood clot), tuberculosis, ulcer (duodenal, fistula, gastric, peptic, stasis, tuberculous, varicose), varicose veins, and wounds (minor).

Discussion: May aid digestion; clear and open bronchial passages; decrease the effect of carcinogens; delay or reduce coagulation of the blood; enhance circulatory system and vascular system functions; increase circulation; promote bowel evacuation, lymphatic drainage, and urine flow; provide dietary supplementation; purify the blood; reduce blood pressure levels; reestablish healthy system functions; serve as a nutritional adjuvant to therapeutic programs; soothe mucous membrane irritation; speed healing.

Cautions/Contraindications: Avoid use if pregnant or breast-feeding, or if you have anemia. Some persons may experience bleeding or increased clotting time when using this herb with anticoagulant drugs or aspirin.

Adverse Reactions: Bleeding (possibly serious), coagulation problems, diarrhea (possibly bloody), gastrointestinal cramps (severe), headache, hematuria (blood in the urine), liver damage (often characterized by jaundice), nausea, stupor, and/or vomiting.

Herb/Drug Interactions: This herb could cause an interaction (possibly severe) when taken with the following drugs: Anticoagulant drugs, Salicylates, and Subsalicylates.

Preparations/Dosage: Crude Herb: 3-6 grams. Crude Herb (powdered): Average dose in substance 3-30 mg ($^1/_{20}$-½ grain). Infusion: ½-1 cup per day.

Milk Thistle (milk this el)

(*Carduus nutans*)

Synonyms/Related Species: Briste Thistle, Creeping Plume Thistle (*carduus arvensis*), Dwarf Thistle (*carduus acaulis*), Field Thistle (*carduus crispus*), Ground Thistle, Holy Thistle (*carduus benedictus*), Marian Thistle (*carduus marianum*), Marsh Plume Thistle (*carduus palustris*), Marythistle, Melancholy Thistle (*carduus heterophyllus*), Musk Thistle, Nodding Thistle, Our Lady's Thistle, Plumeless Thistle (*carduus acanthoides*), Spear Thistle (*carduus lanceolatus*), St. Mary's Thistle, Way Thistle, Welted Thistle, and Woolly-Headed Thistle (*carduus eriophorus*).

Family/Class: Compositae (composite).

Habitat: Asia, Britain, England, Europe, North America, and Scotland.

Flavor: Bitter.

Parts Used: Leaves, root, seeds.

Properties: Alterative, antibiotic, anticarcinogen, antidepressant, antioxidant, antiperiodic, antiphlogistic, antiviral, astringent, cholagogue, demulcent, depurative, diaphoretic, emmenagogue, emetic, hemostatic, hepatic, laxative, lithotriptic, malariacidal, parasiticide, and tonic.

Constituents: Cnicin, fatty acids (oleic, palmitic, stearic), fixed oils (olein, palmitin, stearin), flavonoids, glycosides, and volatile oil.

Historical Uses: Abscess, acne, ague, addiction (alcohol, drug), altitude sickness, Alzheimer's disease, appetite loss, arteriosclerosis, bleeding, cancer (breast, prostate, testicular), cellulite, cirrhosis, constipation, Crohn's disease, cyst (ovarian), depression (mild/moderate), diabetes, fever (ephemeral, intermittent), digestive complaints, flatulence, gallbladder problems, gallstones, gastritis, gastrointestinal problems, glandular problems, headache, hepatitis, hypercholesteremia, indigestion, infection (bacterial, viral), inflammation, irritable bowel syndrome (IBS), jaundice, kidney stones, liver problems, malaria, menopausal/menstrual problems, mucus, nausea, parasites (malarial plasmodia), Parkinson's disease, plague, pleurisy, poisoning (alcohol, amanita mushroom, chemical, drug, radiation), psoriasis, seizure conditions, skin problems, sores, spleen problems, thrombosis (blood clot), tumors, and urinary calculus.

Discussion: May cleanse the liver; decrease insulin resistance in diabetics and the effect of carcinogens; dissolve blood clots and calculi; enhance gallbladder, liver, and spleen functions; increase circulation; inhibit oxidation; improve bilirubin levels, blood platelet counts, and lipid balance; offset the negative effects of chemotherapy and radiation therapy; promote bile flow, bowel evacuation, and lymph node drainage, and perspiration; protect the liver; reduce arterial plaque formation and the toxic effects of various poisons such as alcohol, drugs (various), and chemical solvents; regenerate damaged liver cells; reestablish healthy system functions; restore normal tone to tissues; regulate the digestion of fats; serve as an antidote to the prevention of and/or the treatment of poisoning (amanita mushroom); soothe mucous membrane irritation; speed clearance of pharmaceutical medications; stabilize blood sugar and cholesterol levels; stimulate appetite, the immune system, menstruation, and peristalsis; stop or slow abnormal cell growth.

Cautions/Contraindications: Avoid use if pregnant or breast-feeding, or if you have liver disease. May reduce the effectiveness of oral contraceptives. Some individuals may experience a temporary mild laxative effect that generally lasts from one to three days when taking milk thistle.

Adverse Reactions: Diarrhea, nausea, and/or vomiting.

Herb/Drug Interactions: This herb could cause an interaction (possibly severe) when taken with the following drugs: Acetaminophen, Anesthetic drugs (major), Antibiotic drugs, Antineoplastic drugs, Cardiac drugs, HMG-CoA Reductase Inhibitor drugs, Hormones and Synthetic Substitutes (i.e. conjugated estrogens, contraceptives (oral, etc.), and other hormonal replacement therapy (HRT), and Immune Suppressive drugs.)

Preparations/Dosage: Crude Herb: 3-9 grams. Infusion (leaves, root, and/or seeds): 1-1½ cups per day. Seeds (powdered) of *Carduus nutans*: Average dose in substance 1 teaspoon. Tincture (seeds of *carduus nutans*): 15-30 drops (1-2 cc.) one to three times per day. Flower Heads (*carduus nutans*): Boiled and eaten as a vegetable.

Milk Vetch (milk vech)
(*Astragalus americanus*)

Synonyms/Related Species: Alpine Milk Vetch (*astragalus alpinus*), American Milk Vetch, Astragalus, Bok Kay, Bourgeau's Milk Vetch (*astragalus bourgovii*), Canadian Milk Vetch (*astragalus canadensis*), Drummond's Milk Vetch (*astragalus drummondii*), Elegant Milk Vetch (*astragalus eucomus*), Field Milk Vetch (*astragalus agrestis*), Huang Qi (*astragalus membranaceus*), Indian Milk Vetch (*astragalus australis*), Locoweed (*astragalus mollissimus*), Meolc Veche, Mulgere Vicia, Prickly Milk Vetch (*astragalus kentrophyta*), Pulse Milk Vetch (*astragalus tenellus*), Purple Milk Vetch, Standing Milk Vetch (*astragalus adsurgens*), Timber Milk Vetch (*astragalus miser*), Tragacanth Shrub (*astragalus gummifer*), Woollypod Milk Vetch (*astragalus purshii*), and Yellow Vetch.

Family/Class: Leguminosae (legume).

Habitat: Alaska, the Alpine and Subalpine zones, Asia, North America, and the Yukon Territory.

Flavor: Sweet.
Parts Used: Gum (tragacanth), root
Properties: Anticarcinogen, anticoagulant, antihidrotic, antioxidant, diuretic, emmenagogue, febrifuge, mydriatic, stimulant, and tonic.
Constituents: Bassorin (bassora gum), betaine (lycine), coumarins, glucuronic acid, inulin (starch), monosaccharides, pectic acid, pectin, and vitamins (A, choline).
Historical Uses: Acquired immune deficiency syndrome (AIDS), amenorrhea, angina, anorexia, appetite loss, arrhythmia, arteriosclerosis, bipolar/manic depressive condition, burns (minor), cancer (colorectal, kidney, melanoma), cardiovascular conditions, cirrhosis, diabetes, diabetic retinopathy, diarrhea, digestive complaints, diphtheria, edema, emaciation, ephidrosis (excessive perspiration), fatigue, fever (ephemeral), glandular problems, hemorrhage (metrorrhagia), human immunodeficiency virus (HIV), infection (bladder), infertility, lung problems, lupus, myasthenia gravis, myocarditis, nephritis, prolapse (rectal, uterine), rheumatoid arthritis (RA), shortness of breath, spleen problems, tumors (lymphoma), ulcer (duodenal, gastric, peptic), and wounds (minor).
Discussion: May assist in the production of white blood cells; cause mydriasis (pupil dilatation); delay or reduce coagulation of the blood; decrease the effect of carcinogens; diminish ephidrosis (excessive perspiration); enhance cardiovascular system, digestive system, gallbladder, kidney, liver, pericardium, respiratory system, and spleen functions; increase circulation, energy, interferon production, left heart ventricle action, phagocytic activity, sperm motility and viability, and stamina; inhibit oxidation and protein in the urine; prevent the deposition of fat in the liver; promote urine flow; protect blood-brain barrier and certain brain cells from damage and protect against suppression (immune) caused by cancer treatments; stimulate the immune system, menstruation, metabolism, natural killer (NK) and T cell activity; strengthen intestinal movement and muscle tone; prevent adverse effects during bipolar therapy, heart tissue damage after bypass surgery or heart attack, and immune system damage caused by the use of lithium; restore normal tone to tissues.
Cautions/Contraindications: Avoid use if pregnant or breast-feeding, or if you have a cold, influenza, or hypertension, or if you are taking drugs following a heart attack. Astragalus has a tendency to absorb selenium and molybdenum from the soil. Taking astragalus with hypertension drugs may result in dangerously high blood pressure levels, headache, and nervous conditions. Use with caution when on immunosuppressive therapy.
Adverse Reactions: Anemia, brittle bones, headache, nausea, nervousness, staggering, stroke (apoplectic), and/or vomiting.
Herb/Drug Interactions: This herb could cause an interaction (possibly severe) when taken with the following drugs: Cardiac drugs and Hypertensive drugs.
Preparations/Dosage: Crude Herb: 6-12 grams. Gum (tragacanth): Mixed with water until it forms a gelatinous consistency, the gum can be used to suspend insoluble powders, for the preparation of troches (tablets/lozenges), or as an emollient.
Isolation: Betaine: Average dose of 2-4 grains (0.13-0.26 gm.) for use as an emmenagogue.

Milkweed (milk wēd)

(*Asclepias incarnata*)

Synonyms/Related Species: American Milkweed (*asclepias syriaca*), Bastard Ipecacuanha (*asclepias curas-savica*), Blood-Weed, Butterfly Weed (*asclepias tuberosa*), Canada Root,

Common Milkweed, Common Silkweed, Cottonweed, Indian Milkweed (*asclepias curassavica*), North American Milkweed (*asclepias verticillata*), Orange Milkweed, Pleurisy Root, Redhead, Rose-Colored Silkweed, Showy Milkweed (*asclepias speciosa*), Silkweed, Silky Swallowwort (*asclepias galiodes*), Soma Plant (*asclepias acida*), Swamp Milkweed, Swamp Silkweed, Syrian Milkweed (*asclepias syrica*), Tame Poison (*asclepias vincetoxicum*), Tuber Root, Vermilion Milkweed, Virginia Silk, White Root, Wind Root, and Woolypod Milkweed (*asclepias eriocarpa*).

Family/Class: Asclepiadaceae (milkweed).

Habitat: Africa, Asia, Europe, India, North America, South America, and Syria.

Flavor: Bitter/pungent.

Parts Used: Root.

Properties: Abortifacient, analgesic, antiphlogistic, antispasmodic, cardiant, carminative, diaphoretic, diuretic, emetic, expectorant, insect repellant, laxative, lithotriptic, sedative, stimulant, and tonic.

Constituents: Albumin (albumen), alkaloids, asclepiadin, bitter principle, fatty acids (oleic, palmitic, stearic), fixed oils (olein, palmitin, stearin), galitoxin, glycosides, inulin (starch), monosaccharides, pectic acid, pectin, resin, sterols, and volatile oil.

Historical Uses: Amenorrhea, arthritis, asthma, blindness, bronchitis, calculus, calluses, cardiovascular conditions, colds, contraceptive, corns, cough, debility, diarrhea, digestive complaints, dysentery, dysmenorrhea, edema, emphysema, fever (ephemeral, rheumatic, scarlet, typhus), fleas, gallstones, gastrointestinal problems, glandular problems, headache, infection, inflammation, influenza, kidney problems, kidney stones, lesions (tubercle), leukorrhea, lochia, lung problems, measles, mucus, muscle and joint pain, rash, pleurisy, respiratory conditions, rheumatism, scarletina, scrofula, sexually transmitted diseases (STDs), sinusitis, snakebite, sores, spasmodic conditions, tuberculosis, typhus, ulcer (fistula, tuberculous), uterine problems, vaginitis, and warts (digitate, filiform, fugitive, glabra, mother, plana juvenilis, plantar, seborrhoeic, vulgaris).

Discussion: May aid digestion; clear and open bronchial passages; dissolve calculi; enhance intestinal system and lung functions; increase circulation; induce abortion; produce a temporary sterility; promote bowel evacuation, perspiration, lymph node drainage, perspiration, and urine flow; restore normal tone to tissues; stimulate the cardiovascular system, menstruation, peristalsis, uterine contractions, and the vagus nerve.

Cautions/Contraindications: Avoid use if pregnant or breast-feeding. May cause dermatitis in susceptible individuals.

Adverse Reactions: Anorexia, appetite loss, ataxia, arrhythmia, debility, diarrhea, enteritis, fever, hematuria (blood in the urine), liver damage (often characterized by jaundice), nausea, respiratory distress, seizure conditions, staggering, tachycardia, and/or vomiting.

Herb/Drug Interactions: This herb could cause an interaction (possibly severe) when taken with the following drugs: Cardiac drugs.

Preparations/Dosage: Crude Herb: 3-6 grams. Infusion: 1-2 cups per day. Root (powdered): Average dose in substance 15-60 grains (0.98-4 gm.). Tincture: 5-30 drops (0.333-2 cc.) one to three times per day.

Mint (mint)

(*Mentha officinalis*)

Synonyms/Related Species: Bergamot Mint (*mentha citrata*), Black Mint, Bombay Mint (*mentha incana*), Brandy Mint, Ceylon Mint (*mentha javanese*), Chinese Mint (*mentha glabrata*), Corn Mint, Curled Mint (*mentha acrispa*), English Horsemint (*mentha sylvestris*), Egyptian Mint, European Mint, Field Mint (*mentha arvensis*), Fraun Munze, Garden Mint, German Spearmint, Green Mint, Hairy Mint, Japanese Menthol Plant, Krausemünzöl, Lamb Mint, Marsh Mint, Our Lady's Mint, Peppermint (*mentha piperita*), Red Mint (*mentha rubra*), Round-Leaved Mint (*mentha rotundifolia*), Russian Spearmint, Sage of Bethlehem, Spearmint (*mentha spicata*), True Mint, Water Mint (*mentha aquatica*), White Mint, Whorled Mint, and Wild Mint (*mentha sativa*).

Family/Class: Labiatae (mint).

Habitat: Africa, Asia, Australia, Britain, the Caucasus, Ceylon, China, Egypt, England, Europe, France, Germany, Iceland, India, Japan, the Mediterranean, North America, Russia, and the Yukon Territory.

Flavor: Pungent.

Parts Used: Leaves.

Properties: Alterative, analgesic, antibiotic, antilithic, antiperiodic, antiphlogistic, antispasmodic, aromatic, astringent, carminative, diaphoretic, diuretic, emmenagogue, expectorant, insect repellent, laxative, lithotriptic, malariacidal, nervine, parasiticide, sedative, stimulant, stomachic, tonic, vasodilator, and vermin repellent.

Constituents: Caffeic acid, carvene (limonene), carvone, eucalyptol (cineol), fatty acids (caproic, caprylic), flavonoids, luteolin, menthenone, menthol, menthone, menthyl, minerals (calcium, copper, iodine, iron, magnesium, potassium, silicon, sulfur), phellandrene, pinene, pulegone, resin, silicic acid, tannic acid, vitamins (A, B_1 (thiamine), B_2 (riboflavin), B_3 (niacin), B_5 (pantothenic acid), B_6 (pyridoxine), B_{12}, B_x (para-aminobenzoic acid (PABA), C (ascorbic acid), choline, H (biotin), inositol, M (folic acid), and volatile oil.

Historical Uses: Abdominal pain, ague, allergy (food), amenorrhea, anxiety, appetite loss, arrhythmia, arthritis, bronchitis, calculus, chills, cholera, cirrhosis, colds, colic, colitis, congestion (uterine, vaginal), constipation, convulsions, cough, cramps, Crohn's disease, depression (mild/moderate), diarrhea, digestive complaints, diphtheria, dizziness, dysentery, dysmenorrhea, dysuria (painful/difficult urination), eczema, fainting, fever (ephemeral, intermittent, rheumatic), flatulence, flavoring agent, gallstones, gargle/mouth rinse, gastritis, gastrointestinal problems, gout, halitosis, headache, hepatitis, hysteria, indigestion, infection (bacterial, bladder), inflammation, influenza, insect bites or stings, insomnia, irritable bowel syndrome (IBS), kidney problems, kidney stones, leukorrhea, lithemia, liver problems, malaria, measles, menopausal/menstrual problems, migraine, mosquitos, motion sickness, muscle and joint pain, muscle strain, nausea, nervous conditions, neuralgia, nightmares, pain, parasites (malarial plasmodia, ringworm), periodontal disease, poisoning (food), pruritus, respiratory conditions, rheumatism, shock, sore throat, spasmodic conditions, sprain, toothache, ulcer (duodenal, gastric, peptic, syriac), urethritis, urinary problems, vaginitis, vermin, vomiting, and wounds (minor).

Discussion: May aid digestion; calm the nervous system; cause blood vessel dilatation; clear and open bronchial passages; destroy the listeria and salmonella microorganisms that cause food poisoning; dissolve calculi; enhance gallbladder, liver, lung, and stomach functions; improve mental clarity; increase circulation; inhibit or destroy developement and growth of bacteria and other microorganisms; prevent the deposition of fat in the liver and prevent the development of calculus or stones; promote bowel evacuation, perspiration, and urine flow; reduce excessive levels of lithic acid (uric acid) and urates in the blood, tophi, and urine; reestablish healthy system functions; restore normal tone to tissues; stimulate appetite, peristalsis, and uterine contractions.

Cautions/Contraindications: Avoid use if pregnant or breast-feeding, or if you have acid reflux, cholecystitis, hernia (hiatal), indigestion (chronic), liver disease, an iodine sensitivity, or an obstruction (biliary). Excessive inhalation or ingestion of the oil and/or leaves may be toxic. Infants and small children should never be exposed to products containing menthol, and applying the oil to the faces of children or infants could trigger an asthma-like attack or respiratory failure. May interfere with the effectiveness of certain indigestion medications and thyroid drugs. May cause allergic reactions or dermatitis in susceptible individuals.

Adverse Reactions: Abdominal pain, arrhythmia, asthma-like attack, diarrhea, fever, headache, drowsiness, hypertrophy (thyroid), iodism (iodine poisoning), mucous membrane irritation, nausea, priapism, rash, respiratory failure, seizure conditions, thirst, and/or vomiting.

Herb/Drug Interactions: This herb could cause an interaction (possibly severe) when taken with the following drugs: GI drugs, Medications/Products containing menthol, and Thyroid drugs.

Preparations/Dosage: Crude Herb: ½-9 grams. Infusion: ½-2 cups. Oil of Peppermint (*oleum menthae piperitae*) or Oil of Spearmint (*oleum menthae spicatae*): 1-5 drops (0.066-0.333 cc.) per day in water or on a sugarcube. Tincture: 5-15 drops (0.333-1 cc.) one to three times per day. Tincture: 5-15 drops (0.333-1 cc.).

Isolation: Menthol: Average dose of ½-2 grains (0.033-0.133 gm.) applied topically, for use as an analgesic. Eucalyptol: 5 drops (0.3 cc.) in atomization or inhalation therapy for use in respiratory conditions.

Did You Know? Peppermint (*mentha piperita*) is a hybrid species between spearmint (*mentha spicata*) and water mint (*mentha aquatica*).

Mistletoe (mis el·tō)
(*Viscum album*)

Synonyms/Related Species: All-Heal, Birdlime, Devil's Fuge, European Mistletoe, Herbe de la Croix, and Mystyldene.

Family/Class: Loranthaceae (mistletoe).

Habitat: Africa, Asia, Australia, England, Europe, Sweden, and the United States (primarily California).

Flavor: Bitter.

Parts Used: Leaves, twigs (young).

Properties: Abortifacient, anticarcinogen, antilithic, antiperiodic, antiphlogistic, antispasmodic, cardiant, coagulant, depurative, diuretic, hallucinogen, hemostatic, hypertensive, hypotensive, malariacidal, narcotic, nervine, oxytocic, sedative, stimulant, tonic, vasoconstrictor, vasodilator, and vermifuge.

Constituents: Acetylcholine, betuline, ethylamine, fatty acids (oleic, palmitic, stearic), fixed oils (olein, palmitin, stearin), flavonoids, glycosides, histamine, lignin, mannitol (mannite), minerals (cadmium, calcium, cobalt, copper, iodine, iron, magnesium, potassium, sodium), monosaccharides, mucilage, pinite (pinitol), polypeptides, polysaccharides, proteins, quebrachitol, resin, saponins, syringin, tyramine, ursone (ursolic acid), viscin, viscumitol, and vitamins (B_{12}, choline)

Historical Uses: Ague, amenorrhea, anxiety, arteriosclerosis, arthritis, asthma, bleeding, calculus, cancer (breast), cardiovascular conditions, chilblains, cholera, chorea, convulsions, delirium, diarrhea, digestive complaints, dizziness, enuresis (urinary incontinence), epilepsy, exhaustion, fatigue, fever (ephemeral, enteric, intermittent, rheumatic), gallbladder problems, gallstones, gout, headache, hemorrhage (metrorrhagia), hypertension (mild/moderate), hypoglycemia, hypotension, hysteria, inflammation, insufficiency (venous), kidney stones, lithemia, lung problems, malaria, menstrual problems, mental disturbances, migraine, muscle and joint pain, nervous conditions, neuralgia, pain, parasites (malarial plasmodia), poisoning (amanita mushroom), rheumatism, sciatica, sores, spasmodic conditions, spleen problems, tachycardia, toothache, tumors, typhoid, ulcer (bouveret, duodenal, gastric, peptic, stasis, varicose), urinary problems, varicose veins, vertigo, and whooping cough.

Discussion: May aid digestion; calm the nervous system; cause blood vessel dilatation; decrease the effect of carcinogens; increase muscle and uterine elasticity, the production of beneficial free radicals, and pulse rate; induce abortion; offset the negative effects of chemotherapy and radiation therapy; prevent the development of calculus and stones; promote coagulation of the blood and urine flow; purify the blood; reduce blood pressure levels and excessive levels of lithic acid (uric acid) and urates in the blood, tophi, and urine, and reduce the frequency of nighttime urination; restore normal tone to tissues; serve as an antidote for amanita mushroom poisoning and serve as an adjuvant to cancer therapies; stimulate the cardiovascular system, glandular system, immune system, parasympathetic system, and uterine contractions. This herb directly affects the circulatory system by initially increasing the pressure of the blood on the walls of the arteries and then reducing that pressure to below the initial level.

Cautions/Contraindications: Avoid use if pregnant or breast-feeding, or if taking monoamine oxidase inhibitor (MAOI) drugs, or if you have a chronic infection, depression, Parkinson's disease, protein hypersensitivity, tuberculosis, or an iodine sensitivity. Berries are poisonous. Care must be taken when harvesting as some parasitic plants may take up toxins from their hosts. Do not confuse this herb with American mistletoe (*phoradendron spp.*). May cause allergic reactions in susceptible individuals. May interfere with the effectiveness of certain thyroid medications. Mistletoe, when administered by intramuscular (IM) injection, may produce temporary side effects of abdominal discomfort, flu-like symptoms, elevated body temperature, injection-site inflammation, and/or nausea. Administration of Intramuscular (IM) injection recommended for professional use. Not for long-term use. Use with professional guidance/supervision.

Adverse Reactions: Abdominal pain, angina, arrhythmia, bradycardia, cardiac failure, chills, convulsions, diarrhea, fever, hallucinations, headache, hypertrophy (thyroid), insufficiency (circulatory), iodism (iodine poisoning), nausea, priapism, shock, stupor, thirst, vomiting, and/or possible death.

Herb/Drug Interactions: This herb could cause an interaction (possibly severe) when taken with the following drugs: Cardiac drugs, Hypotensive drugs, Monoamine Oxidase Inhibitor (MAOI) drugs, and Thyroid drugs.

Preparations/Dosage: Crude Herb: 3-6 grams. Infusion (twigs): ¼-1 cup per day. Infusion (leaves): ½-1½ cups per day. Juice (leaves and/or twigs): 1-4 teaspoons per day. Leaves (powdered): Average dose in substance 10-60 grains (0.6-4 gm.). Tincture: 5-10 drops (0.333-0.666 cc.) one to three times per day.

Isolation: Acetylcholine (chloride and bromide salts): Used in a 5% solution, average dose of 0.05-0.20 gm., administered intravenously or subcutaneously, for use to relax the peripheral blood vessels. Histamine phosphate: Used in a 1:1000 solution in an average dose of 5 drops (0.3 cc.) administered intravenously or subcutaneously, for use as a powerful vasodilator, or for use as a stimulant. Mannitol hexanitrate: Average dose of 15-60 mg. for use as a vasodilator.

Morinda (môr in·dā)
(*Morinda officinalis*)

Synonyms/Related Species: Cheesefruit, Great Morinda (*morinda citrifolia*), Indian Mulberry (*morinda indica*), Koonjerung, Mengkudu, Morus, Noni, Painkiller Tree, Polynesian Bushfruit, and Tokoonja.
Family/Class: Rubiaceae (madder).
Habitat: Asia, Australia, China, Fiji, Hawaii, India, Japan, Java, Malaysia, the Pacific Islands, the Philippines, Polynesia, and Surinam.
Flavor: Sour/sweet/bitter.
Parts Used: Bark, flowers, fruit, leaves, seeds, root.
Properties: Alterative, analgesic, anthelmintic, antibiotic, anticarcinogen, antidepressant, antifungal, antioxidant, antiperiodic, antiphlogistic, antispasmodic, cytotoxic, diuretic, emmenagogue, hypotensive, malariacidal, parasiticide, sedative, stimulant, stomachic, tonic, vasodilator, and vermifuge.
Constituents: Alizarin, alkaloids, anthraquinone, chrysophanic acid (rumicin), emodin, fatty acids (caproic, caprylic), glycosides, inulin (starch), lactone, minerals (iron, magnesium, potassium, sodium), monosaccharides, morindadiol, morindaparvin, morindolide (iridoid lactone), morindine, morindone, phosphate, protein, quercetin, resin, ruberythric acid, rubin (fuchsin), sterols, succinic acid, ursone (ursolic acid), vitamins (C (ascorbic acid), and volatile oil.
Historical Uses: Abscess, acne, acquired immune deficiency syndrome (AIDS), addiction (drug), ague, amenorrhea, arthritis, arteriosclerosis, asthma, broken bones, burns (minor), cancer (liver, lung), cardiovascular conditions, colds, colic, constipation, cough, deficiency (autoimmune), depression (mild/moderate), diarrhea, diabetes, digestive complaints, dysentery, erectile dysfunction, fever (ephemeral, intermittent, rheumatic), fractures, gleet, gonorrhea, headache, human immunodeficiency virus (HIV), hypertension (mild/moderate), indigestion, infection (bacterial, bladder, fungal, kidney, sexually transmitted, urinary tract), inflammation, influenza, insomnia, insufficiency (venous), leishmaniasis, lesions (tubercle), leukemia, lumbago, malaria, menorrhagia, menstrual problems, muscle and joint pain, nausea, pain, parasites (leishmania, lice and their nits, malarial plasmodia, roundworm), periodontal disease, premature ejaculation, respiratory conditions, rheumatism, scrofula, sexually transmitted diseases (STDs), sinusitis, skin problems, sore throat, spasmodic conditions, sprain, syphilis, tuberculosis, tumors, ulcer (fistula, gastric, stasis, syphilitic, tuberculous), urethritis, urinary problems, and wounds (minor).
Discussion: May aid digestion; allow the brain to receive more endorphin hormones by opening the brain receptor sites; cause blood vessel dilatation; correct cell and protein structure problems; decrease the effect of carcinogens; ease the effects of drug (various) withdrawal; enhance all body systems; improve sperm motility; increase endurance, energy, fertility, and stamina; increase norepinephrine and serotonin levels; induce cancer cells to destroy themselves; inhibit

oxidation and inhibit development or destroy growth of bacteria and other microorganisms; normalize blood sugar levels; promote urine flow; reduce blood pressure levels; reestablish healthy system functions; restore normal tone to tissues; stimulate male sexual function, menstruation, and the production of xeronine; strengthen bones, ligaments, and the vascular system.

Cautions/Contraindications: Avoid use if pregnant or breast-feeding, or if you have dribbling urine, or dysuria (painful/difficult urination). May cause dermatitis in susceptible individuals.

Adverse Reactions: Edema, nausea, and/or vomiting.

Herb/Drug Interactions: This herb could cause an interaction (possibly severe) when taken with the following drugs: Hypotensive drugs.

Preparations/Dosage: Fruit: May be ingested freely. Juice (fruit): Take before meals or on an empty stomach, as gastric acids tend to destroy the herb's digestive enzymes.

Isolation: Chrysopahanic acid: Average dose of 1-10 grains (0.065-0.666 gm.) for use in skin problems.

Moss, Irish (môs, ī rish)

(*Chondrus crispus*)

Synonyms/Related Species: Carrageen, Chondrus, and Pearl Moss.

Family/Class: Rhodophyceae (red algae).

Habitat: The Baltic, the Cape Verde Islands, Europe, Iceland, Japan, Morocco, North America, Russia, and Spain.

Flavor: Salty.

Parts Used: Thallus (fresh/dried).

Properties: Alterative, antibiotic, anticarcinogen, anticoagulant, antiphlogistic, antiviral, demulcent, expectorant, laxative, nutritive, sedative, and tonic.

Constituents: Fatty acids (arachidonic, linoleic, linolenic), minerals (bromine, calcium, chlorine, iodine, iron, magnesium, manganese, phosphorus, potassium, sodium, sulfur), mucilage, polysaccharides, protein, and vitamins (A, D, E (alpha-tocopheral), K).

Historical Uses: Anemia, bladder problems, bronchitis, cancer, colds, cough, dentifrice, diarrhea, dietary supplementation, digestive complaints, dry skin, dysentery, emaciation, fever, flatulence, gastritis, gastrointestinal problems, glandular problems, glandular swelling, goiter, halitosis, infection (bacterial, viral), inflammation, influenza, insufficiency (venous), kidney problems, laryngitis, lesions (tubercle), lung problems, malnutrition, mucus, mumps, muscle and joint pain, pneumonia, respiratory conditions, rickets, scrofula, sores, sore throat, substitute for gelatin, tuberculosis, tumors, ulcer (duodenal, fistula, gastric, peptic, stasis, tuberculous, varicose), varicose veins, and wrinkles.

Discussion: May clear and open bronchial passages; decrease the effect of carcinogens; delay or reduce coagulation of the blood; enhance digestive and glandular system functions; inhibit or destroy development and growth of bacteria and other microorganisms; promote bowel evacuation; provide dietary supplementation; reestablish healthy system functions; restore normal tone to tissues; serve as a nutritional adjuvant to therapeutic programs; soothe mucous membrane irritation; stimulate peristalsis.

Cautions/Contraindications: Avoid use if pregnant or breast-feeding, or if you have an iodine sensitivity, or an obstruction (intestinal). May interfere with the effectiveness of certain thyroid

medications. Some persons may experience bleeding or increased clotting time when using this herb with anticoagulant drugs or aspirin.
Adverse Reactions: Bleeding (possibly serious), coagulation problems, cold extremities, diarrhea, diminished sex drive, edema, erectile dysfunction, halitosis, headache, hypertrophy (thyroid), nausea, skin problems, sleepiness, and/or vomiting.
Herb/Drug Interactions: This herb could cause an interaction (possibly severe) when taken with the following drugs: Anticoagulant drugs, Salicylates, Subsalicylates, and Thyroid drugs.
Preparations/Dosage: Crude Herb: 3-9 grams. Decoction: 1-2 cups per day. Tincture: 10-15 drops (0.666-1 cc.). Irish Moss (fresh): Wash well to remove any sand. Add one cup of moss to three cups of water. Simmer until most of the seaweed has dissolved. Remove any undissolved fragments and pour into a mold (a jello mold works well) until mixture has jelled. Irish moss may be flavored with other herbs such as cinnamon, ginger, lemon, or licorice.

Moss, Sphagnum (môs, sfag nem)
(*Sphagnum warnstorfii*)

Synonyms/Related Species: Bog Moss (*sphagnum cymbifolium*), Bristly Peat Moss (*sphagnum squarrosum*), Brown Peat Moss (*sphagnum fuscum*), Bushy Peat Moss (*sphagnum angustifolium*), Peat Moss, Red Peat Moss (*sphagnum magellanicum*), Sphagnum, Warnstorf's Peat Moss, White Sphagnum Moss, and Yellow-Green Peat Moss.
Family/Class: Bryophytes (mosses).
Habitat: England, Europe, Germany, Ireland, New Foundland, North America, and Scotland.
Flavor: Bland.
Parts Used: Moss (fresh/dried).
Properties: Absorbent, antibiotic, and astringent.
Constituents: Sphagnol.
Historical Uses: Acne, chilblains, eczema, hemorrhoids, infection (bacterial), insect bites or stings, menstruation (pads), parasites (scabies), pruritus, psoriasis, skin problems, and wounds (minor).
Discussion: May inhibit or destroy development and growth of bacteria and other microorganisms.
Cautions/Contraindications: Avoid use if pregnant or breast-feeding.
Adverse Reactions: None known.
Herb/Drug Interactions: This herb could cause an interaction (possibly severe) when taken with the following drugs: None known.
Preparations/Dosage: External uses only.
Did You Know? Sphagnum moss is highly absorbant and was initially used by medics in the field as a surgical dressing for wounds.

Motherwort (muth er·wûrt)
(*Leonurus cardiaca*)

Synonyms/Related Species: Lion's Tail, Moderwort, and Roman Motherwort.
Family/Class: Labiatae (mint).
Habitat: Asia, Britain, Europe, Germany, Greece, North America, and Russia.
Flavor: Bitter.

Parts Used: Flower tops, leaves.
Properties: Anticarcinogen, anticoagulant, antioxidant, antiphlogistic, antispasmodic, astringent, cardiant, carminative, diaphoretic, diuretic, emmenagogue, hemostatic, hypotensive, nervine, sedative, stimulant, stomachic, tonic, and vasodilator.
Constituents: Alkaloids, betaine (lycine), bitter principle, caffeic acid, flavonoids, glycosides, resin, rutin, tannic acid, vitamin A, and volatile oil.
Historical Uses: Amenorrhea, angina, anxiety, arrhythmia, arteriosclerosis, asthma, bleeding, bronchitis, bruises, cancer, cardiovascular conditions, chorea, convulsions, cramps, debility, delirium, delirium tremens (DTs), depression (mild/moderate), digestive complaints, dizziness, dysmenorrhea, edema, fainting, fever (ephemeral, rheumatic), flatulence, glandular swelling, goiter, headache, hypertension (mild/moderate), hyperthyroidism, hysteria, inflammation, insomnia, lung problems, menopausal/menstrual problems, mucus, muscle and joint pain, nervous conditions, neuralgia, neuritis, premenstrual syndrome (PMS), respiratory conditions, restlessness, rheumatism, sexually transmitted diseases (STDs), shortness of breath, spasmodic conditions, stomachache, tachycardia, thyroid problems, tremors, uterine problems, vaginitis, and vertigo.
Discussion: May aid digestion; balance the hormonal system; calm the nervous system; cause blood vessel dilatation; decrease the effect of carcinogens; delay or reduce coagulation of the blood; enhance circulatory system and stomach functions; inhibit oxidation; prevent hemorrhage in persons with hypertension; promote perspiration and urine flow; reduce blood pressure levels and capillary fragility; restore normal tone to tissues; serve as an adjuvant to alcoholism treatment programs to assist in easing delirium tremens (DTs); slow and strengthen the heartbeat; stimulate the cardiovascular system, immune system, menstruation, and uterine contractions.
Cautions/Contraindications: Avoid use if pregnant or breast-feeding, or if you have a coagulation problem. May cause dermatitis in susceptible individuals. Some persons may experience bleeding or increased clotting time when using this herb with anticoagulant drugs or aspirin.
Adverse Reactions: Arrhythmia, bleeding (possibly serious), coagulation problems, diarrhea, gastrointestinal irritation, hemorrhage (metrorrhagia), nausea, and/or vomiting.
Herb/Drug Interactions: This herb could cause an interaction (possibly severe) when taken with the following drugs: Anticoagulant drugs, Cardiac drugs, Hypotensive drugs, Salicylates, Sedative drugs, and Subsalicylates.
Preparations/Dosage: Crude Herb: 10-30 grams. Crude Herb (powdered): 30-60 grains (½-1 drachm). Decoction: ⅓ cup. Extract (solid): Average dose in substance 5-15 grains (0.324-1 gm.). Infusion: 1 cup per day. Tincture: 5-15 drops (0.333-1 cc.) one to three times per day.
Isolation: Betaine: Average dose of 2-4 grains (0.13-0.26 gm.) for use as an emmenagogue.

Muirapuama (moo·ē rä·poo·ä mä)
(*Liriosma ovata*)

Synonyms/Related Species: Marapuama, Potency Bark, and Potentwood.
Family/Class: Oleaceae (olive).
Habitat: South America.
Flavor: Pungent.
Parts Used: Bark, resin, root, wood.
Properties: Aphrodisiac, astringent, stimulant, and tonic.

Constituents: Alkaloids, behenolic acid, camphene, camphor, pinene, resin, sterols, and ursone (ursolic acid).
Historical Uses: Alopecia, depression (mild/moderate), diarrhea, diminished sex drive, erectile dysfunction, exhaustion, fatigue, frigidity, and gargle/mouth rinse.
Discussion: May arouse sexual impulses; enhance kidney function; increase sperm production in men; restore normal tone to tissues; stimulate the libido and nervous system.
Cautions/Contraindications: Avoid use if pregnant or breast-feeding, or if you have a hypersexual condition. May cause an allergic reaction in susceptible individuals. Not for long-term use.
Adverse Reactions: Nausea and/or vomiting.
Herb/Drug Interactions: This herb could cause an interaction (possibly severe) when taken with the following drugs: None known.
Preparations/Dosage: Crude Herb: 3-9 grams. Capsule: Not recommended as they are poorly assimilated in the stomach and the digestive juices destroy the herb's active constituents. Decoction (bark and/or wood): 1-2 cups per day. Tincture: 5-20 drops (0.333-1.25 cc.) one to three times per day. Aphrodisiac Uses: Tincture: Take 10-60 drops (0.666-4 cc.) two to four times per day. Resin: Place 1 pea-sized pellet in the mouth (about 1-1½ hours before coitus) and let dissolve in the saliva before swallowing. To extract the resin, immerse bark or root in grain alcohol for two weeks (resin will not extract in water). Strain mixture. Put strained liquid into a double boiler and evaporate the solvent (alcohol) until only the resinous mixture remains. Gather this substance from the bottom of the pan, form it into small pea-sized pellets, and refrigerate. The aphrodisiac use of muira puama may include a temporary, unharmful physical effect of chills up and down the spine. This effect, though subtler, is similar to that experienced upon ingestion of yohimbe bark, and generally occurs about two hours after ingestion.

Mulberry (mul ber ē)
(*Morus rubra*)

Synonyms/Related Species: Black Mulberry (*morus nigra*), Chinese White Mulberry (*morus alba*), Common Mulberry, Morberie, Murberie, Purple Mulberry, and Red Mulberry.
Family/Class: Moraceae (mulberry).
Habitat: Asia, China, Britain, Egypt, Europe, Greece, North America, the Caucasus, Persia, and Sweden.
Flavor: Bark/Branches/Leaves: bitter/sweet. Fruit: Sweet.
Parts Used: Bark (inner), branches (young), fruit (ripe), leaves.
Properties: Alterative, analgesic, antibiotic, antiphlogistic, antispasmodic, demulcent, depurative, diaphoretic, diuretic, expectorant, hallucinogen, hypotensive, laxative, nutritive, parasiticide, teniacide, teniafuge, tonic, and vasodilator.
Constituents: Adenine, amylase, arabinose, citric acid, coumarin, disaccharide, fatty acids (arachidonic, linoleic, linolenic, oleic, palmitic, stearic), fixed oils (olein, palmitin, stearin), flavonoids, malic acid, monosaccharides, pectic acid, pectin, protein, rutin, succinic acid, tannic acid, tartaric acid, ursone (ursolic acid), and vitamins (A, B_2 (riboflavin), choline, C (ascorbic acid).
Historical Uses: Anemia, arthritis, asthma, cirrhosis, colds, conjunctivitis, constipation, cough, diabetes, dietary supplementation, diphtheria, dizziness, edema, emphysema, fever (ephemeral, rheumatic), headache, hemoptysis, hyperemia, hypersensitivity, hypertension (mild/moderate),

infection (bacterial), inflammation, influenza, insomnia, insufficiency (circulatory), liver problems, lung problems, malnutrition, mucus, muscle and joint pain, nervous conditions, neuralgia, pain, parasites (ringworm, tapeworm), respiratory conditions, rheumatism, sore throat, spasmodic conditions, thirst, tinnitus, urinary problems, visual disturbances, vomiting, and wheezing.
Discussion: May cause blood vessel dilatation; clear and open bronchial passages; enhance cardiovascular system, glandular system, liver, and respiratory system functions; inhibit development or destroy growth of bacteria and other microorganisms; prevent the deposition of fat in the liver and hemorrhage in persons with hypertension; promote bowel evacuation, perspiration, and urine flow; purify the liver; provide dietary supplementation; reduce blood pressure levels and capillary fragility; reestablish healthy system functions; restore normal tone to tissues; serve as a nutritional adjuvant to therapeutic programs; soothe mucous membrane irritation; stimulate peristalsis.
Cautions/Contraindications: Avoid use if pregnant or breast-feeding, or if you have a weak digestive system or experience frequent bouts of diarrhea.
Adverse Reactions: Drowsiness, hallucinations, nausea, nervousness, and/or vomiting.
Herb/Drug Interactions: This herb could cause an interaction (possibly severe) when taken with the following drugs: Hypotensive drugs.
Preparations/Dosage: Crude Herb (bark/branches): 6-12 grams. Crude Herb (fruit): 3-12 grams. Crude Herb (leaves): 3-9 grams. Fruit: Ingest a small handful daily. Infusion: 1-2 cups per day.

Mullein (mul in)
(*Verbascum thapsus*)

Synonyms/Related Species: Aaron's Rod, Black Mullein (*verbascum nigrum*), Common Mullein (*verbascum thapsiform*), Flannel Leaf, Great Mullein, Jacob's Staff, Jupiter's Staff, Moleyn, Moth Mullein (*verbascum blattaria*), Orange Mullein (*verbascum phlomoides*), Shepherd's Staff, Torchweed, Velvet Dock, Velvet Plant, and White Mullein.
Family/Class: Scrophulariaceae (figwort).
Habitat: Asia, Britain, Europe, the Himalayas, Ireland, the Mediterranean, North America, and the Subalpine zone.
Flavor: Bitter.
Parts Used: Flowers, leaves.
Properties: Analgesic, antibiotic, antiphlogistic, antispasmodic, astringent, expectorant, demulcent, diuretic, hemostatic, narcotic, scabicide, sedative, stimulant, and vulnerary.
Constituents: Arabinose, caffeic acid, coumarin, flavonoids, minerals (iron, magnesium, phosphorous, potassium, sulfur), monosaccharides, mucilage, phosphoric acid, resin, rotenone, rutin, saponins, sterols, tannic acid, verbascose, vitamins (A, B_1 (thiamine), B_2 (riboflavin), B_3 (niacin), B_5 (pantothenic acid), B_6 (pyridoxine), B_{12}, B_x (para-aminobenzoic acid (PABA), choline, D, H (biotin), inositol, M (folic acid), and volatile oil.
Historical Uses: Abscess, allergy (pollen), alkaline urine, asthma, bleeding, bronchitis, bruises, colds, colic, conjunctivitis, constipation, cough, cramps, croup, diarrhea, dysentery, ear infection, earache, edema, emphysema, enuresis (urinary incontinence), fever (ephemeral, hay, rheumatic), flatulence, frostbite, gargle/mouth rinse, glandular problems, glandular swelling, hemorrhage, hemorrhoids, herbal tobacco, hiccups, infection (bacterial), inflammation, influenza, insomnia, laryngitis, lesions (tubercle), lung problems, mastitis, menopausal/menstrual problems, mucous

membrane problems, mucus, mumps, muscle and joint pain, nervous conditions, orchitis, pain, parasites (scabies), pleurisy, pneumonia, rash, rheumatism, respiratory conditions, scrofula, sexually transmitted diseases (STDs), sinusitis, skin problems, sore throat, sores, spasmodic conditions, sprain, sunburn, tonsillitis, toothache, tuberculosis, tumors, ulcer (duodenal, fistula, gastric, peptic, tuberculous), warts (digitate, filiform, fugitive, glabra, mother, plana juvenilis, plantar, seborrhoeic, vulgaris), and wounds (minor).

Discussion: May clear and open bronchial passages; enhance bladder function; inhibit or destroy development and growth of bacteria and other microorganisms; prevent hemorrhage in persons with hypertension; promote urine flow; reduce capillary fragility and the frequency of nighttime urination; soothe mucous membrane irritation; speed healing.

Cautions/Contraindications: Avoid use if pregnant or breast-feeding, or if you have cancer. Mullein seeds are toxic. Not for long-term use.

Adverse Reactions: Diarrhea (possibly bloody), gastrointestinal cramps (severe), hematuria (blood in the urine), nausea, and/or vomiting.

Herb/Drug Interactions: This herb could cause an interaction (possibly severe) when taken with the following drugs: None known.

Preparations/Dosage: Crude Herb (leaves): 3-9 grams. Crude Herb (flowers): 9-12 grams. Crude Herb (powdered): Average dose in substance 3-4 grains (0.2-0.26 gm.). Decoction (root): ¼-½ cup per day. Infusion (flowers and/or leaves): 1-2 cups per day. Oil of Mullein Flowers (*oleum verbascum florum*): Place 2-3 drops (0.133-0.2 cc.) into the ear for earache or apply topically for skin problems. Tincture: 10-20 drops (0.666-1.33 cc.) one to three times per day.

Mushroom, Hoelen (mush room, hō len)
(*Wolfiporia cocos*)

Synonyms/Related Species: Baifuling, Chifuling, China Root, Fuling, Fushen, Indian Bread, Indian Potato, Matsuhodo, Muksheng, Poria, and Tuckahoe.

Family/Class: Basidiomycetes (club fungi).

Habitat: Asia, Australia, and North America.

Flavor: Sweet/bland.

Parts Used: Fruiting body.

Properties: Antibiotic, diuretic, emmenagogue, expectorant, hypoglycemic, nervine, nutritive, sedative, and tonic.

Constituents: Dodecenoic acid, eburica acid, eburicoic acid, fatty acids (arachidonic, caprylic, linoleic, linolenic, oleic, palmitic, stearic), fixed oils (olein, palmitin, stearin), minerals (calcium, copper, iron, magnesium, manganese, potassium, sodium, zinc), monosaccharides, nemotinic acid, nitrogen, pachymic acid, phospholipids, poriatrin, poricoic acids, polysaccharides, resin, sterols, triterpenecarboxylic acids, tumulosic acid, and vitamins (choline).

Historical Uses: Acquired immune deficiency syndrome (AIDS), alopecia, amenorrhea, anxiety, autoimmune disease, cirrhosis, colds, congestion (uterine, vaginal), cough, dietary supplementation, digestive complaints, diphtheria, edema, emaciation, hepatitis, human immunodeficiency virus (HIV), hyperactivity, hyperglycemia, infection (bacterial), insomnia, jaundice, kidney problems, leukorrhea, liver problems, lung problem, lupus, malnutrition, mucus, respiratory conditions, restlessness, survival food, tumors, urinary problems, and vaginitis.

Discussion: May calm the nervous system; clear and open bronchial passages; enhance digestive system, kidney, pancreatic, spleen, and stomach functions; inhibit or destroy development and

growth of bacteria and other microorganisms; prevent antibody formation and the deposition of fat in the liver; promote urine flow; provide dietary supplementation; reduce blood sugar levels; restore normal tone to tissues; serve as a nutritional adjuvant to therapeutic programs; stimulate hair growth, the immune system, and menstruation; stop or slow abnormal cell growth.
Cautions/Contraindications: Avoid use if pregnant or breast-feeding. May cause allergic reactions in susceptible individuals
Adverse Reactions: Dizziness, edema, limb soreness, nausea, and/or vomiting.
Herb/Drug Interactions: This herb could cause an interaction (possibly severe) when taken with the following drugs: Antidiabetic drugs.
Preparations/Dosage: Crude Herb: 8-12 grams. Infusion: 1-3 cups per day.

Mushroom, Kawaratake (mush room, kä·wä·rä·tä·kē)
(*Trametes versicolor*)

Synonyms/Related Species: Trametes, Turkey Tail, and Yun Zhi.

Family/Class: Basidiomycetes (club fungi).
Habitat: Asia, Europe, Japan, and North America.
Flavor: Sweet.
Parts Used: Fruiting body (fresh/dried).
Properties: Analgesic, antibiotic, anticarcinogen, anticoagulant, antihyperlipemic, antioxidant, antiphlogistic, antiviral, diuretic, hypotensive, nutritive, parasiticide, sedative, and vasodilator.
Constituents: Ergosterol, coriolan, glycosides, hydromethylquinoline, monosaccharides, polysaccharide krestin (PSK), polysaccharide peptide (PSP), protein, and sitosterol.
Historical Uses: Acquired immune deficiency syndrome (AIDS), arrhythmia, arthritis, arteriosclerosis, burns (minor), cancer (adenomatosum carcinoma, breast, carcinoma, cervical, colon, endometrial, esophageal, liver, lung, melanoma, ovarian, prostate, stomach, uterine), diabetes, dietary supplementation, eczema, fever (ephemeral, herpetic, rheumatic), glandular problems, hepatitis, herpes, human immunodeficiency virus (HIV), hypertension (mild/moderate), impetigo, infection (bacterial, viral), inflammation, influenza, leukemia, lupus, malnutrition, mucus, muscle and joint pain, pain, parasites (ringworm), rheumatism, rheumatoid arthritis (RA), sclerosis, sexually transmitted diseases (STDs), thrombosis, and tumors (lymphoma, sarcoma).
Discussion: May activate natural killer (NK) cells; boost cellular immunity; cause blood vessel dilatation; decrease the effect of carcinogens; delay or reduce coagulation of the blood; enhance immune system and liver functions; improve blood vessel function; increase energy, interferon and interleukin production, T-cell counts, and the potency of cancer therapies; inhibit development or destroy growth of bacteria and other microorganisms, inhibit oxidation, and inhibit HIV infected cells from binding to lymphocytes; offset the negative effects of chemotherapy and radiation therapy; prevent tumor metastases and decreases in white blood cells; prolong the effects of antibiotics; promote urine flow; protect against heart disease; provide dietary supplementation; reduce blood pressure levels and cholesterol levels; serve as a nutritional adjuvant to therapeutic programs and serve as an adjuvant to enhance chemotherapy, radiation, or immunotherapy; speed healing; stimulate interferon production; stop or slow abnormal cell growth.
Cautions/Contraindications: Avoid use if pregnant or breast-feeding, or if you are on long-term aspirin therapy, or if you have multiple sclerosis (MS), or if you have a known allergy

(mold). Do not use raw kawaratake, boiling the mushrooms prior to use will destroy any bacteria that may have been growing on them. Some persons may experience bleeding or increased clotting time when using this herb with anticoagulant drugs or aspirin.
Adverse Reactions: Bleeding (possibly serious), coagulation problems, nausea, and/or vomiting.
Herb/Drug Interactions: This herb could cause an interaction (possibly severe) when taken with the following drugs: Anticoagulant drugs, Hypotensive drugs, Salicylates, and Subsalicylates.
Preparations/Dosage: Crude Herb: 3-9 grams. Fruiting Body (powdered): 3-12 grams.
Isolation: Polysaccharide Krestin (PSK): Average dose of 3-6 gm. orally (by mouth) per day in conjunction with radiation therapy. Polysaccharide Krestin (PSK): Average dose of 6 gm. orally (by mouth) per day in conjunction with chemotherapy drugs. Polysaccharide Peptide (PSP): Average dose of 1 gm., 3 times per day. Polysaccharide Peptide (PSP): Average dose of 3 gm. per day in conjunction with radiation and chemotherapy.

Mushroom, Maitake (mush room, maī·tä·kē)
(*Grifola frondosa*)

Synonyms/Related Species: Dancing Mushroom, Hen of the Woods, and Sheep's Head.
Family/Class: Basidiomycetes (club fungi).
Habitat: Asia, Europe, and North America.
Flavor: Sweet/bland.
Parts Used: Fruiting body.
Properties: Anticarcinogen, anticoagulant, antiviral, hypoglycemic, hypotensive, and vasodilator.
Constituents: Enzymes, minerals (copper, magnesium, manganese), monosaccharides, polysaccharides, and protein.
Historical Uses: Acquired immune deficiency syndrome (AIDS), bronchitis, cancer (breast, colorectal, liver, lung, prostate, stomach), chronic fatigue syndrome (CFS), colds, diabetes, Epstein Barr Virus (EBV), fibromyalgia, herpes, human immunodeficiency virus (HIV), hyperglycemia, hypertension (mild/moderate), infection (viral), influenza, leukemia, Lyme disease, mononucleosis (infectious), muscle and joint pain, sinusitis, and tumors (Kaposi's sarcoma).
Discussion: May alter fat metabolism by inhibiting accumulation of liver lipids and the elevation of serum lipids; build immunity; cause blood vessel dilatation; decrease the effect of carcinogens; delay or reduce coagulation of the blood; increase energy, longevity, and the potency of cancer therapies; offset the negative effects of chemotherapy and radiation therapy; protect the liver and protect against heart disease; reduce blood pressure levels, blood sugar levels, and cholesterol levels; stimulate the immune system and T cell activity; stop or slow abnormal cell growth.
Cautions/Contraindications: Avoid use if pregnant or breast-feeding, or if you are on long-term aspirin therapy, or if you have multiple sclerosis (MS), or if you have a known allergy (mold). Some persons may experience bleeding or increased clotting time when using this herb with anticoagulant drugs or aspirin.
Adverse Reactions: Bleeding (possibly serious), coagulation problems, nausea, and/or vomiting.

Herb/Drug Interactions: This herb could cause an interaction (possibly severe) when taken with the following drugs: Anticoagulant drugs, Antidiabetic drugs, Hypotensive drugs, Salicylates, and Subsalicylates.
Preparations/Dosage: Crude Herb: 3-9 grams.

Mushroom, Reishi (mush room, rē·shē)
(*Ganoderma lucidum*)

Synonyms/Related Species: Ling-chi, Phantom Mushroom, and Spirit Plant.
Family/Class: Basidiomycetes (club fungi).
Habitat: Asia, Japan, Taiwan, and North America.
Flavor: Sweet/bland.
Parts Used: Fruiting body.
Properties: Anticarcinogen, anticoagulant, antifungal, antiviral, emmenagogue, hypotensive, nervine, nutritive, and vasodilator.
Constituents: Alkaloids, betaine (lycine), coumarin, enzymes, ergosterol, fatty acids (oleic, palmitic, stearic), fixed oils (olein, palmitin, stearin), fumaric acid, ganoderic acids, minerals (calcium, copper, germanium, iron, magnesium, manganese, zinc), mannitol (mannite), monosaccharides, polysaccharides, protein, triterpenes, and vitamins (choline).
Historical Uses: Addiction (alcohol), allergy, altitude sickness, amenorrhea, asthma, bronchitis, cancer (liver), candida, cirrhosis, colds, cough, dietary supplementation, diphtheria, fibroids, herpes, hypertension (mild/moderate), infection (viral), influenza, insomnia, leukemia, liver problems, malnutrition, memory/cognitive problems, moniliasis, nervous conditions, neuralgia, pain, poisoning (mushroom), shingles, and spasmodic conditions.
Discussion: May calm the nervous system; cause blood vessel dilatation; counteract suppression (red and white blood cells); decrease the effect of carcinogens; enhance adrenal, cardiovascular system, liver, and lung functions; delay or reduce blood coagulation; improve cognition and memory; increase natural killer (NK) cell activity, and the potency of cancer therapies; offset the negative effects of chemotherapy and radiation therapy; prevent the deposition of fat in the liver; promote longevity; protect against heart disease; provide dietary supplementation; reduce blood pressure levels and cholesterol levels; serve as a nutritional adjuvant to therapeutic programs; stimulate the immune system, menstruation, and production of bone marrow.
Cautions/Contraindications: Avoid use if pregnant or breast-feeding, or if you are on long-term aspirin therapy, or if you have multiple sclerosis (MS), or if you have a known allergy (mold). Do not use raw reishi, boiling the mushrooms prior to use will destroy any bacteria that may have been growing on them. Some persons may experience bleeding or increased clotting time when using this herb with anticoagulant drugs or aspirin.
Adverse Reactions: Bleeding (possibly serious), coagulation problems, diarrhea (possibly bloody), dryness (mouth), gastrointestinal irritation, nausea, nosebleed, skin rash, and/or vomiting.
Herb/Drug Interactions: This herb could cause an interaction (possibly severe) when taken with the following drugs: Anticoagulant drugs, Hypotensive drugs, Salicylates, and Subsalicylates.
Preparations/Dosage: Crude Herb: 3-6 grams.
Isolation: Betaine: Average dose of 2-4 grains (0.13-0.26 gm.) for use as an emmenagogue. Mannitol hexanitrate: Average dose of 15-60 mg. for use as a vasodilator.

Mushroom, Shitake (mush room, shē·täkē)
(*Lentinus edodes*)

Synonyms/Related Species: Hoang-mo, Japanese Mushroom, and Shitake.
Family/Class: Basidiomycetes (club fungi).
Habitat: Asia, Japan, and North America.
Flavor: Sweet/bland.
Parts Used: Fruiting body.
Properties: Anticarcinogen, anticoagulant, antiphlogistic, antiviral, cytotoxic, hypotensive, nutritive, stimulant, and vasodilator.
Constituents: Eritadenine, lentinan, polysaccharides, and vitamins (B_1 (thiamine), B_2 (riboflavin), B_3 (niacin), B_5 (pantothenic acid), B_6 (pyridoxine), B_{12}, B_x (para-aminobenzoic acid (PABA), H (biotin), M (folic acid).
Historical Uses: Acquired immune deficiency syndrome (AIDS), cancer (breast, carcinoma, prostate, stomach), chronic fatigue syndrome (CFS), colds, dietary supplementation, Epstein Barr Virus (EBV), fatigue, fever, fibromyalgia, heart disease, hepatitis, human immunodeficiency virus (HIV), hypercholesteremia, hypertension (mild/moderate), infection (viral), inflammation, leukemia, Lyme disease, macular degeneration, malnutrition, mononucleosis (infectious), muscle and joint pain, and tumors (hepatoma, multiple myeloma, sarcoma).
Discussion: May activate natural killer (NK) cells; balance cholesterol levels; build resistance to viruses; cause blood vessel dilatation; decrease the effect of carcinogens; delay or reduce blood coagulation; increase the effectiveness of some cancer drugs; induce cancer cells to destroy themselves; increase the potency of cancer therapies; inhibit the replication of the HIV virus; offset the negative effects of chemotherapy and radiation therapy; promote long-term cancer stabilization or remission; protect against heart disease; provide dietary supplementation; reduce blood pressure levels and cholesterol levels; serve as a nutritional adjuvant to therapeutic programs; stimulate the immune system; stop or slow abnormal cell growth.
Cautions/Contraindications: Avoid use if pregnant or breast-feeding, or if you are on long-term aspirin therapy, or if you have cancer (bladder) or multiple sclerosis (MS), or if you have a known allergy (mold). Do not use raw shitake, boiling the mushrooms prior to use will destroy any bacteria that may have been growing on them. Some persons may experience bleeding or increased clotting time when using this herb with anticoagulant drugs or aspirin.
Adverse Reactions: Bleeding (possibly serious), coagulation problems, diarrhea (possibly bloody), digestive complaints, gastritis, hives, indigestion, irritable bowel syndrome (IBS), nausea, and/or vomiting.
Herb/Drug Interactions: This herb could cause an interaction (possibly severe) when taken with the following drugs: Anticoagulant drugs, Antiretroviral drugs, Hypotensive drugs, Salicylates, and Subsalicylates.
Preparations/Dosage: Crude Herb: 3-9 grams.

Mustard, Black (mus terd, blak)
(*Sinapis* (*Brassica*) *nigra*)

Synonyms/Related Species: None Known.
Habitat: Africa, Asia, England, Europe, Germany, Greece, Holland, Italy, North America, Siberia, and South America.

Flavor: Pungent.
Parts Used: Seeds.
Properties: Alterative, analgesic, antibiotic, antifungal, antiphlogistic, carminative, counterirritant, depurative, diuretic, emetic, expectorant, laxative, and stimulant.
Constituents: Alkaloids, erucic acid, fatty acids (behenic, oleic, palmitic, stearic), fixed oils (olein, palmitin, stearin), isothiocyanates, glycosides, minerals (calcium, cobalt, iodine, iron, manganese, phosphorus, potassium, sulfur), mucilage, myronate, myronic acid, myrosin, protein, sinamin, sinapolin, sinigrin, vitamins (A, B_1 (thiamine), B_2 (riboflavin), B_{12}, C (ascorbic acid), and volatile oil.
Historical Uses: Abscess, amenorrhea, appetite loss, arthritis, bronchitis, chilblains, cold extremities, colds, cough, emphysema, fever (ephemeral, rheumatic), flatulence, gout, halitosis, hiccups, indigestion, infection (bacterial, fungal), inflammation, kidney problems, liver problems, lumbago, lung problems, mucus, muscle and joint pain, neuralgia, pain, peritonitis, pleurisy, pneumonia, poisoning (narcotic), respiratory conditions, rheumatism, sciatica, snakebite, sore throat, sores, spasmodic conditions, and sprain.
Discussion: May aid digestion; clear and open bronchial passages; enhance urinary system function; increase circulation; inhibit development or destroy growth of bacteria and other microorganisms; promote bowel evacuation and urine flow; purify the blood; reestablish healthy system functions; stimulate appetite, gastric secretions, and peristalsis.
Cautions/Contraindications: Avoid use if pregnant or breast-feeding, or if you have an iodine sensitivity, or an insufficiency (venous). Do not administer to children under 12 years old. May interfere with the effectiveness of certain thyroid medications. May interfere with iodide metabolism. May cause dermatitis in susceptible individuals. Mustard poultices are to be removed after no more than 15-20 minutes. Not for long-term use.
Adverse Reactions: Abdominal pain, arrhythmia, blisters, cardiovascular conditions, coma, diarrhea (possibly bloody), digestive complaints, fever, gastritis, gastrointestinal problems, hypertrophy (thyroid), indigestion, insufficiency (thyroid), iodism (iodine poisoning), irritable bowel syndrome (IBS), mucous membrane problems, nausea, priapism, respiratory distress, thirst, ulcer, and/or vomiting.
Herb/Drug Interactions: This herb could cause an interaction (possibly severe) when taken with the following drugs: Thyroid drugs.
Preparations/Dosage: Crude Herb: 3-6 grams. Infusion: ¼-½ cup per day. Oil of Black Mustard (*oleum sinapis*): Internal Use: ⅛-¼ drop (0.008-0.0165 cc.). External uses. Dilute with a good quality vegetable oil before use. To help avoid blistering when applied to the skin, mix mustard with egg whites instead of water, and if the external application of mustard is too strong when applied to skin, mix it with a small amount of rye flour.

Mustard, White (mus terd, hwīt)

(*Sinapis* (*Brassica*) *alba*)

Synonyms/Related Species: None Known.
Family/Class: Brassicaceae (mustard).
Habitat: Europe.
Flavor: Pungent.
Parts Used: Seeds.

Properties: Alterative, analgesic, antibiotic, antifungal, antiphlogistic, carminative, counterirritant, depurative, diuretic, emetic, expectorant, laxative, and stimulant.
Constituents: Fatty acids (erucic, oleic, palmitic, stearic), fixed oils (olein, palmitin, stearin), isothiocyanates, glycosides, minerals (calcium, cobalt, iodine, iron, manganese, phosphorus, potassium, sulfur), mucilage, myronic acid, myrosin, protein, sinalbin (white mustard), sinapine (white mustard), sinapolin, vitamins (A, B_1 (thiamine), B_2 (riboflavin), B_{12}, C (ascorbic acid), and volatile oil.
Historical Uses: Abscess, amenorrhea, appetite loss, arthritis, bronchitis, chilblains, cold extremities, colds, cough, emphysema, fever (ephemeral, rheumatic), flatulence, gout, halitosis, hiccups, indigestion, infection (bacterial, fungal), inflammation, kidney problems, liver problems, lumbago, lung problems, mucus, muscle and joint pain, neuralgia, pain, peritonitis, pleurisy, pneumonia, poisoning (narcotic), respiratory conditions, rheumatism, sciatica, snakebite, sore throat, sores, spasmodic conditions, and sprain.
Discussion: May aid digestion; clear and open bronchial passages; enhance urinary system function; increase circulation; inhibit development or destroy growth of bacteria and other microorganisms; promote bowel evacuation and urine flow; purify the blood; reestablish healthy system functions; stimulate appetite, gastric secretions, and peristalsis.
Cautions/Contraindications: Avoid use if pregnant or breast-feeding, or if you have an iodine sensitivity, or an insufficiency (venous). Do not administer to children under 12 years old. May interfere with the effectiveness of certain thyroid medications. May interfere with iodide metabolism. May cause dermatitis in susceptible individuals. Mustard poultices are to be removed after no more than 15-20 minutes. Not for long-term use.
Adverse Reactions: Abdominal pain, arrhythmia, blisters, cardiovascular conditions, coma, diarrhea (possibly bloody), digestive complaints, fever, gastritis, gastrointestinal problems, hypertrophy (thyroid), indigestion, insufficiency (thyroid), iodism (iodine poisoning), irritable bowel syndrome (IBS), mucous membrane irritation, nausea, priapism, respiratory distress, thirst, ulcer, and/or vomiting.
Herb/Drug Interactions: This herb could cause an interaction (possibly severe) when taken with the following drugs: Thyroid drugs.
Preparations/Dosage: Crude Herb: 3-9 grams. Infusion: ¼-½ cup per day. External uses: To help avoid blistering when applied to the skin, mix mustard with egg whites instead of water, and if the topical application of mustard is too strong when applied, mix it with a small amount of rye flour.
Note: White mustard's actions are similar to that of black mustard, but are considered to be much weaker.

Myrobalan (mī·räb e·len)
(*Terminalia officinalis*)

Synonyms/Related Species: Beleric (*terminalia bellerica*) fruit is also called Baheera, Behada, Bhibitaki, and Bishitaki. **Chebule** (*terminalia chebula*) fruit is also called Harad and Haritaki.
Family/Class: Combretaceae (combretum).
Habitat: Asia and India.
Flavor: Bitter/sweet.
Parts Used: Fruit (dried).

Properties: Antibiotic, antiemetic, antioxidant, antiphlogistic, astringent, carminative, demulcent, depurative, erythropoietic, expectorant, hemostatic, hypotensive, laxative, nutritive, stimulant, tonic, and vasodilator.
Constituents: Chebulinic acid, ellagic acid, fatty acids (oleic, palmitic, stearic), fixed oils (olein, palmitin, stearin), flavonoids, gallic acid, glycosides, luteolin, minerals (calcium, magnesium), monosaccharides, oligomeric proanthocyanidins (OPCs), saponins, sennoside, tannic acid, and vitamin C (ascorbic acid).
Historical Uses: Allergy, alopecia, anemia, anorexia, arteriosclerosis, asthma, bronchitis, cardiovascular conditions, colic, congestion (lymphatic, uterine, vaginal), constipation, convalesence, cough, debility, deficiency (vitamin B), depression (mild/moderate), diabetes, diarrhea, dietary supplementation, dysentery, edema, emaciation, ephidrosis, erectile dysfunction, fever, flatulence, frigidity, gastrointestinal problems, gleet, gonorrhea, gout, hemorrhage, hemorrhoids, hypercholesterolemia, hypertension (mild/moderate), hypoglycemia, indigestion, infection (bacterial, sexually transmitted, urinary tract), infertility, inflammation, insufficiency (circulatory, immune), jaundice, leukorrhea, liver problems, malnutrition, melancholy, mucus, nausea, prolapse (rectal), respiratory conditions, sexually transmitted diseases (STDs), skin problems, thirst, urethritis, vaginitis, visual disturbances, vomiting, and weight loss.
Discussion: May aid digestion; cause blood vessel dilatation; clear and open bronchial passages; enhance cardiovascular system, colon, kidney, liver, lung, musculoskeletal system, pancreas, stomach, and uterine functions; promote absorption and utilization of the B vitamins and bowel evacuation; provide dietary supplementation; purify the blood, colon, digestive tract, and liver; improve cardiac muscle and liver mitochondrial functions; increase mental alertness, mobility, the production of red blood cells, and the quality of life; inhibit or destroy development and growth of bacteria and other microorganisms; reduce blood pressure levels; regulate the bowels; rejuvenate and revitalize the whole body; restore normal tone to tissues; serve as a nutritional adjuvant to therapeutic programs and as an adjuvantive therapy to weight loss programs; soothe mucous membrane irritation; stimulate appetite, enzymatic action, and peristalsis; strengthen the cerebral function, respiratory system, male libido, nervous system, vascular system, and vision.
Cautions/Contraindications: Avoid use if pregnant or breast-feeding, or if you have angina or congestive heart failure.
Adverse Reactions: Diarrhea (severe/possibly bloody), gastrointestinal cramps (severe), hematuria (blood in the urine), nausea, and/or vomiting.
Herb/Drug Interactions: This herb could cause an interaction (possibly severe) when taken with the following drugs: Hypotensive drugs.
Preparation/Dosage: Crude Herb: 3-12 grams. Whole Body Rejuvenator/Revitalizer: Combine equal parts of beleric, chebula, and currant/gooseberry (*ribes spp.*). Take ½-3 tablespoons per day.

Myrrh (mûr)

(*Commiphora myrrha*)

Synonyms/Related Species: Arabian Myrrh (*commiphora erythrea*), Didin, Guggul Gum, Indian Myrrh (*commiphora roxburghiana*), Karam, Mirra, and True Myrrh.
Family/Class: Burseraceae (frankincense).
Habitat: Africa, Arabia, Egypt, and India.
Flavor: Bitter/pungent.

Parts Used: Gum resin.
Properties: Analgesic, antibiotic, anticarcinogen, antifungal, antiphlogistic, antispasmodic, astringent, aromatic, carminative, counterirritant, depurative, diuretic, emmenagogue, expectorant, hemostatic, stimulant, tonic, and vesicant.
Constituents: Benzoates, benzoic acid, formic acid, gum, mucilage, myrrhin, sterols, sulfates, sulfuric acid, tannic acid, triterpenes, and volatile oil.
Historical Uses: Abscess, acne, amenorrhea, angina, arteriosclerosis, arthritis, asthma, athlete's foot, bleeding, bronchitis, bruises, cancer, candida, canker sores, colds, colitis, congestion (uterine, vaginal), cough, cramps, cystitis, diabetes, diarrhea, digestive complaints, diphtheria, dysmenorrhea, ear infection, eczema, edema, emphysema, fever (ephemeral, enteric, herpetic, rheumatic, scarlet), flatulence, gangrene, gargle/mouth rinse, halitosis, hemorrhoids, herpes, high triglyceride levels, hypercholesteremia, hypoglycemia, incense, indigestion, infection (bacterial, fungal), inflammation, insufficiency (circulatory), laryngitis, leprosy, lesions (tubercle), leukorrhea, lung problems, menopausal/menstrual problems, moniliasis, mucus, muscle and joint pain, nervous conditions, nipple soreness, pain, perfume, periodontal disease, pimples, pharyngitis, respiratory conditions, rheumatism, rheumatoid arthritis (RA), scarletina, scrofula, sexually transmitted diseases (STDs), shock, sinusitis, skin problems, sore throat, sores, spasmodic conditions, stomatitis, strep throat, syphilis, tonsillitis, toothache, tuberculosis, tumors, typhoid, ulcer (bouveret, duodenal, fistula, gastric, peptic, syphilitic, syriac, tuberculous), uterine problems, vaginitis, weight loss, and wounds (minor).
Discussion: May aid digestion; clear and open bronchial passages; cleanse the colon; decrease the effect of carcinogens; enhance cardiovascular system, liver, and lung functions; increase circulation, endurance, energy, and stamina; improve flexibility and mobility; inhibit or destroy development and growth of bacteria and other microorganisms; promote urine flow; reduce cholesterol and triglyceride levels; speed healing; stimulate appetite, gastric juices, menstruation, peristalsis, the thyroid, and the production of white blood cells; strengthen the bones.
Cautions/Contraindications: Avoid use if pregnant or breast-feeding, or if you have Crohn's disease, inflammatory bowel disease, irritable bowel syndrome (IBS), kidney problem, menorrhagia, stomach pain of unknown origin, or liver disease. Do not use crude gum resin. Not for long-term use.
Adverse Reactions: Appetite loss, arrhythmia, diarrhea, fever, hematuria (blood in the urine), mouth/skin/throat blistering, mucous membrane irritation, nausea, perspiration, skin rash, and/or vomiting.
Herb/Drug Interactions: This herb could cause an interaction (possibly severe) when taken with the following drugs: Beta-Adrenergic Blocking drugs and Calcium Channel Blocker drugs.
Preparations/Dosage: Crude Herb: 3-9 grams. Crude Herb (powdered): 5-30 grains (0.333-2 gm.) diluted with water or combined with other herbs. Infusion: 1 teaspoon one to four times per day. Tincture: 10-30 drops (0.666-2 cc.) one to three times per day.

Nettle, Dead (net l, ded)

(*Lamium album*)

Synonyms/Related Species: Archangel, Bee Nettle, Blind Nettle, Henbit Dead Nettle (*lamium amplexicaule*), Hungary Dead Nettle (*lamium pannonicum*), Purple Archangel, Purple Dead Nettle (*lamium purpureum*), Red Archangel (*lamium rubrum*), Small Dead Nettle, Spotted Dead Nettle (*lamium maculatum*), Stingless Nettle, White Archangel, White Dead Nettle, Yellow Archangel, and Yellow Dead Nettle (*lamium galeobdolon*).

Family/Class: Labiatae (mint).
Habitat: Asia, Europe, Hungary, North America, and Sweden.
Flavor: Bitter/sweet.
Parts Used: Leaves.
Properties: Antibiotic, antiperiodic, antiphlogistic, antispasmodic, astringent, demulcent, depurative, expectorant, hemostatic, malariacidal, and tonic.
Constituents: Caffeic acid, chlorogenic acid, flavonoids, lamine, mucilage, and saponins.
Historical Uses: Abscess, acne, ague, amenorrhea, bleeding, bronchitis, bruises, burns (minor), colds, congestion (uterine, vaginal), cough, digestive complaints, dysmenorrhea, eczema, fever (ephemeral, intermittent), flatulence, gastritis, gastrointestinal problems, gout, hemorrhage, indigestion, infection (bacterial), inflammation, insomnia, insufficiency (venous), irritable bowel syndrome (IBS), leukorrhea, malaria, melancholy, menstrual problems, mucus, muscle and joint pain, nosebleed, parasites (malarial plasmodia), pimples, psoriasis, rash, respiratory conditions, sciatica, skin problems, sores, spasmodic conditions, tumors, ulcer (duodenal, gastric, peptic, stasis, varicose), vaginitis, varicose veins, and wounds (minor).
Discussion: May clear and open bronchial passages; purify the blood; soothe mucous membrane irritation.
Cautions/Contraindications: Avoid use if pregnant or breast-feeding.
Adverse Reactions: Diarrhea (possibly bloody), gastrointestinal cramps (severe), hematuria (blood in the urine), nausea, and/or vomiting.
Herb/Drug Interactions: This herb could cause an interaction (possibly severe) when taken with the following drugs: None known.
Preparations/Dosage: Crude Herb: 3-6 grams. Infusion: 1-1½ cups per day. Leaves (powdered): Average dose in substance 1-3 grains (0.066-0.2 gm.). Tincture: 5-10 drops (0.333-0.666 cc.) one to three times per day.

Nettle, Stinging (net l, stiŋ iŋ)
(*Urtica dioica*)

Synonyms/Related Species: Common Nettle, Great Stinging Nettle, Roman Nettle (*urtica pilulifera*), Noedl, Small Field Nettle (*urtica urens*), True Nettle, and Vrishchikali.
Family/Class: Urticaceae (nettle).
Habitat: Africa, the Andes, Asia, Australia, Austria, Britain, Egypt, England, Europe, Germany, Holland, Japan, North America, Russia, Scotland, the Yukon Territory.
Flavor: Bitter.
Parts Used: Leaves, root, stems (young).
Properties: Anticarcinogen, antihistamine, antilithic, antiperiodic, antiphlogistic, astringent, counterirritant, depurative, diuretic, expectorant, hemostatic, hypoglycemic, hypotensive, lithotriptic, malariacidal, nutritive, stimulant, tonic, and vasodilator.
Constituents: Acetylcholine, ammonia, chlorophyll, coumarin, fatty acids (arachidonic, linoleic, linolenic), fiber, flavones, flavonoids, formic acid, histamine, indoles, lectins, lignin, minerals (calcium, chromium, copper, iron, magnesium, manganese, phosphorous, potassium, silicon, sodium, sulfur, zinc), monosaccharides, mucilage, phosphates, phosphoric acid, polysaccharides, protein, rutin, silicic acid, sterols, tannic acid, and vitamins (A, choline, C (ascorbic acid), D, E (alpha-tocopheral).

Historical Uses: Acquired immune deficiency syndrome (AIDS), ague, allergy (pollen), alopecia, anemia, arthritis, asthma, bleeding, bronchitis, bruises, calculus, cancer, canker sores, colds, cough, cystitis, dandruff, diarrhea, dietary supplementation, diminished sex drive, dysentery, dysuria (painful/difficult urination), eczema, edema, endometriosis, fever (ephemeral, hay, intermittent, rheumatic), fractures, gallstones, gout, hair conditioner, hair rinse, hematuria (blood in the urine), hemorrhoids, hemorrhage (metrorrhagia), hives, human immunodeficiency virus (HIV), hyperglycemia, hypertension (mild/moderate), hypothyroidism, hypertrophy (benign prostatic), infection (bladder, urinary tract), inflammation, insect bites or stings, insufficiency (circulatory), kidney problems, kidney stones, lesions (tubercle), lithemia, lung problems, lupus, malaria, malnutrition, Menier's disease, menopausal/menstrual problems, menorrhagia, mucus, muscle and joint pain, nephritis, neurologic conditions, nervous conditions, nosebleed, parasites (malarial plasmodia), peripheral vascular disease, poisoning (hemlock, henbane, nightshade), prostate problems, pruritus, rash, respiratory conditions, rheumatism, rheumatoid arthritis (RA), rickets, sciatica, scrofula, seborrhea, skin problems, sores, tuberculosis, ulcer (fistula, indolent, tuberculous), urinary problems, vaginitis, warts (digitate, filiform, fugitive, glabra, mother, plana juvenilis, plantar, seborrhoeic, vulgaris), weight loss, and wounds (minor).

Discussion: May cause blood vessel dilatation; clear and open bronchial passages; counteract the effect of histamine; decrease the effect of carcinogens; dissolve calculi; enhance intestinal, lung, stomach, and thyroid functions; prevent the development of calculus or stones, and hemorrhage in persons with hypertension; promote urine flow; provide dietary supplementation; purify the blood; reduce blood pressure levels, blood sugar levels, capillary fragility, creatinine levels, and excessive lithic acid (uric acid) and urate levels in the blood, tophi, and urine; restore normal tone to tissues; serve as a nutritional adjuvant to therapeutic programs and serve as an antidote (via ingestion of the seeds) to hemlock, henbane, and nightshade poisoning; stimulate gastric secretions, hair growth, the immune system, libido, T-cell activity, and white blood cell production; strengthen capillaries.

Cautions/Contraindications: Avoid use if pregnant or breast-feeding, or if you have congestive heart failure (CHF), edema, influenza, kidney disease, or cancer (prostate). Eat potassium rich foods such as bananas or fresh vegetables when taking nettle to replace potassium loss. Avoid using nettles that are old or those that have been harvested late in the season, as they have a tendency to develop microscopic mineral conglomerates and can cause dizziness, fainting, kidney damage, and skin rash. May cause dermatitis in susceptible individuals. Use heavy weight gloves when harvesting as fresh plants sting.

Adverse Reactions: Dizziness, fainting, hematuria (blood in the urine), nausea, skin rash, and/or vomiting.

Herb/Drug Interactions: This herb could cause an interaction (possibly severe) when taken with the following drugs: Antidiabetic drugs, Diuretic drugs, Hypotensive drugs, and Sedative drugs.

Preparations/Dosage: Crude Herb: 9-20 grams. Decoction (root): ¼-½ cup per day. Infusion (leaves and/or seeds): ½-1 cup per day. Leaves (powdered): Average dose in substance 5-10 grains (0.333-0.666 gm.). Leaves/Stems (young): Boiled and eaten as a vegetable. Tincture: 10-20 drops (0.666-1.25 cc.) one to three times per day. Asthma/Respiratory Conditions: Combine leaf and root juice with an equal amount of water. Add honey to taste. Take 1-2 teaspoons one to four times per day.

Isolation: Acetylcholine (chloride and bromide salts): Used in a 5% solution, average dose of 0.05-0.20 gm., administered intravenously or subcutaneously, for use to relax the peripheral blood vessels. Histamine phosphate: Used in a 1:1000 solution, average dose of 5 drops (0.3 cc.), administered intravenously or subcutaneously, for use as a powerful vasodilator, or for use as a stimulant.

Nutmeg (nut meg)

(*Myristica fragrans*)

Synonyms/Related Species: Mace, Muscus Nux, Musky Nut, Myristica, Noiz Muscade, Notemygge, Nux Moschata, and Wild Nutmeg.

Family/Class: Myristaceae (nutmeg).

Habitat: Africa, the Banda Islands, India, Indonesia, and the Molucca Islands.

Flavor: Bitter/pungent.

Parts Used: Seed kernel.

Properties: Abortifacient, analgesic, anthelmintic, antiperiodic, antiphlogistic, aphrodisiac, aromatic, astringent, carminative, demulcent, diaphoretic, emmenagogue, hallucinogen, hemostatic, laxative, malariacidal, narcotic, stimulant, stomachic, teniacide, teniafuge, tonic, toxic, and vermifuge.

Constituents: Elemi oil, elemicin, eucalyptol (cineol), fatty acids (oleic, palmitic, stearic), fixed oils (olein, palmitin, stearin), gum, inulin (starch), lauric acid, lignin, monoterpenes, hydrocarbons, myristicine, myristicol, myristin (myristic acid), pinenes, protein, sabinene, safrol, sterols, and volatile oil.

Historical Uses: Ague, ancylostomiasis, appetite loss, arthritis, asthma, bleeding, bronchitis, cardiovascular conditions, chills, cholera, colic, congestion (uterine, vaginal), cough, digestive complaints, diphtheria, fever (ephemeral, intermittent, rheumatic), flatulence, flavoring agent, diarrhea, headache, hemorrhoids, indigestion, inflammation, insomnia, lesions (tubercle), leukorrhea, malaria, muscle and joint pain, nausea, nervous conditions, pain, parasites (hookworm, malarial plasmodia, pinworm, roundworm, tapeworm), rheumatism, scrofula, sores, tuberculosis, ulcer (fistula, tuberculous), urethritis, vaginitis, vomiting, and wounds (minor).

Discussion: May aid digestion; arouse sexual impulses; enhance colon, spleen, and stomach functions; induce abortion; offset the negative effects of prescription drugs; promote bowel evacuation and perspiration; restore normal tone to tissues; soothe mucous membrane irritation; stimulate appetite, menstruation, peristalsis, and uterine contractions.

Cautions/Contraindications: Avoid use if pregnant or breast-feeding. Ingesting over 7 grams or as few as 1-2 nuts may result in severe poisoning and possible death. Not for long-term use.

Adverse Reactions: Chest tightness, delirium, dizziness, drowsiness, fainting, hallucinations, headache, lowered body temperature, nausea, skin flushing, stomach pain, stupor, visual disturbances, vomiting, weakened pulse rate, and/or possible death.

Herb/Drug Interactions: This herb could cause an interaction (possibly severe) when taken with the following drugs: None known.

Preparations/Dosage: Crude Herb: 1-3 grams. Nutmeg Oil (*oleum myristicae*): 1-3 drops (0.06-0.2 cc.) in atomization or inhalation as an aromatic stimulant. Seed kernel (powdered): Average dose in substance 5-20 grains (0.333-1.333 gm.). Tincture: 5-20 drops (0.333-1.25 cc.) one to three times per day.

Isolation: Eucalyptol: 5 drops (0.3 cc.) in atomization or inhalation therapy for use in respiratory conditions. Safrol: Average dose of 20-30 drops (1.333-2 cc.) for use as an analgesic.

Did You Know? The oil that is used as an ingredient in self-protective aerosal sprays comes from the dried outer covering of the nutmeg. This oil has the combined effects, which are similar to that of a tear gas and a nerve gas, and when sprayed will temporarily blind and stun the attacker.

Nux Vomica (nuks vom i·ke)
(*Strychnos nux vomica*)

Synonyms/Related Species: Brucea Shrub (*strychnos ligustrina*), Curare (*strychnos toxifera*), Egyptian Nux (*strychnos innocua*), False Angostura, Hoang-nan (*strychnos gaultheriana*), Ignatia (*strychnos ignatii*), Indian Nut (*strychnos pseudo*), Nightshade, Poison Nut (*strychnos lethalis*), Quaker's Buttons, Ratsbane, Semen Strychnos, St. Ignatius' Bean, and Upas (*strychnos tieute*).
Family/Class: Loganiaceae (logania).
Habitat: Asia, British Guina, China, Egypt, India, Java, Malay, Pakistan, the Philippines, South America, and Vietnam.
Flavor: Bitter.
Parts Used: Seeds.
Properties: Anesthetic, antispasmodic, cardiant, stimulant, tonic, and vermin poison.
Constituents: Albumen, alkaloids, brucine, caffeic acid, caseanic acid, casein, caseinic acid, curarine, fatty acids (oleic, palmitic, stearic), fixed oils (olein, palmitin, stearin), icajine, iridoide minerals (copper), monoterpenes, loganin, polysaccharides, struxine, strychnicine, strychnine, strychnolethaline, and tannic acid.
Historical Uses: Anemia, appetite loss, cardiovascular conditions, constipation, convulsions, depression (mild/moderate), eye problems, flatulence, gastrointestinal problems, indigestion, inflammation, insufficiency (circulatory), leprosy, migraine, nervous conditions, neurologic conditions, poisoning (chloral, chloroform, lead), pruritus, respiratory conditions, sexually transmitted diseases (STDs), shock, skin problems, spasmodic conditions, syphilis, tetanus, trismus (lockjaw), ulcer (syphilitic), and vermin.
Discussion: May destroy vermin; elevate blood pressure levels; increase reflex excitability (involuntary action or movement); restore normal tone to tissues; serve as an adjuvant in chronic lead poisoning, general anesthesia, and as an antidote in chloral or chloroform poisoning; stimulate appetite, the cardiovascular system, peristalsis, and gastric juices.
Cautions/Contraindications: Avoid use if pregnant or breast-feeding. Not for long-term use. Use with professional guidance/supervision.
Adverse Reactions: Anxiety, cardiac failure, convulsions, enhanced reflexes, equilibrium disturbances, heightened perception, liver damage (often characterized by jaundice), muscular rigidity, nervousness, neural damage, paralysis, respiratory failure, restlessness, spasmodic conditions, and/or possible death.
Herb/Drug Interactions: This herb could cause an interaction (possibly severe) when taken with the following drugs: None known.
Preparations/Dosage: Crude Herb (powdered): 1-4 grains (0.066-0.26 gm.). Extract: 1-3 drops (0.06-0.2 cc.). Extract (powdered): Average dose in substance ¼ grain (15 mg.). Tincture: 5-10 drops (0.333-0.666 cc.) one to two times per day.

Oak (ōk)
(*Quercus alba*)

Synonyms/Related Species: Abram's Oak, Black Oak (*quercus tinctoria*), Blue Oak (*quercus douglasii*), British Oak (*quercus robur*), Common Oak (*quercus pedunculata*), Durmast Oak (*quercus sessiliflora*), English Oak, Evergreen Oak (*quercus ilex*), False Sandalwood (*quercus abelicea*), Fendler's Oak, Gambel's Oak (*quercus gambelii*), Gospel Oak, Guatamala Oak (*quercus skinneri*), Holm Oak, Kermes Oak (*quercus coccifera*), Live Oak (*quercus virens*), Oregon White Oak (*quercus garryana*), Prickly Evergreen, Quebec Oak, Quercuez, Red Oak (*quercus rubra*), Sindian, Tanner's Bark, Turkey Oak (*quercus cerris*), Valley Oak (*quercus lobata*), and White Oak.

Family/Class: Fagaceae (beech).

Habitat: Asia, the Caucasus, Crete, England, Europe, Guatamala, Japan, Java, Libya, the Mediterranean, North America, Persia, South America, and Turkey.

Flavor: Bitter.

Parts Used: Acorns, bark, galls.

Properties: Anthelmintic, antibiotic, anticarcinogen, antifungal, antilithic, antiperiodic, antiphlogistic, antispasmodic, antiviral, astringent, demulcent, diuretic, hemostatic, lithotriptic, malariacidal, nutritive, parasiticide, stomachic, tonic, and vermifuge.

Constituents: Albumin (albumen), carbohydrates, flavones, flavonoids, gallic acid, inulin (starch), minerals (calcium, cobalt, iodine, iron, lead, phosphorous, potassium, sodium, strontium, sulfur, tin), lignin, monosaccharides, mucilage, phosphoric acid, protein, resin, tannic acid, and vitamin B_{12}.

Historical Uses: Acquired immune deficiency syndrome (AIDS), ague, allergy (drug-related), bladder problems, bleeding, bruises, burns (minor), calculus, cancer, candida, canker sores, cholera, congestion (uterine, vaginal), cough, degenerative conditions, diarrhea, dietary supplementation, dysentery, emaciation, enema, epilepsy, fever (ephemeral, intermittent), gallstones, gangrene, gargle/ mouth rinse, glandular swelling, gleet, goiter, gonorrhea, gout, hematuria (blood in the urine), hemorrhage, hemorrhoids, herpes, human immunodeficiency virus (HIV), indigestion, infection (bacterial, fungal, viral), inflammation, insect bites or stings, insufficiency (venous), jaundice, kidney problems, kidney stones, lesions (tubercle), leukorrhea, lithemia, liver problems, malaria, malnutrition, menorrhagia, menstrual problems, moniliasis, mucus, muscle and joint pain, nausea, nephritis, parasites (malarial plasmodia, pinworm, ringworm), periodontal disease, poisoning (strychnine, veratrine), prolapse (rectal, uterine), rheumatism, scrofula, sexually transmitted diseases (STDs), sinusitis, skin problems, snakebite, sore throat, sores, spasmodic conditions, spleen problems, strep throat, substitute for coffee (ground acorns), substitute for quinine, tonsillitits, toothache, tuberculosis, tumors, ulcer (duodenal, fistula, gastric, peptic, stasis, tuberculous, varicose), urethritis, urinary problems, vaginitis, varicose veins, vomiting, and wounds (minor).

Discussion: May clot the blood; dissolve calculi; decrease the effect of carcinogens; enhance intestinal system, lung, spleen, and stomach functions; inhibit development or destroy growth of bacteria and other microorganisms; offset the negative effects of chemotherapy and radiation therapy; prevent the development of calculus and stones; promote urine flow; provide dietary supplementation; reduce excessive levels of lithic acid (uric acid) and urates in the blood, tophi, and urine; restore normal tone to tissues; serve as a nutritional adjuvant to therapeutic programs and serve as an antidote for allergy (drug-related) strychnine poisoning, and veratrine poisoning; soothe mucous membrane irritation; stimulate metabolism; strengthen capillaries.

Cautions/Contraindications: Avoid use if pregnant or breast-feeding, or if you have an iodine sensitivity. May cause dermatitis in susceptible individuals. May interfere with the absorption of atropine (when taken by mouth), codeine, ephedrine, pseudoephedrine, and theophylline drugs. May interfere with the effectiveness of certain thyroid medications.
Adverse Reactions: Abdominal pain, arrhythmia, constipation, diarrhea, edema, fever, hematuria (blood in the urine), hypertrophy (thyroid), iodism (iodine poisoning), liver damage (often characterized by jaundice), nausea, priapism, thirst (excessive), and/or vomiting.
Herb/Drug Interactions: This herb could cause an interaction (possibly severe) when taken with the following drugs: Autonomic drugs, Opiate Agonists/Narcotic drugs, other Medications/Products containing ephedra or pseudoephedrine, Theophylline drugs, and Thyroid drugs.
Preparations/Dosage: Crude Herb: 3-6 grams. Extract (galls): 5-15 drops (0.333-1 cc.) one to two times per day. Galls (powdered): 5-20 grains (0.333-1.333 gm.) applied externally. Infusion (bark and/or galls): ½-1 cup per day. Tincture: 5-30 drops (0.333-2 cc.) one to three times per day. Acorns (ground/powdered): Used as a coffee or flour substitute.

Oak, Poison (ōk, poi zen)
(*Toxicodendron diversilobum*)

Synonyms/Related Species: Eastern Poison Oak (*toxicodendron toxicarium*), Pacific Poison Oak, and Western Poison Oak.
Family/Class: Anacardiaceae (cashew).
Habitat: Asia, British Columbia, Europe, Germany, and North America.
Flavor: Pungent/bitter.
Parts Used: Leaves.
Properties: Antiphlogistic, counterirritant, narcotic, parasiticide, and stimulant.
Constituents: Toxicodendrin, toxicodendrol, and urushiol.
Historical Uses: Arthritis, eczema, edema, fever (ephemeral, herpetic, rheumatic), herpes, infection, inflammation, muscle and joint pain, palsy, paralysis, parasites (ringworm), rash, rheumatism, sexually transmitted diseases (STDs), skin problems, and warts (digitate, filiform, fugitive, glabra, mother, plana juvenilis, plantar, seborrhoeic, vulgaris).
Discussion: May enhance liver function; stimulate the immune system.
Cautions/Contraindications: Avoid use if pregnant or breast-feeding. Berries and root are poisonous. Keep away from eyes and mucous membranes. May cause severe dermatitis in susceptible individuals. Use protective clothing and gloves when harvesting.
Adverse Reactions: Conjunctivitis, corneal inflammation, delirium, diarrhea, dizziness, drowsiness, fainting, fever, gastric irritation, hematuria (blood in the urine), infection, intestinal cramps, pruritus, respiratory distress, severe skin and mucous membrane eruptions, nausea, stupor, vertigo, and/or vomiting.
Herb/Drug Interactions: This herb could cause an interaction (possibly severe) when taken with the following drugs: None known.
Preparations/Dosage: External Uses Recommended: Cover unaffected areas of skin and apply (wearing gloves) in extremely small-diluted amounts. May cause skin irritation, redness, and inflammation upon application. Thoroughly wash affected area afterwards with a soapy solution to remove any resinous residue. Keep away from eyes and mucous membranes. Internal Use: Great care must be taken when using poison oak preparations internally. Initially, those persons

who are not used to ingesting poison oak should begin with *very* small diluted amounts, as the ingestion of large amounts may result in adverse effects, some possibly severe (see above Cautions/Contraindications: Large amounts or overuse). Tincture 1:4 (a dose of 25%): 1-5 drops (0.066-0.333 cc.).

Prevention: Remove affected clothing and place in plastic bag until they can be washed in hot soapy water (wear gloves when removing clothing from bag as contact with the toxic oil can cause severe skin reactions). Washing skin thoroughly within 10 minutes of exposure with hot soapy water may help to remove the toxic (urushiol) oil and prevent skin reactions.

First Aid: Mild to Moderate Cases: Cold soaks in the bathtub for 20 minutes several times daily may help relieve inflammation. Corticosteroid or Corticosterone creams applied topically (avoid genital area) can help to relieve itching and inflammation. Oral (systemic) corticosteroids can also help relieve discomforts. For Severe Cases or affected areas involving the anal or genital area obtain immediate medical attention.

Did You Know? The toxic oil, urushiol can remain active on surfaces for as long as 5 years, and this oil is so potent that as little as a billionth of a gram (nanogram) can cause a rash.

Oat (ōt)

(*Avena sativa*)

Synonyms/Related Species: Avena, Common Oat, Groats, Milky Oat Seed, and Wild Oats.

Family/Class: Graminaceae (grass).

Habitat: Britain, England, France, Germany, Poland, Russia, and North America.

Flavor: Sweet.

Parts Used: Grain/seeds, stalks/straw.

Properties: Antibiotic, antidepressant, antilithic, antiphlogistic, antispasmodic, demulcent, lithotriptic, nervine, nutritive, sedative, stimulant, and tonic.

Constituents: Albumin (albumen), avenin, carbohydrates, fatty acids (oleic, palmitic, stearic), fixed oils (olein, palmitin, stearin), flavonoids, gramine, gluten, glutin, glycosides, gum, inulin (starch), minerals (calcium, copper, iron, magnesium, phosphorus, potassium, silicon, zinc), monosaccharides, peptides, polysaccharides, protein, saponins, silicic acid, sterols, and vitamins (A, B_1 (thiamine), B_3 (niacin), B_2 (riboflavin), E (alpha-tocopheral).

Historical Uses: Abdominal pain, abscess, addiction (morphine, nicotine, opium), anxiety, arthritis, attention deficit disorder (ADD), attention deficit hyperactivity disorder (ADHD), bladder problems, bursitis, calculus, cardiovascular conditions, cold extremities, chicken pox, chilblains, colic, constipation, connective tissue problems, convalescence, cough, debility, depression (mild/moderate), diabetes, dietary supplementation, diminished sex drive, dry skin, eczema, enuresis (urinary incontinence), exhaustion, eye problems, fatigue, fever (ephemeral, rheumatic), food source, frostbite, gallbladder problems, gallstones, gastroenteritis, gastrointestinal problems, gout, hot flashes, hysteria, impetigo, indigestion, infection (bacterial), inflammation, influenza, insomnia, insufficiency (pancreatic), irritability, kidney problems, kidney stones, lithemia, liver problems, lumbago, lung problems, malnutrition, menopausal problems, metabolic problems, muscle and joint pain, nervous conditions, osteoporosis, paralysis, poison ivy/oak, premenstrual syndrome (PMS), rash, rheumatism, seborrhea, skin problems, spasmodic conditions, urinary problems, warts (digitate, filiform, fugitive, glabra, mother, plana juvenilis, plantar, seborrhoeic, vulgaris), and wounds (minor).

Discussion: May balance blood sugar levels; calm the nervous system; dissolve calculi; enhance nervous system, lung, pancreas, spleen, and stomach functions; decrease morphine, opium, and nicotine dependence as well as easing withdrawal symptoms; inhibit or destroy development and growth of bacteria and other microorganisms; increase circulation; prevent the development of calculus or stones; provide dietary supplementation; reduce cholesterol, excessive lithic acid (uric acid) and urate levels in the blood, tophi, and urine, and the frequency of nighttime urination; restore normal tone to tissues; serve as a nutritional adjuvant to therapeutic programs; soothe mucous membrane irritation; stimulate the male libido and uterine contractions.
Cautions/Contraindications: Avoid use if you have a cereal grain sensitivity, Celiac disease, or irritable bowel syndrome (IBS). May cause dermatitis in susceptible individuals.
Adverse Reactions: Diarrhea (possibly bloody), gastrointestinal cramps (severe), headache, hematuria (blood in the urine), nausea, and/or vomiting.
Herb/Drug Interactions: This herb could cause an interaction (possibly severe) when taken with the following drugs: None known.
Preparations/Dosage: Crude Herb: 3-6 grams. Decoction (straw): ½ cup per day. Extract: 5-20 drops (0.333-1.25 cc.) one to two times per day. Grain/Seed (dried): Boiled and eaten or ground into flour. Infusion: ½-1 cup per day. Tincture: 10-30 drops (0.666-2 cc.) one to three times per day.

Olive (ol iv trē)
(*Olea europaea*)

Synonyms/Related Species: Olea and True Wild Olive (*olea oleaster*).
Family/Class: Oleaceae (olive).
Habitat: Asia, Australia, the Caucasus, Chili, Europe, Iran, Italy, the Mediterranean, Peru, South America, Spain, and Syria.
Flavor: Bitter/sweet.
Parts Used: Bark, fruit, leaves, oil (fruit).
Properties: Antibiotic, antifungal, antiperiodic, antiphlogistic, antispasmodic, antioxidant, antiviral, astringent, cholagogue, hypotensive, laxative, lithotriptic, malariacidal, nutritive, vasodilator, vermifuge, and vulnerary.
Constituents: Benzoic acid, fatty acids (arachidonic, linoleic, linolenic, oleic, palmitic, stearic), fixed oils (olein, palmitin, stearin), glycosides, iridoids, ligstroside, luteolin, mannitol (mannite), minerals (calcium), monosaccharides, olease, oleuropein, and vitamin E (alpha-tocopheral).
Historical Uses: Ague, arteriosclerosis, arrhythmia, bruises, burns (minor), calculus, candida, cardiovascular conditions, chills, cholera, chronic fatigue syndrome (CFS), colds, dandruff, diabetes, dietary supplementation, ear infection, eczema, edema, Epstein Barr Virus (EBV), escherichia coli (e-coli), fever (ephemeral, enteric, herpetic, intermittent, scarlet), fibromyalgia, gallstones, glandular problems, hepatitis, herpes, human B-lymphotropic virus, hypertension (mild/moderate), immune system problems, infection (bacterial, fungal, urinary tract, viral), inflammation, influenza, insect bites or stings, kidney stones, lupus, malaria, malnutrition, moniliasis, mononucleosis (infectious), mucus, muscle and joint pain, musculoskeletal problems, neuralgia, nervous conditions, Newcastle disease, numbness, pain, paralysis, parasites (malarial plasmodia), plague, pruritus, psoriasis, respiratory conditions, seizure conditions, sexually transmitted diseases (STDs), sinusitis, skin problems, spasmodic conditions, typhoid, ulcer (bouveret, duodenal, gastric, peptic), visual disturbances, and wounds (minor).

Discussion: May cause blood vessel dilatation; dissolve calculi; enhance immune system function; increase bile secretion, circulation, energy, natural killer (NK) cell activity, white blood cell production; inhibit oxidation and inhibit or destroy development and growth of bacteria and other microorganisms; promote bile flow and bowel evacuation; protect from free radical damage; provide dietary supplementation; reduce blood pressure levels and cholesterol levels; serve as a nutritional adjuvant to therapeutic programs; speed healing; stimulate peristalsis; stop the germination and growth of the bacillus cereus bacteria (a form of food poisoning which is sometimes found in fried rice).

Cautions/Contraindications: Avoid use if pregnant or breast-feeding. Do not confuse this herb with the ornamental Russian olive tree (*elaeagnus spp.*) belonging to the family elaeagnaceae. A temporary detoxification effect may occur in some individuals and is characterized by diarrhea, fatigue, headache, muscle and joint pain, pimples, or skin rash. This detoxification effect is due to the elimination of dead microbes and toxins from the body, which can overburden the kidneys, liver, intestines, and skin. To help ward off detox symptoms, drink 4-6 glasses of water between usages.

Adverse Reactions: Diarrhea (severe), intestinal cramps (severe), muscle and joint pain, nausea, skin problems, and/or vomiting.

Herb/Drug Interactions: This herb could cause an interaction (possibly severe) when taken with the following drugs: Hypotensive drugs.

Preparations/Dosage: Crude Herb: 3-9 grams. Decoction (bark): ¼-½ cup per day. Fruit (ripe/black; unripe/green): Ingest a small handful daily. Infusion (leaves): ½-1 teaspoon one to three times per day. Olive Oil (*oleum olivae*): Cooking or applied topically. Laxative (oil): Take 1-2 tablespoons before bed.

Isolation: Mannitol hexanitrate: Average dose of 15-60 mg. for use as a vasodilator.

Onion (un yen)

(*Allium cepa*)

Synonyms/Related Species: Catawissa Onion, Egyptian Onion (*allium aggregatum*), Geyer's Onion (*allium geyeri*), L'oignon d'Egypte, Nodding Onion (*allium cernuum*), Pissatse'miakim, Potato Onion, Prairie Onion (*allium textile*), Short-Styled Onion (*allium brevistylum*), Spanish Onion, Unio Cepa, and Wild Onion.

Family/Class: Liliaceae (lily).

Habitat: The Alps, Asia, China, Egypt, England, Europe, France, Greece, India, Italy, the Mediterranean, North America, Siberia, Spain, and Sweden.

Flavor: Pungent.

Parts Used: Bulb.

Properties: Alterative, anthelmintic, antibiotic, antifungal, antiperiodic, antiphlogistic, antispasmodic, carminative, diaphoretic, diuretic, expectorant, hypoglycemic, hypotensive, lithotriptic, malariacidal, stimulant, stomachic, tonic, vasodilator, and vermifuge.

Constituents: Allicin, allyl, carbohydrates, flavonoids, fructosans, minerals (arsenic, calcium, iron, manganese, potassium, selenium, sodium, sulfur, zinc), polysaccharides, saponins, and vitamins (A, B_1 (thiamine), C (ascorbic acid), M (folic acid).

Historical Uses: Abscess, acne, ague, allergy, anemia, angina, appetite loss, arteriosclerosis, asthma, athlete's foot, belching, blisters, bronchitis, burns (minor), calculus, calluses, chills, cholera, cold, colic, cough, croup, dehydration, diabetes, diarrhea, digestive complaints, earache, eczema, emaciation, fever (ephemeral, intermittent), flatulence, gallstones, gastritis, gastrointestinal problems, hyperglycemia, hypertension (mild/moderate), hysteria, indigestion, infection (bacterial, fungal), inflammation, influenza, insect bites or stings, irritable bowel syndrome (IBS), laryngitis, malaria, mucus, parasites (malarial plasmodia, roundworm), respiratory conditions, scrofula, sexually transmitted diseases (STDs), skin problems, sore throat, sores, spasmodic conditions, syphilis, tinnitus, ulcer (fistula, syphilitic), warts (digitate, filiform, fugitive, glabra, mother, plana juvenilis, plantar, seborrhoeic, vulgaris), whooping cough, and wounds (minor).

Discussion: May aid digestion; cause blood vessel dilatation; clear and open bronchial passages; dissolve calculi; enhance cardiovascular system and stomach functions; increase sperm count; inhibit or destroy development and growth of bacteria and other microorganisms; promote perspiration and urine flow; reduce blood pressure levels, blood sugar levels, and cholesterol levels; reestablish healthy system functions; restore normal tone to tissues; stimulate peristalsis.

Cautions/Contraindications: Avoid use if pregnant or breast-feeding. Do not confuse this herb with poisonous death camas (*zigadenus spp.*), which does not have that 'onion' smell. May cause dermatitis in susceptible individuals.

Adverse Reactions: Diarrhea (possibly bloody), digestive complaints, edema, acid reflux (esophageal irritation caused by gastric acid), flatulence (excessive), gastritis, gastrointestinal problems, indigestion, irritable bowel syndrome (IBS), nausea, and/or vomiting.

Herb/Drug Interactions: This herb could cause an interaction (possibly severe) when taken with the following drugs: Antidiabetic drugs and Hypotensive drugs.

Preparations/Dosage: Bulb (powdered): Average dose in substance 20 grains (1.333 gm.) Bulb (raw/cooked): Use freely in culinary. Decoction: 1-2 tablespoons one to three times per day. Extract (cold): ½ cup per day. Juice: 1-2 teaspoons in water or mixed with honey three to four times per day. Syrup (*syrupus allii*): 1 drachm (4 cc.).

Orange (ôr inj)
(*Citrus dulcis*)

Synonyms/Related Species: Sweet Orange.

Family/Class: Rutaceae (rue).

Floral Emblem: Florida.

Habitat: Asia, the Mediterranean, and the United States (primarily California and Florida).

Flavor: Sweet.

Parts Used: Fruit, rind (dried/fresh).

Properties: Antiscorbutic, carminative, expectorant, nutritive, and stimulant.

Constituents: Carvene (limonene), citral (geranial), citronellal, flavonoids, coumarin, geraniol (rhodinol), linalyl acetate, nootkatone, sinesal, vitamins (C (ascorbic acid), and volatile oil.

Historical Uses: Appetite loss, bronchitis, colds, cough, dietary supplementation, digestive complaints, flatulence, flavoring agent, indigestion, influenza, gastritis, gastrointestinal problems, malnutrition, mucus, respiratory conditions, and scurvy.

Discussion: May aid digestion; clear and open bronchial passages; provide dietary supplementation; serve as a nutritional adjuvant to therapeutic programs; stimulate appetite and the nervous system.

Cautions/Contraindications: Avoid use if pregnant or breast-feeding. Allergic reactions may occur in children when first introducing them to citrus fruits and/or juice. Do not confuse this herb with bitter orange (*citrus aurantium amara*). May cause allergic reactions, photosensitivity, or photodermatosis in susceptible individuals.

Adverse Reactions: Mucous membrane irritation, nausea, and/or vomiting.
Herb/Drug Interactions: This herb could cause an interaction (possibly severe) when taken with the following drugs: None known.
Preparations/Dosage: Fruit and/or Juice: May be ingested freely. Infusion: 1-2 cups per day. Orange Flower Water: 1 ounce (30 cc.). Syrup: 1-2 ounces (30-60 cc.). Syrup of Orange Flowers: 4-8 drachms (16-32 cc.). Tincture: 15-30 drops (1-2 cc.).

Papaya (pä·pä yä)

(*Carica papaya*)

Synonyms/Related Species: Mamaeire, Melon Tree, Papaw, and Pawpaw.
Family/Class: Caricaceae (papaya).
Habitat: India and South America.
Flavor: Fruit: sweet. Leaves/Seeds: bitter.
Parts Used: Fruit, leaves, seeds.
Properties: Abortifacient, analgesic, anticarcinogen, antiphlogistic, antiprotozoan, astringent, cardiant, diuretic, hemostatic, hypertensive, laxative, parasiticide, stimulant, vasoconstrictor, and vermifuge.
Constituents: Carpaine, enzymes (chymopapain, lysozyme, papainase), glycosides, minerals (calcium, iron, magnesium, phosphorous, potassium, sodium), monosaccharides, papain (caricin), phosphoric acid, saponins, and vitamins (A, B_2 (riboflavin), C (ascorbic acid), D, E (alpha-tocopheral), K).
Historical Uses: Allergy, appetite loss, bleeding, bruises, burns (minor), cancer, Celiac disease, constipation, corns, diarrhea, digestive complaints, diverticulitis, ear infection, edema, fever (ephemeral, herpetic), fractures, flatulence, freckles, gastritis, gastrointestinal problems, hemorrhage, herpes, hypertrophy (benign prostatic), indigestion, infection, inflammation, insufficiency (pancreatic), injury (athletic), insect bites or stings, irritable bowel syndrome (IBS), mucus, muscle and joint pain, pain, parasites (ameba, ringworm), periodontal disease, pimples, sexually transmitted diseases (STDs), shingles, sores, stomachache, ulcer (duodenal, gastric), warts (digitate, filiform, fugitive, glabra, mother, plana juvenilis, plantar, seborrhoeic, vulgaris), and wounds (minor).
Discussion: May aid the digestion of proteins; decrease the effect of carcinogens; elevate blood pressure; induce abortion; promote bowel evacuation and urine flow; reduce heart rate, histamine excretion, and reduce both the rate of growth and the rate of reproduction of protozoa; speed healing and surgical recovery; stimulate appetite, the cardiovascular system, peristalsis, and uterine contractions.
Cautions/Contraindications: Avoid use if pregnant or breast-feeding, or if you have a coagulation problem, hypertension, or a malabsorption disorder. Do not confuse this herb with custard apple (*asimina triloba*). May cause allergic reactions or dermatitis in susceptible individuals. Some persons may experience bleeding or increased clotting time when using this herb with anticoagulant drugs or aspirin.
Adverse Reactions: Bleeding (possibly serious), coagulation problems, diarrhea (possibly bloody), edema, gastrointestinal cramps (severe), hematuria (blood in the urine), nausea, perforation of the esophageal wall, and/or vomiting.

Herb/Drug Interactions: This herb could cause an interaction (possibly severe) when taken with the following drugs: Anticoagulant drugs, Enzymes (pancreatic), Salicylates, and Subsalicylates.

Preparations/Dosage: Fruit (pulp): May be eaten raw, dried, or pickled. Fruit (powdered): Average dose in substance 2-8 grains (0.133-0.5 gm.). Infusion (leaves): ½-1 cup per day. Seeds (powdered): Average dose in substance 1-3 grams.

Isolation: Carpaine: Average dose of $^{1}/_{10}$-$^{1}/_{6}$ grain (0.006-0.01 gm.) administered hypodermically, for use as a cardiant, diuretic, and stimulant. Carpaine's action is similar to that of digitalis. Papain: Average dose of 1-5 grains (0.066-0.333 gm.) for use in digestive complaints, or as a topical application for corns, warts, etc. use in a 5-15% solution in equal parts of vegetable glycerin and water.

Parsley (pärs lē)
(*Petroselinum sativum*)

Synonyms/Related Species: Celery-Leaved Parsley, Common Parsley, Hamburg Parsley (*petroselinum crispum*), Neapolitan Parsley, Persely, Petersylinge, Plain-Leaved Parsley, Rock Parsley, Stone Parsley, and Turnip-Rooted Parsley.

Family/Class: Umbelliferae (parsley).

Habitat: Algeria, England, Lebanon, the Mediterranean, Scotland, and Turkey.

Flavor: Sweet.

Parts Used: Leaves, root, seeds.

Properties: Abortifacient, anticarcinogen, antilithic, antiperiodic, antiphlogistic, antispasmodic, carminative, depurative, diuretic, emmenagogue, expectorant, hypotensive, laxative, lithotriptic, malariacidal, parasiticide, stimulant, and vasodilator.

Constituents: Apiol, apiolin, bergapten, chlorophyll, coumarin, fatty acids (oleic, palmitic, petroselinic, stearic), fixed oils (olein, palmitin, stearin), flavonoids, glycosides, inulin (starch), minerals (calcium, cobalt, copper, iron, magnesium, potassium, silicon, sodium, sulfur), monosaccharides, mucilage, myristicine, pinene, psoralen, resin, silicic acid, terpenes, vitamins (A, B_1 (thiamine), B_2 (riboflavin), B_3 (niacin), C (ascorbic acid), and volatile oil.

Historical Uses: Ague, allergy (pollen), amenorrhea, arthritis, asthma, bronchitis, bruises, calculus, cancer, colic, conjunctivitis, cough, digestive complaints, dizziness, dysmenorrhea, earache, edema, enuresis (urinary incontinence), fever (ephemeral, hay, intermittent, rheumatic), flatulence, flavoring agent, gallstones, gleet, gonorrhea, gout, halitosis, hypertension (mild/moderate), indigestion, infection (bladder, sexually transmitted), inflammation, insect bites or stings, insufficiency (pituitary), jaundice, kidney problems, kidney stones, lithemia, liver problems, lumbago, lung problems, malaria, menorrhagia, menstrual problems, mucus, muscle and joint pain, pain, parasites (lice and their nits, malarial plasmodia), prostate problems, rheumatism, sexually transmitted diseases (STDs), spasmodic conditions, spleen problems, syphilis, thyroid problems, tumors, ulcer (syphilitic), urethritis, urinary problems, wounds (minor).

Discussion: May aid digestion; cause blood vessel dilatation; clear and open bronchial passages; decrease the effect of carcinogens; dissolve calculi; enhance liver function; induce abortion; prevent the development of calculus or stones; promote urine flow; purify the blood; reduce blood pressure levels, excessive lithic acid (uric acid) and urate levels in the blood, tophi, and urine, and the frequency of nighttime urination; stimulate menstruation and uterine contractions; strengthen the optic nerves and vein walls.

Cautions/Contraindications: Avoid use if pregnant or breast-feeding, or if you are allergic to apiole, or if you have nephritis.

Adverse Reactions: Congestion (lung), diarrhea (possibly bloody), convulsions, dizziness, a drastic drop in blood pressure levels, edema, fainting, mucous membrane bleeding, nausea, nerve inflammation, paralysis, and/or vomiting.

Herb/Drug Interactions: This herb could cause an interaction (possibly severe) when taken with the following drugs: Hypotensive drugs.

Preparations/Dosage: Crude Herb: 3-9 grams. Decoction (root): ½-1 cup per day. Infusion (leaves): 1-2 cups per day. Seeds (powdered): Average dose in substance 20-30 grains (1.333-2 gm.). Oil of Parsley Seed (*oleum apiol fructus*): 3-5 drops (0.2-0.333 cc.) in water or on a sugarcube. Tincture: 15-30 drops (1-2 cc.) one to three times per day.

Isolation: Apiol: Average dose of 3-5 drops (0.18-0.333 cc.) for use in menstrual problems. Apiolin: 3 drops (0.18 cc.) for use as an emmenagogue.

Passionflower (pash en·flou er)
(*Passiflora incarnata*)

Synonyms/Related Species: Apple-Fruited Granadilla (*passiflora maliformis*), Blue Passionflower (*passiflora caerulea*), Gourd Passionflower (*passiflora macrocarpa*), Granadilla (*passiflora quadrangularis*), Maypop, Passion Fruit, and Water Lemon (*passiflora laurifolia*).

Family/Class: Passifloraceae (passionflower).

Habitat: England, Europe, India, Jamaica, North America, and South America.

Flavor: Fruit: sweet. Leaves: bitter.

Parts Used: Fruit (mature), leaves.

Properties: Analgesic, anticarcinogen, antioxidant, antispasmodic, diaphoretic, diuretic, emmenagogue, febrifuge, hallucinogen, hypnotic, hypotensive, nervine, nutritive, sedative, stimulant, tonic, and vasodilator.

Constituents: Alkaloids, flavonoids, glycosides, gum, harmaline, harmine, harmol, monosaccharides, passiflorine, sterols, and volatile oil.

Historical Uses: Addiction (cocaine, heroin, opium), angina, anxiety, arrhythmia, asthma, attention deficit disorder (ADD), cancer (thyroid), conjunctivitis, convulsions, diarrhea, dietary supplementation, diminished sex drive, dysentery, encephalitis lethargica, epilepsy, fever (ephemeral), gynecomastia, headache, hyperactivity, hypertension (mild/moderate), hysteria, infection (viral), insomnia, lethargy, malnutrition, menopausal/menstrual problems, nausea, nervous conditions, neuralgia, neurologic conditions, pain, paralysis (cerebral), parkinsonism, Parkinson's disease, restlessness, seizure conditions, shingles, spasmodic conditions, visual disturbances, and vomiting.

Discussion: May aid withdrawal from cocaine, heroin, or opiate addictions; calm the nervous system; cause blood vessel dilatation; conserve testosterone already in the body; decrease the effect of carcinogens; enhance cardiovascular system and liver functions; induce sleep; inhibit oxidation; promote perspiration and urine flow; provide dietary supplementation; reduce blood pressure levels; restore normal tone to tissues; serve as a nutritional adjuvant to therapeutic programs; stimulate menstruation.

Cautions/Contraindications: Avoid use if pregnant or breast-feeding or if you are trying to become pregnant. Passionflower is a monoamine oxidase inhibitor (MAOI) herb. The combined use of passionflower with sedative, tranquilizer, antihistamine, narcotic, or tricyclic antidepressant drugs will cause hypertensive crisis. The combined use of passionflower with amphetamines, cocaine, LSD, alcohol (including wine), avocados, unripe bananas, and dairy products (including aged cheese) will cause hypotensive crisis. It is recommended that no other drugs be used in combination with or within a ten-hour period of the use of passionflower.
Adverse Reactions: Abdominal pain, cardiac failure, confusion, convulsions, debility, depression, dizziness, excitability, exhaustion (extreme), fainting, fatigue, hypertensive crisis (severe rise in blood pressure levels), hypotensive crisis (arrythmias, breathing difficulty, chills, severe drop in blood pressure levels), liver damage (often characterized by jaundice), nausea, paralysis, respiratory failure, vomiting, and/or possible death.
Herb/Drug Interactions: This herb could cause an interaction (possibly severe) when taken with the following drugs: Amphetamine drugs, Antidepressant drugs, Antihistamine drugs, Anxiolytic drugs, Cardiac drugs, Hypotensive drugs, Migraine drugs, Monamine Oxidase Inhibitors (MAOIs), Opiate Agonists/Narcotic drugs, Sedative drugs, and Tranquilizer drugs.
Preparations/Dosage: Crude Herb: 3-6 grams. Leaves (powdered): Average dose in substance 3-10 grains (0.2-0.666 gm.). Extract: 10-15 drops (0.666-1 cc.) one to two times per day. Tincture: 10-30 drops (0.666-2 cc.) one to three times per day.

Pasqueflower (pask flou er)

(*Anemone pulsatilla*)

Synonyms/Related Species: Butterflower, Cut-Leaved Anemone (*anemone multifida*), Easter Flower, May Flower, Meadow Anemone, Northern Anemone (*anemone parviflora*), Prairie Crocus, Pulsatilla, Red-Flowered Anemone (*anemone coronaria*), Thimbleweed, Western Pasqueflower (*anemone occidentalis*), Windflower, Wood Anemone, and Yellow Anemone (*anemone richardsonii*).
Family/Class: Ranunculaceae (buttercup).
Floral Emblem: South Dakota.
Habitat: Alaska, the Alpine and Subalpine zones, Denmark, Europe, Germany, Italy, and North America.
Flavor: Bitter.
Parts Used: Entire plant.
Properties: Alterative, antibiotic, antiphlogistic, antiprotozoan, antispasmodic, astringent, diaphoretic, emmenagogue, emetic, expectorant, hemostatic, laxative, nervine, parasiticide, sedative, and vermifuge.
Constituents: Alkaloids, anemonin, anemonol, protoanemonin, ranunculin, resin, saponins, tannic acid, and volatile oil.
Historical Uses: Ague, amenorrhea, anemia, anxiety, arthritis, asthma, bleeding, bronchitis, cardiovascular conditions, coated tongue, colds, conjunctivitis, constipation, depression (mild/moderate), diarrhea, digestive complaints, dysentery, earache, exhaustion, fever (ephemeral, rheumatic), gastrointestinal problems, gout, headache, indigestion, infection (bacterial, urinary tract), infertility, inflammation, insomnia, measles, menstrual problems, migraine, mucus, muscle and joint pain, neuralgia, neurologic conditions, nervous conditions, parasites (amebas, trichomonas), respiratory conditions, restlessness, rheumatism, skin problems, spasmodic conditions, spermatorrhea, styes, toothache, whooping cough, and windburn.

Discussion: May calm the nervous system; clear and open bronchial passages; enhance intestinal system function; increase circulation; inhibit or destroy developement and growth of bacteria and other microorganisms; promote perspiration; reduce both the rate of growth and the rate of reproduction of protozoa; reestablish healthy system functions; stimulate menstruation.
Cautions/Contraindications: Avoid use if pregnant or breast-feeding. May cause dermatitis in susceptible individuals. Not for long-term use.
Adverse Reactions: Asphyxiation, blistering of the mouth and throat, chills, convulsions, depression, diarrhea (possibly bloody), dizziness, fainting, gastroenteritis, gastrointestinal cramps (severe), hematuria (blood in the urine), kidney failure, nausea, nervousness, paralysis, salivation, slowed pulse rate, vomiting, and/or possible death.
Herb/Drug Interactions: This herb could cause an interaction (possibly severe) when taken with the following drugs: None known.
Preparations/Dosage: Crude Herb: 1-3 grams. Extract: 2-3 drops (0.133-0.2 cc.) one to two times per day. Tincture: 5-10 drops (0.333-0.666 cc.) one to three times per day.

Patchouli (pat·shoo lē)

(*Pogostemon cablin*)

Synonyms/Related Species: East Indian Herb, Indian Mint, Java Patchouli (*pogostemon heyneanus*), Paccilai, Pucha-Pat, and Putcha-Pat.
Family/Class: Labiatae (mint).
Habitat: India and Paraguay.
Flavor: Pungent.
Parts Used: Leaves (oil).
Properties: Alterative, anesthetic (local), antibiotic, antiemetic, antifungal, antilithic, antispasmodic, astringent, cardiant, carminative, diaphoretic, lithotriptic, and stimulant.
Constituents: Anisic aldehyde, carvene (limonene), caryophyllen, chavicol, eugenol (eugenic acid), pinene, pyridine, sesquiterpene, and volatile oil.
Historical Uses: Asthma, calculus, colds, colic, diarrhea, digestive complaints, diphtheria, dysentery, flatulence, gallstones, gleet, gonorrhea, gout, incense, indigestion, infection (bacterial, fungal, sexually transmitted), kidney stones, lithemia, mucus, nausea, perfume, potpourri, respiratory conditions, sexually transmitted diseases (STDs), spasmodic conditions, urethritis, urinary problems, vaginitis, and vomiting.
Discussion: May aid digestion; dissolve calculi; enhance lung, spleen, and stomach functions; inhibit or destroy developement and growth of bacteria and other microorganisms; offset the negative effects of chemotherapy and radiation therapy; prevent the development of calculus or stones; promote perspiration; reduce excessive levels of lithic acid (uric acid) and urates in the blood, tophi, and urine; reestablish healthy system functions; stimulate the cardiovascular system.
Cautions/Contraindications: Avoid use if pregnant or breast-feeding. Keep away from eyes and mucous membranes. May cause allergic reactions or dermatitis in susceptible individuals. Not for long-term use.
Adverse Reactions: Appetite loss, insomnia, mucous membrane irritation, nausea, nervousness, and/or vomiting.
Herb/Drug Interactions: This herb could cause an interaction (possibly severe) when taken with the following drugs: None known.

Preparations/Dosage: External uses only. Oil of Patchouli (*oleum patchouli*): Diluted and applied topically.

Pau D'Arco (paw dē·arkō)
(*Tabebuia heptaphylla*)

Synonyms/Related Species: Ipe-Roxo, Lapacho (*tabebuia impetiginosa*), Purple Lapacho, Tabebuia, and Taheebo.
Family/Class: Bignoniaceae (bignonia).
Habitat: South America.
Flavor: Bitter.
Parts Used: Bark (inner) aged for 1 year.
Properties: Alterative, analgesic, antibiotic, anticarcinogen, antifungal, antiperiodic, antiphlogistic, antiviral, carminative, depurative, hemostatic, hypotensive, malariacidal, parasiticide, tonic, vasodilator, and vermifuge.
Constituents: Lapachol, minerals (iron), and quinic acid.
Historical Uses: Abscess, ague, alopecia, anemia, arthritis, asthma, arteriosclerosis, athlete's foot, bronchitis, cancer, candida, Chagas' disease, colds, colitis, congestion (uterine, vaginal), cystitis, diabetes, digestive complaints, dizziness, eczema, erectile dysfunction, fever (ephemeral, enteric, hankow, herpetic, intermittent, rheumatic), fistula, flatulence, gastritis, gleet, gonorrhea, hemorrhage, hemorrhoids, herpes, Hodgkin's disease, hypertension (mild/moderate), indigestion, infection (bacterial, fungal, sexually transmitted, urinary tract, viral), inflammation, insufficiency (venous), kidney problems, leukemia, leukorrhea, liver problems, lupus, malaria, moniliasis, muscle and joint pain, nephritis, osteomyelitis, pain, paralysis, parasites (malarial plasmodia, ringworm, scabies, schistosoma), Parkinson's disease, polyps (intestinal), prostatitis, psoriasis, respiratory conditions, rheumatism, schistosomiasis, sexually transmitted diseases (STDs), skin problems, sores, spleen problems, syphilis, tumors, typhoid, ulcer (bouveret, duodenal, gastric, peptic, stasis, syphilitic, varicose), urethritis, vaginitis, varicose veins, and wounds (minor).
Discussion: May aid digestion; assist in nutrient assimilation; cause blood vessel dilatation; decrease the effect of carcinogens; enhance liver and lung functions; increase circulation and red corpuscle count; inhibit or destroy developement and growth of bacteria and other microorganisms; offset the negative effects of chemotherapy and radiation therapy; purify the blood; reduce blood pressure levels; reestablish healthy system functions; restore normal tone to tissues; stimulate the immune system; stop or slow the growth of abnormal cells.
Cautions/Contraindications: Avoid use if pregnant or breast-feeding. May interfere with antineoplastic (chemotherapy) drugs.
Adverse Reactions: Bleeding (serious), nausea, and/or vomiting.
Herb/Drug Interactions: This herb could cause an interaction (possibly severe) when taken with the following drugs: Antineoplastic drugs and Hypotensive drugs.
Preparations/Dosage: Crude Herb: 3-6 grams. Decoction: ½-1 cup per day. Tincture: 15-30 drops (1-2 cc.) one to three times per day.

Peach (pēch)

(*Prunus persica*)

Synonyms/Related Species: Amygdalis Persica, Peche, Persian Apple, Persian Fruit, and Pesche.

Family/Class: Rosaceae (rose).

Floral Emblem: Delaware.

Habitat: Asia, China, England, Europe, France, Greece, India, Italy, Persia, and the United States.

Flavor: Bark/Leaves/Inner Seed Kernel: bitter. Fruit: sweet.

Parts Used: Bark (inner), fruit (ripe), leaves, seed (inner kernel).

Properties: Antibiotic, antiphlogistic, antispasmodic, astringent, carminative, demulcent, depurative, diuretic, emmenagogue, expectorant, insect repellant, laxative, nervine, sedative, tonic, and vermin repellant.

Constituents: Amygdalin, emulsin (synaptase), fatty acids (arachidonic, linoleic, linolenic, oleic, palmitic, stearic), fixed oils (olein, palmitin, stearin), glyceric acid, hydrocyanic acid, minerals (magnesium, potassium), phloretin, and volatile oil.

Historical Uses: Bladder problems, bleeding, bronchitis, calculus, cholera, colds, colic, congestion (pelvic cavity), constipation, cough, edema, fever, flatulence, fleas, gastroenteritis, headache, inflammation, insomnia, jaundice, kidney problems, mucus, nausea, nervous conditions, respiratory conditions, sores, spasmodic conditions, stomachache, substitute for quinine (bark/leaves), tumors, uterine problems, vermin, vomiting, whooping cough, and wounds (minor).

Discussion: May aid digestion; calm the nervous system; clear and open bronchial passages; enhance cardiovascular system, colon, and liver functions; increase circulation; promote bowel evacuation and urine flow; purify the blood; restore normal tone to tissues; speed healing; stimulate menstruation and peristalsis.

Cautions/Contraindications: Avoid use of bark, leaves, and inner seed kernel if pregnant or breast-feeding. Peach pits contain hydrocyanic acid and are extremely poisonous; use *only* the inner kernel of the seed.

Adverse Reactions: Arrhythmia, cardiac failure, congestion (spleen), enteritis (severe), hydrocyanism (hydrocyanic acid poisoning), nausea, vomiting, and/or possible death.

Herb/Drug Interactions: This herb could cause an interaction (possibly severe) when taken with the following drugs: Antimalarial drugs.

Preparations/Dosage: Crude Herb (bark/leaves): 3 grams. Inner Seed Kernel: 3-6 grams. Fruit (ripe): May be ingested freely. Infusion (leaves): 1-2 cups per day. Juice (fruit): May be ingested freely. Syrup: 1-4 drachms (4-16 cc.) one to two times per day. Tincture: 2-10 drops (0.133-0.666 cc.) one to three times per day.

Pear (pâr)

(*Pyrus communis*)

Synonyms/Related Species: Pere and Pirum.

Family/Class: Rosaceae (rose).

Habitat: Temperate regions of the Northern Hemisphere.

Flavor: Sweet.

Parts Used: Fruit.

Properties: Astringent, carminative, diuretic, febrifuge, hemostatic, and laxative.
Constituents: Amygdalin, caffeic acid, citric acid, glycosides, malic acid, minerals (iron), pectic acid, pectin, and quinic acid.
Historical Uses: Bleeding, digestive complaints, fever (ephemeral), flatulence, and indigestion.
Discussion: May aid digestion; promote bowel evacuation and urine flow; stimulate peristalsis.
Cautions/Contraindications: Avoid excessive use if pregnant or breast-feeding.
Adverse Reactions: Diarrhea, nausea, and/or vomiting.
Herb/Drug Interactions: This herb could cause an interaction (possibly severe) when taken with the following drugs: None known.
Preparations/Dosage: Crude Herb: 3-9 grams. Fruit (fresh): May be ingested freely. Juice (fruit): May be ingested freely.

Pennyroyal (pen ē·roi el)
(*Hedeoma pulegioides*)

Synonyms/Related Species: American Pennyroyal, Hedeoma, Mock Pennyroyal (*hedeoma drummondii*), Mosquito Plant, Pulex, Squawmint, and Tickweed.
Family/Class: Labiatae (mint).
Habitat: Africa, Asia, Europe, Iran, and North America.
Flavor: Pungent/bitter.
Parts Used: Leaves.
Properties: Abortifacient, analgesic, antispasmodic, aromatic, carminative, counterirritant, diaphoretic, emmenagogue, febrifuge, insect repellent, oxytocic, sedative, sialogogue, stimulant, stomachic, and vasodilator.
Constituents: Flavonoids, hesperidin, menthone, minerals (lead, sodium), piperitone, pulegone, tannic acid, and volatile oil.
Historical Uses: Abdominal pain, amenorrhea, ants, arthritis, bronchitis, bruises, burns (minor), colds, colic, convulsions, cough, cramps, delirium, digestive complaints, dizziness, earache, eye problems, fainting, fever (ephemeral), flatulence, fleas, flies, gallbladder problems, gastritis, gastrointestinal problems, gnats, gout, headache, indigestion, infection, influenza, leprosy, lesions (tubercle), liver problems, measles, menopausal/menstrual problems, migraine, mites, mosquitos, mucus, nausea, nervous conditions, pain, pleurisy, pneumonia, potpourri, pruritus, rash, respiratory conditions, sachets, scrofula, skin problems, small pox, spasmodic conditions, stomachache, stroke (heat), tension, ticks, toothache, tuberculosis, ulcer (duodenal, fistula, gastric, peptic, tuberculous), uterine problems, vertigo, vomiting, and wounds (minor).
Discussion: May aid digestion; cause blood vessel dilatation; enhance female reproductive system, liver, lung, and stomach functions; increase circulation; induce abortion; promote perspiration and saliva secretion; stimulate menstruation and uterine contractions.
Cautions/Contraindications: Avoid use if pregnant or breast-feeding, or if you have a kidney problem. Not for long-term use.
Adverse Reactions: Convulsions, diarrhea, edema, elevated blood pressure levels, liver damage (often characterized by jaundice), nausea, paralysis, respiratory failure, salivation (increased), vomiting, and/or possible death.
Herb/Drug Interactions: This herb could cause an interaction (possibly severe) when taken with the following drugs: None known.

Preparations/Dosage: Crude Herb: 3 grams. Infusion: ½-1 cup per day. Oil of Pennyroyal (*oleum hedeomae*): Recommended for topical uses. Internal: 1-5 drops (0.06-0.33 cc.) per day in water or on a sugarcube. Topical: diluted and applied topically. Tincture: 15-30 drops (1-2 cc.) one to three times per day.
Note: European pennyroyal (*mentha pulegium*) is similar to American pennyroyal in activity and uses.

Peony (pē e·nē)
(*Paeonia officinalis*)

Synonyms/Related Species: Bai-shao, California Peony (*paeonia californica*), Common Peony, Paiōnia, Pione, Red Peony, Tree Peony (*paeonia suffruticosa*), Western Peony (*paeonia brownii*), and Wild Peony.
Family/Class: Ranunculaceae (buttercup).
Floral Emblem: Indiana.
Habitat: Albania, Asia, Europe, Hungary, Portugal, and the United States.
Flavor: Bitter/sour.
Parts Used: Root.
Properties: Abortifacient, alterative, antibiotic, antiphlogistic, antispasmodic, astringent, depurative, diuretic, emmenagogue, emetic, hemostatic, hepatic, hypotensive, laxative, oxytocic, sedative, tonic, vasodilator, and vesicant.
Constituents: Asparagin, benzoic acid, flavonoids, paeoniflorin, paeonin, paeonol, protoanemonin, tannic acid, triterpenoids, and volatile oil.
Historical Uses: Abdominal pain, abscess, allergy, amenorrhea, anemia, angina, arteriosclerosis, arthritis, asthma, bladder problems, bleeding, bruises, burns (minor), cardiovascular conditions, chorea, colds, conjunctivitis, constipation, convulsions, cough, cramps, depression (mild/moderate), diarrhea, dysmenorrhea, eclampsia, epilepsy, fever (ephemeral, rheumatic), gallbladder, gout, headache, hemorrhage (metrorrhagia), hemorrhoids, hypertension (mild/moderate), indigestion, infection (bacterial), inflammation, jaundice, kidney problems, lesions (tubercle), liver problems, melancholy, memory/cognitive problems, menorrhagia, menopausal/menstrual problems, migraine, muscle and joint pain, nausea, nervous conditions, neuralgia, neurologic conditions, nosebleed, orchitis, pain, pneumonia, prostatitis, rheumatism, rheumatoid arthritis (RA), scrofula, sexually transmitted diseases (STDs), sore throat, sores, spasmodic conditions, skin problems, stomachache, tuberculosis, tumors, ulcer (fistula, tuberculous), whooping cough, and wounds (minor).
Discussion: May cause blood vessel dilatation; cleanse the intestinal system; enhance immune system, liver, lung, and spleen functions; enhance immune and nervous system functions; improve memory and cognition; induce abortion; inhibit or destroy developement and growth of bacteria and other microorganisms; promote bowel evacuation and urine flow; protect the liver; purify the blood; reduce lesions (aortic), blood pressure levels, and blood vessel lining inflammation; reestablish healthy system functions; regulate ovulation and testosterone levels in women; restore normal tone to tissues; stimulate circulation, peristalsis, and uterine contractions.
Cautions/Contraindications: Avoid use if pregnant or breast-feeding. May cause allergic reactions or dermatitis in susceptible individuals. Not for long-term use. Use with professional guidance/supervision.

Adverse Reactions: Blistering of the mouth and throat, convulsions, diarrhea, dizziness, fainting, gastroenteritis, hematuria (blood in the urine), kidney failure, nausea, salivation, stomach pain, vomiting, and/or possible death.
Herb/Drug Interactions: This herb could cause an interaction (possibly severe) when taken with the following drugs: Hypotensive drugs.
Preparations/Dosage: Crude Herb: 1-3 grams. Infusion: ½ teaspoon one to two times per day. Tincture: 1-10 drops (0.066-0.666 cc.) one to three times per day.
Isolation: Asparagin: Soluble in hot water, but insoluble in alcohol and ether. Average dose of 1-2 grains (0.066-0.133 gm.) for use as a diuretic.

Pepper (pep er)
(*Piper nigrum*)

Synonyms/Related Species: Black Pepper, Piper, and White Pepper (*piper album*).
Family/Class: Piperaceae (pepper).
Habitat: Asia, the Caribbean, India, Malabar, Siam, and South America.
Flavor: Pungent.
Parts Used: Berry.
Properties: Analgesic, antibiotic, antilithic, antiperiodic, antiphlogistic, aromatic, carminative, counterirritant, diuretic, malariacidal, parasiticide, sialogogue, stimulant, tonic, and vesicant.
Constituents: Alkaloids, albumin (albumen), carvene (limonene), cellulose, chavicine, minerals (magnesium), piperazine, piperine, and volatile oil.
Historical Uses: Ague, arthritis, bronchitis, cellulite, cholera, constipation, diabetes, diarrhea, digestive complaints, fever (ephemeral, intermittent), flatulence, flavoring agent, gallstones, gastroenteritis, gleet, gonorrhea, gout, indigestion, infection (bacterial, sexually transmitted), inflammation, kidney stones, lithemia, malaria, mucus, muscle and joint pain, nausea, neuralgia, pain, paralysis, parasites (malarial plasmodia, scabies), prolapse (rectal, uterine), rheumatism, sexually transmitted diseases (STDs), syphilis, ulcer (syphilitic), urethritis, and vertigo.
Discussion: May aid digestion; enhance kidney, spleen, and stomach functions; increase circulation; inhibit or destroy developement and growth of bacteria and other microorganisms; prevent development of calculus and stones; promote saliva secretion; reduce excessive levels of lithic acid (uric acid) and urates in the blood, tophi, and urine; restore normal tone to tissues; stimulate metabolism.
Cautions/Contraindications: Avoid use if pregnant or breast-feeding. May cause allergic reactions or dermatitis in susceptible individuals. May increase the effectiveness as well as the side effects of propranolol. May increase blood levels of theophylline drugs.
Adverse Reactions: Blistering of the mouth and throat, mucous membrane irritation, nausea, salivation (increased), and/or vomiting.
Herb/Drug Interactions: This herb could cause an interaction (possibly severe) when taken with the following drugs: Beta-Adrenergic Blocking drugs and Theophylline drugs.
Preparations/Dosage: Crude Herb: 2-5 grams. Crude Herb (powdered): Average dose in substance 5-10 grains (0.3-0.65 gm.).
Isolation: Piperazine hydrochlorate: Dose in 2% solution, 5 grains (0.33 gm.), administered hypodermically; or orally (by mouth), 8 grains (0.5 gm.) for use as an antilithic, antisyphilitic, and diuretic. Piperine: Soluble (slightly) in water. Average dose of 1-5 grains (0.06-0.33 gm.) for use as an antiperiodic.

Did You Know? Black and white pepper come from the same plant. Pepper is black, but when the outer coating of the seed is removed, the result is a milder form of the ordinary black pepper called white pepper.

Persimmon (per·sim en)
(*Diospyros virginiana*)

Synonyms/Related Species: Date Plum, Japanese Persimmon, Jove's Fruit, Kaki, Pasiminan, Seeded Plum, and Winter Plum.
Family/Class: Ebenaceae (ebony).
Habitat: Africa, Asia, Ceylon, Japan, and the United States.
Flavor: Sweet.
Parts Used: Fruit (ripe/yellow).
Properties: Astringent, antiperiodic, antiphlogistic, antiscorbutic, carminative, malariacidal, nutritive, and tonic.
Constituents: Arabinose, benzoic acid, carotinoid, lycopene, malic acid, monosaccharides, oxidase, pentosan, tannic acid, and vitamins (A, B, C (ascorbic acid).
Historical Uses: Ague, bleeding, diarrhea, dietary supplementation, digestive complaints, dysentery, colic, constipation, fever (ephemeral, intermittent), flatulence, gastrointestinal problems, hemorrhoids, hiccups, indigestion, inflammation, malaria, malnutrition, parasites (malarial plasmodia), and scurvy.
Discussion: May aid digestion; enhance lung and stomach functions; provide dietary supplementation; restore normal tone to tissues; serve as a nutritional adjuvant to therapeutic programs.
Cautions/Contraindications: Avoid use if pregnant or breast-feeding.
Adverse Reactions: Nausea and/or vomiting.
Herb/Drug Interactions: This herb could cause an interaction (possibly severe) when taken with the following drugs: None known.
Preparations/Dosage: Fruit (fresh/dried): May be ingested freely.

Peruvian Bark (pe·roo vē·en bärk)
(*Cinchona officinalis*)

Synonyms/Related Species: Calisaya (*cinchona calisaya*), Cinchona, Crown Bark, Evergreen Cinchona Tree, Foso Bark (*cinchona lancifolia*), Jesuits' Bark, Quinquina, Red Bark (*cinchona succirubra*), and Yellow Cinchona.
Family/Class: Rubiaceae (madder).
Habitat: Bolivia, Ceylon, the Andes Mountains of South America (generally on the Western exposure at altitudes of 4,000-5,000 feet), Ecuador, India, Java, and Peru.
Flavor: Bitter.
Parts Used: Bark (aged for one year).
Properties: Antibiotic, anticarcinogen, antiperiodic, antiphlogistic, antispasmodic, astringent, diuretic, hemostatic, malariacidal, oxytocic, sialogogue, stimulant, tonic, and vermifuge.
Constituents: Alkaloids, cinchol, cinchonamine, cinchonate, cinchonic acid, cinchonicine, cinchonidine, cinchonine, cinchophen, cinchotine (cinchonifine), inulin (starch), minerals

(potassium), mucilage, quinidine (chinidine), quinine (chinine), quinic acid, quinidamine, quinoline (chinoline), quinone (chinone), quinovin, resin, tannic acid, and vitamin C (ascorbic acid).

Historical Uses: Ague, allergy (food, pollen), anemia, appetite loss, arrhythmia, bleeding, cancer, colds, convalesence, cough, cramps, debility, diarrhea, digestive complaints, dysentery, edema, enteritis, exhaustion, fever (ephemeral, enteric, hay, intermittent, rheumatic), flatulence, gargle/mouth rinse, gastritis, gastrointestinal problems, gleet, gonorrhea, gout, hypertrophy (spleen), hysteria, indigestion, infection (bacterial, sexually transmitted), inflammation, influenza, irritable bowel syndrome (IBS), jaundice, lesions (tubercle), malaria, menstrual problems, muscle and joint pain, nervous conditions, neuralgia, neurasthenia, parasites (malarial plasmodia), pneumonia, rheumatism, rhinitis, scrofula, sexually transmitted diseases (STDs), small pox, sore throat, spasmodic conditions, substitute for quinine, syphilis, tuberculosis, typhoid, ulcer (bouveret, duodenal, fistula, stasis, syphilitic, tuberculous), urethritis, whooping cough, and wounds (minor).

Discussion: May decrease the effect of carcinogens; enhance cardiovascular system, liver, and stomach functions; inhibit or destroy development and growth of bacteria and other microorganisms; promote saliva secretion and urine flow; restore normal tone to tissues; stimulate gastric secretions and uterine contractions.

Cautions/Contraindications: Avoid use if pregnant or breast-feeding, or if you have acidity (gastric) or an ulcer (gastric, peptic). Some persons may experience bleeding or increased clotting time when using this herb with anticoagulant drugs or aspirin.

Adverse Reactions: Arrhythmia, asphyxiation, auditory problems, bleeding (possibly serious), blindness, bradycardia, cholera, coagulation problems, dizziness, eczema, fainting, fever, gastrointestinal irritation, headache, heart failure, nausea, pruritus, reduced body temperature, salivation (increased), tachycardia, tinnitus, vascular problems, visual disturbances, and/or possible death.

Herb/Drug Interactions: This herb could cause an interaction (possibly severe) when taken with the following drugs: Anticoagulant drugs, Salicylates, and Subsalicylates.

Preparations/Dosage: Crude Herb: 3-6 grams. Bark (powdered): Average dose in substance 3-10 grains (0.2-0.666 gm.). Infusion: ½-1 cup per day. Tincture: 5-30 drops (0.333-2 cc.) one to three times per day.

Isolation: Cinchonidine sulfate or Cinchonine sulfate: Average dose of 2½ grains (0.15 gm.) for use as a febrifuge, stimulant, and tonic. Cinchophen: Average dose of 7½-15 grains (0.5-1 gm.) for use as a diuretic. Quinine acetate: Average dose of 1-10 grains (0.065-0.6 gm.) for use as a febrifuge, stimulant, and tonic; locally in spray form for use in fever (hay), rhinitis, and whooping cough. Quinine albuminate: Average dose of 2-15 grains (0.13-1 gm.) for use as a tonic. Quinidine sulfate or bisulfate: Average dose of 3-6 grains (0.2-0.4 gm.) three times per day for use in arrhythmia.

Did You Know? Condurangu (*equatoria garciana*) and Peruvian Bark both originate in the same region and flourish only under identical climactic conditions.

Periwinkle (per e·wing kel)

(*Vinca officinale*)

Synonyms/Related Species: Blue Buttons, Centocchio, Early Flowering Periwinkle, European Creeper, Flower of Death, Greater Periwinkle (*vinca major*), Lesser Periwinkle (*vinca minor*),

Madagascar Periwinkle (*vinca rosea*), Parwynke, Peruince, Pucellage, Sorcerer's Violet (*vinca pervinca*), Vincio, and Virginflower (*vinca pubescens*).
Family/Class: Apocynaceae (dogbane)
Habitat: Africa, Asia, Britain, the Caucasus, Europe, France, India, Italy, Spain, and the United States.
Flavor: Bitter.
Parts Used: Aerial.
Properties: Anticarcinogen, astringent, diuretic, hallucinogen, hemostatic, hypotensive, laxative, lithotriptic, nervine, sedative, tonic, and vasodilator.
Constituents: Alkaloids, flavonoids, glycosides, vindblastine, vincristine, and vinine.
Historical Uses: Bleeding, calculus, cancer (chorionic carcinoma), canker sores, colitis, constipation, cramps, dandruff, diabetes, diarrhea, dizziness, gallstones, gargle/mouth rinse, gout, hematuria, hemorrhage, hemorrhoids, Hodgkin's disease, hypertension (mild/moderate), hysteria, inflammation, insufficiency (circulatory), kidney stones, leukemia, memory/cognitive problems, menorrhagia, mucus, muscle and joint pain, nervous conditions, nosebleed, periodontal disease, skin problems, sore throat, sores, tinnitus, tonsillitis, toothache, ulcer (duodenal, gastric, peptic), and wounds (minor).
Discussion: May calm the nervous system; cause blood vessel dilatation; decrease the effect of carcinogens; dissolve calculi; enhance kidney function; promote bowel evacuation and urine flow; restore normal tone to tissues; stimulate peristalsis; stop or slow abnormal cell growth.
Cautions/Contraindications: Avoid use if pregnant or breast-feeding. Not for long-term use.
Adverse Reactions: Alopecia, ataxia, bone marrow damage, bradycardia, coma, convulsions, drowsiness, dry mouth, hallucinations, hypotension, liver damage (often characterized by jaundice), nausea, psychosis, shock, skin flushing, visual disturbances, and/or possible death.
Herb/Drug Interactions: This herb could cause an interaction (possibly severe) when taken with the following drugs: Hypotensive drugs.
Preparations/Dosage: Crude Herb: 1-3 grams. Infusion: ¼-½ cup per day. Tincture: 5-10 drops (0.333-0.666 cc.) one to three times per day.

Pine (pīn)

(*Pinus officinalis*)

Synonyms/Related Species: Bristlecone Pine (*pinus aristata*), Burma Pine (*pinus khasya*), Cuban Pine (*pinus cubensis*), Deal Pine, Dwarf Pine (*pinus pumilio*), Georgia Pine, Himalayan Pine (*pinus roxburghii*), Hungarian Pine (*pinus mughus*), Jack Pine (*pinus banksiana*), Japanese Pine (*pinus densiflora*), Limber Pine (*pinus flexilis*), Loblolly Pine (*pinus toeda*), Lodgepole Pine (*pinus contorta*), Mediterranean Pine (*pinus halepensis*), Neosa Pine (*pinus gerardiana*), Norway Pine (*pinus sylvestris*), Nut Pine (*pinus sabiniana*), One-Leaved Piñon Pine (*pinus monophylla*), Piñon Pine (*pinus edulis*), Pinyon Pine, Ponderosa Pine (*pinus ponderosa*), Short-Leaved Pine (*pinus echinata*), Soft Pine, Two-Needle Piñon, Western White Pine (*pinus monticola*), Western Yellow Pine, Whitebark Pine (*pinus albicaulis*), White Pine (*pinus strobus*), and Yellow Pine (*pinus ponderosa*).
Family/Class: Pinaceae (pine).
Floral Emblem: Maine.
Habitat: Alaska, the Alpine and Subalpine zones, the Caucasus, Cuba, Europe, the Himalayas, India, Iran, Japan, the Mediterranean, Myanmar (formerly Burma), North America, and Siberia.

Flavor: Bitter.
Parts Used: Bark (inner), buds, needles, pitch.
Properties: Abortifacient, analgesic, antibiotic, antifungal, antiphlogistic, antiscorbutic, antispasmodic, astringent, carminative, counterirritant, depurative, diuretic, expectorant, hemostatic, laxative, and stimulant.
Constituents: Bitter principle, cadinene, camphene, carvene (limonene), coniferin, lignin, minerals (calcium, copper, iodine, manganese, nickel, sodium, zinc), mucilage, myrcene, phellandrene, pinene, proanthocyanidin, resin, tannic acid, tar, terpinolene, vitamins (A, C (ascorbic acid), and volatile oil.
Historical Uses: Abscess, arthritis, bladder problems, bleeding, bronchitis, burns (minor), cardiovascular conditions, colds, cough, croup, debility, diarrhea, digestive complaints, dysentery, fever (ephemeral, rheumatic), gastritis, gastrointestinal problems, gleet, gonorrhea, headache, indigestion, infection (bacterial, fungal, sexually transmitted), inflammation, influenza, irritable bowel syndrome (IBS), kidney problems, laryngitis, lesions (tubercle), measles, mucus, muscle and joint pain, nausea, nephritis, neuralgia, pain, paralysis, pneumonia, psoriasis, rash, respiratory conditions, rheumatism, sciatica, scrofula, scurvy, sexually transmitted diseases (STDs), skin problems, sore throat, sores, spasmodic conditions, strep throat, syphilis, tonsillitis, tuberculosis, ulcer (duodenal, fistula, gastric, peptic, syphilitic, tuberculous), urethritis, vaginitis, and wounds (minor).
Discussion: May aid digestion; clear and open bronchial passages; enhance kidney and liver functions; induce abortion; inhibit or destroy development and growth of bacteria and other microorganisms; promote urine flow; purify the blood; regulate blood pressure levels.
Cautions/Contraindications: Avoid use if pregnant or breast-feeding, or if you have asthma, cardiovascular conditions, whooping cough, or an iodine sensitivity. May interfere with the effectiveness of certain thyroid medications.
Adverse Reactions: Abdominal pain, arrhythmia, central nervous system damage, diarrhea, edema, fever, gastrointestinal cramps, hematuria (blood in the urine), hypertrophy (thyroid), iodism (iodine poisoning), muscle twitches, nausea, priapism, salivation (increased), sore throat, staggering, thirst, vertigo, and/or vomiting.
Herb/Drug Interactions: This herb could cause an interaction (possibly severe) when taken with the following drugs: Thyroid drugs.
Preparations/Dosage: Crude Herb (bark/buds/needles): 3-9 grams. Decoction (bark and/or buds): ¼-½ cup per day. Infusion (buds and/or needles): 1 cup per day. Oil of Pine Needles (*oleum pinus*): Inhale for respiratory conditions. Pitch: Roll into small pea-sized balls and chew one per day or allow it to dissolve in your mouth.

Pineapple (pīn ap el)
(*Ananas sativa*)

Synonyms/Related Species: Bromelia.
Family/Class: Bromeliaceae (pineapple).
Habitat: Tropical and subtropical regions.
Flavor: Sweet.
Parts Used: Fruit.
Properties: Antibiotic, anticarcinogen, anticoagulant, anti-inflammatory, carminative, and vulnerary.
Constituents: Bromelin and minerals (sodium).

Historical Uses: Angina, arthritis, bronchitis, bruises, burns (minor), cellulite, cancer, connective tissue problems, digestive complaints, dysmenorrhea, edema, epilepsy, indigestion, infection (bacterial), inflammation, injury (athletic), insufficiency (pancreatic), mucus, pneumonia, respiratory conditions, scleroderma, sinusitis, thrombophlebitis, trauma (postoperative), and tumors.
Discussion: May aid digestion; decrease the effect of carcinogens; delay or reduce coagulation of the blood; enhance pancreatic function; improve absorption; inhibit development or destroy growth of bacteria and other microorganisms; reduce the effects of postoperative tissue trauma; speed healing.
Cautions/Contraindications: Avoid excessive use if pregnant or breast-feeding. May increase the effectiveness of antibiotic drugs. May cause allergic reactions and dermatitis in susceptible individuals. Some persons may experience bleeding or increased clotting time when using this herb with anticoagulant drugs or aspirin.
Adverse Reactions: Bleeding (possibly serious), coagulation problems, diarrhea, edema, hemorrhage (metrorrhagia), intestinal membrane weakening, menorrhagia, nausea, and/or vomiting.
Herb/Drug Interactions: This herb could cause an interaction (possibly severe) when taken with the following drugs: Antibiotic drugs, Anticoagulant drugs, Salicylates, and Subsalicylates.
Preparations/Dosage: Fruit or Juice: May be ingested freely.

Pineapple Weed (pīn ap el wēd)
(*Matricaria discoidea*)

Synonyms/Related Species: False Chamomile.
Family/Class: Compositae (composite).
Habitat: North America.
Flavor: Sweet.
Parts Used: Flowers, leaves.
Properties: Analgesic, antibiotic, anticarcinogen, anticoagulant, antifungal, antihistamine, antioxidant, antiphlogistic, antispasmodic, aromatic, carminative, counterirritant, diaphoretic, emmenagogue, hemostatic, nervine, sedative, and tonic.
Constituents: Aglycones, coumarin, flavonoids, glycosides, minerals (calcium), mucilage, quercetin, rutin, tannic acid, umbelliferone, vitamins (choline), and volatile oil.
Historical Uses: Acne, allergy, anxiety, appetite loss, arteriosclerosis, asthma, attention deficit disorder (ADD), bronchitis, bruises, burns (minor), cancer (endometrial), cardiovascular conditions, cirrhosis, colds, colic, conjunctivitis, constipation, convulsions, corns, cramps, dandruff, diarrhea, digestive complaints, diphtheria, diverticulitis, dysmenorrhea, eczema, edema, eyewash, fever (ephemeral, enteric, rheumatic), flatulence, flavoring agent, gallbladder problems, gangrene, gastritis, gastrointestinal problems, gout, headache, hemorrhage, hemorrhoids, hives, hyperactivity, hysteria, indigestion, infection (bacterial, fungal), inflammation, influenza, insomnia, irritable bowel syndrome (IBS), jaundice, kidney problems, liver problems, menstrual problems, lumbago, lupus, migraine, mucous membrane problems, mucus, muscle and joint pain, nausea, nervous conditions, neuralgia, pain, periodontal disease, premenstrual syndrome (PMS), pruritus, psoriasis, rash, restlessness, respiratory conditions, rheumatism, sciatica, skin problems, sore nipples, sores, spasmodic conditions, substitute for german chamomile (*matricaria chamomilla*), toothache, typhoid, ulcer (bouveret, duodenal, gastric, peptic), and wounds (minor).

Discussion: May aid digestion; calm the nervous system; counteract the effect of histamine; decrease the effect of carcinogens; delay or reduce coagulation of the blood; enhance stomach, liver, and lung functions; facilitate delivery of the placenta following childbirth; inhibit oxidation and inhibit or destroy developement and growth of bacteria and other microorganisms; prevent the deposition of fat in the liver and hemorrhage in persons with hypertension; promote perspiration; reduce capillary fragility; restore normal tone to tissues; soothe nipple soreness; stimulate menstruation; strenthen the blood.
Cautions/Contraindications: Avoid use if pregnant or breast-feeding. Individuals with ragweed sensitivities may experience allergic reactions when using pineapple weed. Some persons may experience bleeding or increased clotting time when using this herb with anticoagulant drugs or aspirin.
Adverse Reactions: Bleeding (possibly serious), coagulation problems, nausea, and/or vomiting.
Herb/Drug Interactions: This herb could cause an interaction (possibly severe) when taken with the following drugs: Anticoagulant drugs, Salicylates, and Subsalicylates.
Preparations/Dosage: Crude Herb: 3-9 grams. Infusion: 1-2 cups per day.

Pipsissewa (pip·sis e·we)
(*Chimaphila umbellata*)

Synonyms/Related Species: Bitter Wintergreen, Butter Winter, Ground Holly, King's Cureall, Menzies' Pipsissewa (*chimaphila menziesii*), Pipisisikweu, Prince's Pine, Rheumatism Weed, Spotted Wintergreen (*chimaphila maculata*), and Umbellate Wintergreen.
Family/Class: Ericaceae (heath).
Habitat: Asia, Europe, North America, Siberia, and South America.
Flavor: Pungent/bitter.
Parts Used: Leaves.
Properties: Alterative, analgesic, antibiotic, antilithic, antiphlogistic, antispasmodic, astringent, counterirritant, depurative, diaphoretic, diuretic, hemostatic, laxative, lithotriptic, oxytocic, tonic, and urinary antiseptic.
Constituents: Arbutin, chimaphilin, chlorophyll, flavonoids, gum, inulin (starch), minerals (calcium, lime (calcium oxide), magnesium, potassium, silicon, sodium), monosaccharides, pectic acid, pectin, renifolin, resin, silicic acid, tannic acid, ursone (ursolic acid), and vitamin C (ascorbic acid).
Historical Uses: Albuminuria, alkaline urine, appetite loss, arthritis, bladder problems, bleeding, blisters, calculus, cancer, cystitis, diarrhea, dysuria (painful/difficult urination), edema, epilepsy, fever (ephemeral, rheumatic), gallstones, gleet, gonorrhea, gout, hematuria (blood in the urine), indigestion, infection (bacterial, bladder, sexually transmitted, urinary tract), inflammation, kidney problems, kidney stones, lesions (tubercle), lithemia, muscle and joint pain, nephritis, nervous conditions, pain, prostate problems, prostatitis, rheumatism, scrofula, sexually transmitted diseases (STDs), skin problems, sores, spasmodic conditions, substitute for pyrola and bearberry, tuberculosis, tumors, ulcer (duodenal, fistula, gastric, peptic, tuberculous), urethritis, and urinary problems.
Discussion: May cleanse the kidneys and liver; dissolve calculi; enhance bladder, cardiovascular system, intestinal system, and spleen functions; enhance cardiovascular, intestinal, and spleen functions; inhibit or destroy developement and growth of bacteria and other microorganisms; prevent the development of calculus and stones; promote bowel evacuation, perspiration, and

urine flow; reduce excessive levels of lithic acid (uric acid) and urates in the blood, tophi, and urine; reestablish healthy system functions; restore normal tone to tissues; stimulate appetite, peristalsis, and uterine contractions.
Cautions/Contraindications: Avoid use if pregnant or breast-feeding. May cause dermatitis in susceptible individuals. Not for long-term use.
Adverse Reactions: Diarrhea, edema, nausea, and/or vomiting.
Herb/Drug Interactions: This herb could cause an interaction (possibly severe) when taken with the following drugs: None known.
Preparations/Dosage: Crude Herb: 3-6 grams. Extract (powdered): Average dose in substance 1-45 grains (0.666-3 gm.). Infusion: ½-1 cup per day. Tincture: 2-15 drops (0.133-1 cc.) one to three times per day.
Isolation: Arbutin: Average dose of 5-15 grains (0.3-1 gm.) for use as a diuretic and urinary antiseptic. Chimaphilin: Average dose of 2-3 grains (0.13-0.2 gm.) for use as a diuretic and as a potential cancer remedy.
Note: The action of pipsissewa, though gentler, is similar to that of bearberry and pyrola.

Pitcher Plant (pich ·er·plänt)
(*Sarracenia purpurea*)

Synonyms/Related Species: American Pitcher Plant, Common Pitcher Plant, Eve's Cups, Fly-Trap, Gibbosa, Huntsman's Cup, Nepenthes, Purple Side Saddle Flower, Sarracenia, Side Saddle Plant, Smallpox Plant, and Water-Cup.
Family/Class: Sarraceniaceae (pitcher plant).
Habitat: Asia, China, Ceylon, India, and North America.
Flavor: Bitter.
Parts Used: Root.
Properties: Analgesic, astringent, carminative, diuretic, laxative, narcotic, stimulant, stomachic, and tonic.
Constituents: Alkaloid, coniine, enzymes, sarracenin, sarracenic acid, and tannic acid.
Historical Uses: Appetite loss, bleeing, constipation, digestive complaints, flatulence, indigestion, infection (urinary tract), kidney problems, liver problems, pain, small pox, and uterine problems.
Discussion: May aid digestion; enhance stomach function; promote bowel evacuation and urine flow; restore normal tone to tissues; stimulate appetite and peristalsis.
Cautions/Contraindications: Avoid use if pregnant or breast-feeding.
Adverse Reactions: Diarrhea, nausea, stupor, and/or vomiting.
Herb/Drug Interactions: This herb could cause an interaction (possibly severe) when taken with the following drugs: None known.
Preparations/Dosage: Crude Herb (powdered): Average dose in substance 10-30 grains (0.666-2 gm.). Infusion: 1 cup per day. Tincture: 5-15 drops (0.333-1 cc.) one to three times per day.

Plantain (plan tin)
(*Plantago major*)

Synonyms/Related Species: African Plantain (*plantago decumbens*), Alkali Plantain (*plantago eriopoda*), Balatanna, Barguthi, Black Jack, Black Plantain, Blond Psyllium Husk, Broad-Leaved

Plantain, Buck's Horn Plantain (*plantago coronopus*), Cempa Plant, Common Plantain, Cornu Cervinum, Costa Canina, Cuckoo's Bread, English Plantain, Englishman's Foot, Fleaseed, Greater Plantain, Hoary Plantain (*plantago media*), Indian Psyllium Husk, Ispaghul Plantain (*plantago ovata*), Lamb's Tongue, Lance-Leaf Plantain, Long Plantain, Narrow-Leaf Plantain, Psyllium Plantain (*plantago psyllium*), Quinquenervia, Ribwort Plantain (*plantago lanceolata*), Ripplegrass, Sand Plantain (*plantago arenaria*), Sea Plantain (*plantago maritimo*), Sheep's Herb, Snake Plantain, Snakeweed, Soldier's Herb, Spogel Seed, Wendles, Weybroed, and Whiteman's Foot.

Family/Class: Plantaginaceae (plantain).

Habitat: Alaska, Africa, Asia, Britain, the Canary Islands, England, India, North America, Persia, and Spain.

Flavor: Salty/bitter.

Parts Used: Leaves, seeds.

Properties: Alterative, analgesic, antibiotic, antifungal, antilithic, antioxidant, antiperiodic, antiphlogistic, astringent, demulcent, depurative, diuretic, emetic, expectorant, hemostatic, hypoglycemic, hypotensive, laxative, lithotriptic, malariacidal, vasodilator, vermifuge, and vulnerary.

Constituents: Allantoin, caffeic acid, chlorogenic acid, coumarin, enzymes, flavonoids, glycosides, minerals (calcium, potassium, silicon, sulfur), mucilage, polysaccharides, protein, psyllium, saponins, silicic acid, tannic acid, and vitamins (A, C (ascorbic acid), K).

Historical Uses: Ague, allergy, appetite loss, asthma, bladder problems, bleeding, blisters, bronchitis, bruises, burns (minor), calculus, colds, colitis, congestion (uterine, vaginal), constipation, conjunctivitis, cough, Crohn's disease, diarrhea, digestive complaints, diverticulitis, dysentery, earache, edema, enteritis, enuresis (urinary incontinence), epilepsy, eye problems, eyewash, fever (ephemeral, intermittent, rheumatic, septic), flatulence, gallstones, gargle/mouth rinse, gastritis, gastrointestinal problems, gleet, gonorrhea, gout, hematuria (blood in the urine), hemorrhage, hemorrhoids, hepatitis, hyperglycemia, hypertension (mild/moderate), infection (bacterial, fungal, sexually transmitted), inflammation, insect bites or stings, intestinal tract infection, irritable bowel syndrome (IBS), jaundice, kidney problems, kidney stones, laryngitis, lesions (throat, tubercle), leukorrhea, lithemia, malaria, menstrual problems, mucus, muscle and joint pain, pain, neuralgia, parasites (malarial plasmodia, ringworm), pleurisy, pneumonia, poisoning (blood, non-caustic), rash, respiratory conditions, rheumatism, scrofula, sexually transmitted diseases (STDs), skin problems, snakebite, sores, toothache, tuberculosis, ulcer (duodenal, fistula, gastric, peptic, tuberculous), urethritis, urinary problems, vaginitis, and wounds (minor).

Discussion: May cause blood vessel dilatation; clear and open bronchial passages; cleanse the intestinal system; dissolve calculi; enhance digestive system, kidney, and respiratory system functions; increase libido; inhibit oxidation and inhibit or destroy developement and growth of bacteria and other microorganisms; prevent the development of calculus or stones; promote blood coagulation, bowel evacuation, and urine flow; purify the blood; reduce blood pressure levels, blood sugar levels, cholesterol levels, excessive lithic acid (uric acid) and urate levels in the blood, tophi, and urine, and the frequency of nighttime urination; reestablish healthy system functions; serve as an antidote to non-caustic poisons; soothe mucous membrane irritation; speed healing; stimulate appetite and peristalsis.

Cautions/Contraindications: Avoid use if pregnant or breast-feeding, or if you have a bowel problem, chronic constipation, colitis, diabetes, or hypoglycemia. Do not use if you are taking multiple prescription drugs on a daily basis. May reduce lithium blood levels. Refrain from

taking psyllium within one hour of taking any type of prescription drug as the absorption of the drug may be reduced. Drink six to ten glasses of water daily when taking psyllium to avoid obstruction (intestinal).
Adverse Reactions: Diarrhea (possibly bloody), gastrointestinal cramps (severe), hematuria (blood in the urine), nausea, obstruction (intestinal), and/or vomiting.
Herb/Drug Interactions: This herb could cause an interaction (possibly severe) when taken with the following drugs: Antidiabetic drugs, Antimanic drugs, Hypotensive drugs, and other Medications/Products containing psyllium.
Preparations/Dosage: Crude Herb: 3-9 grams. Decoction: ½-1 cup per day. Infusion: 1-2 cups per day. Juice: 1-3 teaspoons per day in water or mixed with honey. Seeds (powdered): Average dose in substance 30-60 grains (2-4 gm.).

Plantain, Rattlesnake (plan tin, rat 'l snāk)
(*Goodyera oblongifolia*)

Synonyms/Related Species: Downy Rattlesnake Plantain (*goodyera pubescens*), Netleaf Plantain, Scrofula Weed, Spotted Plantain, Western Rattlesnake Plantain.
Family/Class: Orchidaceae (orchid).
Habitat: North America.
Flavor: Bitter.
Parts Used: Leaves.
Properties: Antiphlogistic, demulcent, emetic, and vulnerary.
Constituents: Allantoin, enzymes, flavonoids, glycosides, minerals (calcium), and mucilage.
Historical Uses: Animal bites, blisters, bruises, burns (minor), fever (ephemeral, rheumatic), inflammation, insect bites or stings, muscle and joint pain, pain, pleurisy, rash, rheumatism, snakebite, sores, toothache, and wounds (minor).
Discussion: May enhance kidney function; soothe mucous membrane irritation; speed healing.
Cautions/Contraindications: Avoid use if pregnant or breast-feeding.
Adverse Reactions: Nausea and/or vomiting.
Herb/Drug Interactions: This herb could cause an interaction (possibly severe) when taken with the following drugs: None known.
Preparations/Dosage: External uses only.

Plantain, Water (plan tin, wôt er)
(*Alisma plantago-aquatica*)

Synonyms/Related Species: Broad-Leaved Water Plantain (*alisma triviale*) and Mad-Dog Weed.
Family/Class: Alismataceae (arrowhead).
Habitat: Asia, England, Europe, North America, and Scotland.
Flavor: Bitter.
Parts Used: Leaves, root.
Properties: Alterative, analgesic, antibiotic, antiphlogistic, antiscorbutic, astringent, counterirritant, demulcent, depurative, diaphoretic, diuretic, expectorant, hemostatic, laxative, lithotriptic, parasiticide, vasoconstrictor, vesicant, and vulnerary.

Constituents: Alismin, caffeic acid, chlorogenic acid, flavones, resin, sesquiterpenes, triterpenes, vitamins (C (ascorbic acid), and volatile oil

Historical Uses: Abscess, bleeding, bronchitis, bruises, burns (minor), calculus, cardiovascular conditions, chorea, colds, congestion (uterine, vaginal), constipation, cough, cramps, cystitis, diarrhea, digestive complaints, diuria (frequent daytime urination), dysentery, dysuria (painful/difficult urination), edema, eczema, enuresis (urinary incontinence), epilepsy, fainting, fever (ephemeral, septic), flatulence, gastritis, gastrointestinal problems, hematuria, hemorrhoids, hepatitis, hydrophobia (rabies in humans), indigestion, infection (bacterial, bladder, urinary tract), inflammation, influenza, injury (back), insect bites or stings, irritable bowel syndrome (IBS), kidney problems, lesions (tubercle), leukorrhea, lung problems, lumbago, mastitis, menorrhagia, menopausal/menstrual problems, mucus, muscle and joint pain, pain, parasites (ringworm), poison ivy/oak, poisoning (blood), respiratory conditions, scrofula, scurvy, sexually transmitted diseases (STDs), skin problems, sores, stomachache, syphilis, tuberculosis, tumors, toothache, ulcer (duodenal, fistula, gastric, peptic, syphilitic, tuberculous), urinary problems, vaginitis, and wounds (minor).

Discussion: May clear and open bronchial passages; constrict the blood vessles; cleanse the whole system; dissolve calculi; enhance circulatory and glandular system functions; inhibit or destroy development and growth of bacteria and other microorganisms; promote bowel evacuation, perspiration, and urine flow; reduce cholesterol levels, the persistent urge to urinate, and the frequency of nighttime urination; reestablish healthy system functions; soothe mucous membrane irritation; speed healing; stimulate peristalsis; strengthen blood vessels, capillaries, veins, and the urinary system.

Cautions/Contraindications: Avoid use if pregnant or breast-feeding.

Adverse Reactions: Blistering of the mouth and throat, mucous membrane irritation, nausea, and/or vomiting.

Herb/Drug Interactions: This herb could cause an interaction (possibly severe) when taken with the following drugs: None known.

Preparations/Dosage: Crude Herb: 3-9 grams. Infusion: ½-1 cup per day.

Pokeweed (pōk wēd)

(*Phytolacca americana*)

Synonyms/Related Species: American Nightshade, American Spinach, Amerikanische Scharlachbeere, Bear's Grape, Cancer Root, Chongrass, Coakum, Cokan, Crowberry, Inkberry, Kermesbeere, Méchoacan du Canada, Morelle à Grappes, Pakon, Phytolacca Berry, Pigeonberry, Pocan, Raisin d'amérique, Red-Ink Plant, Red Weed, Scoke, Skoke, and Virginia Poke.

Family/Class: Phytolaccaceae (pokeweed).

Habitat: Africa, Chile, Europe, Hawaii, the Mediterranean, and North America.

Flavor: Bitter.

Parts Used: Berries (seeds removed), root, shoots (young).

Properties: Alterative, analgesic, antibiotic, anticarcinogen, antifungal, antiphlogistic, antiscorbutic, antiviral, cardiac depressant, carminative, depurative, emetic, laxative, narcotic, nutritive, parasiticide, sedative, and vasodilator.

Constituents: Amino acids (asparagine), caffeic acid, cyclitols, fatty acids (oleic, palmitic, stearic), fixed oils (olein, palmitin, stearin), formic acid, histamine, lignin, minerals (iron,

phosphorous), mitogens, monosaccharides, phytolaccin, resin, ribosome, saponins, tannic acid, and vitamin C (ascorbic acid).
Historical Uses: Abscess, acne, arthritis, benign breast disease, bronchitis, cancer (breast, uterine), colds, congestion (uterine, vaginal), conjunctivitis, constipation, cough, cysts (breast), dietary supplementation, diphtheria, dysmenorrhea, eczema, fever (ephemeral, herpetic, rheumatic), glandular problems, glandular swelling, goiter, headache, hemorrhoids, herpes, indigestion, infection (bacterial, fungal, viral), inflammation, influenza, laryngitis, lesions (tubercle), leukorrhea, malnutrition, mastitis, Menier's disease, mucus, mumps, muscle and joint pain, nephritis, neurologic conditions, pain, parasites (scabies), polio, pruritus, psoriasis, respiratory conditions, rheumatism, rheumatoid arthritis (RA), tonsillitits, scrofula, scurvy, sexually transmitted diseases (STDs), sinusitis, skin problems, sores, sore throat, spleen problems, substitute for asparagus (young shoots), syphilis, thyroid problems, tonsillitis, tremors, tuberculosis, tumors, ulcer (duodenal, fistula, gastric, indolent, peptic, syphilitic, syriac, tuberculous), urinary problems, vaginitis, weight loss, and wounds (minor).
Discussion: May aid digestion; decrease the effect of carcinogens; dilate the blood vessels; diminish or reduce functional activity of the heart; enhance glandular system, kidney, lung, and spleen functions; inhibit or destroy developement and growth of bacteria and other microorganisms; promote bowel evacuation; provide dietary supplementation; purify the blood and lymphatic system; reduce pulse rate; reestablish healthy system functions; serve as a nutritional adjuvant to therapeutic programs; stimulate gastric secretions, metabolism, and peristalsis.
Cautions/Contraindications: Avoid use if pregnant or breast-feeding. May cause dermatitis in susceptible individuals. Not for long-term use. Use with professional guidance/supervision.
Adverse Reactions: Arrhythmia, bradycardia, breathing difficulties, convulsions, debility, diarrhea (possibly bloody), dizziness, ephidrosis, gastrointestinal cramps (severe), hypotension, nausea, respiratory failure, salivation, spasmodic conditions, thirst (excessive), visual disturbances, vomiting, and/or possible death.
Herb/Drug Interactions: This herb could cause an interaction (possibly severe) when taken with the following drugs: None known.
Preparations/Dosage: Crude Herb: ½-1 gram. Decoction (root): ¼-½ teaspoon per day. Infusion (leaves): ½-1 teaspoon per day. Shoots (young): Cooked and eaten as a vegetable. Tincture: 2-5 drops (0.133-0.333 cc.) one to three times per day.
Isolation: Histamine phosphate: Used in a 1:1000 solution, average dose of 5 drops (0.3 cc.), administered intravenously or subcutaneously, for use as a powerful vasodilator, or for use as a stimulant.

Pomegranate (pum·gran et)

(Punica granatum)

Synonyms/Related Species: Carthaginian Apple, Cortezada Granada, Grained Apple, Grenadier, Lybian Apple, Malicorio, Punicaceous Tree, and Scorzo del Melogranati.
Family/Class: Punicaceae (pomegranate).
Habitat: Africa, Asia, Australia, India, the Mediterranean, Japan, Java, South America, Syria, and the United States.
Flavor: Bark: bitter. Fruit/Rind: sweet/sour.
Parts Used: Bark (root), fruit (seeds removed), rind.

Properties: Abortifacient, antiphlogistic, astringent, hemostatic, laxative, teniacide, teniafuge, tonic, and vasodilator.
Constituents: Alkaloids, gallic acid, granatonin (pseudopelletierine), gum, inulin (starch), isopelletierine, mannitol (mannite), minerals (calcium), monosaccharides, pelletierine (punicine), and tannic acid.
Historical Uses: Bleeding, canker sores, congestion (uterine, vaginal), diarrhea, dysentery, eye problems, fever (ephemeral, rheumatic), gargle/mouth rinse, hemorrhoids, hiccups, infection, inflammation, leukorrhea, muscle and joint pain, parasites (tapeworm), rheumatism, skin problems, sore throat, and vaginitis.
Discussion: May cause blood vessel dilatation; enhance colon, kidney, liver, nervous system, and stomach functions; induce abortion; promote bowel evacuation; restore normal tone to tissues; stimulate peristalsis and uterine contractions.
Cautions/Contraindications: Avoid use if pregnant or breast-feeding.
Adverse Reactions: Amaurosis (blindness) lasting for several hours or days then disappearing, debility, diarrhea, dizziness, chills, cramps, fainting, gastrointestinal irritation, mydriasis (extreme pupil dilatation), nausea, optic nerve inflammation, respiratory failure, strychnine-like poisoning, visual disturbances, vomiting, and/or possible death.
Herb/Drug Interactions: This herb could cause an interaction (possibly severe) when taken with the following drugs: None known.
Preparations/Dosage: Crude Herb: 3-9 grams. Decoction: ½-1 cup per day. Rind (powdered): Average dose in substance 20-30 grains (1.333-2 gm.). Tincture: 5-30 drops (0.333-2 cc.) one to three times per day.
Isolation: Mannitol hexanitrate: Average dose of 15-60 mg. for use as a vasodilator. Isopelletierine: Average dose of 10-20 drops (0.666-1.333 cc.) for use as a teniacide. Isopelletierine sulfate: Average dose of 3-6 grains (0.2-0.4 gm.) for use as a teniacide. Isopelletierine tannate: Average dose of 12-24 grains (0.78-1.55 gm.) for use as a teniacide. Pelletierine tannate: Soluble in water. Average dose of 4 grains (0.25 gm.) for use as a teniacide.

Poplar (päp ler)

(*Populus tremuloids*)

Synonyms/Related Species: American Aspen, Balm of Gilead (*populus candicans*), Balsam Poplar, Black Cottonwood (*populus balsamifera*), Black Poplar, Canadian Poplar, European Aspen (*populus tremula*), Golden Aspen, Large Aspen (*populus grandidentata*), Lombardy Poplar (*populus nigra*), Mountain Aspen, Narrow-Leaved Cottonwood (*populus angustifolia*), Quaking Aspen, Tacamahac, Trembling Poplar, and White Poplar (*populus alba*).
Family/Class: Salicaceae (willow).
Habitat: Alaska, the Alpine and Subalpine zones, Europe, North America, and Siberia.
Flavor: Bitter.
Parts Used: Bark, buds.
Properties: Alterative, analgesic, antibiotic, antifungal, antioxidant, antiperiodic, antiphlogistic, antiscorbutic, antispasmodic, antiviral, astringent, counterirritant, demulcent, depurative, diaphoretic, diuretic, expectorant, hemostatic, insect repellent, laxative, malariacidal, stimulant, stomachic, tonic, vasodilator, and vulnerary.
Constituents: Acurcumen, alkane, caryophyllene, eucalyptol (cineol), gallic acid, glycosides, mannitol (mannite), mucilage, populin (benzyl salicin), resin, salicin, salicylic acid, tannic acid, vitamins (C (ascorbic acid), and volatile oil.

Historical Uses: Abscess, ague, alopecia, appetite loss, arthritis, asthma, bleeding, bronchitis, burns (minor), cardiovascular conditions, colds, congestion (uterine, vaginal), cough, dandruff, debility, diarrhea, digestive complaints, diphtheria, dry skin, dysentery, eczema, fever (ephemeral, intermittent, rheumatic), flies, gargle/mouth rinse, gleet, gonorrhea, gout, headache, hemorrhoids, hypertrophy (benign prostatic), indigestion, infection (bacterial, fungal, sexually transmitted, urinary tract, viral), inflammation, insect bites or stings, kidney problems, laryngitis, leukorrhea, liver problems, lung problems, pain, pruritus, malaria, mosquitos, mucus, muscle and joint pain, muscle strain, neuralgia, parasites (malarial plasmodia), psoriasis, prostate problems, rheumatism, scurvy, sexually transmitted diseases (STDs), skin problems, sores, sore throat, spasmodic conditions, sprain, stomatitis, substitute for peruvian bark, sunburn, tuberculosis, ulcer (duodenal, gastric, peptic, syriac), urethritis, uropenia (scanty urination), vaginitis, whooping cough, and wounds (minor).
Discussion: May cause blood vessel dilatation; clear and open bronchial passages; enhance liver, lung, and stomach functions; inhibit oxidation and inhibit or destroy developement and growth of bacteria and other microorganisms; promote bowel evacuation, perspiration, and urine flow; purify the blood; reestablish healthy system functions; restore normal tone to tissues; soothe mucous membrane irritation, speed healing; stimulate appetite and peristalsis.
Cautions/Contraindications: Avoid use if pregnant or breast-feeding, or if you have a sensitivity to aspirin, balsam of peru, or propalis. May cause allergic reactions and dermatitis in susceptible individuals. Some persons may experience bleeding or increased clotting time when using this herb with anticoagulant drugs or aspirin.
Adverse Reactions: Bleeding (possibly serious), coagulation problems, diarrhea (possibly bloody), digestive complaints, gastritis, gastrointestinal problems, hives, indigestion, irritable bowel syndrome (IBS), nausea, and/or vomiting.
Herb/Drug Interactions: This herb could cause an interaction (possibly severe) when taken with the following drugs: Anticoagulant drugs, Salicylates, and Subsalicylates.
Preparations/Dosage: Crude Herb: 3-9 grams. Decoction (bark and/or buds): ¼-½ cup per day. Infusion (buds): 1 cup per day. Tincture (buds): 5-20 drops (0.333-1.25 cc.) one to three times per day.
Isolation: Mannitol hexanitrate: Average dose of 15-60 mg. for use as a vasodilator. Salicin: Average dose of 5-30 grains (0.333-2 gm.) for use as an analgesic, antiperiodic, and febrifuge. Salicin's action is similar to that of quinine. Eucalyptol: 5 drops (0.3 cc.) in atomization or inhalation therapy for use in respiratory conditions.

Poppy, California (pop ē, kal e·fôrn ye)

(*Eschscholtzia californica*)

Synonyms/Related Species: Golden Poppy and Mexican Poppy (*eschscholtzia mexicana*).
Family/Class: Papaveraceae (poppy).
Floral Emblem: California.
Habitat: Europe, France, and the United States.
Flavor: Bitter.
Parts Used: Aerial.
Properties: Analgesic, antigalactic, antiphlogistic, antispasmodic, cholagogue, diaphoretic, diuretic, emetic, expectorant, hypnotic, nervine, parasiticide, sedative, and tonic.

Constituents: Alkaloids, flavones, glycosides, minerals (zinc), narcotine (non-narcotic), protopine, and sanguinarine.
Historical Uses: Anxiety, asthma, bladder problems, bronchitis, colic, cough, depression (mild/moderate), diarrhea, enuresis (urinary incontinence), fever, headache, hyperactivity, hyperexcitability, inflammation, insomnia, jaundice, lesions (tubercle), liver problems, mania, melancholy, migraine, mood swings, nervous conditions, neuralgia, neuropathy, neurosis, pain, parasites (lice and their nits), psoriasis, respiratory conditions, restlessness, scrofula, sores, spasmodic conditions, stomachache, toothache, tuberculosis, ulcer (fistula, tuberculous), vasomotor dysfunction, and whooping cough.
Discussion: May calm the nervous system; clear and open bronchial passages; diminish or suppress lactation; enhance cardiovascular and liver functions; induce sleep; promote bile flow, perspiration, and urine flow; reduce the frequency of nighttime urination; relax the smooth muscles; restore normal tone to tissues; stimulate uterine contractions; strengthen the urinary system.
Cautions/Contraindications: Avoid use if pregnant or breast-feeding. Do not confuse this herb with opium poppy (*papaver spp.*). Not for long-term use.
Adverse Reactions: Headache, lethargy, nausea, and/or vomiting.
Herb/Drug Interactions: This herb could cause an interaction (possibly severe) when taken with the following drugs: None known.
Preparations/Dosage: Crude Herb: 3-6 grams. Infusion: ½-1 cup per day. Tincture: 5-30 drops (0.333-2 cc.) one to three times per day.
Isolation: Narcotine: Average dose of 1-3 grains (0.066-0.2 gm.) for use as a febrifuge and tonic; or an average dose of 3 $^{4}/_{5}$-15 grains (0.25-1 gm.) for use as a hypnotic. Narcotine has no narcotic effects. Protopine: Average dose of 40-100 grains (2.5-7 gm.) for use as an analgesic and hypnotic. Sanguinarine: Average dose of $^{1}/_{40}$-¼ grain (0.0016-0.016 gm.) for use as an expectorant and tonic.

Poppy, Opium (pop e, ō pē·em)
(*Papaver somniferum*)

Synonyms/Related Species: Arctic Poppy (*papaver lapponicum*), Dwarf Poppy (*papaver pygmaeum*), Field Poppy (*papaver dubium*), Red Poppy (*papaver rhoeas*), and White Poppy.
Family/Class: Papaveraceae (poppy).
Habitat: Alaska, the Alpine and Subalpine zones, Asia, China, England, Europe, Germany, India, the Middle East, North America, Persia, and Turkey.
Flavor: Bitter.
Parts Used: Flowers, capsule (seedpod).
Properties: Analgesic, antibiotic, antiphlogistic, antispasmodic, astringent, counterirritant, diaphoretic, emetic, expectorant, hypnotic, laxative, narcotic, nervine, parasiticide, and sedative.
Constituents: Alkaloids, caoutchouc, codamine, codeine, cryptopine, dimethylnornarcotin, fatty acids (oleic, palmitic, stearic), fixed oils (olein, palmitin, stearin), meconic acid, meconidine, meconine, minerals (calcium magnesium), monosaccharides, morphine, mucilage, narceine, narcotine (non-narcotic), narcotoline, papaveraldine, papaverine, papaveroline, papaverosine, rhoeadine, and thebaine (dimethylmorphine).
Historical Uses: Abscess, anxiety, asthma, bronchitis, burns (minor), cataracts, conjunctivitis, cough, diarrhea, dysentery, erysipelas, eye problems, fever, headache, hives, hyperactivity, infection (bacterial), inflammation, insomnia, lesions (tubercle), mucus, nervous conditions,

pain, parasites (lice and their nits), pleurisy, prostatitis, rash, respiratory conditions, scrofula, sores, spasmodic conditions, substitute for castor oil (seed), sunburn, tinea cruris (jock itch), tuberculosis, ulcer (duodenal, fistula, gastric, peptic, stasis, tuberculous), urethritis, and windburn.

Discussion: May calm the nervous system; clear and open bronchial passages; increase endurance; induce sleep; promote bowel evacuation and perspiration; relax smooth muscle; stimulate nervous system and peristalsis.

Cautions/Contraindications: Avoid use if pregnant or breast-feeding. Do not confuse this herb with California poppy (*eschscholtzia californica*). Excessive use can lead to habituation. Not for long-term use.

Adverse Reactions: Arrhythmia, coma, constipation, diarrhea, digestive complaints, dizziness, edema, euphoria, fainting, gastritis, gastrointestinal problems, habituation, hallucinations, indigestion, irritable bowel syndrome (IBS), meconism (opium poisoning), miosis (pinpoint pupils), nausea, respiratory depression, skin problems, sleep, stupor, visual disturbances, and/or vomiting.

Herb/Drug Interactions: This herb could cause an interaction (possibly severe) when taken with the following drugs: None known.

Preparations/Dosage: Crude Herb: 3-6 grams. Tincture: 5-30 drops (0.333-2 cc.) one to three times per day.

Isolation: Codeine, Codeine phosphate, or Codeine sulfate: Soluble in eighty parts of cold water and seventeen parts of boiling water, and easily soluble in alcohol and ether. Average dose of ½ grain (0.033 gm.) for use as an analgesic, and as a substitute for morphine. Codeine is narcotic, but to a lesser degree than morphine. Cryptopine: Average dose of ⅛ grain (0.008 gm.) for use as an analgesic and hypnotic. Meconine: Average dose of 1 grain (0.066 gm.) administered subcutaneously, for use as a hypnotic. Morphine: Soluble (sparingly) in water, and is generally given in the form of its salts. Average dose of $^{1}/_{6}$ grain (10 mg.) for use as an analgesic. Narceine: Soluble (slightly) in alcohol and water. Average dose of ⅛-½ grain (0.008- 0.033 gm.) for use as a hypnotic. Narceine hydrochlorate: Soluble in boiling water, and soluble (slightly) in cold water. Average dose of $^{1}/_{6}$-3 grains (0.01-0.2 gm.) for use as an analgesic, hypnotic, and sedative. Narceine meconate: Average dose of $^{1}/_{10}$-⅔ grain (0.006-0.04 gm.) by hypodermic administration, for use as an analgesic, hypnotic, and sedative. Narcotine: Average dose of 1-3 grains (0.066-0.2 gm.) for use as a febrifuge and tonic; or an average dose of $3^{4}/_{5}$-15 grains (0.25-1 gm.) for use as a hypnotic. Narcotine has no narcotic effects. Papaverine, Papaverine hydrochloride, or Papaverine sulfate: Average dose of ½-1½ grains (0.03-0.08 gm.) for use as an antispasmodic and hypnotic.

Did You Know? Opium is the juice of the poppy and consists of several alkaloids including codeine, cryptopine, morphine, narcotine, narceine, papaverine, and thebaine. When the petals have fallen from the flowers, incisions are made in the cortex of the capsule, which allows the juice to slowly ooze out and partially dry. The juice is then scraped off the capsule, formed into small cakes, and dried completely in the sun.

Poppy, Prickly (pop'e, prik·le)

(*Argemone polyanthemos*)

Synonyms/Related Species: Bastard Wild Poppy (*argemone torulo*), Corn Poppy, Crested Prickly Poppy, Flatbud Prickly Poppy (*argemone munita*), Long-Codded Wild Poppy (*argemone longiore*), Mexican Prickly Poppy (*argemone mexicana*), and Thistle Poppy.

Family/Class: Papaveraceae (poppy).
Habitat: England, Europe, and North America.
Flavor: Bitter.
Parts Used: Root, seeds.
Properties: Analgesic, antiphlogistic, antispasmodic, astringent, caustic, counterirritant, diaphoretic, emetic, expectorant, hypnotic, laxative, narcotic, nervine, parasiticide, and sedative.
Constituents: Alkaloids, calcium, caoutchouc, fixed oil, flavones, glycosides, minerals (magnesium), monosaccharide, mucilage, narcotine (non-narcotic), and protopine.
Historical Uses: Boils, burns (minor), corns, hives, inflammation, insomnia, pain, parasites (lice and their nits), prostatitis, rash, sores, sunburn, toothache, urethritis, warts (digitate, filiform, fugitive, glabra, mother, plana juvenilis, plantar, seborrhoeic, vulgaris), and wounds (minor).
Discussion: May calm the nervous system; clear and open bronchial passages; increase endurance; induce sleep; promote bowel evacuation and perspiration; relax smooth muscle; stimulate nervous system and peristalsis.
Cautions/Contraindications: Avoid use if pregnant or breast-feeding.
Adverse Reactions: Headache, lethargy, nausea, and/or vomiting.
Herb/Drug Interactions: This herb could cause an interaction (possibly severe) when taken with the following drugs: None known.
Preparations/Dosage: Crude Herb: 3-6 grams. Warts/Corns: Apply plant juice (diluted) directly to affected area and cover with a bandaid. Repeat daily until wart/corn is gone.

Privet (priv it)
(*Ligustrum vulgare*)

Synonyms/Related Species: Common Privet and Prim.
Family/Class: Oleaceae (olive).
Habitat: Africa, Asia, England, Europe, and North America.
Flavor: Bitter.
Parts Used: Bark, leaves.
Properties: Alterative, antiperiodic, antiphlogistic, astringent, carminative, hemostatic, laxative, malariacidal, tonic, and vasodilator.
Constituents: Albumin (albumen), fatty acids (arachidonic, linoleic, linolenic, oleic, palmitic, stearic), fixed oils (olein, palmitin, stearin), inulin (starch), ligustrin (syringin), mannitol (mannite), monosaccharides, resin, and ursone (ursolic acid).
Historical Uses: Ague, appetite loss, bleeding, cataracts, diarrhea, digestive complaints, dizziness, emaciation, eye problems, fatigue, fever (ephemeral, intermittent), flatulence, floaters (eye), gargle/mouth rinse, indigestion, inflammation, lumbago, malaria, muscle and joint pain, nervous conditions, parasites (malarial plasmodia), retinitis, skin problems, tinnitus, vertigo, and visual disturbances.
Discussion: May aid digestion; cause blood vessel dilatation; promote bowel evacuation; reestablish healthy system functions; restore normal tone to tissues and hair color (gradually); enhance adrenal, kidney, and liver functions; stimulate appetite and peristalsis; strengthen the cartilage, ligaments, muscles, and vision.
Cautions/Contraindications: Avoid use if pregnant or breast-feeding, or if you have chronic diarrhea.
Adverse Reactions: Diarrhea (severe), gastrointestinal irritation, nausea, and/or vomiting

Herb/Drug Interactions: This herb could cause an interaction (possibly severe) when taken with the following drugs: None known.
Preparations/Dosage: Crude Herb: 3-6 grams. Decoction (bark and/or leaves): 1-2 cups per day. Tincture: 10-15 drops (0.666-1 cc.) one to three times per day.
Isolation: Mannitol hexanitrate: Average dose of 15-60 mg. for use as a vasodilator.

Pumpkin (pum kin)
(*Cucurbita pepo*)

Synonyms/Related Species: Cucurbita, Field Pumpkin, Pepo, and Pompon.
Family/Class: Cucurbitaceae (gourd).
Habitat: North America and other temperate regions.
Flavor: Inner Flesh: sweet. Seeds: bitter/sweet.
Parts Used: Inner flesh, seeds.
Properties: Anthelmintic, antioxidant, anti-inflammatory, diuretic, hypotensive, nutritive, teniacide, teniafuge, vasodilator, and vermifuge.
Constituents: Amino acids (arginine, glutamic), cholesterol, cucurbitol, cucurbocitrin, fatty acids (arachidonic, linoleic, linolenic, oleic, palmitic, stearic), fiber, fixed oils (olein, palmitin, stearin), minerals (calcium, copper, iron, magnesium, manganese, phosphorus, potassium, selenium, zinc), mucilage, protein, sterols, and vitamins (A, B_3 (niacin), E (alpha-tocopheral).
Historical Uses: Bladder problems, dietary supplementation, enuresis (urinary incontinence), hypertension (mild/moderate), hypertrophy (benign prostatic), inflammation, malnutrition, nausea, nephritis, parasites (roundworm, tapeworm), prostate problems, and urinary problems.
Discussion: May block the action of the hormone dihydrotestosterone on the prostate gland; cause blood vessel dilatation; enhance colon and stomach functions; inhibit oxidation; prevent arteriosclerosis; promote urine flow; provide dietary supplementation; reduce hormonal damage to prostate cells, reduce the risk of developing cancer (prostate), and reduce nighttime urination; serve as a nutritional adjuvant to therapeutic programs.
Cautions/Contraindications: Avoid use if pregnant or breast-feeding.
Adverse Reactions: Nausea and/or vomiting.
Herb/Drug Interactions: This herb could cause an interaction (possibly severe) when taken with the following drugs: Hypotensive drugs.
Preparations/Dosage: Crude Herb (seeds): 30-60 grams. Decoction: ¼-½ cup per day. Inner flesh: Used in baking/cooking. Resin: Average dose in substance 10-15 grains (0.66-0.98 gm.). Seeds (roasted): Chew ½-1 cup or a handful daily. Seeds (crushed): 1-3 ounces (31-93 gm.) for use as a teniacide.

Puncture Vine (punk cher vīn)
(*Tribulus terrestris*)

Synonyms/Related Species: Calcatrippe, Calketrappe, Caltrop, Coltetraeppe, Goat's Head, Hairy Caltrop, Little Caltrop, and Mudar.
Family/Class: Zygophyllaceae (caltrop).
Habitat: Africa, Asia, Ceylon, India, North America, Pakistan, and the Sunda Islands.
Flavor: Bitter.
Parts Used: Bark (root), fruit.

Properties: Abortifacient, alterative, antibiotic, anticarcinogen, antiphlogistic, antispasmodic, aphrodisiac, diaphoretic, diuretic, expectorant, hemostatic, and lithotriptic.
Constituents: Albumin (albumen), alkaloids, calotropin, caoutchouc, keampferol, mucilage, mudarin, saponins, and volatile oil.
Historical Uses: Abscess, amenorrhea, angina, appetite loss, asthma, bleeding, calculus, cancer, colds, cough, cramps, diarrhea, digestive complaints, dizziness, dysentery, dysuria (painful/difficult urination), eczema, elephantiasis, enuresis (urinary incontinence), epilepsy, erectile dysfunction, fever, gallstones, gleet, gonorrhea, gout, headache, hives, hysteria, infection (bacterial, sexually transmitted), inflammation, kidney stones, leprosy, lesions, lochia, mastitis, mucus, nephritis, nocturnal emission, nosebleed, pruritus, seizure conditions, sexually transmitted diseases (STDs), skin problems, snakebite, spasmodic conditions, spermatorrhea, syphilis, toothache, tumors, ulcer (duodenal, gastric, peptic, syphilitic), urethritis, urinary problems, vertigo, vitiligo, and warts (digitate, filiform, fugitive, glabra, mother, plana juvenilis, plantar, seborrhoeic, vulgaris).
Discussion: May arouse sexual impulses; clear and open bronchial passages; decrease the effect of carcinogens; dissolve calculi; enhance liver and lung functions; induce abortion; promote perspiration and urine flow; reduce the emission of semen during sleep; reestablish healthy system functions; stimulate menstruation and uterine contractions.
Cautions/Contraindications: Avoid use if pregnant or breast-feeding. May cause photosensitivity or photodermatosis in susceptible individuals. Not for long-term use. Use with professional guidance/supervision.
Adverse Reactions: Bradycardia, convulsions, diarrhea, nausea, respiratory failure, staggering, vomiting, and/or possible death.
Herb/Drug Interactions: This herb could cause an interaction (possibly severe) when taken with the following drugs: None known.
Preparations/Dosage: Bark (powdered): Average dose in substance 2-5 grains (0.133-0.333 gm.). Fruit: 6-10 grams. Infusion: ½-¾ cup per day. Tincture: 5-15 drops (0.333-1 cc.) one to three times per day.
Did You Know? The spines on puncture vine are so tough, they often damage automobile tires.

Purple Coneflower (pûr pel kōn flou er)
(*Echinacea angustifolia*)

Synonyms/Related Species: Black Sampson, Cockup Hat, Coneflower, Echinacea, Gulf Coast Coneflower (*echinacea sanguinea*), Indian Head, Kansas Snakeroot, Missouri Snakeroot (*echinacea stimulata*), Narrow-Leaved Purple Coneflower, Prairie Coneflower (*echinacea atrorubens*), Purple Kansas Coneflower, Red Sunflower, Rudbeckia (*echinacea purpurea*), Sampson Root, Smooth-Leaved Coneflower (*echinacea laevigata*), Snakeroot, Tennessee Coneflower (*echinacea tennesseenis*), and Yellow Coneflower (*echinacea paradoxa*).
Family/Class: Compositae (composite).
Habitat: The Appalachian Mountains, Britain, Germany, and North America.
Flavor: Bitter.
Parts Used: Leaves, root.
Properties: Alterative, antibiotic, anticarcinogen, antifungal, antiperiodic, antiphlogistic, antiprotozoan, antiviral, aromatic, carminative, depurative, emmenagogue, immunomodulator, malariacidal, parasiticide, stimulant, vermifuge, and vulnerary.

Constituents: Alkaloids, arabinose, betaine (lycine), borneol, caffeic acid, caryophyllin, cynarin, echinacen, echinacein, echinacin, echinacoside, echinolone, fatty acids (arachidonic, linoleic, linolenic, oleic, palmitic, stearic), ferulic acid, fixed oils (olein, palmitin, stearin), flavonoids, galactose, hydrocarbons, inulin (starch), inuloid, minerals (aluminum, calcium chlorine, copper, iodine, iron, magnesium, potassium, sulfur), monosaccharides, monoterpenes, polyacetylenes, polysaccharide, protein, quercetin, resin, rhamnose, rutin, sesquiterpene, sterols, tannic acid, tussilagine, vitamins (A, C (ascorbic acid), E (alpha-tocopheral), and volatile oil.

Historical Uses: Abscess, acne, ague, allergy, amenorrhea, anemia, anthrax, arthritis, burns (minor), cancer (breast, colorectal, liver), candida, cholera, chronic fatigue syndrome (CFS), colds, colic, cough, cramps, diphtheria, ear infection, eczema, Epstein Barr Virus (EBV), eyewash, fever (ephemeral, enteric, herpetic, intermittent, rheumatic, scarlet, septic), fibromyalgia, flatulence, gangrene, gargle/mouth rinse, glandular problems, glandular swelling, gleet, gonorrhea, halitosis, herpes, human immunodeficiency virus (HIV), hydrophobia (rabies in humans), indigestion, infection (bacterial, bladder, fungal, sexually transmitted, urinary tract, viral), inflammation, influenza, insect bites or stings, laryngitis, leishmaniasis, leukemia, leukopenia, Lyme disease, malaria, measles, meningitis, moniliasis, mononucleosis (infectious), mucus, mumps, muscle and joint pain, pain, parasites (leishmania, malarial plasmodia, trichomonas), pelvic inflammatory disease (PID), periodontal disease, poisoning (blood, food), poison ivy/oak, prostate problems, prostatitis, pruritus, psoriasis, respiratory conditions, rheumatism, rheumatoid arthritis (RA), scarletina, scorpion stings, sexually transmitted diseases (STDs), skin problems, small pox, snakebite, sores, sore throat, strep throat, syphilis, tetanus, tonsillitis, toothache, trismus (lockjaw), tumors, typhoid, ulcer (bouveret, duodenal, gastric, peptic, syphilitic, syriac), urethritis, urtecaria, whooping cough, and wounds (minor).

Discussion: May activate the macrophages that destroy both cancerous cells and pathogens; aid digestion; cleanse the whole system; decrease the effect of carcinogens; enhance liver, lung, and stomach functions; halt the recurrence of *candida albicans* moniliasis infection; increase energy, T-cell production, and white blood cell counts; inhibit or destroy development and growth of bacteria and other microorganisms, inhibit the action of hyaluronidase by bonding with it to temporarily increase in the integrity of the barrier against pathogenic organisms, and inhibit protozoa; offset the negative effects of chemotherapy and radiation therapy; prevent hemorrhage in persons with hypertension; purify the blood; reduce capillary fragility and both the rate of growth and the rate of reproduction of protozoa; reestablish healthy system functions; regenerate connective tissues destroyed during infection; speed healing; stimulate the immune system, menstruation, and new tissue growth.

Cautions/Contraindications: Avoid use if pregnant or breast-feeding, or if you have a ragweed or sunflower sensitivity, or if you have acquired immune deficiency syndrome (AIDS), cardiovascular conditions, collagenoses, diabetes, human immunodeficiency virus (HIV), lupus, leukoses, multiple sclerosis (MS), tuberculosis, an iodine sensitivity, or before, during, and after organ transplantation. Do not administer to children under 10 years old. Do not confuse purple coneflower with the poisonous variety also known as coneflower (*rudbeckia laciniata*). May decrease fertility in women. May cause vitamin E depletion. May cause allergic reactions in susceptible individuals. May interfere with the effectiveness of certain thyroid medications.

Adverse Reactions: Abdominal pain, arrhythmia, diarrhea, fever, hypertrophy (thyroid), iodism (iodine poisoning), nausea, priapism, rash, thirst, throat irritation, and/or vomiting.

Herb/Drug Interactions: This herb could cause an interaction (possibly severe) when taken with the following drugs: Antifungal drugs, Antihistamine drugs, Antineoplastic drugs, Corticosteroids, Erectile Dysfunction drugs, and Thyroid drugs.

Preparations/Dosage: Crude Herb: 3-9 grams. Crude Herb (powdered): 1-2 grams. Decoction (root): ¼-½ cup per day. Extract: 5-10 drops (0.333-0.666 cc.) one to two times per day. Infusion (leaves): ½-1 cup per day. Tincture: 10-30 drops (0.666-2 cc.) one to three times per day.
Isolation: Betaine: Average dose of 2-4 grains (0.13-0.26 gm.) for use as an emmenagogue.
Did You Know? A mere 6 mg. ($^1/_{10}$ grain) of echinacoside, an active constituent found in purple coneflower, is comparable to approximately one unit of penicillin.
Note: Purple coneflower often causes a harmless, temporary, tingling sensation on the tongue when taken orally.

Purslane (pûrs lin)
(*Portulaca oleracea*)

Synonyms/Related Species: Garden Purslane, Golden Purslane (*portulaca sativa*), Green Purslane, Portulaca, Procelayne, and Purcelane.
Family/Class: Portulacaceae (purslane).
Habitat: Britain, China, England, India, Ireland, Japan, and North America.
Flavor: Bitter/sour.
Parts Used: Leaves.
Properties: Alterative, antibiotic, antioxidant, antiphlogistic, antiscorbutic, diuretic, and hemostatic.
Constituents: Amino acids (alanine, dopa, glutathione, glutamic), citric acid, fatty acids (omega-3), minerals (calcium, iron, phosphorous), monosaccharides, malic acid, norepinephrine, phosphoric acid, and vitamins (A, C (ascorbic acid), E (alpha-tocopheral), K).
Historical Uses: Abscess, ague, bleeding, bruises, burns (minor), conjunctivitis, cough, debility, dermatitis, diarrhea, dysentery, dysuria (painful/difficult urination), enterorrhagia, earache, fever (ephemeral, scarlet), gout, headache, hemorrhage, hemorrhoids, infection (bacterial), inflammation, insect bites or stings, insomnia, lochia, pain, periodontal disease, scarletina, scurvy, shortness of breath, skin problems, snakebite, sores, stomachache, and thirst.
Discussion: May enhance colon, liver, and spleen functions; increase lung capacity and production of interleukins; inhibit oxidation and inhibit or destroy developement and growth of bacteria and other microorganisms; normalize skin pigmentation; promote urine flow; provide an excellent non-fish source of omega-3 fatty acid; reestablish healthy system functions; strengthen the immune system.
Cautions/Contraindications: Avoid use if pregnant or breast-feeding, or if you have a weak digestive system. May cause photosensitivity or photodermatosis in susceptible individuals.
Adverse Reactions: Nausea and/or vomiting.
Herb/Drug Interactions: This herb could cause an interaction (possibly severe) when taken with the following drugs: Bronchodilator drugs.
Preparations/Dosage: Crude Herb: 3-12 grams. Juice: 1-3 tablespoons in water or mixed with honey. Leaves: Steamed and eaten as a vegetable.

Pyrethrum (pī·rē·threm)
(*Chrysanthemum cinerariaefolium*)

Synonyms/Related Species: Dalmation Insect Flowers and Insect Powder Plant.
Family/Class: Compositae (composite).

Habitat: Africa, Australia, the Caucasus, and the United States.
Flavor: Bitter/pungent.
Parts Used: Flowers.
Properties: Insect repellent and parasiticide.
Constituents: Alumina (aluminum oxide), bitter principle, gum, lignin, minerals (calcium, potassium, silicon), pyrethrine, pyrethrolone, pyrethron, resin, silicic acid, tannic acid, and volatile oil.
Historical Uses: Ants, aphids, bedbugs, cochliomyia fly, cockroaches, fleas, flies, hornworm, lace bug, leafhopper, mosquitos, moths, parasites (crabs and their nits, lice and their nits, scabies, screwworm), tsetse fly, and numerous other bugs/insects.
Discussion: May effectively repel insects.
Cautions/Contraindications: Avoid use if pregnant or breast-feeding.
Adverse Reactions: Headache, respiratory distress, nausea, tinnitus, and/or vomiting.
Herb/Drug Interactions: This herb could cause an interaction (possibly severe) when taken with the following drugs: None known.
Preparations/Dosage: External uses only. Flower (powdered): Sprinkle around doors and windowsills to repel insects (flies). Flowers (burnt/smoldering): Use as a fumigator in the proportion of 1 ounce per 30 cubic feet of air space. Evacuate the room of people and pets. Put pyrethrum in a metal pot (the quantity apportioned to any pot should not exceed 1inch in depth) with a tiny bit of alcohol. Set the pot on a couple of bricks, which will prevent the floor from scorching. Open a window a crack to allow a little airflow. Ignite and allow herb to smolder filling the room with smoke (leave the room once the herb begins to smolder). Fumigate for no less than 4 hours (the smoke is as effective as the powder in repeling insects). Completely air-out the room to get rid of any smoky odor. Tincture: 15-30 drops (1-2 cc.) diluted in water and applied topically as a lotion to repel insects.
Note: Pyrethrum is non-absorbing, non-corrosive, and non-toxic to animals, birds, fish, and humans. The fumes given off from smoldering pyrethrum will not corrode metals, damage paintings, or harm fabrics.
Did You Know? The dried and/or powdered flowers will retain their insecticidal properties for an indefinite period. Each plant yields approximately 80-100 flowers in one growing season.

Pyrola (pī rō·le)
(*Pyrola rotundifolia*)

Synonyms/Related Species: Arctic Wintergreen (*pyrola grandiflora*), Bog Wintergreen, Bracted Wintergreen, Canker Lettuce, Greenish-Flowered Wintergreen (*pyrola chlorantha*), Intermediate Wintergreen (*pyrola media*), Large Wintergreen, Lesser Wintergreen (*pyrola minor*), Liverleaf Wintergreen (*pyrola asarifolia*), One-Flowered Wintergreen (*pyrola uniflora*), One-Sided Wintergreen (*pyrola secunda*), Pear-Leaf Wintergreen, Pink Wintergreen, Round-Leaved Pyrola, Shin-Leaf (*pyrola elliptica*), Shy Maiden, Single Delight, Wax Flower, White-Veined Wintergreen (*pyrola picta*), and Yevering Bells.
Family/Class: Pyrolaceae (wintergreen).

Habitat: Alaska, the Alpine and Subalpine zones, Asia, Britain, the Caucasus, England, Europe,Germany, Ireland, North America, Scotland, and the Yukon Territory.

Flavor: Pungent.

Parts Used: Leaves.

Properties: Analgesic, antibiotic, antiphlogistic, antispasmodic, aromatic, astringent, carminative, counterirritant, depurative, diuretic, expectorant, hemostatic, laxative, stimulant, stomachic, tonic, urinary antiseptic, and vulnerary.

Constituents: Arbutin, methyl salicylate, minerals (magnesium, potassium), and volatile oil.

Historical Uses: Arthritis, bleeding, bruises, canker sores, cough, digestive complaints, ear problems, epilepsy, eye problems, fever (ephemeral, rheumatic), flavoring agent, gargle/mouth rinse, glandular swelling, gleet, gonorrhea, headache, hemoptysis, hemorrhage (metrorrhagia), hyperactivity, infection (bacterial, sexually transmitted), inflammation, insect bites or stings, jaundice, kidney problems, liver problems, menorrhagia, menstrual problems, mucus, muscle and joint pain, nephritis, nervous conditions, pain, respiratory conditions, rheumatism, sexually transmitted diseases (STDs), skin problems, sore throat, spasmodic conditions, substitute for pipsissewa (*chimaphila umbellata*), ulcer (duodenal, gastric, peptic), urethritis, urinary problems, and wounds (minor).

Discussion: May aid digestion; clear and open the bronchial passages; enhance liver, lung, and stomach functions; inhibit or destroy developement and growth of bacteria and other microorganisms; promote bowel evacuation and urine flow; purify the blood; restore normal tone to tissues; speed healing; stimulate metabolism and uterine contractions.

Cautions/Contraindications: Avoid use if pregnant or breast-feeding, or if you have an aspirin sensitivity, or if you have kidney or liver disease. May cause dermatitis in susceptible individuals. Not for long-term use. Some persons may experience bleeding or increased clotting time when using this herb with anticoagulant drugs or aspirin. Using pyrola with willow bark may cause serious bleeding.

Adverse Reactions: Bleeding (possibly serious), coagulation problems, nausea, and/or vomiting.

Herb/Drug Interactions: This herb could cause an interaction (possibly severe) when taken with the following drugs: Anticoagulant drugs, Salicylates, and Subsalicylates.

Preparations/Dosage: Crude Herb: 9-15 grams. Extract (powdered): Average dose in substance 2-4 grains (0.133-0.26 gm.). Infusion: 1-2 cups per day. Tincture: 5-10 drops (0.333-0.666 cc.) one to three times per day.

Isolation: Arbutin: Average dose of 5-15 grains (0.3-1 gm.) for use as a diuretic and urinary antiseptic.

Quebracho (kā·brä chō)

(*Aspidosperma quebracho-blanco*)

Synonyms/Related Species: Aspidosperma, Axe Breaker, Quiebrahacha, Red Quebracho, and White Quebracho.

Family/Class: Apocynaceae (dogbane).

Habitat: South America.

Flavor: Bitter.

Parts Used: Bark.

Properties: Astringent, carminative, emetic, expectorant, febrifuge, and tonic.

Constituents: Alkaloids, aspidosamin, aspidospermatine, aspidospermine, inulin (starch), quebrachamine, quebrachitol, tannic acid, and yohimbine (quebrachin).
Historical Uses: Asthma, cardiovascular conditions, colds, cough, digestive complaints, emphysema, erectile dysfunction, fever (ephemeral), gastritis, gastrointestinal problems, heart disease, indigestion, and respiratory conditions.
Discussion: May aid digestion; clear and open bronchial passages; enhance gastrointestinal function; protect against heart disease; reduce the frequency and severity of asthma attacks; restore normal tone to tissues. Quebrachitol is a sugar that may serve as a sugar substitute for diabetics.
Cautions/Contraindications: Avoid use if pregnant or breast-feeding.
Adverse Reactions: Nausea, priapism, and/or vomiting.
Herb/Drug Interactions: This herb could cause an interaction (possibly severe) when taken with the following drugs: Erectile Dysfunction drugs.
Preparations/Dosage: Crude Herb (powdered): Average dose in substance 10-15 grains (0.666-0.98 gm.). Extract: 5-15 drops (0.333-1 cc.) one to two times per day. Extract (powdered): Average dose in substance 2-8 grains (0.133-0.5 gm.).
Isolation: Yohimbine hydrochlorate: Soluble in water. Average dose of $^{1}/_{12}$-$^{1}/_{10}$ grain (0.005-0.007 gm.) for use in erectile dysfunction and as a carminative.

Queen Anne's Lace (kwēn anz lās)

(*Daucus carota*)

Synonyms/Related Species: Bee's Nest Plant, Bird's Nest Root, and Wild Carrot.
Family/Class: Umbelliferae (parsley).
Habitat: Asia, Britain, Europe, India, North America, and Russia.
Flavor: Root: sweet. Seeds: pungent.
Parts Used: Root, seeds.
Properties: Antacid, anthelmintic, antibiotic, antilithic, antispasmodic, carminative, diuretic, emmenagogue, hypotensive, lithotriptic, stimulant, vasodilator, and vermifuge.
Constituents: Carbohydrates, carvene (limonene), caryophyllin, geraniol (rhodinol), lycopene, minerals (iron, magnesium, potassium), pectic acid, pectin, saccharose, vitamins (A, B, B_2 (riboflavin), B_3 (niacin), B_6 (pyridoxine), C (ascorbic acid), and volatile oil.
Historical Uses: Acidity (gastric), acne, amenorrhea, calculus, colic, contraceptive (female), cough, cystitis, diabetes, diarrhea, digestive complaints, dysentery, edema, flatulence, gallstones, gastritis, gastrointestinal problems, gout, hiccups, hypertension (mild/moderate), indigestion, infection (bacterial), irritable bowel syndrome (IBS), jaundice, kidney problems, kidney stones, lithemia, menstrual problems, parasites (pinworm, roundworm), pimples, prostate problems, rheumatism, skin problems, tonsillitis, ulcer (duodenal, gastric, peptic), and urinary problems.
Discussion: May cause blood vessel dilatation; dissolve calculi; enhance digestive system, kidney, spleen, and stomach functions; inhibit or destroy developement and growth of bacteria and other microorganisms; neutralize acidity; prevent the development of calculus or stones; reduce blood pressure levels and excessive lithic acid (uric acid) and urate levels in the blood, tophi, and urine; serve as a female contraceptive (female; the seeds have an anti-implantation effect on fertilized eggs when taken the morning after); stimulate menstruation.

Cautions/Contraindications: Avoid use if pregnant or breast-feeding. Do not confuse this plant with poison hemlock or other toxic members of the parsley family. May cause dermatitis in susceptible individuals.
Adverse Reactions: Nausea and/or vomiting.
Herb/Drug Interactions: This herb could cause an interaction (possibly severe) when taken with the following drugs: Hypotensive drugs.
Preparations/Dosage: Crude Herb (root): 3-6 grams. Crude Herb (seeds): Average dose in substance 30-60 grains (2-4 gm.). Decoction (root): ½ cup per day. Infusion (seeds): 1 cup per day. Juice: 1-2 cups per day. Root: Cooked and eaten as a vegetable.

Queen's Delight (kwēnz di·līt)
(Stillingia sylvatica)

Synonyms/Related Species: Silver Leaf, Stillingia, and Yaw Root.
Family/Class: Euphorbiaceae (spurge).
Habitat: North America.
Flavor: Pungent/bitter.
Parts Used: Root
Properties: Alterative, anticarcinogen, antiphlogistic, astringent, depurative, diuretic, emetic, expectorant, hemostatic, laxative, sialogogue, stimulant, and tonic.
Constituents: Alkaloids, fatty acids (oleic, palmitic, stearic), fixed oils (olein, palmitin, stearin), inulin (starch), minerals (calcium), resin, stillingine, tannic acid, and volatile oil.
Historical Uses: Acne, amenorrhea, arthritis, bleeding, bronchitis, cancer, colds, congestion (uterine, vaginal), constipation, cough, croup, diarrhea, digestive complaints, eczema, fever (ephemeral, rheumatic), gallbladder problems, hepatitis, inflammation, laryngitis, lesions (tubercle), leukorrhea, liver problems, mucus, muscle and joint pain, pain, respiratory conditions, rheumatism, scrofula, sexually transmitted diseases (STDs), skin problems, sore throat, syphilis, tuberculosis, ulcer (fistula, syphilitic, tuberculous), urinary problems, and vaginitis.
Discussion: May clear and open bronchial passages; decrease the effect of carcinogens; enhance digestive system, glandular system, kidney, liver, and lung functions; offset the negative effects of chemotherapy and radiation therapy; promote bowel evacuation, saliva secretion, and urine flow; purify the blood; reestablish healthy system functions; restore normal tone to tissues; stimulate peristalsis.
Cautions/Contraindications: Avoid use if pregnant or breast-feeding. May cause dermatitis in susceptible individuals. Not for long-term use.
Adverse Reactions: Diarrhea (possibly severe), mucus membrane inflammation, nausea, salivation (increased), and/or vomiting.
Herb/Drug Interactions: This herb could cause an interaction (possibly severe) when taken with the following drugs: None known.
Preparations/Dosage: Crude Herb: 3-6 grams. Decoction: 1 cup per day. Extract: 3-5 drops (0.2-0.333 cc.) one to two times per day. Extract (solid): Average dose in substance 2-5 grains (0.133-0.333 gm.). Root (powdered): Average dose in substance 5-10 grains (0.333-0.666 gm.). Tincture: 5-20 drops (0.333-1.25 cc.) one to three times per day.

Queen of the Meadow (kwēn uv the med ō)
(*Eupatorium purpureum*)

Synonyms/Related Species: Gravelroot, Joe-Pye Weed, Jopi-Weed, Kidneyroot, Purple Boneset, and Trumpet Weed.
Family/Class: Compositae (composite).
Habitat: North America.
Flavor: Bitter/pungent.
Parts Used: Flowers, root.
Properties: Analgesic, anticarcinogen, antilithic, antiphlogistic, aphrodisiac, astringent, carminative, diaphoretic, diuretic, lithotriptic, nervine, parasiticide, stomachic, and tonic.
Constituents: Bitter principle, flavonoids, resin, vitamins (C (ascorbic acid), D), and volatile oil.
Historical Uses: Bursitis, calculus, cancer, cystitis, diabetes, diarrhea, diuria (frequent daytime urination), edema, enuresis (urinary incontinence), fever (ephemeral, enteric, rheumatic), gallstones, gout, hematuria, infection (bladder, urinary tract), inflammation, kidney problems, kidney stones, lithemia, lumbago, menstrual problems, muscle and joint pain, muscle strain, nervous conditions, neuralgia, pain, parasites (ringworm), prostate problems, rheumatism, sprain, typhoid, ulcer (bouveret), urethritis, and urinary problems.
Discussion: May aid digestion; arouse sexual impulses; calm the nervous system; decrease the effect of carcinogens; dissolve calculi; enhance liver, stomach, and urinary system functions; prevent the development of calculus or stones; promote perspiration and urine flow; reduce excessive lithic acid (uric acid) and urate levels in the blood, tophi, and urine, and reduce the persistent urge to urinate; restore normal tone to tissues; strengthen the urinary system.
Cautions/Contraindications: Avoid use if pregnant or breast-feeding.
Herb/Drug Interactions: This herb could cause an interaction (possibly severe) when taken with the following drugs: Diuretic drugs.
Preparations/Dosage: Crude Herb: 3-9 grams. Flowers/Leaves (powdered): Average dose in substance 10-20 grains (0.666-1.333 gm.). Decoction (root): ¼-½ cup per day. Infusion (flowers and/or leaves): 1-2 cups per day. Tincture: 5-15 drops (0.333-1 cc.) one to three times per day.

Raspberry (raz ber·e)
(*Rubus idaeus*)

Synonyms/Related Species: American Blackberry (*rubus villosus*), American Bramble (*rubus odoratus*), Arctic Raspberry, Blackberry, Black Raspberry (*rubus leucodermis*), Bramble (*rubus villosus*), Cloudberry (*rubus chamœnorus*), Dewberry (*rubus cœsius*), Dwarf Raspberry (*rubus articus*), European Red Raspberry, Five-Leaved Bramble (*rubus pedatus*), Garden Raspberry, Goutberry, Hedge Blackberry (*rubus rhamnifolius*), High Blackberry, Red Raspberry (*rubus strigosus*), Roebuck-Berry (*rubus saxatilis*), Salmonberry (*rubus spectabilis*), Thimbleberry (*rubus parviflorus*), Trailing Raspberry (*rubus pubescens*), Western Blackberry, Western Thimbleberry, Whitebark Raspberry (*rubus leucodermis*), Wild English Raspberry, and Wild Red Raspberry.
Family/Class: Rosaceae (rose).
Habitat: Alaska, the Alpine and Subalpine zones, Asia, Australia, Britain, Crete, England, Europe, Greece, North America, and Turkey.
Flavor: Fruit: sweet. Bark/Leaves/Root: bitter.

Parts Used: Bark (root), fruit, leaves, root.
Properties: Alterative, antibiotic, anticarcinogen, anticoagulant, antiemetic, antifungal, antioxidant, antiphlogistic, antiscorbutic, antiviral, astringent, depurative, diuretic, hemostatic, hypoglycemic, laxative, nutritive, oxytocic, sedative, stimulant, stomachic, and tonic.
Constituents: Albumin (albumen), carbohydrates, citric acid, ferulic acid, fiber, flavonoids, fragarine, glycosides, malic acid, minerals (calcium, iron, magnesium, manganese, potassium, sodium), monosaccharides, pectic acid, pectin, salicylic acid, tannic acid, vitamins (A, B_1 (thiamine), B_2 (riboflavin), B_3 (niacin), C (ascorbic acid), E (alpha-tocopheral), and volatile oil.
Historical Uses: Abscess, acne, allergy, anemia, appetite loss, bleeding, bronchitis, burns (minor), calculus, candida, canker sores, cardiovascular conditions, cholera, colds, colic, congestion (uterine, vaginal), constipation, cough, diabetes, diarrhea, dietary supplementation, digestive complaints, dysentery, dysmenorrhea, edema, enteritis, enuresis (urinary incontinence), eyewash, fever (ephemeral, rheumatic), flatulence, gallstones, gargle/mouth rinse, gastritis, gastrointestinal problems, gleet, gonorrhea, gout, hemorrhage, hemorrhoids, hemoptysis (spitting up of blood), hepatitis, hives, hyperglycemia, infection (bacterial, fungal, sexually transmitted, viral), inflammation, influenza, insomnia, jam/jelly (berries), kidney stones, lesions (tubercle), leukorrhea, malnutrition, measles, moniliasis, menorrhagia, menopausal/menstrual problems, mucus, muscle/joint pain, nausea, nervous conditions, pain, periodontal disease, premenstrual syndrome (PMS), prolapse (rectal, uterine), rash, respiratory conditions, rheumatism, rheumatoid arthritis (RA), scrofula, scurvy, sexually transmitted diseases (STDs), sinusitis, skin problems, sores, sore throat, spasmodic conditions, stomachache, thirst, tonsillitis, toothache, tuberculosis, ulcer (duodenal, fistula, gastric, peptic, tuberculous), urethritis, urinary problems, vaginitis, vomiting, whooping cough, and wounds (minor).
Discussion: May aid in the absorption and utilization of vitamin C; decrease the effect of carcinogens; delay or reduce coagulation of the blood; enhance digestive system, immune system, kidney, liver, spleen, and stomach functions; enrich colostrum found in breast milk; increase blood vessel integrity and circulation; inhibit oxidation and inhibit or destroy development and growth of bacteria and other microorganisms; promote bowel evacuation and urine flow; protect against harmful free radicals; provide dietary supplementation; purify the blood; reduce blood sugar levels, the frequency of nighttime urination, and scar formation; reestablish healthy system functions; restore normal tone to tissues; serve as a nutritional adjuvant to therapeutic programs; stimulate appetite, peristalsis, and uterine contractions; strengthen the blood vessels, capillaries, and the urinary system.
Cautions/Contraindications: Avoid use if pregnant or breast-feeding, or if you have a coagulation problem, or if you have cancer (colon, stomach). May interfere with the absorption of atropine (when taken by mouth), codeine, ephedrine, pseudoephedrine, and theophylline drugs. Do not confuse raspberry leaf tea with sweetened raspberry flavored drinks. Some persons may experience bleeding or increased clotting time when using this herb with anticoagulant drugs or aspirin.
Adverse Reactions: Bleeding (possibly serious), coagulation problems, diarrhea, edema, intestinal and kidney irritation, nausea, and/or vomiting.
Herb/Drug Interactions: This herb could cause an interaction (possibly severe) when taken with the following drugs: Anticoagulant drugs, Antidiabetic drugs, Autonomic drugs, Bronchodilator drugs, Opiate Agonists/Narcotic drugs, Salicylates, and Subsalicylates.
Preparations/Dosage: Crude Herb (fruit): 6-12 grams. Crude Herb (bark/leaves/root): 3-9 grams. Decoction (bark or root): ½-1 cup per day. Infusion (leaves): 1-3 cups. Extract (bark or root): 10-15 drops (0.666-1 cc.) one to two times per day. Fruit (fresh): May be ingested freely.

Infusion (leaves): 1-2 cups per day. Juice: 1 cup per day. Syrup: 1-2 tablespoons in water. Tincture: 15-30 drops (1-2 cc.) one to three times per day.
Did You Know? The 'blackberry' of retail markets is actually the black raspberry (*rubus leucodermis* or *rubus villosus*)

Rauwolfia (rô·wol fē·e)
(*Rauwolfia serpentina*)

Synonyms/Related Species: Indian Snake Root, Lu-Fu-Mu, and Sarpagandha.
Family/Class: Apocynaceae (dogbane).
Habitat: Borneo, India, Indochina, Sri Lanka, and Sumatra.
Flavor: Bitter.
Parts Used: Root.
Properties: Antiphlogistic, carminative, hypotensive, sedative, tranquilizer, and vasodilator.
Constituents: Alkaloids, inulin (starch), reserpine, and yohimbine.
Historical Uses: Anxiety, arrhythmia, constipation, debility, diarrhea, edema, erectile dysfunction, fever (ephemeral, rheumatic), gastritis, gastrointestinal problems, hives, hypertension (mild/moderate), indigestion, inflammation, insect bites or stings, insomnia, irritable bowel syndrome (IBS), liver problems, malnutrition, mental disturbances, muscle and joint pain, nervous conditions, reptile bites, rheumatism, snakebite, and tachycardia.
Discussion: May cause blood vessel dilatation; reduce blood pressure levels.
Cautions/Contraindications: Avoid use if pregnant or breast-feeding, or if you have depression (severe). Do not consume alcohol while taking this herb. May enhance the effects of barbiturate and neuroleptic drugs. May exacerbate symptoms of Parkinson's disease. May increase blood pressure levels when taken with sympathomimetics (found in cough, influenza, or appetite suppressant drugs). Not for long-term use. Use with professional guidance/supervision.
Adverse Reactions: Ataxia, erectile dysfunction, lethargy, nausea, stupor, trembling, and/or vomiting.
Herb/Drug Interactions: This herb could cause an interaction (possibly severe) when taken with the following drugs: Amphetamine drugs, Antidepressant drugs, Anxiolytic drugs, Autonomic drugs, Beta-Adrenergic Blocking drugs, Cardiac drugs, Hypotensive drugs, and Selective Serotonin Reuptake Inhibitor (SSRI) drugs.
Herb/Herb Interactions: Do not use with Yohimbe (*pausinystalia yohimbe*).
Preparations/Dosage: Root (powdered): Average dose in substance 600 mg.
Isolation: Yohimbine hydrochlorate: Soluble in water. Average dose of $^{1}/_{12}$-$^{1}/_{10}$ grain (0.005-0.007 gm.) for use in erectile dysfunction and as a carminative.

Red Clover (red klō ver)
(*Trifolium pratense*)

Synonyms/Related Species: Alsike Clover (*trifolium hybridum*), Long-Stalked Clover (*trifolium longpipes*), Purple Clover, Trefoil, Trifolium, White Clover (*trifolium repens*), and Wild Clover.
Family/Class: Leguminosae (legume).
Floral Emblem: Vermont (red clover).
Habitat: The Arctic, Asia, Britain, Europe, Ireland, the Mediterranean, and North America.
Flavor: Sweet.

Parts Used: Flowers.
Properties: Alterative, antibiotic, anticarcinogen, antiphlogistic, antispasmodic, depurative, diuretic, expectorant, laxative, nervine, nutritive, sedative, stimulant, and tonic.
Constituents: Benzyl alcohol, coumarin, daidzein, formononetin, genistein, glycosides, linamarin, lotaustralin, minerals (calcium, cobalt, copper, iron, magnesium, manganese, nickel, selenium, sodium, tin), methyl anthranilate, methyl salicylate, phytoestrogen, protein, resin, vitamins (A, B_1 (thiamine), B_2 (riboflavin), B_3 (niacin), B_5 (pantothenic acid), B_6 (pyridoxine), B_{12}, B_x (para-aminobenzoic acid (PABA), C (ascorbic acid), H (biotin), M (folic acid), and volatile oil.
Historical Uses: Abscess, acne, appetite loss, arthritis, asthma, athlete's foot, bronchitis, burns (minor), cancer, colds, constipation, cough, croup, degenerative conditions, dietary supplementation, eczema, eyewash, fever (ephemeral, rheumatic, scarlet), gout, hepatitis, hot flashes, infection (bacterial), infertility, inflammation, influenza, laryngitis, leprosy, lesions (tubercle), liver problems, lung problems, malnutrition, mastitis, mononucleosis, mucus, muscle and joint pain, nerves, pellagra, pimples, psoriasis, rash, respiratory conditions, rheumatism, rickets, scarletina, scrofula, sexually transmitted diseases (STDs), skin problems, sores, spasmodic conditions, syphilis, tuberculosis, tumors, ulcer (duodenal, fistula, gastric, peptic, stasis, syphilitic, tuberculous), urinary problems, wheezing, whooping cough, and wounds (minor).
Discussion: May calm the nervous system; clear and open bronchial passages; decrease the effect of carcinogens; enhance cardiovascular system lung functions; increase circulation; inhibit or destroy developement and growth of bacteria and other microorganisms; maintain bone health after menopause and the elasticity of large arteries; promote bowel evacuation and urine flow; provide dietary supplementation; purify the blood; regulate estrogen; serve as a nutritional adjuvant to therapeutic programs; stimulate appetite, gallbladder, the immune system, liver, and peristalsis.
Cautions/Contraindications: Avoid use if pregnant, or if you have an abnormally low blood platelet count, a coagulation problem, an estrogen dependant cancer, a history of estrogen dependant cancers, fibroids (uterine), heart disease, stroke (apoplectic), if you have thromboembolism, or thrombophlebitis. May interfere with hormone replacement therapy (HRT) and oral contraceptives. Estrogen containing substances may contribute to abnormal blood clotting, migraine, and could promote the developement of certain types of estrogen dependant cancers. Some persons may experience bleeding or increased clotting time when using this herb with anticoagulant drugs or aspirin.
Adverse Reactions: Bleeding (possibly serious), coagulation problems, diarrhea, edema, nausea, and/or vomiting.
Herb/Drug Interactions: This herb could cause an interaction (possibly severe) when taken with the following drugs: Anticoagulant drugs, Hormones and Synthetic Substitutes (i.e. conjugated estrogens, contraceptives (oral, etc.), and other hormonal replacement therapy (HRT), Salicylates, and Subsalicylates.
Preparations/Dosage: Crude Herb: 6-12 grams. Extract: 2-10 drops (0.133-0.666 cc.) one to two times per day. Infusion: 1-2 cups per day. Tincture: 5-30 drops (0.333-2 cc.) one to three times per day.

Redroot (red root)
(*Ceanothus americanus*)

Synonyms/Related Species: Blue Blossom, California Lilac (*ceanothus thyrsiflorus*), Ceanothus, Fendler's Buckbrush (*ceanothus fendleri*), Jersey Tea, Mountain Sweet, Red-Stemmed Buckbrush (*ceanothus sanguineus*), Snowbrush (*ceanothus velutinus*), Tobacco Brush, Velvety Buckbrush, Walpole Tea, and Wild Snowball.
Family/Class: Rhamnaceae (buckthorn).
Habitat: North America.
Flavor: Bitter.
Parts Used: Bark (root).
Properties: Anticoagulant, antiphlogistic, antispasmodic, astringent, bitter, diuretic, expectorant, hemostatic, hypotensive, laxative, sedative, stimulant, and vasodilator.
Constituents: Alkaloids, ceanothyn, hydrocyanic acid, lignin, malic acid, oxalic acid, resin, saponins, succinic acid, tannic acid, and triterpenes.
Historical Uses: Acne, alopecia, asthma, bleeding, bronchitis, cancer (skin), chills, colds, congestion (uterine, vaginal), cough, cysts, depression (mild/moderate), diphtheria, fever, gargle/mouth rinse, glandular problems, glandular swelling, gleet, gonorrhea, hair rinse, hemorrhage (metrorrhagia), hemorrhoids, hypertension (mild/moderate), infection (sexually transmitted), inflammation, influenza, leukorrhea, liver problems, lung problems, melancholy, menorrhagia, mucus, nosebleed, pimples, respiratory conditions, sexually transmitted diseases (STDs), sinusitis, skin problems, sores, sore throat, spasmodic conditions, spleen problems, stomachache, substitute for black tea, syphilis, tonsillitis, ulcer (duodenal, gastric, peptic, syphilitic, syriac), urethritis, vaginitis, and whooping cough.
Discussion: May cause blood vessel dilatation; cleanse the whole system; clear and open bronchial passages; delay or reduce coagulation of the blood; enhance digestive system, glandular system, liver, lung, and spleen functions; increase assimilation, blood platelet counts, and circulation; promote bowel evacuation and urine flow; reduce blood pressure levels; stimulate hair growth and peristalsis.
Cautions/Contraindications: Avoid use if pregnant or breast-feeding, or if you are taking anticoagulants, or if you have a coagulation problem. Individuals who use large amounts of red root may want to have their coagulation time checked/monitored by their healthcare professional. Some persons may experience bleeding or increased clotting time when using this herb with anticoagulant drugs or aspirin.
Adverse Reactions: Bleeding (possibly serious), coagulation problems, diarrhea (possibly bloody), gastrointestinal cramps (severe), hematuria (blood in the urine), hydrocyanism (hydrocyanic acid poisoning), nausea, oxalism (oxalic acid or oxalate poisoning), and/or vomiting.
Herb/Drug Interactions: This herb could cause an interaction (possibly severe) when taken with the following drugs: Anticoagulant drugs, Hypotensive drugs, Salicylates, and Subsalicylates.
Preparations/Dosage: Crude Herb: 3-6 grams. Decoction: ¼-½ cup per day. Tincture: 5-20 drops (0.333-1.25 cc.) one to three times per day.
Isolation: Ceanothyn: Average dose of 1-2 grains (0.065-0.13 gm.) for use as a hemostatic.
Did You Know? This species contains an abundance of seeds, which after falling to the ground, can lie quietly beneath the soil for hundreds of years before a fire stimulates them to sprout.

Rehmannia (rë mā·ne·ah)
(*Rehmannia glutinosa*)

Synonyms/Related Species: Chinese Foxglove.
Family/Class: Scrophulariaceae (figwort).
Habitat: Asia and North America.
Flavor: Sweet.
Parts Used: Root.
Properties: Alterative, antiphlogistic, antiviral, astringent, demulcent, depurative, diuretic, hemostatic, laxative, tonic, vasodilator, and vulnerary.
Constituents: Amino acids (arginine), glycosides, mannitol (mannite), monosaccharides, resin, saponins, sterols, and tannic acid.
Historical Uses: Acquired immune deficiency syndrome (AIDS), amenorrhea, anemia, anorexia, arrhythmia, autoimmune disease, bleeding, canker sores, cardiovascular conditions, diabetes, dizziness, edema, emaciation, fatigue, fever, hematuria, hemorrhage (metrorrhagia), hot flashes, human immunodeficiency virus (HIV), infection (viral), infertility, inflammation, insomnia, kidney problems, lesions (tubercle), lochia, menopausal/menstrual problems, muscle and joint pain, nephritis, night sweats, nocturnal emission, proteinuria, scrofula, skin problems, sore throat, thirst, tuberculosis, and ulcer (fistula, tuberculous).
Discussion: May cause blood vessel dilatation; enhance kidney function; promote bowel evacuation and urine flow; protect the cardiovascular system, kidneys, liver, and white blood cells during chemotherapy treatments as well as protect the inner ear from chemical induced deafness; purify the blood; reduce nocturnal emisssion; restore normal tone to tissues; soothe mucous membrane irritation; speed healing; stimulate peristalsis.
Cautions/Contraindications: Avoid use if pregnant or breast-feeding, or if you are prone to indigestion, irritable bowel syndrome (IBS), or gastritis.
Adverse Reactions: Arrhythmia, diarrhea (possibly bloody), gastrointestinal cramps (severe), hematuria (blood in the urine), nausea, and/or vomiting.
Herb/Drug Interactions: This herb could cause an interaction (possibly severe) when taken with the following drugs: Cardiac drugs.
Herb/Herb Interactions: Do not use with Foxglove (*digitalis spp.*).
Preparations/Dosage: Crude Herb: 6-30 grams. Decoction: ½-1 cup per day.
Isolation: Mannitol hexanitrate: Average dose of 15-60 mg. for use as a vasodilator.

Rhatany (rat ah·ne)
(*Krameria triandra*)

Synonyms/Related Species: Brazilian Rhatany (*krameria argentea*), Krameria Root, Mapato, Peruvian Rhatany, Pumacuchu, Raiz Para Los Dientes, Ratanhia, Red Rhatany, Savanilla Rhatany (*krameria ixina*), Texas Rhatany (*krameria lanceolata*), and White Rhatany (*krameria grayi*).
Family/Class: Polygalaceae (milkwort).
Habitat: North America and South America.
Flavor: Sour/sweet.
Parts Used: Root.
Properties: Antibiotic, antiphlogistic, astringent, hemostatic, and tonic.

Constituents: Cyanidin (aglycon), gum, inulin (starch), krameric acid, lignin, polymeric, rhatanine (surinamine), and tannic acid

Historical Uses: Bleeding, congestion (uterine, vaginal), dentifrice, diarrhea, dysentery, enteritis, enuresis (urinary incontinence), fever (ephemeral, enteric), gargle/mouth rinse, gastritis, gastrointestinal problems, gleet, gonorrhea, hemorrhage, hemorrhoids, infection (bacterial, sexually transmitted), inflammation, leukorrhea, menorrhagia, periodontal disease, prolapse (rectal, uterine), sexually transmitted diseases (STDs), sore nipples, sore throat, sores, typhoid, ulcer (bouveret), urethritis, vaginitis, and wounds (minor).

Discussion: May inhibit or destroy development and growth of bacteria and other microorganisms; restore normal tone to tissues; soothe nipple soreness.

Cautions/Contraindications: Avoid use if pregnant or breast-feeding. Some persons may experience bleeding or increased clotting time when using this herb with anticoagulant drugs or aspirin.

Adverse Reactions: Bleeding (possibly serious), coagulation problems, hematuria (blood in the urine), mucous membrane irritation, nausea, and/or vomiting.

Herb/Drug Interactions: This herb could cause an interaction (possibly severe) when taken with the following drugs: Anticoagulant drugs, Salicylates, and Subsalicylates.

Preparations/Dosage: Crude Herb: 3-6 grams. Extract (powdered): Average dose in substance 5 grains (0.333 gm.). Infusion: ½-1 cup per day. Root (powdered): Average dose in substance 10-30 grains (0.666-2 gm.). Syrup: ½-4 drachms (2-16 cc.) per day in water. Tincture: 5-15 drops (0.333-1 cc.) one to three times per day.

Rhododendron (rō dō·den dren)

(*Rhododendron hirsutum*)

Synonyms/Related Species: Alpine Rose, Dwarf Rosebay, Great Rhododendron, Lapland Rosebay (*rhododendron lapponicum*), Rosebay Rhododendron, Snow Rose, Western Azalea (*rhododendron occidentale*), White Rhododendron (*rhododendron albiflorum*), and Yellow Rhododendron (*rhododendron chrysanthum*).

Family/Class: Ericaceae (heath).

Floral Emblem: Washington and West Virginia.

Habitat: Alaska, the Alpine and Subalpine zones, the Appalachian Mountains, Asia, Europe, North America, and Siberia.

Flavor: Bitter.

Parts Used: Leaves.

Properties: Antiphlogistic, diaphoretic, diuretic, emetic, hypnotic, narcotic, sialagogue, stimulant, and urinary antiseptic.

Constituents: Alkaloids, andromedotoxin, arbutin, and rhodotoxin.

Historical Uses: Fevers (ephemeral, rheumatic), gout, headache, inflammation, insomnia, muscle and joint pain, pain, rheumatism, sexually transmitted diseases (STDs), syphilis, tinnitus, and ulcer (syphilitic).

Discussion: May promote perspiration, saliva secretion, and urine flow; reduce tissue inflammation.

Cautions/Contraindications: Avoid use if pregnant or breast-feeding. Not for long-term use. Use with professional guidance/supervision.

Adverse Reactions: Abdominal cramps (severe), breathing difficulty, confusion, convulsions, dangerously high blood pressure levels, headache, nausea, paralysis, prickly sensation in the skin, respiratory center inhibition, runny nose, salivation (excessive), severe drop in blood pressure levels, slowed pulse rate, stupor, visual disturbances, and/or vomiting.
Herb/Drug Interactions: This herb could cause an interaction (possibly severe) when taken with the following drugs: None known.
Preparations/Dosage: Crude Herb: ½ -1 gram. Infusion: 1-2 teaspoons per day.
Isolation: Arbutin: Average dose of 5-15 grains (0.3-1 gm.) for use as a diuretic and urinary antiseptic.

Rhubarb (ru barb)
(*Rheum officinale*)

Synonyms/Related Species: Amlavetasa, China Rhubarb, East Indian Rhubarb, English Rhubarb, French Rhubarb (*rheum undulatum*), Garden Rhubarb (*rheum rhaponticum*), Himalayan Rhubarb (*rheum emodi*), Rha, Rheum, Russian Rhubarb, and Turkey Rhubarb (*rheum palmatum*).
Family/Class: Polygonaceae (buckwheat).
Habitat: Asia, China, England, the Himalayas, North America, Russia, Tibet, and Turkey.
Flavor: Sour/bitter.
Parts Used: Stems, root.
Properties: Alterative, anthelmintic, antibiotic, anticarcinogen, antiphlogistic, astringent, cholagogue, hemostatic, laxative, lithotriptic, sialogogue, stimulant, stomachic, tonic, vermifuge, and vulnerary.
Constituents: Aglycones, anthraquinone, chrysophanic acid (rumicin), emodin, flavonoids, gallic acid, glycosides, inulin (starch), minerals (calcium, chlorine, cobalt, iron, nickel, phosphorus, potassium, sodium, sulfur, tin), monosaccharides, oxalic acid, pectic acid, pectin, rhababerone, rutin, sterol, tannic acid, and vitamins (A, B_1 (thiamine), B_2 (riboflavin), B_3 (niacin), B_5 (pantothenic acid), B_6 (pyridoxine), B_{12}, B_x (para-aminobenzoic acid (PABA), C (ascorbic acid), H (biotin), M (folic acid).
Historical Uses: Abscess, acne, addiction (alcohol), amenorrhea, anemia, appetite loss, asthma, bleeding, calculus, cancer, cirrhosis, colitis, constipation, diarrhea, digestive complaints, dysentery, dysmenorrhea, eczema, fever, gallbladder problems, gallstones, gastritis, gastrointestinal problems, headache, hemafecia (blood in the stool), hemorrhoids, indigestion, infection (bacterial), inflammation, influenza, irritable bowel syndrome (IBS), jaundice, kidney stones, leukorrhea, liver problems, menstrual problems, neurasthenia, pain, parasites (pinworm), skin problems, thyroid problems, ulcer (duodenal), vaginitis, and weight loss.
Discussion: May aid digestion; decrease the effect of carcinogens; dissolve calculi; enhance intestinal system, liver, spleen, and stomach functions; increase circulation; inhibit or destroy developement and growth of bacteria and other microorganisms; prevent hemorrhage in persons with hypertension, and the progression of chronic kidney failure; promote bile flow, bowel evacuation, and saliva secretion; reduce capillary fragility; reestablish healthy system functions; restore normal tone to tissues; serve as an adjuvant in the early stages of diabetic kidney disease; speed healing; stimulate appetite, peristalisis, and uterine contractions.
Cautions/Contraindications: Avoid use if pregnant or breast-feeding, or if you have abdominal pain of unknown origin, appendicitis, enteritis, gout, or an obstruction (intestinal). Do not

administer to children under 12 years old. May cause electrolyte/potassium depletion. The leaves are poisonous. Not for long-term use.
Adverse Reactions: Abdominal pain, abnormally low levels of calcium, arrhythmia, bone deterioration, burning sensation in the mouth and throat, coma, confusion, convulsions, diarrhea (severe/possibly bloody), disruption in nervous system function, edema, electrolyte imbalance, headache, hematuria (blood in the urine), liver damage (often characterized by jaundice), muscle cramps and twitches, nausea, oxalism (oxalic acid or oxalate poisoning), salivation (increased), thyroid problems, and/or vomiting.
Herb/Drug Interactions: This herb could cause an interaction (possibly severe) when taken with the following drugs: Laxative drugs.
Preparations/Dosage: Crude Herb: 3-6 grams. Extract: 5-10 drops (0.333-0.666 cc.) one to two times per day. Extract (cold): ½-1 teaspoon per day. Extract (powdered): Average dose in substance 5-15 grains (0.333-1 gm.). Extract (solid): Average dose in substance 2-4 grains (0.133-0.26 gm.). Infusion: ¼-½ cup per day. Root (powdered): Average dose in substance 2-30 grains (0.133-2 gm.). Syrup: 1-4 drachms (4-16 cc.) per day in water. Tincture: 10-30 drops (0.666-2 cc.) one to three times per day.
Isolation: Chrysopahanic acid: Average dose of 1-10 grains (0.065-0.666 gm.) for use in skin problems.

Rice (rīs)

(*Oryza sativa*)

Synonyms/Related Species: Bras, Brown Rice, Dhan, Nivara, Oryza, Paddy, and Tikitiki.
Family/Class: Graminaceae (grass).
Habitat: Africa, Asia, China, India, Malaysia, North America, Spain, and Syria.
Flavor: Grain/Sprouts: bland to nutty. Root: sweet.
Parts Used: Grain, root, sprouts (sprouted rice grain).
Properties: Antigalactic, antiphlogistic, astringent, carminative, demulcent, hemostatic, nutritive, sedative, stomachic, and tonic.
Constituents: Albumin (albumen), amylase, carbohydrates, fatty acids (oleic, palmitic, stearic), fixed oils (olein, palmitin, stearin), gluten, inulin (starch), maltose, monosaccharides, oryzenin, minerals (iron, magnesium, phosphorus, potassium, sodium), prolamin, vitamins (A, B_1 (thiamine), B_2 (riboflavin), B_3 (niacin), B_6 (pyridoxine), C (ascorbic acid), D, E (alpha-tocopheral), and volatile oil.
Historical Uses: Allergy, appetite loss, belching, benign breast disease, bleeding, diarrhea, dietary supplementation, dysentery, ephidrosis, fever (ephemeral, rheumatic), gastrointestinal problems, gout, hepatitis, inflammation, malnutrition, muscle and joint pain, nausea, neuritis, night sweats, pain, rheumatism, and urinary problems.
Discussion: May aid digestion; diminish or suppress lactation; enhance intestinal system, pancreas, spleen, and stomach functions; provide dietary supplementation; restore normal tone to tissues; serve as a nutritional adjuvant to therapeutic programs; soothe mucous membrane irritation.
Cautions/Contraindications: Avoid excessive use if pregnant or breast-feeding, or if you have a weak digestive system.
Adverse Reactions: Edema, nausea, and/or vomiting.

Herb/Drug Interactions: This herb could cause an interaction (possibly severe) when taken with the following drugs: None known.
Preparations/Dosage: Crude Herb (grain/root): 9-30 grams. Crude Herb (sprouts): 10-60 grams. Grains: Boiled in water until cooked. Rice Flour (*oryzae farina*): Ground rice grains used as flour. Rice Water (*aqua oryzae*): ½-1 cup per day. Sprouts: 5-15 grams.
Did You Know? Brown rice and white rice come from the same grain. White rice is obtained when the outer brownish coating of brown rice is removed.

Rose (rōz)
(*Rosa canina*)

Synonyms/Related Species: Briar Rose, Burnet Rose (*rosa spinosissima*), Cabbage Rose (*rosa centifolia*), California Rose (*rosa californica*), Carolina Rose, Cherokee Rose (*rosa laevigata*), China Rose (*rosa roxburghii*), Damask Rose (*rosa damascena*), Dog Rose, Downy Rose (*rosa villosa*), Dwarf Rose, Eglantine Rose (*rosa eglanteria*), Field Rose (*rosa arvensis*), French Rose (*rosa gallica*), Hip Fruit, Musk Rose (*rosa muscatta*), Nootka Rose (*rosa nutkana*), Pale Rose (*rosa centifolia*), Pimpernel Rose, Prairie Rose (*rosa woodsii*), Prickly Rose (*rosa acicularis*), Red Rose (*rosa gallica*), Rodon, Rosa, Rosehip, Scotch Rose, Sweet Briar (*rosa rubiginosa*), Tea Rose (*rosa indica*), Wild Prairie Rose (*rosa woodsii*), Wild Rose, and Wood Rose (*rosa gymnocarpa*).
Family/Class: Rosaceae (rose).
Floral Emblem: Alberta Canada, Iowa, New York, and North Dakota.
Habitat: Alaska, Africa, Algiers, Asia, the Balkans, Bulgaria, the Caucasus, China, Cyprus, England, Europe, France, Germany, Greece, India, Ireland, Italy, Japan, Morocco, North America, Persia, Scotland, South America, the Subalpine zone, Turkey, and Wales.
Flavor: Petals: sweet. Hips: sour.
Parts Used: Hips (seeds removed), petals.
Properties: Anesthetic (local), anticarcinogen, antiphlogistic, antiscorbutic, aromatic, astringent, carminative, depurative, diuretic, emmenagogue, hemostatic, laxative, lithotriptic, nutritive, stimulant, stomachic, and tonic.
Constituents: Anthocyanins, citric acid, eugenol (eugenic acid), fatty acids (oleic, palmitic, stearic), fixed oils (olein, palmitin, stearin), flavones, flavonoids, gallic acid, gum, linalool, malic acid, minerals (calcium, iron, potassium, silicon, sodium, sulfur), monosaccharides, pectic acid, pectin, quercetin, quercitrin, rosein (fuchsin), rutin, saponins, silicic acid, tannic acid, terpene alcohol, vitamins (A, B_1 (thiamine), B_2 (riboflavin), B_3 (niacin), B_5 (pantothenic acid), B_6 (pyridoxine), B_{12}, B_x (para-aminobenzoic acid (PABA), C (ascorbic acid), D, E (alpha-tocopheral), H (biotin), K, M (folic acid), and volatile oil.
Historical Uses: Amenorrhea, appetite loss, arteriosclerosis, arthritis, bleeding, bruises, calculus, cancer, canker sores, chills, colds, congestion (uterine, vaginal), constipation, cramps, diarrhea, dietary supplementation, diuria (frequent daytime urination), dizziness, dysentery, earache, edema, emphysema, enuresis, eyewash, fever (ephemeral, rheumatic), gallstones, gout, headache, infection (urinary tract), inflammation, influenza, insect bites or stings, jaundice, kidney stones, leukorrhea, malnutrition, menstrual problems, mucus, muscle and joint pain, nervous conditions, pain, perfume, potpourri, psoriasis, rheumatism, sachets, sciatica, scurvy, sore throat, spermatorrhea, tea (leaves/root), vaginitis, and wounds (minor).

Discussion: May aid digestion; decrease the effect of carcinogens; dissolve calculi; enhance intestinal system, stomach, and urinary system functions; increase circulation; prevent hemorrhage in persons with hypertension; promote bowel evacuation and urine flow; provide dietary supplementation; purify the blood; reduce capillary fragility and the persistent urge to urinate; restore normal tone to tissues; serve as a nutritional adjuvant to therapeutic programs; stimulate appetite, menstruation, and peristalsis; strengthen the urinary system.
Cautions/Contraindications: Avoid use if pregnant or breast-feeding, or if you have a kidney disease.
Adverse Reactions: Diarrhea (possibly bloody), gastrointestinal cramps (severe), nausea, and/or vomiting.
Herb/Drug Interactions: This herb could cause an interaction (possibly severe) when taken with the following drugs: None known.
Preparations/Dosage: Crude Herb (petals): 1-6 grams. Crude Herb (hips): 3-12 grams. Candied Rose Petals (*confectio rosae*): Eat 3-6 petals or use them for a deliciously edible garnish on cakes. Extract: ½-2 drachms (1.85-8 cc.). Infusion (hips): 1 cup. Rose Water (*aquae rosae*): 1-2 ounces. Syrup (*syrupus rosae*): 1-2 drachms (4-8 cc.).

Rosemary (rōz ma·re)
(*Rosmarinus officinalis*)

Synonyms/Related Species: Common Rosemary, Compass Weed, Polar Plant, and Sea-Dew.
Family/Class: Labiatae (mint).
Habitat: Africa, Asia, Australia, France, the Mediterranean, Morocco, Portugal, Spain, and the United States.
Flavor: Pungent.
Parts Used: Leaves.
Properties: Analgesic, antibiotic, anticarcinogen, antifungal, antioxidant, antiperiodic, antiphlogistic, antispasmodic, aromatic, astringent, carminative, counterirritant, diaphoretic, hemostatic, malariacidal, narcotic, nervine, sedative, stimulant, stomachic, and tonic.
Constituents: Borneol, caffeic acid, camphene, camphor, carvene (limonene), cymene, eucalyptol (cineol), flavonoids, hesperidin, linalool, minerals (calcium, iron, magnesium, phosphorus, potassium, sodium, zinc), myrcene, pinene, quinone, resin, tannic acid, ursone (ursolic acid), verbenol, vitamins (A, C (ascorbic acid), and volatile oil.
Historical Uses: Ague, alopecia, Alzheimer's disease, appetite loss, arthritis, asthma, bleeding, bronchitis, bruises, cancer, candida, colds, congestion (uterine, vaginal), convulsions, cough, cramps, dandruff, depression (mild/moderate), digestive complaints, diphtheria, eczema, edema, eyewash, fever (ephemeral, intermittent, rheumatic), flatulence, flavoring agent, gallbladder problems, gargle/mouth rinse, gastritis, gastrointestinal problems, hair rinse (brunette hair shades), halitosis, headache, herbal tobacco, hypertension (mild/moderate), hypotension, hysteria, indigestion, infection (bacterial, fungal), inflammation, influenza, insect bites or stings, insomnia, insufficiency (venous), irritable bowel syndrome (IBS), leukorrhea, liver problems, malaria, memory/cognitive problems, menopausal/menstrual problems, migraine, moniliasis, muscle and joint pain, muscle strain, nausea, nervous conditions, pain, parasites (malarial plasmodia), perfume, potpourri, prostate problems, restlessness, rheumatism, sachets, sores, sore throat, spasmodic conditions, sprain, sciatica, ulcer (duodenal, gastric, peptic, stasis, syriac, varicose), urethritis, vaginitis, varicose veins, and wounds (minor).

Discussion: May aid digestion; balance blood pressure levels; calm the nervous system; decrease the effect of carcinogens; enhance cardiovascular system, circulatory system, gallbladder, intestinal system, liver, spleen, and stomach functions; improve cognition and memory; inhibit oxidation and inhibit or destroy developement and growth of bacteria and other microorganisms; promote perspiration; protect the liver; reduce cholesterol levels; restore normal tone to tissues; stimulate hair growth and peristalsis; stop or slow abnormal cell growth; strengthen the vascular system.
Cautions/Contraindications: Avoid use if pregnant or breast-feeding, or if you have a coagulation problem. Some persons may experience bleeding or increased clotting time when using this herb with anticoagulant drugs or aspirin.
Adverse Reactions: Bleeding (possibly serious), coagulation problems, coma, edema, gastroenteritis, hematuria (blood in the urine), hemorrhage (metrorrhagia), menorrhagia, kidney failure, nausea, spasmodic conditions, vomiting, and/or possible death.
Herb/Drug Interactions: This herb could cause an interaction (possibly severe) when taken with the following drugs: Anticoagulant drugs, Salicylates, and Subsalicylates.
Preparations/Dosage: Crude Herb: 3-6 grams. Infusion: ½-1 cup per day. Oil of Rosemary (*oleum rosmarini*): 1-2 drops (0.066-0.13 cc.) in water or on a sugarcube, or used topically. Tincture: 5-20 drops (0.333-1.25 cc.) one to three times per day. Herbal Tobacco: Combine rosemary and coltsfoot and smoke for relief of respiratory conditions.
Isolation: Camphor: Average dose of 2 grains (0.12 gm.) for use as a powerful irritant and stimulant, diaphoretic and narcotic. Camphor is toxic in overdoses and sedative in small doses. Eucalyptol: 5 drops (0.3 cc.) in atomization or inhalation therapy for use in respiratory conditions.
Did You Know? Approximately 100 pounds of rosemary are needed to obtain about 8 ounces of oil.

Rue (roo)

(*Ruta graveolens*)

Synonyms/Related Species: Common Rue, Garden Rue, German Rue, Herb of Grace, Rhytē, and Ruta.
Family/Class: Rutaceae (rue).
Habitat: The Alps, the Balkans, Europe, France, Italy, Spain, and North America.
Flavor: Bitter/pungent.
Parts Used: Leaves.
Properties: Abortifacient, anthelmintic, antibiotic, anticoagulant, antifungal, antiperiodic, antiphlogistic, antispasmodic, aphrodisiac, aromatic, counterirritant, emmenagogue, emetic, hallucinogen, hypotensive, insect repellent, laxative, malariacidal, narcotic, oxytocic, sedative, stimulant, stomachic, tonic, vasodilator, and vermifuge.
Constituents: Alkaloids, coumarin, dictamnine, eucalyptol (cineol), fatty acids (caprylic), flavones, flavonoids, harmaline, harmine, lignin, linalyl acetate, menthol, pectic acid, pectin, psoralen, ptelein, rutin, skimmianine, tannic acid, umbelliferone, vasicine, vitamins (choline), volatile oil, and xanthotoxin.
Historical Uses: Ague, amenorrhea, ancylostomiasis, angina, arteriosclerosis, arrhythmia, arthritis, asthma, bronchitis, bruises, chilblains, cirrhosis, colic, congestion (uterine, vaginal), contraceptive (male/female), convulsions, cough, cramps, croup, diarrhea, diphtheria,

dysmenorrhea, earache, encephalitis lethargica, epilepsy, eye problems, eyestrain, fever (ephemeral, enteric, intermittent, rheumatic), flatulence, fleas, gleet, gonorrhea, gout, headache, hepatitis, hypertension (mild/moderate), hysteria, indigestion, infection (bacterial, fungal, sexually transmitted), inflammation, insanity, insect bites or stings, insufficiency (circulatory, venous), jellyfish stings, leukorrhea, liver problems, malaria, menopausal/menstrual problems, muscle and joint pain, muscle strain, nervous conditions, neuralgia, nightmares, nosebleed, palsy (cerebral), parasites (hookworm, malarial plasmodia), parkinsonism, poisoning (non-caustic), rheumatism, rhinitis, sciatica, scorpion stings, sexually transmitted diseases (STDs), skin problems, small pox, snakebite, spasmodic conditions, sprain, tendonitis, toothache, typhoid, ulcer (bouveret, duodenal, gastric, peptic, stasis, syriac, varicose), urethritis, vaginitis, varicose veins, vertigo, whooping cough, and wounds (minor).

Discussion: May aid digestion; arouse sexual impulses; cause blood vessel dilatation, decrease capillary permeability; delay or reduce blood coagulation; enhance liver, nervous system, spleen, and stomach functions; increase ligament flexibility and metabolism; induce abortion; inhibit or destroy developement and growth of bacteria and other microorganisms; prevent the deposition of fat in the liver and hemorrhage in persons with hypertension; promote bowel evacuation; reduce blood pressure levels and capillary fragility; restore normal tone to tissues; serve as an antidote to non-caustic poisons; stimulate menstruation and uterine contractions; strengthen the bones, ocular (eye) muscles, teeth, and vascular system.

Cautions/Contraindications: Avoid use if pregnant or breast-feeding. Rue is a monoamine oxidase inhibitor (MAOI) herb. The combined use of sedative, tranquilizer, antihistamine, narcotic, or tricyclic antidepressant drugs will cause hypertensive crisis. The combined use of rue with amphetamines, cocaine, LSD, alcohol (including wine), avocados, unripe bananas, and dairy products (including aged cheese) will cause hypotensive crisis. It is recommended that no other drugs be used in combination with or within a ten-hour period of the use of rue. May prolong the action of epinephrine. May cause allergic reactions, dermatitis, photosensitivity, or photodermatosis in susceptible individuals. Some persons may experience bleeding or increased clotting time when using this herb with anticoagulant drugs or aspirin.

Adverse Reactions: Abdominal pain, bleeding (possibly serious), coagulation problems, confusion, debility, delirium, dependancy, depression, dizziness, exhaustion (extreme), fainting, hallucinations, hematuria (blood in the urine), hypotensive crisis (arrythmias, breathing difficulty, chills, and a severe drop in blood pressure levels), insomnia, liver damage (often characterized by jaundice), nausea, paralysis, spasmodic conditions, tremors, vertigo, vomiting, and/or possible death.

Herb/Drug Interactions: This herb could cause an interaction (possibly severe) when taken with the following drugs: Amphetamine drugs, Anticoagulant drugs, Antidepressant drugs, Antihistamine drugs, Anxiolytic drugs, Bronchodilator drugs, Cardiac drugs, Hypotensive drugs, Migraine drugs, Monamine Oxidase Inhibitors (MAOIs), Opiate Agonists/Narcotic drugs, Salicylates, Sedative drugs, Subsalicylates, and Tranquilizer drugs.

Preparations/Dosage: Crude Herb: 1-3 grams. Extract (cold): ¾ cup per day. Infusion: ½-1 cup per day. Leaves (powdered): Average dose in substance 15-30 grains (0.98-2 gm.). Oil of Rue (*oleum rutae*): 1-5 drops (0.066-0.333 cc.) per day in water or on a sugarcube. Tincture: 5-30 drops (0.333-2 cc.) one to three times per day.

Isolation: Eucalyptol: 5 drops (0.3 cc.) in atomization or inhalation therapy for use in respiratory conditions. Harmine: Average dose ⅓-⅔ grain (0.02-0.04 gm.) administered intramuscularly or subcutaneously for paralysis (cerebral) and parkinsonism. Menthol: Average dose of ½-2 grains (0.033-0.133 gm.) applied topically, for use as an analgesic.

Safflower (saf low·er)
(*Carthamus tinctorius*)

Synonyms/Related Species: American Saffron, Bastard Saffron, Carthamus, Dyer's Saffron, False Saffron, Flores Carthami, Hoang-tchi, Koosumbha, and Zaffer.
Family/Class: Compositae (composite).
Habitat: Africa, Asia, China, Egypt, Europe, India, Iran, the Mediterranean, and the United States.
Flavor: Pungent/bitter.
Parts Used: Flowers.
Properties: Abortifacient, analgesic, antibiotic, antilithic, carminative, diaphoretic, diuretic, emmenagogue, expectorant, febrifuge, laxative, lithotriptic, and stimulant.
Constituents: Carthamin, chalcones, fatty acids (arachidonic, linoleic, linolenic, oleic, palmitic, stearic), fixed oils (olein, palmitin, stearin), flavonoids, quinone, and vitamins A and K.
Historical Uses: Abdominal pain, abscess, amenorrhea, anemia, angina, arteriosclerosis, arthritis, bronchitis, bruises, calculus, cerebrovascular disease, chicken pox, colds, constipation, coronary artery disease (CAD), cough, delirium, diabetes, digestive complaints, diverticulitis, dysmenorrhea, edema, fever (ephemeral, scarlet), flatulence, gallbladder problems, gallstones, gastritis, gastrointestinal problems, gout, hypoglycemia, hysteria, indigestion, infection (bacterial), influenza, insufficiency (venous), irritable bowel syndrome (IBS), jaundice, kidney stones, lesions (tubercle), lithemia, liver problems, measles, menstrual problems, mucus, mumps, pain, poison ivy/oak, respiratory conditions, rheumatism, scarletina, scrofula, skin problems, substitute for saffron oil, thrombosis (blood clot), tuberculosis, ulcer (fistula, tuberculous), and urinary problems.
Discussion: May aid digestion; clear and open bronchial passages; dissolve blood clots and calculi; enhance cardiovascular system, liver, and spleen functions; increase circulation, energy, and endurance; induce abortion; prevent the development of calculus or stones; promote bowel evacuation, perspiration, and urine flow; protect against brain injury from lack of blood flow; reduce cholesterol levels and excessive lithic acid (uric acid) and urate levels in the blood, tophi, and urine; stimulate menstruation, peristalsis, and uterine contractions.
Cautions/Contraindications: Avoid use if pregnant or breast-feeding, or if you have menorrhagia. Do not confuse this herb with saffron (*crocus spp.*) or meadow saffron (*colchicum autumnale*). Some persons may experience bleeding or increased clotting time when using this herb with anticoagulant drugs or aspirin.
Adverse Reactions: Bleeding (possibly serious), coagulation problems, hemorrhage (metrorrhagia), nausea, and/or vomiting.
Herb/Drug Interactions: This herb could cause an interaction (possibly severe) when taken with the following drugs: Anticoagulant drugs, Salicylates, and Subsalicylates.
Preparations/Dosage: Crude Herb: 3-6 grams. Infusion: 1-2 cups per day. Tincture: 5-20 drops (0.3-1.3 cc.) one to three times per day.

Saffron (saf ron)
(*Crocus sativus*)

Synonyms/Related Species: Crocus, Greek Saffron (*crocus cartwrightianus*), Italian Saffron (*crocus orsinii*), Karcom, Krokus, Persian Saffron (*crocus hausknechtii*), Spanish Saffron, Tree Saffron, True Saffron, Wild Persian Crocus, and Wild Saffron (*crocus pallasii*).
Family/Class: Iridaceae (iris).
Habitat: Asia, the Balkans, China, France, Greece, India, Iran, Italy, the Mediterranean, Persia, and Spain.
Flavor: Bitter.
Parts Used: Stigmas.
Properties: Abortifacient, alterative, analgesic, antilithic, antiphlogistic, antispasmodic, aphrodisiac, aromatic, carminative, diaphoretic, emmenagogue, expectorant, laxative, lithotriptic, sedative, and stimulant.
Constituents: Bitter principles, crocin, glycosides, lactic acid, lycopene, minerals (calcium, phosphorous, potassium, sodium), phosphoric acid, picrocrocin, vitamins (A, B_{12}), and volatile oil.
Historical Uses: Anemia, appetite loss, arthritis, asthma, bronchitis, calculus, colds, colic, cough, depression (mild/moderate), digestive complaints, edema, erectile dysfunction, fever (ephemeral, rheumatic, scarlet), flatulence, flavoring agent, gallstones, gastritis, gastrointestinal problems, gout, headache, heart disease, hemorrhage (metrorrhagia), hyperglycemia, hypertrophy (spleen), hypoglycemia, hysteria, indigestion, infertility, inflammation, insomnia, irritable bowel syndrome (IBS), jaundice, kidney stones, lesions (tubercle), lithemia, measles, menopausal/menstrual problems, mucus, muscle and joint pain, neuralgia, pain, psoriasis, respiratory conditions, rheumatism, scarletina, scrofula, skin problems, spasmodic conditions, stomachache, tuberculosis, ulcer (duodenal, fistula, gastric, peptic, tuberculous), urinary problems, and whooping cough.
Discussion: May aid digestion; arouse sexual impulses; clear and open bronchial passages; dissolve calculi; enhance cardiovascular system, liver, respiratory system, and spleen functions; increase circulation; induce abortion; prevent the development of calculus or stones; promote bowel evacuation and perspiration; protect against heart disease; reduce cholesterol levels and excessive lithic acid (uric acid) and urate levels in the blood, tophi, and urine; reestablish healthy system functions; stimulate appetite, gastric acid secretions, menstruation, peristalsis, and uterine contractions.
Cautions/Contraindications: Avoid use if pregnant or breast-feeding. Do not confuse this herb with meadow saffron (*colchicum autumnale*) or safflower (*carthamus tinctorius*). Not for long-term use. Use with professional guidance/supervision.
Adverse Reactions: Bradycardia, diarrhea (possibly bloody), dizziness, edema, fainting, gastrointestinal cramps, hematuria (blood in the urine), hemorrhage (metrorrhagia, mucous membrane), liver damage (often characterized by jaundice), paralysis, stupor, vertigo, and/or vomiting.
Herb/Drug Interactions: This herb could cause an interaction (possibly severe) when taken with the following drugs: None known.
Preparations/Dosage: Stigmas (dried/powdered): Average dose in substance 10-30 grains (0.666-2 gm.). Tincture: 5-15 drops (0.333-1 cc.) one to three times per day.
Did You Know? It takes over 4,000 stigmas to make 1 ounce of saffron, and over 60,000 stigmas to produce 1 pound of saffron.

Saffron, Meadow (saf ron, med ō)
(*Colchicum autumnale*)

Synonyms/Related Species: Autumn Crocus, Colchicum, Naked Ladies, and Upstart.
Family/Class: Liliaceae (lily).
Habitat: Africa, Asia, England, Europe, and North America.
Flavor: Root: sweet/bitter/pungent. Seeds: bitter.
Parts Used: Bulb (corm), seeds.
Properties: Antimitotic, antiphlogistic, counterirritant, diaphoretic, diuretic, emetic, laxative, and sedative.
Constituents: Alkaloids, colchiceine, colchicine, fatty acids (oleic, palmitic, stearic), fixed oils (olein, palmitin, stearin), glycosides, and inulin (starch).
Historical Uses: Arthritis, fever (ephemeral, rheumatic), gout, inflammation, muscle and joint pain, pharyngitis, rheumatism, and tonsillitis.
Discussion: May inhibit mitosis (the division of active somatic and germ cells); promote bowel evacuation, perspiration, and urine flow; stimulate peristalsis.
Cautions/Contraindications: Avoid use if pregnant or breast-feeding. Do not administer to children. Do not confuse this herb with saffron (*crocus spp.*) or safflower (*carthamus tinctorius*). Not for long-term use. Use with professional guidance/supervision.
Adverse Reactions: Alopecia, burning sensation in the mouth and throat, circulatory collapse, depression, diarrhea, difficulty swallowing, gastrointestinal cramps (severe), hypotension, bone marrow damage, hematuria (blood in the urine), insufficiency (circulatory), kidney failure, liver damage (often characterized by jaundice), paralysis, nausea, respiratory failure, spasmodic conditions, vomiting, and/or possible death.
Herb/Drug Interactions: This herb could cause an interaction (possibly severe) when taken with the following drugs: Colchicine drugs.
Preparations/Dosage: Extract (powdered): Average dose in substance ¼-1 grain (0.015-0.066 gm.). Extract (root or seed): 1-10 drops (0.066-0.666 cc.). Extract (solid): Average dose in substance ⅛-¼ grain (0.008-0.015 gm.). Root (powdered): Average dose in substance 2-5 grains (0.133-0.324 gm.). Tincture: 5-15 drops (0.333-1 cc.) one to three times per day.
Isolation: Colchicine: Average dose of $^1/_{120}$-$^1/_{60}$ grain (0.5-1 mg.) for use in gout.

Sage (sāj)
(*Salvia officinalis*)

Synonyms/Related Species: Apple Bearing Sage (*salvia pomifera*), Asian Red Root Sage (*salvia miltiorrhiza*), Balsamic Sage (*salvia grandiflora*), Black Sage (*salvia mellifera*), Blue Sage, Broad-Leaved Sage, Chia (*salvia columbariae*), Cinnabar Root, Clary Sage (*salvia sclarea*), Common Sage, Crimson Sage, Cyprus Sage (*salvia cypria*), Gallitricum, Garden Clary, Garden Sage, Hardy Sage (*salvia glutinosa*), Horminum, Hummingbird Sage (*salvia spathacea*), Lyre-Leaved Sage (*salvia lyrata*), Meadow Sage (*salvia pratensis*), Muskateller Salbei, Narrow-Leaved White Sage, Oculus Christi, Purple Sage (*salvia dorrii*), Red Root Sage, Red Sage, Red-Topped Sage (*salvia horminum*), Salvia, Sauja, Sawge, Scarlet Sage, Simla Sage (*salvia hians*), Spanish Sage (*salvia candelabrum*), Texas Sage, Thistle Sage, Toute Bonne, True Sage, Vervain Sage (*salvia verbenaca*), White Sage (*salvia apiana*), and Wild Sage.
Family/Class: Labiatae (mint).

Habitat: Asia, Dalmatia, England, Europe, France, Germany, Holland, Italy, Manchuria, the Mediterranean, Mexico, Mongolia, North America, Spain, Switzerland, and Syria.
Flavor: Pungent.
Parts Used: Leaves.
Properties: Alterative, antibiotic, anticoagulant, antifungal, antigalactic, antihidrotic, antioxidant, antiperiodic, antiphlogistic, antisialic, antispasmodic, antiviral, aromatic, astringent, carminative, depurative, diaphoretic, emmenagogue, expectorant, hemostatic, lithotriptic, malariacidal, stimulant, and tonic.
Constituents: Borneol, caffeic acid, camphene, chlorogenic acid, eucalyptol (cineol), flavonoids, formic acid, linalool, luteolin, minerals (calcium, phosphorous, potassium, silicon, sodium, sulfur), mucilage, phosphoric acid, pinene, resin, salviol, silicic acid, sterols, tannic acid, thujone, ursone (ursolic acid), vitamins (A, B_1 (thiamine), B_2 (riboflavin), B_3 (niacin), B_5 (pantothenic acid), B_6 (pyridoxine), B_{12}, B_x (para-aminobenzoic acid (PABA), C (ascorbic acid), H (biotin), M (folic acid), and volatile oil.
Historical Uses: Abscess, addiction (alcohol), ague, alopecia, amenorrhea, angina, appetite loss, arteriosclerosis, arteriostenosis, arthritis, bleeding, bronchitis, calculus, candida, canker sores, chronic fatigue syndrome (CFS), cirrhosis, colds, congestion (lung, uterine, vaginal), coronary artery disease (CAD), cough, cramps, cystitis, dandruff, debility, dentifrice, depression (mild/moderate), diarrhea, digestive complaints, diphtheria, dizziness, dysentery, earache, enteritis, epilepsy, Epstein Barr Virus (EBV), erectile dysfunction, erysipelas, exhaustion, fainting, fever (ephemeral, herpetic, intermittent, rheumatic), fibroids (uterine), fibromyalgia, flatulence, flavoring agent, gargle/mouth rinse, gastritis, gastrointestinal problems, gleet, gonorrhea, hair rinse, headache, hemorrhage (metrorrhagia), hepatitis, herpes, hot flashes, indigestion, infection (bacterial, bladder, fungal, sexually transmitted, viral), inflammation, influenza, insect bites or stings, irritable bowel syndrome (IBS), laryngitis, leukorrhea, malaria, memory/cognitive problems, menorrhagia, menopausal/menstrual problems, moniliasis, mononucleosis (infectious), mucus, muscle and joint pain, nausea, nervous conditions, night sweats, oily hair, pain, palsy, paralysis, parasites (malarial plasmodia), perfume, periodontal disease, pharyngitis, phlebitis, poison ivy/oak, pruritus, psoriasis, rash, respiratory conditions, rheumatism, sexually transmitted diseases (STDs), sinusitis, skin problems, snakebite, sore throat, sores, spasmodic conditions, stomachache, stomatitis, syphilis, tonsillitis, ulcer (duodenal, gastric, peptic, syphilitic, syriac), urethritis, vaginitis, vertigo, warts (digitate, filiform, fugitive, glabra, mother, plana juvenilis, plantar, seborrhoeic, vulgaris), and wounds (minor).
Discussion: May aid digestion; balance blood pressure levels; clear and open bronchial passages; delay or reduce coagulation of the blood; diminish or suppress lacation and saliva secretion; dissolve calculi; enhance cardiovascular system, lung, nervous system, stomach, and thyroid functions; improve cognition and memory; increase circulation; inhibit oxidation and inhibit or destroy developement and growth of bacteria and other microorganisms; promote perspiration; protect the liver, nerve cells, and optic nerve from free radical damage; purify the blood; reduce alcohol absorption from the gastrointestinal tract, alcohol craving, blood sugar and cholesterol levels, the formation of scar tissue, obstruction (intestinal), and triglyceride levels; reestablish healthy system functions; restore normal tone to tissues; serve as an agent for controlling excessive alcohol consumption; stimulate appetite, estrogen production (with long-term use), hair growth, and menstruation.
Cautions/Contraindications: Avoid use if pregnant or breast-feeding, or if you have an estrogen dependant cancer, if you have a history of estrogen dependant cancers, or if you have epilepsy. Do not confuse this herb with wormwood (*artemisia absinthium*). Some persons may

experience bleeding or increased clotting time when using this herb with anticoagulant drugs or aspirin.
Adverse Reactions: Arrhythmia, bleeding (possibly serious), coagulation problems, convulsions, diarrhea (possibly bloody), dryness (mouth), edema, nausea, tachycardia, seizure conditions, vertigo, and/or vomiting.
Herb/Drug Interactions: This herb could cause an interaction (possibly severe) when taken with the following drugs: Anticoagulant drugs, Nonsteroidal Anti-inflammatory Drugs (NSAIDs), Salicylates, and Subsalicylates.
Preparations/Dosage: Crude Herb: 3-9 grams. Infusion: 1-3 cups per day. Leaves (powdered): Average dose in substance ¼-½ teaspoon. Tincture 10-30 drops (0.666-2 cc.) one to three times per day.
Isolation: Eucalyptol: 5 drops (0.3 cc.) in atomization or inhalation therapy for use in respiratory conditions.

Saint John's Wort (sānt jänz wurt)
(*Hypericum perforatum*)

Synonyms/Related Species: Goatweed, Hardhay, Hypericum, Klamath Weed, Large Saint John's Wort (*hypericum majus*), St. John's Wort, Tipton Weed, and Western St. John's Wort (*hypericum scouleri*).
Family/Class: Hypericaceae (saint john's wort).
Habitat: The Alpine to Subalpine zones, Africa, Asia, Britain, Europe, and North America.
Flavor: Bitter.
Parts Used: Aerial.
Properties: Alterative, antibiotic, anticarcinogen, antidepressant, antiphlogistic, antispasmodic, antiviral, aromatic, astringent, diuretic, expectorant, hemostatic, nervine, sedative, and vulnerary.
Constituents: Caffeic acid, caryophyllin, chlorogenic acid, flavonoids, hypericin, oligomeric procyanidines, pseudohypericin, quercetin, rutin, sesquiterpenes, undecane, volatile oil, and xanthone.
Historical Uses: Abscess, acquired immune deficiency syndrome (AIDS), allergy (pollen), anemia, anxiety, arthritis, autoimmune disease, bleeding, bronchitis, bruises, burns (minor), cancer (breast), carpal tunnel syndrome, chronic fatigue syndrome (CFS), chorea, colds, colic, cough, depression (mild/moderate), diabetes, diarrhea, digestive complaints, dysentery, dysmenorrhea, earache, ear infection, enuresis (urinary incontinence), epstein barr virus (EBV), fever (ephemeral, hay, herpetic, rheumatic), fibromyalgia, fibrositis, gastrointestinal problems, glandular problems, headache, hemorrhoids, hemorrhage, hepatitis, herpes, human immunodeficiency virus (HIV), hysteria, indigestion, infection (bacterial, viral), inflammation, insect bites or stings, insomnia, insufficiency (venous), irritable bowel syndrome (IBS), jaundice, laryngitis, lung problems, Lyme disease, lymphangitis, mastitis, melancholy, menopausal/menstrual problems, mood swings, mononucleosis (infectious), mucus, muscle and joint pain, muscle strain, nausea, nervous conditions, neuralgia, neuritis, pain, parasites (trypanosomes), respiratory conditions, rheumatism, sciatica, seizure conditions, sexually transmitted diseases (STDs), skeletal problems, skin problems, sores, spasmodic conditions, sprain, stomachache, trypanosomiasis, tumors, ulcer (duodenal, gastric, peptic, stasis, varicose), urinary problems, varicose veins, vitiligo, warts (digitate, filiform, fugitive, glabra, mother, plana juvenilis, plantar, seborrhoeic, vulgaris), and wounds (minor).

Discussion: May balance serotonin levels; calm the nervous system; clear and open bronchial passages; decrease the effect of carcinogens; ease withdrawal symptoms after tobacco smoking cessation; elevate mood; enhance colon, liver, lung, spleen, and stomach functions; increase circulation as well as the skin repigmentation effects with exposure to natural sunlight; inhibit or destroy developement and growth of bacteria and other microorganisms, and inhibit new virus particles from infecting other cells; prevent hemorrhage in persons with hypertension; promote urine flow; reduce capillary fragility, drug and toxin levels in the blood, and the frequency of nighttime urination; reestablish healthy system functions; serve a potential use as a blood transfusion additive, which could help to inactivate infective viruses; speed healing; stimulate the immune system; stop or slow abnormal cell growth; strengthen capillaries, blood vessles, urinary system, and veins.
Cautions/Contraindications: Avoid use if pregnant or breast-feeding. May decrease the effectiveness of anticoagulant, antipsychotic, chemotherapy, digoxin, contraceptives (oral), and theophylline drugs. May increase the effectiveness of sulfa drugs. May cause photosensitivity or photodermatosis in some individuals. Saint John's Wort acts like a monoamine oxidase inhibitor (MAOI). The combined use of this herb with sedative, tranquilizer, antihistamine, narcotic, or tricyclic antidepressant drugs will cause hypertensive crisis. The combined use of this herb with amphetamines, cocaine, LSD, alcohol (including wine) avocados, unripe bananas, and dairy products (including aged cheese) will cause hypotensive crisis. It is recommended that no other drugs be used in combination with or within a ten-hour period of the use of St. John's wort. May interfere with the absorption of prescription drugs. Some persons may experience bleeding or increased clotting time when using this herb with anticoagulant drugs or aspirin.
Adverse Reactions: Bleeding (possibly serious), cardiac failure, coagulation problems, hypertensive crisis (severe rise in blood pressure levels), hypotensive crisis (arrythmia, breathing difficulty, chills, and a severe drop in blood pressure levels), nausea, respiratory failure, stroke (apoplectic), and/or vomiting.
Herb/Drug Interactions: This herb could cause an interaction (possibly severe) when taken with the following drugs: Amphetamine drugs, Antibiotic drugs, Anticoagulant drugs, Antidepressant drugs, Antihistamine drugs, Antimanic drugs, Antipsychotic drugs, Antineoplastic drugs, Cardiac drugs, Hormones and Synthetic Substitutes (i.e. conjugated estrogens, contraceptives (oral, etc.), and other hormonal replacement therapy (HRT), Immune Suppressive drugs, Migraine drugs, Monoamine Oxidase Inhibitor (MAOI) drugs, Opiate Agonists/Narcotic drugs, Protease Inhibitor drugs, Salicylates, Sedative drugs, Selective Serotonin Reuptake Inhibitor (SSRI) drugs, Subsalicylates, Theophylline drugs, and Tranquilizer drugs.
Preparations/Dosage: Crude Herb: 3-9 grams. Infusion: ½-2 cups per day. St. John's Wort Oil: 10-15 drops (0.666-1 cc.) per day in water or on a sugarcube. Tincture: 10-20 drops (0.666-1.25 cc.) one to three times per day.

Sandalwood (san d'l·wood)
(*Santalum album*)

Synonyms/Related Species: Candana, Chandanam, Indian Sandalwood, Red Saunders (*santalum rubrum*), Sanderswood, Santalonwood, True Sandalwood, White Sandalwood, and Yellow Sandalwood.
Family/Class: Santalaceae (sandalwood).

Habitat: Asia, Australia, and India.
Flavor: Pungent.
Parts Used: Heartwood, oil.
Properties: Analgesic, anticarcinogen, antiphlogistic, aromatic, astringent, carminative, diuretic, expectorant, lithotriptic, and stomachic.
Constituents: Resin, santalin (santalinic acid), santalol, santene, santol, tannic acid, and volatile oil.
Historical Uses: Abdominal pain, angina, anxiety, bronchitis, calculus, cancer (skin), cold, coronary artery disease (CAD), cough, cystitis, depression (mild/moderate), diarrhea, dizziness, fever, gallbladder problems, gallstones, gleet, gonorrhea, hot flashes, incense, indigestion, infection (sexually transmitted, urinary tract), inflammation, liver problems, menopausal problems, nephritis, ozena, pain, perfume (oil), periodontal disease, prostatitis, respiratory conditions, sexually transmitted diseases (STDs), skin problems, stroke (heat), syphilis, ulcer (syphilitic), urethritis, vaginitis, and vomiting.
Discussion: May aid digestion; clear and open bronchial passages; decrease the effect of carcinogens; dissolve calculi; enhance liver, spleen, and stomach functions; increase glutathione activity; promote urine flow
Cautions/Contraindications: Avoid use if pregnant or breast-feeding, or if you have kidney disease. Some persons may experience bleeding or increased clotting time when using this herb with anticoagulant drugs or aspirin. Not for long-term use.
Adverse Reactions: Bleeding (possibly serious), coagulation problems, hematuria (blood in the urine), nausea, and/or vomiting.
Herb/Drug Interactions: This herb could cause an interaction (possibly severe) when taken with the following drugs: Anticoagulant drugs, Salicylates, and Subsalicylates.
Preparations/Dosage: Crude Herb (heartwood): ½-6 grams. Infusion (heartwood/cut pieces): 1-2 cups per day. Heartwood (powdered): Average dose in substance 15 grains (1 gm.). Sandalwood Oil (*oleum santali*): 10-30 drops (0.6-2 cc.) per day in water or on a sugarcube. Tincture: 20-30 drops (1.25-2 cc.) one to three times per day.
Isolation: Santalol: Average dose of 3 grains (0.2 gm.) for use as a urinary antiseptic.

Sarsaparilla (sar sap·e·ril e)
(*Smilax officinalis*)

Synonyms/Related Species: Brown Sarsaparilla, Caracao Sarsaparilla (*smilax papyracea*), Costa Rican Sarsaparilla, Ecuador Sarsaparilla (*smilax febrifuga*), Gray Sarsaparilla, Greenbriar (*smilax aristolochiifolia*), Guatamala Sarsaparilla (*smilax spruceana*), Guayaquil Sarsaparilla, Honduran Sarsaparilla (*smilax regelii*), Jamaican Sarsaparilla (*smilax ornata*), Mexico Sarsaparilla (*smilax mexicana*), Parilla Vine, Red Sarsaparilla, Sacra Briar, Spanish Sarsaparilla, Vera Cruz Sarsaparilla, and Zarzaparilla.
Family/Class: Smilacaceae (sarsaparilla).
Habitat: Asia, Central America, Europe, India, North America, and South America.
Flavor: Sweet/pungent.
Parts Used: Root.
Properties: Alterative, antibiotic, antilithic, antiphlogistic, aphrodisiac, aromatic, demulcent, depurative, diaphoretic, diuretic, laxative, lithotriptic, parasiticide, stimulant, stomachic, and tonic.

Constituents: Aglycones, glycosides, inulin (starch), minerals (calcium, copper, iodine, iron, manganese, silicon, sodium, sulfur, zinc), monosaccharides, parillin, progesterone, resin, saponins, sarsasaparilloside, sarsapogenin, silicic acid, smilacin, sterols, testosterone, vitamins (A, B_1 (thiamine), B_2 (riboflavin), B_3 (niacin), B_5 (pantothenic acid), B_6 (pyridoxine), B_{12}, B_x (para-aminobenzoic acid (PABA), C (ascorbic acid), D, H (biotin), M (folic acid), and volatile oil.

Historical Uses: Abscess, age spots, anemia, appetite loss, arthritis, bodybuilding, calculus, colds, congestion (uterine, vaginal), conjunctivitis, constipation, debility, digestive complaints, diminished sex drive, eczema, edema, epilepsy, erectile dysfunction, eyewash, fever (ephemeral, herpetic, rheumatic), flavoring agent, flatulence, frigidity, gallstones, gastritis, gastrointestinal problems, glandular problems, gleet, gonorrhea, gout, hepatitis, herpes, hormonal imbalances, indigestion, infection (bacterial, sexually transmitted), inflammation, jaundice, kidney problems, kidney stones, leprosy, lesions (tubercle), leukorrhea, lithemia, liver problems, Lyme disease, menopausal problems, muscle and joint pain, parasites (ringworm), poisoning (mercury), pruritus, psoriasis, respiratory conditions, rheumatism, scrofula, sexually transmitted diseases (STDs), skin problems, sores, syphilis, toothache, tuberculosis, ulcer (fistula, syphilitic, tuberculous), urethritis, urinary problems, vaginitis, and wounds (minor).

Discussion: May arouse sexual impulses; bind and remove endotoxins from the bowel; dissolve calculi; enhance glandular system, kidney, liver, and stomach functions; increase circulation and muscle mass; prevent the development of calculus or stones; promote bowel evacuation, perspiration, and urine flow; purify the blood; reduce excessive lithic acid (uric acid) and urate levels in the blood, tophi, and urine; reestablish healthy system functions; restore normal tone to tissues; serve as an alternative to anabolic steroids; slow the heart's action; soothe mucous membrane irritation; stimulate appetite, hair growth, metabolism, and peristalsis.

Cautions/Contraindications: Avoid use if pregnant or breast-feeding, or if you have a prostate problem, or an iodine sensitivity, or if you are taking prescription drugs on a daily basis. Do not confuse this plant with wild sarsaparilla (*aralia nudicaulis*). May increase the absorption and/or excretion of prescription drugs. May interfere with the effectiveness of certain thyroid medications.

Adverse Reactions: Abdominal pain, arrhythmia, diarrhea, edema, fever, gastrointestinal irritation, hypertrophy (thyroid), iodism (iodine poisoning), nausea, priapism, thirst, and/or vomiting.

Herb/Drug Interactions: This herb could cause an interaction (possibly severe) when taken with the following drugs: Thyroid drugs.

Preparations/Dosage: Crude Herb: 3-12 grams. Decoction: 1-2 cups per day. Syrup: 1-4 drachms (4-16 cc.) per day in water. Tincture: 10-20 drops (0.666-1.25 cc.) one to three times per day.

Sassafras (sas e·fras)

(*Sassafras officinalis*)

Synonyms/Related Species: Ague Tree, Cinnamon Wood (*sassafras albidum*), North American Sassafras (*sassafras variifolia*), and Saxafrax.

Family/Class: Lauraceae (laurel).

Habitat: North America and Taiwan.

Flavor: Pungent.

Parts Used: Bark (root), stem (pith).
Properties: Abortifacient, alterative, analgesic, antibiotic, antinarcotic, antiphlogistic, aromatic, carminative, demulcent, depurative, diaphoretic, diuretic, sedative, stimulant, and tonic.
Constituents: Albumin (albumen), alkaloids, camphor, gum, inulin (starch), lignin, mucilage, pinene, resin, safrene, safrol, tannic acid, volatile oil, and wax.
Historical Uses: Abscess, addiction (narcotic), acne, arthritis, bladder problems, bronchitis, colds, colic, diarrhea, edema, eye problems, fever (ephemeral, rheumatic), flavoring agent, flatulence, gleet, gonorrhea, gout, infection (bacterial, sexually transmitted, urinary tract), inflammation, influenza, insufficiency (venous), kidney problems, muscle and joint pain, pain, poison ivy/oak, psoriasis, respiratory conditions, rheumatism, sexually transmitted diseases (STDs), skin problems, spasmodic conditions, stomach cramps, syphilis, toothache, ulcer (duodenal, gastric, peptic, stasis, syphilitic, varicose), urethritis, varicose veins, and weight loss.
Discussion: May aid digestion; enhance kidney and lung functions; induce abortion; inhibit or destroy development and growth of bacteria and other microorganisms; promote perspiration and urine flow; purify the blood and liver; reestablish healthy system functions; restore normal tone to tissues; serve as an adjuvant to narcotism (addiction to narcotics); soothe mucous membrane irritation.
Cautions/Contraindications: Avoid use if pregnant or breast-feeding.
Adverse Reactions: Dizziness, fainting, fatty degeneration of the heart/liver/kidneys, circulatory depression, nausea, pupil dilatation, respiratory failure, stupor, vomiting, and/or possible death.
Herb/Drug Interactions: This herb could cause an interaction (possibly severe) when taken with the following drugs: None known.
Preparations/Dosage: Crude Herb: 3-6 grams. Decoction (bark): ¼-½ cup per day. Extract: 10-15 drops (0.666-1 cc.). Infusion (bark): 1 cup per day. Oil of Sassafras (*oleum sassafras*): 1-5 drops (0.066-0.333 cc.) in water or on a sugarcube. Sassafras Stem Pith (*mucilago sassafras medullae*): Add 60 grains of pith to one pint of boiling water. Take ½-1 cup per day for use as a demulcent in bronchial conditions and gastric problems. Tincture: 15-30 drops (1-2 cc.) one to three times per day.
Isolation: Safrol: Average dose of 20-30 drops (1.333-2 cc.) for use as an analgesic.

Savory (sā ver·ē)
(*Satureja officinalis*)

Synonyms/Related Species: Bean Herb, Bohnenkraut, Bwa nah, Culinary Herb, Satureja, Spanish Savory (*satureja thymbra*), Summer Savory (*satureja hortensis*), Vine Mint (*satureja chamissonis*), Winter Savory (*satureja montana*), and Yerba Buena (*satureja douglasii*).
Family/Class: Labiatae (mint).
Habitat: Africa, England, Europe, France, Greece, India, the Mediterranean, and Spain.
Flavor: Pungent/bitter.
Parts Used: Leaves.
Properties: Antibiotic, antiphlogistic, antispasmodic, aphrodisiac, aromatic, astringent, carminative, diaphoretic, diuretic, emmenagogue, expectorant, hemostatic, stimulant, and stomachic.
Constituents: Caryophyllin, carvacrol, cymene, minerals (potassium), pinene, tannic acid, thymol, and volatile oil.

Historical Uses: Appetite loss, bleeding, colds, colic, cramps, diarrhea, ear problems, fever (ephemeral, rheumatic), flatulence, flavoring agent, gargle/mouth rinse, gas, gastroenteritis, gastrointestinal problems, indigestion, infection (bacterial), inflammation, influenza, insect bites or stings, insomnia, kidney problems, mucus, nausea, respiratory conditions, rheumatism, and spasmodic conditions.
Discussion: May aid digestion; arouse sexual impulses; clear and open bronchial passages; enhance bladder, liver, lung, and stomach functions; inhibit or destroy development and growth of bacteria and other microorganisms; promote perspiration and urine flow; soothe mucous membrane irritation; stimulate appetite and menstruation; strengthen the blood.
Cautions/Contraindications: Avoid use if pregnant or breast-feeding.
Adverse Reactions: Nausea and/or vomiting.
Herb/Drug Interactions: This herb could cause an interaction (possibly severe) when taken with the following drugs: None known.
Preparations/Dosage: Crude Herb: 3-9 grams. Extract: 5-10 drops (0.333-0.666 cc.) one to two times per day. Infusion: 1-2 cups per day. Tincture: 10-30 drops (0.666-2 cc.) one to three times per day.

Saw Palmetto (sô pal·met ō)

(*Serenoa serrulata*)

Synonyms/Related Species: Dwarf Palmetto (*serenoa repens*), Fan Palm, Palmito, Sabal Palm (*serenoa sabal-palmetto*), Sarenoa, and Serenoa.
Family/Class: Palmaceae (palm).
Habitat: India and the United States (primarily Florida).
Flavor: Pungent/sweet.
Parts Used: Berry.
Properties: Anticarcinogen, anti-inflammatory, aphrodisiac, demulcent, diuretic, expectorant, laxative, sedative, and tonic.
Constituents: Fatty acids (arachidonic, capric, caprylic, linoleic, linolenic, oleic, palmitic, stearic), fixed oils (olein, palmitin, stearin), flavonoids, lauric acid, monosaccharides, phytoestrogen, polysaccharides, quercetin, sterol, resin, tannic acid, vitamin A, and volatile oil.
Historical Uses: Appetite loss, acquired immune deficiency syndrome (AIDS), arthritis, asthma, atrophy (testicular), bladder problems, bodybuilding, bronchitis, cancer (prostate), colds, convalesence, cystitis, diabetes, digestive complaints, emaciation, enuresis (urinary incontinence), erectile dysfunction, frigidity, hirsutism, human immunodeficiency virus (HIV), hormonal imbalances, hypertrophy (benign prostatic), inflammation, infection (urinary tract), infertility, influenza, kidney problems, mastitis, menstrual problems, mucus, nephritis, nervous conditions, neuralgia, pain, prostate problems, prostatitis, respiratory conditions, sore throat, urethritis, urinary problems, and whooping cough.
Discussion: May arouse sexual impulses; balance the hormonal system; clear and open bronchial passages; decrease the effect of carcinogens; enhance glandular system, kidney, liver, reproductive system, spleen, and immune system functions; increase endurance, energy, female fertility, male libido, muscle mass, strength, and stamina; promote bowel evacuation and urine flow; reduce the frequency of nighttime urination as well as excessive hair growth in women without reducing estrogen or testosterone levels; restore normal tone to tissues; soothe mucous

membrane irritation; stimulate appetite, the deposit of proteins into the muscle tissue, and peristalsis; strengthen the male reproductive system.
Cautions/Contraindications: Avoid use if pregnant or breast-feeding, or if seeking to become pregnant, or if you have an estrogen dependant cancer, or if you have a history of estrogen dependant cancers, or if taking hormonal replacement drugs or contraceptives (oral). Estrogen containing substances may contribute to abnormal blood clotting, migraine, and could promote the developement of certain types of estrogen dependant cancers.
Adverse Reactions: Diarrhea, nausea, and/or vomiting.
Herb/Drug Interactions: Hormones and Synthetic Substitutes (i.e. conjugated estrogens, contraceptives (oral, etc.), and other hormonal replacement therapy (HRT).
Preparations/Dosage: Crude Herb: 3-9 grams. Berry (powdered): Average dose in substance 15 grains (1 gm.). Extract: 10-15 drops (0.666-1 cc.) one to two times per day. Infusion: 1-2 cups per day. Tincture: 30-60 drops (2-4 cc.) one to three times per day.

Schizandra (skiz'zen·drô)
(*Schizandra chinensis*)

Synonyms/Related Species: Five Flavored Fruit, Gome-si (*schizandra nigra*), and Magnolia Vine (*schizandra sinensis*).
Family/Class: Magnoliaceae (magnolia).
Habitat: Asia, China, Japan, and the United States.
Flavor: Sweet/sour.
Parts Used: Berry.
Properties: Alterative, anticarcinogen, antihidrotic, anti-inflammatory, astringent, hemostatic, sedative, tonic, and vulnerary.
Constituents: Citral (geranial), gomisin, lignin, minerals (calcium, iron, magnesium, manganese, phosphorus, potassium, selenium, silicon, sodium), schizandrin, schizoandrol, sesquicarene, sterol, and vitamins (C (ascorbic acid), E (tocopherol).
Historical Uses: Acquired immune deficiency syndrome (AIDS), arrhythmia, arteriosclerosis, asthma, bleeding, cancer (skin), cirrhosis, coronary artery disease (CAD), cough, depression (mild/moderate), diabetes, diarrhea, digestive complaints, dizziness, emaciation, fatigue, gastritis, headache, hepatitis, human immunodeficiency virus (HIV), hypercholesteremia, infection, inflammation, insomnia, kidney problems, lesions (tubercle), liver problems, lung problems, motion sickness, nervous conditions, neurasthenia, night sweats, nocturnal emission, poisoning (morphine, radiation), restlessness, scrofula, thirst, tuberculosis, ulcer (fistula, tuberculous), uterine problems, visual disturbances, and wheezing.
Discussion: May balance blood pressure and blood sugar levels; decrease the effect of carcinogens; diminish perspiration; enhance cardiovascular system, glandular system, kidney, lung, nervous system, and immune system functions; improve cognition, mental acuity, and visual acuity; increase endurance, energy, and stamina; offset the negative effects of chemotherapy and radiation therapy; reduce glutamic acid and liver enzyme levels in persons with hepatitis; protect against harmful free radicals and stroke (apoplectic); reduce the emission of semen during sleep; reestablish healthy system functions; restore normal tone to tissues; serve as an antidote to morphine drug overdose and radiation poisoning; speed healing; stimulate liver cell regeneration and peristalsis.

Cautions/Contraindications: Avoid use if pregnant or breast-feeding, or if you have acidity (gastric), epilepsy, gallstones, hypertension (mild/moderate), intracranial pressure, obstruction (biliary), or ulcer (peptic). May increase the effectiveness of benzodiazepine and barbiturate drugs.
Adverse Reactions: Edema, nausea, and/or vomiting.
Herb/Drug Interactions: This herb could cause an interaction (possibly severe) when taken with the following drugs: Acetaminophen, Anxiolytic drugs, and Sedative drugs.
Preparations/Dosage: Crude Herb: 3-6 grams. Decoction: ¼-1 cup per day.

Scotch Broom (skäch broom)
(*Cytisus scoparius*)

Synonyms/Related Species: Basam, Besom, Bisom, Bizzom, Breeam, Broom, Brum, Green Broom, Irish Broom, Laburnum Tree (*cytisus laburnum*), Scocchen Brom, Scopa, and True Broom.
Family/Class: Leguminosae (legume).
Habitat: Africa, Asia, the Canary Islands, Chile, England, Europe, North America, Japan, and Scotland.
Flavor: Bitter.
Parts Used: Flower tops.
Properties: Abortifacient, antiphlogistic, cardiant, depurative, diuretic, emetic, hallucinogen, hemostatic, hypertensive, laxative, lithotriptic, oxytocic, stimulant, and vasoconstrictor.
Constituents: Albumin (albumen), alkaloids, bitter principle, chlorophyll, cytisine, flavonoids, lignin, monosaccharides, mucilage, oxytyramine, scoparin, sparteine, tannic acid, volatile oil, and wax.
Historical Uses: Ague, arrhythmia, cardiovascular conditions, edema, fever (ephemeral, rheumatic), gallstones, gout, hemophilia, hemorrhage, herbal tobacco, hypotension, inflammation, insufficiency (circulatory), jaundice, kidney stones, liver problems, lochia, menorrhagia, muscle and joint pain, periodontal disease, rheumatism, sciatica, spleen problems, tachycardia, and urinary calculus.
Discussion: May cause blood vessel constriction; dissolve calculi; elevate blood pressure levels; enhance circulatory system, colon, and kidney functions; improve action of the heart; induce abortion; promote bowel evacuation and urine flow; purify the blood; stimulate the cardiovascular system, peristalsis, and uterine contractions.
Cautions/Contraindications: Avoid use if pregnant or breast-feeding, or with atrioventricular blocks, or if you have hypertension, hypertrophy (benign prostatic), or nephritis. Do not confuse this herb with California broom (*lotus scoparius*) or Spanish broom (*spartium junceum*). Not for long-term use. Use with professional guidance/supervision.
Adverse Reactions: Arrhythmia, bradycardia, cardiac failure, diarrhea, gastrointestinal problems, hypotension, reduced nerve strength, respiratory failure, vomiting, and/or possible death.
Herb/Drug Interactions: This herb could cause an interaction (possibly severe) when taken with the following drugs: Bronchodilator drugs, Cardiac drugs, and Monoamine Oxidase Inhibitor (MAOI) drugs.
Preparations/Dosage: Crude Herb: 3-6 grams. Infusion: ½-2 cups per day. Juice (*succus scoparii*): 1-2 drachms (4-8 cc.) per day in water. Tincture: 1-10 drops (0.066-0.666 cc.) one to three times per day.

Isolation: Sparteine sulfate: Average dose of ½ grain (30 mg.) for use as a cardiant, diuretic, and stimulant. Sparteine's action is similar to that of digitalis.
Note: Spanish broom (*spartium junceum*) possesses actions similar to that of scotch broom, but to a much greater degree.

Self Heal (self hēl)
(*Prunella vulgaris*)

Synonyms/Related Species: Blue Curls, Brownwort, Brunella, Carpenter's Herb, Heal-All, Hercules Wound Wort, Panay, Prunella, Sickle Wort, Woundwort, and Wundwort.
Family/Class: Labiatae (mint).
Habitat: Asia, Britain, England, Europe, and North America.
Flavor: Pungent/bitter.
Parts Used: Aerial.
Properties: Alterative, antibiotic, anticarcinogen, antifungal, antioxidant, antiphlogistic, antispasmodic, antiviral, astringent, diaphoretic, diuretic, hemostatic, hypotensive, stimulant, tonic, vasodilator, and vulnerary.
Constituents: Bitter principle, cellulose, flavonoids, monosaccharides, rutin, saponins, tannic acid, ursone (ursolic acid), vitamins (B_1 (thiamine), C (ascorbic acid), K), volatile oil.
Historical Uses: Abscess, acne, acquired immune deficiency syndrome (AIDS), angina, arrhythmia, arteriosclerosis, bleeding, bruises, burns (minor), cancer, candida, cardiovascular conditions, colds, conjunctivitis, convulsions, cough, diabetes, diarrhea, digestive complaints, dizziness, dysentery, edema, eyewash, fever, flatulence, gargle/mouth rinse, gastroenteritis, glandular swelling, gout, headache, hemorrhage, hemorrhoids, hepatitis, herpes, herpetic keratitis, human immunodeficiency virus (HIV), hypertension (mild/moderate), indigestion, infection (bacterial, fungal, viral), inflammation, insect bites or stings, jaundice, laryngitis, menorrhagia, menstrual problems, moniliasis, muscle and joint pain, nausea, periodontal disease, pharyngitis, sexually transmitted diseases (STDs), shingles, shortness of breath, skin problems, sore throat, sores, spasmodic conditions, stomatitis, tumors, ulcer (duodenal, gastric, peptic), vomiting, and wounds (minor).
Discussion: May block cell-to-cell transmission of the HIV virus and prevent it from binding to T-cells; cause blood vessel dilatation; decrease the effect of carcinogens; enhance cardiovascular system, gallbladder, and liver functions; inhibit oxidation and inhibit or destroy developement and growth of bacteria and other microorganisms; prevent hemorrhage in persons with hypertension; promote perspiration and urine flow; reduce blood pressure levels, capillary fragility, congestion (lymphatic), and scarring; reestablish healthy system functions; restore normal tone to tissues; soothe mucous membrane irritation; speed healing; stimulate peristalsis.
Cautions/Contraindications: Avoid use if pregnant or breast-feeding, or if you have chronic diarrhea, nausea, stomachache, or vomiting. May interfere with anticoagulant drug absorption. Some persons may experience bleeding or increased clotting time when using this herb with anticoagulant drugs or aspirin.
Adverse Reactions: Bleeding (possibly serious), coagulation problems, diarrhea (possibly bloody), gastrointestinal cramps (severe), hematuria (blood in the urine), hypotension, nausea, and/or vomiting.

Herb/Drug Interactions: This herb could cause an interaction (possibly severe) when taken with the following drugs: Anticoagulant drugs, Hypotensive drugs, Salicylates, and Subsalicylates.
Preparations/Dosage: Crude Herb: 3-9 grams. Infusion: 1-2 cups per day.

Senega (sen e·gah)
(*Polygala senega*)

Synonyms/Related Species: Chinese Senega Root (*polygala tenuifolia*), Horned Milkwort (*polygala cornuta*), Mountain Flax, North American Seneca Snakeroot, Polygala, Seneca Snakeroot, Seneka, and Sierra Milkwort.
Family/Class: Polygalaceae (milkwort).
Habitat: North America.
Flavor: Bitter/pungent.
Parts Used: Root.
Properties: Antiphlogistic, diaphoretic, diuretic, emmenagogue, emetic, expectorant, hypoglycemic, laxative, sedative, stimulant, and tonic.
Constituents: Albumin (albumen), cerotinic acid (cerin), fatty acids (oleic, palmitic, stearic), fixed oils (olein, palmitin, stearin), glycosides, gum, minerals (aluminum, iron, lead, magnesium, silicon, tin), polygalin (polygalic acid), senegin, silicic acid, and tannic acid.
Historical Uses: Anxiety, arrhythmia, asthma, bronchitis, colds, cough, croup, depression (mild/moderate), edema, fever (ephemeral, rheumatic, septic), gout, hangover (caused by alcohol consumption), hives, inflammation, insomnia, laryngitis, mental disturbances, mucus, muscle and joint pain, pleurisy, pneumonia, poisoning (blood, non-caustic), respiratory conditions, restlessness, rheumatism, small pox, snakebite, and whooping cough.
Discussion: May clear and open bronchial passages; enhance cardiovascular system, kidney, and lung functions; offset the negative effects of pharmaceutical drugs; prevent alcohol intoxication; promote bowel evacuation, perspiration, and urine flow; restore normal tone to tissues; serve as an antidote for non-caustic poisons; stimulate menstruation, peristalsis, and uterine contractions.
Cautions/Contraindications: Avoid use if pregnant or breast-feeding, or if you have gastritis, a seizure condition, or ulcer.
Adverse Reactions: Depression (possibly severe), diarrhea (possibly bloody), esophageal constriction, gastrointestinal cramps, nausea, respiratory failure, sneezing, vertigo, visual disturbances, and/or vomiting.
Herb/Drug Interactions: This herb could cause an interaction (possibly severe) when taken with the following drugs: None known.
Preparations/Dosage: Crude Herb: 3-6 grams. Extract: 3-5 drops (0.2-0.333 cc.) one to two times per day. Infusion: ½-1 cup per day. Root (powdered): Average dose in substance 6-12 grains (0.4-0.8 gm.). Syrup: 1 drachm (4 cc.) in water per day. Tincture: 5-8 drops (0.333-0.5 cc.) one to three times per day.

Senna (sen e)
(*Cassia acutifolia*)

Synonyms/Related Species: Alexandrian Senna, American Senna (*cassia marilandica*), Cassia Stick Tree, Dwarf Cassia, Egyptian Senna (*cassia obtusa*), Indian Senna (*cassia angustifolia*), Jamaica Senna, Locust Plant, Mecca Senna, Nubian Senna (*cassia ethiopica*), Port Royal Senna,

Prairie Senna (*cassia chamoecrista*), Pudding Pipe Tree, Purging Cassia (*cassia fistula*), Tinnevelly Senna (*cassia elongata*), and Wild Senna.
Family/Class: Leguminosae (legume).
Habitat: Africa, Arabia, China, Egypt, India, Mozambique, North America, and Somali.
Flavor: Bitter/sweet.
Parts Used: Leaves, pods.
Properties: Anthelmintic, antiphlogistic, astringent, cardiant, cholagogue, depurative; diuretic, emmenagogue, hemostatic, laxative, lithotriptic, stimulant, and vermifuge.
Constituents: Cathartin, cathartinic acid, chrysophanic acid (rumicin), emodin, flavones, glycosides, resin, sennatin, tannic acid, tartaric acid, and volatile oil.
Historical Uses: Bleeding, calculus, canker sores, cardiovascular conditions, colic, constipation, fever (ephemeral, rheumatic), gallstones, gout, halitosis, headache, hemorrhoids, indigestion, inflammation, jaundice, kidney stones, menstrual problems, muscle and joint pain, parasites (roundworm), pimples, rheumatism, skin problems, sores, and weight loss.
Discussion: May cleanse the whole system; dissolve calculi; enhance colon function; inhibit intestinal reabsorption; promote bile flow, bowel evacuation, and urine flow; stimulate the cardiovascular system, menstruation, and peristalsis.
Cautions/Contraindications: Avoid use if pregnant or breast-feeding, or if you have appendicitis, ear infection, or an obstruction (intestinal). Do not administer to children under 12 years old. May interfere with the effectiveness of digoxin. May cause electrolyte/potassium depletion. Not for long-term use.
Adverse Reactions: Abdominal pain, arrhythmia, cardiac failure, bone degeneration, gastrointestinal problems, spasmodic conditions, laxative dependency, nausea, and/or vomiting.
Herb/Drug Interactions: This herb could cause an interaction (possibly severe) when taken with the following drugs: Cardiac drugs and Laxative drugs.
Herb/Herb Interactions: Do not use with foxglove (*digitalis purpurea*).
Preparations/Dosage: Crude Herb (leaves): 3-6 grams. Crude Herb (pods): 3-12. Cold Infusion (pods): ½-1 cup per day. Infusion (leaves): ½-1 cup per day. Leaves (powdered): Average dose in substance 5-60 grains (0.333-4 gm.). Tincture: 5-20 drops (0.3-1.3 cc.) one to three times per day.
Isolation: Cathartinic acid: Average dose of 4-6 grains (0.26-0.4 gm.) for use as a laxative. Chrysopahanic acid: Average dose of 1-10 grains (0.065-0.666 gm.) for use in skin problems. Sennatin: Average dose 2 grains (0.12 gm.) administered subcutaneously, for use as a laxative.

Sesame (ses e·mē)
(*Sesamum indicum*)

Synonyms/Related Species: Bene, Benne, Black Sesame Seeds, Gingili, Šūmšemā, Šamaššamu, and Teel.
Family/Class: Pedaliaceae (pedalium).
Habitat: Africa, Asia, Egypt, and India.
Flavor: Leaves: bitter. Oil/Seeds: sweet.
Parts Used: Leaves, oil (seeds), seeds.
Properties: Demulcent, emmenagogue, laxative, nutritive, and tonic.
Constituents: Carbohydrates, fatty acids (arachidonic, linoleic, linolenic, oleic, palmitic, stearic), fixed oils (olein, palmitin, stearin), lecithin, minerals (calcium, manganese,

phosphorous, sulfur, zinc), mucilage, myristin (myristic acid), phosphoric acid, protein, sesamin, stearin, and vitamins (A, B, B_3 (niacin), C (ascorbic acid), choline, E (alpha-tocopheral).

Historical Uses: Bladder problems, cholera, cirrhosis, cough, cystitis, diarrhea, dietary supplementation, diphtheria, dizziness, dryness conditions, dysentery, flavoring agent (seeds), food source (seeds), headache, liver problems, malnutrition, muscle and joint pain, respiratory conditions, spasmodic conditions, substitute for olive oil (oil), tinnitus, urethritis, and visual disturbances.

Discussion: May destroy insects and their larvae; enhance kidney, liver, lung, and spleen functions; nourish the blood; prevent the deposition of fat in the liver; promote bowel evacuation; provide dietary supplementation; restore normal tone to tissues; serve as a nutritional adjuvant to therapeutic programs; soothe mucous membrane irritation; stimulate menstruation and peristalsis.

Cautions/Contraindications: Avoid use if pregnant or breast-feeding.

Adverse Reactions: Diarrhea, nausea, and/or vomiting.

Herb/Drug Interactions: This herb could cause an interaction (possibly severe) when taken with the following drugs: None known.

Preparations/Dosage: Crude Herb (leaves): 1-2 whole leaves. Crude Herb (seeds): 3-30 grams. Infusion (leaves): ¼-1 cup per day. Oil of Sesame (*oleum sesami*): ½ teaspoon-2 tablespoons taken before bed as a laxative. Oil: Used like olive oil in cooking.

Shepherd's Purse (shep erdz pûrs)
(*Capsella bursa-pastoris*)

Synonyms/Related Species: Blindweed, Bourse de Pasteur, Case-Weed, Clappedepouch, Cocowort, Hirtentasche, Lady's Purse, Mother's Heart, Poor Man's Parmacettie, Rattle Pouches, Sanguinary, Shepherd's Bag, St. James' Weed, and Witches' Pouches.

Family/Class: Brassicaceae (mustard).

Habitat: Asia, Britain, Europe, France, Germany, Ireland, and North America.

Flavor: Pungent/bitter.

Parts Used: Entire plant.

Properties: Alterative, antibiotic, antilithic, antiphlogistic, antiscorbutic, aromatic, astringent, diuretic, hemostatic, hypertensive, insecticide, larvacide, laxative, lithotriptic, oxytocic, stimulant, tonic, and vasoconstrictor.

Constituents: Acetylcholine, alkaloid, bursine, bursinic acid, caffeic acid, chlorogenic acid, fatty acids (oleic, palmitic, stearic), fixed oils (olein, palmitin, stearin), flavonoids, glycosides, isothiocyanate, luteolin, minerals (calcium, iron, magnesium, potassium, sodium, sulfur, tin, zinc), monosaccharides, polypeptide, resin, rutin, saponins, sinigrin, tannic acid, vitamins (choline, C (ascorbic acid), E (alpha-tocopheral), K), and volatile oil.

Historical Uses: Amenorrhea, arrhythmia, arteriosclerosis, bleeding, burns (minor), calculus, cardiovascular conditions, cirrhosis, colic, constipation, cramps, cystitis, diarrhea, diphtheria, dysentery, ear infection, edema, endometriosis, fever (ephemeral, rheumatic), gallstones, gastrointestinal problems, gout, headache, heart, hemorrhoids, hemorrhage (metrorrhagia), hypotension, infection (bacterial), inflammation, insufficiency (venous), jaundice, kidney problems, kidney stones, leukorrhea, lithemia, liver problems, lochia, lumbago, menorrhagia, menstrual problems, mosquitos (larvae/seeds), muscle and joint pain, nosebleed, poison ivy/oak, premenstrual syndrome (PMS), rheumatism, scurvy, substitute for ginger (root), substitute for mustard (pods/seeds), tinnitus, ulcer (duodenal, gastric, peptic, stasis, varicose), urinary problems, uterine problems, vaginitis, varicose veins, and wounds (minor).

Discussion: May cause blood vessel constriction; destroy mosquito larvae; dissolve calculi; elevate blood pressure levels; enhance cardiovascular system, liver, and stomach functions; increase blood pressure levels; inhibit or destroy development and growth of bacteria and other microorganisms; maintain retinal health; prevent the deposition of fat in the liver, the development of calculus or stones, and hemorrhage in persons with hypertension; promote bowel evacuation and urine flow; reduce capillary fragility and excessive lithic acid (uric acid) and urate levels in the blood, tophi, and urine; reestablish healthy system functions; restore normal tone to tissues; stimulate peristalsis and uterine contractions.

Cautions/Contraindications: Avoid use if pregnant or breast-feeding, or if you have hypertension, thromboembolism or thrombophlebitis, or a history of heart attack or stroke (apoplectic). Do not use shepherd's purse for vaginal bleeding during pregnancy. May interfere with iodide metabolism. May cause dermatitis in susceptible individuals. Not for long-term use.

Adverse Reactions: Diarrhea (possibly bloody), digestive complaints, edema, gastritis, gastrointestinal problems, goiter, hematuria (blood in the urine), indigestion, irritable bowel syndrome (IBS), nausea, suppression (thyroid), and/or vomiting.

Herb/Drug Interactions: This herb could cause an interaction (possibly severe) when taken with the following drugs: Hypertensive drugs.

Preparations/Dosage: Crude Herb: 3-12 grams. Crude Herb (powdered): Average dose in substance 10-15 grains (0.666-0.98 gm.). Extract (cold): ½-¾ cup per day. Infusion: ½-1 cup per day. Juice: 1-2 teaspoons in water one to three times per day. Tincture: 15-30 drops (1-2 cc.) one to three times per day.

Isolation: Acetylcholine (chloride and bromide salts): Used in a 5% solution, average dose of 0.05-0.20 gm., administered intravenously or subcutaneously, for use to relax the peripheral blood vessels.

Simaruba (sim e·roo be)

(*Simaruba amara*)

Synonyms/Related Species: Bitter Damson, Bitter Wood, Brazilian Simaruba (*simaruba versicolor*), Cuban Simaruba (*simaruba alauca*), Dysentery Bark, Jamaica Quassia, Jamaican Simaruba (*simaruba glauca*), Maruba, Mountain Damson, Quassia Excelsa (*simaruba excelsa*), Simaba (*simaruba cedron*), Slave Wood, Stave Wood, Sumaruppa, Surinam Quassia, and Winged-Leaved Quassia (*simaruba medicinalis*).

Family/Class: Simaroubaceae (quassia).

Habitat: Cuba, Guatamala, India, Jamaica, Martinique, Panama, and South America.

Flavor: Bitter.

Parts Used: Bark (root).

Properties: Alterative, anthelmintic, antiphlogistic, antispasmodic, cholagogue, counterirritant, diaphoretic, diuretic, emetic, insecticide, laxative, stimulant, stomachic, tonic, vermifuge, and vermin repellent.

Constituents: Alkaloids, bitter principle, gallic acid, lignin, malic acid, minerals (calcium, iron, potassium, silicon, sodium), pectic acid, pectin, quassin (quassiin), resin, silicic acid, ulmin (ulmic acid), and volatile oil.

Historical Uses: Addiction (alcohol), appetite loss, arthritis, constipation, dandruff, diarrhea, dysentery, fever (ephemeral, rheumatic), flatulence, flies and their larvae, indigestion, inflammation, insomnia, muscle and joint pain, parasites (pinworm, roundworm), rheumatism, skin problems, snakebite, spasmodic conditions, and vermin.
Discussion: May destroy flies and their larvae; enhance intestinal system, liver, and stomach functions; promote bile flow, bowel evacuation, perspiration, and urine flow; reestablish healthy system functions; restore normal tone to tissues; stimulate peristalsis.
Cautions/Contraindications: Avoid use if pregnant or breast-feeding.
Adverse Reactions: Blindness, depression, edema, mucous membrane irritation, nausea, visual disturbances, and/or vomiting.
Herb/Drug Interactions: This herb could cause an interaction (possibly severe) when taken with the following drugs: None known.
Preparations/Dosage: Crude Herb: 3-6 grams. Bark (powdered): Average dose in substance 10-20 grains (0.666-1.333 gm.). Infusion: ½-1 cup per day. Tincture: 10-30 drops (0.666-2 cc.) one to three times per day.
Isolation: Quassin (quassiin): Average dose of $^{1}/_{30}$-⅓ grain (0.0022-0.022 gm.) for use as a tonic.

Skullcap (skul kap)
(*Scutellaria lateriflora*)

Synonyms/Related Species: Baicalen, Blue Pimpernell, Blue Skullcap, California Skullcap (*scutellaria californica*), Chinese Skullcap (*scutellaria baicalensis*), Dannie's Skullcap (*scutellaria tuberosa*), Greater Skullcap, Helmet Flower (*scutellaria galericulata*), Hoodwort, Lesser Skullcap (*scutellaria minor*), Mad-Dog Weed, Madweed, Marsh Skullcap (*scutellaria epilobiifolia*), Mexican Skullcap (*scutellaria coccinea*), Narrow-Leaved Skullcap (*scutellaria angustifolia*), Quaker Bonnet, Scullcap, Scute-Root, Siberian Skullcap (*scutellaria micrantha*), Side-Flowering Scullcap, Toque, and Virginian Scullcap.
Family/Class: Labiatae (mint).
Habitat: Britain, China, England, Europe, India, Ireland, Mexico, North America, Siberia, and the Yukon Territory.
Flavor: Bitter.
Parts Used: Leaves, root.
Properties: Analgesic, antibiotic, anticarcinogen, antidepressant, antifungal, antiphlogistic, antispasmodic, antiviral, astringent, carminative, diuretic, hemostatic, hypotensive, laxative, nervine, sedative, tonic, and vasodilator.
Constituents: Albumin (albumen), bitter principle, cellulose, chlorophyll, fatty acids (oleic, palmitic, stearic), fixed oils (olein, palmitin, stearin), flavonoids, lignin, minerals (calcium, iron, magnesium, potassium, silicon, zinc), monosaccharides, resin, scutellarin, silicic acid, tannic acid, vitamins (C (ascorbic acid), E (alpha-tocopheral), and volatile oil.
Historical Uses: Abscess, acquired immune deficiency syndrome (AIDS), addiction (alcohol, barbiturate, heroin, meprobamate, morphine, opium, valium), allergy (pollen), anemia, anxiety, appetite loss, arteriosclerosis, asthma, attention deficit disorder (ADD), autoimmune disease, bleeding, cancer (colorectal, lung), cardiovascular conditions, chorea, chronic fatigue syndrome (CFS), colds, colic, convulsions, cough, delirium, delirium tremens (DTs), depression (mild/moderate), diabetes, digestive complaints, diphtheria, drug withdrawal, dysentery, ear

infection, endometriosis, enuresis (urinary incontinence), epilepsy, Epstein Barr Virus (EBV), excitability, exhaustion, fatigue, fever (ephemeral, hay, rheumatic), fibromyalgia, flatulence, gleet, gonorrhea, gout, hangover (caused by alcohol consumption), headache, hepatitis, human immunodeficiency virus (HIV), hydrophobia (rabies in humans), hypercholesteremia, hypersensitivity, hypertension (mild/moderate), hypoglycemia, hysteria, indigestion, infection (bacterial, fungal, sexually transmitted, viral), infertility, inflammation, influenza, irritability, insanity, insect bites or stings, insomnia, jaundice, leukemia, Lyme disease, memory/cognitive problems, menopausal/menstrual problems, mental disturbances, meningitis, mononucleosis (infectious), mucus, multiple sclerosis (MS), muscle and joint pain, nervous conditions, neuralgia, neuritis, pain, Parkinson's disease, palsy, paralysis, pelvic inflammatory disease (PID), periodontal disease, premenstrual syndrome (PMS), pneumonia, prostatitis, respiratory conditions, restlessness, rheumatism, rheumatoid arthritis (RA), rickets, seizure conditions, sexually transmitted diseases (STDs), shingles, snakebite, sores, spasmodic conditions, substitute for quinine, tetanus, thirst, thyroid problems, tremors, trismus (lockjaw), tumors (hepatoma), ulcer (syriac), urethritis, urinary problems, and vomiting.

Discussion: May aid digestion; calm the nervous system; cause blood vessel dilatation; decrease the effect of carcinogens; ease alcohol or drug withdrawal symptoms; enhance cardiovascular system, immune system, intestinal system, liver, and urinary system functions; improve cognition and memory; induce sleep; inhibit or destroy development and growth of bacteria and other microorganisms; prevent damage to DNA; promote bowel evacuation and urine flow; protect the liver; reduce blood pressure levels and the frequency of nighttime urination; serve as an adjuvant to alcoholism treatment programs to assist in easing delirium tremens (DTs), chemotherapy treatments, drug addiction therapy programs to assist in breaking heroin, morphine, and opium addictions, and may assist in weaning persons from barbiturate, meprobamate, and valium abuse; stimulate appetite, collagen growth, menstruation, and peristalsis; strengthen the urinary system.

Cautions/Contraindications: Avoid use if pregnant or breast-feeding. Not for long-term use.

Adverse Reactions: Abnormal pulse rate, confusion, diarrhea, dizziness, excitability, giddiness, insomnia, liver damage (often characterized by jaundice), muscular twitching, nausea, stupor, and/or vomiting.

Herb/Drug Interactions: This herb could cause an interaction (possibly severe) when taken with the following drugs: Hypotensive drugs.

Preparations/Dosage: Crude Herb: 3-6 grams. Extract: 1-3 drops (0.06-0.2 cc.) one to two times per day. Extract (powdered): Average dose in substance 1-3 grains (0.066-0.2 gm.) administered in capsule or pill form. Infusion (leaves): ½-1 cup per day. Tincture: 3-30 drops (0.2-2 cc.) one to three times per day.

Isolation: Scutellarin: Average dose of 1-2 grains (0.066-0.133 gm.) for use as an antispasmodic, nervine, and tonic.

Slippery Elm (slip rē elm)

(*Ulmus fulva*)

Synonyms/Related Species: Indian Elm, Moose Elm, Red Elm, Rock Elm, and Sweet Elm.

Family/Class: Ulmaceae (elm).

Habitat: North America.

Flavor: Sweet.

Parts Used: Bark (inner).

Properties: Antacid, anthelmintic, antibiotic, anticarcinogen, antiphlogistic, astringent, demulcent, diuretic, expectorant, hemostatic, laxative, nutritive, tonic, vermifuge, and vulnerary.
Constituents: Carbohydrates, fatty acids (arachidonic, linoleic, linolenic), flavones, hexosan, inulin (starch), minerals (bromine, calcium, copper, iodine, iron, manganese, phosphorous, potassium, selenium, sodium, zinc), monosaccharides, mucilage, pentosans, phosphoric acid, polysaccharide, protein, tannic acid, ulmin (ulmic acid), and vitamins (E (alpha-tocopheral), K).
Historical Uses: Abscess, acidity (gastric), allergy (pollen), appendicitis, asthma, bedsores, bladder problems, bladder inflammation, bleeding, bronchitis, burns (minor), cancer, colitis, constipation, cough, cramps, Crohn's disease, croup, cystitis, diarrhea, dietary supplementation, digestive complaints, diphtheria, diverticulitis, dryness conditions, dysentery, eczema, enema, enteritis, esophagitis, eye problems, fever (ephemeral, hay, herpetic), flatulence, gangrene, gastritis, gastrointestinal problems, hemorrhage, hemorrhoids, herpes, hernias (hiatal), hot flashes, indigestion, infection (bacterial, urinary tract), infertility, inflammation, influenza, irritable bowel syndrome (IBS), jaundice, laryngitis, lesions (tubercle), leukorrhea, lung problems, malnutrition, menopausal/menstrual problems, mucous membrane problems, mucus, muscle and joint pain, nausea, nephritis, parasites (roundworm), plague, pneumonia, poisoning (food, non-caustic), poison ivy/oak, pruritus, rash, respiratory conditions, scrofula, sexually transmitted diseases (STDs), skin problems, sore throat, sores, syphilis, tonsillitis, tuberculosis, tumors, ulcer (duodenal, fistula, gastric, syphilitic, syriac, tuberculous), vaginitis, whooping cough, and wounds (minor).
Discussion: May clear and open bronchial passages; decrease the effect of carcinogens; enhance digestive system, reproductive system, respiratory system, and urinary system functions; neutralize acidity; promote bowel evacuation and urine flow; provide dietary supplementation; restore normal tone to tissues; serve as a nutritional adjuvant to therapeutic programs and serve as an antidote for food and non-caustic poisoning; soothe mucous membrane irritation; speed healing; stimulate peristalsis.
Cautions/Contraindications: Avoid use if pregnant or breast-feeding, or if you have an iodine sensitivity. May interfere with the absorption of prescription drugs. May interfere with the effectiveness of certain thyroid medications. May cause dermatitis in susceptible individuals.
Adverse Reactions: Abdominal pain, arrhythmia, diarrhea, edema, fever, hypertrophy (thyroid), iodism (iodine poisoning), nausea, priapism, thirst, and/or vomiting.
Herb/Drug Interactions: This herb could cause an interaction (possibly severe) when taken with the following drugs: Thyroid drugs.
Preparations/Dosage: Crude Herb: 9-15 grams. Infusion: 1-2 cups per day.

Snakeweed (snāk wēd)
(*Gutierrezia sarothrae*)

Synonyms/Related Species: Broom Snakeweed, Collàlle, Escoba de la Vibora, Gutierrezia, Matchweed, San Joaquin Snakeweed (*gutierrezia californica*), Snakebroom, Threadleaf Snakeweed (*gutierrezia microcephala*), and Yerba de la Vibora.
Family/Class: Compositae (composite).
Habitat: North America.
Flavor: Bitter.
Parts Used: Aerial.
Properties: Alterative, antiphlogistic, astringent, emetic, hemostatic, laxative, and tonic.

Constituents: Glycoprotein and tannic acid.
Historical Uses: Anxiety, arthritis, bleeding, bruises, canker sores, colds, cough, diarrhea, dizziness, dysmenorrhea, dysuria (painful/difficult urination), earache, eye problems, eyewash, fever (ephemeral, rheumatic), gastrointestinal problems, headache, inflammation, influenza, insect bites or stings, earache, measles, menorrhagia, menstrual problems, muscle and joint pain, rash, respiratory conditions, rheumatism, snakebite, sore throat, sores, sprain, stomachache, and tumors.
Discussion: May promote bowel evacuation; reestablish healthy system functions; restore normal tone to tissues; stimulate peristalsis; strengthen the muscles.
Cautions/Contraindications: Avoid use if pregnant or breast-feeding.
Adverse Reactions: Diarrhea, nausea, and/or vomiting.
Herb/Drug Interactions: This herb could cause an interaction (possibly severe) when taken with the following drugs: None known.
Preparations/Dosage: Crude Herb: 1-3 grams. Infusion: 1-2 cups per day.

Soapwort (sōp wûrt)
(*Saponaria officinalis*)

Synonyms/Related Species: Bouncing Bet, Bruisewort, Crow Soap, Fuller's Herb, Latherwort, Old Maid's Pink, Sweet Betty, and Wild Soapwort.
Family/Class: Caryophyllaceae (pink).
Habitat: Asia, England, Europe, France, and North America.
Flavor: Bitter/sweet/pungent.
Parts Used: Root.
Properties: Alterative, antibiotic, antiphlogistic, cholagogue, diaphoretic, diuretic, emetic, expectorant, laxative, stimulant, and tonic.
Constituents: Aglycone (genin), fiber, gum, flavonoids, quillaic acid, resin, saponetin, and saponins.
Historical Uses: Abscess, acne, bronchitis, colds, cough, dermatitis, eczema, fever (ephemeral, rheumatic), gleet, gonorrhea, gout, infection (bacterial, sexually transmitted), inflammation, jaundice, liver problems, mucus, muscle and joint pain, pruritus, respiratory conditions, rheumatism, sexually transmitted diseases (STDs), skin problems, substitute for sarsaparilla, syphilis, tumors, ulcer (syphilitic), and urethritis.
Discussion: May clear and open bronchial passages; promote bile flow, bowel evacuation, perspiration, and urine flow; reestablish healthy system functions; restore normal tone to tissues; stimulate peristalsis.
Cautions/Contraindications: Avoid use if pregnant or breast-feeding.
Adverse Reactions: Diarrhea (possibly bloody), gastrointestinal cramps (severe), hematuria (blood in the urine), mucous membrane irritation, nausea, and/or vomiting.
Herb/Drug Interactions: This herb could cause an interaction (possibly severe) when taken with the following drugs: None known.
Preparations/Dosage: Crude Herb: 1-3 grams. Decoction: ½-2 tablespoons one to three times per day. Extract (powdered): Average dose in substance 10-20 grains (0.666-1.333 gm.). Snuff (sternutatory): Snuff 2-6 grains to produce sneezing.

Solomon's Seal (sol o·munz sēl)
(*Polygonatum multiflorum*)

Synonyms/Related Species: American Solomon's Seal (*polygonatum biflorum*), Dropberry, Dwarf Solomon's Seal, European Solomon's Seal (*polygonatum odoratum*), Lady's Seals, Scean de Solomon, Scotland Solomon's Seal (*polygonatum verticillatum*), Saint Mary's Seal, Sealwort, Sigillum Salomonis, True Solomon's Seal, and Weusswurz.
Family/Class: Liliaceae (lily).
Habitat: Asia, England, Europe, Germany, the Himalayas, Ireland, North America, Scotland, Siberia, and Switzerland.
Flavor: Sweet/bitter.
Parts Used: Root.
Properties: Antibiotic, antifertilizin, antiphlogistic, aphrodisiac, astringent, cardiant, demulcent, diaphoretic, diuretic, emetic, expectorant, hemostatic, hypoglycemic, laxative, stimulant, tonic, and vulnerary.
Constituents: Asparagin, convallarin, gum, inulin (starch), monosaccharides, mucilage, pectic acid, pectin, and saponins.
Historical Uses: Abscess, acne, amenorrhea, arthritis, bleeding, bronchitis, bruises, cancer, cardiovascular conditions, colds, constipation, contraceptive (female), cough, diabetes, earache, edema, emaciation, fever (ephemeral, rheumatic), glandular swelling, headache, hemorrhoids, hyperglycemia, indigestion, infection (bacterial), inflammation, injury (internal), kidney problems, lung problems, menopausal/menstrual problems, mucus, muscle and joint pain, nausea, pain, pimples, poison ivy/oak, pruritus, rash, respiratory conditions, rheumatism, skin problems, sore throat, sprain, substitute for false solomon's seal (*smilacina spp.*), ulcer (duodenal, gastric, peptic), and wounds (minor).
Discussion: May arouse sexual impulses; clear and open bronchial passages; enhance lung and stomach functions; neutralize fertilizin (fertilization); promote bowel evacuation and perspiration; reduce blood sugar levels; restore normal tone to tissues; soothe mucous membrane irritation; speed healing; stimulate the cardiovascular system.
Cautions/Contraindications: Avoid use if pregnant or breast-feeding.
Adverse Reactions: Arrhythmia, diarrhea (possibly bloody), gastrointestinal cramps (severe), hematuria (blood in the urine), nausea, and/or vomiting.
Herb/Drug Interactions: This herb could cause an interaction (possibly severe) when taken with the following drugs: Antidiabetic drugs and Cardiac drugs.
Preparations/Dosage: Crude Herb: 6-12 grams. Decoction: ¼-½ cup per day. Infusion: ½-1 cup. Shoots (young): Boiled and eaten as a vegetable. Tincture: 10-30 drops (0.66-2 cc.) one to three times per day.
Isolation: Asparagin: Soluble in hot water, but insoluble in alcohol and ether. Average dose of 1-2 grains (0.066-0.133 gm.) for use as a diuretic.

Solomon's Seal, False (sol o·munz sēl, fôls)
(*Smilacina racemosa*)

Synonyms/Related Species: Solomon's Plume, Star-Flowered False Solomon's Seal (*smilacina stellatum*), and Three-Leaved False Solomon's Seal (*smilacina trifolium*).
Family/Class: Liliaceae (lily).
Habitat: Alaska, North America, the Subalpine zone, and the Yukon Territory.

Flavor: Sweet/bitter.
Parts Used: Leaves, root.
Properties: Antifertilizin, antibiotic, antiphlogistic, astringent, cardiant, demulcent, diaphoretic, diuretic, emetic, expectorant, hypoglycemic, laxative, stimulant, tonic, and vulnerary.
Constituents: Asparagin, convallarin, glycosides, inulin (starch), mucilage, pectic acid, pectin, and saponins.
Historical Uses: Abscess, acne, amenorrhea, arthritis, bleeding, bronchitis, bruises, cancer, cardiovascular conditions, colds, constipation, contraceptive (female), cough, diabetes, earache, edema, emaciation, fever (ephemeral, rheumatic), flushing, glandular swelling, headache, hemorrhoids, indigestion, infection (bacterial), inflammation, injury (internal), kidney problems, lung problems, menopausal/menstrual problems, mucus, muscle and joint pain, nausea, pain, pimples, poison ivy/oak, pruritus, rash, respiratory conditions, rheumatism, skin problems, sore throat, sprain, substitute for solomon's seal (*polygonatum spp.*), ulcer (duodenal, gastric, peptic), and wounds (minor).
Discussion: May clear and open bronchial passages; neutralize fertilizin (fertilization); promote bowel evacuation and perspiration; reduce blood sugar levels; restore tone to tissues; soothe mucous membrane irritation; speed healing; stimulate the cardiovascular system.
Cautions/Contraindications: Avoid use if pregnant or breast-feeding. Not for long-term use.
Adverse Reactions: Arrhythmia, diarrhea (possibly bloody), gastrointestinal cramps (severe), hematuria (blood in the urine), nausea, and/or vomiting.
Herb/Drug Interactions: This herb could cause an interaction (possibly severe) when taken with the following drugs: Antidiabetic drugs and Cardiac drugs.
Preparations/Dosage: Crude Herb: 6-12 grams. Decoction: ¼-½ cup per day. Infusion: ½-1 cup per day. Tincture: 10-30 drops (0.66-2 cc.) one to three times per day.
Isolation: Asparagin: Soluble in hot water, but insoluble in alcohol and ether. Average dose of 1-2 grains (0.066-0.133 gm.) for use as a diuretic.

Sorrel (sôr el)
(*Rumex acetosa*)

Synonyms/Related Species: Alpine Sorrel (*rumex paucifolius*), Buckler-Leaf Sorrel, Cuckoo's-Meate, Cuckoo Sorrow, Field Sorrel, French Sorrel (*rumex scutatus*), Garden Sorrel, Gowke-Meat, Green Sorrel, Sheep Sorrel (*rumex acetosella*), Sourgrass, and Surele.
Family/Class: Polygonaceae (buckwheat).
Habitat: The Alpine and Subalpine zones, Arctic, Asia, Barbery, Britain, England, Europe, France, Germany, Italy, North America, Scotland, and Switzerland.
Flavor: Sour.
Parts Used: Leaves.
Properties: Antibiotic, anticarcinogen, antioxidant, antiphlogistic, antiscorbutic, astringent, depurative, diaphoretic, diuretic, hemostatic, laxative, lithotriptic, nutritive, and tonic.
Constituents: Aglycone (genin), chrysophanic acid (rumicin), emodin, flavonoids, glycosides, minerals (calcium, potassium, sodium), monosaccharides, mucilage, oxalic acid, tannic acid, tartaric acid, and vitamin C (ascorbic acid).
Historical Uses: Abscess, age spots, amenorrhea, appetite loss, bleeding, bruises, calculus, cancer, cholera, colds, degenerative conditions, digestive complaints, dizziness, fever (ephemeral, rheumatic), freckles, gallstones, gout, hemorrhage, infection (bacterial), inflammation, jaundice, kidney stones, lesions (tubercle), liver problems, menorrhagia, menstrual

problems, muscle and joint pain, respiratory conditions, rheumatism, scrofula, scurvy, skin problems, sores, thirst, tuberculosis, ulcer (duodenal, fistula, gastric, peptic, tuberculous), and warts (digitate, filiform, fugitive, glabra, mother, plana juvenilis, plantar, seborrhoeic, vulgaris).
Discussion: May cleanse the liver; decrease the effect of carcinogens; dissolve calculi; enhance cardiovascular system function; inhibit oxidation and inhibit development or destroy growth of bacteria and other microorganisms; promote bowel evacuation, perspiration, and urine flow; restore normal tone to tissues; stimulate appetite and peristalsis.
Cautions/Contraindications: Avoid use if pregnant or breast-feeding, or if you have gout or kidney stones. Not for long-term use.
Adverse Reactions: Diarrhea, gastric irritation, hemorrhage, kidney irritation, nausea, oxalism (oxalic acid or oxalate poisoning), and/or vomiting.
Herb/Drug Interactions: This herb could cause an interaction (possibly severe) when taken with the following drugs: None known.
Preparations/Dosage: Crude Herb: 3-6 grams. Infusion: 1-2 cups per day. Leaves: Fresh or boiled as a vegetable. Tincture: 10-30 drops (0.666-2 cc.) one to three times per day.
Isolation: Chrysophanic acid: Average dose of 1-10 grains (0.065-0.666 gm.) for use in skin problems. Oxalic acid: Average dose of ½-¾ grain (0.0333-0.048) for use in amenorrhea.

Sorrel, Wood (sôr el, wood)
(*Oxalis acetosella*)

Synonyms/Related Species: Alleluya, Fairy Bells, Oregon Oxalis (*oxalis oregana*), Oxalis, Paniscuculi, Redwood Sorrel, Sour Trefoil, Stickwort, Stubwort, Three-Leaved Grass, and Wood Sour.
Family/Class: Oxalidaceae (wood sorrel).
Habitat: The Alpine zone, the Arctic, Ireland, and North America.
Flavor: Sour.
Parts Used: Leaves.
Properties: Analgesic, antibiotic, antiphlogistic, antiscorbutic, astringent, counterirritant, depurative, diuretic, emmenagogue, laxative, parasiticide, and stomachic.
Constituents: Enzymes, minerals (iron, potassium), mucilage, oxalic acid, and vitamins (A, B, C (ascorbic acid).
Historical Uses: Abscess, age spots, ague, appetite loss, bleeding, canker sores, cholera, conjunctivitis, digestive complaints, dizziness, eyewash (juice), fever (ephemeral, rheumatic), freckles, gargle/mouth rinse, gastritis, gout, hemorrhage, indigestion, infection (bacterial), inflammation, liver problems, menstrual problems, mucus, muscle and joint pain, nausea, pain, parasites (ringworm), periodontal disease, pruritus, rheumatism, scurvy, sore throat, sores, substitute for spinach (young leaves), thirst, tumors, urinary problems, vomiting, and wounds (minor).
Discussion: May enhance stomach function; promote bowel evacuation and urine flow; purify the blood; stimulate appetite, menstruation, and peristalsis.
Cautions/Contraindications: Avoid use if pregnant or breast-feeding, or if you have gout or kidney stones.
Adverse Reactions: Diarrhea, gastric irritation, hemorrhage, kidney irritation, nausea, oxalism (oxalic acid or oxalate poisoning), and/or vomiting.
Herb/Drug Interactions: This herb could cause an interaction (possibly severe) when taken with the following drugs: None known.

Preparations/Dosage: Crude Herb: 3-6 grams. Infusion: 1-2 cups per day. Leaves: Fresh or boiled as a vegetable. Tincture: 10-30 drops (0.666-2 cc.) one to three times per day.

Soybean (so'i bēn)
(*Glycine soja*)

Synonyms/Related Species: Chinese Bean (*soja hispida*), Shōyū, and Soja.
Family/Class: Leguminosae (legume).
Habitat: Asia, China, India, Japan, North America, and Taiwan.
Flavor: Bland.
Parts Used: Bean, oil.
Properties: Anticarcinogen, antioxidant, depurative, hypotensive, lithotriptic, nutritive, and vasodilator.
Constituents: Albuminoids, carbohydrates, flavones, glycinin, inulin (starch), lecithin, lipids, minerals (iron, magnesium, manganese, phosphorus, potassium, sulfur, zinc), phytic acid, phytoestrogen, protein, saponins, urease, and vitamins (B_1 (thiamine), B_2 (riboflavin), B_3 (niacin), choline, K).
Historical Uses: Addiction (alcohol), Alzheimer's disease, appetite loss, arteriosclerosis, bipolar/manic depressive condition, bone loss, calculus, cancer (bladder, brain, breast, colon, liver, lung, melanoma, ovarian, prostate, skin), cirrhosis, diabetes, diabetic retinopathy, dietary supplementation, diphtheria, fatigue, fibroids, fractures, gallstones, hangover (caused by alcohol consumption), heart disease, hepatitis, Hodgkin's disease, hot flashes, hypercholesteremia, hypertension (mild/moderate), hypoglycemia, kidney stones, leukemia, liver problems, malnutrition, memory/cognitive problems, menopausal problems, multiple sclerosis (MS), neurologic conditions, night sweats, osteoporosis, psoriasis, Tourette's syndrome, and weight loss.
Discussion: May aid calcium absorption; balance blood sugar and estrogen levels; cause blood vessel dilatation; decrease the effect of carcinogens; dissolve calculi; improve cognition and memory; inhibit oxidation and the effects in hormone related cancers; neutralize the breakdown of blood cholesterol; prevent bone loss, the deposition of fat in the liver, the formation of blood vessel plaque, and intestinal iron from generating free radicals; protect against heart disease; provide dietary supplementation; purify the blood and liver; reduce blood pressure levels and cholesterol levels; regenerate damaged liver cells and reverse cirrhosis when alcohol intake is stopped; serve as a nutritional adjuvant to therapeutic programs and serve as an alternative to estrogen therapy programs; stop or slow abnormal cell growth; strengthen bones.
Cautions/Contraindications: Avoid use if pregnant or breast-feeding, or if you have an estrogen dependant cancer, or if you have a history of estrogen dependant cancers, or a thyroid condition. May reduce the effectiveness of oral contraceptives and thyroid hormone drugs. Estrogen containing substances may contribute to abnormal blood clotting, migraine, and could promote the developement of certain types of estrogen dependant cancers.
Adverse Reactions: Diarrhea (possibly bloody), gastrointestinal cramps (severe), hematuria (blood in the urine), nausea, and/or vomiting.
Herb/Drug Interactions: Hormones and Synthetic Substitutes (i.e. conjugated estrogens, contraceptives (oral, etc.), and other hormonal replacement therapy (HRT), Hypotensive drugs, and Thyroid drugs.

Preparations/Dosage: Crude Herb: 3-9 grams. Beans (dried): Cooked and eaten as a vegetable. Soybean Oil (*oleum soja*): Used like olive oil in cooking.

Speedwell (spēd·wel)

(*Veronica americana*)

Synonyms/Related Species: Alpine Speedwell (*veronica alpina*), American Speedwell, American Brooklime, Brooklime Speedwell (*veronica beccabunga*), Buxbaum's Speedwell (*veronica buxbaumii*), Chamaedrys, Common Speedwell (*veronica officinalis*), Culver's Physic, Farewell, Finger Speedwell (*veronica triphyllos*), Fluellin, Germander Speedwell (*veronica chamædrys*), Ground-Hele, Gypsy Weed, Ivy-Leaved Speedwell (*veronica hederifolia*), Low Speedwell, Marsh Speedwell (*veronica scutellata*), Persian Self-Heal (*veronica persica*), Procumbent Speedwell (*veronica agrestis*), Rock Veronica (*veronica saxatilis*), Spiked Speedwell (*veronica spicata*), St. Veronica, Thyme-Leaved Speedwell (*veronica serpyllifolia*), Upland Speedwell, Vernal Speedwell (*veronica verna*), Veronica, Veronique Petit Chêne, Wall Speedwell (*veronica arvensis*), Water Pimpernel, and Water Purslain.
Family/Class: Scrophulariaceae (figwort).
Habitat: Alaska, the Alpine and Subalpine zones, Asia, Britain, England, Ireland, North America, Scotland, and the Yukon Territory.
Flavor: Bitter.
Parts Used: Leaves, stems.
Properties: Alterative, antiperiodic, antiphlogistic, antiscorbutic, astringent, cholagogue, depurative, diaphoretic, diuretic, emmenagogue, expectorant, laxative, malariacidal, stomachic, tonic, vasodilator, and vulnerary.
Constituents: Alkaloid, bitter principle, cinnamic acid, dextrose, glycosides, mannitol (mannite), minerals (magnesium, potassium), monosaccharides, resin, saponins, tannic acid, vitamin C (ascorbic acid), and volatile oil.
Historical Uses: Abdominal pain, ague, amenorrhea, anemia, asthma, calculus, cancer, colitis, constipation, cough, depression (mild/moderate), diarrhea, digestive complaints, dizziness, dysentery, edema, enteritis, fever (ephemeral, intermittent, rheumatic), gallbladder problems, gallstones, gargle/mouth rinse, gastrointestinal problems, gout, headache, homorrhage, hepatitis, indigestion, infection (urinary tract), inflammation, jaundice, kidney stones, lesions (tubercle), liver problems, lung problems, malaria, measles, menstrual problems, mucus, nephritis, parasites (malarial plasmodia), poisoning (food), pruritus, respiratory conditions, rheumatism, scrofula, scurvy, sexually transmitted diseases (STDs), skin problems, small pox, spasmodic conditions, syphilis, tuberculosis, ulcer (fistula, syphilitic, tuberculous), urinary problems, and wounds (minor).
Discussion: May aid digestion; cause blood vessel dilatation; dissolve calculi; enhance liver function; promote bile flow, bowel evacuation, perspiration, and urine flow; purify the blood; reestablish healthy system functions; restore normal tone to tissues; stimulate menstruation, the kidneys, and peristalsis.
Cautions/Contraindications: Avoid use if pregnant or breast-feeding.
Adverse Reactions: Diarrhea (possibly bloody), gastrointestinal cramps (severe), hematuria (blood in the urine), nausea, and/or vomiting.
Herb/Drug Interactions: This herb could cause an interaction (possibly severe) when taken with the following drugs: None known.

Preparations/Dosage: Crude Herb: 1-3 grams. Infusion: 1-1½ cups per day. Juice: 1-2 tablespoons one to three times per day in milk or water. Leaves/Stems: Cooked and eaten as a vegetable. Tincture: 10-20 drops (0.666-1.25 cc.) one to three times per day.
Isolation: Mannitol hexanitrate: Average dose of 15-60 mg. for use as a vasodilator.

Spikenard (spīk nard)
(*Aralia racemosa*)

Synonyms/Related Species: American Spikenard, American Sarsaparilla, Californian Spikenard (*aralia californica*), Indian Root, Life of Man, Old Man's Root, Petty-Morel, Rabbit's Foot, Small Spikenard, Spignet, Spica Nardi, Wild Licorice, and Wild Sarsaparilla (*aralia nudicaulis*).
Family/Class: Araliaceae (ginseng).
Habitat: Japan, New Zealand, and North America.
Flavor: Sweet/pungent.
Parts Used: Root.
Properties: Alterative, antilithic, antiphlogistic, antiscorbutic, aromatic, carminative, depurative, diaphoretic, diuretic, emmenagogue, expectorant, insecticide, lithotriptic, stimulant, and tonic.
Constituents: Acetic acid, albumin (albumen), bassorin (bassora gum), inulin (starch), minerals (iron, magnesium, potassium), pectic acid, pectin, resin, saponins, tannic acid, vitamin C (ascorbic acid), and volatile oil.
Historical Uses: Allergy (pollen), asthma, bladder problems, bruises, burns (minor), calculus, colds, congestion (uterine, vaginal), coronary artery disease (CAD), cough, diarrhea, exhaustion, fever (ephemeral, hay, rheumatic), fleas, gallstones, gout, hemorrhoids, inflammation, leukorrhea, lithemia, menopausal/menstrual problems, mucus, muscle and joint pain, kidney problems, kidney stones, nervous conditions, night sweats, respiratory conditions, rheumatism, scurvy, sexually transmitted diseases (STDs), skin problems, sores, substitute for sasaparilla, syphilis, ulcer (syphilitic), urinary problems, vaginitis, and wounds (minor).
Discussion: May aid digestion; clear and open bronchial passages; destroy fleas and their larvae; dissolve calculi; enhance lung, nervous system, and spleen functions; prevent the development of calculus or stones; promote perspiration and urine flow; purify the blood; reduce excessive lithic acid (uric acid) and urate levels in the blood, tophi, and urine; reestablish healthy system functions; restore normal tone to tissues; serve as a beneficial hormone precursor for women; stimulate menstruation and the renewal of tissue.
Cautions/Contraindications: Avoid use if pregnant or breast-feeding. Not for long-term use.
Adverse Reactions: Diarrhea (possibly bloody), gastrointestinal cramps (severe), hematuria (blood in the urine), nausea, and/or vomiting.
Herb/Drug Interactions: This herb could cause an interaction (possibly severe) when taken with the following drugs: None known.
Preparations/Dosage: Crude Herb: 3-6 grams. Infusion: 1-2 cups per day. Tincture: 5-30 drops (0.333-2 cc.) one to three times per day.

Spirulina (spī roo·lē·nä)
(*Spirulina platensis*)

Synonyms/Related Species: Blue-Green Algae (*spirulina maxima*), Chinampas, Dihe (*spirulina geitleri*), Green Algae, Green Gold, Helix, Manna, Spargein, Speira, Spiralis, Sprangât, and Tecuitlatl.
Family/Class: Cyanophyceae (blue-green algae).
Habitat: Lake Chad (Chad, which is a country in NC Africa, south of Libya), Lake Rudolf and Lake Nakura (Kenya, which is a country in EC Africa, on the Indian Ocean), Lake Texcoco (Mexico City/Teotihuacan Valley).
Flavor: Sweet.
Parts Used: Entire plant.
Properties: Antibiotic, antiphlogistic, demulcent, depurative, erythropoietic, nutritive, tonic, and vasodilator.
Constituents: Amino acids (alanine, arginine, aspartic, cystine, glutamic, glycine, histidine, isoleucine, leucine, lysine, methionine, phenylalanine, proline, serine, threonine, tryptophan, tyrosine, valine), carbohydrates, chlorophyll, cholesterol, cryptoxanthine, echinenone, enzymatic pigments, fatty acids (arachidonic, linoleic, linolenic, oleic, palmitic, stearic), fiber, fixed oils (olein, palmitin, stearin), glycogen, lutein, mesafirine, minerals (calcium, iron, magnesium, manganese, phosphorus, potassium, selenium, sodium, zinc), nucleic acids, phycocyanin, phycoerythrin, phytonadione, polysaccharides, porphyrin, protein, rhamnose, ribosomes, tetrapyrrole, vitamins (A, B_1 (thiamine), B_2 (riboflavin), B_3 (niacin), B_5 (pantothenic acid), B_6 (pyridoxine), B_{12}, B_x (para-aminobenzoic acid (PABA), C (ascorbic acid), choline, E (alpha-tocopheral), H (biotin), inositol, M (folic acid), xanthophylis, and zeaxanthin.
Historical Uses: Acquired immune deficiency syndrome (AIDS), addiction (food), allergy (pollen), Alzheimer's disease, anemia, arthritis, cancer, cardiovascular conditions, cataracts, cirrhosis, constipation, diabetes, dietary supplementation, eye problems, fever (ephemeral, rheumatic), food source, goiter, gout, halitosis, hepatitis, human immunodeficiency virus (HIV), hypoglycemia, hypothyroidism, infection (bacterial), inflammation, liver problems, malnutrition, memory/cognitive problems, mucous membrane problems, muscle and joint pain, pancreatitis, pain, poisoning (chemical, heavy metal), rheumatism, skin problems, thyroid problems, ulcer (duodenal, gastric), visual disturbances, weight loss, and wounds (minor).
Discussion: May aid in the formation of healthy red blood cells, the transmission of nerve impulses that control heart contractions, and the digestion of amino acids; assist in the body's manufacture of prostaglandins, carrying on the metabolic processes throughout the body, and weight loss; balance the flow of enzymatic secretions; boost immunity, break-up cholesterol in the blood stream; cause blood vessel dilatation; coat irritated stomach lining; diminish sensitivity to seasonal allergy (pollen); enhance cardiovascular system and liver functions; improve hair, nail, and skin condition as well as the overall efficiency of the heart; increase circulation, energy, vigor, and overall wellbeing; inhibit ulceration and inhibit or destroy development and growth of bacteria and other microorganisms; normalize cholesterol and the secretion of digestive acids; offset the negative effects of chemotherapy and radiation therapy; prevent pancreatic exhaustion; promote the excretion of heavy metals; protect against cell damage from exposure to radiation or heavy metals; provide the body with all the required nutrients as well as providing energy without burdening the pancreas or precipitating hypoglycemia; purify the blood, colon, and liver; reduce allergic sensitivity, excessive pepsin secretion, food cravings, insulin need, leukocyte loss (reduction of white blood cells), and tissue inflammation; regenerate damaged liver cells and

new tissue; regulate blood pressure levels, blood sugar levels, capillary resilience, and hormones; serve as a nutritional adjuvant to therapeutic programs; sharpen mental capacity; slow the loss of white blood cells; soothe mucous membrane irritation; stimulate peristalsis; strengthen capillaries, blood vessels, and veins; suppress appetite. Spirulina contains such extremely low amounts of sodium that no danger is presented for those individuals who have hypertension and/or are on a salt-restricted diet.
Cautions/Contraindications: Avoid use if pregnant or breast-feeding, or if you have hyperthyroidism. May interfere with the effectiveness of certain thyroid medications.
Adverse Reactions: Abdominal pain, arrhythmia, diarrhea, fever, hypertrophy (thyroid), iodism (iodine poisoning), nausea, priapism, thirst, and/or vomiting.
Herb/Drug Interactions: This herb could cause an interaction (possibly severe) when taken with the following drugs: Thyroid drugs.
Preparations/Dosage: Because spirulina is basically a food, dosage recommendations are inappropriate. Spirulina is available in tablet or powder form and may be taken as a nutritional supplement. Nutritional Supplement: 6-10 grams or 12-20 tablets daily. Hypothyroidism: Take 10 grains (0.666 gm.) of powdered spirulina daily (supplies about 300 mcg. of iodine). To reduce the risk of stomach upset, take spirulina with food.
Did You Know? Spirulina is one of the most naturally hygenic "foods" found in nature. Spirulina grows and thrives in very warm, alkaline environments, and can be found in fresh water lakes and ponds that have a saline range of 8.0-11 pH, and a water temperature of 32° to 60° C (85° to 140° F). This ability ensures its germ-free state, as no other microorganism can stay alive to contaminate the waters in which this alga thrives.

Spruce (sproos)
(*Picea sitchensis*)

Synonyms/Related Species: Black Spruce (*picea mariana*), Blue Spruce, Colorado Blue Spruce (*picea pungens*), Englemann Spruce (*picea engelmannii*), Norway Spruce (*picea abies*), Picea, Pix, Pruce, Prussia, Sitka Spruce, and White Spruce (*picea glauca*).
Family/Class: Pinaceae (pine).
Habitat: Alaska, Europe, North America, and the Subalpine zone.
Flavor: Bitter.
Parts Used: Bark (inner), buds, needles, shoots (young).
Properties: Antibiotic, antiphlogistic, depurative, diaphoretic, diuretic, expectorant, laxative, and sedative.
Constituents: Borneol, camphene, carvene (limonene), myrcene, pinene, santene, and vitamin C (ascorbic acid).
Historical Uses: Abscess, arthritis, bronchitis, burns (minor), cancer, cardiovascular conditions, colds, cough, dermatitis, digestive complaints, dysentery, edema, gargle/mouth rinse, gleet, gonorrhea, headache, infection (bacterial, sexually transmitted), inflammation, influenza, kidney problems, lesions (tubercle), liver problems, mucus, muscle and joint pain, nervous conditions, neuralgia, pain, poisoning (chemical, heavy metal), rash, respiratory conditions, rheumatism, scrofula, sexually transmitted diseases (STDs), skin problems, sore throat, sores, sunburn, syphilis, toothache, tuberculosis, ulcer (fistula, syphilitic, tuberculous), urethritis, and wounds (minor).

Discussion: May clear and open bronchial passages; inhibit or destroy developement and growth of bacteria and other microorganisms; promote bowel evacuation, perspiration, urine flow, and the excretion of heavy metals; purify the blood; stimulate peristalsis and uterine contractions.
Cautions/Contraindications: Avoid use if pregnant or breast-feeding, or if you have asthma, cardiovascular conditions, or whooping cough.
Adverse Reactions: Nausea and/or vomiting.
Herb/Drug Interactions: This herb could cause an interaction (possibly severe) when taken with the following drugs: None known.
Preparations/Dosage: Crude Herb: 1-3 grams. Decoction: ¼-½ cup per day. Infusion: ½-1 cup per day.

Squaw Vine (skwaw vīn)
(*Mitchella repens*)

Synonyms/Related Species: Checkerberry, Deerberry, Hive Vine, One-Berry, Partridge Berry, Twinberry, and Winter Clover.
Family/Class: Rubiaceae (madder).
Habitat: North America.
Flavor: Bitter.
Parts Used: Leaves.
Properties: Antibiotic, astringent, diuretic, expectorant, hemostatic, lithotriptic, nervine, oxytocic, sedative, and tonic.
Constituents: Alkaloids, dextrin, glycosides, inulin (starch), mucilage, resin, saponins, tannic acid, and wax.
Historical Uses: Amenorrhea, bleeding, calculus, colds, colitis, congestion (uterine, vaginal), conjunctivitis, diarrhea, dysmenorrhea, edema, gleet, gonorrhea, hemorrhoids, infection (bacterial, sexually transmitted), insomnia, insufficiency (venous), leukorrhea, menstrual problems, mucus, nervous conditions, respiratory conditions, sexually transmitted diseases (STDs), skin problems, snakebite, substitute for pipsissewa (*chimaphila spp.*), syphilis, ulcer (stasis, syphilitic, varicose), urethritis, urodialysis (suppression of urine), uterine problems, vaginitis, varicose veins, and wounds (minor).
Discussion: May calm the nervous system; clear and open bronchial passages; dissolve calculi; enhance digestive system and liver functions; inhibit or destroy development and growth of bacteria and other microorganisms; promote urine flow; restore normal tone to tissues; stimulate uterine contractions.
Cautions/Contraindications: Avoid use if pregnant or breast-feeding.
Adverse Reactions: Diarrhea (possibly bloody), gastrointestinal cramps (severe), hematuria (blood in the urine), nausea, and/or vomiting.
Herb/Drug Interactions: This herb could cause an interaction (possibly severe) when taken with the following drugs: None known.
Preparations/Dosage: Crude Herb: 3-6 grams. Infusion: 1-3 cups per day. Tincture: 5-20 drops (0.3-1.3 cc.) one to three times per day.

Squill (skwil)
(*Urginea maritima*)

Synonyms/Related Species: African Squill (*urginea altissima*), Epimenidea, European Squill, Indian Squill (*urginea indica*), Maritime Squill, Pyrenees Squill (*urginea lilio-hyacinthus*), Red Squill, Scilla, Scylla, Sea Onion, Siberian Squill (*urginea sibirica*), Skilla, Urginea, and White Squill.

Family/Class: Liliaceae (lily).

Habitat: Abyssinia, Algeria, Asia, the Canary Islands, Corsica, England, France, Greece, India, Italy, Malta, the Mediterranean, Morocco, Nubia, Portugal, the Pyrenees, Spain, and Syria.

Flavor: Bitter/pungent.

Parts Used: Bulb (outer scales and center removed).

Properties: Cardiant, diuretic, expectorant, stimulant, and vermin poison.

Constituents: Glycoside, minerals (calcium), mucilage, scillain, scillin, scillipicrin, scilliroside, scillitin, scillonin, scillotoxin, sinistrin, tannic acid, and volatile oil.

Historical Uses: Arrhythmia, asthma, bronchitis, cardiovascular conditions, colds, cough, croup, edema, insufficiency (venous), kidney problems, lung problems, menstrual problems, mucus, nausea, respiratory conditions, urinary problems, vermin, vomiting, and whooping cough.

Discussion: May clear and open bronchial passages; destroy vermin; enhance digestive system function; lower diastolic pressure; promote urine flow; slow and strengthen the heartrate; stimulate the cardiovascular system and uterine contractions.

Cautions/Contraindications: Avoid use if pregnant or breast-feeding, or if you have an acute inflammatory condition, carotid sinus syndrome, hypercalcaemia, hypokaliemia, hypertrophic cardiomyopathy, tachycardia, thoracic aortic aneurysm, or nephritis. May cause dermatitis in susceptible individuals. Not for long-term use. Use with professional guidance supervision.

Adverse Reactions: Abdominal pain, appetite loss, arrhythmia, asphyxiation, cardiac failure, confusion, convulsions, depression, diarrhea, dramatic reduction in body temperature, gastrointestinal and genitourinary tract inflammation, hallucinations, headache, insufficiency (circulatory), mucous membrane irritation, nausea, psychosis, respiratory distress, stupor, visual disturbances, vomiting, and/or possible death.

Herb/Drug Interactions: This herb could cause an interaction (possibly severe) when taken with the following drugs: Autonomic drugs, Calcium Carbonate, Cardiac drugs, Gluco-Corticoid drugs, and Laxative drugs.

Preparations/Dosage: Crude Herb (powdered): Average dose in substance 0.1-0.5 grains. Extract: 1-3 drops (0.06-0.2 cc.) one to two times per day. Pill Form: Average dose 1-3 grains (0.066-0.2 gm.). Syrup of Squill (*syrupus scilla*): 5-30 drops (0.333-2 cc.) per day in water. Tincture: 5-15 drops (0.333-1 cc.) one to three times per day. Vinegar of Squill (*acetic scilla*): 5-15 drops (0.333-1 cc.) one to three times per day.

Isolation: Scillain or Scillipicrin: Average dose of $^{1}/_{60}$ grain (0.0011 gm.) for use as a diuretic. Scillitin: Average dose of $^{1}/_{65}$ grain (0.001 gm) for use as a diuretic. Scillonin: average dose in substance $^{1}/_{120}$-$^{1}/_{60}$ grain (0.0005-0.001 gm.) for use as a cardiant, diuretic, and stimulant. Scillonin's action is similar to that of digitalis.

Stevia (stē vē·e)
(*Eupatorium rebaudianum*)

Synonyms/Related Species: Guarani.
Family/Class: Compositae (composite).
Habitat: South America (primarily the Rain Forests).
Flavor: Sweet.
Parts Used: Leaves.
Properties: Hypoglycemic and nutritive.
Constituents: Disaccharide, glycosides, minerals (chromium, iron, manganese, phosphorus, potassium, selenium, silicon, sodium, zinc), monosaccharides, rebaudin, silicic acid, and vitamins (A, B_1 (thiamine), B_2 (riboflavin), B_3 (niacin), C (ascorbic acid).
Historical Uses: Addiction (food), diabetes, gargle/mouth rinse, hyperglycemia, hypertension (mild/moderate), substitute for sugar, and weight loss.
Discussion: May enhance pancreatic and spleen functions; increase glycogen (stored sugar) in the liver; reduce blood sugar levels; provide dietary supplementation; serve as an adjuvant to nutritional therapeutic programs, as an adjuvant for hyperglycemia and Type I diabetes, and serve as a noncaloric sweetener, a substitute for sugar, and a sweetener in liquid extracts, tinctures, and teas.
Cautions/Contraindications: Avoid excessive use if pregnant or breast-feeding.
Adverse Reactions: Edema, nausea, and/or vomiting.
Herb/Drug Interactions: This herb could cause an interaction (possibly severe) when taken with the following drugs: None known.
Preparations/Dosage: When using stevia in liquid form, several drops are equivalent to several teaspoons. When using in powder form, use only a few grains. Stevia can be added to hot or cold food or drink. Sweeten to taste (do not use in excess).
Did You Know? Stevia is a nontoxic, nonfattening (contains approximately one calorie per eight to ten leaves), natural sweetener that is several hundred times times sweeter than sugar.

Stone Root (stōn root)
(*Collinsonia canadensis*)

Synonyms/Related Species: Collinsonia, Hardhack, Hardrock, Horsebalm, Horseweed, Knob Grass, Knotroot, Oxbalm, Richleaf, Richweed, and Wild Citronella.
Family/Class: Labiatae (mint).
Habitat: North America.
Flavor: Pungent/sour.
Parts Used: Root.
Properties: Alterative, antispasmodic, astringent, diaphoretic, diuretic, emmenagogue, hemostatic, lithotriptic, sedative, stomachic, tonic, and vulnerary.
Constituents: Alkaloid, caffeic acid, carvene (limonene), caryophyllin, inulin (starch), mucilage, resin, saponins, tannic acid, volatile oil, and wax.
Historical Uses: Amenorrhea, asthma, bleeding, bronchitis, bruises, calculus, colds, colitis, congestion (uterine, vaginal), dermatitis, diarrhea, dysentery, dysmenorrhea, edema, gallstones, gargle/mouth rinse, gastritis, gastroenteritis, gastrointestinal problems, hemorrhoids, hypertrophy (benign prostatic), inflammation, influenza, insufficiency (venous), kidney stones, laryngitis, leukorrhea, menorrhagia, menstrual problems, pleurisy, poison ivy/oak, pruritus, skin problems,

spasmodic conditions, spider veins, sore throat, sores, ulcer (duodenal, gastric, peptic, stasis, varicose), urinary problems, vaginitis, varicose veins, and wounds (minor).
Discussion: May dissolve calculi; enhance colon, liver, lung, and stomach functions; promote perspiration and urine flow; reestablish healthy system functions; restore normal tone to tissues; speed healing; strengthen the vascular system; stimulate menstruation.
Cautions/Contraindications: Avoid use if pregnant or breast-feeding.
Adverse Reactions: Diarrhea (possibly bloody), dizziness, fainting, gastrointestinal cramps (severe), hematuria (blood in the usrine), mucous membrane irritation, nausea, and/or vomiting.
Herb/Drug Interactions: This herb could cause an interaction (possibly severe) when taken with the following drugs: None known.
Preparations/Dosage: Crude Herb: 1-4 grams. Crude Herb (powdered): Average dose in substance 15-60 grains (1-4 grams). Decoction: ¼-1 cup per day. Extract: 5-10 drops (0.333-0.666 cc.) one to two times per day. Infusion: 1 cup per day. Tincture: 5-20 drops (0.333-1.25 cc.) one to three times per day.

Strawberry (strô ber ē)
(*Fragaria virginiana*)

Synonyms/Related Species: Beach Strawberry (*frageria chiloensis*), Fragaria, Mountain Strawberry, Otehimika, Otsistini, Straberie, Streawberie, Wild Strawberry, and Wood Strawberry (*frageria vesca*).
Family/Class: Rosaceae (rose).
Habitat: Alaska, Asia, Britain, California, England, Europe, France, Hawaii, North America, South America, the Subalpine zone, and the Yukon Territory.
Flavor: Fruit: sweet. Leaves/Root: sweet/bitter.
Parts Used: Fruit, leaves, root.
Properties: Antiphlogistic, antiscorbutic, astringent, depurative, diuretic, hemostatic, hypotensive, laxative, lithotriptic, tonic, vasodilator, and vulnerary.
Constituents: Anthocyanin, catechins, citric acid, ellagic acid, fiber, flavonoids, fragarine, malic acid, minerals (calcium, iron, phosphorous, potassium), monosaccharides, mucilage, oligomeric proanthocyanidins, pectic acid, pectin, phosphoric acid, quercetin, rutin, tannic acid, and vitamins (A, B_1 (thiamine), B_2 (riboflavin), B_3 (niacin), B_5 (pantothenic acid), B_6 (pyridoxine), B_{12}, B_x (para-aminobenzoic acid (PABA), C (ascorbic acid), H (biotin), inositol, M (folic acid).
Historical Uses: Acne, arthritis, bleeding, burns (minor), calculus, convalescence, dentifrice, diarrhea, dysentery, eczema, fever (ephemeral, rheumatic), gallstones, gastrointestinal problems, gout, headache, hematuria, hypertension (mild/moderate), infection (urinary tract), inflammation, jaundice, kidney stones, liver problems, muscle and joint pain, nervous conditions, night sweats, periodontal disease, rash, respiratory conditions, rheumatism, rheumatoid arthritis (RA), scurvy, skin problems, sores, sunburn, toothache, ulcer (duodenal, gastric, peptic), vaginitis, vomiting, and wounds (minor).
Discussion: May cause blood vessel dilatation; dissolve calculi; increase acid in the urine; inhibit histamine production; prevent hemorrhage in persons with hypertension; promote urine flow; purify the blood; reduce blood pressure levels and capillary fragiltity; remove discoloration of the teeth; restore normal tone to tissues; speed healing.
Cautions/Contraindications: Avoid use if pregnant or breast-feeding. May increase the effectiveness of antihistamine drugs.

Adverse Reactions: Diarrhea, nausea, and/or vomiting.
Herb/Drug Interactions: This herb could cause an interaction (possibly severe) when taken with the following drugs: Antihistamine drugs and Hypotensive drugs.
Preparations/Dosage: Crude Herb (leaves/root): 3-6 grams. Extract (root): 3-5 drops (0.2-0.333 cc.) one to two times per day. Fruit: May be ingested freely. Infusion (leaves or root): 1-3 cups per day. Juice: 2-4 tablespoons one to two times per day. Tincture (leaves or root): 5-15 drops (0.333-1 cc.) one to three times per day. Dentifrice: To whiten teeth rub a cut strawberry over teeth, allowing the juice to remain on the teeth for five minutes. Add a pinch of bicarbonate of soda to warm water and rinse teeth (do not swallow water).

Suma (soo mä)
(*Pfaffia paniculata*)

Synonyms/Related Species: Brazilian Ginseng and Para Todo.
Family/Class: Amarantheaceae (amaranth).
Habitat: South America.
Flavor: Bitter/sweet.
Parts Used: Root.
Properties: Alterative, anticarcinogen, antiphlogistic, aphrodisiac, demulcent, erythropoietic, nutritive, tonic, and vulnerary.
Constituents: Allantoin, fatty acids (arachidonic, linoleic, linolenic), minerals (germanium, iron, magnesium), saponins, sitosterol, stigmasterol, and vitamins (A, B, C (ascorbic acid), E (alpha-tocopheral).
Historical Uses: Anemia, arthritis, bronchitis, cancer (breast), chronic fatigue syndrome (CFS), colds, diabetes, dietary supplementation, Epstein Barr Virus (EBV), erectile dysfunction, fatigue, fever (ephemeral, rheumatic), fibromyalgia, frigidity, heart disease, Hodgkin's disease, hot flashes, hypercholesteremia, hypoglycemia, infection (viral), inflammation, insufficiency (venous), leukemia, malnutrition, menopausal/menstrual problems, mood swings, mononucleosis (infectious), muscle and joint pain, osteomyelitis, osteoporosis, premenstrual syndrome (PMS), rheumatism, skin problems, tumors, ulcer (duodenal, gastric, peptic), and wounds (minor).
Discussion: May arouse sexual impulses; balance the hormonal system; decrease the effect of carcinogens; enhance immune system, lung, pancreas, and spleen functions; increase circulation, endurance, energy, estrogen levels, and stamina; produce red blood cells; promote new cell growth; protect against harmful free radicals and protect against heart disease; provide dietary supplementation; reduce cholesterol levels; reestablish healthy system functions; regulate blood sugar levels; restore normal tone to tissues and restore sexual function; serve as a nutritional adjuvant to therapeutic programs; soothe mucous membrane irritation; speed healing; stop and/or slow abnormal cell growth.
Cautions/Contraindications: Avoid use if pregnant or breast-feeding.
Adverse Reactions: Diarrhea (possibly bloody), gastrointestinal cramps (severe), hematuria (blood in the urine), nausea, and/or vomiting.
Herb/Drug Interactions: This herb could cause an interaction (possibly severe) when taken with the following drugs: None known.
Preparations/Dosage: Crude Herb: 3-9 grams. Infusion: 1-3 cups per day.
Isolation: Germanium dioxide: Used in 0.2% aqueous solution, for use as an erythropoietic.

Sumac (su mak)
(*Rhus glabra*)

Synonyms/Related Species: Dwarf Sumac, European Sumac (*rhus coriaria*), Fragrant Sumac, Lacquer Tree, Mountain Sumac (*rhus copallinum*), Pennsylvania Sumac, Scarlet Sumac, Sicilian Sumac, Skunkbrush, Smooth Sumac, Squaw Bush (*rhus trilobata*), Staghorn Sumac (*rhus typhinum*), Sugar Sumac (*rhus ovata*), Summāq, Sweet Sumac (*rhus aromatica*), Upland Sumac, Varnish Sumac (*rhus vernicifera*), Velvet Sumac, Venetian Sumac (*rhus cotinus*), and Virginian Sumac.

Family/Class: Anacardiaceae (cashew).

Habitat: China, England, Europe, Japan, and North America.

Flavor: Bitter.

Parts Used: Bark (branch/root), exudation, leaves.

Properties: Alterative, antibiotic, antifungal, antihidrotic, antiphlogistic, astringent, counterirritant, demulcent, diuretic, emmenagogue, emetic, laxative, parasiticide, tonic, and vulnerary.

Constituents: Fatty acids (oleic, palmitic, stearic), fixed oils (olein, palmitin, stearin), gallic acid, malic acid, mucilage, resin, rhusin, tannic acid, and volatile oil.

Historical Uses: Alopecia, angina, appetite loss, asthma, bleeding, candida, canker sores, congestion (uterine, vaginal), cystitis, debility, diabetes, diarrhea, dysentery, dysuria (painful/difficult urination), eczema, ephidrosis, fever, frostbite, gargle/mouth rinse, gastrointestinal problems, glandular swelling, gleet, gonorrhea, hemorrhoids, infection (bacterial, fungal, sexually transmitted, urinary tract), inflammation, influenza, lesions (tubercle), leukorrhea, lochia, lung problems, mercurial conditions, moniliasis, parasites (ringworm), periodontal disease, poison ivy/oak, poisoning (mercury), prolapse (rectal, uterine), pruritus, psoriasis, rash, scrofula, sexually transmitted diseases (STDs), skin problems, sore throat, sores, stomachache, strep throat, sunburn, syphilis, toothache, tuberculosis, ulcer (duodenal, fistula, gastric, peptic, syphilitic, tuberculous), urethritis, urinary problems, vaginitis, and wounds (minor).

Discussion: May diminish ephidrosis (excessive perspiration); enhance liver and urinary system functions; inhibit or destroy development and growth of bacteria and other microorganisms; promote bowel evacuation and urine flow; reestablish healthy system functions; restore normal tone to tissues; soothe mucous membrane irritation; speed healing; stimulate appetite, menstruation, and the immune system.

Cautions/Contraindications: Avoid use if pregnant or breast-feeding. Do not confuse these species of sumac with other more toxic species such as poison sumac (*rhus venenata*). Keep away from eyes and mucous membranes. May cause dermatitis in susceptible individuals. Use protective clothing and gloves when harvesting.

Adverse Reactions: Asphyxiation, conjunctivitis, corneal inflammation, delirium, diarrhea, dizziness, drowsiness, fainting, fever, gastrointestinal cramps, hematuria (blood in the urine), pruritus, respiratory distress, skin and mucous membrane eruptions (possibly severe), nausea, stupor, vertigo, vomiting, and/or possible death.

Herb/Drug Interactions: This herb could cause an interaction (possibly severe) when taken with the following drugs: None known.

Preparations/Dosage: External uses recommended. Great care must be taken when using sumac preparations externally, and internal use (ingestion) of sumac preparations is recommended only for those persons who have long used and are experienced with its uses in

this way. Topical Use: Cover unaffected areas of skin and apply (wearing gloves) in extremely small-diluted amounts. May cause skin irritation, redness, and inflammation upon application. Thoroughly wash affected area afterwards with a soapy solution to remove any resinous residue. Keep away from eyes and mucous membranes. Internal Use: Initially, those persons who are not used to ingesting sumac should begin with extremely small-diluted amounts, as the ingestion of large amounts can cause severe adverse effects resulting in possible death due to asphyxiation. Crude Herb: 3-6 grams. Decoction (bark): ⅛-¼ cup per day. Extract (bark): 3-8 drops (0.2-0.5 cc.) one to two times per day. Exudation (dried/powdered): Average dose in substance 20 grains (1.333 gm.). Infusion (bark or leaves): ¼-½ cup per day. Tincture: 5-10 drops (0.3-0.6 cc.) one to three times per day.
Isolation: Rhusin: Average dose of 1-2 grains (0.06-0.13 gm.) for use as an astringent.
Prevention: Remove affected clothing and place in plastic bag until they can be washed in hot soapy water (wear gloves when removing clothing from bag as contact with the toxic oil can cause severe skin reactions). Washing skin thoroughly within 10 minutes of exposure with hot soapy water may help to remove the toxic oil and prevent skin reactions.
First Aid: Mild to Moderate Cases: Cold soaks in the bathtub for 20 minutes several times daily may help relieve inflammation. Corticosteroid or Corticosterone creams applied topically (avoid genital area) can help to relieve itching and inflammation. Oral (systemic) corticosteroids can also help relieve discomforts. For Severe Cases or affected areas involving the anal or genital area obtain immediate medical attention. Be prepared to administer artificial respiration (CPR) in the event of respiratory failure.
Note: There are many varieties of sumac, and care should be taken to make the distinction between the non-poisonous and poisonous species. Non-poisonous sumac berries are red to reddish orange, densely covered in short reddish or rust-colored hairs, hang in drupes, and have compound, terminal panicles. Poisonous sumac berries are red to reddish orange, smooth, hairless, hang in drupes, and have axillary panicles.

Sumbul (sum bel)
(*Ferula sumbul*)

Synonyms/Related Species: Euryangium Muskroot, Jatamansi, Moschuswurzel, Ofnokgi, Ouchi, Racine de Sumbul, Sambul Root (*ferula suaveolens*), and Sunbul.
Family/Class: Umbelliferae (parsley).
Habitat: Asia, India, Iran, Libya, Persia, Russia, Siberia, and Turkey.
Flavor: Bitter/pungent.
Parts Used: Root.
Properties: Antiphlogistic, antispasmodic, caustic, diaphoretic, diuretic, emmenagogue, expectorant, nervine, stimulant, and vesicant.
Constituents: Acetic acid, alkaloid, betaine (lycine), bitter principle, fatty acids (angelic, arachidonic, cerotinic, linoleic, linolenic, oleic, palmitic, stearic, tiglic), fiber, fixed oils (olein, palmitin, stearin), gum, inulin (starch), monosaccharides, pentosan, protein, resin, sterol, umbelliferon, valerianic acid, vanillic acid, volatile oil, and wax.
Historical Uses: Asthma, bronchitis, colds, corns, cough, delirium, diarrhea, dysentery, dysmenorrhea, fever (ephemeral, rheumatic), gout, hysteria, inflammation, menopausal/menstrual problems, mucus, muscle and joint pain, neurasthenia, nervous

conditions, pneumonia, respiratory conditions, rheumatism, spasmodic conditions, tumors, and warts (digitate, filiform, fugitive, glabra, mother, plana juvenilis, plantar, seborrhoeic, vulgaris).
Discussion: May calm the nervous system; clear and open bronchial passages; promote perspiration and urine flow; stimulate menstruation.
Cautions/Contraindications: Avoid use if pregnant or breast-feeding.
Adverse Reactions: Blistering of the mouth/skin/throat, confusion, nausea, skin tingling, stupor, and/or vomiting.
Herb/Drug Interactions: This herb could cause an interaction (possibly severe) when taken with the following drugs: None known.
Preparations/Dosage: Crude Herb: 1-3 grams. Decoction: ¼-½ cup per day. Infusion: ½-1 cup per day. Extract: 1-3 drops (0.06-0.2 cc.) one to two times per day. Extract (powdered): Average dose in susbstance 2-5 grains (0.133-0.333 gm.). Extract (solid): Average dose in substance 4 grains (0.26 gm). Tincture: 2-5 drops (0.133-0.333 cc.) one to three times per day. Corns and Warts: Apply root juice once a day directly on corn or wart and cover with a bandaid. Reapply daily until corn or wart is gone.
Isolation: Acetic acid (dilute): Used in an aqueous solution containing 6% of the pure acid, average dose of 60-90 drops (4-6 cc.) in water, for use as a caustic. Angelic acid: Average dose of 10-30 grains (0.666-2 gm.) for use in fever (intermittent), gout, and rheumatism. Betaine: Average dose of 2-4 grains (0.13-0.26 gm.) for use as an emmenagogue.

Sundew (sun doo)
(*Drosera rotundifolia*)

Synonyms/Related Species: Dew Plant, Great Sundew (*drosera anglica*), Herba Rosellae, Lustwort, Red Root, Rosée du Soleil, Roundleaf Sundew, Round-Leaved Sundew, Sonnenthaurosollis, and Youthwort.
Family/Class: Droseraceae (sundew).
Habitat: Asia, Britain, China, Europe, India, North America, Russia, and South America.
Flavor: Bitter/pungent.
Parts Used: Aerial.
Properties: Abortifacient, alterative, antibiotic, antifungal, antiphlogistic, antiscorbutic, antispasmodic, antiviral, aphrodisiac, caustic, counterirritant, demulcent, expectorant, laxative, and tonic.
Constituents: Citric acid, enzymes, flavonoids, malic acid, napthoquinone, plumbagin, vitamins (C (ascorbic acid), and volatile oil.
Historical Uses: Arteriosclerosis, asthma, bronchitis, bunions, colds, corns (juice), cough, fever, infection (bacterial, fungal, viral), inflammation, laryngitis, mucus, nausea, pleurisy, pneumonia (lobar), respiratory conditions, scurvy, spasmodic conditions, warts (digitate, filiform, fugitive, glabra, mother, plana juvenilis, plantar, seborrhoeic, vulgaris), and whooping cough.
Discussion: May arouse sexual impulses; clear and open bronchial passages; enhance lung function; induce abortion; inhibit or destroy developement and growth of bacteria and other microorganisms; promote bowel evacuation; reestablish healthy system functions; restore normal tone to tissues; soothe mucous membrane irritation; stimulate the immune system.
Cautions/Contraindications: Avoid use if pregnant or breast-feeding. Not for long-term use.
Adverse Reactions: Blistering of the mouth/skin/throat, diarrhea, nausea, and/or vomiting.
Herb/Drug Interactions: This herb could cause an interaction (possibly severe) when taken with the following drugs: None known.

Preparations/Dosage: Crude Herb: 1-3 grams. Crude Herb (powdered): Average dose in substance 1-3 grains (0.066-0.2 gm.). Extract (solid): Average dose in substance 2-5 grams. Infusion: 1-2 cups per day. Tincture: 2-5 drops (0.133-0.3 cc.) one to three times per day. External Use: Corns/Warts (juice): Mix juice with milk or buttermilk and apply directly to corn or wart once or twice daily. Cover with a band-aid. Repeat as needed until corn or wart is gone.

Sunflower (sun flou·er)
(*Helianthus annuus*)

Synonyms/Related Species: Chrysanthemum Peruvian, Common Sunflower, Corona Solis, Heliosanthos, Marigold of Peru, Nuttall's Sunflower (*helianthus nuttallii*), Russian Sunflower, and Sola Indianus.
Family/Class: Compositae (composite).
Floral Emblem: Kansas.
Habitat: Bulgaria, Chile, China, Denmark, Egypt, England, France, Germany, Hungary, India, Italy, Japan, Manchuria, Mexico, North America, Peru, Poland, Romania, Russia, South America, and Spain.
Flavor: Sweet.
Parts Used: Flowers, flower buds, seeds.
Properties: Antiperiodic, antiphlogistic, astringent, diaphoretic, diuretic, expectorant, hemostatic, hypoglycemic, insect repellent, malariacidal, and nutritive.
Constituents: Campesterol, carbohydrates, cholesterol, fatty acids (arachidonic, behenic, linoleic, linolenic, oleic, palmitic, stearic), fixed oils (olein, palmitin, stearin), inulin (starch), lecithin, levulin, minerals (calcium, iron, magnesium, manganese, phosphorus, potassium, sulfur, zinc), monosaccharides, polysaccharides, protein, vitamins (A, B_1 (thiamine), B_2 (riboflavin), B_3 (niacin), B_5 (pantothenic acid), B_6 (pyridoxine), B_{12}, B_x (para-aminobenzoic acid (PABA), E (alpha-tocopheral), H (biotin), inositol, M (folic acid), and volatile oil.
Historical Uses: Ague, appetite loss, bladder problems, bleeding, blisters, bronchitis, bruises, cardiovascular conditions, colds, constipation, cough, deficiency (EFAs), diabetes, dietary supplementation, dysentery, fever (ephemeral, intermittent, rheumatic), flies, food source (oil/ripened seeds), headache, hyperglycemia, inflammation, insect bites or stings, kidney problems, laryngitis, lesions, lung problems, malaria, malnutrition, mucus, muscle and joint pain, parasites (malarial plasmodia), psoriasis, respiratory conditions, rheumatism, skin problems, snakebite, sores, substitute for artichokes (flower buds), weight loss, whooping cough, and wounds (minor).
Discussion: May clear and open bronchial passages; promote perspiration and urine flow; provide dietary supplementation; reduce blood sugar levels; serve as a nutritional adjuvant to therapeutic programs; stimulate appetite and the immune system.
Cautions/Contraindications: Avoid use if pregnant or breast-feeding. May cause allergic reactions in susceptible individuals.
Adverse Reactions: Elevated triglyceride levels, flatulence, nausea, and/or vomitng.
Herb/Drug Interactions: This herb could cause an interaction (possibly severe) when taken with the following drugs: Antidiabetic drugs.
Preparations/Dosage: Crude Herb (flowers): 3-6 grams. Flower Buds (unopened): Boiled and eaten as a vegetable. Sunflower Seed Oil (*oleum helianthus*): 10-15 drops (0.666-1 cc.) or used

in cooking. Seeds (shells removed): Ground and used as a flour or roasted and eaten freely. Tincture (flowers): 5-20 drops (0.333-1.25 cc.) one to three times per day.
Did You Know? Sunflowers are heliotropic, which means the flower heads turn during the course of the day so they always face the sun.

Sweet Almond (swēt ä mend)
(*Prunus amygdalus dulces*)

Synonyms/Related Species: Almande, Amande, Greek Nuts, Jardin, Jordan Almond, Shakad, Sicilian Almond, and Valentia Almond.
Family/Class: Rosaceae (rose).
Habitat: Africa, Asia, the Balearic Islands, Belgium, Egypt, England, Europe, France, Greece, Italy, the Mediterranean, Morocco, Palestine, Portugal, Spain, Syria, and the United States.
Flavor: Sweet/bland.
Parts Used: Kernels.
Properties: Antiphlogistic, antispasmodic, demulcent, diuretic, expectorant, lithotriptic, and nutritive.
Constituents: Fatty acids (arachidonic, linoleic, linolenic, oleic, palmitic, stearic), fixed oils (olein, palmitin, stearin), protein, mucilage, and volatile oil.
Historical Uses: Acne, bladder problems, calculus, colds, colic, cough, dietary supplementation, digestive complaints, dry skin, fever, gallstones, gastritis, gastrointestinal problems, gout, indigestion, inflammation, kidney problems, kidney stones, laryngitis, malnutrition, mucus, pain, nephritis, pimples, pleurisy, respiratory conditions, skin problems, spasmodic conditions, substitute for olive oil (oil), substitute for peanut butter (the kernels are made into almond butter), and urinary problems.
Discussion: May clear and open bronchial passages; dissolve calculi; promote urine flow; provide dietary supplementation; serve as a nutritional adjuvant to therapeutic programs; soothe mucous membrane irritation.
Cautions/Contraindications: Avoid use if pregnant or breast-feeding. Do not confuse this plant with bitter almond (*prunus amygdala amara*).
Adverse Reactions: Nausea and/or vomiting.
Herb/Drug Interactions: This herb could cause an interaction (possibly severe) when taken with the following drugs: None known.
Preparations/Dosage: Kernels: Handful daily. Oil of Sweet Almond (*oleum amygdalae expressum*): 60-120 drops (4-8 cc.) in water or on a sugarcube.
Did You Know? The annual amount of imported sweet almonds into this country averages over 500 tons.

Sweet Cicely (swēt sis ’lē)
(*Osmorhiza longistylis*)

Synonyms/Related Species: Anise Root, Blunt-Fruited Sweet Cicely (*osmorhiza depauperata*), Mountain Sweet Cicely (*osmorhiza chilensis*), Sweet Anise, Sweet Chervil, Sweet Jarvil, Sweet Root, and Western Sweet Cicely (*osmorhiza occidentalis*).
Family/Class: Umbelliferae (parsley).
Habitat: Alaska, North America, and the Yukon Territory.

Flavor: Sweet.
Parts Used: Root.
Properties: Analgesic, antibiotic, anticarcinogen, antifungal, antiphlogistic, antispasmodic, aromatic, carminative, depurative, diaphoretic, diuretic, emmenagogue, expectorant, insect repellent, laxative, narcotic, oxytocic, parasiticide, stimulant, stomachic, and tonic.
Constituents: Carbohydrates, coumarin, creosol, fatty acids (arachidonic, linoleic, linolenic, oleic, palmitic, stearic), fixed oils (olein, palmitin, stearin), lipids, minerals (calcium, iron, magnesium, potassium), monosaccharides, mucilage, phytoestrogen, pinene, protein, sterols, vitamins (B, choline), and volatile oil.
Historical Uses: Abdominal pain, amenorrhea, anemia, appetite loss, asthma, belching, bronchitis, bruises, cancer (prostate), candida, cholera, cirrhosis, colds, colic, convulsions, cough, cramps, diarrhea, digestive complaints, diminished sex drive, diphtheria, edema, epilepsy, fever (ephemeral, rheumatic), flatulence, flavoring agent, fleas, halitosis, headache, hepatitis, hiccups, indigestion, infection (bacterial, fungal), inflammation, influenza, insomnia, kidney problems, liver problems, menopausal problems, moniliasis, mucus, muscle and joint pain, nausea, nervous conditions, pain, parasites (lice and their nits, scabies), perfume, pneumonia, potpourris, respiratory conditions, rheumatism, sachets, sinusitis, sore throat, sores, spasmodic conditions, substitute for anise, toothache, ulcer (indolent), vomiting, whooping cough, and wounds (minor).
Discussion: May aid digestion; cleanse the intestinal tract; clear and open bronchial passages; decrease the effect of carcinogens; enhance stomach function; inhibit or destroy developement and growth of bacteria and other microorganisms; prevent the deposition of fat in the liver; promote bowel evacuation, perspiration, and urine flow; regenerate damaged liver cells; restore normal tone to tissues; serve as an adjuvant to some cancer (prostate) therapies; stabilize sugar metabolism; stimulate appetite, glandular secretions, libido, menstruation, and uterine contractions.
Cautions/Contraindications: Avoid use if pregnant or breast-feeding, or if you are allergic to anise or anethol, or if you have an estrogen dependent cancer, or if you have a history of estrogen dependant cancers, or if you are taking oral contraceptives. Do not confuse this herb with poison hemlock (conium spp.). Estrogen containing substances may contribute to abnormal blood clotting, migraine, and could promote the developement of certain types of estrogen dependant cancers. Not for long-term use.
Adverse Reactions: Abdominal pain, cancer (breast), coagulation problems, diarrhea, dizziness, edema, insufficiency (circulatory), migraine, nausea, seizure conditions, skin problems, stupor, and/or vomiting.
Herb/Drug Interactions: This herb could cause an interaction (possibly severe) when taken with the following drugs: Hormones and Synthetic Substitutes (i.e. conjugated estrogens, contraceptives (oral, etc.), and other hormonal replacement therapy (HRT).
Preparations/Dosage: Crude Herb: 3-6 grams. Infusion: 1-1½ cups per day. Tincture: 10-15 drops (0.666-1 cc.) one to three times per day.
Isolation: Creosol: Average dose of ½-2 drops (0.025-0.1 cc.) for use as an antimicrobic.

Sweet Cicely, European (swēt sis 'lē, yoor e·pē en)
(*Myrrhis odorata*)

Synonyms/Related Species: British Myrrh, Cerfelle, Chervil, Cow Chervil, Great Sweet Chervil, Shepherd's Needle, Smooth Cicely, Sweet Bracken, Sweet Chervil, Sweet-Cus, Sweet Fern, Sweet Humlock, Sweets, and The Roman Plant.
Family/Class: Umbelliferae (parsley).
Habitat: Britain, the Caucasus, England, the Pyrenees, and Scotland.
Flavor: Sweet.
Parts Used: Leaves, root, seeds.
Properties: Antibiotic, antiphlogistic, aphrodisiac, aromatic, carminative, depurative, diuretic, expectorant, hypotensive, lithotriptic, stimulant, stomachic, and vasodilator.
Constituents: Apiol, apiolin, bergapten, carvene (limonene), coumarins, fatty acids (oleic, palmitic, stearic), fixed oils (olein, palmitin, stearin), flavonoids, minerals (calcium, iron, magnesium, phosphorus, potassium, silicon, sodium, sulfur), phthalides, psoralens, quercitrin, resin, silicic acid, and vitamins (A, B, C (ascorbic acid).
Historical Uses: Abscess, asthma, bladder problems, bruises, calculus, colds, cough, digestive complaints, dysmenorrhea, eczema, edema, fever (ephemeral, rheumatic), flatulence, flavoring agent, gallstones, gout, hiccups, hypertension (mild/moderate), infection (bacterial), inflammation, kidney stones, mucus, muscle and joint pain, pleurisy, respiratory conditions, rheumatism, snakebite, sore throat, thrombosis (blood clot), ulcer (duodenal, gastric, peptic), urinary problems, and wounds (minor).
Discussion: May aid digestion; arouse sexual impulses; cause blood vessel dilatation; clear and open bronchial passages; dissolve blood clots and calculi; enhance stomach function; inhibit or destroy development and growth of bacteria and other microorganisms; promote urine flow; purify the blood; reduce blood pressure levels.
Cautions/Contraindications: Avoid use if pregnant or breast-feeding.
Adverse Reactions: Edema.
Herb/Drug Interactions: This herb could cause an interaction (possibly severe) when taken with the following drugs: Diuretic drugs and Hypotensive drugs.
Preparations/Dosage: Crude Herb: 3-6 grams. Decoction: ½ cup per day. Infusion: ½-1 cup per day. Leaves/Root/Seeds (fresh): May be ingested freely or cooked as a vegetable.

Tamarind (tam'e·rind)
(*Tamarindus indica*)

Synonyms/Related Species: Imlee, Indian Date, and Tamr Hindī.
Family/Class: Leguminosae (legume).
Habitat: Africa and India.
Flavor: Bitter/sweet.
Parts Used: Fruit (pulp).
Properties: Antiphlogistic, antiscorbutic, astringent, laxative, nutritive, and stimulant.
Constituents: Bitartrate, citric acid, fiber, gum, malic acid, minerals (calcium, potassium), monosaccharides, pectic acid, pectin, tartaric acid, and vitamins (B_2 (riboflavin), C (ascorbic acid).

Historical Uses: Asthma, constipation, convalesence, dietary supplementation, dysentery, fever (ephemeral, rheumatic), flavoring agent, inflammation, jam/jelly, jaundice, liver problems, malnutrition, muscle and joint pain, rheumatism, scurvy, and sore throat.
Discussion: May promote bowel evacuation; provide dietary supplementation; serve as a nutritional adjuvant to therapeutic programs; stimulate peristalsis.
Cautions/Contraindications: Avoid use if pregnant or breast-feeding.
Adverse Reactions: Diarrhea, nausea, and/or vomiting.
Herb/Drug Interactions: This herb could cause an interaction (possibly severe) when taken with the following drugs: None known.
Preparations/Dosage: Fruit (pulp): 8-16 grams. Infusion (fruit pulp): ½-2 cups per day.

Tansy (tan ze)
(*Tanacetum vulgare*)

Synonyms/Related Species: Athanaton, Bitter Buttons, Common Tansy, Hindheal, New England Aster, Parsley Fern, Tanacetum, and Wild Tansy.
Family/Class: Compositae (composite).
Habitat: Europe, North America, and Scotland.
Flavor: Bitter/pungent.
Parts Used: Leaves, tops.
Properties: Abortifacient, anthelmintic, antibiotic, antiphlogistic, antispasmodic, carminative, demulcent, diaphoretic, diuretic, emmenagogue, insect repellent, narcotic, nervine, parasiticide, stimulant, stomachic, tonic, vermifuge, and vermin repellent.
Constituents: Borneol, camphor, chlorophyll, citric acid, gallic acid, gum, monosaccharides, pinene, protein, resin, sabinene, stearine, tanacetic acid, tanacetin, tannic acid, thujone, vitamin A, and volatile oil, wax.
Historical Uses: Ague, amenorrhea, appetite loss, bruises, cramps, dysmenorrhea, epilepsy, fever (ephemeral, rheumatic), flatulence, flies, gastroenteritis, gout, hysteria, indigestion, infection (bacterial), inflammation, jaundice, menopausal/menstrual problems, migraine, muscle and joint pain, nervous conditions, neuralgia, parasites (pinworm, roundworm, scabies), pimples, rheumatism, skin problems, sore throat, spasmodic conditions, sprain, tumors, vermin, and wounds (minor).
Discussion: May aid digestion; calm the nervous system; enhance kidney and stomach functions; induce abortion; inhibit or destroy development and growth of bacteria and other microorganisms; promote perspiration and urine flow; restore normal tone to tissues; soothe mucous membrane irritation; stimulate menstruation and uterine contractions.
Cautions/Contraindications: Avoid use if pregnant or breast-feeding. May cause dermatitis in susceptible individuals. Not for long-term use. This herb is extremely potent and it is highly recommended that it be used with professional guidance/supervision.
Adverse Reactions: Abdominal pain, arrhythmia, coma, convulsions, gastrointestinal cramps (severe), nausea, paralysis, pupil dilatation, seizure conditions, severe nervous system damage, respiratory failure, stupor, vomiting, and/or possible death.
Herb/Drug Interactions: This herb could cause an interaction (possibly severe) when taken with the following drugs: None known.
WARNING! ½ ounce of the oil applied topically or ingested is **poisonous** and can result in death in as little as 2-4 hours.

Preparations/Dosage: Crude Herb: ½-3 grams. Extract: 5-8 drops (0.333-0.5 cc.) one to two times per day. Extract (solid): Average dose in substance 3-5 grains (0.2-0.333 gm.). Infusion (weak): ⅛-¼ cup per day. Tansy Oil (*oleum tanacetum*): 1 drop (0.06 cc.) extremely diluted in a good quality vegetable oil.

Tea (tē)

(*Thea sinensis*)

Synonyms/Related Species: Black Tea, Camellia Sinensis, Chinese Tea, Green Tea, Japan Rose, and Thea.
Family/Class: Theaceae (tea).
Habitat: Argentina, Assam, Ceylon, China, India, Indonesia, Japan, Java, Kenya, Malawi, Pakistan, Sri Lanka, and Turkey.
Floral Emblem: Alabama.
Flavor: Bitter/sweet.
Parts Used: Leaf buds and young leaves.
Properties: Analgesic, antibiotic, anticarcinogen, antihistamine, antioxidant, antiviral, astringent, hemostatic, stimulant, and vasodilator.
Constituents: Aglycones, alkaloids, boheic acid, caffeic acid, caffeine, catechins, chlorogenic acid, fluoride, linalool, minerals (aluminum, potassium), polyphenols, protein, quercetin, resin, saponins, tannic acid, theaflavine, theobromine, theophylline, vitamin K, volatile oil, and wax.
Historical Uses: Allergy, arteriosclerosis, asthma, benign breast disease, bleeding, bronchitis, cancer (bladder, breast, colon, liver, ovarian), canker sores, cataracts, Celiac disease, cirrhosis, colds, diabetes, diabetic retinopathy, diarrhea, ear infection, eczema, edema, emphysema, endometriosis, fever (ephemeral, herpetic), gastrointestinal problems, gout, headache, herpes, hives, human immunodeficiency virus (HIV), hypercholesteremia, hypertension (mild/moderate), infection (bacterial, viral), influenza, macular degeneration, migraine, neuralgia, pain, periodontal disease, poisoning (food, opium), polio, prostatitis, rheumatism, sexually transmitted diseases (STDs), shingles, spasmodic conditions, tumors, vomiting, weight loss, and wrinkles.
Discussion: May cause blood vessel dilatation; counteract the effect of histamine; decrease the effect of carcinogens; increase collagen production and energy; induce cancer cells to destroy themselves; inhibit oxidation, the attachment of bacteria to teeth, and inhibit or destroy developement and growth of bacteria and other microorganisms; offset the negative effects of chemotherapy and radiation therapy; protect the eye lens and retinal cells from toxins and the skin from ultraviolet damage; reduce arterial plaque formation, blood pressure and cholesterol levels, the effects of estrogen on the body, and gastric lining erosion; stimulate metabolism; stop or slow abnormal cell growth.
Cautions/Contraindications: Avoid use if pregnant or breast-feeding, or if you have anxiety, hyperthyroidism, kidney disease, a spasmodic condition, stomach sensitivity, or a weakened cardiovascular system. Do not drink green tea within one hour of taking any prescription drug as the drugs effects may be reduced. May interfere with the absorption of antidepressants, atropine (when taken by mouth), codeine, haloperidol, and theophylline drugs. May increase the side effects of ephedrine, pseudoephedrine, theophylline, or ephedra containing drug products. Insomnia and/or overstimulation may occur when taking green tea with beverages or foods

containing caffeine. Some persons may experience bleeding or increased clotting time when using this herb with anticoagulant drugs or aspirin.
Adverse Reactions: Acidity (gastric), appetite loss, arrhythmia, bleeding (possibly serious), coagulation problems, diarrhea (possibly bloody), excitability, gastrointestinal cramps (severe), headache, indigestion, insomnia, irritability, nausea, nervousness, restlessness, tremors, vertigo, and/or vomiting.
Herb/Drug Interactions: This herb could cause an interaction (possibly severe) when taken with the following drugs: Antibiotic drugs, Anticoagulant drugs, Antidepressant drugs, Autonomic drugs, Colchicine drugs, H-2 blocker drugs, Opiate Agonists/Narcotic drugs, other Medications/Products containing ephedra or pseudoephedrine, Salicylates, Subsalicylates, and Theophylline drugs.
Herb/Herb Interactions: Do not use with Ephedra or Ginseng.
Preparations/Dosage: Crude Herb: 3-9 grams. Infusion: 1-3 cups per day (tea is high in tannin content and adding a small amount of milk to the brewed tea will help offset any stomach upset).
Isolation: Caffeine: Soluble in alcohol and water. Average dose of 1-3 grains (0.06-0.2 gm.) for use as a diuretic, nervine, and stimulant, and in poisoning (opium). Theobromine calcium gluconate: Average dose of 0.32-0.65 gm. for use in hypertension. Theobromine salicylate: Soluble (sparingly) in water. Average dose of 15 grains (1 gm.) for use as a diuretic. Theobromine sodiosalicylate: Used in a 5% solution, average dose of 15 drops (1cc.) for use as a diuretic. Theobromine and sodium acetate: Average dose of 15-45 grains (1-3 gm.) for use as a powerful diuretic. Theophylline and sodium acetate: Average dose of 2-5 grains (0.12-0.3 gm.) for use as a diuretic.
Did You Know? Black tea and green tea come from the same plant. Green tea is less processed and retains more of the plant constituents than black tea.

Teasel (tē zel)
(*Dipsacus sylvestris*)

Synonyms/Related Species: Barber's Brush, Brushes and Combs, Card Thistle, Chinese Teasel (*dipsacus asper*), Dipsacus, Fuller's Teasel (*dipsacus fullonum*), Small Teasel (*dipsacus pilosus*), Taesel, Tasel, Venus' Basin, and Wild Teasel.
Family/Class: Dipsacaceae (teasel).
Habitat: Africa, China, England, France, Germany, Italy, and North America.
Flavor: Bitter.
Parts Used: Root.
Properties: Antibiotic, antiperiodic, antiphlogistic, diaphoretic, diuretic, hemostatic, laxative, malariacidal, opthalmic, stomachic, and tonic.
Constituents: Alkaloid, caffeic acid, chlorogenic acid, lamine, and volatile oil.
Historical Uses: Abscess, acne, ague, appetite loss, arthritis, bleeding, eyewash, fever (ephemeral, intermittent, rheumatic), fistula, infection (bacterial), inflammation, jaundice, liver problems, malaria, muscle and joint pain, parasites (malarial plasmodia), pimples, psoriasis, rheumatism, skin problems, sores, warts (digitate, filiform, fugitive, glabra, mother, plana juvenilis, plantar, seborrhoeic, vulgaris), and wounds (minor).
Discussion: May enhance liver and stomach functions; increase circulation; promote bowel evacuation, perspiration, and urine flow; restore normal tone to tissues; stimulate appetite and peristalsis; strengthen bones, ligaments, and tendons.

Cautions/Contraindications: Avoid use if pregnant or breast-feeding.
Adverse Reactions: Nausea and/or vomiting.
Herb/Drug Interactions: This herb could cause an interaction (possibly severe) when taken with the following drugs: None known.
Preparations/Dosage: Crude Herb (root): 3-12 grams. Decoction: ¼-½ cup per day.

Thyme (tīm)
(*Thymus vulgaris*)

Synonyms/Related Species: Caraway Thyme, Creeping Thyme, French Thyme, Garden Thyme, Herbe Baronne, Lemon Thyme (*thymus citriodorus*), Mother Thyme, Mountain Thyme, Orange Thyme, Silver Thyme, and Wild Thyme (*thymus serpyllum*).
Family/Class: Labiatae (mint).
Habitat: Africa, Algeria, the Alps, Asia, Germany, the Mediterranean, and Spain.
Flavor: Pungent.
Parts Used: Leaves.
Properties: Analgesic, anthelmintic, antibiotic, antifungal, antiphlogistic, antispasmodic, aromatic, astringent, carminative, counterirritant, diaphoretic, diuretic, emmenagogue, expectorant, hemostatic, insect repellent, larvacide, laxative, parasiticide, sedative, stimulant, teniacide, teniafuge, tonic, and vermifuge.
Constituents: Borneol, caffeic acid, carvacrol, cumene, cymene, flavonoids, linalool, luteolin, menthone, minerals (iodine, silicon, sodium, sulfur), pinene, saponins, silicic acid, tannic acid, thymene, thymol (thyme camphor), ursone (ursolic acid), vitamins (B_1 (thiamine), B_2 (riboflavin), B_3 (niacin), B_5 (pantothenic acid), B_6 (pyridoxine), B_{12}, B_x (para-aminobenzoic acid (PABA), C (ascorbic acid), D, H (biotin), M (folic acid), and volatile oil.
Historical Uses: Addiction (alcohol), allergy (pollen), amenorrhea, ancylostomiasis, anemia, appetite loss, asthma, athlete's foot, bleeding, bronchitis, bruises, candida, colds, colic, congestion (uterine, vaginal), cough, dentifrice, deodorant, diarrhea, digestive complaints, dysmenorrhea, emphysema, enteritis, epilepsy, fainting, fatigue, fever (ephemeral, hay, rheumatic), flatulence, flavoring agent, gargle/mouth rinse, gastritis, gastrointestinal problems, gout, hangover (caused by alcohol consumption), headache, hysteria, indigestion, infection (bacterial, fungal), inflammation, influenza, insomnia, irritable bowel syndrome (IBS), laryngitis, leprosy, leukorrhea, mastitis, menstrual problems, migraine, moniliasis, mosquitos, mucus, muscle and joint pain, nervous conditions, neurasthenia, pain, paralysis, parasites (crabs and their nits, hookworm, lice and their nits, roundworm, tapeworm), perfume, periodontal disease, premenstrual syndrome (PMS), pruritus, respiratory conditions, rheumatism, sciatica, shingles, sinusitis, skin problems, sore throat, sprain, spasmodic conditions, stomatitis, tonsillitits, tumors, ulcer (gastric, peptic), uterine problems, vaginitis, warts (digitate, filiform, fugitive, glabra, mother, plana juvenilis, plantar, seborrhoeic, vulgaris), whooping cough, and wounds (minor).
Discussion: May aid digestion; clear and open bronchial passages; destroy mosquito larvae; enhance liver, lung, respiratory, and stomach functions; help overcome alcohol addiction; increase circulation; inhibit or destroy developement and growth of bacteria and other microorganisms; promote bowel evacuation, perspiration, and urine flow; restore normal tone to tissues; stimulate appetite, menstruation, and peristalsis.

Cautions/Contraindications: Avoid use if pregnant or breast-feeding, or if you have hyperthyroid, hypothyroid, an iodine sensitivity, or ulcer (duodenal). May interfere with the effectiveness of certain thyroid medications.
Adverse Reactions: Abdominal pain, arrhythmia, diarrhea (possibly bloody), edema, fever, gastrointestinal cramps (severe), hyperemia, hypertrophy (thyroid), iodism (iodine poisoning), mouth corner cracks, nausea, poisoning (phenol-like), priapism, swollen tongue, thirst, and/or vomiting.
Herb/Drug Interactions: This herb could cause an interaction (possibly severe) when taken with the following drugs: Thyroid drugs.
Preparations/Dosage: Crude Herb: 3-9 grams. Extract: 5-10 drops (0.333-0.666 cc.) one to two times per day. Infusion: 1-2 cups per day. Oil of Thyme (*oleum thymi*): 1-5 drops (0.066-0.333 cc.) in water or on a sugarcube. Tincture: 10-20 drops (0.666-1.25 cc.) one to three times per day.
Isolation: Thymol: Average dose of ½-2 grains (0.033-0.133 gm.) for use as an anthelmintic and antimicrobic, or in a 1:1000 solution, applied topically, for use as an antirheumatic and antiseptic.

Toadflax (tōd·flaks)
(*Linaria vulgaris*)

Synonyms/Related Species: Aaron's Beard, Brideweed, Butter-and-Eggs, Buttered Haycocks, Churnstaff, Common Toadflax, Climbing Sailor, Creeping Jenny, Dalmation Toadflax (*linaria dalmatica*), Devil's Head, Dragon-Bushes, Eggs and Collops, Flaxweed, Fluellin, Gallwort, Ivy-Leaved Toadflax (*linaria cymbalaria*), Larkspur Lion's Mouth, Mother of Millions, Oxford Weed, Pattens and Clogs, Pedlar's Basket, Pennywort, Plant of the Madonna, Rabbits, Ramsted, Snapdragon, Toadpipe, Wild Snapdragon, Yellow Rod, and Yellow Toadflax.
Family/Class: Scrophulariaceae (figwort).
Habitat: Asia, Britain, England, Europe, Holland, India, Ireland, Italy, the Mediterranean, North America, Scotland, and South America.
Flavor: Salty/bitter/pungent.
Parts Used: Aerial.
Properties: Alterative, antibiotic, antiphlogistic, antiscorbutic, astringent, carminative, emetic, depurative, diaphoretic, diuretic, hemostatic, hepatic, laxative, lithotriptic, stimulant, and tonic.
Constituents: Alkaloids, citric acid, flavonoids, glycosides, linaracin, linarin, linarosin, monosaccharides, mucilage, pectic acid, pectin, pectolinarian, peganine (vasicine), sterols, tannic acid, vitamins (C (ascorbic acid), and volatile oil
Historical Uses: Bleeding, bronchitis, calculus, cardiovascular conditions, cystitis, diabetes, diarrhea, digestive complaints, edema, fever, gallbladder problems, gallstones, heart disease, hemorrhoids, hepatitis, infection (urinary tract), inflammation, jaundice, kidney stones, liver problems, rash, sciatica, scrofula, scurvy, skin problems, sores, spleen problems, ulcer (duodenal, fistula, gastric, peptic), and wounds (minor).
Discussion: May aid digestion; dissolve calculi; inhibit developement or destroy the growth of bacteria and other microorganisms; normalize bilirubin levels; promote bowel evacuation, perspiration, and urine flow; protect against heart disease; purify the blood; reestablish healthy system functions; restore normal tone to tissues; stimulate the liver and persitalsis.
Cautions/Contraindications: Avoid use if pregnant or breast-feeding.

Adverse Reactions: Nausea and/or vomiting.
Herb/Drug Interactions: This herb could cause an interaction (possibly severe) when taken with the following drugs: None known.
Preparations/Dosage: Crude Herb: 1-3 grams. Infusion: ½-1 cup per day.

Tobacco (te·bak ō)

(*Nicotiana repandu*)

Synonyms/Related Species: Aztec Tobacco, Chinese Tobacco (*nicotiana fruticosa*), Coyote Tobacco (*nicotiana attenuata*), Cuban Tobacco (*nicotiana tabacum*), Indian Tobacco (*nicotiana quadrivalvis*), Nicotiana, North American Tobacco, Orinoco (*nicotiana latissima*), Persian Tobacco (*nicotiana persica*), Tabacum, Tree Tobacco (*nicotiana glauca*), Turkish Tobacco (*nicotiana rustica*), and Wild Tobacco.
Family/Class: Solanaceae (nightshade).
Habitat: Asia, China, Cuba, France, Germany, Greece, Holland, Peru, Portugal, Turkey, and North America (primarily the central and southern areas).
Flavor: Bitter/pungent.
Parts Used: Leaves (cured/dried).
Properties: Analgesic, antibiotic, antiphlogistic, antispasmodic, cardiac depressant, counterirritant, diuretic, emetic, expectorant, insecticide, laxative, narcotic, sedative, and sialogogue.
Constituents: Albumin (albumen), alkaloids, anabasine, fatty acids (oleic, palmitic, stearic), fixed oils (olein, palmitin, stearin), gum, monosaccharides, nicotianin, nicotinamide, nicotine, nicotyrine, resin, solanine, vitamins (B_3 (niacin), and volatile oil.
Historical Uses: Abscess, alopecia, ants, aphids, arthritis, asthma, athlete's foot, bleeding, bruises, colds, constipation, convulsions, cough, croup, dandruff, dysmenorrhea, dysuria (painful/difficult urination), earache, eczema, edema, fever (ephemeral, rheumatic), glandular swelling, headache, hemorrhoids, herbal tobacco (leaves), hives, hysteria, infection (bacterial), inflammation, insects (numerous species), insect bites or stings, laryngitis, lesions (tubercle), measles, mucus, muscle and joint pain, neuralgia, nosebleed, orchitis (testicular inflammation), pain, pellagra, pruritus, rash, respiratory conditions, rheumatism, scrofula, skin problems, snakebite, sore throat, sores, spasmodic conditions, sunburn, tetanus, toothache, trismus (lockjaw), tuberculosis, ulcer (fistula, tuberculous), urinary problems, and wounds (minor).
Discussion: May clear and open bronchial passages; destroy insects and their larvae; increase blood pressure levels; inhibit or destroy development and growth of bacteria and other microorganisms; promote bowel evacuation, saliva secretion, and urine flow; reduce functional cardiac activity; stimulate gastric secretions and peristalsis.
Cautions/Contraindications: Avoid use if pregnant or breast-feeding, or if you have acidity (gastric) or an ulcer (gastric, peptic). Do not administer to children. May reduce the effectiveness of cisapride, famotidine, insulin, nifedipine, ranitidine, and selective serotonin reuptake inhibitor (SSRI) drugs, as well as OTC and prescription drug products containing caffeine. May interfere with conjugated estrogen hormone therapy. Leaf ingestion is toxic and may be fatal. Not for long-term use. Highly addictive when smoked. Use gloves when harvesting as toxins may be absorbed through the skin.
Adverse Reactions: Addiction, arterial deterioration, arrythmia, debility, diarrhea, dizziness, drowsiness, gastrointestinal irritation, fainting, nausea, nicotinism (poisoning by nicotine or by

tobacco), perspiration, respiratory failure, salivation (increased), spasmodic conditions, tremors, vascular problems, vomiting, and/or possible death.
Herb/Drug Interactions: This herb could cause an interaction (possibly severe) when taken with the following drugs: Antidiabetic drugs, Calcium Channel Blocker drugs, GI drugs, H-2 Blocker drugs, Hormones and Synthetic Substitutes (i.e. conjugated estrogens, contraceptives (oral, etc.), and other hormonal replacement therapy (HRT), other Medications/Products containing caffeine, and Selective Serotonin Reuptake Inhibitor (SSRI) drugs.
Preparations/Dosage: External uses only.

Tonka Bean (tän ke bēn)
(*Dipteryx odorata*)

Synonyms/Related Species: Rumara and Tonquin Bean.
Family/Class: Leguminosae (legume).
Habitat: North America and South America.
Flavor: Bitter.
Parts Used: Bean/seed.
Properties: Anticoagulant, aromatic, cardiant, narcotic, stimulant, and tonic.
Constituents: Coumaric acid, coumarin, fatty acids (oleic, palmitic, stearic), fixed oils (olein, palmitin, stearin), gum, inulin (starch), monosaccharides, and stigmasterol.
Historical Uses: Disguises odors, flavoring agent, perfume, and whooping cough.
Discussion: May delay or reduce blood coagulation; restore normal tone to tissues; stimulate the cardiovascular system.
Cautions/Contraindications: Avoid use if pregnant or breast-feeding. Some persons may experience bleeding or increased clotting time when using this herb with anticoagulant drugs or aspirin.
Adverse Reactions: Atrophy (testicular), bleeding (possibly serious), coagulation problems, growth retardation, headache, heart failure, liver damage (often characterized by jaundice), nausea, stupor, and/or vomiting.
Herb/Drug Interactions: This herb could cause an interaction (possibly severe) when taken with the following drugs: Anticoagulant drugs, Salicylates, and Subsalicylates.
Preparations/Dosage: Crude Herb (powdered): Average dose in substance 1-8 grains (0.066-0.5 gm.).
Did You Know? About one pound of tonka beans yields approximately 110 grains of coumarin.

Unicorn Root, False (yoo ne·kôrn root, fôls)
(*Chamaelirium luteum*)

Synonyms/Related Species: Drooping Star Wort, Fairy-Wand, Helonias Root, and Starwort.
Family/Class: Liliaceae (lily).
Habitat: The United States.
Flavor: Bitter.
Parts Used: Root.
Properties: Antibiotic, antiphlogistic, diuretic, emetic, emmenagogue, expectorant, hemostatic, insect repellent, laxative, narcotic, oxytocic, parasiticide, sialagogue, stimulant, teniacide, teniafuge, and tonic.

Constituents: Chamaelirin, glycosides, helonin, minerals (cadmium, cobalt, copper, molybdenum, sulfur, zinc), resin, saponins, turpentine, vitamins (C (ascorbic acid), and volatile oil.
Historical Uses: Albuminaria, amenorrhea, anorexia, appetite loss, benign breast disease, bladder problems, colds, colic, congestion (uterine, vaginal), cough, depression (mild/moderate), diabetes, digestive complaints, dysmenorrhea, edema, endometriosis, enuresis, erectile dysfunction, fever (ephemeral, rheumatic), flatulence, frigidity, gleet, gonorrhea, headache, hematuria (blood in the urine), hemorrhage (metrorrhagia), indigestion, infection (bacterial, sexually transmitted), inflammation, insects (numerous species), kidney problems, laryngitis, leukorrhea, liver problems, lochia, menopausal/menstrual problems, mucus, muscle and joint pain, nausea, nephritis, nocturnal emission, nosebleed, orchitis, pain, parasites (lice and their nits, tapeworm), prostate problems, pruritus, respiratory conditions, rheumatism, sexually transmitted diseases (STDs), sinusitis, sore throat, stomachache, tonsillitis, urethritis, uterine problems, vaginitis, and vomiting.
Discussion: May clear and open bronchial passages; enhance kidney, reproductive system, spleen, and digestive system functions; inhibit or destroy development and growth of bacteria and other microorganisms; produce progesterone; promote bowel evacuation, saliva secretion, and urine flow; reduce the emission of semen during sleep; restore normal tone to tissues; soothe mucous membrane irritation; stimulate appetite, peristalsis, and uterine contractions.
Cautions/Contraindications: Avoid use if pregnant or breast-feeding.
Adverse Reactions: Diarrhea (possibly bloody), gastrointestinal cramps (severe), hematuria (blood in the urine), nausea, stupor, and/or vomiting.
Herb/Drug Interactions: This herb could cause an interaction (possibly severe) when taken with the following drugs: None known.
Preparations/Dosage: Crude Herb: 3-9 grams. Root (powdered): Average dose in substance 10-15 grains (0.666-0.98 gm.). Tincture: 5-30 drops (0.333-2 cc.) one to three times per day.
Isolation: Helonin: Average dose of 2-4 grains (0.133-0.266 gm.) for use as an anthelmintic and diuretic.

Unicorn Root, True (yoo ne·kôrn root, troo)
(*Aletris farinosa*)

Synonyms/Related Species: Bettie Grass, Bittergrass, Black Root, Blazing Star, Colic Root, Crow Corn, Devil's Bit, Star Root, Starwort, and True Unicorn Stargrass.
Family/Class: Haemodoraceae (bloodwort).
Habitat: North America.
Flavor: Bitter.
Parts Used: Root.
Properties: Antiphlogistic, diaphoretic, diuretic, emetic, expectorant, laxative, narcotic, stomachic, and tonic.
Constituents: Bitter principle, inulin (starch), resin, saponins, and volatile oil.
Historical Uses: Acne, amenorrhea, appetite loss, arthritis, bronchitis, colic, debility, digestive complaints, dysmenorrhea, fever (ephemeral, rheumatic), fistula, flatulence, hysteria, indigestion, inflammation, insufficiency (venous), menstrual problems, muscle and joint pain, prolapse (rectal, uterine), rheumatism, skin problems, sores, and warts (digitate, filiform, fugitive, glabra, mother, plana juvenilis, plantar, seborrhoeic, vulgaris).

Discussion: May clear and open bronchial passages, enhance liver and stomach functions; increase circulation; promote bowel evacuation, perspiration, and urine flow; restore normal tone to tissues; stimulate appetite and peristalsis; strengthen bones, ligaments, and tendons.
Cautions/Contraindications: Avoid use if pregnant or breast-feeding. Not for long-term use.
Adverse Reactions: Confusion, diarrhea (possibly bloody), gastrointestinal cramps (severe), hematuria (blood in the urine), nausea, stupor, vertigo, and/or vomiting.
Herb/Drug Interactions: This herb could cause an interaction (possibly severe) when taken with the following drugs: None known.
Preparations/Dosage: Crude Herb: 1-3 grams. Decoction: ½-1 cup per day. Extract: 3-5 drops (0.2-0.3 cc.) one to two times per day. Root (powdered): Average dose in substance 5-10 grains (0.333-0.666 gm.). Tincture: 5-10 drops (0.3-0.6 cc.) one to three times per day.

Valerian (ve·lir ē·en)
(*Valeriana officinalis*)

Synonyms/Related Species: Alpine Valerian (*valeriana montana*), Amantilla, Bengal Valerian (*valeriana jatamansi*), Capitate Valerian (*valeriana capitata*), Elder-Leaved Valerian (*valeriana sambucifolia*), Fragrant Valerian, Garden Heliotrope, Great Wild Valerian, Heart-Leaved Valerian (*valeriana pyrenaica*), Heliotrope, Himalayan Valerian, Indian Valerian (*valeriana wallichii*), Japanese Valerian, Kesso Root, Marsh Valerian (*valeriana dioica*), Mexican Valerian (*valeriana mexicana*), Mountain Valerian, Saliunca (*valeriana celtica*), Setwall, Sitka Valerian (*valeriana sitchensis*), Subalpine Valerian (*valeriana acutiloba*), Tagar, Tobacco Valerian, Vandal Root, Water Valerian (*valeriana aquatica*), Western Valerian (*valeriana occidentalis*), and Wild Valerian (*valeriana edulis*).
Family/Class: Valerianaceae (valerian).
Habitat: The Alpine and Subalpine zones, Asia, Britain, England, Europe, France, the Himalayas, Holland, India, Japan, North America, Prussia, the Pyrenees, and the Yukon Territory.
Flavor: Pungent/bitter.
Parts Used: Root
Properties: Analgesic, antiphlogistic, antispasmodic, aromatic, carminative, hypnotic, hypotensive, lithotriptic, nervine, sedative, stimulant, tonic, and vasodilator.
Constituents: Albumin (albumen), alkaloids, caffeic acid, chlorogenic acid, flavonoids, formic acid, glycosides, inulin (starch), minerals (copper, lead, magnesium, potassium, zinc), monosaccharides, pinene, resin, sesquiterpenes, sterols, tannic acid, valerianic acid, valerol, valerone, and volatile oil.
Historical Uses: Acne, addiction (alcohol, drug), amenorrhea, anxiety, arrhythmia, arthritis, bladder problems, bronchitis, bruises, chorea, colds, colic, constipation, convulsions, cough, cramps, croup, dandruff, depression (mild/moderate), digestive complaints, epilepsy, fainting, fever (ephemeral, scarlet), flatulence, gastritis, gastrointestinal problems, hangover (caused by alcohol consumption), headache, hyperactivity, hypertension (mild/moderate), hysteria, indigestion, inflammation, insomnia, irritable bowel syndrome (IBS), measles, menopausal/menstrual problems, migraine, muscle and joint pain, nausea, nervous conditions, neuralgia, neurasthenia, pain, palsy, panic attacks, paralysis, restlessness, scarletina, shock, spasmodic conditions, ulcer (duodenal, gastric, peptic), and urinary calculus.

Discussion: May aid digestion; calm the nervous system; cause blood vessel dilatation; dissolve calculi; enhance cardiovascular system, circulatory system, liver, and respiratory system functions; increase circulation; induce sleep; reduce blood pressure levels, morning sleepiness, symptoms of angina, and withdrawal symptoms of alcoholism; restore normal tone to tissues; stimulate peristalsis.

Cautions/Contraindications: Avoid use if pregnant or breast-feeding, or if you have a thyroid problem. May increase the effectiveness of barbiturates, benzodiazepine, and sedative drugs. Do not drive or operate machinery after taking valerian. Do not take valerian with alcohol.

Adverse Reactions: Arrythmia, depression, dizziness, drowsiness, fainting, giddiness, hallucinations, headache, liver damage (often characterized by jaundice), morning grogginess, nausea, nervousness, paralysis, restlessness, sleep problems, spasmodic conditions, visual disturbances, and/or vomiting.

Herb/Drug Interactions: This herb could cause an interaction (possibly severe) when taken with the following drugs: Antidepressant drugs, Anxiolytic drugs, Hypotensive drugs, Opiate Agonists/Narcotic drugs, Sedative drugs, and Tranquilizer drugs.

Preparations/Dosage: Crude Herb: 3-6 grams. Extract (solid): Average dose in substance 5-10 grains (0.333-0.666 gm.). Infusion: ½-1 cup per day. Tincture: 10-30 drops (0.6-2 cc.) one to three times per day.

Vervain (vûr vān)

(*Verbena hastata*)

Synonyms/Related Species: Blue Vervain, Burry Vervain (*verbena lappulaceae*), Common Vervain, Dormilón, Enchanter's Plant, European Vervain (*verbena officinalis*), Ferfaen, Herba Sacra, Herbe Sacrée, Herba Veneris, Herb of Grace, Hyssop, Indian Hyssop, Jamaican Vervain (*verbena jamaicensis*), Juno's Tears, Moradilla, Simpler's Joy, Verbana, Verveine, and Wild Hyssop.

Family/Class: Verbenaceae (verbena).

Habitat: Barbary, China, England, Europe, Jamaica, Japan, the Mediterranean, and North America.

Flavor: Bitter.

Parts Used: Aerial.

Properties: Alterative, analgesic, antibiotic, antidepressant, antiphlogistic, antispasmodic, antiviral, aphrodisiac, aromatic, astringent, carminative, demulcent, depurative, diaphoretic, diuretic, emmenagogue, emetic, expectorant, hemostatic, laxative, lithotriptic, nervine, parasiticide, sedative, stimulant, stomachic, and tonic.

Constituents: Alkaloids, bitter principle, caffeic acid, flavonoids, glycosides, gum, luteolin, marrubin, minerals (calcium, manganese), mucilage, pinenes, resin, tannic acid, verbenone, vitamins (C (ascorbic acid), E (alpha-tocopheral), and volatile oil.

Historical Uses: Ague, amenorrhea, anxiety, arthritis, ascites, asthma, bladder problems, bleeding, bronchitis, bruises, burns (minor), calculus, cirrhosis, colds, conjunctivitis, convulsions, cough, cramps, depression (mild/moderate), diarrhea, digestive complaints, dislocations, dysentery, dysmenorrhea, ear infection, earache, edema, epilepsy, exhaustion, eye problems, fatigue, fever (ephemeral, herpetic, rheumatic), flatulence, gallbladder problems, gallstones, gangrene, gargle/mouth rinse, gastrointestinal problems, gout, headache, hemorrhage, hemorrhoids, hepatitis, herpes, hyperactivity, hysteria, indigestion, infection (bacterial, urinary tract, viral), inflammation, influenza, insect bites or stings, insomnia, jaundice, kidney problems, kidney stones, laryngitis, lesions (tubercle), liver problems, lung problems, mastitis, metabolic problems, migraine, menopausal/menstrual problems, mucous membrane problems, mucus, muscle and joint pain, nausea, nervous conditions, neuralgia, pain, parasites (lice and their nits), perfume, periodontal disease, pleurisy, potpourri, pneumonia, premenstrual syndrome (PMS), pruritus, respiratory conditions, rheumatism, scrofula, seizure conditions, sexually transmitted diseases (STDs), shock, skin problems, snakebite, sore throat, sores, spasmodic conditions, sprain, syphilis, tinnitus, toothache, tuberculosis, ulcer (duodenal, fistula, gastric, peptic, syphilitic, tuberculous), wheezing, whooping cough, and wounds (minor).

Discussion: May aid digestion; arouse sexual impulses; balance blood pressure levels; calm the nervous system; clear and open bronchial passages; dissolve calculi; enhance immune system, liver, lung, spleen, and stomach functions; inhibit or destroy developement and growth of bacteria and other microorganisms; promote bowel evacuation, perspiration, and urine flow; purify the blood; reestablish healthy system functions; restore normal tone to tissues; soothe mucous membrane irritation; stimulate menstruation and peristalsis.

Cautions/Contraindications: Avoid use if pregnant or breast-feeding, or if you have asthma or a history of heart disease.

Adverse Reactions: Nausea and/or vomiting.

Herb/Drug Interactions: This herb could cause an interaction (possibly severe) when taken with the following drugs: None known.

Preparations/Dosage: Crude Herb: 3-9 grams. Tincture: 5-30 drops (0.333-2 cc.) one to three times per day.

Violet (vī e·lit)
(*Viola tricolor*)

Synonyms/Related Species: Blue Violet (*viola papilionacea*), Bogbice Violet, Butterfly Violet, Canada Violet (*viola canadensis*), Dog Violet (*viola canina*), Dwarf Violet (*viola calcarea*), Early Blue Violet (*viola adunca*), European Wild Pansy, Garden Violet, Hairy Violet (*viola hirta*), Heartsease, Herba Trinitatis, Hooked Spur Violet, Johnny-Jump-Up, Love-in-Idleness, Marsh Violet (*viola palustris*), Northern Bog Violet (*viola nephrophylla*), Pansy, Pensée, Round-Leaved Yellow Violet (*viola orbiculata*), Stream Violet (*viola glabella*), Sweet Violet (*viola odorata*), Western Dog Violet (*viola adunca*), Wild Pansy, Wild Violet, Yellow Montane Violet (*viola nuttallii*), and Yellow Wood Violet.

Family/Class: Violaceae (violet).

Floral Emblem: Illinois, New Jersey, Rhode Island, and Wisconsin.

Habitat: Africa, Asia, Britain, Europe, France, India, the Middle East, North America, South America, the Subalpine zone, and the Yukon Territory.

Flavor: Bitter/sweet.

Parts Used: Flowers, leaves.

Properties: Alterative, analgesic, anthelmintic, antibiotic, anticarcinogen, antioxidant, antiperiodic, antiphlogistic, antispasmodic, aromatic, demulcent, depurative, diaphoretic, diuretic, emetic, expectorant, hypotensive, laxative, lithotriptic, malariacidal, sedative, vasodilator, vermifuge, and vulnerary.

Constituents: Alkaloids, coumarin, curcumene, flavonoids, luteolin, monosaccharides, mucilage, propionic acid, resin, rutin, salicylic acid, saponins, scoparin, tannic acid, umbelliferone, violin, vitamins (A, C (ascorbic acid), and volatile oil.

Historical Uses: Abscess, acne, ague, anxiety, arrythmia, arteriosclerosis, arthritis, asthma, bladder problems, bronchitis, bruises, calculus, cancer (skin), cardiovascular conditions, colds, constipation, convulsions, cough, cramps, diarrhea, digestive complaints, eczema, edema, enuresis (urinary incontinence), epilepsy, fever (ephemeral, intermittent, rheumatic), flatulence, gallstones, gargle/mouth rinse, gastritis, gastrointestinal problems, glandular swelling, gout, hangover (caused by alcohol consumption), headache, hypertension (mild/moderate), hysteria, impetigo, indigestion, infection (bacterial, urinary tract), inflammation, insomnia, insufficiency (venous), irritable bowel syndrome (IBS), jaundice, kidney stones, laryngitis, lesions (tubercle), liver problems, lung problems, malaria, migraine, mucus, muscle and joint pain, nervous conditions, pain, parasites (malarial plasmodia, roundworm), periodontal disease, pimples, pleurisy, pruritus, psoriasis, respiratory conditions, rheumatism, scrofula, seborrhea, sexually transmitted diseases (STDs), shortness of breath, sinusitis, skin problems, sore nipples, sore throat, sores, spasmodic conditions, syphilis, tuberculosis, tumors, ulcer (duodenal, fistula, gastric, peptic, syphilitic, tuberculous), urinary problems, whooping cough, and wounds (minor).

Discussion: May cause blood vessel dilatation; clear and open bronchial passages; decrease the effect of carcinogens; dissolve calculi; enhance cardiovascular system, liver, lung, metabolic, and stomach functions; inhibit oxidation and inhibit or destroy development and growth of bacteria and other microorganisms; prevent hemorrhage in persons with hypertension; promote bowel evacuation, perspiration, and urine flow; purify the blood; reduce blood pressure levels, capillary fragility, and the frequency of nighttime urination; reestablish healthy system functions; soothe mucous membrane irritation and nipple soreness; speed healing; stimulate peristalsis; strengthen the urinary system.

Cautions/Contraindications: Avoid use if pregnant or breast-feeding. The roots and fruits/seeds are toxic.

Adverse Reactions: Diarrhea (possibly bloody), gastrointestinal cramps (severe), mucous membrane irritation, nausea, nervousness, skin problems, and/or vomiting.

Herb/Drug Interactions: This herb could cause an interaction (possibly severe) when taken with the following drugs: Hypotensive drugs.

Preparations/Dosage: Crude Herb: 3-9 grams. Infusion: ½-1 cup per day. Leaves/Flowers (fresh): Add to salads. Tincture: 2-10 drops (0.133-0.666 cc.) one to three times per day.

Did You Know? The flower petals and leaves of all violets are safe to eat, and make a wonderful addition to salads, or they can be used as decoration on a cake.

Virgin's Bower (ver jinz bou er)
(*Clematis virginiana*)

Synonyms/Related Species: Blue Clematis, Blue Virgin's Bower (*clematis occidentalis*), Clematis, Flammula Jovis, Klēmatis, Leatherflower (*clematis douglasii*), Rocky Mountain Clematis (*clematis pseudoalpina*), Rushwood, Sweet Scented Virgin's Bower (*clematis flammula*), Traveler's Joy (*clematis vitalba*), Upright Virgin's Bower (*clematis recta*), Western White Clematis (*clematis ligusticifolia*), White Virgin's Bower, and Yellow Clematis (*clematis tangutica*).

Family/Class: Ranunculaceae (buttercup).

Habitat: Europe and North America.
Flavor: Pungent.
Parts Used: Flowers, leaves, root, stem.
Properties: Analgesic, antibiotic, antifungal, antiperiodic, antiphlogistic, antispasmodic, counterirritant, diaphoretic, diuretic, malariacidal, stimulant, and vasodilator.
Constituents: Clematine, protoanemonin, and saponins.
Historical Uses: Abscess, ague, arthritis, blisters, bruises, burns (minor), cancer, candida, colds, contraceptive (female), cramps, cystitis, enuresis (urinary incontinence), escherichia coli (e-coli), eczema, edema, eye problems, fever (ephemeral, herpetic, intermittent, rheumatic), gleet, gonorrhea, gout, headache, herpes, infection (bacterial, fungal, sexually transmitted), inflammation, insufficiency (venous), malaria, menstrual problems, migraine, moniliasis, muscle and joint pain, pain, parasites (malarial plasmodia), pruritus, respiratory conditions, rheumatism, sexually transmitted diseases (STDs), skeletal problems, skin problems, sore throat, sores, spasmodic conditions, syphilis, ulcer (duodenal, gastric, peptic, stasis, syphilitic, varicose), urethritis, varicose veins, visual disturbances, and wounds (minor).
Discussion: May cause brain lining constriction and blood vessel dilatation; enhance bladder function; inhibit or destroy the growth of bacteria and other microorganisms; promote perspiration and urine flow; reduce the frequency of nighttime urination; strengthen the urinary system.
Cautions/Contraindications: Avoid use if pregnant or breast-feeding. May cause dermatitis in susceptible individuals. Not for long-term use. Use with professional guidance/supervision.
Adverse Reactions: Asphyxiation, blistering of the mouth and throat, convulsions, diarrhea (possibly bloody), dizziness, fainting, gastrointestinal cramps (severe), hematuria (blood in the urine), kidney failure, salivation, urinary tract irritation, and/or possible death.
Herb/Drug Interactions: This herb could cause an interaction (possibly severe) when taken with the following drugs: None known.
Preparations/Dosage: Crude Herb: 3-9 grams. Extract (root/stem/powdered): Average dose in substance 1-2 grains (0.066-0.133 gm.). Infusion (flowers/leaves): Use 30-40 grains (2-2.666 gm.). Take 1 tablespoon. External Use: Root/Stem (bruised): Boil in water, then combine with a good quality oil and let sit for a few weeks. Apply topically for skin problems.

Wahoo (wä hoo)

(*Euonymus atropurpureus*)

Synonyms/Related Species: Arrow Wood, Asian Spindle Tree (*euonymus japonicus*), Bitter Ash, Bonnet-de-Prêtre, Burning Bush, European Burning Bush (*euonymus europaea*), Fusain, Fusoria, Gadrose, Gatter, Indian Arrow Wood, Pigwood, Prickwood, Skewerwood, Spilboome, Spindle Tree, Strawberry Bush, Ûhawhu, Wanhu, Western Burning Bush (*euonymus occidentalis*), and Western Spindle Tree (*euonymus americanus*).
Family/Class: Celastraceae (staff tree).
Habitat: Asia, Europe, France, Germany, the Netherlands, and North America.
Flavor: Bitter/pungent.
Parts Used: Bark (root).
Properties: Alterative, antiperiodic, antiphlogistic, antispasmodic, cardiant, cholagogue, diuretic, expectorant, hepatic, laxative, malariacidal, stimulant, and tonic.
Constituents: Alkaloids, amines, asparagin, bitter principle, caffeine, frangulin, glycosides, pyridine, resin, saponins, sesquiterpene, and theobromine.

Historical Uses: Ague, appetite loss, asthma, cardiovascular conditions, chills, cholecystitis, colds, congestion (uterine, vaginal), constipation, dandruff, digestive complaints, diphtheria, edema, fever (ephemeral, intermittent), gallbladder problems, gleet, gonorrhea, hypertension (mild/moderate), indigestion, infection (sexually transmitted, urinary tract), inflammation, intestinal problems, jaundice, leukorrhea, liver problems, malaria, mucus, pain, parasites (malarial plasmodia), respiratory conditions, sexually transmitted diseases (STDs), skin problems, spasmodic conditions, substitute for quinine, ulcer (syriac), urethritis, urinary problems, and vaginitis.
Discussion: May aid digestion; clear and open bronchial passages; enhance liver, lung, and stomach functions; promote bile flow, bowel evacuation, and urine flow; protect the liver; reestablish healthy system functions; restore normal tone to tissues; stimulate appetite, the cardiovascular system, and peristalsis.
Cautions/Contraindications: Avoid use if pregnant or breast-feeding. Berries are poisonous. May cause potassium depletion. Not for long-term use.
Adverse Reactions: Arrhythmia, breathing difficulty, cardiac failure, circulatory failure, coma, diarrhea (possibly bloody), dizziness, elevated body temperature, elevated cerebrospinal pressure, fainting, gastrointestinal cramps (severe), nausea, respiratory failure, restlessness, spasmodic conditions, stupor, and/or possible death.
Herb/Drug Interactions: This herb could cause an interaction (possibly severe) when taken with the following drugs: None known.
Preparations/Dosage: Crude Herb: 3-6 grams. Bark (powdered): Average dose in substance 3-10 grains (0.2-0.65 gm.). Extract (powdered): Average dose in substance 2 grains (0.133 gm.). Infusion: ½-1 cup per day. Tincture: 5-10 drops (0.333-0.666 cc.) one to three times per day.
Isolation: Asparagin: Soluble in hot water, but insoluble in alcohol and ether. Average dose of 1-2 grains (0.066-0.133 gm.) for use as a diuretic. Pyridine: Average dose of 2-10 drops (0.133-0.666 cc.) for use as an antimicrobic, antispasmodic, and cardiant, or for use (diluted) in atomization or inhalation therapy. Pyridine tannate: Average dose of 2-10 drops (0.133-0.666 cc.) for use as an antilithic and astringent. Theobromine calcium gluconate: Average dose of 0.32-0.65 gm. for use in hypertension. Theobromine salicylate: Soluble (sparingly) in water. Average dose of 15 grains (1 gm.) for use as a diuretic. Theobromine sodiosalicylate: Used in a 5% solution, average dose of 15 drops (1cc.) for use as a diuretic. Theobromine and sodium acetate: Average dose of 15-45 grains (1-3 gm.) for use as a powerful diuretic.

Walnut (wôl nut)
(*Juglans nigra*)

Synonyms/Related Species: Black Walnut, Butternut Bark, California Black Walnut (*juglans californica*), Carya Persica, Circassian Walnut, English Walnut (*juglans regia*), Jove's Nut, Jupiter's Nut, Nux Regia, Oil Nut, Persian Walnut, Walhhnutu, Wallnuss, Wealh Hnutu, Welsche Nuss, and White Walnut (*juglans cinerea*).
Family/Class: Juglandaceae (walnut).
Habitat: Asia, England, France, Germany, Greece, the Himalayas, Iran, Italy, Lebanon, the Middle East, Persia, Switzerland, and the United States.
Flavor: Bark/Leaves: bitter. Kernels: sweet.
Parts Used: Bark (inner and root), leaves, kernels of the fruit.

Properties: Alterative, anthelmintic, antibiotic, anticarcinogen, antifungal, antigalactic, antihidrotic, antiperiodic, antiphlogistic, antiviral, astringent, demulcent, depurative, insect repellent, laxative, malariacidal, nutritive, parasiticide, teniacide, teniafuge, tonic, and vermifuge.
Constituents: Albumin (albumen), alkaloids, cellulose, ellagic acid, fatty acids (arachidonic, linoleic, linolenic, oleic, palmitic, stearic), fixed oils (olein, palmitin, stearin), juglandic acid, juglone, minerals (calcium, iodine, iron, magnesium, manganese, phosphorus, potassium, silicon), myristin (myristic acid), nucin, oxidase, protein, quercetin, silicic acid, sterols, tannic acid, vitamins (A, B, C (ascorbic acid), E (alpha-tocopheral), inositol), and volatile oil.
Historical Uses: Abscess, acne, ague, anorexia, appetite loss, athlete's foot, cancer, candida, canker sores, colds, colitis, congestion (uterine, vaginal), constipation, dandruff, diarrhea, dietary supplementation, diphtheria, dysentery, eczema, emaciation, enteritis, ephidrosis, eye problems, fever (ephemeral, herpetic, intermittent, rheumatic), flies (leaves), glandular problems, glandular swelling, gout, hemorrhoids, herpes, impetigo, infection (bacterial, fungal, viral), inflammation, influenza, insufficiency (venous), intestinal problems, laryngitis, lesions (tubercle), leukorrhea, liver problems, lupus, lymphedema, malaria, malnutrition, moniliasis, mosquitos (nut meats), parasites (lice and their nits, malarial plasmodia, pinworm, ringworm, scabies, tapeworm), periodontal disease, poison ivy/oak, prolapse (rectal, uterine), psoriasis, rash, rheumatism, scrofula, sexually transmitted diseases (STDs), skin problems, sore throat, sores, syphilis, thyroid problems, tonsillitis, tuberculosis, tumors, ulcer (duodenal, fistula, gastric, peptic, stasis, syphilitic, syriac, tuberculous, varicose), vaginitis, varicose veins, warts (digitate, filiform, fugitive, glabra, mother, plana juvenilis, plantar, seborrhoeic, vulgaris), and wounds (minor).
Discussion: May balance blood sugar levels; decrease the effect of carcinogens; diminish or suppress lactation and perspiration; enhance brain, colon, kidney, and lung functions; increase strength and virility; inhibit or destroy developement and growth of bacteria and other microorganisms; provide dietary supplementation; reestablish healthy system functions; serve as a nutritional adjuvant to therapeutic programs; stimulate appetite.
Cautions/Contraindications: Avoid use if pregnant or breast-feeding, or if you have an iodine sensitivity. May interfere with the absorption of atropine (when taken by mouth), codeine, ephedrine, pseudoephedrine, and theophylline drugs. May interfere with the effectiveness of certain thyroid medications.
Adverse Reactions: Abdominal pain, arrhythmia, diarrhea, fever, hypertrophy (thyroid), iodism (iodine poisoning), nausea, priapism, thirst, and/or vomiting.
Herb/Drug Interactions: This herb could cause an interaction (possibly severe) when taken with the following drugs: Autonomic drugs, Opiate Agonists/Narcotic drugs, other Medications/Products containing ephedra or pseudoephedrine, Theophylline drugs, and Thyroid drugs.
Preparations/Dosage: Crude Herb (bark/leaves): 3-6 grams. Crude Herb (kernels): 6-12 grams. Decoction (bark): ½-1 cup per day. Extract (powdered): Average dose in substance 5-20 grains (0.333-1.333 gm.). Infusion (leaves): 1 cup per day. Syrup (bark): 1 tablespoon in water one to two times per day. Tincture (bark): 5-20 drops (0.3-1.3 cc.).

Watercress (wôt er·kres)
(*Nasturtium officinale*)

Synonyms/Related Species: Indian Cress, Nasturtium, Nasus Tortus, Tall Nasturtium, True Nasturtium, and White Watercress.
Family/Class: Brassicaceae (mustard).

Habitat: Alaska, Asia, Europe, North America, Russia, and the Yukon Territory.
Flavor: Pungent/bitter.
Parts Used: Leaves (fresh).
Properties: Antibiotic, antiphlogistic, antiscorbutic, depurative, diuretic, erythropoietic, expectorant, hypoglycemic, laxative, lithotriptic, nutritive, stimulant, stomachic, and tonic.
Constituents: Bitter principle, flavonoids, isothiocyanates, tropeolin (tropaeolin), minerals (calcium, chlorine, copper, iodine, iron, manganese, magnesium, phosphorus, potassium, sodium, sulfur, zinc), monosaccharides, vitamins (A, B_1 (thiamine), B_2 (riboflavin), B_3 (niacin), C (ascorbic acid), D, E (alpha-tocopheral), and volatile oil.
Historical Uses: Acne, age spots, alopecia, anemia, appetite loss, arthritis, bronchitis, calculus, cardiovascular conditions, cirrhosis, colds, cough, cramps, cysts, deficiency (vitamin C), digestive complaints, dietary supplementation, dizziness, eczema, edema, fever (ephemeral, rheumatic), flatulence, food, freckles, gallstones, gout, hormonal imbalances, hyperglycemia, hypotension, indigestion, infection (fungal), inflammation, kidney problems, kidney stones, lesions (tubercle), liver problems, malnutrition, mental disturbances, mucus, muscle and joint pain, nausea, pimples, pruritus, respiratory conditions, rheumatism, rheumatoid arthritis (RA), scrofula, scurvy, skin problems, substitute for lettuce, tuberculosis, tumors, ulcer (fistula, tuberculous), and urinary problems.
Discussion: May aid digestion; clear and open bronchial passages; dissolve calculi; enhance glandular system and stomach functions; increase endurance, energy, and stamina; promote bowel evacuation, the production of red blood cells, and urine flow; provide dietary supplementation; purify the blood; reduce blood sugar levels; restore normal tone to tissues; serve as a nutritional adjuvant to therapeutic programs; stimulate appetite, glandular function, metabolism, and peristalsis; strengthen the gums.
Cautions/Contraindications: Avoid use if pregnant, or if you have inflammatory kidney disease, ulcer (duodenal, peptic), or iodine sensitivity. Avoid harvesting watercress from polluted waters as heavy metals and pesticides have a tendency to accumulate in the plant. Do not confuse this plant with poisonous water hemlock (*cicuta virosa*). May interfere with the effectiveness of certain thyroid medications. May interfere with iodide metabolism. May cause dermatitis in susceptible individuals. Use for no longer than four weeks.
Adverse Reactions: Abdominal pain, arrhythmia, diarrhea (possibly bloody), digestive complaints, edema, fever, gastritis, hematuria (blood in the urine), hypertrophy (thyroid), indigestion, iodism (iodine poisoning), irritable bowel syndrome (IBS), mucous membrane problems, nausea, priapism, suppression (thyroid), thirst, and/or vomiting.
Herb/Drug Interactions: This herb could cause an interaction (possibly severe) when taken with the following drugs: Antidiabetic drugs and Thyroid drugs.
Preparations/Dosage: Crude Herb: 3-9 grams. Infusion: 1-2 cups per day. Juice: 1-2 ounces (30-60 cc.) per day in water. Leaves (fresh): Eaten in salads.

Watermelon (wôt er·mel en)
(*Cucurbita citrullus*)

Synonyms/Related Species: Cucurbita.
Family/Class: Cucurbitaceae (gourd).
Habitat: Africa, North America, and other temperate, tropical, and subtropical regions worldwide.
Flavor: Pulp/Juice: sweet. Rind/Seed: bitter/bland.

Parts Used: Pulp, rind, juice, seeds.
Properties: Antiphlogistic, diuretic, emmenagogue, hypotensive, sialagogue, and vasodilator.
Constituents: Amino acids (arginine, citrulline), betaine (lycine), cucurbitol, cucurbocitrin, dextrose, disaccharides, lycopene, malic acid, minerals (bromine, phosphorous, potassium, sodium), monosaccharides, phosphoric acid, phytofluene, sterol, and vitamins A and C (ascorbic acid).
Historical Uses: Amenorrhea, dysentery, edema, fever, hypertension (mild/moderate), inflammation, irritability, stroke (heat), thirst, and urinary problems.
Discussion: May cause blood vessel dilatation; enhance stomach function; promote saliva secretion and urine flow; stimulate menstruation.
Cautions/Contraindications: Avoid use if pregnant or breast-feeding.
Adverse Reactions: Nausea, salivation (increased), and/or vomiting.
Herb/Drug Interactions: This herb could cause an interaction (possibly severe) when taken with the following drugs: Hypotensive drugs.
Preparations/Dosage: Crude Herb (rind): 9-15 grams. Crude Herb (seeds): 6-12 grams. Decoction (seeds): ¼-½ cup per day. Fruit (fresh): May be ingested freely. Juice: 1-2 cups per day.
Isolation: Betaine: Average dose of 2-4 grains (0.13-0.26 gm.) for use as an emmenagogue.

Wild Yam (wīld yam)
(*Dioscorea villosa*)

Synonyms/Related Species: Colic Root, Dioscorea, Javanese Wild Yam (*dioscorea hirsuta*), Medicinal Yam, Mexican Yam (*dioscorea mexicana*), Rheumatism Root, Tokoro, and Yuma.
Family/Class: Dioscoreaceae (yam).
Habitat: China, Java, Mexico, and the United States.
Flavor: Sweet/bitter.
Parts Used: Root.
Properties: Analgesic, antiphlogistic, antiprotozoan, antispasmodic, carminative, diaphoretic, diuretic, expectorant, hemolytic, lithotriptic, nervine, nutritive, and parasiticide.
Constituents: Alkaloids, botogenin, carbohydrates, dioscorine, diosgenin, inulin (starch), minerals (chlorine, magnesium, phosphorus, potassium), monosaccharides, mucilage, phytoestrogens, saponins, tannic acid, and vitamins (B_1 (thiamine), B_2 (riboflavin), B_6 (pyridoxine).
Historical Uses: Abdominal pain, abscess, arthritis, asthma, atrophy (ovarian), bronchitis, calculus, cholera, colds, colic, cough, cramps, cysts (ovarian), diabetes, diarrhea, dietary supplementation, digestive complaints, diverticulitis, dysentery, dysmenorrhea, enteritis, enuresis, fever (ephemeral, rheumatic), flatulence, gallbladder problems, gallstones, hiccups, hypercholesteremia, indigestion, infection (urinary tract), inflammation, influenza, irritable bowel syndrome (IBS), jaundice, kidney stones, liver problems, malnutrition, menstrual problems, mental disturbances, mucus, muscle and joint pain, nausea, nervous conditions, neuralgia, pain, parasites (amebas, scabies), poisoning (barbiturate), premenstrual syndrome (PMS), respiratory conditions, rheumatism, sciatica, spasmodic conditions, spermatorrhea, and whooping cough.
Discussion: May aid digestion; balance the glandular system; calm the nervous system; clear and open bronchial passages; dissolve calculi; enhance gallbladder, kidney, liver, lung, pancreatic,

and spleen functions; increase circulation; promote perspiration and urine flow; provide dietary supplementation; reduce both the rate of growth and the rate of reproduction of protozoa; serve as an antidote to poisoning (barbiturate), and as a nutritional adjuvant to therapeutic programs; stimulate peristalsis and uterine contractions.

Cautions/Contraindications: Avoid use if pregnant, or if you have an estrogen dependant cancer, a history of estrogen dependant cancers, or if you have diabetes, hepatitis, hypoglycemia, leukemia, ulcer (peptic), or a thyroid problem. Estrogen containing substances may contribute to abnormal blood clotting, migraine, and could promote the developement of certain types of estrogen dependant cancers.

Adverse Reactions: Central nervous system depression, convulsions, diarrhea (possibly bloody), gastrointestinal cramps (severe), hematuria (blood in the urine), hemolysis, nausea, and/or vomiting.

Herb/Drug Interactions: This herb could cause an interaction (possibly severe) when taken with the following drugs: Hormones and Synthetic Substitutes (i.e. conjugated estrogens, contraceptives (oral, etc.), and other hormonal replacement therapy (HRT).

Preparations/Dosage: Crude Herb: 3-9 grams. Infusion: 1 cup per day. Root: Boiled and eaten as a vegetable. Tincture: 10-30 drops (0.6-2 cc.) one to three times per day.

Isolation: Dioscorine: Average dose of $^1/_6$-¼ grain (10-15 mg.) administered intravenously, for use as an antidote in poisoning (barbiturate). Dioscorine's action is similar to that of picrotoxin.

Willow (wil ō)

(*Salix alba*)

Synonyms/Related Species: Alaska Willow (*salix alaxensis*), American Willow, Arctic Willow (*salix arctica*), Arroyo Willow (*salix lasiolepis*), Barclay's Willow (*salix barclayi*), Barratt's Willow (*salix barrattiana*), Bebb's Willow (*salix bebbiana*), Black Willow (*salix nigra*), Blueberry Willow (*salix myrtillifolia*), Catkins Willow, Drummond's Willow (*salix drummondiana*), Dusky Willow (*salix melanopsis*), Dwarf Willow, European Willow, Farr's Willow (*salix farriae*), Flat-Leaved Willow (*salix planifolia*), Geyer's Willow (*salix geyeriana*), Goat Willow, Grey-Leaved Willow (*salix glauca*), Hoary Willow (*salix candida*), Little-Tree Willow (*salix arbusculoides*), Mountain Willow (*salix monticola*), Narrow-Leaved Willow, Netted Willow (*salix reticulata*), Plain-Leaved Willow, Purple Willow (*salix purpurea*), Pussywillow (*salix discolor*), Red Willow (*salix bonplandiana*), Rock Willow (*salix vestita*), Salicin Willow, Sallow Willow (*salix caprea*), Sandbar Willow (*salix exigua*), Scouler's Willow (*salix scouleriana*), Short-Fruited Willow (*salix brachycarpa*), Silver Willow, Sitka Willow (*salix sitchensis*), Tealeaf Willow (*salix planifolia*), Variable Willow (*salix commutata*), White Willow, Withe Withy, and Yellow Willow.

Family/Class: Salicaceae (willow).

Habitat: Africa, Alaska, the Alpine and Subalpine zones, Asia, Europe, North America, and the Yukon Territory.

Flavor: Bitter.

Parts Used: Bark (inner).

Properties: Alterative, analgesic, antibiotic, antiperiodic, antiphlogistic, aphrodisiac, astringent, counterirritant, diaphoretic, diuretic, hemostatic, malariacidal, parasiticide, and tonic.

Constituents: Flavonoids, glycosides, populin (benzyl salicin), salicin, salicylamide, salicylic acid, salinigrin, and tannic acid.

Historical Uses: Ague, allergy (pollen), alopecia, arthritis, atrophy (ovarian), bleeding, burns (minor), canker sores, chills, colds, corns, cough, cysts (ovarian), dandruff, diarrhea, digestive complaints, dryness conditions, dysentery, earache, eczema, edema, fever (ephemeral, hay, intermittent, rheumatic), gargle/mouth rinse, gastritis, gastrointestinal problems, gleet, gonorrhea, gout, headache, indigestion, infection (bacterial, sexually transmitted), inflammation, influenza, insufficiency (venous), irritable bowel syndrome (IBS), laryngitis, malaria, measles, migraine, muscle and joint pain, neuralgia, nosebleed, osteoarthritis (OA), pain, parasites (malarial plasmodia, scabies), periodontal disease, pruritus, rash, respiratory conditions, rheumatism, sciatica, sexually transmitted diseases (STDs), sore throat, sores, stomatitis, substitute for aspirin, syphilis, tonsillitis, toothache, ulcer (stasis, syphilitic, varicose), urethritis, varicose veins, and wounds (minor).
Discussion: May arouse sexual impulses; enhance cardiovascular system, kidney, and liver functions; inhibit or destroy development and growth of bacteria and other microorganisms; promote perspiration and urine flow; reestablish healthy system functions; restore normal tone to tissues; serve as an alternative to non-steroidal anti-inflammatory drugs (NSAIDs); stimulate hair growth.
Cautions/Contraindications: Avoid use if pregnant or breast-feeding, or if you have gastritis or ulcer (duodenal, gastric, peptic), or if you have an aspirin sensitivity. Due to the high salicin content and the possibility of Reye's syndrome, do not give willow to children who have fever, chicken pox, influenza, or other viral infection. May cause dermatitis in susceptible individuals. Some persons may experience bleeding or increased clotting time when using this herb with anticoagulant drugs or aspirin.
Adverse Reactions: Anemia, asthma, auditory problems, bleeding (possibly serious), canker sores, coagulation problems, diminished sexual interest, dizziness, hives, nausea, salicylism (salicylic acid poisoning), shortness of breath, tinnitus, ulcer, and/or vomiting.
Herb/Drug Interactions: This herb could cause an interaction (possibly severe) when taken with the following drugs: Anticoagulant drugs, Salicylates, and Subsalicylates.
Preparations/Dosage: Crude Herb: 3-9 grams. Bark (powdered): 1-1½ teaspoons. Decoction: ½-1 cup per day. Tincture: 10-20 drops (0.666-1.25 cc.) one to three times per day.
Isolation: Salicin: Average dose of 5-30 grains (0.333-2 gm.) for use as an analgesic, antiperiodic, and febrifuge. Salicin's action is similar to that of quinine. Salicylamide: Average dose of 3-5 grains (0.2-0.33 gm.), applied topically, for use as an analgesic, antirheumatic, and febrifuge.

Wintergreen (win ter·grēn)
(*Gaultheria procumbens*)

Synonyms/Related Species: Alpine Wintergreen (*gaultheria humifusa*), American Wintergreen, Boxberry, Cancer Wintergreen (*gaultheria hispidula*), Checkerberry, Deerberry, Gaultheria, Groundberry, Hairy Wintergreen (*gaultheria hispidula*), Hillberry, Mountain Tea, Partridge Berry, Salal, Sallol Wintergreen (*gaultheria shallon*), Scented Wintergreen, Slender Wintergreen (*gaultheria ovatifolia*), Spiceberry, Spotted Wintergreen (*gaultheria maculata*), Teaberry, and Trailing Wintergreen.
Family/Class: Ericaceae (heath).
Habitat: Alaska, the Alpine and Subalpine zones, Europe, and North America.
Flavor: Pungent.

Parts Used: Leaves.
Properties: Analgesic, antibiotic, antifungal, antiphlogistic, antispasmodic, aromatic, astringent, carminative, counterirritant, depurative, diuretic, expectorant, hemostatic, laxative, nutritive, stimulant, tonic, and vulnerary.
Constituents: Gaultherin, glycosides, methyl salicylate, mucilage, tannic acid, volatile oil, and wax.
Historical Uses: Abscess, amenorrhea, arthritis, asthma, bladder problems, bleeding, calluses, cancer, candida, carpal tunnel syndrome, colds, colic, congestion (uterine, vaginal), corns, cough, cystitis, diabetes, diarrhea, dietary supplementation, digestive complaints, diphtheria, dysmenorrhea, edema, fever (ephemeral, rheumatic), flatulence, flavoring agent, gargle/mouth rinse, gastralgia, gastritis, gastrointestinal problems, gleet, gonorrhea, gout, headache, hematuria (blood in the urine), hemorrhage (metrorrhagia), hyperactivity, indigestion, infection (bacterial, sexually transmitted, urinary tract), inflammation, irritable bowel syndrome (IBS), kidney problems, lesions (tubercle), leukorrhea, lumbago, liver problems, malnutrition, menstrual problems, moniliasis, mucus, muscle and joint pain, nephritis, neuralgia, pain, perfume, periodontal disease, pleurisy, prolapse (uterine), prostate problems, respiratory conditions, rheumatism, rheumatoid arthritis (RA), sciatica, scrofula, sexually transmitted diseases (STDs), skin problems, sore throat, spasmodic conditions, toothache, tuberculosis, ulcer (fistula, syriac, tuberculous), urethritis, vaginitis, warts (digitate, filiform, fugitive, glabra, mother, plana juvenilis, plantar, seborrhoeic, vulgaris), and wounds (minor).
Discussion: May aid digestion; cleanse the kidneys and liver; clear and open bronchial passages; increase circulation; inhibit or destroy development and growth of bacteria and other microorganisms; promote urine flow; provide dietary supplementation; restore normal tone to tissues; serve as a nutritional adjuvant to therapeutic programs; speed healing; stimulate uterine contractions; strengthen bones, joints, and ligaments.
Cautions/Contraindications: Avoid use if pregnant or breast-feeding, or if you have an aspirin sensitivity, or if you have kidney or liver disease. Do not ingest or apply the volatile oil to children under the age of twelve. Do not apply the oil in hot weather, after strenuous exercise, or use it with a heating pad. External application of the oil should be limited to no more than three times a day, and for no longer than three consecutive days within a month. May cause dermatitis in susceptible individuals. Not for long-term use. Some persons may experience bleeding or increased clotting time when using this herb with anticoagulant drugs or aspirin. Using wintergreen with willow bark may cause serious bleeding.
Adverse Reactions: Bleeding (possibly serious), coagulation problems, hematuria (blood in the urine), liver damage (often characterized by jaundice), nausea, and/or vomiting.
Herb/Drug Interactions: This herb could cause an interaction (possibly severe) when taken with the following drugs: Anticoagulant drugs, Salicylates, and Subsalicylates.
Herb/Herb Interactions: Do not use with willow (*salix spp.*).
Preparations/Dosage: Crude Herb: 3-9 grams. Infusion: 1-2 cups per day. Oil of Wintergreen (*oleum gaultheriae*): 5-30 drops (0.333-2 cc.) in water, on a sugarcube, or in capsule form. Tincture: 10-20 drops (0.666-1.333 cc.) one to three times per day.

Winter's Bark (win'terz bärk)
(*Drimy's winteri*)

Synonyms/Related Species: Australian Winter's Bark (*drimy's aromatica*), Chilean Winter's Bark (*drimy's chilensis*), True Winter's Bark, Wintera, and Winter Cinnamon.
Family/Class: Magnoliaceae (magnolia).
Habitat: Australia, Columbia, North America, and South America.
Flavor: Pungent.
Parts Used: Bark.
Properties: Anesthetic (local), antiscorbutic, aromatic, carminative, febrifuge, stimulant, stomachic, and tonic.
Constituents: Eugenol (eugenic acid), drimenin, drimenol, eucalyptol (cineol), minerals (iron), pinene, resin, sesquiterpenes, tannic acid, vitamins (C (ascorbic acid), volatile oil, and winterin.
Historical Uses: Ague, asthma, bronchitis, colic, congestion (uterine, vaginal), dermatitis, diarrhea, digestive complaints, diphtheria, fever (ephemeral), flatulence, gastrointestinal problems, indigestion, leukorrhea, rash, respiratory conditions, scurvy, skin problems, substitute for white cinnamon and peruvian bark, toothache, ulcer (duodenal, gastric, peptic, syriac), urethritis, vaginitis, and wounds (minor).
Discussion: May aid digestion; enhance stomach function; restore normal tone to tissues.
Cautions/Contraindications: Avoid use if pregnant or breast-feeding.
Adverse Reactions: Nausea and/or vomiting.
Herb/Drug Interactions: This herb could cause an interaction (possibly severe) when taken with the following drugs:
Preparations/Dosage: Crude Herb: 3-6 grams. Bark (powdered): Average dose in substance 30 grains (2 gm.).
Isolation: Eucalyptol: 5 drops (0.3 cc.) in atomization or inhalation therapy for use in respiratory conditions.

Witch Hazel (wich hā zel)
(*Hamamelis virginiana*)

Synonyms/Related Species: Hamamelis, Hazel Nut, Snapping Hazel, Spotted Alder, Striped Alder, Tobacco Wood, Winter Bloom, and Wyche-Elm.
Family/Class: Hamamelidaceae (witch hazel).
Habitat: Asia, Europe, and North America.
Flavor: Bitter/pungent/sweet.
Parts Used: Bark (branch and trunk), leaves.
Properties: Antibiotic, antiphlogistic, astringent, hemostatic, sedative, stomachic, tonic, and vulnerary.
Constituents: Flavones, flavonoids, gallic acid, hamamelose, minerals (calcium, copper, iodine, manganese, selenium, zinc), oligomeric procyanidins, resin, saponins, sterol, tannic acid, vitamins (choline, C (ascorbic acid), E (alpha-tocopheral), K), and volatile oil.
Historical Uses: Bleeding, bruises, burns (minor), bruises, cirrhosis, congestion (uterine, vaginal), conjunctivitis, diarrhea, diphtheria, dysentery, ear infection, eczema, fever (ephemeral, herpetic), gargle/mouth rinse, gastrointestinal problems, gleet, gonorrhea, hemorrhage, hemorrhoids, herpes, hypertrophy (pores), infection (bacterial, sexually transmitted), inflammation, insect bites or stings, insufficiency (venous), laryngitis, lesions (tubercle),

leukorrhea, liver problems, lung problems, mastitis, menorrhagia, menstrual problems, mucus, muscle and joint pain, nervous conditions, periodontal disease, poison ivy/oak, prolapse (rectal, uterine), pruritus, rash, scalds, scrofula, sexually transmitted diseases (STDs), sinusitis, skin problems, sore throat, sores, sprain, sunburn, tonsillitis, tuberculosis, tumors, ulcer (duodenal, fistula, gastric, peptic, stasis, tuberculous, varicose), urethritis, vaginitis, varicose veins, wounds (minor), and wrinkles.

Discussion: May enhance cardiovascular system, intestinal system, circulatory system, and stomach functions; inhibit or destroy development and growth of bacteria and other microorganisms; prevent the deposition of fat in the liver; restore normal tone to tissues; soothe discomfort of mucous membrane irritation, as well as soothe discomfort of episiotomy, stitches, and rectal or vaginal surgery; speed healing; stimulate uterine contractions.

Cautions/Contraindications: Avoid use if pregnant or breast-feeding, or if you have an iodine sensitivity. Do not ingest commercial preparations of witch-hazel that contain isopropyl alcohol. Do not confuse this herb with hazelnut (*corylus avellana*). May interfere with the absorption of atropine (when taken by mouth), codeine, ephedrine, pseudoephedrine, and theophylline drugs. May interfere with the effectiveness of certain thyroid medications. Not for long-term use.

Adverse Reactions: Abdominal pain, arrhythmia, constipation, diarrhea (possibly bloody), fever, gastrointestinal cramps (severe), hematuria (blood in the urine), hypertrophy (thyroid), iodism (iodine poisoning), liver damage (often characterized by jaundice), nausea, priapism, thirst, and/or vomiting.

Herb/Drug Interactions: This herb could cause an interaction (possibly severe) when taken with the following drugs: Autonomic drugs, Opiate Agonists/Narcotic drugs, other Medications/Products containing ephedra or pseudoephedrine, Theophylline drugs, and Thyroid drugs.

Preparations/Dosage: Crude Herb: 3-9 grams. Decoction (bark or leaves): 1 cup per day. Extract (leaves): 5-8 drops (0.333-0.5 cc.) one to two times per day. Tincture: 5-20 drops (0.333-1.25 cc.) one to three times per day.

Woodruff (wood·ruf)
(*Asperula odorata*)

Synonyms/Related Species: Master of the Wood, Muge de Boys, Sweet Woodruff, White Woodruff, Woderove, Wood Rova, Woodwrad, and Wuderove.

Family/Class: Rubiaceae (madder).

Habitat: Africa, Europe, France, Germany, and Siberia.

Flavor: Bitter/sour.

Parts Used: Leaves.

Properties: Analgesic, anticoagulant, anti-inflammatory, antilithic, antispasmodic, cardiac depressant, carminative, diaphoretic, diuretic, expectorant, lithotriptic, nervine, sedative, and stomachic

Constituents: Cinnamic acid, citric acid, coumarin, glycoside, malic acid, tannic acid, and volatile oil.

Historical Uses: Abdominal pain, agitation, arrhythmia, calculus, colds, cough, edema, flavoring agent, gallstones, gout, headache, hysteria, inflammation, insomnia, jaundice, kidney stones, liver problems, menstrual problems, migraine, mucus, nervous conditions, neuralgia, pain, perfume, premenstrual syndrome (PMS), respiratory conditions, restlessness, spasmodic

conditions, urinary problems, urodialysis (suppression of urine), whooping cough, and wounds (minor).
Discussion: May aid digestion; calm the nervous system; clear and open bronchial passages; delay or reduce blood coagulation; diminish or reduce functional activity of the heart; dissolve calculi; enhance stomach function; prevent the development of calculus or stones; promote perspiration and urine flow.
Cautions/Contraindications: Avoid use if pregnant or breast-feeding, or if you are taking anticoagulant drugs, or if you have a coagulation problem. Some persons may experience bleeding or increased clotting time when using this herb with anticoagulant drugs or aspirin. Not for long-term use.
Adverse Reactions: Bleeding (possibly serious), coagulation problems, dizziness, fainting, headache, nausea, stupor, and/or vomiting.
Herb/Drug Interactions: This herb could cause an interaction (possibly severe) when taken with the following drugs: Anticoagulant drugs, Salicylates, and Subsalicylates.
Preparations/Dosage: Crude Herb: 3-6 grams. Extract (cold): ½-1 cup per day. Infusion: 1 cup per day. Tincture: 5-15 drops (0.3-1 cc.) one to three times per day.

Wormwood (werm wood)
(*Artemisia absinthium*)

Synonyms/Related Species: Absinthe, Alpine Sage (*artemisia scopulorum*), Annual Wormwood (*artemisia annua*), Artemisia, Biennial Wormwood (*artemisia biennis*), Big Sagebrush, Black Sage, California Mugwort, Chamiso, Chinese Wormwood, Cina, Coast Sage (*artemisia californica*), Common Mugwort (*artemisia vulgaris*), Cudweed, Devil's Liquor, Dragon Mugwort, Drakon, Esdragon, European Wormseed (*artemisia santonica*), Field Wormwood, Fringed Sagebrush, Green Ginger, Herbe au Dragon, Lad's Love, Levant Wormseed (*artemisia cina*), Little Dragon, Michaux's Mugwort (*artemisia michauxiana*), Mountain Sage, Mountain Sagewort (*artemisia arctica*), Moxa, Northern Wormwood (*artemisia campestris*), Prairie Sagewort (*artemisia frigida*), Rocky Mountain Sage, Rocky Roman Wormwood (*artemisia pontica*), Sagebrush (*artemisia tridentata*), Sailor's Tobacco, Santonica (*artemisia maritima*), Sea Wormwood, Silver Sagebrush (*artemisia cana*), Southernwood (*artemisia abrotanum*), Tarragon (*artemisia dracunculus*), Threetip Sagebrush (*artemisia tripartite*), Western Mugwort (*artemisia ludoviciana*), and White Wormwood Sage.
Family/Class: Compositae (composite).
Floral Emblem: Nevada (sagebrush).
Habitat: Africa, Alaska, the Alpine and Subalpine zones, Asia, the Baltic, Britain, the Channel Islands, England, Europe, France, Germany, Hungary, Ireland, the Mediterranean, Mongolia, North America, Russia, Siberia, and South America.
Flavor: Bitter/pungent.
Parts Used: Leaves.
Properties: Abortifacient, alterative, analgesic, anthelmintic, antibiotic, antifungal, antiperiodic, antiphlogistic, antispasmodic, antiviral, aromatic, astringent, cardiant, carminative, cholagogue, depurative, diaphoretic, diuretic, emmenagogue, hemostatic, hypoglycemic, insect repellent, laxative, malariacidal, narcotic, nervine, sedative, stimulant, stomachic, tonic, vermifuge, and vulnerary.
Constituents: Absinthic acid, absinthin, absinthol, acetic acid, aldehyde, bitter principle, borneol, cadinene, coumarin, cumin, eucalyptol (cineol), flavonoids, inulin (starch), malic acid,

minerals (calcium, cobalt, manganese, potassium, sodium, tin), phellandrene, phenol, pinene, resin, santonic acid, santonin (santoninic acid), sesquiterpene lactone, succinic acid, tannic acid, thujone, valerianic acid, vitamins (A, B_1 (thiamine), B_2 (riboflavin), B_3 (niacin), B_5 (pantothenic acid), B_6 (pyridoxine), B_{12}, B_x (para-aminobenzoic acid (PABA), C (ascorbic acid), H (biotin), inositol, M (folic acid), and volatile oil.

Historical Uses: Abscess, ague, alopecia, amenorrhea, anemia, anxiety, appetite loss, arthritis, asthma, beverage (absinthe), bladder problems, bleeding, blisters, bronchitis, bruises, cancer, candida, colds, congestion (uterine, vaginal), constipation, convulsions, cough, cramps, debility, depression (mild/moderate), diabetes, diarrhea, digestive complaints, diphtheria, dizziness, dysentery, dysmenorrhea, earache, eczema, edema, enuresis (urinary incontinence), fatigue, fever (ephemeral, intermittent, rheumatic), flatulence, gallbladder problems, gallstones, gargle/mouth rinse, gastritis, gastrointestinal problems, gout, headache, hemorrhage (metrorrhagia), hepatitis, herbal tobacco, hot flashes, hyperglycemia, hysteria, indigestion, infection (bacterial, fungal, urinary tract, viral), inflammation, influenza, insect bites or stings, irritable bowel syndrome (IBS), jaundice, kidney problems, laryngitis, lesions (tubercle), leukorrhea, liver problems, lung problems, malaria, menopausal/menstrual problems, menorrhagia, moniliasis, moths, moxabustion therapy, mucus, muscle and joint pain, nausea, nervous conditions, neuralgia, nosebleed, pain, palsy, parasites (malarial plasmodia, pinworm, roundworm), periodontal disease, pneumonia, pruritus, rash, respiratory conditions, rheumatism, sciatica, scrofula, sinusitis, sore throat, sores, spasmodic conditions, spleen problems, sprain, stomachache, stroke (heat), substitute for chloroquinine, tonsillitis, toothache, tuberculosis, ulcer (duodenal, fistula, gastric, syriac, tuberculous), urethritis, urinary problems, vaginitis, and wounds (minor).

Discussion: May aid digestion; calm the nervous system; cleanse the liver; enhance gallbladder, liver, nervous system, and stomach functions; increase circulation; induce abortion; inhibit or destroy development and growth of bacteria and other microorganisms; promote bile flow, bowel evacuation, perspiration, and urine flow; reduce blood sugar levels; reestablish healthy system functions; restore normal tone to tissues; serve as a useful remedy for chloroquinine-resistant malaria; speed healing; stimulate appetite, bitter taste bud receptors of the tongue, the cardiovascular system, menstruation, peristalsis, and uterine contractions.

Cautions/Contraindications: Avoid use if pregnant or breast-feeding, or if you have acidity (gastric), a coagulation problem, stomach inflammation, or ulcer (peptic). Do not confuse this herb with sage (*salvia spp.*). Some persons may experience bleeding or increased clotting time when using this herb with anticoagulant drugs or aspirin. May cause an allergic reaction or dermatitis in susceptible individuals. Not for long-term use.

Adverse Reactions: Bleeding (possibly serious), coagulation problems, coma, convulsions, dependency, diarrhea, dizziness, edema, fainting, gastrointestinal problems, headache, impaired reproductive system function, mental disturbances, nausea, nervous system damage, stupor, trembling, and/or vomiting.

Herb/Drug Interactions: This herb could cause an interaction (possibly severe) when taken with the following drugs: Anticoagulant drugs, Antidiabetic drugs, Antimalarial drugs, Salicylates, and Subsalicylates.

Preparations/Dosage: Crude Herb: 3-6 grams. Extract: 3-5 drops (0.2-0.333 cc.) one to two times per day. Infusion: ½ cup per day. Moxabustion Therapy: see "Moxa" under Methods of Preperation. Leaves (powdered): Average dose in capsule form 5-30 grains (0.33-2 gm.), one to two capsules, one to two times per day. Oil of Wormwood (*oleum absinthium*): 2-5 drops per day in water or on a sugarcube. Tincture: 5-10 drops (0.3-0.6 cc.) in water or on a sugarcube one to three times per day.

Isolation: Eucalyptol: 5 drops (0.3 cc.) in atomization or inhalation therapy for use in respiratory conditions. Santonin: Average dose of 1-4 grains (0.066-0.266 gm.) for use as an anthelmintic.
Did You Know? Vermouth comes from the German word wermut, which means wormwood.

Yarrow (yar ō)
(*Achillea millefolium*)

Synonyms/Related Species: Band Man's Plaything, Bloodwort, Carpenter's Weed, Common Yarrow, Devil's Nettle, Field-Hop, Gæruwe, Gearwe, Herbe Militaris, Knight's Milfoil, Millefeuille, Milfoil, Old Man's Pepper, Plumajillo, Sanguinary, Sneezewort (*achillea ptarmica*), Soldier's Woundwort, Staunchweed, Thousand Weed, Western North American Yarrow (*achillea lanulosa*), Wild Yarrow, Woolly Yellow Yarrow (*achillea tomentosa*), and Yerw.
Family/Class: Compositae (composite).
Habitat: Africa, Alaska, the Alpine zone, the Balkans, Europe, North America, Norway, Portugal, Scotland, Sweden, Switzerland.
Flavor: Bitter/pungent.
Parts Used: Flowers, leaves.
Properties: Analgesic, antacid, antibiotic, anticarcinogen, anticoagulant, antiperiodic, antiphlogistic, antispasmodic, aromatic, astringent, demulcent, depurative, diaphoretic, diuretic, hemostatic, hypotensive, malariacidal, stimulant, tonic, vasodilator, and vulnerary.
Constituents: Achillein, azulene, caryophyllin, eucalyptol (cineol), flavonoids, glycosides, gum, luteolin, minerals (copper, iodine, iron, manganese, potassium), monosaccharides, nitrates, phosphates, pinene, resin, rutin, sesquiterpenes, thujone, lactone, tannic acid, vitamins (A, C (ascorbic acid), E (alpha-tocopheral), K), and volatile oil.
Historical Uses: Abscess, acidity (gastric), ague, alopecia, anorexia, appetite loss, asthma, bladder problems, bleeding, bronchitis, bruises, burns (minor), bursitis, cancer, chicken pox, colds, congestion (uterine, vaginal), cough, contraceptive (male), cramps, cystitis, diabetes, diarrhea, digestive complaints, diphtheria, dysentery, dysmenorrhea, dysuria (painful/difficult urination), endometriosis, ear infection, epilepsy, fever (ephemeral, enteric, intermittent, rheumatic), flatulence, gastritis, gastrointestinal problems, headache, hemorrhage (metrorrhagia), hemorrhoids, hot flashes, hypertension (mild/moderate), hysteria, indigestion, infection (bacterial, urinary tract), inflammation, influenza, insect bites or stings, insomnia, insufficiency (venous), irritable bowel syndrome (IBS), jaundice, kidney problems, leukorrhea, liver problems, malaria, measles, menopausal/menstrual problems, menorrhagia, muscle and joint pain, nephritis, nosebleed, pain, parasites (malarial plasmodia), plague, pleurisy, pneumonia, pruritus, respiratory conditions, rheumatism, skin problems, small pox, sore nipples, sore throat, sores, spleen problems, spasmodic conditions, toothache, typhoid, ulcer (bouveret, duodenal, gastric, peptic, stasis, syriac, varicose), urethritis, uterine problems, vaginitis, varicose veins, visual disturbances, and wounds (minor).
Discussion: May cause blood vessel dilatation; decrease the effect of carcinogens; delay or reduce coagulation of the blood; enhance circulatory system, liver, and lung functions; halt sperm production in males; prevent hemorrhage in persons with hypertension; inhibit or destroy developement and growth of bacteria and other microorganisms; neutralize acidity; promote perspiration and urine flow; purify the blood; reduce blood pressure levels and capillary fragility;

restore normal tone to tissues; soothe mucous membrane irritation and nipple soreness; speed healing; stimulate peristalsis; suppress menstruation.

Cautions/Contraindications: Avoid use if pregnant or breast-feeding, or if you have a coagulation problem, gallstones, menorrhagia, pelvic inflammatory disease (PID), or an iodine sensitivity. Persons having sensitivity to aspirin may also have sensitivity to yarrow. May cause photosensitivity or photodermatosis in susceptible individuals. May interfere with the effectiveness of certain thyroid medications. Some persons may experience bleeding or increased clotting time when using this herb with anticoagulant drugs or aspirin.

Adverse Reactions: Abdominal pain, arrhythmia, bleeding (possibly serious), coagulation problems, diarrhea (possibly bloody), fever, headache, hypertrophy (thyroid), iodism (iodine poisoning), nausea, priapism, skin rash, thirst, and/or vomiting.

Herb/Drug Interactions: This herb could cause an interaction (possibly severe) when taken with the following drugs: Anticoagulant drugs, Hypotensive drugs, Salicylates, Subsalicylates, and Thyroid drugs.

Preparations/Dosage: Crude Herb: 3-9 grams. Infusion: 1 cup per day. Juice 1-2 teaspoons in water one to three times per day. Tincture: 5-20 drops (0.333-1.25 cc.) one to three times per day.

Isolation: Eucalyptol: 5 drops (0.3 cc.) in atomization or inhalation therapy for use in respiratory conditions.

Yerba Santa (yer be san te)

(*Eriodictyon californicum*)

Synonyms/Related Species: Bear Plant, Bearsweed, Consumptives' Weed, Gum Bush, Holy Herb, Mountain Balm, Narrow-Leaf Yerba Santa (*eriodictyon angustifolium*), Saintly Herb, and Tarweed.

Family/Class: Hydrophyllaceae (waterleaf).

Habitat: North America (primarily California and Mexico).

Flavor: Pungent.

Parts Used: Leaves.

Properties: Alterative, antiphlogistic, antispasmodic, aromatic, carminative, counterirritant, depurative, diuretic, expectorant, sialogogue, tonic, vesicant, and vulnerary.

Constituents: Aglycone (genin), eriodictyol (eriodictin), flavonoids, formic acid, monosaccharides, resin, sterol, tannic acid, and volatile oil.

Historical Uses: Asthma, allergy (pollen), bronchitis, colds, constipation, cough, dermatitis, diarrhea, dizziness, dryness conditions, dysentery, fever (ephemeral, hay, rheumatic), flavoring agent, gargle/mouth rinse, gastrointestinal problems, gleet, gonorrhea, halitosis, hemorrhoids, indigestion, infection (bladder, sexually transmitted), inflammation, influenza, insect bites or stings, kidney problems, laryngitis, lesions (tubercle), lung problems, mucus, muscle and joint pain, nausea, pain, pneumonia, pleurisy, poison ivy/oak, rash, respiratory conditions, rheumatism, scrofula, sexually transmitted diseases (STDs), sore throat, sores, spasmodic conditions, sprain, stomachache, thirst, tuberculosis, ulcer (fistula, tuberculous), urethritis, vomiting, and wounds (minor).

Discussion: May aid digestion; clear and open bronchial passages; enhance lung and spleen functions; promote saliva secretion and urine flow; purify the blood; reestablish healthy system functions; restore normal tone to tissues; speed healing; stimulate gastric secretions.

Cautions/Contraindications: Avoid use if pregnant or breast-feeding, or if you have acidity (gastric) or an ulcer (gastric, peptic).
Adverse Reactions: Blistering of the mouth/skin/throat, gastrointestinal irritation, mucous membrane irritation, nausea, salivation (increased), and/or vomiting.
Herb/Drug Interactions: This herb could cause an interaction (possibly severe) when taken with the following drugs: None known.
Preparations/Dosage: Crude Herb 3-6 grams. Infusion: ½-1 cup per day. Leaves (powdered): Average dose in substance 15-60 grains (1-4 gm.). Tincture: 10-30 drops (0.6-2 cc.) one to three times per day.

Yohimbe (yo-him be)
(*Corynanthe yohimbe*)

Synonyms/Related Species: Johimbe and Pausinystalia Yohimbe.
Family/Class: Rubiaceae (madder).
Habitat: Africa.
Flavor: Bitter.
Parts Used: Bark.
Properties: Analgesic, antidiuretic, aphrodisiac, cardiant, hallucinogen, and stimulant.
Constituents: Alkaloids, corynanthine, tannic acid, yohimbenine, and yohimbine.
Historical Uses: Angina, arteriosclerosis, diabetes, dieting, diminished sex drive, dysmenorrhea, dyspnea, edema, erectile dysfunction, exhaustion, fever, frigidity, menstrual problems, pain, Parkinson's disease, respiratory conditions, sexual problems, skin problems, and weight management.
Discussion: May arouse sexual impulses; diminish or suppress urine flow; enhance glandular system and kidney functions; increase circulation, erection duration and strength, and adrenal output of norepinephrine (a hormone needed for erection); inhibit serotonin; stimulate the cardiovascular system, central nervous system, and the genitourinary system.
Cautions/Contraindications: Avoid use if pregnant or breast-feeding, or if you have angina, intestinal problems, heart disease, depression (severe), hypertension, hypotension, kidney problems, liver problems, prostate problems, or psychosis. Do not take yohimbe with diet aids or nasal decongestants containing phenylpropanolamine (PPA) as hazardous adverse effects could develop. Elevated levels of norepinephrine may increase blood pressure levels and heart rate. Yohimbe is a monoamine oxidase inhibitor (MAOI) herb. The combined use of yohimbe with sedative, tranquilizer, antihistamine, narcotic, anxiety, blood pressure, nitroglycerin, migraine, viagara, seizure, tricyclic antidepressant, or weight loss aid drugs will cause hypertensive crisis. The combined use of yohimbe with amphetamines, cocaine, LSD, alcohol (including wine) avocados, unripe bananas, and dairy products (including aged cheese) will cause hypotensive crisis. May increase the effectiveness of selective serotonin reuptake inhibitor (SSRI) drugs. Librium and sodium amobarbitol will partially block the effects of yohimbe. It is recommended that no other drugs be used in combination with or within a ten-hour period of the use of yohimbe. Foods to avoid when using yohimbe include chocolate, aged cheese, liver/organ meats, and any foods that contain tyramine. The aphrodisiac use of yohimbe bark may include temporary physical effects of chills up and down the spine. Some persons will occasionally experience slight auditory and visual hallucinations as well as mild nausea. These effects, though more intense, are similar to that experienced upon ingestion of muira puama, and

generally occur about one to two hours after ingestion and can last from two to four hours. Not for long-term use.

Adverse Reactions: Abdominal pain, anxiety, arrhythmia, cardiac failure, confusion, debility, delirium, dependancy, depression, dizziness, excitability, exhaustion (extreme), fainting, hallucinations, hematuria (blood in the urine), hypertensive crisis (severe rise in blood pressure levels), hypotensive crisis (arrythmias, breathing difficulty, chills, and a severe drop in blood pressure levels), insomnia, liver damage (often characterized by jaundice), mania, nausea, nervousness, paralysis, priapism, respiratory failure, salivation, spasmodic conditions, tachycardia, tremors, vertigo, vomiting, and/or possible death.

Herb/Drug Interactions: This herb could cause an interaction (possibly severe) when taken with the following drugs: Amphetamine drugs, Antidepressant drugs, Antihistamine drugs, Anxiolytic drugs, Autonomic drugs, Cardiac drugs, Erectile Dysfunction drugs, Hypotensive drugs, Migraine drugs, Monamine Oxidase Inhibitors (MAOIs), other Medications/Products containing phenylpropanolamine, Opiate Agonists/Narcotic drugs, Phenylpropanolamine drugs, Sedative drugs, Selective Serotonin Reuptake Inhibitor (SSRI) drugs, and Tranquilizer drugs.

Herb/Herb Interactions: Do not use Rauwolfia (*rauwolfia serpentina*) or any other herbs containing yohimbine while taking yohimbe.

Preparations/Dosage: Crude Herb: 3-6 grams. Infusion: 1-2 cups per day. Residue (mainly yohimbine hydrochloride): Soak 1 ounce of bark shavings in grain alchohol for 8-12 hours. Strain the liquid into a bowl. Pour the liquid onto a flat sheet (cookie sheet) and let the alcohol evaporate (to speed the evapaoration process, put the cookie sheet in an oven on low heat (150°-250° F). The residue remaining will result in approximately 1-1½ grams (enough for one person). Snuff the residue or place it under the tongue. The effects are more pronounced and the reaction occurs within ten to twenty minutes versus the hour or two via the infusional method. To help reduce nausea, add 1,000 mg. of vitamin C (ascorbic acid) to the infusion. The vitamin C reacts with the bark to form yohimbine and yohimbiline ascorbate, which makes these two alkaloids very soluble and more easily assimilated by the body. Also, fasting for 16-18 hours prior to ingesting yohimbe may also help reduce nausea.

Isolation: Yohimbine hydrochlorate: Soluble in water. Average dose of $^{1}/_{12}$-$^{1}/_{10}$ grain (0.005-0.007 gm.) for use in erectile dysfunction and as a carminative.

Yucca (yuk e)
(*Yucca glauca*)

Synonyms/Related Species: Adam's Needle, Banana Yucca (*yucca baccata*), Mojave Yucca (*yucca schidigera*), Narrow-Leaved Yucca, Soap Plant, Spanish Bayonet, and Taino.

Family/Class: Liliaceae (lily).

Floral Emblem: New Mexico.

Habitat: Central America, Europe, North America, and South America.

Flavor: Sweet.

Parts Used: Leaves, root.

Properties: Alterative, antifungal, antiphlogistic, depurative, diuretic, hemostatic, laxative, and nutritive.

Constituents: Aglycone (genin), gitogenin, minerals (calcium, copper, iron, manganese, phosphorous, potassium), phosphoric acid, saponins, sterols, tigogenin, and vitamins (A, B_1

(thiamine), B_2 (riboflavin), B_3 (niacin), B_5 (pantothenic acid), B_6 (pyridoxine), B_{12}, B_x (para-aminobenzoic acid (PABA), C (ascorbic acid), H (biotin), inositol, M (folic acid).

Historical Uses: Addison's disease, arthritis, asthma, bleeding, bursitis, cancer (melanoma), cholesterol, dandruff, dietary supplementation, fever (ephemeral, rheumatic), fractures, gallbladder problems, gleet, gonorrhea, gout, hair rinse, hair shampoo, infection (fungal, sexually transmitted), inflammation, liver problems, malnutrition, muscle and joint pain, prostatitis, rheumatism, sexually transmitted diseases (STDs), skin problems, sprain, substitute for soap (root), ulcer (duodenal, gastric, peptic), and urethritis.

Discussion: May enhance liver and stomach functions; promote bowel evacuation and urine flow; provide dietary supplementation; purify the blood; reduce cholesterol levels; reestablish healthy system functions; serve as a nutritional adjuvant to therapeutic programs; stimulate peristalsis.

Cautions/Contraindications: Avoid use if pregnant or breast-feeding. May slow fat-soluble vitamin absorption.

Adverse Reactions: Diarrhea (possibly bloody), gastrointestinal cramps (severe), hematuria (blood in the urine), nausea, and/or vomiting.

Herb/Drug Interactions: This herb could cause an interaction (possibly severe) when taken with the following drugs: None known.

Preparations/Dosage: Crude Herb 3-6 grams. Flowers: Edible in salads. Infusion: 1 cup per day. Seed Pods (immature): Steamed and eaten.

Zedoary (zed ō·er ē)

(*Curcuma zedoaria*)

Synonyms/Related Species: Curcuma, East Indian Arrowroot (*curcuma angustifolia*), Gauri, Haldi, Haridra, Indian Saffron, Indian Turmeric Root, Jadwār, Jiang-huang, Kurkum Saffron, Tarmaret, Terre-Mérite, Tormerik, Turmeric (*curcuma longa*), Yu-jin, and Zadwār.

Family/Class: Zingiberaceae (ginger).

Habitat: Arabia, Asia, Bengal, China, India, Indonesia, Java, the Moluccas, New Guinea, the Philippines, and South America.

Flavor: Pungent.

Parts Used: Root.

Properties: Alterative, analgesic, antibiotic, anticarcinogen, anticoagulant, antifertilizin, antioxidant, antiphlogistic, antiscorbutic, aromatic, astringent, carminative, emmenagogue, hemostatic, hypoglycemic, lithotriptic, stimulant, stomachic, and vulnerary.

Constituents: Alkaloids, curcumen, curcumin, fatty acids (oleic, palmitic, stearic), fixed oils (olein, palmitin, stearin), gum, inulin (starch), minerals (calcium, potassium), monosaccharides, protein, turmerol, vitamins (C (ascorbic acid), volatile oil, and zingiberene.

Historical Uses: Abdominal pain, acquired immune deficiency syndrome (AIDS), amenorrhea, appetite loss, arteriosclerosis, arthritis, bleeding, bronchitis, bruises, bursitis, calculus, cancer (carcinoma, colon, oral, ovarian, skin), cardiovascular conditions, carpal tunnel syndrome, cataracts, cirrhosis, colds, colic, conjunctivitis, cystitis, diabetes, diarrhea, dysmenorrhea, eczema, edema, endometriosis, fever, flatulence, flavoring agent, flushing, gallbladder problems, gallstones, gastritis, gastrointestinal problems, halitosis, headache, hepatitis, Hodgkin's disease, human immunodeficiency virus (HIV), hyperglycemia, indigestion, infection (bacterial, viral), inflammation, irritable bowel syndrome (IBS), jaundice, kidney stones, leech bites, leprosy, leukemia, liver problems, menstrual problems, mucus, muscle and joint pain, pain, nephritis, periodontal disease, poisoning (chemical, radiation), premenstrual syndrome (PMS), psoriasis, scurvy, skin problems, tendinitis, tumors (Kaposi's sarcoma, multiple myeloma), and wounds (minor).

Discussion: May aid digestion and assimilation; balance the hormonal system; decrease the effect of carcinogens; delay or reduce coagulation of the blood; dissolve calculi; enhance cardiovascular system, gallbladder, liver, lung, and stomach functions; increase circulation and T-cell activity; inhibit oxidation and inhibit or destroy development and growth of bacteria and other microorganisms; neutralize fertilizin (fertilization), offset the negative effects of chemotherapy and radiation therapy; reduce blood sugar levels, cholesterol levels, and kidney damage (diabetic); reestablish healthy system functions; protect the liver; serve as an anti-food poisoning agent and serve as an adjuvant to radiation poisoing; speed healing; stimulate gastric secretions, menstruation, peristalsis, and the immune system.

Cautions/Contraindications: Avoid use if pregnant or breast-feeding, or if you have an acidity (gastric), a coagulation problem, colic (acute), gallstones, heart disease, liver problems, an obstruction (biliary), ulcer (gastric, peptic), or if you are seeking to become pregnant. Some persons may experience bleeding or increased clotting time when using this herb with anticoagulant drugs or aspirin. Not for long-term use.

Adverse Reactions: Bleeding (possibly serious), coagulation problems, nausea, and/or vomiting.

Herb/Drug Interactions: This herb could cause an interaction (possibly severe) when taken with the following drugs: Anticoagulant drugs, Antidiabetic drugs, Salicylates, and Subsalicylates.

Preparations/Dosage: Crude Herb: 3-9 grams. Root (powdered): Average dose in substance 8-30 grains (0.5-2 gm.).

Bee Products

The benefits and extraordinary nutritive value of bee products has been known since antiquity. Those skilled workers, the honeybees (*apis mellifica*), produce through their mastership, some of the most precious substances on earth. Collecting nectar to make honey, and pollen to feed their larvae, as well as producing royal jelly to feed and sustain their queen, the worker bees are tireless in their endeavors. Bee products contain amino acids, vitamins, minerals, enzymes, coenzymes, and carbohydrates, and are useful in protecting the body against autoimmune disease and infection. They help boost energy levels and metabolism, reduce build-up or debris in cells, stop or slow abnormal cell growth, strengthen the blood cells, promote nutrient absorption, support the immune system, and reduce inflammation.

WARNING! Do not use bee products if you have a seasonal allergy (pollen), a heart condition, a serious infection, or if you are allergic to bee stings.

<u>Note</u>: Pollen, propolis, and royal jelly are highly concentrated substances and only small amounts may be required to receive their full benefits.

Bee Pollen (bē päl en)

Synonyms/Related Species: Breeches, Hoschen, Miracle Food, Palē, Pel, and Super Food.

Description: Bee Pollen consists of microspores, the dust-like male reproductive cells of flowers and trees that are collected on the hind legs of bees as they brush against the anthers (pollen

producing part) of the plant. There are two classifications of pollen, anemophilous (wind-borne), and entomophilous (insect-borne). Pollen coloring is dependant on the plant species and can cover a wide variety of shades. Bee Pollen is considered to be a complete food, supplying the body with everything it needs to maintain life.
Flavor: Bitter/sweet.
Parts Used: Pollen (raw or micronized).
Properties: Antibiotic, anticarcinogen, antiphlogistic, antiscorbutic, aphrodisiac, astringent, carminative, coagulant, depurative, diuretic, erythropoietic, hemostatic, hypotensive, nutritive, sedative, stimulant, and vasodilator.
Constituents: Amines, amino acids (alanine, arginine, cystine, glycine, histidine, hydroxylysine, hydroxyproline, leucine, lysine, methionine, phenylalanine, proline, threonine, tryptophan, valine), anthocyanins, carbohydrates, chlorophyll, cyanocabalamine, enzymes, flavonoids, lecithin, lycopene, minerals (calcium, chlorine, copper, iron, magnesium, manganese, phosphorus, potassium, silicon, sodium, sulfur, zinc), monosaccharides, protein, quercetin, rutin, silicic acid, vitamins (A, B_1 (thiamine), B_2 (riboflavin), B_3 (niacin), B_6 (pyridoxine), C (ascorbic acid), choline, D, E (alpha-tocopheral), H (biotin), inositol, M (folic acid), xanthophylls, and zeaxanthin.
Historical Uses: Allergy (food, pollen), anemia, appetite loss, arthritis, asthma, bladder problems, bleeding, blemishes, blepharitis (eyelid inflammation), blisters, bruises, burns (minor), cancer, colds, colic, colitis, conjunctivitis, constipation, convalescence, debility, depression (mild/moderate), diarrhea, dietary supplementation, digestive complaints, diminished sex drive, escherichia coli (e-coli), eczema, enteritis, exhaustion, eye problems, fatigue, fever (ephemeral, enteric, hay, rheumatic), flatulence, gallbladder problems, gastritis, gastrointestinal problems, glandular problems, hemorrhoids, hypertension (mild/moderate), hypertrophy (benign prostatic), hypoglycemia, indigestion, infection (bacterial), infertility, inflammation, insomnia, insufficiency (circulatory, venous), irritable bowel syndrome (IBS), kidney problems, liver problems, malnutrition, memory/cognitive problems, muscle and joint pain, nervous conditions, neurologic conditions, periodontal disease, prostate problems, psoriasis, respiratory conditions, rheumatoid arthritis (RA), salmonella, scurvy, sinusitis, skin problems, tumors, typhoid, ulcer (bouveret), and wrinkles.
Discussion: May aid digestion; arouse sexual impulses; cause blood vessel dilatation; cleanse the whole system; decrease the effect of carcinogens; desensitize individuals to plants of which they are allergic; enhance circulatory system, glandular system, and intestinal system functions; improve cognition and memory; increase calcium retention, endurance, energy, the production of red blood cells, stamina, testosterone levels, and vitality; inhibit development or destroy growth of bacteria and other microorganisms; offset the negative effects of chemotherapy and radiation therapy; prevent hemorrhage in persons with hypertension; promote blood coagulation and urine flow; protect against hemorrhage (arterial, cerebral, retinal); provide dietary supplementation; reduce blood pressure levels and capillary fragility; restore equlibrium; serve as a nutritional adjuvant to therapeutic programs; slow heart rate; stimulate appetite, growth, the immune system, and metabolism; stop or slow abnormal cell growth; strengthen the vascular system and heart contractions.
Cautions/Contraindications: Avoid use if pregnant or breast-feeding, or if you have asthma, a seasonal allergy (pollen), a heart condition, a serious infection, or if you are allergic to bee stings. May cause allergic reactions in susceptible individuals.
Adverse Reactions: Anaphylaxis, arrhythmia, asthma, difficulty swallowing, dizziness, hives, itchy/watery eyes, respiratory distress, scratchy throat, skin flushing, and/or wheezing.

Herb/Drug Interactions: This herb could cause an interaction (possibly severe) when taken with the following drugs: Hypotensive drugs.
Preparation/Dosage: Crude Herb: 15-30 grams. Start with 1 grain (0.066 gm.), and if you experience no adverse reactions gradually increase amount by 1-2 grains (0.066-0.133 gm.) daily.
Note: When using pollen, keep in mind that the amount of bee pollen needed can vary from person to person. Start out with a very small amount daily, perhaps only a few granules, then if you experience no adverse effects, very slowly, in increments over days, increase your dosage. Remain vigilant for signs of allergic reactions as you increase the dosage. If possible, stay with a single pollen source once you have determined that you experience no adverse effects, because the pollen content can vary among batches. Each batch of pollen is composed of different pollens that have been collected from a wide variety of flowers. Occasionally, an individual will find they are allergic to certain ones, so be sure to sample a small amount of pollen from each new batch to test for any allergic reactions. Drink plenty of water when taking bee pollen. When taking fresh or powdered/dried bee pollen, try sprinkling it over a bowl of cereal (oatmeal) or other food, or mixing it with apple juice. Store pollen in a dry, moisture free place. Pollen may be refrigerated or frozen.
Did You Know? In a single spring, bees can collect anywhere from sixty to eighty pounds of pollen. If a human were to try and collect pollen by hand, they could only gather approximately ½ gram per hour.

Honey (hun ē)

Synonyms/Related Species: Dew, Honang, Honi, Hunig, Kāñcana, Kenekó, Mel, and Nectar of the Gods.
Description: A thick, sweet, sticky, syrup-like substance produced by bees from the nectar they have collected from flowers. Honey coloring is dependant on the nectar obtained from the flowers and can cover a wide variety of shades. The flavor of honey comes from the aromatic substances found in the flower nectar.
Flavor: Sweet.
Parts Used: Honey.
Properties: Antibiotic, antiphlogistic, aphrodisiac, aromatic, demulcent, expectorant, laxative, nutritive, tonic, vasodilator, and vulnerary.
Constituents: Aldehydes, dextrose, dulcitol, enzymes, mannitol (mannite), minerals (aluminum, calcium, chlorine, copper, iron, magnesium, manganese, phosphorous, potassium, silicon, sodium, sulfur), monosaccharides, phosphoric acid, protein, silicic acid, terpenes, and vitamins (B_1 (thiamine), B_2 (riboflavin), B_3 (niacin), C (ascorbic acid).
Historical Uses: Allergy, arthritis, bladder problems, blisters, bronchitis, burns (minor), colds, constipation, cough, dietary supplementation, digestive complaints, edema, fatigue, fever (ephemeral, rheumatic), food source, flavoring agent, infection (bacterial), inflammation, insomnia, insufficiency (venous), kidney problems, laryngitis, liver problems, malnutrition, mucus, muscle and joint pain, prostate problems, respiratory conditions, rheumatism, rheumatoid arthritis (RA), skin problems, sore throat, and wounds (minor).
Discussion: May aid digestion; arouse sexual impulses; cause blood vessel dilatation; clear and open bronchial passages; enhance the whole system; increase calcium retention, endurance, energy, immunity, and stamina; inhibit development or destroy growth of bacteria and other

microorganisms; offset the negative effects of chemotherapy and radiation therapy; promote bowel evacuation; provide dietary supplementation; restore normal tone to tissues; serve as a nutritional adjuvant to therapeutic programs; soothe mucous membrane irritation; speed healing; stimulate metabolism and peristalsis; strengthen the eyes.
Cautions/Contraindications: Avoid excessive use if pregnant or breast-feeding. Do not use if you have a seasonal allergy (pollen), a heart condition, a serious infection, or if you are allergic to bee stings. May cause allergic reactions in susceptible individuals.
Adverse Reactions: Anaphylaxis, arrhythmia, asthma, difficulty swallowing, dizziness, hives, itchy/watery eyes, respiratory distress, scratchy throat, skin flushing, and/or wheezing.
Herb/Drug Interactions: This herb could cause an interaction (possibly severe) when taken with the following drugs: None known.
Preparation/Dosage: Take 3-6 teaspoons daily (start with a ¼ teaspoon and if you experience no adverse reactions, increase by ½ teaspoon daily). Honey will keep indefinitely since bacteria cannot live in honey. Keep honey in a dry place. Do not store honey in a damp place as honey absorbs and retains moisture. Do not store honey in the refrigerator. Honey may be stored in the freezer. If honey crystalizes (developes harmless crystals) place sealed or capped container in very warm water until crystals dissolve.
Isolation: Mannitol hexanitrate: Average dose of 15-60 mg. for use as a vasodilator.

Propolis (präp e·lis)
Synonyms/Related Species: Bee Glue and Nature's Antibiotic.
Description: Propolis is a mixture of tree resin that is harvested by bees. The bees then combine the resin with their own secretions to produce a glue-like substance used to build, disinfect, and repair their hives.
Flavor: Bitter/sweet.
Parts Used: Propolis.
Properties: Antibiotic, antihistamine, antiviral, nutritive, and stimulant.
Constituents: Amino acids (glycine, histidine), enzymes, flavonoids, quercitin, and vitamins (B_1 (thiamine), B_2 (riboflavin), B_3 (niacin), B_5 (pantothenic acid), B_6 (pyridoxine), B_{12}, B_x (para-aminobenzoic acid (PABA), H (biotin), inositol, M (folic acid).
Historical Uses: Allergy, bronchitis, bruises, colds, dietary supplementation, gargle/mouth rinse, infection (bacterial, viral), malnutrition, respiratory conditions, sore throat, strep throat, and wounds (minor).
Discussion: May counteract the effect of histamine; inhibit development or destroy growth of bacteria and other microorganisms; provide dietary supplementation; serve as a nutritional adjuvant to therapeutic programs; stimulate the immune system.
Cautions/Contraindications: Avoid use if pregnant or breast-feeding, or if you have asthma, a seasonal allergy (pollen), a heart condition, a serious infection, or if you are allergic to bee stings. May cause allergic reactions in susceptible individuals.
Adverse Reactions: Anaphylaxis, arrhythmia, asthma, difficulty swallowing, dizziness, hives, itchy/watery eyes, respiratory distress, scratchy throat, skin flushing, and/or wheezing.
Herb/Drug Interactions: This herb could cause an interaction (possibly severe) when taken with the following drugs: None known.
Preparation/Dosage: Propolis (raw): Chew or suck daily on a small (pea-sized) piece until it breaks down (you can swallow the remainder).

Note: propolis creates a normal, harmless, tingling-type sensation on your tongue and in your mouth. If the tingling sensation becomes too intense, simply remove the propolis from your mouth for about half an hour and then return it again.

Royal Jelly (roi el jel ē)

Synonyms/Related Species: None known.
Description: Royal jelly is a highly nutritional substance secreted from the worker bee's maxillary glands and serves as food for the queen and the larvae.
Flavor: Bitter/sweet.
Parts Used: Royal jelly.
Properties: Antibiotic, antiphlogistic, antiviral, nervine, nutritive, stimulant, tonic, and vulnerary.
Constituents: Amino acids (histidine), and vitamins (B_1 (thiamine), B_2 (riboflavin), B_3 (niacin), B_5 (pantothenic acid), B_6 (pyridoxine), B_{12}, B_x (para-aminobenzoic acid (PABA), H (biotin), inositol, M (folic acid).
Historical Uses: Arthritis, dietary supplementation, fever (ephemeral, rheumatic), hypercholesteremia, infection (bacterial, viral), inflammation, malnutrition, muscle and joint pain, nervous conditions, rheumatism, and wounds (minor).
Discussion: May calm the nervous system; inhibit development or destroy growth of bacteria and other microorganisms; provide dietary supplementation; reduce cholesterol levels; restore normal tone to tissues; serve as a nutritional adjuvant to therapeutic programs; speed healing; stimulate the formation of bone tissue.
Cautions/Contraindications: Avoid use if pregnant or breast-feeding, or if you have asthma, a seasonal allergy (pollen), a heart condition, a serious infection, or if you are allergic to bee stings. May cause allergic reactions in susceptible individuals.
Adverse Reactions: Anaphylaxis, arrhythmia, asthma, difficulty swallowing, dizziness, hives, itchy/watery eyes, respiratory distress, scratchy throat, skin flushing, and/or wheezing.
Herb/Drug Interactions: This herb could cause an interaction (possibly severe) when taken with the following drugs: None known.
Preparation/Dosage: Begin with very small amounts and if you experience no adverse reactions, gradually increase amounts daily.

Healing Food Chemicals

The earliest healing food chemicals or dietary supplements were herbs that people consumed as food, and all medicinal herbs contain amino acids, vitamins, minerals, therapeutic phytochemicals, and trace elements that range in proportion from infintesimal to plentiful. Supplements can make a dramatic impact on an individual's quality of life and health, however, nutritional supplements are just that, *supplementary*. An individual cannot make up for poor dietary habits, a negative attitude, or a lack of exercise by taking pills. Although nutritional supplementation is effective in improving health, in the long run it is essential that one develop a positive attitude, a regular daily exercise routine, and a healthy diet.
Note: The safety of many supplements during pregnancy or breast-feeding has not been verified. As with any supplement not absolutely necessary for health, your safest course is to avoid it

during pregnancy or breast-feeding. If you have any serious illness, only take supplements after consulting with your healthcare professional.

Amino Acids

Amino acids are a group of organic substances that are the building blocks of proteins that enable our bodies to grow. Essential to metabolism, they also help build neurotransmitters (the chemicals that convey messages in the brain); maintain antibodies, blood cells, and tissues; produce hormones such as insulin; they assist enzymes that stimulate bodily functions and certain types of body fluids; they are vital for the repair and maintenance of organs, glands, muscles, tendons, ligaments, skin, hair, and nails. In addition, certain amino acids may help protect against heart disease, reduce blood pressure levels, protect against stroke (apoplectic), alleviate intermittent claudication; help in cancer therapies; reduce sugar cravings; build immunity; and protect the body in a variety of other ways. While the body must get the essential amino acids from foods, it can manufacture the nonessential amino acids on its own if the diet is lacking in them.
Note: Avoid taking higher than recommended doses, as certain amino acids can be toxic in large amounts, causing diarrhea, nausea, and/or vomiting. Take amino acid supplements at least 30 minutes before or after a meal (taking them on an empty stomach eliminates the possibility that they will compete with the amino acids in high-protein foods. The only exception to this is glutathione, which should be taken with food to prevent stomach irritation). If you take an individual amino acid supplement for longer than 30 days, take it with an amino acid complex (contains a variety of amino acids) to ensure that you get the correct balance of all the amino acids. Also, avoid taking individual amino acid supplements for longer than three months unless you are under the guidance/supervision of a physician familiar with their use.

Alanine is a naturally occurring, nonessential, water-soluble amino acid that increases endurance, energy, and strength as well as stimulating the immune system function and supporting thymus gland production.
Supplement/Drug Interactions: This supplement could cause an interaction (possibly severe) when taken with the following drugs: None known.
Adverse Reactions: None known.
Cautions/Contraindications: Avoid use if pregnant or breast-feeding.

Arginine is an essential amino acid produced by the digestion of proteins, and is one of the major building blocks of cartilage and bone. It balances cholesterol levels; enhances cardio, immune system, and vascular functions; promotes production of the growth hormone; and reduces fat absorption.
Supplement/Drug Interactions: This supplement could cause an interaction (possibly severe) when taken with the following drugs: Amphetamine drugs, Antimanic drugs, Anxiolytic drugs, Sedative drugs, and Vasodilating drugs.
Adverse Reactions: Diarrhea, dizziness, imbalance of phosphorous and potassium, nausea, and/or vomiting.
Cautions/Contraindications: Avoid use if pregnant or breast-feeding, or if you have cancer, diabetes, herpes, or schizophrenia. Do not administer to children as it may have an impact on

growth hormone levels. Do not take arginine if you have herpes as this amino acid can trigger outbreaks. May aggravate diabetes, promote the growth of some types of tumors, or worsen psychosis. May reduce the effectiveness of barbiturate and sedative drugs.

Asparagine is a nonessential, water-soluble amino acid that is a monamide of aspartic acid and a constituent of many proteins. It detoxifies the liver of ammonia and supplies the brain with needed energy.
Supplement/Drug Interactions: This supplement could cause an interaction (possibly severe) when taken with the following drugs: None known.
Adverse Reactions: None known.
Cautions/Contraindications: Avoid use if pregnant or breast-feeding.

Aspartic Acid is a nonessential amino acid derived from asparagine and made in the body with the help of pyridoxine (vit. B_6). It is an anticoagulant. It enhances immune system, brain, and nervous system functions; increases stamina; minimizes post-exercise fatigue; produces DNA; promotes mental alertness; rids the body of ammonia; supports the thymus gland; and turns carbohydrates and other foods into energy.
Supplement/Drug Interactions: This supplement could cause an interaction (possibly severe) when taken with the following drugs: None known.
Adverse Reactions: Elevated blood levels of aspartic acid, seizure conditions (possible), and/or possible stroke (apoplectic).
Cautions/Contraindications: Avoid use if pregnant or breast-feeding, ir if you have a history of stroke (apoplectic), epilepsy, phenylketonuria (PKU), or are subject to seizure conditions or excessive brain stimulation. Do not administer to children except under professional supervision. Healthy adults should only use aspartic acid for short periods (a few weeks at a time).

Carnitine, L-acetylcarnitine and L-Carnitine is formed in the body from the amino acids lysine and methionine. Its function is to turn fat into energy, which helps to fuel the heart and other muscles. Its uses include Alzheimer's disease, cardiovascular conditions, diabetes, immune system problems, infertility, liver and kidney problems, and vascular problems.
Supplement/Drug Interactions: This supplement could cause an interaction (possibly severe) when taken with the following drugs: Anticonvulsant/Antiseizure drugs, Antineoplastic drugs, Antiretroviral drugs.
Adverse Reactions: Coagulation problems, elevated blood triglyceride levels.
Cautions/Contraindications: Avoid use if pregnant or breast-feeding, or if you are on hemodialysis. Do not use the 'D' form of carnitine.

Citrulline is a nonessential amino acid that is made in the body from arginine. Its role in the body consists primarily in the processing of nitrogen, and helping to lower cholesterol levels.
Supplement/Drug Interactions: This supplement could cause an interaction (possibly severe) when taken with the following drugs: Amphetamine drugs, Antimanic drugs, Anxiolytic drugs, Sedative drugs, and Vasodilating drugs.
Adverse Reactions: Diarrhea, dizziness, imbalance of phosphorous and potassium, nausea, and/or vomiting.
Cautions/Contraindications: Avoid use if pregnant or breast-feeding. Since this amino acid is closely connected to arginine it is recommended that its use be avoided if you have cancer,

diabetes, herpes, or psychosis. Administration to children is not recommened as growth hormone levels may be impacted. Do not take citrulline if you have herpes as it may trigger outbreaks. Use of this amino acid may aggravate diabetes, reduce the effectiveness of barbiturate drugs and sedative drugs, or worsen psychosis.

Cysteine and N-acetylcysteine (NAC) is a nonessential amino acid produced in the body from the amino acid methionine. It enhances antitumor responses in the body, helps prevent photosensitivity, photodermatosis, infection, and tissue damage, maintains and preserves the body's cells, neutralizes natural and pharmaceutical toxins, protects the cells from damage caused by pollution, heavy metals, alcohol, copper, and cigarette smoke, rids the body of damaging free radicals, strengthens the stomach lining, and it is essential for the adequate use of pyridoxine (vit. B_6).
Supplement/Drug Interactions: This supplement could cause an interaction (possibly severe) when taken with the following drugs: Acetaminophen, Antineoplastic drugs, Antiviral drugs, Corticosteroids, Nitrate drugs, and Vasodilating drugs.
Adverse Reactions: Heart disease, oxidative damage (increased).
Cautions/Contraindications: Avoid use if pregnant or breast-feeding. Avoid high doses. Not for long-term use. Do not use if you are taking any form of prescription or over the counter medication. Monitor blood levels when using this amino acid. Use with professional guidance/supervision.

Cystine is a nonessential amino acid that is converted in the body from cysteine. Cystine strengthens structural proteins in the body and it is essential for the adequate use of pyridoxine (vit. B_6).
Supplement/Drug Interactions: Acetaminophen, Antineoplastic drugs, Antiviral drugs, Corticosteroids, Nitrate drugs, and Vasodilating drugs.
Adverse Reactions: Hematuria (blood in the urine).
Cautions/Contraindications: Avoid use if pregnant or breast-feeding. Avoid high doses. Not for long-term use.

Gamma-Aminobutyric Acid (GABA) is a nonessential alpha amino acid that is made in the body from glutamic acid and pyridoxine (vit. B_6). It enhances the effectiveness of insulin, reduces blood sugar levels, regulates blood pressure, and has a stabilizing effect on brain cells by inhibiting further transmissions instead of triggering them.
Supplement/Drug Interactions: This supplement could cause an interaction (possibly severe) when taken with the following drugs: Anticonvulsant/Antiseizure drugs, Anxiolytic drugs, and Sedative drugs.
Adverse Reactions: Agitation, anxiety (increased), appetite loss, mouth numbness, nausea, and/or tingling of the skin.
Cautions/Contraindications: Avoid use if pregnant or breast-feeding. May enhance the effectiveness of insulin and may increase absorption of sedatives.

Glutamic Acid is a nonessetial amino acid that is referred to as the body's acid pool because it is combined with two other closely connected nonessential amino acids called GABA and glutamine. These amino acids can be found throughout the body in the fluids and blood ready to work at a moments notice. It detoxifys the brain of ammonia and regulates blood sugar levels.
Supplement/Drug Interactions: None known.

Adverse Reactions: Damage to the blood-brain barrier (possible).
Cautions/Contraindications: Avoid use if pregnant or breast-feeding, or if you have a history of stroke (apoplectic), or if you are sensitive to monosodium glutamate (MSG). Avoid high doses or long-term use.

Glutamine is a nonessential amino acid that plays a major role in the synthesis of DNA. It is a source of fuel for the cells lining the intestines, and it regulates the actions of glutamic acid and GABA. Glutamine supports healthy muscle tissue, transforms into energy for the brain and body, and is used by the white blood cells to protect the body from infection.
Supplement/Drug Interactions: This supplement could cause an interaction (possibly severe) when taken with the following drugs: Antibiotic drugs and Antineoplastic drugs.
Adverse Reactions: None known.
Cautions/Contraindications: Avoid use if pregnant or breast-feeding, or if you have cancer, or are undergoing chemotherapy. May interfere with absorption of antibiotics. If constipation occurs, increase daily intake of water by 2-3 glasses.

Glutathione is composed of three amino acids (cystine, glutamic acid, and glycocoll). It helps the liver neutralize toxins, rids the body of damaging free radicals, and may help control red-blood cell damage caused by dialysis.
Supplement/Drug Interactions: This supplement could cause an interaction (possibly severe) when taken with the following drugs: Antibiotic drugs and Antineoplastic drugs.
Adverse Reactions: None known.
Cautions/Contraindications: Avoid use if pregnant or breast-feeding, or if you are undergoing chemotherapy. May interfere with absorption of antibiotics. Take glutathione with food to prevent stomach irritation.

Glycine is one of the simplest essential amino acids. Its role in the formation of creatine is one of the key ingredients in the chemical reaction that powers the muscles. Glycine detoxifies the liver, eliminates lithic acid (uric acid), enhances mental function, increases blood sugar levels and growth hormone secretions, lowers triglyceride levels, and promotes synthesis of glutathione.
Supplement/Drug Interactions: This supplement could cause an interaction (possibly severe) when taken with the following drugs: Antimanic drugs.
Adverse Reactions: Backache, blood pressure fluctuations, dehydration, dysuria (painful/difficult urination), fatigue, inflammation, psychosis (severe), thirst, urination (excessive), nausea, and/or vomiting.
Cautions/Contraindications: Avoid use if pregnant or breast-feeding, or if you have a kidney or liver problem.

Histidine is an amino acid essential for zinc absorption and the conversion to histamine. This amino acid helps to protect the nerve sheaths as well as protecting against radiation and toxic metal contamination, and it supports the immune system and the production of red and white blood cells. It is useful for hypertension and rheumatoid arthritis (RA), and it may increase circulation in the sex organs thereby enhancing sexual pleasure.
Supplement/Drug Interactions: This supplement could cause an interaction (possibly severe) when taken with the following drugs: Antidepressant drugs, Antimanic drugs.
Adverse Reactions: Depression (increased).

Cautions/Contraindications: Avoid use if pregnant or breast-feeding, or if you have any form of a depressive condition.

Isoleucine is an essential amino acid and one of the three branch-chained amino acids (BCAAs) that are the building blocks of protein. Isoleucine assists in the formation of oxygen-carrying hemoglobin, builds muscle mass, provides energy, regulates blood sugar levels, and wards off muscle tremors.
Supplement/Drug Interactions: This supplement could cause an interaction (possibly severe) when taken with the following drugs: None known.
Adverse Reactions: Inhibition of dopamine and serotonin in the brain.
Cautions/Contraindications: Avoid use if pregnant or breast-feeding, or if you have a liver or kidney problem. Do not administer to infants or children except under professional medical supervision. Monitor blood levels when taking this amino acid.

Leucine is an essential amino acid and one of the three branch-chained amino acids (BCAAs) that are the building blocks of protein. Essential for growth, it boosts growth hormone production and helps reduce blood sugar levels. An energy source for the body, it encourages the secretion of insulin, and enhances protein building inside muscle tissue.
Supplement/Drug Interactions: This supplement could cause an interaction (possibly severe) when taken with the following drugs: None known.
Adverse Reactions: Inhibition of dopamine and serotonin in the brain.
Cautions/Contraindications: Avoid use if pregnant or breast-feeding, or if you have a liver or kidney problem. Do not administer to infants or children except under professional medical supervision. Monitor blood levels when taking this amino acid.

Lysine is an essential amino acid that plays an important role in the absorption and conservation of calcium, and it may block the proliferation of the Human B-Lymphotropic Virus (HBLV). It aids in the formation of collagen, helps build muscle, maintains healthy blood vessels, regulates blood sugar levels, and is needed for proper bone formation.
Supplement/Drug Interactions: This supplement could cause an interaction (possibly severe) when taken with the following drugs: None known.
Adverse Reactions: Diarrhea, elevated cholesterol levels (possible), and/or gallstones (possible).
Cautions/Contraindications: Avoid use if pregnant or breast-feeding, or if you have diabetes, a kidney or liver problem, or an allergy (protein). Do not administer to infants or children. Do not drink milk or consume dairy products at the same time you take lysine.

Methionine is a sulfur-bearing, essential amino acid that, along with folate and pyridoxine (vit. B_6), help enhance nail and skin health, keep homocysteine levels in line, rid the body of excess histamine, produce additional lecithin, and ward off liver damage.
Supplement/Drug Interactions: None known.
Adverse Reactions: Heart disease (increased risk).
Cautions/Contraindications: Avoid use if pregnant or breast-feeding. Avoid high doses. Not for long-term use.

Ornithine, Ornithine alpha-ketoglutarate (OKG) is a nonessential amino acid that is transformed into arginine. It aids in the processing of body waste for elimination in the urine, boosts human growth hormone production, heals and repairs damaged tissues, helps rid the body

of ammonia and helps in liver regeneration, promotes weight loss and the growth of white blood cells, stimulates the immune system, and supports liver function.
Supplement/Drug Interactions: This supplement could cause an interaction (possibly severe) when taken with the following drugs: None known.
Adverse Reactions: Cancer or reproduction of cancerous cells, deepening of the voice, elevated blood sugar levels, hypertrophy (joints, larynx), insomnia, seizure conditions, and/or thickening of the skin.
Cautions/Contraindications: Avoid use if pregnant or breast-feeding, or if you have diabetes, herpes, or schizophrenia. Avoid high doses or long-term use. Do not administer to infants or children. May reactivate latent herpes infection.

Phenylalanine, L-Phenylalanine, and D,L-Phenylalanine (DLPA) is an essential amino acid that helps to negate melancholy, relieve pain, and support the production of dopamine, epinephrine, norepinephrine, and phenylethylamine. Phenylalanine and aspartic acid produce aspartame, which is used in the manufacture of some artificial sweeteners.
Supplement/Drug Interactions: This supplement could cause an interaction (possibly severe) when taken with the following drugs: Antidepressant drugs and Monoamine Oxidase Inhibitor (MAOI) drugs.
Adverse Reactions: Blood pressure fluctuations, headache, and/or migraine.
Cautions/Contraindications: Avoid use if pregnant or breast-feeding, or if you have depression, or if you have phenylketonuria (PKU). Do not administer to infants or children. May aggravate anxiety and hypertension.

Proline and Hydroxyproline are nonessential amino acids that boost energy, build muscle tissue, improve cognition, concentration, and memory, reduce blood pressure levels, strengthen connective tissues, and tone the muscles, tendons, and joints.
Supplement/Drug Interactions: This supplement could cause an interaction (possibly severe) when taken with the following drugs: None known.
Adverse Reactions: Cancer (increased risk).
Cautions/Contraindications: Avoid use if pregnant or breast-feeding, or if you have a kidney or liver problem. Antibiotic drugs may reduce absorption of proline. Avoid high doses or long-term use.

Serine is a nonessential amino acid produced in the body from glycine. It suppresses the enzymes that catalyze chemical reactions in the body, the immune system, and the hormones that regulate body processes and neurotransmitters. Serine transforms into antibodies.
Supplement/Drug Interactions: This supplement could cause an interaction (possibly severe) when taken with the following drugs: Immune Suppressive drugs.
Adverse Reactions: Elevated blood pressure levels and mental disturbances.
Cautions/Contraindications: Avoid use if pregnant or breast-feeding. Use with professional guidance/supervision.

Taurine is a nonessential amino acid required for proper brain and nervous tissue development. It helps absorb fats and fat-soluble vitamins, and plays an important role in metabolism and nervous system muscles. Taurine helps increase the excretion of cholesterol; maintain cell membranes; regulate the heartbeat; and rid the body of excess fluids.

Supplement/Drug Interactions: This supplement could cause an interaction (possibly severe) when taken with the following drugs: Antineoplastic drugs.
Adverse Reactions: Diarrhea and/or peptic ulcer.
Cautions/Contraindications: Avoid use if pregnant or breast-feeding, or if you have an allergy (protein). May increase the effects of anticonvulsant/antiseizure drugs.

Threonine is an essential amino acid that assists in the growth and maintenance of body tissues, collagen, and tooth enamel, and is the basis of connective tissues. It supports the immune system and stimulates the production of antibodies.
Supplement/Drug Interactions: This supplement could cause an interaction (possibly severe) when taken with the following drugs: None known.
Adverse Reactions: None known.
Cautions/Contraindications: Avoid use if pregnant or breast-feeding.

Tryptophan, 5-Hydroxytryptophan (5-HTP) is an essential amino acid that assists the body in making melatonin and niacin. It stimulates growth hormone secretion, and triggers the production of serotonin in the brain. Also called proteinochromogen.
Supplement/Drug Interactions: Antidepressant drugs, Antimanic drugs, Carbidopa, Carbidopa/Levodopa, Hypnotic drugs, Monoamine Oxidase Inhibitor (MAOI) drugs, Nonsteroidal Anti-inflammatory drugs (NSAIDs), Selective Serotonin Receptor Agonist drugs, Selective Serotonin Reuptake Inhibitor (SSRI) drugs.
Adverse Reactions: Constipation, debility, diarrhea, grogginess, headache, high fever, muscle and joint pain, nausea, rash, swelling of the arms or legs, and/or vomiting.
Cautions/Contraindications: Avoid use if pregnant or breast-feeding, or if you have asthma, ulcer, Crohn's disease, or lupus. Avoid high doses or long-term use. Monitoring by a healthcare professional is advised while taking this supplement.

Tyrosine, L-Tyrosine is a nonessential amino acid that supplies the raw material needed for the manufacture of dopamine, norepinephrine, and epinephrine. It is used by the thyroid gland to produce thyroxine. Tyrosine assists in the formation of nerve cells, and in the production of adrenaline, enkephalins, noradrenaline, and melanin.
Supplement/Drug Interactions: This supplement could cause an interaction (possibly severe) when taken with the following drugs: Monoamine Oxidase Inhibitor (MAOI) drugs.
Adverse Reactions: Cancer (melanoma), elevated blood pressure levels, hematuria (blood in the urine), liver damge (often characterized by jaundice), nausea, and/or vomiting.
Cautions/Contraindications: Avoid use if pregnant or breast-feeding, or if you have a psychotic condition. Do not administer to infants or children. Do not take the 'D' form of tyrosine. May elevate blood pressure levels or trigger anxiety or insomnia.

Valine is an essential amino acid and one of the three branch-chained amino acids (BCAAs) that are the building blocks of protein. It is a constituent of most of the body's proteins and contributes to energy and muscle growth. Valine encourages growth hormone production; enhances brain and nerve functions; and helps normalize brain chemistry by inhibiting an excess of other amino acids from getting into the brain.
Supplement/Drug Interactions: This supplement could cause an interaction (possibly severe) when taken with the following drugs: None known.

Adverse Reactions: Elevated blood levels of Valine, increased growth hormone production (dramatic).
Cautions/Contraindications: Avoid use if pregnant or breast-feeding, or if you have a liver or kidney problem. Do not administer to infants or children except under professional medical supervision.

Vitamins

Vitamins are unrelated organic substances, which occur in small amounts in many foods, and are necessary in that they enable us to maintain normal metabolic functioning of the body. They may be water-soluble or fat-soluble.

Biotin (Vitamin H) is the most potent and ubiquitous member of the vitamin B family known, is reguired by or occurring in all forms of life, and is necessary for cell growth, the production of fatty acids, and the metabolism of carbohydrates, fats, proteins, and the B vitamins. It assists in the conversion of amino acids from protein into blood sugar for energy; promotes hair and skin health; protects against alopecia; and regulates bone marrow, the nerves, and the sebaceous glands. Depression, dermatitis, dry skin, eczema, fatigue, heart disease, insomnia, mucous membrane ryness, and muscular pain may indicate a deficiency (biotin).
Supplement/Drug Interactions: This supplement could cause an interaction (possibly severe) when taken with the following drugs: Antidiabetic drugs, Anticonvulsant/Antiseizure drugs, and Insulin (animal and human).
Adverse Reactions: None known.
Cautions/Contraindications: Avoid use if pregnant or breast-feeding.

Folic Acid (Folacin, Folate, Vitamin Bc, Vitamin Bc conjugate, Vitamin M) is a B vitamin, an essential growth factor, a coenzyme in DNA synthesis, and is necessary for proper brain function, cell division, embryonic and fetal development, energy production, and the metabolism of protein. It aids in lactation and tissue regeneration; protects against anemia (macrocytic), cancer (lung), hemorrhage (postpartum), menorrhagia, and memory/cognitive problems. It is recommended that pyridoxine (vit. B_6) and cyanocobalamin (vit. B_{12}) be used in conjunction with folic acid.
Supplement/Drug Interactions: This supplement could cause an interaction (possibly severe) when taken with the following drugs: Antacids, Antibiotic drugs, Anticonvulsant/Antiseizure drugs, Antidepressant drugs, Antidiabetic drugs, Antimanic drugs, Antineoplastic drugs, Bile Acid Sequestrant drugs, H-2 Blocker drugs, Hormones and Synthetic Substitutes (i.e. conjugated estrogens, contraceptives (oral, etc.), and other hormonal replacement therapy (HRT), Nitrous Oxide, Salicylates, Subsalicylates.
Adverse Reactions: None known.
Cautions/Contraindications: Avoid excessive use if pregnant or breast-feeding, or if you have epilepsy, or if you have an estrogen dependant cancer, or if you have a history of estrogen dependant cancer, or if you have a convulsive condition. Avoid high doses. Not for long-term use.

Vitamin A and carotenoids are antioxidants that are important for normal growth, reproduction, and sperm formation as well as the development of bones, fetal growth, and teeth. They enhance the immune system; promote gastrointestinal, mucous membrane, respiratory, skin, and vision health; protect against cancer, heart attack (in high risk group), and pollutants; reduces acne, allergy, angina, dry skin, eczema, emphysema, eyestrain, fever (hay), hyperthyroidism, infections, and nightblindness; and speeds healing of abscess and ulcer (gastric). Vitamin A is water and fat-soluble and sensitive to air and heat.
Supplement/Drug Interactions: This supplement could cause an interaction (possibly severe) when taken with the following drugs: Antibacterial drugs, Antidepressant drugs, Antineoplastic drugs, Bile Acid Sequestrant drugs, Colchicine drugs, Corticosteroids, GI drugs, Hormones and Synthetic Substitutes (i.e. conjugated estrogens, contraceptives (oral, etc.), and other hormonal replacement therapy (HRT), HMG-CoA Reductase Inhibitors, Mineral Oil, Modified/Altered Versions of Vitamin A, and other Multi-Vitamin/Mineral Supplements.
Adverse Reactions: Alopecia, amenorrhea, diarrhea, dizziness, dry skin, headache, hypertrophy (liver, spleen), muscle and joint pain, nausea, rash, and/or stunted growth.
Cautions/Contraindications: Avoid use if breast-feeding or during pregnancy as it may cause spontaneous abortion or serious birth defects. Do not use if you have depression or are undergoing chemotherapy.

Vitamin A_1 has similar properties to vitamin A and is found in the eye tissues of marine fish.
Vitamin A_2 has similar properties to vitamin A but with a different absorption spectrum in the ultraviolet. It is found in the livers of fresh water fish.
Vitamin B is a member of the vitamin B complex group.

Vitamin B Complex is a group of water-soluble substances including thiamine, riboflavin, niacin (nicotinic acid), nicotinamide (niacin amide, nicotinic acid amide), the vitamin B_6 group (pyridoxine, pyridoxal, pyridoxamine, alpha pyracin, beta pyracin), biotin (vitamin H), pantothenic acid, folic acid (vitamin M, B_c, or B_c conjugate), paraaminobenzoic acid (PABA), inositol, vitamin B_{12}, and choline. They are useful for allergy, anemia, anxiety, asthma, candida, depression, epilepsy, insomnia, mental disturbances, migraine, nervous conditions, and premenstrual syndrome (PMS), and promote eye, hair, liver, nerve, and skin health.
Supplement/Drug Interactions: This supplement could cause an interaction (possibly severe) when taken with the following drugs: Antibiotic drugs, Antidepressant drugs, and other Multi-Vitamins and Minerals.
Adverse Reactions: Constipation or diarrhea, and nightmares (possible).
Cautions/Contraindications: Avoid use if pregnant or breast-feeding. Antibiotics, AZT (a drug used in the treatment of AIDS), and diuretic drugs may cause a depletion of vitamin B complex group.

Vitamin B_1 (Thiamine) is a member of the B complex group. It enhances cardiovascular, circulatory, digestive, muscular, and nervous system functions as well as the formation of blood; helps in the manufacture of fats, and metabolizes protein in order to provide energy and heat for the body. It is useful for brain damage, confusion, fatigue, heart disease, motion sickness, postoperative pain, and shingles. Vitamin B_1 is water-soluble and sensitive to heat.
Supplement/Drug Interactions: This supplement could cause an interaction (possibly severe) when taken with the following drugs: Antidepressant drugs, Diuretic drugs, and Hormones and

Synthetic Substitutes (i.e. conjugated estrogens, contraceptives (oral, etc.), and other hormonal replacement therapy (HRT).
Adverse Reactions: None known.
Cautions/Contraindications: Avoid use if pregnant or breast-feeding. Alcohol, antibiotic drugs, caffeine, conjugated estrogens, contraceptives (oral), a diet high in carbohydrates, heat, hormonal replacement therapy (HRT), sugar, and sulfa drugs may decrease the effects of thiamine.

Vitamin B_2 (Riboflavin) is a member of the B complex group. It is required for cell metabolism, growth, the absorption of iron, the formation of red blood cells, the metabolism of carbohydrates, fats, and proteins, and the production of antibodies. It prevents alopecia, deficiency (nutritional), dandruff, skin problems, and dryness (vaginal); promotes growth; and protects against birth defects and cancer. Riboflavin is useful for anemia, carpal tunnel syndrome, depression, digestive complaints, eczema, exhaustion, lip/mouth/tongue sores, oily skin, and vision fatigue. Cracks or sores occurring at the corners of the mouth may indicate a deficiency (riboflavin). Vitamin B_2 is water-soluble and sensitive to light.
Supplement/Drug Interactions: This supplement could cause an interaction (possibly severe) when taken with the following drugs: Antibiotic drugs, Antidepressant drugs, Antineoplastic drugs, Hormones and Synthetic Substitutes (i.e. conjugated estrogens, contraceptives (oral, etc.), and other hormonal replacement therapy (HRT).
Adverse Reactions: None known.
Cautions/Contraindications: Avoid excessive use if pregnant or breast-feeding. Avoid high doses if you have cataracts. Alcohol and antibiotic drugs destroy vitamin B_2. Riboflavin may temporarily turn the urine a bright yellow color. Vitamin B_2 supplementation may decrease the effects of some antineoplastic drugs.

Vitamin B_3 (Niacin) is a member of the B complex group and is required for circulatory and nervous system functions. It aids in the metabolism of carbohydrates, fats, and proteins; produces hydrochloric acid, which aids digestion; and reduces blood pressure and cholesterol levels. Niacin is useful for backache, constipation or diarrhea, halitosis, headache, insomnia, stress, and vertigo. Autism, bipolar/manic depressive conditions, hostility, paranoia, personality changes, and schizophrenia may indicate a deficiency (niacin). Vitamin B_3 is water-soluble and is not sensitive to acids, alkalis, or heat.
Supplement/Drug Interactions: This supplement could cause an interaction (possibly severe) when taken with the following drugs: Antibiotic drugs, Antidepressant drugs, HMG-CoA Reductase Inhibitors, Hormones and Synthetic Substitutes [i.e. conjugated estrogens, contraceptives (oral, etc.), and other hormonal replacement therapy (HRT).]
Adverse Reactions: Liver damage (often characterized by jaundice).
Cautions/Contraindications: Avoid use if pregnant or breast-feeding, or if you have glaucoma, gout, high liver enzyme levels, liver problems, or ulcer (peptic). Niacin may cause a harmless, temporary flushing (reddening) and tingling of the skin. Use with professional guidance/supervision if you have diabetes as niacin supplementation may interfere with glucose tolerance.

Vitamin B_5 (Pantothenic Acid) is a member of the vitamin B complex group, and is necessary for growth and weight. It assists in the formation of antibodies; the metabolism of carbohydrates, fats, and proteins; and the production of red blood cells and adrenal hormones.

Pantothenic acid is useful for Alopecia, anemia, anxiety, cataracts, depression, eczema, fatigue, headache, incoordination, respiratory conditions, shock (postoperative), skin problems, thyroid problems, and ulcer (gastric, peptic). Allergy, arthritis, fever (hay), a furrowed tongue, and sinusitis may indicate a deficiency (pantothenic acid).
Supplement/Drug Interactions: This supplement could cause an interaction (possibly severe) when taken with the following drugs: Antidepressant drugs.
Adverse Reactions: Diarrhea.
Cautions/Contraindications: Avoid use if pregnant or breast-feeding.

Vitamin B_6 (Pyridoxine) aids in the formation of red blood cells; enhances brain and immune system functions; metabolizes amino acids; fights infection; plays a part in DNA synthesis; protects against cancer, heart disease, nutritional dermatitis, and toxemia; and regulates certain metabolic processes by assisting in the production of neurotransmitters, prostaglandins, and red blood cells. It is useful for acquired immune deficiency syndrome (AIDS), allergy, anemia, anxiety, arteriosclerosis, arthritis, asthma, debility, diabetes, epilepsy, hypoglycemia, insomnia, irritability, leg cramps, morning sickness, premenstrual syndrome (PMS), and ulcer. Carpal tunnel syndrome may indicate a deficiency (pyridoxine). Vitamin B_6 is water-soluble and sensitive to air and ultraviolet light.
Supplement/Drug Interactions: This supplement could cause an interaction (possibly severe) when taken with the following drugs: Antibacterial drugs, Antibiotic drugs, Anticonvulsant/Antiseizure drugs, Antineoplastic drugs, Carbidopa/Levodopa, Chelating agents, Corticosteroids, Hormones and Synthetic Substitutes (i.e. conjugated estrogens, contraceptives (oral, etc.), and other hormonal replacement therapy (HRT), Hypertensive drugs, and Theophylline drugs.
Adverse Reactions: Nerve damage (reversible), nightmares, and tingling/numbness of hands and feet.
Cautions/Contraindications: Avoid excessive use if pregnant or breast-feeding. Avoid high doses. Diabetics need to monitor blood sugar daily, as pyridoxine supplementation may reduce insulin requirements.

Vitamin B_{12} (Cyanocobalamin, Cobalamin) aids the digestive system, growth, and the reproductive system; assists folate in making DNA and RNA; helps produce myelin, which covers and protects nerve fibers; increases red blood cell formation in individuals with anemia (macrocytic, pernicious) and sprue. It is useful for arrhythmia, asthma, bipolar/manic depressive conditions, depression, fatigue, insomnia, memory/cognitive problems, menstrual problems, nervous conditions, schizophrenia, and skin problems. Vitamin B_{12} is water-soluble and sensitive to acids, alkalis, and light. Cyanocobalamin is not easily assimilated through the digestive tract, and needs to be taken under the tongue or by injections from your health care professional. Anemia, digestive complaints, eye problems, hallucinations, jerky movements, memory/cognitive problems, reduced sensory perception, speech problems, and weakness of the legs may indicate a deficiency (cyanocobalamin).
Supplement/Drug Interactions: This supplement could cause an interaction (possibly severe) when taken with the following drugs: Antibacterial drugs, Antibiotic drugs, Antidepressant drugs, Antidiabetic drugs, Antiretroviral drugs, Colchicine drugs, HMG-CoA Reductase Inhibitors, H-2 Blocker drugs, Hypertensive drugs, and Nitrous Oxide.
Adverse Reactions: None known.

Cautions/Contraindications: Avoid use if pregnant or breast-feeding. Anticoagulant drugs, conjugated estrogens, contraceptives (oral), gout drugs, hormone replacement therapy (HRT), and potassium supplementation may interfere with absorption of vitamin B_{12}.

Vitamin B_{13} (Orotic Acid) is a vitamin found in milk that aids in the metabolism of folic acid and cyanocobalamin, and may be useful for multiple sclerosis.
Supplement/Drug Interactions: This supplement could cause an interaction (possibly severe) when taken with the following drugs: None known.
Adverse Reactions: None known.
Cautions/Contraindications: Avoid use if pregnant or breast-feeding.

Vitamin C (Ascorbic Acid) is an antioxidant that is important for the building of white blood cells and the immune system, and is needed for amino acid metabolism, proper adrenal function, the synthesis of hormones, and tissue growth and regeneration. It assists the body in transforming proline into collagen; destroys harmful free radicals; forms and repairs collagen; produces antistress hormones and interferon; promotes normal formation of bones and teeth; protects against atherosclerosis, cancer, coagulation problems, infection, periodontal disease, phlebitis, scurvy, and toxins. It is useful for allergy, cataracts, colds, conjunctivitis, diabetes, ear infections, gallstones, hepatitis, infection (bacterial, viral), influenza, periodontal disease, sinusitis, tonsillitis, and ulcers. Extra-large doses administered intravenously may serve as an adjuvant to acquired immune deficiency syndrome (AIDS), and may help put the disease into remission; human immunodeficiency virus (HIV), which, if done at initial detection, may help change status from positive to negative; and schizophrenia, which may help to reverse the condition. Periodontal disease, recurrant infections, and scurvy may indicate a deficiency (vitamin C). Ascorbic acid is water-soluble and sensitive to air, alkalis, copper, heat, and light.
Supplement/Drug Interactions: This supplement could cause an interaction (possibly severe) when taken with the following drugs: Acetaminophen, Antibiotic drugs, Anticoagulant drugs, Antineoplastic drugs, Autonomic drugs, Bronchodilator drugs, Corticosteroids, other Medications/Products containing ephedra, pseudoephedrine, or phenylpropanolamine, Nitrate drugs, Nonsteroidal Anti-inflammatory drugs (NSAIDs), Phenylpropanolamine drugs, Salicylates, and Subsalicylates.
Adverse Reactions: Cramps, diarrhea, and/or nausea.
Cautions/Contraindications: Avoid excessive use if pregnant or breast-feeding, or if you are receiving chemotherapy or radiation therapy. Avoid high doses (with the exception of certain conditions). Ascorbic acid may interfere with copper absorption. Because salicylates (i.e. aspirin) deplete ascorbic acid in the bloodstream, take them at least one hour apart. Ascorbic acid may destroy vitamin B_{12}. Notify your healthcare professional *prior* to any lab work if you are taking vitamin C as this supplement can cause false results in some tests. Extra-large doses of vitamin C taken for certain conditions require the supplement to be administered intravenously by a healthcare professional. Vitamin C may reduce the effectiveness of antidiabetic drugs and sulfa drugs. Not for long-term use.
<u>Note</u>: When extra-large doses of ascorbic acid are administered for certain conditions, supplementation of 50-mg. pyridoxine (vit. B_6) or calcium/magnesium tablets three times per day is recommended to protect against the formation of kidney stones.

Vitamin D (Cholecalciferol) is naturally obtained by the body by exposure to sunlight or can be obtained through supplementation, and is needed for the proper development and growth of bones and teeth. It aids in calcium and phosphorous absorption, regulates whether these minerals are deposited into bone or withdrawn out of bone, and signals to the kidneys whether to release calcium and phosphorous or hold on to them. Osteoporosis may indicate a deficiency (cholecalciferol). Vitamin D is fat-soluble.
Supplement/Drug Interactions: This supplement could cause an interaction (possibly severe) when taken with the following drugs: Antibiotic drugs, Anticoagulant drugs, Anticonvulsant/Antiseizure drugs, Bile Acid Sequestrant drugs, Calcium Channel Blocker drugs, Corticosteroids, Diuretic drugs, H-2 Blocker drugs, Hormones and Synthetic Substitutes (i.e. conjugated estrogens, contraceptives (oral, etc.), and other hormonal replacement therapy (HRT), and Mineral Oil.
Adverse Reactions: Diarrhea, elevated blood calcium levels, headache, nausea.
Cautions/Contraindications: Avoid excessive use if pregnant or breast-feeding. Avoid high doses. For proper conversion by the liver and kidneys, vitamin D supplements should be taken with calcium. Some drugs may interfere with absorption of cholecalciferol supplements.

Vitamin E (Tocopherol) is an antioxidant that combines with oxygen and destroys free radicals; helps eliminate plaque from arterial walls; protects polyunsaturated fats as well as other oxygen sensitive compounds from being destroyed by damaging oxidation reactions; protects against arthritis, cancer, cataracts, heart disease, hypertension, muscular dystrophy in children, and toxins; and reduces blood pressure and cholesterol levels. It is useful for amyotrophic lateral sclerosis (ALS) and other degenerative disease therapies; benign breast disease, cancer (breast), cell regeneration, infertility, lactation, menopausal problems, pregnancy, premenstrual syndrome (PMS). Vitamin E is fat-soluble and sensitive to air, alkalis, and ultraviolet light.
Supplement/Drug Interactions: This supplement could cause an interaction (possibly severe) when taken with the following drugs: Antibiotic drugs, Anticoagulant drugs, Antidiabetic drugs, Antifungal drugs, Antimanic drugs, Antineoplastic drugs, Antiretroviral drugs, Anticonvulsant/Antiseizure drugs, Bile Acid Sequestrant drugs, Diuretic drugs, HMG-CoA Reductase Inhibitors, Immune Suppressive drugs, Insulin (animal-source and human), Mineral Oil, Salicylates, Subsalicylates, and Vitamin C.
Adverse Reactions: Bleeding (uncontrolled), coagulation problems, increased risk of stroke (apoplectic).
Cautions/Contraindications: Avoid excessive use if pregnant or breast-feeding, or if you have a coagulation problem, diabetes, or hyperthyroidism. Because tocopherol is only stored for a short time in the body, it should be taken with zinc to maintain levels in the blood. Tocopherol and iron should be taken at least eight hours apart.

Vitamin K is required for blood coagulation and sugar metabolism. It aids in bone formation; converts glucose to glycogen for storage in the liver; and protects against heart attack and osteoporosis. Vitamin K is useful for all bleeding conditions, hemorrhage (postpartum), menorrhagia, metrorrhagia, and prior to surgery. Celiac disease, colitis, diarrhea, and nosebleed may indicate a deficiency (vitamin K). Vitamin K is fat-soluble and sensitive to air, acids, alkalis, and light.
Supplement/Drug Interactions: This supplement could cause an interaction (possibly severe) when taken with the following drugs: Antibacterial drugs, Antibiotic drugs, Anticoagulant drugs, Anticonvulsant/Antiseizure drugs, Bile Acid Sequestrant drugs, Corticosteroids, and Mineral Oil.

Adverse Reactions: Bleeding (uncontrolled), brain damage (possible), coagulation problems, liver damage (often characterized by jaundice), increased risk of stroke (apoplectic).
Cautions/Contraindications: Avoid use if pregnant or breast-feeding, or if you have coagulation problems. Antibiotic drugs, frozen or irradiated foods, mineral oil, pollutants (air), radiation, salicylates (i.e. aspirin), and roentgen rays (x-rays) may destroy vitamin K supplements in the body.

Minerals

Minerals are inorganic substances that are found in the soil and are absorbed by plants. They are contained in every cell of the body and help maintain the structure of living tissue as well as regulating body processes. If you are taking individual mineral supplements, it is best to space them apart from one another throughout the day.

Boron is a nonmetallic element required for calcium metabolism. It may protect against the development of osteoarthritis (OA) and osteoporosis, and it has a beneficial effect on estrogen, which may help to reduce menopausal/menstrual problems. It is also an important mineral for maintaining the health of bones, joints, and teeth.
Supplement/Drug Interactions: This supplement could cause an interaction (possibly severe) when taken with the following drugs: None known.
Adverse Reactions: Diarrhea, nausea, and/or vomiting.
Cautions/Contraindications: Avoid use if pregnant or breast-feeding.

Calcium is a yellowish metal and the basic element of lime. It is an essential mineral for activation of several enzymes, brain function, blood coagulation, DNA and RNA function, enzyme activation, heartbeat regulation, hormonal secretion, menstruation/menopausal, muscle contraction and relaxation, nerve impulse transmissions, and structural system integrity. It aids in the passage of nutrients in and out of cells, builds strong bones and teeth, maintains the strength and vitality of connective tissues as well as new tissues and cells, maintains the body's acid balance, protects against cancer (intestinal) and osteoporosis, reduces blood pressure levels, cholesterol levels, cramps, insomnia, and stress, and strengthens cell membranes. Arm or leg numbness, arrhythmia, brittle nails, eczema, muscle and joint pain, muscle cramps, nervous conditions, periodontal disease, rheumatoid arthritis (RA), rickets, and spasm can indicate a deficiency (calcium). Calcium dissolves in acid and is not affected by heat or light.
Supplement/Drug Interactions: Antacids, Antibacterial drugs, Antibiotic drugs, Antineoplastic drugs, Bile Acid Sequestrant drugs, Biphosphonate drugs, Bronchodilator drugs, Caffeine, Calcium Channel Blocker drugs, Corticosteroids, Digestive Enzymes, Diuretic drugs, Hormones and Synthetic Substitutes (i.e. conjugated estrogens, contraceptives (oral, etc.), and other hormonal replacement therapy (HRT), Hypertensive drugs, Mineral Oil, Nonsteroidal Anti-inflammatory drugs (NSAIDs), and Thyroid drugs.
Adverse Reactions: Appetite loss, constipation, debility, diarrhea, drowsiness, dry mouth, fatigue, headache, hematuria (blood in the urine), kidney failure (possible), kidney stones, and a metallic taste in the mouth.

Cautions/Contraindications: Avoid use if pregnant or breast-feeding, or if you have cancer, hyperthyroidism, sarcoidosis, or if you have a tendency to develop kidney stones. May interfere with the absorption of iron.

Chromium is a whitish, brittle metal that helps improve the body's ability to handle glucose; protects against the buildup of plaque in the arteries and liver; reduces blood pressure levels; regulates the action of insulin; and stabilizes blood sugar levels. Diabetes and hypoglycemia may indicate a deficiency (chromium).
Supplement/Drug Interactions: This supplement could cause an interaction (possibly severe) when taken with the following drugs: Antidiabetic drugs, Insulin (animal-source).
Adverse Reactions: Headache, interference with insulin, kidney or liver problems, vertigo.
Cautions/Contraindications: Avoid use if pregnant or breast-feeding, or if you have a kidney or liver problem. Diabetics taking chromium should monitor their blood sugar levels daily, as less insulin may be required when taking this supplement.

Cobalt is an element whose compounds afford pigments. It is a part of vitamin B_{12}, and helps protect against anemia. It can be obtained through B complex or B_{12} supplementation. Anemia may indicate a deficiency (cobalt).
Supplement/Drug Interactions: This supplement could cause an interaction (possibly severe) when taken with the following drugs: None known.
Adverse Reactions: Depress erythropoiesis (the production of red blood cells).
Cautions/Contraindications: Avoid use if pregnant or breast-feeding.

Copper is a reddish, malleable metal that assists in the absorption and use of iron and vitamin C; helps in the formation of bones, elastin, enzymes, hemoglobin, collagen, protein, and red blood cells; and is an important mineral for energy, healing, the reproductive and nervous system, skin pigmentation, the sense of taste, and hair color. Osteoporosis may be an early indication of a deficiency (copper).
Supplement/Drug Interactions: This supplement could cause an interaction (possibly severe) when taken with the following drugs: Angiotensin-Converting Enzyme (ACE) Inhibitors, Antacids, Antiretroviral drugs, H-2 Blocker drugs, Chelating agents, Hormones and Synthetic Substitutes (i.e. conjugated estrogens, contraceptives (oral, etc.), and other hormonal replacement therapy (HRT), Nonsteroidal Anti-inflammatory drugs (NSAIDs), and Selenium.
Adverse Reactions: Dizziness, headache, heart disease, vascular problems, and vomiting.
Cautions/Contraindications: Avoid use if pregnant or breast-feeding. Avoid high doses. Copper is best obtained from multi-vitamin/mineral supplementation. Not for long-term use.

Fluorine is a halogen, nonmetallic gasous element. It is essential for the development and maintenance of strong bones and teeth. Fluoride is a binary compound of fluorine and is present in fluoridated drinking water and most toothpaste.
Supplement/Drug Interactions: This supplement could cause an interaction (possibly severe) when taken with the following drugs: None known.
Adverse Reactions: Bone problems, liver damage, mottled tooth enamel, and osteoporosis.
Cautions/Contraindications: Avoid use if pregnant or breast-feeding. Avoid high doses. Not for long-term use.

Germanium is a very rare white metal with erythropoietic properties. It is a major aid to the immune system, and increases oxygen to the cells, organs, and tissues; protects against exposure to chemicals and other pollutants; reduces chronic pain; regulates mood; and may serve as an ajuvant to acquired immune deficiency syndrome (AIDS), allergy (food), anemia, autoimmune disease, chronic fatigue syndrome (CFS), high cholesterol, human immunodeficiency virus (HIV), infections (fungal, viral), and rheumatoid arthritis (RA) therapies.
Supplement/Drug Interactions: This supplement could cause an interaction (possibly severe) when taken with the following drugs: None known.
Adverse Reactions: None known.
Cautions/Contraindications: Avoid use if pregnant or breast-feeding.

Iodine is a nonmetallic halogen element with a pungent taste and a somewhat odd odor. It is essential in nutrition; helps maintain thyroid and metabolic balance; and wards off emotional instability and nervous system distress. Goiter, cancer (breast), mental retardation, and obesity may indicate a deficiency (iodine).
Supplement/Drug Interactions: This supplement could cause an interaction (possibly severe) when taken with the following drugs: Thyroid drugs.
Adverse Reactions: Abdominal pain, arrhythmia, diarrhea, fever, glandular swelling, hypertrophy (thyroid), iodism (iodine poisoning), metallic taste in the mouth, mouth sores, priapism, thirst, nausea, and/or vomiting.
Cautions/Contraindications: Avoid use if pregnant or breast-feeding, or if you have sensitivity to iodine. May interfere with the effectiveness of certain thyroid medications.

Iron is a metallic element that enhances immune system health; increases oxygen and mental clarity; is required for enzyme function; produces hemoglobin; promotes stamina; and protects against anemia, debility, and frailty. Alopecia, anemia, arrhythmia, brittle nails, constipation, debility, diarrhea, dizziness, fatigue, indigestion, irritability, memory/cognitive problems, nausea occurring after meals, pruritus, recurrent illnesses, sallow complexion, and verticle ridges in the nails may indicate a deficiency (iron).
Supplement/Drug Interactions: This supplement could cause an interaction (possibly severe) when taken with the following drugs: Antacids, Antibiotic drugs, Anticoagulant drugs, Antiretroviral drugs, Carbidopa/Levodopa, Chelating agents, Hormones and Synthetic Substitutes (i.e. conjugated estrogens, contraceptives (oral, etc.), and other hormonal replacement therapy (HRT), H-2 Blocker drugs, Nonsteroidal Anti-inflammatory drugs (NSAIDs), Salicylates, Subsalicylates, Thyroid drugs, and Vitamin C.
Adverse Reactions: Abdominal pain, constipation, diarrhea, digestive complaints, gastritis, gastrointestinal problems, hemochromatosis, indigestion, irritable bowel syndrome (IBS), nausea, vascular damage.
Cautions/Contraindications: Avoid use if pregnant or breast-feeding, or if you have anemia (cooley's, sickle cell), cancer, hemochromatosis, or an infection (bacterial). Avoid high doses and long-term use. Do not administer to children as fatalities can occur. Iron supplementation may cause a temporary darkening of the stools. Persons with cancer or rheumatoid arthritis (RA) may have difficulty-assimilating iron. Use only hydrolyzed-protein chelate, which is organic iron. Don't use ferrous sulphate, which is a synthetic form of iron. Vitamin E and zinc may interfere with iron absorption, so be sure to space these supplements at least six to eight hours apart from iron.

Magnesium is a white metallic element that is essential in nutrition, and necessary for enzyme action, muscle function, the transmission of nerve impulses, and the use of calcium, phosphorous, and potassium. It aids in bone, nerve, tissue, and tooth growth; balances the body's acid/alkaline levels; enhances metabolism; reduces blood pressure levels; protects the arterial lining, and protects against heart attack and the formation of gallstones and kidney stones; regulates parathyroid hormone function; relieves indigestion and constipation; relaxes the nervous system; and soothes cell and tissue irritations. Arrhythmia, cravings for chocolate, confusion, debility, nervousness, and muscular cramps and twitches may indicate a deficiency (magnesium).
Supplement/Drug Interactions: This supplement could cause an interaction (possibly severe) when taken with the following drugs: Antibiotic drugs, Anticoagulant drugs, Antidiabetic drugs, Antifungal drugs, Biphosphonate drugs, Bronchodilator drugs, Corticosteroids, Diuretic drugs, HMG-CoA Reductase Inhibitors, H-2 Blocker drugs, and Theophylline drugs.
Adverse Reactions: Diarrhea.
Cautions/Contraindications: Avoid use if pregnant or breast-feeding, or if you have diabetes, heart disease, or a kidney problem, or if you have had intestinal surgery, or if you are taking medication to slow intestinal movement.

Manganese is a metallic element that resembles iron, and is needed for the production of breast milk, enzyme activation, Vitamin B, C, and E assimilation, the metabolism of carbohydrates, fats, and proteins, proper connective tissue growth and bone formation; the regulation of blood sugar levels, and nerve and immune system health. Auditory problems, bowed bones, dizziness, elevated blood sugar levels, incoordination, memory/cognitive problems, poor reflexes, and tinnitus may indicate a deficiency (manganese).
Supplement/Drug Interactions: This supplement could cause an interaction (possibly severe) when taken with the following drugs: Antibiotic drugs and Hormones and Synthetic Substitutes (i.e. conjugated estrogens, contraceptives (oral, etc.), and other hormonal replacement therapy (HRT).
Adverse Reactions: None known.
Cautions/Contraindications: Avoid excessive use if pregnant or breast-feeding.

Molybdenum is a hard, silvery-white, metallic element, and is used for cell and enzyme reaction; the utilization of iron and nitrogen; uric acid production, and may serve as an adjuvant to acquired immune deficiency syndrome (AIDS) and cancer therapies. Molybdenum supplementation may be useful in counteracting copper toxicity. Cancer or gum or mouth conditions may indicate a deficiency (molybdenum).
Supplement/Drug Interactions: This supplement could cause an interaction (possibly severe) when taken with the following drugs: None known.
Adverse Reactions: Asthma-like symptoms and gout.
Cautions/Contraindications: Avoid use if pregnant or breast-feeding. May interfere with copper assimilation.

Phosphorus is a nonmetallic, translucent, poisonous, highly inflammable element that works together with calcium, magnesium, and vitamin B_3 (niacin), and is necessary for brain and nerve function. It produces energy for the body, and is important for muscle action and enzyme formation. Anorexia, arthritis, kidney problems, obesity, periodontal disease, poor bone growth,

and uncontrolled appetite may indicate a deficiency (phosphorus). Bonemeal with vitamin D, or a calcium-magnesium-phosphorus supplement is recommended.
Supplement/Drug Interactions: This supplement could cause an interaction (possibly severe) when taken with the following drugs: None known.
Adverse Reactions: Fatty degeneration of the liver, osteoporosis.
Cautions/Contraindications: Avoid use if pregnant or breast-feeding.

Potassium is a soft, silvery-white, metallic element that is crucial in the nerve to muscle message transmission. It alkalinizes and neutralizes acids in the blood chemistry; aids in muscle contraction; balances blood pressure levels; maintains proper pH levels and fluid balance; protects against cysts, fibroids, other benign growths, and stroke (apoplectic); and wards off nervous system agitation. Breathing difficulties, debility, fatigue, cardiovascular insufficiency, constipation, hypoglycemia, insomnia, poor reflex action, and thirst (continual) may indicate a deficiency (potassium). Daily consumption of bananas or orange juice may be helpful in potassium supplementation.
Supplement/Drug Interactions: This supplement could cause an interaction (possibly severe) when taken with the following drugs: Angiotensin-Converting Enzyme (ACE) Inhibitors, Antacids, Antibiotic drugs, Anticoagulant drugs, Antimanic drugs, Colchicine drugs, Corticosteroids, Diuretic drugs, Hypertensive drugs, Laxatives, Nonsteroidal Anti-inflammatory drugs (NSAIDs), and Theophylline drugs.
Adverse Reactions: Arrhythmia, cardiac failure, coma, convulsions, debility, gastrointestinal bleeding, hemafecia (blood in the stool), hypotension, infection, paralysis (limb), and protein breakdown.
Cautions/Contraindications: Avoid use if pregnant or breast-feeding. Use with professional guidance/supervision if you have a heart condition.

Selenium is a nonmetallic poisonous element resembling sulfur that works with vitamin E and functions as an antioxidant. It activates DNA and RNA; creates antibodies; enhances immune system function; protects against free radical cell damage; reduces hot flashes sometimes experienced during menopause; and strengthens the cardiovascular system. Heart disease, infertility, muscular dystrophy, skin problems, and stroke (apoplectic) may indicate a deficiency (selenium).
Supplement/Drug Interactions: This supplement could cause an interaction (possibly severe) when taken with the following drugs: Anticonvulsant/Antiseizure drugs and Antineoplastic drugs, and Copper.
Adverse Reactions: Alopecia, fatigue, nail changes/discoloration, nausea, nervous conditions, and/or vomiting.
Cautions/Contraindications: Avoid use if pregnant or breast-feeding. Avoid high doses. Not for long-term use.

Silicon is a nonmetallic element whose dioxide is silica. It is necessary for bone and tissue fomation, and the absorption of calcium. It balances the emotional and nervous system; brings radiance to the skin and luster to the hair; builds strong bones, ligaments, nails, skin, teeth, and tendons; maintains arterial flexibility; nourishes the brain cells, nerve cells, eyes, and tissues; protects against Alzheimer's disease, coronary artery disease (CAD), osteoporosis, and poisoning (aluminum).

Supplement/Drug Interactions: This supplement could cause an interaction (possibly severe) when taken with the following drugs: Thyroid drugs.
Adverse Reactions: None known.
Cautions/Contraindications: Avoid use if pregnant or breast-feeding.

Silver is a soft, white, malleable, metallic element. Silver is used in preparations only. Colloidal Silver is a well-known preparation of silver that has been used as an antibiotic and immunity booster. Its uses include arthritis, cancer, diabetes, human immunodeficiency virus (HIV), colds, moniliasis, blood and food poisoning, tuberculosis, eczema, athlete's foot, herpes, and prostate problems.
Supplement/Drug Interactions: This supplement could cause an interaction (possibly severe) when taken with the following drugs: None known.
Adverse Reactions: Allergic reactions and possible death.
Cautions/Contraindications: Avoid use if pregnant or breast-feeding, or if you have a sensitivity to silver-based medications. Ingesting amounts of 10 grams or more of silver in a single dose may require immediate emergency medical attention and could result in fatality.

Sodium is a soft, white, alkaline, metallic element that is necessary with potassium to maintain the body's pH levels and fluid balance. It brings youthfulness to body membranes, joints, and tissues, and is essential for promoting healthy digestion, as well as maintaining vascular suppleness, and joint flexibility. Arrhythmia, confusion, debility, hypoglycemia, lethargy, and memory/cognitive problems may indicate a deficiency (sodium).
Supplement/Drug Interactions: This supplement could cause an interaction (possibly severe) when taken with the following drugs: None known.
Adverse Reactions: Edema, heart failure, hypertension, kidney problems, liver problems, and potassium deficiency.
Cautions/Contraindications: Avoid use if pregnant or breast-feeding.

Sulfur is a yellowish, nonmetallic element that exists in many forms, and is a part of the amino acid chemistry. Its antibiotic, diaphoretic, and laxative properties aid oxidation in the body; maintain hair, respiratory, and skin health; protect against pollutants and radiation; and stimulate bile. The best source of sulfur is with complete amino acid supplementation.

Vanadium is a rare, gray, metallic element that is required for bone and tooth formation, and blood sugar, cell, and insulin metabolism. It protects against heart attack and reduces cholesterol levels.
Supplement/Drug Interactions: This supplement could cause an interaction (possibly severe) when taken with the following drugs: None known.
Adverse Reactions: Depression (manic) and metabolism interference.
Cautions/Contraindications: Avoid use if pregnant or breast-feeding. Take vanadium at least one hour apart from chromium. Tobacco smoking greatly decreases assimilation of vanadium.

Zinc is a bluish-white, poisonous, metallic element that is necessary for proper immune system function. It aids in healing and cell regeneration, and the transportation of vitamin A from its storage site in the liver; controls the contraction of muscles; helps in the formation of insulin, and the metabolism of carbohydrates, fats, and proteins; plays a factor in DNA synthesis; protects against diabetes and liver toxicity; reduces body odor, infection, inflammation, and

memory/cognitive problems; and regulates the body's pH levels and enzymatic flow in the cells. White spots on the fingernails may indicate a deficiency (zinc).
Supplement/Drug Interactions: This supplement could cause an interaction (possibly severe) when taken with the following drugs: Angiotensin-Converting Enzyme (ACE) Inhibitors, Antibiotic drugs, Anticoagulant drugs, Anticonvulsant/Antiseizure drugs, Antiretroviral drugs, Bile Acid Sequestrant drugs, Chelating agents, Corticosteroids, Diuretic drugs, Hormones and Synthetic Substitutes (i.e. conjugated estrogens, contraceptives (oral, etc.), and other hormonal replacement therapy (HRT), Salicylates, and Subsalicylates.
Adverse Reactions: Anemia, deficiency (copper), elevated cholesterol levels, immune system depression, scurvy-like symptoms, skin problems, and zincalism (chronic zinc poisoning).
Cautions/Contraindications: Avoid use if pregnant or breast-feeding. Avoid high doses. Not for long-term use.

Miscellaneous Natural Supplements

Algae are single-celled organisms that are full of beneficial nutrients such as amino acids, gammalinolenic acid (GLA), iron, minerals, and vitamins. Algae species balance blood pressure and cholesterol levels; enhance the immune system; protect against allergic reactions and cell mutations; reduce inflammation; and stimulate bile flow.
Supplement/Drug Interactions: This supplement could cause an interaction (possibly severe) when taken with the following drugs: Thyroid drugs.
Adverse Reactions: Edema, iodism (chronic iodine poisoning).
Cautions/Contraindications: Avoid use if pregnant or breast-feeding, or if you have an allergy (seaweed), or if you have an iodine sensitivity, or if you are taking acid reflux drugs. May decrease intestinal absorption.

Brewer's Yeast (Dried Yeast) is the United States Pharmacopeia (U.S.P.) name for the dry cells of any strain of *saccharomyces cerevisiae.* It contains vitamin B complex and is useful for conditions caused by deficiency (vitamin B) in the diet.
Supplement/Drug Interactions: This supplement could cause an interaction (possibly severe) when taken with the following drugs: Antibiotic drugs.
Adverse Reactions: None known.
Cautions/Contraindications: Avoid use if pregnant or breast-feeding.

Choline, Phosphatidylcholine is one of the building blocks of acetylcholine, which is a chemical messenger in the nervous system. Together, choline and inositol make lecithin. It aids in the production of hormones and the transportation of fats into the cells; enhances brain and liver function; controls mood; improves memory/cognition; protects against arteriosclerosis, cancer, circulatory problems, gallbladder problems, glaucoma, heart attack, and thrombosis; reduces cholesterol levels and excess fat in the gallbladder, heart, and liver; and supports the integrity of cell membranes. Choline is sometimes included with the B complex group of vitamins.
Supplement/Drug Interactions: This supplement could cause an interaction (possibly severe) when taken with the following drugs: Antinausea drugs.

Adverse Reactions: Depression (increased), intestinal tract problems, muscle stiffness, nausea, and/or salivation (increased).
Cautions/Contraindications: Avoid use if pregnant or breast-feeding, or if you have depression, Parkinson's disease, or ulcer.

Coenzyme Q_{10} (CO-Q10, Ubiquinone) is a powerful antioxidant and antibiotic, and is necessary for metabolism, and helping to counteract the oxidation of fats in the blood stream. It aids circulation; enhances immune system function; minimizes the amount of micro-traumas that occur to the heart; protects against cancer; reduces cholesterol and triglyceride levels; and strengthens the heart muscle. It is useful for acquired immune deficiency syndrome (AIDS), allergy, Alzheimer's disease, asthma, candida, diabetes, heart disease, hypercholesteremia, hypertension, multiple sclerosis, obesity, periodontal disease, respiratory conditions, and schizophrenia. May serve as an adjuvant in cancer and leukemia therapies to help offset the negative effects of chemotherapy and radiation. Taking coenzyme Q_{10} with olive oil increases absorption. Coenzyme Q_{10} is heat and light sensitive.
Supplement/Drug Interactions: This supplement could cause an interaction (possibly severe) when taken with the following drugs: Anticoagulant drugs, Antidepressant drugs, Antineoplastic drugs, Beta-Adrenergic Blocking drugs, HMG-CoA Reductase Inhibitors, Hypertensive drugs.
Adverse Reactions: None known.
Cautions/Contraindications: Avoid use if pregnant or breast-feeding.

Crude Fiber is raw or unrefined fiber that is used to promote and maintain colon and intestinal system health.
Supplement/Drug Interactions: This supplement could cause an interaction (possibly severe) when taken with the following drugs: Analgesics (narcotic), Calcium Channel Blocker drugs, HMG-CoA Reductase Inhibitors, Laxatives.
Adverse Reactions: Diarrhea (possibly severe).
Cautions/Contraindications: Avoid use if pregnant or breast-feeding, or if you have an intestinal obstrution.

Docosahexaenoic Acid (DHEA), Dehydroepiandrosterone is a powerful hormone made by the adrenal glands that is converted into testosterone in males and estrogen in females. It aids weight loss; enhances immune system function; increases lean muscle mass; improves libido and mood; and slows the aging process.
Supplement/Drug Interactions: This supplement could cause an interaction (possibly severe) when taken with the following drugs: Corticosteroids, Immune Suppressive drugs.
Adverse Reactions: Arrhythmia, cancer (breast, ovarian, prostate) increased risk, heart disease (increased risk), liver damage (often characterized by jaundice), oily skin.
Cautions/Contraindications: Avoid use if pregnant or breast-feeding. Due to the hormonal effects, do not administer to children or teenagers. Use with professional guidance/supervision.

Enzymes are contained in all living tissue and are necessary for metabolism. Each enzyme has its own specialized task. Enzymes break down carbohydrates, fats, and proteins into easier to digest portions; dissolve artery and vein thrombosis (blood clot); and protect against arterial plaque formation. Uses include lactose intolerance, bloating, flatulence, acne, acquired immune deficiency syndrome (AIDS), shingles, inflammatory conditions, cancer, and multiple sclerosis (MS).

Supplement/Drug Interactions: Antibiotic drugs and Anticoagulant drugs.
Adverse Reactions: Abdominal pain, constipation, diarrhea, flatulence, hemafecia (blood in the stool), nausea, and/or vomiting.
Cautions/Contraindications: Avoid use if pregnant or breast-feeding. Avoid use of digestive enzymes if you have gastritis.

Essential Fatty Acids (EFAs, Vitamin F) are vitamin-like lipids with antioxidant properties that are essential to the body, but since the body cannot make them by itself, foods containing them need to be eaten. EFAs aid coagulation of the blood, the endocrine glands, adrenal glands, the nervous, reproductive, and respiratory systems, and thyroid glands; insulate and protect the nerves and tissues; maintain body temperature; provide energy; protect against damage from roentgen rays (x-rays); reduce cholesterol levels; and are vital for proper growth and development of the brain, metabolism, and nervous system. Acne, diarrhea, eczema, gallstones, skin problems, the loss of beneficial intestinal bacteria, and varicose veins may indicate a deficiency (EFAs). EFAs are best taken with vitamin E during meals.
Supplement/Drug Interactions: This supplement could cause an interaction (possibly severe) when taken with the following drugs: Antibacterial drugs, Antibiotic drugs, Anticoagulant drugs, Anticonvulsant/Antiseizure drugs, Bile Acid Sequestrant drugs, Corticosteroids, and Mineral Oil.
Adverse Reactions: None known.
Cautions/Contraindications: Avoid use if pregnant or breast-feeding.

Fish Oil (Cod Liver Oil, Halibut Liver Oil, Shark Liver Oil, and Salmon Oil) is a fixed oil from the livers of various fish, primarily codfish, halibut, shark, and salmon. This oil contains omega 6 and omega 3 essential fatty acids (EFAs), as well as gaduin (a fatty principle), olein, other glycerides, vitamins A and D, and small variable quantities of bromine, iodine, morrhuic acid, phosphorus, and sulfur. These EFAs are necessary for blood vessel dilatation; cell membrane formation and function; prompting the body to produce favorable prostaglandins; protecting against arterial plaque formation, arthritis, bipolar/manic depressive conditions, cancer, depression, endometriosis, heart disease, hypertension, lupus, mania, osteoarthritis (OA), osteoporosis, and schizophrenia; and reducing cholesterol and triglyceride levels.
Supplement/Drug Interactions: This supplement could cause an interaction (possibly severe) when taken with the following drugs: Anticoagulant drugs, Immune Suppressive drugs, Salicylates, Subsalicylates, and Vitamins A or D (high doses).
Adverse Reactions: Alopecia, bleeding (possibly serious), cardiovascular conditions, coagulation problems, headache, hyperglycemia, kidney problems, menstrual problems, and muscle and joint pain.
Cautions/Contraindications: Avoid use if pregnant or breast-feeding, or if you have diabetes, a blood coagulation problem, or a tendency to hemorrhage. Some persons may experience bleeding or increased clotting time when using this supplement with anticoagulant drugs or aspirin. Toxicity may occur in persons who are taking high doses of vitamin A or D.

Gamma-oryzanol assists in building lean muscle tissue; prevents gastrointestinal problems; regulates digestive enzymes; and stimulates the excretion of cholesterol from the body.
Supplement/Drug Interactions: This supplement could cause an interaction (possibly severe) when taken with the following drugs: None known.
Adverse Reactions: None known.
Cautions/Contraindications: Avoid use if pregnant or breast-feeding.

Gammalinolenic Acid (GLA) is an essential fatty acid and a precursor of prostaglandin E1 (PGE1). The cells of all the important tissues and organs of the body efficiently take it up. GLA helps control cholesterol levels and protects against heart disease, hypertension, obesity, and vascular problems. It is useful for alcoholism, allergy, asthma, benign breast disease, cancer, cystic fibrosis, depression, diabetes, eczema, infertility, lithium toxicity, lupus, migraine, multiple sclerosis (MS), premenstrual symptoms (PMS), rheumatoid arthritis (RA), schizophrenia, and numerous other conditions. To prevent oxidation of GLA in the body, take it with vitamin E.
Supplement/Drug Interactions: None known.
Adverse Reactions: Headache, nausea, rash.
Cautions/Contraindications: Avoid use if pregnant or breast-feeding. Initial use of evening primrose oil may cause a temporary headache, nausea, and minor skin rash. To avoid headache, take evening primrose oil with food.

Glucosamine Sulfate is a synthetic version of Glucosamine (a naturally occurring body substance), which plays a significant role in maintaining and repairing cartilage. It can be used as an alternative to nonsteroidal inflammatory drugs (NSAIDs) to reduce the pain of osteoarthritis (OA).
Supplement/Drug Interactions: This supplement could cause an interaction (possibly severe) when taken with the following drugs: None known.
Adverse Reactions: Heartburn, indigestion, and nausea.
Cautions/Contraindications: Avoid use if pregnant or breast-feeding. Not for long-term use.

Inositol is closely related to choline, and together they make lecithin. It is necessary for assimilation of vitamin C and E, and aids in cholesterol an fat metabolism, and in the transportation of fat to cells; helps in the removal of fat from the gallbladder, heart, and liver, and is essential for brain, muscle and nerve functions; protects against arteriosclerosis; reduces cysts and hypercholesteremia; regulates serotonin levels; and supports nerve transmission. Inositol is sometimes included with the B complex vitamins.
Supplement/Drug Interactions: This supplement could cause an interaction (possibly severe) when taken with the following drugs: None known.
Adverse Reactions: Impairment of glucose tolerance.
Cautions/Contraindications: Avoid use if pregnant or breast-feeding, or if you have diabetes, hypertension, peripheral neuropathy, or depression.

Lecithin aids in the transportation of cholesterol and fats throughout the body; improves memory/cognition; protects against heart failure; and reduces cholesterol levels.
Supplement/Drug Interactions: This supplement could cause an interaction (possibly severe) when taken with the following drugs: None known.
Adverse Reactions: Depression (possible), dizziness, nausea.
Cautions/Contraindications: Avoid use if pregnant or breast-feeding.

Lipoic Acid assists in the transformation of carbohydrates to energy; enhances insulin sensitivity; prevents glucose from attaching to red blood cells; protects against acquired immune deficiency syndrome (AIDS), cancer cataract formation, glaucoma, heart disease, human immunodeficiency virus (HIV), kidney problems, liver problems, and memory/cognitive

problems; and the regeneration of damaged nerves. It is useful for diabetic neuropathy and poisoning (mushroom), and may serve as an adjuvant to heavy metal detoxification programs.
Supplement/Drug Interactions: This supplement could cause an interaction (possibly severe) when taken with the following drugs: None known.
Adverse Reactions: None known.
Cautions/Contraindications: Avoid use if pregnant or breast-feeding. Diabetics should monitor blood sugar daily when taking lipoic acid.

Melatonin is a powerful hormone produced by the pineal gland that regulates body rhythms, promotes normal sleep, and is responsible for the regulation of hormones. It enhances immune system function; protects against jet lag, seasonal affective disorder (SAD), insomnia, hypercholesteremia, hypertension, and Alzheimer's disease; reduces blood pressure and cholesterol levels; and strengthens the bones.
Supplement/Drug Interactions: This supplement could cause an interaction (possibly severe) when taken with the following drugs: Anticonvulsant/Antiseizure drugs, Antidepressant drugs, Antineoplastic drugs, Anxiolytic drugs, Beta-Adrenergic Blocking drugs, Corticosteroids, Mood Altering agents/drugs, Nonsteroidal Anti-inflammatory Drugs (NSAIDs), Sedative drugs, and Steroidal drugs.
Adverse Reactions: Depression (increased), disruption in normal sleep patterns, drowsiness, headache, nausea, and/or skin rash.
Cautions/Contraindications: Avoid use if pregnant or breast-feeding, or if you have acquired immune deficiency syndrome (AIDS), osteoarthritis (OA), depression, epilepsy, diabetes, heart disease, multiple sclerosis (MS), allergy (severe), an autoimmune disease, or a glandular problem. Not for long-term use.

Para-Aminobenzoic Acid (PABA) has antioxidant properties, is sometimes included as a member of the B complex vitamin group, is a constituent of pantothenic acid (vitamin B_5), and is required in the formation of folic acid. It aids in the assimilation of protein and the formation of red blood cells; enhances the effects of cortisone and estrogen; multiplies the potency of body-produced hormones; prevents blood vessel constriction; protects against cancer (skin) and sunburn; supports other B vitamins; and suppresses an overactive immune system. Depression, digestive complaints, eczema, fatigue, and irritability may indicate a deficiency (PABA).
Supplement/Drug Interactions: This supplement could cause an interaction (possibly severe) when taken with the following drugs: Antibacterial drugs, Antibiotic drugs, and Antineoplastic drugs.
Adverse Reactions: Appetite loss, fever, hypoglycemia, liver damage (often characterized by jaundice), nausea, skin rash, and/or vomiting.
Cautions/Contraindications: Avoid use if pregnant or breast-feeding. Avoid high doses. May negate the effects of sulfa drugs. Not for long-term use.

Phenethylisothiocyanate (PEITC) is a potent sulfur-containing supplement that detoxifies cancer-causing substances; protects the liver and DNA; and stimulates the production of glutathione.
Supplement/Drug Interactions: This supplement could cause an interaction (possibly severe) when taken with the following drugs: None known.
Adverse Reactions: None known.
Cautions/Contraindications: Avoid use if pregnant or breast-feeding.

Probiotics (Lactobacillus acidophilus [acidophil], Lactobacillus bifidus, Lactobacillus brevis) and Fructo-Oligosaccharide (FOS) are friendly organisms that exist in the intestinal tract and promote a healthy environment. They process food residue and keep unfriendly bacteria in check by preventing overgrowth. Fructo-Oligosaccharides (Fructo = fructose, which is a crystalline sugar found in honey and sweet fruits, and Oligosaccharide = a group of carbohydrates consisting of a small number of simple sugar molecules) are tiny, indigestible carbohydrates that nourish the body's friendly bacteria.
Supplement/Drug Interactions: This supplement could cause an interaction (possibly severe) when taken with the following drugs: Antibiotic drugs.
Adverse Reactions: None known.
Cautions/Contraindications: Avoid use if pregnant or breast-feeding.

S-adenosylmethionine (SAM) is produced in the body and is a combination of the energy molecule known as adenosine triphosphate (ATP) and methionine. It aids in the formation of joint cartilage; encourages the production of dopamine, phosphatidylserine, and serotonin in the brain; enhances nail and skin health, eliminates fat from the liver; promotes the processing of fats within the body; stimulates the body to make extra lecithin; and supports liver function.
Supplement/Drug Interactions: This supplement could cause an interaction (possibly severe) when taken with the following drugs: Antidepressant drugs.
Adverse Reactions: Depression (increased), gastrointestinal problems, nausea.
Cautions/Contraindications: Avoid use if pregnant or breast-feeding, or if you have diabetes, a kidney or liver problem, manic depression, or an allergy (protein). May worsen psychosis. Persons taking antidepressant medication should consult a physician before taking SAM.

Wheat Germ is the embryo of the wheat plant, is rich in calcium, copper, manganese, magnesium, phosphorous, B vitamins, octacosanol, is one of the richest sources of vitamin E, and is necessary for immune function. It aids in controlling glucose and fats in the blood; enhances endurance and reaction time; improves oxygen usage by the body; lowers cholesterol and triglyceride levels; produces normal red blood cells, protects cells against oxidation; supports healthy neuromuscular function, and is a good source of folic acid.
Supplement/Drug Interactions: This supplement could cause an interaction (possibly severe) when taken with the following drugs: None known.
Adverse Reactions: None known.
Cautions/Contraindications: Avoid use if pregnant or breast-feeding. Because wheat germ is a plant-based analog of the female sex hormone estrogen, large amounts, long-term, or overuse may cause testicular degeneration or loss of sex-drive in men.

Therapeutic Phytochemicals

Herbal medicine has been a part of ancient cultures for thousands of years. Indeed the first dietary supplements were herbs that people consumed as food. Today, science is taking a closer look at the therapeutic properties of certain herb chemicals and discovering that many of them may actually help protect against disease. All of the chemicals in herbs work better together than as isolated substances and thus provide enhanced benefits when consumed from the whole herb than supplements. Amongst the most potent of these substances are the antioxidants, carotenoids, flavonoids, phytoestrogens, and polyphenols. Recently, phytochemicals have been found in fruits and vegetables, and these chemicals are currently undergoing various studies by researchers from the National Science Institute. Phytochemicals are not exactly nutrients, but compounds that work closely with each other in complimentary ways to protect the herb from damage due to environmental pollutants and/or excessive sunlight. Scientists speculate that phytochemicals acting as antioxidants in herbs may provide a similar benefit in people, and initial research suggests that they may be valuable in protecting against malignant cell growth.

Antioxidants including carotenoids (especially beta-carotene), the mineral selenium, and vitamins A, C, and E have the ability to destroy free radicals. Antioxidants help protect against heart attack and stroke (apoplectic), halt the actions of carcinogenic substances within the body, and limit the formation of or neutralize free radicals before they can harm the body. Sources include but are not limited to beets, carrots, red peppers, squash, sweet potatoes, tomatoes, turnips, and other yellow to red vegetables; brocolli, brussel sprouts, cabbage, cauliflower, collard greens, kale, lettuce, mustard greens, spinach, watercress, and other leafy green vegetables; apricots, cantaloupe, lemons, limes, melons, nectarines, oranges, peaches, pineapples, and other yellow or orange fruits; blueberries; garlic, leeks, onions, and shallots; seafood; and whole grains.

Carotenoids are responsible for the colors found primarily in vegetables. They're not vitamins, but some of them are converted to vitamin A in the body. The carotenoids that have been studied and show promise are lutein and lycopene. These carotenoids help protect against eye damage caused by excessive sunlight; reduce the risk of certain cancers; and provide antioxidant protection. Sources include but are not limited to brocolli, brussel sprouts, cabbage, cauliflower, collard greens, kale, lettuce, mustard greens, spinach, watercress, and other leafy green vegetables; apricots, cantaloupe, lemons, limes, melons, nectarines, oranges, peaches, pineapples, and other yellow or orange fruits; beets, carrots, red peppers, squash, sweet potatoes, tomatoes, turnips, and other yellow to red vegetables; and algae, bladderwrack, and kelp.

Flavonoids (Bioflavonoids, Vitamin P) are color pigments found in fruits and vegetables that have antiallergenic, anticarcinogenic, and anti-inflammatory activity. By acting as antioxidants, flavonoids may help protect against arterial plaque, platelet aggregation, and some cancers. Different flavonoids, numbering over four thousand, provide varying benefits. For example, those flavonoids occurring in berries act as powerful antioxidants and appear to decrease the destruction of collagen tissue that results from inflammatory conditions. Other flavonoids, such as quercetin, alter the sensitivity response to allergens by inhibiting the release of histamine. Sources include but are not limited to apples, blueberries, brocolli, cabbage, eggplant, grapes, lemons, limes, oranges, peppers, red wine, squash, tea, tomatoes, and yams.

Phytoestrogens are a specific group of hormone-like plant chemicals that act as estrogen antagonists. Isoflavones, a class of phytoestrogens, bind to estrogen receptors and prevent the body's own estrogen from doing so. These compounds may help protect against estrogen dependant cancers. Phytoestrogens may also enhance immune system function and reduce thrombus (blood clot) formation. Sources include but are not limited to lentils, peas, and other legumes; soymilk, tofu, and other soy products; and barley, corn, oats, and other whole grains.

Polyphenols are being intensely studied for their potential ability to improve lipid metabolism, reduce cholesterol levels, protect against some cancers and heart disease, and provide antibacterial protection.

Researchers theorize that polyphenols may be responsible for the reduced rate of heart disease in persons having a high fat diet. Sources include but are not limited to apples, coffee, grapes, green tea, nuts, red wine, strawberries, onions, and yams.

Monographs

FORMULARY

Reigning over the orchard in royal robes, a young cherry tree with its long, narrow leaves glows in colors of carmine and vermilion. The other trees, planted in rows that stretch as far as the eye can see, are as yet green or slightly tinged with red. The wind ceases its stirring and the earth rests in perfect stillness.

Debra Rayburn

Therapeutic

Do you experience the discomforts of arthritis, digestive complaints, or muscle and joint pain? With nature's assistance, many problems can be alleviated. A healthy diet, exercise, fresh air, sunshine, and fresh water are all very important in helping your body to ward off illness, or to facilitate healing when an illness does occur. Sometimes, the best results are achieved when herbal preparations are used both externally and internally. Herbal preparations used in combination therapy can help strengthen the body's response to prescription drugs as well as helping to offset any negative effects. Amazing results may be achieved from using just one specific formula. However , due to individual body differences, that same formula may offer little or no results for another person. Remember that herbs tend to work gradually and they generally take at least two to six weeks to build up in your system, so benefits and/or results may not be noticeable until that time. Also, additional therapeutic practices such as diet, exercise, massage, nutritional/vitamin supplementation, or other healing modalities may help speed up recovery and round out one's treatment plan. The following formulas are given in terms of proportions rather than amounts. This way, any amount of mixture can be prepared to suit one's need. For example, if the formula specifies ginseng (1 part), you could use ½ ounce, 1 cup, or 1 teaspoon of herb for that one-part measurement. The quantity used for the one-part measurement can be adjusted to your convenience as well as to the availability of the herb. Multiple formulas are listed under the condition headings.

Abscess

The formation of an abscess, which is a collection of pus or other infected material within a body cavity formed by the breakdown of tissue, is usually due to an infection caused by the *streptococci* or *staphylococci* bacteria. This bacterium enters through the hair follicles or sweat glands, and can occur anywhere on the body but most often appears in the armpit, groin, or other hairy area, and may be characterized by fever, inflammation, and a painful, reddish nodule with pus forming in the nodule's central core. To relieve the discomfort of an abscess, soak the area with warm compresses for about fifteen minutes every hour until it drains.

Formula 1
Goldenseal (3 parts)
Marshmallow (5 parts)
Oat (5 parts)
Oregon Grape Root (3 parts)
Purple Coneflower (1 part)

Formula 2
Dock (2 parts)
Garlic (1 part)
Ginger (1 part)
Goldenseal (1 part)
Purple Coneflower (2 parts)

Acidity (Gastric)

Gastric acidity, hyperacidity, or sour stomach pertains to the excessive acidity level of the stomach acid, and occurs when there is an alteration of stomach acid due to weak gastric function.

Formula 1
Calamus (¼ part)
Dandelion (1 part)
Goldenseal (¼ part)
Slippery Elm (1 part)

Formula 2
Cayenne (⅛ part)
Marshmallow (½ part)
Raspberry leaves (1 part)
Slippery Elm (1 part)

Acne

Acne is a chronic inflammatory condition of the sebaceous glands, which occurs most frequently on the face, back, and chest, and is characterized by small, inflamed papules that sometimes contain pus (pustules), or as comedomes with black centers (blackheads), which can leave small scars or pits in the skin. Acne commonly occurs around puberty, but can occur in adults, as well, due to excessive oil secretion, certain medications, heredity, hormonal changes such as menstruation or menopause, microbial infections, stress, or chemical irritants. To help reduce or protect against acne, increase your intake of fresh fruits and vegetables and decrease your consumption of fats and sugar. Also, some commercial hair and skin products can trigger outbreaks of acne, especially if you have sensitive skin.

Formula 1
Chaparral (2 parts)
Dock (1 part)
Garlic (1 part)
Ginseng (1 part)
Goldenseal (1 part)
Purple Coneflower (2 parts)
Sarsaparilla (1 part)
Sassafras (1 part)

Formula 2
Burdock (1 part)
Dandelion (1 part)
Kelp or Bladderwrack (1 part)
Licorice (½ part)
Purple Coneflower (2 parts)
Red Clover (1 part)
Sarsaparilla (2 parts)

Alcoholism

Alcoholism is caused by the excessive or repeated and long continued use of alcoholic drinks. Repeated, excessive use of alcohol can lead to chronic alcoholism or craving for intoxication by alcoholic beverages. The following formulas will help to create "distaste" for alcohol, may induce nausea and/or vomiting, and will help to eliminate alcohol toxins from the system.

Formula 1
Combine equal amounts of:
Milkweed
Pennyroyal
Peony

Formula 2
Combine equal amounts of:
Kudzu
Milk Thistle
Mushroom, Reishi

Alzheimer's Disease

Alzheimer's disease is a presenile condition that occurs during middle age, is caused by a buildup of plaque in the brain (yes, the same type of plaque that builds up in the arteries), and is characterized by mental weakness and deterioration.

Formula 1
Blessed Thistle (3 parts)
Cayenne (1 part)
Ginger (1 part)
Ephedra (1 part)
Ginkgo (1 part)
Gotu Kola (3 parts)
Lobelia (½ part)
Vervain (3 parts)

Formula 2
Astragalus (2 parts)
Cohosh, Black (1 part)
Ginger (1 part)
Ginseng (2 parts)
Goldenseal (½ part)
Kelp or Bladderwrack (1 part)
Licorice (1 part)

Amenorrhea

Amenorrhea is an abnormal absence or cessation of the menstrual flow, usually resulting from a deficiency of the estrus-producing (ovarian) or pituitary hormone, poor nutrition, stress, anemia, tumors, or overly strenuous exercise. Adequate rest, a well balanced diet that is rich in iron, and a sensible exercise routine can help maintain reproductive system health.

Formula 1
Combine equal amounts of:
Cohosh, Blue
Life Root
Motherwort
Thyme

Formula 2
Cohosh, Blue (2 parts)
Chamomile (3 parts)
Ginger (¼ part)
Goldenseal (½ part)
Motherwort (4 parts)

Anemia

Anemia is a condition in which the blood is deficient either in quantity, such as compression of a blood vessel or direct loss of blood, or in quality, such as the reduction of the amount of hemoglobin or in the number of red blood corpuscles, or both, and is characterized by, arrrhythmia, depression, fatigue (extreme), headache, irritability, insomnia, lethargy, lightheadedness, murmurs (systolic), paleness of the skin and mucous membranes, poor memory, or restlessness. Extreme cases of anemia, are characterized by cardiac weakness, fever, multiple blood clots in the arteries and capillaries, paralysis, pharyngitis, and vomiting. The elderly and women who are pregnant are at higher risk for anemia.

Formula 1
Astragalus (2 parts)
Cohosh, Black (1 part)
Ginger (1 part)
Ginseng (2 parts)
Goldenseal (½ part)
Kelp or Bladderwrack (1 part)

Formula 2
Buckbean (1 part)
Licorice (1 part)
Red Clover (1 part)
Sarsaparilla (4 parts)
Sassafras (½ part)
Yellow Dock (2 parts)

Arrhythmia
Arrhythmia is a disturbance in the normal rhythm of the heartbeat that causes irregularity in the force, equality, and sequence of the beat, and is characterized by fluttering, throbbing, or pounding, and may be caused by problems including stress, excessive adrenal or thyroid secretion, reduced blood glucose levels, or menopause. Consult your healthcare professional if arrhythmia is accompanied by a history of heart disease, hypotension, and/or lightheadedness.

Formula 1
Ginger (2 parts)
Ginseng (3 parts)
Hawthorn (6 parts)
Motherwort (3 parts)

Formula 2
Bladderwrack or Kelp (2 parts)
Cayenne (½ part)
Hawthorn (4 parts)
Rosemary (2 parts)

Arteriosclerosis
Arteriosclerosis occurs when the arterial and blood vessel walls thicken, harden, and become narrowed by deposits of plaque. Narrowing of the vessels makes blood circulation difficult, and causes the blood platelets to coagulate and form clots. If the clot blocks a coronary artery, it could result in a heart attack, and if the clot blocks an artery leading to the brain, it could result in a stroke (apoplectic). Arteriosclerosis is a condition commonly associated with chronic nephritis, hypertension, or congenital syphilis, and can remain undetected for years with no symptoms. However, advanced stages of this disease are often characterized by a bluish tinge to the skin, drowsiness, dizziness, muscle cramps and tinnitus.

Formula 1
Hawthorn (4 parts)
Plantain (2 parts)
Shave Grass (1 part)
Valerian (1 part)

Formula 2
Cayenne (½ part)
Cohosh, Black (2 parts)
Fenugreek (2 parts)
Hawthorn (2 parts)

Arthritis

Arthritis is a chronic condition that affects the joints, and may occur from an injury received earlier in life. The three main types of arthritis are gout, osteoarthritis (OA) , and rheumatoid arthritis (RA). Arthritis may be caused by a bacterial infection, poor nutrition, or stress. Fatigue, fever, pain, and inflamed, painful, stiff, swollen, misshapen joints characterize arthritis. All forms of arthritis are affected by diet, allergy, nutritional status, and lifestyle.

Formula 1
Ash, Prickly (3 parts)
Cohosh, Black (3 parts)
Ginger (2 parts)
Oregon Grape Root (6 parts)
Parsley (6 parts)
Sassafras (3 parts)

Formula 2
External uses.
Cayenne (1 part)
Lobelia (2 parts)
Mullein (6 parts)
Plantain (2 parts)
Slippery Elm (9 parts)

Asthma

Asthma is a condition generally associated with allergy (food), eczema, and hayfever. These sudden, recurring, and often intense attacks last from as little as a few minutes to several days, and often occur at night, during vigorous exercise, or in times of stress. Sudden, intense coughing, shortness of breath, a sensation of choking, and a feeling of chest constriction characterize an asthma attack. Keeping a daily log will help identify possible causes.

Formula 1
Steam Inhalent.
Combine equal amounts of:
Life Root
Mullein
Thyme
Wormwood

Formula 2
Cayenne (¼ part)
Grindelia (1 part)
Horehound (1 part)
Lobelia (1 part)
Red Clover (1 part)
Slippery Elm (2 parts)

Athlete's Foot

Athlete's foot is a chronic fungal infection of the skin of the foot, primarily occurring between the toes and on the soles, that is caused by the fungi species of *trichophyton* or *epiderinophyton* (the same fungi that causes ringworm), and is characterized by cracked, red, intensly itchy, raw, scaly skin. To protect against athlete's foot and keep the infection from spreading, soak your feet twice daily in a strong infusion of black tea, bearberry, or oak bark. Also wearing cotton socks absorbs perspiration, or spending as much time as possible barefoot or in sandals. Sprinkling cornstarch (not talcum powder) in your shoes also helps absorb perspiration.

Formula 1
Buchu (½ part)
Goldenseal (2 parts)
Juniper (1 part)
Plantain (2 parts)
Purple Coneflower (2 parts)

Formula 2
Combine equal amounts of:
Black Walnut
Calendula
Goldenseal
Thyme

Backache
The back is the posterior portion of the trunk from the neck to the pelvis. Back pain can occur from a wide variety of conditions including poor posture, spinal curvature, muscle strain, kidney infection, or a herniated disk, and is characterized by symptoms, including, but not limited to a dull ache, sharp pain, spasm, and in some cases localized inflammation.

Formula 1
Cabbage, Skunk (1 part)
Carrot (1 part)
Celery (1 part)
Juniper berries (1 part)
Parsley (1 part)
Senna (2 parts)
Wahoo (½ part)

Formula 2
Betony (1 part)
Bladderwrack or Kelp (½ part)
Raspberry leaves (2 parts)
Rosemary (1 part)
Skullcap (1 part)
Vervain (1 part)
Willow (2 parts)

Bleeding
Bleeding is the flow of blood occurring either internally from an ulcer, internal injury, etc., or externally from a wound. Seek immediate medical attention if bleeding is profuse, occurring from the ear or eye, or will not stop. The following formulas are for mild to moderate bleeding only.

Formula 1
Bayberry (1 part)
Calendula (1 part)
Cayenne (½ part)
Ginger (½ part)
Loosestrife, Purple (2 parts)
White Water Lily (1 part)

Formula 2
Combine equal amounts of:
Cayenne
Oak
Potentilla
Shave Grass
Shepherd's Purse

Blood Tonic
Blood is the fluid that circulates through the heart, arteries, capillaries, and veins, carrying nutrients and oxygen to the body tissues. It consists of a colorless liquid called plasma that contains red blood

corpuscles, yellowish disks that contain hemoglobin, which carry oxygen, white blood corpuscles, and blood platelets. If you experience recurrent problems including abscess, colds, infections, or sinusitis, a blood-cleansing program may be of benefit.

Formula 1
Chaparral (2 parts)
Dock (1 part)
Garlic (1 part)
Ginger (1 part)
Ginseng (1 part)
Goldenseal (1 part)
Purple Coneflower (2 parts)
Sarsaparilla (1 part)
Sassafras (1 part)

Formula 2
Blackberry leaves (2 parts)
Burdock (3 parts)
Centaury (2 parts)
Dandelion (1 part)
Elder (2 parts)
Evening Primrose (2 parts)
Licorice (1 part)
Nettle (1 part)
Oregon Grape Root (1 part)

Bronchitis
Bronchitis is an inflammation of the bronchial tubes that may be caused by acute conditions, the aspiration or inhalation of irritant substances, or exposure to cold, and is characterized by chest pain (primarily on coughing), cough, difficult or labored breathing, and fever.

Formula 1
Flax (2 parts)
Marshmallow (1 part)
Licorice (1 part)
Lungwort (1 part)
Mullein (1 part)
Sage (2 parts)

Formula 2
Anise (2 parts)
Cascarilla (9 parts)
Cherry, Wild (4 parts)
Elecampane (6 parts)
Hyssop (2 parts)
Moss, Irish (2 parts)

Bruises
Bruises are injuries situated near the surface of the skin that are produced by some form of impact, which does not cause tearing of the skin. They are characterized by inflammation, a purplish to yellowish discoloration of the skin, and tenderness.

Formula 1
Ash, Prickly (¼ part)
Indigo (1 part)
Myrrh (½ part)
Slippery Elm (1 part)

Formula 2
External Uses.
Calendula (1 part)
Comfrey (½part)
Plantain (½ part)

Burns

Burns are lesions caused by contact with heat. The following formulas are for 1st degree (minor household burns) and for external uses only. If you incur a 2nd degree or greater burn, or a chemical or electrical burn, seek immediate medical attention.

Formula 1

Cayenne (¼ part)
Chapparral (3 parts)
Honey (½ part)
Marshmallow (1 part)
Purple Coneflower (3 parts)
Wheat Germ (½ part)

Formula 2

External uses.
Calendula (1 part)
Comfrey (½ part)
Honey (½ part)
Mugwort (½ part)
Plantain (½ part)
Wheat Germ (½ part)

Calculus

Calculus is an abnormal concretion primarily composed of mineral salts that can occur in numerous places such as the biliary passages or gallbladder (gallstones), near a joint (gout), or in the bladder, intestine, kidney, liver, pancreatic duct, prostate, a seminal vesicle, or urinary tract.

Formula 1

Gravelroot (1 part)
Marshmallow (½ part)
Meadowsweet (½ part)
Uva-Ursi (½ part)

Formula 2

Buchu (1 part)
Gravelroot (1 part)
Parsley (1 part)
Uva-Ursi (½ part)

Cancer

Cancer is a term assigned to a cellular tumor the natural course of which is almost always fatal. A melanoma is a malignant tumor made up of melanin-pigmented cells that has a tendency to metastasize. The formation of secondary tumors, sarcomas, and other malignant tumors are usually associated with cancer. Cancer rates are on the rise in this country, and certain food additives, diets high in fats, hormones [i.e. diethylstilbestrol (DES), and other estrogenic hormones] tobacco smoking, and environmental chemicals, pesticides, and pollutants are just a few of the leading causes. These hormones, as well as other cancer causing substances, are a source of damaging free radicals in the body which suppress the immune system and affect cell reproduction, DNA encoding, and the formation of protein. There are no simple answers, but there are actions one can take to protect against cancer causing substances such as the elimination of as many of the potential causes as possible, switching to a low fat diet, initiating a smoking cessation program, and incorporating more antioxidant herbs and vitamins into your diet to help cleanse your system and boost your immunity.

Formula 1
Chaparral (2 parts)
Dock (1 part)
Garlic (1 part)
Ginger (1 part)
Ginseng (1 part)
Goldenseal (1 part)
Licorice (1 part)
Pokeweed (1 part)
Purple Coneflower (2 parts)

Formula 2
Combine equal amounts of:
Dandelion
Burdock
Ginseng
Goldenseal
Purple Coneflower
Red Clover
Violet
Yellow Dock

Canker Sores
A canker sore chiefly occurs on the inside of the mouth or on the tongue, and may be due to an infection, stress, or by an allergic reaction to certain foods including chocolate, citrus, nuts, or various aged cheeses, and is characterized by a small hard swelling or ulceration, inflammation, and pain.

Formula 1
Bayberry (1part)
Cohosh, Blue (½ part)
Goldenseal (½ part)
Oregon Grape Root (1 part)
Witch Hazel (½ part)

Formula 2
Combine equal parts of:
Bayberry
Pine bark
White Water Lily
Witch Hazel

Cardiovascular System Tonic
Cardiovascular system health is often dependent on genetics, which largely determines blood vessel structure and how cholesterol is processed. A diet high in saturated fats, a sedentary lifestyle, or stress (intense) can result in high cholesterol, hypertension, and other cardiovascular problems. To enhance and strengthen the heart and vascular system, eat low fat foods, incorporate more fresh fruits and vegetables into your diet, initiate a smoking cessation program (if you smoke), exercise daily, and reduce stress levels.

Formula 1
Ginger (2 parts)
Ginseng (3 parts)
Hawthorn (6 parts)
Motherwort (3 parts)

Formula 2
Ginkgo (1 part)
Hawthorn berries (2 parts)
Linden flowers (1 part)
Yarrow (1 part)

Cartilage Tonic

Cartilage is the tough, whitish, elastic, gristly substance (a form of connective tissue) that is attached to bone surfaces at the joints and forms certain parts of the skeletal structure. Cartilage is found in various parts of the body. The cartilaginous framework of the nose consists of five thin flexible plates, two upper, two lower, and the cartilage of the septum, and there are nine cartilages of the larynx (arytenoids-2, cricoid, epiglottis, thyroid, cornicula-2, and cuneiform-2).

Formula 1
Comfrey (6 parts)
Gravelroot (3 parts)
Lobelia (1 part)
Marshmallow (3 parts)
Mullein (3 parts)
Oak (6 parts)
Skullcap (1 part)
Walnut (3 parts)
Wormwood (2 parts)

Formula 2
Burdock (2 parts)
Chaparral (4 parts)
Comfrey (4 parts)
Horsetail (4 parts)
Marshmallow (2 parts)
Oat (3 parts)
Parsley (2 parts)
Plantain (2 parts)
Slippery Elm (2 parts)

Chicken Pox

Chicken pox is an acute, infectious disease that is caused by the *briareus varicellae* virus and is characterized by fever and skin eruptions that rarely burst open or crust over and seldom leave a scar.

Formula 1
Burdock (1 part)
Calendula (3 parts)
Cleavers (1 part)
Haw (1 part)
Oregon Grape Root (1 part)

Formula 2
Combine equal amounts of:
Boneset
Elecampane
Purple Coneflower
Yarrow

Chorea

Chorea is a convulsive nervous disease that is characterized by involuntary jerking movements, depression, irritability, and mental impairment.

Formula 1
Combine equal amounts of:
Feverfew
Lady's Slipper
Skullcap

Formula 2
Combine equal amounts of:
Cohosh, Black
Cramp Bark
Hop

Circulatory System Tonic
The circulatory system contains the blood and lymph vessels and is responsible for the circulation and transport of blood, lymph fluid, and nutrients to all parts and organs of the body. A dysfunction of the circulatory system may cause cold extremities, congestion, or various other problems.

Formula 1
Cayenne (3 parts)
Garlic (1 part)
Ginger (2 parts)
Ginseng (1 part)
Goldenseal (1 part)
Parsley (3 parts)

Formula 2
Foot Soak.
Combine equal amounts of:
Cinnamon
Epsom Salt
Ginger
Pepper

Colds
Colds are viruses that infect the respiratory system and may be characterized by coughing, chills, muscle aches, sneezing, sniffles, sore throat, and runny nose.

Formula 1
Garlic (6 parts)
Parsley (1 part)
Rosehip (6 parts)
Rosemary (1 part)
Watercress (1 part)

Formula 2
Black Haw (1 part)
Burdock (1 part)
Calendula (3 parts)
Cleavers (1 part)
Oregon Grape Root (1 part)

Congestion
Congestion is an abnormal or excessive accumulation of blood that can occur in an organ or any part of the body.

Formula 1
Atractylode (3 parts)
Cardamom (3 parts)
Coix (4 parts)
Cumin (3 parts)
Kudzu (4 parts)
Magnolia (3 parts)
Mint (2 parts)
Mushroom (4 parts)
Orange peel (1 part)

Formula 2
Asafoetida (3 parts)
Atractylode (3 parts)
Black pepper (2 parts)
Caraway (2 parts)
Cumin (2 parts)
Dandelion (2 parts)
Ginger (1 part)
Orange peel (2 parts)
Long Pepper (2 parts)

Conjunctivitis
An acute, infectious condition of the conjunctiva (delicate membrane that lines the eyelids and covers the eyeball), and characterized by inflammation, a pinkish coloring of the conjunctiva, itching, and usually discharge. The following formulas, are for **internal uses** only. *Don't* put into eyes!

Formula 1
Agrimony (½ part)
Blueberry (4 parts)
Buckbean (½ part)
Eyebright (3 parts)
Raspberry leaves (2 parts)

Formula 2
Bayberry (1 part)
Blueberry (3 parts)
Eyebright (3 parts)
Goldenseal (1 part)
Raspberry leaves (2 parts)

Constipation
Acute or chronic constipation is the infrequent or difficult evacuation of the feces due to intestinal sluggishness and may be caused by lack of exercise, excessive use of laxatives, poor eating habits, certain medications, or nervous tension. Regularity of bowel evacuation is extremely important, and though variation in regularity does occur, evacuation of the bowels in any given person should normally take place at the same usual intervals. Consult a healthcare professional if constipation is severe or prolonged. Eating a high fiber diet and getting plenty of exercise can help reduce or eliminate defacation problems.

Formula 1
Cinnamon (1 part)
Fennel (½ part)
Marshmallow (1/2 part)
Rhubarb (6 parts)
Slippery Elm (1 part)

Formula 2
Cayenne (⅛ part)
Dandelion (½ part)
Fennel (½ part)
Ginger (⅛ part)
Marshmallow (½ part)

Cough
Coughing is a sudden, noisy expulsion of air from the lungs that can either be dry or contain expectorant, and may be caused by the inhalation or aspiration of an irritant substance, compression of the bronchi, obstruction (nasopharnyx), or acid reflux.

Formula 1	Formula 2
Anise (8 parts)	Cherry, Wild (4 parts)
Cherry, Wild (8 parts)	Loquat leaves (6 parts)
Cranesbill (8 parts)	Yerba Santa (6 parts)
Licorice (16 parts)	Osha (5 parts)
Lobelia (2 parts)	Coltsfoot (4 parts)
Lungwort (10 parts)	Licorice (3 parts)
Moss, Irish (4 parts)	Mullein (3 parts)

Cramps
Cramps are painful spasmodic muscular contractions that can occur with any muscle (gastrointestinal, leg, uterine, etc.). Cramps occurring in the legs can be quite painful and are sometimes due to a deficiency in calcium, too much or not enough exercise, or stress. To relieve a muscle cramp in the leg, extend the leg out as far as possible with the toes pointing as far backward as possible (this extends and helps relax the calf muscle) and lightly massage the area until the cramp dissipates.

Formula 1	Formula 2
Cardamom (¼part)	Burdock (2 parts)
Cayenne (¼ part)	Chaparral (4 parts)
Cramp bark (1 part)	Horsetail (4 parts)
Horsetail (4 parts)	Marshmallow (2 parts)
Skullcap (½ part)	Parsley (2 parts)
Slippery Elm (2 parts)	Plantain (2 parts)

Cystitis
Cystitis is a urinary tract infection (UTI) caused by a bacteria, that can occur in recurrent bouts, and may be caused by injuries, irritation, gonorrhea, etc., and is characterized by bladder inflammation, granular-like cysts in the bladder and urinary tract, infection, pain an burning sensation on urination, frequent need to urinate, and urethral pain. If left untreated, a UTI can travel to the kidneys where it can cause a range of serious complications. To protect against cystitis, urinate when you feel the need (don't hold it in), and increase your water intake throughout the day to flush the urinary system of any toxins. Decreased estrogen levels, or the use of diaphragms or spermicidal jelly may also cause UTIs.

<u>Formula 1</u>
Chamomile (½ part)
Dandelion (½ part)
Lovage (1 part)
Parsley (1 part)
Uva-Ursi (2 parts)

<u>Formula 2</u>
Buchu (1 part)
Ginger (½ part)
Gravelroot (1 part)
Parsley (1 part)
Uva-Ursi (½ part)

Depression
Depression is an absence of cheerfulness and can take many forms including agitation, panic, the feeling of impending doom, uneasiness, and worry. Seek immediate medical attention if depression is severe and/or associated with suicidal thoughts or tendencies. The following formulas are for mild to moderate depression only.

<u>Formula 1</u>
Astragalus (4 parts)
Bupleurum (1 part)
Ginger (1 part)
Hop (1 part)
Licorice (2 parts)
Lemon Balm (4 parts)
Mint (2 parts)

<u>Formula 2</u>
Betony (1 part)
Cayenne (½ part)
Cohosh, Black (½ part)
Ginger (½ part)
Hop (1 part)
St. John's Wort (4 parts)
Valerian (2 parts)

Diarrhea
Diarrhea is an abnormal frequency of the fecal discharge and is caused by an infection of the gastrointestinal tract, and is characterized by dehydration, electrolyte loss, intestinal cramps, loose watery (sometimes mucous and bloody) stools, nausea, and occasionally vomiting. Drink plenty of fluids to replace lost electrolytes, and make sure to avoid cold drinks as the digestive system's process is assisted by warmth. Drinking warm water sweetened with honey will help replace lost fluids.

<u>Formula 1</u>
Cinnamon (¼ part)
Oak (1 part)
Plantain (3 parts)
Potentilla (4 parts)
Raspberry leaves (½ part)

<u>Formula 2</u>
Birch bark (4 parts)
Cranesbill (4 parts)
Ginger (3 parts)
Oak (4 parts)
Pomegranate (8 parts)

Digestive System Tonic
Digestion is an amazingly complex process by which food is transformed into energy of which the body uses to make it run efficiently. Many digestive complaints can be traced to problems such as insufficient enzyme production or an unhealthy chemical environment that either destroys the enzymes before they have a chance to work or neutralizes them so they can't work, often resulting in indigestion, nausea, and intestinal complaints.

<u>Formula 1</u>
Anise (2 parts)
Calamus (4 parts)
Centaury (2 parts)
Dandelion (2 parts)
Gentian (4 parts)
Goldenseal (¼ part)
Licorice (1 part)
Mugwort (1 part)
Slippery Elm (1 part)

<u>Formula 2</u>
Calamus (4 parts)
Centaury (2 parts)
Dandelion (1 part)
Fennel (1 part)
Gentian (4 parts)
Ginger (1 part)
Goldenseal (2 parts)
Licorice (½ part)
Orange peel (2 parts)

Diphtheria
Diphtheria is an extremely contagious, often fatal, disease caused by the corynebacterium *diphtheriae bacillus* and characterized by anemia, exhaustion (extreme), high fever, insufficiency (cardiac), grayish patches in the mouth and throat, larynx and pharynx swelling, and possible vomiting.

<u>Formula 1</u>
Gargle/mouth rinse.
Combine equal parts of:
Mullein
Oak
Persimmon bark

<u>Formula 2</u>
Agrimony (½ part)
Bayberry (¼part)
Cayenne (⅛ part)
Mullein (½ part)
Myrrh (½ part)
Raspberry leaves (½ part)

Douche
Administered vaginally, a douche will cleanse, disinfect, and soothe vaginal problems. Prepare a decoction or infusion. Strain and cool to body temperature. Fill a douche bulb, insert it into the vagina and squeeze slowly and gently until all the formula is expressed into the vaginal cavity (it is best to do this while straddling the toilet, standing in the bathtub, or lying down with a container such as a bedpan underneath you, as the formula will run back out of the vagina). Avoid using a douche if you are pregnant or suspect you are pregnant.

Formula 1
Birch (1 part)
Moss, Irish (1 part)
Oak (4 parts)
Plantain (1 part)
Sage (1 part)

Formula 2
Alumroot (1 part)
Myrrh (2 parts)
Myrtle (4 parts)
Rosemary (4 parts)
Yarrow (4 parts)

Dysmenorrhea
Dysmenorrhea is painful and difficult menstruation accompanied by congestion in the uterus, and can be caused by blood clots, pelvic lesions, or ovarian problems, and is characterized by spasmodic uterine contractions.

Formula 1
Cohosh, Black (1 part)
Cramp Bark (1 part)
Ginger (½ part)
Lobelia (½ part)
Squaw Vine (1 part)

Formula 2
Angelica (1 part)
Chamomile (1 part)
Cramp Bark (1 part)
Ginger (½part)
Raspberry leaves (2 parts)

Formula 3
Chamomile (1 part)
Cramp Bark (2 parts)
Lily, Yellow Pond (2 parts)
Squaw Vine (4 parts)
Wild Yam (1 part)

Eczema
Eczema is a chronic inflammatory skin disease that can be dry or moist and is generally characterized by small watery blisters, the development of scaly and crusty patches, and scaling, flaking, drying, and cracking of the skin. Eczema is accompanied by a burning sensation of the skin, fever, itching, and restlessness.

Formula 1
Chaparral (2 parts)
Garlic (1 part)
Ginger (1 part)
Ginseng (1 part)
Goldenseal (1 part)
Licorice (1 part)
Purple Coneflower (2 parts)
Sarsaparilla (1 part)
Sassafras (1 part)
Yellow Dock (1 part)

Formula 2
Burdock (1 part)
Centaury (1 part)
Chaparral (2 parts)
Dock (1 part)
Fumitory (½ part)
Garlic (1 part)
Marshmallow (1 part)
Sunflower seeds (1 part)
Yarrow (1 part)

Edema

Edema is due to the decreased excretion of water and electrolytes by the kidneys which leads to an increase of extracellular body fluid or an unusually large amount of fluid in the intercellular tissue spaces of the body, and may be due to congestive heart failure (CHF) (which is one of the most dangerous causes of edema), insufficient lymphatic drainage, deficiency of protein in the blood, and inflammation. Edema is characterized by temporary swelling in any part of the body (i.e. ankles, feet, legs) due to the escape of fluid into a part or tissue. To protect against edema, the use of diuretic herbs that act directly on the kidneys or by inhibiting salt reabsorption in body tissues may prove helpful. Consult a healthcare professional prior to the use of any diuretics if you have congestive heart failure (CHF).

Formula 1
Birch (1 part)
Dandelion (2 parts)
Juniper berries (2 parts)
Nettle (1 part)
Rosemary (1 part)
Shave Grass (2 parts)

Formula 2
Broom (1 part)
Buchu (1 part)
Couch Grass (1 part)
Hydrangea (1 part)
Parsley (8 parts)
Uva-Ursi (1 part)

Enuresis

Enuresis is urinary incontinence or the inability to restrain urine, which results in the involuntary discharge of urine. Nocturnal enuresis or bed-wetting is the involuntary discharge of urine at night or during sleep. For nocturnal enuresis, formulas should be administered prior to 3 p.m. to ensure emptying of the bladder before bedtime.

Formula 1
Combine equal amounts of:
Horsetail
Raspberry leaf
Yarrow
Add one of the following herbs:
Buchu, corn silk, oat straw, or parsley

Formula 2
Ginger (1 part)
Goldenseal (3 parts)
Lily, Yellow Pond (1 part)
Poplar (1 part)
Uva-Ursi (1 part)
Yarrow (1 part)

Epilepsy

Epilepsy is a chronic, functional condition characterized by brief convulsive seizures in which there is often a loss of consciousness. The attacks come in succession, vary in intensity and frequency, and can last from 5 to 20 minutes.

Formula 1
Combine equal parts of:
Bistort
Boneset
Chamomile
Vervain

Formula 2
Bedstraw (1 part)
Mistletoe (3 parts)
Shave Grass (3 parts)
Valerian (2 parts)
Wormwood (1 part)

Erectile Dysfunction
Erectile dysfunction is impotence or the failure to attain an erection. This lack of copulative power or virility is usually due to paralysis of the motor nerves, lesions (central nervous system), a mental complex, a perineal nerve injury, certain medications, or some other condition.

Formula 1
Bee Pollen (3 parts)
Bladderwrack (3 parts)
Gotu Kola (2 parts)
Oat (2 parts)
Sarsaparilla (1 part)

Formula 2
Damiana (½ part)
Ginseng (1 part)
Morinda (2 parts)
Muirapuama (1 part)
Saw Palmetto (½ part)

Formula 3
Astragalus (2 parts)
Ginseng (2 parts)
Licorice (2 parts)
Sassafras (1 part)
Yohimbe (½ part)

Erysipelas
Erysipelas is an infectious skin condition that can occur on various parts of the body, and is characterized by lesions, itching, redness, small blisters, and inflammation.

Formula 1
External Use.
Indigo (5 parts)
Myrrh (2 parts)
Purple Coneflower (2 parts)
Witch Hazel (50 parts)

Formula 2
Bladderwrack or Kelp (½ part)
Cayenne (½ part)
Cohosh, Black (2 parts)
Garlic (4 parts)
Valerian (3 parts)

Eye Tonic
Eyes are the organs of vision and our windows to the world. Within each eye are numerous blood vessels; the optic and ciliary nerves, delicate connective tissues, the cornea, which is composed of five layers; the retina. or internal coat which is primarily composed of nerve tissue, is made up of three layers, and is one of the layers of the cornea; the iris, which varies in color according to pigment; the pupil, which is composed of smooth muscular fibers and dilates or contracts depending on the source of light; the eye lens; and numerous other wonderments. Aging can make us more vulnerable to poor vision due to the fact that the retina responds more slowly to changes in light. Other problems such as cataracts or diabetes can also cause vision disturbances. The following formulas are for **internal use** only. *Don't* put into eyes!

Formula 1
Bayberry (1 part)
Blueberry (4 parts)
Cayenne (½ part)
Eyebright (2 parts)
Goldenseal (1 part)
Raspberry (2 parts)

Formula 2
Combine equal amounts of:
Blueberry
Eyebright
Goldenseal
Lichen, Usnea
Purple Coneflower
Raspberry

Fatigue
Fatigue is usually described as tiredness and feelings of lethargy that often result from overexertion.

Formula 1
Bladderwrack (1 part)
Cayenne (1 part)
Ginger (1 part)
Ginseng, Siberian (2 parts)
Gotu Kola (1 part)
Mint (1 part)

Formula 2
Astragalus (2 parts)
Ginger (1 part)
Ginseng (2 parts)
Goldenseal (½ part)
Kelp (1 part)
Sarsaparilla (1 part)

Fever
A fever is a sign that the body is fervently manufacturing white blood cells to protect against bacterial and viral invaders of the body, and it may be some consolation to know that with each infection successfully conquered, the body' recuperative ability as well as the body's resistance and capacity to withstand any additional invasion increases. Elevation of body temperature, drowsiness, accelerated or feeble pulse rate, clammy or hot dry skin, restlessness, debility, and occasional delirium are characteristic of fever.

Formula 1
Cinnamon (2 parts)
Ginger (2 parts)
Licorice (1 part)
Peony (2 parts)

Formula 2
Cayenne (¼ part)
Centaury (½ part)
Hyssop (½ part)
Raspberry leaves (½ part)

Formula 3
Cayenne (¼part)
Cherry, Wild (1 part)
Cinchona (2 parts)
Cinnamon (¼ part)

Fibroids
Fibroids are benign tumors composed primarily of fibrous tissue that can develop and grow in the mammary glands (breasts), the uterus, and other places such as the lungs or nares (openings to the nasal cavity). The growths of breast and uterine fibroids are usually associated with high levels of estrogen in the body, and their size is often greatly reduced, possibly even disappearing after menopause. Uterine fibroids may be characterized by menorrhagia or pain, and can sometimes grow

so large that they interfere with other organs. Fibrocystic breasts or benign breast disease is a condition affecting the female mammary glands, which may be characterized by tender to painful breasts that feel lumpy due to inflamed fibrous tissue and benign cysts, with symptoms having a tendency to worsen just prior to the onset of menstruation. To protect against or reduce fibroids, avoid alcohol, caffeinated beverages (i.e. coffee, cola, tea), chocolate, dairy products, poultry, red meat, and other mucus encouraging foods, switch to a diet low in saturated fats, and increase your daily intake of fresh water, fruits, vegetables, and whole grains. Also, supplementation with calcium, iodine, magnesium, selenium, and vitamins A, B, C, and E may be helpful.

Formula 1
Cayenne (¼ part)
Licorice (1 part)
Slippery Elm (½ part)
Uva-Ursi (½ part)
White Water Lily (½ part)

Formula 2
Ginger (½ part)
Gravelroot (1 part)
Parsley (1 part)
Purple Coneflower (1 part)
Uva-Ursi (1 part)

Flatulence

Flatulence is characterized by a distention (enlargement) of the stomach or the intestines with air or gases, and often results in the act of expelling air or gas from the rectum. On average, a normal person will pass gas approximately twelve to fourteen times per day. Flatulence may be caused by swallowing air while chewing food or gum with your mouth open, dentures that don't fit well, eating too fast, or excessive talking while eating. Also, if you have recently switched to a diet high in fiber, or have started eating lots of fruits, legumes, and vegetables you may experience more flatulence for the next few weeks while your digestive system adapts. Eating slowly, chewing your food thoroughly with your mouth closed, and avoiding excessive conversation while dining may help reduce episodes of flatulence.

Formula 1
Cayenne (⅛ part)
Dandelion (½ part)
Fennel (½ part)
Ginger (⅛ part)

Formula 2
Chamomile (2 parts)
Fennel (2 parts)
Mint (3 parts)
Valerian (1 part)

Gallbladder Tonic

The gallbladder is the pear-shaped reservoir for the bile which is located on the under surface of the liver. Occasionally the gallbladder can become obstructed, take on a fish-scale-like appearance due to small cysts, or become constricted resulting in increased inflow of bile and decreased outflow.

Formula 1
Alder (1 part)
Cascara Sagrada (2 parts)
Cleavers (1 part)
Gentian (4 parts)
Mint (8 parts)

Formula 2
Cascara Sagrada (2 parts)
Cayenne (½ part)
Celery seed (1 part)
Dandelion (4 parts)
Licorice (2 parts)
Wild Yam (1 part)

Gallstones

Gallstones are biliary concretions, usually of cholesterin (a fat-like pearly substance that crystallizes in the form of needle-like crystals), that form in the bile duct or gallbladder. They are often characterized by inflammation and pain. To protect against gallstones, increase your water intake throughout the day, switch to a low-fat diet, and exercise daily. One of the functions is to produce bile, and a yearly liver cleanse will help it to function more efficiently (see formulas under Liver), and as a result will support and preserve bile duct and gallbladder health, especially if you are exposed to toxins on a continuous basis.

Formula 1
Dandelion (1 part)
Ginger (½ part)
Gravelroot (3 parts)
Lemon Balm (1 part)
Licorice (½part)
Marshmallow (2 parts)
Parsley (1 part)

Formula 2
Cleavers (1 part)
Flax (1 part)
Fringetree (½ part)
Ginger (½ part)
Juniper berries (1 part)
Parsley (1 part)
Wild Yam (½ part)

Gastritis

Gastritis is an inflammation of the stomach that is characterized by abdominal bloating, alteration in the quantity of gastric juice secretion, appetite loss, indigestion, mucus secretion (excessive), nausea, pain, and vomiting.

Formula 1
Agrimony (½ part)
Cayenne (⅛ part)
Marshmallow (½ part)
Raspberry leaves (1 part)

Formula 2
Calamus (¼ part)
Dandelion (1 part)
Goldenseal (¼ part)
Slippery Elm (1 part)

Gastrointestinal System Tonic

The gastrointestinal system is comprised of the stomach and intestine, and there are few problems of the gastrointestinal tract that cannot be prevent by a properly balanced diet. People with gastrointestinal problems often eat too much red meat and too little dietary fiber, consume too much sugar (refined carbohydrates) and too much fat, and/or they abuse substances such as alcohol or drugs. Also, a diet insufficient in essential vitamins, minerals and fatty acids can cause potentially serious problems such as gastroenteritis and gastroduodenitis. To protect against gastrointestinal problems and restore gastrointestinal health, it is important to avoid stress and tension, exercise regularly, eat a diet that is high in fiber, drink plenty of water to flush the toxins from your system, and get plenty of sleep.

Formula 1
Centaury (½ part)
Dandelion (1 part)
Ginger (¼ part)
Goldenseal (½ part)
Motherwort (1 part)

Formula 2
Chamomile (2 parts)
Juniper (1 part)
Lavender (4 parts)
Mint (2 parts)
Thyme (6 parts)

Glandular Tonic
The glands, crucial to a healthy system, are dependant upon the nourishment of vitamins and minerals to maintain their efficient functions. These vitamins and minerals supply the raw substances needed to aid the glands in producing their own hormones (secretions). These vital secretions are necessary for growth and health, and have an effect on the entire system. There are numerous glands located throughout the body including the pituitary gland (located at the base of the brain), the adrenal glands (flattened glands situated near the upper end of each kidney that furnish an internal secretion of epinephrine, which has a strong effect on kidney function and growth); the pineal gland, the endocrine glands (influence metabolism and other body processes); the mammary glands (produce and secrete milk following childbirth in women, in men the mammary or breast is classified as *mammary virilis*); and the thyroid gland, which needs to be kept in perfect balance as it stimulates all of the cells. A deficiency (iodine) is a common cause of thyroid problems as are certain conditions, drugs, genetic disposition, or stress.

Adrenal Glands
Bee Pollen (3 parts)
Bladderwrack (4 parts)
Cayenne (½part)
Ginger (2 parts)
Ginseng (2 parts)
Gotu Kola (2 parts)
Licorice (2 parts)
Moss, Irish (4 parts)
Oat (2 parts)

All Glands
Angelica (2 parts)
Cohosh, Black (1 part)
Ginger (1 part)
Ginseng (2 parts)
Goldenseal (½ part)
Kelp (1 part)
Licorice (1 part)
Lobelia (1 part)
Sarsaparilla (1 part)

Mammary Glands
Chamomile (2 parts)
Cohosh, Black (4 parts)
Haw (1 part)
Licorice (3 parts)
Passionflower (1 part)
Raspberry leaves (2 parts)
Saw Palmetto (1 part)
Squaw Vine (1 part)
Wild Yam (½ part)

Gleet

Gleet is a chronic form of urethritis caused by a gonorrheal infection and characterized by dysuria (painful/difficult urination), inflammation, penile discharge (containing both mucus and pus that can sometimes be black or bloody), and urethral stricture (narrowing).

Formula 1
Chaparral (2 parts)
Marshmallow (1 part)
Oak (2 parts)
Periwinkle (4 parts)
Yarrow (1 part)

Formula 2
Burdock (1 part)
Myrrh (½ part)
Red Clover (1 part)
Slippery Elm (1 part)
Yellow Dock (1 part)

Formula 3
Buchu (1 part)
Cubeb (¼ part)
Juniper berries (¼ part)
Uva-Ursi (½ part)

Gonorrhea

Gonorrhea is a contagious, usually sexually transmitted, venereal disease characterized by genital inflammation of the mucous membranes, pain, dysuria (painful/difficult urination), and a discharge containing both mucus and pus that can sometimes be black or bloody. Gonorrhea is often associated with complications such as cystitis, orchitis, prostatitis, and urethritis.

Formula 1
Burdock (1 part)
Myrrh (½ part)
Red Clover (1 part)
Slippery Elm (1 part)
Yellow Dock (1 part)

Formula 2
Buchu (1 part)
Cubeb (¼ part)
Juniper berries (¼ part)
Purple Coneflower (2 parts)
Uva-Ursi (½ part)

Headache

There are various types of headaches, including nervous tension and regular headache. A nervous tension headache may include symptoms of pain that originates at the back of the head and moves to the front. Common causes include but are not limited to poor posture, stress, or muscle strain. A regular headache may include symptoms of a dull, throbbing of the entire head. Common causes may include but are not limited to temperature or altitude changes, congestion of the nasal passages, or illness. The following formulas are for relief of nervous tension headaches and regular headaches only. For cluster headaches and migraine, see the formulas under migraine. Note: Consult a healthcare professional if a headache does not respond to the usual dosage of an analgesic (i.e. a couple of aspirins), is brought on by physical exertion, is accompanied by dulled senses and a feeling of sedation, or if there is an onset of headaches (severe) after the age of 40, as this may be a chief symptom of an imminent stroke. The majority of strokes (apoplectic) are often preceded by what is called a mini-stroke, and the most common, characteristic symptom of this is a severe headache. If you experience any of these symptoms, prompt treatment could ward off a possible stroke.

Formula 1
Combine equal amounts of:
Catnip
Lady's Slipper
Skullcap

Formula 2
Combine equal amounts of:
Betony
Mint
Rosemary

Heart Disease
Heart disease is a functional, mechanical, or organic condition of the heart. It may originate in the muscular tissue of the heart (myocardial), the nervous system (neurogenic), or va1vular (aortic , mitral, pulmonary, tricuspid). A history of problems early in life such as diabetes, a diet high in saturated fats, hypercholesteremia, hypertension, a sedentary lifestyle, or stress (intense) may put you at risk of developing heart disease later on. To lower cholesterol levels and protect against heart disease, switch to a low fat diet, eat more fruits and vegetables, and exercise daily.

Formula 1
Chamomile (1 part)
Garlic (8 parts)
Lily of the Valley (2 parts)
Parsley (8 parts)
Valerian (1 part)

Formula 2
Arnica (1 part)
Borage (1 part)
Burnet (3 parts)
Lemon Balm (3 parts)
Rue (2 parts)

Hemorrhage
A hemorrhage is the profuse escape of blood from the arteries, blood vessels, kidneys, lungs, uterus, etc. Shock (hypovolemia) can occur with the copious loss of blood, and may be characterized by anxiety, clammy skin, feeble pulse, hypotension, pallor, restlessness, slowed respiration, and unconsciousness (possible) .

Formula 1
Bayberry (1 part)
Calendula (1 part)
Ginger (½ part)
Loosestrife, Purple (2 parts)
White Water Lily (1 part)

Formula 2
Cranesbill (4 parts)
Haw (1 part)
Raspberry leaves (4 parts)
Shepherd's Purse (3 parts)
Witch Hazel leaves (2 parts)

Hemorrhoids
Hemorrhoids are swollen veins in the mucous membranes of the rectum that may extend beyond the anus, and can be caused by poor diet (which often leads to constipation and straining with bowel movements), abdominal muscle weakness, liver problems, a sedentary lifestyle, pregnancy, and/or stress or fatigue (which can cause bowel muscle constriction). Inflammation, itching, pain, a burning

sensation, and occasional bleeding during bowel movements characterize hemorrhoids. Ointments applied topically and cool sitz baths several times daily may help soothe inflamed tissues and reduce discomfort.

Formula 1
Cascara Sagrada (1 part)
Chicory (1 part)
Dandelion (2 parts)
Licorice (½ part)
Oregon Grape Root (1 part)

Formula 2
External Uses.
Bayberry (1 part)
Comfrey (1 part)
Goldenseal (1 part)
Witch Hazel (2 parts)

Formula 3
Goldenseal (1 part)
Mullein (2 parts)
Slippery Elm (3 parts)
Witch Hazel (3 parts)

Herpes

Herpes is an acute, contagious, recurring, inflammatory skin and mucous membrane disease caused by the *briareus varicellae* virus (yes, the same virus that causes chicken pox). Once this virus enters the cells, it becomes integrated with cell DNA, settles in the nerves, and becomes a permanent fixture. After the virus has established itself, acute flare-ups can be triggered by fever, exposure to sunlight, colds, sore throat, stress, or certain foods or supplements. The herpes virus is highly contagious during outbreaks, but in some instances, this virus can transmitted when there are no lesions present.

Formula 1
Combine equal amounts of:
Dock
Gentian
Goldenseal
Lemon Balm
Mushroom, Hoelen
Purple Coneflower

Formula 2
Burdock (1 part)
Calendula (3 parts)
Cleavers (1 part)
Dock (1 part)
Garlic (½ part)
Haw (1 part)
Oregon Grape Root (1 part)

Hyperglycemia

Hyperglycemia is a higher than normal concentration of glucose (sugar) in the blood. The best way to balance the level of glucose in your blood is to maintain a balanced diet by eating small, frequent meals that consist of low sugar foods, and also making sure that all but your final meal of the day includes protein, which slows glucose metabolism.

Formula 1
Birch leaves (6 parts)
Blueberry leaves (7 parts)
Eucalyptus (5 parts)
Fumitory (5 parts)
Milk Thistle (7 parts)
Nettle (1 part)

Formula 2
Birch leaves (5 parts)
Blueberry leaves (6 parts)
Broom (4 parts)
Eucalyptus leaves (4 parts)
Fumitory (4 parts)
Milk Thistle (6 parts)

Hypertension

Hypertension is abnormally high tension, especially high blood pressure levels, and is usually caused by cholesterol plaque, which leads to arterial stricture (narrowing), but can also be caused by lifestyle habits or heredity. According to the American Heart Association, about half of all persons over the age of 55 have been diagnosed with high blood pressure, although it is by no means restricted to the middle and upper age brackets. Often existing unknown for years with no symptoms, hypertension can increase the risk of heart disease, primarily coronary artery disease (CAD), kidney failure, or stroke (apoplectic). To protect against hypertension, lose excess weight, reduce or eliminate salt, exercise daily, switch to a low fat diet, increase your intake of fresh fruits, vegetables, and whole grains, and have your healthcare professional monitor your blood pressure as part of your regular medical care. Consult your healthcare professional if you experience blurred vision, dizziness, facial flushing, headache, tinnitus, and frequent nosebleeds, as these symptoms may be an indication of hypertension (severe). The following formulas are for mild to moderate hypertension only.

Formula 1
Ginger (2 parts)
Ginseng (3 parts)
Hawthorn (6 parts)
Motherwort (3 parts)
Yarrow (1 part)

Formula 2
Anise (1 part)
Caraway (1 part)
Chamomile (2 parts)
Fennel (1 part)
Mint (2 parts)

Hypotension

Hypotension is reduced or diminished blood pressure levels and can be caused by such things as exhaustion, a severe allergic reaction, malnutrition, or profuse blood loss. Orthostatic hypotension sometimes occurs when a person changes from a supine (lying down) to an upright position. If this occurs, simply pause for a moment at a sitting position before standing. Severe hypotension can occur due to an injury resulting in profuse blood loss, or a severe allergic reaction where the histamines cause extreme blood vessel dilation, which could result in cardiovascular collapse. Obtain immediate medical attention if you experience severe hypotension. If blood pressure is low due to malnutrition or lack of nutrients, the following formulas may help balance blood pressure levels, improve circulation, supply needed energy, reduce tension, and improve appetite and digestion.

Formula 1
Ginger (2 parts)
Ginseng (3 parts)
Hawthorn (6 parts)
Motherwort (3 parts)
Yarrow (1 part)

Formula 2
Anise (1 part)
Caraway (1 part)
Chamomile (2 parts)
Fennel (1 part)
Mint (2 parts)

Hysteria
Hysteria is a psychoneurosis that may be characterized by anxiety, choking sensation, convulsions, fever, hallucinations, a lack of control over acts or emotions, morbid self-consciousness, imitation of various diseases, pain and tenderness in the head, paralysis, sensory disturbances, spasm, urodialysis, and vasomotor and visual disturbances.

Formula 1
Astragalus (4 parts)
Bupleurum (4 parts)
Chaste Tree (4 parts)
Cyperus (3 parts)
Ginger (3 parts)
Haw (3 parts)
Licorice (3 parts)
Peony (3 parts)
Poria (7 parts)

Formula 2
Buckbean (4 parts)
Chamomile (1 part)
Fennel (3 parts)
Garlic (1 part)
Lavender (1 part)
Mint (1 part)
Skullcap (1 part)
Valerian (2 part)
Yarrow (3 parts)

Indigestion
Indigestion, both a feeling and a physiological state, is due to a faulty digestive system, and may be caused by poor eating habits, ingesting highly acidic foods such as citrus or tomatoes, stress, eating too fast or chewing with your mouth open and swallowing too much air, consuming foods that are too spicy or foods that are either too cold or too hot, a lack of digestive enzymes, poor food combinations, allergies (food), infection (fungal), ulcers, smoking, hernia (hiatal), gallbladder or liver problems, hypothyroidism, and/or eating a high carbohydrate diet. Cramps, gas, bloating, heartburn, constipation or diarrhea, nausea, pain, and vomiting characterize the feeling of indigestion, and the physiological state is one of defective digestion. Left untreated, indigestion may lead to problems such as gastritis or acid reflux (characterized by a burning sensation in the esophagus). Consult a healthcare professional if you have chronic indigestion, as this may be a symptom of a more serious problem. Keeping track of what you eat, eating smaller portions, and avoiding the consumption of a large or heavy meal prior to bedtime may help reduce indigestion.

Formula 1
Fennel (3 parts)
Ginger (3 parts)
Hawthorn (6 parts)
Marshmallow (2 parts)
Mint (3 parts)
Wild Yam (6 parts)

Formula 2
Angelica (1 part)
Calamus (1 part)
Dandelion (1 part)
Gentian (1 part)
Ginger (½ part)
Valerian (1 part)

Formula 3
Calamus (¼ part)
Dandelion (1 part)
Goldenseal (¼ part)
Orange peel (2 parts)
Slippery Elm (1 part)

Infection
An infection results when pathogenic organisms invade the body tissues. These organisms can transmit infection through the air (air-borne) by means of dust particles, can occur in clinic and hospital settings, can be acquired through the placenta, and can be transferred via small drops of sputum thrown into the air through coughing, sneezing or talking.

Formula 1
Garlic (6 parts)
Parsley (1 part)
Rosehip (6 parts)
Rosemary (1 part)
Watercress (1 part)

Formula 2
Cramp Bark (1 part)
Damiana (1 part)
Purple Coneflower (2 parts)
Saw Palmetto (2 parts)
Yarrow (1 part)

Inflammation
Inflammation is a condition in which tissue reacts to an injury, and is characterized by heat, redness, congestion (or a stoppage of blood in that area), pain, and swelling. A cool compress may ease discomfort and help reduce swelling.

Formula 1
Cayenne (¼ part)
Chaparral (3 parts)
Marshmallow (1 part)
Purple Coneflower (3 parts)

Formula 2
Calendula (1 part)
Comfrey (½ part)
Mugwort (½ part)
Plantain (½ part)

Formula 3
Bayberry (1 part)
Ginger (½ part)
Raspberry leaves (1 part)

Influenza
Influenza or flu is an acute, infectious, epidemic condition caused by a virus. The varieties of influenza viruses are ever changing (mutating), which can make successful vaccination difficult. Flu vaccinations are often recommended for those persons in high-risk groups such as those with chronic cardiovascular, metabolic, or pulmonary conditions; adults over the age of 65; and residents and staff of hospitals, nursing homes, or other chronic care facilities. Persons with known hypersensitivity or anaphylactic reaction to eggs should avoid taking the influenza vaccine. Achiness, chills, cough,

convulsions (possible), debility, delirium, diarrhea, dry throat, fever, gastrointestinal problems, headache, insomnia, muscle and joint pain, nausea, nervous conditions, respiratory conditions, sore throat, and vomiting characterize influenza. To protect against contracting the flu virus, wash your hands thoroughly and often, avoid stress, reduce or discontinue smoking and alcoholic beverages, and boost your immune system by eating a balanced diet, getting plenty of sleep, and exercising daily. At the onset of the flu, taking a hot epsom salt or sea salt bath for about twenty minutes just prior to bed will encourage ephidrosis (heavy perspiration) which aids the body in eliminating toxins.

Formula 1
Cayenne (¼ part)
Ginger (½ part)
Goldenrod (2 parts)
Pleurisy Root (2 parts)

Formula 2
Combine equal amounts of:
Boneset
Purple Coneflower
Yarrow

Insomnia
Insomnia is the body's inability to relax during the night, and is generally caused by stressors during the day. Individual sleep requirements vary, and while six to eight hours of sleep each night is considered to be normal, some people do well with only four or five hours of sleep, while others may need nine or ten to feel rested. It's estimated that nearly 30 million people have chronic insomnia, and nearly everyone at some point in their life has experienced an occasional bout of sleeplessness that lasts a day or even a couple of weeks. The lack of sleep can cause immune system problems, memory/cognitive problems, and affect your overall health. Exercising earlier in the day, learning relaxation techniques, keeping a sleep log to help you identify and correct behaviors and patterns that affect your sleep, reducing or eliminating alcoholic or caffeinated beverages with evening meals, going to bed and waking at the same time every day, and winding down for about an hour or two prior to bedtime may relieve occasional insomnia. Consult your healthcare professional if insomnia is recurrent or lasts for longer than two weeks.

Formula 1
Hop (1 part)
Mint (1 part)
Passionflower (1 part)
Valerian (½ part)

Formula 2
Evening Primrose (6 parts)
Hop (3 parts)
Lavender (4 parts)
Valerian (1 part)

Formula 3
Anise (1 parts)
Chamomile (2 parts)
Dill (1 part)
Hops (1 part)

Intestinal Tonic

The intestine is a membranous tube the extends from the stomach to the anus. The first portion of the intestine is called the small intestine, which is about twenty feet long and includes the duodenum (first portion of the small intestine), the ileum (the lower portion of the small intestine extending from the jejunum to the cecum), and the jejunum (the portion of the small intestine that extends from the duodenum to the ileum). The large intestine is about five feet long and comprises the cecum (the dilated intestinal pouch into which open the appendix, colon, and ileum), the colon (portion of the large intestine that extends from the cecum to the rectum), and the (the lower portion of the large intestine extending from the sigmoid flexure [curved part] to the colon).

<u>Formula 1</u>
Barberry root (1 part)
Cascara Sagrada (2 parts)
Ginger (1 part)
Goldenseal (1 part)
Raspberry leaves (1 part)
Rhubarb (1 part)
Slippery Elm (1 part)

<u>Formula 2</u>
Chamomile (1 part)
Cranesbill (1 part)
Goldenseal (1 part)
Comfrey (1 part)
Marshmallow (2 parts)
Plantain (1 part)
Purple Coneflower (2 parts)

Jaundice

Jaundice, an early indication of liver congestion, is a condition caused by hyperbilirubinemia and the deposit of bile pigment in the mucous membranes and skin, which results in a yellowish appearance.

<u>Formula 1</u>
Agrimony (½ part)
Barberry (½ part)
Cayenne (¼ part)
Cleavers (½ part)
Flax (¼ part)
Raspberry leaves (½ part)

<u>Formula 2</u>
Ash, Prickly (1 part)
Balmony (2 parts)
Elder (2 parts)
Gentian (1 part)
Goldenseal (2 parts)
Wahoo (1 part)

Kidney Stones

Kidney stones occur due to an excessive accumulation of minerals, a buildup of certain acids, various toxins, or a urinary tract infection (UTI). Many smaller stones cause no discomfort and pass easily through the urinary tract; however, those stones that are too large will cause discomfort. To protect against the formation of kidney stones, drink plenty of fresh water through the day to help flush out harmful impurities. Also, when taking calcium supplements, especially in the range of 1,000 to 1,500 mg., be sure to take them with a full eight ounce glass of water as this elevated range can cause kidney stone formation in those persons susceptible to them. If you have a history of kidney stones, consult a healthcare professional before taking any calcium supplementation.

Formula 1
Dandelion (1 part)
Ginger (½ part)
Gravelroot (3 parts)
Lemon Balm (1 part)
Licorice (½ part)
Marshmallow (2 parts)
Parsley (1 part)

Formula 2
Buchu (1 part)
Ginger (½ part)
Gravelroot (1 part)
Lobelia (½ part)
Marshmallow (2 parts)
Parsley (2 parts)
Uva-Ursi (½ part)

Laryngitis
Laryngitis is an inflammation of the vocal chords and may be caused by a sore throat, bad cold, overuse of the voice, or by contact with chemical irritants. To help ease discomfort, it is best to remain at home and rest your voice as much as possible, keep the throat moist with lozenges, drink soups and warm liquids, use a steam inhalant to moisturize and soothe throat irritation. If you have to communicate, use a pen and paper. Obtain immediate medical attention if you experience difficulty breathing or swallowing, or if your symptoms last more than three to four days.

Formula 1
Black Pepper (pinch)
Cardamom (½ part)
Cinnamon (½ part)
Ginger (4 parts)
Licorice (½ part)
Sage (4 parts)

Formula 2
Anise (8 parts)
Cherry, Wild (8 parts)
Cranesbill (8 parts)
Licorice (16 parts)
Lungwort (10 parts)
Moss, Irish (4 parts)

Laxative
Laxatives are mild or drastic substances that promote bowel evacuation. Discomfort or pain from hemorrhoids, certain medications, or poor dietary habits may result in constipation, which may require the occasional use of a laxative. Regular use of some stimulant laxatives can result in dependency. Daily exercise, switching to a high fiber diet, and drinking plenty of fresh water may help eliminate the need for laxatives. Consult a healthcare professional if laxative use promotes vomiting rather than evacuation, if constipation lasts for more than one week, or if abdominal discomfort or rectal bleeding accompanies constipation, as this could be an indication of bowel obstruction or other serious condition.

Formula 1
Anise (½ part)
Buckthorn (2 parts)
Fennel (½ part)
Moss, Irish (⅛ part)
Plantain seeds (1 part)
Sassafras (⅛ part)
Senna (4 parts)

Formula 2
Butternut (4 parts)
Cascara Sagrada (2 parts)
Cayenne (¼ part)
Ginger (½ part)
Rhubarb (1 part)
Licorice (½ part)
Moss, Irish (½ part)

Libido Tonic
The power of sexual desire is an expression of your vitality, and is the energy derived from the primitive impulses. A high protein diet, daily exercise, plenty of fruits and vegetables, and whole grains help to nourish the reproductive glands and boost your sex drive.

Formula 1
Anise (¼ part)
Astragalus (¼ part)
Coriander (¼ part)
Damiana (2 parts)
Ginseng (1 part)
Muirapuama (1 part)
Saw Palmetto (1 part)

Formula 2
Damiana (1 part)
Ginseng (1 part)
Raspberry leaves (¼ part)
Saw Palmetto (½ part)
Wild Yam (½ part)
Yellow Dock (1 part)
Yohimbe (¼ part)

Formula 3
Bee Pollen (3 parts)
Bladderwrack (4 parts)
Cayenne (½ part)
Ginger (2 parts)
Ginseng, Siberian (2 parts)
Moss, Irish (4 Parts)
Oat (2 parts)

Liver Tonic
The liver is one of the hardest working glands in the body, and is continually bombarded by chemicals, heavy metals, medications, and environmental pollutants. Some of its functions include controlling blood coagulation, filtering toxins from the blood, processing estrogen, producing bile and sex hormones, and the extraction and storage of fat, glucose, minerals, and vitamins. Even though this gland is partially self-rejuvenating, a liver that has been excessively damaged cannot support life. Early indications of liver problems can include appetite loss, fatigue, hepatitis, jaundice, nausea, skin problems, and/or vomiting.

Formula 1
Dandelion root (1 part)
Licorice (¼ part)
Mint (10 parts)
Oregon Grape Root (1 part)
Wild Yam (1 part)

Formula 2
Chicory (1 part)
Dandelion (2 parts)
Gentian (5 parts)
Speedwell (2 parts)
Woodruff (1 part)

Longevity

Longevity is the condition or quality of being long-lived. A balanced diet, adequate rest, daily exercise, plenty of fresh water, and protecting the body from chemicals and environmental pollutants may help increase longevity.

Formula 1
Ginkgo (4 parts)
Ginseng (3 parts)
Gotu Kola (2 parts)
Skullcap (1 part)

Formula 2
Bee Pollen (2 parts)
Honey (4 parts)
Propolis (1 part)
Royal Jelly (1 part)

Memory/Cognition Tonic

Memory is that mental faculty by which ideas, impressions, and sensations are recalled. Cognition is that operation of the mind by which we become aware of objects of perception or thought, including reasoning and understanding. Memory/cognitive problems can include conditions such as Alzheimer's disease and amnesia.

Formula 1
Blessed Thistle (3 parts)
Cayenne (1 part)
Ginger (1 part)
Ephedra (1 part)
Ginkgo (1 part)
Gotu Kola (3 parts)
Lobelia (½ part)
Vervain (3 parts)

Formula 2
Astragalus (2 parts)
Bladderwrack or Kelp (1 part)
Cohosh, Black (1 part)
Ginger (1 part)
Ginseng (2 parts)
Goldenseal (½ part)
Licorice (1 part)
Sarsaparilla (1 part)

Menopause

Menopause, caused by the gradual reduction of estrogen and progesterone levels in a woman's body is *not* a disease, it is a natural process that signals the close of the childbearing years and generally occurs in the late thirties to forties with the ceasing of menstruation occurring somewhere in the fifties. Menopausal symptoms, if any, may be characterized by absent or delayed periods, arrhythmia, dryness(vaginal), scanty flow, erratic cycles, mood swings, hot flashes, osteoporosis, weight gain, or depression. Phytoestrogen is an estrogenic substance contained in some plants that is *very* similar in action to the natural estrogen produced by a woman's ovaries. Estrogen protects against heart disease, osteoporosis, or other problems that may occur due to the decline of this hormone during menopause (or following a hysterectomy), which is why healthcare professionals are so quick to prescribe synthetic forms of hormonal therapy (HRT) to women experiencing the "change of life". Although synthetic HRT can be of help to some women, the drawbacks can include the increased risk of breast and endometrial cancers, circulatory problems, benign breast disease, stroke (apoplectic), and fibroids (uterine). Note: Women who have a history of estrogen dependent cancer (i.e. breast, endometrial), or those women who are at a high risk due to genetic predisposition for developing an estrogen dependant cancer should consult their physician before taking any form of HRT.

Formula 1
Angelica (2 parts)
Cohosh, Black (1 part)
Ginger (1 part)
Ginseng (2 parts)
Kelp (1 part)
Licorice (1 part)
Sarsaparilla (1 part)

Formula 2
Bethroot (3 parts)
Bladderwrack (½ part)
Damiana (2 parts)
Quaking Aspen (2 parts)
Red Clover (1 part)
Squaw Vine (2 parts)
Wild Yarn (½ part)

Menorrhagia
Menorrhagia can be caused by fibroids (uterine), hormonal changes such as menopause, or extended strenuous exercise routines all of which can bring on heavier than normal bleeding. If you experience heavier than normal flow, it is best to stay off your feet as much as possible the first day of your period, avoid alcoholic beverages (including wine), avoid any strenuous exercise, and don't lift anything heavier than a gallon of milk. Excessive menstrual flow should be checked out by your healthcare professional before trying any herbal or other alternative remedy, as it could be the symptom of a more serious condition such as cancer (endometrial).

Formula 1
Bayberry (1 part)
Calendula (1 part)
Ginger (½ part)
Loosestrife, Purple (2 parts)
White Water Lily (1 part)

Formula 2
Ash, Prickly (1 part)
Cinnamon (½ part)
Cohosh, Blue (1 part)
Raspberry leaves (2 parts)
Wild Yam (1 part)

Metabolism
Metabolism is the chemical process, transformation, or building up and breaking down of proteins, etc. by which energy is made available for the uses of the living organism. Energy represents the power expended to maintain proper body functions including circulatory, glandular, muscular tone, peristalsis, respiratory, and temperature. There are individual differences in how we metabolize and store the foods we eat, and much of this is attributed to genetics. Before puberty, girls have 10- 15% more fat than boys. After puberty, girls have almost twice the amount of fat as boys. The sex hormones that surge at puberty also seem to encourage fat storage, primarily in females. The reason for this is nature's way of protecting the mother and developing fetus from starvation in times of famine. Women tend to have lower metabolic rates than men. A stronger metabolism in addition to

their greater fat burning musculature is why men are able to lose weight faster than women. Chronic dieting, which is epidemic among women, will also make it much harder in the long run for a woman to lose the weight she wants because, in response to the forced "famine" of a calorie restricted diet, her metabolism becomes even more efficient at storing fat.

Formula 1
Alder (2 parts)
Dandelion (3 parts)
Licorice (2 parts)
Pansy (3 parts)

Formula 2
Cayenne (¼ part)
Gentian (1 part)
Kelp (1 part)
Moss, Irish (1 part)

Migraine

Migraines are due to the irregular constriction or dilatation of the brain blood vessels. The exact cause still remains a mystery, but may include a genetic predisposition, stress (intense), an allergic reaction to certain foods, or an obstruction (circulatory). Intense pain, nausea, seeing auras, sensitivity to light and noise, visual disturbances, and vomiting may characterize a migraine. Note: Consult a healthcare professional if a headache does not respond to the usual dosage of an analgesic (i.e. a couple of aspirins), is brought on by physical exertion, is accompanied by dulled senses and a feeling of sedation, or if there is an onset of headaches (severe) after the age of 40, as this may be a chief symptom of an imminent stroke. The majority of strokes (apoplectic) are often preceded by what is called a mini-stroke, and the most common, characteristic symptom of this is a severe headache. If you experience any of these symptoms, prompt treatment could ward off a possible stroke.

Formula 1
Raspberry leaves (2 parts)
Rosemary (1 part)
Skullcap (2 parts)
Vervain (1 part)
Willow (4 parts)

Formula 2
Cayenne Pepper (1 part)
Culver's Root (1 part)
Meadowsweet (4 parts)
Valerian (2 parts)
Wormwood (¼ part)

Motion Sickness

Motion sickness can occur with any form of movement such as traveling in a vehicle or vessel on land, over water or in the air, or from rides at the amusement park, and is caused when the sensory input from our eyes, inner ears, and joint, muscle, and skin receptors sends conflicting messages to the brain. Appetite loss, cold sweats, dizziness, fainting, nausea, salivation (excessive), sleepiness, vertigo, or vomiting may characterize motion sickness. To protect against motion sickness when riding in an automobile or boat , sit so you are facing the same direction that the vehicle or vessel is moving. Don't read while traveling, and avoid greasy or spicy foods prior to and during travel.

Formula 1
Cayenne (½ part)
Ginger (4 parts)
Licorice (2 parts)

Formula 2
Atractylode (3 parts)
Kudzu (4 parts)
Mint (2 parts)

Mucus

Mucus is a sticky, whitish secretion produced by goblet or chalice cells, which cover the mucous membranes. Vital for respiratory system cleansing, mucus is also present in the bile, bursal and synovial fluids, and umbilical cord. An overproduction of mucus may be associated with allergy, asthma, bronchitis, colds, emphysema, flu, pneumonia, sinusitis, or mucus-producing foods (i.e. dairy, meats, starches).

Formula 1
Cohosh, Blue (1 part)
Comfrey (1 part)
Ginger (¼ part)
Licorice (1 part)
Lobelia (⅛ part)
Pleurisy Root (½ part)

Formula 2
Cherry, Wild (4 parts)
Horehound (2 parts)
Mullein leaves (1 part)
Plantain (2 parts)
Pleurisy Root (6 parts)
Slippery Elm (2 parts)

Mumps

Mumps is an acute contagious condition caused by the *rabula inflans* virus, and is characterized by fever, headache, pain beneath the ear, and inflammation and painful swelling of the parotid gland (and sometimes the mammary glands, pancreas, ovaries, salivary glands, or testicles) which causes interference with and results in painful actions of chewing and swallowing.

Formula 1
Bayberry (1 part)
Ginger (½ part)
Raspberry leaves (1 part)

Formula 2
Cayenne (¼ part)
Marshmallow (1 part)
Purple Coneflower (3 parts)

Muscle Strain

A muscle strain can occur when there is an overexertion or overstretching of some part of the muscular system of the body. Muscles play a vital role in our life and without them we could not move. The muscular system accounts for nearly half of your body's weight, and in order for muscles to become larger and stronger, they require a regular workout. The more intense your exercise regimen, the more your muscles will build and strengthen. The following formulas are for **external use** only.

Formula 1
Combine equal amounts of:
Arnica
Calendula
Cayenne
Wintergreen

Formula 2
Combine equal amounts of:
Arnica
Balsam of Tolu
Chestnut, Horse
Peppermint

Nausea
The queasy feeling associated with nausea is due to neural connections between certain brain centers and the stomach, and may be provoked by problems such as digestive complaints, stomach problems, influenza, gallstones, noxious or strong odors, indigestion, poisoning, an overindulgence of alcohol or food, disturbing sights, ear infection, vertigo, illness such as diabetes or certain cancers, motion sickness, headache, fever, migraine, inflammations, psychological stimuli, nervous tension, loss of equilibrium, and dizziness. Certain deficiencies (nutritional) can make a person more susceptible to nausea. Persons experiencing occasional bouts of nausea may find that eating bland foods such as bread, cheese, plain pasta, or salty crackers are easier to keep down. Eating smaller portions of foods, avoiding acidic foods such as orange juice and tomato products, and staying away from foods that have a strong aroma such as fish may protect against nausea. Obtain immediate medical attention if nausea is accompanied by abdominal pain or a fever of more than 102° F.

Formula 1
Cayenne (½ part)
Ginger (4 parts)
Licorice (2 parts)

Formula 2
Atractylode (3 parts)
Kudzu (4 parts)
Mint (2 parts)

Nephritis
Nephritis is an acute or chronic condition due to a progressive, degenerative lesion that affects the renal tissues, the vascular system of the kidneys and kidney function, and may be characterized by albuminuria, anemia, debility, dysuria, edema, fever, gastrointestinal problems, headache, hematuria, hypertrophy (connective tissue, stroma), inflammation, insomnia, nervousness, and pain in the lumbar region.

Formula 1
Combine equal amounts of:
Cleavers
Juniper berries
Poplar bark
Uva-Ursi

Formula 2
Combine equal amounts of:
Buchu
Cleavers
Juniper berries
Uva-Ursi

Nervous System Tonic

The nervous system controls the circulatory, digestive, and respiratory functions of the body, as well as the emotions. It is the only system in the body that cannot regenerate damaged or destroyed cells. For example, the continued abuse of alcohol or certain drugs, which can damage and destroy the cells of the brain, could result in permanent harm. We've all heard how stress can worsen and even cause problems in the body; therefore, the time has come to seriously consider theories concerning the role of emotions and illness. When the nervous system is not functioning properly, the body can be prone to various types of nervous conditions including anxiety, depression, fatigue, headache, insomnia, migraine pain, or stress.

Formula 1
Catnip (2 parts)
Chamomile (2 parts)
Hawthorn (1 part)
Lady's Slipper (1 part)
Lemon Balm (2 parts)
Valerian (2 parts)

Formula 2
Betony (1 part)
Cayenne (⅛ part)
Cohosh, Blue (1 part)
Goldenseal (1 part)
Rosemary (½ part)
Skullcap (2 parts)

Neuralgia

Neuralgia is characterized by recurring, intense pain that extends along the course of one or more nerves. It can occur anywhere in the body, and may be due to numerous conditions including angina, diabetes, gout, malaria, or syphilis.

Formula 1
Anise (1 part)
Ash, Prickly (1 part)
Lady's Slipper (2 parts)
Lobelia (¼ part)
Pleurisy Root (1 part)
Skullcap (1 part)

Formula 2
Betony (2 parts)
Raspberry leaves (2 parts)
Rosemary (1 part)
Skullcap (2 parts)
Vervain (1 part)
Willow (4 parts)

Neuritis

Neuritis is the inflammation of a nerve, and may be characterized by a disappearance of the reflexes, emaciation, numbness, tenderness and a disturbance of sensation over the nerve area, pain, or paralysis (possible), and may be caused by numerous conditions including alcoholism, diabetes, diphtheria, leprosy, malaria, palsy, pneumonia, poisoning (lead), rheumatism, or syphilis.

Formula 1
Damiana (½ part)
Ginger (½ part)
Lady's Slipper (1part)
Skullcap (1 part)

Formula 2
Cayenne (¼ part)
Chaparral (3 parts)
Marshmallow (1 part)
Purple Coneflower (3 parts)

Formula 3
Calendula (1 part)
Comfrey (½ part)
Plantain (½ part)
Wormwood (½ part)

Night Sweats
Night sweats are troublesome bouts of ephidrosis or excessive perspiration that occurs during the night or while sleeping, and can be so heavy that the bedclothes become soaked with perspiration. Night sweats may be caused by numerous factors including certain medications, illness, menopause, or a buildup of toxins in the system. Eliminating the ingestion of spicy foods just prior to bedtime, increasing your daily intake of fresh water throughout the day, and incorporating more fresh fruits, primarily strawberries, blueberries, and raspberries into the diet may reduce or eliminate night sweats.

Formula 1
Boneset (2 parts)
Buckbean (4 parts)
Rosemary (2 parts)
Sage (12 parts)

Formula 2
Birch (2 parts)
Boneset (2 parts)
Elder flowers (4 parts)
Mint (2 parts)

Osteoarthritis (OA)
Osteoarthritis is a condition appearing when wear and tear on joint structures exceeds repair. This excessive wear causes the damaged tissues to become inflamed and painful, and over time leads to degeneration of the joint. OA may be caused by obesity, or by prolonged overwork, as in athletic training, or can be the result of nutritional deficiency.

Formula 1
Ash, Prickly (3 parts)
Ginger (2 parts)
Guaiacum (3 parts)
Oregon Grape Root (6 parts)
Parsley (6 parts)

Formula 2
External Use.
Cayenne (1 part)
Lobelia (2 parts)
Mullein (6 parts)
Slippery Elm (9 parts)

Osteoporosis
Osteoporosis is a silent condition that often goes unrecognized until a normal everyday activity such as bending, coughing, lifting, or sneezing results in a hip or wrist fracture, or a compression fracture of the spine. Bones that are brittle and porous are directly connected to the decline of estrogen and the loss of bone density. Maximum bone density loss occurs during the first two years after

menstruation has ceased and is chiefly a condition of postmenopausal women; primarily those of Asian and Caucasian bloodlines. However, it can occur earlier in life, and occasionally affects men, too. Anorexia, certain medications that reduce calcium absorption or promote its loss, deficiency (calcium, cholecalciferol, magnesium), poor nutritional habits, and/or a sedentary lifestyle may cause osteoporosis. To protect against bone density loss, increase your daily intake of dairy products or take a calcium/vitamin D/magnesium supplement, and exercise daily (walk, jog, weightlift, pushups, aerobics, crunches, resistance training). Avoid alcoholic and caffeinated beverages, as well as tobacco, which deplete calcium from the bones.

Formula 1
Comfrey (4 parts)
Dandelion root (2 parts)
Horsetail (6 parts)
Lobelia (1 part)
Oat (3 parts)
Slippery Elm (2 parts)

Formula 2
Burdock (2 parts)
Chaparral (4 parts)
Horsetail (4 parts)
Marshmallow (2 parts)
Parsley (2 parts)
Plantain (2 parts)

Pancreatic Tonic

The pancreas is a large, elongated gland located behind the stomach, and is responsible for the internal secretion of the hormone insulin. It contains four principle enzymes: *amylopsin*, *trypsin*, *steapsin*, and *rennin* that pass into the duodenum and is concerned with digestion and helping to control carbohydrate metabolism. This internal secretion is required to transport sugar into cells where the glucose is converted to energy. Without insulin, glucose continues to circulate and accumulate in the blood until it is eventually excreted in the urine. Dangerous symptoms occur when the body attempts to dilute very high blood sugar levels. The water is extracted from the cells and with it comes potassium. A severe deficiency of potassium may produce coma or even death. Insufficient pancreatic insulin production can lead to serious chronic conditions including diabetes, hyperglycemia, or hypoglycemia.

Formula 1
Cayenne (2 parts)
Goldenseal (1 part)
Juniper berries (16 parts)
Licorice (3 parts)
Mullein (3 parts)
Uva-Ursi (6 parts)

Formula 2
Dandelion (4 parts)
Gentian (2 parts)
Huckleberry leaves (2 parts)
Parsley (2 parts)
Raspberry leaves (2 parts)
Uva-Ursi (4 parts)

Parasites

A parasite is an organism that lives upon or within another living organism at whose expense it derives its sustenance. Children often become infected with intestinal parasites such as pinworms, roundworms, and tapeworms when they play in the dirt, and then put their hands into their mouths. Once infected, the eggs of these worms can be passed on to other members of the family through the sharing of bed linens or towels. To protect against intestinal parasites and prevent the spread of infection, hygiene is very important. Make sure all family members wash their hands frequently and thoroughly, especially before eating, and after playing or working outdoors. Launder bed linens, clothing, and towels in hot water with a germicidal detergent. Formulas for intestinal parasites are:

Formula 1
Anise (1/8 part)
Garlic (1/2 part)
Balmony (1/2 part)
Senna (1 part)
Wormseed (1 part)

Formula 2
Combine equal amounts of:
Garlic
Peach leaves
Thyme
Wormwood

External parasites such as fleas and lice are blood-sucking parasites that may act as carriers of disease. To protect against external parasites, especially lice, instruct children to avoid using anyone's hair comb or brush, and to not wear anyone's hat except their own. Lice and their nits must be destroyed to avoid any possibility of reinfestation. Wash all clothing, bed linens, headgear, combs, brushes, towels, and anything else that has come in contact with the hair in *very* hot or boiling soapy water. Fleas and their eggs primarily live in the carpet. To destroy them, sprinkle diametrious earth over the entire carpet. This non-toxic earth works by drying out the fleas and destroying the eggs. Let it remain on the carpet for a full 20 minutes, and then vacuum. Repeat this procedure once a month, especially if you have cats or dogs in the house. The following formula is for **external use** only.

Lice and their Nits
Add a strong larkspur and thyme infusion to shampoo. Wash hair and allow shampoo mixture to remain on hair for 10- 15 minutes, making sure it doesn't get into eyes as it may cause stinging. Rinse and apply conditioner. Rinse well. Repeat daily until parasites are gone.

Parturition
Parturition is the process of giving birth to a child. Numerous prenatal changes, both mental and physical occur in a woman who is expecting. The blood supply and the need for sleep increases, emotions can fluctuate, and there may be bouts of morning sickness. Throughout pregnancy, the uterus contracts, and shortly before the "due date" you may experience contractions that feel like labor has begun. However, these latent of false labor contractions do not increase in intensity, the time between them does not decrease, and they can last as long as two or three days before the start of true labor contractions, which bring about the cervical changes preceding the actual birth. If you experience these contractions before your twenty-eighth week of pregnancy, or if you experience uterine bleeding at any time throughout your pregnancy, contact your prenatal care professional immediately. It is very important to have a supportive environment before, during, and after

parturition, and try to rest as much as you can between true labor contractions, as this reserves your energy and strength for the birth process. After the delivery of your child, you will no doubt be tired and perhaps sore if an episiotomy was necessary. To help speed healing of postdelivery perineum tears or episiotomy sutures, apply ice packs at hourly intervals for the first ten to twelve hours, and then take three to four sitz baths per day until the incision is healed. Also, applying a calendula and comfrey ointment eases discomfort and helps regenerate skin cells damaged by the incision. The following formulas, for use during the last 4 weeks of pregnancy *only*, help strengthen the uterine muscles which can ease discomforts during labor.

Formula 1
Ginger (1 part)
Marshmallow (1 part)
Raspberry leaves (2 parts)
Squaw Vine (3 parts)
Wild Yam (1 part)

Formula 2
Blessed Thistle (2 parts)
Cohosh, Black (4 parts)
Licorice (1 part)
Raspberry leaves (2 parts)
Squaw Vine (4 parts)

Pellagra

Pellagra is a condition due to a deficiency (niacin), and may be characterized by appetite loss, convulsions, debility, emaciation, gastrointestinal problems, idiocy (extreme mental deficiency), melancholy, recurring rash on portions of the body exposed to heat or light, spinal pain, vomiting, and possible death. Wheat germ, roasted and sprinkled over breakfast cereal or used raw in cooking is a high source of niacin.

Formula 1
Combine equal amounts of:
Burdock
Dandelion
Dock
Goldenseal
Red Clover

Formula 2
Combine equal amounts of:
Alfalfa
Dandelion
Lamb's Quarters
Oat
Watercress

Perspiration

Perspiration is the body's way of cooling itself down, and is also a way of ridding the system of toxins. A balanced diet may help correct perspiration problems, as well as wearing clothing made of fabrics, which help to wick excess moisture away from the skin. If body odor (caused by bacteria)is a problem, bathing with an antibacterial soap may help. Also, launder your clothing often. Control ephidrosis, (excessive perspiration) by adding bearberry, oak, tea, or witch hazel to the bathwater (the tannic acid is an astringent). Perspiration problems may be caused by numerous factors including certain medications, illness, or menopause.

Formula 1
Boneset (2 parts)
Buckbean (4 parts)
Rosemary (2 parts)
Sage (12 parts)

Formula 2
Birch (2 parts)
Boneset (2 parts)
Elder flowers (4 parts)
Mint (2 parts)

Pharyngitis

Pharyngitis is an acute or chronic condition of the pharynx due to conditions such as diphtheria, syphilis, tonsillitis, or tuberculosis, and may be characterized by congestion (mucous membrane), degeneration of the submucous tissues, difficulty swallowing, dry throat, exhaustion, fever, gangrenous patches (possible), granular mucous membrane tissues, hypertrophy (pharyngeal glands), inflammation, pain, secretion (excessive), thickening of the submucous tissues, ulceration of the throat (severe), and vesicles (small abscesses).

Formula 1
Black Pepper (pinch)
Cardamom (½ part)
Cinnamon (½ part)
Ginger (4 parts)
Licorice (½ part)
Sage (4 parts)

Formula 2
Flax (2 parts)
Marshmallow (1 part)
Licorice (1 part)
Lungwort (1 part)
Mullein (1 part)
Sage (2 parts)

Pleurisy

Pleurisy is an acute or chronic inflammation of the pleura (the membrane of the lungs and thoracic cavity) that may be due to conditions such as bronchitis or pneumonia, and may be characterized by chills, dry cough, exhaustion, fever, and a side ache (possibly sharp, stabbing pain).

Formula 1
Boneset (2 parts)
Cranesbill (3 parts)
Elder flowers (2 parts)
Licorice (3 parts)
Moss, Irish (1 part)
Pleurisy Root (4 parts)

Formula 2
Anise (2 parts)
Chamomile (3 parts)
Coltsfoot (5 parts)
Nettle (5 parts)
Pleurisy Root (1 part)
Vervain (1 part)

Poison Ivy/Oak

Poison ivy and poison oak both contain the toxic oil called urushiol. This oil is so potent it can remain active on surfaces for as long as five years, and as little as a billionth of a gram (nanogram) can cause a skin reaction. To prevent spreading the toxic oil, remove all affected clothing and place in a plastic bag until they can be washed in hot soapy water (wear gloves when removing clothing from the bag as contact with the toxic oil can cause severe skin reactions). Wash skin thoroughly within 10 minutes of exposure with hot soapy water to help to remove the toxic (urushiol) oil and prevent skin reactions. First Aid for Dermatitis: For mild to moderate cases, soak in a cold bath for 20 minutes several times daily to help relieve inflammation. Creams such as corticosteroid or corticosterone applied topically (avoid genital area) can help to relieve itching and inflammation, and oral (systemic) corticosteroids can also help relieve discomfort. Severe Cases or affected areas involving the anal, genital, or mouth and throat area require immediate medical attention.

Formula 1
Chaparral (1 part)
Dock (2 parts)
Kava (2 parts)
Purple Coneflower (2 parts)
Valerian (1 part)

Formula 2
External Use.
Combine equal amounts of:
Grindelia
Gromwell
Impatiens

Formula 3
Locate impatiens, a natural antidote to poison ivy/oak, which always grows in close proximity to poison ivy. The impatiens flower is spotted, orange, and trumpet-shaped. Mix it into a paste with a bit of water and slather it over the affected area (wash the affected area first to remove as much of the urushiol oil as possible)

Prolapse

A weakening of the supporting muscles and ligaments around a part or organ causes a prolapse. A rectal prolapse is the protrusion of the rectal mucous membrane through the anus in varying degree, and a prolapse of the uterus is a protrusion of the uterus through the vaginal orifice. In some cases of prolapse, bladder or bowel function can be affected. A prolapsed organ can develop slowly over the years or appear suddenly. Uterine prolapse is most commonly caused by vaginal delivery, but can also be caused by the strain of carrying a child in the womb, chronic coughing, or obesity. Excessive straining during bowel movements may cause a rectal prolapse, or it can occur in those persons who regularly practice anal sex. The following formulas are for use as a douche in uterine prolapse, or as an enema in rectal prolapse.

Formula 1
Comfrey (6 parts)
Lobelia (1 part)
Marshmallow (3 parts)
Mullein (3 parts)
Oak (6 parts)
Walnut (3 parts)
Yellow Dock (4 parts)

Formula 2
Combine equal amounts of:
Astragalus
Bupleurum
Cohosh, Black
Oak
Raspberry leaves
Strawberry leaves

Prostate Tonic

The prostate, a gland the size of a chestnut, surrounds the neck of the bladder and the urethra, and is an organ of the male reproductive system. Prostaglandin, which is a pressor (increases blood pressure), stimulant, and vasodilator is obtained from the prostate gland and the seminal vesicles. Prostate problems may include hypertrophy (benign prostatic), infection, obstruction (prostatic), prostate disease, or prostatitis (inflammation).

Formula 1
Goldenseal (1 part)
Gravelroot (1 part)
Juniper berries (1 part)
Licorice (½ part)
Marshmallow (1 part)
Parsley (1 part)
Uva-Ursi (1 part)

Formula 2
Alfalfa (1 part)
Cornsilk (1 part)
Catnip (1 part)
Fennel (2 parts)
Goldenseal (1 part)
Marshmallow (1 part)
Saw Palmetto (3 parts)

Prostatitis

Prostatitis is an inflammation of the prostate gland due to an infection (urinary tract), and is characterized by hypertrophy (enlargement), which leads to obstruction (bladder). This obstruction impedes the flow of urine causing discomfort and frequent urges to urinate. Cancer (prostate) occurs primarily in men over the age of 60, and is the third leading cause of cancer deaths in men.

Formula 1
Buchu (1 part)
Cubeb (¼ part)
Ginger (½ part)
Gravelroot (1 part)
Juniper berries (¼ part)
Parsley (1 part)
Purple Coneflower (1 part)
Uva-Ursi (1 part)

Formula 2
Cornsilk (1 part)
Couch Grass (1 part)
Horsetail (1 part)
Hydrangea (1 part)
Marshmallow (1 part)
Purple Coneflower (3 parts)
Saw Palmetto (3 parts)
Watermelon seeds (1 part)

Pruritus

Pruritus can be symptomatic of a variety of skin problems such as dermatitis or eczema, or it may occur spontaneously as a neurosis such as obsessive-compulsive behavior. It is characterized by itching (often intense) and can involve various parts of the body such as the genitals, anus, or skin.

Formula 1
Bladderwrack (½ part)
Burdock (3 parts)
Chaparral (4 parts)
Dandelion root (4 parts)
Dock (1 part)
Licorice (1 part)
Purple Coneflower (3 parts)

Formula 2
Burdock (4 parts)
Calendula (1 part)
Cayenne (¼ part)
Chaparral (3 parts)
Marshmallow (1 part)
Plantain (½ part)
Purple Coneflower (3 parts)

Psoriasis

Psoriasis is a chronic skin condition in which the epidermis (the top, outer layer of skin) grows too fast, resulting in patches of dermatitis characterized by silvery scales or red areas that may crack and bleed, or ooze and itch. Psoriasis primarily occurs on the arms, back, chest, ears, elbows, knees, legs, and scalp, with pits and ridges developing on the fingernails and toenails. Allergy (food), certain drugs, constipation, deficiency (zinc), infection (bacterial, viral), kidney or liver problems, poison ivy, stress, sunburn, surgery, and/or wounds (minor) may trigger an attack.

Formula 1
Chaparral (2 parts)
Garlic (1 part)
Goldenseal (1 part)
Licorice (1 part)
Purple Coneflower (2 parts)
Sarsaparilla (1 part)

Formula 2
Burdock (1 part)
Centaury (1 part)
Dock (1 part)
Fumitory (½ part)
Marshmallow (1 part)
Yarrow (1 part)

Rash

A rash is an acute, temporary skin condition due to various factors including certain drugs, dermatitis, illness, or one that sometimes follows vaccination, and is usually characterized by inflammation or reddish eruptions on the skin.

Formula 1
Cayenne (¼ part)
Chaparral (3 parts)
Marshmallow (1 part)
Purple Coneflower (3 parts)

Formula 2
Calendula (1 part)
Comfrey (½ part)
Plantain (½ part)
Wormwood (½ part)

Reproductive System Tonic

Once you arrive at sexual maturity, your sense of physical and emotional health is largely determined by the intricate relationship between the nervous system and the hormones produced by the ovaries (in women) or testes (in men), adrenals, and pituitary gland. During the reproductive years, the fluctuating balance between estrogen and progesterone levels influence a woman's menstrual cycle. Testosterone is the male testicular hormone, and its function is the initiation and maintenance of male secondary sex characters, as well as helping in the production of spermatozoa. The male reproductive organs primarily consist of the prostate, penis, testes, and seminal vesicles. The female reproductive organs chiefly consist of the ovaries, clitoris, vulva, ovarian vessels, vagina, fallopian tubes, mammae (breasts), and uterus.

Formula 1
Bladderwrack (½ part)
Damiana (4 parts)
Ginseng, Siberian (4 parts)
Licorice (1 part)
Sarsaparilla (2 parts)
Saw Palmetto (2 parts)

Formula 2
Astragalas (2 parts)
Cohosh, Black (1 part)
Ginseng (2 parts)
Goldenseal (½ part)
Licorice (1 part)
Sarsaparilla (1 part)

Respiratory System Tonic

Of all the systems in the body, the respiratory system is the one most directly affected by the environment. Oxygen is crucial to our physical being, and since the body cannot store oxygen, we must continuously supply this need through breathing. Each breath is taken into the lungs where the exchange of oxygen and carbon dioxide occur. From there, it is transported to all parts of the body through the bloodstream. Although the lungs do aid in the elimination of toxins from the air we breathe, the respiratory system may still be prone to problems such as allergy (pollen), asthma, or infection (viral).

Formula 1
Cherry, Wild (3 parts)
Elecampane (3 parts)
Ginger (2 parts)
Licorice (1 part)
Lobelia (1 part)
Mullein (3 parts)
Thyme (4 parts)

Formula 2
Combine equal amounts of:
Cayenne
Elecampane
Ginger
Horehound
Ivy, Ground
Purple Coneflower

Rheumatism

Rheumatism is a condition due to dysfunction of the body's immune system which causes discomfort throughout the entire body, and may be characterized by inflammation, muscle and joint pain, fungus-like growths on the heart valves, and the presence of nodules on the heart muscle (myocardium) and skin.

Formula 1
Ash, Prickly (3 parts)
Cohosh, Black (3 parts)
Ginger (2 parts)
Guaiacum (3 parts)
Oregon Grape Root (6 parts)
Parsley (6 parts)
Sassafras (3 parts)

Formula 2
Barberry (½ part)
Burdock (1 part)
Buckbean (1 part)
Cayenne Pepper (⅛ part)
Licorice (1 part)
Meadowsweet (½ part)
Yarrow (1 part)

Rheumatoid Arthritis (RA)
Rheumatoid arthritis is a chronic joint condition occurring when the immune system itself attacks the cartilage and damages the joint structure. RA may be characterized by inflammation of the joints, followed by bone deformity and deterioration.

Formula 1
Ash, Prickly (3 parts)
Cohosh, Black (3 parts)
Ginger (2 parts)
Guaiacum (3 parts)
Oregon Grape Root (6 parts)
Parsley (6 parts)
Sassafras (3 parts)

Formula 2
External Use.
Cayenne (1 part)
Ginger (½ part)
Lobelia (2 parts)
Mullein (6 parts)
Rosemary (1 part)
Slippery Elm (9 parts)

Sciatica
Sciatica is usually due to neuritis (nerve inflammation) or an injury to the sciatic nerve, which is the main nerve that runs the length of the back of the leg. An abnormal sensation of burning or prickling of the leg and thigh, intense debilitating pain occurring along the course of the nerve, which is often made worse by gentle touch, but usually feels better by the application of pressure and heat, and occasionally wasting of the calf muscle generally characterizes sciatica.

Formula 1
Angelica (½ part)
Cleavers (½ part)
Burdock (½ part)
Figwort (½ part)
Ginger (¼ part)
Yarrow (½ part)

Formula 2
Anise (1 part)
Ash, Prickly (1 part)
Lady's Slipper (2 parts)
Lobelia (¼ part)
Pleurisy Root (1 part)
Skullcap (1 part)

Formula 3
Betony (2 parts)
Raspberry leaves (2 parts)
Rosemary (1 part)
Skullcap (2 parts)
Vervain (1 part)
Willow (4 parts)

Scrofula

Scrofula is tuberculosis of the lymphatic glands, and occasionally of bone and joint surfaces, and may be characterized by lesions, pustules, and ulcer (fistula) of the skin. During the 1900s, tuberculosis was the leading cause of death in the U.S. Due to advances in public health and medical science, deaths occurring annually from tuberculosis now account for only about 1,800 out of two million.

Formula 1
Bittersweet (2 parts)
Dandelion (2 parts)
Figwort (1 part)
Sassafras (1 part)
Stillingia (2 parts)
Virginia Creeper (1 part)
Yellow Dock (2 parts)

Formula 2
Grindelia (1 part)
Horehound (1 part)
Lobelia (1 part)
Red Clover (1 part)
Slippery Elm (2 parts)
Thyme (1 part)
Yerba Santa (1 part)

Skeletal System Tonic

Bones make up the skeletal system, and are the storehouses for sodium, calcium, magnesium, phosphorus, protein, vitamins C and D, and boron. When there is a deficiency of these elements, the body draws them from the bones, which results in brittleness, thinness, and weakness, and can lead to osteoporosis. Regular exercise helps deter bone loss, minimize discomfort, and strengthens the bones. Calcium rich products such as dairy foods, sunflower seeds and vegetables can help boost calcium levels in the body.

Formula 1
Comfrey (6 parts)
Gravelroot (3 parts)
Marshmallow (3 parts)
Mullein (3 parts)
Oak (6 parts)
Skullcap (1 part)
Walnut (3 parts)

Formula 2
Burdock (2 parts)
Chaparral (4 parts)
Horsetail (4 parts)
Marshmallow (2 parts)
Parsley (2 parts)
Plantain (2 parts)
Slippery Elm (2 parts)

Sore Throat

A sore throat is an inflammation of the mucous membranes of the throat and vocal chords, often the result of an infection, but can be caused by acid reflux, indigestion, postnasal drip, public speaking, shouting, or singing. Avoid using antihistammes or a gargle/mouth rinse that contains alcohol as they have a tendency to dry out and further irritate the delicate tissues of the throat. To protect against a contagious (infectious) sore throat, don't share a kiss or utensils with people who are infected, disinfect telephone receivers by wiping them with alcohol swabs, and wash your hands thoroughly and frequently. Consult your healthcare professional if you experience chills, fever, and white spots inside your mouth and throat which is an indication of strep throat. Seek immediate medical attention if you have difficulty breathing, swallowing, or talking, as this could be an indication of an allergic reaction.

Formula 1
Black Pepper (pinch)
Cardamom (½ part)
Cinnamon (½ part)
Ginger (4 parts)
Licorice (½ part)
Sage (4 parts)

Formula 2
Anise (8 parts)
Cherry, Wild (8 parts)
Cranesbill (8 parts)
Licorice (16 parts)
Lungwort (10 parts)
Moss, Irish (4 parts)

Spasmodic Conditions

A sudden, violent, involuntary, painful contraction of a muscle or a group of muscles, or a sudden but brief constriction of a canal, orifice, or passage is characteristic of a spasm, and can be due to conditions such as asthma, dysmenorrhea, hemiplegia, lesions (cerebral), neurosis, or rickets. A persistent spasm is called a tonic spasm, and when the spasm is characterized by alternate contraction and relaxation, it is called a clonic spasm.

Formula 1
Cayenne (½ part)
Cohosh, Black (1 part)
Ginger (½ part)
Licorice (½ part)
Lobelia (½ part)
Myrrh (1 part)
Skullcap (1 part)
Valerian (1 part)

Formula 2
Combine equal amounts of:
Calendula
California Poppy
Chamomile flowers
Oat
Saint John's Wort
Skullcap
Valerian

Syphilis

Syphilis is a contagious, usually sexually transmitted, three-stage disease caused by the *treponema pallidum* microorganism. Transmission of the disease is usually during coitus by direct contact with the ulcers of a person with an active infection; however, the bacteria can also pass through broken skin on other parts of the body. Stage one of the disease consists of a painless, hard lesion or chancre appearing in or near the vagina within ten to forty days following infection, as well as swelling and hardness of the nearby lymph glands. Stage two includes fever, flu-like symptoms, lesions, severe pain in the head and joints, ulcer (syphilitic), and rash covering the body or on the palms of the hands and soles of the feet. These lesions and ulcers extend to the lymphatic vessels, mucous membranes, skin, and other tissues of the body, and sometimes to the bones and the tough fibrous membrane (periosteum) that surrounds the bone. The third or late stage often results in the disappearance of symptoms, yet the infection (if untreated) remains. Persons infected with the *treponema pallidum* bacteria, even those having mild or no symptoms, can infect others during the first two stages of the disease (up to two years), and if left untreated, the bacteria can cause bone, brain, eye, heart, joint and spinal cord damage, as well as birth defects and miscarriage. Also, the developing fetus can acquire this infection while in the womb, and may experience symptoms later in life.

Formula 1
Bloodroot (½ part)
Burdock (1 part)
Oregon Grape Root (2 parts)
Red Clover (1 part)

Formula 2
Combine equal parts of:
Blue Flag
Dock
Goldenseal
Pokeweed

Tonsillitis
Tonsillitis, often associated with pharyngitis, is an acute or chronic condition of the tonsils due to an infection, and may be characterized by difficulty swallowing (dysphagia), dry throat, fever, headache, hypertrophy (tonsil), inflammation, pain (possibly severe), pustules, and sore throat. A tonsillectomy may be required in chronic tonsillitis.

Formula 1
Black Pepper (pinch)
Cardamom (½ part)
Cinnamon (½ part)
Ginger (4 parts)
Licorice (½ part)
Sage (4 parts)

Formula 2
Anise (8 parts)
Cherry, Wild (8 parts)
Cranesbill (8 parts)
Licorice (16 parts)
Lungwort (10 parts)
Moss, Irish (4 parts)

Tuberculosis
Tuberculosis is a contagious condition caused by the *myobacterium tuberculosis* bacillus and may be characterized by abscess, cerebral symptoms (pulmonary, meningeal, typhoid), cough, diarrhea, difficult breathing, emaciation, fever, hematuria, hemoptysis, infection (septic), larynx and vocal cord ulceration, night sweats, skin nodules, ulcer (tuberculosis), and the formation of lesions (tubercle) in the blood vessels, lymphatic vessels and body tissues, which have a tendency to spread in all directions. Throughout the 1900s, tuberculosis was the leading cause of death in the U.S.A. Due to advances in public health and medical science, deaths occurring annually from tuberculosis now account for only about 1,800 out of two million.

Formula 1
Agrimony (½ part)
Barberry (½ part)
Cayenne Pepper (⅛ part)
Centaury (½ part)
Cleavers (½ part)
Horehound (½ part)
Ivy, Ground (½ part)
Licorice (¼ part)
Raspberry leaves (½ part)

Formula 2
Cayenne (¼part)
Grindelia (1 part)
Horehound (1 part)
Licorice (¼ part)
Lobelia (1 part)
Red Clover (1 part)
Slippery Elm (2 parts)
Thyme (1 part)
Yerba Santa (1 part)

Ulcer

An ulcer is an open sore on the mucous surface, skin, or internal parts of the body that causes disintegration and necrosis (death) of the tissues, and can be due to conditions such as deficiency (nutrient), diabetes, infection (bacterial, fungal, septic), leishmaniasis, stress, tuberculosis, or typhoid, and may be characterized by discharge, foul odor, or pain. Following a low fiber diet, and decreasing the intake of alcohol, nicotine, and protein foods will help speed healing.

Duodenal Ulcer
Chamomile (1 part)
Cranesbill (1 part)
Goldenseal (1 part)
Marshmallow (2 parts)
Meadowsweet (1 part)
Plantain (1 part)
Purple Coneflower (4 parts)

Gastric and Peptic Ulcer
Fenugreek (1 part)
Gentian (2 parts)
Ginger (½ part)
Goldenseal (4 parts)
Moss, Irish (1 part)
Licorice (4 parts)
Papaya leaves (2 parts)

Stasis Ulcer
External uses only.
Blue Flag (1 part)
Clove (1 part)
Goldenseal (1 part)
Marshmallow (3 parts)
Myrrh (½ part)
Purple Coneflower (3 parts)

Syphilitic Ulcer
External uses only.
Burdock (4 parts)
Cayenne (¼ part)
Comfrey (1 part)
Goldenseal (4 parts)
Myrrh (1 part)
Oregon Grape Root (2 parts)

Urethritis

Urethritis is an inflammation of the urethra, and may be due to gonorrhea, gout, or an infection, and is primarily characterized by discharge (occasionally) and itching. The microorganisms causing urethritis are initially transmitted by the male during coitus, and are then passed back and forth between the partners causing reinfection during each session of coitus. Both partners will need to be treated in order to eliminate any possibility of reinfection. It is recommended that one abstain from coitus, or that protection (condom) be used until the infection has been eliminated. The following formulas are to be used as a vaginal douche for women or as a sitz bath for males.

Formula 1
Chaparral (2 parts)
Marshmallow (1 part)
Oak (2 parts)
Periwinkle (4 parts)
Yarrow (1 part)

Formula 2
Burdock (1 part)
Myrrh (½ part)
Red Clover (1 part)
Slippery Elm (1 part)
Yellow Dock (1 part)

Urinary System Tonic
The bladder is a membranous sac, which serves as a reservoir for the urine, and is situated in the front part of the pelvic cavity. A dysfunction of the bladder can cause urinary problems including cystitis. The kidneys are two glands located in the lumbar region that are approximately the size and shape of a kidney bean. They filter out blood impurities, regulate the body's salt and water content, are responsible for the secretion of urine, and maintain the blood's acid/alkaline balance. Dysfunction of the kidneys can result in calculus, cystitis, nephritis, enlarged and deformed kidneys, kidney stones, renal glycosuria, and various other problems. Drinking plenty of fresh water through the day helps flush the urinary system of bacteria and waste.

Formula 1
Buchu (1 part)
Cleavers (1 part)
Ginger (¼ part)
Juniper berries (1 part)
Marshmallow (1 part)
Parsley (1 part)
Uva-Ursi (1 part)

Formula 2
Dandelion (4 parts)
Ginger (1 part)
Gravelroot (1 part)
Marshmallow (2 parts)
Parsley (4 parts)
Rehmannia (3 parts)
Uva-Ursi (½ part)

Vaginitis
Vaginitis is a term assigned to a number of uterine and vaginal infections such as candida, chlamydia, hemophilus, leukorrhea, non-specific vaginitis, and trichomonas which can be passed back and forth between partners during coitus, and may be characterized by itching, inflammation, rash or redness, and discharge with an unpleasant odor.

Formula 1
Chaparral (1 part)
Goldenseal (1 part)
Purple Coneflower (1 part)
Squaw Vine (1 part)

Formula 2
Bayberry (1 part)
Calendula (1 part)
Loosestrife, Purple (2 parts)
White Water Lily (1part)

Formula 3
Buchu (1 part)
Cubeb (¼ part)
Juniper berries (¼ part)
Uva-Ursi (½ part)

Warts
A wart is a localized (limited to a small area), benign (noncancerous), sometimes transmittable, hypertrophy of the skin caused by viruses. The following formulas are for **external use** only.

All Warts
Don't use on venereal warts!
Calendula (2 parts)
Dandelion root (1 part)
Milk Thistle (3 parts)
Oat (1 part)
Plantain (1 part)
Skullcap (1 part)

Venereal Warts
Combine equal amounts of:
Dock
Gentian
Goldenseal
Marshmallow
Mushroom, Hoelen
Myrrh

Weight Loss
Obesity is a condition resulting from the excessive accumulation of fat in the body, which is primarily due to genetics; however, other factors such as certain drugs, excessive alcohol consumption, or glandular problems could also play a role. Granted, the percentage of fat and the way it is distributed in your body is somewhat based on heredity, the final determining factor is often based on your consumption and exercise habits. Being overweight not only puts a strain on the heart and skeletal system, it can also cause elevated cholesterol, blood pressure, and insulin levels, which could lead to the development of arteriosclerosis, diabetes or hypertension. People usually put on weight due to the combination of excessive fat and sugar intake followed by insufficient exercise. To maintain proper blood glucose (sugar) levels and metabolism balance eat five to six small meals per day rather than three large ones, and exercising in the morning hours stimulates your metabolism, which helps burn calories more efficiently throughout the day. Also, increasing your daily intake of fresh water (helps dilute excess sodium), limiting the amount of sodium in your diet (helps reduce fluid retention), switching to a low-fat, high fiber diet and avoiding the intake of empty calorie foods (i.e. soft drinks, sweets) that offer little or no nutritional value protects against obesity. The following formulas aid appetite control, control the discouraging weight gain that often follows dieting, detoxify the digestive system, increase digestion, energy and nutrient absorption, inhibit short-term weight gain caused by excess insulin or the consumption of salty foods, stimulate metabolism, and help to significantly reduce body fat as they add and retain lean muscle tissue. Consult your healthcare professional prior to starting any weight loss program.

Note: This is *not* a crash diet program intended for rapid weight loss, which robs the body of needed nutrients, but a graduated and precise weight loss program that is to be used in conjunction with daily exercise and proper eating habits.

Formula 1
Burdock (3 parts)
Chickweed (6 parts)
Fennel (2 parts)
Hawthorn (1 part)
Kelp (3 parts)
Licorice (2 parts)
Papaya (2 parts)
Parsley (3 parts)

Formula 2
Bladderwrack (½ part)
Burdock (2 parts)
Dandelion leaves/root (2 parts)
Fennel (4 parts)
Hawthorn (1 part)
Licorice (1 part)
Plantain (6 parts)
Rehmania (3 parts)

Whooping Cough
Whooping cough is an infectious cough caused by a bacterial infection that is characterized by episodes of short, violent coughing with episodes of long intakes of breath, which make a whooping sound.

Formula 1
Bayberry (¼ part)
Bloodroot (1 part)
Hyssop (½ part)
Lobelia (¼ part)
Raspberry leaves (½ part)
Red Root (2 parts)
Rhubarb (½ part)
Thyme (½ part)

Formula 2
Cayenne (¼ part)
Grindelia (1 part)
Horehound (1 part)
Lobelia (1 part)
Red Clover (1 part)
Slippery Elm (2 parts)
Thyme (1 part)
Yerba Santa (1 part)

Yeast Infection
Yeast infections are caused by the genus of yeast-like fungus called *candida albicans.* This fungus is common in all individuals to some degree and is often found in the intestinal tract and vagina. Under normal circumstances, this fungus exists harmoniously with other organisms in the body, but when the pH level or acidic environment of the body or vagina changes and becomes unbalanced, this yeast can begin to grow at an unusual rate. Genital itching (sometimes severe), redness, and a thick cottage cheese-like discharge characterize a yeast infection. Douche with ½ part tea tree oil to 4 parts distilled water once per day for 3-4 days to help destroy the yeast. To help reduce vulva itching and redness, add two cups apple cider vinegar to a sitz bath. Soak for 15-20 minutes. Overgrowth of the *candida* fungus can also result in thrush which is a fungal infection of the mouth, and is characterized by thick, white patches in the mouth, fever, and gastrointestinal problems. Dilute

2-3 drops of tea tree oil with 6-8 ounces water and use as a gargle/mouth rinse. Spit it out and follow with a plain water rinse. Don't swallow it! A tea tree oil gargle/mouth rinse may cause a temporary, harmless tingling or slight numbing sensation of the mouth and tongue. Fungal infection of the nails, causes nail bed distortion and thickening and yellowing of the nails. To destroy the fungus, apply tea tree oil neat (nondiluted). Prior to tea tree oil application, clip the nails as short as possible, then topically apply the oil using a cotton swab directly onto the nail surface and under the top edge once or twice daily until the infection is gone (this may take a few months depending on how long you've had the infection). A temporary, harmless darkening of the nail may occur with the application of tea tree oil. Other factors such as antibiotic drugs, chemotherapy or cortisone drugs, high carbohydrate diet, hormonal changes (i.e. contraceptives, menstruation, pregnancy), immune system depression (i.e. AIDS, diabetes), tampon usage, or from wearing tight, non-breathable undergarments can trigger a candida infection. To protect against candida overgrowth, eat low carbohydrate foods, incorporate more fresh fruits and vegetables into your diet, and the daily consumption of plain yogurt containing live lactobacillus cultures will help to keep this fungus in check. The following formulas help boost immunity levels, fight the infection, and protect against candida.
Note: Do not ingest tea tree oil! Pharmaceutical grade tea tree oil (*melaleuca alternifolia*) is antimicrobic, non-sting, and useful for **topical application** or **diluted** for use as a **gargle/mouth rinse or douche.**

Formula 1
Combine equal amounts of:
Angelica
Black Walnut
Calendula
Coltsfoot
Garlic
Goldenrod
Rosemary
Sage

Formula 2
Combine equal amounts of:
Garlic
Goldenseal
Oshà
Mint
Purple Coneflower
Red Root
Usnea

Baby Care

These formulas work well on baby's delicate skin. As with any topical preparation, if you notice rash, redness, or irritation resulting from the use of a particular formula, discontinue its use immediately and consult your healthcare professional. *Don't* internally administer herbal formulas to infants.

Baby Bath
Here's a safe simple way to introduce gentle, mild, dried or fresh herbs into your babys bath. Place 1 tablespoon each of chamomile, lavender, lemon balm and mint into a small cloth/muslin bag and

tie closed. Place this bag into your baby's bath water. Make sure the bath water is not too hot by testing the temperature with your elbow or the inside of your wrist.

Baby Powder
Combine 2-3 ounces of kaolin clay, ½ teaspoon powdered myrrh, and 2-3 drops of chamomile oil. Mix well and store in a small jar. Makes approximately 3-4 ounces. When powdering baby, it is always important to exercise caution and use only small amounts. Apply the powder to your hand first and then to baby to avoid inhalation by either your baby or yourself.

Diaper Rash Ointment
The following formula is naturally fragrant and soothing. It helps protect baby's bottom from getting chapped or dry, reduces redness, prevents irritation, inflammation and infection, helps ward off staph, viral, and yeast infection, and speeds healing. External uses only.

Use 1 cup of sweet almond oil as a base.
To the base add the following powdered herbs:
1 tablespoon calendula
1 teaspoon chamomile
3 tablespoons lavender
1 tablespoon rose petals
2 tablespoons vitamin E oil
1½ teaspoons of jojoba oil
4 drops of chamomile oil
5 tablespoons beeswax

Warm the base oil in a double boiler or a small pan. Add the herbs to the base and cook on low heat for 25-30 minutes to allow the healing properties of the herbs, to be fully released into the oil. Add the jojoba, vitamin E, and the essential oil to the base mixture. Melt the beeswax on low heat in a small pan or double boiler. Add the melted beeswax to the base mixture and whisk until the mixture is thick and creamy. Fill several 2-4 ounce jars (baby food or small jelly jars work well) with the ointment. Label and store in the refrigerator. Warm to room temperature prior to use. Makes approximately 10- 15 ounces and will keep for about three months.

Child Care

Problems such as bad dream, colds, minor wounds, or an upset tummy can be treated safely and effectively at home. Regardless of how effective an herbal formula is, if the child refuses to take the tea, extract, tincture, capsule, or pill, it's not going to work. Here are a few tricks that usually help.

*Dilute extracts or tinctures with apple juice. *Sweeten tea by stirring in a little honey. *For children who refuse to swallow capsules or pills, you can open the capsule or crush and finely powder the pill. Sprinkle the powdered herb onto applesauce (be sure to mix it in well before administering). *For children who will swallow capsules or pills but have difficulty doing so due to the capsule or pill's dryness, give the child a little warm water to drink first. This will relax the throat and help the capsules or pills go down easier. *Consider using alcohol free (glycerite) extracts or tinctures.

Allergy (Pollen)
Helps reduce itchy, watery eyes and sneezing caused by allergy (pollen). Make a paste by combining equal amounts of finely powdered elderflower, mullein, and purple coneflower in a honey base. Administer 1-4 teaspoons daily or as needed, or prepare a warm tea using the above herbs and administer 2-3 cups daily. Use honey as a sweetener in the tea. For maximum effect, the administration of this formula should begin about a month prior to the start of the allergy season and continue on a daily basis throughout the season.

Bad Dreams
Chamomile tea sweetened with honey helps calm and comfort a child after a bad dream.

Colds
A mild decongestant that soothes inflamed mucous membranes, sniffles, sore nasal passages, and runny nose. Combine equal amounts of elderflower, mullein, nettle, purple coneflower, and thyme. Administer 2-3 cups of warm tea daily.

Fever
To reduce fever in children, combine equal parts of elderflower and peppermint. Administer 2-3 cups of warm tea daily.

Hair Shampoo
This mild, gentle shampoo works great for all hair types, and leaves hair shiny and soft.

½ cup shampoo (no tears baby shampoo is great for children)
1 tablespoon calendula
2 tablespoon chamomile
2 teaspoons comfrey
½ teaspoon chamomile or lavender essential oil
2 teaspoons rosemary
1 tablespoon nettle
2 teaspoons orange peel
2 cups water
Prepare an infusion using the herbs. Strain the mixture into a medium-sized bowl and add the oil. Stir vigorously. Add the shampoo and stir until thoroughly mixed. Bottle and store in the refrigerator. Allow shampoo to warm to room temperature prior to use. This shampoo will clean with a minimal amount of suds, as it does not contain any strong foaming agents. Shake bottle lightly prior to use. Follow with a mild conditioner. Use daily or as needed. Makes enough for approximately 30-40 applications.

Immune System Tonic
This tonic is useful for children who experience frequent colds, ear infection, or runny nose. Combine astragalus and purple coneflower. Administer 2-3 cups of warm tea daily.

Lice Preventative
There is always the possibility, through day care, school, etc., that children could contract head lice. To help ward off lice, add 20 drops each eucalyptus or tea tree, geranium, lavender, lemon, and rosemary essential oils to an eight-ounce bottle of any brand children's shampoo. Adding these oils to shampoo will act as an effective repellent. Wash the child's hair 2-3 times a week (avoid getting shampoo into eyes as it may sting), and use a good conditioner afterwards.

Upset Tummy
To help reduce nausea and queasy tummy in children, make a paste by mixing powdered ginger and peppermint with cool water. Add cinnamon or honey to taste. Administer 2-4 teaspoons per day.
~or~
To soothe an upset tummy, combine equal amounts of chamomile, fennel, and ginger. Administer as a warm tea 2-3 times a day.

Wounds
These non-sting formulas help relieve discomfort, halt bleeding, and speed healing of minor abrasions, cuts, scrapes, and other boo-boos. The following formulas are for **external uses** only.

To soothe discomfort, speed healing, and ward off infection, prepare an infusion using equal amounts of aloe and calendula. Let cool and add 10-20 drops of tea tree oil. Gently apply to affected area with a cotton ball.
~or~
To quickly halt bleeding and alleviate discomfort, apply a thick coating of powdered cayenne pepper directly onto the wound. Cover with a band-aid to keep the cayenne in place. Reapply as needed.
~or~
To speed healing and protect against infection of a minor wound, slather honey directly on the affected area after the bleeding has stopped. Cover with a band-aid to keep the honey in place. Reapply as needed.

Skin Care

The skin that covers our bodies is a vital organ and our major sensory contact with the environment. Its functions range from temperature control to waste removal, and its three surface layers (epidermis, dermis, and subcutaneous tissue) serve us throughout our lives helping to guard against infection and protect us from chemical toxins and everyday environmental pollution which can have a major effect on skin causing it to age prematurely. The skin has amazing powers of absorption, and the capillary endings can take in both damaging and healing substances which may pass into the blood stream and affect various organs and body systems. For example, random blood tests have revealed traces of chemical ingredients contained in cosmetics, and some substances as essential oils applied topically during aromatherapy treatments have a direct effect on the nervous system. The skin also reacts to our emotions, which can cause the skin's oil/water layer to change. The sebaceous and sweat glands secrete this unseen layer. It serves as a moisturizer, helping to balance the skin's pH level. Individuals under stress may find their skin becomes dry and taut, and hormonal changes may cause the skin to become oily often resulting in blemishes. Climate affects the skin as well. If you live where it is hot and dry, you may find a few bumps on your skin as well as dryness, fine lines, or wrinkles. And if you live in an area with humid air, you may find yourself with a dewy or oily complexion. The following formulas help stabilize a healthy skin-condition, relieve stress, calm sensitive skin, repair damaged skin, and rejuvenate skin cells.

Bath

Cleansing Bath
This cleansing, relaxing bath helps soothe and soften flaky, itchy skin, and helps restore skin's pH level.
Add ½ cup cider vinegar directly into bathwater.
Combine equal amounts of the following herbs in a muslin bag and place in bathwater: oatmeal, catnip, chamomile, comfrey, elder, hyssop, jasmine, juniper berries, lemon balm, linden flowers, marshmallow, mullein, passionflower, primrose, roses, slippery elm, tansy, valerian, vervain, and violet.

Put equal amounts of the following herbs into a cloth/muslin bag and place into bath water.

Romantic Bath
Lavender
Lemon Verbena
Lovage
Marjoram
Mint
Rosemary
Rose petals

Stress Reliever Bath
Catnip
Chamomile
Fennel
Lemon Balm
Licorice
Raspberry leaves
Rosehip

Bath Gel
Use in bath or shower to soften skin and help you feel relaxed and revitalized.

Moss, Irish (2 pints)
Orange Water (3 tablespoons)
Water (2½ pints)
If using fresh moss, rinse it to remove any debris. If using dried moss, soak overnight in water to soften it. Put moss and water into a pan. Cover and bring to a boil. Reduce heat and simmer for 20 minutes. Remove pan from heat and stir in orange water. Strain, cool, and pour into jars. Makes

enough for several uses.

Bath Salts
Scented bath salts that soften your skin and make the bath smell wonderful.

½ cup liquid dish soap (unscented)
1 tablespoon almond, olive, or sesame oil
Natural food coloring (your choice of color)
6 cups rock salt crystals
2-3 drops of coconut, lavender, orange, peppermint, or rose essential oils.
Mix the food coloring, oil, and soap together. Pour mixture over rock salt in a large bowl, and stir until salt crystals are evenly coated. Spread salts out in thin layer on a wax lined cookie sheet and allow to air dry for at least 24 hours. To scent your bath salts, add a few drops of the essential oils to the salts after they have dried. Put ¼ cup of the salts (enough for 1 bath) into a small bath bag and tie securely or add the salts directly to warm bath water. Store in an airtight container. Recipe makes enough for 24 baths.

Body Pack
Thoroughly cleanse your body prior to applying the body pack. Spread a thick mixture over your body making sure to avoid the genital area (wear panties/underwear). Let the mixture remain on your body for 15-20 minutes or until the mixture is dry and your skin feels tight. Rinse or shower your body with warm water thoroughly until all of the pack is removed. Pat dry. Use a moisturizing lotion if needed. Apply once a month. Due to individual body sizes, and the large amount of ingredients required for a body pack, ingredient amounts have been left blank. Experiment and have fun.

Combine equal amounts of powdered calendula, chamomile, marshmallow, and oatmeal. Add one container of plain yogurt. Mix herbs and yogurt together adding the oatmeal until it makes a spreadable paste. Apply to body. Leave on until dry. Rinse or shower thoroughly with warm water. Pat dry.
~or~
Combine apple, pear, peach, or raspberry fruit juice and unsweetened, unflavored gelatin in an ovenproof, glass container. Heat gently to dissolve gelatin completely by microwaving on high for 35-45 seconds, or heating on low in a pan on the stove. Place mixture in refrigerator and cool for about 30 minutes. Apply to body and leave on until dry. Rinse or shower thoroughly with warm water. Pat dry.
~or~
Combine powdered milk, honey, and your choice of one of following powdered herb: chamomile, fennel, lemongrass, mint leaves, or parsley. Mix all ingredients together until creamy. Apply mixture to the body. Let dry and leave on for an additional 5 minutes. Rinse or shower thoroughly with warm water. Pat dry.

Skin Cleanser
Apply the following formulas to face (avoid eye/mouth areas) using a cotton ball, then rinse face thoroughly with warm water.

All Skin Types
To refresh, moisten, and revitalize skin, make a normal infusion of calendula, chamomile, yarrow, violet, or elder flowers. Cool. Strain. Store in the refrigerator. Use within 3 days.
~or~
For a cleansing, gentle, body soap:
5 ounces unscented soap flakes
3 ounces of fresh herbs such as rosemary or marjoram
10 ounces water
2 tsp. rosemary and sandalwood oil
Place soap flakes in a bowl; make a normal infusion of your chosen herb. Cool infusion for 20-25 minutes. Then using a strainer, pour the infusion over the soap flakes and place the bowl of soap flakes over a pan of simmering water. Whisk until smooth. Remove from heat and mix in oil. Pour into small molds that been previously waxed. Dry for 6-8 weeks (or until hard) in a warm place.

Dry Skin
1-2 tablespoons each almond and soy oil
1 tablespoon beeswax
1 ounce cocoa butter
2 tablespoons orange flower water
⅛ teaspoon borax
5 drops orange essential oil
Warm the oils and mix them together. In a small pan, melt the cocoa butter and stir it into the oils. Melt the beeswax and beat it into the oil mixture. Warm the orange flower water and dissolve the borax in it. Beat this into the main mixture. Leave to thicken. As the mixture starts to thicken, stir in the essential oil. Once mixture has cooled, put it into jars. Leaves skin feeling refreshed and revitalized. Use within 1 week.
~or~
Prepare the following cleansing, moisturizing facial milk that moisturizes dry skin.
½ cup half and half
1-2 tablespoons chamomile flowers (dried or fresh)
Place into a double boiler and warm for 20-25 minutes (do not let half-and-half boil or form a skin). Strain and refrigerate. Use within one week.

Oily Skin
This gentle, deeply cleansing, cooling, facial milk can be used daily.

2 ounces ground almonds
5 ounces water
3 tablespoons calendula, infusion (strong)
1 teaspoon borax
2 tablespoons grape seed oil
5 drops oil of lemon
Soak almonds in water for several hours, remove almonds and reserve the milky liquid. In small container, add the calendula infusion to the borax and set container in a pan of hot water, stirring until the borax has melted. Whisk the grape seed oil into the borax solution, and then add 4 tablespoons of the almond milk and the oil of lemon. Cool and store in a capped bottle. Shake prior to use. Keeps well in the refrigerator. Use within 1 week.
~or~
Prepare the following cleansing facial milk for oily skin.
½ cup buttermilk
2 tablespoons fennel (powdered)
Gently heat the milk and fennel together in a double boiler for 30 minutes. Cool, strain, and bottle. Use within one week.

Sensitive Skin
Cleansing and moisturizing facial milk.

½ cup half and half
1-2 tablespoons chamomile
Place into a double boiler and warm for 20-25 minutes (do not let half-and-half boil or form a skin). Cool, strain, and bottle. Store in refrigerator. Use within one week.

Deodorant
Prepare an infusion of equal amounts of cleavers, lemon peel, orange peel, and orrisroot. Let cool. Apply this deodorant using a cottonball or place in a spray bottle with a fine mist setting. Keeps in the refrigerator for one week. Makes enough for several uses.

Facemask
Cleanse your face thoroughly prior to applying the facemask. Spread a thick mixture over your face, avoiding eye and mouth areas. Let the mixture remain on your face for 10- 15 minutes or until the mixture is dry and your skin feels tight. Rinse your face with warm water thoroughly until all of the pack is removed. Pat dry. Use once a week. The following formulas are for all skin types.

2 tablespoons each calendula, chamomile, elderflower, and violet.
2 tablespoons plain yogurt

Oatmeal (small amount)
Mix herbs and yogurt together adding the oatmeal until it makes a spreadable paste. Apply to face. Leave on until dry. Rinse face thoroughly. Pat dry.
~or~
1 tablespoon powdered milk
1 teaspoon honey
¼ teaspoon one of the following powdered herbs: chamomile, fennel, lemongrass, mint leaves, or parsley.
Whisk all ingredients together (a blender on low speed for 2 or 3 minutes may be used) until creamy. Apply mixture to the face and throat area. Let dry and leave on for 5 minutes. Rinse face with cool water.
~or~
3-4 teaspoons honey
⅓ cup oatmeal
⅛ cup rose petals
1-2 teaspoons rose water
Combine rose petals with oatmeal and honey. Add rose water and mix well. Apply to cleansed face and relax for 15-20 minutes. Rinse face with warm water to remove.

Face Rinse
Use the following formulas as a face rinse after cleansing. Refrigerate formulas and warm to room temperature prior to use. Shake well before use. Use within 1 week.

All Skin Types
Combine 1 tablespoon of powdered fennel, 2 drops rose oil, and 3 cups of water. Bottle.
~or~
Prepare an infusion of equal amounts of alfalfa, comfrey, jessamine, orange peel, and parsley. Cool, strain, and bottle.

Face Steam
Place equal amounts of herbs and 2-4 cups water in a pan. Bring to a boil. Remove from heat. Pour into a glass bowl. Drape a towel over your head to contain the steam. Lean head over bowl (allow at least 6-8 inches between your face and the steam) and steam face for 5 minutes. Rinse face with cool water. Follow with a moisturizer if needed. Each formula makes enough for one use.
Note: Steam no more than 1-2 times a week. Do not steam for longer than 5 minutes.

Moisturizing Steam	Refreshing Steam	Relaxing Steam
Chamomile	Chamomile	Calendula
Elder flowers	Mint	Lavender
Lavender	Rosemary	Peppermint
Yarrow	Yarrow	Rosemary

Foot lotion

Leaves feet refreshed and tingly. Apply after using the foot scrub formula.

½ cup water
½ cup isopropyl rubbing alcohol
3 - 4 drops peppermint essential oil
Put water and rubbing alcohol in a bottle that can be capped tightly. Add oil and shake well. Massage into feet thoroughly.

Foot Odor

To eliminate foot odor, sprinkle powdered sage onto your feet and into your socks.

Foot Scrub

Reduces dry, rough callused feet, and leaves them feeling smooth, soft, and tingly. Mix all together in a small bowl. Massage into feet. Follow with a moisturizing foot lotion. Use daily or as needed. Makes enough for one application.
¼ cup oatmeal
¼ cup cornmeal
1 tablespoon of sea salt (table salt can be substituted)
Mint essential oil
Water

Foot Soak

If you suffer from cold feet, a stimulating soak may be just what you need to chase away those chills. Combine 2 ounces ginger, 2 ounces cinnamon, 4 ounces of epsom salt, and 6 pints of hot water. Strain and cool to body temperature. Pour into a container (a large plastic dishpan works well). Soak feet 2-3 times a day for 15-20 minutes.

Hand Pack

A hand pack is good for dry, sun damaged, or unevenly colored hands. It leaves hands smooth and soft. Use twice a week. Combine 1-2 tablespoons of oatmeal, 1 tablespoon of plain yogurt, 1 teaspoon almond, peanut, or olive oil, and 2 teaspoons of fresh lemon, pineapple, or strawberry juice. Mix until it forms a paste-like consistency and allow it to thicken for 1 minute. If it is too thick, add a small amount of water. Apply mixture to back of hands and let dry for 15 to 30 minutes. Rinse with cool water. Pat dry and apply a good moisturizer or sunscreen. Makes enough for one application.

Moisturizer

<u>All Skin Types</u>

Make an infusion of calendula, chamomile, yarrow, violet, or elderflowers. Cool. Strain. Apply to skin. Rinse with warm water. Use within 3 days.
~or~

1-2 tablespoons each almond and soy oil
1 tablespoon beeswax
1 ounce cocoa butter
2 tablespoons orange flower water
⅛ teaspoon borax
5 drops orange essential oil
Warm the oils and mix them together. In a small pan, melt the cocoa butter and stir it into the oils. Melt the beeswax and beat it into the oil mixture. Warm the orange flower water and dissolve the borax in it. Beat this into the main mixture. Leave to thicken. As the mixture starts to thicken, stir in the essential oil. Once mixture has cooled, put it into jars.
~or~
½ cup half and half
1-2 tablespoons chamomile
Place into a double boiler and warm for 20-25 minutes (do not let half-and-half boil or form a skin). Strain and refrigerate. Use within one week.

Dry Skin
2-3 ounces aloe gel
1 teaspoon each glycerin and vegetable oil
½ teaspoon grapeseed extract
4-8 drops each rosemary and sandalwood volatile oil
Combine all ingredients. Shake well before each use. Apply with a cotton ball. Rinse. Pat dry.

Ointment

All Skin Types
This basic ointment makes a wonderful treatment for hands or feet, and is great for all skin types. Warm oil and shortening in a small pan or double boiler until melted. Remove from heat and stir in essential oil and vitamm E. Cool slightly and then begin whisking until mixture becomes thick and creamy. May be used daily. Store in the refrigerator and use within 30 days. Makes approximately 15-20 treatments. If using as an overnight treatment, be sure to wear gloves or socks to bed.

1 ounce almond, apricot, peanut, or olive oil
4 ounces vegetable shortening (no lard)
3-4 drops vitamin E
5 drops your choice of essential oil

Dry Skin
3 tablespoons lanolin
1 tablespoon sunflower oil
1 tablespoon almond oil
1 teaspoon lavender oil

In a small bowl over hot water, melt the lanolin. Add the first two oils and mix together well. Remove from heat and briskly stir in the lavender oil. Pour into containers and let cool. Cover when the ointment has cooled.
~or~
½ ounce Irish moss
7 ounces water
2 teaspoons lemon juice
2 tablespoons glycerine
½ teaspoon borax
1-2 drops of lemon oil or orange oil
Soak moss for 15-20 minutes. Place moss in a pan with water and bring to a boil, reduce heat and simmer for 20-25 minutes. Remove from heat and allow mixture to cool. Stir in the lemon juice. Warm the glycerine and add the borax until it has dissolved completely. Mix this with the cooled Irish moss mixture and add a few drops of the lemon or orange oil. Pour into jars.
~or~
This ointment is fragrant, healing, and soothing. Use it to protect your skin from getting chapped or dry. It's great for softening dry skin on hands or feet. Begin with 1 cup of sweet almond oil as a base. To the base add the following:

1 tablespoon calendula
1 teaspoon chamomile
3 tablespoons lavender
1 tablespoon rose petals
2 tablespoons vitamin E oil
1½ teaspoons of jojoba oil
4 drops of either lavender, roman chamomile, or rose essential oil
5 tablespoons beeswax
Powder the herbs using an herb grinder (a coffee grinder works well), or a mortar and pestle. Warm the base oil in a double boiler or a small pan. Add the herbs to the base and cook on low heat for 25-30 minutes to allow the healing properties of the herbs to be fully released into the oil. Add the jojoba, vitamin E, and the volatile oils to the base mixture. Melt the beeswax on low heat in a small pan or double boiler. Add the melted beeswax to the base mixture and whisk until the mixture is thick and creamy. Fill several 2-4 ounce jars with the ointment. Store in the refrigerator, and warm to room temperature prior to using. Use within 3 months. Makes approximately 10-15 ounces.

Soap Balls
¼ cup boiling water
3-4 drops lavender or rose essential oil
1 tablespoon powdered chamomile, lavender, peppermint, rosemary, sage, or thyme
2 cups castille or ivory soap (shredded)
Plastic wrap
Pour boiling water over herbs. Add essential oil. Steep for 10-15 minutes. Reheat until bubbly and

pour over soap. Let cool a bit and mix together with hands. Let stand 10-15 minutes. Mix again and divide into 4-6 parts. Roll each part into a ball. Place on plastic wrap and dry for 2-3 days. Use in bath or shower.

Toner

All Skin Types

Witch Hazel
Lemon juice
Flower water of your choice
1-2 drops of either lavender or rose geranium oil
Combine all ingredients together and shake well. Bottle. Shake well prior to use. Apply to face. Rinse face thoroughly with clean water to remove.

~or~

Apple cider vinegar
Raspberry leaves
Rose petals
Rosemary
Sage leaves
Rose water
Heat apple cider vinegar and pour it over the herbs. Put mixture in a plastic container and cap it with a plastic lid (do not use metal). Shake container once a day for 10 days. Strain, and add rosewater to mixture. Store in non-metal covered containers. Apply to face. Rinse face thoroughly with clean water to remove.

~or~

¾ cup rose water
5-6 drops glycerine
⅔ cup witch hazel
Combine all ingredients together and shake well. Bottle. Shake well prior to use. Apply to face. Rinse face thoroughly with clean water to remove.

Dry Skin

Soothing toner that rejuvenates dry skin. Prepare an infusion of equal parts of alfalfa, comfrey, jessamine, orange peel, and parsley. Cool, strain, and bottle.

~or~

2-3 ounces aloe gel
2-3 ounces orange blossom water
1 teaspoon vinegar
4-5 drops rose geranium oil
1 drop each chamomile, jasmine, sandalwood oil
2- 400 IU vitamin E capsules
Combine all ingredients. Open the vitamin E capsules and squeeze the oil into the mixture. Shake before using.

Hair Care

Pollution, medications, chemically laden hair care products, harsh shampoos, and diet can actually cause hair to become dry and straw-like, oily, lifeless, have split ends, or simply be an unruly tangle. As hair is composed of 97% protein, a diet rich in protein goes a long way in promoting healthy, thick, shiny hair, and supplementing your diet with calcium, phosphoric acid, riboflavin, and vitamins A and B will help prevent alopecia (balding, hair loss) and stimulate growth. Clean hair is important not only to make you look good, but also to make you feel good. Maintaining your hair's proper pH level can sometimes be tricky. The pH level of healthy hair ranges from 4.5 to 4.7. Washing the hair with an alkaline shampoo can disrupt this balance resulting in damage. The following formulas will help you regain and maintain your "crowning glory".

Alopecia (hair loss)
To deter hair loss, massage olive oil into your scalp each night. Allow oil to remain on scalp overnight. Shampoo hair the following morning. To eliminate olive oil stains on your pillowcase, cover your hair with a scarf or cap.
~or~
To help ward off further balding or hair loss, stimulate and thicken existing hair, and increase scalp circulation, prepare an infusion of equal parts of cinnamon, ginkgo, and licorice. Massage into hair and leave on for 5 minutes. Rinse.

Dandruff
Make an infusion of burdock root, cleavers, nettles, and wormwood. Massage into hair and leave for 3-4 minutes. Rinse.

Hair Conditioner

<u>All Hair Types</u>
Nettle is well known for its conditioning properties. It promotes a healthy shine when used as a final rinse and is gentle enough for daily use. Also, it has been known to help eliminate alopecia, by using it as a leave-in conditioner and massaging it into your scalp once a day, 2-3 times a week, then combing it through to the ends of your hair. Make a strong infusion using nettles. Cool, strain and bottle. Makes enough for one use. Store in the refrigerator. Use within 1 week.
~or~
Deep conditions and leaves hair shiny, soft, and manageable.
2 tablespoons olive or sesame oil
1 egg yolk
1 teaspoon mayonnaise (not miracle whip)
½ cup heavy cream
Mix all ingredients in a blender until they reach a creamy consistency. After thoroughly washing hair with a deep-cleansing shampoo, towel-blot and distribute the mixture evenly onto hair, wrap head completely with aluminum foil to retain heat. Leave on 30 minutes. Remove foil and wash hair again

with deep-cleansing shampoo until all the mixture is removed. Apply once a month.

Limp Hair
Conditions and adds body to limp hair. Make an infusion of nettle, fennel leaves, parsley, rosemary, and wormwood. Massage into hair and leave on for 3-4 minutes. Rinse.

Hair Dye
Henna, a shrub that grows in the East, is a safe, natural vegetable dye for brunette to red hair shades. It is generally available from your beauty supply store and comes in a dark brown powdered form which, when moistened with water and applied, coats the hair without penetration. The hair color will continue to deepen with the length of time the preparation is left on. Preparation can be somewhat tricky for those not experienced in using it. For those who want to experiment with it, it is important to use pure powdered henna rather than a metallic compound. Pure henna, when used with no modifying agent, will turn the hair a bright orange-red shade, a color for many that's not very flattering to wear. An equal mixture of pure henna and chamomile will produce varying tones of burnished copper to reddish gold. The length of time to leave henna on the hair will vary with each person. It is best to conduct a strand test using your own hair before you proceed, this way you will know the correct length of time it takes to achieve the color you desire. To do an at home strand test, snip a small amount of hair close to the nape of your neck. Tape it together at the cut end so it doesn't fall apart. Wearing gloves (henna stains skin) prepare a small batch of henna mixture in a nonmetallic bowl. Apply some of the pre-made mixture to the test hair strand and set the timer. Rinse the hair strand every few minutes to check the color depth. If it's not the shade you want, reapply the henna mixture and continue with your timing. When it is the shade you want, you're ready to proceed with your entire head. The strand test seems like a bit of fuss to go through, but it will save any embarrassment later on. Note: Because henna stains skin, be sure to wear gloves when preparing and applying the mixture to your hair. Tip: Put a small amount of cold cream or petroleum jelly on your skin just below your hairline. This will keep any mixture from getting on and staining your skin. Caution! *Don't* use henna on shades of white, gray, or blond hair, as a *very* bizarre shade will emerge!

Hair Fragrance
To add a subtle fragrance to your hair, make an infusion of jasmine flowers or lavender and lemon verbena. Cool, and put into a spray bottle. Spritz a fine mist over your hair several times throughout the day.

Hair Growth
To stimulate hair growth, make an infusion of horsetail, catnip, wormwood, and 4-6 drops of tea tree oil. Massage into hair and leave for 3-4 minutes. Rinse.

Hair Highlights
The following formulas enhance and gradually add subtle highlights to hair. Prepare a strong infusion using equal parts of herbs. Cool and apply as a final hair rinse. Use 2-3 times a week.

Blonde Hair Shades (includes white, light brown, and grey hair shades)
Chamomile, elderflower, lime flower, or yarrow. Extended use helps lighten blonde shades of hair.

Brunette Hair Shades (includes medium brown to black hair shades)
Parsley, rosemary, sage, or thyme. Extended use helps darken brunette shades of hair.

Red Hair Shades (includes light copper to dark auburn hair shades)
Calendula. Extended use adds subtle burnished/copper highlights to red shades of hair.

Hair Rinse
Prepare an infusion using equal amounts of herbs. Massage into hair and leave on for 3-5 minutes. Rinse with plain water.

All Hair Types
Elderflower
Horsetail
Nettle
Rosemary

Dry Hair
Arnica
Birch
Calendula
Marshmallow

Hair Shampoo
This gentle, mild shampoo works great for all hair types. Leaves hair shiny and soft. Make an infusion of the herbs. Strain the mixture into a medium-sized bowl and add the oil. Stir vigorously. Add your choice of shampoo and stir until thoroughly mixed. Bottle and store in the refrigerator. Allow shampoo to warm to room temperature prior to use. This shampoo will clean with a minimal amount of suds, as it does not contain strong foaming agents. Shake bottle lightly prior to use. Follow with conditioner and hair rinse. Use daily or as needed. Makes enough for approximately 30-40 applications.

½ cup your choice of shampoo
1 tablespoon calendula
2 tablespoons chamomile
2 teaspoons comfrey
½ teaspoon lavender essential oil
2 teaspoons rosemary
1 tablespoon nettle
2 teaspoons orange peel
2 cups water

Oral Hygiene

Preventative dental care is important to promote and maintain oral health. A daily cleansing program to remove debris from tooth surfaces, between the teeth, gums, and tongue will help prevent tooth enamel decay and ward off periodontal disease. As teeth are composed of calcium phosphate, and a sufficient quantity of this mineral is necessary to serve as a repair material, suplementation of vitamin D is recommended to enhance the body's ability to assimilate calcium. To protect the tooth enamel and prevent gum tissue breakdown, the body also requires vitamms A and C. A deficiency of either of these two vitamins may cause degeneration of the enamel forming cells, which could result in defective tooth enamel. Use a salt-water rinse after cleansing (stir 1 teaspoon of salt in a glass of warm water). Swish around in mouth. Do not swallow rinse water. A healthy diet that includes large quantities of raw, crisp vegetables and fresh friuts will guarantee a super smile!

Dentifrice

The following tooth cleansers help strengthen the gums, freshen breath, and ward off periodontal disease. Dampen your toothbrush and dip it in the powdered herbal mixture. Brush as usual. Make sure to rinse out your mouth after using these cleansers. Store any remaining cleanser in a covered container. Formulas make enough for several uses. Use daily or as needed. Add 10-15 drops clove or peppermint oil (depending on your taste preference) to the following formulas.

<u>Formula 1</u>
Arrowroot (2 tablespoons)
Cinnamon or Baking Soda (1 teaspoon)
Sea Salt (2 teaspoons)

<u>Formula 2</u>
Myrrh (1 tablespoon)
Sage (1 handful)
Sea Salt (1 tablespoon)

Gargle/Mouth Rinse

The following formula is refreshing and has no bitter after-taste. Prepare an infusion of cassia (2 parts), clove (2 parts), cranesbill (6 parts), goldthread (2 parts), mint (6 parts), oak (6 parts), rhatany (2 parts), rosemary (10 parts), and sage (10 parts). Cool and strain prior to use. Gargle or swish around in mouth for 1 minute. Do not swallow liquid. Refrigerate any unused portion and use within two days.

Tooth Brightener/Whitener

Strawberries naturally help to brighten and whiten teeth, and they leave your mouth feeling clean, fresh, and wonderful tasting. Unless you have a strawberry sensitivity, they work well for everyone, especially those with coffee, tea, or tobacco stained teeth. Mash one medium-sized ripe strawberry into a pulp. Dip your toothbrush into the pulp and brush. Follow with a plain water mouth rinse. Use daily or as needed. Makes enough for one use.

Fragrance

Ancient cultures were skilled at using aromatic herbs to delight the olfactory senses. They created scented soaps and fragrant waters to be used on the skin and hair, and they would hang and strew aromatic herbs in their dwellings, thus adding a fragrant scent to their surroundings. The natural aroma of certain herbs is used to make perfumes, potpourri, and sachets. Herbal fragrances are just as easy to create today as those of years gone by and, with a bit of practice, you can create your very own fragrances, too.

Perfume

Homemade perfume is natural, contains no chemicals, and is quite easy to make. To make the following formulas, simply combine all the ingredients in a bottle, shake well to mix, and let it sit. Perfume will be ready to use in 3-4 weeks (with the exception of spice perfume). Store your perfume in a cool place such as the refrigerator to keep it from turning rancid. Take it out of the refrigerator before use and allow it to warm a bit prior to application.

Rose Perfume

½ cup isopropyl alcohol
⅛ cup rose water
½ tablespoon rosemary oil
1 tablespoon rose oil

Herbal Perfume

½ cup isopropyl alcohol
½ teaspoon basil oil
½ teaspoon dill oil
½ teaspoon sage oil

Citrus Perfume

½ cup isopropyl alcohol
½ tablespoon citronella oil
1 tablespoon lemon oil
½ tablespoon lemon verbena oil
½ tablespoon sandalwood oil

Spice Perfume

Ready to use in 2-3 months.
½ cup isopropyl alcohol
½ tablespoon clove oil
1 tablespoon cinnamon oil
⅛ cup orrisroot (powdered)

Potpourri

Potpourri is a wonderful way to fill each room in your home or business with fragrance. Combine equal amounts of dried herbs in an open top container. Add 2-3 tablespoons of orrisroot powder as a fixative. Adding 2-3 drops of essential oil will enhance and revive its fragrance. It's always fun to experiment with different combinations and create your own unique blends.

Citrus Potpourri

Combine equal amounts of cinnamon, lemon leaf, lemon peel, lime peel, nutmeg, orange blossoms/peel, rosemary, and lemon or orange oil.

Country Potpourri

Combine equal amounts of lemon balm, marjoram, mint, rosemary, sage, thyme, and rosemary oil.

Floral Potpourri
Combine equal amounts of carnation petals, chamomile, cranesbill, lavender, lilac flowers, rose petals, and lavender oil.

Forest Potpourri
Combine equal amounts of alder, cedar, lichen, myrtle, pinecones and needles, sandalwood, wormwood, and cedar oil.

Love Potpourri
Combine equal amounts of lilac flowers, rose leaves/petals, tonka beans, violet petals, and rose oil.

Sleep Potpourri
Combine equal amounts of cloves, lavender, mint, rose leaves/petals, and lavender oil.

Sachets
Sachets are easy and fun to make. Place them in your dresser drawers, inside your pillowcase, under the seat of your car, or present them as gifts. They can be made from any piece of solid color or print fabric. Cut two pieces of fabric into a square. Place the pieces of fabric together with the pattern side showing and sew a straight seam (about a ¼ inch in) around three of the edges leaving one end open. Put some hypoallergenic polyester fiberfill in one end so that it fills about half your sachet, then put your dried, crushed herbs into the center and place some more polyester fiberfill on top. Sew the open end closed, and trim the edges with a pinking shear to add a decorative touch. Sizes are generally 4x8, or 8x10, but can be made any size you like.

Dream Sachet
¼ cup dried lemon verbena leaves
¼ cup dried rose petals
¼ cup dried chamomile flowers
¼ cup dried rosemary or lavender
15 drops rose or lavender volatile oil
¼ cup large pieces of orrisroot
1 cup dried hops flowers

Restful Sleep Sachet
Combine equal amounts of:
Catnip
Lavender
Lemon Balm
Lemon Verbena
Saint John's Wort
Valerian

Household Cleaners

Many herbs make excellent, non-toxic bleaches, cleaners, polishes, carpet or fabric shampoos, and floor wax. Be sure to try these formulas on an inconspicuous area first to test for color fastness or the event of possible fading.

Natural Household Bleach

Formula 1
Extract the juice from sorrel leaves. The juice makes bleach that is useful in removing rust spots from linen or white cotton. It will also make ink stains less visible.

Formula 2
To make a natural bleach and cleaner for kitchen surfaces or laundry, add 1 cup of lemon juice to half a bucket of water. Let it sit overnight. Use the next day.

Ceramic Tile Cleaner/Polisher
Cleans and polishes ceramic tile. Pour all ingredients into a spray bottle. Shake gently to mix. Spray onto surface and wipe dry with a clean, soft cloth.

1 teaspoon of borax
¼ teaspoon each eucalyptus and lavender essential oil
3-4 drops of tea tree essential oil
2-3 tablespoons of vinegar
2 cups of very warm water

Cleaning Soap
This gentle skin softening soap produces a rich lather and can be safely used for all types of cleaning.
1 pound of unscented soap flakes
4 tablespoons of corn oil
4 ounces of honey
4 teaspoons clove oil
Mix soap flakes, corn oil, and honey together in a bowl. Soften these ingredients by placing the bowl over a pan of simmering water for about 20 minutes. Stir. Add the clove oil and pour the mixture into a pan. On low heat setting, stir the mixture until it resembles a stiff dough consistency. Put mixture into oiled molds. Drying time is usually between 2-3 weeks.

Furniture Polish

Formula 1
Brazil nuts, hazelnuts, and walnuts make great furniture polish. Using a circular motion, rub the cut edge of the kernel on the surface to be polished. Then go over the surface again in the direction of the wood grain. Once the polish has dried, you can shine it up with a soft cloth.

Formula 2
A good cleaner and polish for dirty and/or dry wood, and the oils will not darken beech or pine. Apply with a cloth. Polish when dry. Put all ingredients in a covered jar and shake well. Shake prior to each use.

10 ounces linseed oil
5 ounces cider vinegar
6 teaspoons lemon oil

Formula 3
To gently polish wood, mix 3 tablespoons olive oil with 1 tablespoon vinegar. Apply using a soft cloth.

Furniture Wax
Apply this wood furniture wax sparingly. Polish with a soft cloth to a beautiful shine.

4 ounces of beeswax
4 ounces of unscented soap flakes
14 ounces of rosemary infusion at normal strength
Put beeswax into a bowl and melt over a pan of barely simmering water. Remove from heat. Dissolve the soap flakes in the rosemary infusion. Cool both mixtures. Stir them together until the mixture resembles a thick cream consistency. Store in a covered jar. Makes enough for several uses.

Metal Polish
Gather a handful of horsetail stems and rub over pots, pans and pewter to clean and shine them. Wash your pots and pans prior to use.

Upholstery Shampoo
Be sure to try these formulas on an inconspicuous area first to test for color fastness or the event of possible fading. To gently clean upholstery and delicate fabrics, make a decoction using the following herbs.

1 ounce of dried soapwort root or 4 handfuls of fresh soapwort
3 pints of water
Cool. Strain. Store in a covered container.

Wood Floor Wax
This wood floor wax polishes up to a beautiful durable shine. Works great for oak and wood block flooring. Using a cloth or a pad, rub the wax into the floor. Let the wax sit for 1-2 hours. Polish with a soft cloth.

4 ounces beeswax
4 tablespoons linseed oil
4 teaspoons cedar oil
Place beeswax and linseed oil in a bowl. Melt over a pan of simmering water. Remove from heat and stir until mixture resembles a heavy cream consistency. Add the cedar oil and stir. Store in a covered jar.

Insect Repellents

The plant kingdom offers a perfectly effective range of natural insect repellents that help deter numerous insects and bugs as well as the evening onslaught of mosquitoes throughout the warm months of summer. The following herbs, when applied to your skin, placed in doorways or on windowsills, or integrated into your garden, will help to repel insects inside and/or outside of the home.

All Insects
Indoor Uses: Combine equal amounts of dried, crushed bay leaves and vetiver root. Place where insect activity has been observed. ~or~ Place pieces of calamus root and a few tonka beans where insects are present. Outdoor Uses: Combine crushed or powdered bay leaves, eucalyptus, pennyroyal, and rosemary. Sprinkle around building perimeter or scatter over ground where insects are present. Repeat every few days or after a rain.

Ants
Indoor/Outdoor Uses: A safe repellent for use on work surfaces. Boil six to eight handfuls of walnut leaves in one pint of water for 25-35 minutes. Cool and apply with a large paintbrush. ~or~ Place pennyroyal, mint, tansy, and/or wormwood on ant trails, near doors, windows, or wherever you see ants entering your home. These plants can also be integrated into your garden and around fruit trees. Indoor Uses: Crush dried catnip and place on ant trails, also near doors, windows, or wherever you see ants entering your home.

Aphids
Integrate anise, chives, coriander, garlic, nasturtium, and petunias into your garden.

Beetles
Bean Beetle (includes Mexican Bean Beetle and Weevils): Integrate potatoes and thyme into your garden. ~or~ Integrate calendula, potato, rosemary, summer savory, and petunia into your garden.
Cucumber Beetle: Integrate radish and tansy into your garden.
Flea Beetle (Fleas): Combine powdered lavender and orange peels with borax. Sprinkle on carpets. Resprinkle onto carpets after each vacuum. ~or~ Combine powdered wormwood, mint, and catnip. Sprinkle on carpets. Resprinkle onto carpets after each vacuum.
Japanese Beetle: Integrate cranesbill, garlic, larkspur, tansy, rue, and white geranium into your garden.
Potato Beetle (Potato Bug, Colorado Beetle): Integrate green beans, horseradish, nettle, flax, catnip, coriander, tansy, and nasturtium into your garden.
Rose Chafer Beetle (Rose Bug): Integrate geranium, onion, and petunia into your garden.

Bugs

Squash Bug: Integrate catnip, nasturtium, and tansy into your garden.
Bedbugs (Chinch): Place leafy branches of mountain mahogany under bed mattress.
Chiggers (Chigoe): Indoor/Outdoor Uses: Mix pennyroyal or eucalyptus essential oil with a sesame oil, olive oil or rubbing alcohol. Smooth this lotion over skin (avoid eye/mouth area) before going outdoors. Reapply as needed.
Cockroaches (Cucaracha): Scatter bay leaves throughout your house and tuck into areas where roach activity has been observed.
Leafhopper: Integrate cranesbill and petunia into your garden.

Flies

Black Fly: Outdoor Uses: Make an infusion of basil, lavender, and nettle. Apply to exposed skin using a spray bottle with fine mist setting. Avoid eye and mouth area.
House Fly: Indoor Uses: Strew (scatter, sprinkle) mint, pennyroyal, rue, tansy, thyme, or wormwood on the floor, place them on windowsills, or simply hang bunches of the herb from the ceiling. Indoor/Outdoor Uses: Combine equal amounts of dried, crushed bay leaves, cloves, clover flowers, and eucalyptus. Put into mesh bags and hang on the inside and the outside of your entrance doors. ~or~ Place cedar, eucalyptus and lavender on windowsills and hang inside and outside of entrance doors. Outdoor Uses: Mix pennyroyal, eucalyptus, or citronella, essential oil with a sesame, olive oil or rubbing alcohol. Smooth this lotion over skin (avoid eye/mouth area) before going outdoors. Reapply as needed.
Whitefly: Outdoor Uses: Plant calendula, and nasturtium near doorways or strew on walkways.

Gnats

Outdoor Uses: Rub arms, legs, and neck with fresh elder leaves or sage. This protection lasts about 25 minutes. Reapply as needed. ~or~ Make a strong infusion of elder leaves or chamomile and dab onto your skin to avoid bites. Fill a small container with the infusion and carry it with you. Shake well before each use and reapply as needed. ~or~ Mix citronella, eucalyptus, lavender, patchouli, or pennyroyal essential oil with vegetable oil or isopropyl rubbing alcohol base. Smooth over skin (avoid eye/mouth area) before going outdoors. Reapply as needed. ~or~ Rub fresh lavender or elder leaves on your skin, and/or wear fresh lavender or elder leaves in your hair.

Mosquitos

Outdoor Uses: Rub arms, legs, and neck with fresh elder leaves or sage. Protection lasts about 25 minutes. Reapply as needed. ~or~ Make a strong infusion of elder leaves or chamomile and dab onto your skin to deter bites. Fill a small container with the infusion and carry it with you. Shake well before each use and reapply as needed. ~or~ Mix citronella, eucalyptus, lavender, patchouli or pennyroyal essential oil with vegetable oil or isopropyl rubbing alcohol base. Smooth over skin (avoid eye/mouth area) before going outdoors. Reapply as needed. Mosquito Larvacide: Sprinkle the seeds of shepherd's purse on the water where mosquitos breed. The mucilage in the seeds will destroy the larvae. About one pound of seeds will destroy approximately ten million larvae. Thyme oil also destroy larvae.

Moths

All Moths: Indoor Uses: In a large bowl combine 2-3 teaspoons each of mugwort, rosemary, chamomile, thyme, wormwood, cinnamon, ground cloves, nutmeg, salt, and orrisroot powder. Add several drops of lavender, clove, or lemon oil to the herb mixture to scent it strongly. Cover the bowl and set in a dark place for 3 weeks. Place the mixture onto small squares of muslin or cotton, gather up corners and tie with string to make small herb filled bags. Place in drawers or closets. ~or~ Combine ground camphor wood, cedar, lavender, rosemary, sassafras and wormwood. Put into a sachet. Place in boxes, dresser drawers, or hang in closets. ~or~ Melt ½ ounce of paraffin. Stir in ¼ teaspoon each of bergamot, clove, and heliotrope oil. Pour into small molds (candy molds work well). Cool. Put in dresser drawers, storage boxes or place in mesh bags and hang in closets. **Cabbage Moth:** Integrate celery, hyssop, mint, nasturtium, rosemary, sage, thyme, and wormwood into your garden.

Slugs/Snails
Integrate garlic, rosemary, and wormwood into your garden.

Worms

Borer Worm: Integrate garlic, onion, and tansy into your garden.
Cutworm: Integrate tansy into your garden.
Hornworm (Tomato Hornworm): Integrate basil, borage, and calendula into your garden.
Nematodes: Integrate asparagus, calendula, dahlia, and salvia into your garden.

Pet Care

Placing dried herbs in with your pet's bedding helps to relieve allergy, arthritis, depression, and those annoying fleas and ticks. The preferred internal administration method of a pet formula is to place the powdered herbs inside of a gel capsule, moisten the capsule with a small amount of water and place the capsule as far back on the pet's tongue as possible. Holding the pet's mouth closed, gently stroke the throat area encouraging the pet to swallow (wrapping the pet's body inside of a large towel helps to avoid one from getting scratched and keeps the pet relaxed). Mixing the powdered formula in with their food is another method of administration, although many pets may refuse this form of administration due to disagreeable smell or taste. Always consult a veterinarian before attempting to treat a pet's condition on your own.

Cats and Dogs

Allergy

Counteracts allergy in cats and dogs.

Combine: aloe (small pinch), catnip (small pinch), dandelion (small pinch), and powdered garlic (equivalent to one clove - per 10 to 20 lbs. body weight). Lightly sprinkle over or mix into food once a week. Caution: Avoid use if pet is less than six months of age, pregnant, lactating, scheduled for surgery, is taking an anticoagulant, or has a bile duct, gallbladder, kidney, or liver problem.

Ear Mites

Place 3-5 drops of mullein oil into ear daily to help alleviate ear mites.

Fleas and Ticks

Combine ½ cup of powdered arrowroot with equal parts baking soda, clay, or cornstarch. Sprinkle on pet as a preventive powder. ~or~ Sprinkle powdered garlic (equivalent to one clove) onto food and mix in well.

Lice

To destroy lice and their nits, bathe pet with a larkspur infusion added to a mild pet shampoo (avoid eye/mouth area). Leave soap on body for 5-10 minutes. Rinse well. Repeat as needed. Do not apply if irritation is more than superficial. Seek veterinarian assistance if pet has large opened reddened areas of skin.

Mange

The antifungal properties of this formula alleviate mange.

Make an infusion of black walnut hulls, chaparral, echinacea, goldenseal, and myrrh. Massage into pet's skin 2-3 times a day until condition clears. Apply 1-2 drops of tea tree oil directly to affected areas.

Parasites (intestinal)

Sprinkle powdered garlic (equivalent to one clove) onto food and mix in well. ~or~ An etremely small pinch of powdered areca nut seed mixed in with pet food may help to expel tapeworms.

Pet Bath

Put cedarwood, eucalyptus, juniper, lavender, or peppermint into a muslin sachet and place into your pet's bath.

Pet Urine

To remove urine odor and stains combine ¼ cup white vinegar and 1 teaspoon liquid dish soap (unscented if possible). Blot and rinse area with cool water. Using a sponge, apply a generous portion of the solution directly to the area. Leave it on for 10-15 minutes, and then rinse with cool water. Note: Be sure to test a small area of fabric or carpet for color fastness prior to use.

Pet Pillow
Pet pillows can be made from any piece of heavyweight fabric such as canvas or denim. Cut fabric into two squares that are the appropriate size for your pet's bed. Sew a straight seam around three sides leaving one side open. Put equal amounts of dried, crushed cedar wood, chamomile, lavender, pennyroyal and/or rue into the square, and sew the opening closed. Insert this pillow inside of, or underneath your pet's bed mattress.

Horses (includes Burros, Donkeys, and Mules)

Colic
An extremely small pinch of powdered areca nut seed sprinkled over feed may help to reduce bouts of colic.

Heaves
Combine licorice, lobelia (pinch), saltpeter, and skunk cabbage. Give 3 times a day mixed in with feed.

Saddle Sores
To prevent saddle sores, slosh an infusion of cinquefoil over their back after removing the blanket, pack, or saddle.

Wounds
To speed healing of a flesh wound, combine powdered elder and wormwood with olive oil. Apply as a dressing to affected area. Apply a new dressing daily.

Plants that are Poisonous to Livestock
Agave (all livestock); Arbutus, Trailing (cattle); Corydalis (cattle, sheep); Cow Parsnip (all livestock); Goat's Rue (sheep); Lycium (cattle, sheep); Milk Vetch (cattle, horses, sheep); Dusty Miller (cattle, horses); Henbane (cattle, horses); Horsetail (horses); Groundsel (all livestock); Horseradish (all livestock); Laurel, Mountain (all livestock, and when pheasants eat the berries, those who feed on the birds absorb the toxins contained in the berries through ingestion of the bird.); Malabar Nut (all livestock); Pennyroyal (dogs, cats); Poppy, Opium (all livestock); Saffron, Meadow (cattle); Unicorn Root, False (cattle).

Dyeing with Plants

Since ancient times, humans have embellished their fabrics and skin with color. The earliest dyes were no more than stains obtained from barks, berries, flowers, fruits, hulls, leaves, nuts, seeds, roots, or the entire plant. Experimentation with earth, which contains iron and various other minerals, helped set the color rendering it more permanent, and either brightened it or gave it new depth. The most common plant shades are blue, brown, gray, indigo, purple, red and yellow. Other color variations may be accomplished by combing different plant materials. Adding a mordant to the dye

bath, while not required, will help the material absorb the color, resist fading, and make the dye permanent. Natural wool yarn is the easiest material to dye, although inexpensive skeins of synthetic off-white or white yarn purchased from your local craft store will work just as well. Whether this is your first time or you are an experienced dyer, it is always best to gather plant material and make small batches of dye which can be used as samples for future reference. The reason for preparing the samples is that dyeing with plants can be unpredictable in as far as variations in color shades and results. Variations are due to the locations in which they grow, the differences in plant chemistry, as well as the time of year. Also, keep in mind that it generally takes quite a large amount of plant material to dye one pound of wool. For example one pound of wool would require (amounts are approximate): 8-10 quarts of bark, 3-6 quarts of flowers, 8-10 quarts of hulls, 2-4 quarts of leaves, or a varied amount of roots.
Note: Cotton, linen, and silk fabrics can be dyed, however due to their complicated preparation methods, this process will not be discussed here.

Plant Dyeing Equipment

1 large stainless container (used for the dye bath)
1 large pair of tongs (stainless steel or wooden)
1 large spoon (stainless steel or wooden)
1 large bowl or bucket (enamel or stainless steel)
Measuring device
Rubber gloves
Stick or wooden dowel (used to lift and turn the yarn in the dye bath)
Timer

Scouring

This is the initial process that will clean and prepare the yarn for dyeing. Wrap yarn skeins snugly in a figure 8 pattern with white cotton string. Dissolve soap flakes in hot water. Add yarn skeins to the soapy water and hand wash to remove any dirt or oil. Remove the skeins and rinse in hot water until all soap is gone. Hang skeins on a dowel rod or gently spread skeins apart (while still tied) and let air dry. The yarn is now ready for the dyeing process.

Dyeing Process

The actual dye process is fairly easy. Place the dye bath onto a stove, or as some still do, over an open fire. Fill the dye bath ¾ full of cold water. You may add powdered plant material directly into the water and stir until it is well dissolved. If you are using dried or freshly gathered plant materials, they will need to be broken, bruised, or pounded just prior to being put into the dye bath in order for the pigment to be released. Place the plant material into a mesh-type bag, making sure the top is tied securely, and put it into the water. Yarn can be re-dyed to darken or intensify the color.

Mordants

Mordants are compounds that when added to the dye bath will help the yarn absorb, intensify, and set the color. Different colors can be achieved by using different mordants. Care and gloves should

be used when handling mordants, as many of them are toxic. Keep them out of the reach of children and pets.
* Cream of Tartar (Potassium hydrogen tartrate) is *not* the same substance used in baking.

Alum Mordant
(Potassium aluminum sulphate)
Added to the beginning of the dye process, alum helps the dye to penetrate evenly and brightens the color.

4 ounces alum (potassium aluminum sulphate)
1 ounce cream of tartar* (potassium hydrogen tartrate)
1 pound wool yarn (in skeins)

Fill dye bath ¾ full of cold water Dissolve potassium hydrogen tartrate and alum in cold water. Add yarn to dye bath. Bring water to a boil. Reduce heat and simmer for approximately ¾ to 1 hour, or until desired color has been reached. Using tongs, lift yarn from water, drain, and gently squeeze out the excess water. Hang yarn over a cord or spread on a flat surface to dry.

Chrome Mordant
(Bichromate of potash)
Added to the beginning of the dye process, chrome sets the color and gives the yarn a nice soft feel.

½ ounce chrome (bichromate of potash)
1 pound wool yarn (in skeins)

Fill dye bath ¾ full of cold water. Dissolve bichromate of potash in cold water. Add yarn to dye bath. Bring water to a boil, reduce heat and simmer for approximately ¾ to 1 hour or until desired color has been reached. Using tongs, lift yarn from water, drain, and gently squeeze out the excess water. Hang yarn over a cord or spread on a flat surface to dry.

Iron Mordant
(Ferrous sulphate)
Added to the end of the dye process, iron darkens the color.

½ ounce iron (ferrous sulphate)
1 ounce cream of tartar* (potassimn hydrogen tartrate)
1 pound wool yarn (in skeins)

Fill dye bath ¾ full of cold water. Add yarn to the dye bath and simmer for 25-30 minutes. Using tongs, remove yarn from dye bath and set it in the enamel or stainless steel bowl or bucket. Dissolve potassium hydrogen tartrate and iron in dye bath. Put yarn back into dye bath and simmer until it has reached the desired color. Using tongs, lift yarn from water, drain, and gently squeeze out the excess water. Hang yarn over a cord or spread on a flat suffuce to dry.

Tin Mordant
(Stannous chloride)
Added to the end of the dye process, tin intensifies reds and yellows.

½ ounce tin (stannous chloride)
2 ounces cream of tartar* (potassium hydrogen tartrate)
1 pound wool yarn (in skeins)

Fill dye bath ¾ full of cold water. Add yarn to the dye bath and simmer for 35-45 minutes. Using tongs, remove yarn from dye bath and set it in the enamel or stainless steel bowl or bucket. Dissolve potassium hydrogen tartrate and tin in dye bath. Put yarn back into dye bath and simmer until it has reached the desired color. Using tongs, lift yarn from water, drain, and gently squeeze out the excess water. Hang yarn over a cord or spread on a flat surface to dry.

Plants that Yield Dye
To help you get started, here is a listing of some plants that yield dye, the mordants used, and the color ranges. Do not let this list limit you on the many color possibilities. Experiment and have fun!
*Tannic acid can be obtained from oak galls or sumac leaves.

Plant	Plant Part	Mordant	Color Range
Acacia	Entire Plant	None	Browns
Agrimony	Entire Plant	None	Yellows
Alder	Bark	Copper	Reds/Browns
Alder	Catkins	None	Greens
Aloe	Leaves	None	Purples/Violets
Angelica	Flowers	None	Yellows
Apple	Bark	None	Yellows/Golds
Barberry	Bark	Alum	Yellows
Barberry	Root	Lye	Yellows
Bayberry	Berries	None	Blues
Bayberry	Leaves	Alum	Yellows/Browns
Bedstraw	Leaves or Stems	None	Yellows
Bedstraw	Root	None	Orange/Reds
Birch	Bark or Leaves	Alum	Yellows
Birch	Bark	None	Tans/Browns
Birch	Bark	Iron	Lavenders/Purples
Blackberry	Berries	Alum	Blues/Greys

Plant	Plant Part	Mordant	Color Range
Blackberry	Shoots	Iron	Greys/Blacks
Bloodroot	Root	Alum	Yellows
Bloodroot	Root	None	Reds
Blueberry	Berries	Alum	Blues/Purples
Blueberry	Berries	Tannic acid*	Browns
Bugleweed	Leaves or Stems	None	Blacks
Calendula	Flowers	Alum or Chrome	Yellows
Cardamom	Fruit	None	Yellows
Cedar	Root	Alum	Purples
Celandine	Root	None	Yellows
Chamomile	Flowers	Alum	Yellows
Chokecherry	Bark	None	Yellows/Oranges/Tans
Chokecherry	Berries or Root	Alum	Reds/Purples
Cinquefoil	Root	None	Reds
Coffee	Beans	Alum	Tans/Browns
Cohosh, Blue	Root	None	Greenish yellow
Coptis	Root	None	Yellows
Cornflower	Flowers (blue variety)	None	Blues
Dahlia	Flowers	Chrome	Oranges
Dandelion	Root	None	Yellows
Dock	Root	None	Yellows
Elder	Berries	Alum	Purples/Violets
Elder	Leaves	Alum	Greens
Fenugreek	Seeds	None	Yellows
Fern	Root	Alum	Oranges/Yellows
Fern	Shoots	Alum	Greens/Yellows
Fumitory	Flowers	None	Yellows
Goldenrod	Entire Plant	Chrome	Yellows/Golds
Goldenseal	Root	None	Yellows/Golds
Goldenthread	Root	Alum	Yellows
Grape	Berries	Alum	Blues/Purples
Groundsel	Entire Plant	Alum	Yellows
Heather	Shoots	Alum or Chrome	Greens/Yellows
Henna	Leaves	None	Orange-red
Hickory	Bark	None	Yellows
Indigo	Leaves	None	Blues/Purples
Juniper	Bark, Berries, or Twigs	None	Tans
Kola Nut	Nuts	None	Reds
Lamb's Quarters	Entire Plant	None	Greens
Lichens	Entire Plant	Various mordants	Pinks/Plums/Golds/Browns

Plant	Plant Part	Mordant	Color Range
Madder	Root	Alum or Chrome	Pinks/Reds
Mandrake	Root	None	Yellows
Maple	Bark	None	Browns
Milkweed	Entire Plant	Various mordants	Greens/Oranges
Mulberry	Berries	Various mordants	Blues/Purples
Mullein	Juice	Alum	Greens/Yellows
Oak	Bark	Alum or Chrome	Yellows/Tans
Olive	Flowers	Iron	Yellows
Olive	Root	Iron	Greys/Blacks
Onion	Skins	Alum or Chrome	Oranges/Yellows
Orris	Flowers	Iron	Yellows
Orris	Root	Iron	Greys/Blacks
Peach	Bark or Leaves	Alum	Golds
Pine	Cones	Alum	Oranges/Yellows
Pine	Cones	Iron	Browns
Pitcher Plant	Root	None	Yellows
Pokeweed	Berries	None	Reds/Purples
Poplar	Leaves	Alum	Yellows
Poplar	Leaves	Chrome	Golds/Browns
Privet	Berries	Alum	Blues/Greens
Privet	Leaves	Alum	Yellows
Ragwort	Entire Plant	Alum	Yellows
Raspberry	Berries	Alum	Greys/Blacks
Raspberry	Shoots	Iron	Blues/Greys
Safflower	Flowers	Various mordants	Pinks/Oranges/Yellows
Saffron	Stigma	None	Yellows
Saint John's Wort	Flowers	Alum	Greens/Yellows
Saint John's Wort	Flowers	Tin	Pinks
Sassafras	Root	Alum	Browns
Sassafras	Root	Chrome	Reds/Browns
Scotch Broom	Flowers	Alum or Chrome	Yellows
Sumac	Berries or Leaves	None	Tans/Browns
Sumac	Leaves	Alum	Yellows
Sunflower	Flowers	None	Yellows
Sunflower	Seeds	None	Purples/Blacks
Tansy	Flowers	Alum	Yellows
Tea	Leaves	Alum or Chrome	Tans/Browns
Tormentil	Root	None	Reds
Uva-Ursi	Berries	Alum	Blues
Uva-Ursi	Leaves	Alum	Greys/Blacks

Plant	Plant Part	Mordant	Color Range
Violet	Flowers	None	Blues
Walnut	Hulls	None	Tans/Browns
Walnut	Leaves	None	Blacks
Woad	Leaves	None	Blues/Indigos

APPENDICES

The tall grasses of vivid green sway in the morning breeze, while a brightly colored hedge, crowned with a garland of hawthorn dressed in delicate pinkish-white flowers flanks a leafy lane. The speedwell, surrounded by fallen petals from the wild cherry, awakens and opens its blue eyes as buttercups tip their golden discs to greet the day.

Debra Rayburn

Appendix I
Herbs by Common Name

A reference listing that will help you find an herb for which you know only the common name.

A

Abscess Root (*Polemonium reptans*), 32
Acacia (*Acacia senegal*), 32
Aconite (*Aconitum napellus*), 33, 52
Adrue (*Cyperus articulatus*), 34
Agave (*Agave americana*), 35, 40
Agrimony (*Agrimonia eupatori*), 36
Alder (*Alnus glutinosa*), 37
Alfalfa (*Medicago sativa*), 37
Allspice (*Pimenta racemosa*), 39
Aloe (*Aloe barbadensis*), 39
Alpine Cranberry (*Vaccinium vitis-idaea*), 41
Alumroot (*Heuchera parvifolia*), 41
Amaranth (*Amaranthus hypochondriacus*), 42
Angelica (*Angelica atropurpurea*), 43
Angostura (*Galipea cusparia*), 44
Anise (*Pimpinella anisum*), 45
Apple (*Pyrus malus*), 46
Apricot (*Prunus armeniaca*), 47
Araroba (*Andira araroba*), 48
Arborvitae (*Thuja occidentalis*), 48
Arbutus, Strawberry Tree (*Arbutus unedo*), 49
Arbutus, Trailing (*Epigaea repens*), 50
Areca Nut (*Areca catechu*), 51, 78
Arnica (*Arnica montana*), 51
Arrowroot *(Maranta arundinacae*), 52
Artichoke, Cardoon (*Cynara cardunculus*), 53
Artichoke, Globe (*Cynara scolymus*), 53
Artichoke, Jerusalem (*Helianthus tuberosus*),54
Asafetida (*Ferula asafoetida*), 55
Ash (*Fraxinus excelsior*), 56
Ash, Mountain (*Sorbus americana*), 56
Ash, Prickly (*Xanthoxylum americanum*), 57
Ash, Wafer (*Ptelea trifoliata*), 58
Ashwagandha (*Withania somnifera*), 59
Asparagus (*Asparagus officinalis*), 60
Avens (*Geum urbanum*), 61
Ayahuasca (*Banisteria caapi*), 62
Azedarach (*Melia azedarach*), 63

B

Bael (*Aegle marmelos*), 63
Balsam of Peru (*Myroxylon pereirae*), 64
Balsam of Tolu (*Myroxylon balsamum*), 65
Bamboo (*Bambusa arundinacea*), 66
Banana (*Musa paradisiaca*), 66
Baneberry (*Actaea spicata*), 67, 222
Barberry (*Berberis vulgaris*), 68
Barley (*Hordeum vulgare*), 69
Basil (*Ocymum basilicum*), 70
Bay (*Laurus nobilis*), 71
Bayberry (*Myrica cerifera*), 72
Bearberry (*Arctostaphylos uva-ursi*), 73
Bedstraw (*Galium aperine*), 74
Beet (*Beta vulgaris*), 75
Belladonna (*Atropa belladonna*), 76, 85
Betel (*Piper betle*), 51, 77
Beth Root (*Trillium pendulum*), 78
Betony (*Stachys betonica*), 79
Bindweed (*Convolvulus arvensis*), 80
Birch (*Betula alba*), 81
Birthwort (*Aristolochia clematitis*), 82
Bistort (*Polygonum bistorta*), 83
Bitterroot (*Lewisia rediviva*), 84
Bittersweet (*Solanum dulcamara*), 85
Black-Eyed Susan (*Rudbeckia hirta*), 86
Bladderwrack (*Fucus versiculosus*), 86
Blessed Thistle (*Cnicus benedictus*), 88
Bloodroot (*Sanguinaria canadensis*), 88
Blueberry (*Vaccinium myrtillus*), 89
Blue Flag (*Iris versicolor*), 91
Boldo (*Peumus boldus*), 92
Boneset (*Eupatorium perfoliatum*), 92, 147
Borage (*Borago officinalis*), 93
Bryony (*Bryonia dioica*), 94
Buchu (*Barosma betulina*), 95
Buckbean (*Menyanthes trifoliata*), 96
Bugleweed (*Lycopus americanus*), 97
Bupleurum (*Bupleurum falcatum*), 98
Burdock (*Arctium lappa*), 98
Burnet (*Sanguisorba officinalis*), 100

C

Cabbage (*Brassica oleracea*), 100
Cabbage, Skunk (*Symplocarpus foetidus*), 101
Cacao (*Theobroma cacao*), 101
Cactus, Mescal (*Lophophora williamsii*), 102
Cactus, Pricklypear (*Opuntia basilaris*), 103
Cactus, Saguaro (*Carnegiea gigantea*), 104
Calamus (*Acorus calamus*), 91, 105
Calendula (*Calendula officinalis*), 106
Camphor Tree (*Cinnamomum camphora*), 107
Canadian Hemp (*Apocynum cannabinum*), 108, 289
Caraway (*Carum carvi*), 109
Cardamom (*Elettaria cardamomum*), 110
Caroba (*Jacaranda procera*), 110
Cascara Sagrada (*Rhamnus purshianus*), 111
Cashew (*Anacardium occidentale*), 112
Castor Oil Plant (*Ricinus communis*), 113
Catalpa (*Catalpa bignonioides*), 114
Catha (*Catha edulis*), 114
Catnip (*Nepeta cataria*), 115
Cat's Claw (*Uncaria guianensis*), 116
Cattail (*Typha latifolia*), 117
Cayenne (*Capsicum annuum*), 117
Celandine (*Chelidonium majus*), 119
Celery (*Apium graveolens*), 120

Appendix II
Herbs by Scientific Name

A reference listing that will help you find an herb for which you know only the scientific name.

V

W

X

Y

Z

Glossary of Medical Terminology

A

Abdominal Hernia: Protrusion of a structure through the abdominal wall.
Abortifacient: A substance that induces abortion.
Abscess: The formation of an abscess, which is a collection of pus or other infected material within a body cavity formed by the breakdown of tissue, is usually due to an infection caused by the *streptococci* or *staphylococci* bacteria. This bacterium enters through the hair follicles or sweat glands, and can occur anywhere on the body, but most often appears in the armpit, groin, or other hairy area, and may be characterized by fever, inflammation, and a painful, reddish nodule with pus forming in the nodules central core. Also called boil, carbuncle, and furuncle.
Absorbent: Promotes absorption.
Acarus: A small mite that burrows under the skin and causes itching, mange, and other skin diseases.
Acidity: An excessive amount of normal acid. See gastric acidity.
Acne: A chronic inflammatory condition of the sebaceous glands, which occurs most frequently on the face, back, and chest, and is characterized by small, inflamed papules that sometimes contain pus (pustules), or as comedomes with black centers (blackheads), which can leave small scars or pits in the skin. Acne commonly occurs around puberty, but can occur in adults as well due to excessive oil secretion, certain medications, heredity, hormonal changes such as menstruation or menopause, infections, stress, or chemical irritants.
Acquired Immune Deficiency Syndrome (AIDS): A weakened immune system caused by a virus that increases susceptibility to cancer and infection.
Acute: A condition that comes on suddenly with severe symptoms and lasts for a short duration.
Addison's Disease: A usually fatal disease caused by hypofunction of the adrenal glands and characterized by anemia (progressive), bronze-colored skin pigmentation, diarrhea, digestive complaints, exhaustion (severe), and hypotension.
Adiposity: An excessive accumulation of fat in the body. See cerebral adiposity and pituitary adiposity.
Adjuvant: An auxiliary or one that aids other remedies.
Adoptosis: The selective elimination of old, damaged, or undesirable cells.
Adrenal Glands: Flattened glands, situated near the upper end of each kidney, that furnish an internal secretion of epinephrine. This secretion has a strong effect on kidney function and growth.
Aerobic: Bacterial microorganisms that grow only in air or free oxygen.
Agglutinin: A substance that acts as an antigen and stimulates the production of agglutinin, which causes agglutination or the clumping of bacteria, red blood corpuscles, or other cells. Also called agglutogenic.
Aglycone: The noncarbohydrate group of a glycoside molecule. Also called genin.
Ague: Chills, fever (intermittent), headache, and nausea associated with malaria.
Albuminuria: Protein in the urine.
Alcoholism: Alcoholism (alcohol poisoning) or the temporary disturbance (drunkenness) is caused by the excessive or repeated and long-continued use of alcoholic drinks. Repeated excessive use of alcohol can lead to chronic alcoholism or a craving for intoxication by alcoholic beverages.
Alimentary Canal: The passage from the mouth to the anus, and composed of the mouth, esophagus, pharynx, stomach, and intestine.
Alimentary Toxemia: Toxemia due to absorption of toxins from the alimentary canal.
Allergy: Allergies occur when the immune system is weakened by an overabundance of toxins in the body. Sensitivities stem from various items such as food, chemical cleaners, or medications, and may lead to an allergic reaction resulting in asthma, fatigue, hay fever, hives, or high blood pressure in some individuals.
Alopecia: Balding or hair loss.
Alterative: A substance that reestablishes healthy system functions.
Alzheimer's Disease: A condition resulting in mental deterioration that occurs during middle age.
Amaurosis: Sudden, transitory blindness occurring without apparent injury of the eye or disease of the brain, optic nerve, retina, or spine.
Amenorrhea: An abnormal absence or cessation of the menstrual flow usually resulting from a deficiency of the estrus-producing (ovarian) or pituitary hormone, poor nutrition, stress, anemia, tumors, or overly strenuous exercise.
Amino Acids: Groups of organic substances, which are the building blocks of proteins that enable our bodies to grow.
Analgesic: A substance that reduces pain.
Anaphrodisiac: A substance that reduces sexual desire.
Anaphylactic Shock: An unusual, often violent reaction produced by anaphylaxis and by a second injection of a foreign matter such as protein, serum, or other substance into an already hypersusceptible person.
Anaphylaxis: A hypersensitivity to proteins that results in a physical reaction.
Ancylostomiasis: A condition caused by the presence of hookworms and is characterized by abdominal pain, anemia, edema, emaciation, fever, gastrointestinal problems, pallor, and skin eruptions.
Andromedotoxin: Inhibits respiratory function and induces sleep.
Anemia: Anemia occurs when the oxygen level in the blood is reduced and is characterized by lethargy, depression, extreme fatigue, headache, irritability, insomnia, lightheadedness, poor memory, or restlessness. Pregnant women and the elderly are at a higher risk for anemia, and anxiety, infection, or heavy menstruation can deplete the level of iron in the body. See Cooley's anemia and sickle cell anemia.
Aneurysm: A sac that is formed by the dilatation of an artery or vein and is filled with blood.
Aneurysmal: Pertaining to or resembling an aneurysm.
Angina: Angina is a reduction of oxygen to the heart muscle and usually characterized by an intense, choking, suffocating, spasmodic pain in the chest area.

Angiogenic: Developing into blood vessels.
Anisakid Worm: A parasite that is sometimes found in raw fish/sushi.
Antacid: A substance that counteracts or neutralizes acidity.
Anthelmintic: A substance that is destructive to worms.
Antibiotic: A substance that inhibits development or destroys the growth of bacteria and other microorganisms.
Anticarcinogen: Decreases the effect of carcinogens.
Anticoagulant: A substance that delays or reduces blood coagulation.
Antidepressant: A substance that counteracts depression.
Antidiabetic Drugs: Substances used to treat or prevent the development of diabetes.
Antidiuretic: Diminish or suppress urine flow.
Antidote: A substance that counteracts poisons.
Antiemetic: A substance that relieves nausea and prevents vomiting.
Antiepileptic: A substance that combats epilepsy.
Antifertilizin: A substance that neutralizes fertilization (fertilizen).
Antifungal: A substance that inhibits fungal organisms.
Antigalactic: A substance that diminishes or suppresses lactation.
Antigen: A substance that when introduced into the blood or tissues incites the formation of an (sensitizing) antibody.
Antihidrotic: A substance that diminishes excessive perspiration.
Antihistamine: A substance that counteracts the effect of histamine.
Anti-inflammatory: A substance that reduces tissue inflammation.
Antilithic: A substance that prevents the development of calculus or stones.
Antimalarial Drug: A substance used to treat or protect against malaria.
Antimanic Drugs: Substances used to treat mania and depression (severe).
Antimitotic: Inhibits the division of active somatic and germ cells.
Antinarcotic: A substance useful against narcotism.
Antineoplastic Drugs: Substances used to treat people with cancer.
Antinephritic: A substance used in kidney disease.
Antioxidant: A substance that inhibits oxidation.
Antiperiodic: A substance used against malaria or periodic recurrences.
Antiphlogistic: A substance that counteracts fever and inflammation.
Antiprotozoan: Inhibits development and growth of protozoa.
Antipsychotic Drugs: Substances used to treat people with schizophrenia and other psychotic conditions.
Antiretroviral Drugs: Substances that block the reproduction of retroviruses.
Antiscorbutic: A substance that counters scurvy.
Antisialic: A substance that diminishes excessive saliva secretion.
Antispasmodic: A substance that counters skeletal and smooth muscle spasm.
Antiviral: A substance that counteracts viruses.
Anxiolytic: A substance used to treat anxiety, insomnia, panic attacks, seizure conditions and other conditions.
Aphasia: A condition due to a disease or injury of the brain, which results in a speech problem.
Aphonia: Loss of voice due to a functional or organic problem.
Aphrodisiac: A substance that arouses sexual impulses.
Apoplectic Stroke: A condition caused by acute vascular lesions of the brain (i.e. embolism, hemorrhage, thrombosis), and characterized by coma followed by paralysis. Also called apoplexy.
Arrhythmia: A disturbance in the normal rhythm of the heartbeat that causes irregularity in the force, equality, and sequence of the beat, and irregularity of the contractility of the heart muscle. Also called palpitations.
Arsenism: Chronic poisoning (arsenic). Also known as arsenicalism.
Arteriosclerosis: Arteriosclerosis occurs when the arterial and blood vessel walls thicken, harden, and become narrowed by deposits of plaque.
Arteriostenosis: The narrowing or stricture of an artery from contraction or the deposit of abnormal tissue.
Artery: Blood vessels that carry blood away from the heart and toward the tissues.
Arthritis: Arthritis is a chronic condition that affects the joints, and may occur from an injury received earlier in life. The three main types of arthritis are gout, osteoarthritis (OA), and rheumatoid arthritis (RA). Arthritis may be caused by a bacterial infection, poor nutrition, or stress. Fatigue, fever, pain, and inflamed, painful, stiff, swollen, misshapen joints characterize arthritis. All forms of arthritis are affected by diet, allergy, nutritional status, and lifestyle.
Ascaris: Intestinal parasites.
Ascites: The accumulation of clear yellowish fluid in the peritoneal cavity, which produces painless abdominal swelling.
Asthma: A condition often associated with allergy (food), eczema, and hayfever, often occurs at night, during vigorous exercise, or in times of stress, and is characterized by recurrent attacks of sudden, intense coughing, shortness of breath, a sensation of choking, wheezing, and a feeling of chest constriction that is caused by spasmodic contractions of the bronchi, which may be a result of direct irritation of the bronchial tube mucous membrane due to allergens. These sudden, recurring, and often-intense attacks can last from as little as a few minutes to several days.
Astringent: A substance that causes tissue contraction and stops or slows discharges.
Ataxia: Failure or loss of muscular coordination.
Athlete's Foot: A chronic fungal infection of the skin of the foot, especially occurring between the toes and on the soles, that is caused by the fungi species of *trichophyton* or *epidermophyton* (the same fungi that causes ringworm), and is characterized by cracked, red, intensely itchy, raw, scaly skin. Also called dermatophytosis, Hong Kong foot, and tinea pedis.

Atrium: One of the upper chambers of the heart, each chamber consisting of a principle cavity and an auricular appendix.
Atropine: A toxic alkaloid that has mydriatic and narcotic properties. It stimulates the sympathetic and depresses the cerebrospinal nerves; increases the heart rate and respiration; checks the action of the secretory glands (salivary, sweat, etc.); produces paralysis; and dilates the pupils.
Atropinism: Poisoning due to the misuse of atropine.
Auditory: Pertaining to the sense of hearing.
Auricle: An atrium of the heart.
Autoimmune Disease: A condition that causes the immune system to attack the body's tissues.
Autonomic Drugs: Parasympathomimetic (cholinergic) and sympathomimetic (adrenergic) agents that affect the autonomic nervous system.
Autonomic Nervous System: Controls functions of the blood and lymph vessels, smooth muscles, and internal organs such as the glands, heart, intestines, and lungs.

B

Backache: The back is the posterior portion of the trunk from the neck to the pelvis. Backaches can occur from a wide variety of conditions including poor posture, spinal curvature, muscle strain, or kidney infection, and are characterized by symptoms including, but not limited to a dull ache, severe pain, spasm, and in some cases localized inflammation.
Bacillus: Bacterial microorganisms that are aerobic, spore bearing, gram positive, and pathogenic to humans.
Bacillus Cereus Bacteria: A form of food poisoning, which is sometimes found in fried rice.
Basal Cell Carcinoma: A carcinoma that develops from the cells of the deepest layer of the epithelium surface and retains the character of these cells.
Bell's Palsy: Facial paralysis caused by a loss of function of the facial nerve resulting in a distortion of the face.
Benign: Not malignant. Noncancerous.
Benign Breast Disease: A condition affecting the female mammary glands which may be characterized by tender to painful breasts that feel lumpy due to inflamed fibrous tissue and benign cysts, with symptoms having a tendency to worsen just prior to the onset of menstruation. Also called fibrocystic breasts.
Benign Prostatic Hypertrophy (BPH): Hypertrophy (enlargement) of the prostate.
Beta-Adrenergic Blocking Drugs: Substances used for angina, hypertension, and the prevention of certain heart conditions and migraine. Also called beta-blockers.
Biliary: Pertains to the bile, the bile ducts, or to the gallbladder.
Bilirubin: A red pigment found in the bile, and that occasionally occurs in the blood tissues and urine.
Bilirubinuria: The presence of bilirubin in the urine.
Birth Palsy: An injury occurring during birth.
Bladder: The bladder is a membranous sac, which serves as a reservoir for the urine, and is situated in the front part of the pelvic cavity. A dysfuntion of the bladder can cause urinary problems.
Bleeding: Bleeding is the flow of blood occurring either internally (i.e. ulcer, internal injury) or externally (minor wound).
Blood: The fluid that circulates through the heart, arteries, capillaries, and veins, carrying nutrients and oxygen to the body tissues is called the blood, and it consists of a colorless liquid called plasma that contains red blood corpuscles, yellowish disks that contain hemoglobin, which carry oxygen, white blood corpuscles, and blood platelets. The blood contained in the arteries is a bright red color, but after passing to the veins it becomes a dark brownish red.
Blood Pressure: The pressure of the blood on the arterial walls is dependant on the energy of the heart action, the artery wall elasticity, the capillary resistence, and the volume and the viscosity of the blood. The maximum pressure occurs at the time of the systole or the period of the heart's contraction of the left ventricle, and is termed systolic pressure. The minimum pressure is felt at the diastole or dilatation stage of the heart ventricle, and is termed diastolic pressure. Proper diet is pertinent in the reduction of high blood pressure. Regular exercise, incorporating more fruits and vegetables into your diet, and consuming less meat, salt, and beverages that contain caffeine will assist in greatly reducing hypertension (high blood pressure). If poor circulation, lightheadedness, fainting, or low energy occurs, you may be experiencing hypotension (low blood pressure).
Bones: Bones are the storehouses for sodium, calcium, magnesium, phosphorus, protein, vitamins C and D, and boron. When there is a deficiency of these elements, the body draws them from the bones resulting in brittleness, thinness, and weakness, which can lead to osteoporosis.
Bouveret Ulcer: Ulcerations due to enteric fever.
Bradycardia: Abnormally slow heartbeat.
Bronchitis: An inflammation of the bronchial tubes caused by acute conditions, the inhalation of irritant substances, or exposure to cold, and is characterized by chest pain (especially on coughing), cough, difficult or labored breathing, and fever.
Bronchodilator: A substance that causes dilatation of the air passages of the lungs.
Bruises: Injuries situated near the surface of the skin that are produced by some form of impact that does not cause tearing of the skin, and characterized by discoloration of the skin and tenderness.
Burns: Lesions caused by contact with heat. Burns are chiefly classified in 4 degrees. 1st degree or minor household: skin shows redness. 2nd degree: skin blisters. 3rd degree: necrosis or death of skin cells occurs through the entire skin. 4th degree: necrosis or death of skin cells and charring of the skin usually resulting in death.
Bursa: A sac or pouch-like cavity filled with a glutinous or sticky (viscid) fluid and situated at places in the tissues where friction would otherwise develop.
Bursal Fluid: The glutinous or sticky (viscid) fluid contained in the bursa.

C

Calcium Channel Blocker Drugs: Substances that treat angina, arrhythmia, and hypertension.
Calculus: An abnormal concretion primarily composed of mineral salts that can occur in numerous places such as the biliary passages or gallbladder (gallstones), near a joint (gout), or in the bladder, intestine, kidney, liver, pancreatic duct, prostate, a seminal vesicle, or urinary tract.
Cancer: A term assigned to a cellular tumor, the natural course of which is fatal. The formation of melanoma, sarcoma, and other malignant tumors are usually associated with cancer.
Candida: A genus of yeast-like fungi that is found in all individuals. When the system is unbalanced, candida overgrowth may result in a fungal infection of the nails (primarily the toenails), intestinal moniliasis (fungal infection of the intestines), monilid (an allergic skin eruption), thrush (fungal infection of the oral mucous membranes), or a vaginal yeast infection. Also called monilia.
Canker Sore: A canker sore chiefly occurs on the inside of the mouth or on the tongue, and is characterized by a small hard swelling or ulceration, inflammation, and pain. Canker sores may be caused by an infection, stress, or by an allergic reaction to certain foods including chocolate, citrus, nuts, or various aged cheeses.
Capillary Endings: Numerous tiny blood vessels into which both beneficial and harmful chemicals can pass and then be distributed by the blood stream.
Carcinoma: New malignant growths made up of epithelial cells (the cells that cover the mucous membranes and skin) that tend to permeate the surrounding tissues and begin to metastasize (form new growths in other parts of the body). See basal cell carcinoma.
Cardiac Asthma: Difficult or labored breathing associated with heart disease that often occurs at night.
Cardiac Depressant: A substance that diminishes or reduces functional activity of the heart.
Cardiant: A substance that stimulates the heart. Also called cardiac.
Cardiomyopathy: A diseased condition of the heart muscle.
Cardiovascular System: Cardiovascular system health is often dependent on genetics, which largely determines blood vessel structure and how cholesterol is processed. A diet high in saturated fats, a sedentary lifestyle, or stress (intense) can result in high cholesterol, hypertension, and other cardiovascular problems.
Carminative: A substance that aids digestion and relieves flatulence.
Cartilage: Cartilage is the tough, whitish, elastic, gristly substance (a form of connective tissue) that is attached to bone surfaces at the joints and forms certain parts of the skeletal structure.
Caustic: A substance that is destructive to living tissue.
Celiac Disease: A condition generally occurring in children that is similar to sprue.
Cerebral Adiposity: Obesity due to cerebral disease.
Cerebral Palsy: A group of conditions affecting control of the motor system caused by a loss of function in various parts of the brain, which occur as a result of birth palsy or a prenatal cerebral defect.
Cerebrospinal Hyperemia: An excess accumulation of blood in the cerebral and spinal areas.
Cervicitis: An infectious inflammation of the uterine cervix.
Cervix: The opening or neck to the uterus.
Chicken Pox: An acute, infectious disease that is caused by the *briareus varicellae* virus and is characterized by fever and skin eruptions that rarely burst open or crust over and seldom leave a scar. Also called varicellae.
Chlamydia: An infection caused by the genus of parasitic chlamydozoa bacteria that are found in the feces of humans. This microorganism can infect the genitourinary tract through improper toiletry habits, and can also be transmitted through coitus. It is characterized by inflammation and itching (possibly severe). For women, it is very important to wipe from the front to the back, as this keeps the bacteria from entering the bladder.
Cholagogue: Increases the flow of bile.
Cholecystitis: Gallbladder inflammation.
Cholelithiasis: The formation of gallstones.
Cholera: An acute, infectious condition caused by the *vibrio comma* organism, and characterized by congestion (lung), cramps, convulsions, dehydration, diarrhea (severe), exhaustion, urodialysis (suppression of urine), and possible death. Also called Asiatic cholera, epidemic cholera, Indian cholera, and pestilential cholera.
Cholinesterase: An enzyme present in all body tissues that hydrolyzes acetylcholine into choline and acetic acid.
Chorea: A convulsive nervous disease characterized by involuntary jerking movements, depression, irritability, and mental impairment. Also called St. Vitus' dance.
Chronic Fatigue Syndrome (CFS): A condition resulting in chronic fatigue or exhaustion caused by the Epstein Barr Virus (EBV).
Circadian Rhythm: Pertaining to or designating those vital processes in plants, animals, and humans that tends to recur in cycles of approximately 24 hours; the body's natural time cycle.
Circulatory System: The circulatory system contains the blood and lymph vessels and is responsible for the circulation and transport of blood, lymph fluid, and nutrients to all parts and organs of the body.
Coagulant: Promotes blood coagulation.
Coitus: Sexual intercourse.
Colchicine Drugs: Substances that reduce inflammation and pain associated with gout due to high uric acid levels.
Cold Sores (herpes simplex): An acute, contagious, recurring, inflammatory condition caused by a virus and characterized by watery blisters that form in clusters and usually appear on the surface of the lips. Also called fever blisters.
Colds: Viruses that infect the respiratory system and are characterized by chills, cough, muscle aches, runny nose, sneezing, sniffles, and sore throat cause colds. Also called common cold.
Colitis: Inflammation of the colon.
Congestion: An abnormal or excessive accumulation of blood that can occur in an organ or any part of the body.
Congestive Heart Failure (CHF): A condition resulting from the inability of the heart to maintain an adequate flow of blood to all the tissues

of the body.
Conjugate: Paired; working in unison.
Conjugated Estrogens: A combination of several (natural) estrogenic hormones that are used to treat menopausal symptoms, prevent osteoporosis, and as a replacement therapy in conditions of inadequate estrogen production.
Conjunctivitis: An acute, infectious condition of the conjunctiva (delicate membrane that lines the eyelids and covers the eyeball), and characterized by inflammation, a pinkish coloring of the conjunctiva, itching, and usually discharge. Also called pinkeye.
Constipation: The infrequent or difficult evacuation of the feces, which can be caused by lack of exercise, excessive use of laxatives, poor eating habits, some medications, or nervous tension. Eating a high fiber diet and getting plenty of exercise can help reduce or eliminate defacation problems.
Contagious: The capability of being transmitted from one person to another.
Convulsant: A substance that produces or causes convulsions.
Cooley's Anemia: Anemia that occurs chiefly in persons of Mediterranean bloodlines, and characterized by lethargy, depression, extreme fatigue, headache, irritability, insomnia, lightheadedness, poor memory, or restlessness. Also called thalessemia.
Coronary Artery Disease (CAD): A disease affecting the coronary arteries, and is characterized by angiospasms and inflammation.
Corticosteroid: Substance that has a powerful anti-inflammatory effect, is used in the treatment of severe allergic reactions, and is used to prevent organ rejection after organ transplantation.
Cough: A sudden, noisy, expulsion of air from the lungs that can either be dry or contain expectorant, and may be caused by the inhalation or aspiration of an irritant substance, compression of the bronchi, obstruction (nasopharynx), or acid reflux.
Counterirritant: A substance applied externally that induces localized irritation and is intended to relieve some other irritation.
Cramps: Cramps are painful spasmodic muscular contractions that can occur with any muscle (gastrointestinal, leg, uterine, etc.). Cramps occurring in the legs can be quite painful and are sometimes due to a deficiency in calcium, to much or not enough exercise, or stress. To relieve a muscle cramp in the leg, extend the leg out as far as possible and lightly massage the area until the cramp dissipates.
Crohn's Disease: Chronic intestinal tract inflammation that often leads to obstruction (intestinal).
Croup: Croup is a respiratory condition characterized by cough, laborious suffocative breathing, and larynx spasm.
Cushing's Disease: An overgrowth of the basophil cells of the anterior pituitary characterized by abdominal and back pain, amenorrhea in females and erectile dysfunction in males, debility, gray complexion with purplish-colored markings, hypertension, hypertrichosis (in females), kyphosis, pituitary adiposity, and polycythemia.
Cyanosis: A bluish discoloration of the skin and whites of the eyes caused by cyanide poisoning.
Cystic Fibrosis: The formation of fibrous and cyst-like tissue.
Cystitis: Cystitis is an inflammation of the bladder caused by injuries, irritation, gonorrhea, etc., and is characterized by burning sensation and inflammation in the bladder, granular-like cysts, infection, pain on urination, and urethral pain.
Cytotoxic: A substance that induces cancer cells to destroy themselves.

D

Deafness: A complete or partial, lack or loss of auditory function (hearing).
Debility: The lack or loss of strength and is characterized by muscle weakness.
Delirium Tremens (DTs): A form of alcoholic psychosis involving a variety of acute mental disturbances characterized by delirium, trembling, and great excitement, attended by anxiety, distress, sweating, and precordial (upper middle portion of the abdomen) pain.
Demulcent: Soothes mucous membrane irritation.
Dendritic Ulcer: Ulceration of the cornea. Also called dendriform ulcer.
Dentifrice: A substance used to clean teeth.
Depressant: A substance that diminishes or reduces functional activity by producing muscular relaxation and profuse perspiration.
Depression: An absence of cheerfulness and can take many forms including agitation, panic, the feeling of impending doom, uneasiness, and worry. Seek immediate medical attention if depression is severe and/or associated with suicidal thoughts or tendencies.
Depurative: A substance that cleanses or purifies.
Dermatitis: Inflammation of the skin caused by contact with an allergen.
Dermis: The middle layer of skin, which consists entirely of living cells. These cells give skin strength and form. The dermis layer contains the oil secreting sebaceous glands, and it is criss-crossed with blood vessels and nerves.
Diabetes: A chronic disease in which the body develops an inability to handle glucose (sugar).
Diabetes Mellitus: A carbohydrate metabolism condition caused by a disturbance of the normal pancreatic activity, and characterized by excessive sugar in the blood and urine. Certain types of diabetes mellitus may require treatment using insulin by means of hypodermic injection or oral administration of antidiabetic medicines, which are taken by mouth. Insulin-Dependant Diabetes Mellitus (IDDM): Also known as Juvenile Onset diabetes and Type I diabetes. Non-Insulin-Dependent Diabetes Mellitus (NIDDM): Also known as Maturity Onset diabetes, Sugar diabetes, or Type II diabetes.
Diaphoretic: A substance that promotes perspiration.
Diarrhea: Diarrhea is an abnormal frequency of the fecal discharge and is caused by an infection of the gastrointestinal tract, and is characterized by dehydration, electrolyte loss, intestinal cramps, loose watery (sometimes mucous and bloody) stools, nausea, and occasionally vomiting. Drink plenty of fluids to replace lost electrolytes and make sure to avoid cold drinks as the digestive systems process is assisted by warmth. Drinking warm water sweetened with honey will help replace lost fluids.
Diastole: The dilatation or stage of dilatation of the heart and especially that of the ventricles.
Diethylstilbestrol (DES): A nonsteroidal synthetic estrogen that was used as a substitute for natural estrogen. It was prescribed in the 1950's to ward off miscarriage and is known to have caused cervical cancer in the daughters born of the women whom it was given to.
Digestive System: The system that transforms the foods we eat into energy for the body. To maintain a healthy digestive system, a diet that is high in fiber, along with an exercise regimen is recommended. Drink plenty of water to help flush toxins from your system, avoid stress, and get

plenty of sleep.
Digitate Warts: Flat warts with finger-like abnormal growths growing from them.
Dilatation: The condition of being dilated or stretched beyond the normal dimensions. Also called dilation.
Dioxide: A molecule that has two atoms of oxygen.
Diphtheria: An extremely contagious often fatal disease caused by the corynebacterium *diphtheriae bacillus* and characterized by anemia, exhaustion (extreme), high fever, insufficiency (cardiac), grayish patches in the mouth and throat, larynx and pharynx swelling, and possible vomiting.
Diuresis: Increased urination.
Diuretic: A substance that promotes urine flow.
Diuria: Frequent daytime urination.
Diverticulitis: Inflammation of diverticulum (small pouches) of the large intestine. These pouches fill with feces, which cause inflammation and irritation.
Dryness Conditions: Dryness conditions are often reversible conditions involving dryness of the mucous membranes, sebaceous glands of the skin, or the cortex of the hair. Some of the more common conditions include: Dry cough is characterized by a tickling sensation and irritation of the throat due to decreased moisture of the mucous membranes, and may be caused by certain medications, dry indoor air, sore throat, or other problems. Moisturizing the throat with lozenges, adding moisture or humidity to reduce indoor air dryness, and increasing daily fluid intake will usually help to remedy a dry cough. Dry eyes, which are characterized by a sensation of grittiness due to decreased tear production, may be caused by certain therapeutic problems, dry indoor air, or medications. Using eyedrops to replace natural tears, adding moisture or humidity to reduce indoor dry air, and (only where possible) a switch in medications may help relieve eye dryness. Dry hair, which is characterized by dull, straw-like, or flyaway hair that breaks easily, may be caused by diet, exposure to salt water or sun, harsh hair products, or heredity. Switching to non-alkaline hair products, wearing a hat when in the sun, and eating a balanced diet with plenty of fresh fruits and vegetables may protect against problems of dry hair. Dry skin, which is characterized by itching, flaking, rash, irritation, or tightness, may be caused by aging, diet, environmental pollutants, harsh skin care products, or heredity. Switching to non-alkaline or glycerin free skin care products, eating a balanced diet with plenty of fruits and vegetables, applying a skin moisturizer or a sun protection product daily, and wearing protective, breathable fabrics when in the sun may protect against skin dryness and wrinkling. See vaginal dryness.
Duodenal Ulcer: Ulceration in the duodenum.
Duodenum: The first portion of the small intestine.
Dysentery: A term assigned to a number of infectious conditions, primarily amebic dysentery caused by the *endamoeba histolytica* bacteria, and bacillary dysentery caused by the *shigella* genus of bacteria. All forms of dysentery are prevalent in tropical countries, but can frequently occur elsewhere and are primarily due to chemical irritants, bacteria, parasites, or protozoa, and characterized by abdominal pain, diarrhea (bloody, mucous), enteritis, toxemia, and occasionally fatality.
Dysmenorrhea: Painful and difficult menstruation accompanied by congestion in the uterus, and may be caused by blood clots, pelvic lesions, or ovarian problems, and is characterized by uterine spasm (cramps).
Dyspnea: Difficult or labored breathing.
Dysphasia: Impairment of speech.
Dysuria: Often caused by spasm of the bladder and characterized by urination that is painful and difficult.

E

Ear: The ears allow us to enjoy the sounds of life and various conditions such as an earache, ear infection, hearing loss, or tinnitus occur in adults and children, and can interfere with our ability to hear well.
Eclamptic Toxemia: Toxemia occurring in late pregnancy that is characterized by a sudden attack of convulsions. Also called eclampsia.
Eczema: An inflammatory skin disease that can be dry or moist and is generally characterized by small watery blisters, the development of scaly and crusty patches on the skin, and is accompanied by a burning sensation of the skin, fever, itching, and restlessness.
Edema: The presence of unusually large amounts of fluid in the intercellular tissue spaces of the body and characterized by temporary swelling in any part of the body (i.e. ankles, feet, legs) due to the escape of fluid into a part or tissue.
Elephantiasis: A condition due to infestation of the filarioidea parasite within the connective tissues and lymphatics and characterized by inflammation and obstruction (lymphatic), and hypertrophy (skin, subcutaneous tissues).
Emaciation: A wasting condition of the body. Also called phthisis.
Embolism: The blocking of an artery or vein.
Emetic: A substance that causes vomiting.
Emmenagogue: A substance that stimulates menstruation.
Encephalitis Lethargica: A disease caused by a genus of viruses characterized by increasing apathy, drowsiness, and lethargy with progressive debility and cranial nerve paralysis.
Encephalomyelitis: Brain and spinal cord inflammation.
Endometriosis: The presence of endometrial tissue in an internal or external situation. See internal endometriosis and external endometriosis.
Endometritis: Inflammation of the membranous lining of the uterus.
Enteric Fever: A contagious fever associated with typhoid that is caused by *salmonella typhosa*, and characterized by hypertrophy (spleen), inflammation, and skin eruptions. Also called Abdominal Typhus, Intestinal Fever, and Typhoid Fever.
Enteritis: Inflammation of the intestines.
Enuresis: The inability to restrain urine resulting in the involuntary discharge of urine. Also called anischuria, incontinence, and urinary incontinence. See nocturnal enuresis.
Ephedrine: An alkaloid from the herb ephedra that is similar in action to epinephrine. It has a direct effect on the circulatory and nervous system, the secretory glands (salivary, sweat, etc.), and the smooth muscles, and is useful for asthma, hypotension, shock, and as a mydriatic.
Ephemeral Fever: Slight fever lasting only a day or two.

Ephidrosis: Excessive perspiration. See night sweats and perspiration.
Epidermis: The top outer layer of skin, which consists of dead cells. These cells are constantly being replaced from beneath. Lotions and skin creams that are applied topically generally affect only this layer.
Epilepsy: A chronic, functional condition characterized by brief convulsive seizures in which there is a loss of consciousness. The attacks come in succession, vary in intensity and frequency, and can last from 5 to 20 minutes.
Episiotomy: A small surgical incision made to the perineum (area of skin between the vulva and anus) just prior to the actual birth of the child, which prevents tearing of the vulva tissue, and is closed with sutures (stitches) after delivery of the child.
Epstein Barr Virus (EBV): A virus responsible for chronic fatigue syndrome (CFS), and infectious mononucleosis.
Erectile Dysfunction: Erectile dysfunction is impotence or the failure to attain an erection. This lack of copulative power or virility is usually due to paralysis of the motor nerves, lesions (central nervous system), a mental complex, a perineal nerve injury, certain medications, or some other condition.
Erectile Dysfunction Drugs: Substances used to treat erectile dysfunction (impotence).
Ergotism: Chronic poisoning caused by eating or using ergot diseased cereal grains (rye, barley, etc.), and characterized by cerebrospinal symptoms, cramps (possibly severe), hypertension (possibly severe), and/or spasmodic conditions.
Errhine: A substance that promotes nasal discharge or secretion.
Erysipelas: An infectious skin condition that can occur on various parts of the body, and is characterized by lesions, itching, redness, small blisters, and inflammation. Also called St. Anthony's fire.
Erythropoietic: A substance that forms red blood cells.
Esophagitis: Inflammation of the esophagus.
Estrogen Dependant Cancers: Estrogen or hormonal dependant cancers (i.e. breast, ovarian, prostate).
Euphoriant: A substance that creates an abnormal or exaggerated sense of euphoria. Also called euphorigenic.
Expectorant: A substance that aids in the expulsion of mucus from the bronchi, lungs, and trachea. Clears and opens the bronchial passages.
External Endometriosis: Endometrial tissue occurring on the external surface of the bladder, intestines, ovary, uterus, or other surface.
Eye: Eyes are the organs of vision and our windows to the world. Within each eye are numerous blood vessles; the optic and ciliary nerves, delicate connective tissues, the cornea, which is composed of five layers; the retina or internal coat is primarily composed of nerve tissue, is made up of three layers, and is one of the layers of the cornea; the iris, which varies in color according to pigment; the pupil, which is composed of smooth muscular fibers and dilates or contracts depending on the source of light; the eye lens; and numerous other wonderments.

F

Fatigue: Fatigue is usually described as tiredness and feelings of lethargy that often result from overexertion.
Febrifuge: A substance that reduces fever.
Fertilizin: The fusion of the spermatozoon with the ovum resulting in fertilization. Also called fertilization.
Fever: A fever is characterized by an elevation of body temperature, drowsiness, accelerated or feeble pulse rate, clammy or hot dry skin, restlessness, debility, occasional delirium, and is sometimes associated with other symptoms. See enteric fever, ephemeral fever, hankow fever, hay fever, herpetic fever, intermittent fever, rheumatoid fever, river fever, Rocky Mountain spotted fever, scarlet fever, septic fever, typhus fever, and yellow fever.
Fibroids: Benign tumors or cysts composed primarily of fibrous tissue that can develop and grow in the mammary glands (breasts), the uterus, and other places such as the lungs or nares (openings to the nasal cavity). Also called fibromas.
Fibromyalgia: A muscular condition often associated with chronic fatigue syndrome (CFS) in which tender nodules develop causing chronic pain, stiffness, a sensation of muscular tension, and headache. Cold drafts, humidity, or stress can aggravate fibromyalgia.
Filaria: Nematode parasites that invade the tissues and body cavities.
Filariasis: A condition caused by the presence of filaria.
Filiform Warts: Warts with thread-like projections.
Fistula Ulcer: A deep, sinuous ulcer that often leads to an internal hollow organ.
Flatulence: A distention (enlargement) of the stomach or the intestines with air or gases, and often results in the act of expelling air or gas from the rectum.
Formulary: A collection or list of formulas, prescriptions, or recipes.
Free Radicals: Highly reactive and unstable disease causing compounds that form when the body metabolizes oxygen. Free radicals, produced increasingly with age within the body, are believed to promote tumor growth and may contribute to atherosclerosis.
Fugitive Warts: Warts occurring on the hands of children that are generally short-lived.
Funicular Hernia: A hernia of the spermatic cord.

G

Galactic: A substance that promotes lactation.
Gallbladder: The gallbladder is the pear-shaped reservoir for the bile, which is located on the under surface of the liver.
Gallstones: Gallstones are biliary concretions, usually of cholesterin (a fat-like pearly substance that crystallizes in the form of needle-like crystals), that form in the bile duct or gallbladder and are characterized by inflammation and pain.
Gastric Acidity: Gastric acidity pertains to the excessive acidity level of the stomach acid. It can occur when there is an alteration of stomach or gastric acid resulting from a feeble or weak state of the functions of the stomach. Also called hyperacidity and sour stomach.
Gastric Ulcer: Ulceration on the inner wall of the stomach.
Gastritis: Inflammation of the stomach characterized by abdominal bloating, alteration in the quantity of gastric juice secretion, appetite loss, indigestion, mucus secretion (excessive), nausea, pain, and vomiting.
Gastrocardiac Syndrome: A disturbance of the circulatory system, particularly the cardiovascular system, which is due to insufficiency

(gastric).
Gastroduodenitis: Inflammation of the stomach and duodenum.
Gastroenteritis: Inflammation of the stomach and intestines.
Gastrointestinal System: The gastrointestinal system pertains to the stomach and intestines. To maintain a healthy gastrointestinal system it is important to get plenty of exercise, eat a diet that is high in fiber, and drink plenty of water to flush the toxins from your system, avoid stress and tension, and get plenty of sleep.
Genital Herpes (herpes genitalis): An acute, contagious, recurring, inflammatory condition caused by a virus and characterized by fever, inflammation, and watery blisters that form in clusters and occur on the mucous surface of the genitalia.
GI Drugs: Substance that block production of stomach acid. Also called gastrointestinal drugs.
Glabra Warts: Smooth warts.
Glandular System: The glands, crucial to a healthy system, are dependant upon the nourishment of vitamins and minerals to maintain their efficient functions. These vitamins and minerals supply the raw substances needed to aid the glands in producing their own hormones (secretions). These vital secretions are necessary for growth and health, and have an effect on the entire system. There are numerous glands located throughout the body including the pituitary gland (located at the base of the brain), the adrenal glands (flattened glands situated near the upper end of each kidney that furnish an internal secretion of epinephrine, which has a strong effect on kidney function and growth); the pineal gland, the endocrine glands (influence metabolism and other body processes); the mammary glands (produce and secrete milk following childbirth in women, in men the mammary or breast is classified as *mammary virilis*); and the thryroid gland, which needs to be kept in perfect balance as it stimulates *all* of the cells. A deficiency (iodine) is a common cause of thyroid problems as are certain conditions, drugs, genetic disposition, or stress.
Gleet: A chronic form of urethritis caused by a gonorrheal infection and characterized by dysuria (painful/difficult urination), inflammation, penile discharge (containing both mucus and pus that can sometimes be black or bloody), and urethral stricture (narrowing).
Gluco-Corticoid Drugs: Substances that elevate the concentration of liver glycogen and blood sugar.
Glycosuria: An abnormally high amount of glucose in the urine.
Goblet Cells: A form of epithelial cells (cells of varying shape that cover the mucous membranes and skin) that are shaped like goblets and contain mucin (a glucoprotein - the chief constituent of mucus).
Gonorrhea: A contagious, usually sexually transmitted, venereal disease characterized by genital inflammation of the mucous membranes, pain, dysuria (painful/difficult urination), and a discharge containing both mucus and pus that can sometimes be black or bloody. Gonorrhea is often associated with complications such as cystitis, orchitis, and prostatitis.
Gout: This degenerative joint condition is caused by a buildup of uric acid accumulating in one or more joints, often the big toe. The acid forms sharp crystals, which provoke inflammation and pain. Diet plays a large role in gout, especially too much red meat and too much alcohol. Deficiency of some minerals, particularly molybdenum, can also contribute to this condition.
Gram-Negative: Loses or does not retain the color stain as per Gram's method.
Gram-Positive: Retains the color stain as per Gram's method.
Gram's Method: A method of staining bacteria for the purpose of classification.
Gynecomastia: Excessive size of the male breasts.

H

H-2 Blocker Drugs: Substances that block or prevent the release of acid into the stomach, and used for the treatment of gastric and duodenal ulcer as well as acid reflux.
Hallucinogen: A substance that causes auditory, sensory, and visual hallucinations, as well as delusions, depression, lost sense of time, and psychosis.
Halogen: An element of a closely related chemical family, all of which form similar salt like compounds in combination with sodium.
Hankow Fever: Fever associated with schistosomiasis.
Hay Fever: Fever associated with seasonal allergy (pollen).
Headache: There are various types of headaches with a wide range of symptoms. See migraine, nervous tension headache, and regular headache.
Heart Disease: A functional, mechanical, or organic condition of the heart that causes problems. It may originate in the muscular tissue of the heart (myocardial), the nervous system (neurogenic), or valvular (aortic, mitral, pulmonary, tricuspid).
Heat Stroke: A condition caused by exposure to extreme heat and characterized by dry skin, headache (possibly severe), muscle cramps, nausea, thirst (excessive), and vertigo. Heat stroke can occur in one of three forms: heat cramps, heat exhaustion (heat stress), or sunstroke (thermic fever).
Hemafecia: Blood in the stool.
Hemagglutinin: A substance that causes agglutination (clumping) of red blood corpuscles.
Hematemesis: The vomiting of blood caused by bleeding in the stomach.
Hematochezia: The passage of bloody stools.
Hematopoietic: Pertaining to or affecting the formation of blood cells.
Hematuria: Blood in the urine.
Hemochromatosis: A condition caused by the body absorbing too much iron and depositing it in the tissues. Symptoms appearing after significant, irreversible damage has occurred include abdominal pain, change in skin color, dark yellow to reddish colored urine, debility, diabetes, diminished sex drive, heart problems, joint problems, liver problems, loss of armpit hair, and weight loss. Also called bronze skin.
Hemolysis: The separation of the hemoglobin from the corpuscles.
Hemolytic: A substance that causes hemolysis.
Hemophilia: Hereditary condition inherited by males through the mother, and is characterized by delayed or reduced coagulation of the blood resulting in difficulty in controlling bleeding or hemorrhage.

Hemophilus: An infection caused by a genus of parasitic parvo bacteria that can be found in the oral cavity and on the genitals, and this microorganism can be transmitted through coitus. It is characterized by cramps, low back pain, and a creamy whitish or grayish discharge with a fish-like odor that becomes stronger when mixed with blood or semen. Hemophilus species are often associated with influenza, pelvic inflammatory disease (PID), and whooping cough. Also called bacterial vaginosis and gardnerella.
Hemoptysis: The spitting up of blood.
Hemorrhage: The profuse escape of blood from the arteries, blood vessels, uterus, etc. There are several types of hemorrhage including arterial, cerebral, retinal, and uterine hemorrhage (metrorrhagia).
Hemorrhoids: Hemorrhoids are swollen veins of the rectum that may protrude beyond the anus, and may be caused by poor diet, which can lead to constipation and straining with bowel movements, sedentary lifestyle, pregnancy, weak abdominal muscles, and/or stress or fatigue, which can cause the bowel muscles to constrict. Inflammation, itching, pain, a burning sensation, and occasional bleeding during bowel movements characterize hemorrhoids.
Hemostatic: A substance that checks bleeding.
Hepatic: A substance that protects the liver.
Hepatic Drugs: Substances used for liver problems.
Hepatoma: A liver tumor.
Hepatotoxic: A substance that causes liver damage.
Herb: An herb is classified as any plant that can be used as a flavoring (seasoning) agent or as a medicine (remedy).
Hernia: The protrusion of part of an organ or tissue through an abnormal opening. See abdominal hernia, hiatal hernia, inguinal hernia (external and internal), and scrotal hernia.
Herpes: An acute, contagious, recurring, inflammatory skin and mucous membrane disease that is caused by a virus and is characterized by small, watery blisters that form in clusters. See cold sores (herpes simplex), genital herpes (herpes genitalis), and shingles (herpes zoster).
Herpetic Fever: Fever associated with herpes.
Herpetic Keratitis: Inflammation of the cornea caused by the briareus varicellae virus and occurring along with shingles.
Hiatal Hernia: Protrusion of a structure through the esophageal opening (hiatus) of the diaphragm. Also called hiatus hernia.
HMG-CoA Reductase Inhibitor Drugs: Substances that block the production of cholesterol in the body and help reduce elevated cholesterol levels.
Hodgkin's Disease: An aneurysmal dilatation of the center portion of the aorta often accompanied by hypertrophy (heart).
Human B-Lymphotropic Virus (HBLV): Human herpes virus.
Human Immunodeficiency Virus (HIV): A sexually transmitted retrovirus that is capable of multiplication in a living susceptible host and may cause acquired immune deficiency syndrome (AIDS).
Human Papilloma Virus (HPV): The virus that causes venereal warts.
Hydrophobia: The usual name for rabies in humans.
Hyperbilirubinemia: Excessive bilirubin (red bile pigment) in the blood. See jaundice.
Hypercholesteremia: An excessive amount of cholesterol in the blood.
Hyperglycemia: A higher than normal concentration of glucose (sugar) in the blood.
Hyperlipoidemia: An excess of lipoids in the blood.
Hypertension: Abnormally high tension, especially high blood pressure levels.
Hypertensive: A substance that raises blood pressure levels.
Hyperthyroidism: A condition characterized by hypertrophy (spleen), accelerated pulse rate, ephidrosis, nervousness, tremors, emaciation, and increased basal metabolism.
Also called Grave's disease.
Hypertrichosis: Abnormal, excessive hair growth.
Hypertrophy: Enlargement or overgrowth of a gland, organ or part.
Hypnotic: A substance that induces sleep.
Hypocalcemia: Blood calcium levels that are below normal.
Hypoglycemia: A lower than normal concentration of glucose in the blood.
Hypoglycemic: A substances that reduces blood sugar levels in the blood.
Hypokalemic: Low blood potassium.
Hypotension: Reduced or diminished blood pressure levels. See orthostatic hypotension.
Hypotensive: A substance that reduces blood pressure levels.
Hypovolemic Shock: Shock due to the diminished volume of blood.
Hysteria: A psychoneurosis that may be characterized by anxiety, choking sensation, convulsions, fever, hallucinations, a lack of control over acts or emotions, morbid self-consciousness, imitation of various diseases, pain and tenderness in the head, paralysis, sensory disturbances, spasm, urodialysis, and vasomotor and visual disturbances.

I

Immune Suppressive Drugs: Substances that suppress the immune system.
Indigestion: Indigestion includes abdominal discomfort (bloating/distention), burning sensation in the esophagus, constipation or diarrhea, gastritis, heartburn, nausea, and/or vomiting. Indigestion may be acute or chronic and is a symptom of a lack or failure of the digestive function, and may caused by poor eating habits, ingesting highly acidic foods such as citrus or tomatoes, stress, eating to fast or chewing with your mouth open and swallowing too much air, consuming foods that are too spicy or foods that are either too cold or too hot, a lack of digestive enzymes, poor food combinations, allergies (food), infection (fungal), ulcers, smoking, hernia (hiatal), gallbladder or liver disease, hypothyroidism, and/or eating a high carbohydrate diet. Keeping track of what you eat, eating smaller portions, and avoiding the consumption of a large or heavy meal

prior to bedtime will help reduce the discomforts of indigestion.
Indolent Ulcer: Painless ulcerations with elevated edges and a nongranulating base, primarily occurring on the legs.
Infection: An infection results when pathogenic organisms invade the body tissues. These organisms can transmit infection through the air (air-borne) by means of dust particles, they can occur in clinic and hospital settings, they can be acquired through the placenta, and they can be transferred via small drops of sputum thrown into the air through coughing, sneezing, or talking. Infectious organisms are everywhere, and to lessen your chances of picking up or spreading these little nasties, be sure to cover your mouth when you cough or sneeze, and wash your hands regularly.
Infertility: The term used to signify the inability to reproduce; sterility.
Inflammation: A condition in which tissues react to an injury and is characterized by heat, redness, an excess or stoppage of blood in that area, pain (occasional), and swelling.
Influenza: An acute, infectious, epidemic condition caused by a virus and characterized by achiness, chills, cough, convulsions (possible), debility, delirium, diarrhea, dry throat, fever, gastrointestinal problems, headache, insomnia, muscle and joint pain, nausea, nervous conditions, respiratory conditions, sore throat, and vomiting (occasional). The varieties of influenza viruses are ever changing (mutating), which can make successful vaccination difficult. Also called flu.
Inguinal Hernia (external and internal): A hernia into the inguinal (groin) canal.
Intramuscular: In the substance of a muscle.
Insect-Borne Diseases: Diseases that are transmitted to humans by insects. See leishmaniasis, malaria, plague, river fever, Rocky Mountain spotted fever, trypanosomiasis, tularemia, typhus fever, and yellow fever.
Insect Repellent: A substance that repels or deters insects.
Insecticide: Destructive to insects.
Insomnia: The body's inability to relax during the night, and is generally caused by stressors during the day. Exercise and learning relaxation techniques may assist in alleviating insomnia.
Interferon Drugs: Proteins that are made from the human immune system and are used to fight viral infection and help regulate cell function.
Intermittent Claudication: A condition due to an obstruction (circulatory) in the limbs, primarily the legs, and characterized by the absence of pain when at rest, and the beginning of pain and weakness in upon walking, with the intensification of pain until walking becomes impossible.
Intermittent Fever: A fever usually associated with malaria that suddenly reoccurs after periods of cessation.
Internal Endometriosis: Endometrial tissue occurring in the wall of the fallopian tube or uterus.
Interstitial: Pertaining to the gaps or spaces in a tissue.
Interstitial Pneumonia: A chronic form of fibrous pneumonia with an increase of the interstitial tissue and a decrease of the lung tissue. Also called cirrhosis of the lung.
Intestine: A membranous tube that extends from the stomach to the anus. The first portion of the intestine is called the small intestine, which is about twenty feet long and includes the duodenum, jejunum, and ileum. The large intestine is about five feet long and comprises the cecum, colon, and rectum.
Iodism: Iodine poisoning marked by abdominal pain, arrhythmia, diarrhea, fever, thirst, priapism, and vomiting.
Irritable Bowel Syndrome (IBS): Irritation of an abnormally sensitive colon characterized by diarrhea and intestinal cramps can be caused by intolerance to certain foods. Keeping a list of all the foods and beverages you consume on a daily basis will help you to eliminate the products that are causing discomfort from your diet.
Ischemia: A temporary blood deficiency that is caused by a constricted or obstructed blood vessel and is characterized by pain.
Ischemic: Affected with ischemia.

J

Jaundice: Jaundice, an early indication of liver congestion, is a condition caused by hyperbilirubinemia and the deposit of bile pigment in the mucous membranes and skin, which results in a yellowish appearance.

K

Kaposi's Sarcoma: A tumorous condition resulting in multiple, soft, bluish, skin nodules with hemorrhage, which under certain conditions can lead to a rare fatal disease called xeroderma of Kaposi or xeroderma pigmentosum characterized by brown spots, skin ulcer, and atrophy (muscular).
Keratitis: Inflammation of the cornea.
Kidneys: The kidneys are two glands located in the lumbar region that are approximately the size and shape of a kidney bean. They filter out blood impurities, regulate the body's salt and water content, are responsible for the secretion of urine, and maintain the blood's acid/alkaline balance. Dysfunction of the kidneys can result in nephritis, enlarged and deformed kidneys, renal glycosuria, and various other kidney diseases.
Kidney Nephron: The tubular secretory portion of the kidney.
Kidney Stones: Kidney stones may occur due to an excessive accumulation of minerals, a buildup of certain acids, various toxins, or a urinary tract infection. Many smaller stones cause no discomfort and pass easily through the urinary tract; however, those stones that are too large will cause discomfort.
Kyphosis: An abnormal curvature of the spinal column due to softening of the spinal bones.

L

Lachrymator: A substance that causes eye irritation and produces tears.
Lactucism: Poisoning by lettuce (*lactuca spp.*).

Larvacide: Destroys insect larvae.
Laryngitis: Laryngitis is an inflammation of the vocal chords and may be caused by a bad cold, sore throat, overuse of the voice, or by contact with chemical irritants. To help ease discomfort, it is best to remain at home and rest your voice as much as possible, keep the throat moist with lozenges, drink soups and warm liquids, use a steam inhalant to moisturize and soothe throat irritation, and if you have to communicate, use a pen and paper. Obtain immediate medical attention if you experience difficulty breathing or swallowing, or if your symptoms last more than three days.
Laxative: A mild or drastic substance that promotes bowel evacuation. Also called aperient, cathartic, and purgative.
Leishmaniasis: A disease transmitted by the bite of the sand fly and characterized by ulcerations of the mucous membranes of the nose and throat.
Lesion: Pathological or traumatic damage of tissue affecting distinct parts or systems of the body resulting in a disturbance or loss of function in those parts. See tubercle lesion.
Leukorrhea: Leukorrhea is symptomatic with uterine and vaginal congestion, and is characterized by itching and a thin whitish discharge that comes from the vagina and uterine cavity.
Leukoplakia: A disease common in tobacco smokers that sometimes becomes malignant, and is characterized by white, thickened, sometimes fissured patches on the gums, tongue, and mucous membranes of the cheeks.
Lithemia: An excessive level of lithic acid (uric acid) and urates (uric acid salts) in the blood, tophi (joint tissues), and urine due to metabolism problems.
Lithotriptic: A substance that dissolves calculi.
Liver: The liver plays a main role in cleansing the blood. A cleansing regimen performed each spring works well in clearing out toxins that have accumulated throughout the year.
Lobar Pneumonia: An acute condition caused by the *diplococcus pneumoniae* organism and characterized by inflammation of one or more lobes of the lungs, chills, fever, rapid breathing, pain, and cough (bloody).
Lochia: Common vaginal discharge that occurs during the first few weeks following postpartum (childbirth).
Longevity: The condition or quality of being long-lived.
Lumbago: Lumbago is pain occurring in the lumbar (loin) region. Ischemic lumbago is pain occurring in the back. Both forms of lumbago are caused by vascular conditions.
Lupus: A tuberculosis disease of the mucous membranes and skin characterized by the formation of brown nodules and lesions of various forms, prolonged fever, and inflammation.
Lymph: A transparent to opalescent, yellowish or rose colored liquid found in the lymphatic vessels.
Lymphangitis: Inflammation of one or more lymphatic vessels.
Lymphatic System: The lymphatic system contains lymph glands and nodes and is the system of absorbent lymphatic vessels, which drain the lymph from various body tissues and return it to the blood stream.
Lymphedema: Edema caused by insufficient drainage of lymph nodes.
Lymphoma Tumor: A painless, progressive enlargement of lymphoid tissue of unknown cause.

M

Macrocytic: An abnormally large erythrocyte (red blood corpuscle).
Malaria: An infectious, febrile disease transmitted by the bites of mosquitoes infected with the plasmodium protozoa and characterized by fever (ague), chills, and perspiration, which can occur on a daily basis, every other day, or every three days.
Malariacidal: A substance that destroys the *malarial plasmodia* protozoa.
Malignant: Having a tendency to go from bad to worse. Cancerous.
Mammary Glands: Breasts.
Mascticated: Chewed.
Masticatory: A remedy that is chewed but not swallowed.
Measles: Measles is an acute, highly contagious (childhood) disease caused by the *briareus morbillorum* virus and characterized by fever, chills, conjunctivitis, bronchitis, cough, headache, runny nose, watery eyes, and small pink skin eruptions that begin on the forehead, cheeks, and back of the neck, then begin spreading over the body. Complications of the measles virus may include bronchitis (severe), ear infection, emaciation, and pneumonia. Also called rubeola.
Media: A variety of materials and combinations of materials used for the cultivation of microorganisms.
Melanoma: A malignant tumor made up of melanin-pigmented cells that have a tendency to metastasize.
Meniere's Disease: A disease of the organs of the inner ear that affect balance characterized by deafness, dizziness, tinnitus, and sometimes vomiting. Also called Meniere's syndrome.
Meningitis: Inflammation of the three membranes that envelop the brain and spinal cord.
Menopause: Menopause, caused by the gradual reduction of estrogen and progesterone levels in a woman's body, is *not* a disease, it is a natural process that signals the close of the childbearing years and generally occurs in the late thirties to forties with the ceasing of menstruation occurring somewhere in the fifties. Menopausal symptoms, if any, may be characterized by absent or delayed periods, arrhythmia, dryness (vaginal), scanty menstrual flow, erratic cycles, mood swings, hot flashes, insomnia, osteoporosis, weight gain, or depression.
Menorrhagia: Menorrhagia can be caused by fibroids (uterine), hormonal changes such as menopause, or extended strenuous exercise routines, all of which can bring on heavier than normal bleeding. If you experience heavier than normal flow, it is best to stay off your feet as much as possible the first day of your period, avoid alcoholic beverages (including wine), avoid any strenuous exercise, and don't lift anything heavy.
Menstrual Toxemia: Toxemia due to the alteration of retained menstrual blood.
Mercurial: Pertaining to mercury or mercury preparations.
Mercurialism: Poisoning from the misuse of mercury.
Mescalism: The habitual use of mescal buttons.

Metabolism: The chemical process, transformation, or building up and breaking down of proteins, etc. by which energy is made available for the uses of the life form (organism). Energy represents the power expended to maintain body temperature, circulation, glandular function, muscle tone, peristalsis, respiration, and other functions.
Metastasize: To form a new part of disease in a distant part away from the point of origin.
Metrorrhagia: An abnormal uterine hemorrhage unrelated to the menstrual cycle.
Migraine: Symptoms of discomfort may include intense pain usually occurring on one side of the head, sensitivity to light and noise, blurred vision, nausea, and seeing auras. Common causes may include heredity or obstruction (circulatory).
Milk Sickness: Poisoning in humans caused by consuming cow's milk that has been contaminated with tremetol (a toxin contained in white snakeroot), and is ingested by cows that graze on the herb.
Miosis: Pinpoint pupils.
Miotic: A substance that causes pupil contraction.
Mitosis: The division of active somatic and germ cells. Also known as karyokinesis.
Mitral Regurgitation: A malfunction of the hearts mitral valve that causes a backward flow of blood from the left ventricle into the left auricle.
Monoamine Oxidase Inhibitor (MAOI) Drugs: Substances used to treat depression when other antidepressant drug therapies fail.
Monograph: A summarized discussion or presentation of data, evidence, facts, or principles and the conclusions based on these.
Monoplegia: A permanent or temporary paralysis of a single limb or a single part of the body.
Monosodium Glutamate (MSG): A flavor enhancer common in many fast foods, packaged foods, processed foods, and frequently used in Chinese restaurants. Persons with MSG sensitivity may experience arrhythmia, chest tightness, flushing, headache, nausea, and occasionally shock (anaphylactic).
Mood Swings: Mood swings are abrupt, usually temporary, changes in mood. Mood is a broad term referring to a particular state of mind or feeling such as happiness, anger, fear, or suspicion. Blood glucose (sugar) levels, certain medications, diet, or hormonal fluctuations can have a direct effect on mood. To balance diet and stabilize blood glucose levels, switch to a low sugar diet with plenty of dairy products, fruits, protein, vegetables, and whole grains.
Mother Warts: Warts that foster other warts.
Motion Sickness: Motion sickness can occur with any form of movement such as traveling in a vehicle or vessel on land, over water, or in the air, or from rides at the amusement park, and is caused when the sensory input from our eyes, inner ears, and joint, muscle, and skin receptors sends conflicting messages to the brain. Appetite loss, cold sweats, dizziness, fainting, nausea, salivation (excessive), sleepiness, vertigo, or vomiting may characterize motion sickness.
Mucus: Mucus, produced by goblet cells, is a glutinous or sticky, whitish or grayish, watery secretion that covers the mucous membranes and is vital for respiratory system cleansing. Mucus is also present in the bile, the bursal and synovial fluids, and the umbilical cord.
Multiple Myeloma: A malignant tumor of the bone marrow characterized by anemia, neuralgia, protein in the urine (proteinuria), spontaneous fractures, and swellings occurring on the ribs and skull.
Mumps: An acute, contagious condition caused by the *rabula inflans* virus, and is characterized by fever, headache, pain beneath the ear, and inflammation and painful swelling of the parotid gland (and sometimes the mammary glands, pancreas, ovaries, salivary glands, or testicles) which causes interference with and results in painful actions of chewing and swallowing.
Muscle Strain: An overexertion or overstretching of some part of the muscular system of the body.
Muscular System: Muscles play a vital role in our life and without them we could not move. The muscular system accounts for nearly half of your body's weight and in order for muscles to become larger and stronger they require a regular workout. The more intense your exercise regimen, the more your muscles will build and strengthen. Some of the causes of muscle discomfort may include things such as tension, strenuous exercise, or disease.
Myasthenia Gravis: Muscular system exhaustion characterized by progressive paralysis that mainly affects the face, lips, neck, throat, and tongue.
Mydriasis: Extreme dilatation of the pupil.
Mydriatic: A substance that causes pupil dilatation.
Myeloma: A slow growing tumor that is composed of cells of the type normally found in bone marrow. Some myeloma tumors are malignant. See multiple myeloma.
Myocarditis: Inflammation of the heart muscle.
Myopathy: A disease of a muscle. See cardiomyopathy.

N

Narcotic: A substance that produces sleep and relieves pain.
Narcotism: Addiction to narcotics.
Nausea: A queasy feeling that may accompany nervous tension.
Necrosis: Death of a cell or a group of cells that are in contact with living tissue.
Nephritis: An acute or chronic condition due to a progressive, proliferative, degenerative lesion that affects the renal interstitial and stroma tissues, the vascular system of the kidneys, and kidney function in varying portions. Also called Bright's disease.
Nerve Endings: These transmit the sensations of touch to the brain, and substances that penetrate the skin layers can sedate or stimulate the nerves, thus influencing our level of relaxation.
Nervine: A substance that calms the nervous system.
Nervous System: The nervous system controls the circulatory, digestive, and respiratory functions of the body, as well as the emotions, and is the only system in the body that cannot regenerate damaged or destroyed cells.
Nervous Tension Headache: Symptoms of discomfort may include pain that originates at the back of the head and moves to the front. Common causes include but are not limited to poor posture, stress, or muscle strain. Also called tension headache.
Neuralgia: Recurring, intense pain that extends along the course of one or more nerves. It can occur anywhere in the body, and is caused by

numerous conditions including angina, diabetes, gout, malaria, or syphilis.
Neuritis: Neuritis is the inflammation of a nerve, and may be characterized by a disappearance of the reflexes, emaciation, tenderness and a disturbance of sensation over the nerve area, pain, or paralysis (possible), and may be caused by numerous conditions including alcoholism, diabetes, diphtheria, leprosy, malaria, palsy, pneumonia, poisoning (lead), rheumatism, or syphilis. See optic neuritis.
Newcastle Disease: A virus occurring in chickens that can be transmitted to humans and is characterized by encephalomyelitis and pneumonia.
Night Sweats: Night sweats are troublesome bouts of ephidrosis (excessive perspiration) occurring during the night, which can be so heavy that the bedclothes become soaked with perspiration. Night sweats may be caused by numerous conditions including certain medications, illness, or menopause. See perspiration.
Nocturnal Emission: The involuntary emission (discharge) of semen at night or during sleep.
Nocturnal Enuresis: The involuntary discharge of urine at night or during sleep. Also called bed-wetting.
Non-specific Vaginitis: A term assigned to a vaginal infection by a healthcare professional when he/she isn't sure what specific name to give it.
Nutritive: Serves as a nutritional adjunct to therapeutic programs; provides dietary supplementation.

O

Obstruction: A blockage.
Opiate Agonists/Narcotic Drugs: Substances derived from opium that has a narcotic effect.
Opthalmic: A substance used for eye problems.
Optic Neuritis: Inflammation of the optic nerve.
Orchitis: Inflammation of the testicles that is usually caused by an infection resulting from gonorrhea, syphilis, or tuberculosis, and is characterized by pain, swelling, and a feeling of heaviness in that area. Also called orchiditis.
Osteoarthritis (OA): Osteoarthritis is a condition appearing when wear and tear on joint structures exceeds repair. This excessive wear causes the damaged tissues to become inflamed and painful, and over time leads to degeneration of the joint. OA may be caused by obesity, or by prolonged overwork, as in athletic training, or can be the result of nutritional deficiency.
Osteomyelitis: Bone inflammation caused by a pyogenic organism that may remain localized or spread through the bone to the cortex, marrow, etc.
Osteoporosis: Osteoporosis is a silent condition that often goes unrecognized until a normal everyday activity such as bending, coughing, lifting, or sneezing results in a hip or wrist fracture, or a compression fracture of the spine. Bones that are brittle and porous are directly connected to the decline of estrogen and the loss of bone density. Maximum bone density loss occurs during the first two years after menstruation has ceased, and is chiefly a condition of postmenopausal women; primarily those of Asian and Caucasian bloodlines, however, it can occur earlier in life, and occasionally affects men too.
Orthostatic Hypotension: This type of hypotension sometimes occurs when a person changes from a supine (lying down), or sitting position to an upright position.
Otitis: Inflammation of the external, internal, and middle ear characterized by pain, swelling, fever, and auditory problems. See deafness, tinnitus, and vertigo.
Oxalemia: An excessive amount of oxalates in the blood.
Oxalism: Oxalic acid or oxalate poisoning.
Oxaluria: An excessive amount of oxalates or oxalic acid in the urine.
Oxytocic: A substance that stimulates uterine contractions.
Ozena: A disease of the nose characterized by a foul smelling discharge, which is caused by periodontal disease, rhinitis, or syphilis.

P

Palsy: A synonym for paralysis that is used only in connection with certain forms. See Bell's palsy, birth palsy, and cerebral palsy.
Pancreas: The pancreas is a large, elongated gland located behind the stomach, and is responsible for the internal secretion of the hormone insulin, which, containing four principle enzymes: *amylopsin*, *trypsin*, *steapsin*, and *rennin*, passes into the duodenum and is concerned with digestion and helping to control carbohydrate metabolism. This internal secretion is required to transport sugar into cells where the glucose is converted to energy.
Pancreatitis: Inflammation of the pancreas characterized by abdominal distention, pain, and tenderness, and vomiting.
Papule: Small, solid, elevated eruptions of the skin.
Paralytic Ileus: Obstruction (intestinal) producing severe colic. Also called adynamic ileus.
Parasites: An animal that lives on or within another living organism and derives its sustenance from its host.
Parasiticide: Destroys parasites.
Parkinson's Disease: A slowly progressive disease of the central nervous system characterized by muscle tremors when at rest and stiffness of movement.
Parkinsonism: A chronic condition characterized by stiffness of movement that is similar to Parkinson's disease, but without the resting tremors.
Parotid Gland: The gland situated near the ear.
Parturition: The process of giving birth to a child. Also called childbirth.
Pellagra: Pellagra is a condition due to a deficiency (niacin), and may be characterized by appetite loss, convulsions, debility, emaciation, gastrointestinal problems, idiocy (extreme mental deficiency), melancholy, recurring rash on portions of the body exposed to heat or light, spinal pain, vomiting, and possible death.
Pelvic Inflammatory Disease (PID): Inflammation of the pelvic cavity resulting in fever and pain.
Peptic Ulcer: Ulceration on the mucous membrane of the duodenum, esophagus, or stomach.
Pericardium: The membranous sac that contains the heart.

Peritoneum: The serous membrane lining the abdominal walls.
Peritonitis: An inflammation of the peritoneum characterized by abdominal pain and tenderness, constipation, fever, and vomiting.
Pernicious: Tending to a fatal issue.
Perspiration: Perspiration is the body's way of cooling itself down, and is also a way of ridding the system of toxins. See night sweats.
Pharmacognosy: The branch of science that deals with the origin, structure, and chemical constitution of medicines of plants, animals, or minerals in their crude form or unprepared state.
Pharmacology: The science dealing with the action and effects of medicinal products, their nature, preparation, and administration (includes materia medica and therapeutics).
Pharyngitis: An acute or chronic condition of the pharynx due to conditions such as diphtheria, syphilis, tonsillitis, or tuberculosis, and may be characterized by congestion (mucous membrane), degeneration of the submucous tissues, difficulty swallowing, exhaustion, fever, gangrenous patches (possible), granular mucous membrane tissues, hypertrophy (pharyngeal glands), inflammation, secretion (excessive), thickening of the submucous tissues, throat dryness and pain, ulceration of the throat (severe), and vesicles (small abscesses).
Pharynx: The musculomembranous sac between the mouth and the openings into the nasal cavity (nares) and the esophagus.
Phenylketonuria (PKU): A genetic condition resulting in an inborn error in which the body cannot metabolize/process phenylalanine, which results in brain damage or mental retardation.
Phenylpropanolamine (PPA): The hydrochloride of racemic-1-phenyl-2-aminopropanol. It has actions similar to ephedrine and is used by spray or instillation as a bronchodilator and local vasodilator.
Photodermatosis: A condition produced in the skin by exposure to light, which causes sensitivity of the skin's epithelial cells, and is characterized by skin rash and lesions.
Photosensitivity: A sensitivity to light, which could possibly lead to photodermatosis, and is characterized by itching and a sunburn-like rash.
Physostigmine: A miotic alkaloid that inhibits the effects of acetylcholine esterase.
Phytotherapy: Treatment by the use of medicinal herbs and plants.
Pituitary Adiposity: Obesity due to pituitary deficiency.
Plague: An acute, febrile, infectious, often fatal, sometimes insect-borne disease transmitted to humans by either the bite of fleas that have been infected with the *pasteurella pastis* bacteria contracted by the fleas when they feed on infected prairie dogs, rats, or other vermin, or by a bite from the animal itself. Chills, delirium, diarrhea, fever, extreme exhaustion, headache, hemorrhage, lesions, lymph node swelling, poisoning (blood), vomiting, and possible death characterize the disease. Also called bubonic plague.
Plana Juvenilis Warts: Small warts that are smooth, slightly raised, and occur in multiples on the back of the hands, face, knees, neck, and wrists. Also called Skin Tags.
Plantar Fasciitis: Footpad inflammation.
Plantar Warts: Warty growths occurring on the soles of the feet.
Pleurisy: An acute or chronic inflammation of the pleura (the membrane of the lungs and thoracic cavity) that may be due to conditions such as bronchitis or pneumonia, and may be characterized by chills, dry cough, exhaustion, fever, and a side ache (possibly sharp, stabbing pain).
Pneumonia: Inflammation of the lungs. See interstitial pneumonia and lobar pneumonia.
Polycythemia: An excessive number of red corpuscles in the blood.
Polyps: Smooth pedunculated (stemmed) growths from a mucous surface such as the bladder, colon, intestines, or nasal passages. Some polyps can be malignant (cancerous).
Postoperative Shock: Shock following a surgical procedure.
Potentiate: Increase.
Preeclamptic Toxemia: Toxemia occurring in late pregnancy that precedes the development of eclampsia, and is characterized by albuminuria, difficult breathing, headache (possibly severe), nausea, sensitivity to light (eyes), and vomiting. Also called preeclampsia.
Priapism: Persistent, painful penile erection unrelated to sexual desire.
Prolapse: Prolapse is the falling down of a part or organ. A rectal prolapse is the protrusion of the rectal mucous membrane through the anus in varying degree. Prolapse of the uterus is a protrusion of the uterus through the vaginal cavity.
Prostate: The prostate, a gland the size of a chestnut, surrounds the neck of the bladder and the urethra, and is an organ of the male reproductive system. Prostaglandin, which is a pressor (increases blood pressure), stimulant, and vasodilator is obtained from the prostate gland and the seminal vesicles.
Prostatitis: Prostatitis is an inflammation of the prostate gland due to an infection of the urinary tract, and is characterized by hypertrophy, which leads to obstruction (bladder). This obstruction impedes the flow of urine causing discomfort and frequent urges to urinate.
Proteinuria: Protein in the urine.
Prurigo: A chronic, usually incurable skin condition that occurs in childhood and lasts throughout life. It is characterized by small papules and intense pruritus.
Pruritus: Itching (possibly intense) due to a variety of skin conditions (i.e. eczema, prurigo, psoriasis) that cause an irritation.
Psoriasis: A chronic skin condition in which the epidermis (the top outer layer of skin) grows too fast, resulting in patches of dermatitis characterized by silvery scales or red areas that may crack and bleed, or ooze and itch. Psoriasis primarily occurs on the arms, back (primarily lower), chest, ears, elbows, knees, legs, and scalp, with pits and ridges developing on the fingernails and toenails. Allergy (food), certain drugs, constipation, deficiency (zinc), infection (bacterial, viral), kidney or liver problems, poison ivy, stress, sunburn, surgery, and/or wounds (minor) may trigger an attack.
Pyelitis: Inflammation of the pelvis of the kidney and characterized by bloody urine, diarrhea, fever, pain and tenderness in the loins and upon flexion of the thigh, and vomiting.
Pyloristenosis: A narrowing of the pylorus, usually existing at or before birth, that causes obstruction (duodenal).
Pylorus: The duodenal aperture (opening) of the stomach.

R

Rash: An acute, temporary, skin condition due to various factors including certain drugs, dermatitis, illness, or a rash that sometimes follows vaccination, and generally characterized by inflammation or reddish eruptions on the skin.
Raynaud's Disease: A vascular (circulatory) system condition that affects the extremities.
Regular Headache: Symptoms of discomfort may include a dull throbbing of the entire head. Common causes may include but are not limited to temperature or altitude changes, congestion of the nasal passages, or illness. Also called common headache.
Reproductive System: Once you arrive at sexual maturity, your sense of physical and emotional health is largely determined by the intricate relationship between the nervous system and the hormones produced by the ovaries (in women) or testes (in men), adrenals, and pituitary gland. During the reproductive years, the fluctuating balance between estrogen and progesterone levels influence a woman's menstrual cycle. Testosterone is the male testicular hormone, and its function is the initiation and maintenance of male secondary sex characters, as well as helping in the production of spermatozoa.
Respiratory Center: Coordinates the respiratory movements.
Respiratory System: Of all the systems in the body, the respiratory system is the one most directly affected by the environment. Oxygen is crucial to our physical being, and since the body cannot store oxygen, we must continuously supply this need through breathing. Each breath is taken into the lungs where the exchange of oxygen and carbon monoxide occur. From there it is transported to all parts of the body through the bloodstream. Although the lungs do aid in the elimination of toxins from the air we breathe, the respiratory system may still be prone to problems such allergy (pollen), asthma, or infection (viral).
Retinitis: An inflammatory condition of the retina that is characterized by distortion of vision, retinal edema, sight impairment, and occasionally hemorrhage (retinal).
Retinopathy: A noninflammatory condition of the retina.
Reye's Syndrome: A condition that sometimes follows a viral infection and causes brain inflammation.
Rheumatic Fever: Fever associated with rheumatism.
Rheumatism: A condition due to dysfunction of the body's immune system, which causes discomfort throughout the entire body, and may be characterized by inflammation, muscle and joint pain, fungus-like growths on the heart valves, and the presence of nodules on the heart muscle (myocardium) and skin.
Rheumatoid Arthritis (RA): A chronic joint condition occurring when the immune system itself attacks the cartilage and damages the joint structure. RA may be characterized by inflammation of the joints, followed by bone deformity and deterioration.
Rhinitis: Inflammation of the nasal passage mucous membranes.
River Fever: An infectious, febrile disease of short duration transmitted by the bite of the sand fly, and characterized by skin eruptions, painful swelling, mucus, severe eye, head, muscle, and joint pain, with symptoms increasing in severity for a few days, then decreasing somewhat, and increasing yet again. Also known as Japanese river fever and pappataci fever.
Rocky Mountain Spotted Fever: An infectious virus transmitted by the bite of a parasitic tick and characterized by bone and muscle pain, headache, high fever, mental disturbances, and a red spotted skin eruption occurring at the area of the bite.
Roentgen Rays: X-rays.

S

Salicylates: A substance that reduces fever, inflammation, and pain.
Salicylism: Salicylic acid poisoning.
Sarcoidosis: A chronic, infectious disease of unknown origin characterized by lesions (bone, eye, lung, lymph node, salivary gland, skin, and tubercle), fever, inflammation, and sarcoma-like tumors.
Sarcoma: The formation of a secondary, highly malignant tumor, which is associated with cancer and made up of closely packed cells embedded in a homogenous substance. See Kaposi's sarcoma.
Scarlet Fever: An acute, contagious disease caused by a specific strain of *streptococcus* and initially characterized by fever, chills, sore throat, vomiting, rapid pulse rate, a scarlet rash or eruption, and possibly nephritis. Also called scarlatina.
Schistosomiasis: A parasitic disease that sometimes occurs in tourists returning to the United States.
Sciatic Nerve: The largest nerve in the body located in the back of the thigh.
Sciatica: An intense, often debilitating pain occurring along the course of the sciatic nerve, usually due to neuritis (nerve inflammation) or an injury, and may be characterized by an abnormal sensation of burning or prickling of the leg and thigh, tenderness along the nerve, and occasionally wasting of the calf muscle.
Scleroderma: A skin condition characterized by thickened, hard, rigid, pigmented patches.
Sclerosis: A hardening of a part (i.e. connective tissue) from inflammation and in diseases of the interstitial substance.
Scrofula: Swelling of the lymphatic gland caused by the tuberculosis bacteria.
Scrotal Hernia: An inguinal hernia that has descended into the scrotum.
Seasonal Affective Disorder (SAD): A form of depression linked to declining sunlight occurring during the winter months.
Seborrhoeic Warts: Flat, greasy-looking warts that are often associated with seborrhea.
Sedative: A substance generally weaker than a tranquilizer that helps to soothe or quiet a person, and lessen excitement, irritation, and nervousness.
Selective Serotonin Reuptake Inhibitor (SSRI) Drugs: Substances that block the CNS neuronal uptake of serotonin into blood platelets. It is used for depression, obsessive-compulsive disorder, and other conditions.
Sepsis: Poisoning caused by the products of a putrefactive (decomposition) process.
Septic Fever: Fever that is associated with blood poisoning (septicemia).
Septicemia: A condition due to infection of pathogenic microorganisms and other poisons in the blood, and characterized by chills, ephidrosis, exhaustion, and fever. Also called blood poisoning and septic infection.

Sexually Transmitted Diseases (STDs): Contagious venereal diseases that are transmitted chiefly through coitus. See gonorrhea, human immunodeficiency virus (HIV), and syphilis.
Sexually Transmitted Infections (STIs): Infections that are transmitted chiefly through coitus. See gleet, herpes, human immunodeficiency virus (HIV), Human Papilloma virus (HPV), and venereal warts.
Shingles (herpes zoster): An acute, contagious, recurring, inflammatory condition of the cerebral ganglia and ganglia of the posterior nerve roots caused by the *briareus varicellae* virus, which is the same virus that causes chicken pox, and is characterized by blisters that form in clusters along the nerve roots, fever, inflammation, and pain of the blistered area.
Shock: A condition of acute circulatory failure caused by the disarrangement of a part or organ or the copious (profuse) loss of blood. See anaphylactic shock, hypovolemic shock, postoperative shock, and toxic shock syndrome.
Sialogogue: A substance that promotes saliva secretion.
Sickle Cell Anemia: A condition occurring chiefly in the African American bloodlines, and characterized by the red blood cells taking on a crescent-like shape and ulcers.
Silacatosis: A pulmonary condition caused by the inhalation of silicate dust.
Sjögren's Disease: Inflammation of the eye cornea and conjunctiva and a deficiency of tears resulting in dryness (eye). Also known as keratoconjunctivitis sicca and Sjögren's syndrome.
Skeletal System: The Skeletal system is comprised of bones, which are the storehouses for sodium, calcium, magnesium, phosphorus, protein, vitamins C and D, and boron. Regular exercise helps deter bone loss, minimize discomfort, and strengthens the bones. Calcium rich products such as dairy foods, sunflower seeds, and vegetables can help boost calcium levels in the body.
Small Pox: An acute, infectious disease caused by the *borreliota variolae* virus and is characterized by papular than pustular skin eruptions that break open, crust over, have a foul odor, and usually leave a scar, chills, fever, lumbar pain, and vomiting. Some forms of small pox cause severe hemorrhaging from the mucous surfaces and possible death. Also called variola.
Solution: A liquid that consists of a mixture of two or more solutes (substances) that is dissolved in a solvent.
Sore Throat: An inflammation of the mucous membranes of the throat and vocal chords, often the result of an infection, but can be caused by acid reflux, indigestion, postnasal drip, public speaking, shouting, or singing. Avoid using antihistamines or a gargle/mouth rinse that contains alcohol, as they have a tendency to dry out and further irritate the delicate tissues of the throat.
Spasm: A sudden, violent, involuntary, painful, contraction of a muscle or a group of muscles, or a sudden but brief constriction of a canal (i.e. alimentary), orifice (i.e. uterus), or passage (i.e. throat) is characteristic of a spasm. A persistent spasm is called a tonic spasm, and when the spasm is characterized by alternate contraction and relaxation, it is called a clonic spasm.
Spasmodic Conditions: Spasmodic conditions include but are not limited to asthma, dysmenorrhea, hemiplegia, lesions (cerebral), neurosis, rickets, tetanus, or trismus (lockjaw). See spasm.
Spermatorrhea: Frequent, excessive, involuntary discharge of semen without copulation.
Splenauxe: Hypertrophy (spleen).
Sprain: Damage of a joint with partial rupture or other injury of its cartilage or muscle, and characterized by rapid inflammation, swelling, and warmth to the area, and temporary disablement of the joint.
Sprue: A chronic, nutritional condition characterized by a sore mouth, raw tongue, gastrointestinal mucus, periodic diarrhea with frothy, fatty, putrid stools, weight loss, loss of strength and energy, and a blood picture resembling that of anemia (pernicious).
Sputum Cruentum: Bloody sputum or in more severe cases, the coughing of blood.
Stasis Ulcer: An ulceration occurring on the lower extremities due to insufficiency (circulatory).
Stenosis: A narrowing of a duct or canal.
Stimulant: A substance that produces stimulation or increases activity.
Stomachic: A substance that promotes or enhances functional activity of the stomach.
Stomatitis: Inflammation of the mouth.
Stricture: The abnormal narrowing of a duct, canal, or passage.
Stroma: The tissue that forms the framework or matrix of an organ.
Subcutaneous: Located beneath the skin.
Subcutaneous Tissue: The layer of fat below the dermis layer of skin. This tissue provides a protective cushion or padding. The subcutaneous tissue contains the sweat glands, and it is criss-crossed with blood vessels and nerves.
Subsalicylates: Substances used to relieve indigestion and to control diarrhea.
Sulfa Drugs: A group of drugs used for treating bacterial diseases.
Suspension: A substance whose particles are dispersed through a fluid or gel-like substance but not dissolved in it.
Synovial Fluid: A glutinous or sticky (viscid), whitish, alkaline fluid secreted from the synovial membrane, and that is contained in the bursa, joint cavities, and tendon sheaths. Also called synovia.
Synovial Membrane: The connective tissue membrane that lines the bursa, joint cavities, and tendon sheaths, and is the source of synovial fluid.
Synovitis: Inflammation of the synovial membrane characterized by pain.
Syphilis: A contagious, usually sexually transmitted, venereal disease caused by the *treponema pallidum* microorganism, and may be characterized by fever, lesions, pustules, severe pain in the head and joints, and ulcer (syphilitic). These lesions and ulcers extend to the lymphatic vessels, mucous membranes, skin, and other tissues of the body, and sometimes to the bones and the tough fibrous membrane (periosteum) that surrounds the bone.
Syphilitic Ulcer: An ulceration due to syphilis.
Syriac Ulcer: Ulceration due to diphtheria. Also called Syrian ulcer.
Systole: The period of the heart's contraction; also the contraction itself.

T

Tachycardia: Abnormally fast heartbeat.
Tendinitis: An inflammation of the tendons and the tendon-muscle attachements characterized by tenderness and lameness.
Teniacide: Destroys tapeworms.
Tetanus: An acute, infectious condition caused by a toxin that is produced in the body by the *clostridium tetani* bacillus, and characterized by spasm of the jaw muscles causing lockjaw (trismus), followed by continuous, steady muscle spasm of the back.
Thromboembolism: The blocking of an artery or vein with a blood clot (thrombus) that has broken loose from its point of formation.
Thrombophlebitis: An inflammatory condition of the vein wall that preceded the formation of the blood clot (thrombus). Also called vein inflammation.
Thrombosis: The formation or presence of a blood clot (thrombus).
Thrombus: A clot occurring in an artery, vein, or heart cavity, formed by coagulation of the blood, and usually remaining at the site of of its formation. Also called blood clot.
Tinea Cruris: A moist dermatitis chiefly caused by a genus of fungi *epidermophyton* and characterized by intense itching, irritation, redness, and inflammation of the groin and thigh area. Also called jock itch.
Tinnitus: A buzzing, ringing, roaring, or ticking sound occurring in the ears.
Tonic: A substance that restores normal tone to tissues.
Tonsil: A small, almond-shaped mass composed primarily of lymphoid tissue and covered with mucous membrane, located between the supporting structures (pillars) of the passage from the mouth to the pharynx (fauces) on either side. The tonsils act as sources for the supply of fixed or free cells (phagocytes) that destroy microorganisms (bacteria) in the mouth and pharynx.
Tonsillectomy: The surgical removal of one or both of the tonsils, often required in chronic tonsillitis.
Tonsillitis: An acute or chronic condition due to an infection, which is often associated with pharyngitis, and may be characterized by difficulty swallowing (dysphagia), fever, headache, hypertrophy (tonsil), inflammation, pain (possibly severe), pustules, redness, and sore throat. A tonsillectomy may be required in chronic tonsillitis.
Tourette's Syndrome: A nervous condition characterized by convulsions, incoordination, and speech problems. Also called Tourette's disease.
Toxemia: A condition due to the absorption of toxins that have formed from a bacterial infection or a chemical intoxication. See alimentary toxemia, eclamptic toxemia (eclampsia), menstrual toxemia, and pre-eclamptic toxemia (preeclampsia).
Toxic: Poisonous.
Toxic Shock Syndrome (TSS): A rare, serious, occasionally fatal, condition that can occur in women who use tampons during menstruation. Women who are under thirty years of age are at a higher risk of contracting TSS. Diarrhea, dizziness or orthostatic hypotension, fainting, fever of 102° F or higher that comes on suddenly, and a sunburn-like rash characterize toxic shock syndrome. If these symptoms appear, immediately remove the tampon and consult a healthcare professional. To reduce the risk of TSS, select a tampon with the minimum absorbency range needed to control menstrual flow, change your tampon every 4-6 hours or as needed, alternate between the use of external sanitary (hygienic) pads and tampons, or simply avoid the use of tampons.
Tracheitis: Inflammation of the trachea.
Trachoma: An infectious disease of the conjunctiva and cornea of the eye that is caused by the virus *chlamydozoon trachomatis*, and is characterized by pain, photophobia, excessive tearing, redness, and inflammation.
Tranquilizer: A substance generally stronger than a sedative that is used to calm, relieve, and control various emotional disturbances such as anxiety, neuroses, and psychoses.
Trichomonas: An infection caused by the parasitic trichomonas bacteria, that can be found in the vagina of women, primarily if the secretion is acidic, and in the bladder and urethra of men. This microorganism can be transmitted during coitus, and is characterized by burning urination, itching (mild to severe), rash, and a frothy, greenish or yellowish discharge with an unpleasant odor.
Trismus: A motor disturbance of the trigeminus (facial) nerve and spasm of the masticatory (jaw) muscles marked by difficulty in opening the mouth, and a characteristic, early symptom of tetanus. Also called lockjaw.
Trypanosomiasis: A disease caused by the trypanosoma parasite that is transmitted to humans by the bite of the tsetse fly, which can last for months or years, and is initially characterized by anemia, chills, fever, headache, hypertrophy (lymph), pain in the extremities, and vomiting with the final results of depression, lethargy, nervous system problems, sleeping sickness, emaciation, and eventually death. Also called African sleeping sickness and sleeping sickness.
Tubercle Lesion: The characteristic lesions produced by the bacillus of tuberculosis and characterized by a nodule or mass of small, rounded, solid, grayish nodules on the skin that are made up of small spherical cells that contain giant cells, which are surrounded by epithelioid cells (spindle-shaped connective tissue cells). Also called gray tubercle and military tubercle.
Tuberculosis: A contagious condition caused by the *mycobacterium tuberculosis* bacillus and may be characterized by abscess, cerebral symptoms (pulmonary, meningeal, typhoid), cough, diarrhea, difficult breathing, emaciation, fever, hematuria, hemoptysis, infection (septic), larynx and vocal chord ulceration, night sweats, skin nodules, ulcer (tuberculous), and the formation of lesions (tubercle) in the blood vessels, lymphatic vessels, and other body tissues, which have a tendency to spread in all directions.
Tuberculous Ulcer: An ulceration occurring at the mucocutaneous borders of the anus, genitals, mouth, or nose
Tularemia: A disease (similar to plague) of rodents caused by the *pasteurella tularensis* bacteria, which is transmitted by the bites of fleas, flies, lice, and ticks, or by a bite from the animal itself, and is characterized by body pain, chills, headache, lymph gland swelling, rapid elevation of body temperature, and ulcerations.
Typhus Fever: An acute disease caused by the parasitic microorganism *rickettsia*, which is transmitted by bites from infected bedbugs, fleas, mites, lice, and ticks, and is characterized by fever and skin eruptions.

U

Ulcer: An open sore on the mucous surface, skin, or internal parts of the body that causes disintegration and necrosis (death) of the tissues, and can be due to conditions such as deficiency (nutrient), diabetes, infection (bacterial, fungal, septic), leishmaniasis, stress, tuberculosis, or typhoid, and may be characterized by discharge, foul odor, or pain. Following a low fiber diet, and decreasing the intake of alcohol, nicotine, and protein foods will help speed healing.
Urethritis: Urethritis is an inflammation of the urethra, and may be due to gonorrhea, gout, or an infection, and is primarily characterized by discharge (occasionally) and itching. The microorganisms causing urethritis are initially transmitted by the male during coitus, and are then passed back and forth between the partners causing reinfection during each session of coitus.
Urinary System: The urinary system includes the bladder, which is a membranous sac situated in the front part of the pelvic cavity that serves as a reservoir for the urine, and the kidneys, which continuously filter and cleanse toxins from the body, flushing them out through urination. Without the kidneys, the accumulated toxins would poison our body.
Urodialysis: Partial or complete suppression of urine.
Uropenia: Deficiency of urinary flow. Also called scanty urination.

V

Vaginal Dryness: Vaginal dryness can be caused by many conditions including estrogen decline due to menopause or hysterectomy, postpartum dryness (primarily if breast-feeding), stress, surgery, or various medications, and is characterized by itching, irritation, and dryness of the vaginal canal due to depletion of vaginal fluids.
Vaginitis: A term assigned to a number of uterine and vaginal infections that can be passed back and forth between partners during coitus, and may be characterized by itching, inflammation, rash or redness, discharge with an unpleasant odor, and painful coitus. See candida, chlamydia, hemophilus, leukorrhea, non-specific vaginitis, and trichomonas.
Varicose Ulcer: Ulcerations due to varicose veins.
Varicose Veins: Surface veins with weakened walls mainly occur in the legs. The veins have a tendency to twist or knot and are visible just below the skin. Pregnancy, heredity, standing for extended amounts of time, constrictive clothing, or obesity may cause this condition.
Vasoconstrictor: A substance that causes blood vessel constriction.
Vasodepressor: A substance that causes vasomotor depression.
Vasodilator: A substance that causes blood vessel dilatation.
Venereal Warts: Venereal warts are contagious, moist, small, pointed warts caused by the human papilloma virus (HPV), and are transmitted by direct skin to skin contact with an infected person during coitus regardless of whether the warts are visible or not. These warts are located on or near the anus or scrotum, or on the penis in men, and in women are located in or near the vagina, and appear within several weeks to as long as nine months after infection. These warts start out as flat or raised, singly or in multiples, and quickly increase in size to a cauliflower-like growth. Often there are no symptoms and the warts themselves are usually painless, but can occasionally cause burning and itching. In men, these warts are easily diagnosed, but in women the diagnosis is a bit trickier, and is usually done through a colposcopy, an examination of the cervix and vagina by means of the colposcope. Infection of this virus is directly associated with cancer (cervical) in women, and left untreated in men, these warts could result in cancer (penile). Also called Genital Warts.
Veneroid Ulcer: Ulcerations or chancres occurring around the vulva and cervix on women not exposed to venereal disease.
Vermifuge: A substance that expels intestinal parasites and worms.
Vertigo: A sensation, mistaken for dizziness, of the world revolving around oneself, which is caused by a disease of the middle ear, or from a gastric, cardiac, or ocular (eye) condition.
Vesicant: A substance that causes blisters or blistering.
Vomiting: The forcible ejection of the contents of the stomach through the mouth. Sometimes associated with nausea, vomiting may be provoked by problems similar to those causing nausea such as digestive complaints, stomach problems, influenza, gallstones, noxious or strong odors, indigestion, poisoning, an overindulgence of alcohol or food, disturbing sights, ear infection, vertigo, illness such as diabetes or certain cancers, motion sickness, headache, fever, migraine, inflammations, psychological stimuli, nervous tension, loss of equilibrium, and dizziness. Unless vomiting is prolonged, severe, projectile, or includes bile or blood, it is best to let it run its course as this process cleanses the system of indigestible foods, microorganisms, and toxins. Drinking clear, sweetened liquids may help in the replacement of salts and sugars lost during emesis. Also called emesis.
Vulgaris Warts: Warts that commonly occur on the skin.
Vulnerary: A substance that speeds healing.

W

Warts: Localized benign, sometimes contagious, hypertrophy (skin) caused by a virus.
Whooping Cough: An infectious cough caused by a bacterial infection that is characterized by episodes of short, violent coughing with episodes of long intakes of breath, which make a whooping sound.

Y

Yellow Fever: An acute, infectious, disease associated with the virus *charon evagatus*, which is transmitted to humans by the bites of mosquitoes, and is characterized by albuminuria, fever, and jaundice.

Botanical Index

A reference list to help you find any of the botanical names included in the book.

A

General Index

A

497, 503, 516, 517, 519, 531, 533, 535, 582
Diabetes Mellitus, 40, 582
Diabetic Retinopathy, 46, 90, 182, 201, 204, 208, 213, 221, 298, 399, 417
Diaper Rash Ointment, 536
Diaphoretic, 32, 33, 43, 45, 48, 51, 56, 57, 60, 61, 70, 71, 72, 75, 78, 79, 81, 82, 83, 85, 86, 88, 91, 93, 94, 95, 98, 100, 101, 105, 106, 107, 108, 111, 115, 117, 119, 122, 123, 133, 134, 141, 142, 144, 145, 150, 153, 155, 160, 161, 162, 163, 164, 165, 169, 174, 175, 176, 177, 178, 179, 188, 190, 195, 198, 200, 202, 203, 209, 210, 216, 217, 222, 223, 224, 229, 231, 232, 234, 239, 240, 241, 242, 245, 248, 249, 253, 254, 260, 261, 272, 273, 274, 277, 278, 282, 284, 290, 292, 293, 294, 296, 299, 300, 306, 307, 320, 326, 330, 331, 332, 335, 342, 343, 346, 349, 350, 351, 353, 355, 362, 368, 372, 373, 375, 376, 377, 378, 381, 383, 387, 388 391, 395, 396, 397, 400, 401, 403, 406, 410, 412, 414, 416, 418, 419, 420, 423, 425, 426, 428, 432, 434, 437, 438, 440, 468, 582
Diarrhea, 2, 3, 23, 25, 30, 32, 33, 34, 35, 36, 37, 38, 39, 40, 41, 42, 43, 44, 45, 46, 48, 49, 50, 52, 55, 56, 57, 59, 61, 62, 63, 64, 65, 68, 69, 70, 71, 72, 73, 75, 76, 77, 78, 79, 80, 81, 83, 84, 85, 87, 88, 90, 91, 93, 94, 95, 97, 98, 99, 100, 101, 102, 103, 104, 105, 106, 107, 108, 109, 110, 111, 112, 113, 114, 115, 117, 118, 120, 122, 123, 124, 126, 127, 128, 129, 131, 132, 133, 134, 135, 136, 137, 138, 139, 140, 141, 142, 143, 144, 145, 146, 147, 148, 149, 150, 151, 152, 154, 155, 156, 157, 158, 159, 160, 161, 162, 163, 164, 165, 166, 168, 169, 170, 171, 172, 173, 174, 175, 176, 177, 178, 179, 181, 182, 183, 185, 187, 189, 190, 191, 192, 193, 194, 195, 197, 198, 199, 200, 201, 202, 205, 208, 209, 210, 211, 212, 215, 216, 217, 218 219, 220, 221, 222, 223, 224, 226, 227, 228, 229, 230, 231, 232, 233, 234, 235, 236, 237, 238, 239, 240, 241, 242, 243, 245, 247, 248, 249, 250, 251, 252, 253, 254, 256, 257, 258, 261, 263, 264, 266, 267, 268, 269, 270, 271, 272, 273, 274, 276, 277, 278, 279, 280, 281, 282, 283, 285, 286, 287, 288, 290, 291, 292, 293, 294, 295, 296, 297, 298, 299, 300, 301, 302, 303, 304, 305, 306, 307, 308, 309, 312, 313, 314, 315, 316, 317, 318, 319, 320, 322, 323, 325, 326, 327, 328, 330, 331, 332, 335, 336, 337, 338, 340, 341, 342, 343, 344, 345, 346, 347, 348, 349, 350, 351, 352, 353, 355, 356, 357, 360, 361, 362, 363, 364, 365, 366, 367, 368, 369, 370, 371, 372, 373, 376, 377, 378, 379, 381, 382, 383, 384, 385, 386, 387, 388, 390, 391, 392, 393, 394, 395, 396, 397, 398, 399, 400, 401, 403, 404, 405, 406, 407, 408, 409, 410, 411, 414, 416, 417, 418, 419, 420,422, 423, 424, 425, 427, 428, 429, 430, 431, 432, 433, 434, 435, 436, 437, 439, 440, 441, 444, 446, 450, 451, 452, 454, 456, 458, 459, 460, 461, 462, 463, 464, 465, 466, 470, 471, 493, 506, 508, 530, 582
Diastole, 192, 582
Dietary Supplementation, 33, 34, 35, 38, 42, 46, 47, 52, 53, 54, 60, 70, 76, 83, 84, 87, 90, 99, 104, 117, 118, 128, 130, 131, 138, 146, 155, 162, 163, 167, 168, 185, 196, 197, 206, 214, 215, 247, 248, 251, 253, 255, 257, 260, 264, 268, 270, 272, 280, 281, 284, 289, 291, 295, 296, 304, 307, 308, 309, 310, 312, 313, 316, 319, 322, 324, 325, 326, 327, 330, 338, 348, 354, 363, 365, 370, 371, 372, 390, 394, 399, 402, 406, 408, 412, 413, 416, 430, 431, 432, 433, 435, 444, 446, 447, 448, 449
Diethyistilbestrol, 487, 582
Digestive Complaints, 6, 32, 34, 38, 39, 40, 43, 45, 50, 53, 54, 55, 57, 58, 61, 64, 66, 68, 70, 72, 73, 78, 79, 83, 87, 88, 90, 91, 92, 93, 94, 95, 96, 98, 99, 100, 102, 105, 107, 108, 109, 111, 114, 115, 116, 117, 118, 121, 122, 123, 124, 127, 131, 132, 133, 134, 135, 136, 137, 139, 140, 141, 146, 147, 149, 150, 156, 158, 159, 160, 161, 164, 166, 167, 170, 172, 173, 176, 177, 183, 184, 185, 189, 190, 191, 197, 198, 199, 200, 202, 206, 207, 211, 212, 216, 219, 228, 229, 230, 231, 232, 233, 238, 240, 243, 245, 248, 251, 254, 259, 261, 262, 263, 264, 265, 266, 274, 278, 281, 282, 285, 287, 290, 295, 296, 298, 299, 300, 302, 303, 304, 306, 309, 313, 314, 315, 317, 318, 320, 326, 327, 328, 329, 331, 332, 333, 335, 337, 338, 341, 342, 344, 345, 347, 350, 352, 353, 355, 359, 360, 361, 363, 369, 372, 375, 376, 378, 379, 382, 384, 385, 387, 391, 392, 394, 397, 398, 400, 403, 413, 414, 415, 419, 420, 423, 424, 425, 427, 429, 431, 432, 434, 435, 436, 439, 440, 446, 447, 459, 460, 465, 473, 480, 494, 516
Digestive System, 38, 59, 70, 85, 87, 89, 93, 122, 131, 141, 146, 172, 173, 191, 195, 206, 211, 235, 251, 266, 286, 295, 298, 308, 309, 345, 357, 360, 361, 363, 366, 370, 394, 404, 405, 423, 460, 493, 499, 506, 533, 582
Digestive System Tonic, 494
Digitate Warts (*see* Warts)
Dilatation, 34, 38, 40, 43, 56, 67, 69, 72, 73, 77, 80, 85, 87, 94, 96, 102, 103, 105, 112, 116, 118, 119, 121, 122, 127, 128, 129, 131, 133, 135, 139, 140, 141, 143, 151, 152, 153, 155, 156, 157, 161, 168, 174, 178, 179, 182, 183, 190, 196, 199, 200, 204, 207, 208, 212, 214, 219, 221, 222, 224, 225, 227, 230, 244, 246, 247, 248, 249, 250, 251, 252, 253, 261, 262, 263, 272, 278, 281, 286, 287, 298, 300, 302, 303, 306, 308, 310, 311, 312, 313, 316, 319, 326, 327, 329, 330, 333, 335, 336, 340, 345, 349, 350, 353, 354, 360, 364, 366, 367, 374, 383, 387, 393, 399, 400, 402, 407, 415, 416, 417, 425, 427, 428, 432, 440, 446, 448, 471, 514, 583
Dilation (*see* Dilatation)
Diminished Sex Drive, 45, 59, 139, 166, 179, 196, 204, 206, 207, 250, 281, 305, 307, 319, 324, 330, 382, 414, 442, 446
Dioxide, 101, 408, 467, 526, 583
Diphtheria, 39, 45, 52, 61, 71, 78, 92, 94, 105, 110, 115, 118, 119, 122, 123, 125, 135, 139, 146, 166, 167, 177, 178, 180, 183, 185, 198, 200, 202, 206, 210 211, 227, 230, 239, 246, 248, 259, 273, 274, 282, 289, 298, 300, 307, 309, 312, 317, 320, 332, 342, 348, 350, 356, 366, 372, 373, 378, 390, 392, 394, 399, 414, 429, 430, 435, 436, 439, 440, 494, 517, 522, 583
Dislocations, 52, 209, 425
Distemper, 32
Diuresis, 249, 583
Diuretic, 33, 35, 36, 37, 41, 42, 43, 45, 48, 49, 50, 51, 53, 54, 56, 60, 61, 64, 65, 66, 68, 69, 70, 71, 73, 74, 75, 76, 77, 78, 79, 80, 81, 82, 83, 85, 86, 87, 88, 89, 90, 91, 92, 93, 94, 95, 96, 97, 98, 100, 101, 102, 103, 104, 106, 108, 111, 112, 115, 117, 119, 120, 121, 123, 124, 127, 130, 131, 132, 136, 140, 141, 142, 143, 144, 145, 146, 147, 148, 150, 151, 152, 153, 154, 155, 156, 157, 158, 159, 160, 161, 162, 165, 166, 167, 168, 170, 172, 175, 176, 177, 178, 179 180, 181, 183, 186, 187, 189, 190, 192, 193, 194, 195, 198, 200, 202, 203, 209, 210, 212, 213, 216, 217, 218, 219, 221, 222, 223, 224, 226, 229, 230, 231, 232, 233, 236, 237, 238, 241, 243, 246, 248, 249, 250, 251, 256, 257, 258, 259, 260, 263, 271, 272, 273, 274, 277, 278, 279, 282, 284, 285, 290, 291, 292, 293, 294, 295, 298, 299, 300, 301, 303, 306, 307, 308, 309, 310, 314, 315, 317, 318, 322, 326, 328, 329, 330, 334, 336, 337, 338, 339, 340, 343, 344, 345, 346, 349, 350, 354, 355, 357, 359, 360, 361, 362, 363, 365, 366, 367, 368, 369, 371, 375, 377, 379, 381, 383, 384, 386, 387, 388, 389, 390, 391, 392, 394, 395, 396, 397, 398, 400, 401, 403, 404, 405, 406, 407, 409, 410, 412, 413, 414, 415, 416, 418, 419,420, 421, 423, 425, 426, 428, 429, 431, 432, 434, 435, 437, 438, 440, 441, 443, 446, 583
Diuretic Drugs, 50, 74, 75, 96, 112, 120, 121, 168, 192, 205, 235,

277, 278, 280, 282, 284, 290, 296, 298, 300, 303, 306, 309, 312, 317, 320 329, 330, 331, 334, 335, 336, 342, 355, 357, 360, 371, 373, 375, 376, 378, 383, 388, 389, 398, 400, 401, 406, 409, 410, 411, 414, 416, 419, 423, 425, 432, 438, 444, 583
Emphysema, 46, 89, 144, 146, 161, 166, 177, 178, 180, 184, 185, 200, 206, 214, 219, 234, 263, 265, 274, 284, 289, 291, 299, 307, 308, 314, 315, 317, 360, 371, 417, 419, 458, 515
Encephalitis Lethargica, 62, 220, 330, 374, 583
Encephalomyelitis, 583
Endocrine System, 196
Endometriosis, 38, 125, 245, 319, 390, 393, 417, 423, 440, 444, 471, 583
Endometritis, 583
Enema, 11, 13, 15, 127, 322, 394, 523
Enfleurage, 15
Enteric Fever (*see* Fever),
Enteritis, 40, 58, 71, 83, 90, 91, 100, 112, 113, 128, 136, 158, 160, 191, 198, 241, 246, 254, 265, 284, 291, 299, 334, 338, 345, 363, 368, 369, 378, 394, 400, 419, 430, 432, 446, 583
Enterorrhagia, 234, 357
Enuresis, 34, 36, 50, 66, 73, 76, 95, 110, 121, 133, 151, 152, 155, 164, 166, 173, 179, 225, 227, 234, 246, 248, 250, 285, 287, 290, 291, 302, 308, 324, 329, 345, 347, 351, 354, 355, 362, 363, 368, 371, 379, 384, 393, 423, 427, 428, 432, 439, 496, 583
Environmental Stress Sensitivity, 207
Enzymes, 4, 6, 46, 53, 54, 60, 69, 91, 101, 111, 113, 122, 167, 288, 304, 311, 312, 328, 329, 344, 345, 346, 398, 411, 445, 446, 447, 448, 450, 455, 463, 464, 470, 471, 494, 506, 519
Pancreatic, 91, 329
Ephedrine, 50, 74, 178, 179, 218, 323, 363, 417, 430, 437, 583
Ephemeral Fever (*see* Fever),
Ephidrosis, 17, 76, 164, 179, 203, 204, 227, 246, 247, 298, 316, 348, 370, 409, 430, 508, 518, 521, 583
Epidermis, 525, 538, 584
Epilepsy, 32, 39, 42, 45, 52, 75, 79, 83, 101, 105, 111, 113, 115, 137, 141, 142, 156, 157, 176, 178, 192, 197, 200, 212, 216, 222, 223, 225, 227, 229, 245, 254, 270, 271, 272, 274, 289, 302, 322, 330, 336, 341, 343, 345, 347, 355, 359, 374, 378, 382, 386, 393, 414, 416, 419, 424, 425, 427, 440, 451, 457, 458, 460, 473, 496, 584
Episiotomy, 437, 521, 584
Epstein Barr Virus, 39, 55, 59, 60, 76, 90, 116, 137, 139, 196, 206, 207, 214, 265, 281, 311, 313, 325, 356, 378, 379, 393, 408, 584
Equivalents, 26
Erectile Dysfunction, 39, 59, 83, 120, 130, 133, 137, 139, 154, 166, 173, 179, 196, 198, 204, 206, 207, 230, 237, 248, 266, 280, 281, 289, 303, 305, 307, 316, 333, 355, 360, 364, 376, 378, 382, 384, 408, 423, 442, 443, 497, 584
Erectile Dysfunction Drugs, 356, 360, 443, 584
Ergotism (*see* Poisoning)
Errhine, 584
Erysipelas, 34, 46, 76, 144, 236, 239, 274, 282, 351, 378, 497, 584
Erythropoietic, 181, 196, 316, 402, 408, 431, 446, 465, 584
Escherichia coli, 43, 50, 68, 73, 132, 134, 170, 214, 250, 290, 325, 428, 446
Esophagitis, 191, 394, 584
Essential Fatty Acids, 94, 182, 471
Euphoriant, 288, 584
Euphorigenic (*see* Euphoriant)
Excessive Perspiration (*see* Ephidrosis)
Exhaustion, 43, 59, 60, 62, 77, 89, 96, 107, 112, 115, 120, 133, 139, 166, 173, 196, 202, 212, 217, 220, 224, 243, 247, 254, 259, 274, 286, 287, 302, 307, 324, 331, 338, 374, 378, 393, 401, 402, 425, 442, 443, 446, 459, 494, 505, 522
Expectorant, 12, 32, 41, 43, 45, 47, 48, 49, 51, 55, 60, 64, 65, 72, 75, 77, 78, 79, 83, 87, 89, 91, 93, 94, 98, 101, 105, 108, 109, 110, 118, 119, 120, 124, 127, 128, 129, 130, 132, 133, 134, 137, 138, 141, 142, 144, 146, 148, 151, 156, 158, 159, 160, 163, 164, 165, 166, 176, 177, 178, 179, 180, 183, 183, 185, 186, 187, 188, 190, 194, 198, 200, 202, 203, 204, 209, 210, 216, 219, 222, 223, 229, 231, 232, 233, 235, 239, 240, 242, 247, 251, 252, 256, 257, 259, 264, 265, 267, 268, 270, 272, 273, 274, 277, 278, 279, 280, 282, 283, 284, 288, 290, 291, 292, 293, 294, 295, 299, 300, 304, 307, 308, 309, 314, 315, 316, 317, 318, 326, 327, 329, 331, 334, 340, 345, 346, 349, 350, 351, 353, 355, 359, 360, 361, 365, 366, 375, 376, 378, 379, 381, 383, 384, 388, 394, 395, 395, 397, 400, 401, 403, 404, 405, 410, 411, 412, 413, 414, 415, 419, 421, 423, 425, 426, 428, 431, 432, 435, 437, 441, 447, 491, 584
External Endometriosis, 584
Extracts, 15, 16, 19, 406, 536, 537
Eye Drops, 15, 175, 245
Eye Infection (*see* Conjunctivitis)
Eye Problems, 43, 56, 76, 152, 155, 156, 162, 173, 175, 184, 190, 204, 212, 229, 244, 274, 277, 278, 288, 321, 324, 335, 345, 349, 351, 353, 359, 374, 383, 394, 395, 402, 425, 428, 430, 446, 460
Eye Tonic, 497
Eyestrain, 176, 183, 374, 458
Eyewash, 16, 41, 68, 122, 136, 149, 150, 152, 173, 175, 183, 208, 211, 234, 255, 269, 270, 288, 291, 342, 345, 356, 363, 365, 371, 372, 382, 387, 395, 398, 418

F

Face Rinse, 543, 547
Face Steam, 543
Facemask, 17, 542
Fatigue, 584
Febrifuge, 584
Ferrous sulphate (*see* Iron Mordant)
Fertilization (*see* Fertilizin)
Fertilizin, 63, 116, 132, 162, 173, 252, 253, 396, 397, 445, 584
Fever, 3, 6, 14, 17, 32, 34, 36, 37, 38, 39, 40, 41, 43, 44, 45, 46, 48, 49, 50, 52, 53, 54, 56, 57, 58, 60, 61, 63, 64, 65, 66, 67, 68, 70, 71, 72, 73, 75, 76, 78, 79, 80, 81, 82, 83, 85, 86, 87, 88, 89, 90, 91, 92, 93, 94, 95, 96, 97, 98, 99, 100, 101, 102, 104, 105, 106, 107, 108, 109, 110,111,113, 115, 116, 117, 118, 119, 120, 121, 122, 123, 124, 125, 127, 128, 129, 130, 131, 132, 133, 134, 135, 136, 137, 139, 140, 141, 142, 144, 145, 146, 148, 149, 150, 151, 152, 153, 154, 155, 156, 157, 158, 159, 160, 161, 162, 163, 164, 166, 167, 168, 169, 170, 171, 172, 173, 175, 176, 177, 178, 179, 180, 182, 183, 184, 185, 186, 187, 189, 190, 191, 193, 194, 195, 198, 200, 202, 205, 206, 207, 208, 209, 210, 211, 212, 213, 214, 215, 216, 217, 219, 220, 221, 222, 223, 224, 227, 229, 230, 231, 232, 233, 234, 235, 236, 239, 240, 241, 242, 245, 247, 248, 249, 250, 251, 252, 253, 254, 256, 257, 258, 259, 260, 261, 262, 264, 265, 266, 267, 268, 270, 271, 272, 274, 275, 276, 277, 278, 279, 280, 281, 282, 283, 284, 285, 287, 289, 290, 291, 293, 294, 295, 296, 298, 299, 300, 301, 302, 303, 304, 306, 307, 308, 310, 313, 314, 315, 316, 317, 318, 319, 320, 322, 323, 324, 325, 326, 328, 329, 330, 331, 333, 334, 335, 336, 337, 338, 339, 341, 342, 343, 345, 346, 347, 348, 349, 350, 351, 353, 355, 356, 357, 359, 360, 361, 362, 363, 364, 365,

I

N

O

427, 430, 445, 446, 525, 591
Pulmonary Hemorrhage (*see* Hemorrhage)
Pyelitis, 50, 74, 96, 155, 591
Pyloristenosis, 246, 591
Pylorus, 591
Pyrexia (*see* Fever)
Pyridoxine, 37, 66, 70, 83, 88, 99, 100, 109, 111, 115, 118, 130, 137, 141, 142, 144, 155, 183, 201, 202, 211, 221, 230, 231, 233, 234, 254, 265, 288, 291, 300, 308, 313, 360, 365, 369, 370, 371, 378, 382, 402, 407, 412, 419, 432, 439, 444, 446, 448, 449, 451, 452, 454, 457, 458, 460, 461

R

RA (*see* Rheumatoid Arthritis)
Radiation Burns/Exposure, 40
Radiation Therapy, 40, 46, 48, 59, 116, 139, 184, 200, 205, 206, 207, 211, 214, 243, 289, 297, 302, 310, 311, 312, 313, 322, 332, 333, 356, 361, 385, 402, 417, 445, 446, 448, 461
Rash, 7, 40, 42, 50, 52, 61, 68, 74, 75, 81, 84, 94, 111, 119, 122, 124, 126, 129, 130, 135, 139, 141, 150, 158, 160, 172, 173, 175, 176, 177, 178, 182, 190, 197, 206, 208, 209, 215, 219, 224, 229, 234, 235, 238, 241, 242, 250, 254, 265, 269, 271, 276, 280, 284, 291, 294, 299, 301, 309, 312, 317, 318, 319, 323, 324, 326, 335, 341, 342, 345, 346, 351, 353, 356, 363, 365, 378, 394, 395, 396, 397, 403, 407, 409, 420, 421, 430, 434, 436, 437, 439, 441, 456, 458, 472, 473, 521, 525, 529, 532, 535, 536, 592
Raynaud's Disease, 69, 104, 592
Rectal Prolapse (*see* Prolapse)
Red Hair Shades, 549
Refreshing Steam, 543
Regular Headache (*see* Headache)
Relaxing Steam, 543
Renal Drugs, 41
Reproductive System. 122, 125, 139, 167, 206, 271, 278, 335, 384, 385, 394, 423, 439, 460, 482, 524, 592
Reproductive System Tonic, 525
Reptile Bites, 364
Respiratory Center, 258, 274, 369, 592
Respiratory Conditions, 12, 18, 32, 33, 34, 39, 42, 43, 45, 47, 48, 49, 52, 55, 57, 60, 61, 64, 65, 67, 68, 69, 70, 71, 72, 75, 78, 79, 82, 84, 85, 87, 88, 89, 90, 91, 92, 93, 94, 95, 96, 97, 100, 101, 105, 107, 111, 118, 119, 121, 122, 124, 127, 128, 129, 130, 132, 133, 135, 136, 137, 139, 140, 142, 144, 146, 148, 153, 155, 160, 161, 162, 164, 166, 167, 172, 175, 176, 177, 178, 179, 180, 181, 182, 183, 184, 185, 186, 187, 189, 190, 191, 194, 198, 200, 202, 203, 204, 206, 207, 209, 210, 211, 212, 216, 217, 219, 220, 224, 229, 231, 232, 233, 235, 239, 240, 241, 243, 245, 246, 247, 248, 249, 250, 251, 252, 256, 257, 259, 261, 263, 264, 265, 267, 268, 270, 272, 273, 274, 275, 277, 278, 279, 281, 283, 284, 289, 290, 291, 292, 294, 295, 296, 299, 300, 301, 303, 304, 306, 308, 309, 314, 315, 316, 317, 318, 319, 320, 321, 325, 327, 331, 332, 333, 334, 335, 341, 342, 345, 347, 348, 350, 351, 356, 359, 360, 361, 363, 365, 366, 373, 374, 375, 376, 378, 379, 381, 382, 383, 384, 388, 390, 393, 394, 395, 396, 397, 398, 400, 401, 403, 404, 405, 407, 411, 412, 413, 414, 415, 419, 421, 423, 426, 427, 428, 429, 431, 433, 434, 435, 436, 437, 439, 440, 441, 442, 446, 447, 448, 460, 470, 508
Respiratory System, 34, 66, 71, 89, 93, 97, 103, 104, 106, 107, 141, 155, 191, 200, 206, 212, 227, 232, 245, 250, 286, 287, 298, 308, 316, 345, 376, 394, 425, 490, 515, 526, 592
Respiratory System Tonic, 526
Restful Sleep Sachet, 553
Restlessness, 34, 77, 98, 115, 122, 123, 140, 142, 143, 178, 179, 190, 205, 221, 227, 230, 247, 250, 254, 263, 268, 270, 275, 286, 287, 306, 309, 321, 330, 331, 342, 351, 372, 385, 388, 393, 418, 425, 429, 437, 482, 495, 498, 503
Retinal Hemorrhage (*see* Hemorrhage)
Retinal Inflammation (*see* Retinitis)
Retinitis, 90, 353, 592
Retinopathy, 46, 90, 182, 201, 204, 208, 213, 221, 298, 399, 417, 592
Reyes Syndrome, 157, 592
Rheumatic Fever (*see* Fever)
Rheumatism, 34, 36, 37, 38, 39, 40, 41, 43, 45, 46, 48, 49, 50, 52, 53, 54, 56, 57, 58, 60, 63, 64, 65, 67, 68, 70, 71, 72, 74, 76, 78, 79, 80, 81, 82, 84, 85, 87, 90, 91, 92, 93, 94, 95, 96, 99, 101, 102, 103, 104, 105, 107, 108, 111, 116, 118, 119, 121, 122, 123, 124, 128, 129, 130, 131, 133, 134, 139, 140, 141, 142, 143, 144, 145, 146, 150, 151, 152, 153, 155, 156, 157, 159, 160, 161, 162, 164, 166, 167, 168, 169, 171, 172, 173, 175, 176, 178, 179, 180, 182, 184, 185, 187, 189, 190, 191, 193, 195, 200, 202, 206, 207, 209, 210, 212, 213, 214, 215, 216, 217, 219, 220, 221, 224, 226, 229, 230, 232, 233, 234, 236, 240, 241, 243, 245, 246, 247, 248, 250, 251, 254, 256, 257, 258, 260, 268, 270, 271, 274, 275, 277, 278, 281, 283, 284, 285, 287, 289, 290, 294, 295, 296, 299, 300, 302, 303, 306, 308, 309, 310, 314, 315, 317, 319, 320, 322, 323, 324, 329, 331, 333, 336, 337, 339, 341, 342, 343, 345, 346, 348, 349, 350, 356, 359, 360, 361, 362, 363, 364, 365, 368, 370, 371, 372, 374, 375, 376, 377, 378, 379, 382, 383, 384, 386, 388, 389, 391, 392, 393, 395, 396, 397, 398, 400, 401, 402, 403, 407, 408, 411, 412, 414, 415, 416, 417, 418, 419, 421, 423, 424, 426, 427, 428, 430, 431, 432, 433, 434, 435, 439, 440, 441,444, 447, 449, 517, 526, 592
Rheumatoid Arthritis (*see* Arthritis)
Rhinitis, 211, 339, 374, 592
Riboflavin (*see* Vitamin B2)
Rickets, 185, 187, 196, 282, 304, 319, 365, 393, 463, 529
Ringworm (*see* Parasites)
River Fever (*see* Fever and Insect-Borne Diseases)
Rocky Mountain Spotted Fever (*see* Fever and Insect-Borne Diseases)
Rodents (*see* Vermin)
Roentgen Rays, 463, 471, 592
Romantic Bath, 539
Rose Bug, 556
Rose Chafer Beetle, 556
Rose Perfume, 552
Roundworm (*see* Parasites)
Royal Jelly, 445, 449, 512
Rubeola (*see* Measles)

S

S-adenosyhmethionine, 474
Sachets, 45, 259, 261, 262, 335, 371, 372, 414, 552, 553
SAD (*see* Seasonal Affective Disorder)
Saddle Sores, 560
St. Anthony's fire (*see* Erysipelas)
St. Vitus' dance (*see* Chorea)
Salicylates, 38, 44, 58, 64, 94, 98, 116, 119, 123, 124, 128, 129, 132, 134, 139, 157, 162, 169, 182, 185, 189, 196, 199, 201, 203, 204, 205, 206, 207, 208, 211, 214, 218, 243, 266, 295, 296, 305, 306, 311, 312, 313, 329, 339, 342, 343, 350, 359, 363, 365, 366, 368, 373, 374, 375, 379, 380, 381, 388, 418, 422, 434, 435, 438, 439, 441, 445, 457, 461, 462, 463, 465, 469, 471, 592

193, 194, 195, 196, 197, 198, 200, 201, 202, 205, 206, 208, 210, 212, 213, 216, 217, 219, 221, 222, 223, 226, 230, 231, 232, 234, 236, 240, 241, 243, 247, 249, 253, 254, 256, 259, 260, 261, 264, 265, 267, 268, 269, 270, 271, 275, 277, 279, 280, 282, 285, 286, 288, 290, 293, 294, 296, 298, 299, 300, 301, 303, 304, 306, 307, 309, 316, 317, 318, 320, 321, 322, 324, 326, 330, 333, 334, 336, 337, 338, 339, 340, 342, 343, 344, 348, 349, 350, 351, 352, 353, 359, 360, 361, 362, 363, 365, 367, 369, 370, 371, 372, 373, 378, 381, 383, 384, 385, 387, 388, 389, 390, 391, 392, 393, 394, 395, 396, 397, 400, 401, 402, 404, 406, 407, 408, 409, 411, 414, 416, 418, 419, 420, 422, 423, 424, 425, 428, 430, 431, 434, 435, 436, 438, 440, 441, 447, 449, 485, 488, 489, 490, 494, 497, 499, 500, 501, 509, 511, 512, 517, 519, 524, 525, 526, 528, 529, 532, 538, 594

Tonsil, 530, 594

Tonsillitis, 34, 57, 75, 99, 118, 137, 144, 146, 158, 176, 190, 211, 212, 217, 224, 239, 243, 268, 274, 284, 291, 309, 317, 340, 341, 348, 356, 360, 363, 366, 377, 378, 394, 423, 430, 434, 437, 439, 461, 522, 530, 594

Tooth Brightener/Whitener, 551

Toothache, 33, 35, 39, 43, 58, 60, 76, 78, 84, 86, 91, 102, 105, 106, 109, 111, 115, 117, 118, 119, 122, 124, 135, 137, 138, 150, 152, 156, 169, 174, 187, 189, 190, 198, 200, 203, 210, 225, 227, 230, 232, 240, 250, 259, 261, 269, 271, 274, 278, 280, 290, 291, 294, 300, 302, 309, 317, 322, 331, 335, 340, 342, 345, 346, 347, 351, 353, 355, 356, 363, 374, 382, 383, 403, 407, 409, 414, 421, 426, 434, 435, 436, 439, 440

Toothpaste (*see* Dentifrice)

Tophi, 36, 50, 74, 78, 90, 92, 96, 99, 121, 131, 160, 181, 184, 249, 250, 294, 295, 301, 302, 319, 322, 325, 329, 332, 337, 343, 345, 360, 362, 375, 376, 382, 391,401

Tourette's Syndrome, 399, 594

Toxemia, 460, 594

- Alimentary, 578
- Eclamptic, 583
- Menstrual, 588
- Preeclamptic, 591

Toxic, 2, 7, 8, 16, 19, 24, 38, 46, 108, 113, 129, 153, 164, 204, 216, 229, 242, 266, 297, 301, 309, 320, 324, 361, 373, 409, 410, 421, 427, 450, 453, 522, 523, 562, 594

Toxic Shock Syndrome (*see* Shock)

Tracheitis, 144, 594

Trachoma, 244, 594

Tranquilizer, 62, 115, 152, 220, 237, 288, 331, 364, 374, 380, 442, 594

Tranquilizer Drugs, 62, 212, 220, 237, 331, 374, 425, 443

Trauma, 52, 128, 129, 146, 166, 208, 342

- Brain, 128
- Postoperative, 52, 129, 208, 342

Tremors, 51, 77, 93, 97, 148, 153, 182, 192, 205, 220, 226, 227, 254, 274, 306, 348, 374, 393, 418, 422, 443, 454

Trichomonas (*see* Parasites)

Trismus, 118, 137, 157, 224, 225, 274, 289, 321, 356, 393, 421, 594

Trypanosomes (*see* Parasites)

Trypanosomiasis (*see* Insect-Borne Diseases)

Tryptophan, 66, 161, 196, 402, 446, 456

Tsetse Fly, 358

TSS (*see* Toxic Shock Syndrome)

Tubercle Lesion (*see* Lesions)

Tuberculosis, 32, 33, 35, 36, 37, 40, 42, 43, 58, 60, 64, 65, 66, 69, 70, 72, 75, 84, 85, 87, 91, 97, 99, 103, 110, 124, 127, 134, 141, 144, 146, 149, 153, 156, 161, 169, 172, 173, 177, 178, 180, 185, 190, 194, 200, 202, 204, 207, 210, 212, 216, 217, 219, 225, 229, 230, 231, 234, 239, 249, 251, 256, 264, 267, 268, 269, 270, 271, 275, 279, 280, 283, 284, 285, 287, 290, 291, 296, 299, 302, 303, 304, 309, 317, 319, 320, 322, 335, 336, 339, 341, 343, 345, 347, 348, 350, 351, 352, 356, 361, 363, 365, 367, 375, 376, 382, 385, 394, 398, 400, 403, 409, 421, 426, 427, 430, 431, 435, 437, 439, 441, 468, 522, 528, 530, 531, 594

Tuberculous Ulcer (*see* Ulcer)

Tularemia (*see* Insect-Borne Diseases)

Tumors, 36, 38, 43, 69, 70, 75, 78, 84, 87, 91, 93, 95, 98, 99, 106, 113, 116, 117, 118, 124, 128, 132, 137, 146, 161, 167, 172, 173, 176, 185, 190, 193, 195, 196, 197, 199, 200, 207, 208, 210, 211, 212, 214, 225, 229, 230, 233, 234, 239, 251, 254, 256, 260, 261, 267, 269, 270, 271, 272, 274, 279, 281, 289, 297, 298, 302, 303, 304, 309, 310, 311, 313, 317, 318, 322, 329, 333, 334, 336, 342, 343, 347, 348, 355, 356, 365, 379, 387, 393, 394, 395, 398, 408, 411, 416, 417, 419, 427, 430, 431, 437, 445, 446, 451, 482, 487, 498

- Brain, 211
- Hepatoma, 313, 393, 586
- Lymphoma, 298, 310, 588
- Non-Hodgkin's Lymphoma, 132
- Myeloma, 589
- Multiple Myeloma,36, 207, 313, 445, 589
- Sarcoma, 310, 313, 487, 592
  - Kaposi's Sarcoma, 116, 207, 311, 445, 587

Type I Diabetes (*see* Diabetes Mellitus)

Type II Diabetes (*see* Diabetes Mellitus)

Typhoid, 33, 36, 43, 46, 58, 69, 70, 76, 82, 90, 93, 103, 105, 107, 117, 122, 124, 141, 151, 158, 174, 180, 194, 200, 211, 217, 231, 239, 245, 249, 254, 259, 260, 277, 285, 287, 302, 317, 325, 333, 339, 342, 356, 362, 368, 374, 440, 446, 530, 531

Typhoid Fever (*see* Enteric Fever)

Typhoid Hemorrhage (*see* Hemorrhage)

Typhus Fever (*see* Fever and Insect-Borne Diseases)

Tyrosine, 161, 176, 196, 402, 456

U

Ubiquinone (*see* Coenzyme Q_{10})

Ulcer, 17, 32, 33, 35, 36, 37, 38, 39, 40, 42, 43, 46, 49, 50, 58, 60, 61, 63, 64, 65, 67, 69, 70, 72, 74, 75, 76, 78, 80, 82, 84, 85, 86, 87, 88, 90, 91, 92, 93, 94, 96, 97, 99, 100, 103, 105, 106, 107, 108, 110, 111, 112, 116, 117, 118, 119, 121, 122, 124, 125, 127, 128, 129, 130, 132, 133, 134, 135, 137, 138, 139, 140, 141, 143, 144, 146, 147, 148, 149, 151, 152, 153, 155, 156, 157, 158, 159, 160, 161, 163, 164, 166, 167, 169, 170, 172, 173, 174, 176, 177, 178, 180, 182, 183, 185, 187, 190, 191, 192, 194, 197, 198, 200, 202, 203, 204, 206, 207, 210, 211, 212, 214, 216, 217, 218, 219, 221, 225, 227, 228, 229, 230, 231, 233, 234, 235, 236, 237, 239, 240, 241, 243, 245, 246, 247, 249, 250, 251, 252, 254, 256, 258, 259, 260, 262, 264, 265, 267, 268, 269, 270, 271, 273, 274, 277, 279, 280, 283, 284, 285, 287, 289, 290, 291, 293, 294, 295, 296, 298, 299, 300, 302, 303, 304, 309, 314, 315, 317, 318, 319, 320, 321, 322, 325, 327, 328, 329, 333, 335, 336, 337, 339, 340, 341, 342, 343, 345, 347, 348, 350, 351, 352, 355, 356, 359, 360, 361, 362, 363, 365, 366, 367, 368, 369, 372, 374, 375, 376, 378, 379, 381, 382, 383, 385, 386, 387, 388, 391, 393, 394, 395, 396, 397, 398, 400, 401, 402, 403, 404, 406, 407, 408, 409, 414, 415, 419, 420, 421, 425, 426, 427, 428, 429, 430, 431, 433, 434, 435, 436, 437, 439, 440, 441, 442, 444, 445, 446, 456, 458, 459, 460, 470, 485, 528, 529, 530, 531, 595

- Bouveret, 33, 36, 43, 46, 58, 69, 70, 76, 82, 90, 93, 103, 105,

345, 346, 347, 348, 350, 353, 356, 359, 363, 365, 368, 371, 372, 374, 378, 379, 382, 387, 391, 394, 396, 397, 398, 400, 401, 402, 403, 404, 406, 407, 408, 409, 412, 414, 415, 416, 418, 419, 420, 421, 426, 427, 428, 430, 434, 435, 436, 437, 438, 439, 440, 441, 445, 447, 448, 449, 485, 525, 536, 538, 560
Wrinkles, 40, 46, 87, 106, 126, 128, 176, 214, 251, 304, 417, 437, 446, 539

X

X-rays (*see* Roentgen Rays)

Y

Yeast Infection, 534, 536
Yellow Fever (*see* Fever and Insect-Borne Diseases)

Z

Zinc, 40, 68, 87, 99, 109, 123, 130, 133, 139, 144, 146, 167, 183, 188, 200, 201, 204, 205, 211, 219, 221, 230, 251, 265, 280, 290, 291, 309, 312, 318, 324, 326, 341, 350, 354, 372, 382, 390, 392, 394, 399, 402, 406, 412, 423, 424, 431, 436, 446, 453, 462, 465, 468, 469, 525

References for Additional Reading

American Association of Naturopathic Physicians (AANP), The. "Nature's Pharmacy." 2001. Publications International, Ltd.
Arky, Ronald. "PDR® Physicians' Desk Reference®, 49 Edition." 1995. Medical Economics Data Production Company.
Balch, Phyllis A. "Prescriptions for Herbal Healing." 2002. Penguin Putnam, Inc.
Behrens, Julie and Slump, Kenneth W. "Window on the Tropics." 1998. Denver Botanic Gardens.
Blumgarten, A. S. "Textbook of Materia Medica." 1930. The MacMillan Company.
Castleman, Michael. "The Healing Herbs." 1991. Rodale Press.
Castleton, Virginia. "The Handbook of Natural Beauty." 1975. Rodale Press, Inc.
Challem, Jack Joseph. "Spirulina." 1981. Keats Publishing, Inc.
Chamberlain, Logan. "What the Labels Won't Tell You." 1998. Interweave Press, Inc.
Chin, Wee Yeow. "A Guide to Medicinal Plants." Singapore Science Center. 1992 (p. 106: description, chemical compounds, uses, photo).
Christopher, John R. "School of Natural Healing." The Reference Volume on Herbal Therapy for the Teacher, Student, or Practitioner. 1976. Christopher Publications, Inc.
Coon, Nelson. "Using Wild and Wayside Plants." 1980. Dover Publications, Inc.
Doane, Nancy Locke. "Indian Doctor Book." 1985. Nancy Locke Doane, Publisher.
Foley, Denise and Neches, Eileen. "Women's Encyclopedia of Health and Emotional Healing." 1993. Rodale Press, Inc.
Foster, Steven. "Herbal Renaissance." Gibbs Smith, Publisher.
Foster, Steven and Hobbs, Christopher. "Western Medicinal Plants and Herbs." 2002. Houghton Mifflin Company.
Freeman, Sally. "Every Woman's Guide to Natural Home Remedies." 1996. GuildAmerica Books.
Gerard, John. "The Herbal or General History of Plants." 1975. Dover Publications, Inc.
Graham, Judy. "Evening Primrose Oil." 1984. Thorsons Publishers, Inc.
Gray, Henry. "Gray's Anatomy." 1995. Barnes & Noble, Inc.
Green, James. "The Male Herbal." 1991. The Crossing Press.
Grieve, M., Mrs. "A Modern Herbal, Vol.I and II." 1971. Dover Publications, Inc.
Hawken, C.M. "St. John's Wort." 1997. Woodland Publishing.
Heinerman, John. "Heinerman's Encyclopedia of Healing Herbs & Spices". 1996. Parker Publishing Company, Inc.
Hobbs, Christopher. "Echinacea, The Immune Herb!" 1996. Botanica Press.
Hobbs, Christopher. "Medicinal Mushrooms." 1995. Botanica Press.
Keith, Velma J. and Gordon, Monteen. "The How To Herb Book." 1984. Mayfield

Publications.
Kershaw, Linda and MacKinnon, Andy. “Plants of the Rocky Mountains.” 1998. Lone Pine Publishing.
Kramer, Jack. “The Old-Fashioned Cutting Garden.” 1979. MacMillan Publishing Co., Inc.
Lininger, Schuyler W., Jr., Gaby, Alan R., Austin, Steve, Batz, Forrest, Yarnell, Eric, Brown, Donald J., and Constantine, George. “A-Z Guide to Drug-Herb-Vitamin Interactions.” 1999. Prima Publishing.
Lust, John B. “The Herb Book.” 2001. Benedict Lust Publications, Inc.
Mabey, Richard. “The New Age Herbalist.” 1988. MacMillan Publishing Company.
McCormick, Marjorie. “The Golden Pollen.” 1984. Busiest Bee Publications
Meyer, Joseph E. “The Herbalist.” 1960. Rand McNally & Company, Conkey Division.
Miller, Richard Alan. “The Magical and Ritual Use of Aphrodisiacs.” 1993. Destiny Books.
Moore, Michael. “Medicinal Plants of the Mountain West.” 1979. The Museum of New Mexico Press.
Mowry, Daniel B. “The Scientific Validation of Herbal Medicine.” 1986. Keats Publishing, Inc.
National Life Extension Research Institute, The. “The Olive Leaf.” 1999. The National Life Extension Research Institute, Inc.
Nurse’s Handbook of Alternative & Complementary Therapies. 1999. Springhouse Corporation.
O’Brien, James. “The Miracle of Garlic and Vinegar.” 1995. Globe Communications Corp.
Ody, Penelope. “100 Great Natural Remedies.” 1999. Barnes & Noble, Inc.
Ody, Penelope. “The Complete Medicinal Herbal”. 1993. D.K. Publishing, Inc.
Passwater, Richard A. “Evening Primrose Oil.” 1981. Keats Publishing, Inc.
Pizzorno, Joseph and Murray, Michael T. “Encyclopedia of Natural Medicine.” 1998. Prima Publishing.
Prevention® Magazine Health Books, by the editors of. “The Secret Healing Power of Garlic.” Rodale Press, Inc.
Reckeweg, Hans-Heinrich. “Homotoxicology.” 1989. Menaco Publishing Company, Inc.
Shuttleworth, Floyd S. and Zim, Herbert S. “Non-Flowering Plants.” 1967. Golden Press.
Sifton, David W. “The PDR® Family Guide To Nutritional Supplements”™.
Smith, Ed. “Therapeutic Herb Manual.” 1999. Ed Smith, Publisher.
Soepadmo, Dr. E, "The Encyclopedia of Malaysia: Plants", Editions Didier Millet, 1998 (p. 16: seasonality).
Solomon, Charles. “Pharmacology, Materia Medica, and Therapeutics.” 1936. J.B. Lippincott Company.
Spoerke, David G., Jr. “Herbal Medications.” Woodbridge Press Publishing Company.
Stein, Diane. “The Natural Remedy Book for Women.” 1992. The Crossing Press.
Tenney, Louise. “Today’s Herbal Health.” 1992. Woodland Books.
Tierra, Michael. “The Way of Herbs.” 1998. Pocket Books.
Tierra, Michael. “Planetary Herbology.” 1988. Lotus Press.
Tillotson, Alan Keith. “The One Earth Herbal Sourcebook.” 2001. Kensington Publishing

Corp.
United States Pharmacopeial Convention, Inc. "The Physicians and Pharmacists Guide to your Medicines." 1981. Ballantine Books.
Wade, Carlson. "Natural and Folk Remedies." 1970. Tower Publications, Inc.
Weil, Andrew. "Spontaneous Healing." 1995. Alfred A. Knopf, Publisher.
Werbach, Melvyn R., and Murray, Michael T. "Botanical Influences on Illness." A Sourcebook of Clinical Research. 1994. Third Line Press.
Wheelwright, Edith Grey. "Medicinal Plants and their History." 1974. Dover Publications, Inc.
Whitaker, Julian. "Anti-Aging Miracles." Your Guide to Health and Longevity. Philips Publishing, Inc.
Willard, Terry. "Edible and Medicinal Plants of the Rocky Mountains and Neighboring Territories." 1992. Wild Rose College of Natural Healing, Ltd.
Zim, Herbert S. and Martin, Alexander C. "Flowers." A guide to Familiar American Wildflowers. 1950. Simon and Schuster.

Websites

Federal Government Agencies

Administration on Aging, Department of Health and Human Services (DHHS): http://www.aoa.gov/
Food and Drug Administration, Department of Health and Human Services (DHHS), Center for Food Safety and Applied Nutrition:
http://www.cfsan.fda.gov/~dms/supplmnt.html , http://www.cfsan.fda.gov/~dms/ds-savvy.html , and http://www.cfsan.fda.gov/label.html
Federal Trade Commission: www.ftc.gov
National Institutes of Health, DHHS:
National Center for Complementary & Alternative Medicine:
http://nccam.nih.gov/ (Clearing house) 1-888-NIH CAM
Office of Dietary Supplements: http://dietary-supplements.info.nih.gov
Office on Women's Health, DHHS, http://www.4woman.gov/owh/aboutowh.htm or 1-800-994-WOMAN
U.S. Department of Agriculture, Food and Nutrition Information Center: www.nal.usda.gov/fnic

Non-Federal Government Organizations and Other Websites

American Dietetic Association: http://www.eatright.org
American Pharmacists Association: www.pharmacyandyou.org
Food Marketing Institute: www.fmi.org
International Food Information Council Foundation: http://ific.org
National Council on Patient Information and Education: http://www.talkaboutrx.org/compliance.html#dietary
AARP: http://www.aarp.org
Memorial Sloan-Kettering Cancer Center - http://www.mskcc.org
Council for Responsible Nutrition - http://www.crnusa.org
Institute for Nutraceutical Advancement - http://www.nsfina.org
American Botanical Council - http://www.herbalgram.org
American Herbal Products Association - http://www.ahpa.org
Herb Research Foundation - http://www.herbs.org
Organic Trade Association - http://www.ota.com
Herbal Materia Medica - http://www.healthy.net/clinic/therapy/herbal/herbic/herbs/

About the Author

Debra J. Rayburn has over 20 years experience in the alternative health field with an emphasis on Phytotherapy as well as the use of other nutritional supplements including amino acids, vitamins, and minerals. She has spent numerous years researching natural approaches to health and wellness, and has collected extensive information about the medicinal properties of plants as well as other natural, noninvasive modalities that enhance the body's natural healing powers. Debra is an accomplished sculptor, a gifted writer of poetry, and a practitioner of various therapeutic modalities including aromatherapy, meditation, relaxation therapy, healing touch, and reflexology, as well as other wellness therapies to include art, music, and color. Her interest in the plant kingdom has stemmed since childhood. Exploring field and forest, she would stop to closely examine the wide variety of plants and flowers she would come across. A miracle indeed, that a creation of such beauty and simplicity can be utilized in the health and wellness of all. Debra currently lives in the Rocky Mountain region.

Other Books by Ozark Mountain Publishing, Inc.

Dolores Cannon
A Soul Remembers Hiroshima
Between Death and Life
Conversations with Nostradamus, Volume I, II, III
The Convoluted Universe -Book One, Two, Three, Four, Five
The Custodians
Five Lives Remembered
Jesus and the Essenes
Keepers of the Garden
Legacy from the Stars
The Legend of Starcrash
The Search for Hidden Sacred Knowledge
They Walked with Jesus
The Three Waves of Volunteers and the New Earth
Aron Abrahamsen
Holiday in Heaven
Out of the Archives – Earth Changes
James Adams
Little Steps
Justine Alessi & M. E. McMillan
Rebirth of the Oracle
Kathryn/Patrick Andries
Naked in Public
Kathryn Andries
The Big Desire
Dream Doctor
Soul Choices: Six Paths to Find Your Life Purpose
Soul Choices: Six Paths to Fulfilling Relationships
Patrick Andries
Owners Manual for the Mind
Cat Baldwin
Divine Gifts of Healing
Dan Bird
Finding Your Way in the Spiritual Age
Waking Up in the Spiritual Age
Julia Cannon
Soul Speak – The Language of Your Body
Ronald Chapman
Seeing True
Albert Cheung
The Emperor's Stargate
Jack Churchward
Lifting the Veil on the Lost Continent of Mu
The Stone Tablets of Mu
Sherri Cortland
Guide Group Fridays
Raising Our Vibrations for the New Age
Spiritual Tool Box
Windows of Opportunity
Patrick De Haan
The Alien Handbook
Paulinne Delcour-Min
Holy Ice
Spiritual Gold
Anthony DeNino
The Power of Giving & Gratitude
Michael Dennis
Morning Coffee with God
God's Many Mansions
Carolyn Greer Daly
Opening to Fullness of Spirit
Anita Holmes
Twidders
Aaron Hoopes
Reconnecting to the Earth
Victoria Hunt
Kiss the Wind
Patricia Irvine
In Light and In Shade
Kevin Killen
Ghosts and Me
Diane Lewis
From Psychic to Soul
Donna Lynn
From Fear to Love
Maureen McGill
Baby It's You
Maureen McGill & Nola Davis
Live from the Other Side
Curt Melliger
Heaven Here on Earth
Henry Michaelson
And Jesus Said – A Conversation
Dennis Milner
Kosmos
Andy Myers
Not Your Average Angel Book
Guy Needler
Avoiding Karma
Beyond the Source – Book 1, Book 2
The Anne Dialogues
The Curators
The History of God
The Origin Speaks

Other Books by Ozark Mountain Publishing, Inc.

James Nussbaumer
And Then I Knew My Abundance
The Master of Everything
Mastering Your Own Spiritual Freedom
Sherry O'Brian
Peaks and Valleys
Riet Okken
The Liberating Power of Emotions
Gabrielle Orr
Akashic Records: One True Love
Let Miracles Happen
Victor Parachin
Sit a Bit
Nikki Pattillo
A Spiritual Evolution
Children of the Stars
Rev. Grant H. Pealer
A Funny Thing Happened on the Way to Heaven
Worlds Beyond Death
Victoria Pendragon
Born Healers
Feng Shui from the Inside, Out
Sleep Magic
The Sleeping Phoenix
Michael Perlin
Fantastic Adventures in Metaphysics
Walter Pullen
Evolution of the Spirit
Debra Rayburn
Let's Get Natural with Herbs
Charmian Redwood
A New Earth Rising
Coming Home to Lemuria
David Rivinus
Always Dreaming
Richard Rowe
Imagining the Unimaginable
M. Don Schorn
Elder Gods of Antiquity
Legacy of the Elder Gods
Gardens of the Elder Gods
Reincarnation…Stepping Stones of Life
Garnet Schulhauser
Dance of Eternal Rapture
Dance of Heavenly Bliss
Dancing Forever with Spirit
Dancing on a Stamp
Manuella Stoerzer
Headless Chicken
Annie Stillwater Gray
Education of a Guardian Angel
The Dawn Book
Joys of a Guardian Angel
Work of a Guardian Angel
Blair Styra
Don't Change the Channel
Who Catharted
Natalie Sudman
Application of Impossible Things
L.R. Sumpter
Judy's Story
The Old is New
We Are the Creators
Artur Tadevlsyan
Croton
Jim Thomas
Tales from the Trance
Jason & Jolene Tierney
A Quest of Transcendence
Nicholas Vesey
Living the Life-Force
Janie Wells
Embracing the Human Journey
Payment for Passage
Dennis Wheatley/ Maria Wheatley
The Essential Dowsing Guide
Maria Wheatley
Druidic Soul Star Astrology
Jacquelyn Wiersma
The Zodiac Recipe
Sherry Wilde
The Forgotten Promise
Lyn Willmoth
A Small Book of Comfort
Stuart Wilson & Joanna Prentis
Atlantis and the New Consciousness
Beyond Limitations
The Essenes -Children of the Light
The Magdalene Version
Power of the Magdalene
Robert Winterhalter
The Healing Christ